Balfour

Balfour

The Last Grandee

R. J. Q. ADAMS (an American).

JOHN MURRAY

First published in Great Britain in 2007 by John Murray (Publishers)
An Hachette Livre UK Company

1

A CIP catalogue record for this title
is available from the British Library

ISBN 978-0-7195-5424-7

Typeset in Bembo by M Rules

Printed and bound by Clays Ltd, St Ives plc

John Murray policy is to use papers that are natural, renewable and recyclable
products and made from wood grown in sustainable forests. The logging and
manufacturing processes are expected to conform to the environmental
regulations of the country of origin.

John Murray (Publishers)
338 Euston Road
London NW1 3BH

www.johnmurray.co.uk

For Joseph and Beverly Dawson

Contents

Illustrations

The author and publishers would like to thank the following for permission to reproduce illustrations: Plates 1 (GD 433/2/101), 3 (GD 433/2/189), 32 (GD 433/2/474), 33 (GD 433/2/462) and 34 (GD 433/2/474), National Archives of Scotland; 2 and 26, © Hulton-Deutsch Collection/CORBIS; 4, 5, 6, 7, 8, 15, 16 and 22, National Portrait Gallery, London; 9, 28, 30 and 31, © Bettmann/CORBIS; 10, © Francis G. Mayer/CORBIS; 11, Harmsworth Archive; 13 and 14, City of Westminster Archives Centre; 17 and 27, © 2007 TopFoto; 18, The National Archives/HIP/TopFoto; 19, 21 and 25, Mary Evans Picture Library; 20, 23 and 24, Hulton Archive/Getty Images; 29, The British Library/HIP/TopFoto.

Preface and Acknowledgements

ARTHUR JAMES BALFOUR was born to privilege and wealth, and with the way to power – if not open – at least cleared of many obstructions. In a political career lasting half a century he experienced both rewarding successes and humiliating defeats, yet when it suited him he could retreat into a comfortable world of family and familiars, as well as of ideas – a world which, when he chose it, insulated him from the hurly-burly of public life. Other men in his time – Lord Rosebery comes readily to mind – enjoyed similar advantages of birth and talent but seem never to have secured what Balfour enjoyed for so long: contentment.

In such a long public life – more than half of it in office – Balfour showed little interest in what his fellow politicians thought of his actions, and profound indifference to what historians after his time would make of him. He did not keep a diary, nor did he make the slightest effort to preserve his private or political papers – the fact that the two collections of Balfour papers in London and Edinburgh are as large and complete as they are is due entirely to admiring family members, particularly his sister Alice and his niece Blanche Dugdale, and to his secretaries, primarily John Satterfield Sandars and Wilfrid Short.

Balfour's character and his actions have often puzzled observers, and historians and popular writers in his time and afterwards have invested much energy and ingenuity in attempting to understand him. Late in his career he joked to Ian Malcolm that he rather enjoyed praise and did not particularly mind abuse, but he added, 'I have moments of uneasiness when being explained.'[1] Too often the explanations have been misleading and very long-lived: to the historian George Dangerfield, writing not long after Balfour's death, he was in politics for the rather destructive fun, treating it as a game which he played 'with a faintly supercilious finesse which belongs to a bachelor of breeding, and with a bitterly polite sarcasm which was quite his own'.[2] The financier-newspaper proprietor Lord Beaverbrook – a gifted publicist and an amateur historian – disliked Balfour.

Straightforward Bonar Law was 'the Beaver's' hero, and the elegant philosopher-aristocrat seemed too slippery a character, neither one thing nor the other: 'Balfour was a hermaphrodite,' he raged. 'No one saw him naked.'[3]

Those who knew Balfour might have laughed at such descriptions – particularly those who served him. However, the number of authors over the past seventy-five years who have concluded that he was a cold and aloof figure, gazing down upon the world of mortals from a great height, is formidable. Leaving aside the caricatures of Dangerfield and Beaverbrook (whose perspectives and purposes were very different), it is understandable why many observers might find him perhaps a bit too much of a Brahmin. He certainly had no 'common touch', and this proved a terrible weakness in a party leader in the twentieth century. Lord Vansittart, when a junior at the Foreign Office, found it 'hopeless to avoid devotion' to him; but the suave diplomat did concede that part of Balfour's charm was that 'he viewed events with the detachment of a choir-boy at a funeral service.'[4] In an increasingly democratic century, this would just not do.

Many studies of Arthur Balfour's life and career have been written, and these are discussed in the Bibliographic Note later in this book. The reader is certainly entitled to enquire why he or she is now holding yet another. Though much effort is invested here in countering enduring misconceptions about the man, the first reason worth mentioning is that his was a life of great significance in Britain's recent history, but also it was a life of great colour and variety and interest. A philosopher, social lion and wit, he would have been recalled, though admittedly not to the same degree, even had he not become a star in the galaxy of politics. It is a noisome cliché, but true all the same, to say that he was a transitional figure in British politics – or at least that his political contemporaries were living in a transitional time. He appeared to glide quite naturally into the powerful place that seemed almost to be reserved for those of his class. This was not the whole story, of course, but it was a significant part of it. Yet later even the most high born of those who rose to the top of politics – Churchill, for example, who was the grandson of a duke – found that their background was not the advantage it had been in his time. Balfour's accomplishments and failures throughout his long political career tell us much about the development of political culture in Britain, why and how that world changed – and why the new models were Bonar Law and Baldwin, not to mention Wilson, Thatcher and Blair.

There is another, more personal, reason why I have written this book, and it is to be hoped that every biographer has felt it: the central character was a profoundly interesting man, and his story is a pleasure to tell. He was at once a proponent of science and of spiritualism, and a philosopher who was master of the ways of the House of Commons; he was 'Prince Arthur' but became 'Bloody Balfour'. His was a personality of remarkable subtlety, which some in his time and after found simply unknowable. There will be no 'definitive' biography of Arthur James Balfour – as there will be none of Gladstone or Lloyd George or Churchill. For as long as there is an interest in Britain and its past, historians will try their hands at explaining Balfour – despite the 'moments of uneasiness' this caused in his time. I have found the task irresistible.

I have written elsewhere that, in many ways, all histories are collaborations, for we all depend on others – not least on those who have come before us. We accrue a store of debt to those who have contributed to our efforts, and it is a great pleasure to record here my thanks to some of those who have helped me. First, I am very pleased to record my thanks to the 5th Earl of Balfour, to John Balfour and Michael Brander, who have provided such generous assistance to me in my researches into the life of their kinsman.

It is impossible for me adequately to thank all who have assisted in the making of this book, but I cannot fail to single out Dr Jane Ridley, the co-editor of the letters of Balfour and Lady Elcho, who read the manuscript and shared her understanding of those loving friends. With the permission of Lady Elcho's great-grandson, Lord Neidpath, I was permitted by Dr Ridley to read photocopies of the original letters. I am grateful also to Professors Thomas Kennedy and William Lubenow and Dr Frank Winters, who also read and commented on the manuscript, so much to my benefit. Other distinguished historians who have shared their insights as well as the produce of their own researches include Professors Paul Addison, David Cannadine, Nancy Ellenberger, Peter Hennessy and John Ramsden. Kenneth Rose and David Gilmour helped me to understand the complicated Balfour–Curzon friendship. I am pleased to say that several of my former research students, Dr Derek Blakeley, Dr David Hudson, Dr J. Lee Thompson, Dr David Freeman and Jeremy Dyes, now historians of important elements of politics in Balfour's time, were very helpful. For their assistance in understanding certain aspects of Arthur Balfour and his world I am grateful to Professor Hugh Freeman, Professor A. W. F. Edwards, and the archivist of Eton College, Penny Hatfield, as well as Jeremy Dyes and Peter Warburton. Three friends with whom I spent many delightful hours discussing Balfour are themselves gone – Alfred Gollin and John Grigg, dear friends for three decades, and Ewen Green, a younger friend, taken so much before his time. I am so very sorry not to be able to present them with this book. I must also add that errors of fact or interpretation are of course my own, as are those which are the result of my failing to take good advice when it is offered.

I am pleased to thank the Department of History and College of Liberal Arts of the Texas A&M University for their support during the writing of this book, and similarly Dr Robert Kennedy, now president of the University of Maine and formerly vice-president for research at Texas A&M. My work has also been aided by friends and generous benefactors of Texas A&M, including Mr Claudius M. Easley, Jr, and Mr Bookman Peters.

Without the help of professional librarians and archivists, research historians are all but helpless, and I particularly wish to thank the staffs of the British Library and the National Archives of Scotland, keepers of the Balfour manuscripts, for their assistance in my use of these and other collections. For their patience and guidance in use of the manuscript collections in their care, I am very grateful to Pamela Clark of the Royal Archives, Colin Harris of the Bodleian Library, Oxford, Stephen Ellison, Clerk of the Records, House of Lords, and Leanne Swallow, principal search-room archivist, Historical Search Room, National Archives of Scotland, as well as the late Dr R. A. H. Smith of the British Library. I am also pleased to record my thanks to the professional staffs of many other institutions I visited in my work. These include the National Archives, Kew; the National Library of Scotland; the National Library of Wales; the Bodleian Library, Oxford; the University of Cambridge Library; the Churchill Archives Centre, Churchill College, Cambridge; the Reading University Library; the West Sussex Record Office; the Wiltshire County Record Office; the Liverpool City Library; and the Harry Ransom Humanities Center of the University of Texas. My gratitude over thirty years to the staff of the Sterling C. Evans Library of Texas A&M University remains boundless.

I must acknowledge the gracious permission of Her Majesty the Queen to quote from materials held in the Royal Archives. For permission to quote from Crown Copyright materials held in the National Archives, the British Library and the National Archives of Scotland, I wish to thank the Controller of Her Majesty's Stationery Office. For their consent to quote from papers to which they hold copyright, I wish to thank Pam Arnold-Forster, Lord Baldwin, Lord Balfour, Michael Brander, Sir Simeon Bull, Edward Rory Carson, the Curzon family, Lord Derby, C. A. Gladstone, Lord Lansdowne, Lord Midleton, Lord Neidpath, Lord Salisbury, the Clerk of the Records, House of Lords, the British Library Board, the University of Birmingham and the Master and Fellows of Churchill College, Cambridge. Quotations from Winston Churchill are reproduced with permission of Curtis Brown Ltd, London, on behalf of the Estate of Winston Churchill, copyright Winston S. Churchill. Quotations from *The Letters of Arthur Balfour and Lady Elcho, 1885–1917*, edited by Jane Ridley and Clayre Percy, appear with the permission of Peters, Fraser & Dunlop Group Ltd. Every effort has been made to clear permissions. If permission has not been granted please contact the publisher who will include a credit in subsequent printings and editions.

Any American who has dedicated a long professional life to the study of a nation many thousands of miles from his own would be helpless without the generous support of British friends who have helped to make Britain a second home to me. Certainly Professor Ian and Dr Sally Craig have done that with great generosity and understanding over more than thirty years. Professors Paul Addison and John Ramsden have often opened their homes to me, and I learned much history therein. The Master and Fellows of St Catherine's College, Oxford, have welcomed me each year for decades, and I am pleased once again to record my thanks to them. In my own university, Professors Walter Buenger, Brian McAllister Linn and David Vaught have shown great support for this project and for me. Without the faith and encouragement of my publisher, Roland Philipps, and of Caroline Westmore of John Murray, as well as Grant McIntyre (who has retired from the publishing wars after a distinguished career, and who originally commissioned this book) and certainly of my literary agent, Andrew Lownie, this book would not have come about. For many years, Professor Joseph and Mrs Beverly Dawson have been loving and supportive friends through times fair and foul. I hope it will please them that this book is dedicated to them with my thanks and affection.

R. J. Q. Adams
Bryan, Texas

I

The Balfours of Whittingehame

A RTHUR JAMES BALFOUR – Arthur for the Iron Duke of Wellington and James for his father – was born in the early hours of 25 July 1848 at Whittingehame in East Lothian. 'Balfour' is an ancient name in Scotland and may have been derived from a settlement called Balfoidh in the Old Scottish, near the junctions of the rivers Ore and Leven near Markinch in Fife.[1] One Peter Balfur of Dovyn was granted lands in Fifeshire in the early thirteenth century. The name of John de Balfure appears on an assize of 1304, and his kinsman William witnessed charters by Duncan, earl of Fife, in 1331 and 1335. Balfours had fought beside Robert the Bruce at Bannockburn, and a pedigree drawn up under the authority of the Lord Lyon King of Arms traced the descent of Arthur Balfour's grandfather in direct line from King Robert II (1371–90), son-in-law of the Bruce.[2] By the seventeenth century the Balfours were established as the lairds of Balbirnie in Fifeshire, and it was a later son of this line who founded the branch that would beget the future prime minister.

This later son was James Balfour, who in 1793 embraced a fate not uncommon for younger sons and accepted exile to India to seek his fortune in the service of the East India Company. Young James laboured hard and rose quickly – by 1800 he was already deputy commercial resident in the Madras residency, but in that year he met with disaster. Virtually sovereign in the subcontinent following Clive's victory at Plassey, in 1757, 'John Company' demanded high standards of propriety among its staff to prevent further accusations of corruption such as those which had tarnished the reputation of even the Conqueror, himself. As a result of accepting an Arabian steed from a local princeling, the ardent young horseman was found to have breached Company standards and was sacked and sent home in disgrace. He had his revenge, however, for within two years he was back in India after talking his way into a fat Admiralty contract (backed no doubt with his father's influence and his capital) for provisioning all ships of the British navy in Indian waters. This was a case of a wise father knowing his own son and knowing a good investment when he saw one, for James was ambitious and single-minded and determined both to erase the stain of his fall and, of course, to enrich himself. Over the next decade he did both, as his enterprise grew from strength to strength. His early transgression was soon forgotten, and his reputation among the Anglo-Indians prospered along with his accounts. By 1812 he surrendered management of the business to an agent and returned to Scotland with a fortune reputed to have been some £300,000 – at least forty times as much in modern value.[3] He also returned with a nickname, 'the Nabob', which clung to him within the family through the generations.

The Nabob wasted no time in making his mark in Scottish and in English society. First he negotiated himself into a socially advantageous marriage to Lady Eleanor Maitland, daughter of the 8th Earl of Lauderdale; then he purchased a substantial London house in fashionable Grosvenor Square in which to keep her.[4] But he was a Scot after all, and drawn to a country seat in his homeland, so he purchased the estate of Balgonie (once the home of the bride of that thirteenth-century Peter Balfur), followed by a more rustic property, Strathconan, in Ross-shire. These were not enough, however, and he meant to build a grand house near the family seat in Fife. But Lady Eleanor would have none of it: a habitually poor sailor (as was her most famous grandson, Arthur), she vetoed any notion of regular crossings of the Firth of Forth. Hence James Balfour's eye fell on East Lothian. After a failed attempt to purchase one historic property, he reached agreement with the impoverished Hay family to buy the Whittinghame estate (pronounced and later spelled Whittingehame, as it is henceforth in this book) and its surrounding 10,000 acres.[5]

Though a striking site on the northern extreme of the Lammermuir Hills, the estate had no suitable house. So James Balfour engaged the popular architect Robert Smirke, who was midway through a career which would lead eventually to a knighthood and immortality as the designer of the British Museum. Smirke was enthralled in this period with rigidly symmetrical neoclassical exteriors, but he also preferred to work with the latest technology in building methods and materials. Hence Whittingehame House was designed in a spare rectilinear style, in what the architect termed the 'stripped cube' form, and was built of Cullalo freestone (in preference to the local red sandstone) quarried in Fife, ferried across the Firth of Forth by barge, and then transported overland by ox-drawn carts. The mansion's classical style concealed the fact that it was constructed on an iron framework, making it the first private house in Britain to be built using this technique.[6] Suitable formal gardens were laid out by the designer William S. Gilpin, lavish interior furnishings were purchased, and the Balfours took possession of the house in 1819. The Nabob clearly wished to demonstrate his success and quite probably to outshine the senior branch of the family, and there is no doubt that he succeeded in both. In its austere classical beauty, Whittingehame pleased its owner: if neither massive nor flamboyant, it was a supremely comfortable and handsome country house in which the new master could establish his line.

Little time was wasted in this latter business, as in 1820 was born James Maitland Balfour, the heir in whom resided the hopes for the future of the Balfours of Whittingehame.[7] After Eton and Cambridge, young James was packed off to London to learn the ways of business and investment, and there he fell in love and at the age of twenty-three married Lady Blanche Gascoigne Cecil, daughter of the 2nd Marquess of Salisbury. His family must have been delighted. The Cecils of Hatfield had been of supreme importance in the political life of the nation in the reigns of Elizabeth I and James I (another Scot who had done well in England). Though their political significance was perhaps not so central in the 1840s, their connections remained both formidable and up to date – Lady Blanche had from childhood been a particular favourite of the great Wellington, the godfather and namesake of her eldest son. (Wellington died when Balfour was four.) It was a remarkably good marriage, for the alliance with the Cecils offered a solid link to the considerable wealth and enormous prestige of one of England's great families, and provided sound evidence that the Balfours of Whittingehame had arrived.

The younger Balfours were married for thirteen years, until James's untimely death in 1856, and it was a happy union. The young husband possessed an amiable, affectionate and generous nature, if occasionally seasoned with bad temper; his popular bride combined gentle beauty with an inner strength which saw her through her duties as chatelaine of Whittingehame, as she became after the death of her father-in-law in 1847. And there were to be many children. The first three were daughters – one stillborn, the others Eleanor (always called Nora) and Evelyn – then on 25 July 1848 arrived the first son and heir, Arthur James. He was followed by another son (Cecil) and a daughter (Alice), and finally by three more sons (Francis – known as Frank – Gerald and Eustace). All but that first unfortunate infant grew to adulthood; two (Cecil and Frank) suffered accidental deaths in young adulthood, and the others lived long and full lives.

Following the death of the Nabob, James Maitland Balfour removed his young family from St James's Square in London, and Whittingehame became their home. By all reports he was a generous landlord and a responsible squire. As several of his Maitland forebears had done before him, he sat in Parliament as Conservative Member for Haddington Burgh, and at his own expense he equipped and commanded the East Lothian Yeomanry. He improved Strathconan, his rather primitive Highland estate, by the building of roads, the improvement of tenant housing, and the appointment of a reforming principal agent who was given orders to plough the first five years of profits of his regime into improvements.[8]

Unlike the Nabob, young James was not destined for long life, and in 1854 he fell ill with the first signs of tuberculosis, that scourge of his time. Lady Blanche, frustrated with his doctors' inability to cure her husband, soon took all nursing responsibility upon herself. Despite all efforts, his lungs grew weaker as the disease tightened its grip. In Victorian medical practice, travel was highly regarded as a restorative, and it took little to convince Lady Blanche that the cold and wet Scottish winters could do her patient little good. Hence evacuation was called for, and in the cold months of 1854–5 and 1855–6 the invalid and his family sailed for Madeira. Neither his doctor's efforts nor Lady Blanche's nursing could stem the disease, however, and in 1856 he died and was buried on the island.

Although he was seven at the time of this family tragedy, Arthur James Balfour insisted late in his life that he had almost no memories either of this illness, of the journey to Madeira – or, for that matter, of his father.[9] To become rather renowned for his poor memory, the future statesman must have been spared much pain by such a lapse. His mother, then only thirty-two, came close to breakdown. She faced more than the loss of a beloved husband after two years of strenuous efforts to stem the debilitating illness: from this point she took on primary responsibility for Whittingehame, the other family properties, her husband's various business interests and, of course, for eight children between the ages of two and eleven.

Lady Blanche did not collapse under the strain, though the demanding life she led from now on was to exact a considerable price of her own health. In his own autobiographical fragment, Arthur James Balfour noted that his first real memory was of witnessing from a window of the Turf Club the fireworks display in celebration of the victorious conclusion of the Crimean War.[10] This would have been in the early spring of 1856, and hence after the death of his father. From that point his memories of his youth grew fuller, and at their centre was always the figure of Lady Blanche – and much the same could be said of her other children, so complete was her dominion in the well-insulated little world of

4

Whittingehame. She conducted the affairs of the household with the help of two Swiss governesses (the Kling sisters), who were partly responsible for the education of the girls, and a handful of servants. There were tutors for the boys – Arthur recalled vividly only one of them, and that because he pulled the lads' ears during Latin recitations and complained of their stupidity when contrasted with his former students, the Percy boys. Finally the mistress could depend absolutely upon a companion who spent much of her time in Scotland during the remainder of Lady Blanche's abbreviated life, the appropriately named Emily Faithfull, daughter of the vicar of the parish church in Lady Blanche's childhood home at Hatfield. Miss Faithfull was adopted into the family by the children, who remained close to her for the rest of her days. A close observer recalled many years later that her arrivals for her regular visits to Whittingehame were 'red letter' days, and the days of her departure were black indeed.[11]

Even if one discounts somewhat the hagiographical recollection of her left by the Presbyterian minister of Whittingehame church, the Rev. James Robertson, Lady Blanche Balfour was a remarkable woman, possessing rather advanced ideas of parenting for her time. She had little faith in corporal punishment and believed in abundant rest, clean water, a variety of healthy foods, fresh air, and plenty of time spent out of doors. As important, she rejected the common and readily available commercial 'cures' for childhood illnesses. Most of all she relied on hands-on mothering, which included direct combat with the regular epidemics of childhood diseases which families so dreaded throughout the nineteenth century. When Arthur was an Eton boy of perhaps fifteen at home for the Christmas holidays, his mother and Miss Faithfull nursed the entire brood through a terrifying battle with diphtheria which nearly claimed the life of the second youngest, Gerald. When the danger point was passed among her own children, she turned to her staff and tenants to nurse them in their own struggles with the dreadful disease.

Lady Blanche supervised her children's education and left her idiosyncratic mark upon it, as she did with the character of each of them. It was a well-established custom of their time and class that, in addition to music, drawing and household management, girls were taught French and perhaps German in the hope that these modern tongues would be of social value in their adult lives. The education of boys, on the other hand, was centred on history, mathematics and, above all, the classical languages, Latin and Greek. When her sons became old enough, Lady Blanche left mathematics and the ancient languages to the tutors – not terribly successfully in the case of young Arthur – and set out herself to engage the faculties that children possess in abundance: curiosity and imagination. She valued literacy above everything, and taught them all to read from the earliest possible moment. Then she introduced them to modern fiction and to the French language – which she adored – through the rather unusual technique at the time of reading adventure novels aloud to them. Arthur recalled that she began with *The Count of Monte Cristo*, by Dumas *père*, then and now guaranteed to seize the interest of the young. With her eight avid pupils at various learning levels, it must have been a daunting task, but if one is to judge by the results she was quite successful. Arthur Balfour was never a master of languages, and his conversational French was always quite imperfect, yet he gratefully recorded that he learned 'to read French and enjoy it' for the remainder of his long life. It was also Lady Blanche whom Arthur credited for encouraging what became a lifelong devotion to music.

While Gerald went on to be a classics scholar and Frank to hold a distinguished science chair at Cambridge, it was history and literature which first captured the imagination of Lady Blanche's eldest son, and soon after that there was kindled an interest in technology – the application of scientific principles to worldly needs. By the start of his university days, all these would become secondary to his love of philosophy. The explanation of the development of this bookishness is one which many will find quite modern in character: with first-hand knowledge of their cleverness and curiosity and believing that reading nearly anything was superior to reading nothing, Lady Blanche coaxed her children to use the well-stocked Whittingehame library. She believed that allowing them great latitude both in what books they chose and how they read them would encourage a love of literature. Arthur Balfour wrote many years later:

> Now, I was fortunate in being born with the germs of many tastes; I was still more fortunate in the wise way in which they were encouraged by my mother. The home influences were thus unusually propitious. I read, idly no doubt, but (for a boy) I read a good deal. There was no question here of lessons. No question of finishing a book because I had begun it; or of mastering the tedious parts of a subject because there were other parts which entertained me. This easy-going procedure, no doubt, had its demoralizing side. But this was somewhat mitigated by my mother's influence. She loved good literature; she taught us to love it; and because she never dogmatized, her guidance was irresistible.[12]

Like his mother, he developed a deep affection for the novels of Jane Austen, then largely out of vogue, as well as for Dryden, Milton and Pope – all read not as components in a set curriculum but because they were sampled and then enjoyed. No doubt other icons of English literature were rejected for opposite reasons. Young Arthur, however, gave special place to the writings of Lord Macaulay – though, he points out in his memoir, he was captivated not by the great *History*, but by the miscellaneous essays, the brief vivid pictures of the past presented in helpings a bright boy could savour and digest. Here Balfour found his first literary hero, admired not for the learning but for the drama. From this point and throughout his life, the reading of history became a source of pleasure for him that might bring satisfaction to some readers of this book.

Lady Blanche – as mothers have been through centuries beyond counting – was ingenious in devising ways to occupy her children, and typically she combined motives both educational and moral. During the recuperation of the children from the diphtheria epidemic, she organized them into the staff of an in-house newspaper they chose to call the *Whittingehame Advertiser*, with Arthur and Eleanor placed in charge. The young journalists were required to gather information from the family and estate, write and submit their reports, and present the latest issue before the gathered household in evening readings. So popular was the exercise that two further volumes appeared over the next two Christmas seasons.

Lady Blanche's idea of a useful educational grounding did not consist entirely of the written word, and she also saw value in leading regular excursions into the greater world. The children were taken occasionally to village market days and shown the lives of those less fortunate than themselves, and they were allowed to attend and even to enter their own exhibits in local agricultural fairs which provided recreation for the tenantry. Perhaps the most remarkable of these expeditions occurred when the brood were still quite young, when mother and children were shepherded by the proprietor into one of the pits of the Drummond Colliery. A moment of delicious terror for the children, no doubt staged for their benefit, was provided when the lights were 'accidently' extinguished and all found themselves in inky darkness. It was not an experience which was typical among the offspring of the genteel classes.[13]

There are no particular mysteries in understanding why so many of the Balfour siblings were seen in later life to be a brilliant lot: the children were intelligent offspring of intelligent parents and disciplined by the practices of this unusual household in relative isolation. In adulthood the siblings displayed a decidedly bookish side – in addition to Arthur, the philosopher, and the two aforementioned dons, Eustace became an architect, Evelyn married a distinguished academic, Eleanor was destined to head a

Cambridge college, and even the retiring youngest sister, Alice, became a published author.

Lady Blanche was no domestic tyrant, yet her strong personality, perseverance and obvious self-sacrifice made her the absolute mistress of her household. Her withdrawal into a pious widowhood spent primarily among her children saw her household largely cut off from the social intercourse enjoyed in the days of her father-in-law or husband. In her world of retainers, tenants and dependants of various sorts, she was only rarely called upon to deal with any adult who could have been considered her peer. In the small universe of Whittingehame House, Lady Blanche was the sun, and her light fell primarily on her children – and most brightly on the eldest son. Arthur seems to have been a loving and easy child, and among the siblings he was judged to have been the most gregarious and openly affectionate.[14]

Visitors from outside the family were rare; most of the public rooms of the house were kept closed, and domestic life centred upon Lady Blanche's sitting room and the nurseries. If she lived for her children, it would be no insult to her memory to suggest that she meant the remainder of her life to be lived through them. The eight young Balfours spent much of their time in each other's company and came to form something of a closed club. To some 'outsiders' it appeared that even in adulthood, with families of their own, when the Balfours gathered at Whittingehame they were most content when undisturbed by others, seemingly dividing humanity into *us* and *them*. It is also true that, though the life of a public man required that he spend much of his time among masses of strangers, Arthur James Balfour throughout his life was most happy with his family or with groups of close friends.

A last element of the character of Lady Blanche Balfour is worth noting: she was deeply religious, but her piety was nearly unspecific in theological terms. As a Cecil, she had of course been received into the Church of England. In her youth she took a decidedly evangelical outlook, and then as a widow and mother she tended towards the Broad Church.[15] When marriage translated her north of the border she quite comfortably made herself at home among the Presbyterians. While strict adherents of the two churches had much about which to disagree, Lady Blanche brushed aside all differences as trifles. Her intense personal piety, based on commitment to good works and acceptance of what she saw as God's mysterious knowledge of how best to place each soul in the world, made her comfortable in either Church. This religious eclecticism had a profound effect on her children, not least on her eldest son. Arthur noted that 'controversial questions between the Churches, which she deemed to be of secondary importance, were quietly ignored. We were all of us christened and confirmed in the Church of England; we all of us, when at home, took part in the services of our Presbyterian Parish Church. I am to this day [he wrote a year before his death] a communicant in both Churches.'[16]

In 1866 Lady Blanche took the children to Cannes, and set 'improving' tasks for them during their travels. Then seventeen, young Arthur wrote two historical essays, one of which dealt with church governance and, in a remarkably mature voice, argued forcefully against the historical proofs of the apostolic succession. His modernism went further, as he concluded that each Church must discover its own system of authority, as 'the only way to prevent useless animosities is by providing each sect with the form of government best suited to its tastes and opinions.'[17] Balfour remained a committed theist throughout his life, but this impatience with ecclesiastical orthodoxy never left him.[18]

Lady Blanche's moral regimen required more than regular sermons on Sunday, Bible reading and daily prayers: it required activity and interaction with a world that could be made better. In her view, the nobility were expected truly to oblige, and she continued her husband's ways as an improving landlord, which they both believed at once bettered the lives of their tenants and improved the income provided by the estates. Also, she insisted with deep conviction that life for her dependants must not be all work and prayer, and she delighted in sponsoring feasts and celebrations for the entire community at Christmas, Easter, harvest time and other occasions during the year. It was at one of these that the twelve-year-old Arthur made his first halting public address, expressing the family's thanks for a season's productive labours.

Lady Blanche Balfour's life at Whittingehame as mother, teacher and unrelenting inspiration to her large brood severely taxed her limited energies, and in that century it is not surprising that she did not live to a great age. There were other costs as well. The size and relative isolation of the family and the singular place of Lady Blanche at its centre created an atmosphere in which the eight children often had to compete for her attentions. It has been suggested that this was the reason for the competitiveness and lack of sympathy in girlhood among the sisters, Eleanor, Evelyn and Alice. While the elder two married both happily and well, Alice had little good to say of most men and chose spinsterhood as Arthur's housekeeper and confidante. Small and spare like her mother, she was capable of a bulldog-like ferocity as her brother's self-appointed protector and jealous guardian of his privacy. Sadly, she became a difficult woman,

9

who possessed Lady Blanche's desire for control without her mother's natural authority or ability to have her own way. She seems to have trusted few outside the family and not even all those within it, and as a result, as Kenneth Young has written, 'In countless small ways, she contrived to make life difficult for her relations.'[19] Arthur, her life's vocation, was the exception – as he seems always to have been in the inevitable disagreements which surfaced among such a large group of siblings.

Frank and Gerald Balfour achieved marked success – the first as a scientific prodigy, and the latter in both academe and politics. Cecil and Eustace both led less than happy lives in quite different ways: Eustace's worldly achievements did not equal those of his better-known elder brothers, and he married the strong-willed, ambitious and intellectually curious Lady Frances Campbell, the daughter of the Duke of Argyll. Not without talent, he became an architect and Territorial soldier, but his life was blighted by a fondness for drink and a marriage gone sour. Cecil's was a different sort of tragedy: he was the family's black sheep. In contrast with the academic achievements of his brothers, Cecil had been a disappointment.[20] After Harrow and Oxford (rather than the path of Eton and Cambridge followed by his brothers) and a brief and hopeless business career, at the age of thirty-one he forged a cheque in Arthur's name to stave off his creditors. His elder brother extracted him from his financial difficulty, and his disgrace was kept within the family – but the price was banishment into Australian exile. As it was, he never returned, for soon after his arrival in early 1881 he broke his neck in a fall from a horse. A different sort of catastrophe claimed the gifted Francis. After a stunningly successful collegiate career, Frank Balfour was widely credited to be the most promising biologist of his generation, and before his thirtieth birthday he was the inaugural holder of a chair in animal morphology at Cambridge created to prevent his being lured away to Oxford. But he was devoted to the dangerous sport of mountaineering, then so much in vogue, and while climbing in the Italian Alps in 1882 he fell to his death.

In 1859, when all these concerns lay in an unknown future, was enacted a ritual common among boys of his class: eleven-year-old Arthur James Balfour was sent away to school. For some children it was and is a wrenching experience, though for young Arthur this does not seem to have been the case, and he recalled in his memoirs that the event, 'though accompanied by all the pains of family separation, was otherwise an unmixed blessing'.[21] He was the favoured child at Whittingehame, the eldest son and heir to its broad acres, and the acknowledged leader of the crowd of

Balfour young. His natural charm was obvious, and grew apace under his mother's indulgent dictatorship. There seems little doubt, if one is to judge by the evidence at hand, that his sense of fun was the most highly developed among his siblings – for the Balfours were generally a serious family, who achieved their air of gravity at a young age. Arthur was an apparent exception, and his self-confidence and sense of humour allowed him to be the major source of light entertainment in a household in which duty to God and man were so vigorously stressed. Yet it was also a household in which the children were indulged in many ways, and no doubt a school miles from Lady Blanche's watchful but tolerant eye might be expected to enforce a stricter regimen.

As it turned out, the young grandee had little to worry about. Balfour was to spend two years at the Grange School in Hertfordshire being 'prepped' for Eton, his father's public school. Life at the Grange reflected the personality of its principal, the Rev. C. J. Chittenden, who happened to be the brother-in-law of Miss Faithfull. The brutal bullying and rough justice common to boarding schools in that time were forbidden. The fierce Victorian heartiness which dominated so many such establishments was tempered by Chittenden's closely held values of openness, nurture and mutual respect.

Young Arthur, though he seems to have suffered no more than usual from the childhood illnesses of his time, was declared 'delicate'. In a famous phrase he noted at age eighty, 'In what, from a medical point of view, my "delicacy" exactly consisted, I have not the least idea.'[22] It may well have been that he suffered from slight anaemia, but, whatever the reason, his energy level was not that of most boys of his age. He also had rather poor vision, no doubt through common afflictions of myopia and astigmatism. This condition could easily have been alleviated with corrective lenses, but the wearing of spectacles was simply not the done thing among ten-year-old schoolboys. Whether his eyesight went unnoticed or was merely misunderstood among adults is unrecorded, and he did not begin to use 'glasses' until just before entering Eton.[23] While the short-sighted could deal with reading by holding books ever closer, the cricket pitch or the football ground must have been largely incomprehensible blurs to him, and hence positive dangers. Because of his 'delicacy' and poor eyesight, Arthur was excused from strenuous games when it became clear that his limited vigour prevented useful participation – though, Chittenden noted, 'He would *endure* a game of cricket conscientiously, as he would anything that was prescribed by lawful authority.'[24]

In the tolerant regime at the Grange, with the headmaster's acceptance

11

of Arthur's 'delicacy', he was spared certain other demands of school routine. When the other boys poured out on to the playing fields in the afternoon, Chittenden's humouring included playing the organ quietly in the hall while Balfour followed his doctor's orders and rested in his room. Balfour had many reasons to recall the headmaster with affection and respect. Chittenden loved music, literature and, above all, philosophy, and his young pupil already shared these interests. If he could not push the boy's physical development, he could cultivate his interests and coax his mind forward – and Balfour never ceased being grateful for it. Chittenden also encouraged his pupil's taste for walking, for when his schoolfellows were charging up and down the football pitch Arthur accompanied him on long rambles during which they enjoyed intense discussions. The man recalled of the boy, 'He was a delightful companion, and his conversation was more like that of an intelligent youth than that of a boy of twelve.' It was in these times that the experienced and sensitive teacher learned the way to encourage his eccentric pupil: the young Balfour revealed the primary intellectual characteristic of the man he would become. His mind worked in a way unlike that of many of his schoolfellows in that he was interested in and therefore retained only information which aided him in reducing both abstract and specific knowledge to some sort of order. It was the developing of a synthesis, rather than the mental warehousing of information, that captured his interest. While children so often seek clear and comprehensive answers, duly certified by authority, Balfour sought explanations which allowed many answers to be considered, refined and eventually made useful to his understanding of the subject at hand. Chittenden remembered it thus: 'His interest in anything he learnt varied in proportion as it gave room for reducing chaos into order.'

One must recall that the teaching method of choice of those times was to stress rote memorizing by means of repetition and, often, punishment, and the principal subjects of preparatory academies training boys for entrance into the great public schools had changed little for generations. In Arthur's case, success was mixed, at best: in his Latin lessons, prose interested him little and poetry not at all; in mathematics, also predictably, only arithmetic logic captured his mind. Chittenden recalled, 'He cared most for history, and this most in its political, social and economic aspects.' The Grange made little headway in teaching him to recall the verse of the Roman poets, but encouraged his emerging sense that a study of the past – of its ideas as well as its examples – could provide a useful source of information for bringing sense and order to the problems of the present. There seems little doubt that he thrived under the Rev. Chittenden's régime.[25]

As with all good things, Arthur Balfour's happy time at the Grange ended, and in 1861 he entered Eton College. His relaxed view of the labour of learning had qualified him only for the upper fourth form, whereas his intelligence and age had led his mother (if not his masters) to expect that he would be placed in remove, the class above it. The practice at the great and ancient school was not so flexible as that of the Rev. Chittenden, but certain modifications in normal practice were made for one so 'delicate' – he was excused the grinding memorization exercises of the 'saying lessons' of early school, for example, and upon physicians' advice he was allowed to take more rest than exercise. He was a schoolfellow of several boys with whom he was to share the centre stage of politics for thirty years, yet he seems hardly to have been acquainted with Lord Dalmeny, who as Lord Rosebery would in later life be his political opponent, or Lord Randolph Churchill, the second son of the Duke of Marlborough and a future Unionist colleague, ally and rival. An exception was Henry Charles Keith Petty-Fitzmaurice, Lord Clanmaurice and the future 5th Marquess of Lansdowne, known to intimates as 'Clan'. Clanmaurice was three years senior to Balfour, who served for a time as the older boy's 'fag', in that antiquated public-school caste system under which older boys supervised and were waited upon by younger ones. Though Clanmaurice had the reputation of being a strict fagmaster, the two got on well, and the young Anglo-Irishman and the even younger Scot established a friendship which survived into their old age.

Balfour seems to have shared the opinion of many of his masters in evaluating his own accomplishments at Eton:

> I was neither very good nor very bad [he wrote]; I distinguished myself neither in the pupil-room nor in the playing fields; I was not a hero among my fellows, nor the subject of hopeful speculation among my teachers. I had, indeed, no difficulty in maintaining an average position among my contemporaries. But I had no great desire to do more; and whether looked at from the scholastic or the athletic point of view, I was quite uninteresting.[26]

His first housemaster, Mr Birch, wrote to Lady Blanche in his first year that her son was producing work only 'among the ordinary – I do not think he is an ordinary boy.'[27] Many years later he recalled Balfour as a boy delicate in appearance, who played with books rather than studied them, and who was, frankly, rather indolent. 'Had you asked me in 1864 what I thought of his future, I should have said: "mind too restless for the frame it is set in, and he will be very short-lived."'[28] While this seems to have been an opinion shared by other masters who taught the intelligent but intellectually undisciplined boy, there was a notable exception. This was William Johnson, the man who has been called the most brilliant Eton tutor of his time. In his own student days, 'Billy' Johnson had amassed a glittering academic record at Eton and King's College, Cambridge, and he later combined his schoolmastering with a fellowship at King's. Author of the 'Eton Boating Song' as well as an admired poet and scholar, Johnson had once been nominated, though unsuccessfully, for the chair of modern history at Cambridge. As a teacher, he earned the admiration of many of the boys who grew to become Britain's great men. Sadly, he was also a sexual predator much attracted to 'boyflesh', and, after a parent found a compromising letter from the master to his son, Johnson was sacked in 1872. Thereafter he took his grandmother's surname of Cory, married, and lived quietly for the remainder of his life – though never forgotten by many of his students.[29]

It would be a mistake to underestimate the impact of this man of, in Balfour's words, 'very marked and somewhat quaint individuality' on many of the sons of the elite whom he taught. Some, for a time at least, he fell in love with, and some of these seem to have responded to his approaches. Balfour – not one of his 'beautiful' boys – seems not to have been invited to the inner circle of the 'Mousetrap', Johnson's name for his private rooms.

Whatever else he was, Johnson was a challenging instructor who was successful in encouraging and broadening the intellectual reach of clever boys not ideally suited to the rigid teaching methods of the public-school system. Balfour was such a boy, and the fact that his underachieving ways were considered a disappointment to most of his masters did not fail to trouble him. He remembered years later: 'I never supposed that my school-work was worse thought of than it deserved. But, however low I might choose to rate scholastic successes, scholastic failures wholly unrelieved by any flashes of appreciation began, as boyhood drew to its close, somewhat to discourage me, and tended to make me doubtful of myself.'[30]

Johnson offered encouragement and recognition when young Arthur needed it most, for in his upper-fifth-form half-year examinations, because of a particularly successful paper (typically of Johnson, on subjects outside the usual curriculum), the schoolmaster rated him second overall in the order of merit – which pleased the boy immensely. Few of his teachers had doubted his talent, but most seem to have pronounced it wasted, due to his indiscipline and abstract manner of thought. Johnson was the exception. The eccentric master did more, according to Balfour's second housemaster, the Rev. A. J. Thackeray, who wrote in 1901, '[Johnson] marked Arthur

Balfour as exceptional, and reported him as such to his friends at Cambridge.'[31] Another Old Etonian, Reginald Brett, later Lord Esher, remained close to Johnson and wrote to Balfour in 1887 that his former teacher continued to refer to him as 'fearless, resolved and negligently great'.[32] Balfour never forgot his debt, and wrote to Johnson's brother after the schoolmaster's death, 'William Johnson, when I was in his Division, formed a very different estimate of my capacities from that which my success in ordinary schoolwork would naturally have justified. It was an immense encouragement to me, and probably of more importance than anything else that occurred to me in those years.'[33] The encouragement may have had some effect, as under Thackeray's guidance Arthur also took another essay prize, this in English constitutional history, later in his fifth-form year.[34]

Despite all that has been said – and the fact that late in his life he rather shocked the Princess of Wales by insisting that in his day no one seemed to take note of whether classrooms were properly heated or boys adequately breakfasted – Balfour would remember his old school for the remainder of his life with affection, regularly attending the annual cricket match with Harrow and cheering lustily. This he did in 1891, when he pleaded a schedule conflict which prevented his attending a lunch for the visiting German Kaiser.[35] When the old school triumphed, Ian Malcolm added, 'there were no bounds to his exultation.'[36] Notwithstanding its failings, more than three decades after leaving Eton he said of the British system of public schools, 'In truth, it is as natural, and, therefore, as inexplicable, a growth as the British constitution itself. For my part, I am a hearty believer in that system.' However, he revealed that he remembered well what he saw as its weaknesses as well as its strengths. 'The merits of the public school are not to be adequately gauged either by the character of its curriculum or the success, however great, of scholars whom it turns out,' he declared, and the traditional curriculum, grounded entirely in the classics, he thought out-dated. On the threshold of the twentieth century, an education preparatory for university must offer greater breadth, and to Balfour this meant modern languages, contemporary philosophy and, most of all, the modern sciences.[37] This heresy against centuries of elite education would be a cause which he would never abandon, and would of course become the new orthodoxy before the end of the next century.

Eton remembered him fondly too. If he left in 1866 with few of the usual honours, Arthur was measured a success all the same. The Rev. Thackeray noted that he was sorry to see him go: 'His tastes are so refined and his conversation so much more intellectual than that of most lads his age, that I shall miss him much as a companion.'[38] His mathematics master added: 'Arthur leaves Eton with great dignity – & much respected.'[39]

With those days behind him, he set out for the larger world of Cambridge, as there had never been any doubt that he would: his father had been a Trinity man, and so should he be. He arrived shortly before the onset of Michaelmas term 1866, with his uncle and friend Lord Sackville Cecil, child of his grandfather Salisbury's second marriage and almost exactly Arthur's age. As James Maitland Balfour had done in his day, the two took their places as 'fellow-commoners', a status long since obsolete, which – in return for paying higher fees – granted the right to wear a short blue gown trimmed with silver, rather than the normal black of most undergraduates. They enjoyed two other special privileges: the guarantee of college rooms for their entire Cambridge careers (Balfour's were at the corner of New Court adjoining the library and facing the famous lime avenue) and the right to dine at high table, 'on a chair instead of a bench', unlike their peers.[40] To Balfour the latter was a priceless gift, for it gave him access to regular informal conversation with the college dons, something which would otherwise have been impossible. While it was usual for the fellow-commoners to arrive for dinner moments after their elders and file in to take their places at the foot of the high table, Balfour ignored precedent and frequently arrived early in the hope of enjoying the talk among some of the best minds Trinity had to offer.

Balfour found that Cambridge suited him, and the mixture of relaxed academic discipline and an exciting intellectual atmosphere gave him great pleasure. As he entered manhood his stamina improved; he grew stronger, and during his university years the delicate boy became a handsome, slim and athletic young man standing over six feet tall. Furthermore, his improved vigour (and the wire-rimmed spectacles he now habitually wore) made it possible for him to enjoy athletics, and he took up the ancient game of tennis – that is, court or royal tennis, not the outdoor game (which he came to love even more, but which was not to be invented for another decade).

He was also fortunate in his tutors, who included such well-known Cambridge figures as Joseph Prior and Percy Hudson, and he joined an informal seminar gathered around the Trinity philosopher Henry Sidgwick, who was destined to figure greatly among the Balfours. Also among the Trinity dons he befriended Frederic William Henry Myers, who would gain fame as the author of *Human Personality and Its Survival of Bodily Death* and, with Sidgwick, would fire the undergraduate's early interest in the paranormal. The talented young scientist John Strutt, also of

Trinity, became one of Balfour's closest friends for the remainder of his life and, like Sidgwick, would one day become his brother-in-law.

Like many youths before and since, Balfour thrived in the heady atmosphere of university life – and one of the principal reasons was that he was thrown together with a wide variety of contemporaries with whom he discovered he shared interests. Through his love for philosophy, music and sport, Balfour for the first time in his life acquired a large circle of friends among his peers, including George Darwin, another devotee of court tennis and the son of the great evolutionary biologist. Other new friends were Walter Durnford and Spencer Lyttelton, as well as Arthur Kinnaird and Hugh Elliot, with whom he was accused by a policeman of maliciously pulling the doorbell of an unpopular don. The young gentlemen were called before the Cambridge police court and fined twenty shillings for the 'crime', which all emphatically denied.[41] Kinnaird shared a more serious Hebridean adventure with Balfour and another Trinity man, Reginald MacLeod, when the three insisted on sailing in Rob Roy canoes along the coast of Skye, then following a portage inland, eventually across the sixteen miles of open ocean to the Isle of Rum. Balfour admitted years later that the scheme was certainly 'harebrained', for the shallow craft could hardly have been less appropriate for even a short sea voyage. The adventurers survived, however, and continued to tell the tale for the rest of their lives, and in his fragment of memoir Balfour noted with joy that at least two of the canoes, including his, remained in use throughout his life.[42]

In an early draft chapter of the *Autobiography*, Balfour referred to his study habits as 'slipshod', by which he meant that he read and wrote largely what he wished and freely mixed his interests – developing not only his knowledge of philosophy, but sampling history, literature and music – without concern for order or method.[43] Music had captured him, and growing up as he did in a house in which it was always valued he willingly submitted to piano lessons in childhood and mastered musical notation. Yet, despite the good-natured derision which it earned from family and friends, he took up a far humbler instrument: the unprepossessing concertina. At one time he owned four concertinas, which he dubbed 'the infernals', and throughout his youth he played them daily, coaxing from the simple reeds and bellows not merely the customary light airs that might be expected, but the themes of Bach, Mozart or the composer to whom he would be devoted for the remainder of his life, George Frederick Handel.[44]

Few of the friendships which he formed at Cambridge proved so intimate or long-lived as those with the two young dons Strutt and Sidgwick. John Strutt, later 4th Baron Rayleigh, was just six years Balfour's senior and had only recently taken up his fellowship at Trinity when the future politician arrived. He was widely touted as a 'coming man' – a prediction that proved fully accurate for a future head of the Cavendish Laboratory and Nobel laureate – and he would encourage the younger man's interest in science. Balfour credited him with opening his eyes to the importance of scientific research to the health, prosperity and security of Britain – a cause which he pursued throughout his political career. The two became known among intimates in those years as the 'Cambridge Inseparables', and remained friends until Strutt's death in 1919. Friendship became a family tie when Strutt married Balfour's sister Evelyn in 1871.

In the young ethicist and political economist Henry Sidgwick, Balfour found a mentor 'who, by accomplishments and temperament, was ideally qualified to give me exactly what I needed, exactly in the way I most needed it'. Sidgwick was by nature a questioner who resisted playing the role of authority for his pupils; a born enemy of dogma, he encouraged the inquiries of students rather than merely sending them away with received solutions. Remembered as one who 'loved truth more than victory', he readily acknowledged the value in his opponents' objections to his own positions and struggled to understand them.[45] Sidgwick was most comfortable in small and informal discussions in his college rooms – just the sort of environment that Balfour found most comfortable and in which his intellect could shine. It was a fortunate happenstance that brought the two men together, for, despite divergences in philosophical matters, teacher and student were mutually encouraging of one another's inquiries. As in the case of the scientist, Strutt, Balfour remained friendly with the philosopher for the remainder of his life, and they shared many interests beyond the world of books – not least of which was the opening of higher education to women. This came also to be a passionate cause of Eleanor Balfour, and after she married Henry Sidgwick, in 1876, the two found their lives' work in creating Newnham College.

Balfour's time at Cambridge was not, of course, limited to tennis and philosophical discussions. Though Cambridge, town and university, was in those years a shadow of what it would become, it already provided the music-loving young man with entertainments which, after the isolated rustic life of Whittingehame and the Grange, must have seemed generous. The university has for centuries been rich in choral music, but there were also chamber performances and the occasional opera – both forms of music which would become favourites for the balance of Balfour's life. As a freshman, he joined the amateur dramatic society and also began his life-long passion for collecting beautiful things (beginning with blue china, which he displayed in his rooms). From his earliest days at Trinity, on Sunday evenings he began to host in his rooms a regular circle of friends, meetings recalled fondly by one regular for 'his excellent claret, with much talk of men and books'.[46] Apparently there was little talk of politics. The son of an MP and nephew of a future prime minister, Balfour joined but did not frequent the Union and the other usual venues of young men of political ambition. It has been suggested that this may have been because his maternal uncle, Robert Cecil, then Lord Cranborne, was in temporary eclipse on account of his violent opposition to Disraeli's Second Reform Bill. Perhaps he simply found parliamentary life a dull game for dull men, as he wrote when just twenty to his sister Eleanor in 1868: 'The first result of the new Reform Bill has been to elect a stupider 650 and odd gentlemen than having ever met in Westminster since the memory of man.'[47] Whatever the reason, there was little room for politics at this point in his life.

Balfour's early interest in the paranormal, no doubt stimulated by the interest of scholars such as Myers and Sidgwick, was keen, and he seems to have joined a group called the Cambridge Ghost Society. Today this would be seen as something entirely frivolous, if not worse, but the nineteenth century was unaffected by the modern world's casual and even sophisticated intimacy with science. Such arcane forces as electricity and magnetism must have seemed little short of magic to many, and it appeared to others as though the powers of science and the human intellect might bring enlightenment regarding the mystery of the next life as they seemed to be conquering the secrets of this one. The Christian faith that Balfour had imbibed at his mother's knee assured him of the existence of life beyond the earthly realm, but his confidence that the living could make contact with the Other Side stopped short of certainty. His curiosity was sincere enough, however, and was shared (and surpassed) by Eleanor and Gerald, who later joined him in founding the Society for Psychical Research, still Britain's most important agency for such inquiries.

It seems odd that Balfour did not gravitate to the Apostles, the justly famous Cambridge Conversazione Society. The secretive club, founded in 1820, was limited to twelve undergraduate members at a time (elected only upon invitation) and dedicated to good conversation about any and all subjects that interested them. Past members included his Eton masters William Johnson and the celebrated 'O.B.', Oscar Browning; also, Henry Sidgwick was one of the most admired of 'angels' (as Apostles referred to those former members who had completed their degrees and hence 'taken wings'). One of Balfour's closest undergraduate friends, Alfred Lyttelton, was an Apostle, as later were his own brothers Frank, Gerald and Eustace. 'Reggie' Brett, another member – contemporary of the three younger Balfours – who would become an intimate of Arthur, wrote to a friend of his university days, 'Arthur used to be looked upon as a curious relic of an older generation, with affectionate pity. I could see his brothers', Frank and Gerald, brotherly patronage extended to him mentally, when he used to come down to Trinity on a visit.'[48] It would appear that one of the causes of his being passed over by the society was his commitment to a Christianity 'of a queer undefined sort', in Brett's words, in a time when many intellectual young bloods tended towards agnosticism. The Apostles were a self-anointed progressive elite of achievers, and Balfour must have appeared to them indolent, conservative and stodgily orthodox. Whatever the reasons, he was not invited to lend his conversation to the society – an oversight that Browning noted years later as one of the greatest mistakes the group ever made.[49]

After three pleasurable years, in 1869 Balfour faced the Moral Sciences tripos. Moral Sciences was then a new honours school, combining modern philosophy and political economy, which had been recently inaugurated by Sidgwick. Balfour had little choice but to be one of the first to pursue this degree, for he had slight interest in the poets and philosophers of the ancient canon and insufficient mastery of Latin, Greek or mathematics to face the traditional examination fields. He much enjoyed reading history and declared that his respect for classical learning was immense, 'But what in fact interested me was not the past, but the present and the future. It was the clash of beliefs held by modern men about the universe, as modern men in their various ways feel driven to conceive it; and naturally, there-fore, it was with modern beliefs that I wished to begin.'[50] His view would not change for the remainder of his life, and, unlike many parliamentary colleagues of later years, he seldom embellished his speeches with quota-tions from the classics in their original languages.

He faced the daunting examinations with his usual relaxed approach, interpreting the papers in ways that suited him and dealing with only the authorities which captured his interest. He always wrote slowly and painstakingly, and, in a century when books were fatter and speeches longer, he valued brevity as a high virtue. Throughout his student days, when he was satisfied that he had written what he wished on any essay topic he stopped, feeling no need to parade whatever other learning he might have possessed. His performance in the tripos, his examiners agreed, merited only a respectable second-class degree. Sidgwick was obviously dis-appointed, and explained to his pupil that it was not the quality of his papers that prevented a higher classification, but rather that there simply was not enough of it. This seems to ring true, given the nature at this time of Balfour's method (or lack of it) in applying his talents. He professed no particular despondency over the result (though 'certainly I should have preferred a First, myself'), but it must have stung.[51]

Not the least important reason for disappointment was that there would now be no offer of a fellowship, and his Cambridge idyll was over. If it had ended differently, if there had been a first followed by a fellowship, as in the cases of his brothers Frank and Gerald, it is quite possible that Arthur Balfour might have been remembered as a distinguished academic rather than a statesman. Had the opportunity presented itself, it is very likely that he would have snatched it. As with many an undergraduate before and since, university life had charmed the twenty-one-year-old completely. In years to come it was not unusual for Balfour, given his dual life of politician and amateur philosopher, to face the question of whether he had chosen the proper order of precedence, with politics as his vocation and the contemplative life of ideas as his avocation. Lady Blanche, as usual, had a strong opinion, for when her son announced at about this time that he was considering the life of a scholar, she replied, 'Do it if you like, but remember that if you do, you will find you have nothing to write about by the time you are forty.'[52] As it was, Balfour produced his last book long after his fortieth birthday. And she was quite correct in the real substance of her remark: her son was likely to have grown bored with academic life long before old age. In fact, Arthur Balfour never lost his passion for metaphysics, and he was swept into politics almost as a birthright. But it enriched his existence to combine the great game at Westminster with a parallel intellectual life as separate from it as is possible to imagine.

In the summer after taking his degree Balfour came into his inheritance, and to mark the great occasion fêtes were held at his principal estates. At Whittingehame a French chef was brought in to prepare the feast, and many Balfours, Cecils and Maitlands were welcomed to dine with the entire tenantry of the estates, as well as neighbours and district notables, at vast outdoor tables.[53] The trustees of his inheritance, his uncles the 3rd Marquess of Salisbury (as Lord Cranborne had become) and his father's brother, Charles Balfour, as well as local dignitaries and representatives of the tenantry, offered speeches to the five hundred guests, to which the young laird responded. All were lustily cheered, and it was reported that a grand time was had by all. In his old age, Balfour recalled this long-ago event: 'It is, I think, just sixty years since I went through a coming of age.

I didn't much like it – there was too much speechifying; and I was shy. I have spent most of the intervening years in making speeches, and would doubtless still be making them if an all-wise Providence had not intervened with my voice. But I am still shy; so the infirmities of old-age have their good side.'[54]

The huge change in the value of money since that time makes it difficult to gauge the size of his newly inherited wealth. However, given that he now possessed the acreage and buildings of the Whittingehame and Strathconan estates and a number of other agricultural properties – more than 180,000 acres – as well as the body of assets and investments founded by his grandfather and supplemented by his father and guardians, he became one of the richest young men in Britain, with an estate worth perhaps as much as £4 million – more than sixty times as much in modern reckoning.[55]

In the following year, at a cost of £20,500, he purchased the lease on the London house which would be his home in the capital for the next sixty years, 4 Carlton Gardens, St James's.[56] Designed by John Nash and built in 1830, the street takes its name from Carlton House, the former mansion of the Prince Regent, pulled down in 1827. The row is separated from the clubs of Pall Mall (built soon afterwards) by what remains of the greenery of Prince's Gardens, and to its back the ground falls away to the Mall and St James's Park. It is a comfortable walk to Buckingham Palace or the Houses of Parliament. This parade of houses has sheltered many of Britain's notables – Balfour's house, for example, had once been owned by Lord Palmerston. In Balfour's time William Ewart Gladstone was his near neighbour, and later Lords Curzon and Kitchener and the 9th Duke of Devonshire had houses nearby, as did 'the Squire', Henry Chaplin, later Balfour's Cabinet colleague. A brisk ten-minute walk from Carlton Gardens would have taken one at various times in Balfour's long occupancy to the homes of Lords Salisbury, Cranbrook and Rosebery, Lord Randolph Churchill, Sir Stafford Northcote, and many others. Estate agents advise their clients that the most significant single factor in the marketplace is location. In political terms, Carlton Gardens could scarcely have been better placed.

With manhood also came sadness, however. Lady Blanche's health was already failing by the time of her son's coming of age, and in May 1872 she died at the age of forty-seven. Frequent childbirths and a demanding life had taxed her far from robust constitution. She developed heart disease, and her last two years were hard – given her nature, it is difficult to gauge whether the pain or the inactivity of an invalid's life was more telling on her. As she had done when nursing her dying husband, she fled the winters of the Scottish Borders for the South of France, though she spent much of her final year as an invalid in her London house in Belgravia. Quite characteristically, she left instructions for a simple funeral and was laid to rest at Whittingehame. Arthur had been her favourite, and he seems not to have exaggerated his feelings when he recalled near the end of his own that all the debts he had accumulated throughout his long life, 'compute them how you will, are as nothing compared to what I owe to her love, her teaching, and her example'.[57] Arthur James Balfour possessed an enviable lineage; he had passed a happy childhood, and enjoyed a remarkably painless education. Now he possessed the independence that came with wealth, youth and intelligence. He was the master of his own fate in a sense that only a few young men would ever know.

2

Young Gentleman

B Y THE TIME his university days were over, Balfour's self-imposed regimen of long walks and court tennis had turned the 'delicate' boy into
a strong and fit young man. He would always enjoy the company and the
conversation to be found at the elaborate dinners which the Victorians
adored, but he ate and drank in moderation – not least of all because he
was repelled by the idea of taking on the rotund shape so common among
gentlemen of this time. Balfour also took up a commission in his father's
beloved yeomanry regiment – which provided him in future years with
fodder for self-deprecatory tales of his limitations as a soldier, though he
certainly looked appropriately gallant in uniform.[1] From the outset of his
London life he patronized a good tailor, bootmaker and barber, and he cut
a handsome figure among the elite of the great capital.

His was a typical Balfour face – the forehead broad and high, the nose
straight and narrow, with prominent cheekbones, deep brows and pointed
chin. His thick hair was dark and curly, and, in the manner of young men
of his generation, he oiled and parted it at the side before a few years later
adopting the more familiar centre parting. Even before leaving Cambridge
he grew the moustache he wore throughout the rest of his life, and lush
side whiskers he did not. Despite years of good-natured abuse by his
mother and sisters, his posture was often careless, and he adopted a sort of
sprawl when seated. In the days of his fame, this became a gift to political
cartoonists.

A handsome man, as were all the Balfour brothers, he took such great
care in his appearance that close friends and family sometimes chided him
for his vanity. In these days he habitually wore the stiff collar and four-in-
hand cravat which were the convention of his sex and class and had not yet
adopted the soft collar and simple black crossed tie which he came usually
to wear. In his good black broadcloth, immaculate white linen and carefully
brushed spats, he appeared – and was – a well-bred, wealthy and very
eligible young gentleman. With his impressive breeding added to the mix,
London society soon took notice of him.

Throughout his life Balfour took great interest in his personal environment, and he never seemed to tire of the redecoration and restoration of his houses (his sister-in-law Lady Frances recalled, 'he would never hear of Utility being subordinated to Preservation'). In this expensive pursuit he was enthusiastically aided and abetted by his architect brother, Eustace.[2] Characteristically, before taking occupancy, he arranged for a thorough renewal of the forty-year-old Carlton Gardens property. The house met several requisites: it was well located in Westminster, and it provided space for a large music room and a generous and very private sanctum for its new master. Further, it offered broad expanses in its public rooms for entertaining and for the display of the pictures and art objects which he meant to acquire. Pleased with the prospects, he took occupancy even before redecorating was entirely complete. Sadly, the bedroom and sitting room prepared for his invalid mother were never to be occupied by her and ultimately came to be the domain first of his eldest sister, Nora, and then of Alice, successive housekeepers to their bachelor brother. His London home for the next six decades, No. 4 today boasts two commemorative plaques, but neither bears his name.[3]

He was always as much a countryman as an urbanite, and some of his earliest and fondest memories were of his country estates, Whittingehame and Strathconan.[4] Soon after coming of age he added to these properties the picturesque thirteenth-century ruin of Hailes Castle in East Linton – famous for its connections to the Scottish wars of independence, to the unfortunate Queen Mary Stuart and to the struggle against Cromwell – for the enormous purchase price of £131,000, selling several smaller Scottish holdings to raise the needed funds. Ultimately, despite his wealth, he could no longer justify the costs of maintaining two country estates, and he was forced in 1885 to lease and then finally to sell Strathconan. He retained Hailes in unaltered form until 1926, when he presented it to the nation.

Arthur Balfour's fortunate situation meant that he possessed the priceless luxuries of time and leisure. At eighty he recalled his life of sixty years earlier:

> I saw something of London society; I heard a great deal of music; I played (court) tennis at Lord's with much enjoyment and some improvement; I invited friends to Whittingehame; I visited them in country houses; I travelled; in short I did the sort of things that other young men do whose energies are not absorbed in learning or practising their chosen professions. I had at that time *no* chosen profession; I had, indeed, no dominant occupations, unless I may apply this honourable description to the habit of

miscellaneous reading . . . or to the meditations intermittently pursued though never abandoned, on the best way of giving effect to my philosophic ambitions.[5]

He always had time for companionship. Throughout his life he attracted and enjoyed the company of circles of close friends – circles in which he invariably occupied the centre. So had it been in his Whittingehame childhood and at Cambridge, and so would it be in the wider world into which he was now successfully launched. It was at this time that he was happily absorbed into a made-to-order clique of the younger generation of the Lyttelton–Gladstone family, a connection which began with his friendship at Cambridge with George William Spencer Lyttelton, son of the 4th Baron Lyttelton. The two young men shared much in common: both came from large county families, shared a deep religious faith and gloried in music (and both had younger brothers who were Cambridge Apostles, though they themselves were not). Spencer Lyttelton's father had in 1839 married Mary Glynne in a double ceremony in which her sister Catherine became the wife of a promising young politician, William Ewart Gladstone. Both couples were to raise large families – the Lytteltons eventually had twelve children, and the Gladstones eight – who formed a close-knit, boisterous and immensely talented company into which Balfour was welcomed from his first visit to the Lytteltons' Worcestershire house, Hagley. He was at home with large families, though this good-humoured and often unruly tribe presented a marked contrast with his more orderly siblings. Lady Frances recalled of the young Balfours, whose family she had just married into, 'They were all older than myself and were old for their years, with a gravity and sedateness I could never hope to emulate . . . [An] austere reserve kept them silent on subjects in which we [her own Campbell family] were vociferous.'[6] How different the young Lytteltons were, and Balfour found them absolutely enchanting. The fact that the Balfours were Conservatives and the Lytteltons and Gladstones Liberals seemed completely unimportant.

The Lyttelton brothers' athleticism rivalled their intelligence – all became celebrated cricketers, and in their student days were members of the Eton side that faced Harrow and of Cambridge versus Oxford; the daughters' intellects were of a similar quality, if their other skills were on a less boisterous plane. Visitors noted that the remarkable music which habitually filled Hagley was as worthy of note as the deadly accuracy of the missiles launched in the bread fights (with Lord Lyttelton as likely as not the principal target) which were prone to erupt at family meals –

something it is certain Arthur never experienced at Whittingehame in Lady Blanche's time. In all, the Lytteltons were quite unlike anything he had ever encountered, and he liked them from the outset; visits between the young of Whittingehame and Hagley were soon exchanged on a frequent and regular basis. Since Balfour's London house was but a few yards away from that of W. E. Gladstone, a kind of unofficial London headquarters for the cousinhood, it was easy for the new friendships to thrive.

Of this period of Arthur Balfour's life there exists a remarkable record in the recollections of Gladstone's third daughter, Mary, one of four close friends among this formidable group. 'Us four', as they called themselves, were Balfour, Mary Gladstone and her cousins Spencer Lyttelton and his sister Mary (always known as May), and above all else they shared a deep passion for music. Those critics and admirers alike who in later years came to see Balfour as an aloof, intellectually superior and somewhat imperial personage would without doubt have been stunned had they seen the youthful friends – with Balfour as the unofficial jester of the group. His advantageous birth allowed him to do precisely as he wished, and what he wished in the early 1870s was to attend every possible concert, ball and country-house weekend, and to insist that his friends share his fun.

Mary Gladstone's record of the time describes all this, and the rather reserved and talented daughter of the four-time Prime Minister came in rapid succession to be curious, then fascinated and eventually deeply in love with this dazzling youth who shone so brilliantly in this colourful company.[7] It was his humour, his 'grand sense of the ridiculous', that shattered her feeble resistance. She attended Balfour's impromptu luncheon party in his coach at the annual Eton–Harrow cricket match in 1871, and recalled:

> [He invited everyone] he knocked up against right and left, till the party swelled to gigantic size. Spencer and I were jammed up at the end, 10 others inside, 5 on the box, and others about the wheels and steps of the carriage. Our host was in mad spirits, shouting choruses [of Handel] between acts, hatless, with a handkerchief round his head, hair flying all over the place. We had great fun, and were very sorry when we had done.[8]

Even in the days of his fame, Balfour had an uninhibited gift for self-mockery which sometimes reached nearly theatrical heights. At this stage of his young manhood he was already conscious of his poor memory for the details of everyday life – names, dates and events of all sorts – a characteristic which was due more to his habit of dismissing from his mind things which simply did not interest him than it was to any cerebral malfunction. Though not uncommon, in his case it was remarkably and sometimes embarrassingly pronounced, and in later years he enjoyed disparaging his poor gift of recall in comparison with contemporaries like Lord Rosebery or Bonar Law (two who seemed to Balfour never to forget anything at all). Similarly, Balfour entertained his friends with tales of what he insisted was his hopeless indecision. More than once he reduced groups of friends to paroxysms of glee by insisting that he could not decide whether to descend from the first floor by the left or right of the two great staircases of his London house – both of which, of course, led only to the same destination. His self-caricature as an indolent young grandee apparently always managed to provoke laughter among his intimates, both at and with this talented performer.[9] The hint of truth behind the joke seems to have made the self-derision all the funnier. His memory was undisciplined, and, while he could hoard in his brain masses of complex ideas, he often simply did not bother to remember specific information and, even worse, frequently confused facts and left it to others to sort them out as they chose. He *was* capable of maddening indecision, and when the mood was upon him his mental and physical lassitude confounded his intimates.

It was his ready intelligence and the privileges of his birth, as well as his personal gifts – the vaunted Balfour charm – that allowed him to pay close attention only to what interested him. The lolling figure of Arthur Balfour, MP, sprawling on the front bench, legs outstretched and eyes drooping, was in part a performance – protective coloration meant to lull opponents into overconfidence. As a political neophyte learning his craft in the Commons, he used it for protection: it was meant to show him as of little consequence and thus undangerous. What lay behind it – then and even later, when he was considered one of the most formidable debaters of his age – was the fact that most of the hours he spent in the House both bored and fatigued him. His mind sought occupation and challenge, and boredom was always the enemy. His poor memory, his ambivalence and indolence, such as they were, were largely rooted in his resistance to fixing his concentration on things which did not engage him.

While still a young man with a world before him, his new friends certainly did engage his interest, and they were invariably prepared to enjoy his idiosyncrasies. 'Us four' were constantly together in those carefree years, in a time when Balfour seemed as likely to be found in the Gladstone house as his own. This suited the great Liberal and his wife, for they too were captivated by their charming young neighbour and apparently encouraged their daughter's friendship with a young man so splendidly qualified as a potential son-in-law.[10] Mary loved him almost from the first: she finally admitted to her mother, 'I do not indeed think I could have helped it[,] for I have tried very hard not to let the feeling grow.'[11] In this she failed, but what good were her efforts before a man whom she insisted 'has but to smile and men and women fall prone at his feet'.[12] Balfour certainly cared for Mary – for her intelligence, her humour, her kindness and of course her love of music. However, he did not love her. There was, Mary was certain, a relatively simple explanation: Balfour loved her cousin, May Lyttelton.

May was nineteen when in 1870 her brother Spencer first brought Balfour to Hagley. She was tall, with masses of dark curls and a stately beauty beyond her years, and her intellect and quick humour rivalled Balfour's own and set her apart from the usual crop of debutantes. In fact May was already more experienced in love than her friends, for by the time she met Balfour she had given her heart to twenty-nine-year-old Edward Denison, a much admired young MP, who already enjoyed her father's approval. An engagement might have been expected, but Denison's health broke down, and he died before this could be arranged. In a cruel jab of fate, in 1872 it happened again as May once more fell in love, this time with Rutherford Graham. The son of a wealthy Glasgow businessman who was a patron of the Pre-Raphaelite painters, Graham was a handsome Oxford undergraduate with a somewhat raffish reputation. Lord Lyttelton was troubled, and insisted that the young lovers remain apart for a year before he would consider a match. Young Graham meant to wait out his exile in America, but on the eve of his departure he was struck down with diphtheria and died after a brief illness. May was disconsolate, her usual vivacity evaporated, and for a time she disappeared from the small circle of boisterous music-lovers.[13]

After almost a year of near isolation May re-emerged, and Mary Gladstone could not fail to note that close attention was being paid to her pretty cousin by Balfour. What might have come of this will never conclusively be known, for tragedy again intervened: at only twenty-five, May contracted typhoid fever and died on Palm Sunday 1875.

Though some historians have accepted the idea that the future premier fell in love and even proposed marriage to May, conclusive proof from the two parties is absent. There exists not one contemporary letter by him indicating such an attachment; nor did May – who appears to have kept no detail of her various infatuations from her cousin Mary Gladstone, or her siblings – indicate that she was in love with him, much less a possible engagement. May's diary testifies to her love for the unfortunate Graham, but not for Arthur Balfour. There are tempting hints from his side, however. In December 1874 the two were among the guests at Lord Chesham's Christmas house party at Latimer, and it is sometimes said that there he expressed his deep feelings for her. This he may have done, but Balfour apparently mentioned nothing of this to his sister and lifelong confidante, Nora; nor did he mention it to his brothers, to his Uncle Salisbury, or to May's brother and his own intimate friend Spencer Lyttelton. This was one of the last times the young couple would meet, for, though May fell ill in January, Balfour seems to have visited her only once in that month – exceedingly curious behaviour for an ardent suitor. Similarly, the loquacious May did not speak in more than a most oblique way of anything that passed between her and Balfour, even though she lived for almost another three months.

The evidence which is frequently cited in support of the tragically romantic tale comes from two sources: one was Lavinia Talbot, May's elder sister and the wife of the Rev. Edward Talbot, warden of Keble College, Oxford, and future bishop of Winchester. Mrs Talbot's recollections many years later indicated her belief that in 1874 Balfour had approached her sister – if not directly confronted her – with the subject of marriage. She recalled that 'there were words on his part which made May have little doubt what they were intended to mean.'[14] After Balfour's death she wrote to Blanche Dugdale, who enshrined the tragic tale in her 1937 biography of her beloved uncle: 'It would have been best if he had proposed to her then, but he was in deadly fear of a refusal, and thought he had spoken quite plainly of his attachment, and would propose at the next opportunity.'[15]

Balfour himself was the other source, though he left clues of the possibility of such plans only well after May's death. Cited frequently was the undeniable fact that he arranged for a keepsake to be buried with her. He learned of May's death from a letter written on the sad day by Edward, another of the Lyttelton brothers, which closed with words hardly suitable for a lover: 'You knew her as well as most and I thought it best to forestall the newspapers.'[16] Balfour asked Edward secretly to place in May's coffin a small emerald ring which had belonged to his mother. Lyttelton complied, and wrote two days later, 'I have done as you asked . . . I have told no one about it except Edward Talbot and his wife, as I was a little puzzled at first.'[17] Edward Lyttelton seems to have asked no questions, and took the secret of the emerald ring with him to the grave.

The Talbots believed that a betrothal had been in the making, and it is clear that Balfour encouraged them in that belief. Years later Lavinia Talbot testified of his being 'staggered to the last degree' by the death, of his having described how he disconsolately wandered the streets of London after hearing the news, and of his deep despair at the funeral service on Maundy Thursday. She also recalled that upon leaving the church after the service he confided to her alone that he had just witnessed the interment of his intended bride. On the sad Easter Sunday which followed, Edward Talbot wrote to console Balfour that if the sadness they shared offered any grace it would be found in their drawing even closer together in friendship – and so they did. For some years Balfour spent part of each Eastertide with the Talbots, and during a visit they made to Whittingehame he spoke of the planned architectural innovations he would have made in the event of his marriage to May.[18] Yet it remains that there is no confirmation that he disclosed any intention to wed before May's death in 1875. Edward Lyttelton, Balfour's agent in the episode of the emerald ring, thought it entirely appropriate to inform him that a loan which Balfour had made to him some weeks following May's death would be used for a visit to the Grahams, the family of her former beloved.[19]

The reason for the mystery may lie in Balfour's being too shy to mention his love and his hopes for May at the time. Perhaps he was so deeply shocked by the tragic death, that he simply could not speak of his desires to others. It is possible that he had never really made his intentions clear to May. There may be another reason entirely: it may be that he never had such a purpose, and employed the agency of the Talbots – who cared deeply for both the young people and wished for a romance to have existed – to act as repositories of a tale that was entirely illusory. A myth of a tragic youthful love could be an excellent means by which an eligible young man who wanted no part of marriage might avoid it entirely. The internal evidence is interesting. There is no doubt that Mary Gladstone deeply loved Balfour before, during and after their friendship with her unfortunate cousin, and a letter to him two years after May's death, now lost, had apparently made this clear. Balfour's reply throws some light on the inner man. He did not mention May Lyttelton or any lingering effect her death might have left. However, he made it clear that the usual exchanges between lovers were impossible for him:

> The only and sole reason why I have not answered your letter was that I knew it to be absolutely impossible that I could express myself in such a manner and to make it worthwhile to do so, or indeed so as to be anything but absurd. To some people it comes, I believe, quite easy to say what they feel on the subject about which they feel a great deal: with me it is not so. I cannot talk, I can still less write, about such things: and therefore can, if it pains you, that such should be the case I hope you will bear with me. I will only add that your letter was & is of the most pathetic interest.[20]

One cannot but wonder if such a man would or could propose marriage, as Mrs Talbot suggested. It is worth pointing out here that, in the years which followed this letter to Mary Gladstone, Balfour's feelings on the subject of commitment did not change. He was merely a fond friend to Miss Gladstone, but he did love another, later in his life. To this woman, Mary Charteris, Lady Elcho, he wrote nearly twenty years later in response to an apparently explicit love letter:

> Your last letter gave me a little pain – but not very much, for I understood the reasons which moved you to write it. Yet I do not regret that I said nothing in my last epistle of the kind which perhaps you wished. Such things are impossible to me: and they would if said *to* me give such exquisite pain, that I could never bring myself to say them to others – even at their desire. Moreover if I am to speak all my mind, the mixture of topics of this kind with shooting invitations, bicycles, cures for obesity and current literature, is to my mind positively repulsive – though I think that in this respect I may be singular. I return the letter.[21]

As for marriage he came right to the point in another letter: 'Whether I have time for *Love* or not, I certainly have no time for *Matrimony*.'[22]

It might be argued that these later obviously painful confessions to these two women were an outcome of the tragic experience with May Lyttelton, but that does not ring entirely true in the light of his behaviour. Why did he not visit May during her obviously serious illness? Then, following the death which supposedly wounded him for life, why did he not mourn as a lover might be expected to do? Soon he was accepting social invitations in the usual way, even to breakfast – a meal which typically he was loath to share as a social occasion – with May's uncle, W. E. Gladstone.[23] He did not stop his joyous concert-going with his friends – including a music-filled trip to Düsseldorf in April, shortly after May's funeral.[24] Then, despite having launched his political career only the year before, he and Spencer Lyttelton set off together in August 1875 on a six-month journey during which, despite their close friendship and connections to May, he seems to have made no mention of her. True love is a curious thing, and young love in which death intervenes is catastrophic to the survivor. It is tempting to embrace the conclusion that the deep wound caused by this tragedy explains the singular life Balfour chose afterwards. His affection for May Lyttelton was genuine, but the idea that he planned a marriage – or that he would have been accepted – while attractive, is only speculation. It seems no less possible that the cruel turn of fate provided him with a shield to turn away annoying questions as to why he never chose a conventional domestic life. It is unlikely that we shall ever know more.

At all events, life went on. Balfour and Spencer Lyttelton had enjoyed each other's company on a brief holiday in Greece and Egypt almost two years before, but their 1875 round-the-world tour was a far more ambitious undertaking.[25] Balfour was a terrible sailor, and remained seasick and bedridden throughout their Atlantic crossing. Their North American itinerary took them from New York City to nearby Lake George and Niagara Falls, neither of which overly impressed the travellers, and then by Pullman car to Chicago, and across the Great Plains to San Francisco – for which the young men also expressed no particular enthusiasm. Lyttelton reported that his companion spent more time reading than sightseeing, though Balfour emerged long enough to be enthralled with the giant California sequoia forests, which he never tired of describing for listeners.

Conversely, he seems to have made a greater impression on the American frontier than even he realized, if one is to believe the tale printed jn a Texas newspaper decades later. According to this journalistic scoop, Balfour returned to Wilbarger County, Texas, in 1884 as a special agent of the Cunard Steamship Company. Posing as a cowboy with 'a wide brimmed hat, boots and the never missing handkerchief of rainbow hue about his neck' and with a 'huge, old-fashioned Colt [pistol], swinging at his hip, bang [ing] the saddle as he rode', he supposedly had been sent to apprehend an embezzling shipping agent. This he is said to have done, then riding off into the sunset in a style worthy of a true Wild West hero. Sadly, Balfour seems to have been nowhere near Wilbarger County, Texas, in 1875 or 1884. If he had ever been a covert agent of the Cunard Company, it remains an unverified secret. But the year 1884 is rather well accounted for, and there were no further voyages to America, and no ten-gallon hats or Colt pistols in evidence. Would that there were.[26]

From San Francisco the young adventurers sailed for New Zealand. There, travelling in miserable weather by coach or on horseback, they spent much of their time cold and wet (and more than once wired London for additional funds), yet Balfour seems to have been more taken with the largely unsettled landscape than he had been with the cities and geographical wonders of North America. Near Christchurch he purchased a sheep run, and unlike the majority of his investments, this annually turned a modest profit for the remainder of his life. In November they continued on to Australia, and by Christmas they sailed for Singapore. There the adventure was cut short, however, when word reached them that Eleanor Balfour had become engaged to Henry Sidgwick; so the travellers – tanned,

33

hardened and exhausted, with a lifetime's worth of tales – embarked for home. Balfour had seen much, and had learned that travel did not suit him. Though he had covered more of the world before the age of thirty than most statesmen of his era would in several lifetimes, this expedition would be his last journey abroad – save for brief holidays to France and Austria – for more than forty years.

Having survived his epic journey, Arthur Balfour preferred to direct his energy in the late 1870s towards the reading and writing of philosophy. This led to the publication in 1879 of his first book, *A Defence of Philosophic Doubt: Being an Essay on the Foundations of Belief*, which he later recalled as 'from a personal point of view the most important event' of this period of his life.[27] The mode of thought and expression that dominates the work is typical of him in that it is concerned as much with ideas contrary to his own as it is with his own conclusions – less didactic than it is dialectical and argumentative.[28]

His subject was the struggle between science and religion in the post-Darwinian intellectual world. Early in the book the young philosopher announces boldly that his essay is intended to be a 'destructive criticism', but – and he argues as a convinced religionist – destructive not of science itself, but of its overzealous defenders who had concluded that religion had had its day and in so doing had substituted their own new faith, which Balfour termed 'Naturalism'. The book's 350 pages therefore encompass spirited attacks on the English empiricists who drew their inspiration from Mill and their 'evidence' for the rejection of theism from their observations – for Balfour, poor stuff on which to base a 'scientific' philosophy which purported to have solved the mystery of the First Cause. The optimistic positivists, and their guide, Comte, suffer as badly, and likewise the transcendentalist Kantians. The 'doubt' of his title was, of course, directed not at theism but towards modernist – Naturalist – intolerance.

Modern 'scientific' philosophies, he contended, were flawed first by their blind confidence in their own fallible methods and, second, by their failure to accomplish what they promised: their own scepticism, he insisted, could deny but could not disprove the existence of God. For Balfour, who doubted neither God nor science, the Creator had not been dethroned, but nor had the author any desire to invalidate science in its own sphere. Instead, he levelled his fire at those so blinded by their own certainty that they did not see what was to him the obvious symbiosis between science and religion. His complaint was aimed at what he judged to be a kind of scientific 'fundamentalism' which utterly rejected theism and, if unchecked, seemed bound to sweep away the moral foundations of society. He explained:

> If the reader, in the interests of speculation . . . feels inclined to complain of the purely destructive nature of the criticisms contained in the preceding pages, I reply that speculation seems sadly in want of destructive criticisms just at the present time. Whenever any faith is held strongly and universally, there is a constant and overpowering tendency to convert Philosophy, which should be its judge, into its servant. It was so formerly, when Theology ruled supreme; it is so now that Science has usurped its place: and I assert with some confidence that the bias given to thought in the days of the Schoolmen through the overmastering influence of the first of these creeds was not a whit more pernicious to the cause of impartial speculation than the bias which it receives at this moment through the influence of the second.[29]

He did not argue for a world in which religious belief denied science, but mankind could not progress in understanding if its enthusiasts made science into an intolerant orthodoxy. To denude the world of religious belief was to make a society that embraced a view of existence which promised in the end only death – of the individual and, in time, of the race itself – and nothingness. In this and all his later philosophical writings it was clear that he believed as he did for at least two reasons: without the existence of a godhead the world made no sense – there could be no truth, no logic, no value – and, furthermore, recognition of this required no torturous exercise of faith or reason but only 'common sense'. However, he feared he was swimming against a powerful tide, and wrote to Lady Elcho years later that the book's conclusions

> are repugnant to most people, because they are antagonistic not only to what we all as a matter of fact *do* believe, but to what it is impossible but that, in our ordinary moments, we *should* believe. Mankind gets not unnaturally rather impatient when they are told, through a whole octavo volume, that there is not the slightest *reason* why they ought to accept as true the most certain conclusion of science and the most solid teaching of common sense![30]

A Defence of Philosophic Doubt was published by Macmillan in an edition of only 1,000 copies 'at the author's risk'. The book is elegantly crafted, though comprehension comes only with careful reading, and it received a handful of generally approving notices, as well as a short and generally positive discussion in *Mind* by Professor John Caird of Glasgow University.[31] However, the first book by a young amateur achieved only a modest impact outside a small circle of thinkers. The author sent copies to a number of philosophers whose works he admired and whose comments he solicited, and also 'perpetrated to be sent' a copy to Gladstone, then Leader of the Opposition. He then received letters of congratulations on its publication from notables such as Asa Grey, Frederick Pollock and Sir Leslie Stephen,[32] and a long, largely epistolary friendship with the Scottish philosopher Andrew Pringle-Pattison resulted when the two met at the Edinburgh Philosophy Society soon after the book appeared.[33] Balfour's publishers maintained the book on their list for several years, though it sold only in small numbers. He eventually arranged for its reprinting, 'without any alteration of text or paging', in 1920, when to his amusement his then fame ensured a brisk sale. As these words are written, more than a century later, it is once again in print.

Though confirmed in his bachelorhood, Balfour led a far from solitary life. There was always plenty of time in his life for family, and he insisted that as his siblings married and had children of their own, all should continue to view Whittingehame as their home. Even when there were no brothers and sisters or nieces and nephews enlivening his existence, a growing circle of friends ensured that he was far from lonely. He delighted in their frequent country-house weekends, or 'Saturday-to-Mondays', at the Elchos' Stanway, the Astors' Cliveden, the Cowpers' Panshanger and, of course, his own estates. He had always been fascinated by competitive games, and this combined with his enjoyment of outdoor exercise when his heart was captured by golf, so appropriate to a loyal Scot. Even earlier, he took up another game, which appeared in 1874, called Sphairistike, which used the equipment of court tennis but was played out of doors on a strange hour-glass-shaped court. This rapidly evolved, of course, into the more familiar lawn tennis. He was introduced to the game in its early days by the daughters of Lord Chesham during a house party at Latimer, and played it with great pleasure and skill for the next fifty years.[34]

Balfour did not take up golf until the 1880s, owing in part, he explained, to 'the fact that I spent the critical years at schools and University, which in those days of darkness . . . knew nothing of golf, and [I] had no opportunity of practising it'.[35] The game was not yet the international obsession it would become, and was not much played outside Scotland. Balfour noticed it during one of his autumn visits to Bradbury's Hotel in North Berwick, where he regularly exiled himself for solitary and restorative quiet, reading and writing. He tried his hand, and, like many before and after, instantly fell in love with the game. With his handicap in his prime hovering around ten, golf soon became a regular part of his North Berwick retreats: he played a full round each morning and another in the afternoon on one or another of several courses in the district. He was particularly adept with the putter, but a long-time golfing companion noted that in those days of niblicks, mashies and brassies his greatest assets were his concentration and his placidity in the face of disaster: 'Usually when he made a bad shot, he turned away & gazed over the Fife, & then turned round smiling!'[36] A few months before becoming prime minister, he found time to comment to the journalist E. B. Iwan-Müller on the fascination of the newspapers with his play: 'My records at golf have been somewhat magnified by the Press. But as I do not contradict the many falsehoods which they say *against* me, I have not thought it necessary to make a solemn protest on one of the (in my opinion) rare occasions on which they exaggerate my merits!'[37] His native East Lothian was to him always 'the paradise of golfers; and Whittingehame lies at its centre.'[38]

There was also in Arthur Balfour a generous helping of the same fervour which burned in the breast of the immortal Mr Toad of Toad Hall, for it seemed no new technological contrivance failed to provoke his attention or his desire. Like Salisbury's, his London house boasted electrical and telephone service as soon as they were available, and he purchased one of the first gramophones in Scotland. In time, he would leap at the chance to become an early passenger in both a submarine and an aeroplane. His passion for the automobile, once it appeared at the turn of the century, became legendary, and he became the first prime minister to possess one. But at this time in his life those modes of transportation lay in the future, and his fascination for mechanics was centred on the bicycle. The reasonably workable 'penny-farthing' bicycle appeared in 1870, and a chain-driven two-wheeler with functioning brakes – the 'Safety' bicycle – appeared not long thereafter. Balfour soon became an avid cyclist, and remained one for many years, and most of his siblings shared his enthusiasm – as did his uncle Salisbury, whose age and girth restricted him to a three-wheeler, rather like a gargantuan child's tricycle. So fervent was Balfour that he regularly took his 'bike' with him when travelling, and he shocked the elderly W. E. Gladstone in 1896 by arriving at Hawarden Castle on two wheels, having pedalled from the railway station.[39]

His passion for music remained with him as well, but after the hectic youthful chasing about with 'Us four' it came to be expressed with a bit more adult decorum. He became a subscriber to the Saturday and Monday 'Pops' concerts at the St James's Hall and the popular orchestral series at the Crystal Palace, and he frequently arranged for professional musicians to perform for his guests at Carlton Gardens. More often than not, these evenings featured a composition by Handel, his perennial favourite. Handel's music captivated Balfour, and he published an essay about him in 1887, and at twenty-five he underwrote the cost of presenting the first complete performance in forty years of the composer's oratorio *Belshazzar*, at the Royal Albert Hall.[40]

He indulged another passion as he began in the 1870s to establish an enviable art collection in his London house. He was particularly drawn to the Pre-Raphaelites, then at the peak of their fame, and engaged his particular favourite, Edward Burne-Jones, to produce a series of pictures based on the legend of Perseus. The rôle of art patron was not for the faint of heart or pocketbook, as the painter's original estimate of the cost was £4,000.[41] As it was, the series of six canvases was never completed, though four eventually hung in Carlton Gardens.[42]

His love of books and his eclectic taste in authors were well founded in youth and did not diminish in manhood. His tastes broadened, though he never abandoned Jane Austen, always his favourite. He believed that art was born and grew to suit its time, and there was no snobbery in him concerning fiction. He developed, for example, an insatiable appetite for detective fiction, a genre born not long before Balfour himself, and became devoted to the works of Conan Doyle, which began to appear in the 1880s. His love of biography and history also remained with him for life, as did his interest in reading science literature – and, of course, always philosophy. Though he tried his hand at it in youth, thereafter he read no poetry, and his reading in the fine arts was confined to music. And, though he would come to develop useful connections to important journalists, he never tired of insisting that for newspapers he had no time at all.[43]

Balfour endeavoured to set aside a part of most days for reading and often for writing, but, as his political career prospered, this became increasingly difficult to arrange. Writing gave him pleasure, but the process always progressed slowly, and at times painfully. His handwriting was terrible and grew steadily worse with age, and he depended upon secretaries who could transform his scrawls to readability. Eventually he accustomed himself to giving dictation to a shorthand writer. A severe critic of his own words, he wrote slowly and pored over early drafts, habitually editing and recasting until he was more or less satisfied with the result. This was invariably a tedious and extended process. However, his satisfaction in the final polishing of his prose was great, though he was never fully content with the end product. Ian Malcolm, who served as his amanuensis during his years as Foreign Secretary, later recalled Balfour saying to a friend, 'What pleases me most is to write something quietly by myself – to touch it up and to complete it with a feeling that one has done one's best.'[44]

His reading and even his writing often took place in the inner sanctum of his bedroom: he seldom appeared in the morning before 11 a.m., though unlike Winston Churchill – another famous late riser, with whom he is sometimes compared – he did not usually write or dictate in his bed. Balfour took to heart the advice he had been given in his school-days: to apportion his energies with care, with time set aside for quiet thought and rest. To some this appeared to be unalloyed indolence, as Ian Malcolm recalled:

> Some supposed that this was a form of laziness; others that it was necessary to rest his back, and I know not what else. But, in reality, it was none of these things. It was the overwhelming desire for a period of undisturbed soli-tude during some period of every day which he declared was 'good for the soul'. In that quiet time apart, he did all of his best thinking, made up his mind and crystallised his conclusions on the important problems that waited upon him for handling or solution.[45]

Balfour carefully guarded his private hours. When he grew older and was often surrounded at Whittingehame for weeks at a time by several gen-erations of the Balfour clan, servants as well as visitors, siblings, in-laws and even the regiments of nieces and nephews who adoringly swirled about him whenever possible, all knew better than to disturb him before he emerged from his bedroom. Typically, only his secretaries were admitted, and then only when summoned.

Certainly much that has been said about the routine of Balfour's life thus far cannot but sound idyllic to modern ears, and it is true that his com-fortable lifestyle freed him from the servitude of income-chasing that shaped the lives of the many. Yet it is also true that when he entered poli-tics at the age of twenty-six he took up an unpaid career in service to an exceedingly demanding master. It seemed quite natural that a talented young patrician in those days, unsure of what to do with his life, should drift into public life at the prompting of a powerful uncle who could pull as many wires as necessary to ensure that the door was open to him. Certainly Lord Salisbury had long been an important influence on the fatherless youth – second only to Lady Blanche – though less as a surrogate father than as a wise older brother. Eighteen years Balfour's senior, Salisbury cared much for his precocious nephew, and strove to nurture both his character and his ambition. The method he chose appealed enormously to young Arthur, for he avoided lecturing the lad but, instead, conversed with him from his Eton days as he might with another adult, 'with no flavour of patronage, no tactful manipulation of the subject-matter, to mar the impression of conversational equality'.[46] Though eventually two of Salisbury's sons would enter Parliament, it was Balfour who became his political heir.

Yet it was not merely an uncle's suggestion that set Balfour's foot on the path that eventually led to Downing Street, for he had begun to consider it even before a significant luncheon at the Cecil home in London's Arlington Street, probably in the late summer of 1873.[47] Salisbury reminded his nephew that the sitting Conservative Member for Hertford intended to stand down at the next election.[48] The Cecils commanded wide influence in the borough, which was virtually in the shadow of Hatfield House, and a victory could be expected for the candidate they favoured. The Marquess suggested strongly that Balfour had much to offer and that his privileged birth made his responsibilities great. He invited the young man to offer himself as candidate, and Balfour accepted, he recalled, 'without hesitation'.[49] Politics was to be his chosen career – if politics would have him.

A public life for Balfour was virtually there for his taking: Salisbury's word was good enough for the local party, and they adopted him as the Conservative candidate. He waltzed through the 1874 general election unopposed after offering a twenty-three-line election address and a brief speech at the Hertford Corn Exchange. This latter oration – his first polit-ical speech – he dreaded more than any other in his long life, and he cited as reasons his poor 'verbal memory' and his lack of any talent for popular rhetoric. The political rostrum was not his natural home, but, with two franchise reform acts passed and more to come, popular politics was more than ever destined to reward the platform spellbinder. Debate, however, was entirely another matter, for Balfour had grown to manhood in a highly articulate family circle in which argumentation was the indoor sport of choice. But politics was a game played increasingly beyond the walls of the Palace of Westminster, and his early speeches could not hide his un-familiarity and anxiety with the set-piece address. Throughout his career he had to guard against the tendencies towards speaking too long and straying down intellectual byways that led him from his primary points, and with these tendencies he would have to struggle if he expected to make a suc-cess of his political life.

To this point, life had been easy for Arthur Balfour, but now he faced a world in which birth, wealth and brilliance were not rare, a world governed by demanding rules, with painful penalties for failure. He would have to school himself in the ways of public speaking, parliamentary debate and the chemistry of party practice. In increasingly democratic politics, Britain proved to be no different from other nations: electorates are most comfortable with aspirants to power whose drive is masked with disarming language but whose ambition can be counted on to keep them hard at their tasks. Naked ambition generates distrust, but a complete absence of 'push and go' ensures failure. It remained to be seen whether Arthur Balfour, MP, duly enrolled as a follower of the great Disraeli, possessed either.

The signs at first did not seem particularly encouraging, as soon after his election he embarked on his round-the-world travels, and on his return he committed much of his time and energy to the completion of *Philosophic Doubt*. However, he responded to the chiding of his Aunt 'Georgie' Salisbury, who reminded him in the spring of 1876 that, with his third session in the House looming, it was time to show some 'overt signs of Parliamentary activity'.[50] What was called for was a maiden speech – that frightening initial performance which all new Members face as they show their wares to colleagues and opponents alike. It finally came in August, and it was a carefully calculated affair: according to Balfour's telling, he chose the highly technical and 'intrinsically dull' subject of Indian currency – a little-known topic which he had meticulously studied well in advance. He carefully selected a time when the House was nearly empty, at the traditional dinner hour.[51] Few of the parliamentary stars were present, and the Chamber was left to the not-yet-known and the perennially obscure who hoped for a chance to say a word that would appear in Hansard: 'They wanted an audience,' Balfour recalled. 'I on this occasion wanted none.'[52] And he got none. But, though his learned plea for bimetallism passed nearly unnoticed, it was delivered to his sparse audience without any major gaffes. At least it could be said that he had been launched.

After a brief and markedly unsuccessful intervention a few months later in which he daringly introduced (and, after a predictable hammering, almost immediately withdrew) an amendment to a university bill to allow the granting of academic degrees to women, Balfour did not speak again for the remainder of the session. Still uncertain in his new trade, he thought that was quite enough calling attention to himself for a while. He became a regular attender, seated just below the gangway with another uncle and mentor, Alexander James Beresford-Hope (who had vigorously opposed his nephew's recent amendment), and remained generally silent.

Beresford-Hope had married Salisbury's sister Mildred, and was MP for

Cambridge University. 'Uncle James' was very close to his nephew and acted as his teacher and adviser in the ways of the House, with frequent winks and nods revealing the coaching and encouragement that the veteran offered the tyro. That eagle-eyed observer of all things parliamentary Sir Henry Lucy observed of the older man a few years later, 'He watches over him as a hen hovers round its last surviving fledgling.'[53] Beresford-Hope was considered a rather progressive Conservative, but he was also a fierce defender of the prerogatives of the Established Church, and this caused another rare (if good-natured) division between them. For in April 1878 Balfour brought his first bill before the House, to amend the ancient law which empowered Anglican clergymen to demand that Dissenters be interred in churchyards only if the burial service of the Established Church was employed. Since secular or Dissenter burial grounds were not always available in the towns and villages of England, this was a cause of bitterness among non-Churchmen which Balfour, whose devoutness did not include a rigid commitment to liturgy, thought easily enough remedied.

He was much mistaken: though a Churchman himself, he failed to reckon with the depth of feeling on all sides of the question. Balfour discovered that many Nonconformists raged against Anglican control of churchyards as part of a greater campaign against all the entitlements of the Established Church. Their interests were little served by such a half-a-loaf reform – better to keep all irritants intact and feelings high. Defenders of the status quo sought absolute rejection of his bill in order to discourage any hope for a broader attack on the Church's prerogatives. Wise Salisbury warned him in characteristic language, 'A very good Bill – if men's minds were in a temper to take good Bills . . . But if you bring it in you will probably find [yourself] fully protected from the curse which attaches to those of whom all men speak well.'[54] The bill did not survive its second reading, being talked to an early death by none other than his doting Uncle James – a useful lesson for a young politician.

More pressing in the minds of parliamentarians in 1878 was the so-called Eastern Question, the Victorian euphemism for the continuing crisis caused by the desire among the Great Powers to hasten the Sick Man of Europe – the Ottoman Turkish Empire – to his grave and divide the leavings. Certainly Salisbury, now India Secretary, was interested. After an unsuccessful conference of the Powers in Constantinople in late 1876, war between Turkey and its most appetitive neighbour, Russia, became inevitable – and, not surprisingly, Russian armies were within sight of Constantinople by the end of 1877. This resulted in the humiliating Treaty of San Stefano of March 1878, which left the Balkans largely in the hands of Russian client states, with the eastern Mediterranean potentially under Russia's sway – and the balance among the uneasy Great Powers in shreds.

At precisely the same time, the hopelessly irresolute 15th Earl of Derby vacated the Foreign Office, and Lord Beaconsfield (as Disraeli had become in 1876) appointed Salisbury in his place.[55] The Marquess recognized the menace of Russian ambitions towards India and the Near East, and informed the Powers that, if the Russo-Turkish treaty stood, it meant war between Britain and Russia. The result was the Congress of Berlin, under the chairmanship of the self-anointed 'honest broker', the German Chancellor, Prince Bismarck. Salisbury attended as Beaconsfield's second-in-command, and he took Balfour with him as his private secretary.

The Foreign Secretary detested such ceremonial affairs. Balfour, on the contrary, enjoyed the opportunity to sample the elaborate theatricality of the great occasion – despite the embarrassment, due to the tardy arrival of his luggage, of having to appear at his first state dinner in borrowed and ill-fitting evening clothes. The hewing of a workable treaty he watched from a discreet distance, being charged as he was only with minor tasks such as deciphering telegrams and delivering Salisbury's most confidential messages – leaving him, he soon found, rather bored and with limited amusements in a rather cheerless capital where most spoke yet another language he did not know. He met all of the grand figures in attendance and remembered particularly the reception at which he was presented to the great Bismarck, who enquired if he was related to that Balfour of Burleigh 'who plays his part in Sir Walter Scott's *Old Mortality*'. Denying close relationship (and suppressing the information that the 'part' was mere fiction), he complimented the statesman on his knowledge of the iconic Scottish novelist. Balfour was delighted by the reply: '"Ah," said the Prince, "when we were young we all had to read Sir Walter. *He was considered so very proper*."'[56] In the end, with Salisbury's help, Beaconsfield returned bearing 'Peace with Honour', and Balfour came home with relief. All the same, he found his first experience on the world stage an intoxicating experience he would never forget.

In fact this was the apogée of Beaconsfield's government, its popularity draining away because of high taxation, a faltering economy and an electorate whose taste for the grandeur of imperialism was for the moment wearing thin. At the same time, an aged and infirm prime minister seemed unable or unwilling to provide a forceful lead. What may have been worse was the fact that Gladstone – whose hasty retirement after his 1874 defeat had served simply to recharge his political batteries – now re-emerged into national politics with his legendary Midlothian Campaign, flaying the government for its abandonment of the Christians of the Ottoman Empire. At the top of his form once again, he hammered the Conservatives over the conduct of the bloody Zulu War and the 'forward' policy in Afghanistan – policies, he thundered, devoid of both morality and success. The dazzling performances by the seventy-one-year-old Gladstone energized the Liberals, while Tory hopes sank. By the spring of 1880 time had run out, and the ensuing election soon proved disastrous for Conservatives.

Balfour's contest in Hertford took place early in the balloting – for elections before 1918 were still spread over several weeks – and he conducted his campaign from his headquarters at the town's principal inn, tellingly called the Salisbury Arms. The seat proved to be not quite so 'safe' as it had seemed in 1874, as a spirited challenge was offered by a Harrow schoolmaster, Edward Bowen. In what he recalled as a 'severe' struggle, Balfour held Hertford by 164 votes – almost exactly, one observer slyly noted, the number of houses that Lord Salisbury owned in the borough.[57] He was honoured to be invited to speak in hostile Midlothian in support of the sitting Member, Lord Dalkeith (son of the Duke of Buccleuch, the local magnate) in his campaign against Gladstone himself. The honour had its limits, however: his audiences were quite Gladstonian in temper, and Balfour made few converts. But there were not many Conservative MPs with local connections to whom Dalkeith might have turned. After the election it was worse: the Grand Old Man (universally shortened to 'GOM') captured the seat, and the north was nearly swept clean of Tories.

The election was a crushing disappointment for the Conservative Party, which was out-polled by the Liberals by more than 400,000 votes; 116 seats were lost, giving Gladstone and his allies a majority of 115 over their principal rivals and 52 over all parties in the Commons. From London, Balfour wrote rather flippantly to Salisbury of the palpable depression at the Carlton Club, the Conservative headquarters then in Pall Mall only a few steps from his front door: 'Nobody talks of anything but the elections and nobody says anything worth hearing about them. The only excitement is to walk into the Carlton to see what our last loss has been, and even that by frequent repetition is losing its edge!'[58] Salisbury's reply illustrates his own deep unease over the change of political climate:

> The hurricane that has swept us away is so strange & new a phenomenon that we shall not for some time understand its real meaning. I doubt if so much enthusiasm & such a general unity of action proceeds from any

sentimental opinions – or from a new academic judgement. It seems to be inspired by some definite desire for change: & means business. It may disappear as rapidly as it came: or it may be the beginning of a serious war of classes. Gladstone is doing all he can to give it the latter meaning.[59]

Beaconsfield, five years Gladstone's senior, retired to the Buckinghamshire countryside and died within a year, leaving his party leaderless, demoralized and facing a rejuvenated enemy. Balfour's political education was about to enter its next phase, as the Conservatives settled into the role of Loyal Opposition.

At thirty-two, Balfour now had a career which required a commitment unlike any he had encountered in his comfortable life, and it was also at about this same time that another corner in his life was turned. Not long before the election he made the acquaintance of Mrs Percy Wyndham and her son and daughter, George and Mary, while attending a musical evening at the home of the painter Sir Frederic Leighton. Like Balfour, the Wyndhams were patrons of the arts, though unlike him they had about them (like Leighton, for that matter) a slight bohemian air, which also characterized the circle who gathered in their estate, Clouds House, near Salisbury. The paterfamilias, Percy Wyndham, MP, commissioned his 'modern' house (which soon burned to the ground and was replicated on the site in every detail) from the architect Philip Webb, a champion of the Arts and Crafts movement; mother Madeline befriended artists of many sorts, painted and potted, and rather scandalously smoked cigarettes in public. Their unorthodoxy was leavened with wealth, charm and spontaneity, however, and Balfour liked them from the first. When they met, George was sixteen and Mary seventeen (Balfour was thirty-one), and in their own ways each began at that moment to fall in love with Arthur Balfour. George – another adored elder son – was also destined for politics, but his promise went unfulfilled, and his career would end in failure. Mary's bond with Balfour would last the remainder of his life, and begs for more explanation.

Mary Wyndham was a striking young girl, tall and athletic, if the least conventionally beautiful of three famously lovely sisters, and even in her teens she possessed a presence imbued by the self-confidence instilled in her by her remarkable parents. She was immediately drawn to Balfour, and wasted no time on coquettish shyness in the presence of the promising politician fourteen years her elder. Madeline Wyndham was a purposeful woman with three daughters to navigate through the marriage market, and she saw the handsome Anglo-Scottish aristocrat as a highly desirable potential mate for her Mary. It also seems that Mary required no particular encouragement from her mother. Balfour, who throughout his life took delight in the company of bright, pretty and outgoing girls and young women, was also attracted, but he was not to be landed easily. With her motherly duty, Madeline could not wait for ever, even if her daughter might – and soon another option hove into sight.

This was Hugo Charteris, Lord Elcho and eldest son of the eccentric 10th Earl of Wemyss and March, who had been Robert Lowe's comrade-in-arms in parliamentary opposition to the 1867 Reform Bill. Hugo was another highly eligible prospect, if hardly a determined suitor, but his wooing was constant enough and his intentions transparent. Despite Mary's hopes, Balfour steadfastly refused to propose ('If only you married me in '81,' she lamented fifteen years later).[60] Finally, with Hugo willing and Balfour not, Mary Wyndham and Lord Elcho were betrothed. They married in 1883, and in that year Hugo also won election as MP for Haddingtonshire, once the seat held by James Maitland Balfour. By the expectations of their social class, the marriage was successful, lasting more than fifty years and producing seven children; but in such marriages there was room for flexibility. Mary's relationship with Balfour continued to grow more intense after her marriage, and she also enjoyed other amorous adventures. Hugo, for his part, was true to her in his fashion, which allowed for a number of romantic liaisons as well as two long-term extra-marital love affairs. Yet all was done with the discretion for which their caste was famous, and their loyalty to each other survived Mary's increasingly idiosyncratic behaviour and her passion for Balfour, as well as Hugo's love affairs and his hopeless financial incompetence.

Balfour's relationship with Mary – Lady Elcho, as she was until 1914, when she became Countess of Wemyss and March – evolved from friendship to intimacy and finally to interdependence over a period that spanned five decades. They saw much of each other, and became central to that glittering pre-First World War social set known as 'the Souls'. The two exchanged hundreds of letters – Balfour's newsy and witty but always punctiliously correct; Lady Elcho's playful, intimate and sometimes passionate.[61]

Many observers have been satisfied to accept that Balfour was essentially sexless – or at least comfortably celibate.[62] It seems undeniable that his aversion to expressing the usual intimacies reserved for lovers did not weaken since the days when he had dashed the hopes of Miss Gladstone – as he demonstrated in that anguished 1894 letter to Lady Elcho quoted earlier. The closest he seems to have come to a conventional love letter reached

Mary in January 1895, when she was engaged in a risky liaison in the Arabian desert with the poet Wilfrid Scawen Blunt: 'Think of what you would like best to hear,' Balfour wrote, 'and have faith that that is what I should like to speak.' But did he speak it to her – ever? If he did, he certainly could not write it. Yet the intimacy between Balfour and Mary Elcho was more than epistolary – Mary noted fondly in 1906, for example, her memory of their 'f–rst k–ss'.[63] His surviving letters (originally to 'My dear Lady Elcho' and later 'My dear Lady Wemyss', while hers for years addressed 'Dear Mr Balfour', though both eventually abandoned any salutation) give no explicit indication of their activities – if any letters ever did, they have been destroyed or lost.

In recent years it has become known that the two shared a taste for mild sado-masochistic sexual excitement, and that this seems to have taken the form of rôle play.[64] Mary, who sometimes decorated her letters with rather mischievous drawings, wrote to him daringly in 1907, 'I must send you a valentine tonight . . . the Valentine objects are somewhat obscure – to the left is a birch rod, to the right a brush and a tin of squirting grease (smells of peppermint!).'[65] These she drew in the margins of the notepaper. Two years earlier she had written to him from Paris, 'I saw a representation of a young ladies school at the theatre Thursday – it reminded me, not that it in any way resembled it, of our school – the one I have aptly named and rather wittily named "the finishing school" – certainly, in many respects you gave that poor young girl a "liberal education" and left no regions of her little body! unexplored, after that night there will have been few surprises left for her.'[66] There are hints that rôles may even at times have been reversed.

It is hard to doubt that Balfour had sexual needs that led in a direction that Mary Elcho was pleased, even anxious, to follow. It is difficult to say how far the relationship went beyond a furtive kiss at teatime, 'when statesmen made love' on the afternoons when the House rose early. She wrote to him a year before his death, as he was dictating his memoirs, to remind him of times long past. It may be surmised that she referred somewhat enigmatically to the occasion on which they first became lovers: 'Early 1887, you became Chief Secretary for Ireland and shortly before that, in the same year, a small very private incident (gear changing!) took place in yr downstairs room at 4 [Carlton Gardens] – me 25, you 39 – but you won't describe this incident in yr Memoirs important tho' it was . . . and so on . . . and so on . . .'[67] The timing seems right: in 1887 he was about to go to a troubled and rebellious Ireland as Chief Secretary. His life would certainly be in danger, and another newly appointed Chief Secretary had been murdered by terrorists in Dublin only five years earlier. It does not overtax the historical imagination to wonder if he and Mary might have become lovers on at least this one occasion, and this raises the possibility that the 'gear changing' event might have been repeated. Yet it is also true that all of this does not constitute an undeniable proof. Whatever may have occurred, the two were satisfied enough with their intimacy to maintain it for half a century.[68]

As he made ready to go to Ireland, Balfour left a letter for his sister-in-law, Lady Frances, relating 'to a matter with which only you can deal', and with it a sealed leather pouch containing another note, to be opened only in the event of his death. If the worst transpired, his letter to Lady Frances continued, his intimates would be able to discuss it – and him – openly, but 'There is however one who will not be in this position. I want you to give her from yourself this little brooch which you will find herewith: and tell her that, in the end, if I was able to think at all, I thought of her. If I was the means of introducing any unhappiness into her life I hope God will forgive me. I know she will.'[69] These letters did not prove necessary in their day, and only after Balfour's death in 1930, did two elderly ladies, the Countess of Wemyss and Lady Frances Balfour, together open the pouch and find the note and a diamond brooch, at last delivered to the one for whom it was meant.

3

Learning the Ropes

⌒⌒

THE POLITICAL LANDSCAPE appeared dismal enough to Conservatives after their defeat in 1880. Their ageing generalissimo, Beaconsfield, was in steep decline, and in the Commons many ambitious younger Tories who had survived the recent battering were spoiling for a fight. Yet Balfour recalled of that time that, in such an unsettled political world, careers might be made by ambitious men.

> When, in the hour of their defeat, they moved from Mr Speaker's right hand to his left they lost greatly in collective power, but they gained in individual freedom. Party discipline is looser; personal initiative finds openings; and the art of attack offers to the ingenious Parliamentarian a greater scope and variety of method than the counter-art of defence. In short, from the point of view of the unofficial members, it is more amusing to criticize than to praise, to expose the blunders of your opponents than the merits of your friends; so, at least, it seemed to me in the year 1880.[1]

The 3rd Marquess of Salisbury, of course, was insulated from this scene in the Lords, as the real political weather was made in the Commons. It is also true that his nephew's usefulness to him as information-gatherer and sounding board would come to be very great – and Balfour, from his side, could scarcely have wished for a better patron. Over the five years that followed, his interest in and commitment to politics grew, for the inveterate gamesman found himself in the midst of the greatest game of all, that of power.

For a time, as the Liberals ruled, Balfour found it amusing and useful to throw in his political lot with three other independent spirits, and together they came to be known as the Fourth Party. Despite their impressive appellation (the label was pinned on them by a sneering Irish Nationalist), this gang of four was even less a party than the political cave of forty years before with which it is sometimes compared, Disraeli's Young England. In fact they possessed neither ideology nor programme, but they shared a wealth of dissatisfaction and disappointment in their official leaders. At fifty-four, the eldest of them was Sir Henry Drummond Wolff, a sometime diplomat and MP for Portsmouth. Balfour remembered him as 'a man of the world by temperament and training, with a great aptitude for amusing and being amused, playing the game of life with gusto, and finding an interlude of Opposition politics, spent in congenial company, an occupation very much to his taste'.[2] Quite different was John Eldon Gorst, QC, then forty-five and since 1875 MP for Chatham. Gorst had done yeoman service with his tireless efforts between 1870 and 1874 as principal agent of the party – but gratitude was not enough for him: he had wanted office. He did not get it, and he nursed a sense of grievance which now found an outlet a half-dozen years later in the Fourth Party. A difficult man at the best of times, in this period he did not merely not suffer fools gladly, but too often dealt with fools and able men with similar impatience.

The acknowledged leader of the group, though the youngest, was Lord Randolph Churchill, the second son of the Duke of Marlborough. It is no revelation to suggest that Lord Randolph possessed talent and ambition beyond the power of his judgement. He was thirty-one, seven months younger than Balfour, and like him, as MP for Woodstock, he sat for what was more or less a family borough. They had been at Eton together – though apparently they knew little of one another there – and both entered the House in 1874. There the similarities ended: Churchill was impetuous and craved excitement – as did Jenny Jerome, the beautiful American heiress he married in 1874. He loved the turf, and dazzled (and quarrelled with, was ostracized by and eventually was reconciled with) the fast and fashionable Marlborough House set of the Prince of Wales. Churchill's ambition to shake off the dreaded spectre of anonymity and to master the greatest legislative body of the world drove him to take risks and collect admirers – and enemies. He and Balfour gravitated together and came to enjoy one another's company, with Balfour enduring with good grace Churchill's playful jibes and pet names (he called Balfour 'Posslethwaite', which he thought somehow appropriate to his colleague's bookishness).[3] There was never any doubt that, among the four, the brightest light always fell on Lord Randolph.

What propelled them for a time into prominence was the dearth of fighting leadership on the Conservative side of the Commons. Balfour himself concluded later, 'There would surely never have been a Churchill had there not also been a Northcote.'[4] By the same token, there might not have been a Fourth Party had there not been a Bradlaugh. The celebrated 'case' of Charles Bradlaugh erupted in the spring of 1880 as Gladstone strove to direct his unruly majority, while Sir Stafford Northcote, the

Conservative leader in the Commons, faced the even more daunting task of leading the wounded and bad-tempered Opposition. Northcote possessed ability, integrity and experience; he was scholarly and quite respectable. However, he was also 'an instinctive consensual centrist',[5] and this was a bad time for such reasonableness. Beaconsfield had chosen Northcote because he was an able man to whom the party owed a debt, but he lacked the gift of inspiration, and hence could never master his ostensible followers. Nor had he the right sort of help. The Tory front bench boasted able parliamentarians, for example Northcote's two senior lieutenants, W. H. Smith and Richard Cross (whose bourgeois origins Churchill unfairly mocked by dubbing them 'Marshall and Snelgrove', after the London department store), but they were as poorly suited to be warriors as was their leader. The restive Tories, missing Dizzy's combative inspiration, faced the GOM with the formidable Harcourt, Dilke and Chamberlain at his back. It was hardly a fair fight, as it was clear that the Liberals had the bigger guns. To the impatient Lord Randolph, if those pillars of middle-class virtue Smith and Cross were 'Marshall and Snelgrove', then his leader, Northcote, was the 'goat'.

Into this drama strode Charles Bradlaugh, self-made man and born contrarian, as well as militant freethinker and unapologetic atheist – and in 1880 duly elected by the voters of Northampton as one of their two MPs – the other being the Radical Henry Labouchere.[6] Bradlaugh's refusal to swear the Oath of Allegiance, professing instead his right to affirm, for a time stopped the business of the House in its tracks. To Churchill and his friends, the atheist was a godsend. They expressed their utter outrage, and caught the spirit of the Chamber – of the Conservative backbenchers and of many Liberals besides. The details belong to a different story, and it is sufficient to say that, despite becoming for a time the most hated man in England, Bradlaugh stood his ground, and so did the electors of Northampton. With Gladstone and his ministers seeking re-election in their constituencies (as was required from the time of the eighteenth century Act of Settlement until after the First World War), Churchill, Drummond Wolff and Gorst raised a hubbub of spectacular proportions. Gladstone was in an unenviable position as the circus raged throughout May, while Churchill and his friends won the admiration of their fellow Tories by merrily flaying a government that seemed neither to endorse nor to condemn Bradlaugh. Soon the Fourth Party took over the front bench below the gangway (with Lord Randolph claiming the corner seat vacated by Alexander Beresford-Hope) and attracted a fellow-traveller in the person of Arthur Balfour.

Balfour did not take a leading part in the Bradlaugh debates, but he did draw close to the three friends, and was soon speaking regularly in their running campaign of distraction, intimidation and mischief-making. However, while he enjoyed their comradeship – Lord Randolph and Drummond Wolff were especially good company, and invitations to their dinners at the Garrick Club were highly prized – he did not become a particularly close friend to any. Nor was he quite so morally outraged at Bradlaugh's politics or lifestyle as his colleagues claimed to be. But he did enjoy the fun and see the value in attempting to drive Northcote to provide the strong leadership their party required, or in revealing his inability to do so. So he acknowledged to Lord Salisbury in the days following the crisis:

> The Govt. have certainly lost ground – but we can hardly be said to have gained it. The condition of the party is even more unsatisfactory than it was when you were [in the Commons]. We are trampled on by the Govt. and we make no sign. We have no organisation. We have no leader: – or rather our leader is (and, what is worse, is very commonly thought to be) a source of weakness rather than strength.[7]

Balfour was ready to take on a more visible role in party affairs, even to the point of calling attention to himself – a far cry from the young man who only four years earlier had to be driven to offer a maiden speech. He felt needed, as he indicated to his uncle in the same letter: 'Things have got to such a pass last week that in order to prevent worse happening . . . I agreed to speak our grievances at a meeting of the party which Northcote held here last Thursday. I never disliked anything more. . . . However, as nobody else could be found I undertook the business.'

He undertook the 'business', as he said, but in a manner devoid of Churchillian sledgehammer tactics, for Balfour addressed the need for greater consultation between leaders and backbenchers and the general desire for a more energetic Opposition. He neither insulted nor indicted Northcote, and this demonstrates the real difference between him and his three co-conspirators. Drummond Wolff sought amusement and diversion, and Gorst the advancement of his career and his own vision of what he referred to as Tory Democracy. Churchill saw their activities as a device to propel himself forward towards his own goal: to sweep Northcote out of his path. Balfour also was disappointed in Northcote's performance and thoroughly disapproved of the Gladstone government and its programmes. He too had tasted ambition, and now relished the fact that he was well on the way to making a name for himself in the House – and there is no doubt that he enjoyed the show. Yet, unlike the others, he had no desire to endanger loyalty among his party's rank and file, and even less to challenge directly the anointed leadership – not least because 'Dizzy's' heir in the Lords was his Uncle Salisbury. Hence he was always unwilling to go to the lengths with which Churchill and Gorst, and even the less intense Drummond Wolff, regularly flirted.

While Beaconsfield lived, his great prestige prevented any open rupture of the uneasy peace within the party. Northcote, who bore the brunt of Fourth Party antics, was far from content, and wrote to Cross in November 1880, 'We shall find the Fourth Party extremely violent and troublesome; and I am secretly uneasy lest they should receive a little too much encouragement from quarters which I need not now mention.'[8] Almost certainly he suspected the aged party leader of coddling, perhaps for some perverse reason even encouraging, the rebels, despite being told only a few months before by him that he – Beaconsfield – had 'means' of ensuring their good behaviour. Yet, if they are to be believed, Dizzy laid only the gentlest of hands on the bomb-throwers. He did summon Gorst (whose managerial skills he wished once again to employ at party headquarters) to Hughenden for a talk, apparently advising him that he might continue to enjoy a certain amount of fun with his friends but to mind his manners towards Northcote. Drummond Wolff reported to Churchill that, far from receiving a reprimand from the old man, he had been told only that they 'must stick to Northcote'; but Dizzy had added, 'He represents the respectability of the party. I wholly sympathize with you because I was never respectable myself . . . Don't on any account break with Northcote but defer to him as often as you can. Whenever it becomes too difficult you can come to me and I will try to arrange matters.'[9] But in April 1881 the great man died.

A half-century later, Balfour noted that, while he had forgotten much of this early period of his parliamentary life, the change in Conservative Party affairs after Beaconsfield's death in April 1881 remained clear enough:

> Such calamities are familiar and inevitable, and had Lord Salisbury been in the Commons, had Sir Stafford Northcote been in the Lords, had there been no independent Conservative Members of Parliament endowed with Lord Randolph's temperament and talents, party politics would, I suppose, have smoothly followed their accustomed course. But with things as they were, what happened was unavoidable.[10]

The Conservative Party had no formal procedure for the choice of a party leader when in Opposition. The Tory peers quickly endorsed

Salisbury's succession as their leader, and Northcote laboured on in the Commons – even though the Queen had assured him that she considered him leader of the entire party. The duumvirate was not a happy compromise, and created an instability which would not be settled until one or the other emerged as paramount. In this confusion of authority a brilliant young man with a great name, who had in only a year made himself a national figure and who sensed that perhaps his time had come early in his career, might thrust himself into the contest. Lord Randolph Churchill's machinations for power would destroy the Fourth Party and drive Balfour to make a choice in his political allegiance. That choice was not difficult for him, and would propel him on towards the top rank in his party.

His own confidence and reputation in the House were growing as a result of the Fourth Party agitation, as he learned parliamentary craft and polished his debating skills. It was in these days after 'Bradlaugh' that he enjoyed his first truly great moment in the Chamber, and it is somehow fitting that the episode should involve Ireland, the great matter that would make a misery of Gladstone's latter days and would be the political making of Arthur Balfour.

'John Bull's other island' was afflicted with poverty, ignorance, superstition and absentee landlordism, and in response a shadowy Irish Land League had been organized. Its chieftains, acting almost as a rival government, now decreed among the peasantry who should and who should not pay rent. The object was to exert economic pressure on the landowning classes and thereby on the London government. In Parliament, an Irish National Party dispensed its co-operation when it wished and at other times conducted a sort of guerrilla campaign against the orderly conduct of business. This party was essentially the creation of the brooding genius, Charles Stewart Parnell, the 'Uncrowned King of Ireland'. An Anglo-American and a Protestant landlord himself, the 'Green Lion of Wicklow' was thoroughly Irish in all but blood and religion and was at once the most admired and hated man in Ireland. He lived for the day when he would bring off the political stroke that would avenge all the English slights and knocks of centuries: Home Rule. These two words embodied the dreams and wishes of his followers and meant the virtual subversion of the Act of Union of 1801 and the establishment of an Irish parliament, sitting in an Irish capital, governing Irish affairs. Some dreamed of a true and separate Irish nation; but first things must come first, and Home Rule was the immediate goal.

Gladstone's sympathy with the Irish people was genuine enough, though he found the unruly Irish party a great nuisance. In 1881 he passed a Land Act which granted the 'Three F's' which Parnell demanded – fair rents, fixity of land tenure and free sale of landholdings – and set up land courts to adjudicate disagreements between landlord and tenant. The bill passed easily, and one cynic noted that had the Grand Old Man asked a frustrated Parliament searching for a way out of its difficulties to pass 'the Koran or the Nautical Almanac as an Irish Land Bill, he would have met with no difficulty'.[11] The Land League, however, was unsatisfied, and forbade the Irish peasantry to petition for redress in Gladstone's land courts, except with its express permission. Gladstone had had enough: in October 1881 Parnell and his senior lieutenants, William O'Brien and J. J. O'Kelly, were arrested for 'treasonable practices' and unceremoniously packed off to Kilmainham Gaol. This led to the declaration of a full-scale national rent strike by day and a bloody campaign by the terrorist bands of 'Captain Moonlight' by night. Ireland was in chaos once again.

Using the good offices as go-between of a rather shady Irish Nationalist MP, Captain William O'Shea (whose wife was Parnell's lover), the government and the Irish leader achieved a truce in May 1882. In this so-called 'Kilmainham Treaty', Gladstone and the Radical President of the Board of Trade, Joseph Chamberlain, agreed to deal with the thorny matter of rent arrears for the strikers, while Parnell pledged to end the strike and use his influence to stop the violence. Parnell and his colleagues were free once again, Ireland rejoiced, and in time the Irish leader did bring his influence to bear on the rent strike. In Britain, however, there was less rejoicing and more outrage. The furious Irish Secretary, W. E. Forster, resigned immediately over the 'treaty' and in debate revealed some of the circumstances of the deal. This was bad enough for Gladstone, but there was worse to come. Forster's successor was Lord Frederick Cavendish, the second son of the Duke of Devonshire, who quipped to Gladstone's daughter just before embarking for Ireland, 'Well, I am in for it.'[12] It was a tragic jest, for, a few days before Forster's attack on Gladstone, Lord Frederick and his undersecretary, Thomas Burke, were set upon by members of a secret terrorist band calling themselves the Invincibles and stabbed to death while they strolled in Dublin's Phoenix Park.[13]

The murder came as the political atmosphere was already superheated, with government supporters divided over the Kilmainham bargain, and the Prime Minister and Forster publicly squabbling. There was more trouble to come, as on 16 May Balfour entered the fray. He rose, he said, to move the adjournment of the House in order that the government might have time to prepare its explanations and the Opposition its criticisms. In the five years since his forgettable maiden speech, he had made great progress in the

House. Owing to his increased visibility and in no small part to his connections, he was now beginning to be seen as one of the younger Members marked out for distinction. His part in the 'Fourth Party' guerrilla campaign had gained him notice and even approval, but he had yet to command the regular attention of the House. Now that changed. His fellow Tories passed the word that his speech might be worth hearing, and Honourable Members drifted back into the Chamber in hope of some entertaining pyrotechnics. He rapidly got to the point: the government had done nothing less than treat with its nation's sworn enemies; even worse, it had made a shoddy and secret deal with them. In response to Gladstone's muttered denials, he thundered on: in their covert negotiations with the Irish leaders the Prime Minister and his colleagues had behaved like the gentleman who allowed his friends to have what they wished from his house and then accepted money from them – but as gifts, not as payment:

> The House seemed to have a tolerably clear notion of what had passed. The Government were to give Hon. Gentlemen their liberty and a Bill with regard to arrears. The Hon. Gentlemen were going to give the Government peace in Ireland and support in Parliament. However that transaction might be disguised in words there was no doubt whatever it was a compact.

Such a bargain, he insisted, was without precedent:

> It stood alone – he did not wish to use strong language but he was going to say – it stood alone in its infamy. They had negotiated alone with treason, and almost worse than all, it appeared that one of the things the Government had, in their own words, reasonable grounds for believing, was that they would obtain the Parliamentary support of men they had put in prison for the gravest crime.

'Infamy' and 'treason' were strong words, and Gladstone was immediately up and counter-attacking, with the cheers of his followers ringing in his ears. The injury the GOM had sustained, however, caused real pain – both political and personal, for it had come in the most public forum at the hands of a young friend of whom he had long been fond. The two men soon returned to cordial relations, but the old avuncular feeling that Gladstone had once enjoyed never quite returned. As for Balfour, taking on the greatest Liberal as he had was of massive importance, and it came as hard evidence that the ghost of Lord Randolph's rather indolent 'Posslethwaite' was exorcized.

No one understood this new departure more than Lord Salisbury, who was already coming to employ his nephew's talents in his political inner circle. As early as April 1880, the Marquess – who could hardly be accused of being a natural flatterer – expressed his gratitude to Balfour for acting as his agent in dealing with Beaconsfield: 'I am much obliged to you for your letter & telegrams, & for all the trouble you have been taking.'[14] In June he wrote again, to thank him for his analysis of Liberal plans for legislation to aid evicted tenants in Ireland.[15] By the time his debating skills were coming to be recognized as a benefit to the party, Balfour had already made a place for himself as his uncle's trusted agent. Unlike his Fourth Party companions Drummond Wolff and Gorst, he had a future; and the powerful among the party were coming to see that, unlike the unstable Lord Randolph, he had 'bottom'.

Recognition brought responsibility. There was grudging agreement among Tory leaders that the humiliating defeat of 1880 bespoke serious ills in party organization, and plans were hastily laid to overhaul the machinery of party management. The tetchy Gorst, whose organizational gifts were needed once more, was called back to party headquarters, Central Office, for a stormy two years as principal agent; and, in one of Beaconsfield's last innovations, a new Central Committee was appointed in August, ostensibly to suggest policy and to oversee needed reorganization of the party in the constituencies. In the chair was W. H. Smith. Admired in the House as 'Old Morality', Smith had turned his father's successful news agency into a commercial colossus and knew something about organization. He was joined by the Chief Whip, Rowland Winn; by Earl Percy, the chairman of the National Union of Conservative Associations (the association of constituency organizations); and by Gorst. It was decided to add a younger man, attractive to the backbenchers and also to the party's grandees. They chose Arthur James Balfour, who soon found the committee in a greater or lesser degree of disagreement over virtually everything and to whom fell the task of peacemaking among his elders. This he did with some success.[16]

While Balfour was establishing himself as a coming man and a party insider, Conservatism's new celebrity was clearly Lord Randolph Churchill, whose impatient ambition seemed to be to displace his official leader, Northcote. Churchill had planned to mount the horse of Tory Democracy, left more or less riderless after Beaconsfield's death in early 1881, and he did so with a force and eloquence that belied his innermost doubts about it. The anxious Northcote was not exactly sure to what such an ideology – if it was an ideology – amounted, but he knew that if Lord Randolph meant to 'ride "Tory Democracy pretty hard"' it almost certainly meant trouble.[17] When himself asked once what exactly it all meant, Churchill responded with remarkable candour: 'To tell the truth, I don't know myself what Tory

Democracy is, but I believe it is principally opportunism. Say you are a Tory Democrat and that will do.'[18]

Lord Randolph needed no tutoring in opportunism. Backed once again by Gorst and Drummond Wolff, he demonstrated it by working at wrenching the National Union from under the thumb of Central Office and declaring it the one true instrument of grass-roots Conservatism. With an eye on duplicating the success of Chamberlain's creation of the Liberal Association, Lord Randolph got himself elected to the Union's Central Council in 1883, and in February 1884 he successfully ousted Earl Percy from the chair. His audacious plan to employ the Union to lay siege to Central Office and the new Central Committee was not in the end entirely successful. It did wonders, however, in establishing his position as a national figure and rival to the official leaders. In fact he soon threatened to eclipse Northcote and – despite insisting that he favoured the Marquess as leader of the party – was breathing heavily down the neck of Salisbury.[19]

In July, 1884, a compromise over Churchill's National Union plan was patched together: Salisbury agreed to the dissolution of the Central Committee, and Churchill would abandon his campaign. The two leaders – two only, for Salisbury ignored Northcote – agreed to a compromise under which ex-Colonial Secretary Sir Michael Hicks Beach would chair the National Union; George Bartley, Gorst's successor as principal agent, would become treasurer; and Churchill's confederate Gorst would become a vice-chairman, as would Aretas Akers-Douglas and Salisbury's nominee, Arthur Balfour.[20] It looked clear enough: Gorst (who disliked the compromise) represented the Churchill faction, and his erstwhile Fourth Party comrade Balfour the Salisburyites. Equally obvious was the fact that Northcote had been left out in the cold. For the moment it was Salisbury or Churchill, and the Marquess understood that he had a formidable rival – but a rival not without weaknesses. More than a particular policy to which he was dedicated, the young Tory rebel had a combination of genius, ambition and charisma, and Salisbury wrote to a friend in the midst of the party crisis, 'Randolph and the [Muslim religious fanatic the] Mahdi have occupied my thoughts about equally. The Mahdi pretends to be half mad, but is very sane in reality. Randolph occupies exactly the converse position.'[21] Lord Randolph, he understood, was unpredictable and therefore dangerous, and the situation could not continue indefinitely.

Balfour was coming to see things in much the same fashion. He and Churchill continued to maintain friendly personal relations, but in political terms they were drawing apart. Churchill's biographer Sir Robert Rhodes James saw this distance as evidence of betrayal: 'There is no doubt that in leaving the Fourth Party Balfour made a shrewd step; what is slightly repellent about him was that he took great care to maintain his links with Churchill until he could destroy him, while at the same time constantly denigrating him to Salisbury.'[22]

In fact Churchill had never considered Balfour much more than an appendage of the Fourth Party and treated him accordingly, even cruelly, saying to him things along the lines of 'Go and take my wife to a concert while I stay here and talk real business.'[23] Of Balfour's commitment to their little insurrection, Gorst noted years later, 'We did not take him very seriously.'[24] Though he came away with a vice-presidency, Gorst feared that Tory Democracy had been betrayed by the National Union compromise – but by Churchill, not Balfour.

It is true that by this time in the correspondence of Salisbury and Balfour there was much wondering and conjecture about what Churchill was up to and what tactics he would choose. Yet, it is difficult to find 'those waspish little remarks' to which Churchill's biographer refers.[25] There is guesswork about his machinations – and about the degree of his party commitment – on the part of both Salisbury and Balfour. In January 1884 Balfour discussed with Churchill his own unease about the National Union controversy that the latter had raised. He wrote to Salisbury in January 1884 that he had laid his cards on Churchill's table:

> I think I fully explained my view of Randolph when you were here. He is I think quite capable of denouncing in a public speech the existing [party] organisation. At least he told me so the other day when, having asked me whether it was to be peace or war between us on this subject, I said that if peace meant yielding to his pretensions, it was war! – We are excellent friends at this moment otherwise!

But relations between the former Fourth Party men had changed for ever. Balfour advised Salisbury, 'My idea is that we ought to do nothing at present and simply let Randolph hammer away.'[26]

The centre stage in Tory affairs now belonged to Salisbury and Churchill. The former seemed to embody the comforting and familiar amalgam of experience, wisdom and indifference to the fray; the latter generated excitement and brilliance on the public stage and possessed courage to the point of foolhardiness. Reality, of course, added its leaven: both men were ambitious, both possessed great political talent and substantial followings. Their differences over the direction their party should follow and how, and by whom it should be led, were profound – so much so, in fact, that it was clear that a long-term working relationship was impossible.

Balfour had well-known ties to each, but they were links of different kinds. He recognized Churchill as a colleague and an asset, if an unreliable one, to their party, and he had enjoyed and learned much in their Fourth Party days. Also, the two agreed that the party leadership in the Commons could not continue as it had. Salisbury, on the other hand, he had known throughout his life; he shared his fundamental values, and was deeply indebted to him as an older kinsman and mentor during his fatherless childhood. The family tie meant much to Arthur Balfour. Furthermore, the two men were repelled by the idea of party revolution – nipping at Northcote's heels was one thing, but Churchill's campaign was something quite different.[27] Balfour was growing sure that his former Fourth Party comrade was capable of causing a rift in the party. He himself was willing to work to prevent such a split and to accommodate Lord Randolph when possible, but was also drawing near to the conclusion that no compromise that involved Churchill could endure indefinitely and that a crash must eventually come. He wrote to Salisbury in January that he was inclined 'to think that we should avoid as far as possible all "rows", until Randolph puts himself entirely and flagrantly in the wrong by some act of party disloyalty which every body can understand and no one can deny. By this course we may avoid a battle altogether; but if a battle is forced upon us we shall be sure to win it.'[28]

Unlike Lord Randolph, Balfour could not energize the public, and, as for the mass of the party membership, he remarked in later years that he would as soon take political advice from his valet as from a meeting of the party. He preferred the counsel of experienced leaders in whom he had confidence; he believed also that kinship deserved loyalty, and the sum of all of this was that it was Salisbury to whose views he paid the most attention. Though Balfour was but thirty-six years of age and had not yet held office, it was also evident that Salisbury listened to and valued what his nephew had to say.

By the time this crisis was resolved it had exacted a toll on the parliamentary party; but in the end it left the Conservatives better off, for the more able Lord Salisbury had eclipsed Northcote and emerged as the likely candidate to lead the next Tory government. The lay of the political land itself was about to undergo a significant change in 1884, for the government announced it would table a bill to bring the county franchise into line with the more democratic practice of the boroughs. With less reluctance than Salisbury, Balfour had made his peace with both the principle and the reality of Disraeli's 1867 franchise law. Yet they and their fellow Conservatives dug in their heels over Gladstone's proposed bill – unless he agreed to reveal his plans for parliamentary redistribution. The Grand Old Man was outraged, complaining of the intolerable behaviour of the Opposition both to the Queen – to whom he linked Balfour's name with Salisbury's for particular complaint – and from the platform. The new franchise bill inevitably passed through the Commons, where the Liberals could do as they wished; but in June in the Conservative stronghold of the Upper House it was crushed. Negotiations with the government ensued, again with Balfour in the midst of things, while Chamberlain rumbled ominously about a possible 'peers against the people' campaign. At last, in the autumn the Liberals agreed to reveal their redistribution plan, the Tories accepted franchise reform, and the two linked bills passed through both houses.

Balfour remarked to Blanche Dugdale in 1928, many years after this extended battle:

> Do you want to know what I thought about Tory Democracy? The words sound all right, but they never meant what *I* mean by them. Democracy. What's Democracy? It's government by the people, and I'm all for that; but in 1883 I was all for the extension of the franchise, though Randolph wasn't, which is comic. But I saw no point in resisting what was bound in logic to come.[29]

While Salisbury too was a realist who saw that franchise reform could not be stopped, by his very nature he assumed the worst possible result. Balfour agreed that resistance was foolhardy, yet he thought it safe, as Disraeli had advised in earlier times, to trust the people. Unlike his uncle and many of their class, Balfour had come to believe that the millions lumped together and labelled as 'the people' were essentially as conservative as their social superiors. Recalling that Lord Macaulay had predicted disaster in 1832 in the event of the broadening of the franchise with the passage of the Great Reform Bill, he continued to his niece: 'I have never believed that for a moment – and in fact the countries where there is real universal suffrage prove my point – look at Switzerland – where the referendum is used and always in a Conservative cause.'

The changes wrought by these bills were profound. As one wry observer noted, 'Few revolutions achieve the aims on their banners; but all revolutions achieve something, and it is usually the unpleasantly expected.'[30] The 1884 Reform Act did effect a vastly important constitutional change, and the new principle was to be 'one man, one value' as the electorate swelled to more than 5 million. Seventy-nine small boroughs lost their representation, plural-member constituencies passed away, and the electoral map was divided into single-member districts. Quite unexpectedly, this did great harm to the uneasy Whig–Radical marriage within the Liberal Party, as the local organizations in the former two-member constituencies could no longer comfortably nominate one candidate of each persuasion. Finally, the franchise was similarly extended in Ireland – solidifying the political hold of Parnell's Irish Nationalists, sweeping away Liberal hopes in the south and west, and leaving the Conservatives and Nationalists to fight it out in the north.

Gladstone's Liberals still had their majority in the Commons, and no doubt many of their number must have enjoyed watching the Tory discomfort. Yet they had worries of their own, for the 1880–85 government had never been a happy one, and foreign policy had caused the most grief, with seemingly insoluble troubles in Afghanistan, Egypt and South Africa. In February, 1885 came a blow which was in itself almost too much: the popular hero General Charles 'Chinese' Gordon had been overwhelmed and slain in Khartoum by the forces of the fanatical Mahdi, the 'Chosen One'. Then the government's two most voluble Radicals, Sir Charles Dilke and Chamberlain – who trumpeted his own 'Unauthorized Programme' up and down the country – resigned in March 1885 in opposition to renewed coercion measures to bring order to Ireland. With Dilke (whose career would soon be crippled when he was named co-respondent in a sensational divorce case), 'Radical Joe' launched a plan for local government for Ireland which the Home Rulers rejected and which the Liberal Cabinet found unappealing for reasons of their own. Sensing an opportunity, Churchill decided to invite Parnell to his house for a private tête-à-tête, suggesting that perhaps a better offer could be secured from the Conservatives than from the dithering Liberals. Parnell listened, while Irish MPs and Irish voters awaited their orders. The command finally came: desert Gladstone.

By this time, of course, the Fourth Party was no more, but the former members came together one last time to conspire to bring the second Gladstone administration to a close. At a lunch at 4 Carlton Gardens during the first week of June 1885, Balfour hosted Churchill, Drummond Wolff and Gorst, as well as Henry Cecil Raikes, MP, a former chairman of the National Union and fellow-traveller of the Fourth Party, and the bluff and steady Hicks Beach, whose stock among Conservatives was rising at the same rate that Northcote's was plummeting. The plan was for Hicks Beach to propose an amendment to the Budget on 8 June, and the conspirators agreed that they might manage a surprise defeat of the divided government that could drive it into retreat and resignation. Balfour described the day:

A somewhat languid debate, apparently leading to its too familiar end, then a slowly growing sense that something unusual was about to happen. Surely the attendance on the Government side was thin. Was an Opposition victory possible? Was it probable? . . . The Division was close. Not till the tellers walked up to the table was the result assured. The Government was beaten by fourteen.[31]

With the assistance of half of Parnell's Nationalists, and the absence from the Chamber of some forty-eight 'unpaired' Liberals, the Budget was defeated and the government finished; with this the Fourth Party was finally laid to rest. Lord Randolph, now seemingly at the top of the party pyramid with Salisbury and Hicks Beach, made ready for the next step on his inexorable rise to national leadership. Balfour, who also moved up the political ladder as he joined Her Majesty's Privy Council a fortnight later, could be confident that his place as a politician with a future was confirmed. Drummond Wolff received the same honour at this time, but it was an exit prize, as he returned to his diplomatic career. Gorst received a knighthood, but could look forward to little more than membership in the party chorus. Their time at centre stage was over.

Gladstone promptly resigned, and in June Salisbury took the gamble that Disraeli had shunned in 1873, forming a minority administration. His selection by a monarch who had once endorsed Northcote for the place confirmed the unfortunate Sir Stafford's eclipse. Characteristically, Salisbury was not much enthused about the prospect, writing to a friend on the very eve of the Liberal defeat, 'To have to govern [for] six months with a hostile but dying Parliament is the very worst thing that can happen to us.'[32] Always known as the 'Caretaker Government', it was so called by those who were confident that a prompt election based on a revised electoral register would return the Grand Old Man to his 'natural' place as premier and the Tories, once again, to the Opposition benches. No one could have predicted what a year of political tumult lay ahead, but in the meantime a government had to be formed. Salisbury intended to serve as both prime minister and foreign secretary – the office which Northcote mistakenly presumed would once again be his. Hicks Beach's status was confirmed as he became Chancellor of the Exchequer and Leader of the House, and Churchill took the India Office – remarkable for a Cabinet novice at the tender age of thirty-six.

Lord Randolph was never averse to pushing his luck, and he demanded that the already eclipsed Northcote be banished from the Commons he once had led. This brought about an exhausting week of delicate negotiation between Salisbury and Northcote, once again conducted largely through the good offices of Balfour; and in the end Sir Stafford surrendered and accepted banishment to the Lords as Earl of Iddesleigh, with the nominal post of First Lord of the Treasury.[33] There were few light moments in the entire affair, but there was at least one: as an announcement of the new administration appeared imminent, pressmen haunted Northcote's house, begging information from his rather haughty butler. What office would his master accept? "'After much consideration," the butler is said to have replied with dignity, "the Cabinet has offered him the private secretaryship to Lord Randolph Churchill.'"[34] Balfour was well aware that no Conservative government could be made without Churchill. The man was popular, and he was also ambitious and dangerous, and Balfour advised his uncle, 'Of course, the line I took tonight with R.C. and the one I suggested for tomorrow, were based on the supposition that it was better to have him with us than against us.'[35]

With neither the experience of Hicks Beach nor the popular following of Churchill, Balfour was quite content with the presidency of the Local Government Board, outside the Cabinet. Though confident in his abilities, Salisbury had preferred at first to keep him close as under-secretary at the Foreign Office, but for the time being it was thought best to give him his own department outside the bright glare of the Cabinet and not advance him too rapidly in this vulnerable government.

The 1884 Reform Act required a new electoral register and a prompt election, hence the 1885 arrangements were never meant to be more than temporary, no matter which party won the next contest. Balfour's five months at the Local Government Board were neither particularly happy nor easy. The work was necessary but unexciting – especially when compared with that of his old comrade Churchill at the India Office, where Lord Randolph was soon enjoying a 'jolly row' with the Queen over the appointment of her military advisers and, despite Salisbury's objections, annexing Upper Burma. Balfour offered up but one noteworthy piece of legislation, a Medical Relief Disqualifications Bill. This got him rather knocked about by Joseph Chamberlain after the new minister had purposely engaged the great radical in debate – a useful lesson that the pinprick tactics of the Fourth Party, so amusing in Opposition, were less so in office.[36] He never made the mistake again.

In fact the ghost that menaced the so-called Caretaker Government and its successors was once again an Irish one. The Conservatives, finding unpalatable Chamberlain's latest initiative of increased local governance, brought in Lord Ashbourne's Act. So called after the Irish Lord Chancellor, this provided to the Irish tenantry increased funds available on generous terms for the further purchase of smallholdings. On 23 November, Parnell issued orders recommending that his admirers forsake the Liberals, which many did. Yet Gladstone's forces won the election without them, with a majority over their Conservative rivals in the Commons of eighty-six seats – precisely the number of Irish Nationalist MPs. The Green Lion now held the balance, and Ireland's 'national aspirations' seemed within his grasp. For the moment, however, he was content to maintain the Conservatives in office.

Balfour had faced an important question on the eve of the 1885 election, and his conclusion had a great impact on his career. His safe constituency of Hertford would not survive redistribution, and he accepted the nomination of the Conservatives of East Manchester for an urban seat of importance with a large majority of working-class voters – as unlike the comfortably obscure Hertford as could be imagined. Balfour had consulted his uncle when the change was first mooted two years earlier. Salisbury's reply was useful advice:

> If I answer as a party leader – my answer is very easy. You will undoubtedly be rendering a great service to the party by standing. I do not think there is any one who could approach the contest with so good a chance of success: & of course, it would be a great victory to win this seat . . .
>
> If you win Manchester your position as a public man will be very much stronger. The time has come when the benefit to you of your connection with me is at all events mixed. The fact that you sit for a seat reputed – quite falsely – to be mine, joined to our other ties, makes many people take you too much as my double: & this detracts, & may detract more, from the natural effect of your powers. My impression, therefore, is that you would gain very perceptibly in force, as compared with the other prominent men of your own standing, if you spoke as the representative of a large working-class constituency.

But Salisbury, being Salisbury, added a cautionary note:

> But this advantage would be purchased by much labour, much discomfort, & some risk – perhaps a considerable risk. Are you disposed to incur these disadvantages? It is a question that no other man can decide for you.[37]

Balfour never feared risk, and if he envisioned a great career this risk was one he did well to take. When the election came, for the first time in his parliamentary life he campaigned hard against formidable opposition, and he won the seat with a majority of 824. He was destined to hold it for the next twenty years.[38]

During the stormy campaign Gladstone had had little to say about

Ireland, and – like Sherlock Holmes's dog that 'did nothing in the night-time' – raised no immediate alarm among defenders of the Union. However, in the summer following his resignation the Grand Old Man had turned his mind towards Home Rule as the solution to the stand-off. His silence during the campaign masked the fact that, though they were agreed that something needed to be done, Liberals were by no means united regarding just exactly what that might be.[39] As for the 'Caretakers', they had passed a generous land act, but there would be no Home Rule from their hands. How long, then, could their amicable relations with the Parnellites last?

In mid-December, with the Tories having been issued with their notice to vacate by the electorate, Balfour found himself part of a jolly house party at Eaton Hall, the country seat of the Duke of Westminster, a Whig admirer of Gladstone. Eaton was very near the Grand Old Man's own Hawarden Castle, and it was not so unusual when the once and future Prime Minister unexpectedly paid a call. Balfour recalled that Gladstone's 'mind was full of Ireland':

> During this very visit to Eaton, in the course of a conversation with Lady Cowper, an old friend and the wife of an old colleague [Lord Cowper had been Irish Lord Lieutenant in 1880–82], Mr Gladstone declared that if terms were to be made with Mr Parnell they must be made 'now or never'; whereupon Lady Cowper (good Whig that she was) smote the table with her open hand, vehemently exclaiming, 'Then let it be never.'[40]

It was Balfour, not His Grace of Westminster, whom Gladstone had come to see, and the concealed thinking behind his visit, once it became public, would cause the Duke in a few months' time to remove the portrait of his friend from the wall at Eaton and bundle it off to an auction house. Gladstone took Balfour aside and confided to him that he had secret information that a campaign of violence and outrage would be brought to England if 'substantial concessions' to Parnell's demands were not forthcoming. According to Balfour, '"In other words," I said to Mr Gladstone, "we are to be blown up and stabbed if we do not grant Home Rule by the end of the next session." "I understand," answered Mr Gladstone, "the time is shorter than that."' Clearly Gladstone had concluded that the way to Salisbury lay through Arthur Balfour.

Events quickened from this point: on 17 December there appeared in the press a delicious scoop revealing the 'Hawarden kite', flown certainly with the knowledge of his father by Herbert Gladstone. The 'kite' was the revelation that the Liberal leader had decided in favour of Irish self-governance. Then, three days later, the elder Gladstone wrote to Balfour:

> On reflection I think that what I said to you in our conversation at Eaton may have amounted to the conveyance of a hope that the Government would take a strong and early decision on the Irish Question. For I spoke of the stir in men's minds, & of the urgency of this matter, to the both of which every day's post brings me new testimony.[41]

The Liberal leader was offering to allow the government to remain in office and to support a Tory Home Rule bill:

> I feel sure the question can only be dealt with by a Government – & I desire specially on grounds of public policy that it should be dealt with by the present Government. If therefore they bring in a proposal for settling the whole question of the future Government of Ireland, my desire will be, reserving of course necessary freedom, to treat it in the same spirit in which I have endeavoured to proceed with respect to Afghanistan & with respect to the Balkan Peninsula.

Balfour (after cautioning Gladstone that he could not imagine that an 'integral part of the United Kingdom' could be dealt with so easily as Afghanistan) wanted nothing to do with the scheme, which in his view could only reward treason as well as divide the Conservatives and save Gladstone from his foolhardiness. He promptly passed the letter along to Salisbury, and advised his uncle that he had learned some things about the Liberals 'which I believe to be accurate'.[42] He believed that Gladstone had put it about within his party that he had encouraged a Conservative Home Rule solution, but that support from certain important Liberals for this or any other policy leading to the creation of an Irish legislature was not forthcoming. Balfour singled out for special mention the grandee Lord Hartington (the future Duke of Devonshire known as 'Harty-Tarty', and brother of the unfortunate Lord Frederick Cavendish) and the former Chancellor G. J. Goschen, as well as Chamberlain and Dilke – and he was right in each case. To Balfour it was clear that, despite his electoral victory, Gladstone's position was precarious, and the best policy was to allow him to stew in the juice of his own creation: the word of his conversion to Home Rule had been leaked, and he must be forced into office and open partnership with Parnell. 'All these considerations', he advised, 'I think go to strengthening the view that we *must* get out of office, and at once. Even if we have to return in consequence of no one being able to fill our places, it is all important that that fact should be driven well into the minds of the public.'

Salisbury needed no convincing. It is true that he was not so philo-
sophically and emotionally dead set against consideration of the *idea* of Irish
autonomy as were most of his party. In a rather dramatic gesture, for
example, he had allowed Lord Carnarvon, the Lord Lieutenant known to
favour some form of Irish self-governance, to meet in secret with Parnell
in early August. The two discussed, parted company, and did nothing.[43] Yet
the Prime Minister understood that such an innovation, in whatever form,
was impossible for the foreseeable future – and if it was destined to be
attempted, it could not be by a Conservative government. He would have
nothing to do with Gladstone's offer of bipartisan support for a bill, muttering only that 'His hypocrisy makes me sick.'[44] Balfour agreed, and
conveyed his uncle's 'curt' conclusion to Gladstone.[45] In January the government met Parliament, the Liberals challenged and defeated them in
the debate on the Queen's Speech, the Irish Nationalists abandoned
the Conservatives, and the Caretaker administration was at an end. The
reluctant Queen had no choice but to call for Mr Gladstone.

Balfour's prediction about the incoming government proved correct.
The Liberal Party existed in an uneasy state at the best of times, with
Whigs clinging to their old traditions and often distrusting the Radical
wing of their own party, and Radicals – not least of all the impatient
Chamberlainites – equally suspicious of the cautious Whigs. Then there
was the Gladstone factor: he was the only leader the Liberals had known,
and a man who inspired great personal loyalty – but who in his party would
embrace Home Rule, who would bolt, and who would sulk in his tent?
He finally revealed his plan to the Cabinet on 16 March; ten days later
Chamberlain resigned the presidency of the Local Government Board,
and G. O. Trevelyan, the Radical Scottish Secretary, followed suit. The
immensely influential Hartington, who had refused to join the government, hardly seemed a natural ally of the Radicals. Now if his friends and
the Chamberlainites could reach some accommodation, it could only mean
greater danger for the Grand Old Man.

But the way was being prepared for other, even more menacing,
alliances. In the midst of this tense atmosphere, Balfour again served as his
uncle's ambassador. He was invited to an intimate 'man's dinner' on 22
March at the London house of Reginald Baliol Brett, a Cambridge contemporary of Frank and Gerald Balfour and a curious, perhaps even
strange, man who possessed intelligence, charm and discretion. A born
courtier (and briefly a Liberal MP), he was uninterested in political power
and responsibility, preferring to influence others who were. He had
many friends, and was 'on the best of terms with mutual enemies like

Chamberlain and Morley, Rosebery and Hartington, Harcourt and Balfour'.[46] His was the ideal safe house where men of disparate party allegiance but mutual antipathy to Home Rule might discuss the political tidal wave that was breaking over them.

Also present were Nathaniel Lord Rothschild, the head of the powerful banking family and a former Liberal MP; Albert Grey, another prominent former Liberal Member and future Governor General of Canada; and, most importantly, Joseph Chamberlain. Balfour, of course, wasted little time in appraising the discussion for his leader, and most of his attention was concentrated on Chamberlain. It was no secret that the great Radical would not stand for Home Rule from Gladstone's or any other hand, and Balfour concluded that, regardless of what had passed between them, Conservative co-operation with Chamberlain and his followers was now possible. Furthermore, he reported to Salisbury Chamberlain's suspicion of the Whig element of the Liberal Party and of Hartington, the Whigs' natural leader, in particular. Balfour was sympathetic, and wrote, 'We shall find in him so long as he agrees with us a very different kind of ally from those lukewarm & slippery Whigs whom it is difficult to differ *from* and impossible to act *with*.' But he added, 'What results will ultimately follow in the impending reconstruction of parties I cannot conjecture. "In politics Ch. [Chamberlain] said on Monday (in words with which in Randolph's mouth I am familiar) there is no use looking beyond the next fortnight"!'[47]

Two days after this letter was written, Chamberlain resigned from the Cabinet, and six weeks thereafter Gladstone introduced his Home Rule bill. At one o'clock in the morning on 8 June, the bill failed on its second reading, as ninety-four 'slippery' Whigs and Chamberlainite Radicals voted against the government.[48] The GOM resigned, and, as predicted, Westminster was once again in turmoil. Lord Randolph Churchill, who had been negotiating over tea in his drawing room with Parnell a few months before and had shown little concern for the Ulster Unionists in the past, now boisterously took up their cause.[49] He made certain Gladstone was aware of his threat to 'agitate Ulster even to resistance beyond constitutional limits', and made ready to play the 'Orange card' for all it was worth.[50] At this time, the always quotable Lord Randolph popularized a sobering political slogan and renamed a party: in 1886 the catchphrase 'Ulster will fight, Ulster will be right' was his; then on 2 March, in a speech in Manchester, he referred to all those who opposed Home Rule, regardless of previous appellation, collectively as the 'Unionist Party', and, as it turned out, the name stuck.[51] Thereafter, Conservatives and anti-Home Rule Liberals would soon come collectively to be known as Unionists.

Despite such fireworks, the election which followed in early July saw a reduced poll compared with that of the previous November, but Balfour retained his seat in East Manchester by 644 votes. The House of Commons was much changed: the Liberal loyalists now numbered only 192, though they could again count on the support of 85 Irish Nationalists; and the Conservatives and their new allies now held 393 seats (315 Tories and 78 anti-Home Rule Liberals or Liberal Unionists), giving them a rock-solid majority over the combined Opposition. As the next decade would show, this was no fluke, as the Irish Question made the Unionists what the Tories alone had not been since 1846: a national party.[52]

A few weeks earlier Balfour had once again served as Conservative emissary to Joseph Chamberlain, meeting him at the country house of Ferdinand de Rothschild on 13 June. Afterwards he told Salisbury that he had asked the great Radical if a Conservative–Liberal Unionist government was possible. For Chamberlain such an offer was premature: 'So far as I am concerned,' he replied, 'it would be impossible for me to form part of such a Government; and though I cannot speak for [Hartington], I doubt he would join one.' His preference was that Salisbury should head a Conservative Cabinet with the external support of the Liberal Unionists, and that is precisely what happened.[53]

Salisbury offered to serve under Hartington, who was seen, owing to rank and experience, as the nominal chief of the Liberal Unionists; but this overture was hardly meant to be accepted. It had to be Salisbury, and the Marquess kissed hands on 25 July. The business of Cabinet-making was the usual delicate dance round the often conflicting aspirations of his colleagues: this time Salisbury bowed to Iddesleigh's desire for the Foreign Office, and Churchill claimed the great prize which could not be denied him and became Chancellor of the Exchequer as well as leader in the Commons. The day that his uncle again became prime minister happened to be Balfour's thirty-eighth birthday, and he passed it quite happily golfing in Great Malvern, attended only by his secretary, F. J. Woods. 'I am rapidly recovering the effect of the general election,' he wrote to Salisbury. 'Fresh air, solitude, and golf are dissipating the last remains of a most obstinate cold. I shall stay here probably till I am wanted in London or until it is safe to go North. Society is at this moment quite intolerable from the unending iteration of the question "what is going to happen next?"'[54] In fact Balfour must have posed to himself the same question regarding his political career.

Mrs Dugdale later pictured him in his hideaway in the Malvern Hills, troubled by doubt, anxious that Salisbury had found his brief performance at the Local Government Board disappointing. He has also been described as troubled by 'virulent self-doubt'.[55] In fact, he was almost immediately offered the Scottish Office – a proposal, self-doubt or not, which he embraced without delay. There was another matter that certainly did trouble Balfour – he wondered if he would be seen by critics merely as the beneficiary of family largesse. He apparently had enquired of his cousin Lord Cranborne (who had held his own parliamentary seat only by five votes) if he detected any hint of nepotism in his uncle's offer. Though a mere twenty-five-year-old political neophyte himself, 'Jem' Cranborne addressed the matter with Cecilian forthrightness: Balfour had been offered a place in the government because there was 'every reason to believe you will be a good appointment in that Office . . . For the rest it was evidently necessary you should have an Office with which you would readily be put into the Cabinet, where Papa, I know, considers you will be most useful to himself and the country. Lastly Papa knows quite well what he is doing – there is, I feel sure, no misapprehension.'[56] As it turned out, Papa undoubtedly did know what he was doing.

The concern about his personal connection to Salisbury continued to trouble him, however, and he wrote to Lady Frances from his retreat:

> I want you, if you can, to find out whether you think it would be desirable, having regard to all the circumstances that I should come back to London at once . . . I feel no natural vocation for being a Great Man's Great Man, still less for being thought to be so, therefore there are obvious motives for not leaving these solitudes; but of course they would not for a moment stand in the way of my coming up if I could be of the slightest use to Uncle R.[57]

He had written similarly to Cranborne's younger brother, Lord Robert Cecil, who was serving as secretary to Salisbury. The two knew each other very well, and the twenty-two-year-old looked upon his cousin as an admired older brother. Despite his youth, he too answered in plain language: 'You say you are quite ready to come to town when any one asks for you. You ought to know your uncle [well enough] to be aware that when he asks for you, you will already be too late.'[58] As it was, Balfour decided not to wait to be asked. Perhaps it was inevitable that critics would murmur that his primary political qualification was that he was 'Prince Arthur' to 'King' Salisbury – for, as the popular saying went, 'Bob' was in fact his uncle. In the end he chose to test both these critics and himself.

★

Despite the urging of Lord Randolph Churchill – of all people – Salisbury did not at first offer Balfour a place in the Cabinet in appointing him Secretary for Scotland. His reputation in the party was advancing, but if he was to prove himself worthy of Cabinet rank it was imperative that he make a success of his new opportunity. The Scottish Office was a new department, launched only in 1885; it was headquartered in hand-me-down premises in Dover House, Whitehall, and saddled with formidable responsibility, inadequate executive power, and uncertain prestige. In his new office, Balfour inherited a struggle which had been generations in the making. At its centre lay the troubling matter of rural poverty in the Highlands and in the Hebridean islands, where a capital-poor and techno-logically backward agriculture was carried on by chronically impoverished and landless crofters. Understandably, some had learned of and embraced the methods of their Irish opposite numbers – so there were rent strikes, intimidation and often open violence, all in the face of inadequate police authority. Parliament seemed agreed that something must be done to aid the crofters while maintaining law and order, but three Scottish Secretaries in hardly more than a year had made little progress discovering what that something should be.

Balfour's Liberal predecessor, Lord Dalhousie, had concentrated his attentions on the small island of Tiree, owned for the most part by the Duke of Argyll, the father of Lady Frances Balfour. Troops and a turret ship were sent to enforce the collection of rents and to prevent violence, but the show of force accomplished little: there were not enough soldiers for a full-scale occupation, and the rebellious population would not allow the satisfaction of an open confrontation. Without any constructive plan – save, perhaps, of pleasing the Duke – the troops contributed nothing to a solution. Balfour quickly reduced the force and returned the ship to the navy, with his thanks. While an irritant and even an embarrassment, Tiree was not to be the centre of concern in the north, and the new Scottish Secretary decided that it was the Isle of Skye where the rebellious move-ment was at the moment most dangerous. And it was to be the Isle of Skye that proved to be his first test in his new office.

In late August, Balfour sent to the Cabinet a memorandum outlining his plans: the violence and disregard for law among the island's crofters were real, frequent and, though on a smaller stage, greater at that time than those in Ireland. Yet the Scottish Secretary lacked the police powers or resources of his Irish counterpart, which in the Scottish case lay primarily with the Home Office.[59] He reminded the Home Secretary, Henry Matthews, of this in a letter of 7 September:

I do not wish to be troublesome, but the question of 'Who is to govern Scotland' is really pressing. Little or nothing is being done in the Western Highlands and Islands to restore the beginnings of law and order: The Lord Advocate declines to move; I cannot move; and I apprehend that the Officials at the Home Office are not troubling their heads about the matter one way or the other.[60]

Balfour got his way, and – with trouble obviously brewing and many other difficulties to worry over – Matthews may well have been relieved to pass the problem along. Action followed soon afterwards, as the police force on Skye was armed and reinforced by a detachment of forty Royal Marines. The Scottish Secretary's policy was made clear: violence would not be tolerated and, where found, would be punished severely. Rent arrears would be paid, or evictions would follow. Finally, as evidence of his even-handedness, he announced that unpaid rates would also be collected from the landlords (many of whom considered themselves exempt from the rates during the rent strikes) at the same time – it was to be law and order for all, without exception.

This was by no means an easy policy to enforce, but Balfour persevered despite a sullen peasantry who hated paying rents and a landlord class who came to revile the Scottish Secretary for forcing them to pay tax before they had collected the full measure of rents owed them. Balfour's problems were made no easier, he insisted to his cousin Robert, by a local bureaucracy accustomed to fitting the laws to the needs of their social betters.[61] Yet by 19 October he felt confident of success, writing to the Prime Minister that, though it was yet early in the game, 'The Skye business has *so far* gone exceedingly well. A considerable number of Crofters have paid up: – and the organisation of the expedition seems to have worked well as my most sanguine anticipations led me to expect.'[62] This, he was pleased to report, came without the use of even one gunboat.

Balfour's early administrative and political success in Scotland was neither unremarked nor unrewarded. On 17 November, Salisbury sent him a hasty note of only two paragraphs. The first brought joy: 'I informed the Cabinet today', the Prime Minister announced, 'that in view of the fact that much of our impending legislation has a Scotch side – & Scotland being in no way represented in the Cabinet – I thought it expedient that you should become a member of it. The announcement was very cordially received.'[63] Certainly Lord Cranborne had revealed to Balfour that Salisbury had expectations of his nephew, presumably if he made a success of his Scottish appointment – and apparently Salisbury was satisfied. In conventionally modest terms Balfour accepted his promotion, adding, 'I do not take a very sanguine estimate of my own political capacities, but if I am able to be of any use in the House it can only be as a Cabinet Minister.'[64]

The remainder of his letter gives a hint of why Balfour's time at the Scottish Office would be brief and the completion of his work there would be left to another:

> And also, it may be, that I shall prove of some use as a counterpoise, even though a feeble one, to Randolph. But this I say not as rating myself high, (Heaven knows!) But as rating the rest of my colleagues, from this point of view, low. – This however is a speculation which if not wholly visionary relates to the 'dim and distant future': by that time we may all be too sick of politics to find further courage to take part in them.

Salisbury had great need of such a counterpoise, for Lord Randolph was proving difficult. He had learned that when he wished to have his way a resignation threat worked wonders, and some must have wondered if he was beginning to see himself as an alternative, perhaps even inevitable, premier. Balfour's prediction of the 'dim and distant future' was optimistic, for the crisis between Salisbury and Churchill came sooner rather than later. The Chancellor quarrelled frequently with his colleagues, and it seemed he took an interest in what some colleagues thought was not necessarily his business. Even those who deferred to him often did so without actually sharing his point of view. Salisbury's patience seemed endless, but it was not, and the divide between the premier and his brilliant but increasingly demanding colleague soon became a chasm. On 2 October 1886, in a speech at Dartford, Churchill announced his own agenda for the government. Among other things, this included ambitious plans to alleviate hardship among the agricultural classes, to change the practice of tithing within the Established Church, and to reform county governance – all of this to be accomplished while significant economies were to be achieved in government spending. Perhaps even more alarming to Salisbury, the Chancellor had his own plans for reshaping foreign policy, calling for greater co-operation with Germany and Austria–Hungary, particularly in regard to policy in the endlessly convoluted struggle for power in the Balkans. Churchill confidently noted to Chamberlain that his speech had caused a 'profound change' in the direction of the nation.[65]

In fact, the 'profound change' was not at all what he anticipated, for when he forced a crisis at the end of the year the result was that he found himself not in Salisbury's place but out of office entirely, amid the ruins of his political career. The object of his ire once again was W. H. Smith, now Secretary of State for War. The military budget was outrageously high,

Churchill insisted, and he called for drastic and immediate reductions. He wrote rather high-handedly to Smith on 15 December, pressing his case and adding, 'I own I do not look for much assistance in this matter from the Govt. generally or from the [Prime Minister], but nothing will induce me to give way on the matter and if I cannot get my way I shall go.'[66] Smith stood firm, and Salisbury backed him – and waited for Churchill's next move. The Cabinet coldly received Lord Randolph's proposals three days later, and refused to endorse them. Churchill, finding himself isolated, chose the grand gesture: he would find out once and for all if they could govern without him. He cheerfully composed his rather ungenerous letter of resignation on the stationery of Windsor Castle, where he was a guest of the Queen – writing while making pleasant conversation with another guest, Lord George Hamilton, the India Secretary, who was one of those whom he blamed for the government's ills. He would never hold office again.

Salisbury, unperturbed at the stroke, held his course, the Cabinet backed him to a man, and the Queen agreed. The Prime Minister seized the opportunity and secured another Chancellor in the person of the Liberal Unionist George Joachim Goschen. An ironic touch was lent by the fact that W. H. Smith, whom he had so long disparaged, replaced Lord Randolph as Leader of the House. Salisbury also wished once again to combine the Foreign Office with the premiership, and saw his opportunity in the crisis. Lord Iddesleigh's health was failing, and again he gave way to Salisbury – sadly, he died of heart failure under Salisbury's roof just as agreement had been reached on his resignation. There was another significant change in the government, as the formidable Hicks Beach faced prolonged medical treatment. Fearing he might be losing his sight, 'Black Michael' resigned office and withdrew for the time being from active politics. To the surprise of many, Arthur Balfour took his place as Chief Secretary for Ireland.

4

Bloody Balfour

❧

O N 7 MARCH 1887 Balfour became Irish Secretary, the tenth man in a decade to take his place in what must have seemed the graveyard of ambitions. One had been murdered, and several had retired with damaged health; the Liberal G. O. Trevelyan broke down under the strain, and his hair was said to have turned white in his year in the post. It is little wonder that Sir Frederick Pollock wrote to Balfour, 'The Chief Secretaryship can hardly, as things go now, be much cause for congratulations to the man who has to undertake it.'[1] Another friend, Walter Pollard, added, 'I don't know whether to congratulate or condole you – perhaps "delighted condolences" is not far from the mark.'[2]

Doubtless there were many who doubted the ability of the willowy young aristocrat to survive the inevitable battles with the case-hardened Irish Nationalists, and at least one journalist lamented that the appointment was akin to throwing a wounded bird 'among a congregation of angry cats'.[3] Though their leaders had informed the Prime Minister that Balfour was one of a handful of aspirants they would tolerate at the Irish Office, among Nationalist backbenchers the reaction was nothing less than 'incredulous laughter'.[4] The Irish *Freeman's Journal* concluded that Balfour was merely 'an elegant, fragile creature, a prey to aristocratic languor, which prevents him from taking any but the limpest attitude', and possessing only three qualifications for the job: 'He was the Prime Minister's nephew, he had no statesman-like reputation to injure, and he was totally ignorant of Ireland.' The Liberal *Pall Mall Gazette* joined in the fun: 'Lord Salisbury may be anxious to avoid the charge of nepotism; but this is nepotism the other way about – nepotism not of the patronizing but of the murderous order. To offer Mr Balfour the Irish Office is like the presentation of a silken bowstring to the doomed victim of the Caliph.'[5] Another Nationalist was said to have got right to the point: 'We have killed Forster, blinded Beach, and smashed up Trevelyan – what shall we do with this weakling?'[6] There was much more of the same, and on none of it did the new Chief Secretary offer a comment.

The indisposed Hicks Beach reflected on the list of recent Chief Secretaries and advised the Prime Minister, 'Physique is, in this office, quite as important as ability – perhaps more . . . If he breaks down, after me, how much does that strengthen the Home Rule argument . . . A fourth failure would almost prove that no man could do the work.'[7] Balfour apparently agreed, recalling many years later:

> Putting all personal considerations aside it surely would be very inexpedient that yet another Chief Secretary should be driven from office by the combined effect of tireless obstruction, bitter invective, and administrative perplexities. From my youth up I had never been robust. It therefore seemed wise, before undertaking new and onerous duties, to show myself to Sir William Jenner.[8]

The eminent physician concluded that Balfour possessed, 'in insurance office language . . . a first class life'.[9] The new Chief Secretary immediately sailed for Ireland to inaugurate what would be remembered as one of the most controversial Irish administrations of the century. He understood that he accepted a dangerous assignment and therefore left behind with his sister-in-law the sealed pouch with its secret glimpsed in an earlier chapter. Consequently, while Chief Secretary his steps would be dogged by two detectives of Scotland Yard's Irish Special Branch, formed in 1883 for just such a purpose, and when he remembered to do so he carried a pistol in the pocket of his coat. Balfour accepted the presence of the policemen, but there were limits to his docility. He rebelled against their tracking on his rambles about his Whittingehame estate and their proximity as he practised golf strokes on the lawns. 'So, he would slip out a side door,' his niece recalled, 'mashie in hand, leaving the detectives stolidly watching the front.'[10]

Balfour's initial stay in Dublin was brief – long enough only to be sworn to his office by the thirty-four-year-old Lord Lieutenant, Charles Vane-Tempest-Stewart, 6th Marquess of Londonderry. The Marquess had once been Balfour's fag at Eton and, despite his grand office, he still knew his place. The office of Chief Secretary for Ireland had once in fact been and was officially still subordinate to that of the Lord Lieutenant. No Lord Lieutenant, however, had sat in the Cabinet since Carnarvon in Salisbury's short-lived Caretaker administration – and none would again. While Londonderry longed for a more active role, he realistically accepted that Balfour was the responsible minister and would not tolerate interference. During his own premiership, Balfour made very clear to another Lord Lieutenant, 'There can be but one head of Irish Administration,' and it was the Chief Secretary.[11]

The new Chief Secretary had a less easy time with Lord Ashbourne, the Irish Lord Chancellor. It was not to be an easy partnership, not least because Ashbourne considered himself supremely expert on all matters Irish and was unimpressed with young Balfour. The Lord Chancellor also possessed a strong voice, which grated on Balfour, who wrote to Salisbury only a day after arriving in Dublin, 'I had rather carry on serious business in the middle of a Manchester Cotton Mill than within reach of that man's voice!'[12] Dublin-born, Ashbourne (as Edward Gibson) had once been MP for Trinity College, Dublin, and was the author of the eponymous 1885 legislation which had provided a fund of £5 million for loans to the Irish tenantry to facilitate land purchase. He was unused to being challenged within his party on Irish affairs and, unlike Londonderry, he enjoyed the advantage of a seat in the Cabinet.[13] It was not a happy match, and Balfour managed it simply by ignoring the Lord Chancellor as much as possible.

From his predecessor Balfour inherited as permanent under-secretary Major General Sir Redvers Buller, a capable and experienced officer whose reputation would one day be broken on the South African veldt. Sympathetic to the trials of the tenantry – perhaps too sympathetic for the taste of many Unionists – Buller was nearing the end of his term in Ireland, and was anxious to return to the army. As his successor, Balfour chose a retired Indian Army officer, Sir Joseph West Ridgeway, whose intellect, administrative experience and quiet zeal for the enforcement of law appealed to his new master. Ridgeway had another qualification which pleased Balfour: he explained to his prospective employer that, while he was of Irish birth, he knew little of the country and had no friends there. The combination Balfour found irresistible: 'Then that is a great qualification for the post, for you will not be besieged by your friends in search of employment.'[14] Balfour would come to consider the choice a happy one, and the two worked well together.

As his under-secretary, Balfour chose Colonel Edward King-Harman. The appointment was provocative to the Nationalists, for the Irish Unionist landlord had in his youth been a supporter of the proto-Home Ruler Isaac Butt, and thus was loathed by them as a turncoat. To Balfour's delight, King-Harman demonstrated absolute indifference to all harangues and insults. Henry Lucy considered him 'rather more distinguished for muscle than brains', but King-Harman was an unflappable subordinate who could be trusted with the minor sparring in the House at question time – which his opponents, vainly crying 'Balfour, Balfour!', angrily (and accurately) judged was an expression of the Chief Secretary's contempt for their disruptions.[15]

Balfour took as his personal secretary his young friend George Wyndham. Schooled like the Balfour brothers at the Grange and at Eton, young Wyndham was an indifferent scholar, excelling more on the playing fields than in the schoolroom. Percy Wyndham was forced to relinquish his hopes of academic distinction for his son, who was allowed to choose Sandhurst over Oxford and to take a commission in the Coldstream Guards. By 1887 he had already seen action in Egypt, been mentioned in dispatches, and seemed to have found his place; but, it proved not suitable enough – as so much in his life seemed not suitable enough.[16]

Wyndham was extraordinarily handsome and deeply patriotic, and his charm and romantic, rather poetic, sentimentality were admired during his young manhood. Much is given to some, for in addition he was also a gifted athlete who cut a splendid figure on horseback. As Balfour assembled his staff, Wyndham had just completed the successful wooing and winning of Sibell, Lady Grosvenor, the beautiful widow of the son of the Duke of Westminster. Ten years older than Wyndham, Lady Grosvenor (who retained that style over being plain Mrs Wyndham) was said to have broken the hearts of many suitors who wished to comfort her in her loss, including that of Balfour's fellow Soul George Curzon.

Yet Wyndham was not a man destined to happiness and contentment. He turned his back on his army career in favour of politics, and made a 'good' marital connection over one founded on an enduring love. Ultimately, the first decision would bring him humiliation, and the second disappointment – perhaps he was too sentimental for the life he chose and too ambitious for the one he rejected. Whatever the reason, Wyndham became something of a tragic figure, for whom life's brilliant beginnings would fade away in anticlimax and drink.

From boyhood, Wyndham had hero-worshipped Arthur Balfour, the philosopher-politician. The Irish Secretary's mix of artistic and intellectual gifts with political success dazzled the young lieutenant, and that admiration endured for the remainder of his life, even years later when the two became politically divided. With what was surely spectacularly poor timing, Balfour wrote to the newly-wed Wyndham offering him the unpaid post of private secretary while the happy couple were still on their wedding travels in Italy.[17] It was an offer too good to ignore, and, at twenty-three, Wyndham abandoned both his army career and his honeymoon and accepted at once.

Salisbury, pessimist that he was, had no romantic notions about Ireland and suspected that in the end it was not assimilable into the British system – perhaps, as he put it, an 'Irish Republic of the future' lay at the distant end of things.[18] But if this ultimately came about, it certainly would not be for a very long time – and it would not be because of any failure of heart of any government he led. In the meantime, he was sure that what Ireland needed was not what he considered Gladstone's pandering and politicking, but rather a generation of 'resolute' governance. In the face of the Nationalists' recently launched Plan of Campaign and of the parliamentary obstructionism by the Irish party, as well as what he feared was the weakness of the Irish police and judiciary, the Prime Minister concluded that both Hicks Beach and Buller had failed to see obvious necessity. 'I agree with Buller', he wrote, 'that you cannot govern the Irish, or anybody else, by severity alone; but I think he is fundamentally wrong in believing that conciliation and severity must go together. The severity must come first. They must "take a licking" before conciliation will do them any good.'[19]

Balfour believed deeply in the Irish Union not merely because he was a Conservative and Conservatives believed such things, but also because Home Rule meant political subdivision of an island kingdom with a large empire to hold. 'Surely we should be mad', he told the House on 9 April 1889, 'if at a time when every nation in America and Europe is drawing closer the bonds which unite separate parts, we were to scatter and divide.' He believed equally strongly that a political nostrum such as Home Rule simply could not solve Ireland's great problem, its poverty. In fact, if self-government would allow Ireland to be more Irish, then this was, to his mind, precisely the antithesis of what was needed – prosperity. To him, the only hope was for the Irish to embrace modernizing Anglo-Saxon ways.[20] This deeply held belief led Balfour to his greatest success in Ireland, his programme of social legislation to uplift the most dreadfully poor districts of that nation. Yet it also reflected his greatest failure, his inability to understand the reality of Irish nationalism in a century perhaps more committed to that heady draught than any other. It also caused him, with somewhat greater success, to strive to undo for a time the success achieved by Charles Stewart Parnell in shaping an effective Irish National Party. To Balfour, even when on their best behaviour, the Parnellites were never more than a party of revolutionaries who wished ultimately to break up the United Kingdom and cared little for what it might take or with whom it would require them to co-operate.[21]

Balfour agreed with his uncle that an Irish policy based on 'platitudes and rose-water' would be useless, but what was his policy to be? In the first place, he agreed with the March 1887 conclusions of the commission on the land question, appointed by Gladstone and chaired by Lord Cowper, that the various Irish land acts passed had so far solved nothing; and he was certain that further initiatives would have to be taken to alleviate the enduring poverty of rural Ireland. Some Irishmen, however, were disinclined to await his solutions. The Plan of Campaign, created by the Nationalists John Dillon, William O'Brien and Timothy Harrington, had been announced in October 1886 and, by means of withholding rents on some 100 targeted estates and paying them instead into a maintenance fund for evicted tenants, was meant to bring the landlords and the administration to their knees. Operating illegally (and without the active participation of Parnell), it proved a formidable challenge, but could not function without the use of selective intimidation – of landlord and tenant alike. To frustrate the authorities further, whether due to principle or coercion, juries often refused to convict those charged with offences under existing laws. This cycle Balfour meant to break.

Economic and social reform also must come, he believed, and unreasonable landlords – those 'who act like lunatics' – must be brought to heel as much as rebellious tenants. First, however, order had to be restored.[22] The primary problem, in his view, was economic rather than political; and in Ireland economic questions resolved themselves into questions about the land.[23] A definitive solution to this problem would then eventually ensure accommodation between Britain and Ireland. He was quite willing to impose a 'stern, though paternal despotism' to accomplish this goal, and, in cases where amelioration of rents offered no long-term hope, he was already considering such seemingly unconservative measures as mandatory state purchase of economically hopeless estates, while encouraging the migration of excess population. He wondered: could such a 'scheme be carried out through the instrumentality of a very strong Land Commission, sitting in Dublin, with powers to purchase compulsorily from the Landlord; to emigrate a portion of the inhabitants; and to resell the land to the remainder?'[24] In the meantime, recalcitrant landlords might well be subdued, he thought, by being forced into the bankruptcy courts.[25]

While willing to dose landowner and peasant with strong medicine, he did not covet the role of conqueror: his concern was not obedience to himself, but obedience to the law for the purpose of working a constructive policy. The use of coercion to exact mere compliance, he thought, was where Cromwell's policy had foundered. Likewise, to greet lawlessness with generosity was simply giving way to extortion. He believed that Britain had vacillated between these two policies, relying first upon one and then the other, and solved nothing. 'That mistake I shall not imitate,' he pledged to the House of Commons:

> I shall be as relentless as Cromwell in enforcing obedience to the law, but at the same time, I shall be as radical as any reformer in redressing grievances, and especially in removing every cause of complaint in regard to land.

And he indicated that he was not entirely in agreement with the Prime Minister on the matter of the provision of the carrot and the application of the stick:

> It is on the twofold aspect of my policy that I rely for success. Hitherto English Governments have stood first upon one leg and then upon the other. They have either been all for repression, or all for reform. I am for both; repression as stern as Cromwell: reform as thorough as Mr Parnell or anyone else can desire.[26]

Balfour was pleased to consider any option which might strengthen his hand, including enlisting the assistance of the papacy itself. Employing the good offices of several prominent Catholic Unionists, including the Duke of Norfolk and Sir John Ross of Bladensberg (the secretary to the British mission to the Vatican), the case against the Plan of Campaign was put before Pope Leo XIII, who in April 1888 issued a papal rescript condemning both the practice of boycotting and the Plan of Campaign itself.[27] While something of a public relations triumph, the papal stricture had little effect in Ireland.

Though it made overzealous Protestants uncomfortable, co-operation with the Holy See was not the only extra-political front on which the Chief Secretary waged his war against the Plan of Campaign. Plan strategists chose a vulnerable target in the financially rickety estates of Charles Ponsonby in Youghal, County Cork, and by late 1888 the rent strike had almost destroyed him. Balfour was much concerned and wrote to Salisbury, 'Ponsonby is "broke", and has lost all nerve . . . If Ponsonby gives in, it will be the worst thing that has happened to us for some time past. This and Clanricarde [under a similar attack] . . . are the most dangerous rocks ahead.'[28] Frustrated that the landlord's neighbours offered no assistance and that arbitration had been rejected by Plan leaders, Balfour even considered using 'secret service money' to keep Ponsonby afloat. Finally he hit upon the idea of covertly encouraging the formation of a syndicate of wealthy landlords of the district, each putting in £10,000 both to rescue Ponsonby and to thwart the Plan of Campaign. The strategy saved Ponsonby, but the secret of the syndicate – or at least part of it – leaked, and its leader, Arthur Smith-Barry, was soon contending with rent stoppages on his estates in Tipperary. Smith-Barry's pockets were deep, however: the treasury of the Plan of Campaign was nearly exhausted in the battle, and the struggle ended in stalemate. Balfour was anxious that his name and the initiative taken by his office remain veiled, which they did – save in rumour. The syndicate strategy was, if expensive, successful enough to be used on a smaller scale elsewhere in Ireland.[29]

The most effective device to which London had turned in the past to suppress lawlessness had been special legislation – ad-hoc 'Crimes Acts' to increase the powers of the police and the courts to crush disorder. Legislation of this kind was nothing new: Gladstone had passed such a bill as recently as 1882, and Hicks Beach was in the early stages of bringing in another at the time of his resignation. Balfour ignored this and introduced his own Criminal Law Amendment Bill on 28 March 1887, which predictably was met with uproar by the Irish Nationalists. Gladstone added his own special brand of drama by condemning the exercise in the Commons and storming out of the Chamber, and Lord Hartington despaired of Balfour's chances of shepherding his bill through Parliament.[30] In a long and detail-laden speech much interrupted by his Parnellite antagonists, Balfour doggedly laid out the plan: powers of the resident magistrates to examine witnesses under oath would be increased, and the Irish Attorney-General would be empowered to transfer trials from unsettled districts to others where 'fair and impartial' proceedings could be carried out – though on Hartington's advice Balfour abandoned a clause to provide for the removal of such trials to England.[31] The Lord Lieutenant was authorized to 'proclaim' entire districts in violation of the law and within them to create courts of summary jurisdiction to deal with cases of rent conspiracy, riot, resistance to eviction and incitement to violation of any provision of the law. Justice would be swift in proclaimed districts, with up to six months' hard labour for violators of the act. Unlike certain of his predecessors, Balfour did not seek to suspend habeas corpus; but, unlike the efforts of his predecessors, he established the act as part of the permanent legal code of Ireland – hence obviating the need ever to repeat the process.[32]

The new Chief Secretary's speech introducing the long and complicated bill was pedestrian at best, and was made worse by the endless heckling of the Nationalists. Balfour himself admitted to his sister Lady Rayleigh that, exhausted by the late hours and lack of sleep required to rush the bill along, he had stumbled badly, and he added playfully that his own side called out 'our man has failed!'[33] But he had not, and confidence was soon restored. It was usually a mistake to judge either his knowledge or his resolution from set-piece speeches – even those made in better circumstances than these.

The next few years were to be the making of him as a politician. In his first important office and leading a crucial fight for the first time since entering the House, he quickly developed the style and method for which he would become legendary. Sprawling on the front bench in his usual languorous and untroubled fashion, feet upon the table, eyes hooded, and long hands folded casually, he missed not a word of debate and was on his feet in an instant when challenged. He possessed a lightning wit polished in the Balfour family school of dining-table debate, and he quickly developed the invaluable gift he shared with Joseph Chamberlain of 'making capital out of interruptions that would embarrass a less ready speaker'.[34] It was a pose, of course, and while it was true that his memory was notoriously unreliable, he was blessed with a dependable staff who regularly supplied him with the masses of data for his defence which he had no hope of carrying in his head. This was a Balfour neither the Irish nor the Liberals – nor, without doubt, many Unionists – expected. Taking personal charge of the struggle night after night, he made regular use of the parliamentary procedural weapon of closure, which allowed the majority to limit debate and force a bill to a vote. Known as the 'guillotine', it had been originated by Gladstone five years earlier and strengthened by the Unionists for the express purpose of dealing with Irish obstructionism.

He did not miss a day of debate, and his campaign was carried out through a mixture of leaving the minor annoyances to King-Harman (who was usually instructed merely to respond with cursory prepared remarks) and taking on the dangerous ones himself. The hope among the Parnellites that he would prove easy prey was crushed. Salisbury had once counselled him: 'You will soon by experience learn the precise limit of your powers – & then within those limits you will be able to inflict an intolerable amount of annoyance.'[35] He bore this advice in mind. In fact his style of debate was both purposely irritating and stunningly effective – apparently, to judge from the results, more irritating and more effective than his opponents. Winston Churchill recalled of a debate a few years later that when an Irish MP, irritated to the point of losing his temper, shook his fist in Balfour's face, he stood his ground, showing no emotion whatever, gazing down upon the red-faced attacker 'with no more and no less than the interest of a biologist examining through a microscope the contortions of a rare and provoked insect'.[36] The observant Henry Lucy recalled his parrying 'with light rapier the bludgeon blows rained upon him, and then stepping forward and pinking an adversary with a sharp, clear thrust . . . He is the most perfect living example of the mailed hand under the silken glove.'[37] In future years, observers could look back on these scenes as a sort of prototype of a 'Balfour debate'. Without ever showing his very real exasperation or raising his voice, he declared victory on 8 July when his bill passed its final reading in the House.

After sailing through the Unionist-dominated Lords, the Crimes Act received the royal assent ten days later, and Balfour found himself in the strongest legal position of any Chief Secretary in living memory – and all waited to see exactly what he would do with his new authority. From the outset, he reminded friend and foe alike that those who opposed government policy could do so within the broad constitutional channels available to them, but violation of the law – whatever the reason – was another matter altogether. He explained his position to a sympathetic audience in Manchester, but his words were directed as much towards the radical Home Rulers: 'Mere abuse will be treated with contempt, but when it comes to open advocacy of crime, when men who come over here and speak softly to the English people, go back to Ireland and urge the excitable peasantry of that country to resist the law, then I say you have ceased to be politicians, and you have become criminals, and as criminals I shall proceed against you.'[38] There was, in his mind, no distinction between political and non-political crime, as there would be no distinction among perpetrators. And his deeds were the guarantees of his words: within a year of the passage of the bill more than twenty Irish Nationalist MPs had experienced prison time as results of the Crimes Act – and there were more to come.

Much was made of this, as the imprisonment by the government of the day of political opponents had not been a common British political practice for some long time. Salisbury and Balfour shared the belief that a dose of the plank bed and prison garb was a sovereign prescription even for MPs who flirted with revolution, and the Irish Secretary wrote in September, 'I have left word that [Irish magistrates] are to proceed against any Member of Parliament in every case in which there is a serious incitement to lawlessness given, and a clear prospect of getting a conviction.' Celebrities who courted political martyrdom were to be accommodated: if convicted under the Crimes Act, they were to be imprisoned:

> with general instructions that they are to be treated in every respect like ordinary prisoners, but that most careful watch is to be kept on their health. I am going to have a Prison Inspector over from England to take a general survey of Prison management on the other side of St George's Channel as to enable me to state with confidence in the House of Commons that the systems are identical in both Countries, not merely in theory, but also in practice.[39]

Several prominent Liberal Unionists, Chamberlain among them, had expressed concerns about the treatment of Crimes Act convicts, and Balfour consistently replied that he could not 'see my way now anymore than I have on previous occasions to admit a distinction between "Crimes Act crime" and ordinary crime'. He refused to bend to demands that prisoners be allowed to wear their own clothes, though he did end the 'idiotic rule related to their hair clipping'.[40] Though severe – and meant to be – by the standards of the time the treatment of Crimes Act convicts was humane and even privileged.[41]

Not all those who fell foul of the act were MPs, of course – nor for that matter were they all Irish. Balfour believed in a remarkable degree of equality when it came to the new act, which in its first year resulted in nearly 700 arrests, and almost as many convictions. Those caught in the snare of the law included, at one time or another, not only many of Parnell's party, but also the gentleman poet and adventurer Wilfrid Scawen Blunt, a kinsman of Lady Elcho and George Wyndham. This 'drawing room revolutionary and bedroom subversive' in 1887 contrived to get himself arrested for encouraging the rent strike against the notorious Lord Clanricarde. Balfour wrote to Lady Elcho, 'We are trying to put your cousin in gaol. I have not heard whether we have succeeded: I hope so, for I am sure Blunt would be horribly disappointed at any other consumma-tion.'[42] The Prime Minister was more to the point: 'I was delighted to see you had run Wilfrid Blunt in.'[43] Blunt knew Balfour slightly, but was a close friend of Wyndham, and he hoped his own arrest would bring maximum embarrassment to the Chief Secretary. However, he had mis-calculated. Balfour described him to Lady Elcho as a 'goodish poet a goodish lawn tennis player and a goodish fellow', but that did not deter him in the slightest from ordering his arrest. In the end, only Wyndham was discomfited, and Blunt served his eight-week sentence.[44]

A postscript to this affair provides a tale worth repeating: four years later, when Balfour was Leader of the House, Wyndham invited him to dine and asked, given these earlier events, if he could forgive and forget, and meet Blunt again. The invitation elicited a reply both priceless and characteris-tic: 'My dear George, I don't know that I am very forgiving, but I do know that I am very forgetting, and not having the least idea to what you refer, I can only say that I shall be delighted to dine with you to meet Wilfrid Blunt.'[45] The ex-convict noted in his diary that the dinner conversation was apolitical, and that Balfour was very kind to him and drove him home in his brougham.[46] A further five years later, Blunt would seek his revenge against Balfour in another way.

There were more serious challenges than any that could be posed by Wilfrid Blunt. Soon after Balfour's appointment, an official order went out to the Royal Irish Constabulary barracks at troubled Youghal in County Cork from the local magistrate, Captain Plunkett, meant to embolden the local police unit: 'Deal very summarily with any resistance to lawful authority,' it indicated. 'If necessary do not hesitate to shoot them.' The Chief Secretary supported the magistrate, the order was leaked to the press, and Nationalists were outraged – but careful to keep their protests verbal. As might be expected, Home Rulers saw their opportunity to brand the new régime as plotters of 'wholesale butchery'.[47] Buller, on the other hand, advised his master that his endorsement was 'that sort of support that Irish officials have so long needed'.[48] The contest of wills between Nationalists and the new Chief Secretary was on.

It exploded in the autumn of 1887 and immortalized the village of Mitchelstown when, on 9 September, a riot broke out at what was to be the trial of William O'Brien and John Mandeville for inciting disobedience of the Crimes Act. A protest was announced, and a crowd of several thousand gathered to be addressed by John Dillon, and the English Radical, Henry Labouchère – O'Brien and Mandeville were as yet nowhere to be seen. The badly outnumbered police reported that, when they attempted to clear a way though the crowd so their recorder could take down the words of the speakers, men armed with stout blackthorn sticks attacked them. Badly mauled, the constables retreated to their barracks – but not before shots were fired and three of the crowd lay dead, with several more wounded. No fewer than fifty-four police were injured. As a result, Balfour was attacked in Parliament with all the force the Parnellites and their Liberal allies could muster – Labouchère described the scene of a 'massacre' in which armed police coldly opened fire on unarmed men, women and children, and Gladstone himself thundered 'Remember Mitchelstown!' The Chief Secretary faced two full days of verbal assaults and gave not an inch, supporting, even commending, the Royal Irish Constabulary for their courage and loyalty in the face of intimidation and armed assault.[49]

His critics were not limited to Parliament and the rent-strike villages of Ireland, for on 13 November a huge protest rally was held in Trafalgar Square. Harangued by some of the most famous radicals of the day, including at least one future Liberal Cabinet minister, John Burns, the demonstration erupted into violence, the police were thrown back, and several mounted Guards units were summoned. This 'Bloody Sunday' produced plenty of injuries on all sides – several of which proved fatal – and Burns, among others, drew a six weeks' sentence for incitement to riot, adding immeasurably to his growing fame. Again, Balfour did not recant a syllable of his support for the police. The law must be obeyed, he insisted, and its officers must be expected to defend themselves by whatever means possible 'in the last necessity'. He reminded those who would consider violence that 'when that last necessity occurs' there were means which 'no officer should shrink from using'. From this point, his enemies never again likened the Chief Secretary to a wounded bird thrown among angry cats: after Mitchelstown and Bloody Sunday he was 'Bloody Balfour'. He gloried in the cognomen, writing (in red ink) to Lady Elcho on Christmas Eve: 'Greetings from Bl—dy B-lf-r. I write to you in the hue appropriate to my sanguinary character.'[50]

Though the constables at Mitchelstown were indicted by the local coroner's jury, the charge was struck down by the Dublin Court of Queen's Bench, while the Chief Secretary again publicly praised their bravery and commended their forbearance. His unswerving public support of the police – though within the confines of his headquarters at Dublin Castle he demanded that the service be improved – had an extremely positive effect on morale within the force. He insisted that what he expected was honesty, courage and efficiency, and in return the constabulary would receive the full support of the state.[51]

Balfour soon discovered, however, that the police constituted only one of his problems, and that the Irish judiciary presented yet another. The central and circuit courts and the local magistracy were notoriously undependable in carrying out prosecutions under the Crimes Act. Some, particularly on the lowest levels, were intimidated by threats of violence, while others were openly sympathetic to the Nationalist cause; some he suspected of simple corruption. He informed Salisbury, 'With Packed Benches of [Nationalist] Magistrates; & with corrupt coroners juries we shall have to deal with a somewhat high hand. – I wish to Heaven we could deal with the Dublin Magistrates in an equally effective manner.'[52] The Irish judiciary constituted a problem that he never fully solved during his time in Ireland. He paid close attention to the performance of individual magistrates, to the transfer whenever possible of those he suspected of excessive leniency, and to the appointment of competent judges when vacancies occurred.[53] The Legal Department of Dublin Castle – the 'Law Room' – was crucial to making the Chief Secretary's plans a success. Salisbury warned him to expect little: 'You have the stupidest lot of lawyers in Ireland any Govt was ever cursed with.'[54]

Balfour himself had no particular love for lawyers.[55] There were exceptions, however, and one was the forty-five-year-old Irish Solicitor

General, Peter O'Brien. Called 'Peter the Packer' because of his ability to impanel juries likely to return guilty verdicts, he could usually be depended upon to ensure that indictments led to convictions. A Catholic Unionist, O'Brien's long and successful service in the Law Room made him one of the most unpopular men in Ireland – it also ensured his rise to become Attorney-General and then Lord Chief Justice of Ireland and a peer of the realm.

More significant for the future of Irish and also British politics was another Dublin lawyer, Edward Henry Carson. Only thirty-three when he caught the Chief Secretary's eye, Carson was a natural prosecutor if ever there was one, and he first earned Balfour's respect and admiration by agreeing to take on the case which led to the infamous Mitchelstown affray. Carson's courage was as formidable as his will: he strode through the angry crowd who knew he was there only to ensure that their heroes went to prison. The bravery of the tall, saturnine advocate had for the moment gained their respect and with it their undying enmity – and the latter would long outlast the former. He also acquired the admiration of the Chief Secretary, and, in the four years that followed, Balfour in turn earned the respect of the unflinching young prosecutor. Carson recalled to Mrs Dugdale long after Balfour's death that his fearless consistency and steady public support of his officials made him a hero to that habitually dispirited and reviled class: 'It was Mitchelstown that made us certain we had a man at last. That affair was badly muddled. But Balfour never admitted anything. He simply backed his own people up. After that there wasn't an official in Ireland who didn't worship the ground he walked on.' In years to come the two would have their political differences, but in these dangerous days the Chief Secretary had discovered a ruthless and loyal ally. Carson found steady employment, becoming the busiest of Crown prosecutors and Ireland's most famous and controversial lawyer. In his eightieth year Balfour had not forgotten: 'I made Carson and Carson made me,' he told Mrs Dugdale. 'I've told you how no one had courage . . . On the whole it was an impossible state of affairs. Carson had nerve, however. I sent him all over the place, prosecuting, getting convictions. We worked together.'[56] Balfour also 'made' Carson in another way, for in 1890 he recommended him as Unionist parliamentary candidate for Trinity College, Dublin, a seat which he won two years later and held for twenty-six years.[57] If the Chief Secretary became 'Bloody Balfour', his favourite lawyer soon gained the sobriquet 'Coercion Carson'.

In Balfour's first months in office another bizarre episode unfolded in London which would shake the government and blemish the reputation of the world's most famous newspaper. This involved a series of articles in *The Times* published between March and June 1887 under the provocative title 'Parnellism and Crime' and meant to link Parnell and his lieutenants firmly to the violent outrages which regularly punctuated the Anglo-Irish struggle. On 18 April, the day of the second reading of Balfour's Crimes Bill, the most inflammatory article appeared linking Parnell to the gruesome 1882 Phoenix Park murders of Lord Frederick Cavendish and Thomas Burke. The chief piece of evidence was a letter of 15 May 1882 over Parnell's signature to a known Fenian, Patrick Egan, expressing his regret over the 'accident of Lord F. Cavendish's death'; but, the message continued, 'I cannot refuse to admit that Burke got no more than his deserts.'[58]

While his followers raged against the accusation that he would approve of murder, Parnell denounced the letter as a 'barefaced forgery' but refused to take action against the newspaper. One F. H. O'Donnell, who insisted he had been libelled in the articles, thought differently and sued *The Times*. The tale of the scandal is long and complicated and has been much examined by historians. It is sufficient to say here that, once the battle was engaged, the Irish leader – who knew the letter to be a forgery for the simple reason that he had not written it – meant to fight it out to the greatest political advantage.[59] Denied by Salisbury the select committee of the House he demanded, Parnell accepted the offer of a special judicial commission, which Salisbury intended to investigate not merely the veracity of the newspaper articles but the accuracy of the charges against Parnell and his friends.

To carry out their investigation, this panel of distinguished jurists endured excruciating months filled with exhibits, testimony, accusation and counter-accusation, and in February 1889 the affair reached its climax. In what F. S. L. Lyons has called 'the best traditions of Parnellite melodrama', testimony to the commission revealed that agents of *The Times* had advanced money to a disreputable anti-Home Rule clique that had provided the 'evidence' on which the exposé was based.[60] Richard Pigott, an unsavoury Irish journalist and sometime pornographer 'who looked like a Pickwickian but was a blackmailer', confessed to having forged the letter.[61] After this revelation – and Pigott's flight to Madrid and subsequent suicide – the newspaper was appropriately humiliated, and the charge that Parnell had been stupid enough to record on paper his approval of daylight murder was ground underfoot. After such theatrics the appearance of the commission report a year later at first seemed anticlimactic in the extreme, even though the Irish leaders stood charged – if not with Cavendish's murder – certainly with incitement of violence in Ireland. Parnell is said to have replied to his friends, 'Well, really, between ourselves, I think it is just about what I would have said myself.'[62]

Parnell and his Nationalist and Liberal supporters endeavoured to keep interest focused on the infamous letter, and for a time succeeded. The 'Uncrowned King of Ireland', after the Pigott revelations, was greeted in the House on 1 March 1889 with a huge ovation led by the Grand Old Man himself. He was granted the freedom of the City of Edinburgh and elected a life member of the National Liberal Club. He was warmly received by Gladstone at Hawarden, as his fame reached its apogee.

In public, Salisbury offered no satisfaction to his enemies: the revelations regarding the letter, he insisted, proved only that the uncovering of the activities of rascals led to the discovery of further mischief by other rascals. Yet he understood that the prestige of his government was badly shaken by the affair, as a sought-after triumph had been for the moment reduced to a great public humiliation. But to him this was only a battle lost, and there was a war to win.

Balfour agreed. Dublin Castle might be for the moment demoralized, and the entire Irish administration in need of 'gingering up', but the cause was more important than any setback. He wrote to his under-secretary in the dark days of February:

> To a person of cynical mind there is something extremely entertaining in the present posture of affairs with regard to the Parnell Commission. That the 'Times' has been stupid beyond all that history tells us of stupidity is surprising enough. It is perhaps even more surprising that the results of their stupidity should have spread such dismay among our people . . . I shall make it clear that the Government are not going out of office over Pigott which appears to be the settled conviction.[63]

He added a month later, 'I have never felt personally discouraged, and hope that you will try to explain to our weak-kneed brethren in Dublin that the Government are not likely to dissolve for many years to come.'[64]

In the House, he faced some of the most brutal assaults of his entire tenure as Irish Chief Secretary and tirelessly led the counter-attack night after night, giving his opponents no satisfaction. The struggle also saw the end of the last vestiges of co-operation between Churchill and his former colleagues, as Lord Randolph's persistence in criticizing the creation of the commission and tying it in the strongest language to the Pigott scandal ('A ghastly, bloody, rotten foetus – Pigott!! Pigott!! Pigott!!') divided him from Balfour – and from almost all his old friends – for the remainder of their careers.[65]

The thirty-five volumes that made up the report of the judicial commission did not appear until a year after the Pigott affair, by which time the remarkable career of Charles Stewart Parnell was all but ruined. The costs to the government were great: the Opposition insisted that the administration had behaved in a blatantly partisan fashion in creating a quasi-judicial body that was a constitutional innovation and sidestepped the normal course of justice. The injury to the reputation of *The Times* was enormous, as was the financial damage: though Parnell was awarded only £5,000 in damages, its total outlay for the entire affair exceeded £200,000.[66] Unable to deny its support of the newspaper (whose leading counsel was none other than the Attorney-General, Sir Richard Webster), the government also shared in some of that humiliation. The financial burden remained the newspaper's alone, for, though Salisbury was tempted to respond to the request for assistance from G. E. Buckle, the editor, Balfour was adamantly opposed to the idea, as was the balance of the Cabinet.[67]

The episode of the special commission was an embarrassing defeat for the Unionists – and well deserved, many historians have concluded, for such witch-hunting.[68] And so it may have been. But recently other observers have suggested that, despite the curse of Pigott, the daily press reports of the hearings and the massive final report accomplished more than these earlier critics allowed: 'For while Parnell was triumphantly vindicated, links between other ostensible constitutionalists and criminality had been firmly established, and a wider relationship between the Home Rule movement and militancy had been posited.'[69] Despite its obvious heavy-handedness, the Unionist strategy against the Nationalist leadership drew blood, damaging severely the respectability so valued by Parnell. Balfour never indicated enthusiasm over the creation of the judicial commission, but he never wavered in his support of it – even when the tactic seemed to have failed – and in the end it played a useful part in damaging the credibility of the Home Rule party.[70]

As it was, the joy of the Home Rulers was short-lived. It was true that the Protestant 'Green Lion' had managed to establish a modus vivendi with the Catholic hierarchy in Ireland. Likewise, there were British Liberals, believers in the 'union of hearts' of the right-thinking, who preferred to concentrate their thoughts on Parnell's high-minded goal of a more just Ireland rather than on the methods of some of his supporters. These linkages were vulnerable, however, and if they could be impugned, perhaps Parnell and the Home Rule movement could be crippled for another generation. Only weeks after the commission report was released, the public-relations tide turned in favour of the Unionists. In warfare, whether among armies or political parties, victory seldom comes without luck, and an enemy's blunder sometimes provides a triumph that neither leadership nor bravery could have produced. So it was that, at this crucial point, the Unionists were handed the prize they had failed to achieve on their own, the destruction of Charles Stewart Parnell – for which he had only himself to blame.

The details of this romantic and tragic story belong to another life, and we need take account only of the barest outline. On Boxing Day 1889, the dubious go-between Captain O'Shea surfaced once again. After consulting with Joseph Chamberlain, of all people, he wrote to Balfour explaining that he had instituted divorce proceedings against his wife, Katherine, and that Parnell would be named as co-respondent.[71] Though he played the part of the wronged husband, he had been aware for years of his wife's liaison with Parnell, and of the children she had borne the Irish leader.[72] By bringing suit in open court, O'Shea managed to make known to the world the damaged lives of all three principals and ensured their mutual destruction. Balfour, though well aware of the obvious political advantage in the development, was repelled by the sordidness of the affair and answered O'Shea's letter coldly. As a comparative stranger, he said, it would be impertinent of him to comment on the deeply personal matter.

> It deals [he wrote] with a subject necessarily painful, and of which the painfulness must, I fear, necessarily be increased by the publicity which would seem to be now forced upon you. I sincerely trust that no aggravation of inevitable suffering may be brought about by the unwarrantable introduction of political and party feeling into private affairs, from which, in my opinion, they should be wholly dissociated.[73]

Balfour accordingly made no public statements about the affair and left the low road to others – and few derived such pleasure from it as the Liberal Unionist leader Lord Hartington, who, as Professor Curtis reminds us, was 'perhaps the least qualified of all to throw stones at adulterers'. Harty-Tarty wrote to the Queen that he 'never thought anything in politics could give me as much pleasure as this'.[74] Even Gladstone, who must have known of the Parnell–O'Shea liaison, abandoned his former ally in the face of Nonconformist displeasure at the sordid news. The GOM, in a public letter to his colleague John Morley, called upon Parnell to resign the leadership of the party he had done so much to create, and vaguely threatened his own retirement if the Irish leader did not own up and leave politics. Despite impossible odds in the climate of opinion of those

Victorian days, the Green Lion roared defiance at his critics, and in so doing he ensured that his party – rapidly dividing into Parnellites and anti-Parnellites – would tear itself to pieces.

The distance which Balfour maintained from the tawdry affair has set some historians to wondering, and at least one has presumed that his silence may have been evidence that he 'apparently felt some empathy for Parnell'.[75] Another sternly advises that, while Salisbury possessed the most caustic tongue in British politics, at least he expressed some admiration for the courage of a beleaguered opponent: 'This much could not be said for his nephew, who watched the entire drama unfold without betraying any emotion save a smile.'[76] It is worth recalling that by this point, for nearly three years the Irish Secretary had been battered nightly in the House of Commons by the Parnellites. His name was cursed regularly in Irish tavern and pulpit alike. At least one assassination plot against him had been hatched among the Fenians, and his intelligence operatives who had penetrated the revolutionary Irish Republican Brotherhood learned that Parnell may even have taken the oath of the secret organization in 1882.[77] It would not have been surprising if Balfour had been more heated and more public in his language, and yet he did not join in the feeding frenzy. Little in his life annoyed Arthur Balfour more than witnessing clever people behaving stupidly, and this was precisely what it seemed Parnell had done.

Balfour's comments on the affair were confined entirely to politics. He wrote to his under-secretary of the struggle within the Irish National Party which erupted in 1890, predicting correctly what lay ahead: 'My own private belief is that Parnell's back is up, that he will stick to his guns as long as he can, and that nothing but *force majeure* will turn him out.' The letter continues, revealing Balfour's pleasure at his own silver lining in the dark cloud that overhung the Nationalists:

> How all this is to end I do not know, and I do not much care. It is extraordinarily amusing while it lasts, and, at all events, it enables us to get through our business in a reasonable time – now the rapidity with which Parliament does its work is almost embarrassing, and we do not know how to spend our evenings after 8 o'clock! Loving deputations of priests come to me every day, and altogether the situation is so novel that I feel quite out of my element.[78]

It is a rare political leader, immersed in a continuing battle with much at stake, who cannot derive warm solace in observing the nearly hysterical self-destruction of a ruthless opposition. Balfour was no exception, yet in the end he bore no grudges: 'You cannot sit opposite to people who accuse you of murder every night', he once said to his friend 'Willie' Desborough, 'without getting rather to like them!'[79]

The uncontested divorce petition was granted to O'Shea, and in June 1891 Parnell and his 'Kitty' married in the registry office at Steyning. By then, more than a year had passed since the revelations of their private life; Parnell led only a portion of his broken party, and he had been abandoned by his clerical allies in Ireland and his political allies in Britain. Never robust at the best of times and weakened by his struggle to hold on to a political movement that was falling to bits all around him, Parnell's health declined, and he was dead by the end of the year.

In the meantime, Arthur Balfour got on with the business of governing Ireland. In 1887 he had promised that strict law enforcement would be only a part of his policy, and that he would not lose sight of Ireland's needs – in the phrase of the day, with coercion must come conciliation. Though the harrowing tales of Bloody Balfour, the 'tyrant in the guise of a dilettante, who enjoyed arresting newsboys, jailing priests or members of Parliament, and harrying innocent tenants off Plan estates', provided useful fodder for Irish Nationalists, they constituted only one aspect of the story, and there was another part to Balfour's plan.[80] This came to be characterized as the policy of 'killing home rule with kindness'. He hoped to create a new social and economic order with a law-abiding peasantry resistant to separatism and violence because they were reconciled to the Union with Britain. This reconciliation was to be based on a sense of a more uniform justice under the law, but also on a more general economic prosperity. He hoped the key to success in all this would be to implement a programme that went beyond previous reforms and would move the landless tenantry towards a new role as landowning smallholders – as a sort of 'West British' agrarian class.[81]

This scheme was to be advanced through a series of parliamentary acts which owed much to Gladstone's 1880 law which promised much and delivered substantially less, and to Ashbourne's 1885 act which modestly extended the practice of public funding of land purchase by tenants.[82] In his first Land Act, in 1887, Balfour carried on from the previous acts, extended the coverage to include leaseholders, and provided additional money to the loan fund. He advised his uncle to press the idea that 'The Government regard the passing of the Land Bill as second only in importance to that of the Crimes Bill and in order to pass it, are prepared to sacrifice the time that they would have desired to give to English measures.'[83]

Despite his criticism of what he considered the ambiguity of Gladstone's legislation, this land bill was merely a stopgap extension of those earlier laws which had established the land courts for the resolution of disputes and pioneered state-funded land purchase by tenants. Balfour believed that Ireland's problems were rooted in the country's poverty, and that an effective assault on this was also a blow against both lawlessness and Irish Nationalism. The district of Connaught and counties Donegal, Kerry and West Cork were traditionally the poorest parts of the island, the poverty belt of the so-called 'congested districts' defined by Ridgeway as those 'estates or districts where the holdings are too small by subdivision etc to support the occupiers'.[84] Balfour believed that land legislation which encouraged a peasant proprietorship was one path to a cure; another was to take advantage of any opportunity to encourage emigration – in effect, to export surplus population and, with it, poverty. A third approach was through economic development, and to this end in 1889 he introduced legislation to provide for the construction of nearly 300 miles of light railway to facilitate the movement of goods and passengers. Building the railway also provided employment in a time of bad harvests, and was one of a number of public works projects begun in Balfour's time.[85]

In 1891 he introduced his second Land Act, perhaps the most important and ambitious measure of his reform programme. Owing to a resistant Opposition and to Unionist suspicion, its passage was a slow and torturous process which dragged on for many months. Balfour defended the bill through long days of negotiation and even longer nights of wrangling on the floor of the Chamber. Perhaps the most significant advantage which fell to him grew from the fact that Irish MPs were at the time meeting daily in Committee Room 15 of the House, locked in the divisive struggle which followed the Parnell divorce scandal – the mischief these ruthless warriors could inflict, while still formidable, was less than it might have been had they not been preoccupied with battling among themselves. The immensely complex 1891 bill included the most generously funded land-purchase scheme to that point (creating a fund of some £33 million), and was meant to encourage more tenants to seek landownership rather than merely lower rents.

With the concerted campaign against it of 'Nationalist agitators', the distrust of many landlords regarding the method of payment for sale (by government bonds), and the surprising apathy towards purchase among the peasantry, the scheme enjoyed only moderate success. There was an additional reason that damaged the policy in the widely shared assumption that Salisbury's government was nearing its end and that Gladstone's return – presumably with a new Home Rule bill in hand – was not far in the future. All these factors hampered the bill from enjoying the impact for which Balfour hoped. A recent close observer of the period has concluded rather persuasively, 'The problem was that no easy way had yet been found to make real reform an experienced reality in the anarchic political, social, and economic worlds which collectively constituted late-nineteenth-century Ireland.'[86]

More successful was the second part of the bill, which created a Congested Districts Board. 'No doubt', Balfour wrote to Ridgeway in 1889, 'the congested districts supply us with the most insoluble part of the Irish difficulty. In other parts of Ireland it would probably be enough to restore obedience to the law and to facilitate the Freehold of their tenancies by the farmers – in the congested districts something more is required, and what that something more is shall be a most perplexing question.'[87] As the land-purchase plan got off to its sluggish start, much of Balfour's hope for an answer to the question of Irish rural poverty came to be vested in this creation.

The Congested Districts Board was an independent body comprised of two land commissioners and five 'experts', with the Chief Secretary serving *ex officio*. It enjoyed almost complete autonomy, in that it was funded by the state but not directly under the control of the Chief Secretary. Its primary responsibilities were to promote local industry through subsidy and education, to amalgamate uneconomic landholdings through purchase, to encourage migration from impoverished districts, and to improve the efficiency of farming practices in the area under its authority.[88] In Balfour's time the Board exercised authority over more than 3 million acres and more than half a million people. The role that the Board developed, largely due to its remarkable first secretary, W. L. Micks, was 'essentially that of a benevolent (and autocratic) landlord'.[89] It was remarkably successful, and continued its work until the Union with Ireland was finally dissolved three decades later.

Internal improvements and relief measures, under the direct authority of either Dublin Castle or the Board, included the dredging of rivers and the construction and repair of bridges, roads and piers. Following the seemingly inevitable failures of the potato crop (as occurred again in 1890), emergency relief measures were organized, followed often with public works to provide temporary employment. Exasperated by the unreliability of the homely tuber, Balfour once exclaimed to the pioneer agricultural scientist Sir James Caird, 'I wish to Heaven we could induce the Irish to grow some food of a more trustworthy character than the potato. I doubt, however, whether any attempt to induce them either to cultivate lentils or to eat them would be successful.'[90] In this same year, Balfour and the new Lord Lieutenant, the Marquess of Zetland, sponsored a private aid fund which eventually raised more than £50,000 for immediate relief of distress caused by the crop failure.[91]

If the Congested Districts Board was one of his successes, Balfour was disappointed in his inability to establish in Ireland a state-sponsored Roman Catholic university college as a component of the system of Queen's Colleges created by Peel a half-century earlier. When the idea of the papal rescript was first under discussion in 1888, a delegation of Catholic Unionists led by the Duke of Norfolk called upon the Chief Secretary to encourage such a foundation. Balfour pursued the idea with Salisbury, writing to him in plain language of their call for a 'direct bribe to Rome (in the shape of a Catholic College, endowed by the state & governed in the first instance by nominees of the state) to be given when, by the efforts of the Holy Father, the Irish Priesthood shall have learnt the ten commandments'.[92] Balfour needed no convincing that increased access to higher education among the Roman Catholic majority was among Ireland's greatest needs, and he understood the value of the 'bribe' of a university college in exchange for the abandonment by the Irish bishops of aggressive nationalism. He realized also that, while he might receive some support in the Cabinet, scepticism was the best he could hope for among most of his colleagues. In the end the plan foundered on the rock of sectarianism, with the Catholic hierarchy seeking maximum independence and state funding, and zealous Protestant Unionists equally determined that no good could emerge from a papist institution funded from the public purse.

In the autumn of 1890, in the midst of these tumultuous matters, Balfour faced a particularly unappealing and much-postponed prospect: a tour of Connemara and Donegal, the heart of the Congested Districts. Balfour never understood the need of enduring any discomfort that could be avoided; nor did he enjoy the prospect of dealing with the crowds, be they adoring or hostile, that would inevitably greet him at each stop along the way. Yet, good Victorian that he was, he quietly accepted that duty must be fulfilled – he must 'show himself' to the people; but, if he must, then he would do so without the trappings of an imperial proconsul. There would be no mounted guards, no entourage, no evidence of grandeur of any sort. 'I can certainly give you ten days for my tour,' the Chief Secretary allowed, and he suggested his security might be entrusted to a single plain-clothes officer, 'if that is thought desirable'.[93] Despite her brother's scepticism, his intrepid sister and housekeeper, Alice, insisted on going as well. Hence, in October 1890, the two Balfours set off with a small expedition in two closed carriages, accompanied by Ridgeway and a secretary, Thomas Browning. The final member of the group was George Wyndham, now Balfour's parliamentary secretary and recently elected MP for Dover. Balfour agreed to having two Special Branch men, who acted as drivers. His reason for rejecting an elaborate entourage was simple: the grander the procession, the grander the cost – and the grander the temptation to local officials, 'beggars by profession', to present their demands for public monies. The protests of Constabulary headquarters that the Chief Secretary needed more protection Balfour summarily waved aside.

The Nationalist press called for energetic protest wherever the travellers paused, but little was in evidence. When he heard of the cheers that greeted the Chief Secretary in Donegal, 'Willie' Redmond, MP, attributed the warm reception to Balfour's cowardice: 'Mr Balfour's tour is one of the meanest of his acts. He dare not go to face the men of Mayo without his sister, for he knew that no matter in what light they regarded him, they would not do anything discourteous to a lady.'[94] But the reason behind the warm reception given at most of the villages where the party called was more than mere gallantry: it often expressed appreciation for 'Bloody Balfour's' efforts to relieve the curse of poverty which had so long plagued the island. An elderly Irish priest and keen Home Ruler expressed to Sir Sydney Parry of the Treasury a troublesome ambivalence where Balfour was concerned: he knew that his own politics demanded that he should hate the Chief Secretary like the devil, but 'as a mere man, I can't deny that he has done more for Ireland than any of his predecessors, Saxon or otherwise . . . Sure it's like Balaam I am, blessing when I want to curse.'[95]

By the time the 1891 Land Act came into effect, Balfour's tenure in Ireland was nearly over. For four years he had faced challenges which had proved too much for many able and experienced men, and the consensus in Westminster seemed to be that he had, on balance, been a surprising success. By the time he left Dublin Castle, boycotting, rent-striking and violent demonstrations had dropped to negligible figures, and it had become safe to lift the sanctions on the 'proclaimed' districts. Among the Unionists, 'Pretty Fanny' (as his detractors once called him) had been forgotten, and he was welcomed as a hero. Henry Lucy considered how delighted Balfour's uncle and mentor Alexander Beresford-Hope would have been had he lived to see the 'marvellous development of the genius and capacity in which he was a fervid believer':

It is doubtful whether even the prophetic soul of Mr Balfour's uncle ventured to forecast the brilliant Parliamentary success to be achieved in an incredibly brief space of time . . . The fair-faced, languid youth, too indolent to stand bolt upright, was the very last person likely to develop into a civil Cromwell, the most unbending, thorough administrator of iron rule Ireland had known since '98.

In Lucy's judgement, 'He is undoubtedly the favourite minister of the day.'[96]

On 6 October 1891, both Charles Stewart Parnell and W. H. Smith died. Balfour, recently returned from the annual Wagner festival in Bayreuth, wrote to Ridgeway two days later, 'I am much upset by this announcement of Smith's death – it is a great personal blow. Parnell's death which we heard [rumoured?] this way in one sense produces more startling political results, but Smith's loss is irremediable.'[97] In fact 'Old Morality' had proven to be a far more effective leader in the Commons than many had expected, but the cost to his strained constitution had been high. Three years earlier, his health once again uncertain, it had appeared as though Smith might be unable to go on. This caused Balfour to put down for the Prime Minister some 'stray thoughts, [with] most of which you are probably familiar':

> If Smith goes there are so far as I can see only two men now on the Bench who can possibly succeed him: – Goschen & myself. There are many grave objections to the latter. But there is one which is insuperable. Goschen would certainly object, & be right in objecting to serve under one who was not in Parliament when he first became a Cabinet Minister.

Goschen was officially a follower of Hartington and Chamberlain – a Unionist, but not a Conservative. Balfour noted in his letter to Salisbury that in discussing the situation with the editor of *The Times*, G. E. Buckle, 'I added that Goschen could hardly lead the Conservative Party in the House of C unless he consented to call himself a Conservative and to join the Carlton.' He himself could see no alternative to a formal 'fusion' of the two Unionist parties into a true coalition government, with Hartington leading in the Commons.[98]

This letter to Salisbury is marked 'not sent', and it is unclear whether the writer thought better of his conclusions or simply communicated them to his uncle by other means. Salisbury cannot have failed to consider the same factors. It was the usual practice in British politics at this time for even the most ambitious of men (except to their most trusted familiars) to deny interest in office and in promotion. The danger of being labelled overtly ambitious, a 'self-advertiser', was quite real. Yet here was Balfour, a Cabinet minister for only two years, saying quite unequivocally to the Prime Minister that, despite the claims of more experienced colleagues, the highly respected Goschen was only a remote possibility for the leadership and in reality there was only himself. These were the thoughts of a man both self-confident and ambitious.

Self-advertising or not, over the next few years Balfour's conclusion remained, and his reasoning proved to be sound.[99] Lord Salisbury knew that there would be muttering about nepotism and the 'family firm', but he realized how limited were his options: Balfour was correct, for Goschen was unacceptable to the Conservatives. Hicks Beach had seniority and experience and was now recovered from his ailments. 'Black Michael' was a Tory through and through, but he was admired rather than loved among backbenchers – and, besides, he made clear to the Prime Minister that he had no interest in leading the Commons.[100] Goschen presented a somewhat stickier problem, and Balfour in characteristic manner argued the case for the older man's right to feel aggrieved if passed over ('I think there must be exaggeration in the estimates I have heard of his unpopularity'); but there was that insuperable matter of party affiliation. Balfour advised his uncle:

> Of all the objections which I understand are urged against him the only one with which I have any sympathy . . . [is] that he will not formally, or at least *has* not formally, admitted that he is a member of the Party which he has claims to lead in the Commons. If you do not choose to put him there this is the point on which I should be rely [*sic.*]: – for it implies nothing which is not highly creditable to his honour, if not to his prudence.[101]

As it turned out, Goschen did his duty and obeyed Salisbury's nudging to make it known the next day that he acquiesced to the choice of Balfour. Hartington, a fanatical devotee of the turf, had kept his colleagues waiting for his answer: 'Hartington is at Newmarket,' Salisbury wrote to Balfour, '& all political arrangements have to be hung up till some quadruped has run faster than some other quadruped.'[102] But by 16 October it was settled: the Queen was rather enthusiastic (and irrationally wished Balfour to combine the offices of Leader of the House and Irish Secretary), and both the Tories and the Liberal Unionists, Salisbury wrote, 'expect you to take Smith's place'. There were duties as well as dangers, however, and it would have been unlike Salisbury to minimize them to a colleague – particularly to one who was also a nephew as dear to him as a son: 'It will make you the target for very jealous & exacting criticism. But I do not think that you can avoid or refuse it as matters stand – The feeling is so general that it would require a strong personal reason to justify you in declining it.'[103]

'I am too much of a fatalist', Balfour replied on the following day, 'to trouble myself about possibilities when the path seems quite clearly marked out.'[104] He wrote to Ridgeway in Dublin denying any concern over the business (though he was well aware that he was the inevitable choice): 'With regard to the leadership of the House, I know nothing, nor have I taken any pains to make myself acquainted with the feeling of the Party.'[105] Then, once the news became known, his theme was that taking the leadership was his duty and that he was pleased – but not overly so. Lady Frances, his sister-in-law, friend and drawing-room antagonist, both believed in and yet was infuriated by the pose, and added her usual note of diminuendo to the episode. In her memoir she sniffed:

> Ambition is an ambiguous word, it usually implies one who will advance himself over others. It is a word often used of one who feels his own power, while other men do not see it as clearly . . . There is no grit in a man who does not want to produce what is best in himself, and do honour to the Cause he upholds. Arthur's opportunities were all made for him.[106]

Balfour was fond of Lady Frances, as he was fond of their frequent verbal sparring. However, when she announced that she was keeping her correspondence for future publication, it was matters such as this that he had in mind when he told his sister, 'Then I shall leave it in my will that no one is to believe a word she says.'[107] Lady Frances seems to have missed a point or two regarding her brother-in-law's Irish service: to ally and opponent, it was clear that 'Bloody Balfour' had proven his 'grit'; and his conclusion in the matter of the leadership of the House of Commons illustrates that he possessed as much ambition as most other office-holders. If he was, as Henry Lucy declared, the 'favourite minister', he would have to prove himself once again in his new and ever more significant post.

Leaving Dublin Castle behind for ever saddened Alice Balfour, who had grown to love the Irish countryside as she grew to enjoy having her brother to herself, without the interference of sisters-in-law or Balfour's many friends – who stayed away from Dublin in droves. He also admitted that he had enjoyed his Irish years: 'I feel as if I [have] had a good time which has for ever come to an end, and the thought is not agreeable.'[108] To Lady Elcho he wrote similarly: 'It does not seem a very attractive place, nor does the life seem a very attractive life. Yet we have all had a very good time, and I hate to see it coming to an end.'[109] Balfour always insisted that the constructive achievements of his administration justified his efforts in Ireland, and that it was in these, not in his efforts as a 'policeman', that he took pride. Long after the Irish Union had been dissolved, Mrs Dugdale asked her uncle what remained of those achievements: "'Everything, everything!" he answered. "What was the Ireland the Free State took over? It was the Ireland that we made, though the Liberals went back on our policy . . . They could have done nothing – nothing with Ireland but for our work."'[110] There was truth in this, though the debate over 'how much?' will not end any time soon.

5.

Friends and Ideas.

◆◆

LADY RAYLEIGH ONCE noted a conversation with her brother not long after he became Leader of the House of Commons: 'He remarked that his mind did not naturally turn to politics. He never thought about them in bed, which was the test . . . There was Goschen; he got quite worried if anything went wrong, and as for Chamberlain, he thought of nothing else.'[1] Certainly during the trying time of his premiership, and in the tumultuous years when he led the Opposition, his political troubles crept into his thoughts as he retired for the evening. Yet, among those who enjoyed long careers in the top levels of British politics, few were more gifted at juggling several lives at once. If his working days were dedicated to exercising or seeking power, no one said of him that he 'thought of nothing else'.

He had been born into a time when a tiny portion of the population combined property, education and family connections in a whirl of privilege and comfort, when national leadership was still treated as though it were a service only they could provide. In that long-past gold-sovereign world, Arthur Balfour was a true grandee – 'Prince Arthur' he was dubbed by 'Toby' of *Punch*, and the name stuck.[2]

Balfour's family life had changed since his days as a music-mad young heir. Unlike Arthur and Alice, Gerald and Eustace Balfour had married, as had their sisters Eleanor and Evelyn. Despite the early demise of both of their parents and with two exceptions, this generation of Balfours were long-lived, and all but one of these marriages (the Sidgwicks') were fruitful, producing six sons and eight daughters among them.

Sadly, two of the brothers died long before their time. The name of Cecil Balfour hardly appears in the surviving mountain of family papers. When the sordid evidence surfaced that he had forged Arthur's name to a cheque to stave off creditors, he was apparently banished from the family to Australia.[3] Only a few brief references to his death remain: a telegram to Balfour from one John Clark in Boggabri, Australia, reported in April 1881: 'Mr Balfour died at Henriendi this morning at four o'clock

[. . .] fell off his horse yesterday.' Neither his body nor his ashes were returned to Whittingehame, as Clark reported that he was buried at the outpost of Gullendaddy on the day of his death.[4] A rather puzzling bit of evidence survives in a letter to Arthur Balfour of 5 April from Lord Salisbury:

> The news is very sad indeed: but if there was no hope of a cure – & there seemed no hope of that – it was better that it should end. A prolongation of life would only have been a prolongation of utter misery – & worse. Whatever the cause – the latter part of his life was passed under aggravated cerebral disease: – from which he could never have recovered.[5]

It remains unclear whether Cecil Balfour had been medically diagnosed with a 'cerebral disease' that explained his conduct or whether his uncle's reference is merely a suggestion that his behaviour was explicable only as a sort of mental illness; however, it certainly was 'very sad indeed' for the family.

Little more than a year later, on 19 July 1882, came the death of Professor Francis Maitland Balfour in a mountaineering accident – while attempting to climb the Italian face of Mont Blanc. The news reached England a day later, and the family gathered in their grief at Carlton Gardens. All were devastated, and Eustace and Gerald (himself a keen mountaineer who might well have been a member of the ill-fated expedition) were dispatched to arrange the return of the body. The Balfour siblings were a close circle, but humour among them was often pointed, for Arthur had joked when the climbers left London, 'Don't get killed – it would be such a bore,' at which all present had laughed heartily. Privately, however, Arthur had expressed to Gerald and Lady Frances his concerns for the safety of the climbers. It is revealing that the latter noted in her reminiscence of Frank's death: 'It was the first time that a violent and sudden death had come into our ken.'[6] This comment, of course, neglected the death of Cecil – certainly both 'violent and sudden' – a year earlier – demonstrating, perhaps, the depth of his disgrace.

His extended family, with its roots deep in the soil of Whittingehame, remained the vital centre of Arthur Balfour's life. He had settled comfortably into the role of bachelor head of the clan, and he teased Lady Frances when, on the birth of her first son, Frank, she exclaimed her joy that the day would come when he would proudly wear the tartan of her own Campbell clan. He replied in mock horror:

> As for my nephew, he may (Heaven help him) clothe himself, for anything I care, from head to foot in the Campbell tartan. He may have his shirt made

of it, and his boots made of it. He may tattoo himself with it, and he has my leave to play 'The Campbells are Coming' in every key, and on every instrument under Heaven . . . But I cannot agree with your view as to his *rights*. He is a Balfour, not a Campbell; and has, therefore only a *right* to wear the Strathconan mixture and to play Handel; exceedingly badly on the pianoforte. Everything else is by favour.[7]

What moved him was not blood pride in the clan or its symbols – as Lady Frances knew well – but the pleasure he took in the people who bore the name. He was never happier than during the annual four or five months (typically from September to January) when much of the family decamped for Whittingehame. By the early 1890s, life in the great house had been shaped to a pattern suited to its master. Balfour remained close to his surviving brothers, Gerald and Eustace. Gerald had himself begun a political career in 1885, when he was returned for the Central Division of Leeds, and in 1887 he married Lady Elizabeth (Betty) Lytton, the daughter of the Earl of Lytton. Eustace, the youngest Balfour sibling, had established an architectural practice in London and, as we have seen, had married Lady Frances. The two couples were themselves very close, and for some years lived as neighbours in London, where they produced a bumper crop of Balfour cousins. In the nineties these children formed a boisterous tribe who regularly spilled out of the Whittingehame nursery and into the lives of their elders – by all accounts Uncle Arthur was indulgent to a degree that pained his spinster sister Alice. The children repaid the debt with nothing short of adoration of their beloved 'Nunky'.[8]

Lady Elcho's daughter, Cynthia, a contemporary of the Balfour children and frequent visitor to Whittingehame, remembered that 'Nunky' could be as affectionately patient with dogs as he was with children. She recalled fondly his solemnly intoning to her mother's imperious chow, 'Oh Ching, how greatly I love you!'[9] There is no record of whether the haughty Ching returned Balfour's affection, but the Balfour nieces and nephews certainly did, and no less so in adulthood. Despite the Victorian belief that children should be seen and not heard, he always made time to listen to them with the same attention he gave their elders. He then addressed them in turn as miniature adults. Mrs Dugdale recalled a typical conversation when she was a little girl which took place during a minor seaside disaster: while she was in 'Nunky's' care, the two were inspecting a small tidal pool, and 'Baffy' slipped into the water in a 'sitting posture'. Her uncle lifted her to her feet and asked if she was hurt:

'No,' I answer, 'but my drawers are very wet.'

'What can we do about that?' he asks, obviously concentrating upon the problem, but with a certain helplessness which fills me with astonishment in one of his age. It seems that the control of the situation lies with me, and a keen anxiety to keep the mishap from my mother's knowledge inspires my next remark.

'Sea-water never gives cold,' I assert sententiously. The statement would have been powerless to avert 'a fuss' among my Campbell relatives, but it worked like magic on the speculative Balfour mind.

'Is that really so?' he asks, and then, not suspiciously, but with a real desire for information, 'How do you know?'

At this moment voices from the beach call us to tea . . .

'Uncle Arthur,' I say.

'Yes, my dear?'

'Don't let's speak about it at tea.'

There was a short pause. No doubt reviewing a situation for which his own share of responsibility may have occurred to him for the first time. At any rate, he appeared to grasp my point. I do not recall that he made any comment in words, but as we approached the picnic fire we were conversing gaily on some subject quite unconnected with the cold and clammy condition of my drawers.[10]

It is easy to understand why children would cherish such an uncle. Balfour – who was not particularly drawn to certain boyish things such as football or cricket – seems to have shone his most brilliant light on the nieces. Lord Esher (with some exaggeration) wrote to his son during a visit to Whittingehame a decade later, when the nieces and some friends were in attendance, 'There are 10 girls here and all sit at AJB's feet and adore him. All nieces. Only one boy – a nephew.'[11] The attachment – and the adoration – held fast throughout the remainder of Balfour's life.

With the adult women in his family circle, Balfour's pleasures were more mixed. Eleanor he recognized as his intellectual peer, and she remained a trusted confidant throughout his life. Nora Sidgwick was an austere woman and, free of the duties of motherhood, she devoted her energies to the interests which touched her heart and her intellect. The cause dearest to the Sidgwicks' hearts was the extension of higher education to women, and the two founded what would become Newnham College, Cambridge, in the 1870s. A generous and steadfast supporter of their efforts was her brother Arthur. Balfour and the Sidgwicks also enjoyed a deep interest in psychic phenomena, and were among the founders of the Society for Psychical Research.

Balfour also enjoyed the close friendship of his sister Evelyn and her husband, his friend of Cambridge days John Strutt, Lord Rayleigh. 'Evie' Rayleigh was always noted as the exception among the sisters in that she delighted in the company of new and old friends from beyond the family. Apparently an amusing menace to pedestrians as she hared about Cambridge in her pony cart, she was much loved in and outside the Balfour family circle for her sunny disposition.

There was, however, occasional discord in the household, particularly in the extended guerrilla war between sisters-in-law Alice, mistress of Whittingehame, and Lady Frances Balfour. Immensely clever and often tactless, Lady Frances found Alice priggish, peevish and mean, and she often upbraided her about what she saw as her pinch-penny household management. Alice, thin-skinned and jealous of her position, carefully accounted for every slight and hurt, and meticulously planned her counterblasts against her adversary. The skirmishing between these two strong-willed women ebbed and flowed, and many colourful tales have survived. In 1897, for example, Alice single-handedly arranged with the Postmaster General and the Inspector of the Ordnance Survey to change the spelling of the local village (and with it the family house) from Whittinghame to Whittingehame, to end the annoying mispronunciation 'Whitting-ham'. Lady Frances promptly announced she would never accept the change, and stuck to her guns for the rest of her life – to her sister-in-law's immense irritation.[12]

Occasionally even the patient Balfour could stand it no more: confrontation was business as usual in Westminster, but he would not have it under his own roof. Periodically he would intervene with a brief lecture or a sharp note to one or both combatants, and discipline would for a time be restored – but only for a time. Lady Elcho, who knew the Whittingehame women intimately, wrote to Balfour after he had sent a stiff letter to Lady Frances about her treatment of Alice:

> I thought you were very uneasy that things below the surface were not going well, and that perhaps [Frances] was pursuing a pinprick policy and that you were in mortal dread of a *row* and had therefore chosen the opportunity of her letter to send her a warning . . . I think that writing to her as you did, makes her hate Alice a million times more and that in her present state upsets [Frances] much more than you'd think possible . . . I fear they will always hate each other, the fact that Alice is mistress is in itself an affront to Frances (most wrongly so) and I suppose Alice's old-maidishness annoys her. It's very sad and certainly is one of the drawbacks of yr life.[13]

And so it remained for the balance of Balfour's days, for both women out-lived him.

Country-house life could not be enjoyed without the labour of many ser-vants, and Balfour's comfortable existence was no exception. The home farm was managed by a factor, and Alice Balfour supervised a large indoor staff and for many years depended upon two familiar Whittingehame fig-ures: Baker, the butler, and Mrs Anderson (called 'Fairy' by the adoring young Balfours), the housekeeper. Valets came and went until Balfour dis-covered a treasure in James Coleman, who remained with him for many years. Another retainer entered Balfour's service after the repeal in 1896 of the archaic 'red flag' law, which limited motor cars to a speed of four miles per hour and required that they be preceded by a man waving a red flag. Fascinated with any new technology, Balfour quickly purchased one of these 'boneshakers' and engaged the services of Frederick Mills to drive his deDion–Bouton roadster – nicknamed 'the Hornet'. Mills too became a household fixture.[14]

Two other invaluable additions took their places in Balfour's professional life in the early 1890s. When he became Leader of the House, Balfour engaged as his political private secretary a fascinating character, John Satterfield Sandars. 'Jack' Sandars had recently left his appointment as a clerk in the Home Office, where he had acted as a liaison with the Irish Office, and had met Balfour during his term as Chief Secretary. Five years younger than his new master, Sandars had been educated at Repton and Magdalen College, Oxford, and was called to the bar in 1877. In 1886 he became secretary to Sir Henry Matthews, Salisbury's Home Secretary, remaining with him until 1892, when he stood unsuccessfully for Parliament in the Unionist interest. Later in the year, Balfour's amanuen-sis, F. J. Woods, left his service after six years, and Sandars took his place. He was intelligent, tireless, ambitious and self-confident. Balfour recog-nized several other qualities in Sandars that made him an ideal secretary. In the first place he was a keen golfer – though it was also true that Sandars enjoyed a passion for the turf which thoroughly bored his employer. More importantly, Sandars was very well connected, and was already friendly with most Unionist notables – and also useful to Balfour was that he was liked by the Prince of Wales, who, as Edward VII, was later pleased to have Sandars as his master's go-between with the court.

Unlike Balfour, Sandars had a practised eye for administrative details, and the two complemented each other from the outset. He was also good company, and they quickly became comfortable with one another. Sandars was soon addressing his correspondence to 'My dear Chief', closing always with 'Yrs. Affly, Jack'. To Balfour, Sandars's enthusiastic willingness to take from his employer's shoulders as many responsibilities as were allowed to him was a great quality, though it would earn them both criticism in the difficult days after Balfour became leader of the party. Balfour soon came to trust the secretary's loyalty, kept no political secrets from him, and depended on him to act in situations which most senior politicians might never have left to even the most trusted secretary. Sandars relished the dual roles of agent and, eventually, gatekeeper to his patron; and Balfour ignored or perhaps was unconcerned about the jealousy among his colleagues to which this gave rise.[15] Sandars remained in Balfour's service until 1912, and in close touch with him until 1915. When he returned to office in the first wartime coalition, Balfour showed a kindness to a former political opponent whom Sandars hated, and for this the former secretary never forgave the generous patron from whose hand he had received so much. Sandars, as we shall see, rejected Balfour's repeated gestures of friendship, and nursed his grievance until Balfour's death.

Another vital addition to the Balfour circle was made in 1894, when Wilfrid Short became Balfour's principal clerical secretary, and it is his flawless copperplate hand with which all who have searched the Balfour papers are familiar. He came to his position only after Balfour had expelled his predecessor 'at a half hour's notice' after it was discovered that he was frequenting public houses in the company of Irish Nationalist MPs.[16] There were no such complaints about 'Shorty', and he remained happily in his master's service for twenty-six years. He became a Balfour family favourite, and deftly maintained friendships that crossed the lines even of the sisterly feuds. Short supervised the scriveners and typists who came and went, and Balfour trusted only him with his confidential correspondence. Unlike Sandars, Short remained in Balfour's service until 1920, and they remained on very friendly terms.

An admirer once said of Balfour that he would 'dine with almost anyone who asked him', and this seems very nearly to have been the case.[17] Few provided better table talk than he, and, Lady Elcho's daughter recalled, 'No conversation could be too unambitious, too personal, or too frivolous for his taste. Still less could it be too technical. No one equalled him at drawing out by intelligent cross-examination experts on their own subjects, whatever they might be – gunnery, chemistry, medicine, golf – what you will.' In recalling such occasions in his letters, Balfour said little of food, preferring to concentrate on the quality of the conversation and the guests who provided it. While he valued privacy to read and write and think,

Balfour enjoyed the company of others to discuss 'motor cars with a mechanic, crops with a farmer, corns with a chiropodist' in the hope of staving off the boredom that he so dreaded.[18]

It is not surprising that such a man was a born joiner, ever receptive to companionship that showed signs of providing amusement. Though it is difficult to imagine him as 'pubbable', he was decidedly 'clubbable'. In 1885 he became a member of Grillions, the celebrated political dining club, which boasted among its members many of the most prominent parliamentarians of all parties. He was elected to membership in another dining society of celebrated men of the arts and public life founded in 1763 by Dr Johnson, known simply as the Club.[19] While still a young man he discovered the pleasures to be found in London's gentlemen's clubs – within whose walls all men, even the most domesticated, for a few hours were bachelors. His London house was just a few steps from Pall Mall, ideally placed for a clubman, and it was in this celebrated avenue that his favourites were located, including the Travellers', which he joined soon after coming to London, and frequented more than any other.[20] Next door was the sombre Athenaeum, with its well-earned reputation as the meeting ground of the learned and eminent, of which he also remained a member for more than forty years. He also joined the Garrick Club, whose membership included citizens of the worlds of politics, the arts and the press. After becoming MP for the City of London, in 1906, he joined the City Carlton, a popular lunchtime haunt of Tory politicians and businessmen. Though he had no taste for racing, he enjoyed the elegant Turf Club, as his father had done before him. He was also elected to several of London's ancient livery companies, of which the Company of Grocers, which traced its origins to the fourteenth century, was his favourite.

When in Edinburgh he habitually stayed at the New Club, another favourite, and as a long-time Manchester MP he joined the Manchester Tennis and Racquet Club and maintained his membership long after his political association with the city ended. Also worthy of note was his long membership in the Roxburghe Club, a society of wealthy lovers of literature. Each new member was required to underwrite the cost of printing a lavish facsimile edition of a classic volume, and Balfour presented several.

Then, of course, there were the political clubs: membership of the Carlton – at that time located at the corner of Pall Mall and Carlton Gardens, minutes from Balfour's door – was a necessity from his first days as a Tory MP.[21] But visiting it was for him often a trying experience, and he wrote to George Curzon (who had recently been elected to the House), 'The Carlton is a beastly club: infested by the worst of the species viz: – the political bore. But you are quite right to belong to it. It must be suffered, like late hours and constituents, as a necessary, though disagreeable, accompaniment of a political career.'[22]

More to his liking was the St Stephen's Club, whose membership included not only many Unionist MPs but also, rather curiously, a sizeable contingent of electrical engineers – with 4 Carlton Gardens, their clubhouse was one of the first buildings in St James's to be electrified.[23] He also was a long-time member of the Unionist Constitutional Club. Perhaps he found this less tiresome than the more 'official' Carlton – there are, at any rate, no complaining references to infestations there of 'political bores'. Given his devotion to his favourite games, it is no surprise that he became a member of the All England Lawn Tennis and Croquet Club, and the legendary Royal and Ancient of St Andrews (which Balfour served as captain in 1894–5), the centre of the golfing universe.

He was pleased in 1888 to be elected a fellow of the Royal Society, like Salisbury a few years before. In 1879, its final year of existence, he had been elected a member of the celebrated Metaphysical Society, a 'talking club' founded by Tennyson, which boasted among its members many of Britain's most admired minds (including Gladstone, Bagehot, Ruskin, Manning, Huxley and Sidgwick) and thrived in the 1870s, until the members seem to have agreed that they had begun to repeat themselves – evidence to them that they had exhausted the supply of topics. Fifteen years after the group disbanded, the Roman Catholic editor Wilfrid Ward discussed with Balfour the possibility of forming another society as 'a kind of successor to the Metaphysical Society', of which Ward's father had been a founder.[24] In January 1896 Balfour and Ward met at the Junior Carlton Club with the Canon of Westminster, Charles Gore, and Balfour's old friend warden Edward Talbot to form what they eventually agreed to call the Synthetic Society.[25] They hoped that by bringing together many minds they could achieve a mutually acceptable definition of the theistic position: according to their by-laws, they aimed 'to consider existing Agnostic tendencies, and to contribute toward a working philosophy of religious belief'.[26] With philosophical dons such as Sidgwick and Hastings Rashdall, High Churchmen like Lord Hugh Cecil, Catholic laymen including Ward, Baron Friedrich von Hügel and G. K. Chesterton, Unitarians like the Rev. James Martineau, spiritualists like Professor Myers, and scientists like Lord Rayleigh and Sir Oliver Lodge – with a leavening of metaphysicians, Hegelians, socialists and intellectual politicians, including James Bryce,

Gerald Balfour, Alfred Lyttelton, and R. B. Haldane – the desired synthesis eluded them. The members shared sympathy for religion, 'if not by conviction at least by aspiration', and enjoyment in their common effort was apparently interesting enough to ensure the survival of the society for a decade.

Balfour read the first paper, a familiar indictment of materialism and positivism for ignoring the need for a First Cause, without which, he argued, science and logic became untenable. To the amusement of some of their fellows, he and the other Privy Counsellors present turned up in court uniform, as they were expected at the Speaker's levée on the same evening. It was a strain to find time to produce even a thirty-minute lecture, as he noted to Ward: 'I will do my best about the paper, though more unlucky circumstances under which to ask a philosopher to compose a philosophical paper I cannot imagine, as I can hardly get through my day-to-day tasks, which are hardly philosophical.'[27] While leading the Commons, the demands on his time were great, and he read only two more papers to the Society. He made every effort to attend and participate in most of the monthly dinner meetings of the group during the Synthetic's January–May calendar, and its spirited discussions offered a brief escape from his other life of politics and responsibility. He was one of the half-dozen men elected chairman of the Society, ultimately serving for three of the thirteen years of the club's lifespan. When it was finally wound up, he had all the papers of the Society printed, and presented a copy to each of the members.[28] Dubious though he might have been that the Society, with its diverse and brilliant membership, could achieve its stated goal of synthesizing a belief in God, Balfour took delight in the collective search.

Balfour always insisted that he was no metaphysician, but he never doubted that life consisted of more than earthly existence, and he shared with many others a deep interest in what lay beyond it – and his interest was not confined to mere acceptance of a more-or-less orthodox afterlife. Fascination with what would come to be called the paranormal was extremely high during these years, and he shared in the questioning. London, it seemed, was positively awash with spirit mediums, and, though most were unsubtle charlatans, some were more convincing – and it is not difficult to imagine the entertainment value in the séances they conducted. Balfour and a number of friends sought something more substantial, however, and in 1882 he was joined by his siblings Eleanor and Gerald, by Lord Rayleigh and Professor Sidgwick, his academic brothers-in-law, as well as by

scientists Sir William Crookes and Sir Oliver Lodge and psychologist
F. W. H. Myers in founding the Society for Psychical Research (SPR).
Many of these, of course, would also go on to become members of the
Synthetic Society. Sidgwick became the first president of the SPR (as he
was later of the Synthetic), and each of these worthies eventually held that
office, Balfour in 1894.[29] Eleanor and Gerald were perhaps the most complete believers within the Balfour circle in the possibility of contact with
the spirits of the departed. After his retirement from politics in 1906,
Gerald Balfour gave much of his time and energy to the Society, while
Professor Sidgwick, much troubled by his increasingly shaky faith in the
eternal, was nearly as relentless a pursuer of proofs of an afterlife. From
the outset Balfour was less convinced of the possibility of a happy result;
but he always maintained an open mind, writing to Lady Elcho in 1894, for
example, of her brother George Wyndham's experiences with a seer who
told him 'everything he ever did' and who had prophesied that the young
politician would die at fifty – which, curiously enough, he did.[30] In the
same letter he reported the 'extraordinary results of the furniture-moving
description under the most stringent tests' carried out by SPR members
Lodge and Myers with Professor Charles Richet, the distinguished French
physiologist. Not all the family approved of this enthusiasm, however, and
Lady Frances's Presbyterian conscience was particularly troubled by such
goings-on. She expressed her dire judgement in a letter to Gerald's wife,
Lady Betty, complaining that 'the thing [is unholy], & profane . . . I wish
Gerald was out of it, for no good can come of such traffic.'[31] The other
Balfours, of course, ignored her warnings.

Arthur Balfour always had time for a good séance – he hosted many over
the years, even in Downing Street, and participated in others in his brother
Gerald's home. At the height of the political crisis of 1911, he found time
to invite the famous spiritualist (and companion of Charles Bradlaugh)
Annie Besant to dine at Carlton Gardens 'to talk occultism with Gerald and
me'.[32] Yet, unlike many in the SPR, he never expressed complete confidence in the reports of communications with the dead. He had many
messages from the 'astral plane' over the years, transmitted by mediums of
every sort – one of the earliest seemingly (and incorrectly) predicting
Balfour's imminent marriage.[33] If the mediums were to be believed, May
Lyttelton was an occasional communicator, as was his mother, Lady
Blanche, and later Sidgwick and Salisbury. There seems to be no evidence
that he believed in any of them.[34] He certainly was unimpressed with the
available evidence of 'ectoplasmic manifestations' – ghosts – but quite sincerely pressed for more research into all questions of the unexplained. In his

presidential address to the SPR in January 1894, he took as his topic the hostility among most scientists towards 'obscure psychical phenomena'. Most scientists, he insisted, were wedded to proofs based upon the five senses – but what of the 'cases in which not the normal five or six senses, but some abnormal and half-completed sense, so to speak, comes into play; in which we have to work, not with the organisations of an ordinary and normal type, but with certain exceptional organisations who can neither explain, account for, nor control the abnormal powers they appear to possess'?[35]

If SPR investigators could not 'put our phenomena in a retort and boil them over a spirit lamp and always get the same results', this did not, he insisted to the Society, invalidate the search. Scepticism of such intensity demonstrated a 'most unphilosophic view of the question', which he considered typical of scientists. However, since these searches unearthed what were undeniably 'odd facts' that simply did not 'fit in' with the rules of the universe as laid down by science, they were not necessarily rendered invalid by the simple act of denying them. He particularly had in mind phenomena such as telepathy or extrasensory perception, which simply could not happen under the rules of science – yet seemed to, nonetheless. The search must go on, he concluded, and orthodox science and psychical research must continue in parallel paths, neither invalidating the other.

How far would he go in justifying psychical research?

It does seem to me that there is at least strong ground for supposing that outside the world, as we have, from the point of science, been in the habit of conceiving it, there does lie a region, not open indeed to experimental observation in the same way as the more familiar regions of the material world are open to it, but still with regard to which some experimental information may be laboriously gleaned; and even if we cannot entertain any confident hope of discovering what laws these half-seen phenomena obey, at all events it will be some gain to have shown, not as a matter of speculation or conjecture, but as a matter of ascertained fact, that there are things in heaven and earth not hitherto dreamed of in our scientific philosophy.

The pleasure for Balfour was in the inquiry itself. Furthermore, psychical research satisfied that part of his restless intellect that was offended when the majority of the intelligent and the educated rejected any kind of question out of hand. Finally, the thrust of his philosophical writings from beginning to end never varied from the premise that, despite their great triumphs, scientists too often ignored what they could not quantify. For him, in psychical research as in religion were to be found profound questions worthy of open-minded consideration, and adamant rejection of the inquiry he found intellectually sterile.

An inherently social being, Arthur Balfour seemed to operate his life as a series of concentric circles of associates that usually revolved around him, and it was apparent that he needed them and they him. Of course, not all of them were like the Synthetic Society or the SPR, or, early in the new century, the Unionist Party, concentrated on intellectual inquiry or political power. Some – perhaps the most important – were purely social. By the time he began his reign among the Unionist MPs, what today might be called his social 'support group' was well established, and it centred on a group of friends immortalized as 'the Souls'.

Many cliques existed within London society in the later Victorian years, perhaps the most celebrated being the Marlborough House Set of the Prince of Wales, famed for its dedication to lavish entertaining, high-stakes gambling and the 'fast' life. Coming together in the late 1880s, the Souls were a loosely organized group of some three dozen friends whose interests lay with other things – books, ideas, Conservative politics, intellectually challenging games, and 'good talk' – above all things, the Souls valued talk.[36] Contrary to the usual practice, Souls women did not retire from the table following dinner, gentlemen did not linger over port and cigars, and there was more than leisurely bridge to follow: in their society the sexes partook equally in discussion and recreation – which most of the time were one and the same. Their name apparently originated with Admiral Lord Charles Beresford, who is said to have commented at a dinner where several were present that they seemed to talk rather a lot about their souls – and an undying appellation was born.[37]

The Souls orbited around a collection of famous country estates and London houses, of celebrated hosts and hostesses and political luminaries; but, once embraced by the group, members were equals, regardless of their ability to return the hospitality of the Cowpers, Brownlows or Ribblesdales. Perhaps the most celebrated of all Souls gatherings were the two great dinners given by George Curzon, the son of Lord Scarsdale, who lived in lodgings in London while waiting out his inheritance – hence the feasts of July 1889 and 1890 were held at the celebrated Bachelors' Club, often said to prefigure P. G. Wodehouse's uproarious Drones' Club. Curzon produced for his guests' amusement a verse of doggerel about each Soul, published thirty years later (without his permission) by the irrepressible Margot Tennant (by that time Mrs H. H. Asquith). Curzon was only thirty in 1889, and his brilliant career as explorer, viceroy of India, chancellor of Oxford and Cabinet minister lay before him. Yet he was the ideal Souls man: brilliant (though a first-class degree eluded him at Balliol, as it had Balfour at Trinity), dedicated to the Empire, and possessed of a stunning wit far keener than his critics would later credit. In his mock epic, here were the Elchos:

> From kindred essay
> LADY MARY to-day
> Should have beamed on a world that adores her,
> Of her spouse debonair
> No woman has e're
> Been able to say that he bores her.

Margot and her sisters, and their baronet father, Sir Charles Tennant, Curzon managed to fit into one stanza:

> Here a trio we meet,
> Whom you never will beat,
> Tho' wide you may wander and far go;
> From what wonderful art
> Of that Gallant Old Bart.,
> Sprang CHARTY and LUCY and MARGOT.

And on it went, with verses for the Grenfells, the Lytteltons, the Brodricks and the rest. Pride of place, however, Curzon gave to the group's premier celebrity:

> There was seen at that feast
> Of this band, the High Priest,
> The heart that to all hearts is nearest;
> Him may nobody steal
> From the true Common weal,
> Tho' to each is dear Arthur the dearest.[38]

Balfour was not so much the leader of the clique – a group that he and others insisted had no organization – as he was their hero and the centre around which their circle turned.[39] Souls were generally Unionist in politics and imperial in outlook; they were drawn to books and 'serious' conversation, and committed to play that taxed the intellect rather than the sinews. To a greater or lesser degree they shared Balfour's religious faith, though they were also adept practitioners of high-voltage flirtation, which only occasionally lapsed (within the group, at any rate) into actual adultery. Most were scions of wealth and possessed good looks to complement their fortunate births; they loathed boredom, and possessed the means to pursue their tastes. In all Souls virtues, Balfour was unsurpassed.

The celebrated group began among the close friends of another Tennant sister, Laura, the wife of Balfour's friend Alfred Lyttelton. Pretty, flirtatious and charmingly eccentric, with her childlike exuberance Laura captured the hearts of men and women alike. It had once been rumoured (without substance) that she would marry Arthur Balfour, and she actually considered marrying Gerald; despite legions of other suitors, she married Lyttelton in 1885. Sadly, the adored Laura died soon after giving birth the following year at the age of twenty-four, and the group seems to have been formed from those friends who came together around her grieving widower, Alfred, and sisters, Margot and Charlotte (or 'Charty').[40] The grief was real. Balfour wrote to Lyttelton, 'You will not, I know, mind my writing to you: for I do not write to offer vain condolences and worthless consolations; I am wretched on my own account . . . [She was] one of the very few perfect friends which in this weary desert of existence a specially fortunate man hopes to have.'[41]

And so the group was forged in sadness, and Balfour acted as a sort of unifying force among the living. Joy returned, however, at least in part due to his inspiration. Margot wrote to him in August 1886 of a tiresome gathering, 'I remember you said everyone was dull "but we weren't!" wh. was true when you are with us.'[42] Then barely out of her teens and already the toast of London society, Margot thus testifies to what was to be a key element of Souls identity: the inspiration of the older and more established Balfour. This coterie added more friends until the group came to number between thirty and forty, including Gerald and Lady Betty and Lady Frances Balfour (but not necessarily Eustace), Lord and Lady Ribblesdale (the former 'Charty' Tennant), St John and Hilda Brodrick (the sister of Lady Elcho), and the American Souls, Henry and Daisy White. The list also included Alfred Lyttelton's second wife, 'D.D.' (born Edith Balfour but unrelated to the Whittingehame Balfours), George Wyndham and Lady Grosvenor, Harry Cust, Lord and Lady Windsor, and the unofficial limner of the Souls, Lady Granby (the future Duchess of Rutland). Other significant Souls were Sir John and Lady Horner (he was said to be descended from the legendary 'Little Jack' Horner, and she was the sister of the late Rutherford Graham) and always William and Ettie Grenfell, later Lord and Lady Desborough.

Their country-house parties sometimes included 'occasional Souls', often from the worlds of fine arts and letters, who amused the regulars. Burne-Jones was a favourite, as was John Singer Sargent; writers included H. G. Wells, Edmund Gosse and the Anglo-American Henry James. Raffish figures such as Wilfrid Blunt and Oscar Wilde or earnest socialists like William Morris or the Webbs were included at one time or another.[43] Their generally Tory predilections did not prevent the Souls from including a sprinkling of interesting members of the Opposition. The Tennants were Liberals, and the rising stars R. B. Haldane and H. H. Asquith (a young widower destined to wed Margot Tennant in 1894) enjoyed their hospitality. As did the arch-Gladstonian John Morley, though in a positively puritanical mood he declared the privileged atmosphere 'most blighting to one's democracy'.[44]

The 'Saturday-to-Mondays' at the great Souls' houses were not usually given over to the all-too-common shooting, hunting, gluttony and dozing, which they scorned. The Souls assembled not to shoot things, or to gamble or vegetate, but to play clever games, to exercise their brains and, of course, to talk. Conversation was often of politics, but just as often was about books, religion, society or aesthetics. Evenings were given over to the 'pencil games' to which they were devoted, and their favourites they themselves invented (or adapted). One was a sort of ancestor to modern Scrabble, just as likely to be played using German or French instead of English; another was 'Clumps', requiring opposing teams to cross-examine as in 'twenty questions' with the goal of discovering an obscure object ('a lost cause', 'the last straw' or 'the last golf ball Mr Arthur drove into a bunker'). Another game was 'Styles', in which players were to write parodies of famous authors in rhyme or prose; in still another, players were challenged to identify a Soul from the title of an imaginary book. On one evening the mysterious title was *Three Girls and a Horse*, and for some reason known but to them the answer was Arthur Balfour. Their games stressed a nimble wit, literary knowledge, a generous sense of humour and, above all, great facility with words – for the power of words was what amused the Souls above all things.[45]

Margot defended what seemed to be childish merriment: 'These games were good for our tempers and a fine training,' she recalled; 'any loose vanity, jealousy or over-competitiveness were certain to be shown up; and those who took the buttons off the foils in the duel of argument – of which I have seen a good deal in my life – were instantly found out.'[46] Perhaps this was so, but the clever competition was real enough, and outsiders welcomed for a time into the charmed circle could not be blamed if they saw all of it as an elaborate system for exclusion – which the Souls vehemently denied. Of course the Souls were exclusive: most were privileged and well-born; they were clever and good-looking, and unburdened with concerns about making their ways in the world. They delighted in their own slang, pet names and abbreviations – collectively a sort of Souls lexicon which excluded the uninitiated. Wilfrid Blunt, who hated their most deeply held political beliefs, did not seem to mind and concluded, 'No section of society was better worth frequenting, including as it did all that there was most intellectually amusing and least conventional.'[47] But some thought all the cleverness a bit much, and, as Lord Robert Cecil accurately noted in his memoirs, 'such a group will never be popular with those who are left outside . . . and it was the fashion with certain people to sneer at and criticise the "Souls".'[48] R. B. Haldane, who knew many of them well, suggested that the problem may have been that they 'sometimes took themselves much too seriously'.[49]

Some certainly did, though it is unlikely that Haldane thought Balfour was one of them, yet Margot recalled in her memoirs that he once said, 'No history of our time will be complete unless the influence of the Souls upon society is dispassionately and accurately recorded.'[50] However, when her book appeared, he noted to Lady Wemyss (as Lady Elcho had become), 'All the things that people quote to me from it as containing observations of mine seem to be quite untrue, but not intentionally malevolent.'[51] Whatever he might have believed about their 'influence', he highly valued the Souls' companionship. Associations such as the Synthetic Society exercised his intellect, but the Souls were fun. Balfour was pleased to be their 'Adored Gazelle', the ridiculous nickname they gave him, because they were amusing and seldom boring.[52] The clever and beautiful Souls helped to stave off the deadening mundaneness that he dreaded in society. Even though he knew it to be the case, the idea that other ambitious politicians thought of nothing but politics he thought positively doleful.

As in his youth, the bachelor Balfour continued to enjoy and even depend upon the friendships he established with women – not all of them were Souls, but all were attractive and intelligent. Most of his flirtations were with female friends quite safely wed (and therefore not a matrimonial threat). Not all, however: before his days at the Irish Office he seems to have enjoyed the companionship of Jenny Lindsay, daughter of the Earl of Crawford and sister of Lady Granby. There were even delicious rumours of marriage, which of course came to nothing.[53] For a time it was rumoured that Balfour was on the verge of proposing marriage to the lovely D.D. Balfour, before her marriage to Alfred Lyttelton, but this too was never a genuine possibility.

A more typical Souls flirtation diverted Balfour in 1901 – with the delicately beautiful wife of another Soul, the Viceroy of India, George Curzon. While her husband remained behind to rule the subcontinent, his

Because he was a queer

Homo

Gay

get real

a big

hong

queer

Vicereine returned for several months to Britain. The American-born Mary Curzon was not only lovely but also intelligent and very amusing company – as well as a prime source of information about the thoughts of her George, who was at the moment giving fits to the government. Ever loyal, Mary reported back to Curzon, apparently including her admiration for the Leader of the House. The Viceroy, who was certainly capable of jealousy but did not fear his friend's intentions, replied, 'He is a tepid though charming lover. So Pappy does not feel seriously afraid.'[54] 'Pappy' had nothing about which to be fearful, as for Balfour – and also for Lady Curzon – this was merely a diversion. Mary returned to India, and all remained friends.

Few of his women friends were so clever, colourful or eccentric as Margot Tennant. Though not a great beauty, she did not lack for male admirers. It was not merely the dowry she might bring to a marriage: Margot was a brilliant and ambitious young woman, with an entertaining, almost theatrical, manner. Her uninhibited sense of fun also made her amusing to be with. When the Tennant sisters burst on the London scene in the mid-1880s, they shocked and delighted society; and if Laura became the first darling of what would become the Souls, Margot became their sharp-tongued jester, sometime ringleader, and self-appointed conscience.

In 1882 she met Balfour at a dinner party, where she was seated between him and the Earl of Pembroke, both experienced veterans of London society. She more than held up her end of the conversation with her dinner companions – remarkable in itself for a mere teenager: 'It was an achievement', her biographer notes, 'few girls of her age could claim so early in her first season.'[55] Within a year or two her conquests were legion. But, they did not include Arthur Balfour. A friendship began which, despite many impediments, evolved and survived for many years; but he was not destined to become the brilliant and wealthy husband that she may well have wished him to be.

In the mid-1880s a London newspaper erroneously announced that the two were engaged to be married. It was not the only time this sort of thing happened, and when a similar story linked her name with Rosebery's it nearly snuffed out their friendship. Balfour was not so tetchy, and soon after the story broke the two met at a London ball. Sensing the opportunity for some fun, he strode prominently across the room to her side. 'He asked me to sit down next to him in a conspicuous place', she recalled, 'and we talked through two dances.' Taking the display as confirmation, another guest reportedly asked the smiling Balfour if it was true that he was to wed Miss Tennant. 'No, that is not so,' he is said to have replied. 'I rather think of having a career of my own.'[56] The tale seems almost too good to be true - and probably was just that – but when Margot popularized it in her memoirs, Balfour never denied it.

More important to Balfour was another society belle, Ettie, the wife of 'Willie' Grenfell, MP. Born Ethel Fane, she had been orphaned young and brought up by her uncle and aunt, Lord and Lady Cowper. Beautiful and intelligent (and heiress to the Cowper fortune), she possessed social gifts that made her an ideal hostess – in many ways the ideal Souls woman. At twenty, she married the strikingly handsome and athletic Grenfell, later ennobled on Balfour's recommendation as Lord Desborough. The six-foot-five-inch scion of a wealthy merchant family, Grenfell had rowed and fenced and swum his way to glory at Oxford. He dedicated his life to public service and to Ettie, and had the curious distinction of having read his own obituary erroneously printed in *The Times* twenty-five years before his death. Lady Desborough became an object of infatuation for many men, which seems not to have prevented her marriage from being both successful and happy.

The Desboroughs hosted as many summertime weekend parties as possible, first at Willie's Taplow in Buckinghamshire, and later at Panshanger, the great house in Hertfordshire inherited from the Cowpers. During the London season there were balls and dinners at their house in St James's Square. Tall and slim, Ettie had been a pretty young girl and became a strikingly attractive woman; combined with her charm and gift for conversation, this made her truly a society legend in her own time. She violated many of the Souls' prime strictures with impunity: her appreciation of music or painting was scant, and she was devoted to racing, which other Souls disdained. In her case it did not seem to matter, and falling in love with her was a popular activity among male Souls – the habitual womanizer Harry Cust was among them, as were George Wyndham, Lord Revelstoke and Evan Charteris, Lord Elcho's brother. If Balfour was not, he certainly delighted in her company.

Lady Desborough's lifelong friendship with Mary Elcho masked a kind of rivalry. In her letters to Balfour, Lady Elcho usually playfully referred to Ettie as 'Delilah' – but at times, jealousy showed itself in a less jocular way. Here is an example of 1895:

> I must say that I *did* appreciate your coming to see me three times in one week and it got me over some *very* agitating conversations with D[elilah] that put me in a flutter, but you certainly gave me the impression that you still cared for me in London and that kept me happy and confident, tho' I must say that unless you are the wickedest humbug which I won't and don't

believe, that Delilah does use you as a blind partly or at any rate is so proud of the intimacy that she makes the most of it in some directions, she talks of [your] letters as though they came *constantly*.[57]

Lady Elcho's annoyance lay in the fact that Balfour quite obviously enjoyed the company of the vivacious Ettie, who sent him no soul-searching letters and pleas for proof of affection. Her vitality and buoyant optimism charmed him, and he never grew tired of her ability to make him smile. At the Desboroughs' house parties there was always much variety among the guests, and Balfour was always the first to be invited. At Taplow, visitors were billeted where Ettie thought best, and bachelors received the lowest priority. But Balfour had his own room – located on the first floor in the curious corner turret which dominated the austere façade of the house – and, despite the many demands on his time, he made every effort to attend as many of Ettie's 'Saturday-to-Mondays' as possible. His friendship with the Desboroughs thrived for the remainder of his life, and for Ettie he felt real affection. But, despite Lady Elcho's fears, there was no love affair. The friendship was real, and there was love, but it was platonic.

These friendships were important to him, but Balfour was simply incapable of being swept away by them. Like Lady Elcho, in her youth the headstrong Margot craved pledges of affection and signs of commitment, and she once upbraided him for not really caring for the women who adored him: 'If Mary, Etty and I died you would not miss us,' she challenged. 'I know that you are devoted to Mary Wemyss, but for us others, you don't care two hoots! You have a taste for us as you might have in clocks and furniture.' Balfour is said to have reflected on the accusation and replied: 'I should mind if you all died on the same day.'[58] In fact he would have cared very much, as his sincere mourning for Margot's sister, Laura Lyttelton, indicates. Yet he simply could not or would not give what certain of them might have wished for – marriage, or even a love affair of the conventional sort.

Even the self-absorbed Margot realized that Mary Elcho enjoyed the place closest to Balfour's heart. By the time he had become Leader of the House of Commons, Mary too had grown from a pretty, clever girl, flattered by his attentions, into a beautiful, charming and mature woman. She had strength of character as well, and needed it. She not only managed a sizeable household (eventually including seven children), based at picturesque Stanway in Gloucestershire and in a large house in Cadogan Square, but did so with the most precarious finances. Lord Elcho had a long wait before coming into his inheritance in 1914, and with a large establishment to maintain, and no fortune of his own, he was a willing prey to one investment scheme or another. These usually turned out badly, and when they did the Elchos often veered dangerously close to bankruptcy. In the end, the family established a trust outside Hugo's control to underpin the Elchos' prosperity, and, ironically, Arthur Balfour became one of the trustees. This Elcho accepted with characteristic good humour. The Souls' tastes in recreation often bored him, yet, when his mood was right, Hugo displayed a roguish sense of humour that captivated even that demanding audience.

Lord Elcho took several mistresses during his marriage, and – fair-minded sportsman that he was – he was untroubled by his wife's affection for Arthur Balfour, whose friendship he valued. There were lines that a gentleman did not cross, however, and both Balfour and Elcho respected them. Wilfrid Blunt, a philanderer of positively legendary repute, crossed and recrossed these as a matter of course; and he invited Lady Elcho to visit his Egyptian desert hideaway, Sheykh Obeyd, in January 1895 – her husband happened to be staying with his mistress Hermione, Duchess of Leinster, at the time. Mary's beauty and charm made her attractive to the poet, as did her connection to Balfour: Blunt, of course, had once been imprisoned by him, and perhaps he saw his opportunity to even the score. He was handsome and exotic, a swashbuckling poet-revolutionary, in a setting worthy of a Valentino silent film, and Mary Elcho gave in to the temptation. Despite the presence of his wife, his own as well as the Elcho children, and various nannies, maids and valets, Blunt's seduction plan prospered during an expedition into the desert. Eventually an unhappy Hugo arrived unexpectedly, the ailing Duchess having died, and the spell was broken. Soon all returned to England, where Mary discovered she was pregnant with Blunt's child and apparently confessed her misdemeanour. Though he raged against Blunt by mail, Hugo embraced the child – a daughter, also called Mary – as his own, and no more was made of the affair.[59]

Mary's purpose in the escapade is difficult to fathom – perhaps it was to punish Hugo for his devotion to his mistress; or perhaps it was related to Blunt's relationship with her own mother, whom he had seduced years before. It was also possible that her purpose was to touch Balfour's heart, to force him to take more notice of her, to drive him to act, to be a more conventional lover. Or perhaps it was nothing more than a romantic fling, as Mary confronted the passing of her youth. Whatever the reasons may have been, the historians of the episode have suggested that, at thirty-one, it was a cathartic experience for her: 'She returned with a new confidence. Crazy though her Egyptian adventure was, it made her grow up. Before, she wrote to Arthur as to a superior being; after Egypt she was no longer "little Mary".[60]

It is unclear how much Balfour knew of the Egyptian escapade at this busy time in his life. If it caused tensions between him and Lady Elcho, they were temporary, and the two quickly returned to their usual ease with one another. Mary soon resumed her incessant entertaining; Balfour, whenever possible, continued to grace the guest list. She wrote to him in June 1895 from Stanway that his 'little visit before dinner made me happy tho' it *is* tiresome to be made to eat one's dessert first and then [to be] stuffed with batter afterwards . . . I was stodged with Batter (Asquith and Morley etc etc) all the evening while *you* were having a fine time at the other end of the room.'[61]

During her pregnancy with Blunt's child, her letters often became more insistent, demanding attention and confirmation of her position as first in Balfour's heart. Sometimes they took the form of further barbs aimed towards 'Delilah', as in May 1895:

> I get haunted sometimes that you *must* be more amused in her talk than mine, before it was different you were very foolish about me once and I was young and good looking . . . but she has so much to say and she delights you so, and incipient love even if quite unexpressed *must* be more exciting than stale love, even if warmly expressed. Today you'll go and see her and yr eyes will burn and your cheek will glow and you'll say lots of nice things to her, that I should not like to hear – never mind you are very nice to me and I'll not let you go![62]

If Balfour replied – and it is unlikely that he did – his letter has not survived. Mary's passive-aggressive campaign eventually tapered off and gave way to a manner much more friendly and less demanding. Balfour's letters, whether scribbled late at night on the Treasury bench or composed at leisure in his private sanctum, remained unfailingly correct and newsy but never approached the ardent commitment for which she hoped. Eventually, tensions such as these passed away and the two kinds of love they felt evolved into a comfortable and loving friendship.

His expanding political responsibilities and his complex social life among the Souls enriched portions of Balfour's life. He needed more, however, and to provide his restless intellect with the stimulation that it demanded he continued to depend on the writing of philosophy. He smiled at his own expense about his books – typically referring to any work in progress as the 'immortal work' – but he took his writing, both the subject and the process, very seriously. As the Unionist government was approaching its end in 1892, he began writing a second book, eventually published in February 1895 as *Foundations of Belief, being Notes Introductory to the Study of Theology*. Then as now, it was a brave thing for even the most brilliant layman to venture into a field so congested with learning as theology, and in the preface of the book he was quick to point out that he had no intention of blundering into such a rarefied discipline. His goals, he insisted, were more modest: 'What I have tried to do', he cautioned, 'is not write a monograph about, or a series of monographs, upon Theology, but to delineate, and, if possible, to recommend, a certain attitude of mind; and I hope that in carrying out this less ambitious scheme I have put in a few touches that were superfluous and left out none that were necessary.'[63] Unlike *A Defence of Philosophic Doubt*, the new work sold well, requiring five additional printings before the end of the year. Balfour insisted that it was intended not for philosophers or theologians but for the lay reader, and its brisk sale indicates that it found its audience. However, though the language is powerful throughout, and even beautiful in parts, it is also extremely complex. The book required of the reader not only some knowledge of logic, ethics and theology, but considerable powers of concentration. Balfour wondered, with reason, how well it would have fared in the bookshops had the author not been one of Britain's most celebrated parliamentarians. Its curiosity value must have been considerable: even in those days, when few MPs had escaped a classical education, it was rare for those on the front benches to produce works of this sort.

Despite joking to Haldane – another philosopher-statesman – before publication that he was sure that it would be found 'equally repulsive when finished, to the philosopher, the theologian and the man of the world', the book was reviewed generously.[64] Certainly the philosopher and social scientist William James was favourably impressed, writing to his novelist brother, Henry, 'I have been reading Balfour's "Foundations of Belief" with immense gusto . . . There is more real philosophy in such a book than in fifty German ones of which the eminence consists of heaping up subtleties and technicalities about the subject.' The American's conclusion was most complimentary: 'B. is a great man.'[65] Though well aware that Balfour was far from sympathetic to their faith, Catholic critics were among the most enthusiastic defenders of the work, among them his Synthetic Society colleagues Wilfrid Ward and the Jesuit George Tyrrell.[66] It had its critics too, however – particularly among the flinty-eyed social engineers who followed Herbert Spencer, and the more-Darwinian-than-Darwin circle of T. H. Huxley.[67]

Balfour's object in this new book was essentially the same as that of *A Defence of Philosophic Doubt*: to counter the increasingly powerful modernist doctrine of rationalist disbelief, which placed faith in empiricism alone. As he had said in another context, to the Society for Psychical Research, he believed that to suspect all that could not be quantitatively verified was to limit fatally any search for understanding. While his respect for science was both deep and broad, he saw a potentially destructive flaw in its power to close the mind towards all other forms of knowledge, including the holy. Modernist sceptics, he argued, ultimately found themselves as blindly faithful to a demanding and restrictive body of belief as the most orthodox of religionists. In the world they defined, there could be at the end of things only darkness and death. The single best-known passage of the book, in his most powerful and terrifying language, addresses this awful possibility. It is still mistakenly paraded as evidence of the author's belief in the hopelessness of the human condition. It was quite the reverse, and for that reason is worth quoting at length. The key to understanding his point is, of course, in the first few words, and those most often misused are found at the end:

> *Man, so far as natural science by itself is able to teach us, is no longer the final cause of the universe, the Heaven-descended heir of all the ages.* His very existence is an accident, his story a brief and transitory episode in the life of one of the meanest of the planets. Of the combination of causes which first converted a dead organic compound into the living progenitors of humanity, science, indeed, as yet knows nothing. It is enough that from such beginnings famine, disease, and mutual slaughter, fit nurses of the future lords of creation, have gradually evolved, after infinite travail, a race with conscience enough to know that it is vile, and intelligence enough to know that it is insignificant. We survey the past, and see that its history is of blood and tears, of helpless blundering, of wild revolt, of stupid acquiescence, of empty aspirations. We sound the future, and learn that after a period, long compared with the divisions of time open to our investigation, the energies of our system will decay, the glory of the sun will be dimmed, and the earth, tideless and inert, will no longer tolerate the race which has for a moment disturbed its solitude. Man will go down into the pit, and all his thoughts will perish. The uneasy consciousness, which in this obscure corner has for a brief space broken the contented silence of the universe, will be at rest. Matter will know itself no longer. 'Imperishable monuments' and 'Immortal deeds', death itself, and love stronger than death, will be as though they had never been. Nor will anything that *is* be better or be worse for all that the labour, genius, devotion, and suffering of man have striven through countless generations to effect.[68]

Such was the only possible fate of the world according to what Balfour called 'Naturalism', his term for any system of belief which 'ultimately profits by any defeats which Theology may sustain, or which may be counted on to flood the spaces from which the tide of Religion has receded'.[69] For him, Naturalism lumped together agnosticism (a term coined by Huxley in 1859), positivism and empiricism, and was the modern scourge that prevented a full understanding of existence and man's place within it.

Balfour agreed that reason was a human faculty of the highest importance, yet if reliance on empirical reasoning as the exclusive guide to understanding the world led, as he insisted it did, only to belief in a universe of randomness and ultimately of purposelessness, then what was the value of existence? In effect, what was the use of anything? In a crucial portion of his argument, he offered as a guide what he termed 'Authority'. This is sometimes misunderstood simply as his synonym for coercive power, but it was not this at all. 'Authority, as I have been using the term,' he argued, 'is in all cases contrasted with Reason, and stands for that group of non-rational causes, moral, social and educational, which produces its results by psychic processes other than reasoning.'[70] This 'group' included traditions and social mores, as well as both taught and customary wisdom tested over time – which he suggests gave a human community its character. In a practical 'real world' sense, understanding for him was based far more on this than on pure reason – which, given human weakness, had led sometimes to great errors. When the development of society is examined, he insisted, Authority will be found to be the basis of ethics, social life, politics, even of reason itself; for society, it is Authority not reason that 'cements its superstructure', and its importance is both subtle and great:

> At every moment in our lives, as individuals, as members of a family, of a party, of a nation, of a Church, of a universal brotherhood, the silent, continuous, unnoticed influence of Authority moulds our feelings, our aspirations, and what we are more immediately concerned with, our beliefs. It is from Authority that Reason itself draws its most important premises. It is in unloosing or directing the forces of Authority that its most important conclusions find their principal function. And even in those cases where we may most truly say that our beliefs are the rational product of strictly intellectual processes, we have, in all probability, only got to trace back the thread of our inferences to its beginnings in order to perceive that it finally loses itself in some general principle which, describe it as we may, is in fact due to no more defensible origin than the influence of Authority.[71]

On what, then, was the validity of Authority based? Balfour's answer was that this, as all else, depended upon a Creator. Yet this was the God as much of reason and science as of the most sincere and simple piety, for all validity, he argued, ceased without that God. 'What I have so far tried to establish is this,' he writes: 'that the great body of our beliefs, scientific, ethical, aesthetic, theological, form a more coherent and satisfactory whole if we consider them in a Theistic setting, than if we consider them in a Naturalistic one.'[72] To theorize any other First Cause was to accept that terrifying end time in which all that was – the noble and vile alike – would pass away, leaving behind only nullity. While Balfour scrupulously avoided an evangelical tone, he left the reader in no doubt that, after years of 'destructive criticism' in the age of science (he had, after all, read David Strauss and Ernest Renan), only Christianity was best fitted to 'minister to our ethical needs', and he added confidently, 'I find it hard to believe that [the reader] will arrive at any different conclusion.'[73] In short, to posit a Godless 'Naturalist' world was to endorse an existence without purpose or meaning – built only upon incomplete understanding.[74] Balfour sought to hasten the two faiths – theism and science – towards the unity which he was certain would one day be achieved.[75] To his disappointment, scientific unbelievers were unimpressed by his willingness to include them in the moral synthesis he defined.

Carefully crafted (even Huxley praised Balfour's prose) *Foundations of Belief* was meant not for the theologian but for the ordinary believer confronted with the aggression of scepticism and unyielding empiricism. Like Burke, Balfour sought to remind his reader that the old truths had not been rendered invalid simply because they were old. And, though he scrupulously denied that the work was anything more than an introduction to the study of theology, he argued powerfully his belief that the marvels of discovery were not possible in any other than a world created by a personal God 'to whom men may pray'. The book remains in print as these words are written, and, successful or not, his case was among the most powerful ever made in the language.

6

Leader in the Commons

———∼———

ARTHUR JAMES BALFOUR was forty-three years of age when he became
First Lord of the Treasury and Leader of the House of Commons.
Unlike some of his predecessors as Chief Secretary, his Irish trials had left
no traces in his appearance. His hair was still dark and thick, though the
luxuriant curls had long been sacrificed, and he continued to affect the
moustache and side whiskers that were much in style. His figure remained
slim, due in large part to his continued passion for golf and tennis. By this
time he had adopted the soft collar and simple crossed tie that would
remain signatures of his dress for the remainder of his life, but his posture
on the Treasury bench was as careless as it had been when he was a backbencher, years before.

His predecessor, the tireless W. H. Smith, had set a high standard of diligence as Leader of the House, arriving in the Chamber early each evening
and staying late. 'Old Morality,' one observer recalled, 'foregoing the
luxury of dining at [his home in] Grosvenor Place, had a chop or a cut off
the joint served in his room behind the Speaker's chair . . . He was always
ready to rush into the House at the sound of the division bell or on the
arrival of a messenger with news of gathering complications.'[1] There
would be no chop eaten hastily in his room for Balfour, and, when he
appeared in the Chamber in dinner dress, many Members noted 'a rare
departure from the unwritten law that controls fashion in this matter'.[2]
What they witnessed proved to be the new order of things. As we have
seen, the often torpid pace of parliamentary business and the droning on
of speakers whose earnestness or determination sometimes outmatched
their talents bored him to distraction. He wrote to Lady Elcho in 1899 in
'praise' of the newly installed Liberal leader, Sir Henry Campbell-
Bannerman, that, while less able than his predecessor, Sir William
Harcourt, 'C-B' at least 'kept me awake'. He continued, 'Nobody who
has not had (as I have) to get up about seven o'clock in a tired and hungry
House and reply to a two hour speech about nothing in particular, knows
how great is the relief. Harcourt used really to *hypnotize* me on these

occasions: I was almost too bored to speak!'[3] Too often, the Leader did a poor job of concealing his ennui.

Yet, as in his days as Irish Secretary, when the hard work of politics needed to be done, he delegated the donkey work to subordinates and took upon himself what he considered important matters. Lord Curzon, his friend and sometime rival over four decades, once confided to an intimate that Balfour's style obscured the substance: 'Balfour has raised political nonchalance to the dignity of a fine art, but it is largely superficial, and behind it all he is as patriotic and as capable of strenuous – though not detailed – work as any man.'[4] Balfour would not have been offended by this, and he soon discovered in his new dignity that superficial nonchalance was not always easily achieved.

The transition required considerable effort. As Irish Secretary he faced battle daily, and 'every parrying stroke or skilful thrust was watched with keen delight and hailed with rousing cheers.'[5] Veteran parliament-watcher that he was, Henry Lucy stressed that the skills of a successful Leader of the Commons were very different – qualities of compromise and calm, and an 'unaggressive nature'. He noted that the transition from Chief Secretary to Leader of the House was hard on Balfour, and that soon he looked 'aweary' and strained. Lucy wrote of Balfour that, only weeks after taking up his new duties: 'The light is fading from his eye, the ready smile from his lips; his temper is growing short, and his face grey.'[6] The reporter feared that the youthful hero's early performance might presage a failure and a poor comparison with giants like Disraeli and Gladstone, or even Smith.

It was true that after years as a warrior for the Irish Union, and now faced with the new burden of leading the House and a front bench that had largely worn out their welcome, Arthur Balfour was fatigued. Laughing at himself, he once said to Lord Balcarres, 'I have one faculty of statesmanship, namely the power of taking a perfect holiday . . . Rosebery can't sleep or eat in moderation owing to his impotence for holidaymaking. In this matter I am quite perfect! It is the first requirement of the public man.'[7] As it was, there was little time for holidays, and for the moment he tried to cut corners, often entering the Chamber well after the session had begun. His habit at question time of delegating responses to subordinates so that he might slip into his place later to deal only with weightier matters was not always welcomed by opponents or supporters.

For Balfour there also remained unfinished business, as he rather than his successor as Irish Secretary, W. L. Jackson, took charge of a bill to redeem his pledge to establish county councils in Ireland like those already in place in Britain. The authority of these bodies was to be limited to the maintenance of highways and appointment of local officials, with the franchise to include women and peers in addition to parliamentary electors, and with clauses included to safeguard minority representation.[8] The bill, introduced in February 1892, was much unloved: Home Rulers thought it offered too little, and many Unionists feared that it held out too much. In defending an energetically criticized feature of the bill, Balfour identified English school board election law as his model: 'I think', he mused, 'that there are great advantages in doing a stupid thing that has been done before, rather than a wise thing which has not yet been done.'[9] But humour did not save the unpopular bill, which was quietly withdrawn by the government after its second reading – and perhaps the fatigued House was past caring. Many suggested that the mandate of this Parliament had run its course; the Opposition could smell blood, and an election could not be long delayed. The Unionist leaders agreed, and Parliament was dissolved on 28 June, with polling to begin a week later.

Balfour agreed that resignation was the best political decision, and it also appealed to him personally, as he contemplated having time not merely for leisure, but for the delicious possibility of turning once again to his writing. In the early days of polling, as the prospect of electoral defeat seemed increasingly likely, he admitted to his uncle, 'This is provoking from some points of view but makes it at all events tolerably certain that we shall have a long holiday! I shall be able to prepare my new edition of "Philosophic Doubt"!'[10] As we have seen, it was not a revision of his earlier book that claimed his attention, but the preparation of a new one, *Foundations of Belief.* When, a week later, it was certain that the Unionists would be turned out, he wrote to Lady Salisbury, 'With the total result I am well pleased: and feel like a boy on the first days of the holidays.'[11]

East Manchester polled early, and Balfour held his seat, though with a majority reduced by a third, to 398. His cousin Cranborne lost his seat at Darwen ('I suppose it was those confounded [Roman Catholics],' Balfour noted to Salisbury), but Balfour took some joy in the fact that in Midlothian Gladstone's previous majority of more than 4,600 fell to under 700.[12] The overall results were curious: the total poll rose from 2.75 million to 4.4 million votes, and the Unionists were the largest single party in the new House of Commons, winning 313 seats and more than 2 million votes. The Liberals received only slightly fewer votes and won only 272 seats; but their allies, the Irish Nationalists, held the balance with their 81 seats, giving Gladstone a surplus of 40 – their 'motley majority', Salisbury grumbled.[13] Salisbury chose to meet Parliament – offering the shortest Queen's Speech, only a few lines, in living memory – and face defeat. It came in the Commons on 11 August, when an amendment to the Queen's Speech was passed by the Liberal rising star H. H. Asquith, and on the following day Salisbury made his way to Osborne House to offer his resignation to the sovereign. The Queen unhappily summoned Gladstone, and Parliament adjourned.

Salisbury's annoyance over his defeat passed slowly, but Balfour was quite content. Though he continued to lead his party in the Commons, the flow of red boxes was staunched, and the pace of work slowed. After the House rose, he fled to Scotland to clear away the mental clutter of six years in office, and he knew no better short-term prescription for his ills than a fortnight of golf at North Berwick – where he struggled mightily (and largely unsuccessfully) to ignore claims for places in the resignation honours list, which kept his secretaries busy.

His peace was soon disturbed, as he discovered that an election petition had been brought against his return in East Manchester charging that his supporters had violated the law by providing free beer to his constituents. Twenty-eight-year-old Lord Robert Cecil was one of the lawyers briefed for the defence, and recalled years later, 'The evidence showed that there had been a good deal of beer drunk in the course of the election. But there was nothing to show that Balfour or any agent of his had provided the beer.'[14] Balfour wrote to Lady Salisbury at the time, 'I am not (yet) a prisoner at the bar,' but he added, 'Bob is looking beautiful in his wig – : I am cursing & swearing at being kept here over this infernal petition instead of being at Stanway where I have long been promised for this week.'[15] Lady Elcho, however, did not despair long at the absence of her favourite guest: the case was dismissed, and Balfour soon joined her party.

The Christmas holidays were passed as usual among the family at Whittingehame. Alice Balfour had been much saddened at the sale of Strathconan in the previous year, but had apparently stifled her deep disappointment. Perhaps in part as a reward, Balfour acceded to her wish to flee to warmer climes for a few days.[16] Immediately following the new year, brother and sister travelled to Pau in the South of France, where the ex-First Lord of the Treasury strove to concentrate his thoughts for a while on philosophy rather than politics. The mental furlough was brief, however, for when he returned to London in time for the new parliamentary session on 31 January he knew that a renewed battle over Irish Home Rule was inevitable.

The Grand Old Man, now in his eighty-fourth year, faced a formidable struggle, backed only by his forty-seat majority. Alvin Jackson has rightly

noted that for the Prime Minister 'Home Rule was a matter of both justice and obligation, but it was a duty that, given the inscrutability of the
Almighty and the intractability of Parliament, Gladstone accepted with
diminished enthusiasm.'[17] Not only the Almighty was inscrutable, for
Gladstone kept his colleagues in the dark about the Irish legislation which
would make or break their administration. As late as three days before his
bill was to be introduced, most of the government had little idea of its
details. On the appointed day, 13 February 1892, and despite his advanced
age, the GOM delivered himself of a two-and-a-half-hour speech in his
usual extravagant mode. The Home Rule plan called for a bicameral legislature and a representation of eighty Irish MPs at Westminster, and, as in
the 1886 bill, Ireland would be expected to pay its share of imperial costs,
based upon its income from customs duties. Gladstone brushed aside the
outrage of the restive Ulster Protestants at his proposal that there be one
Irish administration in Dublin for all of Home Rule Ireland. For the
Unionists the gauntlet lay conspicuously on the ground, and now the test
would be whether Gladstone could pilot the bill through the House.

It was in this fight against the man whom he later ranked among the
greatest Members the House had known that Balfour demonstrated that he
was constructed of the stuff of which parliamentary leaders are made.
From the outset, all knew that if Gladstone's majority in the House stuck
by him, Balfour could not prevent the passage of the bill. However, he
could make that progress as difficult and controversial and divisive as possible. He savaged what he called this 'abortion of a measure' from its
introduction. Despite the Prime Minister's guarantees, it could lead, he
insisted, only to the disintegration of the United Kingdom and the Empire.
It was neither one thing nor the other, he argued, but a destructive hotch-
potch of disparate notions. 'A Federal Government may be good,' he
argued. 'Colonial Government may be good. The British Constitution as
it now stands may be good; but this bastard combination of the three is
ludicrous and impossible.' As he had written in another context a year
earlier, the gentlemen who had for five years supported Salisbury's government were before all else a Unionist party, and now the Union must be
defended.[18] In the seven months that followed, he defended it with all the
strength and craft he could muster.

Although it was hardly necessary, Balfour was reminded of the vehemence of opposition to Home Rule among the Irish Unionists when he
travelled to Belfast in early April, standing in for an ailing Salisbury. It was
not a visit to which he looked forward: he cared little for the Ulster capital, and as usual he dreaded crossing the North Channel. 'As you know,'

he warned, 'I am an indifferent sailor and shall require all my time to [recover] after the night's journey.'[19] He survived the rough crossing, and the reception that he received exceeded anything he had ever encountered. Alice accompanied him, and recorded what she witnessed. The Unionist leader arrived by coach with the Lord Mayor and the Lord Lieutenant, the Marquess of Zetland. A vast crowd had been waiting for hours in the city centre, and their reception took on the atmosphere of a Roman triumph. Alice was already in her place among the honoured guests, and recalled:

> Every house was decorated with flags; every window was full of spectators, and the streets were packed with men, women and even children, so that it seemed impossible that carriages would ever get through them . . . The pressure must have been terrific, shouts of men and screams of women coming up at every moment, till one became so possessed with fear that some horrible accident would take place that one could hardly give attention to the oncoming procession.[20]

The ceremonies went on for several hours, as the dignitaries condemned Home Rule and pledged their support for the Union, and then reviewed a march-past of loyal Unionists. They continued so long that Balfour grew weary, and a tall stool was fetched upon which he could lean. Alice was amazed by the near-hysteria of the meeting, and described the difficult negotiation through the adoring throng of her brother's coach:

> I afterwards saw a Doctor who had attended a man who had his leg rather badly injured by the wheel of the carriage Arthur was in going over it in a crowd. The Doctor said the man stoutly declared he didn't care – he'd be run over again only to shake hands with Balfour.

A few days later, Balfour was back in the House as the second-reading debate began. It ended on 21 April with the government victorious, by 347 votes to 304. The struggle continued into the committee stage, and Gladstone increasingly relied on frequent use of the parliamentary guillotine. To the amusement of the Liberals, Balfour himself was among its victims, forced into silence on 6 July in the midst of a spirited condemnation of the bill. So heated was the atmosphere that three weeks later a violent demonstration broke out among Honourable Members, and one participant recalled that the next morning the cleaners swept up 'a broken arm of a bench, some buttons, several shirt studs, and a false tooth'.[21]

Despite everything, on 2 September, by a vote of 307 to 276 the Home Rule bill passed. It then was handed on to the Upper House, where the Unionists, of course, held a massive majority. Their lordships began their considerations three days later, and on 9 September crushed the bill on a vote of 419 to 41 – the largest total of votes ever cast in the House of Lords.[22] Rather than go to the country, the bruised Liberals soldiered on, and Gladstone retired from the premiership in the following March. Instead of calling for the new Leader of the House of Commons, Sir William Harcourt, the Queen chose to summon Lord Rosebery, the Foreign Secretary. The new premier promptly crushed the hopes of the Irish by announcing that the Liberals would squander no more political capital on Home Rule until he was certain that such a measure could command the adherence of a majority of English MPs. This, of course, was not likely to happen any time soon, and Home Rule thereafter lay dormant, at least in parliamentary terms, for the next seventeen years.

Archibald Philip Primrose, 5th Earl of Rosebery, was a year older than Balfour, and the two seemed to share much in common – they had been schoolfellows, both were Scottish aristocrats, and both entered political life early and combined politics with 'serious' writing. And both would lead brief and troubled governments. Rosebery is said to have announced as a young man that his ambitions were to win the Derby, marry an heiress, and become prime minister.[23] He achieved all three, but these were the aspirations of a character unlikely to appeal to Balfour. Rosebery was emotional and Balfour controlled. Rosebery could become overpowered by his own feelings, exacerbating the depression which sometimes haunted him. Balfour was satisfied to gaze sceptically upon himself and his comfortable world.

Balfour's niece wrote of the two men that they shared 'genuine respect and affection', though 'they were not formed to be perfectly at ease with each other.'[24] In fact they disliked one another. Balfour suggested to Lady Rayleigh in 1894 that he was unaware of any particular quality the new premier had demonstrated, save a talent for self-advertisement.[25] For his part, Rosebery sniffed to Sir Frederick Ponsonby that Balfour had done wonderfully – 'for an amateur politician', and Sir Edward Hamilton recalled his saying that 'in spite of his personal charm he considered [Balfour] an ungenerous foe.'[26] The prickliness long survived: can Rosebery have been aware years later that in 1911 Balfour had cautioned the palace against the practice of granting the Order of Merit to 'literary' politicians? – and if it had to be done, he rated Rosebery's histories only on the level of the essays and legal volumes of Augustine Birrell – a comparison the Earl would not have found flattering.[27] And did Balfour learn that when he was himself inducted into the Order, five years later, Rosebery opposed the award 'to the last'?[28]

As it was, Rosebery's government was fatally wounded from the outset by a lack of sympathy between the Prime Minister – hero of his party's imperialist wing – and such Gladstonian loyalists as Harcourt and Morley, the Irish Secretary. The unhappy Cabinet staggered along for little more than a year under Rosebery, and finally succumbed in June 1895, defeated by seven votes on the censure motion of St John Brodrick. Rosebery resigned immediately, and left the matter of an election to the Unionists. Perhaps Rosebery's heart was not in the task, but no matter what he did he simply could not be another Gladstone to his party. Balfour would himself discover in his own time how difficult it was to succeed a colossus.

The battle over Home Rule had been draining, yet Balfour had found the years of leading the Opposition in the Commons quite agreeable. After all, he had a bit more time for his non-political life – time to write *Foundations of Belief*, time for the Souls, and time also for golf and tennis. He did not long to return to office, but with Rosebery's resignation the choice had been made for him.[29] He was again appointed Leader of the House and First Lord of the Treasury, which led this time to his taking a new London address. The famous house in Downing Street which has become synonymous with the premiership held no appeal to Salisbury, who was quite content to remain in Arlington Street. In fact No. 10 was by tradition at the disposal of the First Lord of the Treasury (not technically of the prime minister, who usually held that older ceremonial office as well), and had been since Walpole first occupied it – as the brass plaque on its imposing black door indicates to this day. Unlike his uncle, Balfour was willing to give it a try, and he removed his household (including a part of his art collection and two pianos) from Carlton Gardens to the historic house which would be his London residence for a decade. For a time, 4 Carlton Gardens was let to the newly-wed George Curzon, who was so pleased with the area that he purchased the adjoining house in Carlton House Terrace.[30]

The composition of the new government seemed to indicate that the two principal Unionist parties were well on the way to formal unification – certainly Balfour expected it.[31] On 24 June, Salisbury and Balfour met in Arlington Street with the Duke of Devonshire (as Lord Hartington had become in the previous year) and Joseph Chamberlain, and it was clear that there would be no fusion of parties at this point. There would be close co-operation, however: no time would be wasted in a symbolic offer by Salisbury to serve under the Duke – which apparently Devonshire regretted – but, more importantly, the Liberal Unionists agreed that they would serve in the new government.[32] Salisbury would again combine the Foreign Office with the premiership, and Balfour would continue to lead the Commons; Devonshire accepted the Lord Presidency of the Council, with supervisory responsibility for education and national defence. Chamberlain's importance was underscored by the offer to him of any other office he wished, and to the surprise of the others he brushed aside traditionally more prestigious appointments and chose the Colonial Office. Salisbury gave him a day to reconsider, but Joe got precisely what he asked for – and with it came Lord Wolmer, Salisbury's son-in-law, as his under-secretary. Hicks Beach became Chancellor, while Goschen (who, unlike Chamberlain, had apparently joined the Carlton Club) accepted the Admiralty, with Chamberlain's eldest son, Austen, as his second-in-command. Balfour's old schoolfellow Lord Lansdowne took the War Office, and Gerald Balfour became Chief Secretary for Ireland, outside the Cabinet.

It is not surprising that Balfour favoured party unification, for management of the Unionist coalition raised problems that were spared those who led a single unified party. Three years earlier he had had to quell a rebellion among Conservatives in East Worcestershire, good Churchmen all, who balked at supporting a Unitarian nominee, Austen Chamberlain. Balfour wrote to the local party chairman:

> But it must be recollected that the party which has with such unswerving loyalty supported the [Salisbury] Government through five stormy sessions is not a Conservative Party but a Unionist Party: – a Unionist Party in which no doubt the Conservative element greatly predominates, but one nevertheless of which the Liberal element forms an essential and most important part.[33]

If the principal offices were distributed with relatively little friction in 1895, the distribution of secondary appointments stirred up trouble. This was owing at least in part to the fact that some of the far more numerous Conservatives were resentful that the Liberal Unionists seemed to be receiving more than their share of the spoils of office.[34] If all were members, once and for all, of a single party this might be settled. In April, Balfour had revealed to the Liberal Unionist Sir Henry James the direction in which his mind was moving. In an upcoming speech he would 'hint at closer fusion in the future . . . I shall take care not to make my acknowledgment too definite or explicit.'[35] He was even more frank with Sir George Bartley: Liberal Unionists and Conservatives, he insisted, were unalike only in name.[36] There were those on both sides of Unionism who were receptive to the idea of a merger, but the majority were not ready to surrender their historic labels. Formal amalgamation of the two organizations would not come for another sixteen years, after Balfour had retired from the party leadership.

The first order of business for the new government was to fight and win an election, and the results in July justified Unionist confidence. Balfour was easily returned for East Manchester, and he was joined by 410 other Unionists, forming a majority of 152 over the combined Opposition. He and Chamberlain took the lead in the electoral battle, and Balfour never campaigned more vigorously, speaking widely and often to large and enthusiastic audiences. Wyndham wrote to him in the later stages of the contest, 'Let me congratulate you on the victory & on the long series of speeches you have been making. I have watched your career with awe & wonder & hope you are not half dead.'[37] After more than three weeks of rushed banquets, thrice-daily speeches, endless shaking of hands, and unremitting railway and coach journeys, there was no doubt in Balfour's mind that he had earned a brief respite at Whittingehame.

Balfour was one of the three figures who dominated Unionist politics for the lifespan of this government; the others were Salisbury and Chamberlain. As we have seen, Salisbury and Balfour formed a natural partnership, and they stayed in such close touch that Salisbury arranged for a private telephone line between their houses. They shared the important link of blood, for family connection meant much to them both; but perhaps even more important was the fact that Salisbury and Balfour were both natural conservators, committed to the defence of what they saw as the best elements of the society they thought beyond compare in the world. It is true that Salisbury was forever dogged by a deep pessimism regarding how much success in this endeavour could be expected, and a dark fear that, in the end, it was almost certainly a losing battle. Balfour's scepticism, his instinct for philosophical questioning, was well established; but perhaps more than his uncle he saw long-term value in the alleviation of the weaknesses in the nation as he found it.

They had at least one similar weakness in that they both had wretched memories for data: Salisbury once asked Edward VII if he could identify the clergyman they had met earlier in the day. When the King related the story to the Bishop of London (the cleric in question) the latter was shocked, for the Prime Minister had apparently forgotten that he had himself introduced the other two men earlier that same afternoon. 'You need not mind, Bishop,' His Majesty replied, 'for he took up a photograph of me this morning and thought it was [Sir Redvers] Buller.' Balfour's recollection of faces and names was better, but he cared little for facts. St John Brodrick recalled that his fellow Soul could easily 'substitute counties for provinces; squadrons for regiments, and the like, with happy disregard of the marred effect'.[38]

Balfour and Chamberlain could hardly have been more unalike in their origins, style and manner of carrying out their works. The Anglo-Scottish grandee was conservative and intellectual, and he approached government as a series of problems to be solved, one after the other. The Birmingham screw manufacturer was intuitive, impatient and drawn to grand long-range programmes for reform in both domestic and foreign affairs. Thinking him the most powerful speaker in politics, Balfour said of Chamberlain that he was one of only two men whose speeches he really cared to hear (the other was H. H. Asquith). 'Radical Joe' was sixty years old in 1896, though his appearance belied it, and he was conscious that time was not on his side. If the two men were too unalike for genuine friendship, each understood the other's strengths and struggled with what they thought were his weaknesses. Their co-operation was forged in necessity, and was to be tested time and again over the next decade.

Balfour did not feign the omniscience that admirers insisted on seeing in Gladstone, nor would he have been able to bear the adulation with which the Grand Old Man was comfortable. His mind was too restless, and he lacked the patience of 'Old Morality' Smith to stick to his last, day after day, without complaint. Balfour depended heavily on his party whips and the famous Central Office machine directed by the incomparable 'Skipper' – Conservative chief agent Captain Richard Middleton. Unlike his predecessors, or Salisbury for that matter, Balfour was always comfortable using Christian names with colleagues whom he knew well – and there were many – yet he saw no reason at all to appear particularly 'accessible' to the many he did not. Lord Balcarres, the great political diarist and later Balfour's chief whip in the Commons, thought it significant enough to note in his diary in 1895 that 'To my infinite surprise Arthur Balfour spoke to me this evening.'[39] This reaction was apparently not unusual. Balfour did not frequent the renowned Members' smoking room, where leaders so often rubbed elbows with followers, and he avoided the Commons dining room whenever possible. As we have seen, if there was no pressing business, he disliked remaining on the front bench throughout question time, much less during the hour after hour of uninspiring speeches, which he considered of interest only to the speakers. To many MPs, all of this was evidence of his legendary aloofness from all but a sort of inner circle of colleagues – and there was some (though incomplete) truth in this.

As Salisbury's lieutenant, Balfour led the Unionists in the Commons for more than a decade, and established patterns which seldom varied. Few had a more unobstructed view of him than Sir Sydney Parry, who in 1897 left the Treasury to become Balfour's departmental private secretary for five years. In that year Parry was surprised to be summoned to an interview in the imposing Cabinet Room at No. 10, which served as Balfour's office – Salisbury preferring to meet his colleagues at the Foreign Office. He was received by the Leader of the House himself, and years later he recalled meeting an immaculately dressed figure – he was always struck by the whiteness of Balfour's spats – whose smile and disarming manner defused the secretary's anxiety. The two got on well from the outset, and Parry joined the staff immediately.[40]

Balfour continued his habits of rising late and taking breakfast in his bedroom, during which time he conducted business after Parry and his secretaries had 'invaded' him. It was a regular part of this ritual for Jack Sandars to offer a detailed abridgement of the morning newspapers, for Balfour insisted that he never read them if he could avoid it ('and never for mere relaxation').[41] In fact he paid close attention to the press and to certain important journalists, though he cultivated the myth that he cared not at all about the great London dailies, then at the height of their influence: 'There is no need for the newspapers to tell me my faults,' he once joked. 'I know them all, but I can't alter them.'[42] He slyly chided Winston Churchill, who supplemented his income through occasional journalism, by declaring apropos the morning papers, 'I have never put myself to the trouble of rummaging through an immense rubbish-heap on the problematical chance of discovering a cigar band.'[43] In fact he had been friendly since their Cambridge days with the influential leader writer E. B. Iwan-Müller of the *Daily Telegraph*, and he frequently employed his services in trying to shape press opinion. He also co-operated frequently with J. L. Garvin, the influential editor of *The Observer*, and he once offered (unsuccessfully) a baronetcy to G. E. Buckle, the editor of *The Times*. He did the same (quite successfully) for Alfred Harmsworth, the 'greatest figure who ever strode down Fleet Street', and followed it up a year later with a peerage.[44] Balfour frequently employed Sandars as his confidential agent with the Unionist newspapers.[45]

After Sandars's report, Balfour typically faced the morning's correspondence. He was always comfortable dictating letters, usually to Wilfrid Short and habitually before his bath and while still in his dressing gown. Though he always found the physical act of writing taxing, many times dictation would not do. In such cases, like many tall men, Balfour employed a 'stand-up' desk at which to draft his letters – and all but the most private correspondence was then copied before being sent – after 'Shorty' had repaired the Balfourian curiosities of spelling.

Balfour's relations with his secretaries were candid and quite relaxed, and Parry witnessed his master's habits almost daily for five years. The secretary noted Balfour's method of dealing with the residual anxiety and the fatigue of high office by clearing his mind once he had stepped from the political line of fire. If time allowed, this might mean bicycling, tennis or golf. If only an hour was available, it meant refreshing himself mentally by throwing himself into a book. Balfour developed complete confidence in his secretary's gift for choosing a diverting volume: 'Do ring for tea,' Parry remembered him commanding, '& find me a good novel from the side table.' Sir Sydney recalled, 'I once administered A. E. W. Mason's *Four Feathers* which had just been published, & he pronounced it a splendid tonic and one of the best yarns he had ever read.'[46] When the interlude was over, the Leader of the House declared himself refreshed, and returned to parliamentary business.

This openness with his personal assistants had its amusing side. Once, during the dark days of the South African War, Parry recalled, an urgent message requiring an immediate reply arrived at No. 10 while Balfour was still in his bath. Sir Sydney tapped at the door to inform his master that the message had come, and to the secretary's surprise he was invited to enter immediately to read the dispatch. Parry did so, and was amused by the minister's rising from the tub to dictate his reply while towelling himself dry.

Balfour was inclined to 'see the best' in people, the secretary testified, adding, 'I have never heard him make a cruel or venomous remark, & I can't remember seeing him really out of patience more than once – it was after months of provocation from a very high, self-sufficient & senile dignitary.' Yet Parry understood the well-known view of Balfour as 'hard and unemotional', and added that he certainly never wore his 'heart on his sleeve'.[47] When implored for help, Sir Sydney recalled, Balfour gave it if he could and 'did not make a song of it'. And if he could not, rather than purchase a moment's peace with promises he could never fulfil, 'he was apt to switch off entirely.' It requires little imagination to gather that such a treatment would elicit varying reactions. A colleague mused to Parry what his 'chief's' public image might have been, but for a detail or two:

But, ye gods! If he only knew, he might be the most popular Prime Minister on record. Give him a wife and half a dozen kiddies. Then let them walk to church every Sunday morning with his wife on his arm and a big prayer-book in his hand, the kiddies two & two behind, and let him stop at intervals & pat a girl on the head. Talk of old Gladstone reading the lessons! He wouldn't be in it with your chief.

Parry does not indicate whether he shared this prescription with Balfour – it is highly unlikely – but his boss certainly had heard such advice before. This did not change the fact that following it was for him inconceivable.

Balfour's generosity was legendary among his staff, and they strove mightily to protect him from the many 'begging letters' he received regularly. Their concern was not so much that these annoyed Balfour, but that he was too often inclined to respond to them. In one case a notorious scoundrel had slipped through the cordon of secretaries, and his sad tale netted him a fat cheque. When the villain ended up in the dock, the cheque surfaced as an exhibit and Balfour was among those summoned to the witness box to testify when the malefactor was apprehended and tried for his crimes.

Like his one-time mentor and sometime antagonist, W. E. Gladstone, Balfour carried out some fine tuning of the rules of the House of Commons which challenged the ingenuity of the minority party. Sandars noted with admiration that Balfour's revision of the rules for voting Supply (funding) defused a useful Opposition weapon for making difficulties for the government: to this point it was relatively easy to delay Supply votes until the rushed final days and hours of the parliamentary session. According to Sandars, 'On one occasion, under the leadership of Sir W. Harcourt, all the Army Votes were passed in a single sitting.'[48] Balfour's solution was to place Supply at the beginning of each session, thus snatching away from his opponents a useful delaying tool (which he had, of course, himself employed in the past). Despite the undoubted dreariness to him of the subject of parliamentary procedure, he gave it his full attention, mastered the necessary details, and pushed his changes through the House.

Though many Conservatives were wary of the Chamberlainite drive for social reform, Balfour insisted throughout his career that such reform had long been the 'work of the Unionist party, as distinguished from the Radical or Socialist Party'.[49] With the exception of a knot of reactionaries within the party, most Unionists understood by this time that, after the great franchise reforms of the past century, further social legislation of some kind was unavoidable, and that absolute resistance meant eventual surrender to the Liberals. When he became prime minister, Balfour wrote to a colleague about the debates then swirling around them concerning fiscal and social reform. Many traditional beliefs – dogmas, he called them – might have served in the past but 'in many respects are unsuited to our present industrial & national position'.[50] Yet in 1895 he warned a Manchester audience that there must be limits to such thinking and that the Unionist Party did not place its sole faith in legislation. The state could do much to ameliorate want and suffering, but, he cautioned:

> I am not one of those who suppose that legislation can cure all the ills to which flesh is heir. I am not one of those who think that, if ministers are clever enough, and Parliaments only industrious enough, we can so remodel this world of ours that it shall blossom as the rose. I put before you no extravagant promises, I ask you to entertain no extravagant hopes; but I do believe that a Government and House of Commons should devote themselves . . . to the way in which their action would actually benefit their fellow countrymen.[51]

Socialism, he believed, erred in that to work the changes it promised it required a state which must first confiscate, in order to give – and, he declared, 'No class is ultimately benefited by robbing any other classes.' Furthermore, it postulated that the state must assume the role of both initiator and arbiter of social improvement – another dangerous fallacy, he suggested, for 'the free individual . . . working, co-operating with his fellows in freely organised associations, which as in the past, so in the future, must do a great share of the work of raising the standard of life, of happiness, of cultivation, and of prosperity'.[52]

However, there was a role for the state to play in such matters, and Balfour was content that this government should act accordingly – and there is little reason to doubt that he and most Unionist leaders accepted that, if they did not act, the next Liberal administration would do so and would make a worse job of it. Hence, following the recommendations two years earlier of the Royal Commission on Labour, in 1896 a Conciliation Act was passed which created machinery to provide arbitration between workers and management in the event of trades disputes. In the same year the government's response to the growing economic crisis in the countryside was an Agricultural Rates Act which reduced the tax burden on landholders by one-half (compensating the local authorities for the lost revenue through Exchequer grants). In 1897 the government passed an Employers' Liability Act indemnifying workers against workplace injury. In defending the measure in a Manchester speech, Balfour took on all critics –

The Balfour brothers, *c.*1870: Eustace and Cecil (*seated left to right*), Arthur (*standing*), Gerald and Frank. With them is their mother, Lady Blanche, who disliked being photographed and defaced most likenesses of herself

Gerald Balfour, *c.*1910: brother and lifelong confidant

May Lyttelton: one of 'Us Four' of Balfour's youth and perhaps his first love

Robert Gascoyne-Cecil, 3rd Marquess of
Salisbury

Lord Hugh (Gascoyne-)Cecil (later Lord
Quickswood)

Lord Robert (Gascoyne-)Cecil (later Lord
Cecil of Chelwood)

James Gascoyne-Cecil, 4th Marquess of
Salisbury

Balfour at forty, while Chief Secretary for Ireland

Lady Frances Balfour: sister-in-law, friend and drawing-room antagonist

The Wyndham sisters by John Singer Sargent, 1910: Mary, Lady Elcho (*left*), Pamela, Lady Glenconner and Madeline, Mrs Charles Adean

Left: Lord Northcliffe and Balfour witness an early flight of the Wright brothers' 'flyer' at Pau, France, 1909. Balfour's smile speaks of his lifelong love of technology

Below: Balfour at the dispatch box, August 1892. On the front bench are: C. T. Ritchie (*second from left*), G. J. Goschen (*in top hat*), Sir M. Hicks Beach (*reading*) and Sir J. Gorst (*standing at the end of the bench*). On the second bench is G. Wyndham (*fifth from left*) and G. N. Curzon (*standing in the background to Balfour's left*)

Right: The first prime minister to own a motorcar, Balfour sets off on an expedition from 10 Downing Street in 1905

Below: Following the Unionist disaster in the 1906 election, removal vans collect Balfour's 'goods and chattels' to return them to Carlton Gardens

'Ettie' Grenfell (later Lady Desborough), Sir William Harcourt and Balfour in fancy dress, 1897

Balfour and Mary, Countess of Wemyss, with one of her beloved chows, photographed by Lady Ottoline Morrell in 1925. 'You have only loved me little yet . . . you have loved me long'

Balfour at seventy-four on the tennis court with Princess Alice, Countess of Athlone, 1922

Balfour, with Hugo, Lord Elcho (*left*) and F. G. Faithfull, on the links in East Lothian, 'the paradise of golfers', 1888

Balfour as a stained-glass 'Arthurian', as seen by Francis Carruthers-Gould, 1901

not least those Tories who saw such a measure as 'contrary to the traditions of the conservative party'. For as long as Parliament had taken up such things, he insisted:

> we, the Conservatives, have borne the heat and brunt of the battle . . . To us . . . is due the great and beneficial factory legislation, which has done so much for the working man . . . and when its effects are thoroughly under-stood, it will be added to that long list of measures passed by Conservative Governments which, passed indeed, in the interests chiefly of the working classes of this country, have nevertheless, received the hearty and enthusias-tic support of the capitalists and employers also.[53]

In fact this broad 'support' took longer to achieve than Balfour might have hoped, and he may well have had social reform in mind when he joked to Margot Asquith about the similarities between himself and Salisbury: 'There is a difference,' he said. 'My uncle is a Tory . . . and I am a Liberal.'[54]

There might have been more. The subject of old-age pensions was dear to the heart of Chamberlain and other 'progressive' Unionists, and when the matter was pressed by the Opposition in early 1899 Balfour was pre-pared to press ahead with it. Though a select committee under Henry Chaplin reported in July that orthodox funding sources could not support such a plan, Balfour and Chamberlain continued to argue that a rudimen-tary system might still be possible. In December, Balfour distributed a Cabinet paper on the subject; but by this time the South African War had begun, and in a miracle of bad timing the memorandum was distributed in the midst of the infamous 'Black Week' of battlefield defeats.[55] In early February Balfour explained to King Edward's secretary Lord Knollys that, despite the sovereign's support for a pension programme, the costs of the war now rendered it impractical: 'It is, I think, hardly possible at such a moment to ask the Chancellor of the Exchequer to find anything more – even for so valuable a domestic reform as that for which the King is so properly anxious.'[56] Pensions – with the problem of funding still unsolved – would be left to the future, and to the innovative mind of Lloyd George.

After the eclipse of Gladstonian Home Rule in 1893, Balfour referred to that contentious movement as the ominous 'Sleeping Beauty' of Westminster politics, which might awake at any time.[57] Balfour, of course, never believed that the Irish Union could be preserved through power alone, and the new Chief Secretary, his brother Gerald, enthusiastically agreed. The first evidence of this, in 1896, was yet another Land Act, which the brothers agreed improved on Arthur's 1891 law by simplifying the purchase of land by tenants and empowering the land courts to sell the bankrupt estates which came under their jurisdiction.[58] The new bill, which the landlord interest in the Unionist Party held in great suspicion, caused a generous share of trouble for the party, and therefore for the Leader of the House.

In 1892 the Irish Unionist contingent in the House was bolstered by the powerful voice of the newly elected Edward Carson. Strong ties had been forged between them when Carson had served Balfour in Ireland, and Balfour recommended the talented advocate as a parliamentary candidate and nominated him to be Irish Solicitor-General. While battling the Gladstone and Rosebery administrations, Balfour frequently turned to Carson for advice on Irish affairs. But now the dour prosecutor rounded on Gerald Balfour and his land bill with all his formidable skills. Carson allied himself with Colonel Edward Saunderson, the Ulster Unionist leader, and the two men burdened the bill with amendments and led their little band into the Not Content lobby in each division. Gerald shared his brother's philosophical outlook and his intellectual power, but his political skills were not so polished as Arthur's, and the elder sibling frequently was forced to come to his aid. Carson, whose formidable talents were submerged in a melancholy nature, was fiercely independent and inflexible when his principles were challenged, but he was not guilty of ingratitude. When the battle was over, and he was beaten – as he knew he would be – he wrote to his former master reminding him of those earlier Irish days when they had struggled side by side. He told Balfour that he felt deeply his electoral pledge to defend the side of landlord rights in Ireland, but that 'I hope it will not lead you to think that I am the less grateful or devoted to you whom I owe so much and whom alone I would ever consent to follow.' The Leader was touched by this sentiment from a proud man. Balfour knew that politics was a high-stakes game, in which men fought with the weapons that came to hand, for those things in which they believed. Yet he held that there was more to life than politics, and he answered, 'I have ever felt confident that a friendship like ours, tried as it has been both by adversity and prosperity, was not destined to vanish and become as if it had never been. We have too often had to rely on each other in circumstances of difficulty and perplexity to permit our mutual confidence to be easily disturbed.'[59] Carson went so far as to reject the party whip for a time, but all was eventually forgiven. In 1900 Balfour would secure for him the English Solicitor-Generalship, and years later, when Balfour's leadership was under attack within the party, Carson refused to join in.

Lady Frances Balfour, with her gift for creating tension within the family, also opposed her brother-in-law's bill. Curiously, she couched her opposition in a vociferous defence of the Irish landlord class, which she insisted Gerald meant to destroy. She attacked Gerald within the family circle at any opportunity, and exceeded even her usual quota of turmoil. Her regular confidante Lady Betty soon had had enough, and wrote in September 1896, 'God knows I am sick of this whole wretched business and long to say Pax . . . but your attack on Gerald was on a different footing.'[60] Once again Balfour felt it necessary to take matters in hand, and he wrote a chastening letter to Frances calling for a cessation of hostilities and reminding her that she was making family life at Whittingehame impossible.[61]

Gerald had other problems: he was less successful in 1897 with a bill, withdrawn after a month, to create an Irish Board of Agriculture. In 1899, however, the failure was redeemed when the two brothers successfully passed legislation creating an Irish Department of Agricultural and Technical Instruction, under the 'Progressive Unionist' Sir Horace Plunkett. The new office took control of fisheries, disease prevention and technical research, and offered instruction in scientific agriculture to farmers and farm managers. Like Balfour's earlier constructive Irish legislation, it was popular with the Irish and hated by the right-wing Unionists – the so-called Die-hards – who managed to unseat Plunkett in the next election with a candidate of their own. The bill would not have passed without Arthur Balfour's strong hand on it, and its unhappy reception by the right wing of his own party helped to seal Gerald's decision to accept the offer of the Board of Trade in October 1900.[62]

In May 1897 Gerald had introduced a far more successful Irish Local Government Bill, and the brothers once again shared the leadership of the effort to bring the bill successfully to the law books. An improvement on the inadequate 1892 bill, the new legislation stripped the grand juries of their administrative and fiscal powers and vested these in county councils, borough corporations, and urban and district councils, elected with a wide franchise, including women and peers. The bill proved to be a success, and this and the land legislation enacted by Ashbourne and the Balfours were perhaps the stoutest examples of the Unionist policy of 'killing Home Rule with kindness'.[63] In the end, 'kindness' did not smother Home Rule, but the bill doomed the long political dominance in Ireland of the ancient Protestant Ascendancy.

With this behind him, a related Irish matter which had defeated Balfour's efforts during his time as Irish Secretary was again much in his mind, and this was the Catholic higher-education question. Hoping for inter-party support, in late 1898 he turned to his friend and fellow philosopher the Liberal R. B. Haldane.[64] The two agreed that, despite the dangerous political quagmire in which the idea had perished in 1889, another attempt should be made, and Haldane undertook a secret mission to Dublin to seek the support of the Roman Catholic hierarchy. 'The rest', in Haldane's words, 'Balfour said that he would himself see to.'[65] The plan to create two predominantly Catholic teaching colleges in Belfast and Dublin was laid before the Cabinet in November, but it foundered owing to the continuing opposition among many Unionists.[66] Lord Cadogan, the Irish Lord Lieutenant, predicted nothing but trouble ahead for Balfour's 'bolt from the blue'.[67] Devonshire agreed, and took the lead in Cabinet in opposing the plan; while Walter Long, the President of the Board of Agriculture, opposed any idea of state-funded Catholic higher education and, in his usual way, forwarded a litany of complaints.[68] An interesting exception was Carson, who at that time was refusing the government whip in protest against Gerald's Irish land bill. He enquired of the House, 'Do you think that the Catholics of Ireland will be worse off with the enlightenment of a university education than they are now when they are deprived of it? ... Speaking for myself, I have no fears of a Catholic University.'[69] But no such university was created – nor would it be until the next century.

Ireland was not everything, however, and Balfour and Haldane had more success with a plan which the Liberal suggested to his Unionist friend, thinking him 'virtually prime minister so far as social questions were concerned ... and because the Liberals were not up to the mark about questions of higher education'.[70] Haldane knew and respected Balfour's deep interest in higher education – he had, after all, been an energetic Chancellor of Edinburgh University since 1891. The partners agreed that the University of London should no longer serve merely as an examining body granting external degrees. With surprisingly little support from within the institution, a plan was shaped with the help of the Fabian socialist Sidney Webb to remake it into a teaching university. A bill was crafted under Balfour's guidance and passed into law in 1898, and the university was on its way to greatness.

There was, of course, much else that came to fruition under Balfour's leadership in the Commons: the Telegraphy Act of 1899 prepared the way for the creation of a national telephone system, under the wing of the state. In the same year a bill for the creation of a tier of administrative bodies below that of the London County Council was to have been managed by Chaplin but was in fact steered past energetic opposition by Balfour. It reached the law books as the London Government Act, which returned to Westminster its historic designation of 'city' and created the twenty-eight metropolitan boroughs which outlived the County Council itself.[71]

It would be misleading to suggest that these and other similar bills constituted a coherent blueprint of Balfourian 'constructive' legislation – broad-brush programmes might have interested the Chamberlainites, for Balfour saw proposals as nothing more than reasonable solutions to identifiable needs. It is true that throughout his political life he remained deeply attached to certain ideas. At least one of these, the Irish Union, he was forced to abandon late in his career when it ceased to be viable. Others, like women's suffrage, eventually found acceptance and political success. Another favourite cause was education reform on all levels – particularly scientific and technical training in the schools – as well, of course, as the broadening of the availability of higher education, both areas in which he agreed with the 'educationist' reformers that Britain was well behind the other industrial nations. In his years as Salisbury's lieutenant he would find himself more than once deeply embroiled in the debate over change in the schools, and this brought him face to face with both frustrating failure and heady success.

Put most simply, the problem which faced the government was that, while the need for improvement in the provision of primary and secondary education was self-evident to many, two important factors made any response politically dangerous: one was cost; the other was religious feeling. The previous Unionist administration had made an effort, passing a bill in 1891 to eliminate fees from the state elementary schools. Two years later, further acts were passed by the Liberals to raise the school-leaving age to eleven and to extend education to blind and deaf children through the creation of special schools. Primary-school education in Britain proceeded, of course, along two separate tracks: in the tax-supported board schools and in those schools funded by private sources. The law provided no significant aid to the so-called 'voluntary' or privately funded schools, the majority of which were denominational, with most of those under the Church of England. When the board schools were created by W. E. Forster's 1870 act, the problem of sectarianism was avoided through its famous Clause 14, the Cowper-Temple amendment, barring sectarian religious instruction in the tax-supported schools.[72]

To Balfour, the Old Etonian, 'the normal machinery for education required alike by the parent and the community is the voluntary school.'[73] He had little if any particular understanding of the lower schools, either state or voluntary; nor was he, unlike his Cecil cousins, particularly sympathetic to strengthening the impact on the young of the Established Church, thus undercutting Cowper-Temple. He accepted that the more financially precarious denominational schools should not be allowed to founder and disappear – which appeared to be their fate in the last decade of the century – and said so in July 1895: 'In my opinion the Voluntary schools must be saved.'[74] 'I shall *not* be content if we fail in this object,' he wrote to Bernard Mallett; 'in my opinion, the whole question should be looked at from this point of view, and no extraneous provisions should be introduced into it except with the object of smoothing the passage of an effective measure through the House.'[75] In the event, the passage proved to be anything but smooth.

In early 1896 a bill was drafted to dissolve Forster's elective school boards and vest authority for the rates-supported schools in education committees of the county and borough councils, and also to provide aid to the voluntary schools. The architect of the bill was Balfour's former Fourth Party collaborator Sir John Gorst. Though unpopular and difficult at the best of times, Gorst was deeply interested in and knowledgeable about educational reform, but his parliamentary skills were not up to the task of piloting the measure through the House. There was grumbling over the potential cost of the improvements promised under the bill, which many educationists believed did not advance the cause far enough. The bill also raised the spectre of state aid to Anglican schools, angering pious Dissenters and raising the possibility of a Church-versus-chapel conflict. Other detractors were satisfied with the 1870 act and suspicious of the need to disturb a potentially dangerous sleeping dog.[76]

The religious issue was brought sharply into focus by the fact that the bill, with the approval of Salisbury and other Churchmen, promised to jettison Cowper-Temple and allow religious instruction, which satisfied what was termed a 'reasonable' number of parents in each school – which seemed quite acceptable to Balfour. The matter of direct state aid to the denominational schools energized many Nonconformists, and Chamberlain's efforts at making the bill palatable to them – he was, of course, a Unitarian – did little good. Among the Unionists, the High Church element disliked the bill because they feared that the price of state assistance to their schools would be the transfer of Church authority into the hands of secular officials. Balfour could not allow Gorst to sink without making every effort to save him and his bill. It came to be as he had feared when he had written to Cranborne months before, 'I suppose I shall turn out to be the member of the Cabinet who has got to help Gorst in the matter.'[77] So in fact he was. But, even though by his own estimate he 'expended treasures of ingenuity on this most thankless task', he could not save the bill.[78] The government surrendered as the bill expired in the committee stage, by which time it had collected more than 1,000 proposed amendments. It was not a great political disaster, but it was a disaster all the same, and both Balfour and Salisbury felt it deeply.

In the following year a compromise measure was passed which provided small aid (five shillings per pupil) to the denominational schools, and even this required all Balfour's considerable powers as Leader. This was followed by a less contentious bill to increase aid to the most hard pressed of the board schools, and over the next two years further bills granted pension rights to teachers and raised the school-leaving age to twelve. These were not solutions to the problems of Britain's antiquated educational system, but they would have to do until the problem could be dealt with in the next Parliament. When that time came, it fell to Balfour to ensure that the government would not face another failure such as that of 1896.

As Leader of the House, Balfour was concerned not solely with domestic affairs. However, it had been decades since his round-the-world expedition, and his recent knowledge of foreign lands was limited to favourite hotels in France and occasionally Germany. In 1889 he chaffed George Curzon, a confirmed world traveller then preparing for a tour of Persia. 'I am grieved, but not surprised, at your preference of Persia to Scotland . . .' he wrote. 'But I know there is no use in preaching to you. Travelling is worse than drink.'[79] Perhaps it was, but Balfour could not afford to be a mental Little Englander. He understood that Britain possessed the greatest empire in the world, that its prosperity depended upon worldwide trade, and that it was without major defensive alliances as the balance of power among the nations had undergone dramatic changes in his lifetime. Modern Germany and Italy had come into being; the United States had emerged from the crucible of its Civil War as a wealthy and powerful republic; alliance systems among the European Great Powers had emerged, creating potentially adversarial clusters. Related was the undeniable fact that Britain, the first great industrial power, was no longer the only one. The world had become a more competitive and dangerous place for a small but wealthy island state whose foreign policy had for years been based on 'splendid isolation'. Salisbury's eldest son asserted to the House of Commons in 1901 that 'Britain does not ask for treaties. It grants them.'[80] But realists understood that things were no longer quite so simple – if they ever had been.

Soon after the Unionists returned to power in 1895, friction arose between Britain and two powerful economic rivals. In mid-December, President Grover Cleveland saw the domestic political advantage of twisting the British lion's tail and invoked the Monroe Doctrine in the heated boundary dispute between Venezuela and British Guiana. A fortnight later, Cecil Rhodes's henchman Dr Leander Starr Jameson led a filibustering force from British Bechuanaland into the small neighbouring Republic of the Transvaal, founded by Dutch-speaking Afrikaners or 'Boers' who had fled British rule two generations earlier. With the purpose of raising rebellion among the *uitlanders* (resident foreigners) against the Boer government, which denied them full political rights, Jameson's raiders presumed that the Boer regime could be easily toppled by the *uitlanders*, who outnumbered the Boers. The results of the raid were more farcical than heroic: there was no uprising, and the marauders were in the hands of local authorities within three days. The aged and unwell High Commissioner, Sir Hercules Robinson, had had some prior knowledge of the scheme, and Chamberlain had known something of it and had tried to derail it, but a later parliamentary inquiry held neither of them to be culpable.[81] However, Liberals and anti-imperialists of all stripes never surrendered their belief that 'Joe' was the secret force behind the plot. Whatever was known and by whom, Jameson was handed over to the British authorities for trial. He gallantly assumed full responsibility for the raid, was found guilty, and was sentenced to a fifteen-month prison term.[82]

Though Robinson had been appointed by Rosebery's administration, with the raiders imprisoned and the 'Colossus' Rhodes (who was premier of Cape Colony at the time) politically ruined, the repercussions of the affair caused unavoidable embarrassment to the Unionist government. There was more: the German Kaiser, Wilhelm II, sent a telegram of encouragement and approval to the Transvaal President, Paul Kruger, which immediately became world news. Germany, like the United States, for the moment became widely unpopular in Britain, and a major crisis seemed possible. Balfour, as was his custom, at once saw both sides of the issue – and viewed them with his usual ironic humour. Lady Frances reported that he shocked Alice by informing her that in cases of this sort what was obviously piracy to one side was seen as rebellion on the other, a view he repeated when the famous Houdon statue of George Washington was erected in front of the National Gallery. He added too, 'Jameson's character was the only attractive feature in the matter tho' he ought to be hung all the same.'[83]

The Venezuela disagreement with the United States was dealt with through arbitration, and the war scare dissipated as quickly as it had erupted. It was, however, an occasion for a rare difference between uncle and nephew, as Salisbury, joined only by Chamberlain, stood out for firmness against a Cabinet, including Balfour, strongly for compromise. The Prime Minister, Andrew Roberts has written, 'had no sympathy with the increasingly popular concept that there was some sort of romantic, special relationship between the two English-speaking peoples.'[84] The possibility of an Anglo-American war, he believed, was as conceivable as one with the Russians or the French. Balfour disagreed, and in Manchester on 15 January he delivered a major speech that reaffirmed acceptance of the Monroe Doctrine and expressed his belief that any such conflict 'carried with it something of the unnatural horror of a civil war'.[85] Troubles there might be from time to time, but, as he indicated in 1911, culture was thicker than water:

> There may have been difficulties . . . between the two branches of the English-speaking people of the world; but the realities in history, the foundations of history, are still stronger, and we cannot help being considered as one nation. The bonds go too deep into the history of the people, into the thought, language, literature and everything which gives characteristic expression to the people.[86]

His sense of the kinship between the two English-speaking powers would be put to a further test in 1898, for early in the year the sixty-eight-year-old Salisbury's health began to fail, which required several extended periods of recuperation in the South of France. At the end of February the premier left Balfour in charge of the Foreign Office and of some crucial unfinished business.[87] Russia had coerced the listless Chinese government into conceding control of Port Arthur, and Britain was offered a similar concession at Wei-hai-wei. Salisbury had rejected the overture, as his policy had always been to support the idea of an 'open door' to Chinese trade rather than the creation of Great Power spheres of influence. In March a Sino-Russian agreement was signed (despite Salisbury's scepticism), granting Moscow a long-term lease on the warm-water port, as well as on Talienwan in Liaotung. Though he agreed with his uncle that war with Russia over such a matter would be a grave error, as acting Foreign Secretary Balfour in the end fell into line with the rest of the Cabinet – and with Curzon, then under-secretary at the Foreign Office – and accepted that the lease on Wei-hai-wei must be taken up. This was done, and a crisis with Russia was avoided.[88] A balance of influence among the European Great Powers in China was maintained, as Germany soon afterwards was granted a lease of its own on Kiaochow. Balfour saw the Wei-hai-wei incident as significant but not pressing, as he made clear in a cable to Sir Frank Lascelles: 'We could not of course occupy till Japanese have left the port, and it is a matter of indifference to us when this event occurs.'[89] This solution, he believed, was no more than a stopgap measure.

Balfour's niece tells us of his recollection late in life that whenever he deputized for Lord Salisbury at the Foreign Office 'he found himself dealing with a crisis.'[90] This was not a bad summary, for the China affair was one of a series of difficulties in these months. A source of anxiety closer to home once again was Germany, led since 1888 by the youthful and capricious Wilhelm II, whose widowed mother was the daughter of Queen Victoria. The Germans, divided for centuries into many states, had more often than not been Britain's allies in the struggles among the European nations. After the unification of the nation by Bismarck in 1871, Germany's foreign policy, like the Kaiser himself, became ambitious. To Balfour, the possibility of greater accord with such a rival was worth exploration.

In March, as the China crisis was fading, the German ambassador, Count Hatzfeldt, induced Alfred Rothschild to bring him together for an informal chat with Balfour. Hatzfeldt desired to smooth the rough patches of Anglo-German colonial relations in Asia and Africa, and when they met he gained Balfour's permission to speak informally to Joseph Chamberlain, whose mind was moving speedily in a similar direction. The ambassador met the Colonial Secretary at Rothschild's house on 29 March, and was overwhelmed by Radical Joe's enthusiastic suggestion of further talks, to include even consideration of an Anglo-German alliance.[91] The Germans fought shy of any such hasty embrace, which suited Balfour: Chamberlain had moved too swiftly, and without either authorization or Cabinet consultation – as Balfour intimated to the troubled Hatzfeldt when the two spoke privately later. Reporting the outcome of Chamberlain's 'amateur negotiation' to Salisbury in France, Balfour stressed his caution in contrast with the Colonial Secretary's haste, concluding:

> although I am inclined to favour an Anglo-German agreement, it must, if possible, be made on equal terms. Of this loving couple I should wish to be the one that lent the cheek, not that implanted the kiss. This, I take it, is not the German view; and they prefer, I imagine, reserving their offers until they are sure of being well paid for them.[92]

At the same time that he was pressing his alliance ideas on Hatzfeldt and Balfour, Chamberlain was mentioned as a possible viceroy of India – an impossible suggestion from any side. Perhaps recent events were in Balfour's mind when he noted to St Loe Strachey that, regardless of his years, it was well to remember that Chamberlain possessed a store of 'youthful impulsiveness'.[93] The difference between them, Balfour explained – and it must be recalled that Chamberlain was twelve years his senior – was one of youth and age. 'I', he said, 'am age.'[94]

Balfour's experiment with Chamberlain had not been a success, as Salisbury agreed – though it was always difficult to imagine how Chamberlain could be held back. In this case the matter was swept under the diplomatic rug, but Balfour got his way with the Germans in a related matter. In June the financially desperate Portuguese were engaged in negotiations for a large loan from Britain, which wanted as security the colonies of Delagoa Bay and Angola.[95] Delagoa Bay provided port facilities to the Transvaal, and Angola bordered the German colony of South West Africa. When they got wind of the proposal, the Germans demanded that they should be a party to any agreement. Salisbury, at first, was equally adamant that they should not, and only reluctantly agreed in July to explore possibilities. When in August the premier again fell ill, Balfour again took charge. Dealing patiently with the German government – and without Chamberlain's help – Balfour concluded an agreement with Hatzfeld under which simultaneous loans were to be offered to the Portuguese by the two Powers, with Lisbon's shaky empire as collateral. As it was, the nervous Portuguese backed away from the loan and the two more powerful empires, but Balfour was satisfied that in the negotiations Berlin had relinquished any interest in the South African republics. He informed Salisbury in late August that the terms of agreement were fixed and that he had signed them 'for better or worse'.[96]

Balfour faced another American crisis when the republic declared war against Spain on 25 April 1898. Convinced, as it seemed were the majority of the public, that co-operation with America was more important than remaining in step with the European Powers, Balfour ordered the British ambassador, Sir Julian Pauncefote, to avoid joining in any multi-nation initiative for 'international morality'.[97] While Balfour (and the government) remained punctiliously neutral during the four-month war, he was satisfied with the rapid American victory. Though, in contrast once again to Chamberlain, he did not yearn for a formal alliance with Washington, his hopes for Anglo-American co-operation remained great.

In the midst of the crisis, the attention of the nation was turned away from foreign affairs by a melancholy event, as on 18 May 1898 William Ewart Gladstone died at the age of eight-nine. Balfour at the time was once again suffering from influenza and had taken to his sickbed on the sad day, but he roused himself to attend the House on the following day to offer the respects of the government. David Lloyd George, then a young Radical whose fame was already spreading outside his native Wales, noted in a letter to his brother, 'Balfour is seriously ill, but he staggered into the House and with painful feebleness got up and delivered a glowing and unreserved pan-egyric.'[98] Balfour denied his ability to abstract a life of such achievement, variety and duration, but, of the man who had been over many years mentor, friend and, of course, opponent, he said, 'If I venture to say any-thing, it is rather of Mr Gladstone as the greatest Member of the greatest deliberative assembly, which, so far, the world has seen.' A week later he joined the party of notables who bore the Grand Old Man to his final rest-ing place in Westminster Abbey.

This sad duty performed, the acting Foreign Secretary turned to the final act of the Spanish–American crisis. In August he was faced with a bellicose gesture by a Spain humiliated by its swift defeat by the United States and resentful towards Britain for its unofficial support of the republic over its European neighbour. Madrid's gesture was to begin to construct artillery emplacements to menace the British fleet at anchor in Gibralter Bay. Supported by Salisbury, then taking a cure in Germany, Balfour telegraphed immediately to the British ambassador in Madrid, his old comrade Sir Henry Drummond Wolff, to inform the Spanish that the fortification must stop immediately and that Britain would 'shrink from no consequences' to gain this result. Drummond Wolff was to communicate in as gentlemanly a manner as he wished, but should make absolutely clear 'the settled policy of this country'. Spain climbed down, and in return secured the next year the British promise of support in the unlikely event of an attack on Algeciras.[99]

More dangerous in the event were matters in the Sudan. Under the command of the sirdar (commander) of the Egyptian army, General Sir Horatio Herbert Kitchener, an Anglo-Egyptian force had been dispatched to secure control in the Sudan and to avenge the grisly fate at the hands of the fanatical Mahdi's forces in Khartoum in 1885 of the popular hero General Sir Charles 'Chinese' Gordon. Meeting with initial success, Kitchener's army (including Salisbury's son Lord Edward Cecil) completed its task with a celebrated and bloody victory at Omdurman in September 1898. This came on the heels of the Spanish crisis, and was greeted by more bellicose Britons as further evidence of the irresistible nature of their nation's arms. The government knew, of course, that there was more to the Sudanese crisis merely than this.

Over British objections, the French had sent a much smaller force under Major Jean-Baptiste Marchand from the Congo into the region, and by July 1898 he had laid claim to much of the south Sudan and paused near the village of Fashoda to await reinforcements. To counter this, fresh from his victory at Omdurman, Kitchener proceeded up the Nile to Fashoda and raised the British flag over the village a fortnight later. The French accepted the failure of their gamble and abandoned their claims, and Marchand withdrew. The commanders who faced one another in the so-called 'Fashoda Incident' never countenanced the possibility of a fight, and in the end their governments wisely resisted popular jingoism and chose compromise (the French accepted compensation in North Africa).

When Kitchener − now doubly the hero of the hour − returned to Britain in November, he sought out Balfour for advice. No orator, the soldier wanted help with the speech he was to deliver at a great banquet in his honour at the Guildhall. Balfour wrote to Lady Elcho, 'I did my best to clothe his ideas or some of them in suitable language, but whether he will reproduce it when the time comes, and whether if he does it will harmonize with the portions of his harangue in which my valuable assistance has not been vouchsafed, remains to be seen.'[100] While he dutifully wrote down Balfour's words, on the day the general abandoned them and returned to his original 'harangue'. But it was the hero and not his speech that London's notables had come for, and he was cheered lustily by his audience. Balfour came away from the meeting with mixed feelings, thinking the hero courageous and resolute, but wondering 'how far he could adapt himself to wholly different and perhaps larger problems than those with which he has been dealing'.[101]

It fell to Balfour in June 1899 to propose to the House a grant of £30,000 to Kitchener − who had already received a peerage − which outraged the Liberals. An angry Morley and his colleagues raised the ominous rumours then circulating in London of atrocities on the part of Kitchener's Egyptians which rivalled those of the 'dervishes', and of the decision of the commander himself to desecrate the tomb of the Mahdi. Wilfrid Blunt witnessed the debate, and admitted in his diary that Morley was completely outmanoeuvred:

> His arguments were weak to fatuity . . . So much was this the case that Balfour already found himself in sympathy with the House before he rose to reply. He did this in a speech of great skill and eloquence, which, as mere oratory, it was a relief to listen to, and he succeeded even to taking a high moral line with the wretched Morley, and in proving to him conclusively that Kitchener was absolutely justified, indeed bound by every principle of right feeling to blow up the tomb, dig up the body, chuck it into the Nile, and what he called 'disperse the remains.' . . . I doubt if Morley will ever make a speech again in the House, I should not if I were he.[102]

The sirdar visited Whittingehame following this debate, and Balfour listened to his denials that his troops had misbehaved ungenerously to their adversaries. Alice Balfour was sure that her brother was unconvinced that Kitchener had managed the affair well and that 'the good effects could have been obtained without the unfortunate shocking of the taste of some people'. Of her own opinion she was very clear: 'I don't think Ld. Kitchener is a model of good taste.'[103]

In 1899 personal tragedy touched the Cecils, for in November Lady Salisbury died after an extended illness. All of the Balfours cared deeply for Aunt 'Georgie', and her influence on Arthur had been considerable – she had, after all, played a rôle early in his career in spurring him towards a more active political life. Salisbury was crushed at the loss of his lifelong confidante, and, at seventy, his own health was not good. He would depend increasingly on his nephew, and there were many who wondered if the great man could remain in harness much longer.

7

Inheritance

—◦—

THE ARRIVAL OF the new century was greeted with pleasure by many Europeans, confident of the dawning of a new and better age. All in Britain did not share this elation, for the nation concluded the old century mired in a noisome war in South Africa. Relations between the British authorities in Cape Colony and the Boer republics of the Transvaal and Orange Free State had never been good. A brief British annexation of the Transvaal in 1877 led to the so-called First South African (or Boer) War and then to a British disaster at Majuba Hill in 1881. The two Boer republics were officially recognized, but with the condition of British 'suzerainty' over their foreign relations. Much changed after 1886, as the greatest gold discovery in history was made in Witwatersrand, near Pretoria. Within months, the white population of the Transvaal swelled with an influx of gold-hunters from across the world, not least from Britain. These *uitlanders* were soon complaining that, while they produced the fabulous wealth dug from the earth, the tax they paid to the Boer governments did not seem to bring political rights; and it was they whom Dr Jameson had wished to lead in revolt with his abortive raid of 1895. The Boers, fearing cultural and political inundation, insisted that the outsiders were transient fortune-seekers, uninterested in and undeserving of membership in their community. From this point, few observers thought that further trouble in southern Africa could be avoided.

Colonial policy was in Chamberlain's hands, and his primary lieutenant in Cape Colony was the brooding and charismatic High Commissioner, Sir Alfred Milner, born in 1854 in Hesse-Darmstadt of Anglo-German parents. Scholarships saw Milner through a glittering Oxford career and propelled him on to great fame in the civil service; and in 1897 Chamberlain supported his appointment as high commissioner of Cape Colony. When the Boer republics showed no signs of natural disintegration as Milner had hoped, and tensions over Boer treatment of the *uitlanders* (who had petitioned the Queen for protection) did not slacken, Milner met the Transvaal President, Paul Kruger, at Bloemfontein in May 1899. The two equally stubborn men found little on which to agree, and the situation deteriorated from merely critical to dangerously explosive.

While deputizing again for Salisbury at the Foreign Office, Balfour offered his own analysis to the Cabinet. Warning against haste in turning to force, he argued that the case in the Transvaal was without modern precedent, as the influx of *uitlanders* constituted a new majority in the republic, 'alien in blood, different in language, superior in cultivation and wealth, to a minority which constitutes the original national stock to which the country belongs' – adding that, if he were a Boer, he too would resist what was clearly a call to turn the nation and its culture over to the immigrants. A sabre-rattling policy, he suggested, would be premature and would certainly be seen as unwise by the Powers.[1]

The Milner–Kruger negotiations predictably were doomed from the outset, and conflict soon looked all but certain. The fiercely independent 'Oom Paul' Kruger reasoned that faraway Britain could not subdue a determined people fighting for their way of life – particularly when they possessed the modern weapons that their great wealth had purchased. Balfour could only hope for the best, writing rather enigmatically to Lady Elcho in August, 'I somehow think that war will be avoided – though whether this will in the long run be for the good of mankind is another question.'[2] In September and October, Chamberlain and Kruger (joined by President Steyn of the Orange Free State) had exchanged ultimatums – the Colonial Secretary demanding the recognition of political rights for British subjects in the Boer states, Kruger insisting that Britain withdraw all troops from their borders within forty-eight hours. These expired without action, and Boer forces invaded Cape Colony on 12 October 1899.

Soon the British learned how poorly prepared they were for war. Command was vested in Balfour's former Irish under-secretary, Sir Redvers Buller. A member of the 'African Ring' of admirers of the Commander-in-Chief, Lord Wolseley, the sixty-year-old Buller possessed a distinguished reputation but no adequate plan of campaign, now that his great moment had arrived. With the first body of British reinforcements still on the high seas, the Boers struck quickly and effectively: Sir George White's force was defeated at Nicholson's Nek, and then the key towns of Ladysmith, Mafeking and Kimberley came under siege. Buller's uncertain attempts to seize the initiative led to the disasters of 'Black Week', 10–15 December, at Stormberg, Magersfontein and Colenso. The situation appeared to be little short of disastrous, and, with Salisbury still indisposed, Balfour was in effective charge of the government.

Exhausted and outmanoeuvred, Buller sent an over-hasty telegram to the War Office recommending that Ladysmith be surrendered while he took a defensive posture to safeguard Natal. It was too much for Lansdowne, who summoned an old friend, the sixty-nine-year-old Field Marshal Lord Roberts, from his Dublin command. On the night that news of Colenso reached London, Balfour was called away from a dinner party to the War Office to receive the desperate news. Something had to be done, and, like Lansdowne, he concluded that Buller had to go.

Balfour, Lansdowne and the diminutive 'Little Bobs' met on the following morning. Without consulting either the Queen or Wolseley, Balfour ordered Buller to resign his command to Roberts and take up the defence of Natal – decisions confirmed by the Cabinet's Defence Committee that evening. On his return to Downing Street, Balfour related the events to Sir Sydney Parry. Despite his age, Roberts sought one last great command: '"I've avoided evening parties. I go to bed early, I think I ride to hounds as well as I did a dozen years ago," adding after a moment's hesitation, "You see, I've always felt the country might some day have need of me."'[3] The old soldier's resolve deeply touched both statesmen, particularly as Lansdowne was forced to inform him that, while his son was to receive the Victoria Cross for his heroism at Colenso, it would be the first posthumous VC awarded. Roberts received the news without flinching, and quickly turned to the matter of how to reverse British fortunes in the war. Balfour was impressed: 'Thank God!' he told Parry. 'I've seen a man, and a man who knows his mind.' Within a fortnight, Roberts, with Kitchener heading his staff, took command in South Africa.

Balfour was summoned immediately to Windsor to face his sovereign. Once she had heard his explanations, the Queen gracefully accepted his protestations of the need for haste in the change of command: 'Indeed, she was wonderfully good-humored,' he wrote to Salisbury, 'and wonderfully cheerful. With a very wise self-control she insists not only upon being serene herself, but on everybody round her keeping their serenity also. "I will have no melancholy in this house" is her formula – and not a bad one either in moments of anxiety.'[4] Now it was up to Roberts.

Acting for the Prime Minister, Balfour took on the task of countering the bad news of 'Black Week' which blared from every newspaper hoarding in the country. In January 1900, in his constituency of East Manchester, he delivered a series of speeches, but these proved anything but successful. Even the admiring Mrs Dugdale indicated that her uncle lacked the 'instinct for gauging the popular mind', and he had concluded early in life that, if such a thing existed, it was essentially unknowable, and not to be worried over.[5] His platform speeches, typically delivered spontaneously and with little preparation, were often too long and flawed by too many digressions. As he digressed, his arguments often became too complex for his listeners, and they were nearly as difficult to comprehend when they appeared in print. The mass politics of the twentieth century were made for Lloyd George or Winston Churchill, but for Balfour they were foreign terrain through which he struggled unenthusiastically – and then only when it was absolutely necessary.

The Manchester speeches demonstrated his weaknesses. Though received well enough by his loyal constituents, and widely reported, they suffered withering criticism in the press. On the controversial matter of preparation for war, Balfour explained that the government judged it unwise to take a menacing posture by rushing more troops to South Africa while negotiations with the Boer governments were in train. Would the public have approved? he asked. And what of the Parliament: 'What would have been said by that great mass of moderate opinion both on the other side and on our side of the House if we had made such a proposition?' He had nothing but praise for Lansdowne and the War Office, then the objects of a barrage of criticism regarding manpower, armaments and supply that had not been equalled since the worst days of the Crimean War a half-century earlier. As for the question of manpower, in his view the 25,000 men initially dispatched on the eve of war would have been sufficient had it not been for what he unfortunately termed the 'unhappy entanglement of Ladysmith'. Things were proceeding apace, he assured his listeners, and there had been 'no great reverses' in this war.[6]

Two days later he again defended the War Office:

> Now I understand that we are charged with undue concealment of unpleasant truths. Well, everything is possible which is not self-contradictory; and it is possible that there are facts to be elicited with regard to the War Office administration of this war with which I am not acquainted, which, if revealed to the public, would produce an unpleasant impression. Surely there never has been any war . . . in which the War Office were readier with instantaneous and immediate information upon every incident in that war, whether that incident was pleasant or unpleasant.

When in war, he asked, were there not some problems?

> If an angel from Heaven were to come and tell me that in any great war carried on on that scale it were possible that everything should be done, in fact, as you might write it out on paper, I should know that that angel, with all his credentials, was drawing upon his imagination. The thing is impossible.[7]

The speeches failed in their object – to reassure the public that the administration understood the crisis it faced, had made all reasonable preparations for the worst, and acted promptly when the crisis was upon it. Rather, he found himself pilloried for being overly optimistic and less than candid. He sensed that he might have warded off criticism by turning to the stopgap of offering up scapegoats to public anger. 'I have said in these speeches', he answered a friend's criticisms, 'not all that I thought, but nothing that I did not think. I cannot give my full opinions without blaming gallant men whom I do not wish to blame; but I entirely decline to make a scapegoat of people who I do *not* think deserve any such fate. Far rather would I leave public life for ever.'[8] Though perhaps chivalrous in its own way, this was politically costly, as even the usually supportive *Times* reminded its readers that Balfour's explanation was no explanation at all. In the case of military disasters the chain of responsibility was obvious, and the Government (and the military experts) must be held accountable 'for serious errors, both in policy and warlike preparation'.[9] Balfour was stung by these reproaches, and avoided making the same mistake for the balance of the war.

Balfour's own criticisms of the army and the War Office – primarily regarding advance planning and command decisions in the field – he confined to government circles. He did not, however, suggest that he knew better what to do. Balfour remained a member of the Cabinet Defence Committee, but he did not take a leading part in direction of the conflict after Salisbury's return. He emerged from the sobering experience of war convinced that the military establishment suffered from several glaring weaknesses, among them a surfeit of incompetent senior officers and an absence of machinery to prepare in peacetime for the advent of the next war, whenever it might be.

The appointment of Roberts appeared to be a masterstroke, and did more for the credibility of the government than all ministerial explanations together. 'Bobs' raised the siege of Kimberley within a month of his arrival, and won swift victories at Paardeberg and Poplar Grove. He entered the Orange Free State capital, Bloemfontein, on 13 March 1900. In June, Mafeking was relieved – to riotous delight at home – and Johannesberg fell, as did the Transvaal capital, Pretoria. This was followed by the collapse of Kruger's government and his flight into exile. The final set-piece battle of the war, at Bergendahl Farm, the British won decisively on 27 August. With the Boer armies defeated and their major cities and railway system in his hands, Roberts cabled to the War Office on 17 September for permission to relinquish his command. Kitchener remained to 'mop up', and the aged hero returned to London in December to a conqueror's bounty: an earldom, the Garter, the succession to his rival Wolseley as commander-in-chief – and a £100,000 grant by a grateful Parliament. Few could see at the time that only the traditional war was over, and that nearly two years of guerrilla resistance lay ahead. Peace did not come until the conclusion of the Treaty of Vereeniging on 1 June 1902.

Pleased with what seemed to be brilliant light at the end of what had only recently appeared to be a very dark tunnel, the relieved Unionist leadership requested a dissolution. Could there be a better time? – the Parliament was in its sixth year, and Liberals were deeply divided between the anti-war Pro-Boers and the more belligerent Liberal Imperialists. Patriotic fervour had reached its peak, as Roberts rolled from victory to victory, and Salisbury was convinced that Boer resistance would not be fully broken until all hope of a possible Pro-Boer government was crushed by a sound electoral defeat.[10]

Although he had been dubious about an election six months earlier, Balfour was now convinced and advised his uncle that a 'July Dissolution would be better than [an] Autumn one, and Autumn better than Spring ... We have evidently got before us a long stretch of troubled waters, which it would be much easier to navigate with a new House of Commons than with an old one.'[11] Chamberlain and Central Office agreed; Salisbury found Her Majesty willing, and polling was set to begin on 28 September 1900.

Balfour was quite happy to concede centre stage in the 'Khaki election' to Chamberlain, for, to admirers and critics alike, it was, after all, 'Joe's War'. Though the Unionists fought together, the 'Separatists', as Balfour referred to the Liberals, lived up to that appellation. Some followed the Pro-Boers Harcourt, Morley or the thirty-nine-year-old MP for Carnarvon Boroughs, David Lloyd George; the so-called Liberal Imperialists or 'Liberal-Imps' looked to Asquith, Haldane and Sir Edward Grey. A small third faction uneasily occupied the party centre with the beleaguered party leader, Campbell-Bannerman – a disastrous way to fight an election against a government which appeared finally to be winning its war. Liberals did agree on their animosity towards Chamberlain, however, for it 'was one of the few things Liberals did not have to pretend to have in common: it came naturally.'[12] The Liberals pounced on him when it came to light that his family's business interests included holdings in a major War Office contractor, the armament-maker Kynoch's. Stung by the attacks, Chamberlain fought back savagely ('A seat lost to the Government is a seat gained by the Boers!'), and Balfour backed him.[13] To indict a distinguished public servant falsely was bad enough, Balfour told the House on 10 December, but the Radicals wished to destroy him merely because his kinsmen had engaged in a legal business from which he himself drew no benefit. They demanded, he thundered, the impossible: 'Wanted, a man to serve her Majesty, with no money, no relations, and inspiring no general confidence.' The Colonial Secretary was stung by the onslaught, and wrote warmly to Balfour, 'I want in the first place to thank you for the kind things you said in my defence during the recent Election. I am grateful to you and other friends for the constant loyalty of your friendship. The attacks made upon me . . . are all on private character, and hardly at all on public policy or actions.'[14]

Balfour held East Manchester with a majority of 2,453 (three times that of 1895). The Unionists won an enormous victory with 402 seats, while the Liberals won 184, the Irish Nationalists won 82, and the political committee soon to call itself the Labour Party won 2. The inevitable Cabinet reshuffle followed, and not without some drama. It was obvious to Balfour that Salisbury's age and health would not allow him to continue to combine the premiership and the Foreign Office, and the nephew found himself in the delicate position of engineering his uncle out of the office which he loved and which the Queen wished he would retain. The stalwart Aretas Akers-Douglas described his ghastly assignment as 'negociator' as a 'difficult and unpleasant mission'.[15] In a letter to the former Chief Whip, meant for the Queen's benefit, Balfour wrote:

> It requires no doctor to convince his family that the work, whenever it gets really serious, it is too much for him. I have twice had to take the Foreign Office, and three times, if I remember rightly, he has been obliged to go abroad at rather critical moments in our national affairs . . . If the Queen desires (as I am sure She does) to keep him as Prime Minister, I feel sure She would be well advised not to insist on his being Foreign Minister.[16]

The elderly sovereign acquiesced, as did her first minister. Lansdowne gladly abandoned the War Office to become Foreign Secretary. Her Majesty insisted, incidentally, that he should operate under the Prime Minister's 'personal supervision', and that is how it must have seemed to him, as Salisbury continued to maintain his office and to meet the Cabinet in the Foreign Office.

Balfour was growing impatient with a government largely made up of ageing veterans, and had already written to Salisbury of the need to inject new blood into the Cabinet, singling out his fellow Soul St John Brodrick as the most deserving of the under-secretaries. As a result, Brodrick replaced Lansdowne at the War Office. Balfour also put forward for prefer-ment his former secretary George Wyndham, as well as Chamberlain's son Austen. Wyndham was appointed Irish Chief Secretary – outside the Cabinet – and the younger Chamberlain became Financial Secretary to the Treasury.[17]

The reshuffle also raised another matter too sensitive to mention openly among Unionists: this was the question of exactly how many members of the Cecil family in the government were too many. To the Opposition (and to some Unionists) the government was the 'Hotel Cecil', so called after the luxurious establishment built on the site of the London home of the 1st Earl of Salisbury.[18] Some fire accompanied the smoke: nephew Evelyn Cecil served as the premier's parliamentary sec-retary, and now it was proposed to elevate Salisbury's eldest son, Lord Cranborne, as under-secretary at the Foreign Office. A son-in-law, Lord Selborne, got the Admiralty, and another nephew, Gerald Balfour, became President of the Board of Trade (he barely missed getting the Home Office). Balfour was aware of the criticism, and characteristically refused to take note of any danger in it, arguing to his uncle that appoint-ing one was not much less an offence than appointing all.[19] A motion of censure charging nepotism was tabled – which predictably died a rapid death – and Lord Rosebery roused himself to score on the premier when the new Cabinet was announced in the Lords, but the appointments went ahead as planned.[20]

The new Parliament met on 3 December, and was prorogued twelve days later. It was unexpectedly recalled on 25 January 1901, with the death of the Queen at the age of eighty-one. Having come to the throne as a young girl, she had reigned for more than sixty years. Her name adorned thoroughfares, railway stations and public institutions of every kind – and, of course, the era itself. She was Britain's first empress, and the only sov-ereign that most of her subjects had ever known. Balfour's relations with her had been good, and his admiration for her genuine. He was once again recuperating from influenza, but as Leader of the House it fell to him to eulogize the iconic monarch. His secretary, Sydney Parry, recalled, 'I had hunted up the materials for his speech, and produced a list of epoch-making changes and discoveries that had marked that long reign. But he gave it back to me. "No," he said. "That won't do. I want to speak of her personality, and you can't help me there."'[21]

In the end, his speech struck just the right note and was much admired. Speaking of her ancestors, he told the House:

It has been their less happy destiny to outlive, as it were, their fame, to see other people's love grow cold, to find new generations growing up around them who knew them not, and problems awaiting solution with which they felt themselves incapable to deal. Such was not the destiny of Queen Victoria. She passed away with her children, and her children's children, to the third generation around her, beloved and cherished of all. She passed away without – well, I believe – a single enemy in the world, for even those who loved not England loved her . . . No such ending has been known in our history before.[22]

He did not feel the same about her successor, the fifty-nine-year-old Edward VII. Distrusted by his mother, the new King had been denied responsibility throughout his life, and turned his attentions to his own pleasures. Succeeding Victoria was no easy task in any case, but in Balfour's opinion the new monarch distinguished himself neither for his insight nor for his attention to duty. King and minister got along, but the relationship was neither easy nor warm on either side.[23]

The nation mourned their great Queen as the war in South Africa was still in its second painful phase, but life and the public business must go on. Balfour soon found himself again embroiled in the education question, unresolved after his 1896 disappointment. Though in 1901 Balfour could not imagine 'a less convenient season' for taking up the thorny matter, his hand was forced by a legal ruling.[24] In 1899 the infamous Cockerton judgement by the Board of Trade had denied local school boards the power to fund secondary schools – which many had been doing without authorization – and this was upheld by the courts in 1901.[25] Balfour was disappointed that the schools – primary and secondary, state and volun-tary – presented a disorganized and antiquated picture when compared to the French, German or American systems, and he continued to be con-cerned that technical education generally lagged behind these rivals.[26] Starving such programmes of funds hardly seemed the way towards improvement.

The question, as always, was exactly what was to be done? The Duke of Devonshire presided over the new Board of Education, with Gorst as his second-in-command. Both were enthusiastic educationists, but neither offered much promise for piloting a bill through Parliament. Gorst offered up a bill in May, and it was doomed from the outset – 'Well, Gorst,' Devonshire unceremoniously brought the news when the bill was with-drawn, 'your damned Bill's dead.'[27] A Cabinet committee of Balfour, Devonshire, Long and Gorst met in Balfour's room in the House in August 1901 to pick up the pieces.[28] Robert Laurie Morant, a brilliant senior official of the Board of Education, would play a significant rôle in the drama. His friend Beatrice Webb recalled him as 'a strange complex of mysticism and cynicism, of principle and opportunism, of quixotic affection and swift calculation'.[29] If true, none of this seemed to bother Balfour, as the two men worked well together. Had they not done so, the 1902 education bill would have been as ill-starred as its predecessors. Yet his keenest supporters have been overly enthusiastic in declaring the act to be essentially Morant's creation.[30]

Morant, in fact, placed his hope in Balfour: 'Unless you are going to take the helm in Education next Session and before the Session,' he wrote soon after their first education committee meeting, 'nothing will be done successfully.'[31] It was not precisely what Balfour wished to hear: he complained to Devonshire in July that he had again been 'dragged (much against my will)' into the education question, and a few months later to St Loe Strachey that the education question was 'worse than any metaphysics'.[32] Reluctant he may have been, but the Cabinet agreed with Morant. Though Devonshire – who proved in this struggle to be more useful than his reputation allows – took precedence on the committee, Balfour led the campaign.

If a bill to improve the education system was to work, it would have to address more than the Cockerton judgement and the status of the secondary schools. As in 1896, if local government were to be granted authority over all schools, as the majority of the Cabinet finally accepted, the sensitive issues of religious training in the schools and the provision of local public funds to the voluntary elementary schools would have to be faced. In practical terms the greater controversy was over religion. Unlike Devonshire, Balfour initially preferred a cautious, legislatively piecemeal approach, but he finally came to the conclusion that a big bill was required. By December he insisted that he could not be responsible for a bill conceived on 'narrow and half-hearted lines'.[33]

Dragging behind him the powerful but cautious trio of Salisbury, Chamberlain and Hicks Beach, and an uncertain Cabinet, Balfour came forward with a bill in March 1902. Just as five years earlier, he called for the transfer of the powers of the school boards to new education committees of the county and borough councils, and for rate aid to the financially needy voluntary schools (in exchange for their acceptance of the authority of the local councils). Balfour and Devonshire deflected some initial criticism by agreeing on the latter's plan that the bill should first mandate control over only the secondary schools, allowing local government the option of taking over the primary schools. In July, Balfour supported a free vote on an amendment by the Liberal Unionist Henry Hobhouse to remove the elective principle from the bill, thus placing all schools under county and borough authorities. Hobhouse demonstrated that most local authorities agreed with his plan, as did Balfour, the Duke and the education reformers, and the House accepted it.

The new education bill brought with it renewed religious controversy, and Balfour had recently had his fill of battling clerics and laymen as Anglicans argued among themselves over the controversial matter of 'ritualism' within their denomination. He longed for 'moderate' Churchmen to seize the debate from the Anglo-Catholics on one side and Low Church 'Protestants' on the other, and refused to become embroiled in sectarian battles.[34] Occasionally his exasperation over the endless argumentation burst out: 'It is now equally clear to me that the Clergy, of whatever school, are equally stupid. I had thought the range of stupidity more limited.'[35]

Among Nonconformists there seemed to be no disagreement over the iniquity of the education bill. Even more politically dangerous to the Unionists was that this legislation did what no Liberal alone could: it reunited the Loyal Opposition, which had been tearing itself apart since the retirement of Gladstone.[36] The Liberals, who depended on the support of the nation's diverse Nonconformist community, were unrelenting in their characterization of the bill as both an attack on local representation by abolishing the school boards and a violation of the right of parents to educate their children in their own faiths. Many enraged Nonconformists again pointed to the fact that most voluntary schools operated under the aegis of the Established Church, and therefore the bill was simply a ploy for putting 'the Church on the rates'. Their anger found a spokesman in the Baptist leader Dr John Clifford, and in the fiery Welshman Lloyd George, who raged against the bill with a passion comparable to his pro-Boer campaign.[37] Balfour found it all very trying, noting to Wyndham in September, 'I wish I were with you fighting Irish Nationalists instead of English Nonconformists. The former is a much more congenial employment.'[38]

But there was more: the Churchmen in Balfour's own party – not least his cousin Hugh – were displeased that the education bill failed to guarantee Anglican predominance in education in all schools. Balfour would have none of it, telling Lord Hugh, 'To create in the face of immense opposition a body of Managers with a denominational majority, and then to leave the Anglican parson or Roman Catholic Bishop in uncontrolled supremacy over all that pertains to denominational teaching appears to me to be a very clumsy contrivance.'[39] The zealots failed to derail a final compromise which placed control of religious instruction in the hands of school managers rather than with the local clergy. Most enthusiastic Churchmen and Nonconformists grudgingly accepted the compromise, though some most unhappily.

After a draining forty-nine days in the committee stage, in December the bill was finally passed on to the Lords, where it was promptly approved, and from this point the long-needed revision of British primary and secondary education (including the teacher training colleges) began. By the time the bill received the royal assent, on 20 December, Balfour was heartily sick of the struggle, complaining to his sister Evelyn that it made him 'hate both religion and education'.[40] Chamberlain, who feared the alienation of the 'chapel' Unionists, had had his fill too, and scolded Devonshire in September 1902: 'I told you that your Education Bill would destroy your own Party. It has done. Our best friends are leaving us by scores and hundreds and they will not come back.'[41] Sidney Webb, the bourgeois socialist, saw it quite differently: the act would do much good, because 'For the first time we have made education a public function, simply as education without definition or limit, and without restriction of age, or sex, or class, or subject, or grade.'[42] In this case both pessimist and optimist were more or less correct.

The government's difficulties, however, did not end with the passage of the Education Act. Many Nonconformists proved tenacious in their complaints against it, as rallies and protests continued, with Wales and its Baptist majority at the centre of resistance. Lloyd George championed the 'passive resistance' movement which encouraged opponents of the act to withhold the payment of local rates. The new plan of campaign created a stir, and eventually thousands of resisters faced prosecution. More than 300 had their goods seized for public sale, and eighty were jailed for non-payment.[43] In Wales, county councils illegally withheld rate support or otherwise harassed the voluntary schools with whose welfare they had been unwillingly saddled. Balfour would not back down, Lloyd George could not, and the problem still festered when the Liberals replaced the Unionist government in 1905. It is interesting to note that this did not embitter the two antagonists against one another. Despite their monumental battles over the Boer War and the Education Act, the aristocrat and the cottage-born solicitor each came to respect the other's courage, determination and skill, without giving the other so much as an inch in their skirmishes. 'Fittingly,' John Grigg has noted, 'the next major legislative advance in British education was effected when Lloyd George was Prime Minister and Balfour a member of his Cabinet.'[44]

Webb was correct: the Education Act proved to be a remarkably

effective law with a long and productive lifespan. Yet Chamberlain's prediction was proved right also, in that the immediate political costs were
high, and Balfour made little headway with his attempts to defuse the
anger of the Nonconformist Unionists. The party had made considerable
inroads among those voters since the 1890s (in large part because of the
Home Rule controversy), but the education row played a significant part
in curtailing this trend.[45] In the eight contests that followed the introduction of the bill (but preceding Chamberlain's conversion to Tariff Reform)
the Unionists gained one seat but lost the rest – and were out-polled by
their opponents in all nineteen by-elections that followed. The
Nonconformist vote was significant in many of these defeats.

In the final stages of the education battle, Balfour again took up the
matter of higher education. Working once more with R. B. Haldane, he
served on the inter-party committee which created the Imperial College of
Science and Technology in London. In December 1902 he inspired a committee of the Privy Council, chaired by Devonshire, to take up the matter
of the scarcity of university places in Britain, and this played an important
part in furthering the 'red-brick' university movement, with charters issued
to the universities of Manchester and Liverpool in 1903, and then to Leeds
(1904) and Sheffield (1905), with others to follow.

The coronation of Victoria's heir was planned for 26 June 1902, and Lord
Salisbury had intended to retire immediately afterwards. The King, however, fell seriously ill two days before, and the ceremony was postponed –
but the resignation was not. Salisbury had been premier three times, for a
total of more than thirteen years. He felt all his seventy-two years, and a
few years earlier he had declared his intention never to consent 'to be in
politics the Dowager Lord Salisbury'.[46] On 11 July 1902 King Edward
received him for a final time as first minister, and the Marquess accepted
from his sovereign the Grand Cross of the Victorian Order – he did not
bother to glance at the insignia and absent-mindedly dropped it into his
pocket, noticing only later that it was richly embellished with diamonds.[47]
The following day the succession was complete: Balfour was summoned
and commissioned to form a government. His days as heir apparent were
finally over.

Despite Devonshire's great prestige and the fact that he seemed to enjoy
being offered and declining the premiership, the only other conceivable
Unionist premier was Chamberlain.[48] A few days before Salisbury's resignation, the sixty-six-year-old Colonial Secretary had been injured in a cab
accident in Whitehall, and he was still recuperating when Balfour called on

him immediately after kissing hands. For weeks, rumours had circulated in Whitehall that the Colonial Secretary, whose popularity was at its height as 'Joe's war' at last reached its conclusion, would challenge the heir apparent for the premiership. Balfour knew that this was not the case, for Chamberlain had invited Sandars to his room in the House for a fifteen-minute talk four months earlier: according to the secretary, the great imperialist had insisted that, despite all the press speculation and the wishes of some of his friends, 'he was "not a candidate" for that office.' Sandars knew he was being employed as a conduit: 'All this was said with great earnestness and almost passionate emphasis, and the impression he made on me was that he was talking through me not only to A.J.B. but to other persons who might be interested in the political drama.'[49] Others were less suspicious: Lord Esher wrote to his son that the Colonial Secretary had been 'excellent' over the matter, and the courtier purred, 'It is a pretty story, and quite true.'[50]

As Queen Victoria demonstrated when she called for Rosebery rather than Harcourt in 1894, she still chose her premiers. Certainly the Unionists in those days had no formal machinery to choose one, even if it had been entirely up to them. Things were simpler in 1902, for Balfour was recommended by his predecessor, and as Leader in the Commons he was the presumptive and anticipated candidate in his party. Since Walpole's day, the office of prime minister had existed in practice but not in law, though by this time the PM ruled while the sovereign merely reigned. In a speech at Haddington in September, Balfour reminded his listeners that he now held:

> an office which has no existence in law at all, which is not recognized by any statute, and which does not form part of the British Constitution, as understood by lawyers. The Prime Minister of the day has no salary as Prime Minister. He has no statutory duties as Prime Minister, his name occurs in no acts of Parliament, and though holding the most important place in the Constitutional hierarchy, he has yet no place which is recognized by the laws of his country.[51]

All in his party realized that for decades he had been groomed for the part by Salisbury, and it was as close to an inheritance of the office as modern politics would ever witness. He was a popular as well as an inevitable choice, and India Secretary Lord George Hamilton described to Curzon the party meeting that endorsed the succession: 'I have seldom been present at a meeting as unanimous and enthusiastic as that composed of the Peers and House of Commons members of the Unionist Party, at which his promotion was announced.'[52] When he faced the Commons a few hours later, he found a crowded House. He was roundly cheered, and dealt with the demonstration as he usually did – behaving with his habitual look from side to side as if the display were for someone else. Campbell-Bannerman offered the congratulations of the Opposition, and the cheering began anew. Yet Balfour was clearly moved, and Sir Henry Lucy noted that he responded only briefly, 'speaking in halting voice that threatened a breakdown. But he managed to get on to the end, closing with the touching sentence, spoken in faltering voice, "In fact, I am", he said, "quite incapable of saying what I feel."'[53]

Like Gladstone, Salisbury had retired from politics, and no election was necessary; and Balfour continued with essentially the Cabinet he had inherited. There were some changes: Hicks Beach insisted on retirement from the Exchequer, and, though Balfour had long since ceased to be an admirer, the retreat from office of the much-trusted veteran was a political loss. 'Black Michael' refused Balfour's appeals and agreed to remain only until the end of the session in August.[54] Chamberlain refused to consider a move from the Colonial Office, and the Exchequer went to Charles Thomson Ritchie, the sixty-four-year-old Home Secretary. His former place was taken by Akers-Douglas, always a Balfour favourite, while Devonshire continued as Lord President, gladly relinquishing the Board of Education to Lord Londonderry. Balfour found places for the two men whom he had designated as 'most promising' younger Unionists: George Wyndham, the Irish Secretary, was promoted to the Cabinet, and Austen Chamberlain joined as Postmaster General. The seventy-year-old Chancellor of the Duchy of Lancaster, Lord James of Hereford, was retired in August and replaced by Sir William Walrond. Otherwise the administration remained substantially the same. It is interesting to note, however, that to strengthen the debating power of the front bench a Glasgow businessman became Gerald Balfour's parliamentary secretary at the Board of Trade. This was Andrew Bonar Law, who, though barely known to him at the time, would eventually succeed Balfour as party leader.

The machinations of Cabinet-making always troubled Balfour. Unlike some leaders, he did not know his backbenchers well, and the need to deal with the ambitions of the competent and incompetent alike he found simply repellent. On the busy day he became prime minister he found time to write to Lady Elcho of his predicament:

> I have seldom passed so unhappy a 5 days! – I am utterly unsuited to the kind
> of work into which I have been dragged: and the thought of all the pain
> which those (alas! Too many) who will get nothing must suffer, and the

unsatisfied appetites of those who will not get enough, gives me a sort of perpetual mental toothache which I cannot get away from.

Nor could he resist a rhetorical flourish:

> Why was I born to do this kind of work? What have I done that it should be thrust upon me? If I could retire from public life, and if my place could be cut up into pieces to satisfy all the world and scattered like crumbs among the starving throng how happy should I be. I should stay at Stanway as long as you and Hugo allowed me, and start another book.[55]

Most of this, of course, was charming nonsense – and Mary Elcho knew it. Only a few days later he wrote more seriously to her brother: 'I regard Cabinet rank as the highest sphere in which any man can be called upon to serve the King. It is laborious, and, no doubt, often unpleasant: yet the honour is so great that it seems to me diminished rather than enhanced by any addition which it is possible to make for it.'[56] This may be taken at face value, for despite his eloquent denials, Balfour took the obligations of high office very seriously. Many years later, Lloyd George said of him that Balfour enjoyed office, 'a different thing to liking power'.[57] This is a tempting characterization and contains elements of truth, even if it oversimplifies. Like the 'Welsh Wizard', Balfour thought of executive office as a vast responsibility – the greatest in the nation – yet there is no evidence that the exercise of power over men and institutions gave him much pleasure, as it did Lloyd George. He formulated no visionary designs for remaking the nation, as did Lloyd George or Chamberlain or Churchill. Yet, despite his offhand rhetoric, in office or Opposition – accepting both success and failure along the way – he strove to make the nation secure and content, and to maintain the primacy of the party he thought best suited to lead it. It was his challenge and ultimately his misfortune to assume national leadership in a time when deep divisions in his party and the nation made it nearly impossible to achieve most of what he wished. Lloyd George's quip came late in his own life, and it must be recalled that the two men did not serve together in Cabinet until Balfour was nearly seventy – perhaps by 1931, when the great Welshman implied that Balfour took it all very lightly, he had forgotten the earnest battles the two had fought in opposition and then side by side, in peace and in war.

In 1902 there was much for the new Prime Minister to do – in the eyes of many, there was much that was overdue. Over the previous generation the world economy had changed, and Britain's once advantageous position as 'workshop of the world' was now under challenge from formidable industrial rivals. Balfour now led the nation in a period saddled with an economic recession and faced with the great ailments feared in all industrial states – unemployment and inflation. In a democratic century, the masses had the vote and many looked to the state for redress – for social reform. And, unlike their grandfathers, they were organized. The trade unions that emerged from the Victorian years had grown large, well organized and well funded, and in 1901 several had allied themselves with socialist societies such as the Fabians, the Social Democratic Federation and the Independent Labour Party in the new Labour Representation Committee (the LRC, soon to become the Labour Party), which sought political solutions to workers' demands. By the time of Balfour's resignation, in 1905, the affiliated unions represented nearly 1 million members.

As the Education Act irritated the Nonconformists, so were the trade unions infuriated by two key legal decisions in 1901, both eventually upheld by the House of Lords: the judgement in *Quinn* v. *Leatham* outlawed the use of strikes to force employers to dismiss non-union employees, and a second legal decision held the railwaymen's union liable for strike-related damages against the Taff Vale Railway. These cases energized the labour movement and brought withering criticism on the government and on Balfour. He did not abandon his position that the courts expected no more of the unions than of any other corporate body 'such as a Railway or a Bank', though he admitted to the King, 'it will no doubt put those Members of the Unionist Party who have a large trade union element in their constituencies (as Mr Balfour himself has) in a considerable difficulty, and may lose them many votes.'[58] How correct he was: government supporters promptly lost three by-elections to LRC-backed candidates at North East Lancashire in 1902, and at Woolwich and at Barnard Castle in 1903.

Though, as noted earlier, there would be no old-age-pensions legislation from his government, Balfour did endorse a 1902 bill authorizing the London boroughs to create offices to attempt to bring the unemployed together with potential employers. Then in 1905 Gerald Balfour passed an Unemployment Act which authorized the creation of employment committees in the major cities for similar purposes and, as both brothers had done in Ireland, to encourage emigration among the chronically unemployable. However, the Prime Minister resisted programmes of public employment such as those he had once created in the west of Ireland. Ireland was a special case, he insisted, with its chronic poverty and underdeveloped economy – and, he might well have added, its revolutionary history. In a developed economy like that in Britain, he equated further state intervention with the assumption of state responsibility, and thus the creation of a dependent social class. This for him was the fatal flaw of all socialist theory and practice. 'I do not think', he told a deputation of trade unionists in February 1904, 'it is in the best interests of the community . . . to induce any large class of the community to believe that they have a right to claim at any moment they choose employment from the State or some public body, and become dependent directly or indirectly on rate aid.'[59] On the eve of the resignation of his government and under considerable labour pressure, Balfour did create a Royal Commission on the Poor Law, with Lord George Hamilton in the chair. Its justly famous majority and minority reports would not materialize for four more years, and thus came to be the business of the Liberal administration of H. H. Asquith.

There was one matter in which the Unionists were able to satisfy organized labour, and that was in regard to the restriction of immigration, justified largely with the economic argument of protecting the livelihood of British workers. Such limitations had also been sought for more than a decade by a knot of 'restrictionist' Unionist MPs, and a bill was finally presented in 1904, withdrawn, and passed in revised form in the following year.[60] The Aliens Act of 1905 stipulated that 'undesirable immigrants' be denied entry into the country: these included those judged 'lunatics' or 'idiots', and others could be turned away owing to health or physical condition, or if they appeared likely to become economically dependent. The bill passed easily, though opponents pointed out that in debate 'undesirable alien' had become a code word for Jew, and there is little doubt that many sought to decrease the intake of Eastern European Jews. Balfour was himself much troubled by such accusations, telling the House:

> I have regretted that at intervals throughout the debate there have appeared some allusions to what on the Continent has attained unenviable fame as the Jewish question . . . I cannot imagine anything more disastrous than that any legislation by this House or speech in the House should attempt to join a measure which I shall presently attempt to show is consistent with every sound system of statesmanship with the bigotry, the oppression, the hatred the Jewish race has too often met with in foreign countries. This is a question wholly distinct from the Jewish question.[61]

Due largely to the 1917 Balfour Declaration on the creation of a Jewish homeland, he has often been described as possessing an uncharacteristically enlightened understanding of world Jewry. Certainly Mrs Dugdale, herself a keen Zionist, encouraged this view, and there was much to it.[62] In earlier times, Balfour had been an enthusiastic supporter of the unfortunate Captain in the infamous Dreyfus case, and he deplored its scarcely hidden anti-Semitic subtext.[63] While he was certainly guilty from time to time of expressing the sort of 'polite' anti-Semitic remarks then all too common in Western society, he felt a genuine admiration for Jewish culture and history: 'I like them for their history,' Lady Frances once quoted his table talk, '[from] a Tory point of view for its length, & I am so grateful to them for what they did.'[64] Yet his understanding of that history at this point was neither deep nor broad, as evidenced by his naïve surprise that Zionists were unimpressed by Chamberlain's bizarre brainwave in 1903 of offering land in East Africa as a Jewish homeland.[65] The chairman of his Manchester constituency committee at this time, Dr Dreyfus, happened to be Jewish, and Balfour sought his advice on the matter. Dreyfus's reply was to introduce him to the scientist and Zionist leader Chaim Weizmann, beginning a friendship and a political connection with far-reaching consequences.[66]

Balfour addressed a completely different social issue in 1904, when he brought in a new licensing bill to reduce the number of public houses in Britain. There was a fervent strain of teetotalism among Balfour's old antagonists in the Nonconformist community, and to them the Unionists had long been the 'brewers' party'. It was quite true that those in the distilling and brewing trades often preferred Unionism, where prohibitionist sympathy was thin on the ground. To complicate matters further, the majority of patrons of public houses were working-class men, among whom there was no interest in either decreasing the number of pubs or putting up the price of beer. Balfour recognized the danger inherent in tolerating an over-abundance of public houses, but he rejected the demonization of the publicans and what he insisted was the short-sighted nostrum that the solution to drunkenness lay in legislating law-abiding businessmen out of their livelihoods.[67]

Since 1891 the state had assumed the power to limit the term of licences for the sale of drink, and in 1902 Parliament established standards for licence renewal. The 1904 bill was meant gradually to reduce the number of licences while compensating licensees for the loss of what was, after all, a valuable property. To avoid the charge of its being a 'Tory ramp' or 'brewers' bill', Balfour's draft provided for the creation of a compensation fund drawn from a tax on 'the trade' itself. Austen Chamberlain recalled, 'That the bill was wholly his work I can testify, for I was a member of the Cabinet Committee which was appointed to draft a Bill and the draft which the committee produced bore no resemblance to Balfour's scheme which replaced it.'[68] To Nonconformist prohibitionists it seemed clear whom to blame for putting the 'brewers on the rates', while many workers who looked to the pub as the centre of social life held Balfour responsible when a favoured 'local' shut down or the price of a pint rose. The 1904 act was both necessary and effective, but for a government growing daily more vulnerable it was not helpful to have the Liberals trumpeting the 'licensing of sin'.[69]

Of the many issues which occupied Balfour's mind, few concerned him as much as national defence, and few needed more attention. Unlike his immediate predecessors (or successors, for that matter), his interest was keen. The Boer War came as a sharp reminder that the twentieth-century world was a perilous place, especially for a nation that possessed much and therefore had much to lose. The Royal Navy, under Selborne as First Lord of the Admiralty, was off to a good start, and much of this was due to the tireless Admiral Sir John Fisher. Born in Ceylon, 'Jackie' Fisher was an unlovely little man whose hooded eyes gave rise to cruel tales of an illegitimate birth and an Asian father. His head was full of brilliant innovations, but his studied indiscretions, love of intrigue and ruthless disregard for all opposition came to divide not only the navy but much of official Britain into pro- and anti-Fisher camps. By the time Balfour left office, the Unionists and much of the nation were firmly in the former category, and Fisher had become a seemingly unstoppable force.

From 1902, as Second Sea Lord, the admiral proposed a series of plans which began with a radical overhaul of officer training (the so-called 'Selborne Scheme') and eventually led not merely to the redistribution of the fleet but also to the adoption of new technology such as wireless telegraphy and to radical new vessels including submarines and the 'all big gun' ships, pioneered by his revolutionary *Dreadnought* and *Invincible*. Fisher became First Sea Lord in 1904, and in that powerful position he made even more powerful converts. Balfour and Selborne, like most parliamentarians – like most Britons – were 'navalists', believers in the 'blue-water' doctrine that the nation's security and interests depended on its sea power.[70] Though there were constant concerns over expenditure – for modern warships were far from inexpensive – Fisher generally got his way, and by the time of his retirement in 1910 he was hailed by his admirers as the greatest naval figure since Nelson himself.

The army, particularly after the revelations of the 1899–1902 war, was a different matter, and its many needs occupied much more of the premier's attention. There was no Fisher for the land forces, and Balfour turned to several Royal Commissions for advice. The first of these, appointed in October 1902 under Lord Elgin, was charged with examining matters of military preparation, manpower, supply and operations in the South African War.[71] The Commission heard 114 witnesses in fifty-five days and in the following August concluded, not surprisingly, that the nation's rusty war machine had been badly organized and poorly prepared for the conflict. It was especially worrisome to be reminded by the Commission that the nation had been largely denuded of regular troops: Balfour had himself revealed to the House on 16 May 1901 that on that day there were but 17,000 regulars remaining in Britain. Unlike the Continental forces, the British army depended upon voluntarism for manpower, and the commissioners warned ominously that 'no military system will be satisfactory which does not contain powers of expansion outside the limit of the regular Forces, whatever that limit might be.'[72] To some this sounded very like a call for some sort of mandatory service.

In April 1903 another Royal Commission, under the Duke of Norfolk, was charged to inquire into the condition of the auxiliary forces, the Militia and Volunteers. Eleven months later it announced equally troubling conclusions, warning that these traditional organizations no longer had the 'strength or efficiency required' to fulfil their functions in wartime.[73] Their advice went beyond the Elgin Commission, as they concluded that the time had come for Britain to consider the Continental practice of obligatory military training.[74] Navalist that he was, Balfour was unsympathetic to the idea of expensive mass armies raised on the basis of compulsory service. In 1905 he insisted to Lord Roberts, by then the nation's foremost proponent of mandatory training, that the nation simply would not be persuaded to accept this revolutionary notion. He objected on the grounds that it would produce a mass of ill-trained citizen-soldiers, rather than the well-trained troops that skilful recruiting could bring forth.[75] His ideas did not change after he left office: he wrote in 1911 that even if the army continued as it was, the British Isles were not imperilled, but if the navy ceased to be strong 'we perish.'[76]

The most powerful argument that Roberts and his allies could muster for mandatory training was based on the possibility of unprovoked invasion – the much discussed 'bolt from the blue'. In 1903 Balfour initiated a study of the possibility of such an attack by an army of 70,000 men – according to Roberts, the smallest conceivably effective force. The conclusion of Balfour and the new Committee of Imperial Defence was that no such invasion could succeed, primarily because of the strength of the British navy.[77] Roberts and his National Service League kept up the fight, but for the moment conscription was a dead letter.[78]

★

St John Brodrick, War Secretary since 1900, had been appointed to improve the army without resort to conscription or, given the costs of the Boer War and the projected expense of Fisher's programmes, to increased spending. Balfour was largely responsible for his appointment, and had been confident that 'if any man can reform the army it is St John.'[79] Brodrick revealed his plans in March 1901: he wished to retain the 'linked battalion' system of the regular army, and proposed the reorganization of the home forces into six corps, each of 40,000 men: three, made up of regulars, to form a 'striking force' for foreign service and three, largely of troops drawn from the traditional auxiliary forces, charged primarily with home defence. There were problems: his plan required an increased annual intake of volunteers of more than 11,000, with shortened terms of active service and increased pay — and at least £5 million added to the annual budget — and he would need the co-operation of the auxiliary forces in his ambitious reorganization plan. When his ideas became known, Brodrick's design was not popular with the officer corps, War Office officials or the press. The reorganization plan gained little support in the Cabinet, and it was not long before the King had had enough of Brodrick. There was also much disapproval among MPs, most damagingly among a group of clever young Unionists, the 'Hughligans', led by Balfour's cousin Lord Hugh Cecil and including the fledgling MP for Oldham, Winston Churchill.[80] Balfour unburdened himself to Lady Elcho: 'Never has [Brodrick's] stock been so low. I really do not think it is his fault; but whether his fault or not, his unpopularity is a most serious menace to the Government . . . Many good observers think the feelings against St John are so violent that we shall not get through Army Estimates without a fall!'[81] Chief Whip Sir Alexander Acland-Hood put it as bluntly to Sandars two days later: if they continued to back Brodrick, 'it will end in disaster in the House, and we shall have the country and the Press against us.'[82]

With his government already disrupted, as we shall see, by Chamberlain's tariff campaign, the Prime Minister chose to save Brodrick but not his proposals. In September he moved him to the presumably more sympathetic environs of the India Office, and in October he appointed H. O. Arnold-Forster in his place. The grandson of Rugby's Dr Arnold, and foster son of the educational reformer W. E. Forster, Hugh Oakley Arnold-Forster's 'zeal for reform and knowledge of Army matters', as well as his acknowledged success as Selborne's parliamentary secretary at the Admiralty, were encouraging.[83] But he was a stiff and difficult man, impatient, intellectually arrogant, and unsympathetic towards dissent. He was not popular in the House, and the palace was not particularly pleased with the nomination.[84] Many other names were discussed — Esher, Wyndham, Akers-Douglas and Walter Long among them — but none was possible. Chamberlain endorsed Arnold-Forster, as did 'Willy' Selborne, and it appeared that Balfour had no other choice — Arnold-Forster got the job.[85]

The new war minister inherited a sea of troubles, with the Norfolk Commission about its work and the troubling Elgin report and Brodrick's failure before the public. Furthermore, Balfour was preparing to appoint another committee to recommend improvements in the organization of the War Office — all this as he was struggling to right his political ship, endangered by the tariff debate. Arnold-Forster ignored all and, unlike Brodrick, proposed a 'clean sweep', beginning with the dissolution of the linked-battalion system and substituting a new 112-battalion long-service regular army for imperial and foreign service, with volunteers enlisted for nine-year intervals.[86] In addition, he planned to replace the centuries-old Militia with a short-service home defence force of thirty battalions available to reinforce the regulars in wartime. The remaining auxiliaries would be reorganized for home defence. He proposed also to do away with the office of commander-in-chief and replace it with a modern general staff — a long-overdue innovation which Balfour himself had long favoured.[87]

The Prime Minister soon discovered that his new war minister met any criticism of any part of his complex plan with cold rigidity. And there was no shortage of criticism: despite Balfour's hopes, Arnold-Forster's plan, like Brodrick's, called for increased expenditure, and this earned him the unrelenting opposition of the Chancellor, C. T. Ritchie. The socially and politically well-connected mainstays of the traditional auxiliary forces, the 'militia colonels', hated his plan to destroy the old system, and fought him every inch of the way — and this number included both his former admirer Selborne and 'Jem' Salisbury (who had succeeded his father as marquess in August 1903). Many of the generals disliked the new proposals as much as they had Brodrick's, who himself heaped criticism on his successor's design. To make matters worse, Arnold-Forster's health was not good, and the strain of the political battle made him all that much more difficult.

Arnold-Forster's goals were laudable: to improve the quality of men recruited to the colours; to raise the level of preparation and efficiency of the forces; and to ameliorate procedures to expand the regular forces in wartime. He soon learned that, while his own interest was concentrated on the possibility of European war, the Prime Minister's first priority was the defence of India. The war minister was unable to convince Balfour, the Cabinet, Parliament or the public of his view. When faced with the additional scepticism of the Crown, the Treasury and the officer corps, Arnold-Forster simply became more determined to have his plan. Sadly for him, his gifts in defence thinking were far more creative than any he possessed for practical politics.

The war minister held Balfour largely responsible for his lack of success.[88] It is true that the Prime Minister allowed him to continue in office after he, Balfour, had indicated to him that he had serious misgivings about important elements of his plans and after the Cabinet had lost faith in the proposed reforms. Balfour simply had come to distrust his colleague's judgement as well as his political skills, noting to Esher:

> He has another curious habit of carrying away from an interview in which he has done all the talking an impression that the person to whom he has talked entirely concurs with him: so that he is perpetually quoting eminent soldiers to me as being the most ardent among his supporters, though I suspect they look with considerable coldness on many parts of his scheme.[89]

He wrote similarly to Austen Chamberlain: 'I am never quite sure with A–F whether all his cards are on the table . . . His own temperament is so sanguine that he never sees the difficulties of his own position; and I am seriously afraid lest there prove to be a case against him of which we know little or nothing.'[90]

Arnold-Forster offered his resignation more than once. Why, then, did Balfour not accept it? The reason was that by 1904 Balfour's administration was in great difficulty – he had already weathered a number of resignations due to the corrosive tariff controversy. After Brodrick's failure, it had not been easy to secure an able successor in 1903; in 1904 or 1905 it would have been virtually impossible. In a wounded government, another resignation might well have been fatal. Balfour continued to express his personal confidence in Arnold-Forster's ability – even as he faced the impossibility of his policies and his methods of persuasion – when under more hopeful circumstances he would have parted with him. He did so in order to hold his government together while he struggled to prevent his party from splitting apart. The unfortunate Secretary of State for War became a kind of human sacrifice, and he never entirely forgave Balfour for it.[91]

Balfour did not make Arnold-Forster's path any easier with his decision in 1903 to create a small War Office (Reconstitution) Committee to propose improvements in the operation of the War Office. To chair the so-called 'Triumvirate' Balfour chose his old friend Reginald Brett, 2nd Viscount Esher, who had been a member of the recent Elgin Commission. Perhaps the ultimate insider and master of influence, and considered by many an expert on defence matters, Esher had recoiled from Balfour's offer of the War Office in September 1903.[92] At fifty-one, he preferred the role of courtier, and the exercise of influence rather than the power and responsibility that accompanied political office.[93] Yet Esher was a clever man, and much respected in Westminster – certainly he held the ear of the King and, as an ostensible political 'neutral', of other powerful men of both major parties.

Esher was far from neutral on defence questions, however, and possessed his own vision of an improved army. Though he initially supported Arnold-Forster's appointment, he soon concluded that he and his plan were hopeless. As Balfour's faith in his inflexible minister eroded, he drew closer to Esher. In 1904 a powerful report was released by the committee of Esher, Admiral Fisher, and Sir George Sydenham Clarke, and their advice hastened the retirement in February 1904 of Lord Roberts, the last officer to hold the rank of commander-in-chief.[94] A modern command structure was to be created under a new Commander of the General Staff, and appointed was Balfour's long-time friend, Lieutenant General Sir Neville Lyttelton. Roberts was to be compensated with appointment as a salaried member of the new Committee of Imperial Defence (CID). Another Triumvirate innovation, an Army Council of civilian and service chiefs modelled on the Board of Admiralty, was also created. Esher and his colleagues emerged from their labours with vast credibility and increased influence – as poor Arnold-Forster seemed only to flounder.

Balfour did not create the Committee to divert Arnold-Forster's plans, but it is also true that he could not have chosen more ideal appointees had obstruction been his purpose.[95] He wrote to Sandars early in October 1903 expressing his desire that the Committee and the minister should work co-operatively and his hope that the triumvirs would keep Arnold-Forster informed of their deliberations: 'With a little good will on both sides, there ought to be no difficulty in carrying out this policy, which on the whole is the one which I am inclined to recommend.'[96] It was not to be: Arnold-Forster clung to his plan, while Esher and Clarke were soon intriguing assiduously to substitute their own alternatives – as Balfour's patience ran out.

With his war minister in deep water, by the close of 1904 Balfour was considering Esher's idea of creating a second committee with the charge of offering amendments to Arnold-Forster's scheme. The Secretary of State – no match for the wily courtier – had no choice but to accept such 'help' in February 1905, with Balfour (who seldom attended) chairing a CID sub-committee of Esher, Roberts, Clarke and George Murray of the Treasury.[97]

Peter Fraser does not exaggerate when he suggests, 'The two "triumvirs" [Esher and Clarke] were in short fixing up the Esher committee again, but dressing it up as an extension of the C.I.D.'[98] The committee met behind closed doors at 10 Downing Street, and very soon after its creation Arnold-Forster was complaining to Balfour of its interference.[99] Balfour's replies to the contrary offered little comfort. Please, he wrote to the war secretary, 'dismiss from your mind all the misgivings which appear, for what I hope is but a brief moment, to have found lodgement there.'[100]

The Prime Minister allowed Esher and Clarke such latitude because he could neither accept Arnold-Forster's programme *in toto* nor sack his War Secretary. In particular, Balfour was frustrated that Arnold-Forster ignored the expressed concerns of the Cabinet and paid no attention to the alarms raised by the public and the press, for much of his plan – inevitably – had been leaked to the newspapers. By early 1905 Balfour had grown weary of his colleague, and in a letter of 14 February he recommended reconsideration of the proposed size, period of enlistment and disposition of the long-service army and the substitution for his potentially expensive home-service army of an improved Militia. He implored Arnold-Forster to reconsider: 'Inasmuch as it is clear that your scheme in its entirety is impracticable, even a suggestion may prove of value.'[101] Within a month, he wrote to the King that there was no reason to hope that a viable plan for army reform would emerge from his government.[102] When he accepted office, Arnold-Forster had told the Prime Minister, 'Of course I do not expect you to back me unless I convince you.'[103] By April 1905, he had stiffened considerably, writing to Balfour:

> All the world knows by this time that the Prime Minister has propounded a plan of Army Reform which differs fundamentally from that of the Secretary of State for War. It is quite obvious that such being the case, there can be neither certainty nor progress. No Secretary of State is justified in attempting to further a policy to which his Chief is opposed. Nothing but evil could come of such an attempt.[104]

In such an atmosphere, gridlock was inevitable, and the army remained unreformed while Balfour's political problems destroyed his government. If he was not entirely without success in other areas of national defence, the Prime Minister spoke candidly when he wrote to Lord Roberts that the entire matter of 'Army Reform is a heart-breaking question'.[105]

While this was an all too accurate assessment, his new creation for the co-ordination of defence planning, the Committee of Imperial Defence, proved to be a stunning success. As early as 1888, the Hartington Commission had recognized the absence of something of the sort as one of the major weaknesses in the national defence structure and advised the creation of a permanent defence council. Little was accomplished as a result, however.[106] A joint services committee was tried, as was a Colonial Defence Committee. As noted earlier, Hartington (now Duke of Devonshire) chaired the latter committee, and Balfour hoped this would 'decide all questions of importance connected with Imperial Defence, which involve the co-ordination of Army and Navy'.[107] It did much less, and Devonshire admitted in November 1900 that the Committee 'met rarely, without any definite agenda . . . No minutes have been left, and in general there have been no definite decisions to record.'[108] By the time Balfour succeeded Salisbury, there had been no progress towards the co-ordination of defence planning. There were glimmers of hope, however: in October 1902 Arnold-Forster, though only parliamentary secretary at the Admiralty, circulated a paper supporting the idea, and, more importantly, in November the political heads of the services, Selborne and Brodrick, presented a memorandum of their own calling for action to be taken at last.[109]

Balfour had his new CID in place by December 1902, and it consisted initially of the premier, the service chiefs, the senior military advisers to the government, and certain other senior officers. Roberts and Esher soon became permanent 'independent' members, and the politically inevitable Devonshire took the chair. A secretary was seconded from the Foreign Office, regular meetings were scheduled, and minutes were kept. Balfour, who attended virtually every meeting, took the chair after Devonshire's resignation in October 1903 – as from that point did most prime ministers. Strengthened by the recommendations of the Esher committee, he also established the practice that the chairman summoned any other members he thought necessary, with the proviso that membership should remain as small as possible. Despite some criticism, the CID quickly began to build an infrastructure of its own, nursed to life by Esher with Balfour's support – years before the Cabinet itself would gain a permanent secretariat, in 1916.[110]

Balfour never claimed credit for being the sole parent of the innovative committee, and both Brodrick and Selborne, whose important 1902 memorandum Balfour accorded high praise, claimed parental credit. The unhappy Arnold-Forster asserted exclusive authorship, 'down to the selection of the very man I proposed as secretary'.[111] Yet other significant voices are worth hearing. Austen Chamberlain was certain that the credit for the innovation belonged to Balfour: 'The conception was his; the form and manner of its constitution was his, and his was the direction given to its first steps, to be developed indeed later but never to be changed in any material respect.'[112] Colonel Hankey, the long-time secretary to the Committee, had no doubt that Balfour alone brought the CID 'into existence'.[113] Many years later, Prime Minister Stanley Baldwin told Balfour that the Committee 'is your own child and would indeed feel an orphan without you'.[114]

Balfour defined his new committee to the House on 5 March 1903. Its purpose was not, he said, merely to take up questions referred to it by the Cabinet, as with other committees; rather he intended that it would:

> survey as a whole the strategical needs of the Empire, to deal with the complicated questions which are all essential elements in that general problem, and to revise from time to time their previous decisions, so that the Cabinet shall always be informed and always have at its disposal information upon these important points.

It was the ad-hoc nature of defence thinking within the government that frustrated Balfour, and in his mind this was the blackest mark against it in the run-up to the South African conflict. The new CID, he argued, would strive to provide ministers with information and proposals in advance of trouble, therefore:

> [The Cabinet] should not be left to the crisis of the moment, but when there is no special stress or strain the Government and its advisers should devote themselves to the consideration of these broad and all-important issues. So much for the change in subject, scope and design between the new Defence Committee and the old.

Balfour's defence thinking did not stray from the navalist perspective: the security of the home islands rested with the navy, while the purpose of the army was the protection of the British Empire. To Balfour this meant India – the sole great colony (save Canada) which shared a land frontier with another Great Power, Russia. The implications of this he laid out in two papers to the CID in the spring of 1904.[115] To Lansdowne, he summarized his view in plain language: 'There is only one policy which will prevent wild schemes developing into dangerous acts – the policy, I mean, of a big Navy, an efficient Indian Army, and a perfectly clear intimation to Russia that the invasion of Afghanistan means war with England.'[116] And it was the security of India and the Empire that drove him to seek – without success – a reformed army, with 'powers of expansion'.[117]

In a world of Great Power alliance systems, the drawn-out conflict in southern Africa was a further reminder that, even if it might once have been, isolation was no longer particularly splendid. Even earlier, in 1898, he had been willing to consider closer ties to Germany, but not at any price the Kaiser might require. What, then, were the alternatives? Even before his old schoolfellow succeeded to the premiership, Lansdowne had taken steps of his own at the Foreign Office and negotiated a peacetime defensive alliance – though with Japan, rather than a European Great Power. Balfour was sceptical, and wrote to him in December 1901:

> I do not think we ought ever to have offered to enter into an offensive and defensive alliance with Japan without considering how such a course affects our relations with Germany, and the Triple Alliance [Germany, Austria–Hungary and Italy]. Hitherto we have always fought shy of any such engagements, and whether we have been right or wrong, we could at least say that we were carrying out a traditional policy of isolation which had proved successful in the past . . . The momentous step has been taken, and if the Japanese accept our proposals, we may find ourselves fighting for our existence in every part of the globe against Russia and France, because France has joined forces with her ally over some obscure Russian–Japanese quarrel in Corea [sic].[118]

Though inclined to believe that 'the dangers are less and the gains are greater from joining the Triple Alliance', Balfour also understood that relations between the '[British and German] peoples are at present so hostile as to make negotiations impossible'. There was ample evidence: in 1902 Venezuela became an annoyance by refusing to honour its European debts, and Britain joined with Germany in blockading (in Balfour's famous phrase) the 'disreputable little republic'.[119] This troubled the American President, Theodore Roosevelt, ever mindful of the Monroe Doctrine, and the United States recommended arbitration – which suited Balfour and led to promises of good behaviour from Caracas. The government learned, however, that even minimal co-operation with Berlin was anything but popular with a growing anti-German press in Britain.[120] In the end, Balfour reasonably accepted the Anglo-Japanese treaty as the best arrangement available under the circumstances. In 1905 he presided over its renewal and expansion.

The significance of the Japanese alliance was underscored when war erupted between Russia and Japan in February 1904. Though it did not require British participation under the 1902 treaty, the conflict was closely watched by all the Great Powers, and by none more than France and

Britain, who were allied to the opposing sides. Contrary to much European opinion which anticipated a decisive Russian victory, Balfour had speculated some weeks earlier to Selborne that, even if the Japanese did not win, they were capable of inflicting damage that would leave Russia 'innocuous for some little time to come'.[121] And with India in mind he noted to the Cabinet, 'There could be nothing better for us than that Russia should involve herself in the expense and trouble of a Corean adventure.' Were the Russians foolish enough to engage in such a conflict, he calculated that it would turn out to be a costly enterprise which would ensure that Japan would give the Tsar no peace in Asia.[122] There might well be benefits closer to home, not least because Russia's 'value to France in a war with us would be greatly reduced', and its entire foreign policy reduced to one of 'sweet reasonableness'.[123] Despite arguments to the contrary by Lansdowne, Balfour insisted that there was nothing to be gained by consideration of intervention in the conflict: the war should be kept at arm's length, and he went so far as to oppose Japan's request for a loan of £20 million.

For a brief time it appeared that Britain might be dragged into the conflict after all, as in October ships of the Russian Baltic fleet inexplicably fired on unarmed British fishing vessels (presuming them to be Japanese gunboats) on the Dogger Bank in the North Sea, killing two seamen and injuring several others. Word of the improbable incident reached Balfour in Scotland early on the 23rd, and, Balcarres recalled, his first reaction was that any report so improbable must be a hoax.[124] As soon as he had ascertained that the bizarre episode had in fact truly happened, he telegraphed orders to mobilize the fleet and authorized a public announcement to this effect. Balfour did not hide his cold fury, telegraphing to Lansdowne, 'I shall be sorry to see so gross and gratuitous a blunder left to the slow methods of diplomacy.'[125] To the Cabinet he was even more pointed, informing them that what he intended to say in a speech scheduled at the National Union in Southampton in five days would 'sound very like a declaration of war' but that he could not 'at present see that any other course is consistent either with our national honour or with the fixed sentiments of the country'.[126] After the usual period of bluster, however, the Russians climbed down – though word of this did not reach the Prime Minister until 28 October, literally as he stepped from his train in Southampton.[127]

Britain remained well out of the Russo–Japanese conflict – a war which resulted in stunning Japanese victories both on land and at sea, culminating in the devastation of the Russian fleet in the Tsushima Strait in May

1905.[128] The diplomatic end of the brief conflict was orchestrated by President Theodore Roosevelt, with a treaty signed in Portsmouth, New Hampshire, in the following September. Russia's problems were not at an end, as its defeat was followed by political and social upheaval at home, and it appeared that for the time being any threat it posed to British India was neutralized.

Even before their respective allies battled in Asia, Britain and France began cautiously to draw closer together. As in the case of the Fashoda episode several years earlier, the rivals found that they could profitably defuse their rivalry in a world in which there were other, greater, dangers than each other. Balfour had long believed that the tradition of Anglo-French antagonism constituted a genuine danger, but one rooted in tradition rather than national interests. He supported continuing negotiations which had led in October 1903 to an Anglo-French arbitration treaty. Leaving the key negotiations to the Francophile Lansdowne and the French foreign minister, Théophile Delcassé, 'he interested himself primarily in the key *quid pro quo*: British Egypt for French Morocco. He insisted that France formally recognise the British occupation of Egypt, diminish international financial control, and help gain the assent of the other Great Powers.'[129]

The result was the celebrated *Entente Cordiale*, completed by April 1904. Balfour supported the cautious new direction of the two old rivals, but he did not exaggerate the immediate usefulness of the *Entente*, nor did he presume that France's enemies necessarily were Britain's. The arrangement would, of course, lead to the reshaping of British and European foreign relations in the decade that preceded the Great War, but its full significance would not be known until the ambitious intentions of a restless Germany became clear over the decade that followed.

Berlin's often reckless adventuring brought a new challenge in March 1905. Remembered as the First Morocco Crisis, this was sparked by a provocative speech in Tangier by the Kaiser – thought by all to be a test of French will and the growing Anglo-French co-operation. Though he was disappointed at what he considered initial French fragility in the face of German bluster, Balfour's policy was consistently to support the *Entente* partner.[130] This he continued long after his government passed out of office in December 1905.

The Unionists had been in power for twenty-two of the thirty years that preceded Balfour's resignation in 1905, though his own government lasted little more than three years. There would be no 'Age of Balfour' to rival that of Salisbury. The legislative and administrative accomplishments and failures of his administration, before his first year in office was over, were carried out on borrowed time. The principal reason for this was the internecine Unionist Party battles over fiscal policy.

8

'Cutting each other's throats'

A RTHUR BALFOUR SUCCEEDED to the premiership a fortnight before
his fifty-fourth birthday, and, save for the respiratory infections and
influenza to which he occasionally fell victim, his health was generally very
good. However, while perhaps stopping short of the hypochondria of Sir
Edward Carson, his former Dublin Castle henchman, Balfour's fascination
with the subject of his own health and with medical lore in general seemed
endless. He enjoyed 'talking shop' with physicians, who were often surprised at the extent of his technical knowledge. The royal physician Lord
Dawson wrote years afterwards, 'In all that pertained to medicine, [he]
showed abiding interest; he understood its problems, followed its progress
and appreciated the difficulties which beset its path.'[1] Lord Balcarres put it
somewhat more bluntly: 'The Chief fancies his internal organization differs
from that of everybody else, and he likes going from doctor to doctor discussing symptoms. His bedroom is like a chemist's dispensary.'[2] He
delighted in hearing of and frequently sampling the latest remedies, as the
Cabinet secretary Tom Jones recalled of a lunch in 1924. The poet and
dramatist John Drinkwater enthusiastically extolled the virtues of 'Doctor
Johnson's Tablets', so Balfour took one, examined it, and swallowed it
immediately. 'Could politeness', Jones concluded, 'go any further?'[3] Any
results of the self-medication went unrecorded.

His love affair with mechanics was also undimmed by his new dignity,
and he had recently acquired a large Napier touring car (to which he had
new coachwork fitted, replacing the 'disappointing' body with which it
had been delivered) – the first automobile owned by a prime minister. He
also purchased a motorcycle, which he wisely kept at Whittingehame.[4] He
presumed that his social routine of country-house weekends with the Souls
and other friends, and long family gatherings at Whittingehame, would not
be impeded. Nearly as important were his golfing excursions, for by this
time he was completely committed to the game. 'As a Scotchman', he told
an audience of fellow devotees in 1903, 'my heart swells with pride when
I reflect that it is from Scotland that the infection has spread, not merely

throughout the whole of the United Kingdom, but through every part of the world where the English tongue is spoken.'[5] On a bicycling holiday in Scotland in 1904, A. C. Benson discovered how relaxed the usually immaculate Balfour could be on his private course at Whittingehame:

> [We] saw the Prime Minister approaching across the grass, swinging a golf club – in rough coat and waistcoat, the latter open; a cloth cap, flannel trousers; and large black boots, much too heavy and big for his willowy figure. He slouched and lounged as he walked. He gave us the warmest greeting, with a simple childlike smile which is a great charm.[6]

As we have seen, the achievements of Balfour's brief government were not inconsiderable; yet, blighted by disunity, it survived for less than four years. St John Brodrick wrote insightfully to Selborne in November 1905, 'It is a terrible pie but Arthur is sick of it. I have no doubt he will resign before [the] end of December . . . It is a long way back to 1895 and you will remember the high hopes with which we took office. I am sorry it should flicker out.'[7] The 'terrible pie' in which the Unionists found themselves by the end of 1905 was the product of a series of disasters of their own creation which not only destroyed Balfour's ministry, but ensured that there would never be another.

The Balfour administration was sometimes criticized as a ministry of friends and family, and to a large degree it was. It was also true that many of Balfour's difficulties could be traced to certain of these very intimates. Not the least troublesome was his fellow Soul George Curzon, who in 1898, at the remarkably young age of thirty-nine, had been given an Irish peerage and appointed viceroy of India. None who held the post had ever had better credentials for it: he had travelled widely in Asia, written several substantial books about his experiences and served as under-secretary at both the India Office and the Foreign Office. It might be added that few viceroys had wanted the post more than he.[8]

Curzon was a controversial figure to whom historians generally have not been kind, and it is quite true that a powerful and impatient intellect combined with driving ambition and a soaring ego made him an exceedingly difficult man. The fact that throughout his life he suffered from a painful spinal condition made him no easier to deal with. He was capable of maddening arrogance, and too often he seemed to consider those who opposed him to be not merely wrong, but stupid at best and ill-intentioned at worst. Only those close to him knew that he was also capable of warmth and generosity – and only they experienced the often earthy sense of humour and the passionate nature so at odds with his public self.

There was wide praise in his time for the record he left behind in India of administrative reforms, preservation of public treasures, and settlement of old disputes, but he was admired rather than loved. Not surprisingly, the long friendship of men so fundamentally unalike as Balfour and Curzon did not always run smooth. Curzon thought Balfour's charisma hid deep-seated cynicism, and that his unhurried style and frequent ignorance of details smacked of irresoluteness and, too often, of pure indolence. Balfour admired Curzon's intellect, diligence and unparalleled knowledge of his business, but he thought that the Viceroy's legendary haughtiness detracted from his political effectiveness and that his ambition made him incapable of loyalty. This ambition was sometimes a source of dark humour to Balfour, who laughed at Curzon behind his back as 'the purple emperor'.[9]

Balfour and Curzon had virtually ignored each other during the first years of the latter's viceroyalty. This came to an end in July 1902, when Curzon protested in the strongest terms against the government's expectation that India would bear the expenses of its delegation to the royal coronation in August – especially, he insisted, since India had made British victory in South Africa possible.[10] The government capitulated, though Balfour protested that the language of the Viceroy's letters seemed very like an 'indictment' – and a rather personal one at that – of the Cabinet.[11] Curzon, still in a truculent mood, crowed to his wife that 'by a little courage, I have defeated them all.'[12]

Curzon pressed his advantage: in December, a magnificent durbar – a grand levée of Indian notables – was to be held to celebrate the coronation, and he wrote to the Prime Minister requesting permission to announce reductions in taxation, including the unpopular salt tax. The India Secretary, Lord George Hamilton, pointed out that, though he favoured the reductions, it was unwise to associate the King's name with tax matters, and he withheld his agreement. Balfour and the Cabinet agreed. Curzon replied angrily and at length.[13] The Viceroy reminded them that he had planned every detail of the pageant, including 'the width of the roads, the placing of the tents, the planting of the flower-beds. He also chose the hymns for the church service.'[14] If the government refused his grand gesture, perhaps the great spectacle should be abandoned entirely. He particularly annoyed Balfour by forwarding his complaints directly to the King's secretary, Lord Knollys – who of course passed the correspondence on to the Prime Minister. Balfour held his ground, and the durbar went ahead as planned; but Curzon unhappily had to make do with offering a general promise of relief, without particulars.[15] Hoping to avoid further strife, Balfour sent a conciliatory letter of lavish praise which also contained a rebuke: 'You seem', he wrote, 'to think that you are injured whenever you do not get exactly your own way! But which of us gets exactly his own way!' He reminded his old friend not to commit the deadly error of taking 'any difference of opinion as a personal slight, or as indicating any want of confidence among colleagues'. As for himself, he insisted, 'I have differed from you on this or that point . . . But nothing will for a moment diminish either the warmth of my friendship or the enthusiasm of my admiration.'[16] The Viceroy would not be admonished, and replied reminding Balfour of the grandeur of what none denied was 'his' durbar: 'In half an hour I shall be getting up, & donning uniform & orders, and in less than 3 hours shall be on an elephant, heading what I suppose the newspapers will describe as the most wonderful procession of the century.' He added that Balfour's letter had painted a picture of a petulant self-willed colleague, and had drawn from him 'more than a smile'.[17] The Viceroy was slow to forgive, insisting to his wife that he meant to treat the rebuke with the 'silent disdain' that it deserved.[18] Mary Curzon was convinced that her husband was deeply angered, and that the struggle among old comrades would 'leave a scar'.[19]

So it appeared, as Curzon refused the sovereign's offer of the GCB.[20] Yet, with his health endangered by overwork, in February 1903 he proposed the renewal of his appointment after a leave of six months at home – this despite the wishes of his wife, who had had quite enough of India, and of political friends who worried that his party needed him at home.[21] Balfour was not enthusiastic about extending the appointment and suggested that, even if it were possible, the King and he felt strongly that a furlough of no more than six to eight weeks could be considered.[22] However, the Viceroy would not bend and Balfour could not produce a suitable alternative, so Curzon got his way over both reappointment and the six-month home leave. He arrived in London in April to congratulations and honours, adding the Lord Wardenship of the Cinque Ports to his collection of trophies. Years later Balfour would recall to friends that agreeing to the reappointment was the greatest mistake of his political life.[23] After these events and those that followed in the next two years, Curzon might have been justified in thinking similarly. Whatever else occurred, certainly nothing would ever be quite the same afterwards between the two old friends.[24]

With neither his health nor his peace of mind restored, Curzon returned to India following his leave and set about remaking imperial policy towards the neighbouring states that lay beyond its frontiers. Curzon had long been a proponent of the 'forward' policy in South Asia, leading Salisbury himself to grumble late in his life: 'My difficulty with Curzon is that he always wants me to negotiate with Russia as if I had 500,000 men at my back, & I have not.'[25] Balfour and the Viceroy were agreed that the Russians posed the greatest threat to British imperial interests, but the question of how best to deal with them only increased the friction between the two men. Curzon had long argued, for example, for a restructuring of relations between Delhi and Afghanistan, and during his leave he aggressively pressed this on the government.[26] His plan was to exact a treaty from Kabul granting Britain military access to the border state in the event of a Russian invasion; but, despite his arguments to Balfour and Brodrick – Curzon's oldest friend, now India Secretary – a new treaty signed in 1905 left the British guarantee of Afghan independence in the vague state with which both governments were for the moment satisfied.[27]

Curzon also clashed with the government over relations with neighbouring Tibet, the isolated theocracy which existed under loose Chinese suzerainty. Concerned once again about the Russian menace, in late 1903 the Viceroy exacted permission from London to dispatch a trade mission to Lhasa, led by the soldier-explorer Colonel Francis Younghusband. Balfour was wary, particularly given the tensions then mounting between Russia and Japan. He wrote to Brodrick that he 'strongly deprecate[d] permanent entanglements in Tibet, partly because I think we have as much on our hands as we can look after, partly because if we "Manchurianize" what is technically a part of the Chinese Empire, we may greatly weaken our diplomacy in the Far East'. Yet, he recognized that the home governments were always disinclined to overrule 'people on the spot who say & often with truth, that their policy is the only one which will save bloodshed & money in the long run'. In the end he gave in, but 'I do it reluctantly.'[28]

The mission, as it turned out, soon appeared to have more to do with conquest than with commerce, as Younghusband's small force fought their way into the Forbidden City in 1904, while Curzon was still on leave in Britain. The Prime Minister had defended the Viceroy and the mission in the House, but privately he was uneasy with events. He believed from the outset that Younghusband was gallant enough, but that he had disobeyed explicit instructions and placed the government in a difficult and even dangerous position: by this time Russia and Japan were at war, and entanglements with Tibet and perhaps with China, he believed, presented more risks than advantages for Britain.[29] The Cabinet agreed, and the treaty that the colonel had forced on the Dalai Lama's government in September was rewritten in milder terms. When Younghusband returned to London he was received quite predictably as a popular hero and awarded the KCIE, though he was not so popular with Balfour or Brodrick. Curzon, meanwhile, nursed yet another annoyance with a government that, he insisted, had failed to back their 'man on the spot'.[30]

Curzon took part in one further contest of wills during Balfour's ministry, and his adversary in this struggle was the equally headstrong former hero of the South African War, recently ennobled as Lord Kitchener of Khartoum. Rivalled in popularity only by Lord Roberts himself, 'Lord K of K' was Curzon's choice as commander-in-chief of the Indian Army – which he became in October 1902. Brodrick knew both men well and had advised against the appointment, recalling years later that at the time he would have 'wagered half my fortune that there would be a clash between them'.[31] The troubles were rooted in the fact that the Commander's powers were limited, in that he shared authority over the Indian Army with the Military Member of the Viceroy's Council, an officer junior to him. To K of K, this arrangement was both inefficient and insulting, and he meant to bring it to an end – even though the Viceroy opposed any change. The explosion between the two men came soon after Curzon's return to India in 1904.

Kitchener's plan to end dual control appealed to Balfour, who saw the system of divided authority as impractical, bad for morale, and needlessly expensive. Brodrick agreed, and so did the Cabinet. Curzon, who did not relish a commander of such independent authority, absolutely did not. Balfour preferred to effect a compromise between the two great figures, but this proved impossible. The Viceroy resisted the general with a flood of memoranda and correspondence, while Kitchener blustered about resignation, conducted his own propaganda campaign, and employed his epistolary friendship with Lady Salisbury to attempt to influence the Prime Minister. Balfour's patience was soon exhausted, and he insisted to Brodrick, 'I don't give a damn whether Curzon resigns or Kitchener resigns or they both resign.'[32] He wrote similarly to Sandars: 'I do not easily think ill of mankind; but upon my word, these two old friends of mine are gradually compelling me to take a very dark view of our poor fallen nature.'[33]

In the end, Brodrick backed Kitchener, Balfour backed Brodrick, and the Cabinet backed Balfour – with inevitable results. The resignation of the popular hero Kitchener would be a more dangerous blow to a government already nearly crippled by political problems. Curzon, for all his accomplishments, had become expendable, and he, not the general, cabled his resignation in August 1905. Balfour had had enough of his old friend

George Curzon for the time being, and wrote to Brodrick, 'There is I think no use in fighting him further. If he will go he must go.'[34] Curzon also had had his fill: after this indignity he became a lifelong critic of Kitchener, and his friendship with Brodrick was also ruined. His relationship with Balfour remained chilly for many months, and he never entirely forgave him the episode.[35] The Prime Minister told Lady Salisbury in 1906 that he had insisted to Curzon from the outset that this was a battle he could not win: 'George says that, if he had known this, he would not have returned to India: to which I replied that, if I had not supposed he was well acquainted with it, I should never have allowed him to go back.'[36]

Balfour had been prepared to seek a British peerage for Curzon in 1904, and the Viceroy assumed that an offer now would be made upon his return.[37] In this government's last days, the King wished to offer Curzon an earldom (hoping 'to soothe his feelings'), but Balfour now thought differently, reasoning that to grant such an honour to an official in such open disagreement with the government he served was impossible.[38] He added further that 'it was equally impossible for me to suggest anything in the nature of a bargain, which should give him a peerage as the price of silence. He would not accept it, and certainly I could not offer it.'[39] Though the King suggested that he would be pleased to offer an earldom without his ministers' recommendation, Balfour rejected this as unconstitutional and, contrary to his words to Knollys, indicated with a sly mile to Salisbury: 'I am pretty confident he would take it gladly.'[40]

Fearing the worst, Knollys assured the Prime Minister that he had warned Curzon to 'keep quiet'.[41] For a time this did not seem likely, as Balfour's journalist friend Iwan-Müller met with Curzon on his return and reported his fury towards Brodrick ('his blackest lies'), Kitchener ('blackest liar and worse') and Balfour himself ('foul conspiracy of A.J.B.').[42] The fact that no ministers greeted Curzon when he finally returned to London in December did not help his temper – however, this was the very day that Balfour resigned his government. For a time the ex-Viceroy negotiated with Unionists in the City regarding his possible parliamentary candidacy, but according to Sandars he would consider sitting only as an independent Conservative, rejecting both Balfour's leadership and the Unionist whip.[43] This was not to be, however, as the King, among others, advised against it as inappropriate for the former Viceroy. Furthermore, both Curzon and his wife were in poor health at the time, which ended any hopes of entering the 1906 election. Despite the encouragement of the King, Balfour's Liberal successor, Campbell-Bannerman, would have nothing to do with ennobling Curzon.[44] He finally entered the Lords in 1908 – but as an Irish representative peer, and did not receive his earldom until 1911.[45]

If the battle of wills with Curzon embarrassed his government, the misfortunes of another intimate, George Wyndham, created an even greater political difficulty for the Prime Minister. When he joined Balfour's Cabinet, Wyndham's popularity was at its apogee, and he was certainly a rising star – perhaps *the* rising star – of the Unionist Party. Once Balfour's secretary, he had entered the House at twenty-six, and acquitted himself well as Lansdowne's under-secretary at the War Office a decade later. As we have seen, he was appointed Irish Secretary at thirty-seven and was elevated to the Cabinet when Balfour became premier in 1902. He was only thirty-nine, and there was every reason to believe that he was bound for even greater things.

Wyndham meant to settle the vexed Irish land question, with which both Balfour brothers had recently battled with some success, and the moment was perhaps more promising than any for a generation. A private initiative by certain moderate Irish landlords inspired an extra-governmental conference in Dublin in December 1902 of landowners, tenants and politicians under the chairmanship of Lord Dunraven, which recommended the most ambitious programme of voluntary land purchase yet proposed. It seemed as though the 'centrist moment' had come, and that a moderate solution amenable to all was on the table.[46] Wyndham responded in 1903 with the last great Irish Land Act, offering attractive purchase terms designed to coax participation by landholders (payment in cash rather than state bonds, with a 12 per cent bonus upon sale) and tenants (68½-year mortgages, serviced by purchase annuities to keep payments as low as possible). It won the approval of many landowners, led by the Orangeman Colonel Edward Saunderson, and of many of the Irish Nationalists, now led by John Redmond, as well as of the United Irish League and the independent nationalist William O'Brien.[47] Though he worried about the costs of such a scheme in the post-Boer War economic climate, Balfour warmly supported it.[48]

The conference and the land bill had equally determined Irish opponents, however, such as the hard-line Nationalist John Dillon, who feared that the success of conciliation would do just as moderate Unionists hoped and neutralize the land question, weakening Irish nationalism. Closer to home for Balfour and Wyndham was opposition within the Unionist Party itself. Balfour's former bulldog Sir Edward Carson was now Solicitor

General and the obvious man of the future among Irish Unionists. He did not trust the land conference or Wyndham's bill, and attacked it as ferociously as he had Gerald Balfour's earlier act. For a time he even abandoned the front bench, though he stopped short of resignation from the government.[49] The more militant of the Irish Unionist MPs shared Carson's distrust and opposed the bill with a fervour that matched that of the Dillonites – to these zealots, the generous terms amounted to nothing less than bribery of the landlords and undeserved charity to the Irish Nationalists.

For his own reasons, Joseph Chamberlain, who had been in South Africa for several months, disliked any bill that seemed to him to reward the Irish landlord class that he held in contempt and thereby saddle the government with additional debt. The great Irish landholders, including Londonderry and Lansdowne, were sceptical too, sensing the beginning of the end of their kind. Balfour was unmoved by the critics and told the King that, despite all, the 'far reaching measure' would finally settle the land question once and for all.[50] Wyndham confided to his staunch Home Ruler cousin Wilfrid Blunt that had it not been for Balfour's 'splendid support' the bill would never have emerged from the Cabinet.[51]

The Land Act proved to be the high point of Wyndham's career, but suspicion of him among the Unionist sceptics did not pass away easily – and their memories were very acute. Their revenge came when he blundered into a destructive snare which would for ever link his name with that of the famous civil servant, Sir Antony MacDonnell. After a long and distinguished career in the Indian Civil Service, the fifty-eight-year-old 'Bengal Tiger' returned to London in 1902 to join the Secretary of State's Council of India. As his permanent under-secretary, Sir David Harrel, was scheduled to retire, Wyndham set his heart on MacDonnell as his replacement.[52] An Irish Catholic, Sir Antony's brother was a Nationalist MP, and MacDonnell himself made no secret of his own desire for some degree of constitutional reform of the Union. Balfour learned of MacDonnell's reputation and warned his Irish Secretary, 'I have heard nothing but good of Sir Antony MacDonnell as a man and an administrator: – *but* is he not a H. Ruler? . . . I think you ought to consider well before you take a step which most of your colleagues in the Cabinet and most of your friends in Ireland would regard with the gravest misgivings.'[53] Wyndham promised he would be cautious, and consulted a friend (and former viceroy of India), Lord Lansdowne, who was certain that MacDonnell's hopes for Ireland did not lie with a Home Rule parliament. Wyndham was satisfied, Balfour again allowed a colleague to have his own way – Wyndham got his under-secretary.[54]

In his letter of acceptance of the post, MacDonnell reminded the Chief Secretary that he was 'an Irishman, a Roman Catholic and a Liberal in politics'. Furthermore, the man who had once ruled the Indian north-west with an iron hand had no intention merely of being Dublin Castle's chief enforcer: 'I should be willing to take office under you provided there is some chance of my succeeding,' he informed Wyndham. 'I think there is a chance on this condition – that I be given adequate opportunities of influencing the action and policy of Irish Government, and (subject of course to your control) am allowed freedom of action within the law.'[55]

Nervy and emotional at the best of times, Wyndham was left close to nervous and physical exhaustion by his struggle to pass his land bill, and his resort to drink and 'bracing exercise' made the situation that much worse.[56] Rest was prescribed, and in August 1904 he set off for Germany, leaving the Irish administration to MacDonnell, with instructions not to disturb him for any but the most crucial reasons. With Wyndham out of the country, Dunraven and a delegation from his Irish Reform Association called on MacDonnell, whom they knew through their efforts at the land conference. The deputation of reformers and the Under-Secretary quickly saw eye to eye and settled on a blueprint for 'devolution' – the orderly transfer of authority over Irish local affairs to the Irish. On 26 September the Reform Association announced a scheme – designed largely by MacDonnell – calling for the creation of a national council of twenty-five elected and appointed members (including the Chief Secretary) to be chaired by the Lord Lieutenant and charged with control over Irish fiscal policy, and a second council of Irish MPs and peers to be given responsibility for preparing future Irish-related legislation for Parliament.

Their manifesto was soon published and, predictably, inspired a tidal wave of denunciation by Unionists of all stripes over what they insisted was a proposal as wicked as any from the pen of Gladstone himself. When word reached Wyndham, he roused himself, publicly denied any knowledge or involvement in the 'conspiracy', but refused the demand of the Unionist extremists to sack MacDonnell – it is possible that Wyndham may not have been clear in his own mind whether he did or did not know of the development of the plan.[57] The reason was that the Chief Secretary, ill in spirit and body and plagued by stress and depression, was close to a complete breakdown. When the House assembled in February, the most ferocious knot of Irish Unionists and their British allies showed the 'turncoat' no mercy. His speaking style – often opaque even when he was at his best – became nearly incomprehensible under such stress. The Cabinet sensed that Wyndham was doomed, but what was to be done about the unrepentant MacDonnell? There were accusations aplenty, yet Balfour pointed out to the King that Sir Antony was, after all, merely a civil servant.[58] The steadfast Under-Secretary refused any rebuke, insisting that he had done nothing behind the back of his minister, and therefore nothing wrong.[59] With Wyndham's reputation in tatters, it was his career that was ruined. Balfour feared the worst and wrote to Lady Grosvenor in January 1905, imploring her to entrust his friend's health to a physician: 'His nerves seem to me – nay are – (for the moment) utterly ruined. He is hardly sane.'[60]

Balfour's position, and that of his government, soon became impossible. In the House of Lords, Lansdowne attempted to defend Wyndham by suggesting that MacDonnell had been granted greater latitude for 'initiative' than most under-secretaries could have expected; at the same time, in the Commons, Balfour seemed to deny it. When portions of the correspondence between Wyndham and MacDonnell somehow appeared in the newspapers, the most extreme anti-Home Rulers seemed in danger of bolting the party. Though Balfour wrote to an angry Lord Londonderry of his desire to make it 'unmistakeably [sic.] clear that the Cabinet and every member of the Cabinet disapprove of that [MacDonnell] scheme and consider it to be altogether inconsistent with Unionist principles', it was still not clear enough for many Unionists.[61]

Balfour had tried to stiffen his Irish Secretary, writing in late January: 'We may possibly have a tightish time in the House over it; but I do not think you need worry yourself.'[62] It proved 'tightish' indeed. Several times Balfour rejected Wyndham's resignation offers, but by March the Prime Minister gave in: Wyndham insisted on surrender, and Balfour accepted his decision. 'In my opinion,' he wrote rather ambiguously, 'what is best for you is best for the Party, and what is best for the Party is best for you. Though', he could not resist adding as a classic Balfourian addendum, 'I am clear in this point, I am not so clear as to what that best case is.'[63] Actually, he knew very well what the best case was – at least for the government. Wyndham, who, like his admirers, had once presumed he was the 'next prime minister but three', never held office again. Unlike some others, he never blamed the Prime Minister for his fall, as Lady Grosvenor indicated in a generous letter: 'I want to send you my love dear Mr Balfour,' she wrote, 'for I have a great deal to thank you for. George says "tell him I love him."'[64]

Amid the ruins of Wyndham's career, Balfour laid out for Sandars the 'real facts' of the case: '(1) that George had a nervous breakdown, (2) that the consequences of the MacDonnell controversy, of Lansdowne and George's speeches, of Irish gossip etc etc was to create a kind of atmosphere of mistrust, quite fatal for the moment to George's power for good in Ireland.'[65] All quite true. Yet so was it true that Balfour was distracted by his other political battles and allowed his Irish Secretary more than enough political rope to hang himself.[66] The Prime Minister wrote years later to an old friend of both Wyndham and himself, 'I personally did all I could to dissuade him from appointing Sir Antony to the position of Under-Secretary; not the least because I doubted Sir Antony's ability or integrity, but because I felt the gravest fears lest the appointment of a Roman Catholic Home Ruler would weaken George's hand in dealing with one set of politicians, without strengthening them in dealing with another.'[67] For his own political good, for Wyndham's and for that of his government, he would have been well advised not to give in on such a sensitive policy matter to a minister in his first Cabinet appointment.[68]

In part because of this melancholy episode, the Unionist position on Ireland was captured by the most uncompromising elements of the party. It was in the month of Wyndham's resignation that the shadowy Ulster Unionist Council was formed to defend the connection of Protestant Ulster to Britain. At the same time, Balfour admitted the defeat of concili-ation by appointing as his new Irish Secretary the former leader of the Irish Unionist MPs, Walter Long, though only after offering the post unsuccessfully to Carson (who first accepted and then declined the invita-tion) and to the Irish Attorney General, John Atkinson. MacDonnell quietly shelved his devolutionist schemes and got on well under Long – certainly the two bluff, plain-spoken men were more alike than either resembled Wyndham.[69] If Long, perhaps surprisingly, came to accept MacDonnell as a civil servant who had acted in accordance with what he thought were his minister's wishes, the new Chief Secretary remained furious with Wyndham for causing the crisis and could not bring himself to forgive him for several years.[70]

The poisonous atmosphere created by the Wyndham–MacDonnell affair encouraged the circulation of the absurd rumour among the Unionist extremists that 'Bloody Balfour' had gone 'soft' on Home Rule. 'I think it perfectly outrageous', he fumed, 'that I, for instance, should be suspected of tampering with Home Rule upon evidence on which you would not hang a cat.'[71] Many years later, Murray Hornibrook, Wyndham's former secretary, wrote of the absurdity that any Unionist could accuse the Prime Minister and his closest colleagues of supporting 'watered Home Rule for

Ireland'.[72] Critics seized on Balfour's refusal to allow the publication of all correspondence among the principals relating to the case. Long led the fight, and Balfour was unsuccessful in deflecting his anger.[73]

Balfour's refusal to continue sifting through the wreckage was due largely to his desire to shield Wyndham from further reproof.[74] He wrote to the Chief Whip that, though publication would clarify his own reservations about the appointment of the Under-Secretary, 'I do not see how these letters can be published, for though there is nothing in them to which anybody, except MacDonnell, would object, they are so clearly letters among intimate friends that it seems absurd to bring them before the public.'[75] Some of those Unionists who took the most critical view of their leader in this episode later became the core of the 'Die-hard' faction of the party, who opposed him once again in the House of Lords crisis of 1911. In a monstrous irony, one who joined them in the latter quixotic campaign was George Wyndham. The corrosive climate of opinion created by the Wyndham–MacDonnell affair played a crucial part in the intransigent position taken by Balfour and his party in the Home Rule crisis that preceded the coming of the Great War.[76]

These challenges of imperial and domestic policy would have taxed the resilience of any Cabinet. However, it is impossible to believe that even collectively they would have split the Unionist Party, shortened the lifespan of the government, and destroyed it so utterly at its end. The force which finally did this was the debate over what came to be called Tariff Reform, and the creative genius behind that movement was Joseph Chamberlain. At the time Balfour became prime minister, the Colonial Secretary was sixty-six years of age; he had once been Britain's most famous radical, and then became its greatest imperialist. Twenty years earlier he had been a power in the Liberal Party and a potential prime minister; but he had thrown that potential away when he made war on Gladstone over Irish Home Rule and played his part in splitting that party. Lord Blake has suggested that Chamberlain 'wanted to *do* things rather than *be* someone'.[77] This was once so, but by this time no one doubted that he already *was* 'someone'; and they learned that what he wanted to *do* in the twilight of his career would make him the most dangerous man in British politics.

Chamberlain's political passions were the Empire and social reform, and for him the first could not be great without the second. By the dawn of the twentieth century he had concluded that the danger to achieving his goals lay in the economic as well as the political competition among the Great Powers. He believed that greater unification of the Empire, particularly between Britain and the self-governing colonies, could best be fostered through the creation of an imperial trading union which would bring with it greater imperial unity, prosperity and security. The closer union he envisioned would depend on mutual economic self-interest as well as imperial patriotism, as mother country and colonies would be joined in a kind of customs union like the German *Zollverein*, protected against rivals by tariff barriers. It was a vision of grand proportions, but it would be received as nothing less than fiscal heresy by those in Britain who believed that Free Trade was the bedrock on which Britain's prosperity was constructed.[78]

Chamberlain had begun to reveal his passion for imperial unity as early as 1896, with a speech before the Imperial Chambers of Commerce, and he made another a year later at the London Colonial Conference. At the Conference, the Canadians announced a unilateral 25 per cent reduction of tariffs on British goods, increased to 33 per cent in 1900.[79] Then in April 1902, on the eve of another such conference, the Chancellor, Hicks Beach, levied a small registration duty on all corn imported into Britain. His goal was narrower than Chamberlain's: he argued that the innovation was meant only to broaden the tax base and increase revenue to deal with the enormous costs of the South African War.[80] 'Black Michael' was no friend to Chamberlain's grand vision and intended the duty to be no more than an ad-hoc revenue measure – a fact which the Colonial Secretary conveniently ignored.[81] The Canadians, understandably, made known at the 1902 Colonial Conference that they expected a gesture of reciprocity for their tariff reduction, and the other colonial delegations joined them in calling upon London for preferential treatment for their exports to the mother country in regard to 'duties now or hereafter imposed'.[82]

Seeing these as steps in the right direction, on 21 October 1902 Chamberlain proposed to his colleagues that they remit the new registration duty for Canadian corn and came away satisfied that his great plan was well begun. Then, on 19 November, Joe wrung from the Cabinet endorsement of the corn tax and of his proposal that preferential remission 'should be made in favour of the British Empire'.[83] The Colonial Secretary, pleased with his Cabinet victory but nearly exhausted from overwork, set off to recoup his strength on a four-month tour of South Africa.

If Chamberlain assumed that the basic principal of colonial preference was now settled, he did not reckon with the stiff opposition mounting in the Cabinet in his absence – despite what had seemed to be their earlier agreement. This was led by C. T. Ritchie, successor to Hicks Beach as Chancellor, who had already warned the Cabinet against endorsing any measure of imperial preference.[84] Once the Colonial Secretary was safely out of the country, Ritchie set about organizing the opposition to the Chamberlain initiative.[85] In a curious twist of fate, the Chancellor had been a 'Fair Trader' twenty years earlier, arguing in favour of retaliatory tariffs – and he had crossed swords then with the Liberal President of the Board of Trade, Joseph Chamberlain. That episode (though not his distrust of the man who was now his colleague) was conveniently forgotten by Ritchie, who was emboldened in his opposition to Chamberlain by his Treasury advisers, the Permanent Under-Secretary, Sir Charles Mowatt, and his deputy, Sir Edward Hamilton – both fervent believers in Free Trade ortho-doxy. The Chancellor also found allies in his Cabinet colleagues Lord Balfour of Burleigh, the Scottish Secretary, and Lord George Hamilton, the India Secretary, and together they hoped to enlist the Duke of Devonshire on their side. They also gained the support of two former Chancellors, Goschen and the father of the corn duty himself, Hicks Beach. Their boldness increased in Chamberlain's absence, but the extreme danger in this apparently escaped the eye of Balfour, who was engaged with Devonshire in the final stages of the struggle over the education bill.

Three weeks before the Colonial Secretary was due to return, Ritchie revealed to the Prime Minister that, despite what had passed before, he would not accept Chamberlain's preference scheme. If the government backed Joe, he would resign immediately – two months before his scheduled Budget speech.[86] The popular Chamberlain arrived at Victoria station to a tumultuous welcome on 14 March 1903: the premier, much of the Cabinet and a cheering crowd were there to welcome him, but the trappings of a great triumph were illusory. He had been warned of Ritchie's ultimatum when a message from his son Austen (who had been briefed by Balfour) reached his ship en route, and he arrived spoiling for a fight. The Cabinet were torn: if they appeased Chamberlain and pressed on with the preference experiment, they must face the loss of the Chancellor at a crucial time. On 15 March the Cabinet capitulated to Ritchie, and Chamberlain agreed to postpone the preference offer, 'almost petulantly', adding that without preference the corn duty itself must for the moment be abandoned, in order to lessen the offence to the Canadians.[87] Ritchie agreed, and his May Budget speech proceeded on traditional Free Trade lines, but the matter was far from closed. Chamberlain wrote afterwards to Devonshire that the Cabinet had allowed Ritchie to prevail only for the moment, and he him-self had 'decided to use the summer in further investigation of the questions that had been raised'.[88] In his view, this was no more than a setback that he meant to overcome.

Balfour, premier for only eight months at this point, now faced the unhappy prospect of having two of his most powerful colleagues, the Chancellor and the Colonial Secretary, in open disagreement over a potentially explosive principle. To make matters worse, recent by-election results were disappointing (with Woolwich lost to Labour only days before the contentious Cabinet meeting), and the sage of Central Office, 'Captain' Middleton, was due to retire.[89]

As the divisive tariff debate took shape, a popular matter for debate came to be 'What does Arthur Balfour believe?' Thrust into a difficult position between the contending sides, he often despaired, writing to his cousin Hugh Cecil in 1905, 'I really do not know which is worst – the right or left wing of the Party, which I have the melancholy privilege of leading! As a rule, I find myself for the time being taking the gloomiest view of the last speaker.'[90] If he and his party were to have any hope of continuing to rule Britain, he believed, his task was to maintain a semblance of peace and to find common ground acceptable to all Unionists. Historians have understandably paid more attention to his spectacularly unsuccessful tactics than to his own ideas about tariff policy.[91]

The general direction of the Colonial Secretary's thinking had much appeal for Balfour. He did not fear fiscal reform – from the earliest days of his career he had championed bimetallism, which horrified most economic traditionalists. In the early 1880s, while Chamberlain was still Gladstone's colleague, Balfour had declared in print that there was no maxim of political economy 'which I for one am not prepared to question', and he branded orthodox Free Trade as a creaky ideology rooted in class antagonism and entangled in half-century-old assumptions.[92] He was drawn to the thinking of the 'historical economists' such as W. A. S. Hewins and later W. J. Ashley (who became a close adviser during his premiership), who emphasized the necessity of development of the national economy and the creation of national wealth through production, in contrast to the internationalism – or 'cosmopolitanism', as he termed it – of Cobdenite thought.[93] He was troubled that traditional economics had no response to the question of what Britain was to do to produce and sell its products in the autarkic world of tariff barriers that had grown up beyond Britain's borders since Free Trade had been installed. In short, Arthur Balfour had long been certain that the day would come when something would have to be done to reform Britain's fiscal policy, and that that 'something' would have to be done by Parliament in a climate in which 'Cobdenism' remained popular in the country and in both national political parties. To change the nation's mind would require time, which he thought he had – until the spring of 1903.

If Balfour was generally sympathetic to Chamberlain's imperial and economic goals – even if unclear on the extent of his plans – he was less patient with Ritchie: the Chancellor adhered to the most orthodox Free Trade arguments in his attack on the corn duty and imperial preference, and this Balfour found sterile and unconvincing. Even worse, with his resignation threat, Ritchie had resorted to bullying to get his way. Years later, Balfour recalled, 'Ritchie – he was the villain of the piece in the Tariff Reform affair.' While Chamberlain set off for South Africa, 'in his absence the extreme Free Trade intrigue was set in foot, and Ritchie got deeply involved, and declared he would never consent[;] of course, if he had held any other office than Chancellor of the Exchequer it would not have mattered.'[94] But Chamberlain, bested in the skirmish, was not about to lose the war, and Balfour found himself struggling to prevent his government from being torn to bits.

Though he remained cautious, the Prime Minister was willing to show his hand after the anxious Cabinet on 12 May finally agreed that he should announce his willingness to revive the corn tax as one component of a comprehensive revision of the 'fiscal system', despite the fact, Balfour told the King, that it would 'cause some disquiet in certain circles'.[95] This he planned to do three days later before a Unionist deputation led by the 'Squire' – the convinced protectionist Henry Chaplin. Coincidentally, Chamberlain on the same day was scheduled to address his adoring constituents in Birmingham. Balfour was so cautious in his language to the deputation that Chaplin and his friends came away from their meeting unclear in exactly what direction their leader meant to lead them. But in his speech Chamberlain left no doubt regarding where he stood, calling on his countrymen to take courage and grasp the hand of imperial unity offered by the Canadians. A Free Trade Britain in a world of high tariffs stood on the precipice, with the choice before it of great opportunity or horrible decline. Free Trade belonged to the past, and what he would soon christen Tariff Reform and Imperial Preference was the future.[96] The Colonial Secretary stirred the pot further by acknowledging in the House on 21 May that old-age pensions, a long-range goal which Balfour and he had endorsed, would be impossible unless the government could identify a source of funds to pay for them. This, he announced, would surely require a review of the 'fiscal system' as he had recently outlined – including tariffs. This he followed a week later with another speech in the Chamber reiterating his position and asserting that the system he envisaged would necessitate import duties on foodstuffs.

Balfour did not need to be told of the danger in a fight over fiscal policy, and he wrote to his Free Trader cousin Lord Hugh Cecil, 'I have never quite made up my mind as to which of the two [sides in the tariff debate] are the more unreasonable or which are the least worth the trouble I take to prevent them cutting each other's throats!'[97] In the fiscal debate of 28 May, the Prime Minister endorsed the Colonial Secretary's goal of imperial unity and indicated his willingness to consider a policy of tariff retaliation against trade rivals. This he balanced, however, by adding that he thought it unwise to implement import duties on either food or raw materials without the endorsement of the electorate. He also reminded the zealots on all sides that such a weighty matter must in the end be resolved by the people: it was not 'a question that this House will have to decide this session or next session or the session after. It is not a question that *this* House will have to decide at all.'[98] For the moment (at Chamberlain's insistence) he could promise only a committee of 'enquiry' into the matter, adding that he would propose no policy until their work was done. Chamberlain seemed satisfied, but patience was seldom to be counted among the Colonial Secretary's virtues. The anti-tariff ministers also seemed willing to keep the peace for the time being – at least in public. While Balfour reminded the King of his keen interest in fiscal reform, he added, 'It is imprudent to attempt to "rush" it, either in the Cabinet or in the Country.'[99] The increasingly nervous Cabinet managed on 9 June only to agree to postpone any conclusions and to authorize the Chancellor to announce that the question was being 'enquired into'.[100] Balfour noted to Lady Elcho that only the 'first act' of the tariff drama seemed to have ended satisfactorily, 'but there are many more to come, and the plot promises to be complicated.'[101]

The Liberals, more united than they had been in years by their resistance to Balfour's Education Act, now smelled blood. Free Trade was among the most sacred canons of their party, and tarring the Unionists with the brush of protectionism – particularly if it divided the ruling party against itself – provided them with the best opportunity of regaining office they had had in nearly a decade. Balfour was acutely aware that, as the parliamentary session waned, his own best hope was to postpone a decision until a solution could be found. He wrote to cheer an anxious Devonshire in early June, acknowledging that Chamberlain's impulsiveness had not helped matters: 'Yet surely nothing has happened which ought to make it difficult for us all . . . to act cordially together during the natural term (not, of course, necessarily, or probably the legal term) of the present Parliament.'[102]

Despite this pious hope, he understood how critical the situation was for his government, and knew that sooner rather than later he would face more than one ministerial resignation.[103] He would face more than that, for opponents of Chamberlain's preference ideas were forming a Free Food League, initiated in July by fifty-four Unionist MPs; at the same time, the reformers were organizing a Tariff Reform League to press Chamberlain's case on the party and the country. Balfour had to wonder if there was a middle ground between the polarizing sides, and, if so, could he find it? While he insisted that he rejected the idea that 'a man cannot be a good Unionist although he differs from me upon fiscal matters', his tactics for keeping the Unionist antagonists under a single party umbrella laid him open to attack.[104] In his speech of 28 May he stumbled uncharacteristically in stating that, speaking for himself, he had as yet no 'settled convictions' on the tariff question. A clever Liberal, Sir Wilfrid Lawson, seized on this to score on the Prime Minister by 'quoting' his words:

> I'm not for Free Trade, and I'm not for Protection;
> I approve of them both, and to both have objections.
> In going through life, I continually find
> It's a terrible business to make up one's mind.
> And it's always the best in political fray
> To take up the line of the Vicar of Bray.
> So, in spite of all comments, reproach, and predictions,
> I firmly adhere to Unsettled Convictions.[105]

But, Balfour had mused to Devonshire in his letter of 4 June, despite all, why could his policy of delay not serve to see them through a difficult time? There was much at risk, and much still undone – the education and Irish land bills as examples. Surely it was not 'a felicitous moment for putting the party fortunes to the hazard'. In the previous century, Catholic Emancipation and Free Trade had been open questions in the party, as Disestablishment currently was among the Liberals; why could Unionists not agree to 'allow ourselves a liberty of difference which we allow to our opponents, & which is in strict conformity with constitutional tradition'? Chamberlain had committed only himself, Balfour reminded the Duke, though he admitted that he himself was 'probably more in sympathy with [the Colonial Secretary's arguments] than you or Ritchie'. For the moment, he hoped the party would be willing to treat the matter as just such an open question; that time would be allowed to gather necessary information about the possible effects of the proposed policy; and that, during the balance of the session, explicit statements on the matter would be discouraged. Finally, he requested that the Duke and the Chancellor, as the ranking tariff sceptics, should confine themselves in public to expressions of doubt about the practicality of the policy and assure their friends that their minds remained open. In the meantime, the inquiry under the direction of his brother Gerald, at the Board of Trade, would go about its fact-gathering, and Balfour would formulate a longer-term strategy.[106]

Balfour's tactics carried great danger, not all of it created by his feuding fellow ministers. Many Unionists wondered exactly what their party policy was to be – what, after all, were party leaders for? He also risked losing the loyalty of backbenchers on either side of the question whose opinions were as strong as those of their leaders. Lord Hugh Cecil and his 'Hughligan' compatriots did not fear their own front bench – most were staunch Free Traders, several would cross the floor, and two, J. E. B. Seely and Winston Churchill – eventually would become Liberal ministers. Vehemence came quite naturally to 'Linky' Cecil. 'If we have to turn Arthur out,' he wrote to Winston Churchill, 'I want him & his friends to understand that I do it on purely public grounds – just as I should have sent him to the stake in an earlier age!'[107] Balfour somehow managed not to lose his patience with his young friends, writing to Lord Hugh in July 1903:

> I heard you have been using rather violent language about me in the Lobby: but as I know you easily get your nerves 'on edge' under the stress of controversy, I did not mind . . .
>
> The more serious mistake in which I think you have fallen is that of supposing that the Unionist party were put into office for the purpose of preserving, in every particular, a version of Free Trade doctrine which, as an economist, I, at all events, have never accepted. From this theory of our political obligations I must explicitly dissent.[108]

During the few remaining weeks of the parliamentary session he gathered information of his own, relying not on the Treasury, which he considered hostile to fiscal reform, but on Gerald's Board of Trade and on sympathetic 'imperialist' economists such as Percy Ashley.[109] He retreated to Scotland to prepare his own scheme, which was in Devonshire's hands by 30 July.[110] He also leaked copies of his plan to friendly journalists Iwan-Müller and Charles Cooper of *The Scotsman*.[111] A week later he circulated a paper to the Cabinet, in advance of their final meeting of the session, scheduled for 13 August 1903.

The Cabinet actually received two documents: one (essentially what Devonshire had received) was a lengthy argument in favour of retaliatory tariffs titled 'Economic Notes on Insular Free Trade'.[112] Though the longer of the two papers, it was the simpler, calling for what Balfour argued was true freedom of trade in which Britain was not forced to compete in protected markets while its own was entirely open to all comers. No case was made for general protection, nor was there any argument in favour of imperial preference.

The second, untitled, memorandum of little more than four pages became known as the 'Blue Paper', from the pale colour of the paper on which it was printed.[113] It was cast as a kind of introduction to 'Economic Notes', but in reality it introduced several other ideas into play, thus alarming the Cabinet's Free Trade faction. 'If', Balfour wrote, 'a tax put on for other purposes – say, to discourage "dumping" or to encourage a closer union with our Colonies – has incidently some relatively insignificant Protective effect, it need not on that account be necessarily barred.' He went on to note that there was much sympathy for protection among the working classes, and it had, 'as an abstract theory, *few* energetic enemies'. If done with care, he was confident that a 'readjustment' of fiscal policy to make Britain more competitive would be 'neither impossible nor even difficult'; and that 'two methods of obtaining freer trade for this island are contemplated, namely, "preference" and what has been very infelicitously described (by myself among others) as "retaliation".' The Blue Paper was more speculative and very general, and, depending on the ideological baggage the reader brought with him, could be interpreted as an endorsement of the mildly retaliationist 'Economic Notes' or as a first step towards protection, including duties on imported foodstuffs. Not surprisingly, the wary Unionist Free Traders took the latter view.

Devonshire voiced his fears in a memo of his own, which raised the key issue behind Free Trade anxieties: of the two possibilities, imperial preference and retaliation, could the first, he wrote, be achieved without 'some' food taxes, and the second without 'some' duties on manufactured goods? How far was the Prime Minister recommending that his government go; and were they not in danger of leading the country into a full-scale protectionist system? What was the purpose of the Board of Trade inquiry – and what, His Grace seemed to be saying, was the hurry?[114] These concerns were only heightened by the Blue Paper. The Cabinet meeting of 13 August reflected this and, predictably, was a fractious affair. Balfour and the Duke agreed afterwards that all sides should take time for consideration and declared a one-month moratorium before the Cabinet would again take up the subject: 'What say you', he wrote to Devonshire, 'to 14 Sept.?'[115] The Duke said, 'Yes.'

The angry Free Traders – Ritchie, Sir Edward Hamilton and Balfour of Burleigh – directed their fire at what they saw as the Chamberlainite Blue

Paper, which they believed would open the door to food duties. They looked to the much trusted Devonshire to lead them. But, while the Duke knew he was not a protectionist, he was not at all sure that he was as doctrinaire a Free Trader as were they. He was still confused by what he was sure were the different approaches of 'Economic Notes' and the Blue Paper. Like Balfour, he wanted time to consider, time for the Prime Minister to work some kind of acceptable compromise with adequate safeguards against 'whole-hog' protection, and time to find an escape from the role of Cabinet-breaker into which his friends seemed to be pushing him. Fortified with information assiduously gathered by Sandars, the Prime Minister was certain that the three doctrinaire Free Traders could not be reconciled, so he concentrated his efforts on keeping the Chamberlainites quiet and holding tight to Devonshire. In this way he hoped to steady and preserve his government.

The crucial question that Balfour was avoiding was this: Was he willing, like Chamberlain, to accept duties on imported foodstuffs as part of fiscal reform? At this point, because of what he rightly sensed was the danger to his government of a party flirting with schism, he employed every wile to avoid being forced to give a direct answer. However, he had spoken openly in favour of imperial unity through colonial preference, and had supported the abortive 1902 corn duty. To Austen Chamberlain he indicated that he was 'not going to pretend that I have any objection in principle to a shilling or two shilling tax on corn or on beef or on anything else'.[116] Arthur Elliot, the anti-tariff Financial Secretary to the Treasury, noted in his journal that Gerald Balfour had told him that his brother had admitted to the horrified Ritchie that he was prepared to accept a small duty on foodstuffs in order to implement some degree of colonial preference.[117]

Perhaps this was not enough testimony on which to 'hang a cat', but it was enough to suggest that, in order to increase revenue without adding to an income tax he judged already at its limits, to increase Britain's competitiveness with its tariff-girded commercial rivals, and to foster imperial unity, Balfour meant that the speculations in the Blue Paper should be given serious consideration. In the end, however, all this was set aside and even denied by the Prime Minister. His reason was that he concluded that the political climate of the autumn of 1903 made calm debate impossible, and this became clear to him in the month between the distribution of the documents and the crucial Cabinet meeting of 14 September. He decided that the best course was to keep his conclusion to himself for fear, on the one hand, of putting himself in the hands of the Tariff Reformers and risking an election fought on a 'whole-hog' tariff programme, or, on the other, of binding himself to the Free Traders and driving Chamberlain and his followers into open opposition. His political bête noire was Sir Robert Peel, whose conversion to Free Trade in 1846 had broken the Tory Party over an economic principle he believed more important than party unity. Balfour would risk much to avoid such a step. It is also true that he had always resisted what he considered dogmatic positions. He said once to Chamberlain while this battle raged, 'I know people accuse me of hair-splitting and finessing, but I can't help it if they do. My mind works that way. To me the differences are real and substantial.'[118] Therefore he chose for the time being to play the sphinx – a decision which he realized carried much risk.

Devonshire's mind worked differently, and the anxious Duke wrote to Balfour in late August calling for a set of 'definite proposals' to place before the Cabinet, and an 'open discussion' in Parliament, albeit without a binding resolution.[119] This letter crossed another of prodigious length in which Balfour argued that the proposals of 'Economic Notes' and the Blue Paper were meant to open the subject of fiscal reform and were offered under the assumption that, given the initial approval of the corn duties in November 1902, the Cabinet had already abandoned the old orthodoxy of the Cobden Club. He implored the Duke to strive with him to prevent the debate from falling into the hands of extremists of both sides. Finally, he reminded him that to fail ensured that the governance of the nation would come under the control of the Radicals sooner rather than later.[120] In fact the many pages of the letter seem to have left the Duke even more troubled than he had been. Two days later Balfour rushed another letter to Devonshire imploring him further not to become entrapped by pledges to Ritchie, Balfour of Burleigh and Hamilton, for this 'would be having a Cabinet within a Cabinet with a vengeance'.[121]

The Prime Minister was right to be concerned, for the Free Traders were relentless in their efforts to pressure the Duke into leading the Free Trade faction. The former Chancellor Goschen also dipped his oar into the water and advised the Lord President, 'We shall have to *make* him speak, if he shows any sign of hesitation . . . Devonshire's cautious common sense is scarcely a match for Chamberlain's unscrupulous enthusiasm.'[122] Meanwhile, the Chamberlainite campaign was rapidly coming together, with broad support in the Unionist press to beat the drum for Tariff Reform.

In the midst of this fractious debate, Balfour and his family suffered a great loss when Lord Salisbury died on 22 August, 1903.[123] For many Britons – certainly for loyal Unionists – 'Old Sarum' was nearly as iconic a figure as Victoria herself, and like her he now seemed to belong to another time. The sad event came at a time when Balfour's relations with his Cecil cousins were much strained because of the fiscal controversy. But blood was thicker than the water of politics, and he was welcomed to the old statesman's deathbed to take his leave of the man who had been not only a beloved uncle but his political mentor. He wrote to Lady Elcho a few days later that the great man 'peacefully breathed his last with all his children . . . and myself whom he had ever treated as one of his children, round him'.[124]

Much of Salisbury's life had been devoted to his party, and perhaps he would have been pleased that even in death he could perform one final service for the Unionists: a week later, Balfour and Chamberlain came together at Westminster Abbey at the memorial service for the late Prime Minister and discussed a strategy to extricate the Cabinet from the crisis. Chamberlain laid out his proposal in a letter on 9 September: he offered to resign to support the government from outside and lead the Tariff Reform propaganda campaign, thereby easing Devonshire's anxieties and allowing him to remain in office. In this case, the possible loss of the other ministers would be far less significant; Balfour could carry on with a reshuffled Cabinet, while Chamberlain would be free to devote himself to making his tariff case to the nation.[125] Balfour wrote to Selborne that it was as good a deal as he was likely to get. Besides, he might lose them all: Devonshire still might go, as his friends most certainly would, and the way would be clear for a moderate retaliatory-tariff proposal. Furthermore, if he graciously allowed the Ritchie–Hamilton–Balfour of Burleigh right wing of the government to take flight, 'it is not so certain that we should not do better without the [Chamberlainite] left wing also.'[126] Perhaps, the Prime Minister reasoned, a thorough house-cleaning might have to be faced.

Balfour's surmise seemed to be correct, as the Duke – much pressured by the Free Traders – had more or less decided by the eve of the 14 September Cabinet meeting to resign. Balfour wished to rid himself of the Ritchie–Hamilton–Balfour of Burleigh faction and keep Devonshire, but he did not yet divulge Chamberlain's offer to the Duke, thereby making certain that the information was not leaked to the three Free Traders, giving them an excuse not to resign. An hour before the meeting, Balfour, his brother Gerald and Chamberlain met privately and agreed that the Colonial Secretary should proceed with his resignation. Once in the Cabinet room, the Prime Minister announced to his colleagues that tariff policy was no longer an 'open question' and insisted on their agreement that the time had come for 'fiscal reform'. Accordingly, he added that, on the basis of their public objections, Ritchie and Balfour of Burleigh must retire from the Cabinet – he had 'never heard anything more summary and decisive' was Devonshire's reaction.[127] Chamberlain reiterated his support for complete imperial preference and merely implied that anything short of this would lead to his resignation. Yet neither he nor Balfour mentioned that he had already resolved to resign, while the 'resignations' of Ritchie and Balfour of Burleigh (as Balfour expected, Hamilton and Elliot followed suit a day later) were immediately accepted.[128]

Despite what must to the assembled ministers have been a breathtaking 'summary and decisive' stroke, Balfour still refused to offer up the detailed fiscal plan that Devonshire had requested of him: the Prime Minister demanded his colleagues' acquiescence only to a general resolution in favour of the need for fiscal reform.[129] Balfour was prepared to gamble that this tactic would hold the majority of his Cabinet (including, he hoped, the Duke) and drive out the zealots of both sides until he was ready to announce his own position. In preparation for this, he had charged Acland-Hood with confidentially measuring party opinion in the constituencies on the fiscal question, and this was done by mid-August. The Chief Whip reported that there was much feeling in favour of retaliatory tariffs ('every man is a protectionist of his own industry') and less for colonial preference; food duties were unpopular in the towns, and met with only partial approval in agricultural districts. However, the Chief Whip concluded that, while a policy of retaliation might prove popular, for the foreseeable future food duties would probably lead to electoral disaster.[130] On the envelope which held this document, Sandars minuted, 'It was this report that probably decided the P.M.'s attitude at the Cabinet on Sept 13 [sic.] 1903.'[131]

It was difficult for the Prime Minister to disagree with this analysis, and in the month that followed receipt of the report, Balfour's policy was revealed. He pledged to the King that he would 'do his best to steer between the opposite dangers of making proposals so far reaching . . . *that the people of this country could not be expected to acquiesce in them* – and . . . of ignoring, in a spirit of blind optimism, the signals which indicate approaching perils to our foreign and to our colonial trade'.[132] Now it appeared that the only way to achieve this would be to suspend any effort towards imperial preference until Chamberlain's campaign had been put to the test: for the time being, the government's policy would be limited to tariff retaliation as outlined in 'Economic Notes on Insular Free Trade'.[133] Balfour would not make this public, however, until he had made every effort to retain the allegiance of the Duke.

The struggle for Devonshire's soul intensified: Balfour confided to him alone after the 14 September Cabinet that Chamberlain definitely would resign to conduct his propaganda campaign, while continuing to support the government. Then he called on Devonshire on the following day and pressed him further to remain in the Cabinet. The troubled Duke was still unsure and, after meeting with the sacked Free Trade ministers, he sent in his resignation that evening.[134] Balfour went again to Devonshire's Mayfair mansion on 16 September, and this time, with the other resignations safely in hand, finally read to him Chamberlain's formal resignation letter – which he said had now been accepted. The relieved Duke reconsidered, withdrew his own resignation, and appealed – fruitlessly, of course – to the Prime Minister to welcome back the other resigning ministers.[135] It appeared, therefore, that Balfour had survived the immediate danger caused by the right and left wings of dissent, and he had also held Devonshire, thus depriving any Unionist Free Trade revolt of its greatest possible figurehead.

The Cabinet Free Traders, supported by Goschen and Hicks Beach, simply increased their pressure on the unfortunate Duke. Their cause apparently was aided by the ambitious Duchess, who hoped that the result of his resignation might at last propel her husband into the premiership.[136] Letters poured in on him from the ex-ministers, convinced still that Balfour and Chamberlain were engaged in a plot to bring in general protection – the vaunted whole hog. When Chamberlain's letter of resignation and Balfour's reply (which revealed that Chamberlain's son Austen would take Ritchie's place as Chancellor) were published on 18 September, the ex-ministers saw them as thinly cloaked evidence of collusion. Devonshire's discomfort increased, though he was able to joke to Sandars that as a result of the imbroglio 'he supposed his plumage would be rather ruffled, but that he could survive it.'[137]

Balfour, still hopeful that Devonshire was 'safe', went off to Balmoral to attend upon the troubled King, who was much annoyed that he seemed once again to be the last to know what was taking place within his government. Meanwhile, the Duke, stung by his former colleagues' implications of disloyalty, pleaded for peace while he awaited the Prime Minister's speech before the National Union in Sheffield on 1 October. Balfour knew that each word would be assiduously weighed, so this address, contrary to his usual practice, was carefully crafted. Before an enormous audience, he described the abandonment of protection as 'appropriate and indeed necessary' in 1846, but, he said, times had changed. He declared the independence of his party from the 'Cobdenite' past that dreamed of 'prophecies that have been falsified'. The new economic world was irretrievably riven with barriers to trade, and Free Trade Britain faced a 'wall of hostile tariffs growing up', even including those within the Empire itself. On such a system he blamed the development of the monopolistic trusts in Europe and America which threatened to strangle British trade, endanger capital, and place 'the heaviest weight upon the artizan [*sic*.] and labour classes of this country'.[138]

His duty as leader of the governing party, he insisted, was not to 'paint an imaginary picture of the blessings to follow from any remedy which I have to propose'. Neither the manufacturing nations nor the self-governing colonies could be made to surrender their tariffs. 'My answer, I am afraid, will be a disappointing one. I know of no cure, but I do know a palliative.' His 'request' was 'that the people of this country should give the Government of this country . . . that freedom of negotiation of which we have been deprived, not by force of circumstances, not by the action of overmastering forces, not by the pressure of foreign Powers, but by something which I can only describe as our own pedantry and self-conceit'.

As Britain needed a navy to protect its shores, he argued, it needed the power of tariff retaliation in order to negotiate trade agreements which allowed fair competition. Such power was necessary lest its prosperity winnow away, and with it its Empire, as the self-governing colonies were drawn into the economic spheres of other trading partners. Given the uneasiness that he knew existed in the Cabinet and the nation, he reiterated his belief that general protection was neither desirable nor necessary at the moment, 'because I believe the country will not tolerate a tax upon food'. Yet there could be no doubt about his direction. Did he mean to 'alter fundamentally' the fiscal tradition established since 1846? 'Yes,' he answered, 'I do.' All this, of course, was already known to those who had read 'Economic Notes on Insular Free Trade'.

The speech seemed to be well received by an audience sympathetic to fiscal reform and to their leader. He wrote to an influential backbencher that he realized that the fiscal question had the potential to split the Unionist Party – the very opposite of what he wished. However, if an election were held that day, he declared, these would be the views on which he would stand. 'But', he added, 'I have neither the desire, nor the power, to reduce the views of every Member of the Party to a particular shape, although that shape be the one which, in the present temper of public opinion, seems to me most likely to serve the interests of the country.'[139]

After Sheffield, however, Balfour's painstaking plan to excise only the most troublesome elements of his Cabinet soon began to fall apart, for the next morning brought a telegram from the Duke announcing that he must resign after all. In a letter which followed, Devonshire explained that the Sheffield speech went beyond their discussions and had made his position impossible. However, Lord Stanley, son-in-law of the Duchess and the future Earl of Derby, told Sandars that he had seen Devonshire on the day of Balfour's speech, that he had already drafted a letter of resignation, and that 'the Sheffield speech had nothing whatever to do with the ultimate decision.'[140] The reason, 'Eddy' Stanley was certain, was simply a trouble-some conscience: a gentleman of the old school, Devonshire could not bear the accusations of Ritchie and his friends that he was abandoning them and their cause. The old Whig did fear any strides towards protection, but perhaps Sheffield merely provided an excuse for an exit from circum-stances that had become distasteful.[141]

This disappointment broke Balfour's customary serenity. He was furious, and fired off to the Duke a letter, in his own description, 'distinctly acid in tone' to tell him so.[142] 'If any other man in the world but yourself', he wrote, 'had expended so much inquisitorial subtlety in detecting imaginary heresies I should have surmised that he was more anxious to pick a quar-rel than particular as to the sufficiency of its occasion.'[143] 'Pitiable' was the word he chose to describe the Duke's actions to the King:

> Nor is it possible to excuse, or even to understand, his vacillations without remembering that he without doubt put himself somehow in the power of Mr Ritchie and his friends. He is forced to behave badly to me lest he should be publicly taxed for behaving badly to them. – His loss administra-tively is nothing . . . Mr Balfour's confidence that he can successfully carry on the Government is in no way shaken by the Duke's defection.'[144]

He soon regained his humour, writing to Walter Long a day later, 'That silly old duke! Fancy him resigning after all!!!'[145]

Even before leaving Sheffield, Balfour attempted to minimize the divi-sive effect of the ministerial resignations. At a lunch speech on 2 October he showered praise on the Free Traders, whose exit he announced had 'in no substantial sense divided the party', and who were 'sincerely devoted to the fortunes of the great party for which they have done such admirable service'. On the other side of the dispute he singled out Chamberlain for special tribute, calling him the 'greatest Colonial Minister which this coun-try has seen . . . [whose place] none could fill'.[146] While such generous words might have helped to mend a minor rift, they had little effect on the fissure that was opening within his party. Four years previously he had written to his sister-in-law Lady Frances of the strong feelings that could surface in politics:

> What I do resent, and what I think myself perfectly justified in resenting, is being treated by one's friends as if they were one's enemies. Differences of opinion there must be in any Party. Sometimes, though by no means always, when they exist they ought to be expressed, but they should never be expressed with the accompaniment of imputations either on character or motives. Such a course does infinite mischief to a party. And, in my opinion, is inconsistent with party loyalty.[147]

The two years of life that remained to his administration did not alter those sentiments, and the Unionist Party was certainly in for 'infinite mischief'. But the press of governmental business was great, and Balfour's first duty was the reconstruction of his Cabinet. He did not have an easy time filling the vacant places: in addition to settling the War and India offices, he strove to secure the services of Milner in place of Chamberlain, but the proconsul declined. The Colonial Office went instead to Alfred Lyttelton on Milner's recommendation.[148] Devonshire's place as Lord President was taken by Lord Londonderry, and Balfour's cousin James ('Jem') Cecil, now the 4th Marquess of Salisbury, replaced Londonderry as Lord Privy Seal (despite more 'Hotel Cecil' sneers).[149] Graham Murray became Scottish Secretary in succession to Balfour of Burleigh, and Devonshire's nephew and heir, Victor Cavendish (Financial Secretary to the Treasury), and son-in-law, Lord Stanley (Postmaster General), were given non-Cabinet posts. The grandest promotion of all went to the new Chancellor, thirty-nine-year-old Austen Chamberlain, who, despite his growing reputation, was seen by many as little more than his father's agent – or Balfour's hostage – in the government camp. All regarded the revised Cabinet as weaker than the old team, which it was in experience and certainly in debating strength. The King was not particularly happy with the changes, and Lord Esher – who, as usual, had refused to serve – noted ungenerously that 'the method of giving places in this Government is wholly irresponsible. The names might as well be taken out of a hat!'[150] They certainly were not, but the criticism stuck.

Balfour wasted no time in reminding his colleagues of the danger inherent in the tariff controversy, circulating a memorandum advising that the programme to which his administration was now committed was that enunciated at Sheffield: retaliatory tariffs, but neither a general protection of industry nor food taxes. He acknowledged that differences existed among Unionists and that 'these are pious opinions, which may be legitimately entertained by Members of the Administration'. He was amenable to ministers expressing their own opinions regarding food duties, so long as they adhered *at the present* to the Sheffield Programme that he expected to place before the electorate. He thought the government's position a strong one, he said, but warned, 'All these advantages will be compromised if we expend our chief energies in defending or attacking some *other* position to which, as individuals, we attach importance, in developing or refuting theories not relevant to any immediate issue.'[151]

The gravest danger to his government, however, no longer emanated from within the Cabinet. Soon after his resignation, the reluctant Devonshire found himself conscripted into the presidency of the Unionist Free Food League. Far more potential was obvious in the new Tariff Reform League, from the outset a much larger, richer and more energetic organization, with a far greater following at constituency level. Though the Duke of Sutherland became chairman, with the newspaper proprietor Arthur Pearson as president, the heart and mind of the League was Joe Chamberlain. Though ostensibly extra-party organizations, the two leagues waged their propaganda campaigns to influence the government. Most of the battles were won by the Tariff Reformers, whose numbers and influence swelled, while the Free Food Unionists were unable to rival them in the size of their membership or their audience. Remarkably, given what had passed, within a year Chamberlain was appealing to Devonshire for party unity, mourning to the Duke that it appeared that 'war to the knife' had broken out among the opposing sides of Unionism. The former business magnate knew that game well, however, and a few days after writing these words he displaced Devonshire as president of the Liberal Unionist Association.[152]

Even before the tariff controversy erupted, Wyndham had warned his cousin Wilfrid Blunt that only loyalty to Balfour kept the younger Unionists from gravitating towards the charismatic Chamberlain.[153] There is no doubt that Chamberlain and Tariff Reform had magnetic appeal to many Unionists, young and old, with the message of imperial unity and national revitalization. But they did not attract all youth and talent, and several of Balfour's younger followers were energized to resist 'Chamberlainism' to the point of rebellion. While his 'Free Fooder' Cecil cousins did not leave the party, some other disapproving anti-tariff young bloods joined Churchill and Seely and did just that – with eleven Unionist MPs crossing the floor by the January 1906 election.[154]

Balfour's position between the two battling sides was difficult enough, but there was also the emboldened Opposition to deal with. Campbell-Bannerman, whom Balfour and many other Unionists were often guilty of underrating, saw the opportunity that lay before his Liberals when

Chamberlain thrust tariffs into the limelight: 'All the old warhorses about me . . . are snorting with excitement,' he wrote to a friend. 'We are in for a great time.'[155] The orthodox Free Traders certainly meant to have a 'great time', insisting that Balfour's Sheffield Programme was simply a Tariff Reform Trojan Horse. Sandars noted in February 1904 that it seemed that any man who followed Balfour's retaliation plan and avowed even 'a modicum of sympathy' for considering food duties, while avowing that they lay in some indefinite future, was accused of being a 'protectionist in disguise'. Retaliation, Free Traders insisted, was a ruse, and those who hewed to Balfour's line were in their hearts 'hankering for Joe's scheme which is Protection; [and] for his 10 per cent tariff [;] and [the Chamberlainite] Tariff Commission's operations manifestly point to protection'. Sandars perceptibly concluded that the Opposition had begun successfully to cast the debate simply as that of Free Trade versus Protection, 'and they have labelled your timid followers with the latter designation, and they in their turn hasten to try to tear it off.'[156]

The Unionists were reminded in February 1904 how indispensable the Prime Minister was, for, in the face of a furious Liberal assault during the debate on the King's Speech, Balfour was once again laid low by influenza. Wyndham and Akers-Douglas soldiered on in his place, but the absence was painfully obvious on all sides, as more than twenty Free Trade Unionists voted in favour of the defeated Opposition amendment. Evidence of Balfour's remarkable personal popularity, Henry Lucy noted, was supplied in the enthusiastic (and perhaps relieved) applause that greeted his return on the 25th.[157] But personal regard counted for little in rough-and-tumble politics. While historians have made much of Balfour's difficult position as leader in such dangerous times, his authority over his government remained strong.[158] 'We surely have', he noted in late 1905, 'the most extraordinary Cabinet that this country has ever seen. Every other Cabinet I have known carried on an unending internecine conflict within closed doors, but put a decent face upon it in public. Within our Cabinet room there reigns eternal calm, and it is only on the platform that these regrettable instances occur.'[159] The political situation was worse than this blithe analysis indicated: in the final two years of his ministry the Unionists lost fifteen seats. In these months the struggle to hold his government together and conduct government business eventually proved to be too much for even so seasoned a leader as he.

The Prime Minister clung fast to his contention that his differences with the Tariff Reformers were not so great as they thought, but, given the passions that the great question excited, the Chamberlainites remained unconvinced. He wrote to Austen Chamberlain in late 1904 that, from his own perspective, any disagreement he had with them was minor: they agreed so closely, he insisted, and 'one difference that seems to divide us obtains an undue prominence.' This, of course, concerned general preference and food duties, and Balfour argued at length that the matter depended not only on British party politics but on US–Canadian relations, the development of the Australasian economy, and defence requirements, as well as the willingness of the colonies to participate in a system of imperial preference. 'All of these considerations', he insisted, 'point to the extreme desirability of having a full and free discussion with our colonies on the present position and future organization of the Empire.' For the moment, however, the party must remain united behind the Sheffield speech and leave protection where it was: an idea 'largely held in the party but with no place in its official creed'.[160] The Chancellor remained unconvinced: 'I am afraid', he lamented, 'that the difference in our points of view is greater than I had thought or that you supposed.'[161] Undeterred, Balfour responded by insisting that he saw their differences as 'neither so great nor irreconcilable as you suppose. Time will shew it.'[162]

In fact time did not, despite Balfour's efforts. He attempted another compromise in a major speech at Edinburgh on 3 October 1904.[163] He reiterated the points of his Sheffield Programme of tariff retaliation, adding that 'I still believe that they are consistent with the most scientific teaching of political economy, as well as with the instincts of practical statesmanship.'[164] To them he now grafted the innovation that, following the next election, a conference with the self-governing colonies and India should be held to hammer out an acceptable plan for imperial preference:

> My view, therefore, is that the policy of this party should be, if we come into power after the next election, to ask the colonies to join in a conference on those lines – a conference whose discussions shall be free, but whose conclusions shall not commit any large plan of Imperial union on fiscal lines or other lines unless their various electorates have given their adhesion to the scheme.

The same held true, he indicated, for Britain. Therefore his new plan was to fight and win the rapidly approaching election behind the Sheffield Programme of retaliation. Then, imperial preference, including the inevitable food duties, would be implemented only after endorsement by the colonies and by the British electorate in a second victorious election.

While he spoke of the 'high and disinterested patriotism' necessary to achieve agreement, his complicated plan only irritated the Tariff Reformers. Joseph Chamberlain attacked two days later in a speech at Luton, calling the Edinburgh plan 'a great advance in the programme of the Unionist party', but then he insisted that all the elections would render the plan useless. Sandars wrote hopefully that it might be possible to induce the Tariff Reformers to accept the new plan, though Devonshire, titular leader of the Free Fooders, remained in a state of 'profound suspicion'.[165] In fact he was wrong on all counts – the Tariff Reformers were contemptuous of the Edinburgh plan, and the Duke and his friends were not merely suspicious, they were adamantly opposed to it. The Dogger Bank episode came along just in time to provide Balfour with a riveting non-tariff-related subject for his featured address at the annual party conference soon after this. The crisis provided no more than a brief respite, however, as the Chamberlainites continued to beat their drums for tariffs. They were now openly challenging Unionist Free Food candidates in the constituencies, and they captured control of the National Union. It was obvious that a government with its nominal supporters so divided against themselves had very little future.

Balfour continued throughout the controversy to insist that Tariff Reformers and Free Fooders alike shared in the responsibility for the declining fortunes of their party, as he wrote to his cousin Lord Hugh:

> Just as I think Chamberlain has done much injury to what I believe to be his fundamental objective – Imperial Unity – by his attempts to harness all sorts of particular and selfish interests to his Imperial car; so do I think the free-fooders have also done great injury to free trade by appeals to ignorance and prejudice, and by the exaggerated importance they have given to any objections that may have been made to a re-arrangement of our duties on food.

But, he concluded with typical humour, 'What all this comes down to, however, is perhaps not much more than that I think I have been right, and that everybody else to the right or left of me, has been wrong, – a frame of mind that will cause you no surprise!'[166]

The battle for the middle ground witnessed one last skirmish, as in January 1905 the Liberal John Morley strove to embarrass the premier by offering a reward to any who could define the Prime Minister's fiscal policy on a 'half-sheet of notepaper'. On the premise that one good taunt deserves another, Balfour responded before his own Manchester electors that nothing could be simpler: he wanted true 'freedom of action' in trade through tariff retaliation, closer commercial union with the colonies, an imperial conference devoted to this goal, and, finally, 'I do not desire to raise home prices for the purpose of aiding home production.'[167]

On the imaginary notepaper the dual-election policy was not mentioned, and, when he met Balfour for the first time in months in February, Chamberlain seized on this innovation as the weakness in the Prime Minister's resistance. Joe was not in the best of form: his health was not good, and he was still shaken by the death of his youngest daughter, weeks before. Balfour was friendly but would not budge on food taxes, and he was more certain than ever that the electorate simply would not accept them at the present time.[168] One need only observe the results of recent by-elections, he argued, to be usefully instructed. Sandars worried a few weeks later that the two Unionist leaders were close to the breaking point in their co-operation, yet in the latter weeks of May they were again closeted and appeared to be striving for common ground.[169] Balfour agreed to place Tariff Reform at the centre of the Unionist campaign at the next election, and added that, if the current government survived until after the proposed Colonial Conference, he might give up the two-election pledge.[170] Yet, when revolt among the Unionist Free Fooders seemed imminent, he edged away from the second part of the proposal, though he did announce in the House and in a speech at the Albert Hall the primacy in the Unionist programme of fiscal reform and imperial unity.

Though Balfour manoeuvred the government out of a snap defeat on an Irish bill in July, his administration was running out of time. With the end of the parliamentary session in sight, the major questions that confronted the Cabinet were when and how to leave office. They would not face Parliament again. As the summer waned, the Prime Minister patiently called again for party unity, while Chamberlain chose defiance: at the November meeting of the National Union at Newcastle, Henry Chaplin's strong tariff-reform resolution was carried by a vote of 698 to 2, while a Balfourian amendment endorsing the 'half-sheet of notepaper' garnered only 8 votes.[171] Joe emerged in fighting form once again a week later in a speech in Bristol, declaring his loyalty and admiration for the Prime Minister and then pointing out that success in battle could not come based on the principle that the 'lamest man should govern the march of the army'. It may well be, his biographer has noted, that the insult was meant for 'Linky' Cecil, but much of the audience – and the nation – presumed that it referred to the Prime Minister.[172] Whatever it may have meant, Balfour had had enough and wrote to Chamberlain, 'I find that 10 years of leading the House of Commons has given me an unutterable desire for a change, and I never go upstairs to bed without thanking heaven that, in a very brief period, I shall have left my official residence and gone back to the comfort and repose of my own house!'[173] He resigned office on 4 December 1905.

9

Divided Opposition

RATHER THAN REQUEST a dissolution and an election, Balfour chose to ignore established constitutional practice and force the Liberals to form a government in December 1905. With his government in disarray and his party rowing over Tariff Reform, while accusations of 'clinging to office' were hurled at them by the Opposition and the press, many wondered why he had waited this long. Certainly he did mean to ensure that completion of the army's new model field and horse artillery (not popular with the Liberals) was well under way.[1] There were also significant foreign-policy matters in which Balfour took a proprietary interest, including the renewal of the Japanese treaty in August and the fallout from the Russo-Japanese War. Closer to home, March had brought the German-inspired 1905 Moroccan Crisis, leading to the Algeciras Conference in the following January. All these have correctly received attention from historians, but also on Balfour's mind was his distrust of what he believed to be a Liberal Party under the sway of its Radical wing. He outlined to Devonshire in October 1905 what contemporary Liberalism meant to him: increased direct taxation, the diminution of military strength, payment of Members of Parliament, disestablishment of the Welsh Church and, not least, Home Rule.[2] He might well have added that his concern for the future of the infant Committee of Imperial Defence under a Radical government was so great that he had already met at Balmoral with the King, Esher, Knollys and Haldane to ensure the Committee's survival.[3] While he thought well of the Liberal Imperialists Asquith and Grey, and certainly his regard for his friend Haldane was high, he feared that the left wing of their party would dominate a Campbell-Bannerman administration.

Like most Unionists, he underrated the bluff Glaswegian 'C.B.' ('No parody . . .' he said, 'can exceed the reality'), considering him no more than a 'mere cork, dancing on a torrent which he cannot control'.[4] The Liberal chief, the regular target of his more agile antagonist's stinging strikes in debate, was immune to Balfour's charm, finding him and his policies 'immoral, dishonest & contemptible'.[5] After the matter had lain dormant among Liberals for a decade, Balfour was alarmed when, in November 1905, C.B. seemed to raise the contentious matter of Irish Home Rule in a rather ambiguous speech. His commitment to an unspecified 'great advance on the Irish question' was enough to rouse the ex-leader Lord Rosebery, who promptly denounced his successor for thus endangering Liberal unity.[6] At this same time, Balfour reasoned to the Cabinet that arguments against resignation were dissolving, and that it must come soon. Reading of the Rosebery–Campbell-Bannerman squabble, he hoped that the Liberals might again fall to quarrelling, prove unable to form a credible government, and foul their opportunity. With few other choices and with time running out, it was as good a reason as any for resignation.

In the end, Balfour's hopes for Liberal division came to nothing. Resignation day was 4 December, and Campbell-Bannerman immediately assembled a strong Cabinet representing all the Liberal factions. The election was set to begin on 12 January, and, while no Unionist expected victory, few anticipated the disaster that swept over them. The tariff question dominated the contest, and the Liberals made a thorough job of tarring the Unionists with the brush of 'dear food', which seemed to impress more voters than did 'Tariff Reform means work for all.' The Unionists also suffered from another miscalculation, which had first gained notoriety two years before, when in late 1903 Lord Milner had approved the importation of Chinese workers into South Africa to supplement the insufficient supply of unskilled mining labour.[7] Brought in on short-term contracts, the labourers were barred from bringing their families and were housed in wretched barracks, under the watchful eyes of overseers. The Opposition attacked the policy both as inhumane to the 'coolies' and as threatening to the prospects of British labour; but interest eventually died away. Then, in an appalling error of judgement in 1905, Milner authorized the use of corporal punishment to control the Chinese, and 'Chinese slavery on the Rand' became a lurid element of the Liberal electoral campaign. Balfour was aghast at Milner's 'amazing blunder', and referred privately to its 'inexplicable illegality . . . which seems to violate every canon of international morality.' He promptly saw to it that Selborne, Milner's successor as high commissioner, put a stop to it, but the political damage had been done.[8]

Manchester polled early, and Balfour lost the seat – the only prime minister of modern times to do so – he had held for twenty years to the Liberal Thomas Horridge, who was destined to hold it only until the next election. Balfour continued the fight until the end, campaigning up and down the country, almost always in losing efforts.[9] Many Unionist front-benchers were beaten, Brodrick, Lyttelton and Bonar Law among them. Both Cecil brothers were defeated, as was Gerald Balfour, who soon abandoned politics to devote his energies to scholarship and psychical research. The final results were staggering: the Unionists won only 157 seats to the Liberals' 400, while the Irish Nationalists held the usual 83, and the infant Labour Party surprisingly captured 30. It was the greatest single-party victory in history, and a stunning defeat for the Unionists. After the ghastly results began to pour in, Lady Salisbury wrote to Balfour with eloquent simplicity what must have been felt in many a Unionist heart: 'D—n, D—n, D—n!!'[10]

Balfour had not expected such annihilation, and his thoughts on the magnitude of the defeat were dark but insightful. After observing first hand the growth of broad-based working-class political consciousness, and the more ominous rise of what he saw as the foreign threat of socialism, he insisted to Austen Chamberlain:

> We are dealing with forces not called into being by any of the subjects about which parties have been recently squabbling, but rather due to a general movement of which we see the more violent manifestations in Continental politics . . . I am profoundly interested in this new development, which will end, I think, in the breakup of the Liberal Party, and, perhaps, in other things even more important.[11]

This uncharacteristically dramatic sentiment was meant in part to make it clear that the ex-premier did not intend to attach the blame for the defeat to Tariff Reform. But Balfour was deeply apprehensive about the rise of what seemed to him to be a 'for us alone, by us alone' party claiming sole responsibility to speak for the working classes. His prophecy proved true enough, as, despite their great victory, the Liberals would never again single-handedly win an election, and within little more than a decade they would find themselves divided and ruined.

Though defeated and exhausted, the philosophical Balfour had always insisted that life goes on, no matter what the disaster of the moment.[12] Electoral facts were electoral facts, and he fled in February to Whittingehame, where the family had gathered to succour the two conquered Balfour brothers. Mrs Dugdale remembered his arrival on a dark winter night, when she and the rest of the regiment of nieces and nephews rushed to engulf him. 'As the car drew up, children of all ages swarmed upon it like bees, and its door opened, to disclose a huge gramophone trumpet of shining brass. Behind this object . . . was the beaming face of

A.J.B.'[13] 'Nunky' allowed the young Balfours to play the machine whenever they wished – like Queen Victoria, he announced he would have no
depression in his house. Balfour's ability to set aside his political worries
proved a priceless gift in January 1906, but for the leader of a beaten and
divided party, the Scottish idyll could not last.

Balfour was well aware that the majority of his reduced parliamentary
party was made up of enthusiastic Tariff Reformers. Yet he felt certain that
even most of those Chamberlainites who rejected his misgivings about the
whole-hog programme preferred that he remain as party leader. The
cranky Unionist Free Fooders were far fewer in number, but they had
already proved that they could cause a disproportionate amount of difficulty.[14] It would all make leading the party difficult, and Balfour confessed
'some reluctance in remaining leader' in such circumstances.[15] But this
'reluctance' soon passed.

Confident of his own position, Joseph Chamberlain demanded a party
meeting in order to wipe away any ambiguities in the Unionist commitment to Tariff Reform.[16] Balfour always disliked such meetings, and, while
certain of the need for fiscal reform, he believed that Chamberlain's intensity for the whole-hog programme was dangerous – particularly when
displayed before an admiring crowd. Balfour wrote to Lord Cawdor in
February:

> The difficulty arises not from a wanton ambition on the part of Joe, but from
> his absolute concentration upon one idea. He desires that the party at the
> end of this Parliament should find itself absolutely united, not merely on the
> broad question of Fiscal Reform, but on Fiscal Reform as he individually
> conceives it, and he desires nothing else. For this he would sacrifice all
> other interests, which he regards as mere dust in the balance.[17]

His concerns were well founded. On 2 February, Balfour met with the
two Chamberlains, father and son, and Joe made his position clear: he
wanted the party meeting, with a choice made between his Tariff Reform
and Balfour's more cautious approach – something Balfour bitterly
opposed. If the party rejected his programme, Joe threatened, he might
separate his followers from official Unionism, while Balfour insisted that if
Chamberlain did this the party was sure to 'occupy a position of which it
is difficult to say whether it partakes more of the tragic or comic'.[18]
Realizing that his followers needed to 'blow off steam' after the electoral
catastrophe and hoping to achieve peace among the factions, Balfour summoned a conference of the parliamentary party for 15 February.[19] Balfour
and Chamberlain were soon labouring to find a patch of common ground

on which both could stand; but this was not made easier by the appearance in the press a few days later of an uncompromising Tariff Reform manifesto published over Joe's signature.[20]

In the two days preceding the party meeting, the Balfour brothers and the Chamberlains met with Lansdowne, Akers-Douglas and Acland-Hood. Gerald recalled on 14 February that, working from Chamberlain's draft proposal, 'we fought over again the battle of yesterday, *we* objecting to a revolution, *they* content with nothing short of it.'[21] Hoping to stave off a heated battle in the meeting, Balfour continued to resist Joe's whole-hog ultimatum. The disagreement was resolved, at Austen's suggestion, when it was decided to emphasize in a public exchange of correspondence the ideas on which they did agree. Drafted on the 14th (they appeared in the press on the following day), these became known as the 'Valentine letters'. The basis of their understanding was in Balfour's letter:

> I hold that Fiscal Reform is, and must remain, the first constructive work of the Unionist Party.
>
> That the objects of such reform are to secure more equal terms of competition for British trade, and closer commercial union with the Colonies.
>
> That, while at present unnecessary to prescribe the exact methods by which these objects are to be attained, and inexpedient to permit differences of opinion as to those methods to divide the Party, though other means may be possible, the establishment of a moderate general tariff on manufactured goods, not imposed for the purpose of raising prices or giving artificial protection against legitimate competition, and the imposition of a small duty on foreign corn, are not in principle objectionable, and should be adopted if shown to be necessary for the attainment of the ends in view or for the purposes of revenue.[22]

Chamberlain replied, 'I entirely agree with your description of the objects which we both have in view, and gladly accept the policy which you indicate as the wise and desirable one for the Unionist Party to accept.' The language of the letters allowed both leaders to claim a moral victory: the words were largely Chamberlain's, and yet did not violate Balfour's public position.

When, on the 15th, several hundred MPs, unsuccessful candidates and peers crowded the magnificent ballroom of Lansdowne's Berkeley Square mansion – the venue was Chamberlain's suggestion – the result was, if not harmony, at least relief. The Balfourian loyalist Lord Balcarres concluded that, while the publication in the morning papers of the Valentine letters 'deprived the meeting of dramatic interest', they offered hope: 'There is ample time and opportunity to restrict or extend our proposals before we shall be called upon to formulate any precise scheme.'[23] The pro-tariff atmosphere at the meeting was undeniable, and Chamberlain received the most enthusiastic reception, while Balfour's was more subdued. The Free Fooders, when a few spoke, were heard with muted hostility. Yet Balfour's party leadership was unanimously endorsed, even by his sulky cousin Lord Hugh, and Chamberlain was deputized to act for Balfour in the House until his return (to the discomfort of the Free Fooders). An immediate crisis was avoided, and with this Balfour expressed his satisfaction. To Goschen, however, Balfour revealed that his patience was not endless:

> I am very weary of leading a Party which either cannot, or will not, under-
> stand what seems to me to be quite plain statements, and if it were not for
> the fact that to abandon my post now would be little short of desertion, I
> should take my doctor's hard-pressed advice and throw up the leading part
> in what is too pretty to be called 'tragedy' and too dull to deserve the name
> 'comedy'.[24]

This, however, was no time to consider an extended rest.[25] Rather, Balfour secured his return to the House of Commons on 27 February, when he was overwhelmingly elected to the City of London parliamentary seat vacated somewhat reluctantly by a distant cousin, Alban Gibbs.[26] However, he took to his bed nonetheless, for, like Chamberlain, he imme-diately succumbed to an influenza epidemic sweeping through London and could not take his place in the House for several weeks.[27]

His return to the Chamber finally came on 12 March and was greeted with cheers on the Unionist benches. There was more delight when he promptly launched an attack on the government in the polished and sly dialectical style that had long served him so well. The Liberals, many of them new to the House and unfamiliar with such craft, were in no temper for wordplay. A veteran Yorkshire MP, Sir James Kitson, launched a sting-ing counter-assault against the Unionist flirtation with tariffs, and Balfour elicited much laughter when he noted the unprecedented nature of this 'novel Parliamentary operation – a censure of the Opposition'. A day later, when Balfour returned to the attack, an unsmiling Campbell-Bannerman rose and advised him that the game had changed:

> The right hon. Gentleman is like the Bourbons. He has learned nothing. He
> comes back to this new House of Commons with the same airy graces – the
> same subtle dialectics – and the same light and frivolous way of dealing with
> great questions . . . I say enough of this foolery! It might have answered very
> well in the last Parliament, but it is altogether out of place in this Parliament.
> The tone and temper of this Parliament will not permit it. Move your
> amendments and let us get to business.[28]

The government benches erupted with delight, and Balfour was momentarily silenced. The Liberals must have wondered, with such a prime minister leading their unprecedented majority, if perhaps nothing could prevent them from doing whatever they wished, in any way they wished. The new weapon of choice seemed to be the bludgeon and not the rapier; and if this was to characterize the new style, it was not one with which Balfour was either familiar or comfortable. Yet, if he intended to continue leading his wounded party, he would have to fashion a way to fight back in a House of Commons like none he had ever before experienced.

He faced problems other than the massive Liberal majority, for among the Unionists the Valentine letters represented no more than an armistice over the fiscal question. Chamberlainites already dominated the parliamentary party and the National Union, and they appeared to be bent on subjugating Central Office to solidify their ascendancy over Unionism.[29] Fellow-travellers in this quest were the Confederates, a secret league mostly of frustrated younger 'whole-hoggers' who came together at the end of 1906 around the colourful figures of Henry Page Croft and Lord Winterton, taking as their goal the eradication of all opposition to the full Chamberlainite programme – and, if this meant driving out the party leader, then they appeared to be prepared even for that.[30] The Carlton Club itself seemed to have become 'a hotbed of intrigue' between Tariff Reform and Free Trade Unionists.[31]

Though Balfour meant to resist handing over control of the Unionist infrastructure to the ardent whole-hoggers, the awful defeat and consequent disarray in the party made some degree of modernization irresistible. He consented to the creation of a committee to increase co-operation between the National Union and party headquarters, and another to examine the question of party reorganization.[32] The Tariff Reformers were delighted that the Unionist press was sympathetic to their cause and that the Free Fooders had been routed – now perhaps Balfour could be brought to heel or superseded by another, more compatible, leader. Surely, they seemed to believe, the tide was with Chamberlain.

It was not to be – at least not yet – as tragedy intervened. In July, a great public celebration was held in Birmingham to celebrate Chamberlain's seventieth birthday and thirtieth year in Parliament, and of course to exalt the virtues of Tariff Reform. It was a Roman triumph, as an adoring audience cheered him wildly while a colossal 'fire portrait' of their hero floated above them, suspended from a huge hot-air balloon. On the following evening he collapsed after suffering a massive cerebral haemorrhage.

He was left partially paralysed and, in a supremely cruel blow to the great rhetorician, barely able to speak.[33] For such a man, this was death without release.

The Chamberlain family strove to keep the awful truth veiled, and Balfour learned the worst only through Sandars's detective work. The secretary could not confirm until months later that 'Mr C.' suffered from 'severe hemiplegia' and that 'recovery is *very very* doubtful.'[34] Leadership of the Tariff Reform movement devolved on Austen, who – with his eyeglass and orchid buttonhole – looked remarkably like his sire. He also possessed both intelligence and parliamentary skill, but he lacked the intuition and the ruthless predatory instinct that characterized his father.

For the time being, the pressure of the tariff zealots on Balfour was lessened. Their fallen leader had been the hand behind the demands for party reorganization – something Balfour always instinctually distrusted – but, with Chamberlain off the scene and his henchmen temporarily shaken, the party leader could safely sidetrack a genuine overhaul of the outdated party apparatus. Initiatives to combine the separate Conservative and Liberal Unionist organizations died, as did the effort to absorb the Tariff Reform League into the party. Rather than being brought into much needed closer alignment, the National Union and Central Office were allowed to drift even further apart.[35] Balfour's half-hearted efforts, John Ramsden has written, left behind 'a perfect recipe for institutional confusion, overlap and inefficiency', and they did nothing to stem the decline of morale within the divided party.[36]

Unlike the fervent Chamberlainites, Balfour refused to accept the idea that the purpose of the Loyal Opposition was to generate detailed alternative legislative programmes, for such schemes he thought were the duty and the prerogative of the administration of the day.[37] The Opposition, on the other hand, must go about their proper business and *oppose* the government by whatever means the constitution allowed.[38] In the heat of the election campaign and only days after his own defeat, Balfour had thundered to a delighted audience in Nottingham that, whatever the Liberals might concoct, the Unionists 'should still control, whether in power or opposition, the destinies of this great Empire'.[39] This rather ferocious sentiment has, of course, fascinated historians, for language of such truculence from the master of parliamentary subtlety seemed most out of character. What can he have meant? Certainly he was in part 'gingering up' a party whose confidence was already badly shaken, with worse to come. But the politically astute among his listeners understood fully: like Balfour, they knew that the reduced Unionist host in the Commons had powerful allies on the opposite side of the Palace of Westminster. No matter how great the Liberals' electoral victory might be, the Unionist Party held unchallenged control of an Upper House which could stop much of the Liberal legislative agenda in its tracks – if it dared.

Of the 602 peers at that time, at least 475 were Unionists of one stripe or another, while fewer than ninety were Liberals.[40] This imbalance, of course, was not lost on the cautious Lansdowne, who was aware that they must tread carefully:

> The Opposition is lamentably weak in the House of Commons, and enormously powerful in the House of Lords. It is essential that the two wings of the army should work together, and that neither House should take up a line of its own without carefully considering the effects which the adoption of such a line might have upon the other House.[41]

Balfour had been thinking on similar lines: 'There has certainly never been a period in our history', he replied, 'in which the House of Lords will be called upon to play a part at once so important, so delicate, and so difficult.' Yet he conjectured that under Radical pressure the new government would bring in bills in a more extreme form than moderate ministers could accept, and that they willingly would trust to the Lords to modify 'the most outrageous measures'. But he also anticipated that the Radicals would be 'gradually accumulating a case against the Upper House, and that they will be able to appeal at the next election for a mandate to modify its constitution'. If they had such an 'ingenious' plan, he advised, it was one that 'it will be our business to defeat'.

Despite the political risks in employing the Upper House in this way, he saw no way that their lordships could avoid making 'serious modifications' in the extreme legislation that was bound to pass the Commons. If they acted with 'caution and tact', as with the 1893 Home Rule bill, he thought the Lords would emerge from 'the ordeal strengthened rather than weakened by the inevitable difficulties of the next few years'.[42] Lord Lansdowne agreed, and their strategy was settled. Both leaders anticipated that some sort of change in the Upper House was inevitable and favoured a modernized House of Lords, perhaps made up of life peers and representatives chosen by and from the large body of hereditary lords on the principle of 'birth plus acknowledged services'.[43] Exactly how repeated clashes with the Commons majority could strengthen the Lords Balfour left unexplained.

Balfour knew that, after the rejection by the Upper House of the 1893 Home Rule bill, the Unionists had argued that the Lords' actions were vindicated by the Unionist electoral victory fifteen months later. The situation in 1906 was quite different: the new government majority was much greater than Gladstone's had been, and popular sympathy for the aristocratic principle was much less both in the Commons and in the country. Because neither could see any other outcome but surrender, however, Balfour and Lansdowne proceeded with their hazardous policy.

The first meaningful test came in the autumn of 1906 over the Liberals' education bill, passed by the Commons in July, which sought to undo the religious-training provisions of Balfour's 1902 law.[44] The peers ruinously amended the new bill, and a furious Campbell-Bannerman led his massive majority in rejection of the Lords' amendments. This stand-off became a model for the next three years – if Balfour believed that the House of Lords could be an arena of compromise, he seemed to have been much mistaken.

Thus several significant components of the government programme were destroyed in the next parliamentary sessions, including bills to undo past Unionist designs on plural voting, Irish local government and the licensing of public houses. Yet the peers by no means rejected all Liberal legislation, particularly regarding bills dealing directly with what were seen as working-class interests: the most famous example was the 1906 Trades Disputes Act, which overturned the Taff Vale judgement and virtually exempted the trade unions from financial liability in disputes with employers. On Balfour's command the Lords allowed it through – though not before Lansdowne had reminded the small knot of Liberal peers that the bill was not only wrong, but dangerous.[45] The Lords also acquiesced to the Trade Boards Act and the Old Age Pensions Act of 1908. Other examples, such as Lloyd George's Patent and Merchant Shipping bills as well as his pioneering bill creating the Port of London Authority, appealed to 'efficiency' Unionists and were also passed by the peers without difficulty.[46] However, the government could not save a large part of their programme between 1906 and 1908, and they knew whom to blame. The fertile mind of Lloyd George produced a brilliant epigram that made even Balfour smile: though defended as the watchdog of the constitution, what, he roared, was the House of Lords? 'It is the right hon. Gentleman's poodle. It fetches and carries for him. It barks for him. It bites anybody that he sets it on to.'[47]

Campbell-Bannerman rejected calls for an election, as he declined also the suggestion by a Cabinet committee to avoid legislative deadlock by instituting a system of joint meetings of the Commons with representative peers. C.B. preferred to threaten confrontation, and on 24 June 1907 he offered a resolution declaring that 'it is necessary that the power of the other House to alter and reject Bills passed by this House should be so restricted by law as to secure that within the limits of a single Parliament the final decision of the Commons shall prevail.' This was made necessary, he stormed, by the Opposition leader who made use of the Lords as an 'annexe of the Unionist party'. The frustrated Liberals were delighted, and the resolution passed overwhelmingly.[48] As it was, this was among C.B.'s last triumphs, for in April 1908, after suffering a series of heart attacks, he became the only prime minister to die in 10 Downing Street.[49] Leadership of the government passed to H. H. Asquith, the husband of the irrepressible Margot, and the showdown between Lords and Commons was necessarily postponed – though not for long.

Despite the growing cross-party animosity in these years, Balfour and Asquith had long shared a far greater mutual respect than had ever existed between the Unionist leader and Campbell-Bannerman.[50] Not the least important reason was that Asquith, while he did not share Balfour's interest in defence questions, had a far greater sense of the usefulness of the Committee of Imperial Defence, which C.B. had ignored. This led to a remarkable episode: in response to prompting by Lord Roberts in July 1907, Balfour agreed to write to the Committee enquiring if recent German armaments programmes made further consideration of the invasion question necessary.[51] Campbell-Bannerman reluctantly agreed to create a subcommittee of the CID, with Asquith in the chair. In May 1908, Prime Minister Asquith called Balfour to give evidence to a meeting of the full CID. Having been briefed confidentially by Esher, he reiterated his belief that, so long as the navy remained significantly stronger than the German fleet, there was no credible invasion threat. He spoke without notes for more than an hour, Esher told the King, delivering a tour de force 'quite perfect in form and language . . . Not a question was put to him, and this was perhaps the greatest tribute which the members of the Committee could pay to the masterly performance to which they had listened.'[52]

Balfour also took a close interest in Haldane's efforts at reshaping the army, something his own War Secretaries had failed miserably to do. Balfour saw the value of Haldane's plan to designate part of the regular forces for imperial service, and create a British Expeditionary Force, primarily for use abroad.[53] As a second-line force, the Militia was reorganized into a Special Reserve, while the Yeomanry and Volunteers were recast as the Territorial Army. The formidable Militia colonels, who had savaged Brodrick and Arnold-Forster's efforts, were at least as suspicious of Haldane; but the far more adept War Secretary managed to get his plan through Parliament.

Before presenting his 'little Bill' in 1907, Haldane met with Balfour while the two old friends were guests of King Edward.[54] Haldane came right to the point and asked his friend for assistance, and later recalled, '[Balfour] said that as his Unionist government had not succeeded in disposing of the Army problem it was only right that we should have our chance.' More importantly, Haldane continued, 'He knew our difficulties and he got Lord Lansdowne to agree to give us the like chance in the Lords.'[55] Balfour did more than that, as Haldane quietly saw to it that the Leader of the Opposition received classified War Office information, and Balfour discreetly supported passage of the bill.[56]

Despite the suspicions of the anti-militarist Liberals and the many Unionists who – unlike Balfour – actively distrusted Haldane, army reform was at last begun. The navy was another matter. Twentieth-century naval reform had been initiated under Balfour's government, and the welfare of the redoubtable Admiral Lord Fisher and his building programmes remained high priorities with Unionists. Liberals, once again, were divided, with the social reformers begrudging every shilling spent on warships. Furthermore, the field of play among the naval powers was shifting: perhaps it was not so worrying that the United States was building a great navy, but more alarming was the fact that Germany, under the ambitious and unstable Wilhelm II, had served notice with its ambitious naval construction programme that the Reich was determined to have a high-seas fleet second to none.

There had been reductions in the naval budgets of 1906–7, but Campbell-Bannerman had managed to prevent the 'economists' in his party from crippling the 1908 estimates – though even minor reductions displeased Balfour and his party. The Kaiser's personal assurances to Lord Tweedmouth, the Liberal First Lord, that the very idea that his fleet was meant to challenge Britain was 'nonsensical', may have satisfied the credulous baron, but it did nothing to reassure the pro-navy Unionists, and a good many Liberals, as well.[57]

Balfour's confident testimony during the 1908 invasion inquiry was based soundly on the assumption that the superiority of the fleet over all credible rivals would be maintained. A year earlier, he had dragged from a reluctant C.B. a renewed public commitment to the traditional two-power standard.[58] With the invasion inquiry and the apparent challenge of the accelerated German dreadnought-building programme made public in 1907 (and much sensationalized in the press), the Unionists ferociously demanded that the government respond with a shipbuilding programme of its own.[59] In the following spring, Asquith rose to

Balfour's bait and acknowledged in the House that the government would do just that.[60]

The new Prime Minister faced a public and press aroused and anxious over the perceived German threat, a sizeable element of his own party (the 'economists') equally determined on substantial cuts in naval expenditure, and, finally, a skilfully led Opposition united in its belief that naval budgets must be limited only by the size of the German challenge. In March 1908 the Cabinet became embroiled in a battle between navalists and economists in their own party over the naval estimates of the new First Lord, Reginald McKenna, which provided for six new dreadnoughts. His antagonists, led by Lloyd George, now Chancellor, and Churchill (transformed into a Radical) would accept no more than four. As word of German battleship-building captivated Westminster, it was a golden opportunity for Unionists to tar the administration with the brush of being 'soft' on defence. For Unionists, even six ships were not enough, and a re-energized Wyndham coined their battle-cry of 'We want eight, and we won't wait' – over which the Unionist press became almost hysterical.

Balfour's belief in the importance of the navy was real, but he also knew a tactical opportunity when he saw one.[61] Fortified with information supplied by Fisher and Esher, Balfour led the fight for dreadnought-building in the House with all his old skills: for the moment, Unionist internecine squabbles were forgotten.[62] The deadlock broke only in April 1909, with the curious compromise that four battleships (grudgingly accepted by the economists) would be laid down immediately, with the construction of four more to be authorized if needed – and they soon were, exceeding the plan for the original six. Though Esher confidentially assured Sandars that the Cabinet really wanted to 'surrender their virtue' all along, to most Unionists it all felt very much like a victory.[63] Balfour was much praised for his conduct of this campaign, and, as Carson wrote to a friend, he 'seems to be the hero of the hour'.[64]

Commitments to build dreadnoughts were all well and good, Lloyd George warned his colleagues, but now he was expected to devise a plan to pay for them, as well as for the government's ambitious social agenda – including the recently passed old-age-pensions scheme. It was a critical moment for the Liberals, for in recent by-elections they had lost six seats (including Churchill's in Manchester) to Unionists and another four to Labour, as well as their majority on the London County Council. To make matters worse, 1908 brought an economic downturn, which was grist for the Chamberlainite mill and led to a renewed campaign of 'Tariff Reform means work for all!'

It fell to Lloyd George to pay the bills and to recapture the government's political momentum, all within a Free Trade framework. His answer was revealed in his new Budget, and this he presented in an uncharacteristically dull address on 29 April. For five agonizing hours – with a thirty-minute interval graciously suggested by Balfour when the Chancellor's voice failed – he outlined his proposals, and his treatment of taxation, of course, became the centre of controversy. Income tax was to be raised, with a 'supertax' added for annual incomes over £5,000; death duties and stamp taxes were to be put up, as were imposts on luxuries such as alcohol and tobacco; and new duties were to be collected on the sale of petrol and the mandatory licensing of motor vehicles. More controversial were the proposed taxes on the unearned increment of land, to be collected on inheritance or sale, a capital tax to be levied on undeveloped land and minerals, and a reversion duty on benefits enjoyed by a lessor at the retirement of a lease.[65] Finally, he included provisions to revalue landholdings. Needless to say, the entire edifice was constructed on the purest of Free Trade foundations – and if it produced the needed revenue to pay for social reform and defence without import duties, it would destroy the economic justification of Tariff Reform. Landowners – many of them Unionists, of course – immediately concluded that it was a battle plan to do nothing less than destroy their social class.

Lloyd George insisted that his 'People's Budget' was a declaration of war against 'poverty and squalidness', and so at its best it was. But was it also a declaration of war against the Unionists, and bait to tempt Balfour and the Lords to throw it out and challenge the constitution? In his classic *The Strange Death of Liberal England*, George Dangerfield argued persuasively that the Budget offered the Liberals three advantages:

> It invested the whole party with an aura of progress which was badly needed after three none too progressive years in office; it was a loud champion of Free Trade; and it was a wonderful trap to catch the House of Lords in. To humble the House of Lords was the devout, vindictive wish of all good Liberals.[66]

There is no doubt that the Liberal Cabinet very much wished to end Balfour's power to wield the Lords' legislative axe, but there is no evidence to support the contention that Lloyd George was hatching a plot to tempt their lordships to self-destruction. A Budget was a splendid device to advance a sluggish political agenda and wrong-foot the Unionists, but that Lloyd George would risk the future of the government and his ambitious reform plans entirely on such a wager is unlikely.[67] However, if the Lords chose to gamble and destroy the Budget, the Chancellor was quite willing to fight it out in a monumental battle of 'the peers versus the people'. The decision, so Lloyd George insisted, lay with Arthur Balfour.

The parties were quickly galvanized into action. Liberals generally approved of the Budget, many with wild enthusiasm, a few without – while Rosebery again dissented from the sidelines. The Irish Nationalists were suspicious of the possible ill effects on the Irish economy of increased taxes on distilled spirits. All Unionists furiously condemned the Lloyd George plan from top to toe and, in this golden age of leagues and associations, soon had in place a Budget Protest League, led by the perennially indignant Walter Long. 'The City', Neal Blewett has written, 'protested by letters and meetings, wealthy landlords cut subscriptions to charities and football clubs, and threatened to dismiss employees. Several dukes were unwisely vituperative about Lloyd George, his Budget, and his socialist allies.'[68] It might be added also that the press on all sides of the argument worked themselves into paroxysms of hyperbole. The Budget soon made all else in politics seem irrelevant.

Balfour, of course, led the attack against these wicked Budget 'innovations' in the debates that devoured the next six months of parliamentary time: the bill was not, he insisted, meant to enrich those without property, but rather to impoverish those with it. It 'distinguished arbitrarily' among kinds of wealth, and singled out and unfairly punished landowners, brewers and distillers. Steeped in partisan malice, it aimed not to meet fiscal needs but to redistribute the nation's property and thereby drive wealth out of the country. Furthermore, he argued that by incorporating provision for land revaluation within a finance bill it was unconstitutional. It is not difficult to see why the committee stage of the Budget, begun on 21 June, pushed other Commons business aside for forty-two days.[69]

Lord Jenkins, himself a former Chancellor, has suggested that the Unionists' reborn unity and energy were remarkable: 'They talked about everything that could be talked about, and they divided against everything that could be divided against.'[70] So much talk was there, and so many divisions, that Asquith once again amended the standing orders of the House to make it possible to move forward at all.[71] While such harmony within his party was welcome to Balfour, it in no way changed the fact that the Budget would pass through the Commons no matter what the Opposition did. The great question was, What exactly did he plan to do about it?

All wondered, would he recommend that the Lords, for the first time in more than two centuries, veto a Budget duly approved by the Commons?

Lloyd George made this decision somewhat easier on 30 July with the most famous speech of his career – delivered in an East London mission that had once been an alehouse – that was instantly immortalized simply as 'Limehouse'. It was inflammatory, it was theatrical, and it was brilliant: the purpose of his Budget, he insisted, was in part to build the battleships which the rich had demanded, and for which the workers had graciously dropped their pennies in the hat. As for the rich, 'We went round Belgravia, and there never was such a howl.' As for the landlords, he contended, what was unjust about the fact that they profited handsomely and were asked to pay tax on what land was worth when sold? If the Duke of Northumberland sold his acre for £900, 'All we say is this . . . let him pay taxes on £900.' The dukes ('Oh these dukes – how they harass us!') received special and painful attention in generous measure – each was, after all, as costly as two dreadnoughts, and dukes, he insisted, 'last longer'.[72]

Limehouse offended the King and enraged the Unionists; but it did more than that, for in the logical and systematic mind of Arthur Balfour it shifted the debate from details of national expenditure and income to something different. To him, Lloyd George's evening of dazzling invective, with its titillating elements of class antagonism and the redistribution of wealth, showed the direction in which the Radicals meant to go – to Balfour, the Budget was about socialism. Only a week earlier he had told Esher that he thought it 'not unlikely' that the Lords might reject the Budget; after Limehouse, it became very likely indeed.[73] Yet Balfour was not goaded into a policy of rejection in the Upper House by Lloyd George's rhetoric: it was not the case at all that, 'had he been master of events', he would have preferred to let the Budget through.[74] Balfour believed that using protected legislation to effect a fundamental redistribution of national wealth was both unwise and dishonest. Lloyd George's diatribe raised the temperature of the debate for all parties, and if anything it strengthened the unity of Balfour's party. It did not, however, cause Balfour's decision for rejection – it simply made it easier.[75]

The entire Budget episode was a series of risks – the government wagered that Lloyd George could make his radical plan work and breathe life into the flagging administration, and Balfour and his colleagues gambled that the electorate would endorse rejection by the Lords and reward the Unionists with an electoral victory. On 13 August the editor of *The Observer*, J. L. Garvin, dined with Sandars, who revealed that his master had concluded that the Budget had to be stopped and that he had to act to draw his party as closely together as possible: in the electoral campaign to come, the Unionist alternative would be 'Tariff Reform – full steam ahead!'[76] In response to a speech by Asquith, on 24 September Balfour spoke in Birmingham, the heart of Chamberlain country, and made that very case – the destructive Budget must not go forward, and Tariff Reform was the only non-socialist alternative. Austen Chamberlain, now his father's eyes and ears, wrote joyously to his stepmother that Balfour now 'holds that there is "only one policy for us", and thinks that if the Lords did not reject the [finance] Bill, he could not continue to lead the Party'.[77] There was more good news on 28 October, as a Tariff Reformer took yet another Liberal seat in the Bermondsey by-election.

After seventy-three gruelling days, the 'Red Budget' passed from the Commons on 4 November 1909, with a vote of 379 to 140, and the exhausted House rose for three weeks. With Balfour's approval, six days later Lansdowne announced that at the proper time he would move that the peers could not approve such a Budget without its having been sub-mitted 'to the judgement of the country'. On 30 November, therefore, the bill failed its second reading in the Lords by 350 votes to only 75, with Balfour of Burleigh as the only Unionist in support. The *Daily News* had red rockets fired into the London sky; but Lord Knollys saw no reason for celebration, and was certainly not alone when he concluded that 'he thought the Lords mad.'[78]

Asquith secured a dissolution four days later, and began the longest electoral contest in British history – some twenty-six days – on 14 January 1910. The results of the campaign offered hope to the Opposition, if not outright victory: the Liberals won 275 seats – a drop of 125 from the 1906 contest – on a popular vote of 2.88 million, while the Unionists secured 273 seats, gaining 122, with a total vote of 3.1 million. The Irish Nationalists won 82 seats, and Labour 40. This was not far off Acland-Hood's forecast of 300 Unionist seats, though it fell short of Sandars's prediction that the Unionists would 'practically destroy' the government.[79] They certainly destroyed the Liberal single-party majority, and Balfour and Lansdowne agreed that Asquith, now dependent on the Irish, would be forced to resurrect Gladstonian Home Rule and pave the way for a Unionist victory in the next election.[80] However, such sanguine talk did not hide the fact that the political gamble of rejecting the Budget had failed to break the government, as it was meant to do.

In this heated and somewhat confused political atmosphere the sover-eign hoped that the major parties would somehow see the virtue in compromise. He was to be disappointed, as Sandars told him on 14 February that the Unionists looked upon the election as vindication of the Lords, and that Balfour could not be expected to 'volunteer any offer of assistance' on the Budget without a direct appeal from Asquith – who, of course, meant to make no such request.[81] Balfour promptly forwarded a memorandum to King Edward in similar terms.[82] The Unionist leaders – joined by Rosebery – met at Lansdowne House on 3 March to address the future of the Lords. Certain that they understood the handwriting on the wall, Lansdowne, Newton and several other peers had for some while been labouring to produce a design for reform of the Lords into a second chamber suitable for the twentieth century. Balfour showed little enthusiasm for all this, admitting that he preferred things as they were – which he also admitted now seemed increasingly impossible. If the question before them was how to craft an effective second chamber, he observed:

> I don't think you can in our democratic days unless you admit an elective element, and though I at first thought that the elective and non-elective elements would at once clash and the remaining hereditary element be thrust out I have come to the conclusion on reflection that this danger is not as great as I at first thought and that such a house as we are discussing might stand at any rate for fifty years.[83]

No plan resulted, however, and for several weeks Balfour fled the cold weather and the unreformed House of Lords for the sunshine of Cannes. The government secured final passage of the Budget in April, but by that time the Prime Minister had already revealed that he would proceed with a bill to limit the powers of the Lords – and should the peers be so unwise as to interfere, there would be another election, and the government would make absolutely certain that the bill would pass through the Upper House.[84] This amounted to the warning that, if need be, the King would be asked to create enough peers to overwhelm any Unionist majority. Such a threat had defeated the Lords eighty years earlier, and Asquith believed it would certainly beat them now.

In response, a noisy band of Unionists – the Die-hards – came together to demand that Balfour lead an uncompromising resistance to the bill. Predictably, he remained noncommittal. Then, once again, tragedy intervened as King Edward VII died suddenly on 6 May, in his sixty-ninth year. Balfour had not been among his admirers, finding the monarch's intellectual powers (and his conversation) both limited and underdeveloped; yet, by necessity, the two had managed to work together. In a curious way, the late King now performed a last service to his country, for the shock of his sudden death seemed to freeze the constitutional crisis in place.

The new King was the forty-four-year-old George V, a second son (trained as a sailor) and an infinitely more serious and conventional man than his royal sire. Balfour liked his new sovereign and considered him (along with the Kaiser) 'the only royal prince to whom I can talk man to man'.[85] King George soon discovered that he had inherited a constitutional crisis in which the Crown could not avoid playing a role – though he had no idea what that role might be. The reign was only two days old when the dextrous Garvin offered a lead in *The Observer*, calling for a political 'Truce of God' while the nation mourned, and an inter-party conference to seek political compromise before conflict erupted 'on terms of war to the knife'.[86] The idea, which had been talked about informally for some months, aroused enthusiasm among the public, but the Unionist leaders were wary – Balfour certainly had disregarded the old King's wish that he make the government's way the slightest bit easier. Garvin laboured hard to bring them round with appeals to their patriotic desire to spare the new sovereign from being embroiled in the 'fiercest' of partisan fights.

Finally, with nothing better to suggest and seeing some use in again playing for time, in early June Balfour accepted Asquith's proposal for discussions, and a 'constitutional conference' was hastily organized.[87] The forum met more than twenty times from mid-June into July, and then again in October and November 1910. Balfour was joined by Lansdowne, Austen Chamberlain and Lord Cawdor in meeting Asquith and Lloyd George, as well as Lord Crewe, Leader of the House of Lords, and Augustine Birrell, the Irish Secretary.[88] These eight spent many hours managing more or less to agree in broad terms on the virtues of a viable Upper House, a definition of its powers vis-à-vis the Commons, and an acceptable definition of 'constitutional' versus ordinary legislation. They talked much but agreed on little else, and it is difficult to avoid John Grigg's conclusion that the conference was 'an essentially futile exercise, tediously prolonged and more or less doomed to fail'.[89]

While the conference was in recess in late summer, Lloyd George offered up his own startling solution to the deadlock, and it was a characteristic stroke – expansive, adventurous and completely unexpected. As the talks drifted fruitlessly, he produced a brief paper identifying a host of significant questions: housing, national insurance, unemployment and poor-law reform, as well as mandatory military training, imperial reorganization, Home Rule and the tariff debate. At a time when the parties were at daggers drawn, the device to respond to these challenges was a coalition government: 'The time', he suggested, 'has arrived for a truce, for bringing the two Parties into joint stock in order to liquidate arrears which . . . may end in national impoverishment, if not insolvency.'[90] It was an astonishing document, and Austen Chamberlain's reaction when he learned of it, hardly overstated the case: 'What a world we live in and how the public would stare if they could look into our minds and our letter bags!'[91]

As his emissary to Balfour, Lloyd George chose a brash young Unionist MP, Frederick Edwin Smith ('F.E.' to nearly everyone), whom he had met through Churchill. In October, Smith handed the justly famous 'Lloyd George memorandum' to Balfour, and the two politicians initiated a series of private discussions. At some point in the next few weeks Balfour informed his three conference colleagues of the contents of the mysterious memorandum, though apparently neither they nor the Liberal conferees – probably excepting Asquith – actually saw it at this stage.[92] Sandars, Garvin and Bonar Law were also informed of the Balfour–Lloyd George talks. No Liberal had battled Balfour with more ferocity than Lloyd George, and they were as unalike as two men could be – the intellectual and the intuitive, the thoughtful philosopher and the passionate innovator. Yet they could not help liking each other, and, despite all, admiring each other's talents. Perhaps the Chancellor believed that somehow coalition could be made to work – he apparently suggested to Balfour that Asquith would remain premier and go to the Lords, Balfour would lead the Commons, and there would be imperial preference, joint sittings of the Houses over controversial legislation, and 'a reasonable federal solution to the Irish difficulty'.[93] The plan, had it been put into effect, would have revolutionized British politics, but in the end it came to nothing.

There was much in it to tempt the Unionists, including Empire unity, tariffs and a strengthened defence establishment based on mandatory service; yet there was one element which Balfour knew that neither he nor most of his party could bear. In their discussions, Lloyd George had revealed to Balfour (but probably not to his fellow Liberals) his own discomfort with his party's commitment to Gladstonian Home Rule and placed himself in the camp of those who thought local government could be 'devolved' upon Ireland without the need for a Home Rule bill, 'and that this might form a nucleus for the Federation of the Empire at some future date'.[94] There were Unionists – Austen Chamberlain, Smith and Garvin among them – who were at least willing to consider such innovations. The overwhelming majority of the party rank and file, and Arthur Balfour, were not.

Balfour ended the discussions in late October, and Lloyd George reported the Unionist leader pleading, 'I cannot become another Robert Peel in my party.' But the Chancellor insisted that the decision was much influenced by the trusted ex-Chief Whip Akers-Douglas, now Lord Chilston, and he could not resist adding, 'It was not rejected by the real leaders of the [Unionist] Party, but by men who, for some obscure reason best known to political organisations, have great influence inside the councils of a party without possessing any of the capabilities that excite general admiration and confidence outside.'[95] His great plan, according to this explanation, was torpedoed by the party 'fixers' acting through the party leader.

Balfour, however, thought from the beginning that the scheme was 'improbable' at best.[96] When reminded of this episode by Mrs Dugdale in 1928, the eighty-year-old Balfour admitted that he might well have made the celebrated reference to Peel, and might do so again under similar circumstances. But, he added later, 'Ireland must have been the point – otherwise the remark about Peel would not apply.'[97] More than any single thing, Ireland *was* the point that brought these negotiations to a close, as Balfour at the time of his decision wrote to the 'federalist' Garvin:

> Ireland had a 'subordinate Parliament' till 1782. It took advantage of England's misfortunes to turn it into an 'independent Parliament'. And why? Because, said Grattan and Flood, anything less than this is inconsistent with Irish freedom. This was the argument of loyalists and protestants 140 years ago – is it going to be forgotten by Nationalists and Roman Catholics, merely because Redmond, in order to obtain an instalment of what he considers England's debt to Ireland, promises on behalf of posterity that the instalment shall be forever accepted as payment in full?[98]

If a 'devolution' local government were in place in Ireland, he asked, what was to prevent them from defying the Imperial Parliament? 'They will have money, police, and organisation: In Ireland the imperial Parliament will have none of these things.'

To Balfour, the innovative memorandum was typical of its author, and he mused many years later:

> Now isn't that just like Lloyd George . . . He says to himself at any given moment: 'Come on now – we've all been squabbling too long, let's find a rea- sonable way out of the difficulty' – but such solutions are quite impossible for people who don't share his outlook on political principles – the great things.[99]

The Irish Union was one of the greatest of the 'great things' of Balfour's political life, and had brought the Conservatives and Liberal Unionists together after the first Home Rule bill. He would abandon it only when it became absolutely unavoidable; and that would take place only a decade later, in a world so changed as to be unimaginable in 1910.

The Lloyd George proposal died quickly, the inter-party conference fol- lowed it to its grave on 10 November, and five days later Asquith called for another dissolution.[100] Determined now on a bill to break the Lords' veto power over Commons legislation, the Prime Minister privately demanded from George V the promise that he had not secured from Edward VII: that the sovereign would, if needed, create enough Liberal peers to guarantee passage of the bill in the Upper House once the government had won the coming election. After an unpleasant scene, the Prime Minister secured his 'contingent guarantee', and the inexperienced King never truly forgave him for the 'browbeating' employed to secure it – but it was given all the same.[101]

King George knew that he could not resist his ministers unless he could find alternative advisers, and he was cautioned by Lord Knollys that this was impossible. His other royal secretary, Sir Arthur Bigge, disagreed, but the more experienced man's counsel prevailed. What His Majesty was not told was that, nine days before the death of his royal father, Balfour had been invited to meet at Lambeth Palace with Archbishop Davidson, Knollys and Esher, and had indicated his willingness to consider the possibility of the sovereign's rejection of Asquith's ultimatum.[102] Esher recalled afterwards, '[Balfour] pointed out that if the King refused the Prime Minister's proposal the Government would resign, and that he, Mr Balfour, would then form a Government, and immediately ask the King to grant him a dissolution.'[103]

Knollys dutifully informed the King of the conversation, but the monarch perished apparently without informing his heir either of these developments or of his own intentions. If Edward VII had dismissed his government in this way and called for Balfour, it is impossible to project exactly what would have transpired – but it is certain that, had the Opposition leader tried to form a government, it would have been a great gamble by the Unionists and an even greater one by the King. With three decades of parliamentary experience, Balfour knew in April 1910 that his only hope would have been to win an immediate election – and this was highly unlikely. By October, however, he had surrendered this notion and embraced the inevitable. At Esher's request, on the 9th he prepared a memorandum in which he acknowledged that any attempt by him to form a government, even if Asquith were to choose to resign, would have been hopeless.[104] King George was not told of Balfour's conjecture of April, though Knollys surely told him of the Unionist leader's more resigned opinion outlined in the October memorandum. What mattered most, of course, was that Asquith had the indignant King's 'contingent guarantee' safely in his pocket, but the premier spoke of it only to his most trusted advisers. First Asquith meant to win the second election of 1910.

Balfour's position was more difficult, for the unity his party had achieved over the 'Radical Budget' was showing signs of disintegration. Many Unionists were frustrated with the party truce and the rather secretive inter-party conference. Carson joked to his friend Lady Londonderry in August that the summer had been long and boring: 'I wish the Conference was over or the King would fall in love or Arthur Balfour get into the divorce Court.'[105] The Die-hard Lord Willoughby de Broke saw no humour in all this, however, and insisted in a mid-July letter to the *Morning Post* that Unionists wanted less 'tactics' and more 'frontal assault' from their leaders.[106] He was not alone as rumours of Unionist concessions and 'federalist solutions' made the rounds in Whitehall, and by early autumn Carson's humour also had faded away, and he reminded Balfour of the displeasure of the Ulster Unionists at the slightest hints of compromise over Home Rule.[107]

At the same time, Balfour was subjected to equally earnest but contrary advice from other Unionists, who insisted that an Irish devolution or federal compromise might well save Unionism from continuing to back a doomed horse.[108] Even Sandars reminded him that voters in 1910 could not necessarily be roused by an anti-Home Rule campaign as their predecessors had been in earlier days.[109] Balfour, however, remained unpersuaded by 'back-door' schemes to make Home Rule palatable and to barter it for other parts of the Unionist programme. He also remembered the near hysteria over the Wyndham–MacDonnell affair, and once the constitutional conference had collapsed he made it clear that whatever devolution schemes the Liberals might have conceived had perished without trace. Carson was satisfied, writing to Lady Londonderry, 'My own belief is that there is nothing to fear of AJB being likely to concede anything on Home Rule.'[110] In early November, Balfour sent Sandars to inform Garvin – the major Unionist proponent of devolution at this time – that his campaigns in the *Observer* must cease, and the editor obeyed.[111]

The eclipse of federalism did not end Balfour's party troubles in the autumn of 1910, as the tariff question, and particularly the sensitive question of food duties, continued to hang over Unionism. Though Balfour had publicly accepted Tariff Reform as the 'first constructive work' of the party, most zealous Chamberlainites remained dissatisfied that he had not publicly endorsed either a general tariff or food duties. At the same time, with another election looming, other pro-tariff Unionists were having second thoughts about the whole-hog programme as a vote-getter. Garvin, a Tariff Reformer of independent mind, decided again to intervene, this time to save Balfour and the party from the onus of food taxes. To this end, he met late into the night on 14 November with Lord Ridley, Acland-Hood, Bonar Law, Carson, Edward Goulding, F. E. Smith and Sandars. Only Carson and Sandars agreed with the editor that the idea of food duties ought for the moment to be shelved, and the meeting adjourned without reaching agreement.

During the prolonged deadlock, many Unionists were drawn to the idea of employing a popular referendum to allow the electorate to settle matters insoluble by normal parliamentary methods.[112] Lansdowne, its most committed advocate, raised the idea in the constitutional conference and included it in an abortive November plan for reform of the Upper House. Asquith, of course, rejected the idea out of hand. His India Secretary, Lord Crewe, hectored the Unionists: if their faith in the referendum was so strong, they ought to submit their panacea, Tariff Reform, to the test.[113]

Balfour accepted the challenge on 29 November at the Albert Hall before 10,000 people: 'I have not the least objection', he proclaimed, 'to submitting the principles of Tariff Reform to a Referendum,' and he dared the Liberals to do the same with Home Rule. A voice in the crowd bellowed, 'That's won the election!'[114] This was his pledge: before implementing a full tariff programme, the next Unionist government would hold a national plebiscite to seek the endorsement of the electorate. It was a stunning turn of events, and Austen Chamberlain telegraphed his firm opposition immediately. To all good Chamberlainites who had not forgotten the Valentine letters, this was nothing less than betrayal.[115] To deflect their anger in the direction of one of their own, Balfour craftily referred to this referendum pledge as 'Bonar Law's proposal'; but, though the Glaswegian had written to him of the attractions of the idea to tariff sceptics, it had been pressed more strongly by Lansdowne, Sandars, Brodrick and Garvin, among others. The decision, however, was Balfour's, and identifying it with another Tariff Reformer was merely a device to hold the Chamberlainites in place.[116] Days later he told a cheering audience in Reading that the party's stand on Tariff Reform had not weakened and that 'The Referendum . . . will end many great political controversies. It will make the people's will manifest on many disputed questions.'[117] The referendum pledge was another dangerous gamble by Balfour, and it could be considered successful only if the coming election resulted in a Unionist victory – and even then the Chamberlainites were unlikely to be pacified.[118]

The preceding months had taxed Balfour's stamina, but he now campaigned relentlessly up and down the country, striving to turn the focus of the contest away from the Liberals' theme of 'peers versus people' and towards the democratic virtues of the referendum, as well as the defence of the Irish Union.[119] During the seventeen days of balloting, Unionist hopes remained high – talk in the Carlton Club was of gains of up to thirty-five seats – but the results were almost precisely as in January, with Unionists and Liberals each securing 272 seats with a much reduced poll for all parties. Only outright victory could have saved the House of Lords from Liberal-orchestrated emasculation, and the referendum scheme failed to secure this. Sandars had warned that another defeat would open the floodgates to additional problems, and now the Tariff Reformers held Balfour responsible for the referendum pledge, and the pledge for the election loss.

After yet another electoral disappointment, Balfour had again to face demands for effective reorganization of the machinery of the party. As in 1906, pressure from many quarters was great, and half-solutions would not do after a third successive electoral beating; therefore another committee was appointed in January under the trusted Chilston.[120] This Unionist Organization Committee worked swiftly, and in June submitted its recommendations, including modernization of the operation of Central Office, the creation of the new posts of party chairman and treasurer, and the integration of Central Office and the National Union. Acland-Hood was retired to the Upper House as Lord St Audries, and replaced by Balcarres. These were far more meaningful proposals than those of 1906, but because the prolonged political warfare over the House of Lords would end with Balfour's resignation, completion of the reform agenda was left to his successor.

Attention now focused on the question of exactly what Asquith would do next. On 9 January 1911 Balfour and Esher dined with Knollys at the Marlborough Club, and the Unionist leader suggested they put their 'cards on the table'. With the two 1910 elections behind them, Balfour admitted that if he were King and the government asked him to create enough peers to ensure passage of a Parliament bill, he would be unable to refuse. Esher recalled, 'In Mr Balfour's opinion, the whole situation is governed by the fact that there is no alternative administration possible at the present time. A third general election was impossible, and if Asquith were to resign, and if the King called for him, Balfour could think of no circumstances under which he could secure a majority.' It was impossible, Balfour continued, to foresee what exactly the Liberals would do, but the King must assume that no other government was possible; and, while he should remonstrate strongly against the government's 'unconstitutional' practice, the sovereign had no choice but to acquiesce. To the question of whether he would himself have accepted a summons to attempt to form a government before the December election, Balfour answered that, if asked by the sovereign, 'in the interests of his own party' he might have felt constrained to try. In the 'interests of the King and of the Monarchy', however, he considered that it would have been 'imprudent and unwise' for the King to have taken such an action.[121] At the end of the evening, Knollys revealed that the Prime Minister had approved the meeting in advance, which infuriated Balfour, who presumed that his words would be reported to Asquith. To him, this was hardly putting their 'cards on the table', and he angrily took his leave – still unaware that the Prime Minister had already secured the King's pledge of the previous November to create peers, if called upon.

Only in July 1911 was Esher allowed to tell Balfour of the facts that Knollys had withheld at the Marlborough Club.[122] Though he might well have done, Balfour did not hold Esher responsible, telling Balcarres that he got 'more information out of Esher than Esher out of [him].'[123] It was Knollys ('a regular jackal') whom he blamed, as he wrote to the King's other private secretary, Lord Stamfordham, the former Sir Arthur Bigge:

> Lord Knollys seems therefore to have endeavoured to extract from me general statements of policy . . . while studiously concealing the most important elements in the actual concrete problem which had to be solved . . . one of the most singular examples of domestic Diplomacy of which I have ever heard.[124]

While Balfour and Knollys managed a modus vivendi, their friendship never truly recovered from the episode.[125]

The Parliament bill was finally introduced in the Commons on 21 February 1911, and after a gruelling battle it passed finally on 15 May. The bill called for the reduction of the lifespan of parliaments from seven years to five, and specified that any legislation designated a money bill could not be vetoed by the Lords and that all other legislation passed by the Commons three times within two years would become law regardless of the action of the Upper House. It also provided, to Balfour's horror, for the payment of Members of Parliament – thus neutralizing the Osborne judgement which barred trade unions from mandatory levies of their members for political purposes.

In this combustible atmosphere and with the day of reckoning approaching in the Lords, the Unionist leadership faced the question of what precisely to do next. Balfour had summoned the ex-ministers – the Shadow Cabinet – to Carlton Gardens on 7 July and informed them that Asquith held the King's pledge to create peers. While there was agreement

that the sovereign had been 'duped and jockeyed' into his impossible position, there seemed to be consensus on little else. Lord Halsbury called for
uncompromising resistance to the bill in the Lords, and the brothers-in-law
Salisbury and Selborne supported the octogenarian former Lord
Chancellor. Wyndham and Austen Chamberlain agreed in principle, but
stopped just short of advising the peers to resist to the end. Viscount
Midleton (as Brodrick had become in 1907) recommended that the Lords
meet to determine their own course of action. The discussion meandered
until it was quite clear that the Unionist chieftains were far from agreed on
what to do – or about how to do it.

With time running out, the Shadow Cabinet met again a fortnight later
at Carlton Gardens. For Balfour, the choice lay between acquiescence or a
show of defiance which could lead only to the madness and mockery of an
irrelevant Upper House swollen by as many as 500 peers. He knew when
he was beaten and recommended capitulation, and, after all that could be
said was said, a vote was taken. Balfour and Lansdowne officially recommended allowing the bill to pass, and were joined by Chilston, Curzon,
Londonderry, Midleton, Chaplin, Long, Lyttelton, and the recently
appointed party chairman, Arthur Steel-Maitland. Supporting them,
though unenthusiastically, were Ashbourne, Derby, Finlay, and Bonar Law.
Those preferring resistance included Salisbury, Selborne, Halsbury,
Balcarres, Carson, Chamberlain, Smith and Wyndham. It was Wyndham
who christened those peers willing to 'die in the last ditch' as 'Ditchers',
while the moderate majority he thought were 'liable to trimming', and
were therefore 'Hedgers'.[126] Later that day, more than 200 peers met at
Lansdowne House, and their confused discussions reflected those of the
Shadow Cabinet.[127]

The Commons were to deal with the Lords' proposed amendments to
the bill on 24 July, and on that day the frustration of a group mostly of
younger Unionist MPs boiled over: the Prime Minister stood frozen at the
dispatch box for thirty minutes amid deafening cries of 'Traitor!' and 'Who
killed the King?' Finally surrendering to the tumult, he sat down. This was
the disgraceful 'Cecil Scene', so called because it seems that Lord Hugh,
F. E. Smith, Carson and some thirty of their friends were behind it.[128]
Balfour was disgusted with his cousin's day's work – as ineffectual as it was
boorish – and was all the more embarrassed by the government benches
receiving in silence what was meant to be his reply to the speech Asquith
had not suffered to deliver.

Resistance coalesced around the ancient Halsbury, and a great dinner
of some 600 rapturous supporters (held ironically at the Hotel Cecil)

honoured him on 26 July. With more than 100 peers and MPs present, a large crowd heard their eighty-eight-year-old hero, as well as Milner, Selborne, Wyndham, Smith and Chamberlain, denounce the Parliament bill. Unionist whip William Bridgeman attended the affair and recalled in his diary that, while not 'a word of disloyalty' was spoken towards Balfour, 'there would have been open revolt' if the party leader had forbade the dinner.[129]

Until this point, neither Ditchers nor Hedgers among the backbenchers were precisely sure what Balfour believed. Privately he came close to losing his temper, suggesting that he might well tell the Ditcher peers, '[You] object to your tailor being made a peer, so you mean to vote in such a way that your hatter and barber shall be ennobled into the bargain!'[130] On 22 July he had drafted an angry memorandum to the party. He did not, he wrote, object absolutely to the creation of peers: this had been survived in other times, and the 'creation of 50 or 100 new peers is a matter of indifference.' But broad resistance among the Lords to a determined government holding the King's unconditional guarantee might well lead Asquith to 'swamp' the Lords and render the Upper House a constitutional cipher. As for talk of 'fighting to the last', it was 'essentially theatrical': 'It does nothing, it can do nothing; it is not even intended to do anything, except advertise the situation. The object of those who advocate it is to make people realise what (it is assumed) they will not realise otherwise, namely, that we are the victims of a revolution.' Such talk, replete with military metaphors, of the heroism of resistance seemed to him 'purely for Music Hall consumption'.[131] To Lady Elcho he put it more simply: some Unionists 'seem to have gone temporarily crazy . . . and I see at present no signs of returning sanity'.[132]

Lansdowne and Curzon persuaded Balfour to compose for publication a document, written in milder terms and addressed to an 'imaginary correspondent' (Lord Newton was chosen). Balfour had neither the right nor the desire, he argued, to dictate to their lordships, and he advised simply that he agreed with their leader that there was no alternative to submission: 'With Lord Lansdowne I stand; with Lord Lansdowne, I am ready, if need be, to fall.' He closed with a warning to the Ditchers: any majority they could muster in the Upper House would be met with an even greater creation of peers, by the inevitable passage of the bill, and by virtual destruction of the Upper House. 'It would in my opinion be a misfortune if the present crisis left the House of Lords weaker than the Parliament Bill by itself would make it, but it would be an irreparable tragedy if it left us a divided Party.'[133]

To make matters worse, August 1911 was the hottest month on record; London had become nearly unbearable, with temperatures reaching 100 degrees Fahrenheit. In such an atmosphere, at four-thirty in the afternoon on the 11th, the peers began their final debate of the Parliament bill.[134] Feelings ran high in the normally somnolent House, with the uncharacteristically restive galleries full to overflowing. Selborne spoke last for the Unionists: 'The question is,' he insisted, 'shall we perish in the dark, slain by our own hand, or in the light, killed by our own enemies . . . ?' His answer came at 10.40 p.m., when the bill passed by 130 votes to 114, with the mass of Unionist peers following Lansdowne's lead (and Balfour's order) and abstaining. Most humiliating to the party leadership was the fact that the Die-hard peers would have defeated the bill had not thirteen bishops and thirty-seven Unionist peers joined the Liberals to create the small majority. 'We are beaten', was Wyndham's bitter judgement, 'by the Bishops and the Rats.'[135]

The Die-hards were furious with Lansdowne as well as with Curzon and the 'rats', but had they not acted on Balfour's orders? Many moderates also concluded that their leader had erred by waiting until so late in the game to show his hand and overrule the dissenters. All agreed that the humiliation was made greater by the fact that some of their own men had voted to ensure passage of the hated legislation.[136] Who, some angry Unionists asked openly, was responsible for all of this, if not Arthur Balfour?

Wilfrid Short was candid in his evaluation of his master's predicament, writing to Alice Balfour of the doleful scene as the peers 'cut their own throats, and held themselves up to ridicule by their own action'. He spoke of the deep bitterness among the party towards the bishops and Unionist peers who had voted with the government, concluding, 'It is all very sad and honestly I really do not see how Mr Balfour and Lord Lansdowne can regain their leadership . . . [for] when the forwards of the Party desire a more determined leadership and definite action, they will seize the occasion for breaking away.'[137]

But Balfour, for the moment at least, could not hear the indictments against him, for on the day before the vote he had set out to escape both the meteorological and the political heat of the capital for the more temperate climes of Bad Gastein in Austria. Just before decamping for the Continent, he allowed Balcarres and Sandars a glimpse into his inner thoughts. All seemed clear in his mind: he had striven to keep peace among the factions, he had sought and transmitted to the party his recommendation, endorsed by a majority of the Shadow Cabinet, and many in the party chose stubbornly to ignore that lead. He had no intention, as he once wrote, of going 'about the country' justifying his virtue as leader: 'If people cannot find it out for themselves, they must, so far as I can see, remain in ignorance.'[138] As in the time of the Wyndham–MacDonnell affair, he was deeply wounded by the fact that so many blamed him personally for the humiliating defeat. 'I can never forget', he confided to the Chief Whip, 'the attacks made upon me by those who have charged me with cowardice and disgrace . . . Their publicity, the press campaign, and the speeches render their action unforgettable *and unforgivable*.'[139] To Sandars he confessed to 'feeling I have been badly treated' and that, even more to the point, 'I have no wish to lead the party under these humiliating conditions.'[140] He was even more forthcoming in a letter to Lady Elcho on the day of the Lords' vote, describing politics at that moment as 'quite unusually odious'. He admitted that of late he had 'felt the situation more acutely than any in my public life – I mean from the *personal* point of view. As you know I am very easy going, and not given to brooding over my wrongs. But Friday and Saturday . . . I could think of nothing else . . . On Saturday night the cloud lifted; yet it *has* not, and perhaps *will* not wholly disappear til recent events are things barely remembered.'[141]

Austen Chamberlain lamented, 'Was ever a Party so badly led as ours on this occasion?'[142] Balcarres noted that some critics went further, insisting that Balfour's flight to Bad Gastein was evidence of 'complicity in its most naked form'.[143] The Chief Whip understood the Ditchers' anger, but he could not agree with Short that these quarrels could have any decisive effect on the party leadership. He had written some months earlier, 'When somebody complains of Arthur Balfour's attitude a simple query as to his possible successor brings the conversation to an abrupt close . . . To talk of a change in the leadership is futile when no potential substitute can be found.'[144] Rows there might be, but surely the Unionists would not dare to suggest another leader.

On the back benches and in the press there were those who disagreed. Sir William Bull, a model party loyalist, confided to his diary in July his discomfort that 'Balfour keeps shilly shallying about – first for giving in – then for fighting.' He wondered if backbenchers were not simply 'getting sick of A.J.B.'[145] Garvin, who had co-operated so closely with Balfour in the past, attacked him bitterly in *The Observer* immediately after the Lords' vote. More dedicated to Balfour's overthrow was another old friend, Leopold Maxse, who at this time launched in his *National Review* a ruthless anti-Balfour campaign under the slogan 'B.M.G.': Balfour Must Go![146] But, while backbenchers and editors could be irritating, they could not, in

Balfour's words, 'evict' him from the leadership.[147] The Unionist Party was not a democracy; there was no formal machinery to dismiss a leader, and the inchoate disquiet in 1911 could not easily dislodge him if he did not wish to go.

In September he retreated to Whittingehame for golf and contemplation, and on the 30th he welcomed Balcarres and Steel-Maitland to hear his thoughts. He had already told the Chief Whip that he understood that acquiescence to the Parliament bill might doom his leadership, and that he was quite 'ready to contemplate this as a distinct possibility'.[148] Balfour now reminded his guests that he had led the party in the House for twenty years; he was in less than perfect health, and would be sixty-six if the party came into power in three years' time – 'too old to survive a long ministry'. Ahead lay gruelling battles over Home Rule and Church disestablishment. A change must come sooner or later, and now, he insisted, was 'the best moment'. Steel-Maitland protested: there was no one on their side who could match his talents. But Balfour brushed this aside: W. H. Smith had led successfully and did not possess them. 'I think', he added, 'a slower brain would often be welcome to the party as a whole.' There would be great tumult as a result of his resignation, but 'the atmosphere would be cleared in the process and the party would ultimately come to its own.'

Anticipating the question of who, after all, could replace him, he had a ready answer: Austen Chamberlain (Walter Long's claims he promptly dismissed). He added that, if Lansdowne chose to go, Curzon could lead in the Lords. He assured his friends that he would not abandon politics and would loyally support his successor from the front bench. Their pleas he waved aside; he would act promptly, for delay would leave him feeling like 'a mere warming pan for his successor'.[149]

On the day following this meeting, Balfour received a memorandum from the volatile Long which angered and offended him, and which he considered further evidence that the course he had outlined was the correct one. In it, the former Irish Secretary bluntly presented his bill of indictment against his leader: 'I am honestly convinced', he wrote, 'that the situation is so grave as to call for action on the part of those who are your personal supporters and the true friends of the Party, and to necessitate a complete change in policy and tactics on your own part.' This 'personal supporter' continued, 'You know my views generally, for I have frequently placed them before you. I think you will admit that during the last three years your policy, your tactics, and your leadership have received the most loyal support; but I am sorry to say we are forced to the conclusion now that the results are by no means satisfactory.'

The memorandum continued in this vein for several pages: the party was in 'unsatisfactory condition' and characterized by 'discontent, want of unity, desire for distinct, unqualified guidance'. Long warned his leader, 'It is quite true that you are Leader, and on the principle of *"J'y suis, j'y reste,"* you can retain the position; but this, while proving unsatisfactory to yourself, would surely involve disaster to the Party, and therefore, in my judgement, disaster to the country.'[150]

Balfour's troubles continued to mount in early October, when the former Ditchers and their fellow-travellers formed a Die-hard league they called the Halsbury Club.[151] It was an odd group, Sandars noted, that seemed to 'differ on all constructive questions, but they are united in disapproval of their Leader's advice'.[152] Also in late 1910 the former Confederate Page Croft and his pro-tariff friends had founded another hostile ginger group they called the Reveille, which was more or less dedicated to ridding the party of its leader.[153] Long's hostile memorandum came as a blow upon a bruise, and formation of the two political clubs could have constituted genuine threats to Balfour's leadership; but these were at best 'last straws', for Balfour was already firm in his decision to retire.[154]

On 2 October he reiterated his decision to Balcarres, insisting that these examples of party discontent simply 'confirmed and amplified his deductions'. He proposed to announce his decision in Edinburgh on the 21st and threatened to make public his anger against those in the party who claimed to value leadership while disregarding the lead that had been shown them. 'Hence', he added, 'a fresh leader is imperative who can begin securing closer discipline, etc.'[155] Balcarres talked him out of this plan. He returned to Whittingehame a fortnight later, and came away convinced that Balfour's mind could not be changed – though inevitably, the leader added, an announcement would bring a much dreaded 'cohort of politicians crawling on their bellies and imploring him to retain his post'.[156]

On 8 October, Balfour wrote to Lady Elcho that he was ready to announce a decision on resignation but that 'Bal has persuaded me not to do it before the autumn session but I hope to do it soon after.'[157] Over the next few weeks the circle of those who knew of Balfour's intentions grew – he informed his family and Lord Lansdowne; and soon Lords Curzon, Chilston, Derby, Londonderry, Rothschild and St Aldwyn, as well as Austen Chamberlain, Bonar Law, Long and Lyttelton, were told. On the morning of the 24th a hastily organized meeting of thirteen anxious party notables, including Balcarres, Bonar Law and Long, was held at Devonshire House to attempt to consider a strategy to deflect Balfour from his path, but they soon accepted that his decision was unshakeable.[158]

On 6 November the Halsbury Club grudgingly voted their 'confidence' in their party chief, but only after Chamberlain and Halsbury himself had threatened to resign if they did not. It meant nothing, for on the following day Balfour wrote to the King to inform him of his decision. He made the resignation public at 4 p.m. on 8 November in a few brief remarks to the City of London Conservative Association – according to an onlooker, 'in a grubby little city office at the end of a squalid passage' before some twenty or thirty observers.[159] He had held the leadership of his party longer than anyone since the Younger Pitt, and now, he told them, it was time for a new man. There was talk of 'unrest' in the party, he acknowledged, but he added that there was nothing 'especially exceptional' in that:

> Remember that parties are made up of human beings . . . and there will always be people, when things are not going right, who grumble and criticise . . . Such critics are like the microbes which (as doctors tell us) always dwell within our organism. If we sit in a draught or lower our vitality by fatigue, we get a violent cold or slight fever, but when our strength is recovered the microbe resumes its proper place.[160]

His remarks lasted only a few minutes, and Sandars estimated that the momentous event had taken him away from Carlton Gardens for little more than an hour. Only a few – those perhaps with some interest in the political history of their nation – realized that for the first time in nearly a quarter-century a member of the Cecil connection would not lead the Unionist Party.

IO

The Lamps Go Out

FOLLOWING HIS BRIEF announcement, Balfour made no further public statements about his resignation and fled from London to avoid the intrusions of the press and the sympathy of well-wishers. As he had predicted, letters of regret poured in from all quarters, and in his replies he insisted that his resignation be treated as something less than a national tragedy. He wrote to his old friend (and recently a vociferous Die-hard) Midleton, an antagonist in the Parliament Act fraças: 'To-day marks the end of my political Leadership, not the end of my interest in politics, or of my work for political causes. Do not let us, therefore, take it more seriously than is necessary.'[1]

Though genuinely relieved to be freed from struggling to lead a fractious party, Balfour was understandably hurt over the manner in which the end had come. As he so often did, he turned for comfort to his intimate circle, and, after a brief stay at Fisher's Hill, his brother Gerald's house near Woking, he set off on a round of visits to familiar country houses – among them Stanway (Elcho), Taplow (Desborough), Hackwood (Curzon) and Cliveden (Astor).[2] This was followed by an extended stay on the French Riviera – and, as sunshine and golf usually did, this restored him both physically and spiritually. He did not return to politics for five months.

Balfour expressed great pleasure that his political responsibilities were now much diminished, and he would have more time for his private life. Lady Elcho, his most intimate friend, was quick to share her own opinion on the matter. In a letter written immediately after his resignation, she said that it was all very well for politicians to lay down their burdens, but 'a woman and a *mother* never goes out of office'. However, in one of those enigmatic asides which sometimes crept into her letters, she added, 'It seems to me a pretty tribute that upon yr attaining yr liberty a certain (white) slave should also be liberated. What think you?' No direct answer to the query survives, and possibly none was ever written. Was she hinting at a change in the nature of their association? If she was suggesting an end to their long connection, she soon thought better of it, and there were no more references to 'liberation'. A year later and in a somewhat different key, she wrote, 'I'll give you this much, tho, for although you have only loved me little yet I must admit you have loved me long.'[3] And so did they both.

There was an important change in Balfour's political inner family, however, as Jack Sandars announced that the time had come for him to leave Balfour and the political life. He wrote in January, 'The truth is the small part I have taken in the political drama is gone whether I like it or not; and age and other considerations make it impossible that another should be assigned to me.'[4] The two continued to exchange letters for several years, but they seldom met. Though Balfour returned to politics, Sandars devoted his energies primarily to racing and to writing.[5]

The political squabbles of the preceding half-dozen years seem not to have cost Balfour any meaningful friendships, as old comrades temporarily alienated during the long fiscal debate or the battle over the Parliament Act seem to have returned to intimacy. Soon he suffered other losses, more important to him than politics: on 8 June 1913, George Wyndham died suddenly of coronary thrombosis in a Paris hotel room. Their connection was an old one, and their mutual affection had not been dimmed by political disagreements.[6] His vitality damaged by drink and depression, the unfortunate Wyndham, just as a seer had once predicted, had not lived to see his fiftieth birthday.

Especially painful for Balfour was the tragic death a month later of Alfred Lyttelton, his closest friend among those remarkable siblings. Lyttelton was widely popular in the House and for a time was thought to be a possible successor to Balfour. He was the most gifted in that family of athletes, and perhaps this was his undoing: at the age of fifty-six, he was struck by a cricket ball, and the injury proved fatal. Certainly few had led lives of greater emotional self-discipline than Arthur Balfour, but the senseless death of the much-loved Lyttelton was too much. He broke down at the bedside, and Lyttelton's cousin and Balfour's old friend Mary Gladstone, now Mrs Drew, recalled later 'the pathetic and painful scene when Mr Balfour lost self control and was mastered by emotion'. Later, as he drove her home, Balfour's car broke down near Knightsbridge Barracks. As the two friends sat in the immobilized Napier in the pouring rain, Balfour deeply regretted showing his feelings. Mrs Drew recalled his words: '"I am so bitterly ashamed," he said, "but I have no power of self-control."' She added, 'I could not describe the poignancy of his regret.'[7]

Death made a further claim on Balfour five months later, when Alfred's older brother died. Spencer Lyttelton had been Balfour's friend since

Cambridge days, and had brought him into that remarkable family circle. He had been Balfour's companion on their world tour four decades earlier, and one of 'Us four', with his sister May, Mary Gladstone and Balfour, when they had all been young and devoted to music and merrymaking. These losses, coming in such rapid order, had stunned her beloved friend, and Lady Elcho wrote to him, of Spencer, 'I always think of him in connection to you, trusty loving old friend.' Yet she understood her correspondent so very well: 'There is nothing to be written,' she added, 'nothing to be said.'[8] Balfour lost other old friends and colleagues in these years – among them Arnold-Forster, Lord Percy (both in 1909) and Lord Cawdor (1911).

One of the unavoidable elements of party leadership which Balfour never relished was the regular interaction with the court, and particularly with the courtiers who surrounded the sovereign. Soon after his resignation he was asked, as were many of the statesmen who had served the late King Edward, to grant an interview to Sir Sidney Lee, the editor of the *Dictionary of National Biography*, who was to write about the monarch for the great reference work. Reluctantly, Balfour saw Lee at Carlton Gardens in November 1911, and the historian drafted an essay which he said he based in part on that interview.

Many at court – though not the King's friend Esher – insisted that Sir Sidney's essay left the impression that King Edward's life had been dedicated to his pleasures and had contributed little to the achievements of his governments.[9] Lee defended himself in part by citing his conversation with Balfour, and insisted that he was 'amazed' when he was shown Balfour's official recollection of the reign, full of conventional platitudes.[10] In his own defence, Balfour insisted that the historian had exaggerated his comments. Lee's notes of his talk with Balfour indicate that the former premier observed frankly that the King had not made his celebrated visits to France as part of a government initiative to bring about the *Entente*, and that no discussion he may have held with French officials 'had much effect on policy'. Balfour's conclusion, according to Lee's notes, was mild: the King 'did not interfere in foreign politics'.[11] The storm passed, however, and ultimately it was concluded at the palace simply that Sir Sidney had 'misconstrued the interviews accorded to him'.[12]

Balfour thought the entire affair a royal tempest in a teapot and, according to Sandars, suggested to Sir Sidney that all might be satisfied if he were simply to omit the offending passages from his essay, leaving behind a picture of a 'great Constitutional King, eminently fitted to be Ruler of a great

Empire'.[13] In fact Sir Sidney had reason to be somewhat confused by Balfour's behaviour. When in 1915 a new book credited Edward VII with a part in the formation of the 1905 *Entente*, Balfour bristled at such 'a foolish piece of gossip' and wrote to Lansdowne, 'Now, so far as I remember, during the years which you and I were his Ministers, he never made an important suggestion of any sort on large questions of policy.'[14] Then he wrote to the author, F. Holland Rose, that, while he did not wish to minimize the 'excellent effect' of King Edward's popularity among the French, 'I never remember his making any important suggestion with regard to large questions of policy, foreign or domestic, either by way of initiation or criticism.'[15] This remained his opinion.

Balfour played no part in the choice of his successor, and, as Lansdowne chose to continue to lead the Lords, the Chief Whip announced an election for the post of Unionist leader in the Commons.[16] The two principal candidates were Austen Chamberlain and Walter Long, with the surprising addition to the race of a very dark horse in the person of Andrew Bonar Law. Despite their differences over Tariff Reform, Balfour expected and favoured the selection of Chamberlain, whose intelligence and parliamentary skills he admired. Chamberlain also had certain grave disadvantages, however: the majority of Unionists were Conservatives, but Chamberlain, like Lansdowne, was a Liberal Unionist. He was, of course, the darling of the Tariff Reformers, and in the eyes of some Conservatives the mark of the 'Birmingham gang' was difficult to accept.

Long was the choice of the Tory squirearchy and the party's traditionalists: a former Irish Secretary and a substantial Wiltshire landholder, he bore all the earmarks of his class and position – and he was a moderate on the tariff question. Yet he was also notoriously thin-skinned and tactless, and possessed a volatile temper which sometimes got the better of him in debate. As Balfour knew from experience, Long frequently irritated colleagues and opponents alike by his alternating of harsh criticism with fulsome flattery, and many came to see this as insincerity of the worst sort. Finally, though he must certainly have been the sole Privy Counsellor in his time who could deftly handle a four-in-hand coach at speed, his health was indifferent. If Chamberlain was the favourite of the front bench, Long seems to have been the choice of the majority of Tory backbenchers – and Balcarres had decreed a ballot on the basis of one man, one vote.

In an unprecedented turn of events, neither front-runner was chosen, for when the parliamentary party met on 13 November there was only one name before them, and it was that of Bonar Law. The Glaswegian had confessed that he expected to garner few votes and anticipated a Chamberlain victory. However, to the surprise of the entire party, Chamberlain put it to Long that a fight to the finish between them could only deepen the divisions in their party. With a compromise candidate readily available, the favourites stood down to allow the less divisive man to assume the post without a contest.[17]

When 232 Unionist MPs met in the smoking room of the Carlton Club, they accepted the fact that the choice had been made for them. Bonar Law had never served in a Cabinet and had only recently become a Privy Counsellor, a record which paled beside that of his two rivals and was positively transparent when compared to that of his predecessor. However, he had earned a reputation for probity and for fierce courage in a political fight – and, unlike his predecessor, for an uncannily flawless memory. The party seemed pleased to have a warrior in charge in place of a dialectician and intellectual, as junior whip William Bridgeman confided to his diary: 'We all parted with the feeling that "we are jolly good fellows" & so we really are.'[18] Perhaps it was a good omen that, on the same day, the Unionist in the Oldham by-election reversed a Liberal majority of 3,500, and a week later a similar result was reported at South Somerset.

Despite their Scottish antecedents, the old and the new Unionist leaders could not have been less alike: one was the offspring of wealth and the traditional leadership class, the other a son of the Presbyterian manse in far-away New Brunswick, brought up among the Glasgow mercantile class; one the product of Eton and Trinity, the other of the commercial curriculum of the Glasgow High School.[19] Balfour had sought the middle way on the fiscal question, and Bonar Law was a Tariff Reformer. Despite their differences, the two men liked each other. Bonar Law was a modest man in a position where modesty was often rare. He quite sincerely declared Balfour to be the greatest parliamentarian of his time, and wrote to him on the eve of the succession, 'No one realises more strongly than I how impossible it is for me to fill your place but I know that you will help me.'[20] Bonar Law usually got the help he sought, and the two worked well together in their new roles. Unlike Balfour, Bonar Law slept little and drove himself without relent, and it is not surprising that Balfour worried aloud that the new leader – a man to whom holidays and diversions were unnatural – bore the anxieties of his new office too deeply and constantly courted exhaustion.[21] Despite all, the two men became friends, and Balfour once said to Lansdowne, 'I like Bonar Law.' With a smile, he added that his successor had but two faults: he did not always speak loudly enough to be heard easily in the Commons Chamber and, more importantly, 'he lived in the wilds of Kensington.'[22]

Esher was horrified at the idea that a bourgeois like Bonar Law could be selected to lead the Unionists, but Balfour gently chided him: 'But do not be pessimistic, and do not despair of the party. I think it quite possible that Bonar Law may surprise you.'[23] Lord Derby, ever hostile towards Tariff Reform, soon begged Balfour to seize again what had once been his: 'I know you are loyalty itself,' he wrote, 'but could you not come back with a policy that did not include food taxes?'[24] Balfour refused even to consider such a possibility, and told Derby so in the plainest language.[25] Derby would have been horrified to learn that Balfour even flirted with the idea of leaving Parliament at the next election, but he abandoned this notion quickly enough – if he ever seriously considered it at all.[26]

One of the regrets that plagued Balfour in his years of party leadership was that there never seemed to be time to devote to the philosophy that continued to hold his interest. Certainly there had been little time for writing, though it amused him that he was regularly invited to lecture on philosophical questions. He wrote to Curzon in 1908, 'The public have a sort of idea that the task of lecturing is congenial to me, and that I have appropriate Addresses stocked away in pigeon-holes. They are, in consequence, perpetually appealing to me to deliver them, and I am as persistently refusing to do so.'[27] Some invitations could not be refused, however: even in a time of heated political battle, he honoured his late brother-in-law and devoted friend when he delivered the Henry Sidgwick Lecture at Newnham College, Cambridge, in January 1908. He gave his talk the provocative title 'Decadence' – a word much discussed in those pre-war years.[28] Unlike others who pursued the theme at this time, his concern was neither materialism nor moral probity, but rather the decline of world cultures. Why, he enquired: 'should civilisations thus wear out and great communities decay?' He concluded that there was no discoverable formula which explained the decline and collapse of great nations, and he reiterated his old belief that the races of mankind were unalike in their abilities and weaknesses – this, he felt sure, had as much as anything to do with shaping their histories. He asked, had Britain the capacity to escape the fate of former great empires, such as Rome or Persia? His reply demonstrated that he remained confident in the conclusions reached in his earlier books: if reasonable hope existed, it could only be rooted politically in Western institutions, intellectually in modern science, and morally in theism. Balfour, as always, had no guarantees to offer, and warned that decay was unavoidable 'unless the character of the civilisation be in harmony both with the acquired temperament and the innate capacities of those who had been induced to accept it'. But he did offer some hope, for, 'whatever be the perils in front of us,' he said, 'there are so far no symptoms either of pause or of regression in the onward movement which for more than a thousand years has been characteristic of Western civilisation.'

Several years earlier he had declined the invitation to give the Romanes Lecture at Oxford, and when the offer was pressed upon him again in 1909 by the Chancellor of the university, Lord Curzon, he replied that he would consider it only because it came from his old friend.[29] Curzon insisted, Balfour acquiesced, and in November 1909 he chose as his subject 'Beauty: And the Criticism of Beauty', addressing the question of whether aesthetic criticism was useful to understanding.[30] Always uncomfortable with taxonomy, he proposed that it was true that critics of the arts had their faults:

> For in proportion as criticism has endeavoured to establish principles of composition, to lay down laws of Beauty, to fix criterions of excellence, so it seems to me to have failed: its triumphs, and they are great, have been won on a different field . . . [Critics] have demolished the dogmas of their predecessors, but have advanced few dogmas of their own. So that, after some twenty-three centuries of aesthetic speculation, we are still without any accepted body of aesthetic doctrine.

For two hours he delighted his audience, concluding what many may well have entered the room believing: the search for an immutable standard of beauty was essentially sterile. He advised, 'Let us be content, since we can do no better, that our admirations should be even as our loves.' Predictably for Arthur Balfour, beauty remained where it had always been: not in the mandate of the critics, but in the eye of the beholder.

As the political turmoil of these years became increasingly frenzied, Balfour found that he had little time for philosophical presentations. His most ambitious such efforts came on the eve of war in 1914, when he delivered the Gifford Lectures at Glasgow University. Established by the Scottish jurist Lord Gifford two decades earlier, their purpose was to address for the layman what the founder termed 'natural theology' – that is, to offer an understanding of God through modern thought, without reliance on dogma, mysticism or miracles. Balfour had declined an invitation to deliver the lectures while still prime minister, pleading the pressure of duty and insisting that he had had his 'say' on the subject in his earlier books.[31] In 1913, free of government or party office, he agreed to deliver ten lectures in the following year, with a second series planned for 1915.[32]

The preparation of the lecture series, which he titled 'Theism and Humanism', apparently did not proceed easily, and when Lady Elcho enquired of their progress he insisted, 'I have no idea!'

> I do nothing else: but that does not mean that I work at them as I feel I should. Meditation is apt to degenerate into day-dreaming; and solitary rambles, which are very delicious, take up long hours, and leave a very small residue of useful work. But I suppose something is being done; at least I hope so.[33]

Despite his protestations, the lectures were ready on time, and the first was delivered to an audience of two thousand. From the outset he meant to approach his great task as Lord Gifford had decreed, from the viewpoint of the 'plain man'. There would be no dazzling metaphysics, Balfour promised: rather, in the best-known lines of his lectures, he explained:

> [The] argument of these lectures has a narrower scope: and when, in the course of them, I speak of God, I mean something other than an Identity wherein all differences vanish, or a Unity which includes but does not transcend the differences which it somehow holds in solution. I mean a God whom men can love, a God to whom men can pray, who takes sides, who has purposes and preferences, whose attributes, howsoever conceived, leave unimpaired the possibility of a personal relation between Himself and those whom He has created.[34]

This theme, the involved and knowable God, ran throughout the ten lectures, in which he once again took up such complicated subjects as natural selection and what would come in a later time to be called 'intelligent design', as well as aesthetics, ethics, and another favourite Balfourian theme: the usefulness of 'common sense' as the foundation of understanding. The lectures broke no new ground for Balfour, as these were all matters he had addressed before in his books. The same can be said of what was perhaps the intellectual theme that underlay most of his writings: that science was impossible without intuition inspired by the Divine. 'The source of knowledge must be rational,' he argued. 'If this be granted, you rule out Mechanism, you rule out Naturalism, you rule out Agnosticism; and a lofty form of Theism becomes, as I think, inevitable.'[35]

Readers of *Foundations of Belief* were familiar with his conclusion:

> [God] is Himself the condition of scientific knowledge. If he be excluded from the causal series which produces beliefs, the cognitive series which justifies them is corrupted at its root. And as it is only in a theistic setting that beauty can retain its deepest meaning, and love its brightest lustre, so these great truths of aesthetics and ethics are but half-truths, unless we add to them

yet a third. We must hold that reason and the works of reason have their source in God; that from Him they draw their inspiration; and that if they repudiate their origin, by this very act they proclaim their own insufficiency.[36]

It seems likely that the founder would have been pleased with the lectures; certainly Balfour was satisfied with their warm reception.

In these pre-war years he also found time to devote considerable attention to his duties as chancellor of the University of Edinburgh, and he became a trustee of Wellington School and joined the boards of several charitable institutions. One of these was the Garton Trust, underwritten by the industrialist Sir Richard Garton, and guided by none other than Norman Angell.[37] Dedicated to the idea that general war was an economically and socially obsolete concept, the foundation was championed by Esher, who apparently persuaded his old friend to join the board. The irony of the organization claiming these two champions of military preparedness is more apparent than real: as Balfour wrote in 1912, the idea of aggressive war in the twentieth century for the purpose of national aggrandizement was 'not only wrong but silly . . . Under modern conditions of industry and finance civilised nations, and, most of all, the great Powers, have interests so intimately bound together, that the violent disruption of friendly relations must produce disasters to all concerned, which no indemnities, no gains in territory, no triumphal arches, can ever compensate.' But Balfour's belief that those who sought peace must be prepared for war remained keen, and it was the duty of the Trust, he insisted, 'to see that in furthering one of the greatest of all causes – the cause of peace – they neither endanger national defence nor weaken national sentiment'.[38]

Balfour's interest in the paranormal continued, though, unlike for his siblings Gerald and Eleanor, by this point it seems to have become more about entertainment than science. He continued to take part in séances, often at Fisher's Hill, in which the Balfours' favourite spiritualist, Mrs Willett (Winifred Coombe-Tennant), claimed to communicate with the dead. During at least one session held there Mrs Willett 'contacted' the spirit of the long-lost May Lyttelton and delivered messages to Balfour, her 'faithful knight'. Balfour obviously enjoyed these affairs, and certainly he played his part, even sending messages to the 'other side'. Yet he seems always to have stopped short of expressing his belief in such mysticism, even to humour his siblings.[39]

Somewhat less romantic was his interest during these years in human genetics. The late nineteenth and early twentieth centuries witnessed enormous enthusiasm for the subject among intellectuals, particularly in

Europe, where there was grave concern about static or falling birth rates, and America, where immigration and a sizeable non-white population exercised those troubled by the racialist bogey of the 'rising tide of colour'.[40] While his thinking on matters of racial characteristics and classification would nowadays be considered quaint or something worse, by the standards of his time it was thought to be both humane and progressive. Though he held out little hope that all the world's races could progress at the same rate towards similar results, or were equally endowed with the same aesthetic, political, and intellectual tools, he would not accept the crude racialism that was widely popular in his world. 'Race discrimination', he wrote plainly to Lady Frances, 'is really quite wrong.' [41]

Their concern led some thinkers to eugenics – more or less, the study of selective breeding. Balfour could not have imagined the twisted science and the resultant horror of twentieth-century genocide, and he viewed the weaknesses visited upon humanity by nature as purely scientific problems – he certainly was quite willing to consider what science could do to understand and even to intervene to strengthen the human race. He became a member of the Linnaean Society, founded in 1788, which brought together scholars and laymen sharing interests in biology, genetics and natural history, and also of the English Eugenics Education Society, formed in 1907. These organizations became forums for discussion of the social as well as the biological impact of eugenics. Of the 'difficult problems that Eugenics raises', he wrote in 1913:

> It is most important that these should be treated with a careful regard, not merely to what science has to tell us about heredity, but to what social sentiments have to teach us about the most important of all social arrangements. There seems prima facie evidence that in the case of the feeble-minded some element really has been omitted: and, if it be a Mendelian characteristic, it will [illegible] continue to be omitted in a certain portion of all descendants. If this be so, there seems a fairly clear case for interference, but I do not think that in our present state of knowledge other clear cases are very numerous. However, I must own that I have not kept myself abreast of the most recent literature on the subject.[42]

Balfour was invited to address the International Congress on Genetics in 1912, when he insisted that the crude Social Darwinist view of human breeding must be considered a thing of the past. He added that 'even if there be, which most [scientists] greatly doubt, any such thing as the inheritance [by the various races] of acquired gifts or acquired qualities, we cannot count upon that as being worthy of estimation in dealing with the causes which are to produce the future improvement or future deterioration of mankind.'[43] To mark his pioneering enthusiasm for this branch of science, Lord Esher led the successful effort to establish the Balfour Professorship in Genetics established at Cambridge in the same year.[44] Happily, the professorship continues to the present day.

Balfour often joked that he would dine with anyone who asked him, but it certainly was the case that after resigning the party leadership he had more time to meet (and often dine) with acquaintances old and new. He enjoyed his occasional attendance at the meetings of the 'Coefficients', the intellectual advance guard of the efficiency movement led by Haldane and the Webbs. He met and befriended the philosopher of the 'vital spirit', Henri Bergson, during his 1911 visit to Britain, and even contributed an appreciative article on him to the *Hibbert Journal*. Balfour indulged his interests in music and art, developing at this time a keen interest in the Italian 'Futurist' painters, and seeking out the pioneering American art historian and critic Bernard Berenson. He also continued the apparently endless renovations and revisions of his beloved Whittingehame.

As Balfour grew older his interest in technology and invention grew no less ardent, and he was delighted with the mechanical wonders that the twentieth century offered. In February 1909, while still party leader and only months before Blériot successfully flew across the Channel, Lord Northcliffe, the proprietor of *The Times*, invited him to France to witness a demonstration by Wilbur Wright of the famous 'Wright Flyer'. He leaped at the opportunity, announcing that he could not resist 'taking part in the miracle'. With his coat-tails flying behind him, the former Prime Minister participated in sending the fragile craft into the air, running alongside while steadying one of the fragile wings. 'It is the most wonderful sight . . .' he said. 'I wish I could be flying with him.'[45] Balfour loved the sensation of speed no less than in his youth, and in this the aircraft surpassed even the motor car. He experienced his first flight in 1911, declaring it exhilarating.[46] Unlike Churchill, who shared his fascination with aircraft, he did not pursue pilot training.[47]

A demonstration of a different sort awaited Balfour in May 1912 at the royal naval review at Weymouth, when he joined His Majesty and the Prince of Wales for a brief excursion in a submerged submarine. On the following day, he and the seventy-four-year-old Lord Morley were taken by Churchill, now First Lord of the Admiralty, into the cramped confines of a gun turret on the *Orion*, one of the latest super-dreadnought battleships.[48] Balfour, who combined an unshakeable commitment to sea power with a thorough distaste for the sea, happily clambered through the great ship's hatches and passageways and announced that he had enjoyed the experience immensely.

During these pre-war years, Balfour finally began to show concern about another matter which was to trouble him for the remainder of his life – his financial affairs. There is no doubt that he spoke from the heart when he commiserated with a friend some years later, reminding him of what he doubtless knew already: 'Money may not be "the root of all evil"; but it certainly is the root of most bothers.'[49] His inherited fortune included large holdings in agricultural land and in investments nurtured by his canny forebears. Like his father, he was a generous landlord, and he lived at a time when agriculture in Britain struggled to be profitable. Not surprisingly, this portion of his patrimony steadily decreased in real value through much of his long life. By the ostentatious standards of his time, Balfour did not live on a particularly lavish scale, yet his properties in Scotland and England, and his style of living – and his public life – required large sums to maintain. Like many of his class, he was much interested in bolstering and diversifying the sources of his wealth. In matters of finance, however, Balfour did not inherit the gifts of his father or grandfather. He was always drawn to the shares market, and particularly to investments in new and technologically innovative ventures, and it did not help matters at all that risk attracted him. Lady Elcho, who frequently chided him about his taste for games of chance, had suffered the disastrous effects of her husband's financial ventures. She was quick to caution her friend. 'I have often noticed', she wrote, 'that the handling . . . of huge sums has a strange & lurid & very great charm in your eyes – & wonder if you call it aesthetic.'[50] Max Aitken, then a wealthy Canadian financier new to London, called on Balfour in 1911, hoping for practical political advice. 'I was not only disappointed,' he recalled. 'I was startled. He would talk of nothing but the stock markets, with special reference to the chances of making a big killing on the New York stock exchange.'[51]

By the end of the nineteenth century Balfour was beginning to realize that his fortune was diminishing, and an alarmed Alice Balfour was already warning her brother that, if something was not done to bring income and expenditure into line, 'it could not last.'[52] Hence the idea of the 'big killing' came to fascinate Balfour, and periodically he invested sizeable sums in one enterprise or another. Few seem to have yielded a profit, and some were nothing less than frauds designed to relieve investors of their money. American mining companies, insurance combines, railways in North and South America, and various innovative technologies all caught his eye – and his money. None cost him so dearly as his passion for the development of an inexpensive household fuel from common peat. In the years before the Great War, he (and later Gerald) became convinced that a process called 'wet carbonising' was the answer both to the need for cheap fuel and to the Balfours' financial concerns. As it was, the problem was not that the method did not work, but that it could not be made profitable, particularly in the hands of the shady entrepreneurs in whom he trusted. Balfour's enthusiasm simply overpowered his caution. He wrote to Lady Elcho in 1915, 'The family fortunes are critical. But it is a real satisfaction to know that the [carbonizing] process is now an assured success; and that whoever reaps the money profit[,] the world is richer by a discovery which will prove of immense economic importance.'[53]

The Balfour brothers poured hundreds of thousands into the process – Sir Max Aitken estimated in 1914 that Arthur Balfour's investment alone was £180,000 – before the Wet Carbonising Company finally failed during the Great War. Then, proving that their faith exceeded their best interests, the Balfours poured additional thousands into a succeeding company, which also collapsed.[54] Certainly his losses, and those of his brother, were massive – the equivalent of millions in modern values.[55] Of incidental interest is the fact that the inventor of the process, an eccentric genius called Martin Ekenberg, died in Brixton Prison awaiting extradition to his native Sweden for attempted murder, for he was apparently also the inventor of the letter bomb.

Though he talked of it, Balfour did little to economize on his lifestyle, and neither the investing nor the expenditures were curtailed. The head of a large family, he had endless opportunity to demonstrate his generosity, and expenses cannot have grown less as the many nieces and nephews grew into young adulthood. There is no doubt that the pleasure he took in his generosity was quite real. In June 1912, for example, he insisted on presenting to society the new version of 'Us four', Gerald's daughters, Ruth and Eleanor, and Eustace's, Joan and Alison, with an elaborate ball at Carlton Gardens. The event was reputed to have cost thousands, and was a delight to the press. A reporter amused the elder statesman by impudently enquiring whether he had waltzed with the girls and, if so, had he taken lessons for the occasion.[56]

Balfour 'officially' returned to the House of Commons on 14 March 1912, and Balcarres wondered if he had chosen that day because he had been summoned from the Riviera for the christening of the Elchos' grandson, to whom he was to be godfather.[57] Whatever the reason, at Bonar Law's request he threw himself immediately into parliamentary business, offering a motion to reject the government plan to establish a national wage for miners. These were the years of the great 'labour unrest' in which millions of work-hours were lost in trade disputes, and the nation was at that moment in the midst of a crippling miners' strike. So exercised was Balfour that he told Balcarres that he might volunteer for a day of coal portering if the dock workers refused to handle 'blackleg' coal – a notion, advantageously for the sixty-four-year-old, which was soon forgotten.[58]

At the same time, supporters of the extension of political suffrage to women were raising their own demonstrations. The idea was not unknown in Britain, but a new energy infused the campaign in these years, due at least in part to the ferocity of the small but zealous Women's Social and Political Union, led by Mrs Emmeline Pankhurst and her daughters, Cristabel and Sylvia. These were the 'suffragettes', so called to differentiate them from the more moderate 'suffragists', whose measured protests the militants pushed to the back pages of the newspapers. Balfour's sisters-in-law, Frances and Betty, were both keen suffragists and fought the good fight within the family, often trying his patience with their appeals that he take an active part in securing the prize.[59]

Balfour was among the minority of Unionists who looked favourably on women's suffrage, but he refused to involve himself directly in the struggle beyond declaring his support – he would do no crusading. He wrote to Lady Betty in 1911, 'I am, and have always been, a steady, though not vehement, supporter of the Movement; and I do not think my opinions have undergone any very substantial change during the years in which the subject has been before the country and the House.' His support, he insisted, was not based on any notion of abstract right, but rather on logic and the responsibility of any dutiful representative government. He believed that the franchise was not an inalienable entitlement of either sex, though he added that it seemed to work well enough as it was. However, once there was evidence that a popular majority desired the change, then it was the duty of the state to see that it was promptly effected. He added the personal complaint that, while he expected to be abused by anti-suffragists, he was particularly annoyed with the suffragists, including the ladies of his own family: 'What I do complain of is that I should be expected to act as if I took the same view of the importance of this subject as those who think it is a vital question.'[60] He could not resist adding, in a letter to the veteran militant Annie Kenney, that he had difficulty believing that 'any great improvement in the social and industrial position of women would follow from an extension of the franchise'.[61]

Suffragette violence he found absolutely repellent, and Balcarres noted that, despite Balfour's long advocacy of women's suffrage, he had become 'disgusted at the hysteria and antics of the militant group but he is aghast at the condonation which the latter receive from the non-militant section.'[62] His repulsion reached its zenith when militant suffragettes burned the ancient church at Whitekirk, near Whittingehame.[63] However, he did not change his convictions, as he wrote to Curzon, president of the National League for Opposing Women's Suffrage, 'I have been a consistent supporter all through my political life, and now that the cause of the reasonable moderate women is under so deep a cloud of unpopularity owing to the violence of the extremists, I do not feel disposed to desert them.'[64] He held fast, and was pleased when female suffrage finally arrived in 1918; and in 1919 he was one of the two supporters who presented to the House the first female MP to take her seat, the American-born Viscountess Astor.[65]

These movements were disturbing and divisive, but the unfinished battle over Tariff Reform still held far greater power to shake Unionism to its foundations. Bonar Law attempted in late 1911 to clarify one element of the debate by abandoning Balfour's 1910 referendum pledge – the Liberals, after all, had not responded to his challenge to reciprocate with a Home Rule plebiscite. The change was announced at the party conference in November, to the ecstatic delight of the tariff enthusiasts who crowded the Royal Albert Hall. The joy was not shared uniformly in the party, particularly among the pro-tariff moderates, who worried over the electoral cost of abandoning the pledge and feared the Liberals' cry of 'Food taxes!'

Balfour was unconvinced that his successor's tactic was the right one, and confessed to a friend: 'The old [tariff] difficulty, of course, remains, and, so far as I can see, must for the present remain without any complete or satisfactory solution. It is, however, no longer for *me* to solve it.'[66] He had always sought, and seldom won, flexibility in the fiscal debate, and thought that Bonar Law had made a terrible miscalculation. He insisted that he had 'always begged them, if they could, to leave a loop-hole . . . I am afraid Bonar Law is having a great deal of worry over this.'[67] In the end, the Unionists wished to keep Balfour's referendum pledge. An accommodation was hammered out, and the party chose to keep both the pledge and the two leaders, Bonar Law and Lansdowne, who acquiesced to the reversal of their policy. Balfour supported the pledge *and* the leaders, so, as he wrote to the Earl of Derby (the former Lord Stanley), he was quite satisfied. But Eddy Derby liked neither tariffs nor Bonar Law, and longed from the day of his resignation for his old leader's return. Balfour, as noted earlier, crushed this hope and called his friend to order: if Derby and his friends resisted the compromise, only the worst could be expected. He warned his admirer in the plainest language, 'Remember that if Bonar Law goes the Party, as far as I can see, is doomed.'[68] Derby was silenced, Bonar Law did not go, and Balfour continued to give him his full support.

Politics in the years immediately after the passage of the Parliament Act were fought with a bitterness unequalled in Balfour's recollection. No advantage, no matter how real or illusory, went unexploited; no weakness or wound was left unprobed. A rather lurid example was the Marconi scandal, which burst on the scene in the spring of 1913 and involved accusations that the Chancellor of the Exchequer, Lloyd George, and the Attorney General, Sir Rufus Isaacs, had taken advantage of confidential information to conduct personally profitable dealings in Marconi Company shares. Of this long and untidy story, it need only be noted here that the ministers had indeed purchased stock in the American Marconi Company while the government was negotiating with the British Marconi Company to establish a worldwide wireless network. When rumours of the dealings inevitably leaked, Isaacs denied their involvement in 'that company' – meaning British Marconi. For as long as possible he remained silent about the affiliated US firm, and when the full story became known the Liberal ministers were publicly embarrassed and the Unionists were outraged. When unscrupulous newspapers in Britain and France exaggerated the details of the affair, the ministers sued for libel. By the summer of 1913 the rather unsavoury details became known, and the public was treated to an unseemly and entertaining season of political theatre.[69]

While Unionist backbenchers howled for their heads, the accused struggled to avoid the charge of improper behaviour and pressed ahead with their libel case against the newspapers that had exaggerated the story.[70] Asquith created a select committee of the House – with a Liberal majority – which in June exonerated the ministers. Bonar Law tabled a motion of censure, which was predictably defeated on party lines. Balfour did not play a major role in the affair, and at its climax, in June, he told the House that he had no desire to see the offending ministers driven from public life but thought they ought publicly to express regret for their actions.[71] Churchill in private marvelled that the Unionist leaders did not press the scandal to greater advantage: 'Some of them', he said, 'were too stupid . . . frankly some of them were too nice.'[72] Balfour he included in the latter category.

Balfour's own appetite for investment adventure was not unknown, and as a distraction from his own difficulties Lloyd George a few months later attempted to tar the former Prime Minister with a similar brush by dredging up an old embarrassment.[73] Years before, Balfour had invested in the enterprises of Whitaker Wright, then acclaimed as the financial wizard of his day. His wizardry was revealed to be mere sleight of hand when, in 1901, his London & Globe Finance Company collapsed, and Wright was shown to be little more than a clever swindler. He was tried and convicted, and escaped prison only when he swallowed poison following his sentencing.

Balfour had held shares in London & Globe, and like most other investors he lost every shilling. He wrote to Lord Robert Cecil that he had thought at the time that the Wright case might be suitable for further prosecution by the Attorney General, but was advised that it should be left to the criminal courts. Lloyd George's strained imputations of conflict of interest, which Lord Robert saw as libellous, Balfour waved aside simply as 'childish'.[74] Besides, he noted, he had forgotten the investment entirely and had to be reminded of it by Wilfrid Short – and also of the not inconsiderable amount lost: some £1,000. The entire episode he simply brushed off as politics as usual.[75]

Even the endless tariff debate gave way to an older struggle, which now reached what appeared to be its ultimate crisis: on 11 April 1912 Asquith introduced the new Irish Home Rule bill. With the Parliament Act in place, the Liberal–Irish–Labour alliance had only to pass it through the Commons in three successive sessions, and nothing the Unionist-dominated Lords could do would keep it from the statute books. Anti-Home Rule passions ran highest in Protestant-dominated Ulster, and on Easter Sunday 1912, beneath the largest Union Jack ever flown, Bonar Law and Carson addressed an enormous crowd near Belfast. Carson, once the most feared prosecutor in Ireland, glowered and challenged the throng to raise their hands to swear 'Never under any circumstances will we submit to Home Rule.'[76] Thousands shouted out their oaths, and that chilling ceremony would come to symbolize the battle over the third Home Rule bill: the key issue was to be the 'Protestant Province' of Ulster. Lord Milner would soon write to a disciple, 'To my mind there is only one road to Salvation for Unionists now, and it is to shout "Ulster, Ulster", all the time . . . No running after Lloyd George, no mention of Tariff reform . . .'[77]

Balfour never doubted that the British electorate would vote to preserve the Union, if an election contested unambiguously over Home Rule could be brought about – something he was convinced the Liberal government meant to resist to the end. He and his colleagues also insisted that the

Asquith administration had failed to complete the revision of the constitution pledged in the Parliament Act itself, which called for reforming the House of Lords 'as a Second Chamber constituted on a popular instead of a hereditary basis'. Therefore, they raged, the ancient constitution was 'suspended', and the government was acting in a kind of constitutional limbo, on an 'interim' basis.[78] They demanded that Asquith immediately present his design for a reformed second chamber and consult the electorate. In the House, they hammered away at the government night after night, but Asquith was unmoved – Home Rule must come first, he insisted, and then there would be time for other important matters.

Balfour accepted at face value that both sides in Ireland meant business. He dreaded the possibilities: a sort of private army, the Ulster Volunteers, had already been formed by the Ulster Unionists, and the nationalists followed suit with their own National Volunteers. His mind was filled with dark thoughts, and he wondered if the old rules of the game were breaking up. 'I look with much misgiving upon the general loosening of the ordinary ties of social obligation,' he wrote to Bonar Law in September 1913. 'The behaviour of the Suffragettes and Syndicalists are symptoms of this malady, and the government, in its criminal folly, is apparently prepared to add to these a rebellion in Ireland.'[79] He had recently returned from a brief stay at Balmoral, where the King seemed desperate to identify a path towards compromise. Balfour kept his anxieties to himself, and continued to advise the monarch that the government should request a dissolution – 'the only thoroughly satisfactory course' – adding that, if they continued to refuse, one should be forced on them.[80] This cannot have been much comfort to George V, to whom things looked more menacing with each passing day.

A few weeks later Balfour forwarded to the palace his advice that the King should consider going so far as to change his ministers on 'his own motion', concluding that under the 'present interim constitution' it certainly could be done. Accepting that the appropriate circumstances must be rare, he suggested that one such might arise if a government unwisely pursued a course without the 'express concurrence' of the electorate – as he thought was the case with Home Rule.[81] He had already considered to whom the King might turn for advice if he took such a step, and suggested that an elder statesman might serve as premier for the sole purpose of carrying out an election focused on the Home Rule question. Rosebery would do, or perhaps himself (or even the two acting jointly), though he admitted that, as he himself was still 'identified' with party politics, Rosebery was probably the better choice.

This was a hazardous plan, and the King had no intention of adopting it.[82] It is unlikely that Balfour saw it as anything but a design for a last desperate act, and, as we shall see, he was at the very same time suggesting a possible compromise to Bonar Law. No more was heard of this scheme. Balfour was well aware of its volatility, and cautioned Sandars that it would be 'fatal' if it became public knowledge – and in this, if not in the scheme itself, he was quite correct.[83]

The Unionists continued to press the case for a dissolution and a Home Rule election – insisting that the recent trend in by-elections demonstrated the will of the electorate. Since the second 1910 election, Unionists had taken seat after seat from the Liberals, while losing only one. By the outbreak of the Great War, the Unionists were the largest party in the Commons by some thirty seats, and Central Office calculated that these represented an average turnover in voting totals of 1,300 per constituency. Surely, the managers were confident, they were on the path to a great Unionist victory in the next general election.[84] But, unless an election could somehow be forced, Asquith would continue to govern so long as he held the allegiance of the Irish Nationalists. All the Opposition could do was to maintain unrelenting pressure and hope that the administration's alliances or its resolve would break.

The government majority held, however, and hope of stopping the Home Rule bill became more faint with each day. And, as Milner had predicted, the crisis came more and more to be about 'Ulster, Ulster, all the time'. At the time of the 1910 inter-party constitutional conference, devolution or 'Home Rule all round' caught the attention of certain Unionists as a possible answer to their difficulties – to them, it still made sense that if Nationalist Ireland was to have Home Rule, why should Ulster not enjoy the right to reject it? Curiously, it was an independent-minded Liberal MP who brought the idea of Ulster exclusion into the debate over the new Home Rule bill. On 11 June 1912 Thomas Agar-Robartes introduced an amendment to exclude four Protestant-majority Ulster counties (Antrim, Armagh, Down and Londonderry) from the authority of the proposed Home Rule parliament.[85] Faced with an outbreak of Nationalist anger, Asquith travelled to Dublin a few weeks later to assure a large audience that Agar-Robartes spoke only for himself and not for the government.

Though unqualified opposition to any form of Home Rule continued to be their official policy, the Unionists supported Agar-Robartes's amendment on the reasoning that it was unlikely to pass, and in the implausible event that it did it might break up the Liberal–Irish alliance and force the longed-for election. Balfour and certain other Unionists also realized that, as private armies drilled in warehouses and public parks in Ireland, the Home Rule struggle had reached a point at which compromise of some kind might be the only device to prevent bloodshed.[86]

Predictably, the Agar-Robartes amendment failed, but the Ulster exclusion jinn was out of its bottle. On Ulster Day, 23 September 1912, more than a quarter-million Ulstermen, some in their own blood, signed a Solemn League and Covenant pledging themselves to employ 'all means which may be found necessary to defeat the present conspiracy to set up a Home Rule parliament in Dublin'. And if such a government were created, they pledged further to reject its authority. Not to be outdone, nearly as many Ulsterwomen signed a similar pledge of their own. This was strong talk, and, much as he disliked Home Rule, Balfour hated even more the possibility that, because of it, Britain might slip into violence and perhaps even civil war. As preparations for the Covenant went forward, Balfour was at Balmoral worrying the King about forcing a dissolution. Winston Churchill was in attendance too, and their informal discussions also revolved around the Irish crisis. Afterwards, Balfour wrote to Bonar Law that an election still remained the best solution, but added that, after talking with Churchill, he believed if this proved unattainable perhaps a compromise – Irish Home Rule with Ulster exclusion – was the only realistic solution to their dilemma.[87] He was not optimistic, however, noting that at the moment all prospects appeared gloomy.

The King hoped for some sort of inter-party talks, and by early October the deft Churchill was working to this same end: the plan was for Asquith and Bonar Law to meet privately. Any talk of compromise was fraught with political danger for either side: Asquith's government would be doomed if it lost the allegiance of the Irish Home Rulers. Bonar Law needed the Ulster Unionist MPs, and sympathy for their cause ran deep among the British Unionists in both Houses.

All eyes seemed to be turned towards Northern Ireland, as the idea of Ulster exclusion gained momentum, and even Carson concluded confidentially that the Southern Unionists would accept it if the Home Rule bill could not be stopped.[88] Among the Liberals, Churchill favoured exclusion, and Lloyd George purposefully leaked to a Scottish journalist (who passed it on to Bonar Law) that allowing Ulster to 'contract out' of Home Rule was preferable to violence, but that it was for the Unionists to suggest a scheme before negotiations could begin.[89]

Asquith did invite Bonar Law to meet him, and the venue chosen was Cherkley Court, Aitken's house in Surrey.[90] Three meetings were held between mid-October and early December, and they centred on the Ulster question – and on that rock they foundered. There were many questions and few answers. Which counties might be excluded? Would religiously mixed Fermanagh and Tyrone be included, or perhaps subdivided? Would exclusion be permanent or temporary? Would there be plebiscites? Very few of any party knew of these secret discussions, and Bonar Law sent full reports of each meeting to only two colleagues: Lansdowne and Balfour. In reply, Balfour praised Asquith for his 'boldness and foresight', but added that he himself was certain that the Unionists would accept the Home Rule bill, even with Ulster excluded, only if they were absolutely certain that the Liberal government could hold the allegiance of the Nationalists, making passage of the bill unstoppable. In the meantime, two more by-elections fell to the Unionists, and Balfour was certain that so long as this trend continued it would be difficult to convince their colleagues to surrender their hope for a dissolution and a parliamentary defeat of Home Rule.[91]

After the failure of the Asquith–Bonar Law talks, Asquith met privately with Carson on 16 December and tried without success to convince the Ulster leader to accept a plan granting Ulster limited autonomy under the authority of a Dublin parliament. Carson had heard this before, and rejected it out of hand. A second meeting in early January 1914 achieved nothing. Bonar Law even met secretly with the Nationalist MP William O'Brien – predictably without success.[92] Balfour praised these efforts to show the party as open-minded and resist Liberal and Irish efforts to portray them as 'bigots'. Nevertheless, none of these discussions produced a solution. In early 1914 Balfour concluded with monumental understatement, 'The New Year is likely to be a troubled one.'[93]

January found Balfour in Glasgow for the Gifford Lectures, and in Westminster Bonar Law was raising the political stakes even higher. He produced a plan to amend the Army Annual Act in the Lords to forbid use of the army to quell resistance in Ulster following passage of Home Rule until three months after the seating of a new parliament.[94] This tactic had been raised by the Unionists in 1911 and 1913, and it would have been disastrous then, as it certainly would have been in 1914.[95]

Bonar Law, as always, turned for counsel to his predecessor.[96] Balfour was disturbed by the scheme, and replied in early February noting its 'extraordinary interest and importance'; but, he added, might it not leave the party open precisely to the charges of religious bigotry which they insisted were unjust? One-third of the population of potentially explosive Belfast were Catholic, and if the forces could not be called upon to protect this minority from possible molestation by Protestant extremists, how could the Unionists continue to call themselves the party of law?[97] He admitted to Lansdowne that, while the whole idea 'went against the grain', he accepted that in 'revolutionary times I suppose revolutionary measures are necessary'.[98] On 12 March 1914 an unsettled Shadow Cabinet gave reluctant approval to the scheme.[99]

Balfour did not attend this meeting, and remained pessimistic about the plan. He need not have worried, however, as it died soon after this point – not because of opposition from among the party leaders, but because backbench opinion adamantly opposed it.[100] The very existence of such a dangerous scheme is evidence of the superheated atmosphere of politics in these months. Rumours circulated among Unionists that arrest warrants had been issued for Carson and his lieutenants, and some believed that martial law would soon be applied to Ulster and that a 'pogrom' would soon lay waste to the province. These were fantastic tales. Yet it was true that Major General Sir Nevil Macready had been given a precautionary 'sleeping' commission (another secret leaked to the Unionists) as military governor of Belfast, and Churchill stirred the waters by combining provocative speeches with orders summoning the Third Battle Squadron to Lamlash, on the Isle of Arran. Certainly Balfour feared that the government might be up to something.[101]

A week after the Shadow Cabinet discussed the abortive Army Act scheme, another blow was struck against the national peace of mind as the mass resignation of army officers at the Curragh camp near Dublin launched a far greater crisis. For centuries, Ulstermen had had a strong presence in the British Army, and in the poisonous atmosphere of early 1914 some chose to end their careers rather than risk playing a part in forcing Home Rule on Ulster. The so-called 'Curragh Mutiny' was no mutiny at all, and arose only because of the lawful order to certain army units to advance into Ulster to protect arms stores from possible seizure by Unionist militants.[102] It is necessary here only to say that owing to the bungling of the War Secretary, Sir John Seely, and the army commander in Ireland, Lieutenant General Sir Arthur Paget, officers with a 'direct family connection' to Ulster were offered the unprecedented choice of obeying orders to move north or remaining behind, while other dissenting officers were to be decommissioned with no questions asked. As a result, some sixty officers of the 3rd Cavalry Brigade, led by Brigadier Sir Hubert Gough, immediately chose dismissal. It seemed that the warnings of Lord Roberts might well prove true: to expect the army to force Home Rule on a reluctant Ulster would threaten the very existence of the Regular Forces – and an army without officers is merely a company of armed men.[103] Balfour thought the government's order to move troops might well have had darker motives than the securing of arms depôts. Whatever they may have been, he concluded to Chamberlain, for the moment 'by his blundering, [Paget] has saved us from a great disaster.'[104]

Asquith and his government were shocked by the Curragh affair; the War Secretary who had allowed it to happen, Seely, resigned, and Asquith temporarily took the post. The resignations of the Commander of the Imperial General Staff, Field Marshal Sir John French, and the Adjutant General, Lieutenant General Sir John Ewart, followed; Paget was disgraced, and, in an incredible compromise in London, Gough and his officers were reinstated with guarantees from Seely that they would not be called upon to take action in Ulster. The ink was hardly dry on this bizarre agreement before Bonar Law, Balfour and their colleagues knew of it, probably from their principal source of information at the time, Major General Sir Henry Wilson, the Director of Military Operations. Wilson was a good soldier flawed by an unquenchable appetite for political intrigue; he was also a violently anti-Home Rule Anglo-Irishman who had been meeting covertly for months with Balfour, Bonar Law and other Unionists.[105]

Once Paget had made his fatal offer, and the recalcitrant officers returned to duty with their written guarantee – the 'peccant paragraphs', as Balfour labelled them – the government had every reason to fear that they might not have the means to enforce Home Rule in the north of Ireland. Asquith accepted the errant War Secretary's resignation, appointed himself to the post, and promptly quashed the agreement he had forged with Gough, but the damage had been done.[106] Soon army headquarters in Dublin reported that as much as one-third of the officer corps in Ireland would be likely to resign or accept dismissal rather than march north.[107] Yet the government proceeded with the Home Rule bill, and the Opposition with its demand for a dissolution. The political divide seemed unbreachable, and respected statesmen and citizens alike wondered about the possibility of open violence, of civil war in Ireland in 1914. Asquith announced that he could go no further than the offer he had explored in his secret talks with Bonar Law: to exclude Ulster from Home Rule for six years only. Even if Redmond and the Nationalists could be made to swallow it, the Unionists, let alone the Ulstermen, would not. Nonetheless, the Prime Minister said it was his final offer.

The Irish Union had been a pillar of Balfour's political life. As 'Bloody Balfour' decades earlier, his unbending resolution to pacify the island without Home Rule had made him a hero among Unionists. In the years that followed, he had risen to defend the Union against all challenges. Now, in his sixty-sixth year, he was prepared to embrace compromise – but, as he had told a London audience in February, it must be the right compromise. He wanted nothing to do with United Kingdom federalism, and he rejected Asquith's six-year interim plan. Ulster was right, he insisted, and it should not be assumed that Ulster would not fight – besides, he added, 'If I were an Ulsterman I would do as the Ulstermen are doing.' But a Home Rule plan that stopped at the borders of the province of Ulster would save the nation from the 'evils of what cannot be undone' – that is, civil war. There must be 'a clean cut, and nothing but a clean cut will do it'. If the government refused, there lay ahead only 'irremediable and hopeless disaster'.[108] In his view, if blood were shed, it would be on the heads of Asquith and his colleagues.

Balfour continued to play his part in making certain that the government remained as uneasy as possible – sometimes in unprecedented ways. In early April, Hyde Park witnessed what certainly must have been one of the largest political rallies ever held ('Against British Forces being used to Shoot Ulster Loyalists'). Temporary platforms were erected throughout the park, and from these the most celebrated Unionist orators harangued hundreds of thousands of listeners. Carson, Milner, Long and F. E. Smith were among the speakers, and so was a rather uncomfortable Arthur Balfour – wearing the same flamboyant 'Support Loyal Ulster' badge as these celebrated firebrands.[109] He spoke from the back of a lorry, and was cheered wildly – so much so that he was certain no one could hear his words. Balfour did his best to play the demagogue, but it certainly did not suit him. Chamberlain recalled him saying afterwards, 'I usually do a great deal of my thinking on my legs, as you know, but I *couldn't* think under those conditions.'[110]

By this point the Unionist chieftains saw that the possibility of dissolution was slipping away and tied their hopes to permanent Ulster exclusion. This was not surrender, they insisted, and the Shadow Cabinet agreed on 5 May that they would never give actual support to the Home Rule bill, no matter what compromises might be wrenched from Asquith. Yet they also accepted that it would be impossible – when they won the next election, as they expected – to repeal any Home Rule Ulster-exclusion arrangement that had become law. Balfour believed there could be no going back: if the government intended to 'cut up the United Kingdom . . . then there cannot be a more obvious, a more necessary, or a more inevitable division than the division between the North-east of Ireland and the rest of Ireland'.[111] The tragedy of violence in Ulster must be avoided, and he was prepared to accept the end of the historic Union for which he had fought throughout his public life. Now, he told Chamberlain, they must 'cut Nationalist Ireland wholly adrift and give it full colonial self-government'.[112]

But this was not within their power, and permanent exclusion had not been offered by the government. Bonar Law and Carson met with Asquith on 5 May without result: the Unionists demanded unconditional Ulster exclusion or dissolution, but the Prime Minister would not be moved from his offer of Home Rule coupled with an amending bill granting only temporary exclusion. More desperate men took matters into their own hands, for a few days earlier the Ulster Volunteers had successfully landed 35,000 rifles and 3 million rounds of ammunition at Larne. In July, the Irish Volunteers conducted their own gun-running adventure in broad daylight at Howth, only to be intercepted by the authorities. The chaotic aftermath that followed brought a tragic confrontation in nearby Bachelor's Walk, which resulted in three dead and thirty-eight injured civilians.[113]

As Home Rule crept towards the statute books, in the Lords the government introduced its promised amendment bill, offering to each Ulster county a six-year exemption from Home Rule (to be decided locally by plebiscite), to be followed by reversion to the authority of the planned Dublin parliament – a mere 'six year stay of execution', Carson growled. The Unionist majority in the Lords sent the bill to the Commons only after striking out any reference to the six-year time limit. The question was no longer simply Home Rule 'yes' or Home Rule 'no', but Home Rule for whom, and for how long?

The King, desperate for a peaceful solution, again pressed for an inter-party conference, and Asquith finally agreed.[114] On 17 July the Prime Minister met his sovereign in the palace gardens to settle arrangements, and noted later to his mistress, Venetia Stanley, that King George 'was anxious' that Balfour be included; but Asquith refused the royal request because, he insisted: 'A.B. in this matter is a real wrecker.'[115] In the end, those attending were Asquith and Lloyd George (Liberal), Bonar Law and Lansdowne (Unionist), Redmond and John Dillon (Irish Nationalist) and Carson and James Craig (Ulster Unionist). At the King's suggestion, Speaker James Lowther presided.

For three days the conferees met in the '1844 Room' at Buckingham Palace, and for three days they wrangled without reaching compromise: Asquith and Redmond hinted that they might be willing to give way over the time-limit for exclusion, but the Irish would not accept the exclusion of all the six counties (Antrim, Armagh, Down, Fermanagh, Londonderry and Tyrone) demanded by the Ulstermen. Over this, Carson and the Ulstermen would not budge. And there the conference deadlocked. With Balfour's complete agreement, Bonar Law had sought a settlement. Asquith had as well – but they apparently did not wish for the same settlement. Neither man would proceed further than his Irish allies would allow, and neither Redmond nor Carson could face their supporters if they 'deserted' their people. Perhaps each side thought the other was bluffing.[116] The doomed conference collapsed on the 24th, two days before the tragic affair at Bachelor's Walk. There appeared to be nothing left but to press ahead. Debate on the six-year amending bill was rescheduled for 30 July, and the possibility seemed very real to many that it would all end in bloodshed.

August dawned in violence, but not precisely the violence which some in Britain had feared. At the end of June the heir to the throne of the Dual Monarchy of Austria–Hungary, the Archduke Franz Ferdinand, and his wife had been assassinated by Bosnian nationalists in distant Sarajevo. On the day that the Buckingham Palace conference collapsed, as the participants made ready to take their leave of their King, newspapers were brought in telling of the harsh demands by the Austrians upon the Serbs, whom they held responsible for the terrible murders. At the same time, Arthur Balfour was presiding over an informal committee to discuss a memorial for Joseph Chamberlain, who had died earlier in the month. All these gentlemen now read the same newspapers. Despite all that had gone before, the Irish Question was for the moment put aside in Britain, and the passion and bellicosity it aroused was subsumed for a time into a greater, bloodier, conflict.

But first there was some unfinished Irish business. When war came in August, a political truce was agreed at Westminster. Under the strictures of the Parliament Act, however, Asquith was obliged to do something about the unresolved Home Rule bill. At Redmond's urging, it was decided to complete passage of the bill and at the same time announce that Home Rule would be suspended for the duration of hostilities. This plan he announced on 7 September, and the Unionists – who had pledged to set aside formal opposition for the duration – protested that this was a resumption of the Liberal political agenda.[117]

The government's intentions cannot have come as a surprise, as Balfour had learned of them in outline from Haldane and the Foreign Secretary, Sir Edward Grey, on 12 August. Balfour told Bonar Law that he had argued with the two ministers for at least a ninety-day interim before Home Rule took effect after the end of the war.[118] Asquith was unmoved by any protest and went forward with the bill, under the protection of the Parliament Act.

'How is it possible', Balfour wrote, 'to let political warfare run riot within the [House of Commons] and proclaim a truce of God everywhere else? Such a policy is unthinkable.'[119] On 15 September, the day designated for debate on the matter, Bonar Law spoke only briefly for the Opposition, hurled his malediction at the heads of ministers, and stalked from the Chamber.[120] Balfour and the rest of the Unionists silently followed. Though in suspense until peacetime, Home Rule was now the law of the land

The decision to enter the war in August 1914 was, of course, in the hands of the government, and the Unionists could do no more than offer their advice. Their leader, Bonar Law, had little experience with matters of foreign or defence policy, while Balfour was viewed among Unionists (and many Liberals) as one of his party's wise men on such matters. Certainly he and Winston Churchill had had their differences since the younger man's days as the *enfant terrible* of Unionism, yet the two shared a common goal to strengthen a navy both thought seriously challenged by Germany.[121] The same, of course, could be said of Balfour's co-operation with Admiral Fisher. Churchill had gone so far as to arrange for Balfour to receive official Admiralty papers.[122]

Grey, who would not have considered doing the same with Bonar Law or Chamberlain, also consulted him on Foreign Office matters. As early as 1908, for example, the Foreign Secretary (with Asquith's approval) sought Balfour's opinion on defence policy and 'offered him all the papers'. Balfour preferred an oral briefing, which the Prime Minister left to Esher.[123] Grey continued to seek Balfour's views from time to time during the international crises that punctuated those pre-war years.[124] In 1912 Balfour was comfortable enough with their relationship to send Grey a lengthy memorandum stressing the need to strengthen the French *Entente* by refashioning it into a real alliance.[125]

Haldane, whose respect for Balfour's opinions on defence policy also defied the political antagonism of the time, in 1912 sounded out the former Unionist leader on the possibility of resuming membership of the Committee of Imperial Defence.[126] Anxious over the fractious political situation, Balfour wisely declined. However, when Seely in the same year requested the appointment of a CID subcommittee once again to study the nation's vulnerability to invasion, Balfour agreed to serve.[127] As always, behind the inquiry lay the question of mandatory military service, for which Lord Roberts and his National Service League had tirelessly beaten their drums for more than a decade. Once again their campaign failed, and the committee found mandatory service to be unnecessary.[128] Balfour remained convinced that compulsory service was not the British way of war. A supremely powerful navy was the key to security against invasion.[129] And, as he pointed out to a mandatory-service sympathizer:

> Now it seems certain that, whatever else we have, we must have a volunteer Army. You cannot raise soldiers by conscription, and then send them in large numbers to tropical countries on the other side of the world; and, if ever we come to conscription, one of the most serious dangers that will have to be faced is the effect of conscription upon voluntary enlistment.[130]

Balfour could not know in 1912 that two years later Britain would find itself at war, and that soon thereafter he would once again be in office and immersed in a bitter political struggle over conscription.

Balfour's role as a sage on defence questions sometimes led to odd circumstances in these politically divisive times. In a celebrated instance he strolled in rather tardily to the last meeting of the invasion subcommittee, having returned from a Unionist meeting in his constituency. The committee had been making little progress, and Colonel Hankey recalled, 'Almost immediately he grasped the points at issue, and there and then, with inimitable skill, he drafted paragraphs which brought the whole subcommittee together.' Then, as the two walked out together, Balfour added, 'I spent the first part of the afternoon abusing the government in the City, and the second part in solving their difficulties at the House of Commons.'[131] 'Abuse' the government he might do, but they seemed to consider it worth the price. The historian of Unionist defence policy in this period has described him as a kind of 'cross-bench guru' where such matters were concerned – and so indeed he was.[132]

On 1 August 1914 the Continental Great Powers began the first general conflict since the defeat of Napoleon. The pieces fell easily into place: Austria declared war on Serbia; Russia, 'Big Brother' to the Slavs, mobilized; and Germany, ally of the Austrians, demanded that Russian mobilization cease and that France pledge its neutrality in the event of a Russo-German war, which demand Paris of course rejected. Ultimata crossed counter-ultimata, all of which were ignored, the alliance systems were activated, and German troops were soon on Belgian soil. Italy clung to its escape clause in the Triple Alliance and declared neutrality; while Britain, legally obligated to none of the combatants, stood apart for the moment – its government divided, and its Prime Minister undecided.

On the same day, the Unionist chieftains, Bonar Law, Balfour, Lansdowne and Chamberlain (with Major General Sir Henry Wilson),

THE LAMPS GO OUT

gathered at Lansdowne House to decide what to do. All agreed that Britain must support France in what would surely be a brief and intense war. Balfour continued to believe, as he had cautioned Grey in June 1912, that the British people would never countenance the nation's standing aside while the Germans had their way with France. Now the worst had happened, and the Unionists were in agreement on war: Bonar Law notified Asquith that they were at his disposal. When, on 2 August, there was no reply, a letter (drafted by Chamberlain) was sent to No. 10 strongly encouraging support of Britain's *Entente* partners and pledging Unionist support. Asquith remained publicly noncommittal; but the next day, in the House, Grey made the most celebrated speech of his life, coming down on the side of war at the side of France. Bonar Law reiterated Unionist support, and Redmond and Carson, in rare agreement, did the same for their people. While pro-war crowds demonstrated in Parliament Square, the famous ultimatum passed from London to Berlin: the Germans must withdraw from Belgium. Of course they did not, and Britain found itself at war with Germany and its allies from 11 p.m. on Tuesday 4 August. 'The lamps', as Grey feared, were indeed 'going out all over Europe'.[133]

In the end, only Morley, the Lord President, and John Burns, President of the Board of Trade, left the Cabinet in opposition to the decision for war, and a government singularly thin on military experience waited for the traditional British war machine to function as it always seemed to have done in the past. Few on any side in the conflict could have guessed the kind of war that lay before them. Balfour had no doubts, and wrote to Haldane (now Lord Chancellor and temporarily in charge at the War Office) on that anxious Tuesday that 'as regards Germany, we have burnt our boats. We have chosen our side, and must abide by the result.' It was, he advised, no time for hesitation: 'Is it not a fundamental principle of strategy of this particular kind either to keep out of the conflict altogether or to strike quickly and to strike with your whole strength?'[134] As the British ultimatum expired and the nation passed into a state of war, Balfour met with Haldane. He pressed his case for the immediate dispatch of the British Expeditionary Force and came away somewhat troubled by what he thought was a certain 'indecision of purpose' in the Government.[135] Nonetheless, Asquith summoned a war council of senior ministers and commanders which met over the next two days – their decision was to send four infantry and one cavalry division of the BEF to link up with the French – the remainder of the force soon joined them – and if ever a die was cast, this was one.[136] The troops were in transit on the 9th, and were in action a fortnight later.

For the moment, there was little else for a 'cross-bench guru' to do. On 11 August he motored with his niece to Blackdown Camp to join the family send-off for young Oswald Balfour, Eustace's youngest son, whose regiment was off to France. Another nephew, Arthur Strutt, Lord Rayleigh's second son, would soon be on active service with the Royal Navy, and a young cousin, William Balfour of Balbirnie, in France with his cavalry regiment. Mrs Dugdale recalled the military pageantry of the day at Blackdown, and Balfour's patience with his admirers. The strain upon him was greater than it seemed, she witnessed, for once in the car and free of prying eyes he once again was overcome by emotion. No one could know the scope of the horror that lay ahead, but Balfour knew well enough that all war was terrible. By the evening he had recovered his humour, and when family and friends gathered for dinner at the Royal Automobile Club, he enquired of the waiter, 'Have you still got any German beer? . . . Let's have it while we still can.'[137]

I I

First Lord

IN AUGUST, 1914, Bonar Law pledged his party to 'Patriotic Opposition' –
essentially no opposition at all – and the party whips hammered out an
agreement which was to remain in effect until 1 January 1915 or for the
balance of the conflict.[1] A joint Parliamentary Recruiting Committee was
organized to encourage enlistments; and a Central Committee for National
Patriotic Organizations soon followed, with Asquith and Bonar Law as
president and vice-president. As a symbol of the new order, the two –
rather uncomfortably, it must be said – soon appeared for the first time on
a platform together. At the King's suggestion and Asquith's persuasion,
Balfour became president of a new Prince of Wales Fund for the Relief of
Distress, meant to alleviate the economic hardships which were expected
to accompany a short, intense war among Great Powers. Given the bitterness of British politics in 1914, this show of co-operation must have been
easier for Liberals and Unionists to accept in the context of the expectation
that the conflict would be 'over by Christmas'.

The government itself remained largely unchanged, with one important
exception.[2] In the last days of peace Lord Haldane had temporarily taken
charge of the War Office, but full-time war required a full-time war minister: the premier nominated the sixty-four-year-old hero of Omdurman,
Lord Kitchener of Khartoum. Save for Lord Roberts, now in the twilight
of his life, 'K of K' had no rival as Britain's greatest general, and the
appointment was wildly popular.[3] These were extraordinary times as a
Liberal government thought by many only days before to be tainted with
pacifism now embraced as war minister the first serving officer to hold the
post since General Monck, in the time of Charles II.

Kitchener's presence at Whitehall was universally applauded: 'He was a
national institution . . .' Asquith's daughter wrote. 'The psychological effect
of his appointment, the tonic to public confidence was instantaneous and
overwhelming. And he at once gave, in his own right, a national status to
the government.'[4] Balfour knew Kitchener all too well, and had in the past
found him a perplexing character. Yet he did not deny the Field Marshal's

prowess as a military commander or as a symbol, and he even encouraged Churchill to press the appointment with Asquith.[5]

Kitchener did not desire the job – and drove a hard bargain for his services – but he was prevailed upon by Asquith.[6] Much was expected of Lord K, but in the end his considerable talents were the wrong ones for the job he had accepted. His life had been devoted to the army, and he believed in the absolute responsibility and isolation of supreme authority. Now he found himself a member of a Cabinet, surrounded by politicians – a breed he neither understood nor trusted. His tenure got off to a remarkable start, as he stunned his new colleagues at his first Cabinet meeting by telling them that they had undertaken a war likely to last not for months, as they expected, but for several years, by which time it would require an army of Continental proportions. The Liberal statesmen heard him out, though few believed his 'calculated hunch'.[7] He was, of course, absolutely correct, and this vision was what Lloyd George recalled when he remarked after the great soldier's death that his mind was like a lighthouse beacon, at one moment illuminating all in a blinding light, but then turning away, leaving 'unutterable darkness'.[8] For the moment the beacon, if misunderstood, shone brilliantly.

Bonar Law and Balfour, and certainly Asquith, sought to crush all gossip that the political truce would soon evolve into a coalition government.[9] If not coalition, there were signs that party animosities were being shelved, and the Prime Minister was pleased once again to invite Balfour to dine at No. 10, cheerfully informing Miss Stanley of the great success of the gathering.[10] Asquith took a more meaningful and certainly unprecedented step a few days later when he asked the former Unionist premier to serve again on the Committee of Imperial Defence. Balfour accepted, and attended the first wartime meeting on 7 October, and soon he was meeting privately 'to talk naval "shop"' with Churchill and Fisher.[11] The Prime Minister decided that a Cabinet of twenty-one busy men was too many to assemble at short notice and too numerous to reach decisions efficiently. He chose to assemble a War Council, and on 25 November he summoned Lloyd George, Grey, Churchill, Crewe and Kitchener, as well as the CIGS, Sir James Wolfe Murray, and the seventy-three-year-old Lord Fisher, recently recalled as First Sea Lord.[12] The only Unionist appointed was Arthur Balfour.[13]

Bonar Law, with whom Balfour was in daily contact, did nothing to hold him back, but some weeks later he published letters in the press insisting that these developments and certain offhand statements by senior Liberals in no way rendered his party responsible for wartime decisions made by the government. He did not mention that Lloyd George had already sounded him on the feasibility of an inter-party coalition at some time in the future, and stressed publicly that his party did not seek collaboration with the Liberals, preferring a loosening of the gag of the party truce.[14] It was clear that Balfour was on his own.

In securing Balfour's services, Asquith gained not only his knowledge and experience of military matters, as well as his prestige, but also the immediate benefit of giving the government an inter-party gloss. A party man through and through, Balfour soon had second thoughts about his position. He accepted the appointment because he was deeply patriotic and only too conscious that his age barred him from active service – and the role of Opposition senior statesman when his party was muzzled by the party truce could only mean idleness and frustration. Nonetheless, his mind was troubled, as he wrote to Lansdowne in early January 1915:

> I slid into this by insensible degrees . . . I am rather a curious addition to this collection, and the question arises 'ought I, or ought I not, to say to Asquith that my presence on it puts me in a position so delicate and difficult that I am reluctant to continue my services.'

Yet, he reflected, was his discomfort reason enough to resign?

> At the same time, if I can be of any use, I do not see how I can refuse my services. I am too old to fight, and this is all I can do for the general cause.[15]

Serving on relief committees and making patriotic speeches were simply not enough, and he remained a member throughout the lifespans of the War Council and its two successors. Balfour soon complained, however, that Asquith had not gone far enough: the Council was hampered because it lacked the authority to take decisions without reference to the Cabinet. Asquith dominated the Cabinet, and direction of the war remained with him – and at his right hand was Kitchener of Khartoum, who was intent on building what he considered a proper army.

On 1 August 1914 the principal army recruiting station in London enrolled eight volunteers. Six days later Kitchener issued his first call for the men he insisted the army would need, and recruiting sergeants required police escorts to fight their way through mobs of volunteers to get to their desks. Soon the nation was blanketed by 2 million examples of the famous poster of Kitchener, in field marshal's uniform, insisting, 'Your Country Needs You.' The illustration guaranteed his immortality long after his own victories were all but forgotten. Yet, as his reputation in Whitehall declined in 1915, the ubiquitous image made him the butt of the cruel quip that, if not a great man, Lord K was at least a great poster.[16]

The recruiting campaign achieved remarkable success, with nearly half a million enlistees signed up in September – and these men became the core of the 'Kitchener armies', the flower of British voluntarism. Soon enlistments began to decline, and, with no end of the conflict in sight, the problem of manpower – of the need for men to fight and men to manufacture the things with which others fought – plagued British policymakers. Balfour was among the first to understand the dilemma.

By January 1915 Kitchener had concluded that military victory would require virtually every fit man in Britain between the ages of nineteen and thirty-five.[17] At the same time, Balfour was certain that this was impossible – Kitchener's way might win battles, but would this not undermine industry, making it impossible to win the war? Like Kitchener, who believed that the volunteer was by far the better soldier than the conscript, Balfour had not changed his opinion that the National Service League's panacea of mandatory service was not the answer to the manpower question. Hankey agreed, and in mid-December 1914 he encouraged Balfour to act to resist the conscriptionist position.[18] Balfour needed no inducement, and was already at work on a War Council paper which argued against the army's unqualified appetite for manpower. He reasoned that the labour requirements of the munitions and export industries were crucial for the industrial economy to support the Allied war effort, and that the unrestricted recruiting campaign should be concentrated on 'unproductive' men and those engaged in producing 'luxuries' for domestic consumption. Kitchener and his generals remained unconvinced, and the memorandum made no converts among those who accepted the War Office position. In effect, it was merely Balfour's first salvo in a prolonged struggle over the vexed question.[19]

Like Balfour, Hankey was soon deeply troubled by the realities that lay behind the conscription debate: the development of trench warfare on the Western Front and the reliance on mass infantry assaults to break the resulting deadlock. Though officially only a retired officer and civil servant, Hankey was a trusted Whitehall insider; and at the end of 1914 he produced a paper of his own, immortalized as the 'Boxing Day memorandum'.[20] This argued for consideration of alternatives to the bloody 'deadlock' on the Western Front, and Balfour, equally alarmed at the blood tariff of trench warfare, paid close attention. Among other considerations, Hankey touched on the uses of technology to break the developing stalemate, and for this line of argument Balfour always had time. The most significant result of this initiative was, of course, the development of the 'landship' or, as it eventually came to be known, the tank.

Hankey had already begun a campaign within the military establishment to drum up enthusiasm for such a 'machine gun destroyer', and, while Asquith expressed qualified support, Hankey later wrote: 'Balfour bit at once.'[21] Thanks to Churchill's intervention, the Admiralty played an early part in the development of the revolutionary weapon, and by the time prototypes were in place Balfour had succeeded him as First Lord. The first two prototypes ('Big Willie' and 'Little Willie') were operable by February 1916, and secret tests were held in the parklands of Hatfield, the home of Balfour's cousin Lord Salisbury. Nothing could prevent the sixty-seven-year-old Balfour from squeezing himself into the cramped confines of 'Big Willie' as it churned up the lawns of the historic estate. 'Mr Balfour's delight was as great as my own,' Lloyd George recalled, 'and it was only with difficulty that some of us persuaded him to disembark from H.M. Landship, while she crossed the last test, a trench several feet wide.'[22] Ignoring Kitchener's scepticism, Balfour remained a powerful supporter of the revolutionary invention, which in 1916 went into production with Lloyd George's new Ministry of Munitions.

The Boxing Day memorandum also raised the idea that the developing impasse on the Western Front might be relieved by the creation of an alternative theatre of war, particularly one in which naval power could be brought to bear – Hankey pointed to Turkey, Germany's ally, as a possible object for such an attack. In this lay the origins of the controversial Dardanelles campaign. Balfour replied immediately, and in his customary fashion parsed out the strengths and weaknesses of the case.[23] He agreed that the possibility of driving the Germans from their position on the Western Front by massive attacks was 'a hopeless affair', adding that if the Tsar's armies were 'as strong as they profess to be' there was some hope of their success in the East, though the Russian humiliation by a smaller German force at Tannenberg early in the war cannot have been encouraging.[24] Yet the idea of the alternative front also troubled him. For example, if Constantinople fell, who would then possess it and control the Bosporus? For that matter, would a campaign to topple Turkey, or a successful Russian assault in the East, really 'finish the war'? Might it not be 'regarded as merely subsidiary', inflicting its wounds but leaving Germany undefeated and the Western Front essentially as it was?

The desire to identify a different path to victory attracted other adherents at this stage of the conflict, including Churchill and Lloyd George; and even Kitchener, though still committed to the Western Front, was willing to consider some limited diversion of resources from the main theatre of war. Fisher, the 'septuagenarian sea-dog' (as Asquith called him), for a brief time supported 'Hankey's Turkey Plan', and on 4 January 1915 he wrote to Balfour insisting that it was 'vital and imperative and very pressing'.[25] On 7 January, Kitchener, Balfour, Lloyd George and Churchill were charged to consider the alternatives to the Western Front, and, with the positive recommendation of the naval chief in the eastern Mediterranean, Admiral Carden, they advised pressing ahead with a plan for a naval attack on the Dardanelles fortresses.[26] Later in the month, the War Council endorsed the idea. But all was not well: in a letter to Venetia Stanley, Asquith noted that Fisher had revealed to him privately his misgivings about the strategy.[27] In fact Fisher was deeply troubled about the idea, but, as his scepticism grew, Churchill became more ardent about the plan with each day.[28]

Asquith noted in his letter to Venetia Stanley that Balfour was 'enthusiastic' in his support of the Dardanelles plan, and this seems correct in the sense that at this point he supported a purely naval operation as an alternative to the Western Front. Fisher seems to have judged Balfour to be the most articulate and dangerous proponent of a Dardanelles scheme, and on 29 January he sent him a paper which he insisted had been suppressed because 'they [Asquith and Churchill] don't wish it' and which argued not against the likelihood of success of the plan but against the cost to the navy, given the limited advantages that could be gained.[29] Balfour immediately composed a reply enumerating the advantages to be had if such a naval operation were successful.[30] Fisher held his fire for the moment, but he was far from mollified.

The tragic story of the Dardanelles campaign has been told often and well, and perhaps it is sufficient to note here that in mid-February the War Council authorized the concentration of troops already in the eastern Mediterranean in case they were needed for the Dardanelles operation – they totalled only 10,000 men, all Kitchener would allow at this point.[31] By the time of the War Council meeting of 24 February, after the bombardment of the Turkish forts had begun, the idea that the operation should be entirely a naval operation was already being questioned.[32] The major antagonists were Churchill, now the principal champion of the campaign, and Kitchener, whose growing scepticism was not overcome by the First Lord's eloquence. Both Asquith and Lloyd George refused the proffered seats on Churchill's bandwagon, but they continued their qualified support. Balfour now came down on the side of army reinforcement of the naval operation if necessary, which the War Council assumed at this stage would render the operation successful. In a three-page memorandum circulated on the same day, he argued for the dispatch of 'as many troops as may be required to make the Bosphorus operation, to which we are now committed, a success'.[33] Balfour remained convinced that the goal of relieving pressure on the Western Front and thus hastening the end of the bloody conflict seemed a worthy enterprise. 'We are all agreed,' he concluded, 'whatever else is done, the Bosphorus operation must be carried through to a successful termination.' As it turned out, all members of the Council were not in fact agreed.

By early April a decision could no longer be postponed: either a sizeable ground force had to be committed in support of the attack or the naval operation must be abandoned. The key figure in the debate was the enigmatic Kitchener, and he finally suppressed his scepticism: the army would enter the operation. The bloody result was the Gallipoli offensive. Balfour, who had been supportive to this point, was not about to abandon either the campaign or his colleagues, but he did caution the enthusiastic Churchill that primary responsibility for gaining the planned objective must continue to lie with the fleet and that a broad military attack 'upon a position so inherently difficult . . . was a different matter'.[34] But the First Lord, with Kitchener – compliant for the moment – persisted, with the anxious support of the War Council, including Balfour. By the time the campaign was abandoned in failure, the War Council and the Liberal Cabinet had been swept away, and a different First Lord ruled at the Admiralty.

Not surprisingly, the decision to persevere in the Dardanelles and the reshaping of the government were closely related; yet other important matters played their parts in poisoning the political atmosphere. Of great importance was the growing perception in Whitehall that the British army was being hampered by shortages of warlike stores of all kinds. As the Kitchener armies were being trained for deployment, the supply of ammunition for the guns and men already in the field was becoming a cause of anxiety in the War Office. In October 1914 Kitchener had already cautioned the British commander, Sir John French, 'Do not think we are keeping munitions back. All we can gather is being sent, but at the present rate of expenditure we are certain before long to run short, and then to produce more than a small daily allowance per gun will be impossible.'[35] While large orders for munitions were accepted by the established arms-makers, they could not increase production fast enough to satisfy the demands of the Western Front, and soon the War Office turned to rationing the expenditure of shells – against which French continually railed. Lloyd George soon adopted munitions production as his personal cause, and at his inspiration in October 1914 chairmanship of an ad-hoc Shells Committee to increase production was forced on an unwilling Kitchener. Lloyd George served on the Committee, and pressed the War Office and the manufacturers to act to overcome the shortages. The unsatisfied Chancellor soon presented a paper to the War Council complaining that the greatest manufacturing nation in the world was being beaten at its own industrial game: 'All the engineering works of the country ought to be turned to the production of war material,' he insisted. 'The population ought to be prepared to suffer all sorts of deprivations and even hardships whilst this process is going on.'[36] Only the organization of industry under the leadership of the state, he concluded, would win the war and return the government to the peacetime agenda he had in mind.[37]

Like Lloyd George, Balfour was losing confidence in Kitchener, and he too was concerned about munitions production. After reading Lloyd George's memorandum, he spoke privately with him and was impressed by his zeal and vision. He wrote to him in early March 1915:

> I most earnestly trust that you are not letting slide the matter about which we had a talk the day before yesterday. Putting labour troubles altogether on one side, the position seems to me to be most unsatisfactory, and, unless you will take in hand the organisation of the Engineering resources of the country in the interests of military equipment, I do not see how any improvement is to be expected.[38]

Lloyd George's pressure brought about the creation of the War Office Armaments Output Committee, made up of soldiers and businessmen with Kitchener unhappily in the chair, charged with encouraging the engineering industry to increase armaments production. More significantly, on 22 March Asquith met with Balfour, Lloyd George, Churchill and the Financial Secretary to the Treasury, Edwin Montagu; as a result, the Prime Minister informed a dubious Kitchener that what came to be known simply as the Treasury Committee, chaired by Lloyd George, would come to his assistance to organize industry and labour for war production.[39] The news, Asquith wrote, created a 'royal row on the stocks between Kitchener & Ll. George in regard to the proposed Committee on munitions. Neither is disposed to give way: K. threatens to give up his office, and Ll.G. to wash his hands of the whole business.'[40] Balfour had approved of Kitchener's appointment in August 1914, but after eight months of war he chose to back Lloyd George. At the end of 1915 Balfour dined with Mrs Dugdale, who enquired about 'K's' failings. Her uncle replied, 'He is not a great organiser – he is not a great administrator, nor a great soldier, – and what is more, he knows it. He is not vain. He is only great when he has little things to organise.' But was he not 'rather a great man'? she asked. 'He is in a way,' Balfour said. 'But our language has no word for the subtleties I would like to express about K. I must call his greatness *personality*.'[41] More to the point, he wrote to Lloyd George, 'I cannot help suspecting that K. has only an imperfect grasp of the problem with which he has been faced for seven months.'[42]

The Chancellor was pleased to have Balfour on his committee, and also serving were Montagu, the Labour Party's Arthur Henderson, and several expert members.[43] The panel achieved limited success, but it lacked executive authority and served most of all to convince Lloyd George and Balfour that authority over war production could not remain with the War Office. Lord Kitchener's reputation in the country remained high, but within the confined world of Whitehall it was sinking fast – particularly among the Unionists.

By this time a Unionist Business Committee of influential backbenchers had been organized to press for what they insisted was a more energetic prosecution of the war. Like Balfour, these frustrated men were intensely patriotic but were too old to fight; but unlike him they played no part in wartime policymaking, and felt themselves gagged by the party truce. Their leader, W. A. S. Hewins, noted in his diary on 6 May 1915 that they had concluded of the administration: 'It is quite discredited and the sooner it is reconstituted, the better.'[44] By early May they had prepared a motion of censure against the government, and only the authority of the Unionist leadership defused this direct attack on the Whitehall truce. Bonar Law, Balfour and the other party chieftains believed an open battle in the House would divide the nation and harm the war effort, but they knew also that the silent status quo could not be maintained indefinitely. Balfour's own experience had taught him that backbenchers could not be made to accept the direction of their leaders simply because they were leaders.

The debates over the Dardanelles campaign and the munitions shortage came together in the volatile atmosphere in May 1915 to destroy the last Liberal government. Balfour played only a minor part in the drama, leaving centre stage to Asquith, Lloyd George and Bonar Law. In brief, the episode involved Sir John French, who laid the blame for the failure of his recent attack at Neuve-Chapelle on the shortage of artillery munitions. On the advice of Lord Northcliffe, he sent two trusted officers to London in early May with confidential information for Lloyd George, Bonar Law and Balfour which he presumed would make his case that the fault lay with the

War Office and the government.[45] Then on 14 May Northcliffe struck with a leader in *The Times* laying the blame for the failure at Neuve-Chapelle at the door of the War Office. On the following day the furious Hewins informed Asquith that he intended to raise this in the House, and revolt on the back benches seemed imminent.[46] Bonar Law and Lansdowne, fearing a loss of control of their party followers, hastily produced a letter of their own to the premier expressing their firm judgement that serious changes were needed.[47]

In the afternoon, the War Council met for the first time in five weeks and debated the possibility of strengthening the force in the Dardanelles, with a conflicted Kitchener averse to committing more troops but concerned that a withdrawal would lead to broad revolt in the Muslim population. Balfour had concluded that by this point they had little choice but to carry the campaign through to its conclusion: 'Our immediate course seemed perfectly clear, namely, to maintain our troops in the Peninsula up to the full strength, to make them as comfortable as possible, and to prepare landing places.'[48] The committee decided to ascertain from the army commander 'on the spot', Sir Ian Hamilton, exactly what he would need to ensure his success. By the time the general replied, it was to a different government.

Admiral Lord Fisher played his brief but crucial part in the political drama in the early hours of the following morning, as he dashed out a bizarre letter of resignation to the First Lord. Churchill had recalled him from retirement, and the two had time and again proclaimed their mutual admiration. That was now forgotten, as Fisher could no longer stomach the Dardanelles affair, for which he blamed the First Lord. The admiral's message informed Churchill that his resolve was unshakeable and that he would not discuss the matter, announcing, 'I am off to Scotland at once so as to avoid all questionings.'[49] This time, however, Fisher had gone too far, for he was in effect abandoning his post in wartime.[50] Neither Asquith nor Churchill at first took the resignation seriously, but they soon learned that it was very serious indeed. Asquith ordered Fisher 'in the King's name' to return to the Admiralty – without success. When the admiral was located and brought to him the next day, Fisher was genial but adamant. Then, on 17 May, Bonar Law and Lloyd George met at 11 Downing Street and discovered that they had reached the same conclusion: the Unionists would abandon the party truce if Churchill remained at the Admiralty without Fisher. The Liberal government could not continue, and a coalition was the only answer to their problems. According to the Chancellor, he went immediately to the Prime Minister, and in 'less than a quarter of an hour' the two men agreed that there must be coalition.[51] What was actually said among these men remains obscure, but the result is not: the opposing party leaders agreed to forge a multiparty administration.[52]

As Asquith, Lloyd George and Bonar Law were meeting, Churchill alerted Balfour to the Fisher resignation, but neither knew yet that a revised government was in the planning. Bonar Law called the Shadow Cabinet together on the following day to outline these events, and all agreed to accept the invitation to enter a coalition – with the proviso that they receive a fair share of the available offices.[53] In return for their co-operation they demanded that Churchill surrender the Admiralty. Likewise they blackballed Haldane, whom they disliked nearly as much and had never forgiven for his casual expression years before of his passion for German culture. Balfour fumed at the 'wide-spread stupidity' that the Lord Chancellor was 'pro-German', but his defence of the creator of the British Expeditionary Force fell on determinedly deaf ears.[54] The vengeful Unionists got their way on both counts.

The sixty-three-year-old Prime Minister accepted that coalition was the unavoidable price of his remaining in his office and retaining control of the government and the war.[55] The Cabinet he formed reflected his determination: he wished to hold on to Kitchener. The press campaign against the war lord backfired badly – his popularity as a national symbol remained untarnished and invaluable to the government, and so Kitchener remained at the War Office. Asquith's potential rival, Lloyd George, would be kept busy with a new Ministry of Munitions, with the loyal McKenna 'temporarily' at the Exchequer. Bonar Law was fobbed off with the Colonial Office and Chamberlain the India Office, while Curzon became Lord Privy Seal. Long took the Local Government Board, Carson became Attorney General, and Lansdowne became Minister without Portfolio. Other significant offices remained in the hands of men whom the Prime Minister was certain he could trust.[56]

One of these was Balfour, who gained the most important post among the Unionists: he became First Lord of the Admiralty – an appointment which pleased the King and an otherwise disappointed Churchill (though not the disapproving Lord Fisher).[57] Balfour had spoken privately to Asquith on 18 May expressing his willingness to serve in any way possible, and he followed this with a letter the following morning. 'I am quite indifferent as to what office I take,' he insisted, 'except that I do not think I could usefully be responsible for any heavy administrative office, *except the Admiralty*.'[58] He would be quite satisfied, he added, with a minor responsibility, the Duchy of Lancaster, for example – which in the end was allotted to Churchill. Asquith had held the most powerful office in the land for seven years, and he knew his business. Though the two had been adversaries for many years, he respected Balfour as he did no other Unionist, and was confident he could run the navy without desiring, as did Churchill, to run the war. He also knew him to be without ambition for the premiership, and he did not think the same could be said of Lloyd George or Bonar Law.[59]

Balfour wrote to a friend that he certainly did not envy the Prime Minister's position: 'Thank Heaven', he wrote, 'I am not now, nor ever shall be, again responsible for making a Government.'[60] Asquith's manipulations did not particularly trouble him at this point. Most senior Liberals seemed satisfied that the Prime Minister had managed the crisis as well as could be hoped for. Lord Crewe was pleased that 'our plan' was to deprive the Unionists of the most sensitive offices, with one exception – Balfour – 'and him not one of their inner circle as it now exists'.[61] Crewe was correct in that Asquith had outmanoeuvred the Unionists, but quite wrong in his presumption that Balfour's importance in his party could be discounted.

The Admiralty crisis was quickly settled, as the new First Lord installed in Fisher's place the 'scientific sailor', Admiral Sir Henry Jackson, FRS. Despite the failure of his resignation coup, however, the old admiral was far from ready for a seemly retirement, and quickly offered his services.[62] Balfour knew that Fisher's prestige, his connections and his intelligence remained formidable, but he had no intention of allowing him to interfere in Admiralty business. He was therefore pleased a few weeks later to offer him only the chair of a new Admiralty Board of Inventions and Research.[63] Fisher accepted the job from Balfour, 'with whom my relations are most cordial', but it was not the door to renewed power for which he longed, and their relations soon grew less harmonious.[64]

The 1915 political crisis cost Balfour an alliance he had valued for many years, as Jack Sandars terminated their friendship at this same time – and the reason was Winston Churchill. Sandars had long disliked the former First Lord, whom he thought untrustworthy and self-seeking, and he disapproved of Balfour's habitual tolerance of his ways.[65] When the news leaked that the coalition ministers (with the exception of Asquith) had agreed to pool their salaries, with each taking an equal share, Sandars bitterly condemned this as a 'Churchill Relief Fund'.[66] The final blow seems to have come when Balfour – who remained in Carlton Gardens – allowed the Churchills the continued use of Admiralty House.[67] This kindness Sandars could not bear, and he declined Balfour's request that he return to his service and thereafter ended all communication with his former patron. Balfour's attempts over the following months to rekindle the friendship were fruitless, and he appears to have given them up in 1916.[68] With the assistance of Miss Constance Bliss, Wilfrid Short continued as his master's principal secretary, and seems to have maintained his own friendship with Sandars.[69]

Under Balfour, the pace of life and work at Admiralty House was significantly different from in Churchill's day, and Lord Riddell noted that restless energy had given way to 'marked calm'.[70] The Earl of Crawford, as Balcarres had become, called on the First Lord soon after his installation and noted similarly that his room reflected order and calm: 'There is a writing table, two or three other tables, all very orderly . . . But no sign of or symbol of its being an office: no files or papers lying about, none of the ordinary paraphernalia or equipment of the government workroom.' The former Chief Whip added, however, 'Yet he gets through much business, and has the genius for never being concerned with anything except the essentials.'[71]

Balfour found the Admiralty an agreeable billet, and the officials and officers with whom he was in close contact for the next nineteen months generally found him an agreeable master.[72] In marked contrast to Churchill, Balfour did not think it his duty to initiate detailed strategic or tactical plans for the conduct of the war, and he noted in May 1915 that his predecessor suffered from being perceived as overshadowing his advisers. 'It is a pity,' he added, 'for, with all his shortcomings, he has industry, resources, and above all courage.'[73] He believed that policy decisions were the responsibility of ministers, but that the planning and fighting of campaigns were the preserve of the professionals. This 'hands-off' attitude would lead to criticism, most famously by Lloyd George, of what was seen as a lack of energy and initiative.[74] At sixty-seven, Balfour was unlikely to compete with Lloyd George for sheer activity, and the Welshman had always been bemused by what he saw as a sort of typically Balfourian indolence. Yet, Wilfrid Short informed Sandars, others saw things differently: 'He is very fit; & I have not known him so alert, virile and active for many years: indeed, I hardly remember his being so "wide awake" as he appears to be at present. He is now called at 9!!'[75] Hankey was at first concerned that Balfour lacked the physical vigour for the appointment – a view which Asquith ridiculed. 'This proved correct,' Hankey admitted in his memoirs: 'Balfour seemed rejuvenated by office.'[76]

The creation of the coalition was in part brought about by the criticism that perhaps there was too much 'calm' about Asquith's government, and the Prime Minister decided to show his determination on victory by recasting the War Council as the Dardanelles Committee. It met for the first time on 7 June in Asquith's room in the House, and included Asquith and Balfour, as well as Lansdowne, Curzon, Kitchener, Bonar Law, Grey, Crewe, Selborne and Churchill. Another important member, Lloyd George, was unable to attend the first meeting. The service chiefs became members, and Hankey continued as secretary. Despite his distaste for the Ulster Unionist, Asquith soon added Carson to the committee.[77]

The highest immediate concern of the Dardanelles Committee was the controversial campaign from which it took its name. Despite his initial scepticism, Balfour was convinced that, once it had been undertaken, the campaign had to be seen through to success. In this he soon found himself in disagreement with Lloyd George and Bonar Law, with whom he usually agreed on war matters, and on the same side as Curzon, so often his adversary over the years. At its initial meeting, spurred on by Churchill and Kitchener, the Committee managed to agree to strengthen the military presence and thus the commitment in the Dardanelles. In early August, five British and colonial divisions led by Sir Frederick Stopford landed at Suvla Bay, to join the seven already in position. By the end of the month, this initiative proved to be yet another failure. Hankey had been sent to the war zone to observe operations, and, after reading his reports, the Prime Minister uncharacteristically lost his temper: 'I have read enough to satisfy me', he wrote to Kitchener, 'that the generals and staff engaged on the Suvla part of the business ought to be court-martialled and dismissed from the Army.'[78] Yet General Hamilton remained optimistic (Bonar Law grumbled that he was 'always *nearly* winning') and the Dardanelles Committee, including Balfour, agreed to press on.[79]

By October, the situation in the East had grown more dire: Serbia was obviously doomed, its capital occupied by the Austrians and its eastern provinces menaced by the Bulgarians. The Allied reaction was to consider a second Mediterranean front at Salonica in western Thrace. A recommendation by Admiral Wemyss, second-in-command in the 'Med', for a renewed naval attack was rejected, as it was again in December. Save for the expedient of removing the unfortunate Hamilton and replacing him with Sir Charles Monro, the government seemed paralysed over the Dardanelles question. The new commander arrived on 28 October, and within three days telegraphed Kitchener recommending immediate evacuation.[80]

The Dardanelles Committee met for the last time on 6 November, its purpose – like the ill-fated campaign itself – undermined by Monro's powerful advice. Balfour advised the Cabinet to weigh carefully the costs of withdrawal against what were to him the benefits of retaining a foothold on the Gallipoli peninsula. In a memorandum of 19 November, he granted that he had not favoured the invasion and that now it appeared likely that neither the army nor the navy, 'nor the two in combination, can either drive the Turks from the Peninsula or compel them to surrender'. Why, then, remain? he enquired.

> Our position on the Peninsula resembles a beleaguered fortress, and I am as reluctant to abandon it as I should be to abandon any other fortress which is well-garrisoned, well provisioned, and has no practicable breach in its defences. By such an abandonment we should lose credit in our own eyes, and those of our friends. Quite apart from its effect on our prestige in the East (about which so much has been said in the Cabinet) we have a character to lose in the West. To Russia the blow would be staggering. Even those who rate at the lowest our military organisation and training have never denied us the qualities of tenacity and courage. What will they say when they see us deserting a position so important and so hardly won?[81]

To press on was a gamble, he admitted, but 'some risks must be run and some possibilities must be faced.'

His argument did not convince his colleagues. Before this, Asquith had sent Kitchener off to see the situation for himself, and the war lord cabled on 15 November that the campaign must be abandoned. This trumped Balfour's arguments, and the Cabinet resolved on withdrawal – without Carson, who had resigned in October in disgust over the failure to aid Serbia. The Dardanelles interlude was at an end, and Balfour, as always, accepted political reality when he confronted it. Quite remarkably, the evacuation in December and early January was carried out without the loss of a single life.

Asquith now presided over a troubled and divided government. The Cabinet, with Lord Crewe substituting for an ailing premier, had met on 21 October and recommended the creation of a new four- or five-member war committee in place of the expiring Dardanelles Committee.[82] After Kitchener had left the room, several ministers remained behind and expressed their nearly unanimous view – McKenna was a notable exception – that the War Secretary must be replaced. Only when Kitchener was on his inspection tour of the Dardanelles a fortnight later did the Prime Minister act. He did not sack the still popular Field Marshal. Instead, Asquith plundered Kitchener's authority, delegating much of it to a new CIGS, Sir William Robertson, a bluff-speaking former squaddie who was now to be the chief military adviser to the government as well as the principal conduit of their decisions to the high command in France. 'Wully' Robertson found a co-operative partner in

Sir Douglas Haig, destined in a few weeks to replace the British commander, the unfortunate Sir John French.

The new War Committee was in place by mid-November: with Asquith were Bonar Law, Lloyd George, McKenna, Lord Kitchener – 'if and when he returned' – and Balfour.[83] His Dardanelles strategy in tatters, Churchill was excluded, and this final blow drove him to resign to take command of a battalion in France. Some ministers grumbled that the new committee was not the true war executive they had wanted, for like its predecessors it functioned only as a committee of the Cabinet. To elevate the political temperature even higher, the continuing quarrel of two old antagonists, Lloyd George and McKenna, was such that they could barely tolerate each other's presence. However, the creation of the new committee did diffuse some criticism of his war management, and the Prime Minister's power was to survive for another year.

The sad spectacle in the Dardanelles served to reinforce the belief of many in Britain that victory in the war was possible only through the massive frontal assaults of the Western Front. This 'Westerner' strategy was certainly believed by most of the generals and accepted by their political masters – and after bloody Gallipoli it was never again meaningfully challenged. There were some, however, who did not give up the pursuit of another way and another place where the enemy could be mortally wounded. Lloyd George and the temporarily eclipsed Churchill remained the most famous of these 'Easterners'. Balfour was committed to neither camp. However, like most ministers, if not 'L.G. and Winston', he accepted that his task was to manage his military department so that the experts could get on with fighting the war. Yet he was never comfortable with the idea that the only way Britain could contribute to victory was to supply men for the continual slaughter of what came to be called the war of 'attrition'. He had written to Hankey in January 1915 that it seemed a hopeless strategy to try to drive the Germans out of Belgium by 'assaulting one line of trenches after another'. Yet, after the Dardanelles, neither had the confidence in the alternative suggestions offered by the doughty 'Easterners' to defeat Germany by attacking her perimeters.[84]

The decision, of course, did not lie with Arthur Balfour. In early July he accompanied Asquith, Kitchener, Crewe and Hankey to Calais to meet their French allies, and the Field Marshal on his own authority pledged to the French commander, Joseph Joffre, that Britain would put into the field an army of seventy divisions – more than ten times the force with which Britain began the war, and double the army it could field at the time. Apparently he also agreed with the necessity of a great offensive later in the year – though this he kept from his Cabinet colleagues.[85] Once the war lord had given his word, there was little to do but make it national policy; and a seventy-division army became the goal. Few in Whitehall can have believed with Kitchener that this was either prudent or even possible while relying on voluntary recruitment, particularly as the Ministry of Munitions was engaged in a struggle of its own against Kitchener and the generals to prevent the continued migration of skilled workmen into the forces. Lloyd George, once assumed to be a pacifist, became the most outspoken proponent of managing manpower through mandatory service; and, with Churchill on active service, his strongest allies in the Cabinet were the Unionists.

Balfour was a significant exception, as he continued to be convinced that conscription – either for industry, as Lloyd George and Churchill advised, or for the army – would prove to be a mistake. He submitted several memoranda arguing against both the Westerner perspective and conscription, to which the war of attrition, he reasoned, inevitably would lead. Asquith feared that the conscriptionists were attempting to stampede a nation unready for a dangerously divisive policy.[86] In September 1915 he turned to Balfour for help:

> It has become quite clear that the question of 'compulsion' cannot and will not be discussed in Parliament & the country merely, or perhaps mainly, on its merits . . . Further, it is now indisputable that any attempt at this moment to establish compulsion, either military or industrial, wd. encounter the practically united & passionately vehement opposition of organised labour.

The Prime Minister added that, even if he threw himself behind such a policy, he feared that he could not hold the allegiance of 'some of the best, and in the country some of the most powerful elements of the Liberal Party'. He closed with a plea: 'I have come to think that it is only by our joint efforts that a bridge can be constructed over a yawning & perilous chasm.'[87]

Balfour had already begun to draft a paper which seemed to support Asquith's view. He questioned the assumption that a seventy-division force was necessary or even possible, and argued instead in favour of the traditional British way of war, with the balanced use of fleets, money and, only thirdly, land armies. Like Asquith, he feared that there were other dangers in a conscription policy. In this war, he argued, 'there is a moral contribution which is of incalculable military value, because it adds so enormously to the efficiency of the other three – and this is national Unity.'[88] Was it possible, he asked, to preserve this unity and also implement mandatory service?

As Balfour confronted his colleagues with these arguments, the British army in support of their French allies launched the Battle of Loos on the Western Front, fought in a cramped district of coal-pits and miners' cottages. Though they vastly outnumbered their German opponents, the British lost 50,000 casualties (twice the German losses) and gained nothing of strategic value.[89] Sir John French blamed the failure on the commander of the First Army, Sir Douglas Haig, who in turn blamed French for withholding reserves. As it was, the government had heard enough of French's explanations, and in December it replaced him as commander-in-chief with Haig.

The conscriptionists were unswayed by Balfour's arguments and were contained only by Asquith's gambit in early October of appointing 'the soldier's friend', Lord Derby, to organize a scheme under which men of military age were asked to 'attest' that they would serve when called upon. It was nothing less than a kind of voluntary conscription, and Derby – himself a convinced conscriptionist – had little faith that it would succeed.[90] The exercise did not allay War Office manpower ambitions, and succeeded only in buying time for the voluntarists – it was already beginning to be perceived as hopeless when, on 2 November, Asquith announced unexpectedly in the House that, if conscription came, it would be applied first to bachelors and extended to married men only after 'the unmarried men are dealt with'. In so doing, the premier limited the options of his government when the unsuccessful Derby Scheme was wound up in December, and the now inevitable Military Service Act, promptly nicknamed the 'Bachelors' Bill', was passed in January. On 27 December, the new CIGS, Robertson, was demanding no fewer than 130,000 men per month to fight a war that could be won 'only by attrition or by breaking through the German line'.[91] Balfour counter-attacked with a forceful memorandum of his own on the same day, arguing that commitment to continued massive assaults on the Western Front would lead simply to more unproductive slaughter. Why not, he suggested, play a waiting game in the West, amass needed weaponry and manpower, and force the Germans to take the initiative? When the enemy had attempted their own predictably disastrous frontal assaults and lost massive numbers of casualties, 'then', he insisted, 'will be the time to attempt the general offensive.'[92]

This argument did not deter the generals or the conscriptionists – or the War Committee – and forty-eight hours later the Cabinet acquiesced to compulsory service. Asquith's 'bachelor' qualification succeeded only in making necessary another political battle over the subject in May 1916, when a second Military Service Act applicable to all men between the ages of eighteen and forty-one was passed.

Balfour's reasoning was not powerful enough to overcome the fact that the Allied generals had already agreed at Chantilly in the first week of December that the war could be won only in the West or on the Russian or Italian fronts, and that plans for further offensives must go forward. Hankey noted that, when confronted with this 'rare and remarkable unanimity of military opinion', the politicians – having no better ideas – acquiesced.[93] Despite Balfour's continued opposition, the War Committee agreed in principle on 27 December to preparations for a spring offensive in the West. Nonetheless, he pressed his argument further at a meeting of 13 January, and wrenched out of Asquith the clarification that final approval had not yet been given to proceed with an attack.[94] Yet he was already isolated among the Unionists and within the War Committee, and he finally gave in.

The result of all this was the ill-starred Battle of the Somme. At Chantilly, Haig and Joffre had agreed that any German attack would trigger assaults by the Allied armies in their own sectors. The Germans obliged by launching in February the murderous Battle of Verdun, and Robertson and Haig made ready to fulfil their commitment. This was to happen in Picardy, the 'hinge' between the British and French lines, chosen to provide the opportunity for the Allies to fight side by side. The tragic results at Verdun, however, where the French and Germans each sustained nearly half a million casualties, meant that the British would now have to shoulder the greater load. Haig, as always, was optimistic, and the first British Tommies went 'over the top' at dawn on 1 July 1916 – the bloodiest single day suffered by any army in that very bloody war. By nightfall, Haig had lost 57,000 casualties, more than one-third of them dead, with many battalions at the end of the day fewer than a hundred strong. When the effort was finally abandoned, in November, British casualties numbered 420,000, the French nearly 200,000, while enemy losses approached half a million. After Verdun and the Somme, 1916 proved to be the most murderous year of the war, with – as Balfour had warned – little appreciable gain on any side.

In addition to his participation in the debates and decisions of the Cabinet and the Dardanelles and War committees in this period, Balfour was much occupied as the political head of one of the fighting services. As has been noted above, his always keen interest in technology was turned to wartime needs, and in this he found a kindred spirit in Sir Henry Jackson, the First Sea Lord. Like Balfour, Jackson was cautious in his leadership, and their partnership soon came under fire from their more adventuresome predecessors, Churchill and Fisher. The two former 'naval persons' also found some support in the press and among certain MPs, as criticism was voiced that neither Balfour nor Jackson demonstrated sufficient 'energy' in pressing the naval war. The bitter Fisher shared his complaints with editors as unalike as the Liberal C. P. Scott and the Unionist J. L. Garvin, as well as certain politicians among his still substantial body of admirers. Most bizarre was the fact that in the spring of 1916 Churchill and Fisher seemed to put their own quarrel behind them and bury the hatchet – firmly, it seemed, in the back of Arthur Balfour.

In early March, Fisher laid an inventory of complaints before the War Committee, but Balfour handily demolished these by pointing out to the House that the deficiencies in supply and dockyard manpower to which the old admiral referred had been the results of decisions in the Churchill–Fisher era.[95] In this Naval Estimates debate, Balfour counterattacked against Churchill – recently returned from his brief trench experience – who wasted no time before pouring out his own criticisms of his successor's leadership of the Admiralty. His line was not entirely unlike Fisher's: shipbuilding was proceeding too slowly, the German submarine threat had not been solved, and the navy in general showed insufficient initiative. Churchill's attacks were always formidable, but he stumbled badly when he presented his demand for the reinstallation 'without delay' of Fisher at the Admiralty. Honourable Members had not forgotten what had passed between Fisher and Churchill, and Balfour reminded those who might have done. By emphasizing this eccentric call for Fisher's return, Balfour deflected his predecessor's assault – as Churchill himself later admitted. But, as Lloyd George's henchman Christopher Addison noted, the master debater won the day but failed to 'leave the House satisfied with the Admiralty'.[96] Lloyd George agreed, grumbling of Balfour and the Prime Minister: 'As long as the Germans were not actually defeating us, they thought everything was going on splendidly.'[97]

Then came the Battle of Jutland. On 1 June 1916 it seemed that what had been anticipated and feared and longed for had arrived when the German navy under Admiral Scheer ventured into the North Sea to meet Sir John Jellicoe and the British Grand Fleet (including the twenty-year-old future King George VI, then a junior officer serving on HMS *Collingwood*). The greatest naval engagement of the war lasted until dark, and when it was over the German fleet abandoned the field and fled. Jellicoe's force lost fourteen ships and the Germans eleven, and the Kaiser was quick to declare a German victory. More important, however, was that after Jutland the German fleet never re-emerged to challenge the British, and saw out the conflict in port. The war of the great ships, predicted for a generation, was over in an afternoon.

Balfour spent the entire time monitoring the information that came all too slowly into the Admiralty – Hankey found him in 'a state of very great excitement' – though the disappointing bulletins did not paint the picture of the glorious new Trafalgar for which all longed.[98] On 2 June the Admiralty issued its official communiqué on the action. It remains unclear who wrote the text, but certainly there was no lofty Balfourian language – only a skeletal report, amounting to little more than the sum of sinkings and damage reports. The admirals were unhappy, the politicians dismayed, and the public confused. A second, similar, bulletin was issued a day later, and finally on 4 June a more palatable report, drafted at Balfour's request by Churchill, of all people, appeared; but by then it was too late.[99] In a speech a few days later, Balfour took the unusual and ultimately futile step of addressing the criticism heaped on the dispatches, explaining that the slight available information and the haste to inform the nation lay behind the public-relations faux pas.[100] Only well after Balfour had left the Admiralty for the Foreign Office would the importance of what happened at Jutland become more clear, but by then the political damage had been done.

This affair took some of the lustre from the announcement later in the month in the Birthday Honours List that Balfour would receive the Order of Merit. He continued to believe, as he had warned five years earlier, that the Order had been bestowed upon too many politicians. Now he expressed his gratitude, but added a caution:

> I am certain [he wrote to Stamfordham on the day of Jutland] that there is a real danger lest the Order should be regarded as another reward open to Party Statesmen who combine literary or other interests with their political work. I have just looked through the list of the civil members of the Order, and I find that when I am added to their number, we shall be 13 – and of these 13, no less than 5 will be ex Cabinet Ministers.

He added a postscript:

> If I must appear in the Honours list it will be much better (I venture to think) to describe my qualifications for the O.M. as 'services to Philosophy & Literature'. This seems simple and better than what was proposed this afternoon ['philosophy, theology and scientific research'].[101]

Lord Fisher, successfully sidetracked by Balfour into his inventions committee, had once noted with poisonous wit that Balfour collected honours while 'I got the order of the boot!'[102] Sandars (whom Balfour had recommended for a Privy Counsellorship) was too infuriated by the announcement for wit. He was busying himself at this time writing anonymous articles savaging the politicians, and in November 1916 he managed to get his needle into both Balfour and Churchill:

> In earlier days Mr Balfour's aversion to titles and honorific distinctions was widely known . . . It is, however, unbecoming to express more than surprise.
> Under Mr Balfour's nominal rule and gentle sway civilian clerks may misconstrue dispatches and misread a naval engagement; but what is important is that the Sea Lords in Whitehall and Admirals at sea have resumed their authority, and amateur strategy has ceased.[103]

More important to the war than these personal quarrels was the question of air power in wartime. In August 1914 the 200 aircraft in Britain were regarded typically as little more than curiosities, and only a few visionaries foresaw their immense military potential. The Great War, of course, accelerated technology at a phenomenal rate, and certainly this was true in what was then called aeronautics. In 1916 the First Lord found himself in the midst of a political skirmish among government departments over control of the innovative new weapons.

As important as the remarkable machines themselves was the question of how to organize their use for war. By 1912 the government had approved the creation of the Royal Flying Corps and the Royal Naval Air Service; and predictably the two units became rivals. With the advent of war, questions of mission, of tactics and strategic purpose, and of provision of aircraft required attention; and Lord Curzon took an interest in the problem.[104] In February 1916 Asquith could no longer avoid intervention and created an advisory Joint War Air Committee under Derby, which merely 'concluded that some degree of co-ordination might be achieved through a reconstituted committee with wider powers'. But it had no idea how the necessary co-operation of the rival services could be brought about.[105] Balfour's admirals saw the efforts of the committee as nothing but interference with their preserve, and were reluctant to co-operate – and they were supported by the First Lord. Competition rather than compromise between the air services continued, and the next attempt at overcoming this was the creation in May of the Air Board, under Curzon – undoubtedly a more formidable figure than Derby. Haig once rather cruelly described Derby as being like a feather pillow, bearing the mark of 'the last person who sat on him'.[106] George Curzon had been compared to many things, but never to a feather pillow.

Several factors clouded any hope of an easy solution to the problem: the professionals of the military departments – particularly the airmen themselves – were disinclined to part with their independence, and the imposing figures of Balfour and Kitchener backed their commanders. Also important was the undeniable reality that when Balfour and Curzon disagreed, fireworks could be anticipated – and that was precisely what happened. Curzon sought a Cabinet-level air department with appropriate powers; Balfour, supporting his admirals, opposed this.[107] Balfour objected to Curzon's interpretation of the responsibility of the Air Board, 'over which', Hankey observed at the time, 'the Admiralty are being very sticky'.[108] To the admirals, the Board was simply another example of interference with their efforts to do their duty; Curzon, naturally, resented this and gave fire of his own.

The Board issued its first report in late October 1916. This severely criticized the Admiralty for its failure to co-operate in the creation of a better integrated and more effective air service and called upon the navy to adopt what the Board judged to be the more efficient organizational practice of the army in its air wing.[109] Balfour's replies, privately to Curzon and officially to the Cabinet, brushed aside the reproach and counter-attacked.[110] Hankey observed the contest at close range, recalling later, 'No one who read them will ever forget the series of Memoranda that were exchanged between Balfour and Curzon – an amazing dialectical duel, rapier versus bludgeon . . . but the main controversy could not get itself settled in spite of much discussion and the preparation of many formulae, and still remained unsolved when the Government fell.'[111] By the time the problem was again raised in Lloyd George's War Cabinet, both Balfour and Curzon had moved on to other responsibilities.

Though Jutland meant the virtual retirement of the German surface fleet, German submarines and mines seemed to be everywhere. None, it seemed, was safe: on 5 June Lord Kitchener, on the first leg of a 'fact-finding' mission to Archangel, was killed when the cruiser *Hampshire* was cut in half by a mine only a mile and a half off Marwick Head. After a few tense days, Asquith unhappily capitulated to Lloyd George's demands to succeed the obsolete hero at the War Office.

The 'U-boats' killed many and destroyed thousands of tons of goods en route to and from Britain. And, while he informed the Cabinet in October of the efforts of the navy in countering the German menace, Balfour admitted that the 'most formidable and the most embarrassing [problem faced by the Admiralty] is that raised by the submarine attacks on merchant vessels.' He was not optimistic: 'We must for the present be satisfied with palliation.'[112] The answer, all know now, lay with the convoy system; but Balfour – like Fisher, Jackson, and most of their colleagues – remained unconvinced that this was the case, and Balfour once again supported his admirals. Much criticism fell on Jackson, on whom the responsibility of his high command weighed heavily by late 1916. In November, when the submarine campaign was particularly severe, the exhausted admiral departed to take charge of the Royal Naval College, and Balfour announced that he would be replaced by Jellicoe – who was every bit as suspicious of the convoy system as his predecessor. Like the reorganization of air power, the introduction of convoys would not come until after the fall of the Asquith government and Balfour's translation to the Foreign Office.

Amid these military problems, the Irish Question had little occupied ministers since the passage and suspension of Home Rule in August 1914, but that respite ended on 24 April 1916. This was Easter Monday, and the Prime Minister returned to Downing Street that evening from a restful weekend in the country only to be informed that an armed insurrection had broken out in Dublin. Hankey recalled, 'Asquith merely said "well, that's something", and went off to bed.'[113] The Easter Rising proved to be 'something' indeed. Led by a former schoolmaster turned revolutionary, the Irish 'republican force' enjoyed a surfeit only of dreams – of all else it was in want, including men, guns, ammunition and, at first, public sympathy. Britain was engaged in the greatest war of modern times, and its leaders were in no frame of mind to treat lightly the armed challenge of what they considered a rag-bag company of traitorous adventurers. Within a very few days, the republican tricolour was torn down from the General Post Office in what was then Sackville Street, and 64 rebels lay dead, with 200 wounded. Yet 134 soldiers were also dead and another 400 injured – nearly all of them Irish, as were almost all the 200 dead and the 600 wounded civilians tragically caught up in the firefight. The uprising did not ignite the national revolution that was the hope of the rebels and seemed for a time to be just another tragic episode in a national history awash in tragic episodes.

At first the outbreak hardly impressed Dubliners, but Irish perceptions of the episode began to change after fifteen rebel leaders were summarily convicted in drumhead courts and shot as traitors. The trials and punishments appeared to the Irish to be arbitrary and unjust, with some key conspirators spared the firing squad, and at least one innocent shot on orders of an officer later deemed to be mad.[114] Thus were those first perceived as tragic cranks elevated to the status of martyrs to Irish freedom, and the episode remade into the pivotal event of modern Irish history.

With war worries aplenty, Asquith needed a prompt settlement, and once again turned to Lloyd George to search for a compromise – the Wizard of Wales took this as a charge to solve the Irish problem once and for all. He was not deflected from his purpose by the initial suspicions of the contending parties of British Unionists, Irish Nationalists, Ulster Protestants and Southern Irish Unionists. Lloyd George shuttled back and forth among these until, in early June, he had drafted a plan combining immediate Home Rule with exclusion of the six counties of Ulster – all to be subject to review after the war, though he apparently assured Carson privately that the exclusion would be permanent.[115] Redmond hated the idea of Ulster exclusion as much as in 1914, but he knew that this could be the last hope of his Home Rule party, faced as it was with the separatist movement energized by the Rising.[116] The minister revealed his plan on 12 June, and for a brief while it appeared that he was in sight of achieving a political miracle. While most of the senior Unionist ministers seemed resigned to the Lloyd George plan, there were ominous exceptions, including Balfour's old comrades Lansdowne, Selborne and Long.[117] Furthermore, on 22 June a meeting of eighty angry Unionist MPs courted their leaders' disapproval by denouncing the scheme; but Lloyd George, Carson and Redmond, backed by Bonar Law, held firm. The leaders of both major parties were also too far committed to back away.[118]

Balfour had not been consulted by Lloyd George and played no part in fashioning the compromise plan, nor did he serve on the Cabinet committee Asquith appointed on 27 June to save it. His personal history with Irish affairs was both long and deep, and few had fought harder to defend the Union. He had supported the firm suppression of the Rising; but, as he considered the arguments of Die-hard and moderate alike in the weeks that followed, his mind began to clear.[119] The cost in blood and money to shore up the old system would almost certainly be too great to justify. Perhaps the future which Salisbury had once predicted – when the Union could no longer be maintained – had arrived. Winning the war as rapidly as possible, Balfour concluded, was more important even than preserving the Irish Union. Like Lloyd George, he was impressed by the reports of the British ambassador in Washington, Sir Cecil Spring-Rice, of the 'beneficial effect' an Irish settlement would have in the United States (with a presidential election coming in November), and he and his colleagues hoped passionately for American entry into the war.[120] For the former Chief Secretary the cost of holding the twenty-six Catholic counties simply could no · longer be justified – if Protestant Ulster could be protected.

On 24 June he circulated a Cabinet paper making his case. Lloyd George's proposed settlement of immediate Home Rule for nationalist Ireland, balanced by the guarantee of exclusion for the six Ulster counties, was the best possible arrangement. The only alternative was more bloodshed. 'Very strong, therefore,' he confessed to his colleagues, 'must be the arguments which would induce me to run the hazard of civil war, when *we have offered to us voluntarily* all that successful civil war would give'.[121] For the Die-hard argument that a Home Rule Irish government would be pro-German he had little time, reminding the Cabinet that, even if this were possible, any such government would be ineffectual and, given the preponderance of British power, probably suicidal. Besides, he added, the Nationalist leaders were not to be confused with the small knot of separatist revolutionaries.[122] The veteran Home Ruler T. P. O'Connor must have smiled when he told John Dillon of Lloyd George's judgement that 'Bloody Balfour' fought for the plan 'as if he had been a Home Ruler all of his life'.[123]

Bonar Law would not openly endorse the plan until he had secured the support of the rank and file, and a meeting at the Carlton Club was scheduled for 7 July. There were few men in the Unionist Party who had fought Home Rule with greater ferocity than Balfour, Carson and Bonar Law, and now the three made the case for compromise.[124] No vote was taken, but William Bridgeman – who opposed the Lloyd George scheme – admitted in his diary that, had there been, the leaders would have carried the day.[125] Yet, it all came to nothing, for four days later Lansdowne – who remained in the government – spoke powerfully in the Lords, demanding that the permanency of Ulster exclusion be spelt out clearly before any pen was put to paper. The Die-hards made the same case in the Commons, and Redmond had no choice but to take up the challenge. Exclusion, he insisted, must remain provisional until the proposed post-war conference took it up. With the battle once again engaged, any hope of settlement fell to bits. The Cabinet admitted defeat and agreed to postpone further consideration until the return of peace. There seemed nothing else to do but to restore Dublin Castle government – Lord Wimborne returned as Lord Lieutenant, and a Unionist Chief Secretary, H. E. Duke, replaced the disgraced Birrell, as Asquith sacrificed yet another long-time comrade.

Balfour's decision to support the Lloyd George plan was based on what he considered to be the undeniable logic of the case for compromise. To Sandars, now an embittered critic, his former master stood convicted of nothing less than 'apostasy'.[126] Others in the party were equally shocked that Balfour, Bonar Law and Carson were prepared to 'betray' the Union. Balfour was in the end correct in his fears that more blood would be spilt if Lloyd George's compromise plan were ignored – though he certainly took no solace when proved correct in the years immediately after the war.

The terrible year of 1916 passed without concrete progress towards a victorious peace. Frustration among the Unionists at Westminster was enormous, and many, though unsure of what exactly to do, were certain that change must begin at the top. Balfour had no role in initiating the fall of Asquith, but his actions helped to make it possible to bring together an alternative government. The first signs of political crisis could be seen when Carson – angry as usual, and unmuzzled by his resignation in 1915 – openly attacked the government on 8 November over a minor bill dealing with captured German assets in Africa. The so-called Nigeria debate was not about Africa at all: it was about the Ulster leader's frustration with what he branded a hopeless administration, and with his own party for prolonging its life. Sir Edward Carson was a brilliant and dangerous opponent at any time, but among the restive Unionist backbenchers in the unstable atmosphere of late 1916 he posed a threat to the leadership of the Unionist Party and therefore to the coalition. Bonar Law was shaken by the episode, and cautioned the Prime Minister that serious changes again would have to be made and that he would return when he had a 'definite plan'.[127]

Five days after Carson's assault, Lansdowne circulated a paper to the Cabinet. In this he suggested an alternative to Lloyd George's recent public call for a 'fight to the finish – to a knock-out', arguing instead for consideration of a compromise peace, rather than continuing the bloody stalemate on the Western Front.[128] To his Unionist colleagues – despite their sympathy for a man who had lost a son in the conflict – this was sheer defeatism, and it played its part in bringing the discontented Bonar Law and Carson closer to Lloyd George.[129] Balfour also opposed any talk of a compromise peace, and only a month earlier had circulated a memorandum of his own, confident in its prediction of ultimate victory.[130]

By late November, a meeting between Bonar Law, Lloyd George and Carson was engineered by Aitken, who laboured tirelessly at this time to be rid of the hated 'Squiff'. The trio had proved in the past that they could damage one another – but could they work together? The answer was not long in coming, for by Saturday 25 November they had hammered out a proposal calling for the creation of a small 'Civilian General Staff' of ministers with supreme control over war policy. The document they had drawn up for Asquith's signature called for a committee of three – presumably themselves – with Lloyd George as chairman and the premier only as a sort of external president.[131] Bonar Law took the draft to Asquith that afternoon, warning him that he would survive only if he acted quickly. Confident that he could stand against this rebellion, the Prime Minister rejected both the plan and Bonar Law's advice.[132]

Though the new triumvirate struggled to prevent it, rumours of a government reshuffle inevitably circulated in Westminster and soon appeared in the press. As party leader, Bonar Law could not avoid facing his colleagues, and the Unionist ministers met on the afternoon of Thursday 30 November. The plan for the proposed war directorate was laid out, and Lord Robert Cecil muddied the waters by elaborating his own scheme, revealed earlier in Cabinet, for dual executive committees – one each for war and civilian affairs.[133] The meeting broke up without resolution, and Walter Long expressed the feelings of several who had been present when he wrote to Bonar Law that he did not care which new approach found favour: 'What I care is that we should act together, act promptly, and use our combined strength to save the country from a grave danger.'[134]

Balfour attended but said little that afternoon, for he was again developing a case of influenza.[135] Laid low by a fever, he took to his bed later in the day and remained there for the next three days. While most of the Cabinet fled to the country for the weekend, Bonar Law gathered the available Unionist ministers on Sunday, and they agreed to force Asquith to act by demanding that he restructure the government immediately.[136] Unlike Carson, who did not attend, all seemed quite willing to retain Asquith as head of the government but not of the war. Furthermore, according to Bonar Law, they also seemed willing to stifle their suspicions and give Lloyd George control of the proposed war executive, 'and if the Prime Minister could not see his way to adopt this course, *then we should resign*.'[137] This was put into the form of a resolution which Bonar Law took to No. 10 later in the day and read to Asquith.[138] Events, the Unionist ministers declared, had made a simple reshuffle impossible: 'We therefore urge the Prime Minister to tender the resignation of the government. If he feels unable to take that step, we authorize Mr Bonar Law to tender our resignations.'[139] If Asquith would not remake the government, they were prepared for Lloyd George to try.[140]

Meanwhile, Lloyd George presented Asquith with his demand for a supreme war council free of departmental duties – and of prime-ministerial interference. Asquith was unmoved, insisting that, as premier, he must retain final supervisory authority over any such committee. Lloyd George also indicated that Balfour should be moved from the Admiralty to another office – to which the Prime Minister also objected.[141] The War Secretary did this knowing that Bonar Law would disapprove, but the two rebellious ministers met afterwards and agreed that they would stand together.[142] The Unionist chieftains met again the next day and renewed their demand that Asquith immediately submit the resignation of the government. Fuelled by newspapers gorged on rumours, the political crisis seemed very near the point of detonation.

Later in the day, Asquith and Lloyd George met once again, and the Unionists' threat seemed to have worked: the Prime Minister indicated that he had changed his mind and agreed to the proposed war executive, with himself as external president and Lloyd George as chairman. But it was not to be. Angered by what he considered an insulting anti-government article in *The Times* on Monday morning – which, because of the details it contained, he mistakenly thought inspired by Lloyd George – Asquith reverted to his former position and informed the King that he would reconstruct the government in his own way.[143] The following day, emboldened by Liberal colleagues who advised resistance, he informed Lloyd George by letter (having refused to see him) that he would himself chair any new war committee, whatever its form, and that he would not have Carson on it at any price. He also returned to the matter of the Admiralty: thinking Balfour the sole Unionist minister not hostile to him, he intended to cling to him: 'I cannot (as I told you yesterday) be a party to any suggestion that Mr Balfour should be displaced . . . I believe Mr Balfour to be, under existing conditions, the necessary head of the Board [of Admiralty].'[144]

Still very much *hors de combat*, Balfour knew little of these developments; and it is unclear whether he knew yet that the 'little man' (as he called Lloyd George) was adamant that there must be a change at the Admiralty.[145] Bonar Law's respect and admiration for his former chief were undiminished, and he insisted that he would 'take no part in any attempt to get rid of Mr Balfour from the Admiralty' – but Lloyd George refused to back down. Despite his liking for Balfour and his great admiration for his intellect and tact, he had his reasons for wanting Balfour out of the Admiralty. Lloyd George believed that the war required the qualities of decisiveness, energy and action, and few ministers had been more decisive, energetic or active in office than he – sometimes to his cost. After more than two years of conflict, he was convinced that Asquith's indecisive methods of administration were ill-suited to the demands of a great war. Balfour, brilliant, contemplative and philosophical, certainly did not appear to him to be a spur to a premier reluctant to act. Moreover, Lloyd George's experience at the Ministry of Munitions and the War Office had convinced him that most generals and admirals did not know their business, and Balfour, he believed, was altogether too steadfast in his support of his admirals.

Lloyd George needed his fellow rebel Carson back in the government, but he had learned that the Unionist ministers were not enthusiastic at the idea of having the Ulster leader as a member of the new war executive. Lloyd George wisely surmised that it would be safer to have such a volatile figure in, rather than outside, a new government, and the Admiralty might therefore be the ideal place for him.[146]

On Sunday and Monday 3–4 December, on his sickbed, Balfour learned 'something of what the Unionists have been doing in the meanwhile' from his Admiralty secretary, Masterton Smith, and from Lord Robert Cecil.[147] On Tuesday he felt well enough to entertain Lansdowne at lunch.[148] Possibly from one of them Balfour learned of the stand-off between Lloyd George and Asquith and concluded 'that the dispute about personnel . . . really centred round me: L.G. wanted a change at the Admiralty, which was being resisted by the Prime Minister.'[149] This moved him to act, and at midday he called for Masterton Smith and dispatched him to No. 10 with a letter to the Prime Minister. This endorsed Lloyd George's plan for a war executive and recognized the fact that it 'would work more satisfactorily if the Admiralty were not represented by me. In these circumstances I cannot consent to retain my office, and must ask you to accept my resignation.'[150] Resignation threats by ministers were nothing new to Asquith, but he was chilled by the thought that Balfour meant business. The letter continued:

> I am quite well aware that you do not personally share Lloyd George's view in this connection. But I am quite clear that the new system should have a trial under the most favourable circumstances; and the mere fact that the new Chairman of the war Council *did* prefer and, as far as I know, *still* prefers a different arrangement is, to my mind, quite conclusive, and leaves me no doubt as to the manner in which I can best assist the Government which I desire to support.

By return messenger, Asquith sent a copy of his own letter of 4 December to Lloyd George, featuring the Prime Minister's defence of Balfour as First Lord. This did not weaken Balfour's resolve to resign, however, and in the afternoon he sent yet another letter to Downing Street. He was grateful for Asquith's sentiments, but added:

I do not, however, feel much inclined to change my views. I still think (a) that the break-up of the government by the retirement of Lloyd George would be a misfortune, (b) that the experiment of giving him a free hand with the day-to-day work of the War Committee is still worth trying, and (c) that there is no use trying it except on terms which enable him to work under the conditions which, in his own opinion, promise the best results. We cannot, I think, go on in the old way. An open breach with Lloyd George will not improve matters, and attempts to compel co-operation between him and his fellow-workers with whom he is in but imperfect sympathy will only produce fresh trouble.

I am therefore still of opinion that my resignation should be accepted, and that a fair trial should be given to the War Council à la George.

Balfour sent copies of these letters to Lloyd George and Bonar Law, and they were ushered into his sickroom on the morning of Wednesday the 6th. Asquith's words left no doubt that he absolutely rejected any idea of remaining as a figurehead Prime Minister while Lloyd George ran the war. Yet the three wished somehow to retain Asquith's services and his still formidable prestige in a new government – perhaps this would be possible, Balfour suggested, under Bonar Law's leadership. Bonar Law revealed to his host that on the previous evening, Tuesday 5 December, he had been summoned to the palace and asked by the King whether he felt able to form a government. He had agreed to 'consult his friends', and reiterated his desire for a Cabinet including all of the key ministers. He had then gone to Lloyd George, who expressed similar hopes. One of the possible configurations they discussed was a coalition led by Balfour, with the thought in mind that this might lure Asquith to serve in an undemanding senior post. His night's work not yet complete, Bonar Law then called on Asquith to present this plan. As Unionist leader, he said, he was the constitutional alternative to Asquith, but he added, 'If he [Asquith] thought it would be easier for him to serve under Mr Balfour I would be delighted to fall in with such an arrangement. Mr Asquith, after a moment's consideration, said he would not agree to this.'[151] There seemed little else to do except request – as Bonar Law had suggested to His Majesty on Tuesday evening – that the King summon the contenders to the palace for an 'all-round talk'.

At 3 p.m. on Wednesday, King George received the coalition party leaders – Asquith, Bonar Law and Arthur Henderson of the Labour Party – and, of course, Lloyd George. He also summoned the convalescing Balfour, whom he had requested to come for a private conversation half an hour before the others. In their brief talk, Balfour reiterated to the King his desire for a Cabinet of all the talents, including Asquith, adding that he thought it 'quite impossible for the same man effectively to carry out the ordinary duties of a Prime Minister and Leader of the House of Commons, in addition to those of Chairman of the War Committee'.[152] The King agreed, and asked Balfour to begin the discussion when the others arrived.

This he did, emphasizing the importance of maintaining the national character of any new government while refining the machinery of administration in light of the experience of the previous two years. Each leader had his say in a discussion, Balfour recalled, 'moderate in form, but, in so far as Asquith and L.G. were concerned, with a sub-acid flavour'. Balfour summed up, noting that the only three possible premiers were present at the table – he excluded Henderson and himself – and that it appeared to him that if either Lloyd George or Bonar Law formed a government, Asquith would refuse to serve.[153] At that point the others interrupted simultaneously, protesting that things had not 'gone quite so far as I seemed to suppose'. Of course, they had, and all present knew it. Nonetheless, Asquith insisted that he could commit to nothing without again consulting his colleagues. Given the Prime Minister's resignation, according to Balfour, 'it was understood' that the King would charge Bonar Law to attempt to form a government, if possible including Asquith. There the meeting ended.

It is difficult to imagine that Balfour, who was still quite ill, had not surmised how the crisis would conclude, but perhaps his restless mind wandered. Interestingly, with his diary of the day, King George preserved a piece of paper with a simple pencil drawing of a three-arched bridge in a pastoral landscape. On this he noted, 'This sketch was made by Mr Balfour on blotting paper during the conference, at Buckingham Palace during the political crisis on Dec. 6th 1916 at which I presided.'[154]

On that bitterly cold afternoon, Bonar Law returned with Balfour to Carlton Gardens and on the way enquired if he thought anything could be done to convince Asquith to take office in a Bonar Law or Lloyd George administration. Balfour did not mince words: 'I replied in the negative.'[155] The Prime Minister settled the question by writing to Bonar Law later in the day that his Liberal colleagues would not serve under any other prime minister: 'They think, & I agree with them, that I, and probably they, can give more effective support from outside.'[156] By 7 p.m. both Bonar Law and Lloyd George were back at the palace, where the Unionist leader informed the King that he felt unable to form a government. King George then received Lloyd George and charged him to try – and within a few minutes the two politicians had gone their separate ways to ensure that this attempt at cabinet-making would be a success.

The inter-party constitutional conference, July 1910. *Clockwise around the table*:
H. H. Asquith (*facing away*), D. Lloyd George, A. Birrell, Lord Cawdor, Lord Lansdowne,
Balfour, A. Chamberlain and Lord Crewe

The Fourth Party as seen by 'Spy' (Leslie Ward) in 1910: Churchill speaks while Balfour dozes, Drummond Wolff scribbles and Gorst ruminates

'Joe' Chamberlain and Balfour as colleagues on the front bench, by Sydney Pryor Hall, 1895

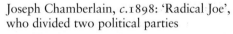

Lord Curzon, with Viscount Peel, emerging from a Cabinet meeting at 10 Downing Street, November 1923

Lord Lansdowne leaving a meeting of Asquith's coalition Cabinet, at the time of the Easter Rising in Dublin, April 1916

Walter Hume Long (later Lord Long of Wraxall): perennially indignant, in 1911 he presented Balfour with a notice to vacate the party leadership

Joseph Chamberlain, c.1898: 'Radical Joe', who divided two political parties

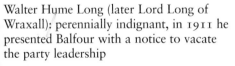

Lloyd George and Churchill:
'The Terrible Twins' on their
way to the House of Commons
on Budget Day, 1910

Balfour at the Department of
State during his first mission to
Washington, April 1917

Foreign Office,
November 2nd, 1917.

Dear Lord Rothschild,

I have much pleasure in conveying to you, on
behalf of His Majesty's Government, the following
declaration of sympathy with Jewish Zionist aspirations
which has been submitted to, and approved by, the Cabinet.

"His Majesty's Government view with favour the
establishment in Palestine of a national home for the
Jewish people, and will use their best endeavours to
facilitate the achievement of this object, it being
clearly understood that nothing shall be done which
may prejudice the civil and religious rights of
existing non-Jewish communities in Palestine, or the
rights and political status enjoyed by Jews in any
other country".

I should be grateful if you would bring this
declaration to the knowledge of the Zionist Federation.

The Balfour Declaration of 1917 which played its part in making the modern world

Balfour speaks at the dedication of the University of Jerusalem, April 1925. He was less welcome in Damascus

Balfour signs the Five Power Treaty at the Washington Naval Conference, February 1922

Balfour and friends enter the British Academy luncheon to honour his eightieth birthday and his seven-year presidency of the organization he helped to found, July 1928

Balfour and Lloyd George at Whittingehame soon after the fall of the coalition government, October 1922. They are followed by Mrs Lascelles and Sir Robert Horne

King George V receives Balfour's seals of office for the final time, May 1929. This was Balfour's last public appearance: 'This is the end,' he wrote. 'Quite time too!'

At 9.30 Bonar Law was once again at Carlton Gardens, this time with his Chief Whip, Lord Edmund Talbot. Balfour – feverish and feeling much the worse for his demanding day – received them in his nightclothes and dressing gown. The Unionist leader brought an offer from the Prime Minister-designate. Balfour recalled:

> He now brought a formal request that I would undertake the position of minister for Foreign Affairs. If I consented, it would in the view of both L.G. and himself, greatly help with the rest of our Unionist colleagues. I agreed to the proposal provided it was understood that I might have a reasonable time to recuperate from the sharp attack from which I was still suffering. To this he very gladly agreed.[157]

Though Bonar Law had at first firmly resisted Lloyd George's veto of Balfour's continuing at the Admiralty, he was impressed with the war minister's idea that 'the proper place for Mr Balfour was at the Foreign Office.'[158] Bonar Law's anxiety that he might become trapped between irreconcilable loyalties passed away. Bonar Law and Lloyd George certainly agreed that Balfour would be the most important acquisition the fledgling administration could make, as his enduring prestige among his party made it easier for those Unionists sceptical of Lloyd George's embrace to support the new experiment.[159]

In one of the most dramatic scenes in his immortal version of these events, Lord Beaverbrook (as Aitken became a few days later) insisted that the offer came as a surprise to Balfour. According to this telling, Balfour 'jumped' to his feet and replied, 'Well you hold a pistol to my head – I must accept.' The press lord had heard an account of this from his friend Bonar Law.[160] Mrs Dugdale insisted that her uncle had already learned from Bonar Law that he was meant to succeed Grey as Foreign Secretary. She added, 'More than once in after years Balfour pointed out to me, and to others, the spot near Buckingham Palace where Bonar Law suggested to him, as they left the Conference together, that he should be Foreign Minister in a new Administration.'[161] This rings true – but does it rule out the colourful scene? Balfour certainly used the 'pistol to the head' phrase from time to time, and employed it in another context in his memorandum of the crisis. As for the question of when the offer of the Foreign Office was first made, in 1928 Beaverbrook sent Balfour a draft of portions of his forthcoming *Politicians and the War*, including this episode. By then approaching eighty and in indifferent health, Balfour declined the offer to vet the entire typescript, insisting, 'My recollection of the sequence of events is a little hazy. I rather think that Bonar Law sounded me with regard to the Foreign Office as we walked away from Buckingham Palace after the Conference; but this is quite immaterial. The general tenor of your statement entirely agrees with my remembrance of it – *though I cannot speak for the details*.'[162] After the Buckingham Palace conference Balfour knew that the government was doomed, that Asquith would serve under no other prime minister, and that the Liberal ministers would not take office without him – and it appears certain that he learned from Bonar Law that the Foreign Office would be placed at his disposal. Few spun a better yarn than Beaverbrook, but in this case it appears he spun it a bit too far.[163]

Asquith never entirely forgave Balfour for backing Lloyd George, with whom the Unionist seemed to have so little in common, against himself, an old friend.[164] It was even more perplexing to the Prime Minister in light of the fact that Lloyd George had openly worked to dislodge Balfour from the Admiralty, while Asquith was adamant that he be allowed to remain. The crucial point was that Asquith's leadership, despite his undeniable ability, was not winning the war nor did it provide any reason to believe it ever would. Asquith's great talents were simply not the ones that were most needed at the moment. Reflecting on the premier and his critics a year earlier, Balfour told Mrs Dugdale:

> They hate Asquith. Well – he has his faults, and they are the worst kind for the present crisis. He is an arbitrator, an eminently fair-minded judge – the best-tempered man I ever knew – a splendid chairman of a committee, and, after all a Cabinet is only a committee; but I never heard him originate or suggest. If he were in this room now and heard us talk, he would still be incapable of understanding that more is required of him than the admirable balance he can give.[165]

Once the political dust had settled, Balfour told his sister-in-law Lady Betty, 'I am sorry Asquith is not still P.M. That was what I wanted – But I was all for Lloyd George to be given a free hand. Since the war began he has done two big things – [by] far the biggest things that have been done – & he alone could do them.' 'L.G.'s' accomplishments that most impressed Balfour were the organization of munitions supply and, after his move to the War Office, of military transportation at the Western Front. He went on to caution Lady Betty that, while she might hear that one businessman or another – the so-called 'men of push and go' – deserved the credit, she should recall who chose them. The acclaim belonged to Lloyd George.[166] Lady Betty also recalled a similar anecdote heard from a friend who claimed as her source 'an Admiralty man'. According to this, when Balfour heard the accusation that Lloyd George wanted to be nothing less than a 'dictator', "'Let him be," sd. A.J.B. "If he thinks he can win the war I'm all for his having a try.'"[167]

There seems to be little doubt that Balfour was disappointed to be expelled from the Admiralty by Lloyd George. Yet this was soon put aside, and it seems to have detracted not at all from the close co-operation of the two men over the lifespan of the new government. This was a case in which Balfour forgave as well as forgot. He wrote in the following September to Lord Robert Cecil, who joined the new government despite his lingering suspicion of Lloyd George:

> You see Lloyd George's faults, and they are not difficult to see. But do you think he can be improved upon out of our existing material? Is there any one of his colleagues in the present War Cabinet you would like to see in his place? Is there any member of the late Government you would like to see in his place? Do you believe there is in the House of Commons any genius on the Back Benches fit for the place? Do you think there is somewhere in the undistinguished mass of the general public some unknown genius to whom, if we could but find him, we might entrust the most difficult, and the most important, task with which British statesmanship has ever been confronted?
>
> For myself I am inclined to answer all these questions in the negative, and, that being so, the most patriotic course appears to me to be to provide the man whom we do not wish to replace with all the guidance and help in our power.[168]

This he did during the remaining two years of war – and, as it turned out, for some time thereafter.

12

Foreign Secretary and Lord President

HAVING PUSHED ASQUITH aside, Lloyd George now created an inno-vative War Cabinet of himself and four colleagues: the Unionists Bonar Law, Curzon and Milner, and Labour's Arthur Henderson, who had abandoned Asquith to give 'L.G.' his chance. Only Bonar Law as Chancellor of the Exchequer held a departmental portfolio, and the heads of the traditional departments of state found themselves subservient to the War Cabinet.[1] Churchill, then out of power and out of sorts, commented of Balfour, now Foreign Secretary: 'He passed from one Cabinet to the other, from the Prime Minister who was his champion to the Prime Minister who had been his most severe critic, like a powerful graceful cat walking delicately and unsoiled across a rather muddy street.'[2] He meant that Balfour had no heart and no loyalty, but neither played a part in his decision – more important were the facts that Asquith had failed and Lloyd George might succeed. The new Prime Minister had insisted that Balfour surrender the Admiralty and did not select him for the War Cabinet, yet he summoned him to virtually all its meetings – and Lord Robert Cecil, his under-secretary, typically took his place when he was unavailable.[3] It is little wonder that Balfour often spoke privately of the war executive as 'we'. During the new government's first week, however, Balfour remained in his sickbed and under his physician's care. Lady Betty Balfour paid him a brief visit, and reported that her sixty-eight-year-old brother-in-law looked very tired, 'much older' and 'very feeble'.[4]

Balfour was barely recovered from his influenza attack when the first crisis of the new regime broke, as the American ambassador, Walter Hines Page, transmitted to the Foreign Office a 'peace offer' by the Germans.[5] This was given to Lord Robert Cecil on 18 December, and was followed a day later by a brief paper by President Wilson calling on all belligerent powers to suspend military operations and make public their war aims. Thomas Woodrow Wilson, a scholar and university president turned politi-cian, had recently been re-elected after a campaign stressing his determination to remain out of the 'European' war. The US was much divided over the conflict, with opposing factions favouring the Allies or the Central Powers, and the apparent majority alarmed at the prospect of participation on any side. American opinion was certainly on the minds of British leaders, whose fondest wish it was that the great English-speaking republic would come to the aid of what had been, after all, its mother country. Certainly Balfour was among them.

Wilson's brilliance was undeniable, but his was a rigid intellect, and it was coupled with a moralist streak, strengthened by his inherent stubbornness. The President seemed to believe that the Great Powers had somehow chosen war in the same way and sought the same goal – European dominance, no matter the cost. The British reply to the German note therefore required careful handling – as did the President. Balfour had met Wilson's confidant Colonel Edward Mandell House when the Texan had visited London in early 1915, and the two men got on well from the outset. House recalled in his journal:

> I took a liking to him at once, and have a sincere desire that it should be reciprocated. I like the quality of his mind. It is not possible to allow one's wits to lag when one is in active discussion with him . . . I am inclined to rank him along with the President and Mr Asquith in intellectuality, and this, to my mind, places him at the summit.[6]

The official Allied reply to Wilson in early January contrasted German aggression with the righteousness of the Allied defence, and stressed the Allies' commitment to a just peace. It carefully sidestepped their outrage at being addressed in the same way as the Germans, whose armies continued to fight on the French and Belgian soil they had occupied since August 1914. Balfour, ever hopeful that the Americans would see that their own interest and that of the Allies were the same, sent a private reply through the British ambassador Spring-Rice. In his view, genuine peace depended on three factors:

> The first is that the existing causes of international unrest should be as far as possible removed or weakened. The second is that the aggressive aims and the unscrupulous methods of the Central Powers should fall into disrepute among their own peoples. The third is that behind international law . . . some form of international sanction should be devised which would give pause to the hardiest aggressor.[7]

Balfour did not know the President, but assumed that surely he must have felt the same. Yet the Foreign Secretary also understood Wilson's delicate position, and never allied himself with those who thought that somehow the great republic could be pushed into war. As it was, the

Americans' eventual abandonment of neutrality had far more to do with German mistakes than with British persuasion. For example, on 16 January 1917 British naval intelligence intercepted a secret communication from the German Foreign Minister, Arthur Zimmermann, to the German ambassador in Mexico City. The infamous 'Zimmermann telegram' indicated that submarine warfare against merchant shipping was to be escalated, and that if this drove the US to join the Allies 'we make Mexico a proposal of alliance on the following basis: make war together, make peace together, generous financial support and an understanding on our part that Mexico is to reconquer the lost territory in Texas, New Mexico, and Arizona.'[8]

On 24 February, Balfour handed the evidence to Ambassador Page. While the bizarre telegram was a blow to German–US relations, the stepped-up submarine-warfare campaign did much greater harm, resulting in March in the destruction of a number of American vessels with many civilian lives lost. This was too much, even for the fence-sitters, and certainly for Wilson: on 2 April 1917 he called for war.

To Wilson, war against Germany did not necessarily mean war in lockstep with Britain and France. However, the War Cabinet understandably wished to forge as close a partnership as possible, and, after considering the possibilities, Lloyd George proposed that the Foreign Secretary himself lead a delegation to Washington to 'place at the disposal of the United States government the experience we have gained in this country during the war'.[9] House enthusiastically advised the President, 'I would like Balfour to get to know you and to take back his impressions so they might come from a less partisan voice than mine.'[10] Wilson agreed, and a French delegation was also invited.[11] Balfour stoically accepted his fate: 'I cannot say I look forward with much pleasure to such an undertaking,' he wrote to Stamfordham, 'for I am a most abominable sailor; but in these days we do what we must, not what we like.'[12]

Balfour; Ian Malcolm, his parliamentary secretary; Lord Cunliffe, the governor of the Bank of England; and some two dozen others on 10 April began their journey on a private train for Scotland. No effort was spared to frustrate prying eyes, and remarkably it was Balfour himself who breached security when he gave his autograph to the lift boy at the hotel in Dumfries where the party passed the night.[13] The Foreign Secretary quickly confessed his misdemeanour, but fortunately no harm came of it.

Balfour's voyage aboard RMS *Olympic*, sister ship of the ill-fated *Titanic*, was uneventful, and Malcolm reported that his master felt 'seedy' only on the first day at sea, and thereafter did not fail to turn up at meals in a private dining room set aside for his party.[14] Balfour ignored the special rubber life-preserver suit that was provided him, noting to Malcolm that 'on the whole, he preferred to drown in his night-shirt.'[15] The ship arrived safely in Halifax on 20 April, when the chief passenger enjoyed his first view of North America in forty-two years. Two days later the party received a tumultuous welcome in Washington, then suffering an enervating spring heatwave.[16] Malcolm wrote to Alice Balfour that, despite all, her brother was 'in the pink', and noted that 'none of this tired the Chief in any way. He went off for a solitary drive in the woods for a couple of hours which greatly refreshed him, and then dined with Spring-Rice at the Embassy.'[17]

On the following day Balfour began an intensive round of discussions and 'events' (none, if possible, before 11 a.m., he requested) which occupied nearly every waking moment for the next five weeks. He charmed leaders and crowds alike, who turned out in force to see the great man. Balfour and his party joined the French as special guests at a celebration at George Washington's home, Mount Vernon, and he returned to town to receive a delegation of Irish-Americans, which he 'weathered . . . splendidly', and went on to dine with a large party of Washington notables – which he did nearly every evening.[18] Despite his age and the demands of his merciless schedule, 'the Chief' slept well every night, Malcolm recorded, and this invariably 'put him right' for the next day. Perhaps his greatest public triumph was his address to the American Congress, the first by a British parliamentarian since his old adversary Parnell had taken the American capital by storm nearly thirty years earlier. The British were delighted when the President left his seat and came down to the floor of the chamber to shake the hand of his guest. 'The pundits', Malcolm noted proudly, 'have ransacked Congressional history, and can find no record of any President having done such a thing before.'[19]

Balfour found time to receive an honorary doctorate from Columbia University, and much enjoyed a visit to the former president Theodore Roosevelt, but his primary purpose was to establish a working relationship with Woodrow Wilson. Balfour got on well with the austere President, and his frankness in their conversations appeared to be much appreciated. He stressed London's deep concern over British finances, following the strain of acting as banker to the Allies for nearly three years. He also discussed fears of the U-boat threat to Britain's food supply, and emphasized the critical need for munitions and warships – particularly for destroyers to protect the North Atlantic convoys, which were finally to begin in earnest in May.[20] At their private dinner on 30 April, Balfour explained to the President Britain's confidential treaty obligations to its allies, France, Russia and Italy – despite the President's insistence that the United States was an 'associated' rather than an 'allied' power.[21]

On 22 May the party boarded a special train for a week's stay in Toronto, Quebec and Ottawa, before arriving home on 9 June – no doubt with Balfour's sincere hope that this was his last Atlantic crossing. It is unlikely that he agreed with Hankey, who wrote to the Prime Minister on the following day, 'I have just seen Mr Balfour, who looks extraordinarily benefited by the sea voyage! I told him so!'[22] There is no record of what, if anything, Balfour replied to Hankey's cheery remark. While he might have disputed that he 'benefited' from the voyage, he did think the mission a success. The substantive discussions with the President, combined with the success of his 'charm offensive', seemed to have ensured Balfour's credibility with the Wilson administration and a new-found popularity with the American people. He had often spoken of Anglo-American co-operation as a 'natural' development, and now it seemed at last achievable. Alice Balfour also noted in her diary that he returned 'with a much pleasanter view of the U.S.A. nation than he had before . . . and twice I heard him say that if you scratched the American you found the Briton'.[23]

There was little time for celebration, however, for Balfour returned to find that much required his attention. His instinct always to support his subordinates was energized by the report of a parliamentary commission which inquired into the mismanagement of the dismal military campaign in Mesopotamia. Lord Hardinge, the viceroy of India during the offensive, had recently returned to the Foreign Office as permanent under-secretary, and Balfour refused to allow him to resign and accept any significant responsibility for the débâcle (as did the India Secretary, Austen Chamberlain, who insisted on resigning). Though Hardinge was now once again a civil servant, Balfour unfortunately encouraged him to address the issue in what turned out to be a poorly received speech to the Lords.[24] Balfour's own speech on the matter was received as no more than a further example of Balfourian loyalty to his underlings, and even the sympathetic Crawford noted that it showed him 'really at his worst'.[25]

Balfour's return from America was also followed by an internecine battle between the Foreign Office and the new Minister of Information, Lord Beaverbrook. 'The Beaver', whose preserve was to be propaganda in enemy countries, demanded unrestricted access to all military and diplomatic intelligence, including that of the secret services. The Foreign Office predictably resisted, and in June the financier-minister (and, since November 1916, proprietor of the *Daily Express*) threatened resignation. Balfour held his ground, Beaverbrook pressed his demands, and the War

Cabinet backed Balfour, but there was 'no surrender by the Foreign Office', the Canadian's biographer has written, 'and no resignation by Beaverbrook'.[26] Balfour and the Foreign Office, however, were not free of their antagonist until October 1918, when – still denied the secrets he wanted – he finally resigned. Beaverbrook – who gloried in being thought a man of action and a rough-edged outsider – did not like Balfour and hated his philosophical method of argumentation: 'Balfour was a hermaphrodite,' he raged. 'No one saw him naked.'[27] Perhaps what the formidable Canadian hated most was Balfour's success in brushing him aside as little more than an annoyance.

This was not the Foreign Secretary's only battle with one of 'L.G's' press lords, for, as he sailed from North America in June, Lord Northcliffe was arriving to take charge of Allied propaganda. Northcliffe – whose newspapers had opposed the inclusion of Balfour in the government – was full of plans, particularly regarding the national aspirations of what would after the war become the 'successor states' to the European empires. As with Beaverbrook, Balfour resisted these incursions into what he insisted was the preserve of the Foreign Office.[28] Again, Lloyd George backed Balfour.

While in 1917 the Allies gained a powerful partner in America, they lost an ally with the collapse of Russia in the same year. The war had brought to that enormous nation little but hunger, discontent and death – and finally it brought revolution. The ineffectual Nicholas II, the last Romanov, finally abdicated the imperial throne on 15 March, and for the next few months a provisional reformist government (under first Prince Lvov and then Alexander Kerensky) attempted to establish a new régime while remaining at war. It failed on all counts, and eventually was shoved aside in November by the Bolsheviks.[29] Considerations by the War Cabinet of ways to bolster the provisional régime and keep Russia in the war proved fruitless, as the largest army in the world began simply to melt away. Balfour was not optimistic. In the unsettled days of March 1917 he wrote to the British ambassador in Moscow, Sir George Buchanan, that, if a republic were declared, he anticipated violence, the eclipse of the moderates and eventual victory of a new autocracy, and finally that 'a disgraceful peace will be patched up with Germany.' He added, 'These gloomy forebodings represent only my personal fears. I hope they are ill founded, and that Russia the country of surprises will give us the greatest surprise of all.'[30] His 'gloomy forebodings' proved true enough, though the 'surprise' eventually revealed by the Bolsheviks proved to be far greater than any that Balfour could have anticipated.

Following the abdication, the Moscow government was faced with the question of what to do with the increasingly unpopular Romanovs. Like the Kaiser, the former Tsar was King George's cousin, and in mid-March the Russians proposed that the former imperial family be relocated to Britain. While this at first seemed to meet with the approval of Lloyd George, the Foreign Office suggested that perhaps a more neutral nation might be more suitable – Denmark or Switzerland, for example. If they would not have the ex-Tsar and his family, then Britain might offer asylum.[31] However, the possible ramifications of welcoming the former Autocrat of All the Russias soon caused the King, despite his 'deep personal friendship' with Nicholas II, to question whether this would be a wise step. Balfour replied that, though the Russians had reached no decision, the British government could not retract its offer, and King George seemed prepared to accept this.[32]

The fate of the Romanovs soon became a matter of public debate, and the King grew troubled by the chorus of voices opposing asylum, particularly among the working classes and the Labour Party.[33] On 6 April, Stamfordham alerted the Foreign Office that the sovereign had concluded that popular feeling against receiving the Tsar was so great that it 'would compromise the position of the King and Queen from whom it is already generally supposed the invitation emanated'. Therefore, 'Buchanan ought to be instructed to tell [Foreign Minister] Milyukoff that the opposition to the Emperor and Empress coming here is so strong that we must be allowed to withdraw from the consent previously given to the Russian Government's proposal.'[34] By this time Balfour and his colleagues were coming to share the monarch's concerns, and on 13 April Lord Robert Cecil noted to Buchanan that, on balance, France might be the best place for the former Tsar.[35] Buchanan replied that he now agreed that granting asylum to the Tsar would have serious 'consequences' at home.[36] The moment of opportunity, if in fact there had ever been one, had passed. Discussions dragged on at least until September, and in the end no solution was found.[37] The Tsar and his family finally fell into the hands of the Bolsheviks and eventually were murdered in July 1918.[38]

None of the great events of 1917 remains more closely linked with Balfour's name than the famous 'Declaration' made public on 2 November in the form of a brief letter from Balfour to Lord Rothschild, the head of the British Zionist movement.

I have much pleasure in conveying to you, on behalf of His Majesty's Government, the following declaration of sympathy with Jewish Zionist aspirations which has been submitted to, and approved by the Cabinet.

> His Majesty's Government view with favour the establishment in Palestine of a national home for the Jewish people, and will use their best endeavours to facilitate the achievement of this object, it being clearly understood that nothing shall be done which may prejudice the civil and religious rights of existing non-Jewish communities in Palestine, or the rights and political status enjoyed by Jews in any other country.

I should be grateful if you would bring this declaration to the knowledge of the Zionist Federation.

Yours sincerely,
Arthur James Balfour[39]

Balfour, of course, had long been interested in Jewish history and culture, and he was pleased in late 1914 to renew his acquaintanceship with the British Zionist leader Chaim Weizmann. A distinguished chemist soon to be engaged on war-related research, Weizmann sought out Balfour in December for the first time since pre-war days to raise the question of the post-war fate of the Jews.[40] According to the scientist: 'He said that, in his opinion, the problem would not be solved until either the Jews became completely assimilated here or a normal Jewish society came into existence in Palestine, and moreover, he was thinking more of the Western European Jews than those of Eastern Europe.'[41] With his party out of office, however, Balfour cautioned that he could promise nothing; but he did invite the Zionist to come again for further talk.

Balfour believed in the existence of national identity and character, and he observed that the assimilation into societies of those of another culture was not always a simple or natural phenomenon.[42] He understood also that centuries of demographic instability had made the European 'races' what they had become by modern times, and that arguments about racial purity – and the discrimination they inspired – were nonsense.[43] Yet he was convinced that for political and economic reasons entirely open borders were impossible. The 1905 Aliens Act of his government had been inspired in large part by anxieties over the immigration into Britain of large numbers of Eastern European Jews. Yet to Balfour anti-Semitism was a horror, and he accepted the profundity of the debt owed to the Jews by Christian civilization – but he also believed that Jews shared a cultural identity beyond their religion, which made it difficult for many to 'become British'. The first point provided spiritual inspiration for what became the Declaration policy, while the latter to him made hard political sense. If a place were provided for them in the land of their historic origins, the Jews would be given the choice of assimilation in their adopted countries or 'Jewish citizenship' in the ancient homeland. 'Thus,' he told the War Cabinet in October 1917, 'any danger of a double allegiance or non-national outlook would be eliminated.'[44] Assuming that Jews who resisted assimilation in their host countries longed for a homeland, and that Palestine was readily available for the purpose, he saw the creation of that homeland under Great Power protection as a way to resolution of a thorny problem.

By 1916 Weizmann was a scientific consultant to the Admiralty, and Balfour, as First Lord, met with him on several occasions. Not surprisingly, the scientist raised the subject of Zionist aspirations. The British Zionists had already raised the matter of a Jewish homeland with Grey and the Foreign Office, and had received some encouragement – including being granted permission to transmit their communications abroad through the Foreign Office, using official ciphers. When Balfour met Weizmann, however, he did not tell him all that he knew – for example, of the promise in 1915 by the British High Commissioner in Egypt, Sir Henry MacMahon, to the Sharif of Mecca of support for Arab ambitions of nationhood. Nor did he discuss the secret 1916 Sykes–Picot Agreement with the French, calling for a post-war division of power in the Near East. The Zionists, however, possessed a sophisticated information-gathering apparatus, and hearing of these things through their own sources did not deter them. By the spring of 1917 Weizmann learned at least as early as did the British that the Vatican, as well as the French and Italian governments, was prepared to lend some support to the Zionist agenda.[45] Success seemed within their compass.

While to Lloyd George 'the idea of reuniting the Jewish people with the land of their forefathers' may have been appealing, he was more concerned that British security would be enhanced if the Holy Land were securely under British sway – and the Zionists looked to him rather useful for this purpose.[46] Hence he also became an important supporter from the earliest days of his government. He approved of Balfour meeting with Weizmann and Lord Rothschild on 13 June 1917, when the Foreign Secretary agreed to consider a statement drafted by them endorsing the creation of a Jewish homeland. Both Lloyd George and Balfour approved the draft in principle, and the War Cabinet discussed it first on 3 September.[47] The reaction was generally sympathetic, and several possible versions of a homeland proposal were considered. But all was not harmony: a powerful case against the Zionist dream was put by India Secretary Edwin Montagu. Himself a Jew, Montagu and his fellow 'assimilationists' believed passionately that the establishment of a Zionist preserve in the Near East would endanger the position of Jews already integrated into the national fabric of the established states, and thus inadvertently serve the cause of anti-Semitism. The two most prominent advocates of the Zionist case, Lloyd George and Balfour, were absent from this meeting, however, and the matter was postponed until October.

Another critic of the scheme was Lord Curzon, Lord President of the Council, member of the War Cabinet and a far greater political force than Montagu. The former Viceroy was the only senior minister who had actually travelled in the East and possessed experience in governing a large Muslim population. Had his colleagues considered, he wondered, whether the arid lands of the Levant could support the population which it was presumed they would attract? Were they aware that the Jews of Palestine were massively outnumbered by their Arab neighbours, whose roots in that land had been established for 1,500 years? What of Jerusalem (which General Allenby was poised to occupy as these discussions took place), sacred to three ancient faiths – would the adherents of two of them timidly accept that the third would take it for its capital?[48] Privately, Curzon thought the Foreign Secretary was 'pressing upon the Cabinet the unfortunate Zionist Declaration' merely – and perhaps cynically – to 'placate the Jews' and purchase their loyalty.[49]

Balfour insisted that the Jewish national genius could overcome these practical challenges. As for the Arabs, he later commented that he was not without sympathy for their character, their history and their rights. The Jewish–Arab demographic imbalance in the Holy Land would continue for many years to come, but like President Wilson, Balfour's confidence in national determination encompassed exceptions. He explained in 1920:

> The deep, underlying principle of self-determination really points to a Zionist policy, *however little in its strict technical interpretation it may seem to favour it*. I am convinced that none but the pedants or people who are prejudiced by religious or racial bigotry, none but those who are blinded by one of these causes would deny for one instant that the case of the Jews is absolutely exceptional, and must be treated by exceptional methods.[50]

There was much else on the minds of these statesmen in September. The combined Allied spring offensive led by General Robert Nivelle had left the French Army reeling. Haig's response, the fruitless Third Battle of

Ypres – Passchendaele – which would eventually cost another 300,000 British casualties, was in its concluding stages. And power in Russia was falling into the laps of the Bolsheviks. By the end of the month President Wilson finally (if covertly) endorsed the idea of a Jewish homeland, and Lloyd George agreed that the plan should be pressed to a conclusion. Perhaps the War Cabinet were also influenced by Balfour's argument that a Zionist policy would edge out the Germans, said to be considering a similar step, and bind worldwide Jewry to the Allied cause.[51] In an effort to make the Declaration more palatable to critics, the final version on which the government agreed struck from the draft the phrase 'Palestine should be reconstituted as the national home of the Jewish people', in favour of calling for the 'establishment in Palestine of a national home for the Jewish people' – which was thought less contentious. To placate the assimilationists and Curzon, there was added the formulation that 'nothing shall be done which may prejudice the civil and religious rights of existing non-Jewish communities in Palestine, or the rights and political status enjoyed by Jews in any other country'.[52] With Lloyd George's recent additions to the War Cabinet of the pro-Zionists Carson and the South African General Jan Smuts, a majority was never in doubt. The assimilationists and Montagu were routed. In the end, as David Vital has written, 'No one had agreed with him, not even Curzon.'[53]

On 31 October the final Declaration was ready for publication, but, with the war in full cry, it was unclear exactly what political changes it would bring in Palestine. The document offered no guidance, and Balfour insisted at this time that a sovereign state was not necessarily called for.[54] If some sort of protectorate were to be created in the region, Balfour was not so certain as the Prime Minister that Britain should accept supervisory authority: even as the peace conference was under way, he was still hoping that the United States could be convinced to take it on.[55] However, in November 1917 he and his colleagues were for the moment satisfied that all that could be done had been done.

Balfour's enthusiasm for Zionism was rooted in his belief that it provided solutions to a number of problems: it would solve the problem of Jewish assimilation in the West, strike at the worldwide curse of anti-Semitism, and revitalize Palestine. Furthermore, it would reunite the Jews in the land of their origins, which he believed in a spiritual as well as a historic sense was in fact theirs. To believe they could make a success of the great experiment, he admitted, required faith; but, as he said after the war, no one 'who is incapable of understanding idealism is capable either of understanding the Zionist Movement or effectually contributing to its consummation'.[56]

Yet, while Balfour was from the outset the most dedicated supporter of the Declaration policy, it is equally true that it would have been doomed had not the War Cabinet for their own reasons supported it. Had the Prime Minister, an enthusiastic pro-Zionist, chosen to sign the famous letter in November 1917, it would have been remembered as the Lloyd George Declaration.[57] But neither Lloyd George nor Milner nor any other leader equalled Balfour's experience with, or zeal for, the Zionist plan. The Zionists, for their part, were sure they knew whom to thank, and Weizmann later wrote to him in 1919 seeking his permission to call one of the first new post-Declaration Jewish agrarian settlements 'Balfouria'.[58]

Balfour's reasoning failed him as he allowed his romanticized visions of the Jewish and Arab peoples to overcome his willingness to face the hard question of whether all sides in Palestine could peacefully be reconciled to the policy. In his 1920 speech he reminded the Zionists that building a Jewish homeland in the Holy Land would not be easy: 'It will require tact, it will require judgement, it will require above all sympathetic goodwill on the part of Jew and Arab.'[59] In the end, the solution embodied in the Declaration required more of these estimable qualities than flesh and blood could muster. Balfour's inclination to see all sides of complicated questions also failed him. He simply could not fathom that the sceptical Arabs might not be satisfied with the creation of the client Arab states of Arabia and Iraq, and therefore smile on the 'small notch . . . in what are now Arab territories being given to the people who for all these hundreds of years have been separated from it'.[60] The addition to the Declaration of a phrase endorsing 'the civil and religious rights of existing non-Jewish communities in Palestine' did nothing to placate them. Even when, in 1925, he travelled in the Near East and witnessed the gratitude of the Jews contrasted with the fury of the Arabs, he did not fully comprehend. It is only a very incomplete defence to recall that, among the decision-makers of 1917, in this he was not alone.

Only weeks after the publication of the Declaration, the press carried another message in which Balfour took far less satisfaction and which for a time divided him from an old friend. This was the famous Lansdowne 'peace letter' published in the *Daily Telegraph* on 29 November.[61] It came at a bad time for the government, coming on the heels of the bloody battle of Passchendaele. Lloyd George had lost patience with 'Wully' Robertson; furthermore, the Central Powers had decided to test the Allies' (and particularly President Wilson's) perseverence with more 'peace feelers'. The Labourite, Henderson, had been sacked from the War Cabinet in August after making known his intention to support an international socialist conclave planned for Stockholm. His place was taken by the Minister of Pensions, George Barnes.[62]

Lansdowne had resigned his leadership of the Lords in March, and brooded over events.[63] By this point, he was certain that the Great Powers were committed to mutual destruction, and in his letter he raised the question that haunted him:

> We are not going to lose this War, but its prolongation will spell ruin for the civilised world, and an infinite addition to the load of human suffering which already weighs upon it . . . but what will be the value of the blessings of peace to nations so exhausted that they can scarcely stretch out a hand with which to grasp them?

The time had come, he insisted, to face hard questions: 'What are we fighting for? . . . What, then, is it we want when the war is over?' Unlike in the case of his November 1916 Cabinet memorandum, now he acted in a public forum, and the reaction was explosive. Certainly there were those who felt as Lansdowne did, and said as much, but they were nearly drowned out by the massive condemnation his gesture provoked – and the harshest voices rose from within his own party. Many who knew the Marquess during his years in office were simply stunned that, in Sandars's words, 'he screwed himself up to do it.'[64]

Lloyd George acted quickly to distance the government from Lansdowne and issued a statement the next day insisting that ministers had read the letter 'with as much surprise as did anyone else'.[65] This was not entirely the case, for Lansdowne had poured out his anxieties to the Foreign Secretary in early November. On the 16th he sent Balfour a memorandum and a series of questions which he 'thought might be put to H.M.G., in either House', all of which prefigured the arguments in the letter. Balfour replied on 22 November, advising that the intention of the government was not the destruction of any nation and that it was only the continued abuse of power on land or sea by the Central Powers which the Allies were fighting to suppress. He also offered some advice: 'I do not think', he wrote, 'that this is a suitable time for discussing peace matters.'[66] Lansdowne, however, was not convinced, and ignored the warning.

In an undated memorandum written 'after publication of his letter', Lansdowne recalled that on 26 November he met Balfour by chance in the street and was once again advised by him not to press his case; but the Marquess had decided to publish a letter, noting that Balfour's opposition 'did not dissuade me'. He offered to provide a draft for his old friend's consideration, but Balfour put him off, pleading that he was leaving for Paris that evening for an Allied conference. Lansdowne recalled asking, 'Did he object to my showing the draft to Hardinge, in order that he might tell me if the letter contained any inaccuracies? [Balfour] agreed, adding "Hardinge knows my thoughts."'[67] The King's secretary, Stamfordham, later spoke to Lord Burnham, proprietor of the *Daily Telegraph*, who was in Lansdowne's confidence and who agreed that Balfour had not seen the actual draft of the letter. At the foot of Stamfordham's memorandum dealing with the affair it is noted in red ink: 'It subsequently transpired that it was Lord Lansdowne not Mr Balfour that suggested submitting the letter to Lord Hardinge.'[68]

According to Lansdowne, the Under-Secretary offered only 'one or two' non-substantial suggestions, declared the draft 'statesmanlike', and added that it 'would do good' (a recollection which Hardinge could not corroborate).[69] After the storm had burst, however, Hardinge wrote to Lansdowne to comment on the statement by Burnham that Balfour had known of *a* letter in advance and that Hardinge had approved it: 'I said that it was so in the main & that it was on the understanding that Mr Balfour approved of my doing so that I criticised some points in the letter chiefly on technical grounds.'[70] Beyond this he would not go.[71] But he need not have worried that Lansdowne meant to share the notoriety: 'Your responsibility for the letter was, as you point out, strictly limited & infinitesimal,' the Marquess replied. 'Balfour was not responsible at all.'[72]

Balfour seems to have paid scant attention to the affair as it unfolded, and said nothing of it in public. Mrs Dugdale indicates her belief that, had he known that Lansdowne 'might be suffering some injustice', he would have revealed all.[73] Perhaps so, but his sole 'official' comment was in a cursory Cabinet paper shortly after the letter appeared, and in this he stated only that in their chance meeting he told Lansdowne that if a letter was to go forward despite his advice, he – Balfour – 'raised no objection' to the inclusion of parts of Lansdowne's November 1916 memorandum. 'It was, of course,' he continued, 'only in reference to the subject thus restricted that I authorised any appeal to Lord Hardinge while I was absent in Paris.'[74]

This affair meant the end of Lansdowne's political life, particularly after Bonar Law's condemnation of the letter at a party conference held the day after publication.[75] Some injuries healed, however, and a few weeks after publication Lansdowne wrote to Balfour, 'How long is it since we have met, and are we ever going to meet again? I hope so, altho I suppose I must be reckoned among the infidels.'[76] And so he remained, but the two men soon resumed their friendship.

As 1917 drew to a close, the Russian situation was again thrust before the War Cabinet, with the overthrow of the Kerensky government by the Bolsheviks in November. Balfour, of course, had had little faith from the outset in the ability of the earlier March Revolution to produce an effective government – nor, for that matter, had he felt much confidence in Allied efforts to keep the Russians in the fight.[77] The coming of the Bolsheviks held his attention, however, particularly after talks began in early December between Leon Trotsky, now commissar for foreign affairs, and the Germans. In a memorandum, 'Notes on the Present Russian Situation', of early December, Balfour found the prospect of the government of commissars rather ominous:

> They are fanatics to whom the Constitution of every State, whether monarchial or republican, is equally odious. They are dangerous dreamers, whose power be it great or small, transitory or permanent, depends partly on German gold, openly on the determination of the Russian Army to fight no more; but who would genuinely like to put into practice the wild theories which have so long been germinating in the shadow of the Russian autocracy.

What was to be done? he asked:

> Now, contrary to the opinion of some of my colleagues, I am clearly of opinion that it is to our advantage to avoid, as long as possible, an open breach with this crazy system. If this be drifting, then I am a drifter by deliberate policy.

Balfour was sure of what the new regime would not do:

> It is certain, I take it, that, for the remainder of this war, the Bolsheviks are going to fight neither Germany nor anyone else. But, if we can prevent their aiding Germany we do a great deal, and to this we should devote our efforts. If we drive Russia into the hands of Germany, we shall hasten the organisation of the country by German officials on German lines. Nothing can be more fatal, it seems to me, both to the immediate conduct of the War and to our post-war relations.[78]

In the struggle only beginning in Russia, Balfour saw little virtue in either the Reds or the Whites, who were to slaughter each other for several years before the Soviets finally established their primacy. He opposed at first the active Allied intervention, championed by the War Office, though the announcement of the Russo-German Treaty of Brest-Litovsk changed his perspective somewhat.[79] While he did support the right of the small Baltic states to free themselves from Russian domination, his support for intervention was never of the fire-breathing Churchillian variety – and the extreme anti-Bolsheviks were not satisfied until he had left the Foreign Office.[80]

Optimists who anticipated in early 1918 that the war might soon end were dealt a rude shock in March. On the 21st General Ludendorff commanded his 6,000 guns to launch his last desperate throw, the fearsome Kaiser Offensive, and by June the British had sustained 350,000 casualties and fallen back 40 miles. As it appeared that the Germans were bearing down on Paris, the irrepressible Sir Henry Wilson, who Lloyd George had installed as CIGS in place of Robertson in February, imagined the unimaginable – that, after all, the war might actually be lost.[81] It was not to be, however, and, with American troops playing their first major role in the conflict, the German offensive soon began to falter. With his last great venture in ruins, Ludendorff would declare 8 August the 'black day' of the German Army, and twelve weeks later the killing finally stopped.

As the conflict wound down, the political question of what to do about the extraordinary wartime administration had to be faced. In July a plan had begun to come together under which the government parties – Unionists, Lloyd George Liberals and a handful of 'National' Labourites – would continue their coalition partnership.[82] Though they were confident they would not be threatened either by Asquith's 'Wee Free' Liberals or by Labour (who left the coalition), the Unionist leaders agreed that it would be unwise to separate themselves from the hugely popular Lloyd George, the Man Who Won the War. Certainly Balfour needed no convincing, as he noted to Bonar Law, 'Our friend is, I think, the most remarkable single figure produced by the Great War.'[83] The Unionists fell into line in October, and a party meeting on 2 November endorsed the plan.[84] The result was the 'coupon election' on 14 December 1918 – the first general election in British history confined to a single day.[85]

The contest got its name because of the letter – the 'coupon' Asquith derisively called it – signed by the three party leaders and sent to authorized coalition candidates.[86] The result was a coalition landslide, with 335 Unionists, 133 Lloyd George Liberals and 10 coalition Labourites returned; the Irish Unionists (independently supporting the coalition) won 25 seats. In opposition were the official Labour Party with 63 seats, the Asquith

Liberals with 28, and all others with 33. Candidates of the Irish separatist party Sinn Féin ('Ourselves Alone') won 73 seats, which they refused to occupy, while the once powerful Nationalists held only 7. This was the first contest under the newly passed Representation of the People Act, which enfranchised all men over twenty-one (nineteen if on active service) and property-holding women at thirty, and increased the electorate to more than 20 million. Another important evidence of change came a year later, when an American-born Unionist, Lady Astor, became the first female MP and entered the House supported by none other than Lloyd George and Arthur Balfour.[87]

Balfour was handsomely returned by his City electors and played little part in the election, and the seventy-one-year-old statesman ignored the unfounded rumours that he might take a peerage. Though he complained of fatigue (at the peace conference, like Clemenceau, he was occasionally seen 'resting his eyes' during the long sessions), he remained in his general good health and continued his devotion to golf and tennis, with Ian Malcolm arranging regular matches throughout the long months of treaty-making in Paris.[88] There was at least one sign of physical decline which troubled him, as his sense of hearing was becoming much less acute. Lloyd George described how he dealt with it in a matter-of-fact way. If he had trouble hearing a speaker in Cabinet or at the peace conference, 'Mr Balfour would rise from his place and stand by the speaker, and when the latter finished his observations he returned to his seat.'[89] His colleagues apparently became accustomed to the unusual practice.

Lloyd George, Balfour, Bonar Law, Milner and Barnes headed the British delegation that arrived in Paris in January to craft the settlement which President Wilson piously hoped would for ever banish the spectre of war.[90] Bonar Law would return to London to manage the administration, and Curzon took temporary charge of the Foreign Office. Once the British entourage – some 300 strong – was in place, Balfour arrived with a personal staff headed by the indispensable Wilfrid Short, and his political secretary, chief fixer and self-appointed Boswell, the tireless Ian Malcolm.[91] The headquarters of the British delegation was the Hotel Majestic, but the Prime Minister and Foreign Secretary were installed in flats, one above the other, in the rue Nitot – Balfour's made ready for him (including a con-cert-worthy piano), of course, by Malcolm.[92] Short remained at Balfour's side throughout the conference and for the remainder of his time as Foreign Secretary, and parted from him only to seek a more lucrative post in 1920.[93] Miss Constance Bliss took his place as Balfour's private secretary.

Balfour was quite comfortable playing second fiddle to the Prime

Minister – and even third fiddle on those occasions when Bonar Law, who remained in London as Lloyd George's deputy for much of the time, was in Paris. The Foreign Secretary got on well with what the press dubbed the 'Big Four': Lloyd George, of course, and Orlando of Italy, Clemenceau of France and, the object of fascination of the Western world, Woodrow Wilson.[94] Like the others, Balfour easily grew weary of the President's 'Sermon on the Mount' perorations.[95] The careworn 'Tiger' of France was another matter, and Balfour never tired of the quick wit and charm that seldom seemed to fail him. Clemenceau once took Balfour by the arm and introduced him as the 'Richelieu' of the peace conference. Malcolm recalled the scene:

> 'But what, then, may I call you, M. le President?'
> 'Call me your friend,' said Clemenceau softly.[96]

Each of the Big Four had his own agenda and bargained at the uttermost limits of his skill to achieve it, but all shared a common desire to make impossible another devastating conflict of the sort they had just – only just – survived. Unlike the French, Balfour believed that destroying Germany would not secure this. He had told the War Cabinet in October 1918, 'I don't want to go beyond making Germany impotent to renew the war, and obtaining compensation. I don't want to trample her in the mud.'[97] Yet the Germans had to be made to accept that their defeat was absolute, even at the cost of 'their colonies, their principal ally, and European provinces which they had vowed never to surrender'. Only after paying this terrible price for its militarism and aggression, Balfour reasoned, would Germany learn its lesson and put militarism behind it in the future.[98] Hence, like Lloyd George, he often found himself caught between the visionary Wilson and the revanchist Clemenceau. It was no surprise to the Foreign Secretary, who had observed to Lord and Lady Wemyss on the eve of his departure for Paris, 'As I have always told you, it is not so much the war as the peace that I have always dreaded.'[99]

Balfour's critics, then and later, have suggested that the Foreign Secretary failed in his duty to make a better peace than that which emerged from Paris. Curzon was predictably severe, noting that to his mind Balfour had 'abdicated all power in favour of Lloyd George . . . The Foreign Minister of Great Britain from that moment dated the practical supersession of the Office and the fatal domination of Lloyd George, which was later to have such deplorable results.'[100] Robert Vansittart of the Foreign Office, who adored Balfour, simply thought he viewed these events 'with the detachment of a choir-boy at a funeral service'.[101] A modern critic concludes that the fault lay not in what he did, but what he was: 'The detachment of Balfour was the expression not so much of the philosophical sceptic, or of even the self-distancing, conscious ironist, still less of the useful disinterestedness of the active critic, but rather of a feckless indifference bordering on the inhuman.'[102] In truth, as Curzon, Milner, Smuts and many others discovered, Britain's part in the peace conference was Lloyd George's show. To recognize this is not simply to shift responsibility (which, of course, it does do) but to recognize what Balfour and millions of others did: at that moment, Lloyd George remained the Man Who Won the War.

Balfour considered himself a realist, and it is true that 'his policy was "a free hand for the little man."'[103] As Leader of the House of Commons a generation earlier, he had understood that the government in the end was Salisbury's; and when he himself had led the Cabinet and the party he had expected others to behave accordingly. When they did not and it all went wrong, he accepted the consequences. When controversy arose in Paris, he spoke frankly to Lloyd George and accepted that final responsibility belonged to the little man.[104] It is true that he accepted this more easily than Curzon, Milner or Smuts, but the result was the same for all.

Balfour wanted a peace made as swiftly as possible in a Europe menaced by revolution and starvation and in which the exhausted Allied forces grew less formidable with each passing day.[105] He refused any part of the popular nonsense about hanging the Kaiser or making the Germans pay until 'the pips squeaked' – slogans with which even Lloyd George toyed briefly. He also thought it bad business to establish the contentious reparations policy without specific parameters, and he believed that grossly selective enforcement of self-determinism of national groups (always excepting Palestine) amounted to handing a hostage to fate. Shifting borders and populations to fit a map based on ideals and not demography and geography was dangerous, as he told the Cabinet: 'What it all comes to is that we have to guard against the danger of being supposed to use our principles to further our fancies.'[106]

Without consulting Balfour, Lloyd George did press ahead with a draft Anglo-French guarantee treaty (meant to soothe Paris after the failure of the French plan for a Rhenish buffer state between France and the Germans), but the Foreign Secretary inserted a clause which made the pact conditional on US ratification of a similar Franco–American treaty.[107] He was also uncomfortable with Wilsonian high rhetoric about 'collective security', and would soon see how empty it was, once the United States had repudiated Wilson and retreated again into isolation.[108] He was equally suspicious of the theory that substitution of short-term volunteer armies for the former system of conscription in the defeated Powers was of itself a guarantee of peace.[109] Yet in the end he accepted all and, with millions of others, hoped for the best. In a very few years, confidence in the treaties and in Lloyd George himself began to erode, but, despite everything, Balfour remained certain that the little man was the peer of Pitt, Castlereagh and Palmerston as the greatest statesman since Napoleon.[110] He recalled to H. A. L. Fisher that the War Cabinet worked in greater harmony than any other within his memory, and that in those years the Prime Minister was at the 'summit of his brilliant powers'.[111]

On 28 June – a dismal Saturday that was also the fifth anniversary of the Sarajevo murders – the Treaty of Versailles was signed in a hastily improvised ceremony.[112] Balfour signed with the gold fountain pen given him by the Prime Minister, which he carried for the remainder of his life. After the formalities were over, rather than retire to his flat he escaped his Special Branch minders and, with Malcolm, strolled through the Paris streets 'bareheaded', reminiscing about earlier days in the City of Light.[113] Afterwards the Big Four withdrew, and Balfour and the other foreign ministers were left to prepare the treaties with the lesser defeated powers.

Even a supporting rôle at the Paris conference demanded much of a man of seventy, but it certainly did not prevent him from enjoying a social schedule that would have exhausted men half his age. His sense of fun remained as acute as his wit, and Lloyd George recalled particularly a lunch at Balfour's flat to honour the celebrated Queen Marie of Romania. She regaled all with a tale of purchasing a pink chemise, and asked her host what she should discuss at her forthcoming meeting with Woodrow Wilson – the League or her chemise? '"Begin with the League of Nations," said Mr Balfour, "and finish with the pink chemise. If you are talking to Mr Lloyd George, you could begin with the pink chemise!"'[114]

In fact by the summer of 1919 he was planning his escape from the Foreign Office, and in August he prevailed on Curzon to deputize for him while he set off for the holiday that his doctor had long recommended.[115] Churchill wondered – perhaps hoped – that this time Balfour was finally on the verge of retirement, but he was quite wrong.[116] Balfour was tired of the Foreign Office (he was 'heartily sick' of it, according to Curzon) but not of politics, and in September – as the Treaty of Saint-Germain with Austria was safely executed – he arranged with the Prime Minister and with Curzon to exchange offices with the Lord President.[117] This became official in October when Lloyd George announced the return to a traditional Cabinet.[118] The new government was largely a Unionist affair, and Balfour found himself surrounded by old comrades Bonar Law (continuing as

Leader of the House and Lord Privy Seal), Chamberlain (Chancellor of the Exchequer), F. E. Smith (now Lord Chancellor, as Viscount Birkenhead), Milner (Colonial Secretary), Long (First Lord of the Admiralty) and, of course, Curzon.

It was customary for the Lord President to hold a peerage, and the King hoped that his trusted friend would accept the honour.[119] Balfour, however, asked that he (like Lord John Russell sixty years earlier) be allowed to remain in the Commons and avoid the Upper House, where he would feel 'in a strange country'.[120] He got his way, but there was more to the refusal than this. Curzon had offered to stand aside to allow the new Lord President to lead the House of Lords, a prospect Balfour declared 'uncongenial' and which in reality horrified him.[121] Balfour wrote to his sister Alice that he was certain Lloyd George and Bonar Law had this up their sleeves, but he wanted nothing to do with it.[122] For the time being he remained plain Mr Balfour while the overworked Curzon was left to combine the Foreign Office with leadership of the Upper House.

Others had their own plans for Balfour. Before the 1918 election, the mastership of Trinity College fell vacant, and there was murmuring among some friends that he might be captured for the appointment. Quite sensibly, nothing came of this.[123] In October 1919, however, he did agree to become chancellor of Cambridge University in succession to his brother-in-law the late Lord Rayleigh.[124] Balfour was reluctant at first – he already held the chancellorship at Edinburgh, and another such honour meant another great claim on his time and energy. However, when Cambridge called he could not fail to answer, and he served enthusiastically for the rest of his life.

Despite their rout in the 1918 election, the Opposition parties soon showed signs of recovery: in the two years after March 1919, thirteen seats that had been held by 'couponed' coalitionists were lost, eight of them to Labour. Among government supporters a coalitionist New Members Committee was organized, and these newcomers concluded that the answer to further decay lay in the 'fusion' of the coalition parties.[125] Some of their elders had believed in this for some time, and by October Bonar Law once again sought Balfour's advice, suggesting 'our Party on the old lines will never have any future again in this country.'[126] Balfour had expressed reservations about the idea of a merger – the major wings of the coalition, after all, were still Liberals and Conservatives, and were not without their ideological differences.[127] On balance, however, he concluded that the potential for benefits was worth the risk. Early in the new year he drafted a letter to

Lord Aldenham, his constituency chairman, declaring, 'In my judgment the time has now arrived in the history of the present Government when its unity of purpose should be supported in the constituencies by a unity of organisation.'[128]

Lord Crawford mused in his diary, 'Fusion is the order of the day. We are to fuse Lloyd George or Ll.G. is to fuse us – I am not sure which.'[129] The former Chief Whip need not have worried, for the plan was promptly strangled – not by the Unionist majority, but by Lloyd George's coalition Liberals. The premier met in March with his followers, and learned that they had no wish to be gobbled up as the Liberal Unionists had been a decade earlier.[130] Word of the scheme was leaked to the press, and plans for fusion were scuttled.[131] Balfour and Bonar Law saw no reason to press the matter, and it was fortunate that they did not.[132] The temper of the June 1920 meeting of the National Union was much against any talk of amalgamation, and Robert Sanders, the deputy chairman, noted that only a slight majority of the delegates favoured continuation of the current coalition at all, much less a merger.[133] Balfour abandoned his fusion letter, and, though his confidence in Lloyd George remained, if neither party desired amalgamation at this point he was content.

Though released from the peace conference and the Foreign Office, Balfour was not free of diplomatic responsibilities in these post-war years. He agreed to attend the Council of the League, the shining hope of those who longed for a durable peace based on a 'new diplomacy'. He played no part in creating the League, but lent generous rhetorical support in public, even becoming a vice-president of the British League of Nations Union, headed by Lord Robert Cecil. In a celebrated speech on the first anniversary of Armistice Day he told the Union that he could not discuss 'with any man what the future of international relations should be unless he is prepared either to accept the League of Nations in some form, or tell me what substitute he proposes for it'.[134] He was unprepared to abandon all scepticism, however, and was shocked at the attacks being made in the US Senate on the Versailles Treaty in 1919 and even considered whether Britain should follow the American lead and abandon the League.[135]

From the outset he had cautioned that an organization with such ambitions as the League's would be endangered if any Great Power had 'reservations' about participation. Long before the war ended, he put his view before the Cabinet in plain terms. 'I am by no means sure', he warned, 'that [a league] is practicable; but I am sure that it is quite impracticable unless the USA takes a leading part.'[136] If the Americans wanted an international league, he was quite satisfied – but he had little hope that it could succeed without strong Anglo-American leadership.[137] Then, on 19 November 1919, the Senate rejected both Versailles and the League, and for the first time refused to ratify a treaty signed by the American president.[138]

Balfour made the best of it, but the hopes of internationalists that the talking shop at Geneva would somehow render obsolete the traditional methods of diplomacy did not resonate with him. He had always been suspicious of pious dreams, and in his experience agreements benefiting nations and world peace were the products of judicious men dealing with one another in reasonably candid fashion. The idealistic passion for 'open covenants, openly arrived at', he found naïve; and the idea that somehow 'open' diplomacy would bring better results was not only illusory, but foolish. What success he had while speaking for his country in the League Council he put down not to the 'new diplomacy' but to his good working relations with the other members and to simple hard bargaining.

Peace, Balfour continued to believe, could be enjoyed only if nations were prepared to defend themselves. The popular talk in these years of 'collective security' meant nothing, he believed, if peaceful nations placed their fates in the hands of others. The champion in earlier days of battleships and field artillery could easily be detected in Balfour's opposition to Churchill's infamous 1919 'Ten-Year Rule', that no major war could be expected over the next decade.[139] Nearly a decade later, when Churchill proposed to the CID that the Rule should be renewed automatically, the ailing eighty-year-old Balfour roused himself to attack: 'To suggest that we could be nine and a half years away from preparedness', he argued, 'would be a most dangerous suggestion.'[140] He preferred, when possible, to put his trust in strength and preparedness; and if an organization such as the League were to do some good, he thought it could do so only if saved from rabid enthusiasts who expected too much of it.[141]

When the Committee of Imperial Defence was re-established in July 1920, Balfour was pleased to serve as its only returning member of pre-war days. A standing subcommittee was formed under Balfour to advise the full committee (which seldom met) as well as the Cabinet. Balfour was a busy man – perhaps far too busy: he was often away at the League Council, he was a member of the Prime Minister's emergency Irish Situation Committee, and he chaired a new Committee on the Co-ordination of Scientific Research. Then there were the inevitable ad-hoc committees, including, rather interestingly, in 1920 yet another on House of Lords Reform.[142] Hankey – still, it seemed, secretary to every important committee – noted to Lloyd George that Balfour's attendance at his committees was far too irregular; nor was it improved, he added pettishly, by the many claims on the Lord President's time and his occasional complaints of illness and fatigue.[143]

At this time, much of Balfour's time and ingenuity came again to be directed towards Ireland. After the failure of his own efforts following the Easter Rising, as Prime Minister himself in 1917 Lloyd George had summoned an Irish Convention of all parties in Dublin. It was, of course, boycotted by the separatist Sinn Féiners.[144] Sadly, a year's deliberation again failed to produce a successful compromise plan.[145] By the time of the 1918 election, Redmond was dead, his National Party was in ruins, and the Sinn Féin MPs refused to occupy the parliamentary seats they had won and instead set up an illegal Irish assembly of their own (the Dáil Éireann) under Éamon de Valera, which declared Irish 'independence' in 1919.[146]

Far worse was the fact that by this time Ireland was the scene of brutal guerrilla warfare, as the British Army and the Royal Irish Constabulary (supported by the notorious 'Black and Tans' and Special Auxiliaries) faced the shadowy Irish Republican Army, supported by de Valera's unrecognized government. The long-suspended 1914 Home Rule Act was a dead letter, yet, as Bonar Law reminded Balfour in October 1919, it would take effect with ratification of the last peace treaty. The government's response, in March 1920, was to propose permanent division: a bill was drawn up providing for two Home Rule parliaments in Ireland, one in Belfast for the much-discussed six Ulster counties, another in Dublin for the rest, with a joint Council of Ireland to resolve questions of mutual concern.[147]

In June, 1920, the Prime Minister appointed his Irish Situation Committee to find a way to pacify the island and allow the plan to work, and with him were Balfour, Birkenhead, Churchill, Long and Fisher, the Liberal education minister. While Balfour enthusiastically supported their apparent resolve to take a firm stand against Sinn Féin, he was not swayed by arguments favouring full-scale martial law.[148] His position was certainly not rooted in any tenderness of heart towards the rebels, but rather reflected his firm judgement that further and bloodier coercion would make any peaceful solution even less likely.

Though Balfour found distasteful the possibility of gaining peace through negotiation with the Sinn Féin separatists, recommended by some Irish and British moderates, he did accept that the Union as it had existed was finished.[149] Ulster was another matter, however, as he made clear to Carson in the last year of war:

I, like you, detest both Home Rule and Federation.

If we cannot retain the broad outline of the existing system (and the Irish Question has been so grossly mismanaged since 1906 that I fear this may be impossible), the solution I should prefer would be to keep Ulster as she is, and to disinterest ourselves completely from the South and West of Ireland, except in so far as it may be necessary to prevent its coast line being used by Enemy Powers.[150]

By 1920 he believed that it was time for reasonable men to cut their losses: if the 'existing system' could not be retained, then federalism would have to do. Lloyd George wondered whether any solution would work, confiding to his wife in the autumn that Ireland was nothing less than a 'Hell's broth'.[151] There seemed nothing to do but to go ahead with the proposed bill, which became law in November. It was ignored outside Ulster, and the 'murder duel' continued in the South.

The King opened the Northern Irish Parliament in Belfast on 22 June 1921, delivering a conciliatory speech meant to open the way towards negotiations. It succeeded, and, despite their scruples, the government spirited de Valera into London in July for secret talks – with Lloyd George particularly insisting that Balfour play a part because of his 'implacable' stand against surrender.[152] Balfour was not implacable at all: he found de Valera distasteful, but his reservations had given way to the realities of the desperate situation. He joined the Prime Minister, Chamberlain and Lloyd George's confidant Sir Edward Grigg in drafting a plan – essentially granting self-governance or Dominion status to the South and West, with the exclusion of Ulster – that would be offered to the separatists.[153] Lloyd George's secretary and mistress, Miss Stevenson, noted that, in Lloyd George's view, Balfour accepted 'gracefully' a settlement that violated all he had stood for through his career – the reason was that to him the alternative was a renewal of violence, with no end in sight.[154]

A ceasefire was achieved in October, and a treaty calling for partition along the lines discussed in June was agreed in early December and was soon ratified by all sides. The result was the hardening of the line between a Northern Ireland within the United Kingdom and the new Dominion of the Irish Free State virtually independent of it. The historic Irish Union, which Balfour had defended for much of his political life, was dissolved – and the Unionist Party once again became the Conservatives.

Balfour was not present for this last act of the drama, for he was in Geneva on League business in the autumn, and then was off to America to lead the British delegation at the Washington Naval Conference convened by President Warren Harding. The prospect of another Atlantic crossing certainly did not appeal to him, and he promoted Bonar Law for the assignment. On his doctors' advice, Bonar Law had retired from office in March 1921, and Balfour wrote to Curzon that he thought that the

Cle ques ?

Glaswegian – now 'one of the unemployed' – a far better choice: 'Moreover he has not been an exile for two months as I have.'[155] In fact Bonar Law had gratefully exiled himself from politics since March; and Lloyd George, occupied with the Irish Question, had no intention of sending anyone but Balfour.

Balfour accepted his fate. Leading a delegation which included Lord Lee, the British ambassador (whose wife was American), First Lord Sir Auckland Geddes, and of course Hankey, he embarked for North America on 2 November. The voyage met Balfour's worst expectations – he took to his bed for much of the trip – and he was grateful to reach dry land a week later. With the American Secretary of State, Charles Evans Hughes, in the chair, the Conference also included delegations from France, Japan and Italy and a number of smaller states.[156] Hughes revealed the American proposal on 12 November, calling for a ten-year naval building 'holiday' and limitations on the size of the great capital fleets. This was not to be 1919 Paris redux. There was no Lloyd George on the scene, and Balfour was virtually without instructions from the Cabinet. He acted accordingly, and scribbled out his reply to Hughes's proposals that afternoon – as usual, on the back of an envelope – and on the following afternoon he delivered a speech Hankey recalled to Lloyd George as nothing less than 'perfect in structure'.[157] Britain, he declared, was prepared to accept the restriction of its navy so long as its own security was not compromised. Like the Prime Minister, Balfour realized that the traditional two-power standard was no longer realistic, and a naval building race with the United States was politically and financially out of the question.

With full support from the government, Balfour announced that Britain would accept the American proposals, and the result was the famous five-nation pact which specified that Britain, the United States, Japan, France and Italy accepted restrictions on the size, armament and number of capital ships, with their total fleets limited in the ratio of 5:5:3:1.75:1.75. Balfour, a lifelong 'blue-water' man, found himself putting his name to the agreement which brought to a close the era of British naval supremacy – in practical terms, like the Irish treaty, to Balfour it was the best deal to be had.

The problem of US hostility towards the Anglo-Japanese alliance, long a pillar of British policy in Asia, required an even more delicate touch.[158] During the war, Balfour had proposed that an Anglo-American–Japanese naval agreement might 'ensure the peace of the world', though his suggestion was not taken up.[159] Before the opening of the Washington Conference, he tried again, drafting a 'tripartite' agreement by which any

Later chief justice

two of the three Powers would be free to ensure its interests in Asia 'by entering into a military alliance provided (a) this arrangement is purely defensive in character and (b) that it is communicated to the other High Contracting Party.'[160] As a substitute for the Anglo-Japanese agreement this may have suited Balfour, but the Americans desired no hard-and-fast military commitments in Asia, and the Japanese cannot have been drawn to the possibility that their own ambitions could lead to an Anglo-American alliance against them. In the end a Four-Power Treaty (the three Powers and France), essentially endorsing the status quo in Asia, replaced the earlier Anglo-Japanese pact. It has been quite fairly called 'a loose arrangement of the anodyne variety' that was hammered out with a minimum of offended sensibilities.[161] Perhaps the best that may be said is that it too was all that was possible at the time, but in the long run it did nothing to prevent war in the Pacific.

The pace and intensity of the negotiations cannot have been easy for the septuagenarian. Oswald Balfour visited his uncle in Washington, and wrote to Lady Frances that 'Nunky' seemed absolutely dedicated to his task and worked every day from 10 a.m. until 'then or later at night'.[162] At Washington there was no grumbling into their diaries by members of his delegation about inattention to duty on the part of their leader. Hankey insisted that he had never seen Balfour in better form, and wrote to his deputy, 'A.J.B. has really achieved a very great position – he is such a gentleman, so different from the crowd, and so very adroit. A really great figure. Unless we get a really bad setback – and there are traps innumerable – we can get through with A.J.B.'[163] In a secret memorandum written soon afterwards, Curzon composed a litany of Balfour's shortcomings, but he had only praise for his 'tact and intellectual superiority' at the conference, where he established 'indisputable ascendancy'.[164]

Balfour returned to a hero's welcome, and when his party alighted at Waterloo station on 15 February 1922 they were met by a cheering crowd led by the Prime Minister and the Cabinet.[165] Alice Balfour recalled the glorious day in her diary, noting that at the station he was handed a letter from the palace which informed him that His Majesty 'had bestowed on him' the Garter and an earldom – it was extraordinary, he later noted to her, that King George seemed to have done so without the 'usual preliminaries'.[166] Balfour knew that his long career was nearing its end, but, save for the Order of Merit, he had always refused all offers of honours.[167] The King, who had known and admired Balfour throughout his own life, pressed his offer personally later in the day, though he feared that the peerage would once again be rejected.[168] Tired, content, and touched by his sovereign's overture, Balfour asked for time to contemplate and fled to France to recuperate.

He did not keep the King waiting long, and accepted the offer of the Garter on the following day. The peerage was another matter, however, and he requested more time until he could 'clearly see his way through the problems, personal and political with which he seems at the present moment to be faced'.[169] The decision was not an easy one: he had been a Member of the House of Commons since 1874, and had long insisted that being an MP and the King's minister were the highest honours to which a statesman could aspire. Yet he was now nearly seventy-four, and a peerage offered the attraction of extending his political life a bit longer without the need to face another election.

In the end he accepted.[170] He wrote to King George expressing at once his gratitude and his sadness at parting from the Commons, but adding, 'he nevertheless fares to hope that he need not, as yet, wholly withdraw from further participation in public affairs. It may well be that in the House of Lords he can be of more use to Your Majesty and the Public than in the more familiar scene of the House of Commons.'[171] By October, with his party once again embroiled in an agonizing internecine struggle, Balfour was certain that he had made the correct decision and wrote to Lady Wemyss that his translation to the Upper House was nothing less than a 'blessing'.[172]

Miss Balfour was deeply concerned that her brother would become merely Earl Balfour, the sound of which she disapproved – besides, she insisted, there was already a Lord Balfour of Burleigh. An ancient site in Fifeshire that bore the family name, owned by his cousin James Balfour of Balbirnie, provided a solution, and Sir Arthur now became the Earl *of* Balfour, and Viscount of Traprain.[173] The family discussion over titles bored him, and Balfour wrote to his sister, 'So far as I am concerned I am indifferent.'[174] Because of his bachelor status, he requested and was granted a special remainder in the interest of his brother Gerald and the 'heirs male of his body'. Finally Lord Balfour took his place in the scarlet-and-gilt chamber on 30 May, flanked by two of his oldest friends, Lords Midleton and Selborne. The irreconcilable Sandars growled that 'the change of the sober broadcloth of the House of Commons for the scarlet robe of a gartered earl, will long be to the minds of those who had given him their admiration and respect a disappointment and regret.'[175] Few, however, seem to have agreed.

Ennoblement did not mean inactivity in the remaining months of the coalition. During the course of the Great War Britain had incurred a mountainous liability to the United States of some £900 million, and was itself owed an even greater sum by the other Allies – much of it by the Russians, whose new rulers had no intention of paying up. By early 1922 Washington appeared to want its money back and created a War Debts Commission to arrange procedures for repayment. In London, an alarmed Cabinet charged Balfour, who was substituting at the Foreign Office for the ailing Curzon, with drafting a response to the American position.[176] The result in early August was the Balfour Note (actually several notes: one to the US and others to the debtor Allies), which pointed out that, after so great a mutual sacrifice, it was unacceptable to 'regard the monetary aspect of this great event as a thing apart, to be torn from its historical setting and treated as no more than an ordinary commercial dealing between traders who borrow and capitalists who lend'. Hence it proposed that Britain would collect from its debtors only the amount demanded by the United States.[177]

Stanley Baldwin, then President of the Board of Trade, insisted that the document was so beautifully written that he wanted it published simply because it deserved to be 'given to the world'.[178] No matter how skilfully composed, the Note was not popular in the City, and it angered the American administration and Wall Street, who correctly saw it as an attempt to place responsibility for the entire question on the United States. The proposal, like the government, had no future, however, and the war–debt issue was left to Bonar Law's subsequent administration. In fact the new premier agreed with the spirit of Balfour's plan, unlike either his party or the City – but like much else in the world of international finance it was swept away by the world depression.

A few weeks later Balfour rushed off once again to the League Council to deal with the Austrian economic crisis, and he returned to London in early October to find the coalition government in the midst of a final political debacle. Lloyd George, the irreplaceable man in 1918, was in trouble. As a possible solution, he had for some months been considering another coalition election campaign, but there was disagreement among his Conservative partners. Austen Chamberlain, who had succeeded Bonar Law as party leader, and most senior ministers remained in step with the Prime Minister; but the party chairman, Sir George Younger, and the Chief Whip, Sir Leslie Wilson, insisted that this was unacceptable to the party rank and file.[179]

Lloyd George's formidable skill and luck were running out: the promises in 1918 of a prosperous Britain 'fit for heroes to live in' appeared rather hollow by 1922. His summit diplomacy had gone sour – most recently at the conferences in Cannes in January and at Genoa in April 1922, as tensions among the wartime allies seemed to endanger post-war co-operation. Then on Easter Sunday the Russians and Germans shocked the West by announcing their mutual recognition and co-operation in the Treaty of Rapallo. Also in April, the dissatisfaction among the anti-treaty faction in Ireland had erupted in further bloody civil conflict, for which many in Britain who had accepted the Irish treaty only in the interest of peace blamed the Prime Minister. The murder in London in June by Irish assassins of the former CIGS Sir Henry Wilson, by then a fire-breathing Ulster MP, added to anti-Lloyd George resentment on the right wing of the Conservative Party.[180] In June a tawdry 'honours scandal' erupted with the revelations in the press of the shady activities of Lloyd George's chief honours tout, J. Maundy Gregory, and rumours of the premier's mysterious secret political fund further damaged his reputation. By mid-1922, plans for a quick coalition electoral victory had to be re-evaluated.

The retirement in March 1921 of the loyal Bonar Law, much loved and trusted by his party's backbenchers, had also been a severe blow to the Prime Minister.[181] Chamberlain was not held in the same high regard, nor had he the skills to make his own loyalty as useful to Lloyd George. By March 1922 the Prime Minister was coming to the conclusion that the former Liberal Unionist might not be able to control the Conservatives – perhaps, he pondered, only Balfour could do it?[182] Chamberlain was anxious as well: perhaps the party was dividing beneath the feet of its own leaders. 'What a kettle of fish!' he wrote to his sister, Ida. 'Envy me my job!'[183]

The final nail was poised to be driven into the coffin lid of the coalition by the eruption of the Chanak affair. This involved the decision of the Cabinet to resist the Turks, who had ignored the 1920 Treaty of Sèvres and driven the Greeks from Smyrna in violation of the Peace of Paris. Under the nationalist Mustapha Kemal, they continued their advance in Asia Minor, and by September 1922 they were menacing the small British force representing the Allies near the village of Chanak on the Asian shore.[184] Balfour returned to London only after the political crisis was under way. Lloyd George and Churchill had resolved to resist the Turks by force, while the British electorate and the Dominions – Canada, South Africa and Australia – inclined towards appeasement. To many Conservatives, this was the absolute last in a lengthy series of last straws – besides, many of them were pro-Turkish and had long grumbled at the Prime Minister's infatuation with the Greeks.[185] By the end of September, what appeared to be the threat of war passed only when the British commander at Chanak,

Sir Charles Harington, ignored his instructions and began negotiations with the Kemalists, which led eventually to an armistice on 12 October. To many it appeared that the 'soldiers at Chanak had kept their heads, but the statesmen in Downing Street had pulled the trigger.'[186] The Chanak crisis passed, but the government's credit had been fatally damaged.

Balfour had written to Churchill from Geneva a few weeks earlier, admitting that he was much out of touch with party politics, but, given what he did know of the current situation, 'whatever be the [Cabinet] decision arrived at I shall neither criticise nor complain.'[187] He returned to London on 5 October, and the atmosphere among his colleagues was volatile.[188] The National Union was to meet on 15 November, and Chamberlain meant to settle matters well beforehand. At a meeting of party leaders on 10 October, he insisted that the coalition must be continued with Lloyd George at its head. Birkenhead spoke similarly, and Balfour agreed, stressing the need for a dissolution before the party conference. Curzon disliked the election plan, and Arthur Griffith-Boscawen, the Minister of Agriculture, openly opposed continuation of the coalition on any terms. Baldwin also spoke up, declaring Lloyd George an 'albatross around our neck' that very much needed getting rid of. Crawford confided quite correctly to his diary, 'The problem of our party is to shed Lloyd George, the problem of ministers [is] how to keep him.'[189]

Chamberlain believed that an election would bring the party to its senses, and advised Birkenhead, 'I am not sure that it may be necessary to call a Party Meeting & to tell them bluntly that they must follow our advice or to do without us in which case they must find their own Chief *at once*. They would be in a d– – – –d fix.'[190] On Sunday 15 October the leading Conservative ministers – with Curzon and Baldwin ominously absent – dined together at the Sussex Gardens home of their coalitionist Liberal colleague Winston Churchill and agreed to a policy of the firm hand.[191] Balfour agreed wholeheartedly, and wrote to his sister that it was his suggestion that a meeting of the parliamentary party (and peers who held office) be convened at the Carlton Club to clear the air.[192] This was planned for the 19th. 'It will not be a pleasant meeting,' he told Alice, 'though a necessary one.'[193]

On the afternoon of 18 October, Lloyd George met his senior colleagues in an 'informal sort of Cabinet' to which Archibald Salvidge, the Conservative political boss of Liverpool, brought the news that Bonar Law had been convinced by the anti-coalitionists to abandon his retirement and attend the Carlton Club meeting. This was a declaration that he was available again to lead the party – and to lead it away from Lloyd George –

and it appeared also that Curzon would support him. According to Salvidge, 'When I had finished my tale [Balfour] banged the table with his fist and shouted, "I say fight them, fight them, fight them! This thing is wrong . . . This is a revolt and must be crushed." Nothing could have been less like the dreamy Balfour of tradition.'[194]

On the designated day, Balfour walked down Carlton Gardens to the great Tory club, arriving only moments before the meeting began at 11 a.m. The coalitionists' hopes had been shaken that morning by press reports of the recent Newport by-election, won by an anti-coalition Conservative over a coalitionist Liberal with government support and a Labourite. The coalitionists had anticipated a victory by the Labour man as evidence of the need for the continued partnership of the non-socialist parties.[195] Chamberlain had been relying on the fact that, no matter how many warriors the insurgents could muster, they had no chiefs – but with the re-emergence of Bonar Law, the darling of the backbenchers, everything was changed.

Chamberlain bravely argued the case for coalition to an audience that listened with courtesy, but without belief. Balfour spoke late in the proceedings, emphasizing that no differences of principle existed among them and pleading for an end to divisiveness. He was accorded polite attention, but Crawford – one of the few peers in attendance – noted that, while 'delightful', his words were 'too subtle to count'. Violently anti-coalition Leopold Amery recorded that Balfour was heard 'with patience but without conviction'.[196] He took his seat to polite applause.

The day belonged to others. First came Baldwin, who argued powerfully that the Prime Minister certainly was the 'dynamic force' of which his admirers spoke. He added, however, 'It is owing to that dynamic force, and that remarkable personality, that the Liberal Party, to which he formerly belonged, has been smashed to pieces; and it is my firm conviction that, in time, the same thing will happen to our party.'[197]

As cries of 'Bonar Law!' filled the air, the meeting quickly took on the appearance of a revolt. The hero of the hour rose at last, seemingly rejuvenated by his long rest. Bonar Law spoke for a mere fifteen minutes, recommending that the Conservatives face the next election without hostility to any coalitionist allies, but as an independent party. He was cheered wildly, and the vote on a motion to do just that passed by 187 votes to 88, with one abstention.[198] The stunned Cabinet (again without Curzon or Baldwin) met at once and resolved to resign. The King called for Bonar Law who found, just as he had feared, that none of the 'birds of paradise' – Balfour, Chamberlain, Birkenhead, Long, Crawford and the Chancellor,

Robert Horne – would serve under him. These notables now found themselves in the strange position of standing against the party majority and identified most of all by their loyalty to the renegade Liberal Lloyd George. In their defeat, they issued a brave statement to the press, while the new premier went about constructing a government without them. Balfour signed the statement, but, unlike some others, he was not at all unhappy at finding himself out of office after seven strenuous years. As he reminded his sister Alice days before the Carlton Club meeting, 'whether we are in or out', he had other things to do.[199]

13

Last Things

———

B ALFOUR WAS CONTENT to put aside the rebuff at the Carlton Club and turn to the long-postponed second set of Gifford Lectures. Delivered in December and January 1922–3 and published soon thereafter as *Theism and Thought*, the ten largely extemporaneous lectures were a further defence of the philosophical position Balfour had occupied since publishing *In Defence of Philosophical Doubt* more than four decades earlier.[1]

Balfour returned to his familiar argument that truth and therefore understanding were impossible without belief in the Divine. 'For I do not argue', he insisted, 'that because certain beliefs are inspired, therefore they must be true. I argue that because they are true (or on the way to truth), therefore they must be inspired. Both arguments in their proper context may be valid. But the second, not the first, is the one on which, in these lectures, I have steadily insisted.' Belief, and therefore understanding, for him did not require mysticism, but mere 'common sense'. And 'common sense' revealed, he continued, that without 'Divine guidance . . . the three great virtues – knowledge, love and beauty' – were impossible, as was truth itself.[2]

Ordinary understanding, he argued, overpowered both 'naturalist' scepticism and mystical neo-idealism, both of which miss the point: the world is as it seems, and is not better understood by over-intellectualizing. The ordinary senses and an open mind are all that is necessary to understand the nature of truth:

> The postulate therefore on which, according to my contention, knowledge and other great values depend, involves conceptions which are somewhat alien to those speculations which strive to embrace the whole of things in some vast intellectual network, but on the other hand are closely akin to the modes of thought and feeling which, in the familiar language of theology, depend on the relation between man and his Maker.[3]

The second set of 'Giffords' were heard by a large and appreciative audience, and after seven stressful years in office Balfour found the exercise

357

intellectually stimulating and mentally refreshing.[4] He also enjoyed the intellectual discipline of editing and expanding the lectures for publication.[5] *Theism and Thought* appeared in December 1923, and his celebrity – possibly more than his subject – ensured that it enjoyed a rather brisk sale.

Balfour had not, however, lost interest in politics. The consensus among the former coalitionists was that Bonar Law would be able only to assemble a Cabinet of 'second-class brains' – a political 'second eleven'. Balfour agreed that the new government would suffer from a shortage of parliamentary stars, but, unlike certain of the exiled ministers, he was confident that 'men of sense with some official experience I should imagine [Bonar Law] could easily find among the Under-Secretaries etc., who have abandoned the Coalition.'[6] In any event, he believed, for the moment there was nothing to be done about it.

On 23 October Bonar Law was officially elected leader of his party, and that same evening the ex-coalitionists put on a brave face as they dined together at the Victoria Hotel to honour the deposed Austen Chamberlain. The former leader's speech was free of bitterness, Crawford noted in his journal, and 'justified his action and that of his co-signatories on high lines'.[7] Balfour also spoke, following the same 'high lines' and avoiding the harshness evident in the table talk of many of the diners. However, Crawford considered that Balfour left no doubt that he did not approve of the actions of former colleagues whom he thought had turned their coats in the recent Cabinet crisis. He had the new Chancellor of the Exchequer, Baldwin (and undoubtedly Curzon also), in mind when he noted to Lloyd George, 'It is the sort of thing gentlemen don't do.'[8]

A week later Balfour welcomed to Whittingehame a brains trust of former coalition ministers, including Lloyd George, Birkenhead and Robert Horne, to contemplate their immediate political future. There was laughter at Curzon's expense – something always dear to the heart of the Man Who Won the War – and talk of Bonar Law's poor prospects in the coming election. Balfour insisted to Horne that all was far from lost:

> Let us all wait . . . to see what this Parliament will bring forth. It is too soon to give up the idea of remaking the Coalition. Say to Bonar – 'well it is rather soon, and I cannot desert Austen.' Sit on the conservative side. The moment – which will be nearly always when B.L. is not there, and the Government are getting worsted in debate – then you or Austen or L.G. answer Simon or Sidney Webb.[9]

They agreed that the coming election would deny any party a majority, and that the Conservative exiles' indispensability to the party would be apparent soon enough – and Balfour added that 'by Christmas we will know where we are.'[10] And in this he would prove to be very correct indeed.

The campaign was rather colourless – issues failed to excite the electorate, and all seemed to turn on the person of the new Prime Minister. Polling day was 15 November, and the results dashed the hopes of the former ministers and certainly deflated their assertions 'that they had a monopoly on brains'.[11] Conservatives captured 345 seats, Labour 142, Lloyd George Liberals 62 and Asquithians 54. With less than 40 per cent of the total vote in a four-party race, a Conservative government had established itself with a comfortable majority, and the coalition loyalists' hopes were crushed. For the time being there seemed nothing else for Chamberlain, Balfour and their friends to do but support the Conservative government – and wait.

Playing Muhammad to Balfour's mountain, Bonar Law came to see him at Whittingehame on the morning of 22 December. The meeting was more than a symbolic gesture of reconciliation, for the Prime Minister's difficulties in assembling his team made clear to him that it must be a high priority to bring the ex-coalitionists back into the government.[12] The two old comrades spoke frankly of the party schism, and Bonar Law insisted he had acted to 'liquidate the situation' only because others would not, adding that in any event he had no intention of remaining in office more than a year. Balfour recorded his reaction: 'This I replied, was impossible. He was there, and there, so far as I could see, he would have to remain.'[13] Balfour could not know it, but there he would not remain for long.

While Chamberlain, Birkenhead and Horne remained aloof, Balfour had already made his own gesture of reconciliation in agreeing to Bonar Law's request that he remain at the head of the British delegation to the League Council.[14] According to Bonar Law's emissary, Sir Eric Drummond, Balfour even indicated that he might be willing to return to office 'for a year'.[15] In their December meeting, Balfour had raised with the Prime Minister the matter of what he thought was the rather unsatisfactory status of the post being offered him, insisting that the chief British representative to the League should hold ministerial rank, as only a Cabinet member could know 'the trend of opinion' of the government.[16] Furthermore the worldwide visibility of the post required a man whose reputation gave him 'personal weight' in British and international affairs, yet who was a loyal team player unlikely to diverge from government policy and tactics. He was, of course, describing himself.

So it seemed to Bonar Law, at any rate, and this intensified his discomfort in his position. He wanted the ex-ministers – or at least some of them – back in harness, and Balfour seemed to be presenting him with the opportunity to begin the process. The Prime Minister recalled another time, in December 1916: perhaps if Balfour came in, as in that wartime crisis, the others would follow. When Bonar Law learned of Balfour's apparent willingness to take office 'for a year', he told Hankey that 'he would sooner have Balfour than all the rest put together.'[17] However, he also knew that it was simply too soon, for his own Conservative loyalists would need more time to forgive and forget. As for Balfour's suggestion that the status of the British representative on the League Council should be raised, Balfour noted, 'I did not gather that B.L. dissented from these general principles; though he seemed to think that there was nobody *in his Government* who exactly answered to this ideal description.'[18] For the time being, Bonar Law would have to confine his government to those who had supported him at the Carlton Club – and it appeared that Balfour's chance, at the age of seventy-four, had passed.

Nonetheless, in January 1923 he travelled to Paris for the League Council meeting hoping to wind up some unfinished business, 'which is trying to get Austria financially on her legs'.[19] However, the crisis caused by the recent French and Belgian occupation of the Ruhr in order to coerce Germany into meeting its reparations obligations took centre stage.[20] The meetings of the Council were predictably divisive and inconclusive, and Balfour announced that his health would not allow him to continue as chief British representative.[21]

When he returned to Britain in March, he found the Conservatives no closer to reunion, and when he was honoured with a dinner a few weeks later it was attended almost exclusively by disgruntled ex-coalitionists. Yet, despite all, Balfour continued to maintain good relations with Bonar Law and the government, and he soon agreed to join the principal CID subcommittee on National and Imperial Defence, chaired by 'Jem' Salisbury. At its first meeting, he was asked to lead an inquiry into the deep division that had opened up between the air force and the navy over control of British air power.[22] Put most simply, the navy wanted complete authority over its own air arm, while the air marshals feared that sharing control of military air services with the other branches would be the beginning of the end for the young RAF. As First Lord, Balfour had taken the side of the admirals in 1916 against what they saw as the interference of Curzon's Air

Board. He remained sympathetic to the senior service, but for a few months before the fall of the previous government he had chaired another short-lived subcommittee on air power, which had increased his awareness of the importance of the RAF.[23]

His contribution to his new subcommittee was diminished by the fact that he was soon laid low with a circulatory disorder, and his committee colleagues, Lords Peel and Weir, conducted much of their inquiry without him. In mid-July, in a lengthy meeting in the Sheringham hotel suite of their recuperating chairman, his colleagues (and Hankey, secretary to both the Salisbury and the Balfour committees) persuaded him to amend his instinctive pro-navy viewpoint in favour of a 'clean cut' between the services over air power – navy at sea, RAF on land. A compromise was worked out, recommending that the air force be charged with primary authority over naval as well as land-based air forces, and from his sickbed Balfour drafted their report which gained Cabinet approval on 31 July. This happily ensured the survival of the endangered RAF but, it must be added, also impeded the development of the Naval Air Arm in the inter-war years.[24]

Balfour's stay at the Grand Hotel in Sheringham, on the Norfolk coast, was originally meant to be devoted to the pleasing company of his oldest friends, including the Wemysses and the Desboroughs – and, of course, to golf – but what turned out to be a severe attack of phlebitis left him bedridden. Though he was annoyed at his enforced inactivity, Balfour's convalescence was made more bearable by the continuing stream of family and friends to his bedside to amuse the patient with books and talk – and there was much to talk about. Bonar Law's government had recently survived a bruising internal battle over Britain's war debt to the United States, and this Cabinet crisis was followed by several particularly humiliating by-election losses.[25]

Balfour was not Whitehall's only convalescent in the spring of 1923. To make matters worse, when MPs returned from the Easter recess it was obvious to all that Bonar Law was seriously ill. He looked drawn and enervated, and was troubled by a throat ailment that stubbornly refused to respond to treatment. He was unable to talk in more than a hoarse whisper, and was forced to allow Baldwin to speak for him in the House. By the end of April he acceded to his doctors' advice that he take a holiday – if that did no good, he informed a startled Cabinet, he would have to consider resignation.[26] In the hope that the sunshine and sea air would restore him, he set off on 1 May for a Mediterranean cruise, leaving Curzon as his deputy and Baldwin in charge in the Commons.

In fact the austere Bonar Law, prey to the tobacco that was his only fleshly indulgence, was dying of cancer of the throat. He abandoned the voyage after only a week, pausing in Paris long enough to be examined by a distinguished physician who diagnosed the fatal affliction. The mission of carrying the shocking news to the capital fell to Amery and to the Prime Minister's secretary, J. C. C. Davidson, who left immediately for London.[27] It did not take long for the account to make its way to Balfour's bedside in Norfolk, and his thoughts mirrored those of politicians and citizenry alike: who would succeed to the premiership? The ailing Bonar Law wanted no part of recommending a successor, and took heart from the cases of other premiers – particularly the gravely ill Campbell-Bannerman in 1908 – who had been excused the duty. He returned to London on 19 May and was told that the King had consented to his wish and that his resignation had been made public.[28] The royal family were in Aldershot for Whitsuntide, and the letter of resignation was taken to King George by Bonar Law's son-in-law, Major General Sir Frederick Sykes, and private secretary, Sir Ronald Waterhouse.

The King, denied the advice of his departing Prime Minister, was faced with a difficult decision: the Conservative Party had no procedure in place to offer a recommendation, and there were two obvious candidates for the premiership – an improbable third runner, Derby, scratched immediately. The choice was his, and King George noted in his diary that it was 'not easy to make up my mind whether to send for Curzon or Baldwin'.[29] His government required a leader immediately, and King George acted quickly to seek what counsel he could on the holiday weekend, when the men of power were scattered throughout the countryside. The task of gathering information fell to the tireless Stamfordham, and the first name on his list was that of Salisbury, who hastened to London on Monday in frock coat and silk hat, in the guard's van of the dawn milk train. He met the royal secretary at the Palace at 9 a.m., and his advice was unambiguous: the King should send for Curzon.[30]

His Majesty was pleased to know Salisbury's mind, but asked Stamfordham also to consult Lord Balfour. Well aware of his old friend's infirmity, the secretary was hesitant to call on Balfour but nonetheless dispatched a telegram: 'I hope you will kindly come to London tomorrow so that I could see you in the afternoon. The matter', Stamfordham emphasized, 'is most urgent.'[31] Hence, despite his doctors' disapproval, Balfour decamped for London, 140 miles away, reclining in the back seat of his motor car. Balfour met Stamfordham twice on Monday 21 May, at Carlton Gardens, and made it clear that he believed he would be put 'in a difficult and invidious position', since he was neither a minister nor a party leader, if he offered advice directly to the King.[32] He was willing, however, to tell Stamfordham 'that my first impression and personal view was that the King should follow the obvious, though not the inevitable, course, and, in the first instance, ask [Baldwin as] the Leader of the House of Commons to form a Government. If for any reason this failed, the situation would, of course, have to be reconsidered.'[33]

Matters were complicated, Balfour added, by the fact that Curzon had served for many years in high office and enjoyed a reputation that far exceeded that of Baldwin, whose own 'experience of Cabinet work was relatively insignificant, and who, so far as I was aware, had no special capacity as a Parliamentarian'.[34] Nonetheless, he believed that the weight of circumstance was all on Baldwin's side: especially delicate, he told Stamfordham, was the fact that the Cabinet already contained an 'unusual proportion' of peers.[35] He feared it would be unpopular also to have the premier in the Upper House, and would make the position of the Leader of the House of Commons difficult. Balfour was also troubled by the additional fact that the Labour Party, now the official Opposition, was unrepresented in the Upper House.

By the end of the day, Stamfordham had summoned both Baldwin and Curzon. In a rather poignant episode, the Marquess – in Somerset for the holiday and isolated from events because there was no telephone at his beloved Montacute House – passed the time on his rail journey to London planning his new government. At their meeting the following afternoon, however, Stamfordham crushed these dreams by informing him that the King had chosen Baldwin, who was in effect already prime minister.[36] Curzon, whose talent and tireless sense of duty were unsurpassed in British politics, was an ambitious, passionate and proud man, and among those whom he came to hold responsible for dashing 'the cup of honourable ambition' from his lips was Arthur Balfour. The pain was somehow made worse by the fact that Balfour 'did not deny it when my wife challenged him later, but said he thought he had done me a good turn in saving me from such a detestable office'.[37]

In fact Baldwin was chosen by the King, not by Balfour, Salisbury, Stamfordham or any other adviser.[38] The sovereign's reasoning, Stamfordham later wrote to Geoffrey Dawson of *The Times*, was not complicated: King George was sure that his responsibility to the nation made it necessary to select an MP, and 'were he not to do so, and the experiment failed, the country would blame the King for an act which was his own and which proved that the King was ignorant of, and out of touch with the public.'[39] Put most simply, Baldwin was selected because he led the majority in the elected House. The fact that the monarch did not much like Curzon was not a factor in the decision.[40] It was also true that in his few months as Chancellor, Baldwin had not much impressed the sovereign, but King George made the best of it. Years later, Hankey told the historian Harold Temperley that Balfour's advice 'as much as anything' made Baldwin prime minister, but it seems that the most that can be said is that Balfour simply reinforced a decision towards which the King was already moving.[41]

After his discussions with Stamfordham, Balfour returned to Sheringham and was welcomed by his friends. According to Churchill, a certain lady immediately enquired if 'dear George' would become prime minister. 'No,' Balfour is said to have replied, 'dear George will not.' Years later, Lord Blake completed the tale:

> To understand the point one must bear in mind the Christian name of Curzon's rich second wife, Grace Duggan. The guest who had asked the question went on, 'Oh I am so sorry. He will be terribly disappointed.' Balfour replied, 'I don't know. After all, even if he has lost the hope of glory he still has the means of Grace.'[42]

True or not, the quip certainly has a Balfourian timbre. Curzon, who never forgot or forgave his disappointment, pulled himself together, agreed to serve under the new premier, and did so until his death two years later.[43] Only days afterwards, at a meeting of the Conservative Party, he generously nominated Baldwin for election to the leadership.

Like the unfortunate Bonar Law, Baldwin wished for the return of the former coalitionists, but he too was sensitive to the fact that the Tory rank and file who had raised him up did not want them back. For their part, the ex-ministers (most of whom had supported Curzon for the premiership) had not yet forgiven Baldwin for their humiliation. He could well have used their talents, for he saw troubles on many fronts: relations with France, now led by the ultra-nationalist Raymond Poincaré, continued to be strained; economic recovery in Europe was stalled; the German and Austrian republics teetered on fiscal collapse, and this did no good to the British economy – dependent as ever on foreign markets. Unemployment was worrisome, and profits, interest rates and investment in the former 'workshop of the world' lagged badly. To combat these troubles and reinvigorate his party, Baldwin turned to the nostrum that had long excited and tormented Conservatives: Tariff Reform. His patron, Bonar Law, had pledged that there would be no tariffs without the consent of the electorate, and Baldwin felt bound to honour the promise. Hence, when he announced a tariff programme (devoid of food taxes) on 25 October, it meant a second general election within a year.

Polling day was 6 December, and the result was a stunning surprise to most government supporters – and, in truth, to most of the country.[44] The government, Tariff Reform and certainly Baldwin all appeared to have lost, but it was less clear who exactly had won. The Conservatives claimed 248 seats, Labour came second with 191, and the various Liberals won 159. It was unclear at first exactly what the government would do, but one thing seemed positively crystalline: the responsibility was Baldwin's. Balfour had known both victory and defeat over his long career, but he averred that he had never witnessed anything quite like this. Austen Chamberlain must have smiled when he quoted Balfour's reaction: 'Obviously Baldwin is an idiot – the only question is whether he is an inspired idiot!'[45] Others agreed, but one can only wonder how many thought that the lame-duck Prime Minister was in any way 'inspired'.

It was unclear whether Baldwin would simply resign, or face Parliament to dare the Liberals to join with Labour to defeat him and pave the way for a socialist government, or challenge them to co-operate with him to prevent it. Among the confused Tories, rumours flew about of a conspiracy, supposedly led by the press lords Rothermere and Beaverbrook, to drive Baldwin from the leadership, and the former coalitionists Chamberlain, Birkenhead and Derby were said to be among the intriguers – as was Arthur Balfour.[46] Certainly Derby, spurred on by Birkenhead, pushed forward the idea that the King should be encouraged to call on Balfour, who would then step aside in favour of Chamberlain.[47] In the end, all this talk came to nothing.

The King again sought Balfour's advice, and summoned him to Ascot on Sunday 9 December. They were again of one mind: the best course would be for the Prime Minister to meet Parliament, rather than resign immediately, and clear the way for Ramsay MacDonald and Labour. Balfour believed Baldwin had acted stupidly in his election ploy, but thought it best that he continue as leader of the Conservative Party.[48] The King agreed and asked the Prime Minister to remain at his post.[49] When Birkenhead complained to Balfour that he wanted the erring Baldwin out and another Conservative in his place before Parliament met, Balfour disagreed: a socialist administration would be nothing short of 'a national disaster'; the need for stability required that Baldwin stay on and that he face the new Parliament.[50] 'Simple arithmetic' dictated that the traditional parties would have to co-operate: 'An arrangement between the two [non-socialist] Parties it must be – or the general feeling of insecurity will be intolerable.' He knew the Liberals disliked Baldwin and that Chamberlain might be more acceptable to Asquith, once again leader of a united Liberal Party. Perhaps Chamberlain was 'incomparably the superior' man, but it was no time to be seen carrying out 'something in the nature of an "intrigue"' to undercut Baldwin. It would even be better, he told Birkenhead, to put Asquith and the Liberals in with Tory support than to stand aside for a socialist government. But 'I am very far from being wedded to the scheme I have outlined,' he added, 'if only someone would shew me better.'[51]

In the midst of the crisis, Balfour reminded Stamfordham, 'Little, however, is likely to be gained by prematurely endeavouring to anticipate every eventuality. As we all know, it is the unexpected that happens.'[52] And so it did. Baldwin faced the House, and on 21 January 1924 he resigned after being defeated by Labour and Liberal votes. The King did his duty and called upon MacDonald, who with Liberal support formed the first socialist Cabinet in British history. Balfour thought the precedent ominous, though at that moment it was unclear exactly how socialist the new minority government would or could be – dependent as it was on the Liberals – or how long it could last.

Their strange defeat finally nudged the Conservatives towards reconciliation. Baldwin had survived all efforts to dislodge him as leader, and now seemed willing even to have Birkenhead and Horne, whom he found distasteful, if they were the price of the return of Balfour, Chamberlain and Crawford, whom he did want. On 7 February all but Horne – who chose to return to his business career – were welcomed into the Shadow Cabinet.[53] Baldwin's protectionist plans were shelved with Chamberlain's benign approval, and for the moment all appeared calm. Four days later, at the Hotel Cecil, Baldwin announced all to an approving Conservative Party meeting.

If several of the returned prodigals – Chamberlain and Birkenhead, for example – continued to have political ambitions, Balfour did not. He preferred playing a part in reuniting the party to being excluded, but at seventy-five he had no illusions about the political future. Yet even an elder statesman who had traded the hurly-burly of the Commons for the somnolent dignity of the Lords ('like talking to a lot of tombstones', he told Riddell) could not avoid political controversy.[54] Winston Churchill was in the process of shrugging off his Liberal identity and edging closer to his original political home among the Conservatives, but he was far from uniformly welcome. In March he announced his candidacy in the by-election in the Abbey Division of Westminster as an independent opposing the official Conservative, Captain Otho Nicholson. Baldwin grumbled to Davidson, now his secretary, 'Just when I thought we were pulling together again. Leading the Party is like driving pigs to market!'[55]

Churchill appealed for help to Baldwin and to Balfour, who was a resident of the constituency, but the party leader had already decreed Shadow Cabinet neutrality in the contest and replied that his hands were tied.[56] Balfour, however, surrendered to the pleas of friendship and drafted an endorsement letter. When a fatigued Baldwin returned home a few days later, after 'a really worrying day', he found the draft letter and a cover note from Balfour enquiring, 'What would you like me to reply to him?'[57] At 11 p.m. the leader rushed to Carlton Gardens to quash the letter, and Balfour, who was leaving for Cannes on the following day, agreed to drop the matter. However, the next morning *The Times* included a letter from Amery in support of Nicholson, and Churchill immediately cried 'foul' to Balfour. There seemed nothing to do but send another note to No. 10 pointing out that Amery's published letter seemed to change everything – which Balfour did, adding that he left the final decision to Baldwin. The party leader acquiesced, and Balfour's letter appeared the next day (forcing Baldwin publicly to take Nicholson's side), though Churchill still lost – albeit by a mere forty-eight votes.[58] In the meantime, Balfour had indeed gone to Cannes, leaving Baldwin to get his pigs to market in his own way.

MacDonald's minority government collapsed after eight months, and, after a third election in two years, Baldwin returned to power in October 1924. This time there was no confusion, as the Conservatives captured 419 seats to 191 for Labour and a mere 40 for the ruined Liberals. The new Cabinet demonstrated that all appeared to be forgiven, as Chamberlain (Foreign Secretary) and Birkenhead (India Secretary) returned to office, as did the rehabilitated Churchill (a Conservative again, as well as Chancellor of the Exchequer). Balfour was not offered a Cabinet post, which Hankey insisted was because the Prime Minister felt a sense of '*gaucherie* and inferiority' in the older man's presence.[59] So Balfour had this effect on many people, Lord Jenkins commented – though he might have added that, even if true, it was never by intent.[60] He might have added too that few premiers wish to have a living monument among their subordinates. It is also true, however, that Balfour's age, health and impaired hearing were much on Baldwin's mind. Whatever the reason, within a short time the two men came to appreciate each other's talents, and Baldwin would soon invite him to rejoin the Cabinet after all. Balfour, who had judged Baldwin so harshly in 1923, also changed his view, noting near the end of his own life that the Prime Minister always 'managed to say and do the right thing at the right moment'; he was, Balfour concluded, a political 'genius'.[61]

When forming his second government, Baldwin invited Balfour to return to the Committee of Imperial Defence and to direct special attention to the 'tiresome and embarrassing' matter of the French-inspired Geneva Protocol on disarmament, endorsed by MacDonald during his brief administration.[62] Balfour found the invitation agreeable: he was pleased that the Committee would provide interesting activity without demanding ministerial duties, and he was not averse to being handed the chance to throttle the controversial Protocol, which he thought at best unnecessary and at worst misleading. In his mind, Britain and its neighbours had signed enough solemn accords since 1919 to pledge them to peace. One more would do no additional good, and what was needed was to breathe life into those that already existed.[63] In the end, the CID and the Cabinet agreed.

Balfour and Curzon, the Lord President, were essentially in agreement in opposing both the Protocol and Chamberlain's proposed mutual assistance treaty, intended to ease French anxieties regarding Germany. It would be one of Curzon's last skirmishes, for on 5 March 1925 the Marquess suffered a severe internal haemorrhage. Surgery was unsuccessful, and a fortnight later he died at the age of sixty-six. George Curzon's long association with Balfour was a curious sort of friendship – if that was what it was – in which mutual respect for one another's talents was diminished by competitiveness and jealousy on Curzon's side and by insensitivity and impatience on Balfour's. Now, after forty years, it was over. Baldwin may have believed only a few months before that Balfour's long career was all but over, but now he thought better of it and turned to him as Curzon's successor.

As Curzon lay on his deathbed, Balfour was at sea, on his way to inaugurate the new Hebrew University in Palestine, and his party included his old friend Chaim Weizmann, now the leader of world Zionism. After a particularly rough passage, during which Balfour was predictably miserable, he was relieved when their ship safely reached Alexandria. The honoured guest quickly pulled himself together, and the party travelled on to Cairo, Tel Aviv and finally Jerusalem.[64] There was much pausing at kibbutzim and townships where Jewish settlers wished to cheer the man they identified as their benefactor, and Balfour smilingly endured the unwonted part of popular hero.

The highlight of the visit was the formal inauguration on 1 April of the new university, and, before an assembly of ten thousand gathered at the

foot of Mount Scopus, Balfour did the honours garbed in the gown of the
chancellor of Cambridge University. Like Weizmann, he found the long
speeches trying – most were in Hebrew, a language of which he knew
nothing – but he endured them, and the ceremony concluded to tumultuous applause. Fatigued by the extended ceremonies, he was pleased to
spend a few days as the guest of Lord Samuel, since 1920 the high commissioner in Jerusalem. He revived quickly, and was soon enjoying tennis
with his host on the clay courts of the residency.[65]

The British authorities and the Jewish defence force, the Haganah, provided security for the official party, but Balfour wished to continue on to
view the historic sites of Syria, where the protection of the visitors became
the responsibility of the French administration, already anxious over a
recent insurrection. Their plans soon went awry as in Damascus a hostile
Arab crowd – infuriated by the presence of the author of the hated 1917
Declaration – advanced on his hotel, only to be received by French cavalry
who fired volleys of warning shots.[66] General Sarrail, the military governor,
was anxious to bundle the party out of his city, and Balfour and his friends
were packed off to Beirut and kept on board ship for three days before their
vessel was allowed to sail. Though Balfour brushed aside his adventure,
insisting he had faced worse times in Ireland, later he would speak only of
the Palestinian days of his adventure.[67] Certainly it in no way shook his
confidence in the rightness of the famous Declaration, and he steadfastly
discounted any signs of racial and religious strife in Palestine, writing in
1927, 'Nothing has occurred during that period to suggest the least doubt
as to the wisdom of this new departure.'[68]

Balfour's post carried few departmental duties, and he was assured by
Baldwin that he was free to take up the matters which interested him.
Science and technology fascinated him as much as they had fifty years
earlier, and he continued his advocacy of the Department of Scientific and
Industrial Research, founded in 1915, which came under his authority as
Lord President. So did the Medical Research Council, of which Balfour
had also long been a champion and which, in a remarkable irony, Curzon
only a few months before had invited him to chair.[69] Though now Lord
President once again, he surrendered to requests that he continue as chairman, and found himself in the odd position, as both responsible minister
and chairman, of reporting to himself – a curiosity which did not seem to
bother Baldwin, the Cabinet or the Research Council in the slightest.[70]

Balfour also took up an idea originally suggested by Haldane some years
earlier and which he himself had raised before Curzon's death: to create a
central body 'for organising and advising on any problems – economic,

hygienic and scientific – which affect the different fractions of the Empire', modelled on the CID.[71] He wished to advance original research, but also to bolster commercial technology with an eye towards increasing the competitiveness of the British export industries. This led to the creation of the Committee of Civil Research, which met first in June 1925 and under Balfour's leadership examined such disparate matters as the tsetse-fly infestation in East Africa, the Indian railways, locust control, rural electrification, and the supply of medical radium.[72] Amery, who served on the committee, was encouraged by the chairman's vision, and hoped that it might 'get the whole spirit of research animating the public life of the Empire'.[73] It was an ambitious undertaking, but after Balfour's retirement in a time of world economic depression the Committee found no other powerful patron. It faded away, and the idea would rise again only after another great war.

Pleading the demands of office, Balfour had declined the presidency of the Royal Society in 1920, but in the following year he agreed to preside over the British Academy – and he continued to do so for seven years. Though his leadership of the organization he had helped to create in 1902 lasted longer than that of any other incumbent, Balfour never found time to deliver the customary presidential address. At the end of 1925, however, he presented the Academy's annual Hertz Philosophical Lecture, speaking on 'Familiar Beliefs and Transcendent Reason'.[74] Once again an argument to faith, it is the only one of his lectures of which a sound recording exists (re-created for the purpose by him in 1927). A hearing today reveals that, at seventy-nine, Balfour's voice remained full and mellifluous.[75]

In Cabinet he continued his interests in defence and foreign policy, supporting completion of the on-again-off-again Singapore naval base and continuing to oppose reductions in the naval budget proposed by the Treasury.[76] Despite his initial scepticism about the proliferation of treaties after the war, Balfour in the end supported the 1925 Treaty of Locarno, the great triumph that brought Chamberlain the Garter and the Nobel Peace Prize.[77] Closer to home, in the unsettling days of the May 1926 General Strike, he stood behind Baldwin in his efforts to curb trade-union influence and held to a policy of firmness, even contributing to Churchill's bellicose anti-strike *British Gazette*.[78]

Balfour's last turn at centre stage came that autumn. Since the 1917 Imperial War Conference, Britain and the self-governing Dominions had been pledged to meet in peacetime to consider 'constitutional relations' within the Empire. A great Imperial Conference was planned for October 1926, and Baldwin called on Balfour – who seemed to the premier to care about such things – to take charge of a crucial Inter-Imperial Relations Committee.[79]

The task the Committee faced was to clarify the relationship between the mother country and the Dominions.[80] The need had been obvious for years, and the 1865 act which reserved the right of the British government to overrule the legislation of the colonial parliaments was almost never enforced – yet its existence was an irritant in Ottawa and Cape Town, not to mention Dublin. The contributions of Dominion forces to the 1918 victory were undeniable, as was the presence of the Dominions' individual delegations at the peace conference and the signatures of their representatives on the treaties.[81] At the Imperial Conference in 1921 their representatives had made known their anxieties about the continuation of the Japanese alliance, which, as we have seen, was abandoned after the Washington naval agreements. Their Cabinets had openly opposed Lloyd George's Chanak gamble in 1922, and they expressed their scepticism over Locarno three years later. No one denied that the Dominions conducted their affairs as though they were independent nations.

All this cannot have particularly cheered the 'Pan-Anglican' Balfour, but he realized that Britain had very little choice in the matter except to make the best of it. The world was changing, and the Empire must change with it. He continued to believe, however, that Empire patriotism could co-exist happily with Canadian or Australian or South African nationalism. Pan-Anglican he may have remained, but he harboured no daydreams that London could ever again 'rule' those young nations.[82]

It is attractive to believe that the role that Balfour was called upon to play in the Imperial Conference was especially satisfying for him – that it was precisely his desire. Mrs Dugdale showed the way: 'Balfour', she wrote of her uncle, 'had been getting ready for this Conference for some fifty years.'[83] In reality it was the elder statesman's conviction that too much clarification would somehow destroy that bifurcated loyalty that he believed was still felt throughout the Empire. Balfour believed that too much precision in defining the Commonwealth connection might very well be a danger, and, as Jason Tomes has written, 'Letting a committee of lawyers loose on it would be a disaster.'[84] The question was, Could any committee hope to craft a definition that would satisfy the Empire sceptics among the Irish Free Staters and the South African Boers and still be acceptable to Empire-minded New Zealanders and Newfoundlanders – as well as to the mother country?

On 26 October, Balfour explained his view to his committee. The British Empire in its parts, he said, was unlike any entity in history, appearing in its diversity to be the 'frailest of structures . . . not competent to enlist a single recruit or impose a shilling of taxation'. Its many components shared two attributes 'with each other and with nobody else': they were all under one Crown and all part of one Empire. On their continued unity depended world peace, he argued, and on world peace depended the future of civilization. Each part of the Empire shared in the contributions and glories of all: 'I at least as a Scotsman', he reminded them, 'am not going to surrender my share of Magna Carta and Shakespeare on account of Bannockburn and Flodden.' Perhaps an Empire foreign policy of consensus was too much to hope for, but he added (with Locarno in mind) so long as the Old World remained the centre of 'difficulty', and while consultation among the governments of the Empire must be improved, in matters of defence and foreign policy he hoped that the Dominions would continue to follow the lead of the mother country.[85]

To hammer out the desired document, Balfour finally turned to meeting privately with the heads of the Dominion delegations.[86] The South African premier, J. B. M. Hertzog, an Afrikaner nationalist and former Boer War general, whose scepticism of British imperial policy ran deep, hammered away at what was to him the key point: Britain and its Dominions, 'freely associated', must each accept the equal independence of all others. Three days later the Committee discussed Balfour's draft statement, written to this design.[87] Balfour had no quarrel with mutual recognition of uniqueness and self-governance, but, for him, any definition must emphasize unity rather than separateness. In the hope of pacifying both Hertzog and the strong Empire-minded premiers like Joseph Gordon Coates of New Zealand, and the moderates Mackenzie King of Canada and Sir Stanley Bruce of Australia, Balfour presented his own variant of Hertzog's draft – which, unlike the South African's, included the word 'Empire'. With only detail changes, this version was accepted by the committee on 9 November and became immortalized as the Balfour 'Definition' of the relationship among the self-governing states of what became in fact as well as in practice the British Commonwealth: 'They are autonomous Communities within the British Empire,' he wrote, 'equal in status, in no way subordinate one to another in any aspect of their domestic or external affairs, though united by a common allegiance to the Crown, and freely associated as members of the British Commonwealth of Nations.'[88]

He accepted that, just as colonies became Dominions, and Dominions matured into nations, so the Empire had evolved into a Commonwealth. Despite such evolution, the Dominions' shared experience and their common 'political instincts', he believed, would endure because most wished them to.[89] At Balfour's insistence, the Definition was included in the opening section of the report of the Conference, much of which he also drafted and which contained some of the most unambiguous language the elder statesman had ever composed. 'Every self-governing member of the Empire is now the master of its destiny . . . Equality of status, so far as Britain and the Dominions are concerned, is thus the root principle governing our Inter-Imperial Relations.'[90]

After long experience in world affairs, his faith in the rightness of Anglo-Saxon institutions remained unimpaired. Perhaps he would have been happier if the Definition had been worded in stronger terms of unity; almost certainly he would have been happiest if it had not been necessary at all. But it was, and in the end his confidence remained. When the Conference ended, his farewells to the imperial leaders were friendly and heartfelt. As for the South African premier, he forgave rather than merely forgetting, and wrote to Alice, 'I took a tender farewell of Hertzog after dinner last night. He really is a very nice man; and I hope left these shores with somewhat different feelings about the British Empire to those he entertained on his arrival.'[91]

The Definition is frequently celebrated as the last great step towards the celebrated 1931 Statute of Westminster, which recognized the legislative primacy within their borders of the Dominion parliaments, and so it was. It goes too far, however, to suggest that the Statute represented the enactment of Balfour's far-sighted design. Rather, what he saw was what the Empire had become, and it had to be accepted. 'We must', he wrote to Sir Samuel Hoare in November 1926, 'take things as we find them!'[92]

The Conference had been a draining experience for Balfour, but, except for his irksome deafness, Balfour told the Asquiths when he met them in Scotland the following spring that he continued to feel 'pretty well'. Margot – now Lady Oxford and Asquith – noted with amazement that Balfour, though four years older than her invalid husband, continued to play both tennis and golf.[93] He also still enjoyed his part as elder statesman, as in 1927, when he sought to alert his Cabinet colleagues to Moscow's anti-British disinformation campaign in China – he was concerned about the civil war and the disintegration of order that threatened anarchy in that vast nation. Chamberlain resolved on watchful waiting, while, not surprisingly, Amery and Birkenhead – the Colonial and India Secretaries – preferred action and called for troops to be dispatched to Hong Kong.[94] To the Foreign Secretary's consternation, America and Japan offered no support, and neither did his colleagues. Balfour wrote to Baldwin that Chamberlain deserved their sympathy, 'navigating unsound waters in the worst possible weather', and perhaps needed their support rather than additional advice.[95] Nonetheless, despite the Foreign Secretary's wishes, the Lord President advocated a naval blockade of the harbour of Soviet-influenced Canton to isolate the danger.[96]

His interest in the navy remained particularly keen. In the summer of 1927 a British delegation took part in the unsuccessful naval conference in Geneva, which foundered primarily due to the inability of London and Washington to agree on limitations of their cruiser fleets (left unspecified by the 1921 treaties), and in the autumn the CID Naval Programme Committee took up the struggle between the Treasury and the Admiralty over Churchill's demands for reductions in the building of cruisers. Balfour finally accepted the economies, acknowledging that another naval building race was to be avoided. Besides, he argued, if Japan were so ill-advised as to attack Britain's Asian colonies, he was confident that America would come to Britain's aid.[97]

Though he would remain in office until the 1929 election, Balfour's public life was drawing to a close. Time was exacting its price: he had recently had most of his remaining teeth removed, his hearing was nearly gone, and his sight was growing poor. In January 1928 his circulatory system began finally to fail, and as Lord Dawson noted, 'This was due not to disease but to wear.'[98] He was also troubled by difficulties in swallowing, and he found he could speak only in a sort of exaggerated whisper – to Baldwin he wrote that politics for the moment was impossible.[99] With rest he seemed to recover, and by March he was visiting the Desboroughs at Taplow once again and enjoying old friends in agreeable surroundings. There he suffered a mild cerebral haemorrhage, though its effects seemed to pass rapidly and without residual damage. His convalescence he spent with the Wemysses, 'a heap of books at his feet and the faithful Baffy by his side' at Mary's beloved Stanway.[100]

By the summer he felt much recovered, and according to Lord Dawson he once again seemed to enjoy activity 'without let or hindrance'. He returned to Carlton Gardens and a limited social life, and attended several Cabinet meetings. In response to an offer by the London publisher Cassell, in February he had agreed to take on the task of producing his memoirs in two large volumes.[101] A few years earlier he had noted to Mrs Dugdale, 'If I remembered all I've seen I should be very interesting and amusing', but despite his typical complaints about his faulty memory he apparently enjoyed dictating his recollections to her, declaring himself 'not in the least bored'.[102] Sadly, his health collapsed after dictating only enough material for the brief *Chapters of Autobiography*, published after his death.

In July, 1928 Balfour's admirers agreed that the statesman's eightieth birthday required special commemoration. Festivities began on the eve of the great day, with the British Academy organizing a lunch to celebrate both the birthday and the culmination of his presidency. After the laudatory speeches had ended the Prince of Wales offered the toast and brought special joy to Balfour's heart by reminding his audience that, despite his own years of dedication to the game, the guest of honour had for decades maintained a golf handicap lower than his own. Balfour's response was heartfelt but brief, for his voice remained weak and it had been a joyous but tiring afternoon.

The following morning brought a personal birthday message from the King, and there was much more to come.[103] Derby and Churchill had organized a special remembrance: 'I have found', Churchill wrote to their political friends, 'that there exists a wish to give him on that birthday some token of the personal regard and affection in which he is held, such presentation to come from old friends and colleagues in the two Houses of Parliament. The idea is to collect a sufficient sum to present him with a new Rolls Royce Motor, the cost of which can roughly be estimated at £3000.'[104] The response was generous, and the car was purchased. Balfour was delighted both by the sentiment and, given his abiding love affair with automobiles, with the beautiful motor car itself.[105]

The presentation was made that afternoon before a large audience in Speaker's Court, with Baldwin, Lloyd George and J. R. Clynes of the Labour Party doing the honours. Balfour roused himself and delivered a reply full of anecdotes of the wartime coalition. 'At one time Balfour described certain aspects of ministerial cooperation "when I was at the Home Office",' Lord Crawford recalled in his diary. '"Foreign Office" whispered someone close by. Ah yes, went on Balfour – Foreign Office – I should have said Foreign Office – and went serenely on to another serious blunder – but how like him it all was, and how disappointed we should all have been if he had given us a precise, accurate, and documented analysis of sentiments.'[106] To his oldest friends it was only to be expected: only a few years earlier he was to present a portrait of Louis Botha to the Empire Parliamentary Association and, forgetting entirely his purpose, delivered an 'eloquent and moving speech' expressing his thanks for the picture.[107] He was forgiven then, and he was forgiven now by an audience that appreciated a precious and unalloyed Balfourism. Churchill elicited a rousing 'Three cheers for A.J.B.' Balfour departed in the Rolls-Royce, driven by the faithful Mills – still his chauffeur after three decades – and the crowd dispersed having heard the last speech he would ever make.[108]

Balfour had hoped to return to the Cabinet after a rest at Whittingehame, but his circulatory problems were growing worse. 'Nobody of my age has the smallest right to grumble about his health', he wrote to Baldwin, 'but all the same I feel rather ill-used at getting an attack of phlebitis just as my throat trouble seemed drawing to a close.'[109] His sense of humour seemed unimpaired, however, as he also noted to the Prime Minister a recent unflattering newspaper picture of a colleague. 'Though I am something of a crock,' he noted, 'even a photographer would not suggest that I looked at death's door.'[110] By the autumn his condition remained unimproved, and he offered his resignation – though Baldwin would not hear of it.

As the autumn waned and his vigour declined, his spirits remained good, and he felt strong enough in September to welcome an unexpected visit to Whittingehame by Mlle Alvarez, the celebrated tennis player.[111] Though for a time he enjoyed daily drives in the Rolls-Royce, which had become the apple of his eye, even this small exertion soon proved exhausting. His voice was growing weaker, and it was discovered that his throat was ulcerated. He suffered periodic coughing fits, and standing and walking grew increasingly difficult and painful. Yet he continued to think of returning to London and the Cabinet; but Alice wrote to Baldwin to discourage any unrealistic expectations. Not surprisingly, speech was the facility he missed most: 'His voice is still bad,' she wrote, 'and the specialist wants him not to speak at all. He does try and refrain, but not thoroughly.'[112] With the coming of the new year he continued to express optimism, insisting to Baldwin in January 1929, 'Even the hope shows that my health is better.'[113] But hope was not enough. His strength continued to ebb, and a few days after writing this he agreed to continue his convalescence at Fisher's Hill, under Gerald's roof.

By this time Baldwin's government had run its course, and a general election was planned for May 1929. The Prime Minister had long been planning to jettison his older colleagues, and Balfour smoothed the way by informing him that he would be unable to continue in office.[114] Baldwin requested, however, that he remain a member of the CID ('which would indeed feel an orphan without you'), adding, 'Few things are more awkward than an Englishman trying to uncover his feelings but I hope you will recognise under these base words something of the gratification I feel to you and of the affection in which I hold you.'[115]

The King was himself recovering from a serious lung infection and had gone to Bognor to recuperate. On 11 May the Lord President mustered his strength to attend his last Privy Council, held at Craigwell House, where the sovereign was recuperating, and (insisting on standing in the King's presence) delivered his seals of office one last time.[116] This event he contemplated with good humour, afterwards writing to Lady Wemyss that he had thought in the dark days of November 1911 that his public career was over.[117] 'But this is the reel [sic.] end. Quite time too!'[118] The day was warm and pleasant, and sovereign and subject – old friends and fellow convalescents – enjoyed lunch together and a pleasant chat in the garden.

A few days later he suffered a 'cerebral clot', and by the end of June, Lord Dawson recalled, 'The phases of enfeebled circulation became more pronounced and with them bodily fatigue increased, and the vital forces ebbed.'[119] His health improved somewhat over the weeks that followed; a last visit to Whittingehame was contemplated, though never undertaken, and he continued to follow closely the Senior Golfers International Match at St Andrews.[120] In October there was a final psychical experience – actually two, as Mrs Willett, Gerald Balfour's friend and favourite medium, was taken to see the dying statesman on the 16th and announced that his room 'was full of presences'; then, two days later in Balfour's sitting room she fell into an apparent trance and made 'contact' with the spirits of Frank Balfour and May Lyttelton, who had died so many years ago, and May's brother Alfred. From May, the medium brought a reassuring message: 'Tell him he gives me Joy.' Later, Lady Betty recalled that Balfour 'said he was profoundly impressed'. Beyond this he would not go, and whether he believed the message or simply admired the performance will never be known.[121]

He was never to leave his rooms at Fisher's Hill, and for the remainder of the summer he dictated more recollections to Mrs Dugdale and discussed his medical condition – with 'acumen and detachment' – with his physicians. On the days when his strength allowed it, he received a regular succession of old friends: there were the politicians Lloyd George, Chamberlain, Churchill, even Philip Snowden, the Labour Chancellor, and Hankey, the perfect secretary. He was also pleased to see the few surviving Souls, among them Lady Desborough, Lord Midleton, 'D.D.' Lyttelton, the widow of his friend Alfred, and of course Lady Wemyss.[122] Stanley Baldwin paid his last visit to Balfour in February 1930, and they talked quietly for nearly two hours about past politics. Baldwin reported to Tom Jones that, through it all, the wit – and the mischief – that had made Balfour's conversation so memorable still shone. Their conversation turned to the great figures he had known, and the ex-Prime Minister wondered aloud why the punctilious Sir Austen Chamberlain, KG, had not risen to the top, as his father meant him to do. Baldwin recalled the scene: 'With his eyes rounded to their widest limit, he [Balfour] said: "Don't you think it is because he is a bore?"'[123]

Soon speech grew difficult and painful, and his deteriorating eyesight meant he could no longer read. On 9 March 1930 he suffered a seizure, and thereafter he was conscious for only a few hours each day. Chaim Weizmann was the last visitor outside the family to see the dying statesman – it was a silent farewell, with Balfour too weak and the great Zionist too overcome to speak. On the 16th Balfour whispered a few words to Eleanor, who replied to his apparent question that they could not be certain if the end had come. 'Well, soon or not,' he whispered, 'I do not mind which it is –.'[124] Balfour had spoken of death many times to his intimates, and his view remained constant through his life: it would be, he was certain, like 'passing from room to room'.[125] The passage came early on the morning of 19 March 1930, as Arthur Balfour died with one hand in that of Gerald and the other held by Eleanor.[126]

Letters of condolence poured in from the great and the small – many from the Jewish communities of Palestine who revered the Declaration's author – correspondents shared their reminiscences in the columns of the newspapers, and political leaders eulogized him in and out of the Houses of Parliament.[127] The family declined the honour of a state funeral and interment in Westminster Abbey, and honoured his wish for a private service and burial at Whittingehame, next to his mother and his brothers Eustace and Frank.[128] Memorial services were held in Edinburgh and Cambridge as well as at the Abbey, where members of the royal family and the nation's leaders paid their final respects, and where there were also, *The Observer* reported, 'a remainder of elderly men and women who, long ago, in the brilliant audacity of their youth, had been "Souls" with him in the days when the time to dream . . . seemed endless'.[129]

His funeral was attended only by family, close friends and estate workers. Under hazy sunshine on the cold afternoon of 22 March, the simple service at Whittingehame church was conducted by the Rev. Marshall Laing, the brother of the Archbishop of Canterbury. The plain oak coffin was borne by family retainers to a farm cart drawn by a brace of Whittingehame's great Clydesdale horses. The procession moved slowly along the one-mile lane to the grave site, followed on foot by the male mourners, led by Gerald, now the 2nd Earl. After the final prayer, the only flowers cast into the grave were those of family members, the sole exception being a small posy of thyme and rosemary sent from France by Lady Wemyss. This done, Arthur James Balfour was laid to rest.[130]

When her brother-in-law had been raised to the peerage, Lady Frances observed sharply to her son, 'Poor Nunky, he will leave little to the family but a title!'[131] Her estimate – given the decades of decline in agricultural prices, a veritable revolution in taxation, and the devastating economic effects of the Great War and the slump that followed it – was closer to the mark than anyone outside his family would have guessed. Balfour had lived an extraordinarily long life and had enjoyed a lifestyle of great comfort and of open-handed generosity to family and friends. His almost uniformly unfortunate investment decisions had further diminished his capital. Gerald's eldest son, Robert – known as 'Ral', and destined to be the 3rd Earl – had managed the affairs of the Whittingehame estate for some years, and now turned his accountant's eye on the wreckage. Ral soon wrote to Lady Betty to confirm that Arthur Balfour's vast fortune was largely gone.[132] Many of his possessions – furniture, automobiles and *objets d'art* – were sold almost immediately to settle debts and duties, and much of Balfour's art collection, including the beloved Burne-Jones pictures, was sold over the following years.

No. 4 Carlton Gardens was sold immediately and converted into offices. Every effort was made to retain Whittingehame as a family residence, but the expense of maintaining the huge property soon proved to be too great. In 1935, the house was closed, and three years later most of the remaining contents were sent to auction. The ancient Whittingehame Tower, restored so lovingly by Alice Balfour, was retained, and is today once again occupied by members of the family. The Nabob's great Whittingehame House in 1939 became a residential training centre for Jewish refugees from Nazism; then, beginning in 1942, it became an institution for troubled boys. In the 1950s it again became a home for political refugees – this time from the Hungarian uprising of 1956 – and in 1963 it was finally sold and for a time became the Holt School for Boys. It was eventually sold again and sank into disuse until in 1980, after careful restoration and conversion into flats, Whittingehame House once again became a home.[133]

Whatever else it was, Balfour's life was remarkable in so many ways – one that could not be lived in our century, no matter how brilliant or rich or well-bred the principal. Balfour was born a Victorian, twenty years before the Second Reform Act, and was fifty-three years old and First Lord of the Treasury when the great Queen died. Nearly three decades later, in an age of one-man (or woman) one-vote, he surrendered his seals of office for the last time to Victoria's grandson. He was born long before the telephone or the internal combustion engine, and lived well into a time when aircraft and automobiles were accepted as commonplace, the radio was ubiquitous, and the first successful demonstration of television had been conducted. Balfour first entered the Cabinet when living memory still encompassed Wellington and Peel, and a Unionist premier ruled quite comfortably from the House of Lords; at the time of his death, the illegitimate son of a labourer and a housemaid was ensconced at No. 10. The list of such contrasts in his lifetime seems nearly endless.

He was a true grandee, the descendant of two great families and heir to a large fortune, born in a time when high birth could still open the path to power. Unlike his friends Curzon or Elcho, his great legacy was his to do what he liked with from the moment he reached his majority. He was brilliant and handsome, and possessed personal charm that became legendary. His father's family had property and influence, and his mother's wealth and national power, and it appeared to many that 'Prince Arthur' was born with all the glittering prizes already at his fingertips. His intellect was such that in public life the broad consensus was that by this measure he had few, if any, peers. He was the vital centre of a large and supportive family, and of a refulgent circle of admiring friends. Though he remained unmarried, he delighted in the role of adoring and adored 'Nunky' to a veritable regiment of nieces and nephews. Nor did his bachelor life preclude love, and particularly the love and friendship over fifty years of Mary Elcho. He became a political and social celebrity long before middle age, and lived long enough to become a sort of national monument and one of the most famous men in the world.

Deeply committed to his religious vision, he placed relatively little stock in dogma and argued powerfully in his books not merely for the compatibility but for the unity of science and theism. He saw no contradiction in being a communicant of both the Anglican and the Presbyterian faiths, nor was he troubled by the fact that Judaism, or Islam or Hinduism – rather than Christianity – seemed to provide sufficient moral underpinnings for millions. He concluded early in life and never wavered from an unshakeable belief that man could do much, but that without God nothing beautiful, good or true was possible.

His rise to the top of the 'greasy pole' of politics seemed to have been almost effortless. Though in subordinate office he more than proved himself in Unionist eyes, in large part he did 'inherit' the premiership from his Uncle Salisbury, who had carefully groomed him for the post from the time the young man entered the House at the age of twenty-five. When he became premier in July 1902 he had no true rivals for the place – not even 'Radical Joe', who many in the Conservative wing of Unionism saw as a sort of brilliant sojourner lodged among them. However, despite genuine triumphs in the important areas of education, foreign affairs and defence, its very brevity and the crushing electoral defeat of his divided party in 1906 stained his leadership with failure. The problems that haunted Balfour's ministry were too powerful for any Unionist – and it certainly did not help that the party had been in office for a very long time. But the central difficulty lay in the fissure within the party caused by the tariff debate, and Balfour's struggle to identify the middle way failed completely.

If there existed any leader capable of driving the pro- and anti-tariff Unionists somehow to put aside their internecine battle for the good of the party, it was not Arthur Balfour. With the intellectualized and public 'Economic Notes on Insular Free Trade' and the contradictory and secret 'Blue Paper', combined with the overly subtle machinations leading to the resignations from the Cabinet of the most troublesome leaders of both sides, he did no more than postpone the day of reckoning and make it more bitter when it came. By his nature unable to seek, much less to find, black-and-white solutions, Balfour finally found himself at the head of a party which did not really know what their leader believed. It is worth recalling his sincere plea at the time: 'I know', he said to Austen Chamberlain, 'people accuse me of hair-splitting and finessing, but I can't help it if they do. My mind works that way. To me the differences are real and substantial.'[134] So they were, but in the short term it all led only to a humiliating electoral débacle, in which Unionist representation in the Commons fell by nearly 250, and Balfour suffered the embarrassment of becoming the only modern prime minister to lose his parliamentary seat.

In his six-year leadership of the Opposition he turned from 'finessing' and towards a harder partisan strategy in allowing the Unionist Lords to savage the Liberal legislative agenda. The beginning of the end of his party leadership came with the rejection by the Lords of the 1909 Budget – a great gamble predicated on the hope that the electorate would see the Budget as unconstitutional and the Unionist peers' action as justified. The only suitable vindication of their course would have been an electoral victory – and the two near-wins of 1910 were simply not good enough. The final collapse for him came, of course, with the battle over the Parliament Act, and Balfour's realism in accepting unavoidable defeat succeeded only in convincing his infuriated party that they needed a new fighting leader. If that was what they wished, then the exhausted Balfour was amenable, and relinquished the reins to Bonar Law.

But, to the surprise of none more than himself, Balfour's ministerial career was far from over, and he was recalled to office in the two wartime coalitions and remained until the age of eighty. With the exception of Lord

Home (and Neville Chamberlain for a mere five months), he was the only Conservative ex-premier of the last century who returned to subordinate Cabinet office.[135] To some observers, also recalling his successful years under Salisbury, this was further evidence that Balfour was excellently equipped to be a minister but not a party leader in the twentieth century. It is true that in Asquith's coalition he was an able if undistinguished First Lord, committed (and eschewing Churchillian 'interference') to meeting the needs outlined by his admirals. After December 1916 he shone more brilliantly as Lloyd George's Foreign Secretary for the balance of the Great War and, as the Prime Minister's staunch number two at the peace conference that followed. His initiative at the age of seventy-three at the Washington Naval Conference was masterful. Then, under Baldwin in 1926, his last bow led to the celebrated Balfour Definition, which eased the refashioning of the Empire into the Commonwealth.

To some critics in his own time and afterwards, Balfour seemed a man more suited to the eighteenth century than to the twentieth, and it is true that much in his elegant lifestyle and tastes was grounded in that earlier age – in the novels of Miss Austen, perhaps, and the music of Handel.[136] But it is also true that Balfour patronized the Pre-Raphaelites and their successors, came to love the 'thrillers' of crime and Wild West fiction, delighted in motor cars and gramophones, and never tired of installing modern conveniences in his houses. His economic thinking, though it did not pacify the battling pro- and anti-tariff partisans, certainly owed nothing to old orthodoxies; and, as a Fellow of the Royal Society for over thirty years and champion of the Medical Research Council and the Committee of Civil Research, his lifelong commitment to scientific research was tireless. In many ways he was far-sighted: keen automobilist that he was, he advised after the First World War, and long before the creation of modern motorways, in favour of an improved highway system. Yet near the end of his life he also cautioned of the dangers of air pollution from combustion emissions.[137]

His philosophical works placed him in the midst of a modernist debate of a different sort. He published his first works in a time when the battle lines between the champions of a so-called 'Darwinist' world view and the proponents of traditional Christianity were still hard and fast. Balfour's plea was not merely for a ceasefire, but for recognition of what was to him quite obvious – that the two world views were not antithetical at all. He argued that without a Creator ('to whom men may pray') there was no knowledge, and that all manner of learning led to an understanding of God. Like Newton's, his system was orderly but left plenty of room for mystery – yet he insisted throughout his life that all that was required of the scientist or the theologian was 'common sense'.

Certainly he is not an easy character for moderns to embrace, and contradictions are plentiful. He was both admired and loved by his various circles of friends, but was never at peace as a public figure in a democratic age. Hence, in his public life the world of the Commons was a home of which he was master for more than thirty years; but the political stage outside the Chamber made him uncomfortable, and his struggles to make himself understood by a wide audience often failed. It is not surprising that a man to whom the crowd was so foreign should have gained a reputation for distance, for aloofness from the more common order of men. Neville Chamberlain found him simply too lofty for ordinary mortals: 'I have always believed that behind his courtesy and affability A.B. is profoundly indifferent to the rest of the world.'[138] Yet this was directly contradicted by Alfred Lyttelton, who insisted that his friend was 'deeply interested in the human comedy'.[139] Austen Chamberlain, who had sparred often with Balfour in their long political careers, disagreed with his brother and cautioned Blanche Dugdale not to let her uncle's biographer 'fall into the too common error that he has not a heart'.[140] The platform and the cheering crowd were foreign territory to Balfour – he had no 'common touch', and was satisfied that this was more the province of Joseph Chamberlain, or Lloyd George or Baldwin.

Yet his undeniable advantages and his frank understanding of himself allowed him in most things to live as he wished – and his long life was remarkably contented. Many of Arthur Balfour's contemporaries outlived the world into which they were born and were uncomfortable in the one in which they eventually found themselves. Perhaps he adapted more easily than many, because of his deep belief that the world was 'as it was'.

Notes

ABBREVIATIONS

AB – Alice Balfour
AJB – Arthur James Balfour
BB – Lady Elizabeth (Betty) Balfour
BCB – Lady Blanche Balfour
BD – Blanche (Baffy) Dugdale
EB – Eleanor Balfour (later Sidgwick)
FB – Lady Frances Balfour
GB – Gerald Balfour
ME – Lady Mary Elcho
JSS – J. S. Sandars
WS – Wilfrid Short

ACP – Austen Chamberlain Papers
A-FP – Arnold-Forster Papers
AJBP/BL – Balfour Papers, British Library
AJBP/NAS – Balfour Papers, National Archives of Scotland
BBK – Beaverbrook Papers
BLP – Bonar Law Papers
CAB – Cabinet Papers
CBP – Campbell-Bannerman Papers
CDP – Dilke Papers
CHAR – Chartwell Trust (Churchill) Papers
CHP – Chandos (Lyttelton) Papers
DAV – Davidson Papers
DP – Derby Papers
ECP – Carson Papers
EHP – Hamilton Papers
EP – Esher Papers
FO – Foreign Office Papers
FP – Fisher Papers
GNCP – Curzon Papers
HH – Hatfield House (Cecil) Papers

HH QUI – Hatfield House (Quickswood) Papers
HHAP – Asquith Papers
HP – Haldane Papers
I-MP – Iwan-Müller Papers
JCP – Joseph Chamberlain Papers
JP – Jellicoe Papers
JSSP – Sandars Papers
KP – Kitchener Papers
LGP – Lloyd George Papers
LMP – Maxse Papers
LONP – Londonderry Papers
LP – Lansdowne Papers
MGP – Mary Gladstone Drew Papers
MP – Midleton Papers
RA – Royal Archives
RCP/BL – Lord Robert Cecil Papers, British Library
RP – Roberts Papers
SBP – Baldwin Papers
SLP – Lee Papers
SP – Selborne Papers
STP – J. St Loe Strachey Papers
TP – Templewood Papers
WBP – Bull Papers
WEGP – W. E. Gladstone Papers
WLP – Long Papers, British Library
WO – War Office Papers
WP – Wrench Papers
WSP – Steed Papers

PREFACE AND ACKNOWLEDGEMENTS

1. Sir Ian Malcolm, *Lord Balfour: A Memory* (London, 1930), p. 95.
2. George Dangerfield, *The Strange Death of Liberal England* (New York, 1961 edn), p. 13.
3. A. J. P. Taylor, *Beaverbrook* (London, 1972), p. 154.
4. Lord Vansittart, *The Mist Procession: The Autobiography of Lord Vansittart* (London, 1958), p. 218.

CHAPTER 1: THE BALFOURS OF WHITTINGEHAME

1. For this period, the author has drawn upon Blanche Dugdale, *Arthur James Balfour: First Earl of Balfour, K.G., O.M., F.R.S., Etc.* (2 vols, London, 1936); Max Egremont, *Balfour: A Life of Arthur James Balfour* (London, 1980); Paul

Harris, *Life in a Scottish Country House: The Story of A. J. Balfour and Whittingehame House* (Whittingehame, 1989); E. T. Raymond, *Mr Balfour: A Biography* (London, 1920) and Kenneth Young, *Arthur James Balfour* (London, 1963). See also George F. Black, *The Surnames of Scotland: Their Origins, Meaning and History* (New York, 1946).

2. This document, apparently lost for sixty years and rediscovered in 1906 in an old dispatch box, is dated 9 Dec. 1840 and was recovered by the Rev. Walter Crick, who returned it to the Balfours. AJBP/NAS GD 433/2/226. See also 29 Jan. 1861, evidence prepared by William Fraser, AJBP/NAS GD 433/2/186/4.

3. All references to comparative money values over time are drawn from Lawrence H. Officer, 'Comparing the Purchasing Power of Money in Great Britain from 1264 to 2005' on the EH.net website, Economic History Services, 2004, URL: http://eh.net/hmit/ppowerbp/.

4. The Earls of Lauderdale were hereditary bearers of the flag of Scotland, and the Maitlands descendants of King Robert II.

5. The alteration in spelling was effected to reinforce the pronunciation of the 'g' in Whittingehame as it is in 'gem', rather than as in 'golf'.

6. Harris, *Whittingehame House*, pp. 17–38.

7. James Maitland was a second son; an elder child, John, died in infancy. Another son, Charles, would inherit Balgonie and establish his own seat at Newton Don, near Kelso – another country house that had been designed by Smirke, originally for the Don family.

8. See the brief and exceedingly pious tribute by the minister of Whittingehame church, Rev. James Robertson, *Lady Blanche Balfour: A Reminiscence* (Edinburgh, 1897).

9. Arthur James, First Earl of Balfour, *Chapters of Autobiography* (London, 1930), pp. 1–3.

10. Ibid., p. 1.

11. Lady Frances Balfour, *Ne Obliviscaris* (2 vols., London, n.d.) [1930], I, p. 356. See also the recollection of her mother by Eleanor Sidgwick, Sept. 1922, AJBP/NAS GD 433/2/145/1.

12. Balfour, *Autobiography*, p. 10.

13. For this see Bernard Alderson, *Arthur James Balfour: The Man and His Work* (London, 1903). Published in the first year of Balfour's premiership, this is a virtual campaign biography, but does contain useful information gleaned from interviews with his contemporaries.

14. N.d. May 1856, BCB to Emily G. Faithfull, AJBP/NAS GD 433/2/157.

15. AJBP/NAS GD 433/2/145/1.

16. Balfour, *Autobiography*, p. 18.

17. AJBP/NAS GD 433/2/195/22.

18. Accompanied by Cecil and by Dr Thackeray, his Eton housemaster, Arthur returned to the Continent in the summer of 1866 to tour the Roman antiquities of Italy. Thackery recalled that while he and Cecil tramped through the historic ruins, Arthur remained at their hotel, his nose pressed in a book, and

on their return asked nothing of their adventures, posing philosophical questions instead. See the files of recollections of Balfour's youth by teachers and
boyhood friends, AJBP/NAS GD 433/2/195/2–8.

19. Young, *Balfour*, p. 11.
20. In 1867, Cecil's disappointed tutor, Mr Carruthers, was charged with preparing him for Oxford and wrote of him and his brother to Lady Blanche,
'Arthur is the most favourable specimen I know so that the comparison is
unfair, but putting aside intellect, judgment & manner, there appears to be a
radical difference between their standard of morality.' 25 Apr. 1867,
AJBP/NAS GD 433/2/240/45.
21. Balfour, *Autobiography*, p. 5.
22. Ibid., p. 6.
23. This seems to have been at Chittenden's insistence, and a pair of spectacles
was dispatched from Whittingehame. 7 Mar. 1861, BCB to Chittenden,
AJBP/NAS GD 433/2/239/12–13.
24. See the undated recollections of Rev. C. J. Chittenden, AJBP/NAS, GD
433/2/195/2–8, which are also the source for the quotations in the following paragraphs.
25. See BCB to Emily G. Faithfull, 20 Dec. 1862, AJBP/NAS GD 433/2/157.
26. Balfour, *Autobiography*, p. 7.
27. 19 Apr. 1862, AJBP/NAS GD 433/2/239/24.
28. 17 Dec. 1895, Augustus F. Birch to Miss Balfour, GD 433/195/2/16–17;
Dugdale, *Balfour*, I, p. 25.
29. Leo McKinstry, *Rosebery: Statesman in Turmoil* (London, 2005), pp. 18–30.
30. Balfour, *Autobiography*, p. 20.
31. Dec. 1901, 'Notes referring to Mr A. J. Balfour by the Rev. A. J.
Thack[e]ray', AJBP/NAS, GD 433/195/2/25.
32. 21 Dec. 1887, AJBP/BL Add. MSS. 49718/18/5.
33. 13 July 1897, AJB to Canon Furse, AJBP/BL Add. MSS. 49852/122–3.
34. AJBP/NAS, GD 433/195/2/25.
35. Kenneth Rose, *King George V* (London, 1984), p. 58. 16 July 1891, AJB to
ME, Jane Ridley and Clayre Percy, eds., *The Letters of Arthur Balfour and Lady
Elcho, 1885–1917* (London, 1992), p. 73.
36. Ibid.; Malcolm, *Balfour*, p.16.
37. This in a speech at Leys School, 16 June 1899. See Alderson, *Balfour*, pp.
13–16.
38. 30 July 1866, Thackeray to BCB, AJBP/NAS GD 433/2/239/41.
39. 2 Aug. 1866, Rev. Stephen Hawtrey to BCB, AJBP/NAS GD
433/2/239/44–5.
40. 1–5 Nov. 1868, AJBP/NAS GD 43/2/195/13.
41. For Elliot's version of this famous tale, see his letter of 3 Sept. 1893 to Alice
Balfour, AJBP/NAS 433/2/195/2/9–12.
42. Balfour, *Autobiography*, pp. 41–50.
43. N.d., 'Cambridge I', AJBP/NAS 433/2/85/5–6. The published memoir
does not contain this frank terminology.

44. See 'Mr Balfour', the recollection of Mary Gladstone Drew, MGP Add. MSS. 46270/184.
45. For these recollections of his friend, see Balfour, *Autobiography*, p. 55.
46. Aug. 1893, Walter Durnford to AB, AJBP/NAS GD 433/2/195/2/13–15.
47. 3 Dec. 1868, AJBP/NAS GD 433/2/195/15.
48. Brett to the Duchess of Sutherland, 11 Feb. 1894. Maurice V. Brett, ed., *Journals and Letters of Reginald Viscount Esher*, vols. 1 and 2 (London, 1934), I, p. 182.
49. For this I am grateful to Professor William C. Lubenow, the historian of the Apostles. See *The Cambridge Apostles, 1820–1914* (Cambridge, 1998).
50. Balfour, *Autobiography*, p. 54.
51. N.d., Balfour's recollection, 'Cambridge', AJBP/NAS GD 433/2/85/7.
52. Dugdale, *Balfour*, I, p. 19.
53. See the exchange of correspondence between AJB and M. A. Smith (estate manager) of 13 July 1869, AJBP/NAS GD 433/2/27.
54. 1 Jan. 1931, John [Strutt, 4th Baron Rayleigh?] to BD, AJBP/BL Add. MSS. 49833/58–9.
55. See J. Bateman, *Great Landowners of Great Britain and Ireland* (Leicester, 1973 edn), p. 23, and Catherine B. Shannon, *Arthur J. Balfour and Ireland, 1874–1922* (Washington, DC, 1988), p. 2. Essential records have been lost over the years, and all figures are estimates.
56. With fifty years remaining at the time of purchase, the lease would be renewed in 1920. The leasehold was sold at the time of Balfour's death, and the building was completely refaced and reconfigured into offices by Sir Reginald Blomfield in 1933.
57. Balfour, *Autobiography*, p. 68.

CHAPTER 2: YOUNG GENTLEMAN

1. To his amusement, until giving up his commission in 1880 he was addressed in the House of Commons as Captain Balfour. Kenneth Rose, *Superior Person: A Portrait of Curzon and his Circle in late Victorian England* (London, 1969), p. 133.
2. F. Balfour, *Ne Obliviscaris*, I, p. 214.
3. One plaque honours Palmerston and the other Charles de Gaulle, whose Free French forces were headquartered there during much of the Second World War.
4. See Balfour's personal ledger for 1880. AJBP/BL Add. MSS. 49962.
5. Balfour, *Autobiography*, pp. 68–9.
6. F. Balfour, *Ne Obliviscaris*, I, p. 172.
7. N.d. [1918], 'Recollection of Mr Balfour', MGP Add. MSS. 46270/174–200.
8. Lucy Masterman, ed., *Mary Gladstone (Mrs. Drew), Her Diaries and Letters* (London, 1930), p. 65.
9. Few knew her brother so well as Nora Sidgwick, who saw through the disguise from the first. See her response to Mary Gladstone's 'Recollection', EB

to AB, 6 Sept. 1918, AJBP/NAS GD 433/2/80. His talent for self-mockery was developed even during his schooldays; see AJBP/NAS GD 433/2/195/2–8.

10. Sheila Gooddie, *Mary Gladstone: A Gentle Rebel* (London, 2003), p. 78.

11. Ibid., p. 82.

12. MGP Add. MSS. 46270/174–200.

13. There are many tellings of this sad tale, but the most complete version is to be found in Gooddie, *Mary Gladstone*, ch. 8.

14. Egremont, *Balfour*, p. 37.

15. Dugdale, *Balfour*, I, p. 33.

16. 21 Mar. 1875, AJBP/NAS GD 433/2/189/4. May's brother Spencer Lyttelton also sent two photographs of his sister to Balfour; see AJBP/NAS GD 433/2/189/8, 9 & 10.

17. AJBP/NAS GD 433/2/189/5.

18. Egremont, *Balfour*, p. 38.

19. 27 July 1875, AJBP/NAS GD 433/2/189/18.

20. 14 Sept. 1877, MGP Add. MSS. 46238/1.

21. N.d., Jan. 1894. Ridley and Percy, eds., *Balfour–Elcho Letters*, pp. 98–9.

22. 31 Jan. 1892, ibid., p. 86.

23. [10 June 1875], AJB to W. E. Gladstone, WEGP Add. MSS. 44785/33.

24. Gooddie, *Mary Gladstone*, p. 86.

25. Balfour experienced other travels in his youth, including a journey with Salisbury and Lord Eustace Percy to Paris on the first train into the city following the bloody suppression of the Paris Commune in 1871. AJBP/NAS GD 433/2/85/22.

26. The newspaper cutting, forwarded by A. H. Bowie on 26 July 1917, survives, as do the comments of Mrs Sidgwick and of Balfour's secretary, W .S. Short. AJBP/BL Add. MSS. 49832/170. This fiction appeared not long after Balfour's triumphal 1917 mission to Washington.

27. Balfour, *Autobiography*, p. 117. Much of the argument in the book appeared in two articles published in 1878 and 1879 in the journals *Mind* and the *Fortnightly Review*, the latter edited by John Morley.

28. For this see John David Root, 'The Philosophical and Religious Thought of Arthur James Balfour', *Journal of British Studies*, 19, 2 (spring 1980).

29. Arthur James Balfour, *A Defence of Philosophic Doubt: Being an Essay on the Foundations of Belief* (London, 1920 edn), pp. 293–4.

30. 21 Jan. 1888, Ridley and Percy, eds., *Balfour–Elcho Letters*, pp. 46–7.

31. Balfour, *Autobiography*, p. 63.

32. AJB to W. E. Gladstone, 16 June 1879, WEGP Add. MSS. 44460/150. AJBL/BL Add. MSS. 49838/63–75.

33. Pringle-Pattison to AJB, 5 Aug. 1928, AJBP/BL Add. MSS. 49798/87. Pringle-Pattison was known as Andrew Seth until 1898.

34. N.d., 'Country house visiting', AJBP/BL GD 433/2/85/21.

35. Balfour, *Autobiography*, pp. 227–8.

36. [Feb. 1932], unattributed letter, AJBP/BL Add. MSS. 49833/297–306.

37. 14 Oct. 1901, AJBP/BL Add. MSS. 49796/68–9. Several of his paeans to the game are reprinted in Wilfrid M. Short, ed., *Arthur Balfour as Philosopher and Thinker* (London, 1912), pp. 268–79.
38. Balfour, *Autobiography*, p. 228.
39. 1–2 Sept. 1896, AJB to ME, Balfour, *Autobiography*, pp. 73–83.
40. The essay appeared in the *Edinburgh Review* in Jan. 1887, and was reprinted in part in Short, ed., *Balfour as Philosopher and Thinker*, pp. 326–38. See also Dugdale, *Balfour*, I, p. 48.
41. [1875] Burne-Jones to AJB, AJBP/BL Add. MSS. 49838/18–19.
42. They hang today in the Staatsgalerie in Stuttgart.
43. 22 June 1931, Sir Sydney Parry to AB, 'Memories of Number 10, Downing St., 1897–1902', AJBP/NAS GD 433/2/81.
44. Malcolm, *Balfour*, p. 101. The friend was the press lord Lord Riddell.
45. Ibid., p. 102.
46. Balfour, *Autobiography*, p. 22.
47. Ibid., p. 84.
48. 19 July 1873, Salisbury to AJB, Robin Harcourt Williams, ed., *The Salisbury–Balfour Correspondence, Letters Exchanged between the Third Marquess of Salisbury and his nephew Arthur James Balfour, 1869–1892* (Hertfordshire, 1988), p. 15. The retiring MP for Hertford was Robert Dimsdale, 6th Baron Dimsdale in the Russian peerage.
49. Balfour, *Autobiography*, p. 86.
50. Ibid., p. 91.
51. *Parliamentary Debates, House of Commons* [Hansard], 3 s, vol. 231, cols. 1033–4.
52. Balfour, *Autobiography*, p. 93.
53. Henry W. Lucy, *A Diary of Two Parliaments*, vol. 2: *The Gladstone Parliament, 1880–1885* (London, 1886), p. 85.
54. AJB to Salisbury, 19 Mar. 1878, Harcourt Williams, ed., *Salisbury–Balfour Correspondence*, p. 25.
55. Derby opposed his Cabinet colleagues' decision to send the British Mediterranean fleet through the Dardanelles and resigned on 24 Jan.
56. Balfour, *Autobiography*, p. 110. Emphasis in the original.
57. Raymond, *Balfour*, p. 21. The total poll was 964.
58. 7 Apr. 1880, Harcourt Williams, ed., *Salisbury–Balfour Correspondence*, pp. 37–8.
59. 10 Apr. 1880, ibid., p. 40.
60. 12 June 1896, ME to AJB, quoted in Angela Lambert, *Unquiet Souls: Indian Summer of the British Aristocracy, 1880–1918* (London, 1984), p. 57.
61. Balfour was careless about his correspondence but, to the gratitude of historians, retained many of Lady Elcho's letters, which were included when his papers were deposited in the British Library. After the publication of Kenneth Young's biography of Balfour in 1963, her family reclaimed them, and, with his letters to her, they remain at Stanway to this day. Some of their correspondence is among the Balfour Papers at the National Archives of Scotland. The Stanway letters were published by Jane Ridley and Clayre

Percy, in their edition of the *Balfour–Elcho Letters*, where this is explained on p. viii.

62. Ruddock MacKay has concluded that 'He evidently experienced no urgent sexual drive' (*Balfour: Intellectual Statesman* (London, 1985), p. 8). Egremont, *Balfour*, pp. 82, 121; and Ridley and Percy, eds., *Balfour–Elcho Letters*, p. 231, lean in the other direction. Mrs Dugdale does not deal with the subject.

63. ME to AJB, 1 Feb. 1906, Ridley and Percy, eds., *Balfour–Elcho Letters*, p. 231. This letter is marked 'Burn!', though Balfour kept it.

64. See ibid. and Egremont, *Balfour*, pp. 120–21.

65. 14 Feb. 1907, Ridley and Percy, eds., *Balfour–Elcho Letters*, p. 236.

66. 25 June 1905, ibid., pp. 223–4. Lady Elcho's typically quixotic punctuation appears as it was written.

67. 7 Mar. 1929, ibid., pp. 353–4.

68. On 2 Jan. 1903, Mary wrote to Balfour: 'I also think that the sex question and a vexed conscience accounts for things I feel with you and show and I think I understand it more now. I also *think* that life has improved me more than not? I think my methods of dealing with things, tho' perhaps peculiar have been disciplined by practice.' Ridley and Percy, eds., *Balfour–Elcho Letters*, p. 193.

69. See Ridley and Percy, eds., *Balfour–Elcho Letters*, p. 34. A discreetly edited portion of the first letter, omitting the phrase quoted, was published by Mrs Dugdale in her official life of her uncle; the second note was not mentioned. *Balfour*, I, p. 127.

CHAPTER 3: LEARNING THE ROPES

1. Balfour, *Autobiography*, p. 134.
2. Ibid., p. 136.
3. See Robert Rhodes James, *Lord Randolph Churchill* (London, 1986 edn), p. 82.
4. Balfour, *Autobiography*, p. 140.
5. John Ramsden, *An Appetite for Power: A History of the Conservative Party Since 1830* (London, 1998), p. 139.
6. See Walter H. Arnstein, *The Bradlaugh Case* (Columbia, Mo., 1983).
7. 25 Aug. 1880, Harcourt Williams, ed., *Salisbury–Balfour Correspondence*, pp. 49–50.
8. Robert Blake, *Disraeli* (New York, 1967), p. 730.
9. Ibid., p. 729.
10. Balfour, *Autobiography*, p. 151.
11. Quoted in Dugdale, *Balfour*, I, p. 64.
12. Gooddie, *Mary Gladstone*, p. 149.
13. See Tom Corfe, *The Phoenix Park Murders: Conflict, Compromise and Tragedy in Ireland, 1879–1882* (London, 1968). The assassins, whose invincibility was much exaggerated, were subsequently captured, tried and hanged.

14. 10 Apr. 1880, AJBP/BL Add. MSS. 49699/22.
15. 16 June 1880, AJBP/BL Add. MSS. 49688/27.
16. See W. H. Smith to AJB, 5 Oct. 1881, AJBP/BL Add. MSS. 49696.
17. Northcote to Salisbury, 19 May 1884, Rhodes James, *Lord Randolph Churchill*, p. 152.
18. Ramsden, *Appetite for Power*, p. 144.
19. See David Steele, *Lord Salisbury: A Political Biography* (London, 2001 edn), pp. 158–9.
20. Akers-Douglas replaced Winn as chief whip. Within the year, 'Captain' Richard Middleton, a former naval officer who had never reached the rank of captain, was appointed principal agent. The legendary 'Skipper' went on to become the most famous figure to hold that position.
21. Robert Blake, *The Conservative Party from Peel to Thatcher* (London, 1985), p. 154.
22. Rhodes James, *Lord Randolph Churchill*, p. 120.
23. Raymond, *Balfour*, p. 25.
24. Ibid.
25. Rhodes James, *Lord Randolph Churchill*, p. 123.
26. 8 Jan. 1884, Harcourt Williams, ed., *Salisbury–Balfour Correspondence*, p. 103.
27. See F. Balfour, *Ne Obliviscaris*, I, 381.
28. 14 Jan. 1884, ibid., p. 104.
29. Dugdale, *Balfour*, I, p. 82. Emphasis in original.
30. Young, *Balfour*, p. 78.
31. Balfour, *Autobiography*, p. 173. He takes the description from Winston Churchill's life of his father. The actual majority was twelve, with the amendment passing by 264 votes to 252.
32. 7 June 1885, Salisbury to Lady John Manners, in Lady Gwendolen Cecil, *Life of Robert, Third Marquis of Salisbury* (4 vols., London, 1921–32), III, p. 133.
33. See Salisbury's early drafts of a possible Cabinet, n.d., AJBP/NAS GD 433/2/654/12. The arrangement at least gave Northcote formal precedence over Churchill, as India Secretary.
34. Rhodes James, *Lord Randolph Churchill*, p. 190.
35. 15 June 1885, Harcourt Williams, ed., *Salisbury–Balfour Correspondence*, p. 121.
36. See Dugdale, *Balfour*, I, p. 89.
37. 16 Dec. 1883, AJBP/NAS GD 433/2/28/4.
38. In the same election Gerald Balfour entered Parliament as Conservative Member for the Central Division of Leeds.
39. Alvin Jackson, *Home Rule: An Irish History, 1800–2000* (London, 2004 edn), pp. 65–6.
40. Balfour, *Autobiography*, p. 211, from which also is drawn the quotation that follows.
41. 20 Dec. 1885, AJBP/BL Add. MSS. 49692/7.
42. 22 Dec. 1885, AJB to Gladstone, WEGP Add. MSS. 44493/263–4. 23 Dec. 1885, Harcourt Williams, ed., *Salisbury–Balfour Correspondence*, pp. 127–8. An important source of information was Sir Charles Dilke, with whom Balfour

had met privately. See AJB to Dilke, n.d. [late 1885], CDP Add. MSS. 47877/1.

43. See Steele, *Salisbury*, p. 190.

44. Ramsden, *Appetite for Power*, p. 155.

45. Balfour recalled the episode in a letter to Churchill twenty years later, quoted in Young, *Balfour*, p. 93.

46. Peter Fraser, *Lord Esher: A Political Biography* (London, 1973), p. 13. See also James Lees-Milne, *The Enigmatic Edwardian, the Life of Reginald, 2nd Viscount Esher* (London, 1986).

47. 24 Mar. 1886, Harcourt Williams, ed., *Salisbury–Balfour Correspondence*, p. 138.

48. The number is commonly reported incorrectly. See William C. Lubenow, *Parliamentary Politics and the Home Rule Crisis: The British House of Commons in 1886* (Oxford, 1988), pp. 250–53 and Appx I, p. 304.

49. For Churchill's realignment with the Ulster party, see Alvin Jackson, *Colonel Edward Saunderson: Land and Loyalty in Victorian Ireland* (Oxford, 1995), pp. 74–80.

50. Ramsden, *Appetite for Power*, p. 155.

51. Ibid., p. 156; Rhodes James, *Lord Randolph Churchill*, p. 234.

52. Numbers of MPs for Unionists and Liberals are murky because of the unclear and often shifting positions of various Members throughout the crisis. The best source for this remains Lubenow, *Parliamentary Politics and the Home Rule Crisis*, ch. 7.

53. N.d., Balfour memorandum to Salisbury, Harcourt Williams, ed., *Salisbury–Balfour Correspondence*, pp. 143–4.

54. 24 July 1886, ibid., pp. 153–5.

55. See Dugdale, *Balfour*, II, pp. 107–8; the latter description is in Young, *Balfour*, p. 98.

56. 23 July 1886. This letter is printed in its entirety in Dugdale, *Balfour*, II, pp. 107–8.

57. Ibid., p. 72.

58. 28 July 1886, AJBP/BL Add. MSS. 49737/4.

59. 21 Aug. 1886, CAB 37/18/42. See James Hunter, *The Making of the Crofting Community* (Edinburgh, 2000 edn); Dugdale, *Balfour*, I, pp. 108–16; and Egremont, *Balfour*, pp. 78–9.

60. Copy to Salisbury. Harcourt Williams, ed., *Salisbury–Balfour Correspondence*, p. 160.

61. AJB to R. Cecil, 4 Oct. 1886, Dugdale, *Balfour*, I, p. 113.

62. 19 Oct. 1886, Harcourt Williams, ed., *Salisbury–Balfour Correspondence*, p. 162. Emphasis in original.

63. 17 Nov. 1886, AJBP/BL Add. MSS. 49688/129.

64. 17 Nov. 1886, Harcourt Williams, ed., *Salisbury–Balfour Correspondence*, p. 165.

65. See Rhodes James, *Lord Randolph Churchill*, p. 274. For the impact of the 'Dartford Programme' see Ramsden, *Appetite for Power*, pp. 166–7.

66. Rhodes James, *Lord Randolph Churchill*, pp. 284–5.

CHAPTER 4: BLOODY BALFOUR

1. 7 Mar. 1887, AJBP/BL Add. MSS. 49839/63–4. Pollock was Corpus Professor of Jurisprudence at Oxford.
2. 8 Mar. 1887, AJBP/BL Add. MSS. 49839/69.
3. Lord Ribblesdale, *Impressions and Memories* (London, 1929), p. 198.
4. Other 'acceptables' were Sir William Hart-Dyke, Sir Henry Holland, and Robert Bourke, but the Nationalists sought to blackball 'the Squire', Henry Chaplin. Andrew Roberts, *Salisbury: Victorian Titan* (London, 1999), pp. 328–9. See also F .S. L. Lyons, *John Dillon: A Biography* (London, 1968), p. 87.
5. For these and other examples see David R. C. Hudson, *The Ireland That We Made: Arthur and Gerald Balfour's Contributions to the Origins of Modern Ireland* (Akron, O., 2003), ch. 5 and p. 222, and Raymond, *Balfour*, pp. 39–40. See also L. P. Curtis, Jr., *Coercion and Conciliation in Ireland, 1880–1892: A Study in Conservative Unionism* (Princeton, 1963), pp. 175–6.
6. Cecil, *Salisbury*, III, p. 347.
7. 5 Mar. 1887, Curtis, *Coercion and Conciliation*, p. 170.
8. Dugdale, *Balfour*, I, p. 126.
9. Egremont, *Balfour*, p. 82. Sir William was the nephew of the pioneer immunologist Edward Jenner.
10. Blanche E. C. Dugdale, *Family Homespun* (London, 1940), p. 57.
11. 15 Aug. 1905, AJB to Lord Dudley, AJBP/BL Add. MSS. 49802/223–5.
12. 9 Mar. 1887, Harcourt Williams, ed., *Balfour–Salisbury Correspondence*, pp. 179–80.
13. See Curtis, *Coercion and Conciliation*, pp. 188–9. Ashbourne demonstrated endurance, serving throughout Salisbury's second and third administrations and proving impossible to dislodge by Balfour in his – in all, a total of sixteen years.
14. Ibid., p. 187.
15. Henry Lucy, *A Diary of the Salisbury Parliament, 1886–1892* (London, 1892), p. 75. King-Harman died in 1888, and his place was taken by William Hayes Fisher.
16. See Nancy W. Ellenberger, 'Constructing George Wyndham: Narratives of Aristocratic Masculinity in Fin-de-Siècle England', *Journal of British Studies*, 39 (Oct. 2000).
17. J. W. Mackail and Guy Wyndham, *Life and Letters of George Wyndham* (2 vols., London, 1925), I, p. 203.
18. Salisbury to Goschen, 5 Oct. 1890, Steele, *Salisbury*, p. 212.
19. Salisbury to Hicks Beach, 28 Feb. 1887, Curtis, *Coercion and Conciliation*, pp. 168–9.
20. See Shannon, *Balfour and Ireland*, p. 53.
21. See Margaret O'Callaghan, *British High Politics and a Nationalist Ireland* (Cork, 1994), pp. 118–20; and A. Jackson, *Home Rule*, p. 81.
22. 13 Mar. 1887, AJB to Buller, AJBP/BL Add. MSS. 49826/27.
23. AJBP/BL Add. MSS. 49897/1-28-146b, *Land, Land Reformers and the Nation* (London, n.d.). See also Mackay, *Balfour*, pp. 32–3.

24. N.d. [1887], 'Series of Queries on Irish Land', AJBP/BL Add. MSS. 49822/1–6.

25. 13 Mar. 1887, AJB to Buller, AJBP/BL Add. MSS. 49826/27. The intractable Lord Clanricarde drove Balfour to consider threatening to withdraw protection from his Portumna estate to force his greater co-operation. 30 Oct. 1889, AJB to Henry White, AJBP/BL Add. MSS. 49845/143–5. Ridgeway insisted that this was, of course, impossible, though the Chief Secretary continued to rail against Clanricarde's 'selfish stupidity'. 13 Nov. 1888, Ridgeway to AJB, AJBP/BL Add. MSS. 49809/17.

26. Raymond, *Balfour*, p. 41.

27. See Shannon, *Balfour and Ireland*, pp. 42–3.

28. 18 Jan. 1889, Harcourt Williams, ed., *Salisbury–Balfour Correspondence*, p. 278.

29. See Curtis, *Coercion and Conciliation*, pp. 248–55, and A. Jackson, *Home Rule*, pp. 82–3.

30. Patrick Jackson, *The Last of the Whigs: A Political Biography of Lord Hartington, Later Eighth Duke of Devonshire* (London, 1994), pp. 270–1.

31. Ibid. See also Roberts, *Salisbury*, p. 445.

32. For a digest of the Crimes Act see Curtis, *Coercion and Conciliation*, pp. 180ff. See also Hudson, *Ireland That We Made*, pp. 75–6, and Shannon, *Balfour and Ireland*, pp. 36–7.

33. Quoted in Egremont, *Balfour*, p. 84.

34. Lucy, *Salisbury Parliament*, p. 271.

35. 20 Oct. 1887, AJBP/BL Add. MSS. 49688/153–4.

36. Winston S. Churchill, *Great Contemporaries* (Chicago, 1973 edn), p. 240.

37. Lucy, *Salisbury Parliament*, pp. 76, 424–7.

38. See Alderson, *Balfour*, p. 78.

39. AJB to Salisbury, 21 Sept. 1887, Harcourt Williams, ed., *Salisbury–Balfour Correspondence*, pp. 208–9.

40. N.d. [1887], AJB to Ridgeway, AJBP/BL Add. MSS. 49834/145–6.

41. Wilfrid Blunt insisted that he had overheard Balfour cheerfully announcing that imprisonment would surely kill John Dillon, MP. Yet the latter's biographer points out that care was taken at Balfour's order to ensure Dillon's health. Blunt, *The Land Campaign in Ireland* (London, 1912), p. 301; Egremont, *Balfour*, p. 89; Lyons, *Dillon*, pp. 97–8.

42. 27 Oct. 1887, Ridley and Percy, eds., *Balfour–Elcho Letters*, pp. 42–3.

43. 26 Oct. 1887, Salisbury to AJB, Harcourt Williams, ed., *Salisbury–Balfour Correspondence*, p. 217.

44. Blunt claimed that he feared for his safety if he fell into Balfour's clutches, and the Chief Secretary replied publicly that he need not fear any official vengeance. Balfour admitted privately to W. H. Smith that he was concerned not about Blunt's guilt but about the certainty of his conviction – which in the end was secured. Lord Chilston, *W. H. Smith* (London, 1965), p. 271.

45. Young, *Balfour*, p. 110.

46. Entry of 10 June 1891, Wilfrid Scawen Blunt, *My Diaries* (2 vols., New York, 1921), I, pp. 53–4.

47. Curtis, *Coercion and Conciliation*, pp. 196–7.

48. 16 Mar. 1887, AJBP/BL Add. MSS. 49807/35–7.

49. A. Jackson, *Home Rule*, p. 81.

50. Ridley and Percy, eds., *Balfour–Elcho Letters*, p. 46. For Balfour's stern words of 10 Sept. 1887, and his support for the RIC, see Dugdale, *Balfour*, I, p. 100.

51. In order to prevent another Mitchelstown, Balfour formulated a revised policy for police units called upon to deal with hostile crowds, and ordered resident magistrates in the most volatile districts to prepare in advance for possible confrontations. AJB to Salisbury, 21 Sept. 1887, Harcourt Williams, ed., *Salisbury–Balfour Correspondence*, pp. 206–8. See also Curtis, *Coercion and Conciliation*, pp. 199–200.

52. 16 Oct. 1887, Harcourt Williams, ed., *Salisbury–Balfour Correspondence*, p. 213.

53. For this see Curtis, *Coercion and Conciliation*, pp. 193–4.

54. 14 Oct. 1887, ibid., p. 212.

55. Balfour admiringly told a youthful John Simon that he did not know Simon was a lawyer. The future Lord Chancellor cherished the remark as 'the greatest compliment ever paid to me in my early days in the House'. David Dutton, *Simon: A Political Biography of Sir John Simon* (London, 1992), p. 330.

56. Dugdale, *Balfour*, I, p. 147.

57. 20 June 1890, AJB to Dr Glynn Whittle, AJBP/BL Add. MSS. 49847/37. He wrote to Carson a month earlier advising him to 'feel free to say you have my good wishes' for his adoption for the Trinity College seat. 12 May 1890, AJBP/BL Add. MSS. 49709/93. Carson sat for Trinity from 1892 until 1918, and since he was still ostensibly an anti-Home Rule Liberal was technically the only member of that party ever to hold the seat.

58. F. S. L. Lyons, *Charles Stewart Parnell* (London, 1977), pp. 374–5. See also Roberts, *Salisbury*, p. 446.

59. There are many studies which deal with the case, including Curtis, *Coercion and Conciliation*, pp. 277–300; Lyons, *Parnell*; Conor Cruise O'Brien, *Parnell and His Party, 1880–1890* (Oxford, 1977); O'Callaghan, *British High Politics* and, most recently, A. Jackson, *Home Rule*.

60. F. S. L. Lyons, *Ireland Since the Famine*, (London, 1973 edn), p. 192.

61. A. Jackson, *Home Rule*, p. 86.

62. Lyons, *Ireland Since the Famine*, p. 193.

63. AJB to Ridgeway, 2 Feb. 1889, AJP/BL Add. MSS. 49827/710–12.

64. AJB to Ridgeway, 4 Mar. 1889, AJBP/BL Add. MSS. 49827/854–62.

65. Rhodes James, *Lord Randolph Churchill*, p. 345.

66. Roberts, *Salisbury*, p. 455; Curtis, *Coercion and Conciliation*, p. 298.

67. AJB to Salisbury, 22 Feb. 1890, Harcourt Williams, ed., *Salisbury–Balfour Correspondence*, p. 306.

68. See, for example, Curtis, *Coercion and Conciliation*, p. 299.

69. A. Jackson, *Home Rule*, p. 87.

70. For the attack on Parnellite 'respectability' see O'Callaghan, *British High*

Politics, pp. 118, 120, and A. Jackson, *Home Rule*, p. 81.

71. AJBP/BL Add. MSS. 49845/244–5. Chamberlain forwarded a copy of Captain O'Shea's letter to Balfour. AJBP/BL Add. MSS. 49845/250–2.

72. O'Shea was said to have discovered that he would not benefit from a long-anticipated inheritance by his wife, thus obviating any reason for prolonging the marriage.

73. 27 Dec. 1889, AJBP/BL Add. MSS. 49845/254–5.

74. Curtis, *Coercion and Conciliation*, p. 328.

75. Sydney Zebel, *Balfour: A Political Biography* (London, 1973), p. 75. Mrs Dugdale recalled only that Balfour forty years later expressed 'utter incredulity' at the suggestion that he had had the opportunity to capitalize on Parnell's troubles. *Balfour*, I, p. 182.

76. Curtis, *Coercion and Conciliation*, p. 329.

77. Roberts, *Salisbury*, pp. 456–7.

78. 27 Nov. 1890, AJBP/BL Add. MSS. 49829/451–4; see also Dugdale, *Balfour*, I, pp. 183–4.

79. AJBP/NAS GD 433/2/77/16.

80. Curtis, *Coercion and Conciliation*, p. 331.

81. See A. Jackson, *Saunderson*, p. 109.

82. To Balfour's eye, Gladstone's 1881 act compromised the ownership rights of landlords without actually granting full ownership to tenants. See 1 May 1890, AJB to Northcote, AJBP/BL Add. MSS. 49828/869–71.

83. 21 Apr. 1887, Harcourt Williams, ed., *Salisbury–Balfour Correspondence*, pp. 186–7.

84. Ridgeway to AJB, 14 Feb. 1890, AJBP/BL Add. MSS. 49810/224–7.

85. He did not pass this legislation without concern that it furthered the principle of using public works to create employment and was likely to lead to excessive public expenditure and increased dependence on the state. 20 Nov. 1890, AJB to Ridgeway, AJBP/BL Add. MSS. 49829/442–4.

86. Hudson, *Ireland That We Made*, p. 88.

87. 15 May 1889, AJBP/BL Add. MSS. 49827/946–52.

88. Lyons, *Ireland Since the Famine*, pp. 205–6.

89. Hudson, *Ireland That We Made*, p. 89.

90. 5 Sept. 1890, AJBP/BL Add. MSS. 49829/218. Sir James had also been a member of the Cowper Commission. See also Curtis, *Coercion and Conciliation*, p. 368.

91. Curtis, *Coercion and Conciliation*, p. 369. Balfour was annoyed at rumours that the office of Lord Lieutenant had been 'begging round the peerage, as has been absurdly stated'. The Duke of Portland and Lord Brownlow had refused it before Zetland accepted. 30 May 1889, AJB to Ridgeway, AJBP/BL Add. MSS. 49828/39–43.

92. 28 Oct. 1887, Harcourt Williams, ed., *Salisbury–Balfour Correspondence*, pp. 219–20. See also his letter to William Hayes Fisher, Colonel King-Harman's successor as under-secretary, 19 Sept. 1889, AJBP/BL Add. MSS. 49828/343–5.

93. 8 Oct. 1890, AJB to Ridgeway, AJBP/BL Add. MSS. 49829/321–2.

94. Alderson, *Balfour*, p. 90.
95. 2 June 1931, Parry to AB, AJBP/NAS GD 433/2/81.
96. Lucy, *Salisbury Parliament*, pp. 78–80, 26.
97. 8 Oct. 1891, AJBP/BL Add. MSS. 49830/266–7.
98. 23 Nov. 1888, AJBP/BL Add. MSS. 49689/38. Curiously, Mrs Dugdale reproduced the entire letter but does not mention the significant super-script: 'not sent'. *Balfour*, I, pp. 201–2.
99. Hartington asked Balfour to ascertain whether, with Smith's health failing, Salisbury contemplated the appointment of Churchill as his successor! Balfour diplomatically replied that no such thought had entered Salisbury's mind, that the only possible alternatives were Hartington, Goschen and himself, and that the best hope for the immediate future was a continuation of Smith's leadership. 28 July 1890, AJB to Salisbury, AJBP/BL Add. MSS. 49869/89.
100. Roberts, *Salisbury*, p. 563.
101. 15 Oct. 1891, Harcourt Williams, ed., *Salisbury–Balfour Correspondence*, p. 361.
102. 15 Oct. 1891, ibid., p. 362.
103. 16 Oct. 1891, ibid., p. 363.
104. 17 Oct. 1891, ibid., p. 363.
105. 15 Oct. 1891, AJBP/BL Add. MSS. 49830/284–6.
106. F. Balfour, *Ne Obliviscaris*, II, p. 199.
107. N.d., AB diary, AJBP/NAS GD 433/1/1/372.
108. 27 Oct. 1891, AJB to Goschen, AJBP/BL Add. MSS. 49834/208.
109. 27 Oct. 1891, Ridley and Percy, eds., *Balfour–Elcho Letters*, p. 83.
110. Dugdale, *Balfour*, I, p. 181. For Balfour's case, see Hudson, *Ireland That We Made*, passim.

CHAPTER 5: FRIENDS AND IDEAS

1. Quoted in Dugdale, *Balfour*, I, p. 218. In his memoirs, Lord Vansittart, who as a young man had served Balfour in the Foreign Office, added, 'or women'. *The Mist Procession*, p. 384.
2. Toby was in fact the 'Lobby' correspondent, Henry Lucy.
3. See Egremont, *Balfour*, pp. 17–18, 61.
4. 4 Apr. 1881, AJBP/BL Add. MSS. 49838/86, 91.
5. 5 Apr. 1881, Harcourt Williams, ed., *Salisbury–Balfour Correspondence*, p. 66.
6. For this episode, see F. Balfour, *Ne Obliviscaris*, I, pp. 349–54. Similarly, Cecil Balfour's name appears only once in Mrs Dugdale's study of her uncle, and that in a brief reference to his death in 'an accident in Australia'. Frank Balfour's triumphs and tragic death are explained fully. *Balfour*, I, p. 70.
7. Dugdale, *Balfour*, I, p. 412.
8. Like the Cecils, the Balfours were irresistibly attached to nursery nicknames. Despite their reputation for formality before guests, the siblings often

addressed their eldest brother as 'Artie' or 'Arthie'. To the nieces and nephews he was always 'Nunky' or simply 'Nunk'.

9. Cynthia Asquith, *Haply I May Remember* (London, 1950), p. 28. Her pet name for Balfour was 'Mr Rabbit', which her mother thought rather appropriate.

10. Dugdale, *Family Homespun*, pp. 52–3.

11. 9 Jan. 1910, Brett, ed., *Esher Journals*, II, p. 435.

12. Harris, *Whittingehame House*, p. 81.

13. 11 Dec. 1898, Ridley and Percy, eds., *Balfour–Elcho Letters*, p. 157.

14. For a recollection of an early harrowing ride in the Hornet, see Lady Cynthia Asquith, *Remember and Be Glad* (New York, 1952), pp. 15–16.

15. Walter Long, later Irish Secretary under Balfour, was among the most adamant in advising Balfour to limit the autonomy he accorded to Sandars. See 20 Jan. 1911, Long to AJB, AJBP/BL Add. MSS. 49777/79–81, 82–9.

16. 10 Jan. 1894, AJB to ME, Egremont, *Balfour*, p. 131. The discharged secretary was H.C. Baker.

17. See C. Asquith, *Remember and Be Glad*, pp. 28–9.

18. Ibid.

19. 13 Feb. 1895, Lansdowne to AJB, AJBP/BL Add. MSS. 49727/4–5.

20. For his club subscriptions, see the undated list in AJBP/NAS GD 433/2/179/1.

21. In those days the Carlton, the Travellers' and the Athenaeum clubs stood in an impressive row in Pall Mall, broken only by the soundly Liberal Reform Club.

22. 17 Jan. 1887, quoted in Rose, *Superior Person*, p. 134.

23. Balfour was pleased to be elected an honorary member of the Institution of Civil Engineers.

24. Maisie Ward, *The Wilfrid Wards and the Transition*, vol. 1: *The Nineteenth Century* (London, 1934), p. 305; William C. Lubenow, 'Intimacy, Imagination and the Inner Dialectics of Knowledge Communities: The Synthetic Society, 1896–1908', in Martin J. Daunton, ed., *The Organization of Knowledge in Victorian Britain* (Oxford, 2005). See also Root, 'Philosophical and Religious Thought'.

25. Talbot became bishop of Rochester a few months later, and Gore became Bishop of Worcester in 1902. Root, 'Philosophical and Religious Thought', and Young, *Balfour*, pp. 160–62.

26. Lubenow, 'Synthetic Society'.

27. 5 Mar. 1896, quoted in Root, 'Philosophical and Religious Thought'.

28. *Papers Read Before the Synthetic Society, 1896–1908* (London, 1909).

29. For the variance in Balfour's and Sidgwick's visions of the purpose of the Society, see Bart Schultz, *Henry Sidgwick: Eye of the Universe* (Cambridge, 2004), ch. 5.

30. 20 Aug. 1894, Ridley and Percy, eds., *Balfour–Elcho Letters*, pp. 110–11.

31. N.d., AJBP/NAS GD 433/2/341/21.

32. Quoted in Young, *Balfour*, p. 319.

33. 8 Nov. [1870s?], Margaret Guerlain [?] to AJB, AJBP/BL Add. MSS. 49838/767. After several days of crystal-gazing, the spiritualist incorrectly revealed Balfour's coming 'down the aisle' with a golden-haired young lady in a white dress.

34. For an interesting argument to the contrary, see Janet Oppenheim, *The Other World: Spiritualism and Psychical Research in England, 1850–1914* (Cambridge, 1985), pp. 131–4.

35. The presidential address of 24 Jan. 1894 is printed in Short, ed., *Balfour as Philosopher and Thinker*, pp. 424–32.

36. See Nancy W. Ellenberger, 'The Souls and London "Society" at the End of the Nineteenth Century', *Victorian Studies*, 25, 2 (1982); Jane Abdy and Charlotte Gere, *The Souls* (London, 1984); and Lambert, *Unquiet Souls*. On 17 Jan. 1929 there appeared in *The Times* an anonymous letter by a self-identified former Soul explaining and defending them against what the author insisted were the inaccuracies which appeared in Lord Haldane's newly published memoirs. This letter was generally attributed to Lady Desborough, and remains a useful description of how the circle viewed themselves.

37. Margot Tennant, later the wife of H. H. Asquith, preferred the name 'the gang', but the more evocative title stuck. Daphne Bennett, *Margot: A Life of the Countess of Oxford and Asquith* (New York, 1985), p. 68. See also Ellenberger, 'Souls and London "Society"'.

38. The entire thirty verses may be found in Margot Asquith, *An Autobiography* (2 vols., New York, 1920), II, pp. 17–24.

39. See Abdy and Gere, *Souls*, p. 173.

40. Ellenberger, 'Souls and London "Society"'.

41. 'Easter Eve' 1886, CHP, 2/2.

42. 21 Aug. 1886, AJBP/BL Add. MSS. 49794/16–17.

43. Lambert, *Unquiet Souls*, p. 50.

44. The Earl of Midleton, *Records and Reactions, 1856–1939* (London, 1939), p. 51.

45. For analyses of the Souls at play, see Ellenberger, 'Souls and London "Society"', and Lambert, *Unquiet Souls*, ch. 6. Despite reports to the contrary, Margot Asquith denied that the Souls ever played 'Breaking the News', a cruel game credited to them which required players to pretend to inform loved ones of the death of someone present. *Autobiography*, II, p. 13.

46. Quoted in Lambert, *Unquiet Souls*, p. 93.

47. 2 June 1891, Blunt, *Diaries*, I, p. 53.

48. Viscount Cecil of Chelwood, *All the Way* (London, 1949), p. 45.

49. Richard Burdon Haldane, *An Autobiography* (London, 1929), p. 120. He added that 'on the whole it is doubtful whether their influence was on balance good.' It is worth recalling that at the time this was written Haldane was a former Labour Lord Chancellor.

50. M. Asquith, *Autobiography*, I, 207. Lady Oxford and Asquith (as Mrs Asquith became) tells a slightly different version of the tale in another book of

recollections, *Off the Record* (London, 1943), p. 51. Balfour also suggested to Lady Elcho that she record her recollections of the group.

51. 17 Nov. 1920, AJBP/NAS GD 433/2/229/1/12.
52. He complained of boredom continually to intimates, writing in a note to Lady Elcho of an evening on the Treasury bench, 'I was almost too bored to speak.' 8 Feb. 1899, Ridley and Percy, eds., *Balfour–Elcho Letters*, p. 158.
53. See Abdy and Gere, *Souls*, p. 38.
54. Nigel Nicolson, *Mary Curzon* (London, 1977), p. 147. See also, Lambert, *Unquiet Souls*, p. 68.
55. Bennett, *Margot*, p. 44.
56. M. Asquith, *Autobiography*, I, pp. 251–2.
57. 3 Dec. 1895, Ridley and Percy, eds., *Balfour–Elcho Letters*, p. 134.
58. This version of the tale is in Lady Oxford and Asquith's memoir *Off the Record*, p. 52.
59. See Ridley and Percy, eds., *Balfour–Elcho Letters*, pp. 113–22, and Elizabeth Longford, *Pilgrimage of Passion: The Life of Wilfrid Scawen Blunt* (London, 1979), pp. 311–13.
60. Ridley and Percy, eds., *Balfour–Elcho Letters*, pp. 123–4.
61. 17 June 1895, ibid., p. 125.
62. 15 May 1895, ibid., p. 125.
63. Arthur James Balfour, *Foundations of Belief, being Notes Introductory to the Study of Theology* (New York, 1895 edn), p. 4.
64. Dugdale, *Balfour*, I, p. 222.
65. 26 Apr. 1895, Root, 'Philosophical and Religious Thought'.
66. Ibid.
67. Huxley's last work published in his lifetime was an attack on *Foundations of Belief*, which appeared in *The Nineteenth Century*, Mar. 1895. Spencer's critical review of *Foundations of Belief* appeared in the same year in *Fortnightly Review*, 63 (1895). Gladstone, to whom Balfour sent a copy of the work, declared it 'clever but . . . wanting in depth & solidity'. 25 Mar. 1895, Angus Hawkins and John Powell, eds., *The Journal of John Wodehouse, First Earl of Kimberley, for 1862–1902* (London, 1997), p. 434.
68. Balfour, *Foundations of Belief*, pp. 30–31. Emphasis added.
69. Ibid., p. 6.
70. Ibid., p. 227.
71. Ibid., pp. 236–7.
72. Ibid., p. 344.
73. Ibid., p. 352.
74. In this regard see Oppenheim, *The Other World*, p. 131, and Schultz, *Sidgwick*, p. 293.
75. He wrote to Wilfrid Ward in Dec. 1895 that 'in some way or other future generations will, each in its own way, find a practical modus vivendi between the natural and the spiritual.' Young, *Balfour*, p. 160.

CHAPTER 6: LEADER IN THE COMMONS

1. Lucy, *Salisbury Parliament*, p. 458.
2. Ibid., p. 491. The 'departure' occurred on 27 May 1892.
3. 8 Feb. 1899, Ridley and Percy, eds., *Balfour–Elcho Letters*, p. 158.
4. 12 Mar. 1900, Curzon to Mrs Craigie, quoted in Rose, *Superior Person*, p. 352.
5. Lucy, *Salisbury Parliament*, p. 455.
6. Ibid.
7. Diary entry of 26 Oct. 1898, John Vincent, ed., *The Crawford Papers: The Journals of David Lindsay, Twenty-Seventh Earl of Crawford and Tenth Earl of Balcarres, 1871–1940, during the Years 1892 to 1940* (Manchester, 1984), p. 52.
8. See Curtis, *Coercion and Conciliation*, p. 384, and Shannon, *Balfour and Ireland*, p. 61.
9. Raymond, *Balfour*, pp. 70–71.
10. 5 July 1892, Harcourt Williams, ed., *Salisbury–Balfour Correspondence*, pp. 423–4.
11. N.d. [July 1892], ibid., p. 425.
12. N.d. [July 1892], AJB to Salisbury, ibid., p. 424.
13. Roberts, *Salisbury*, p. 578.
14. Cecil, *All the Way*, p. 70. Another of the juniors was Alfred Lyttelton, and they were led by Sir Robert Finlay – both of whom were Balfour's Cabinet colleagues.
15. 15 Nov. 1892, Harcourt Williams, ed., *Salisbury–Balfour Correspondence*, p. 438.
16. See 28 May 1891, BB to FB, AJBP/NAS GD 433/2/303/42–3.
17. A. Jackson, *Home Rule*, p. 94.
18. N.d. [Feb.–Mar. 1892], AJB to Col. Milward, AJB/BL Add. MSS. 49850/44–51.
19. 6 Mar. 1893, AJB to W. S. Wrench, WP, Add. MSS. 59541/35.
20. Dugdale, *Balfour*, I, pp. 214–15.
21. A. S. T. Griffith-Boscawen, *Fourteen Years in Parliament* (London, 1907), pp. 32–3.
22. Roberts, *Salisbury*, p. 589.
23. By the age of forty-seven, Rosebery had married Hannah Rothschild (1878); had won the Derby three times, with Ladas II (1894), Sir Visto (1895) and Cicero (1905); and had, of course, been prime minister (1894–5).
24. Dugdale, *Balfour*, II, p. 244, and *Family Homespun*, p. 184.
25. Egremont, *Balfour*, p. 128.
26. Sir Frederick Ponsonby, *Recollections of Three Reigns* (New York, 1952), p. 69; 16 June 1902, Hamilton diary, EHP Add. MSS. 48679. See also McKinstry, *Rosebery*, p. 24.
27. 25 May 1911, AJB to Lord Knollys, RA PS/GV/J 149A/2.
28. 16 July 1929, Lord Stamfordham to Lord Crewe, RA PS/GV J 2234/5.
29. 25 Jan. 1895, AJB to Goschen, AJBP/BL Add. MSS. 49706/161–3.

30. During his long residence in No. 10, Balfour used as his study what is now the White Drawing Room, in which he installed one of his pianos. Anthony Selden, *10 Downing Street* (London, 1999), p. 192.

31. He had indicated as much to the Conservative Primrose League in Dec. 1894. Ramsden, *Appetite for Power*, p. 178.

32. See Peter T. Marsh, *Joseph Chamberlain: Entrepreneur in Politics* (New Haven, 1994), p. 367, and P. Jackson, *Last of the Whigs*, pp. 294–5. Chamberlain had indicated six months earlier that he would join the next Salisbury Cabinet. Ramsden, *Appetite for Power*, p. 178.

33. N.d. [Feb.–Mar. 1892], AJB to Colonel Milward, AJBP/BL Add. MSS. 49850/50–51.

34. June 1895, AJB to Salisbury, HH, 3/M Class E.

35. 14 Apr. 1895, AJBP/BL Add. MSS. 49850/200–203.

36. 28 Aug. 1895, AJBP/BL Add. MSS. 49850/253–4. See also E. H. H. Green, *The Crisis of Conservatism* (London, 1995), pp. 6–8.

37. 27 July 1895, AJBP/BL Add. MSS. 49803/56–7.

38. Midleton, *Records and Reactions*, pp. 109–11.

39. Diary entry of 26 Aug. 1895, Vincent, ed., *Crawford Papers*, p. 31.

40. 22 June 1931, Sir Sydney Parry to AB, 'Memories of Number 10, Downing St., 1897–1902', AJBP/NAS GD 433/2/81, from which all quotes by Parry in this chapter are taken.

41. Ibid.

42. Stephen Koss, *The Rise and Fall of the Political Press in Britain*, vol. 2: *The Twentieth Century* (Chapel Hill, NC, 1984), p. 7.

43. C. Asquith, *Remember and Be Glad*, p. 31.

44. 5 Dec. 1905, Buckle to AJB, AJBP/BL Add. MSS. 49797/42–3. 25 Dec. 1903, the King to AJB, AJBP/BL Add. MSS. 49683/242–5.

45. C. Asquith, *Remember and Be Glad*, pp. 29–30.

46. Lady Elcho's daughter recalled that, on that occasion, Balfour became so absorbed in the book that he read on until 3 a.m. to finish it. Ibid., p. 116.

47. Neville Chamberlain saw only the 'hard' exterior, recalling, '[He] always seemed to me to have a heart like a stone.' 22 Mar. 1930, N. Chamberlain to Ida Chamberlain, Robert Self, ed., *The Neville Chamberlain Diary Letters* (4 vols., Aldershot, 2000–2005), III, pp. 169–72.

48. N.d., memorandum: 'As First Lord of the Treasury', JSSP Mss. Eng. hist. c. 771/321–31.

49. Matthew Fforde, *Conservatism and Collectivism, 1886–1914* (Edinburgh, 1990), p. 5.

50. 27 Aug. 1903, AJB to Devonshire, AJBP/BL Add. MSS. 49770/82–132.

51. *Standard* (London), 9 July 1895.

52. *Manchester Courier*, 17 Jan. 1895. See also Fforde, *Conservatism and Collectivism*, p. 29.

53. *The Times*, 11 Jan. 1898.

54. M. Asquith, *Autobiography*, I, p. 236.

55. 12 Dec. 1899, CAB 37/51/95–6.

56. 9 Feb. 1901. See also Mackay, *Balfour*, p. 88.

57. Dugdale, *Balfour*, I, p. 240.

58. Hudson, *Ireland That We Made*, p. 115.

59. 24 July 1896, Carson to AJB, AJBP/BL Add. MSS. 49709/94–5; H. Montgomery Hyde, *Carson: The Life of Sir Edward Carson, Lord Carson of Duncairn* (London, 1953), p. 149.

60. 6 Sept. 1896, Hudson, *Ireland That We Made*, p. 117.

61. N.d. (draft), AJBP/NAS GD 433/2/195/3/12.

62. Shannon, *Balfour and Ireland*, pp. 106–8; Hudson, *Ireland That We Made*, pp. 130–32.

63. Lyons, *Ireland Since the Famine*, p. 212.

64. Much of their correspondence may be found in AJBP/BL Add. MSS. 49724.

65. Haldane, *Autobiography*, p. 130.

66. See Balfour's Cabinet memorandum of 12 Nov. 1898, CAB 30/60/21.

67. 18 Nov. 1898, AJBP/BL Add. MSS. 49831/5–6.

68. 27 Nov. 1898, AJBP/BL Add. MSS. 49776/10–12. See also Shannon, *Balfour and Ireland*, pp. 108–11.

69. See Hyde, *Carson*, pp. 157–8.

70. Haldane, *Autobiography*, p. 124.

71. For this, see Balfour's correspondence with Salisbury of July 1899. HH 3/M Class E.

72. The compromise was proposed by William Cowper-Temple, later Lord Mount-Temple, the stepson of the great Palmerston, whose natural son he is generally reckoned to have been.

73. Manchester, *The Times*, 19 Jan. 1895.

74. In Manchester, *Standard*, 9 July 1895. See also 12 Sept. 1895, AJB to Cranborne, HH 4M/10/172a.

75. 21 Dec. 1895, AJBP/BL Add. MSS. 49781/57–8.

76. See Steele, *Salisbury*, p. 309.

77. 12 Sept. 1895, HH 4M/19/172.

78. 23 Nov. 1896, AJB to ME, Ridley and Percy, eds., *Balfour–Elcho Letters*, p. 152.

79. 9 Sept. 1889, Rose, *Superior Person*, p. 217.

80. Henry W. Lucy, *The Balfourian Parliament, 1900–1905* (London, 1906), p. 43.

81. Marsh, *Chamberlain*, pp. 382–3.

82. One of his junior counsels was Edward Carson.

83. 7 Jan. 1897, FB to BB, AJBP/NAS GD 433/2/316/9. Upon his release, Jameson returned to South African politics, took the place of Rhodes at the head of the Progressive Party, and became prime minister of the Cape Colony in 1904, and a baronet in 1911.

84. Roberts, *Salisbury*, p. 617.

85. *The Times*, 6 Jan. 1896; Jason Tomes, *Balfour and Foreign Policy* (London, 1997), p. 181.

86. Short, ed., *Balfour as Philosopher and Thinker*, p. 294. Balfour was never confident that the so-called 'non-white races' were capable of the technological

or political development of the European nations and their offshoots, and in this, in modern terms, he was certainly a racist. Yet any exaggerated idea of Anglo-Saxon racial purity and superiority he thought nonsense. He presumed that Britons and Anglo-Americans might have inherited from their ancient ancestors the smallest 'trace of inherited aptitude of blood', but believed that it was primarily their history and their hard-won accomplishments that bound them together. See Tomes, *Balfour and Foreign Policy*, pp. 36–7. For his scepticism about theories of race purity in the British Isles, see 4 Dec. 1912, AJB to FB, AJBP/BL Add. MSS. 49831/246–8.

87. Balfour wrote to Salisbury on 14 Apr. 1898 that he might well consider leaving that office in the hands of himself or another colleague for a month each year when 'Some real holiday is really desirable.' HH 3/M Class E.
88. Tomes, *Balfour and Foreign Policy*, pp. 248–9.
89. 2 Apr. 1898, Dugdale, *Balfour*, I, p. 255.
90. Ibid., p. 182.
91. Marsh, *Chamberlain*, p. 435.
92. 14 Apr. 1898, AJBP/BL Add. MSS. 49691/6–19. This letter is printed in Dugdale, *Balfour*, I, pp. 258–61.
93. 14 Apr. 1898, AJBP/BL Add. MSS. 49797/16–7.
94. Peter Clarke, *Hope and Glory: Britain 1900–1990* (London, 1996), p. 26.
95. See J. A. S. Grenville, *Lord Salisbury and Foreign Policy: The Close of the Nineteenth Century* (London, 1970 edn), ch. 8.
96. 30 Aug. 1898, HH 3/M Class E.
97. See Tomes, *Balfour and Foreign Policy*, pp. 181–2.
98. W. R. P. George, *Lloyd George, Backbencher* (Llandysul, 1983), p. 271.
99. Roberts, *Salisbury*, p. 696.
100. 2 Nov. 1898, Ridley and Percy, eds., *Balfour–Elcho Letters*, p. 156.
101. Ibid.
102. 5 June 1899, Blunt, *Diaries*, I, p. 324.
103. Diary entry of 6 June 1899, quoted in Denis Judd, *Balfour and the British Empire* (London, 1968), p. 278. The vastly outnumbered British troops were accused of having, supposedly with Kitchener's approval, behaved brutally towards the so-called 'dervishes' and particularly of having desecrated the tomb of the Mahdi – which in fact they had done.

CHAPTER 7: INHERITANCE

1. 1 May 1899, CAB 37/49/29. See also Judd, *Balfour and the British Empire*, pp. 164–6.
2. 27 Aug. 1899, quoted in Young, *Balfour*, p. 185.
3. AJBP/NAS GD 433/2/81. He described the meeting in similar terms to Lord Salisbury, 18 Dec. 1899, HH 3/M Class E, and to Lady Elcho, adding, 'Don't you like it?' 23 Dec. 1899, Ridley and Percy, eds., *Balfour–Elcho Letters*, p. 163.

4. 19 Dec. 1899, HH 3/M Class E.

5. Dugdale, *Balfour*, I, p. 303. N.d., 'Introduction to Science of Politics: Miscellaneous Notes', AJBP/BL Add. MSS. 49961/196–206.

6. *The Times*, 9 Jan. 1900; see also Dugdale, *Balfour*, I, p. 305.

7. *The Times*, 11 Jan. 1900.

8. Dugdale, *Balfour*, I, pp. 306–7. Emphasis in original.

9. *The Times*, 11 Jan. 1900.

10. Ramsden, *Appetite for Power*, p. 185; Roberts, *Salisbury*, p. 774.

11. Dec. 1899, AJB to GB, AJBP/BL Add. MSS. 49831/9–11; 5 July 1900, AJB to Salisbury, HH 3/M Class E.

12. Thomas Pakenham, *The Boer War* (New York, 1979), p. 492.

13. Judd, *Balfour and the British Empire*, p. 179.

14. 21 Oct. 1900 (copy), HH 3/M Class E.

15. 3rd Viscount Chilston, *Chief Whip: The Political Life and Times of Aretas Akers-Douglas, 1st Viscount Chilston* (London, 1961), p. 287.

16. 18 Oct 1900, ibid., p. 288.

17. 27 Mar. 1900, AJB to Salisbury, HH 3/M Class E. He had expressed the same thoughts to Lansdowne, 10 Oct. 1898, AJBP/BL Add. MSS. 49727/64–72.

18. Several different wits have been credited with the tag, among them Henry Labouchère and George Bartley. The hotel had been begun by the rather notorious financier and property developer 'unfortunately named Jabez Balfour'. Kenneth Rose, *The Later Cecils* (London, 1975), p. 71. After the collapse of Jabez Balfour's financial empire in 1892, work on the hotel ceased, and it was completed by the official receiver only in 1896. Synonymous with extravagant luxury, the Hotel Cecil was demolished in 1928 to make way for the now familiar Shell-Mex House. David McKie, *Jabez: The Rise and Fall of a Victorian Scoundrel* (London, 2004), pp. 107–8, 196.

19. 17 and 20 Oct. 1900, HH 3/M Class E.

20. Salisbury was untroubled by the controversy. See Roberts, *Salisbury*, pp. 789–90.

21. AJBP/NAS GD 433/2/81.

22. 25 Jan. 1901.

23. See Balfour's appreciation of the contributions of King Edward in the papers of Sir Sidney Lee, 24 Nov. 1911, Add. MSS. 56087A/7–9, in which he insisted that the monarch's part in policymaking was negligible.

24. 25 June 1901, AJB to the Bishop of Coventry, AJBP/BL Add. MSS. 49854/119–20. See also Zebel, *Balfour*, p. 118.

25. The case took the name of the Auditor of the Board of Trade, T. B. Cockerton.

26. Speeches at New Cross and Manchester, *The Times*, 13 Dec. 1901 and 16 Oct. 1902. For Balfour's interest in these weaknesses, see Mackay, *Balfour*, pp. 98–9, 102–3.

27. P. Jackson, *Last of the Whigs*, p. 315.

28. In Nov., the committee was reconstituted: Gorst was dropped. Selborne

and Lord James of Hereford were added, and Robert Morant replaced Sir
George Kekewich, his ostensible superior at the Board of Education, as their
key expert adviser.

29. Entry of 18 Mar. 1920, Margaret I. Cole, ed., *Beatrice Webb's Diaries,
1912–1924* (London, 1952), p. 178.

30. Compare, for example, B. M. Allen, *Sir Robert Morant: A Great Civil Servant*
(London, 1934), and J. E. B. Munson, 'The Unionist Coalition and Education,
1895–1902', *Historical Journal*, 20, 3 (1977), Mackay, *Balfour*, pp. 89–110, and P.
Jackson, *Last of the Whigs*, pp. 309–19. See also Eric Eaglesham, *The Foundations
of Twentieth Century Education in England* (London, 1967).

31. Dugdale, *Balfour*, I, p. 320. See also Allen, *Morant*, p. 158.

32. 25 July 1901, AJBP/BL Add. MSS. 49765/191–2; 11 Dec. 1901, STP,
ST/2/4.

33. Munson, 'Unionist Coalition and Education'.

34. 5 Aug. 1898, AJB to Colonel Sandys, AJBP/BL Add. MSS. 49853/1–3; 22
June 1900, Add. MSS. 49853/210–11.

35. [1904?], 'Remarks on Dr E. S. Talbot's Memorandum', AJBP/BL Add.
MSS. 49837/20.

36. It strained the Liberal–Irish alliance, however, as Irish Members supported
the bill in the interest of the Roman Catholic schools. Alan O'Day, *Irish
Home Rule, 1867–1921* (Manchester, 1998), p. 195.

37. He had at first expressed his conditional approval of the bill but soon changed
his mind. Lloyd George to his wife, Kenneth O. Morgan, ed., *Lloyd George:
Family Letters, 1885–1936* (London 1973), pp. 131–2.

38. 3 Sept. 1902, Mackail and Wyndham, eds., *Wyndham Letters*, II, pp. 753–4.

39. 15 Sept. 1902, HH QUI 1/79–81.

40. Entry of 10 July 1902, Lady Rayleigh's diary, quoted in Mackay, *Balfour*, p.
102.

41. 22 Sept. 1902, quoted in P. Jackson, *Last of the Whigs*, p. 317.

42. Quoted in G. R. Searle, *The Quest for National Efficiency* (Oxford, 1971), p.
208.

43. Zebel, *Balfour*, 120; Egremont, *Balfour*, p. 152.

44. John Grigg, *Lloyd George: The People's Champion, 1902–1911* (London, 1978),
p. 52. The reference is to H. A. L. Fisher's 1918 Education Act.

45. Anthony Selden, 'Conservative Century', in Anthony Selden and Stuart
Ball, eds., *Conservative Century: The Conservative Party since 1900* (Oxford,
1994), p. 21.

46. Roberts, *Salisbury*, p. 823.

47. Ibid., p. 826.

48. Devonshire, who succeeded Salisbury as Unionist leader in the Lords, was not
'quite pleased at not being consulted at all' over the succession, but his relations with Balfour at this point were good. Lord Newton, *Lord Lansdowne: A
Biography* (London, 1929), p. 241; P. Jackson, *Last of the Whigs*, p. 322.

49. 25 Feb. 1902, 'Conversation with Mr Chamberlain', AJBP/BL Add. MSS.
49835/87.

50. 15 July 1902: Brett, *Esher Journals*, I, p. 340.
51. *The Times*, 22 Sept. 1902, The law was changed in 1905, when Campbell-Bannerman became formally the first prime minister.
52. 17 July 1902, GNCP MSS. Eur. F 111/161. Hamilton incorrectly predicted to Curzon that Balfour's first administration would be short-lived and succeeded by a brief 'mongrel and immoral' Cabinet of Rosebery, Asquith and the Liberal Unionists, itself to be succeeded by a Conservative one. 22 May 1902, GNCP MSS. Eur. F 111/161.
53. Henry W. Lucy, *The Balfourian Parliament, 1900–1905* (London, 1906), p. 189.
54. 11 July 1902, AJB to Hicks Beach, AJBP/BL Add. MSS. 49835/92.
55. 12 July 1902, Ridley and Percy, eds., *Balfour–Elcho Letters*, p. 186.
56. 25 July 1903, AJB to Wyndham, AJBP/BL Add. MSS. 49804/137–45.
57. 21 Dec. 1933, Colin Cross, ed., *Life with Lloyd George: The Diary of A. J. Sylvester, 1931–45* (London, 1975), p. 102.
58. 19 Apr. 1904, AJB to King Edward, JSSP MSS. Eng. hist. c. 716/135–7.
59. 8 Feb. 1905, *The Times*. See also Zebel, *Balfour*, p. 123.
60. See Jill Pellew, 'The Home Office and the Aliens Act, 1905', *Historical Journal*, 32, 2 (June 1989).
61. 2 May 1905, *National Union Gleanings*, 24 (1905), pp. 463–7.
62. See Dugdale, *Balfour*, I, pp. 432–6.
63. See, for example, 2 Nov. 1898, AJB to ME, AJBP/BL Add. MSS. 49834/331–2.
64. 2 Sept. 1895, S. H. Butcher, quoting Lady Frances, to BB, AJBP/NAS GD 433/2/314/8–9.
65. Oct. 1903, Lansdowne to AJB, AJBP/BL Add. MSS. 49728/101–3.
66. See Egremont, *Balfour*, p. 205; Young, *Balfour*, p. 255.
67. See his draft letter [1904?], AJBP/BL Add. MSS. 49856/51–2.
68. Sir Austen Chamberlain, *Down the Years* (London, 1935), p. 209.
69. Grigg, *Lloyd George: People's Champion*, p. 71.
70. See, for example, Rhodri Williams, *Defending the Empire: The Conservative Party and British Defence Policy, 1899–1915* (New Haven, 1991), p. 19.
71. 17 July 1902, AJB to King Edward VII, RA VIC/R 22/101. The chair of the Commission was not easy to fill, and Balfour turned to Elgin only after being turned down by Lord Spencer and by H. H. Asquith.
72. *The Report of the Royal Commission on the War in South Africa*, Cd 1789–1792 (1903).
73. Williams, *Defending the Empire*, p. 46. *The Report of the Royal Commission on the Militia and Volunteers*, Cd 2061–2063 (1904).
74. R. J. Q. Adams and Philip P. Poirier, *The Conscription Controversy in Great Britain, 1900–1918* (Basingstoke, 1987), p. 8.
75. 18 Nov. 1905, RP 7301 – 33/8, and similarly 18 Sept. 1905, AJB to Knollys, AJBP/BL Add. MSS. 49685/39–41.
76. 30 Mar. 1911, AJB to Midleton, AJBP/BL Add. MSS. 49721/271–2.
77. 11 Nov. 1903, CAB 3/1/18A; Adams and Poirier, *Conscription Controversy*, p. 14.

78. See Adams and Poirier, *Conscription Controversy*, chs. 1–3.

79. Diary entry of 29 Dec. 1900, Vincent, ed., *Crawford Papers*, pp. 63–4.

80. See Williams, *Defending the Empire*, pp. 12–16, and Lowell Satre, 'St John Brodrick and Army Reform, 1901–1903', *Journal of British Studies*, 15, 2 (spring 1976).

81. 27 Feb. 1903, Ridley and Percy, eds., *Balfour–Elcho Letters*, p. 198.

82. 1 Mar. 1903, Acland-Hood to Sandars, JSSP MSS. Eng. hist. c. 738/185–90.

83. 4 Oct. 1903, AJB to Arnold-Forster, A-FP Add. MSS. 50335/45.

84. 21 Sept. 1903, Akers-Douglas to Sandars, JSSP MSS. Eng. hist. c. 742/48–9, and 14 Oct. 1903, Sandars to AJB, AJBP/BL Add. MSS. 49761/108–115

85. 19 Sept. 1903, J. Chamberlain to AJB, JSSP MSS. Eng. hist. c. 741/7–10; 27 Sept. 1903, Selborne to AJB, JSSP MSS. Eng. hist. c. 742/217–21; 25 May 1905, AB diary, AJBP/NAS GD 433/1/374. See also Williams, *Defending the Empire*, p. 42.

86. 29 Feb. 1904, Brodrick to AJB, MP, Add. MSS. 50072/108–17.

87. 8 Sept. 1903, AJB to Brodrick, AJBP/BL Add. MSS. 49720/217–20.

88. 22 Sept. 1905, Arnold-Forster to AJB, A-FP Add. MSS. 50350/111–14.

89. 30 July 1904, EP 10/32.

90. 6 Jan. 1906, AJBP/BL Add. MSS. 49735/161–3.

91. For the most pointed criticism of Balfour in his handling of Arnold-Forster, see Fraser, *Esher*, pp. 117–18.

92. 24 Sept. 1903, Esher to Maurice Brett, Brett, ed., *Esher Journals*, I, p. 18; similarly, 28 Nov. 1903, Esher to AJB, JSSP MSS. Eng hist. c. 742/166–7.

93. Esher's only official position was constable and governor of Windsor Castle. He had supervised Queen Victoria's Diamond Jubilee and her state funeral, and planned the coronation of Edward VII. He had succeeded his father as Viscount Esher in 1899.

94. There was great difficulty in finding an army officer thought suitable for the Esher committee, and Balfour's compromise choice of Lord Grenfell finally was abandoned for the ex-engineer-officer Clarke. 23 Oct. 1903, AJB to King Edward VII, AJBP/BL Add. MSS. 49683/211–12; 4 Nov. 1903, Knollys to Sandars, AJBP/BL Add. MSS. 49683/219–20.

95. 4 Oct. 1903, AJB to Arnold-Forster, A-FP Add. MSS. 50335/45.

96. 14 Oct. 1903, AJBP/BL Add. MSS. 49761/120–25.

97. In his invitation to Roberts to join the committee, Balfour 'diplomatically' expressed more confidence in Arnold-Forster's plans than he felt. 2 Feb. 1905, RP 7101/23–8.

98. Fraser, *Esher*, pp. 134–5.

99. 3 Feb. 1905, A-FP Add. MSS. 50344/13–18.

100. 10 Feb. 1905, A-FP Add. MSS. 50344/60–61.

101. 14 Feb. 1905, A-FP Add. MSS. 50309/67–74; for a fuller version see also his paper of 24 Feb. 1905, later distributed to the Cabinet. A-FP Add. MSS. 50309/83–4.

102. 10 Mar. 1905, RA VIC/R 25/93.

103. 5 Oct. 1903, A-FP Add. MSS. 50335/11.

104. 5 Apr. 1905, A-FP Add. MSS. 50346/17–21.

105. 12 July 1904, RP 7101–23/8. By the time of his retirement from the prem-iership, Balfour lamented to his sister Alice that his troubles might have been lessened had Wyndham accepted the War Office in 1903, and won-dered if the stress of the political battle had not affected the balance of Arnold-Forster's mind. Dec. 1905, AB diary, AJBP/NAS GD 433/1/374.

106. The Commission anticipated the Esher committee in recommending the abolition of the office of commander-in-chief, but at the time this wilted under disapproval, not least of all from the monarch. P. Jackson, *Devonshire*, pp. 281–2.

107. See his paper on the Cabinet Defence Committee, circulated 4 Dec. 1895 but written some months earlier. CAB 37/40/64.

108. Judd, *Balfour and the British Empire*, p. 28.

109. 20 Oct. 1902, CAB 37/63/145; 10 Nov. 1902, CAB 37/63/152.

110. Sir George Clarke was the first regular secretary of the CID, serving from 1904 to 1907.

111. Midleton, *Records and Reactions*, p. 141; 2 Aug. 1904 Arnold-Forster diary, A-FP Add. MSS. 50339/107–8.

112. Chamberlain, *Down the Years*, p. 207.

113. Lord Hankey, *The Supreme Command, 1914–1918* (2 vols., London, 1961), I, p. 45. See also Egremont, *Balfour*, p. 157.

114. 25 Mar. 1929, AJBP/BL Add. MSS. 49694/12–13. See also P. Jackson, *Devonshire*, p. 303; Judd, *Balfour and the British Empire*, pp. 24–8.

115. 30 Apr. 1904, CAB 6/1/12D; 20 May 1904, CAB 6/1/19D. These were adopted by the CID as a provisional report on 1 June 1904. See Mackay, *Balfour*, p. 157.

116. 20 Oct 1904, AJBP/BL Add. MSS. 49835/163. This is a copy, probably by Mrs Dugdale.

117. 19 Dec. 1904, CAB 3/1/28A. See also Tomes, *Balfour and Foreign Policy*, pp. 55–6.

118. 12 Dec. 1901, AJBP/BL Add. MSS. 49727/159–79.

119. 21 Oct. 1902, AJB to King Edward VII, CAB 41/27/31. A German naval squadron at one point actually opened fire on the Venezuelan fleet.

120. No anti-German voice was louder in this campaign than that of the editor of the *National Review*, Leo Maxse, brother of Lady Edward Cecil. An old friend and occasional tennis partner of Balfour, he was destined to become one of Balfour's bitterest antagonists in the press. See John A. Hutcheson, Jr., *Leopold Maxse and the National Review, 1893–1914* (New York, 1989), pp. 135–6.

121. 29 Dec. 1903, SP, MSS 34/53–8.

122. 22 Dec. 1903, CAB 37/69/92. Balfour employed essentially the same argu-ment with the anxious King on 28 Dec. 1904. Judd, *Balfour and the British Empire*, p. 69.

123. 29 Dec. 1903, CAB 37/67/97.

124. Diary entry of 24 Oct. 1904, Vincent, ed., *Crawford Papers*, pp. 78–9.

125. 24 Oct. 1904, LP Lans F 1/115.
126. Dugdale, *Balfour*, I, pp. 384–5.
127. Diary entry of 24 Oct. 1904, Vincent, ed., *Crawford Papers*, pp. 77–8.
128. CAB 37/67/97; Mackay, *Balfour*, 170–71; Tomes, *Balfour and Foreign Policy*, pp. 122–3.
129. Tomes, *Balfour and Foreign Policy*, p. 121.
130. 8 June 1905, AJB to King Edward VII, CAB 41/30/21.

CHAPTER 8: 'CUTTING EACH OTHER'S THROATS'

1. N.d. [*c*.1935], memorandum by 'D of P' [Lord Dawson of Penn], AJBP/BL Add. MSS. 49833/396–9.
2. Diary entry of 4 Aug. 1911, Vincent, ed., *Crawford Papers*, p. 212.
3. Entry of 24 June 1924, Thomas Jones, *Whitehall Diary*, ed. Keith Middlemas (3 vols., London, 1969–71), I, p. 284.
4. 4 Feb. 1902, 13 Feb. 1903, AJB to ME, Ridley and Percy, eds, *Balfour–Elcho Letters*, pp. 183–4, 196–7; 19 Aug. 1900, AJB to Frank Balfour (nephew), AJBP/NAS GD 433/2/477/2.
5. Short, ed., *Balfour as Philosopher and Thinker*, p. 157.
6. Quoted in Abdy and Gere, *Souls*, p. 42.
7. 24 Nov. 1895, D. George Boyce, ed., *The Crisis of British Unionism: The Domestic Political Papers of the Second Earl of Selborne, 1885–1922* (London, 1987), p. 41.
8. The confident and ambitious Curzon offered himself for the post. David Gilmour, *Curzon* (London, 1994), p. 136.
9. Entry of 14 Oct. 1938, N. J. Crowson, ed., *Fleet Street, Press Barons and Politics: The Journals of Collin Brooks, 1932–1940* (London, 1998), p. 225. Balfour was not alone in his view: when honours were distributed after the Great War, the British ambassador in Paris, Lord Derby, remarked that when he said to an Englishman that 'the chain of the [French Legion of Honour] was only given to Crowned Heads and to George Curzon he was quite satisfied'. 27 Nov. 1918, Derby to AJB, AJBP/BL Add. MSS. 49744/166.
10. 16 July 1902, GNCP MSS. Eur. F 111/161.
11. 31 July 1902, AJB to Curzon, GNCP MSS. Eur. F 111/172.
12. Gilmour, *Curzon*, pp. 238–9.
13. 20 Nov. 1902, Curzon to AJB, AJBP/BL Add. MSS. 49732/87–97.
14. Gilmour, *Curzon*, p. 140.
15. 10 Dec. 1902, Curzon to AJB, AJB/BL Add. MSS. 49732/103–5; Judd, *Balfour and the British Empire*, p. 233.
16. 12 Dec. 1902, GNCP MSS. Eur. F 111/233.
17. 29 Dec. 1902, AJBP/BL Add. MSS. 49732/110–16.
18. Judd, *Balfour and the British Empire*, p. 234; Gilmour, *Curzon*, p. 242. Lord Knollys believed that Lady Curzon, who died in May 1906, was partly responsible for keeping the 'wound open', and Brodrick wrote similarly to

Mrs Dugdale after Balfour's and Curzon's deaths. 26 Nov. 1905, Knollys to AJB, AJBP/BL Add. MSS. 49685/56; 9 Dec. 1930, Midleton to BD, AJBP/BL Add. MSS. 49833/42–5.

19. Gilmour, *Curzon*, p. 242.
20. Curzon sent two telegrams to Balfour on 21 Dec. 1902, GNCP MSS. Eur. F 111/172. The first declined the proffered honour, and the second explained that he could not accept the same decoration given to the Nizam of Hyderabad. It did not sway Curzon that, even though he was viceroy, the Nizam was a monarch in his own right.
21. 5 Feb. 1903, Curzon to AJB, GNCP MSS. Eur. F 111/162.
22. N.d. [Mar. 1903], AJB to Curzon, GNCP MSS. Eur. F 111/233.
23. Brodrick told the story in several letters to Mrs Dugdale – 21 May 1927, AJBP/BL Add. MSS. 49836/187, and 9 Dec. 1930, Add. MSS. 49833/42–5 – as well as in his memoirs, Midleton, *Records and Reactions*, p. 204. Balfour repeated it to others, including Lord Morley: Countess of Minto, *India, Minto and Morley, 1905–1910* (London, 1934), p. 115. See also Egremont, *Balfour*, pp. 170–71.
24. Gilmour, *Curzon*, p. 259.
25. 1930, BD, 'Events Leading to Lord Curzon's resignation, 1905', AJBP/BL Add. MSS. 49837/49–67.
26. Balfour wrote in a waspish mood to Brodrick that, though he was sorry to hear that Curzon's health was not improving, the Viceroy had no one but himself to blame: 'He has had nothing whatever to do since he came home except the work he has made for himself . . .' 6 Sept. 1904, MP Add. MSS. 50072/127–8.
27. See Judd, *Balfour and the British Empire*, pp. 238–9.
28. 28 Oct. 1903, AJBP/BL Add. MSS. 49720/255–6.
29. 28 Oct. 1903, AJB to Brodrick, AJBP/BL Add. MSS. 49720/255–6; Judd, *Balfour and the British Empire*, p. 243.
30. 'KCIE' designated the Knights Cross of the Most Eminent Order of the Indian Empire, an award which faded away after Indian independence in 1947. Balfour expressed his admiration of Younghusband's intentions and his courage but declared his actions disobedient and stupid. See 4 Oct. 1904, AJB to Lansdowne, AJBP/BL Add. MSS. 49729/1. For Curzon's view see Gilmour, *Curzon*, pp. 273–7.
31. Midleton, *Records and Reactions*, p. 201.
32. 9 Dec. 1930, Midleton to BD, AJBP/BL Add. MSS. 49833/42–5.
33. 20 Oct. 1905, AJBP/BL Add. MSS. 49764/64–71.
34. 16 Aug. 1905 [?], MP Add. MSS. 50072/170.
35. Following Curzon's death in 1925, Lord Midleton (as Brodrick had become) released a critical paper, 'Relations of Lord Curzon as Viceroy of India with the British Government, 1902–5', the title page of which declares, 'Seen and approved by the Earl of Balfour, June 1926'. AJBP/BL Add. MSS. 49833/46–54.
36. 24 Apr. 1906, AJBP/BL Add. MSS. 49758/119–21.

37. Gilmour, *Curzon*, p. 356.
38. N.d., Knollys to AJB [?], MP Add. MSS. 50072/171. Copy, forwarded to Brodrick, 7 Oct. 1905, AJB to Knollys (copy), MP Add. MSS. 50072/195–8; 15 Oct. 1905, AJB to Brodrick, MP Add. MSS. 50072/183–92. Brodrick, not surprisingly, strongly agreed. 12 Sept. 1905, Brodrick to AJB, AJBP/BL Add. MSS. 49721/170–71.
39. MP Add. MSS. 50072/183–92.
40. 25 Sept. 1905, HH 4M 56/143–50.
41. 10 Oct. 1905, Knollys to AJB, AJBP Add. MSS. 49685/50–51.
42. 13 Dec. 1905, JSS to AJB, AJBP/BL Add. MSS. 49764/131–2. Sandars, whose liking for Curzon was slight, could not resist adding, 'All this corroborates your general impression of G.C.'s demeanor towards yourself, but I fear it also shows that his attitude of mind does not improve in the English climate.'
43. 15 Dec. 1905, JSS to AJB, AJBP /BL Add. MSS. 49764/136–8; 17 Dec. 1905, JSS to Iwan-Müller, I-MP Add. MSS. 51316/63.
44. Balfour gave lukewarm approval to the Liberals' granting Curzon his peerage. 24 Feb. 1906, AJB to Knollys, AJBP/BL Add. MSS. 49685/95–7.
45. See Rose, *Superior Person*, pp. 366–7.
46. See A. Jackson, *Home Rule*, pp. 104–5; Curtis, *Coercion and Conciliation*, pp. 420–3.
47. See A. Jackson, *Saunderson*, ch. 13.
48. See Mackay, *Balfour*, p. 134.
49. Hyde, *Carson*, p. 188.
50. Mackay, *Balfour*, p. 134.
51. 31 Mar. 1903, Blunt, *Diaries*, II, p. 45.
52. 25 Aug. 1902, Wyndham to AJB, AJBP/BL Add. MSS. 49804/22–6.
53. 26 Aug. 1902, AJB to Wyndham, AJBP/BL Add. MSS. 49804/26–7. Emphasis in original.
54. 24 Aug. 1902, Wyndham to AJB, AJBP/BL Add. MSS. 49804/30–32; 11 Sept. 1902, Lansdowne to Wyndham; and for MacDonnell's permanent appointment to the India Council and secondment to the Irish Office, 24 Sept. 1902, and 27 Oct. 1902, Mackail and Wyndham, eds., *Wyndham Letters*, II, pp. 754–5, 763. 24 Sept. 1902, AJB to Wyndham, AJBP/BL Add. MSS. 49804/63–4.
55. 22 Sept. 1902, Mackail and Wyndham, eds., *Wyndham Letters*, II, pp. 760–61; 24 Sept. 1902, Wyndham to AJB, AJBP/BL Add. MSS. 49804/65–8.
56. See Max Egremont, *The Cousins: The Friendship, Opinions and Activities of Wilfrid Scawen Blunt and George Wyndham* (London, 1977), p. 244.
57. He had, in fact been informed by MacDonnell that the Under-Secretary was 'helping Dunraven in this business'. He took the letter with him on his holiday, and either did not read it or misplaced it. It turned up only years later in his papers. 10 Sept. 1904, MacDonnell to Wyndham, Mackail and Wyndham, eds., *Wyndham Letters*, II, pp. 764–5.
58. Though he categorically rejected the Reform Association plan, Balfour's

defence of MacDonnell was remarkably generous, stressing his record of distinguished service. 11 Dec. 1904, AJB to King Edward VII, CAB 41/29/42; see also 23 Feb. 1905, AJB to Lord Dudley, AJBP/BL Add. MSS. 49802/194–9.

59. 14 Dec. 1904, MacDonnell to Wyndham; Mackail and Wyndham, eds., *Wyndham Letters*, II, pp. 771–2. 8 Feb. 1905, memorandum by Sir Antony MacDonnell, AJBP/BL Add. MSS. 49857/147–55.

60. 26 Jan. 1905, quoted in Egremont, *The Cousins*, pp. 249–50.

61. 17 Feb. 1905, AJBP/BL 49802/96–100. Balfour wrote to Lord Dudley at this time that, regardless of Wyndham's lapses or MacDonnell's presumptions, no part of the devolution scheme 'had, or could have, the approval of the Government'. 23 Feb. 1905, AJBP/BL Add. MSS. 49802/194–9.

62. 3 Jan. 1905, AJBP/BL Add. MSS. 49805/18.

63. 3 Mar. 1905, AJBP/BL Add. MSS. 49805/33–6. For Wyndham's offer of resignation, see 2, 3 March 1905, AJBP/BL Add. MSS. 49805/20–24, 25–6.

64. 5 Mar. 1905, AJBP/BL Add. MSS. 49805/51–2.

65. 26 Apr. 1905, AJBP/BL Add MSS. 49763/116–20. Wyndham acknowledged this, writing to Gerald Balfour, 'If only I had not failed Arthur by breaking down at a critical moment.' 8 Mar. 1905, AJBP/NLS GD 433/2/281/18.

66. See the letter of St John Brodrick [Lord Midleton] to Blanche Dugdale of 21 May 1927, arguing that the only quality that kept Balfour from greatness as a party leader was that 'he never would tell us when he thought we were going wrong before the mischief was done.' This is a fair criticism, though curious coming from Brodrick, who was not fond of being told when he was 'going wrong'. AJBP/BL Add. MSS. 49836/187.

67. 2 Oct. 1913, AJB to Wilfrid Ward, AJBP/BL Add. MSS. 49863/11–15. Ward, like MacDonnell, was a Roman Catholic.

68. 25 May 1905, AB diary, AJBP/NAS GD 433/1/374. In this entry Alice Balfour noted her view that Arthur overrated Wyndham's ability, and quoted Gerald, who believed that Wyndham neither worked hard enough nor paid sufficient attention to detail. Both evaluations are at least partially correct.

69. Hudson, *Ireland That We Made*, pp. 172–3. See also Balfour's Cabinet letter to the King, 23 Mar. 1905, CAB 41/30/11.

70. 7 Sept. 1906, AJB to Acland-Hood, AJBP/BL Add. MSS. 49771/148–52, 153–63.

71. 8 Oct. 1906, AJB to A. Chamberlain, AJBP/BL Add. MSS. 49735/237–8.

72. 16 Jan. 1932, Hornibrook to Mrs Dugdale, AJBP/BL Add. MSS. 49833/273–6. The secretary's explanation centred on the need of Ulster Unionist MPs for a 'good Home Rule scare' to divert the attention of voters from the appeals of a growing Labour Party.

73. 5 Sept. 1906, AJB to Long, AJBP/BL Add. MSS. 49776/169–71.

74. See the two drafts of Balfour's memorandum reviewing the affair. [C. 1906], AJBP/BL Add. MSS. 49859/1–48, 49–79.

75. 7 Sept. 1906, AJB to Acland-Hood, AJBP/BL Add. MSS. 49771/148–52.

See also his further correspondence with Long on the matter. AJB to Long, 7 Sept. and 1 Oct. 1906, AJBP/BL Add. MSS. 49771/153–63 and 179–80.

76. See Shannon, *Balfour and Ireland*, p. 133.

77. Blake, *Conservative Party*, p. 167. Emphasis in original.

78. Lord George Hamilton – hardly a disinterested bystander in the Tariff Reform battles – insisted that Chamberlain wished to create a great distraction for Liberal Unionists disillusioned over Balfour's Education Act. Lord George Hamilton, *Parliamentary Reminiscences and Reflections* (2 vols., London, 1917), II, p. 315.

79. Richard Rempel, *Unionists Divided: Arthur Balfour, Joseph Chamberlain and the Unionist Free Traders* (Newton Abbot, 1972), p. 17.

80. The registration duty was to be 5*d.* on imported flour and 3*d.* on imported grains.

81. Hicks Beach was particularly opposed to old-age pensions – one of Chamberlain's most desired reforms, and endorsed, if less enthusiastically, by Balfour. Hicks Beach to AJB, 11 July 1902, JSSP MSS. Eng hist. c. 736/100–101.

82. Dugdale, *Balfour*, I, 338–9. See also Alan Sykes, *Tariff Reform in British Politics, 1903–1913* (Oxford, 1979), pp. 30–1.

83. Sykes, *Tariff Reform*, p. 32; Marsh, *Chamberlain*, pp. 540–42.

84. 15 Nov. 1903, CAB 37/63/155.

85. 31 Dec. 1922 (notes by Mrs Dugdale of conversation with AJB), AJBP/BL Add. MSS. 49836/81–2. For Ritchie's position, see Alfred Gollin, *Balfour's Burden: Arthur Balfour and Imperial Preference* (London, 1965), pp. 29–30 and *passim*.

86. Lady Victoria Hicks Beach, *Life of Sir Michael Hicks Beach, Earl of St. Aldwyn* (2 vols., London, 1932), II, p. 188.

87. Marsh, *Chamberlain*, p. 561.

88. Dugdale, *Balfour*, I, p. 343.

89. Ramsden, *Appetite for Power*, p. 179. Middleton was a masterful manager of the party machine, but even he could not prevent the loss of three seats in March, to Labour, Liberal and Independent opponents.

90. 11 July 1905, HH QUI 4/3–4.

91. An excellent exception is E. H. H. Green, whose insightful essay on the subject of Balfour's economic thought is necessary reading to understanding the Prime Minister's position in this crisis. E. H. H. Green, *Ideologies of Conservatism: Conservative Political Ideas in the Twentieth Century* (Oxford, 2004), ch. 1.

92. 'Politics and Political Economy', *National Review*, May 1885; 'Cobden and the Manchester School', *Nineteenth Century*, Jan. 1882. Balfour reprinted these in his *Essays and Addresses* (London, 1893).

93. See Green, *Ideologies of Conservatism*, ch. 1. Richard Cobden, usually identified with his like-minded colleague John Bright, was a mainstay of the Anti-Corn Law League in the 1840s, and a Cobden Club was formed in 1866 to further his Free Trade principles.

94. AJBP/BL Add. MSS. 49836/81–2.
95. 12 May 1903, AJB to King Edward VII, CAB 41/28/8; 16 May 1903, AJB to Knollys, RA VIC/R 23/64. Midleton, who thought the free-standing corn duty politically dangerous, was more sanguine about proposing it as part of a broader programme of 'fiscal reform'. 4 Sept. 1902, JSS to AJB, AJBP/BL Add. MSS. 49761/26–9.
96. Balfour reminded Devonshire later that Chamberlain had told his colleagues on 12 May that he would follow the same line as the Prime Minister promised, 'only in a less definite manner'. 27 Aug. 1903, AJBP/BL Add. MSS. 49770/82–132.
97. 27 May 1905, HH QUI 3/162.
98. See Rempel, *Unionists Divided*, p. 34, and Mackay, *Balfour*, p. 145.
99. 27 May 1903, CAB 41/28/9. See also Gollin, *Balfour's Burden*, pp. 63–4.
100. 9 June 1903, AJB to King Edward VII, CAB 41/28/10.
101. 12 June 1903, AJBP/BL Add. MSS. 49835/118.
102. 4 June 1903, AJBP/BL Add. MSS. 49770/10–23.
103. 9 June 1903, Esher to M. V. Brett, Brett, *Esher Journals*, I, p. 412.
104. 20 July 1903, AJB to H. Cecil, AJBP/BL Add. MSS. 49759/40.
105. The lines were much-printed in their day, and may be found in Sir Charles Petrie, Bt., *Walter Long and His Times* (London, 1936), p. 99.
106. AJBP/BL Add. MSS. 49770/10–23.
107. 10 Nov. 1903, CHAR 2/9/31–3.
108. 16 July 1903, HH QUI 1/108–12.
109. See Gollin, *Balfour's Burden*, pp. 89–90. For Balfour's voluminous correspondence with Ashley, see AJBP/BL Add. MSS. 49780.
110. AJBP/BL Add. MSS. 49770/29–33; Rempel, *Unionists Divided*, p. 50; P. Jackson, *Last of the Whigs*, p. 329.
111. Koss, *Political Press*, II, pp. 29–30, 32.
112. JSSP MSS. Eng. hist. c. 740/129–45.
113. JSSP MSS. Eng. hist. c. 740/123–5. Marked 'Confidential'.
114. 12 Aug. 1903, AJBP/BP Add. MSS. 49770/34–57.
115. Rempel, *Unionists Divided*, p. 52.
116. 9 Nov. 1931, A. Chamberlain to BD, AJBP/BL 49833/151–6. The date of this recollection is unclear: Chamberlain recalls it as Feb. 1902, and the paper forwarded to Mrs Dugdale is dated Nov. 1904.
117. 5 Aug. 1903, quoted in Rempel, *Unionists Divided*, p. 51.
118. 9 Nov. 1931, A. Chamberlain to BD, AJBP/BL Add. MSS. 49833/151–6.
119. 27 Aug. 1903, AJBP/BL Add. MSS. 49770/66–81. On 6 Sept. 1903, Balfour sent the Duke a paper further advocating imperial preference and tariff retaliation, and two days later Gerald Balfour forwarded a Board of Trade scheme outlining a system to implement preference, including food taxes. Devonshire was unconvinced. Rempel, *Unionists Divided*, p. 55.
120. 27 Aug. 1903, AJBP/BL Add. MSS. 49770/ 82–132.
121. 29 Aug. 1903, JSSP MSS Eng hist. c. 740/199–202.
122. 15 Aug. 1903, quoted in P. Jackson, *Last of the Whigs*, p. 330.

123. Roberts, *Salisbury*, pp. 831–2.
124. 25 Aug. 1903, AJBP/BL Add. MSS. 49835/123; Ridley and Percy, eds., *Balfour–Elcho Letters*, pp. 204–5. Ironically, Balfour was called away just before the Marquess expired, in order to attend the funeral of Salisbury's sister, Lady Galloway.
125. 9 Sept. 1903, JSSP MSS. Eng. hist. c. 741/91–8. There is an earlier draft of this letter in the Sandars Papers, MSS. Eng. hist. c. 741/85–90. For Chamberlain's position see Marsh, *Chamberlain*, pp. 575–7.
126. 11 Sept. 1903, JSSP MSS. Eng. hist. c. 741/128–31. See also his related letter to Sandars, 11 Sept. 1903, JSSP MSS. Eng. hist. c. 741/125–6.
127. 15 Sept. 1903, Devonshire to AJB, AJBP/BL Add. MSS. 49770/182–7; 15 Sept. 1903, AJB to King Edward VII, RA VIC/R 23/84. See also Rempel, *Unionists Divided*, pp. 58–9.
128. Rempel, *Unionists Divided*, p. 57; Gollin, *Balfour's Burden*, pp. 23–6.
129. 14 Sept. 1903, Cabinet Resolution, JSSP MSS. Eng. hist. c. 741/154–5. This is written in Balfour's hand.
130. 12 Aug. 1903, Acland-Hood to AJB, JSSP MSS. Eng. hist c. 740/164–8.
131. JSSP MSS. Eng. hist. c. 740/163.
132. 14 Aug. 1903, CAB 41/28/14. Emphasis added.
133. On 15 Sept. 1903 Balfour explained his conclusion to the King that, desirable as imperial preference might be, it almost certainly would break up his party and even destroy any hope of securing tariff retaliation. RA VIC/R 23/84. At the dramatic Cabinet meeting, he also requested acquiescence to the publication of 'Economic Notes'.
134. JSSP MSS. Eng. hist. c. 764/233–42. Sandars's narrative memorandum is in two parts: the initial portion of this paper is dated 14 Sept. 1903 but deals with events on subsequent days; the latter part is undated.
135. 21 Sept. 1903, JSS to Selborne, SP 1/20–25.
136. Randolph S. Churchill, *Lord Derby, 'King of Lancashire': the Official Life of Edward, Seventeenth Earl of Derby, 1865–1948* (London, 1959), pp. 79–81; P. Jackson, *Last of the Whigs*, p. 338.
137. JSSP MSS. Eng. hist. c. 764/233–42.
138. *The Times*, 2 Oct. 1903.
139. 5 Nov. 1903, AJB to Sir Samuel Hoare, AJBP/BL Add. MSS. 49856/11. Sir Samuel was Unionist MP for Norwich and the father of the future Lord Templewood.
140. JSSP MSS. Eng. hist. c. 764/233–42.
141. John Dunville, Devonshire's secretary, wrote to Sandars, 3 Oct. 1903, denying that the resignation was hastened by pressure from the Free Trade ministers. Sandars rejected this contention, and quoted Stanley as testifying that Dunville also advised the Duke to resign. JSSP MSS. Eng. hist. c. 743/83–4.
142. 'But', he added, 'I suppose that's written in some book.' 31 Dec. 1922, notes by Mrs Dugdale, AJBP/BL Add. MSS. 49836/81–2.
143. P. Jackson, *Last of the Whigs*, p. 340.

144. 4 Oct. 1903, JSSP MSS. Eng. hist. c. 715/140–45.
145. N.d. [4 Oct. 1903?], WLP Add. MSS. 62403/135–8.
146. *National Union Gleanings*, vol. 21 (1903), p. 293.
147. 23 May 1899, AJB to FB, AJBP/BL Add. MSS. 49831/227–33.
148. Milner remained the darling of imperialists and was admired by the King. His Majesty was upset with him, however, for refusing the Cabinet appointment. 1 Oct. 1903, King Edward VII to AJB, RA VIC/R 23/100.
149. The Lord Presidency demanded a politician of suitable social as well as political rank, and, though Londonderry was not considered a strong appointment, Balfour had few options. The Marquess, a known tariff sceptic, therefore required the Prime Minister's firm pledge that there would be no food duties in the near future. 11 Oct. 1903, AJB to Londonderry, LONP D 2846/3/9/45.
150. 11 Oct. 1903, Esher to M. V. Brett, Brett, ed., *Esher Journals*, II, p. 27.
151. 13 Oct. 1903, CAB 37/66/64. Emphasis in original.
152. P. Jackson, *Last of the Whigs*, p. 343.
153. 28 May 1899, Blunt, *Diaries*, I, p. 322.
154. Mackay, *Balfour*, p. 198. Six more Unionists defected during Balfour's leadership of the Opposition.
155. David Dutton, *His Majesty's Loyal Opposition: The Unionist Party in Opposition, 1905–1915* (Liverpool, 1992), p. 7.
156. 21 Feb. 1904, AJBP/BL Add. MSS. 49762/75–81. The Tariff Commission, with W. A. S. Hewins as its secretary, was the pioneering information-gathering agency of the Tariff Reform campaign.
157. See Lucy, *Balfourian Parliament*, pp. 296–8.
158. See Remple, *Unionists Divided*, p. 121.
159. 3 Nov. 1905, AJB to A. Chamberlain, AJBP/BL Add. MSS. 49735/207.
160. 10 Sept. 1904, AJBP/BL Add. MSS. 49735/103–11.
161. 12 Sept. 1904, AJBP/BL Add. MSS. 49735/112–16.
162. 22 Sept. 1904, AJBP/BL Add. MSS. 49735/134–5.
163. He had outlined portions of this to Austen Chamberlain on 10 Sept. 1904, leaving out the plan for a second electoral test of tariffs. Add. MSS. AJBP/BL Add. MSS. 49735/103–11.
164. *The Times*, 4 Oct. 1903.
165. 16 Oct. 1904, JSS to AJB, AJBP/BL Add. MSS. 49762/162–3.
166. 9 Dec. 1904, AJB to H. Cecil, HH QUI 2/148–55.
167. *The Times*, 27 Jan. 1905.
168. 18 Feb. 1905, AJB to J. Chamberlain, AJBP/BL Add. MSS. 49794/61–5.
169. Rempel, *Unionists Divided*, p. 127.
170. Sykes, *Tariff Reform*, pp. 88–9.
171. Rempel, *Unionists Divided*, p. 133.
172. Marsh, *Chamberlain*, p. 625.
173. 2 Nov. 1905, AJBP/BL Add. MSS. 49774/94–101.

CHAPTER 9: DIVIDED OPPOSITION

1. Mackay, *Balfour*, pp. 192–3.
2. 27 Oct. 1905, AJBP/BL Add. MSS. 49770/205–14.
3. Mackay, *Balfour*, pp. 185–6.
4. 2 Feb. 1901, AJB to Iwan-Müller, I-MP Add. MSS. 51316/29; AJB to AB, Dugdale, *Balfour*, II, p. 438.
5. 10 Nov. 1903, Campbell-Bannerman to John Ellis, CBP Add. MSS. 41214/131. See John Wilson, *CB: A Life of Sir Henry Campbell-Bannerman* (New York, 1974), p. 414.
6. Leo McInstry, *Rosebery: Statesman in Turmoil* (London, 2005), pp. 469–70; Mackay, *Balfour*, pp. 224–5.
7. 14 Nov. 1903, memorandum by A. Lyttelton, JSSP MSS. Eng. hist. c. 746/17–20.
8. 21 Sept. 1905, AJB to Selborne, SP 1/66–7; 20 Oct. 1905, AJB to A. Lyttelton, AJBP/BL Add. MSS. 49775/51; 15 Sept. 1905, AJB to Salisbury, AJBP/BL Add. MSS. 49758/46–8. Balfour acknowledged the electoral cost to the Unionists, 17 Jan. 1906, AJB to Knollys, RA VIC/W 64/73.
9. 8 Jan. 1906, AJB to R. Cecil, AJBP/BL Add. MSS. 49737/136–8.
10. 14 Jan. 1906, AJBP/BL Add. MSS. 49758/91.
11. 17 Jan. 1906, ACP AC 7/2/1. He wrote similarly on the same day to Lady Salisbury, AJBP/BL Add. MSS. 49758/92–3, and to Esher, AJBP/BL Add. MSS. 49719/52; and Knollys, 17 Jan. 1905, AJBP/BL Add. MSS. 49685/94.
12. Regarding Balfour's fatigue after a decade in office, see the recollection of Lord Midleton to Mrs Dugdale, 9 Dec. 1930, AJBP/BL Add. MSS. 49833/42–5.
13. Dugdale, *Balfour*, II, p. 13.
14. AJB to R. Cecil, HH CHE 84/93.
15. 26 Jan. 1906, AJB to JSS, JSSP MSS. Eng. hist. c. 751/124–6.
16. Diary entry of 26 Jan. 1906, Vincent, ed., *Crawford Papers*, pp. 88–9.
17. 7 Feb. 1906, AJBP/BL Add. MSS. 49709/26.
18. 5 Feb. 1906, JSS to Iwan-Müller, I-MP Add. MSS. 51316/77–81; 6 Feb. 1906, AJB to Lansdowne, LP (5) 13.
19. 8 Feb. 1906, AJB to J. Chamberlain, AJBP/BL Add. MSS. 49774/128–30; 6 Feb. 1906, AJB to J. Chamberlain, AJBP/BL Add. MSS. 49774/120–24.
20. Marsh, *Chamberlain*, pp. 635–6.
21. 10 Feb. 1906, J. Chamberlain to AJB, AJBP/BL Add. MSS. 49774/133–41; AJB to J. Chamberlain, AJBP/BL Add. MSS. 49774/142–3. 14 Feb. 1906, GB to BB, AJBP/NAS GD 433/2/117/8. Emphasis in original.
22. 14 Feb. 1906, AJB to J. Chamberlain, AJBP/BL Add. MSS. 49774/147–53. The reply of the same date is AJBP/BL Add. MSS. 49774/154.
23. Diary entry of 15 Feb. 1906, Vincent, ed., *Crawford Papers*, p. 92.
24. 15 Feb. 1906, AJBP/BL 49706/317–18.
25. Diary entry of 10 Feb. 1906, Vincent, ed., *Crawford Papers*, p. 92; Egremont, *Balfour*, p. 210.

26. The son-in-law of Alexander Beresford-Hope, Gibbs succeeded his father as
Lord Aldenham eighteen months later. Though Balfour wished that no
pressure be placed on Gibbs to vacate the seat, from the day of his
Manchester defeat he himself had been pursued by influential City men
about taking it. 23 Jan. 1906, Sir Joseph Lawrence to AJB, AJBP/BL Add.
MSS. 49791/173–6; 17 Jan. 1906, AJB to Acland-Hood, AJBP/BL Add.
MSS. 49771/132–3; 20 Jan. 1906, AJB to Salisbury, AJBP/BL Add. MSS.
49758/96–7.

27. 2 Mar. 1906, AJB to Morley, AJBP/BL Add. MSS. 49778/153.

28. 13 Mar. 1906; J. Wilson, *CB*, p. 497.

29. 5 Feb. 1906, Akers-Douglas to JSS, JSSP MSS. Eng. hist. c. 751/181.

30. For the 'Confederacy', see Larry L. Witherell, *Rebel on the Right: Henry
Page Croft and the Crisis of British Conservatism, 1903–1914* (Newark, Del.,
1997), chs. 4–5. Though insufficiently powerful to topple their leader, the
candidates caused him much annoyance. See, for example, his letter to
Austen Chamberlain, whom many erroneously thought to be a Confederate,
of 23 Oct. 1907, AJBP/BL Add. MSS. 49736/18–20.

31. Dutton, *His Majesty's Loyal Opposition*, p. 27.

32. Appointment of the latter committee enjoyed Sandars's and Akers-Douglas's
support. 25 Dec. 1910, JSS to AJB, Jan. 1906, Akers-Douglas to AJB,
AJBP/BL Add. MSS. 49772/38–40, 49767/58–61.

33. Marsh, *Chamberlain*, pp. 644–7.

34. 4 Mar. 1907, JSS to WS, AJBP/BL Add. MSS. 49765/33. Emphasis in original.

35. Dutton, *His Majesty's Loyal Opposition*, p. 130.

36. Ramsden, *Appetite for Power*, p. 206.

37. See 'Introduction to Science of Pol.[itics]: Miscellaneous Notes', AJBP/BL
Add. MSS. 49961/196–206.

38. 24 Jan. 1907, AJB to JSS, AJBP/BL Add. MSS. 49765/23–5.

39. 15 Jan. 1906. Regarding his aversion to alternative legislative programmes,
see Dugdale, *Balfour*, II, pp. 43–5.

40. See Roy Jenkins, *Mr Balfour's Poodle: An Account of the Struggle between the
House of Lords and the Government of Mr Asquith* (London, 1954), p. 24.

41. 5 Apr. 1906, memorandum by Lord Lansdowne; Newton, *Lansdowne*, p. 353.

42. 13 Apr. 1906, AJB to Lansdowne, AJBP/BL Add. MSS. 49729/228–30;
Newton, *Lansdowne*, p. 354.

43. N.d. [1907], unsigned and unaddressed, but AJB to Lansdowne, AJBP/BL
Add. MSS. 49729/303. To the King, Balfour advocated the granting of life
peerages for distinguished public service, in place of the extant hereditary
system. 1 Dec. 1905, AJBP/BL Add. MSS. 49865/70–72.

44. Balfour would not budge from his conviction that there must be 'no change
in any school except on the initiative of the parents of the requisite number
of children'. 10 July 1906, AJB to Salisbury, HH 4M 58/64–6.

45. Newton, *Lansdowne*, p. 359.

46. See Zebel, *Balfour*, pp. 151–2.

420

47. 26 June 1907, Grigg, *Lloyd George: People's Champion*, p. 154.

48. J. Wilson, *CB*, pp. 562–3.

49. He was no longer premier when he died, having resigned in favour of Asquith shortly before.

50. 2 Mar. 1908, AJB to the Poet Laureate [Alfred Austin], AJBP/BL Add. MSS. 49859/232.

51. Adams and Poirier, *Conscription Controversy*, pp. 34–5.

52. 29 May 1908, Esher to the King, Brett, ed., *Esher Journals*, II, pp. 316–17. He wrote similarly to Sandars on the following day, JSSP MSS. Eng. hist. c. 756/156–7.

53. In Nov. 1905, before he knew that responsibility for army reform would soon fall to him, Haldane admitted, 'I don't envy the man who has got that job.' Edward M. Spiers, *Haldane: An Army Reformer* (Edinburgh, 1980), p. 47.

54. Mackay, *Balfour*, pp. 185–6.

55. Haldane, *Autobiography*, pp. 193–4.

56. See, for example, 11 Mar. 1909, Haldane to AJB, AJBP/BL Add. MSS. 49724/100–103. For Balfour's support for Haldane's reforms, see 30 June 1908, draft letter by AJB, marked 'not sent', AJBP/BL Add. MSS. 49859/253–5.

57. J. Wilson, *CB*, pp. 547–8. The letter became public and, predictably, very unpopular. Lord Tweedmouth's mind was failing, and he would soon be replaced by Reginald McKenna.

58. Britain traditionally sought to maintain a fleet of strength equal to that of its next two largest naval rivals combined. See Balfour's unconvincing qualification of his 'blue-water' views to Lord Roberts. 27 Oct. 1908, RP 7101–23/8. For the Unionist campaign on naval policy, see Williams, *Defending the Empire*, ch. 7.

59. Ibid., p. 89.

60. Journal entry of 14 Mar. 1907, Brett, ed., *Esher Journals*, II, p. 295.

61. For example, see 20 Oct. 1904, AJB to 'Clan' (Lansdowne), AJBP/BL Add. MSS. 49835/163.

62. With the political battle over shipbuilding in the offing, in late 1907 Fisher forwarded to Balfour secret Admiralty reports on the sea trials of *Dreadnought* and wished him 'a happy Christmas and the pulverisation of all your enemies'. 23 Dec. 1907, J. A. Fisher to AJB, AJBP/BL Add. MSS. 49712/23–7.

63. 15 Mar. 1909, AJBP/BL Add. MSS. 49719/76–7, memorandum by Sandars, marked 'Secret'.

64. N.d. [8 July 1909?] Carson to Lady Londonderry, ECP D/2846/1/32. Britain retained its lead in dreadnought-building, and when war came its force stood at nineteen – three more than the German navy's.

65. Jenkins, *Mr Balfour's Poodle*, pp. 74–5.

66. Dangerfield, *Strange Death of Liberal England*, p. 20.

67. See Grigg, *Lloyd George: People's Champion*, pp. 79–80.

68. Neal Blewett, *The Peers, the Parties and the People: The British General Elections of 1910* (Toronto, 1972), p. 74.

69. For the painful progress of the bill through the House, see Jenkins, *Mr Balfour's Poodle*, pp. 80–84.

70. Ibid., p. 81.

71. Ibid., p. 83.

72. See Grigg, *Lloyd George: People's Champion*, pp. 203–6.

73. Diary entry of 24 July 1909, Brett, ed., *Esher Journals*, II, p. 395.

74. Raymond, *Balfour*, p. 139.

75. See Bruce K. Murray, *The People's Budget 1909/10: Lloyd George and Liberal Politics* (Oxford, 1980), p. 210 and ch. 8. See also Alfred M. Gollin, *The Observer and J. L. Garvin: A Study in a Great Editorship* (Oxford, 1960), pp. 115–16.

76. Gollin, *Garvin*, p. 117.

77. 20 Sept. 1909, ACP AC 4/1/449.

78. Grigg, *Lloyd George: People's Champion*, p. 231; Almeric Fitzroy, *Memoirs* (2 vols., London, 1925), I, p. 389.

79. 9 Sept. 1909, Esher to JSS, Brett, ed., *Esher Journals*, II, p. 407; Murray, *People's Budget*, p. 217.

80. Murray, *People's Budget*, p. 219.

81. Egremont, *Balfour*, p. 222.

82. 15 Feb. 1910, JSSP MSS. Eng. hist. c. 760/47–50.

83. 3 Mar. 1910, Sir Austen Chamberlain, *Politics from Inside: An Epistolary Chronicle, 1906–1914* (London, 1936), p. 220.

84. See Blewett, *Peers, Parties and the People*, pp. 108–9.

85. Journal entry 9 May 1909, Brett, ed., *Esher Journals*, II, pp. 386–7. Balfour added, 'He is really clever.'

86. Gollin, *Garvin*, p. 185; R. J. Q. Adams, *Bonar Law* (London, 1999), p. 40.

87. 9 June 1910, Asquith to AJB, AJBP/BL Add. MSS. 49692/101. Austen Chamberlain retained his notes of the proceedings and other related papers. ACP AC 10/2/35–85.

88. For the conference see John D. Fair, *British Interparty Conferences: A Study of the Procedure of Conciliation in British Politics, 1867–1921* (Oxford, 1980), and Corinne Comstock Weston, 'The Liberal Leadership and the Lords' Veto, 1907–1910', *Historical Journal*, 11 (1968). Neither the Labour Party nor the Irish Nationalists were invited to send delegates, but the presence of Lloyd George and Birrell, the Irish Secretary, presumably was meant to ensure that their interests were represented.

89. Grigg, *Lloyd George: People's Champion*, p. 264.

90. Several early drafts of the memorandum, as well as copies of the final version, dated 17 Aug. 1910, may be found in LGP C/16/9.

91. 21 Oct. 1910, A. Chamberlain to Lord Cawdor, ACP AC 10/2/15.

92. 29 Jan. 1915, memorandum by Austen Chamberlain, ACP AC 13/2/2. Sandars preserved an empty envelope inscribed, 'Coalition proposals by Lloyd George', JSSP MSS. Eng hist. c. 762/300. Certainly Austen Chamberlain informed his father of the famous memorandum; Acland-Hood probably knew of it, as did Akers-Douglas. For the Liberals who were

informed, see Grigg, *Lloyd George: People's Champion*, pp. 267–8, and also *War Memoirs of David Lloyd George* (London, 2 vol. edn, 1936), I, p. 22. Chamberlain did not receive a copy of the memorandum until 1915, and it was later published for the first time in Sir Charles Petrie, *The Life and Letters of Austen Chamberlain* (2 vols., London, 1939–40), I, pp. 381–8.

93. This, from the recollections of Major J. A. Hills, MP, in Dugdale, *Balfour*, II, p. 75.

94. Grigg, *Lloyd George: People's Champion*, p. 271. For the federalist movement, see John Kendle, *Ireland and the Federal Solution: The Debate over the United Kingdom Constitution, 1870–1921* (Kingston, Ont., 1989), and Jeremy Smith, *The Tories and Ireland, 1910–1914* (Dublin, 2000), pp. 22–30.

95. Lloyd George, *War Memoirs*, I, p. 23. Akers-Douglas insisted that, while Balfour sought his advice, the leader had had no trouble reaching the decision to reject the memorandum. Chilston, *Chief Whip*, pp. 344–5.

96. 22 Oct. 1910, AJB to AC, AJBP/BL Add. MSS. 49736/97–9.

97. Dugdale, *Balfour*, II, p. 76.

98. 22 Oct. 1910, AJB to Garvin, AJBP/BL Add. MSS. 49795/100–109. He wrote similarly to A. Chamberlain on the same day, AJBP/BL Add. MSS. 49736/97–9.

99. Dugdale, *Balfour*, II, p. 77.

100. 10 Nov. 1910, 'The Constitutional Conference, Memorandum by Mr Balfour', CAB 37/104/60.

101. Harold Nicolson, *King George the Fifth: His Life and Reign* (New York, 1953), pp. 138–9; Kenneth Rose, *King George V* (New York, 1984), pp. 124–5, where it is noted that the monarch harboured a 'lifelong grievance' over the affair.

102. 25 Apr. 1910, Esher to AJB, AJBP/BL Add. MSS. 49719/143.

103. 27 Apr. 1910, memorandum by Esher, Brett, ed., *Esher Journals*, II, pp. 457–9.

104. 9 Oct. 1910, RA PS/GV/K/2552/2/88; G. H. L. LeMay, *The Victorian Constitution* (London, 1979), p. 201; Rose, *George V*, pp. 123–4.

105. 29 Aug. 1910, ECP D/2846/1/52.

106. Quoted in J. Smith, *Tories and Ireland*, p. 31. His letter to Selborne of 17 Aug. 1911 was even less restrained and called upon the former First Lord to form an alternative party organization. SP 74/182–3.

107. 25 Oct. 1910, Hyde, *Carson*, p. 279.

108. See, for example, 16 Oct. 1910, Alfred Lyttelton to AJB, AJBP/BL Add. MSS. 49736/106–7.

109. 18 Oct. 1910, AJBP/BL Add. MSS. 49767/13–17.

110. N.d. [6 Nov. 1910], ECP D/2846/1/57.

111. Gollin, *Garvin*, pp. 229–30.

112. Adams, *Bonar Law*, pp. 43–4. For the referendum idea see Corinne Comstock Weston, *The House of Lords and Ideological Politics: Lord Salisbury's Referendal Theory and the Conservative Party, 1846–1922* (Philadelphia, 1995).

113. Blewett, *Peers, Parties and the People*, p. 177.

114. Adams, *Bonar Law*, p. 44.

115. 29 Nov. 1910, AJBP/BL Add. MSS. 49736/122–4.

116. Adams, *Bonar Law*, pp. 44–7.

117. *The Times*, 2 Dec. 1910.

118. The editor Leopold Maxse wrote to Bonar Law that the pledge was 'nothing less than a crime', while Lansdowne argued to Balfour that, if the whole-hoggers believed in both Tariff Reform and the referendum theory, 'can they reasonably object to test the one by the other?' 14 Dec. 1910, BLP 18/6/145; 28 Nov. 1910, AJBP/BL Add. MSS. 49730/132–3.

119. He did fall ill near the close of the campaign. 17 Dec. 1910, AJB to JSS, AJBP/BL Add. MSS. 49767/42–3, and 26 Dec. 1910, AJB to Long, AJBP/BL Add. MSS. 49777/77.

120. John Ramsden, *The Age of Balfour and Baldwin, 1902–1940* (London, 1978), pp. 58–61. The committee included Lords Selborne and Willoughby de Broke; MPs Long, Arthur Steel-Maitland, Edward Goulding, Ralph Glyn and George Younger; and regional party leaders Sutton Nettlefold and Archibald Salvidge.

121. 10 Jan. 1911, AJBP/BL Add. MSS. 49719/179–82, 'Note of the conversation after Dinner at the Marlborough Club on January 9th 1911'; this is printed in Oliver, 3rd Viscount Esher, ed., *Journals and Letters of Reginald Viscount Esher*, (vols. 3 and 4, London, 1938), III, pp. 40–44. He expressed the same thought in a letter to Lansdowne of 27 Dec. 1910, LP Lans (5) 83. Balfour's anger was rooted in his belief that he had been manipulated by Knollys. See 9 Aug. 1911, AJB to Stamfordham, RA PS/GV/K 2552/2/56, and 18 Aug. 1911, Stamfordham to King George V, RA PS/GV/K 2553/3/77.

122. This was confirmed in a talk with Lloyd George. 18 July 1911, AJBP/BL Add. MSS. 49730/243–8.

123. 6 July 1911, memorandum by Balcarres, Vincent, ed., *Crawford Papers*, p. 190. Balfour's learning of the King's guarantee from Esher is confirmed by Balcarres's diary entry of 18 July 1911, ibid., p. 194.

124. 9 Aug. 1911, RA PS/GV/K 2552/2/56.

125. For a time, Knollys contemplated that in future the two would 'meet as strangers'. The most heated letters between them, of 7–8 Sept. 1911, are in AJBP/BL Add. MSS. 49686/77–82. They did, however, finally agree to end the quarrel. 10–11 Sept. 1911, AJBP/BL Add. MSS. 49686/83–91; 9 Nov. 1911, WS to AB, AJBP/BL Add. MSS. 49832/209.

126. Diary entry of 21 July 1911, Vincent, ed., *Crawford Papers*, p. 196. Ditchers were also known as 'Blue Blooders' and Hedgers as 'White Flaggers' or 'Blue Funkers'. 16, 24 July 1911, Bull diary, WBP 4/4.

127. Even his sympathetic biographer Lord Newton concluded that Lansdowne failed to give a strong lead to his colleagues and that the meeting was rather confused. Newton, *Lansdowne*, p. 423.

128. Diary entry of 24 July 1911, Vincent., ed., *Crawford Papers*, pp. 198–9; Philip Williamson, ed., *The Modernisation of Conservative Politics: The Diaries and Letters of William Bridgeman, 1904–1935* (London, 1988), p. 46. Balcarres had

heard rumours of the demonstration in advance, but his 'hurried interviews' with the militants had not deterred them.

129. 25 July 1911, P. Williamson, ed., *Bridgeman Diaries*, p. 46.
130. 1 Aug. 1911, Balcarres's 'Notes', Vincent, ed., *Crawford Papers*, pp. 208–9.
131. 22 July 1911, AJBP/BL Add. MSS. 49767/206–7.
132. 30 July 1911, AJBP/BL Add. MSS. 49836/80–81.
133. *The Times*, 26 July 1911. Lansdowne circulated a similar memorandum to the Unionist peers on 24 July. GNCP MSS. Eur. F 112/89.
134. See Dangerfield, *Strange Death*, pp. 61–5.
135. Nicolson, *George the Fifth*, p. 155. The act was enforced only seven times during the twentieth century.
136. See 27 July 1911, Arnold Ward to Curzon, forwarded to AJB, GNCP MSS. Eur. F 112/89; 11, 14 Aug. 1911, JSS to AJB, AJBP/BL Add. MSS. 49767/152–4, 155–61; and diary entry of 8 Aug. 1911, Vincent, ed., *Crawford Papers*, p. 214.
137. 14 Aug. 1911, AJBP/BL Add. MSS. 49832/204–8.
138. 6 July 1907, AJB to Lord Dalkeith, AJBP/BL Add. MSS. 49859/158–9. In the same vein, see 16 July 1907, AJB to [James?] Wanklyn, AJBP/BL Add. MSS. 49859/160–61.
139. 9 Aug. 1911, Note: 'Conversation with A.J.B.', Vincent, ed., *Crawford Papers*, p. 215. Emphasis in original.
140. Sept 1911, 'A Diary of the Events and Transactions in connection with the passage of the Parliament Bill of 1911 through the House of Lords', AJBP/BL Add. MSS. 49767/184–259.
141. Ridley and Percy, eds., *Balfour–Elcho Letters*, pp. 269–70.
142. 19 Aug. 1911, A. Chamberlain to Mary Chamberlain, ACP AC 4/1/674.
143. Diary entry of 16 Aug. 1911, Vincent, ed., *Crawford Papers*, p. 219. Short concluded similarly, choosing the word 'connivance'. AJBP/BL Add. MSS. 49832/204–8.
144. 6 Feb. 1911, Balcarres to Lady Wantage, Vincent, ed., *Crawford Papers*, p. 175.
145. 24, 25 July 1911, Bull diary, WBP 4/4.
146. For the campaign, see Hutcheson, *Maxse*, ch. 9. The editor's final judgement of Balfour was that he was a 'cynical philosopher'. 29 July 1911, Maxse to Derby, R. Churchill, *Derby*, pp. 123–5.
147. During the entire period of his party leadership, Balfour believed that much harm had been done by hostility within the Unionist press. See 5 Nov. 1907, AJB to William Kenyon-Slaney, AJBP/BL Add. MSS. 49859/201–2.
148. 25 July 1911, 'Note' by Balcarres, Vincent, ed., *Crawford Papers*, pp. 200–201.
149. 30 Sept. 1911, memorandum by Lord Balcarres, ibid., p. 224.
150. 29 Sept. 1911, JSSP MSS. Eng. hist. c. 764/128–37. The memorandum is printed in Petrie, *Long*, pp. 165–7.
151. Carson, Austen Chamberlain, Robert and Hugh Cecil, Milner and Wyndham were members, and the Club's chief organizers were Selborne and Willoughby de Broke. SP 75.
152. 8 Nov. 1911, JSSP MSS. Eng. hist. c. 764/157–73.

153. For Croft's campaign, see Witherell, *Rebel on the Right*, ch. 8.
154. 8 Oct. 1911, AJB to ME, Ridley and Percy, eds., *Balfour–Elcho Letters*, p. 278.
155. 2 Oct. 1911, memorandum by Balcarres, Vincent, ed., *Crawford Papers*, pp. 228–9. Balfour denied to Sandars on 5 Oct. that his mind was absolutely resolved on resignation, but confessed that he was 'extremely anxious' to do so. JSSP MSS. Eng. hist. c. 764/124–5.
156. Diary entry of 15 Oct. 1911, Vincent, ed., *Crawford Papers*, pp. 231–2.
157. Ridley and Percy, eds., *Balfour–Elcho Letters*, p. 278.
158. Also present were St Aldwyn, in the chair, the Duke of Devonshire and Lords Chilston, Curzon, Derby, Londonderry and Midleton, as well as Chaplin, Lyttelton and Steel-Maitland. N.d., memorandum by Walter Long, WLP Add. MSS. 62415/224.
159. Diary entry of 9 Nov. 1911, Vincent, ed., *Crawford Papers*, p. 243. Balcarres's informant was Claude Hay, MP for Hoxton. Short accompanied Balfour, but Sandars could not bear to witness the proceedings. 9 Nov. 1911, WS to AB, AJBP/BL Add. MSS. 49832/209
160. The speech may be found in *Opinions and Arguments from Speeches and Addresses of the Earl of Balfour*, ed. Blanche Dugdale (London, 1927), pp. 1–11.

CHAPTER 10: THE LAMPS GO OUT

1. 8 Nov. 1911 AJB to Midleton, AJBP/BL Add. MSS. 49721/293–4. Examples of the flood of letters of condolence may be seen in the Balfour Papers. AJBP/BL Add. MSS. 49862. The Prime Minister's wife, Margot Asquith, insisted that she was in tears at the news. 9 Nov. 1911, AJBP/BL Add. MSS. 49794/129030.
2. 9 Nov. 1911, WS to AB, AJBP/BL Add. MSS. 49832/209.
3. 10 Nov. 1911, 19 Nov. 1912, Ridley and Percy, ed., *Balfour–Elcho Letters*, pp. 285, 293.
4. 11 Jan. 1912, AJBP/BL Add. MSS. 49768/14–15. In this letter, Sandars also requested Balfour's intercession with Lord Rothschild regarding a seat on the board of directors of one of the Rothschild companies. See also 8 Jan. 1912, JSS to AJB, AJBP/BL Add. MSS. 49768/12–13.
5. AJBP/BL Add. MSS. 49768 contains their later correspondence.
6. 8 Nov. 1911, Wyndham to AJB, AJBP/BL Add. MSS. 49806/102–104; 15 June 1913, Percy Wyndham to AJB, BL Add. MSS. 49806/106–10. See also Mackail and Wyndham, *Wyndham Letters*, II, pp. 124–5.
7. MGP Add. MSS. 46270/174–200. Balfour corroborated this sad episode in a note to Lady Elcho written later on 5 July 1913. Ridley and Percy, eds., *Balfour–Elcho Letters*, p. 303.
8. 6 Dec. 1913, Ridley and Percy, eds., *Balfour–Elcho Letters*, p. 307.
9. In a letter to Lord Morley, Esher insisted: 'There are no serious misstatements of fact in Sir Sidney Lee's article.' 16 Aug. 1912, Esher, ed., *Esher Journals*, III, pp. 104–5

10. 3 Dec. 1912, Sir Arthur Davidson to Sir Dighton Probyn, RA GV/GG 9/183.
11. 24 Nov. 1911, SLP Add. MSS. 56087A/7–9.
12. 4 Dec. 1912, Fritz Ponsonby to Probyn, RA GV/GG 9/188; 22 Nov. 1913, Sir Arthur Davidson to JSS, RA GV/GG 9/331. Balfour's correspondence concerning the affair may be found in AJBP/BL Add. MSS. 49685/128–202.
13. 20 Nov. 1913, JSS to Davidson, RA GV/GG 9/330.
14. 11 Jan. 1915, AJBP/BL Add. MSS. 49730/275–6.
15. 25 Jan. 1915, AJBP/BL Add. MSS. 49863/286–9.
16. See 8 Nov. 1911, Balcarres to JSS, JSSP MSS. Eng. hist. c. 764/153. At that time, only a current or former premier was designated as leader of the entire Unionist Party, so Balfour's successor technically led the party only in his own House of Parliament.
17. For an hour-by-hour record of the events of 8–13 Nov. 1911, see Balcarres's journal, Vincent, ed., *Crawford Papers*, pp. 242–50. For Bonar Law's part in the episode, see Adams, *Bonar Law*, pp. 57–65. Sandars wrote to Balfour, 'It was rather a clever move on Austen's part, because he forced Walter's hand.' 10 Nov. 1911, AJBP/BL Add. MSS. 49767/318–20. Marked 'Very Confidential'.
18. 13 Nov. 1911, P. Williamson, ed., *Bridgeman Diaries*, p. 54. Copies of the minutes of the meeting may be found in BLP 24/3/69. Sandars retained the record of events kept by Henry Chaplin, who chaired the meeting. To this the secretary attached his own comment that these perpetrated a 'gross travesty' about the details of the Chamberlain–Long compromise. AJBP/BL Add. MSS. 49772/285–9.
19. New Brunswick did not become a part of Canada until Confederation in 1867. Bonar Law, who was adopted as a child by his late mother's Glasgow relatives, remains the only British premier born outside the UK. It is also worth noting that both he and Campbell-Bannerman were graduates of the famous Glasgow High School.
20. 11 Nov. 1911, BLP 117/1/17.
21. Diary entry of 29 Mar. 1912, Vincent, ed., *Crawford Papers*, p. 269. After becoming leader, Bonar Law continued his habit of writing frequently to his predecessor in his own hand; when Balfour insisted he abandon this courtesy and revert to using dictation, Bonar Law gladly complied. 19 Dec. 1911, AJB to BL, AJBP/BL Add. MSS. 49693/21–2.
22. 5 Dec. 1916, AB diary, AJBP/NAS GD 433/1/374.
23. 15 Nov. 1911, Esher, ed., *Esher Journals*, III, p. 73.
24. 22 Dec. 1912, AJBP/BL Add. MSS. 49743/36–7.
25. 20 Dec. 1912, AJBP/BL Add. MSS. 49743/33–5.
26. Diary entry of 22 Oct. 1912, Vincent, ed., *Crawford Papers*, p. 281.
27. 17 Oct. 1908, AJBP/BL Add. MSS. 49733/98–100.
28. The Rt Hon. Arthur James Balfour, *Essays Speculative and Political* (London, 1921), pp. 13–53.
29. AJBP/BL Add. MSS. 49733/98–100. The Romanes Lecture, founded in

1891 by the biologist George Romanes, had been given the previous year by Curzon himself, and two years after Balfour it was given by the former US president Theodore Roosevelt.

30. Balfour, *Essays Speculative and Political*, pp. 57–95.

31. 25 Feb. 1905, AJB to Principal Donaldson, University of Glasgow, AJBP/BL Add. MSS. 49857/186–7.

32. Arthur James Balfour, *Theism and Humanism: Being the Gifford Lectures Delivered at the University of Glasgow, 1914* (London, 1915). For the place of the lectures in Balfour's thought see also Root, 'Philosophical and Religious Thought', and Peter J. Bowler, *Reconciling Science and Religion: The Debate in Early Twentieth-Century Britain* (Chicago, 2001), pp. 370–71.

33. 29 July 1913, Ridley and Percy, eds., *Balfour–Elcho Letters*, p. 303.

34. Balfour, *Theism and Humanism*, p. 21.

35. Ibid., p. 250.

36. Ibid., p. 274.

37. This was Ralph Norman Angell-Lane, a future Nobel peace laureate and author of the influential *The Great Illusion*, which appeared in 1910 and eventually sold over 2 million copies.

38. 12 Oct. 1912, AJB to Esher, AJBP/BL Add. MSS. 49719/235–8. See also Fraser, *Esher*, p. 257. Balfour found time to acquiesce to Esher's request that he write an anonymous essay in support of Angell's arguments. See Esher, ed., *Esher Journals*, III, pp. 111–12.

39. Gerald Balfour seems to have had great faith in Mrs Willett, and she apparently became a friend to him, Lady Betty Balfour and Mrs Sidgwick. See G. W. Balfour, 'A Study of the Psychological Aspects of Mrs Willett's Mediumship, and of the Statements of the Communicators concerning Process', *Proceedings of the Society for Psychical Research*, 40, 139 (1935). See also Jean, Countess of Balfour, 'The Palm Sunday Case', *Proceedings of the Society of Psychical Research*, 52, 189 (1960); Oppenheim, *The Other World*, pp. 132–4; Egremont, *Balfour*, pp. 248–50.

40. For the place of the movement in Britain, see Richard Soloway, *Demography and Degeneration: Eugenics and the Declining Birthrate in Twentieth-Century Britain* (London, 1990).

41. 4 Dec. 1912, AJBP/BL Add. MSS. 49831/246–8.

42. 24 Oct. 1913, AJB to Professor Poulton, AJBP/BL Add. MSS. 49863/26–7.

43. Short, ed., *Balfour as Philosopher and Thinker*, p. 210.

44. William Watson of Maypole Dairies ('the munificent milkman', as Asquith called him) anonymously donated £50,000 to establish the trust supporting the chair. The first professorial grace-and-favour house, called Whittingehame Lodge, was later burned by suffragettes. Lees-Milne, *Esher*, p. 225.

45. Alfred Gollin, *No Longer an Island: Britain and the Wright Brothers, 1902–1909* (London, 1984), pp. 438–40; J. Lee Thompson, *Northcliffe: Press Baron in Politics, 1865–1922* (London, 2000), p. 161.

46. Alfred Gollin, *The Impact of Air Power on the British People and their*

Government, 1909–14 (London, 1989), pp. 171–2. This took place at a demonstration of aerial bombing. Unlike Asquith, Reginald McKenna also accepted the invitation for a brief flight.

47. Young, *Balfour*, p. 284.
48. See Randolph S. Churchill, *Winston S. Churchill*, vol. 2: *Young Statesman, 1901–1914* (Boston, 1966), p. 552.
49. 8 Oct. 1915, AJB to Wilfrid Ward, AJBP/BL Add. MSS. 49864/150.
50. 26 Mar. [1920?] AJBP/NAS GD 433/2/229/1/14. Balfour much enjoyed playing baccarat, and when criticized about it by Lady Elcho he replied, 'I don't for a moment suppose that I shall lose more than old Haldane spends annually upon tobacco!' [Mar. 1913], Ridley and Percy, eds., *Balfour–Elcho Letters*, p. 300.
51. Taylor, *Beaverbrook*, p. 60. In 1911, Aitken was knighted on Balfour's recommendation.
52. Harris, *Whittingehame House*, p. 98.
53. 17 Jan. 1915, Ridley and Percy, eds., *Balfour–Elcho Letters*, p. 317.
54. 8 July 1914, Aitken to Sarah Tugander, BLP 33/1/14; Harris, *Whittingehame House*, p. 98. Balfour continued investing heavily in the process throughout the Great War. AJBP/NLS GD 433/2/179/3.
55. Regarding their losses, see the consoling letter to Gerald Balfour of another disappointed investor, Lord Finlay. 24 Nov. 1924, AJBP/NAS GD 433/2/120/14.
56. 28 June 1912, FB to Frank Balfour (son), AJBP/NAS GD 433/2/344/56. The *Sunday Times* noted that the thought of Balfour giving a ball was akin to the Archbishop of Canterbury dancing a hornpipe in Piccadilly. N.d., note by Mrs Dugdale, AJBP/NAS GD 433/2/344/52.
57. Diary entry, 14 Mar. 1912, Vincent, ed., *Crawford Papers*, p. 267.
58. 26 Mar. 1912, Balcarres to Lady Wantage, ibid., p. 269.
59. Balcarres, whose sympathies appeared not to lie with the suffragists and certainly not with Lady Frances, was amused that her daughter, Alison, had a pet parrot that had been taught to cry out: 'Votes for women? No never, no never.' Diary entry of 14 Oct. 1911, ibid., p. 231.
60. 26 Apr. 1911, AJBP/BL Add. MSS. 49831/110–12. He reminded the same correspondent a few days later that he did not think 'I can say or do anything beyond what I have said and done a hundred times.' 8 May 1911, AJBP/BL Add. MSS. 49831/114–15.
61. 3 Jan. 1910, AJBP/BL Add. MSS. 49793/121–3.
62. Diary entry of 23 Jan. 1913, Vincent, ed., *Crawford Papers*, p. 306.
63. Harris, *Whittingehame House*, pp. 95–6.
64. 26 Mar. 1912, AJBP/BL Add. MSS. 49733/147–8.
65. The other supporter was Lloyd George. The first woman actually elected to Parliament, in Dec. 1918, was Countess Markiewicz, a Sinn Féiner, who refused to take her seat.
66. 21 Nov. 1912, AJB to Colonel Denny, AJBP/BL Add. MSS. 49862/198.
67. 8 Jan. 1913, AJB to Sir Robert Finlay, AJBP/BL Add. MSS. 49862/228–9.

68. 20 Dec. 1912, AJBP/BL Add. MSS. 49743/33–5.

69. Soon after the initial revelations the Liberal Chief Whip, Alexander Murray, was implicated when it was revealed he had speculated in Marconi stock using party funds. For the entire affair see Frances Donaldson, *The Marconi Scandal* (London, 1962). For the parts played by the politicians see Bentley Brinkerhoff Gilbert, *Lloyd George, a Political Life: Organizer of Victory, 1912–1916* (London, 1992), pp. 32–55; John Grigg, *Lloyd George: From Peace to War* (London, 1985), ch. 2; H. Montgomery Hyde, *Lord Reading* (London, 1967), pp. 120–67; and Adams, *Bonar Law*, pp. 119–23.

70. The ministers – including Herbert Samuel who had negotiated the contract with British Marconi – sued the French journal *Le Matin*, which had picked up and garbled the story. Curiously, all the leading barristers in the case were Unionists, including James Campbell, for the newspaper, and F. E. Smith and Carson, for the plaintiffs.

71. 19 June 1913. The Liberal C. F. G. Masterman was certain that Balfour's moderation was part of a double game, seeking some parliamentary note of 'regret' for the ministers' behaviour and thereby causing their resignations. There is no evidence of this. See B. B. Gilbert, *Lloyd George: Organizer of Victory*, p. 49.

72. Duff Cooper, *Old Men Forget* (London, 1953), p. 35.

73. He warned Sir George Riddell in advance that he intended to counter-attack a number of Unionists with accusations of stock-dealing while they had been in office. 21 May 1913, John M. McEwen, ed., *The Riddell Diaries, 1908–1923* (London, 1986), p. 65.

74. Oct. 1913, AJBP/BL Add. MSS. 49737/122–3.

75. On the resumption of good relations between Balfour and Lloyd George following the Marconi affair, see Riddell's diary entry of 14 July 1912, McEwen, ed., *Riddell Diaries*, p. 47.

76. Adams, *Bonar Law*, p. 103.

77. 23 Oct. 1913, quoted in Sykes, *Tariff Reform*, p. 284.

78. 10 Sept. 1913, AJB to JSS, AJBP/BL Add. MSS. 49768/48–61. For the constitutional argument see J. Smith, *Tories and Ireland*, p. 91, and Adams, *Bonar Law*, pp. 106–7.

79. 23 Sept. 1913, BLP 30/2/20. Syndicalism, derived from the French word for trade unionism, was the philosophy of a radical, violence-prone working-class movement seeking to place government and property in the hands of the unions.

80. Ibid.

81. N.d., 'The Constitutional Question', RA PS/GV/K 2553/2/50. See also Nicolson, *George the Fifth*, p. 230. Esher apparently acted as courier for the memorandum, and by the end of the year recommended it to Stamfordham. 28 Dec. 1913, Esher to Stamfordham, Brett, ed., *Esher Journals*, III, pp. 147–8.

82. Sandars advised against the plan. See Egremont, *Balfour*, p. 254, and Shannon, *Balfour and Ireland*, pp. 178–9.

83. 10 Sept. 1913, AJBP/BL Add. MSS. 49768/48–51.

84. Ramsden, *Age of Balfour and Baldwin*, pp. 85–6.

85. Agar-Robartes, MP for Bodmin, Cornwall, was so independent-minded that he had been unseated by petition from his previous seat at St Austell.

86. See Adams, *Bonar Law*, pp. 111–12.

87. 23 Sept. 1913, AJBP/BL Add. MSS. 49693/48–54. See 21 Sept. 1913, Churchill to Asquith, HHAP 38/198.

88. Bonar Law to Lansdowne, 8 Oct. 1913, LP 1/41.

89. 30 Sept. 1913, Kinchin to Bonar Law, BLP 30/2/35. Through T. P. O'Connor, Lloyd George also encouraged the Irish Nationalists to consider this possibility. Patricia Jalland, *The Liberals and Ireland* (London, 1980), p. 150.

90. 8 Oct. 1913, Asquith to Bonar Law, BLP 30/3/11; 10 Oct. 1913, Bonar Law to Asquith, HHAP 38/24.

91. 8 Nov. 1913, AJB to Bonar Law, BLP 30/4/16.

92. 22 Dec. 1913, Bonar Law to Lansdowne, BLP 33/6/115; 27 Dec. 1913, Bonar Law to O'Brien, BLP 33/6/120.

93. 13 Jan. 1914, AJB to Bonar Law, AJBP/BL Add. MSS. 49693/138.

94. This formula was largely the work of Sir Robert Finlay, Balfour's former Attorney General and a future Lord Chancellor. 2 Feb. 1914, 'Proposed Clause in Army (Annual) Bill', BLP 31/2/2.

95. Bonar Law had publicly suggested the use of such a tactic as early as July 1911 in the debate over the Parliament bill, and Milner, Selborne, Lord Hugh Cecil and others had publicly raised the idea in 1913. Adams, *Bonar Law*, p. 147.

96. 30 Jan. 1914, AJBP/BL Add. MSS. 49693/139–40.

97. 3 Feb. 1914, AJBP/BL Add. MSS. 49693/146–51.

98. 1 Mar. 1914, AJBP/BL Add. MSS. 49730/270. The Marquess presumed that amendment was inevitable. 6 Mar. 1914, Lansdowne to AJB, AJBP/BL Add. MSS. 49730/268–9.

99. Diary entry of 12 Mar. 1914, Vincent, ed., *Crawford Papers*, p. 328.

100. 20 Mar. 1914, Bonar Law to J. P. Croal, BLP 34/2/44. Croal, a trusted friend of Bonar Law, was editor of *The Scotsman*. See also the entry of 19 Mar. 1914, John Ramsden, ed., *Real Old Tory Politics: The Political Diaries of Sir Robert Sanders, Lord Bayford, 1910–1935* (London, 1984), p. 74. Sanders was a junior whip, and reported that even the 'Orangemen' opposed the step as 'they had no quarrel with the army'.

101. Even some members of the Liberal Cabinet had suspected the First Lord of planning a *coup de main* against Ulster in 1914, relying on naval power. Entry of 20 May 1915, Edward David, ed., *Inside Asquith's Cabinet: From the Diaries of Charles Hobhouse* (London, 1977), p. 246. Such generally reasonable Unionists as Balcarres and Chamberlain believed in the possibility of an Ulster 'pogrom'.

102. For the complicated incident, see I. F. W. Beckett, ed., *The Army and the Curragh Incident* (London, 1986); Sir James Fergusson, *The Curragh Incident* (London, 1964); A. P. Ryan, *Mutiny at the Curragh* (London, 1956); and Jalland, *Liberals and Ireland*, ch. 7.

103. Hankey dared to intervene with Balfour, asking him to strive to settle the Home Rule battle before, in his view, it destroyed the army, and perhaps the navy too. Balfour advised Bonar Law of this, and added that he wished Hankey would stay out of politics. Stephen Roskill, *Hankey: Man of Secrets* (3 vols., London 1970–74), I, pp. 132–3.
104. 23 Mar. 1914, A. Chamberlain to M. Chamberlain, Chamberlain, *Politics from Inside*, pp. 629–31.
105. Keith Jeffrey, ed., *The Military Correspondence of Field Marshal Sir Henry Wilson, 1918–1922* (London, 1983), p. 8.
106. The agreement with the officers was soon leaked to the press. An Army Order forbidding all such arrangements was issued on 27 Mar. 1914. BLP 93/2/21.
107. Dutton, *Loyal Opposition*, p. 223; Jalland, *Liberals and Ireland*, p. 239.
108. *The Times*, 18 Feb. 1914. For this, see also Shannon, *Balfour and Ireland*, pp. 194–5.
109. Other speakers at the event included Lord Londonderry, Admiral 'Charlie' Beresford, and Balfour's kinsmen Lord Selborne and Lord Robert Cecil, but not Bonar Law. A copy of the bill announcing the event was preserved by Long. WLP Add. MSS. 62436/82.
110. 8 Apr. 1914, A. Chamberlain to M. Chamberlain, Chamberlain, *Politics from Inside*, p. 638. Emphasis in original.
111. 15 Jan. 1913, *Gleanings and Memoranda*, 40 (1913).
112. 5 May 1914, A. Chamberlain to M. Chamberlain, Chamberlain, *Politics from Inside*, pp. 643–4. Balfour had long argued that if the day came when Home Rule could not be resisted, full self-government was inevitable. 19 Sept. 1912, AJB to W. W. K. Robinson, AJBP/BL Add. MSS. 49862/186–7.
113. For a useful brief discussion of these events, including the intriguing question of 'who knew what?', see A. Jackson, *Home Rule*, pp. 154–8. There seems no doubt that Balfour knew nothing in advance and disapproved of both episodes.
114. Asquith advised his mistress that, after the Unionist demonstration in Hyde Park, correspondence from the King was 'rather hysterical'. 7 Apr. 1914, Asquith to V. Stanley, Michael and Eleanor Brock, eds., *H. H. Asquith: Letters to Venetia Stanley* (Oxford, 1982), p. 63.
115. Asquith to Venetia Stanley, ibid., pp. 105–6. Asquith retained the King's notes putting forth the names of Asquith, Lord Crewe (Liberal), Redmond and John Dillon (Irish Nationalists), Carson and James Craig (Ulster Unionists) and Bonar Law (Unionist), with the names of Lloyd George and Balfour followed by '?'.
116. See A. Jackson, *Home Rule*, pp. 162–4.
117. Bonar Law to Asquith, 10 Sept. 1914, HHAP 13/210.
118. 13 Aug. 1914, AJB to Bonar Law, BLP 34/3/36. 15 Aug. 1914, Grey to AJB, AJBP/BL Add. MSS. 49731/21–2.
119. N.d., BLP 34/3/16.
120. Asquith made light of what he portrayed as a comically over-dramatic

gesture, but William Bridgeman confided to his diary that it was hardly that, 'as everyone else was coming out too'. Both on 15 Sept. 1914: Asquith to V. Stanley, Brock and Brock, eds., *Asquith–Stanley Letters*, p. 239; P. Williamson, ed., *Bridgeman Diaries*, p. 83.

121. See R. Churchill, *Churchill*, II, p. 553.

122. Numerous examples may be found in AJBP/BL Add. MSS. 49694.

123. Diary entry of 28 Dec. 1908, Brett, ed., *Esher Journals*, II, pp. 364.

124. See 23 Oct. 1911, A. Chamberlain to M. Chamberlain, Chamberlain, *Politics from Inside*, p. 363.

125. 12 June 1912, AJB to Grey, FO 800/105. See also Samuel R. Williamson, *The Politics of Grand Strategy: Britain and France Prepare for War, 1904–1914* (London, 1990 edn), p. 275.

126. Mackay, *Balfour*, p. 242; Williams, *Defending the Empire*, pp. 105, 202.

127. 21 Jan. 1913, Hankey to AJB, AJBP/BL Add. MSS. 49703/1. While still a Unionist, Seely had been a member of Roberts's National Service League. The committee met until May 1914, and members included Asquith, Lloyd George, Grey and Churchill. Seemingly inevitably, Hankey acted as secretary. See S. Williamson, *Grand Strategy*, pp. 307ff.

128. CAB 38/26/13. See also Mackay, *Balfour*, p. 245.

129. 2 Nov. 1912, AJB to Bonar Law, BLP 27/4/49.

130. 14 Dec. 1912, AJB to Colonel William Thorburn, AJBP/BL Add. MSS. 49862/213–21.

131. Hankey, *Supreme Command*, I, p. 151.

132. Williams, *Defending the Empire*, p. 203.

133. In his memoirs, Grey does not claim to recall having said this, his most famous utterance. Rather, he quotes the recollection of an unnamed friend. Viscount Grey of Fallodon, KG, *Twenty-Five Years*, vol. 2 (London, 1925), p. 20.

134. 4 Aug. 1914, HP 5909/242–8. This is printed in Dugdale, *Balfour*, II, pp. 116–17, and Mackay, *Balfour*, p. 250.

135. See Balfour's memorandum, 5 Aug. 1914, AJBP/BL Add. MSS. 49724/170–77. Haldane, to the contrary, insisted later that 'there was never the slightest foundation for the suggestion . . . that I had wished to delay the sending of the Expeditionary Force.' *Autobiography*, p. 277. In her evaluation, Mrs Dugdale was generous to Haldane (*Balfour*, II, p. 118), but see also Williamson, *Grand Strategy*, p. 363.

136. See S. Williamson, *Grand Strategy*, p. 364.

137. Dugdale, *Balfour*, II, pp. 122–3.

CHAPTER 11: FIRST LORD

1. The party truce was embodied in a memorandum of 28 Aug. 1914, signed by party whips Percy Illingworth (Liberal), Lord Edmund Talbot (Unionist) and Arthur Henderson (Labour), under which the parties agreed not to contest by-elections. The Irish Nationalists did not participate. HHAP 26/13.

2. Lords Beauchamp and Morley, as well as John Burns and John Simon, offered their resignations, but only Morley and Burns persisted.

3. At the age of eighty-two, the gallant 'Little Bobs' died in Nov. 1914 while visiting troops in France.

4. Lady Violet Bonham-Carter, *Winston Churchill As I Knew Him* (London, 1959), p. 257.

5. A. Chamberlain, 'Diary of England's Intervention, 3 August 1914', ACP AC 14/2/2; 3 Aug. 1914, Asquith to V. Stanley, Brock and Brock, eds., *Asquith–Stanley Letters*, p. 152.

6. Kitchener continued to receive his army salary as well as that due him as a Secretary of State, and a special allowance of £1,140 per year. He anticipated, after the successful conclusion of the war, a parliamentary grant for his services. Philip Magnus, *Kitchener: Portrait of an Imperialist* (London, 1959), p. 278.

7. George H. Cassar, *Kitchener: Architect of Victory* (London, 1977), p. 196.

8. He made the remark to George Booth at the memorial service after Kitchener's death at sea in 1916. Duncan Crow, *A Man of Push and Go: The Life of George Macaulay Booth* (London, 1965), p. 137.

9. See the 'Note of a talk with Bonar Law, 20 December 1914', by Geoffrey Robinson [Dawson], editor of *The Times*. MSS. Dawson 119–22.

10. 7, 8 Sept. 1914, Brock and Brock, eds., *Asquith–Stanley Letters*, pp. 224–5.

11. 10 Nov. 1914, AJB to AB, AJBP/BL Add. MSS. 49832/245–51.

12. Fisher replaced the German-born Prince Louis of Battenberg, who was driven from his post by a hysterical anti-German press campaign. Prince Louis later anglicized his name to the now familiar Mountbatten. Wolfe Murray was called 'Sheep' Murray by Churchill because of his subservience to Kitchener, whom he was unable to forget was a field marshal.

13. 24 Nov. 1914, Asquith to LG, LGP C/6/11/22. See also B. B. Gilbert, *Lloyd George: Organizer of Victory*, pp. 139–40. Soon Haldane, McKenna, Lewis Harcourt and Admiral Arthur Wilson were added to the War Council. George H. Cassar, *Asquith as War Leader* (London, 1994), p. 54. Hankey, of course, became secretary.

14. 9, 12 Jan. 1915; 29 Jan. 1915, memorandum by Austen Chamberlain, LGP C 3/14/8. For Bonar Law's unease about Balfour's co-operation with the government, see Adams, *Bonar Law*, p. 177.

15. 9 Jan. 1915, AJBP/BL Add. MSS. 49730/272–3.

16. The famous poster was created by commercial artist Alfred Leete and appeared first as a magazine cover in Sept. 1914; it became the model for the well-known American recruiting poster featuring 'Uncle Sam'. The immortal remark about Kitchener has been attributed both to Asquith and to his wife, but probably was first uttered by his daughter-in-law, Lady Cynthia Asquith.

17. 27 Jan. 1915, CAB 42/1/25.

18. 19 Dec. 1914, AJBP/BL Add. MSS. 49703/121–2.

19. 1 Jan. 1915, 'The Limits of Enlistment', CAB 42/1/7. See David French, *British Economic and Strategic Planning, 1905–1915* (London,1982), p. 156.

20. Though written on Christmas Day, the paper was actually dated 28 Dec. 1914 and sent first to Asquith and then to other members of the War Council, including Balfour. AJBP/BL Add. MSS. 49703/126–36.
21. This recollection appeared in a letter to the historian of the tank, Sir Basil Liddell Hart, 3 Apr. 1948. Roskill, *Hankey*, II, p. 147.
22. Lloyd George, *War Memoirs*, I, p. 383. The prototype was later given to Lord Salisbury. Rose, *Later Cecils*, pp. 85–6.
23. 2 Jan. 1915, HP 4/7; Roskill, *Hankey*, I, pp. 150–51.
24. At Tannenberg in Aug. 1914, the Russians lost more than 90,000 prisoners, and the Russian commander, Sasanov, chose suicide over disgrace. This was the first great success of Hindenburg and Ludendorff, and initiated their rise to become dictators of Germany later in the war.
25. Martin Gilbert, *Winston S. Churchill*, vol. 3: *1914–1916, The Challenge of War* (New York, 1971), p. 237.
26. Casser, *Kitchener*, pp. 274–5.
27. 28 Jan. 1915, Brock and Brock, eds., *Asquith–Stanley Letters*, p. 405.
28. M. Gilbert, *Churchill*, III, pp. 270–72.
29. Fisher's paper is printed in Martin Gilbert, ed., *Winston S. Churchill, Companion Vol. 3*, Pt 1 (Boston, 1973), pp. 452–5. See also Mackay, *Balfour*, pp. 258–60.
30. 1 Feb. 1915, AJBP/BL Add. MSS. 49712/144–7.
31. M. Gilbert, *Churchill*, III, p. 303.
32. 24 Feb. 1915, CAB 22/1/2. Hankey, *Supreme Command*, I, p. 283; Mackay, *Balfour*, pp. 262–3.
33. CAB 42/1/44.
34. 8 Apr. 1915, AJB to Churchill, AJBP/BL Add. MSS. 49694/105–7; M. Gilbert, *Churchill*, III, p. 389.
35. Sir George Arthur, *The Life of Lord Kitchener* (3 vols., London, 1920), III, p. 74.
36. 22 Feb. 1915, 'Some further considerations on the conduct of the war', CAB 42/1/39.
37. Lloyd George invited Balfour to a meeting with trade union representatives in March, which the Chancellor recalled gleefully was eye-opening for his patrician colleague – his first confrontation with workmen 'on a basis of equality'. This was substantially true. Lloyd George, *War Memoirs*, I, p. 177.
38. 5 Mar. 1915, LGP C/3/3/1.
39. 23 Mar. 1915, Asquith to Kitchener, KP PRO 30/57/82.
40. 28 Mar. 1915, Brock and Brock, eds., *Asquith–Stanley Letters*, pp. 513–14.
41. Dugdale, *Balfour*, II, p. 157.
42. 27 Mar. 1915, LGP C/3/3/3. See also 16 Apr. 1915, AJB to Lord Robert Cecil, RCP/BL Add. MSS. 51071A/31–2.
43. 8 Apr. 1915, Asquith to Kitchener, 30/57/82. The other members were Major General von Donop of the War Office, Admiral Tudor and Sir Frederick Black of the Admiralty, and industrialist George Macaulay Booth. Sir William Beveridge was added soon thereafter.

44. W. A. S. Hewins, *The Apologia of an Imperialist: Forty Years of Empire Policy* (2 vols., London, 1929), II, p. 29.

45. Adams and Poirier, *Conscription Controversy*, pp. 76–7. See also Viscount French, *1914* (London, 1919), pp. 358–61.

46. Hewins, *Apologia of an Imperialist,* II, pp. 30–31.

47. 15 May 1915, Bonar Law to Asquith, BLP 117/1/9.

48. 14 May 1915, CAB 42/1/19. See also Hankey, *Supreme Command*, II, pp. 305–7; M. Gilbert, *Churchill*, III, pp. 431–3.

49. The brief letter has been frequently printed, for example in Adams, *Bonar Law*, p. 183.

50. Balfour concluded to Selborne, 'I am afraid Jacky is really a little mad.' 20 May 1915, SP 1/1512; AJBP/BL Add. MSS. 49708/249 (copy).

51. Lloyd George, *War Memoirs*, I, p. 136.

52. This version of events, essentially Lloyd George's, was popularized by Lord Beaverbrook in his *Politicians and the War* (London, 1960 edn), pp. 106–7. See A. Chamberlain, 'Memorandum of Events of 17–18 May 1915', ACP AC 2/2/25. See also Adams, *Bonar Law*, p. 185.

53. ACP AC 2/2/25.

54. See the diary entry of Asquith's daughter-in-law, 22 May 1915, E. M. Horsley, ed., *Lady Cynthia Asquith Diaries, 1915–1918* (New York, 1969), p. 27.

55. In his life of the Prime Minister, Lord Jenkins first explained that at this same time Venetia Stanley announced the end of their relationship and her engagement to Asquith's colleague Edwin Montagu. It is there suggested that his unhappiness over the loss played a part in his 'surrender' to Lloyd George and Bonar Law. Roy Jenkins, *Asquith: Portrait of a Man and an Era* (New York, 1966), pp. 363–6. On balance, Asquith's disappointment seems to have had little or nothing to do with his decision for coalition.

56. At Cabinet level, all were Liberals except for Arthur Henderson of the Labour Party, who now headed the Board of Education.

57. Rose, *George V*, p. 189.

58. 19 May 1915, AJBP/BL Add. MSS. 49692/148. Emphasis added. The following day he wrote to Selborne, 'I do not envy the new First Lord, and I hope it won't be me.' AJBP/BL Add. MSS. 49708/249.

59. Stamfordham noted for the King, 'He admits that there are very few who can add to the strength of the Government always excepting Mr Balfour.' Memorandum, 19 May 1915, RA PS/GV/K 770/3.

60. 21 May 1915, AJB to Lord Alverstone, Alverstone Papers Add. MSS. 61739/98.

61. Crewe to Lloyd George, LGP C/4/1/22.

62. [10?] June 1915, Fisher to AJB; 21 June 1915, AJB to Fisher, AJBP/BL Add. MSS. 49712/170, 172.

63. 26 June 1915, AJB to Fisher, AJBP/BL Add. MSS. 49712/175.

64. 29 May 1915, Fisher to Prince Louis, CHAR 13/53/1. Balfour made clear to Jellicoe that the new Fisher committee was to be 'separate from the depart-

ment, housed elsewhere, and without executive authority'. 4 July 1915, JP Add. MSS. 48990/201–3.

65. Sandars was particularly enraged in 1912 when Churchill replaced Admiral Sir Francis Bridgeman as First Sea Lord with Prince Louis of Battenberg, as Sandars admired Bridgeman almost as much as he hated Churchill. Diary entry of 5 Dec. 1912, Vincent, ed., *Crawford Papers*, p. 291. Balfour agreed with Sandars that Bridgeman had been badly treated by the First Lord.

66. [J. S. Sandars], *Studies of Yesterday by a Privy Councillor* (London, 1928), p. 36.

67. See 2 June 1915, JSS to WS, AJBP/BL Add. MSS. 49768/156. The Churchills had no London house at the time.

68. Sandars's last refusal of a proffered lunch engagement was on 6 Apr. 1916, JSS to AJB, AJBP/BL Add. MSS. 49768/164. See Egremont, *Balfour*, p. 269.

69. At the outbreak of war, the resourceful Miss Bliss was travelling on the Continent and made her way to Belgium and, finally, to England. 5 Aug. 1914, W. Short to AB, AJBP/BL Add. MSS. 49832/216–19. She succeeded Wilfrid Short as Balfour's secretary in 1920, and continued in his employ for the remainder of his life.

70. Egremont, *Balfour*, p. 270.

71. Diary entry of 27 Oct. 1916, Vincent, ed., *Crawford Papers*, p. 362.

72. In 1934 Sir William Graham Greene, the permanent under-secretary, penned his recollections of Balfour's time as First Lord. See Mackay, *Balfour*, pp. 274–5.

73. 20 May 1915, AJB to Sir George [Hamilton], AJBP/BL Add. MSS. 49778/110.

74. No doubt recalling the criticisms aimed at Chamberlain during the Boer War, Balfour wrote to Asquith soon after taking office informing him that he, Balfour, owned shares in the chemical firm Cashner, Kellner, with whom the Liberal government had placed contracts early in the war. Balfour realized the potential for trouble in this, and asked Asquith's advice. There is no reply among Balfour's papers, and it is likely that he retained the shares. 25 June 1915, AJB to Asquith, HHAP 14/68–9.

75. 3 June 1915, JSSP MSS. Eng. hist. c. 768/64; and similarly 30 Nov. 1915, JSSP MSS. Eng. hist. c. 768/106–9. Of the effect of Balfour's being again in harness, Short wrote to Lady Wemyss in August that if she wished for him to live to be an energetic eighty, 'you will hope that he may remain a cabinet minister for many years to come!' Egremont, *Balfour*, p. 270.

76. Hankey, *Supreme Command*, I, pp. 333–4.

77. Ibid., pp. 336–7.

78. 20 Aug. 1915, KP PRO 30/57/76.

79. M. Gilbert, *Churchill*, III, p. 522.

80. He repeated his recommendation in even stronger terms on 2 Nov. An embittered Churchill wrote of him later, 'He came, he saw, he capitulated.' Ibid., p. 563.

81. 19 Nov. 1915, CAB 37/137/36. This is printed in Dugdale, *Balfour*, II, pp. 153–5.

82. 28 Oct. 1915, 'Conduct of the War', H. H. Asquith, CAB 37/136/36.
83. These were Asquith's words to his friend Mrs Sylvia Henley, the sister of Venetia Stanley. Casser, *Asquith as War Leader*, p. 134. Lansdowne declined appointment to the committee.
84. 2 Jan. 1915, Dugdale, *Balfour*, II, p. 130.
85. M. Gilbert, *Churchill*, III, p. 303. See also Casser, *Kitchener*, p. 381, for the influences on the Secretary of State.
86. See his paper 'National Service and the Nation', CAB 37/133/7.
87. 18 Sept. 1915, AJBP/BL Add. MSS. 49692/157–60.
88. 19 Sept. 1915, 'Efficiency in War and Compulsion', CAB 37/134/25.
89. Among the dead were Fergus Bowes-Lyon, the brother of the future Queen Elizabeth, the Queen Mother, and John Kipling, the son of the poet.
90. Derby advised Asquith to have a conscription bill in hand in the event that his efforts failed. Adams and Poirier, *Conscription Controversy*, p. 121.
91. 27 Dec. 1915, WO 106/368.
92. CAB 37/139/55.
93. Hankey, *Supreme Command*, II, pp. 468–9.
94. 27 Dec. 1915, CAB 37/139/55; 13 Jan. 1916, CAB 42/7/5; entry of 15 Jan. 1916, Brett, ed., *Esher Journals*, IV, p. 1. See also David R. Woodward, *Field Marshal Sir William Robertson, Chief of the Imperial General Staff* (Westport, Conn., 1998), p. 112.
95. 8 Mar. 1916, CAB 42/10/8; Mackay, *Balfour*, p. 290. Several weeks earlier, Balfour had made it clear to the editor of the *Manchester Guardian*, C. P. Scott, that if Fisher were returned to the Admiralty he himself would resign. Entry of 18 Feb. 1916, Trevor Wilson, ed., *The Political Diaries of C. P. Scott, 1911–1928* (London, 1970), p. 183.
96. Quoted in Egremont, *Balfour*, p. 273.
97. This to C. P. Scott. Entry of 8 Feb. 1916, Wilson, ed., *Scott Diaries*, p. 181.
98. Hankey, *Supreme Command*, II, p. 491.
99. Jellicoe wrote to Balfour on 6 June that, if the fleet had reason to be 'disappointed over the public attitude', that feeling had dissipated with the Churchill communiqué. 'Opinion has undergone a revolution, both rapid and complete.' JP Add. MSS. 48992/29–30. Lloyd George was not mollified, however. See his harsh comment to his friend Lord Riddell, 3 June 1916, McEwen, ed., *Riddell Diaries*, p. 157.
100. 6 June 1916. Balfour had held a rare but generally successful press conference in April, but any goodwill that it may have created seems to have been dissipated by Jutland. 27 Apr. 1916, McEwen, ed., *Riddell Diaries*, p. 154.
101. 1 June 1916, AJB to Stamfordham, RA PS/GV/J 926/9; 31 May 1916, RA PS/GV/J 926/1.
102. 7 Jan. 1916, Fisher to Bonar Law, FP 1/21/1131.
103. 'Ministers and the Coalition', [Sandars], *Studies of Yesterday*, pp. 185–211.
104. See his Cabinet paper of 14 Feb. 1916, CAB 37/142/37.
105. Malcolm Smith, *The Birth of Independent Air Power: British Air Policy in the*

First World War (London, 1986), p. 47.

106. 14 Jan. 1918, Haig to his wife, quoted in R. Churchill, *Derby*, p. 348.

107. The duelling memoranda were submitted by Curzon on 16 Apr. 1916, CAB 37/146/6, and by Balfour on 29 Apr. 1916, CAB 37/146/25.

108. Roskill, *Hankey*, I, p. 271.

109. 23 Oct. 1916, CAB 42/25/10.

110. 26 Oct. 1916, AJB to Curzon, GNCP MSS. Eur. F 112/170; 6 Nov. 1916, CAB 42/25/10.

111. Hankey, *Supreme Command*, II, pp. 550–51; Lloyd George, *War Memoirs*, II, p. 1126. The Air Board was continued, and responsibility for aircraft design and supply was assigned to the Ministry of Munitions, while the air defence of London was transferred from the navy to the fledgling RAF.

112. 14 Oct. 1916, CAB 37/157/31; Mackay, *Balfour*, p. 299.

113. Hankey, *Supreme Command*, II, p. 475.

114. John Turner, *British Politics and the Great War: Coalition and Conflict, 1915–1918* (New Haven, 1992), p. 91.

115. B. B. Gilbert, *Lloyd George: Organizer of Victory*, p. 23; Hyde, *Carson*, p. 403.

116. Fair, *British Interparty Conferences*, p. 134.

117. John Kendle, *Walter Long, Ireland and the Union, 1905–1920* (Montreal, 1992), p. 115; B. B. Gilbert, *Lloyd George: Organizer of Victory*, pp. 322–3. Selborne resigned over the Irish negotiations, but Lansdowne remained.

118. 27 June 1916, Bonar Law to St Audries (Acland-Hood), quoted in Beaverbrook, *Politicians and the War*, pp. 267–8. Austen Chamberlain, to Balfour's disappointment, threw in his lot with the Die-hard faction. See his letter to Balfour, 2 June 1916, AJBP/BL Add. MSS. 49736/229–31.

119. 10 May 1916, AJB to John Bernard, AJBP/BL Add. MSS. 49864/275. See also Shannon, *Balfour and Ireland*, pp. 213–14.

120. Shannon, *Balfour and Ireland*, p. 217.

121. CAB 37/150/17. Emphasis added.

122. Shannon, *Balfour and Ireland*, pp. 219–21.

123. 28 June, 1916, O'Connor to Dillon (copy), LGP D 8/14/3/44. See also Lyons, *Dillon*, p. 399, and 27 June 1916, Stamfordham's memorandum, RA PS/GV/K 953/6.

124. 7 July 1916, 'Notes', Meeting of the Unionist Party. BLP 63/C/64.

125. Entry of 7 July 1916, P. Williamson, ed., *Bridgeman Diaries*, pp. 107–8.

126. 6 July 1916, JSS to Devonshire, JSSP MSS. Eng. hist. c. 769/171–2.

127. 30 Dec. 1916, Bonar Law's confidential memorandum on the December 1916 political crisis, BLP 85/A/1.

128. 13 Nov. 1916, CAB 37/159/32.

129. B. B. Gilbert, *Lloyd George: Organizer of Victory*, pp. 376–8.

130. 4 Oct. 1916, CAB 37/157/6.

131. 25 Nov. 1916, HHAP 31/1. See also BLP 63/A/3.

132. 26 Nov. 1916, Asquith to Bonar Law, BLP 53/4/24. He noted also that, even if such a committee were desirable, he would not consider passing over Balfour, Curzon or McKenna in favour of Carson.

133. See The Earl of Oxford and Asquith, *Memories and Reflections 1852–1927* (2 vols., London, 1928), II, pp. 175–8.
134. 2 Dec. 1916, Long to Bonar Law, BLP 53/4/28. Beaverbrook printed the letter in his influential study of the period, where it is erroneously dated '2.10.16'. *Politicians and the War*, pp. 368–9.
135. For his actions during the crisis, see 'Government Crisis Dec. 1916, Memorandum by Mr Balfour', 7 Dec. 1916, AJBP/BL Add. MSS. 49692/179–215. This was dictated to Wilfrid Short, and in his hand is added, 'Not revised by Mr B.' This is the principal source of Balfour's actions during the December 1916 political crisis.
136. Crawford, who attended, produced a memorandum following the meeting and in it recalled that, besides Bonar Law and himself, also at the meeting were Curzon, Chamberlain, Duke, Long and Smith. 3 Dec. 1916, Vincent, ed., *Crawford Papers*, pp. 369–70.
137. BLP 85/A/1. Emphasis added.
138. Curiously, Bonar Law did not leave the actual resolution with Asquith – nor apparently did the Prime Minister request that he do so. For this see Adams, *Bonar Law*, p. 232.
139. [3 Dec. 1916] BLP 64/H.
140. BLP 85/A/1. See also Lord Crawford's memorandum of 3 Dec. 1916, Vincent, ed., *Crawford Papers*, pp. 369–72.
141. Maurice Bonham Carter, Asquith's private secretary and son-in-law, knew of this and told his new bride. 1 Dec. 1916, Bonham Carter to Violet Asquith Bonham Carter, Mark Pottle, ed., *Champion Redoubtable: The Diaries and Letters of Violet Bonham Carter, 1914–1945* (London, 1998), p. 97.
142. 1 Dec. 1916, Asquith to Lloyd George, BLP 53/4/27; Lloyd George wrote to Bonar Law on the following day, 'The life of the country depends on resolute action by you now.' BLP 117/1/30.
143. N.d., 'Memorandum on the Circumstances Relating to the Fall of Mr Asquith's Administration December 1916', RA PS/GV/K 1048/A/2. The source for the article was Carson.
144. 4 Dec. 1916, LGP E/2/23/14.
145. Grigg, *Lloyd George: From Peace to War*, p. 456.
146. Lloyd George later denied this line of thought, but see Grigg, *Lloyd George: From Peace to War*, p. 477, and Mackay, *Balfour*, p. 309.
147. 3 Dec. 1916, AB diary, AJBP/NAS GD 433/1/374. Balfour later mistakenly noted that Masterton Smith came to him on 5 Dec.
148. 5 Dec. 1916, AB diary, AJBP/NAS GD 433/1/374, and AJBP/BL Add. MSS. 49692/179–215. Balfour incorrectly recalled 5 Dec. as Monday.
149. AJBP/BL Add. MSS. 49692/179–215.
150. The text of this and the following letters are included in Balfour's memorandum, AJBP/BL Add. MSS. 49692/215. Emphasis in the original. Balfour sent a copy of this letter to Bonar Law, and in a cover note added that Lloyd George's design for a war government deserved to be given a chance, and that he must have a First Lord of his choice – thus relieving the party leader

of the need to champion him against Lloyd George. 5 Dec. 1916, BLP 53/4/32.

151. BLP 85/A/1.

152. AJBP/BL Add. MSS. 49692/179–215. See also n.d. [Dec. 1916], RA PS/GV/K 1048 A/2, 'Memorandum on the Circumstances Relating to the Fall of Mr Asquith's Administration, December 1916'.

153. On this point see Lady Asquith's angry letter to BD, 22 June 1933, AJBP/BL Add. MSS. 49833/356–8.

154. RA GV/GVD/1916: 6 Dec.

155. AJBP/BL Add. MSS. 49692/179–215.

156. 6 Dec. 1916, Asquith to Bonar Law, BLP 81/1/1.

157. AJBP/BL Add. MSS. 49692/179–215.

158. BLP 85/A/1.

159. N.d., 'Memorandum of Conversation between Mr Lloyd George and certain Unionist ex-ministers, December 7th, 1916', ACP AC 15/3/6. In this meeting, which secured the services of Lord Curzon, Lord Robert Cecil, Austen Chamberlain and Walter Long, Lloyd George made clear that Balfour, as Foreign Secretary, would have full access to the new War Cabinet.

160. Beaverbrook, *Politicians and the War*, p. 502. Bonar Law's version in his memorandum was 'Mr Balfour rose from his seat, and without a moment's hesitation, said: "That is indeed putting a pistol to my head, but I say at once yes."' BLP 85/A/1.

161. Dugdale, *Balfour*, II, p. 181.

162. 17 July 1928, AJBP/NAS GD 433/2/1/44, AJB to Lord Beaverbrook. The emphasized phrase was added to the original draft of the letter.

163. Bonar Law's memorandum of the crisis neither confirms nor denies an earlier offer of the Foreign Office. In addition to Aitken, he also told the 'pistol to my head' anecdote to Chamberlain and to the editor Robert Donald. Adams, *Bonar Law*, p. 414, n. 110. For Lord Beaverbrook's writing of history, see J. O. Stubbs, 'Beaverbrook as Historian: "Politicians and the War, 1914–1916" reconsidered', *Albion*, 14, nos. 3–4 (1982); Peter Fraser, 'Lord Beaverbrook's Fabrications in *Politicians and the War*', *Historical Journal*, 25 (1982).

164. For the remainder of her life Margot Asquith insisted that Balfour had deserted her husband and thus brought about his resignation. 2 June 1933, Lady Oxford and Asquith to BD, AJBP/BL Add. MSS. 49833/356–8.

165. Dugdale, *Balfour*, II, pp. 156–7.

166. 30 Dec. 1916, BB to FB, AJBP/BL Add. MSS. 49831/250.

167. 21 Dec. 1916, BB to FB, AJBP/BL Add. MSS. 49831/249. Though Lady Betty's hand is difficult to decipher, the source seems to be identified as 'Vie' – probably Violet, Lady Edward Cecil and later Lady Milner. See also Mackay, *Balfour*, p. 310, n. 27.

168. 12 Sept. 1917, AJBP/BL Add. MSS. 49738/155–61.

CHAPTER 12: FOREIGN SECRETARY
AND LORD PRESIDENT

1. Lloyd George relished being the new broom and, among other changes, he ended for ever the practice of writing Cabinet letters to the sovereign. He created a Cabinet secretariat under Hankey who for the first time recorded minutes of Cabinet meetings. For the King's reaction, see 5 Apr. 1917, Stamfordham to LG, LGP F/29/1/36. See also Stamfordham to AJB, 6 Apr. 1917, FO 800/199/3–4.
2. W. S. Churchill, *Great Contemporaries*, p. 249.
3. 22 Oct. 1917, AJB to Mrs Lascelles, AJBP/BL Add. MSS. 49831/276–8. See 29 May 1934, Hankey to BD, AJBP Add. MSS. 49833/364–6, noting the few meetings from which Balfour was absent. See also Dugdale, *Balfour*, II, p. 241.
4. 30 Dec. 1916, BB to FB, AJBP/BL Add. MSS. 49831/250.
5. Hankey explained to Mrs Dugdale many years later that, though still on the 'sick list', he participated in most of the early War Cabinet meetings which dealt with the German proposal and Wilson's note to the warring Powers. 29 May 1934, AJBP/BL Add. MSS. 49833/364–6.
6. 4 Mar. 1915, Charles Seymour, ed., *The Intimate Papers of Colonel House* (3 vols., Boston, 1926–28), II, p. 387. House, the son of an English immigrant and originally a Houston businessman, was not a colonel – the title was purely honourary. For his friendship with Wilson, see Alexander L. and Juliette L. George, *Woodrow Wilson and Colonel House* (New York, 1956).
7. Dugdale, *Balfour*, II, pp. 189–90.
8. William F. Friedman and Charles J. Mendelsohn, *The Zimmermann Telegram of January 16, 1917, and its Cryptographic Background* (Laguna Hills, Cal., 1994), p. 1 and *passim*. The telegram also proposed that Mexico approach Japan about detaching itself from Britain and joining the Central Powers. See also Barbara Tuchman, *The Zimmermann Telegram* (New York, 2nd edn, 1966).
9. 5 Apr. 1917, Sir Eric Drummond to House, Seymour, ed., *House Papers*, III, p. 33.
10. 6 Apr. 1917, House to Wilson, ibid., p. 35.
11. This was headed by Premier René Viviani and General Joseph Joffre.
12. 5 Apr. 1917, RA PS/GV/Q 1102/5. According to Lord Beaverbrook, Lloyd George pressed Bonar Law – who had no intention of making the trip – to go to Washington. 22 Apr. 1953, Beaverbrook to Robert Blake, BBK C/44.
13. Malcolm, *Balfour*, p. 44.
14. Most of Malcolm's collection of diary letters of the mission may be found in AJBP/BL Add. MSS. 49832.
15. Malcolm, *Balfour*, p. 46.
16. See Charles Hanson Towne, *The Balfour Visit* (New York, 1917).
17. 24 Apr. 1917, AJBP/BL Add. MSS. 49832/321–2.
18. 6 May 1917, Malcolm to R. Cecil, 49738/64–6; Shannon, *Balfour*, p. 229. Balfour was rather taken aback at the emotional outpourings of his French

colleagues, and joked that there should be no tears and kissing of cheeks among his own delegation.

19. AJBP/BL Add. MSS. 49738/64–6.
20. By 28 June 1917, Balfour was insisting that the potential for financial 'calamity' was very real: 'You know I am not an alarmist,' he wrote to Sir William Wiseman in America, 'but this is really serious.' FO 800/209/174.
21. Balfour later recalled to Curzon: 'I handed to the President, if I remember rightly, copies of all the Treaties which had been, at my request, sent me from London.' He admitted, however, that he may have forgotten the agreement with Japan to transfer German concessions in the Shantung Peninsula. 14 Oct. 1919, AJBP/BL Add. MSS. 49734/193–5. See his letter to Wilson of 18 May 1917, four days before he left Washington. FO 800/208/8.
22. 10 June 1917, LGP F/23/1/10.
23. 17 June 1917, AJBP/NAS GD 433/2/136. See also Tomes, *Balfour and Foreign Policy*, pp. 173–4, 187.
24. 6 July 1917, Ramsden, ed., *Sanders Diaries*, p. 87.
25. Quoted in Gilmour, *Curzon*, p. 480.
26. Taylor, *Beaverbrook*, p. 153.
27. Ibid., p. 154. For the humorous reaction of Balfour's former secretary, Sir Sydney Parry, see June 1931, AJBP/NAS GD 433/2/81.
28. See their testy exchange of letters, 6 and 8 June 1918, FO 800/212, 329. For Balfour's reaction to Northcliffe's appointment, see J. Lee Thompson, *Politicians, the Press, and Propaganda: Lord Northcliffe and the Great War, 1914–1919* (Kent, O., 1999), p. 144.
29. The imperial government adhered to the obsolete Julian calender, which placed the two phases of revolution in Feb. and Oct. The new regime adopted the Gregorian system.
30. 17 Mar. 1917, FO 800/205/46–7.
31. 2 Apr. 1917, AJB to Stamfordham, RA PS/GV/M 1067/44. See also Rose, *George V*, p. 210.
32. 30 Mar. 1917, Stamfordham to AJB, FO 800/ 205/63; 2 Apr. 1917, Foreign Office to Stamfordham, FO 800/205/65–6; 3 Apr. 1917, Stamfordham to AJB, FO 800/205/66.
33. 6 Apr. 1917, Stamfordham to AJB, RA PS/GV/M 1067/51.
34. FO 800/205/80. This note included the suggestion that Spain or France might be agreeable as places of exile.
35. 6 Apr. 1917, AJB to Lloyd George, LGP F/3/2/19; 13 Apr. 1917, FO 800/205/87–8.
36. 15 Apr. 1917, FO 800/205/90–91.
37. 8 Sept. 1917, Buchanan to AJB, RA PS/GV/M 1067/74. This was sent two months before the Soviet seizure of power, and the British embassy remained convinced that the imperial family would still be allowed to leave the country.
38. The executions were confirmed by the British ambassador in Copenhagen, Ralph Spencer Paget. 27 July 1918, Paget to AJB, AJBP/BL Add. MSS.

51256/122. The matter of the German origins of the royal family also troubled the monarch, who in July 1917 announced that they would thereafter be known as the House of Windsor.

39. BL Misc. 41178/3. The historical literature regarding the Declaration is, of course, enormous. A useful beginning may be made with Leonard Stein, *The Balfour Declaration* (London, 1961). For Balfour's public position on the question, see The Earl of Balfour, *Speeches on Zionism*, ed. Israel Cohen (London, 1928). Blanche Dugdale, a fervent Zionist herself, published her own explanation, *The Balfour Declaration: Origins and Background* (London, 1940). Very useful also is Tomes, *Balfour and Foreign Policy*, ch. 8.

40. 14–15 Dec. 1914, Weizmann to Ahad Ha'am, Leonard Stein, ed., *The Letters and Papers of Chaim Weizmann*, vol. VII, series A (London, 1975), pp. 81–2. Weizmann became a scientific adviser to the Admiralty and then to the Ministry of Munitions, and pioneered the production of synthetic acetone, necessary to the manufacture of cordite.

41. Chaim Weizmann, *Trial and Error* (New York, 1949), pp. 152–3.

42. See Tomes, *Balfour and Foreign Policy*, pp. 203–5.

43. 4 Dec. 1912, AJB to FB, AJBP/BL Add. MSS. 49831/246–8.

44. Quoted in Tomes, *Balfour and Foreign Policy*, p. 205.

45. See David Vital, *Zionism: The Crucial Phase* (London, 1987), pp. 247–50.

46. John Grigg, *Lloyd George: War Leader, 1916–1918* (London, 2002), p. 349.

47. CAB 23/4.

48. Gilmour, *Curzon*, p. 481.

49. Dec. 1922–Jan. 1923, 'Confidential Memos written by me at Lausanne concerning the fall of the Lloyd George Govt. and other cognate matters for the use of my biographer', GNCP MSS. Eur. F 112/319.

50. This in his speech to the English Zionist Federation, 12 July 1920, reprinted in Balfour, *Speeches on Zionism*, p. 26. Emphasis added.

51. CAB 23/4. The British Zionists also laboured hard at this point to undercut Montagu's assimilationist case and to strengthen Balfour's commitment. See 3 Oct. 1917, Rothschild to Balfour, Stein, ed., *Weizmann Letters and Papers*, vol. VII, series A, pp. 521–2. See also Zebel, *Balfour*, p. 243.

52. CAB 24/24/12. See Tomes, *Balfour and Foreign Policy*, p. 210. Leopold Amery, then on Hankey's War Cabinet staff, later claimed to have written the final form of the Declaration. This seems unlikely, though he contributed to it. See William R. Rubinstein, 'The Secret of Leopold Amery', *History Today*, Feb. 1999, and Grigg, *Lloyd George: War Leader*, p. 356.

53. Vital, *Zionism*, p. 286. Beaverbrook agreed to press the anti-Zionists' case with Lloyd George, to no avail. Anne Chisholm and Michael Davie, *Lord Beaverbrook: A Life* (London, 1993), p. 167.

54. Though by 1921 he seems to have indicated that this had always been his understanding – another example of the fallible Balfour memory? Mackay, *Balfour*, p. 328.

55. 26 June 1919, AJB to Lloyd George, FO 800/217/96–9. See also Mackay,

Balfour, p. 327, and Stein, *Balfour Declaration*, p. 618.

56. Balfour, *Speeches on Zionism*, p. 28.
57. See Grigg, *Lloyd George: War Leader*, p. 346.
58. 14 Aug. 1919, AJBP/BL Add. MSS. 49687/17. Located in the Jezreel Valley, the small *moshav* or communal settlement still exists today.
59. Balfour, *Speeches on Zionism*, p. 23.
60. Ibid., p. 24.
61. A most recent study of Lansdowne is the as yet unpublished Ph.D. thesis of Dr Frank Winters, 'Gentlemen's Diplomacy, The Foreign Policy of Lord Lansdowne, 1845–1927 (Texas A&M University, 2006). The letter was refused by *The Times* and appeared in the *Daily Telegraph* under the heading 'Co-ordination of Allies' War Aims'.
62. Barnes had been general secretary of the Amalgamated Society of Engineers and was MP for Glasgow, Blackfriars – once Bonar Law's constituency. After the war, he headed the coalitionist National Democratic Party.
63. [25] Mar. 1917, Lansdowne to Bonar Law, BLP 81/4/28; 26 Mar. 1917, Bonar Law to Lansdowne, LP Lans (5) 88.
64. N.d., JSS to Newton, JSSP MSS. Eng hist. c. 771/70–72.
65. *Daily Telegraph,* 1 Dec. 1917.
66. The memorandum is dated 6 Nov. 1917, AJBP/BL Add. MSS. 49730/291–9. This and the other documents referred to in this context were printed in a brief article, 'The "Peace Letter" of 1917', by Lansdowne's son, the 6th Marquess, published in *The Nineteenth Century and After*, March 1934. The 6th Marquess knew nothing of the background of the letter and, on active service in 1917, distanced himself from its conclusions while protesting against the 'scurrilous abuse' aimed at his father. *Daily Telegraph*, 17 Dec. 1917. See Winters, 'Gentlemen's Diplomacy', p. 412, and Grigg, *Lloyd George: War Leader*, p. 331.
67. 6th Marquess of Lansdowne, 'Peace Letter'.
68. 2 Dec. 1917, memorandum by Lord Stamfordham, RA PS/GV/Q 1985/41.
69. Many years after the fact, Hardinge wrote to the 6th Marquess that he recalled Lansdowne saying that he had secured Balfour's approval to publish such a letter, which Hardinge thought an error based on Lansdowne's misunderstanding of Balfour's remark 'Hardinge knows my mind.' 27 Dec. 1933, LP Lans (5) 88; 6th Marquess of Lansdowne, 'Peace Letter'.
70. 3 Dec. 1917, LP Lans (5) 85.
71. 27 Dec. 1933, LP Lans (5) 88.
72. 3 Dec. 1917, LP Lans (5) 85.
73. Dugdale, *Balfour*, II, p. 252. Lady Frances Balfour wrote to Lansdowne expressing her regrets that he was 'so hopelessly misunderstood'. 3 Dec. 1917, LP Lans (5) 85.
74. Dugdale, *Balfour*, II, pp. 250–51. Lord Newton, Lansdowne's biographer, years later wrote to the 6th Marquess that, though he believed Balfour and Hardinge had not behaved well towards Lansdowne, neither they nor any Foreign Office official had indicated approval of the letter. 29 May 1933, LP

Lans (5) 88. See also Winters, 'Gentlemen's Diplomacy', p. 426.

75. Adams, *Bonar Law*, p. 263. Bonar Law wrote to Lansdowne in advance of the meeting that their differences would not 'diminish the feeling of personal friendship and of respect' they shared, but it did precisely that. 30 Nov. 1917, BLP 84/6/133.

76. 5 Feb. 1918, AJBP/BL Add. MSS. 49730/300. Lansdowne continued to close his letters 'Your afft, L'; for example, 16 Feb. 1922, AJBP/BL Add. MSS. 49730/301.

77. See Tomes, *Balfour and Foreign Policy*, pp. 218–20.

78. 9 Dec. 1917, CAB 24/35. This paper is printed in Lloyd George, *War Memoirs*, II, pp. 1545–7.

79. Seymour, ed., *House Papers*, III, pp. 409–10; Tomes, *Balfour and Foreign Policy*, pp. 224–5.

80. For the displeasure of the activists, particularly Lord Milner, see Amery's diary entry of 5 June 1918, and his letter to Lloyd George of 8 June. John Barnes and David Nicholson, eds., *The Leo Amery Diaries*, vol. 1: *1896–1929* (London, 1980), pp. 221–2. See also the discussions in Tomes, *Balfour and Foreign Policy*, pp. 223, 229, and Mackay, *Balfour*, pp. 319–22.

81. Balfour was despatched by Lloyd George and the War Cabinet to negotiate with 'Wully' to give up his unprecedented powers as CIGS or accept appointment to the Supreme War Council at Versailles. Robertson refused to do either, and was sacked. See Balfour's notes of the meeting, 15 Feb. 1918, AJBP/BL Add. MSS. 49726/90–92. See also Woodward, *Robertson*, p. 201, and the same author's *Lloyd George and the Generals* (London, 2003), p. 305; also Hankey, *Supreme Command*, II, pp. 777–8.

82. See Adams, *Bonar Law*, p. 275. The official Labour Party left the coalition at war's end. Negotiations were necessarily delicate and, interestingly, the Lloyd George Liberal (and Churchill's cousin) F. E. Guest wrote to the Unionist Robert Sanders that he and his friends were pleased to work with Bonar Law, Chamberlain and Lord Cave, but not Long or Balfour – a linkage which would have amused the latter. 21 July 1918, Ramsden, ed., *Sanders Diaries*, p. 107.

83. 31 July 1919, BLP 97/5/32. Balfour acknowledged, however, that Lloyd George's 'method, or lack of method, of doing business' were trying. See AJB to Derby, 3 Sept. 1918, AJBP/BL Add. MSS. 49744/9–11.

84. For the report of the meeting, see BL 95/3. For reports of dissatisfaction among rank-and-file Conservatives, see 20 Sept. 1918, Younger to Bonar Law, BLP 95/2.

85. For the coalition election manifesto, see BLP 95/1.

86. Bonar Law retained his 'coupon': see BLP 21/6/64 (21).

87. John Grigg, *Nancy Astor: A Lady Unashamed* (Boston, 1980), p. 80. For Lady Astor's deportment during the ceremony, see 2 Dec. 1919, McEwen, ed., *Riddell Diaries*, p. 296.

88. 4 Jan. 1919, Malcolm to AB, AJBP/BL Add. MSS. 49832/275–6; 27 Feb.–3 Mar. 1919, BB to FB, AJBP/BL Add. MSS. 49831/251–63. See Lord

Vansittart, *The Mist Procession*, p. 218; Harold Nicolson, *Peacemaking 1919* (London, 1945 edn), p. 269.

89. Lloyd George, *War Memoirs*, I, p. 605.

90. The most recent comprehensive study of the conference is Margaret Macmillan, *Peacemakers: The Paris Conference of 1919 and its Attempt to End War* (London, 2002).

91. AJBP/BL Add. MSS. 49831/251–63. Bonar Law's secretary, J. C. C. Davidson, complained to Stamfordham of the vast expense of maintaining the delegation 'eating their heads off at the Hotel Majestic' and reducing the available manpower of the home departments. 17 Jan. 1919, RA PS/GV/Q 1098/75.

92. As well as arranging for Balfour's flat, Malcolm planned to sell the contents for him at a profit following the conference, 27 Feb.–3 Mar. 1919 BB to FB, AJBP/BL Add. MSS. 49831/251–63.

93. For the correspondence between them see AJBP/NAS GD 433/2/22. Short became secretary to Lord Dunraven, and remained on friendly terms with Balfour for the rest of his life.

94. They became the 'Big Five' with the arrival in mid-1919 of the Japanese Prince Saionji. See Zebel, *Balfour*, p. 259.

95. The comment was reported by Venetia Montagu, after a dinner party attended by Balfour. Chisholm and Davie, *Beaverbrook*, p. 171. The Italian Foreign Minister, Baron Sonnino, who found Wilson's moralizing exhausting, described the President as 'specie de clergyman'. 28 Dec. 1918, Sir Rennell Rodd to AJB, AJBP/BL Add. MSS. 49745/7–9.

96. Entry of 17 Apr. 1919, AB diary, AJBP/NAS GD 433/2/136; Malcolm, *Balfour*, pp. 73–4. When they disagreed, however, Clemenceau was quite capable of turning his wit against Balfour. According to Lloyd George, '"Take this," he said to Balfour, handing him some iced cake. "It is good for perfidy."' Entry of 15 Dec. 1919, A. J. P. Taylor, ed., *Lloyd George: A Diary by Frances Stevenson* (London, 1971), pp. 192–3.

97. 15 Oct. 1918, Jones, *Whitehall Diary*, I, p. 69.

98. Tomes, *Balfour and Foreign Policy*, p. 153.

99. Dugdale, *Balfour*, II, p. 263. See his similar remark to Alice Balfour, 4–5 Dec. 1918, AB diary, AJBP/NAS GD 433/2/136. See also Tomes, *Balfour and Foreign Policy*, p. 153.

100. Nov. 1924, Curzon, 'Memo on some aspects of my tenure at the Foreign Office', GNCP MSS. Eur. F 112/319.

101. *The Mist Procession*, p. 218.

102. A. Lentin, *Lloyd George, Woodrow Wilson and the Guilt of Germany* (Baton Rouge, La., 1984), p. 125.

103. Kenneth O. Morgan, *Consensus and Disunity: The Lloyd George Coalition Government, 1918–1922* (Oxford, 1979), p. 113, quoting Mrs Dugdale.

104. See Macmillan, *Peacemakers*, pp. 178–9.

105. See Tomes, *Balfour and Foreign Policy*, p. 164.

106. 1 Apr. 1919, FO 800/216/10–12. He also opposed, for example, the ban

preventing union between Germany and the German-speaking Austrians. 11 Nov. 1918, AJB to Stamfordham, FO 800/200/164–5. Some 'fancies' were quite remarkable, as, for example, the suggestion of Grey of Fallodon to turn Heligoland into a bird sanctuary. June 1919, Grey to AJB, AJBP/BL Add. MSS. 49731/184–5.

107. Balfour found the French idea impossible, and had to be persuaded to accept even a temporary French military occupation of the Rhineland. 18 Mar. 1919, AJBP/BL Add. MSS. 49749/39. For the treaties, see Tomes, *Balfour and Foreign Policy*, p. 159, and Vansittart's breezy recollection in *The Mist Procession*, p. 163.

108. See his memorandum of 11 Jan. 1919, FO 800/215/67–78.

109. 5 May 1919, 'Notes on Military Peace Proposals', Balfour memorandum, FO 800/216/181–4.

110. John D. Fair, *Harold Temperley: A Scholar and Romantic in the Public Realm* (Newark, Del., 1992), p. 145.

111. H. A. L. Fisher, *An Unfinished Autobiography* (London, 1940), p. 135. See also Grigg, *Lloyd George: War Leader*, p. 573.

112. Malcolm described the German delegates as 'the two most depraved specimens of humanity', while the Allied delegates 'looked like a row of clerks attending to customers when there was a run upon the bank'. The ceremony he found without 'decorum or dignity . . . merely slipshod'. 28 June 1919, Malcolm to AB, AJBP/BL Add. MSS. 49832/286–8.

113. Malcolm, *Balfour*, p. 80.

114. 10 Mar. 1919, Taylor, ed., *Stevenson Diary*, p. 171.

115. 16 Aug. 1919, AJB to Curzon; 20 Aug. 1919, Curzon to AJB, AJBP/BL Add. MSS. 49734/149–53, 154–60. See also Gilmour, *Curzon*, pp. 504–5.

116. 26 Dec. 1918, Churchill to Lloyd George, LGP F/8/2/49.

117. Nov. 1924, 'Memo on some aspects of my tenure at the Foreign Office', GNCP MSS. Eur. F 112/319. 8 Sept. 1919, AJB to Curzon, AJBP/BL Add. MSS. 49734/164–7.

118. 16 Oct. 1919, AJB to Curzon, AJBP/BL Add. MSS. 49734/196–200. As Lord President, he was no longer entitled to the higher salary of a Secretary of State, to which Curzon now laid claim. He complained to Bonar Law, 'I see no reason, on the merits, why I should get less! Though I do not say I deserve it.' 2 Feb. 1920, BLP 98/7/2; 1, 3 Mar. 1920, BLP 101/4/9 and 98/7/1. He did not press the point – to Bonar Law's relief.

119. See 23 Oct. 1919, Stamfordham to AJB; 24 Oct. 1919, Stamfordham to the King; and 25 Oct. 1919, Stamfordham to Lloyd George, RA PS/GV/J 1525/2, 1, 6.

120. 24 Oct. 1919, AJB to Stamfordham, RA PS/GV/J 1525/5.

121. 16 Oct. 1919, AJB to Curzon, AJBP/BL Add. MSS. 49734/196–200. Gilmour, *Curzon*, p. 505.

122. 15 Oct. 1919, AJB to AB, AJBP/NAS GD 433/2/231/120; 16 Oct. 1919, AJB to Curzon, AJBP/BL Add. MSS. 49734/196–200.

123. For this impossible plan, see 28, 29 Jan. 1918, Horsley, ed., *Cynthia Asquith Diaries*, pp. 403–5.
124. Malcolm, *Balfour*, p. 81; Dugdale, *Balfour*, II, p. 298. As he had long been for the University of Edinburgh, he was an enthusiastic agent for Cambridge, throwing his prestige and popularity in America in 1928 into the quest for a gift of £700,000 from the Rockefeller family for a new library building – though certainly not securing the grant single-handedly, as is often reported.
125. The chairman of the committee was Oscar Guest, Churchill's cousin, and the secretary was the not-yet-infamous Oswald Mosley. For the 'fusion' question in the coalition see Morgan, *Consensus and Disunity*, ch. 7
126. 5 Oct. 1919, AJBP/BL Add. MSS. 49693/272–80.
127. 9 Feb. 1920, AJB to Lloyd George, LGP F/3/5/1. This was inspired by a confidential paper by the Liberal H. A. L. Fisher, advocating a merger of parties and advocating a Liberal agenda, including proportional representation, nationalization of the railways and the drink trade, and establishment of the eight-hour work day. Balfour did not send his own letter on to Lloyd George for at least a week after drafting it.
128. For various drafts of the proposed letter see AJBP/BL Add. MSS. 49791/133–4, 135–55; AJBP/NAS GD 433/2/15/21–8.
129. 15 Mar. 1920, Vincent, ed., *Crawford Papers*, p. 406.
130. See BL to AJB, 12 Mar. 1920, AJBP/NAS GD 433/2/1/33.
131. 24 Mar. 1920, BL to AJB, AJBP/NAS GD 433/2/1/36. 18 Mar. 1920, Taylor, ed., *Stevenson Diary*, p. 206.
132. AJBP/NAS GD 433/2/1/36.
133. 10 June 1920, 'Minutes of the National Union Convention', 23 June 1920, Ramsden, ed., *Sanders Diaries*, p. 139. A news release was quickly prepared rejecting all talk of fusion and denying the rumour that the National Union would elect Lloyd George leader of a new 'fused' party. N.d., BLP 96/4.
134. 11 Nov. 1919, London. See Dugdale, *Balfour*, II, p. 302.
135. See Zebel, *Balfour*, p. 264.
136. 19 Jan. 1916, CAB 37/141/11. For the entire question, see the discussion in Tomes, *Balfour and Foreign Policy*, ch. 11, on which this discussion draws. This may be contrasted with Dugdale, *Balfour*, II, ch. 15.
137. AJBP/BL Add. MSS. 49831/251–63.
138. See John Milton Cooper, *Breaking the Heart of the World: Woodrow Wilson and the Fight for the League of Nations* (New York, 2001).
139. 15 Aug. 1919, CAB 23/15.
140. 5 July 1928, Martin Gilbert, *Winston S. Churchill*, vol. 5: *The Prospect of Truth, 1922–1939* (Boston, 1977), p. 278.
141. See Cecil, *All the Way*, p. 187. Balfour finally resigned his vice-presidency of the League of Nations Union in 1923. 4 June 1923, AJB to R. Cecil, RCP/BL Add. MSS. 51071A/87–9.
142. Shannon, *Balfour and Ireland*, p. 258; Searle, *National Efficiency*, pp. 84, 144; John Campbell, *F. E. Smith: First Earl of Birkenhead* (London, 1991 edn), pp. 596–7.

143. 1 Apr. 1921, Roskill, *Hankey*, II, pp. 156–7.
144. 5 May 1917, AJB to Lloyd George, LGP F/60/2/15.
145. See Robert B. McDowell, *The Irish Convention, 1917–1918* (London, 1970), and Fair, *British Interparty Conferences*, ch. 10.
146. Balfour reminded F. S. Wrench, on 28 Oct. 1918, that he admitted to no 'personal responsibility for Irish Policy'. WP Add. MSS. 59543/19–20.
147. This was the advice of a Cabinet committee chaired by Long, who by this point saw federalism as a possible solution to the Irish stand-off. The committee reported on 4 Nov. 1919. CAB 27/68. See also Kendle, *Ireland and the Federal Solution*, pp. 226–30.
148. See entries of 12 May and 2 June 1921, Jones, *Whitehall Diary*, I, pp. 157–8, 162; Shannon, *Balfour and Ireland*, pp. 259–60, 264–7.
149. Shannon, *Balfour and Ireland*, p. 261.
150. 2 Mar. 1918, AJBP/BL Add. MSS. 49709/166. See also 25 Nov. 1919, CAB 24/93.
151. 11 Sept. 1920, Morgan, ed., *Lloyd George Family Letters*, p. 193.
152. Inspired largely by Smuts, the King's Speech was drafted by Edward Grigg. For Balfour's part in the episode, see 17 June 1921, CAB 27/107. See also Jones, *Whitehall Diary*, I, p. 162; Mackay, *Balfour*, p. 333.
153. Shannon, *Balfour and Ireland*, p. 278. See Balfour's memorandum, 15 July 1921, LGP F 3/5/15.
154. Entry of 22 July 1921, Taylor, ed., *Stevenson Diary*, pp. 230–31.
155. 28 Sept. 1921, AJBP/BL Add. MSS. 49734/225. See also Roskill, *Hankey*, II, p. 236.
156. The historical literature dealing with the conference is large, and an excellent beginning may be made with Stephen Roskill, *Naval Policy Between the Wars: The Period of Anglo-American Antagonism, 1919–1929* (London, 1968), and Erik Goldstein and John Maurer, eds., *The Washington Conference, 1921–22: Naval Rivalry, East Asian Stability and the Road to Pearl Harbor* (Ilford, Essex, 1994).
157. Roskill, *Hankey*, II, pp. 241–2. For Balfour's lack of guidance from the Lloyd George government, see Erik Goldstein, 'The Evolution of British Diplomatic Strategy for the Washington Conference', in Goldstein and Maurer, eds., *The Washington Conference*.
158. For the position of the Pacific Dominions in regard to the question of the Anglo-Japanese Treaty, see Michael Graham Fry, 'The Pacific Dominions and the Washington Conference, 1921–22', in Goldstein and Maurer, eds., *The Washington Conference*.
159. 5 July 1917, [Balfour] to Consul General Bayley, FO 800/209/188–93. President Wilson, however, was not tempted by the offer; 13 July 1917, notes by Wiseman, FO 800/209/203.
160. Balfour's draft was dictated on shipboard while en route. AJBP/BL Add. MSS. 49749/218–22.
161. Tomes, *Balfour and Foreign Policy*, pp. 254–5. The Conference produced a third agreement, the Nine-Power Treaty of the five naval powers as well as

Belgium, China, the Netherlands and Portugal, essentially making the American policy of the Open Door to China international law.

162. Alice Balfour transcribed the letter into her diary, 'Xmas Day' 1921, AJBP/NAS GD 433/2/136.

163. 5 Dec. 1921, Hankey to Thomas Jones, Jones, *Whitehall Diary*, I, p. 182.

164. Dec. 1922–Jan. 1923, 'Confidential Memos . . . concerning the fall of the Lloyd George Govt. . . .', GNCP MSS. Eur. F 112/319.

165. Among the enormous outpouring of congratulatory letters Balfour received was one from Lord Lansdowne – bygones had indeed become bygones. 16 Feb. 1922, AJBP/BL Add. MSS. 49730/301.

166. 14 Feb. 1922, King George V to AJB, AJBP/NAS GD 433/2/10/6/1; n.d., AB diary, AJBP/NAS GD 433/2/136. His Majesty did write that it gave him great pleasure to 'confer' the honours, though he did not intend this to be taken as a royal command.

167. 'It is a subject I so greatly detest', he wrote to Sir Almeric Fitzroy in 1919, 'that I am always apt to put it off too long.' 6 Dec. 1919, AJBP/NAS GD 433/2/10/1/1.

168. RA GV/GVD/1922: 15 Feb.; 12 Feb. 1922, Stamfordham to Lloyd George, RA PS/GV/J 1768/4.

169. 16 Mar. 1922, AJB to King George V, RA PS/GV/J 1768/6.

170. 16 Mar. 1922 (Paris), AJB to George V, RA PS/GV/J 1768/15; 16 Mar. 1922, AJB to Lloyd George, LGP F/3/5/18. Balfour consulted Lord Derby, among others, who offered the unwelcome advice that he consider leading the House of Lords. R. Churchill, ed., *Derby*, p. 429. When official notification of the peerage arrived from the Prime Minister's office over the signature of G. Shakespeare, Balfour's secretary noted on the letter, 'Mr B. thinks that this might be bound up with the rest of Shakespeare's works.' 11 Apr. 1922, AJBP/NAS GD 433/2/10/6/11.

171. 16 Mar. 1922, RA PS/GV/J 1768/15.

172. 21 Oct. 1922, AJB to ME, GD 433/2/229/2.

173. For the correspondence on the matter of the style of Balfour's peerage, see 27 Mar. 1922, James Balfour to AB; 10 Apr. 1922, AJB to Balfour of Burleigh; 11 Apr. 1922, Balfour of Burleigh to AB, AJBP/NAS GD 433/2/206/3, 1, 2.

174. 12 Apr. 1922, AJB to AB, AJBP/NAS GD 433/2/206/4; 17 Apr. 1922, AJBP/NAS GD 433/2/206/5. In 1914, antiquaries digging at Traprain Law, the great dome-shaped hill near Whittingehame, began to unearth evidence that the area had been occupied since pre-Roman times, which delighted Balfour. Harris, *Whittingehame House*, pp. 100–101.

175. [Sandars], *Studies of Yesterday*, p. 182.

176. 16 June 1922, Hankey to Balfour, FO 800/201/358.

177. *The Times*, 2 Aug. 1922. See Tomes, *Balfour and Foreign Policy*, p. 191.

178. Thomas Jones, *A Diary with Letters, 1931–1950* (London, 1954), p. 32.

179. For the crisis, see Beaverbrook's highly coloured but invaluable *The Decline and Fall of Lloyd George* (London, 1963), and Michael Kinnear, *The Fall of Lloyd George: The Political Crisis of 1922* (Toronto, 1973).

180. Salisbury had foreseen the repercussions among the Conservatives of failure of the Irish treaty. 18 Nov. 1921, BLP 107/1/71.

181. '[Lloyd George] is very low at B.L.'s retirement,' Stamfordham wrote to the King. 18 Mar. 1921, RA PS/GV/K 1681/3. His Majesty noted to Lloyd George the pity of Balfour's being away at this time, 'as he could give such valuable advice'. 19 Mar. 1921, LGP F/29/4/40.

182. 2 Mar. 1922, Wilson, ed., *Scott Diaries*, p. 421. Lloyd George had offered to resign in Chamberlain's favour a few days before, though it is difficult to imagine that he thought the loyal Austen would accept – and he did not. 27 Feb. 1922, Lloyd George to A. Chamberlain, LGP F/7/5/6.

183. 24 Sept. 1922, ACP AC 5/1/249.

184. See David Walder, *The Chanak Affair* (London, 1969).

185. 2 Oct. 1922, Sir Arthur Griffith-Boscawen to A. Chamberlain, ACP AC 23/2/28.

186. Walder, *Chanak Affair*, p. 282.

187. 14 Sept. 1922, CHAR 2/124 B/173–7.

188. See diary entry of 6 Oct. 1922, Vincent, ed., *Crawford Papers*, p. 444.

189. Diary entry of 10 Oct. 1922, ibid., pp. 449–50. See also Curzon's 'Notes on Events Attending break-up of the Lloyd George Govt. Written by me in Oct. 1922', GNCP MSS. Eur. F 112/319.

190. 12 Oct. 1922, ACP AC 33/2/52.

191. Churchill insisted years later that, in the presence of Lloyd George, Chamberlain and others including himself, Curzon had agreed to an early coalition election with the words 'All right, I'm game.' 29 Nov. 1929, Churchill to Lord Ronaldshay, GNCP MSS. Eur. F 112/319.

192. Though eligible to attend, Curzon absented himself from the meeting, he said, because of its being 'limited' mainly to MPs. 18 Oct. 1922, Curzon to A. Chamberlain, GNCP MSS. Eur. F 112/319.

193. 16 Oct. 1922, Mackay, *Balfour*, p. 340. Chamberlain told his sister, Hilda, that the meeting was his idea. 20 Nov. 1922, ACP AC 5/1/251.

194. Stanley Salvidge, *Salvidge of Liverpool* (London, 1934), p. 239. Salvidge's published recollections are unreliable, which makes the tale no less appetizing.

195. A recent study of the by-election clarifies the misconceptions that have long been associated with it. See John Ramsden, 'The Newport By-election and the Fall of the Coalition', in Chris Cook and John Ramsden, eds., *By-Elections in British Politics* (London, 1997).

196. 19 Oct. 1922, Vincent, ed., *Crawford Papers*, pp. 453–4; 19 Oct. 1922, Barnes and Nicholson, eds., *Amery Diaries*, I, pp. 299–300. For the meeting see 'A.F.K.-F.' [Keith-Falconer?] to Curzon, GNCP MSS. Eur. F 112/319.

197. Keith Middlemas and John Barnes, *Baldwin* (London, 1969), p. 123.

198. This vote was reported incorrectly in the official *Gleanings and Memoranda*, vol. 56 (1922), p. 495, and has been frequently misreported since 1922. The ballot cards were retained by Davidson and are preserved among his papers. Adams, *Bonar Law*, p. 328.

199. Mackay, *Balfour*, p. 340.

CHAPTER 13: LAST THINGS

1. Arthur James Balfour, *Theism and Thought* (London, 1923). The volume includes several chapters not encompassed in the lectures and another from the earlier *Theism and Humanism* as an Appendix. The text may be found on the website of the Gifford Trust, www.giffordlectures.org, with an introduction for the layman by the philosopher Michael W. DeLashmutt.

2. Balfour, *Theism and Thought*, p. 248. He had written to Pringle-Pattison a decade earlier that to him the 'schism between the God of the metaphysician and the God of ordinary piety' was more apparent than real. 'Personally,' he added, 'I accept *both* aspects of the one God, and believe both are necessary. But I have never seen any purely rational way of completely fusing them, so that I remain in this matter something of a mystic.' 13 Jan. 1914, AJBP/BL Add. MSS. 49798/74–5.

3. Balfour, *Theism and Thought*, p. 251.

4. For his efforts, Balfour received the 'free income of [the Gifford] Trust for the Session 1922–23', amounting to £580 8s. 30 July 1923, Hill Hoggan to AJB, AJBP/BL Add. MSS. 49868/135.

5. Having delivered the lectures from only brief notes, Balfour edited and expanded the shorthand notes of others for publication.

6. 21 Oct. 1922, AJB to ME, AJBP/NAS GD 433/2/229/2.

7. 24 Oct. 1922, Vincent, ed., *Crawford Papers*, p. 459. The new government included Chamberlain's half-brother, Neville, as Postmaster General.

8. 26 Apr. 1934, Taylor, ed., *Stevenson Diary*, p. 270.

9. 19 Nov. 1922, AB diary, 1917–28, AJBP/NAS GD 433/2/136. Copy of notes by Balfour's niece, Mrs Joan Lascelles, who was present.

10. Ibid.

11. Kinnear, *Fall of Lloyd George*, p. 165. On the constituency level the Lloyd George Liberals and the Conservatives often co-operated, and they actually opposed each other in only fifty-five races. Ibid., p. 144 and, for the election, chs. 7–8.

12. Adams, *Bonar Law*, p. 333.

13. Balfour dictated a recollection of this meeting, 'Memo. of a conversation with Mr Bonar Law at Whittingehame, Dec. 22/22', and the only complete copy may be found in AJBP/NAS GD 433/2/19. Partial copies are in the Balfour Papers in the British Library, Add. MSS. 49693/300–305, and in the Beaverbrook Papers, BBK/13/VI, perhaps a copy supplied by Bonar Law.

14. 16 Dec. 1922, AJB to A. Chamberlain, AJBP/NAS GD 433/2/120/26.

15. 5 Feb. 1923, Jones, *Whitehall Diary*, I, p. 226; Hankey's diary entry of 28 Dec. 1922, quoted in Roskill, *Hankey*, II, p. 328. Drummond was Balfour's former secretary at the Foreign Office and was at this time Secretary General of the League. Balfour saw him in the second week of December. 14 Dec. 1922, AJB to GB, AJBP/NAS GD 433/2/120/16

16. He wrote to Bonar Law about this matter, and raised it also with Austen Chamberlain. 16 Dec. 1922, AJBP/NAS GD 433/2/120/26.

17. Hankey had already learned of this from Drummond. Diary entry, 28 Dec. 1922, quoted in Roskill, *Hankey*, II, p. 328. Diary entry of 21 May 1923, Vincent, ed., *Crawford Papers*, p. 482.
18. AJBP/NAS GD 433/2/19. Emphasis added.
19. 14 Dec. 1922, AJB to GB, AJBP/NAS GD 433/2/120/16.
20. The occupation did not end until mid-1925, and led eventually to the so-called Dawes Plan for revising the schedule of reparations payments.
21. Mackay, *Balfour*, p. 343.
22. 2, 15 Mar.1923, Barnes and Nicholson, eds., *Amery Diaries*, I, p. 323. His two colleagues were the India Secretary, Viscount Peel, and Lord Weir, the former minister of munitions and president of the Air Board under Lloyd George.
23. 29 May 1922, 'Continental Air Menace: Note by Lord Balfour', CAB 3/3. See also Geoffrey Till, *Air Power and the Royal Navy, 1914–1945* (London, 1979), pp. 34–6.
24. Amery, as First Lord, opposed the recommendations as being destructive to the navy, and concluded that the Cabinet finally agreed to them not least because Balfour had drafted the document. 31 July 1923, Barnes and Nicholson, eds., *Amery Diaries*, I, pp. 337–8. See Mackay, *Balfour*, pp. 343–5, and, for the entire issue, Till, *Air Power and the Navy*, ch. 2. The Salisbury committee, with Balfour's support, disastrously recommended against the creation of a unified defence ministry.
25. In January Baldwin had returned from Washington with an agreement for the repayment of war debts to America, which the Prime Minister – almost alone in his Cabinet – found absolutely unacceptable. He considered resignation, but drew back in the face of the appeals of his colleagues. Also, in the first week of March, three members of the government – Griffith-Boscawen, George Stanley and J. W. Hills – were all defeated in by-elections, according to Central Office, influenced by former Tory ex-coalitionists. Adams, *Bonar Law*, pp. 347–54.
26. 26 Apr. 1923, Barnes and Nicholson, eds., *Amery Diaries*, I, p. 325.
27. 19 May 1955, memorandum by Davidson, DAV 310; 18–19 May 1923, Barnes and Nicholson, eds., *Amery Diaries*, I, pp. 326–7.
28. Adams, *Bonar Law*, pp. 361–3. For the King's position, see Rose, *George V*, pp. 266–8.
29. RA GV/GVD/1923: 29 May. Derby noted in his diary that Philip Sassoon had told him that Beaverbrook and Rothermere wished to encourage his candidacy. The cautious Earl wisely remained out of the contest. 20–22 May 1923, DP 29/1.
30. 21 May 1923, memorandum by Lord Stamfordham, RA PS/GV K 1853/8. Salisbury was suggested as a source of counsel by Bonar Law. Major General Sir Frederick Sykes, *From Many Angles: An Autobiography* (London, 1942), p. 317.
31. 20 May 1923, Stamfordham to AJB, RA PS/GV K 1853/6.
32. Memorandum 'Dictated by Lord Balfour to Miss Bliss May 22/23 – Conversation with Lord Stamfordham', AJBP/BL Add. MSS. 49686/145–6.
33. Stamfordham excused himself for several hours in the late afternoon in order

to meet with several others, including Geoffrey Dawson of *The Times*; the chairman of the Conservative Party, Colonel Jackson; the retired Treasury Permanent Under-Secretary, Sir George Murray; and Waterhouse. 21 May 1923, memorandum by Lord Stamfordham, RA PS/GV/K1853/8.

34. Ibid.
35. In addition to nine MPs, Bonar Law's Cabinet had included seven peers, among them the Secretaries of State at the Foreign, Colonial, India and War Offices.
36. 22 May 1923, memorandum by Lord Stamfordham, RA PS/GV/K 1853/18.
37. N.d., 'Note on the Events of May 1923 when I failed to become PM', GNCP MSS. Eur. F 112/319.
38. There was also unsolicited advice: Amery and Bridgeman, both strong Baldwinites, waylaid Stamfordham in St James's Park on 21 May 1923 to press their case. Barnes and Nicholson, eds., *Amery Diaries*, I, p. 327. Sir Ronald Waterhouse, without Sykes's knowledge, gave Stamfordham a mysterious unsigned memorandum, purporting to be inspired by Bonar Law and expressing his preference for Baldwin. It was, in fact, a fabrication written without Bonar Law's knowledge by Davidson and Waterhouse, and in the end it seems to have had no effect on the final decision. See Adams, *Bonar Law*, pp. 363–9.
39. Quoted in Rose, *George V*, p. 269.
40. Ibid., pp. 269–73; Gilmour, *Curzon*, p. 583. The King's relationship with Bonar Law certainly stopped well short of friendship, but this did not prevent the latter from becoming prime minister. Had Curzon been an MP rather than a peer, he would have been chosen in 1923.
41. Fair, *Temperley*, p. 238. See also Rose, *George V*, p. 269.
42. Blake, *Conservative Party*, p. 213. Lord Blake cited only 'private information' as his source.
43. See, for example, his letter to Lady Curzon in which he expressed his hope that she would avoid Whittingehame, 'for reasons well known to both of us', and described his old adversary, Derby, as 'that snake'. 29 Aug. 1923, GNCP MSS. Eur. F112/797/109–10.
44. See the diary of Robert Sanders, who shared the surprise and also lost his seat. 12 Dec. 1923, Ramsden, ed., *Sanders Diaries*, pp. 210–11.
45. 14 Dec. 1923, A. Chamberlain to Lord Lee, ACP AC 35/3/18.
46. 9 Dec. 1923, Bridgeman to M. S. Bridgeman, P. Williamson, ed., *Bridgeman Diaries*, p. 174; David Dutton, *Austen Chamberlain: Gentleman in Politics* (Bolton, 1985), p. 213. Certainly the two press lords and the former ministers wished to be rid of Baldwin. See Taylor, *Beaverbrook*, pp. 218–21.
47. Campbell, *F. E. Smith*, p. 651; R. Churchill, *Derby*, pp. 546–8; Nicolson, *George the Fifth*, p. 383.
48. 10 Dec. 1923, Balfour memorandum, AJBP/NAS GD 433/2/1/1.
49. RA GV/GVD/1923: 9, 10 Dec.
50. 11 Dec. 1923, AJB to Birkenhead, AJBP/NAS GD 433/2/1/7; Egremont, *Balfour*, p. 329.
51. 11 Dec. 1923, AJB to Birkenhead, AJBP/NAS GD 433/2/1/7. On the same

day, according to Curzon Derby put forward the suggestion that Balfour might be called upon 'in the emergency', something to which neither Balfour nor the party leaders paid the slightest attention. Curzon to Lady Curzon, GNCP MSS. Eur. F 112/797/207–9.

52. 2 Jan. 1924, Balfour memorandum, RA PS/GV/K 1918/107. This was requested by Stamfordham, 27 Dec. 1923, Stamfordham to AJB, AJBP/NAS GD 433/2/1/5.
53. 7 Feb. 1924, Barnes and Nicholson, eds., *Amery Diaries*, I, pp. 367–8; Campbell, *Smith*, p. 658.
54. 19 July 1922, *Lord Riddell's Intimate Diary of the Peace Conference and After, 1918–1923* (London, 1933), p. 379.
55. Middlemas and Barnes, *Baldwin*, p. 263.
56. 6 Mar. 1924, Churchill to AJB, AJBP/NAS GD 433/2/1/20.
57. 7 Mar. 1924, AJB to Baldwin, AJBP/NAS GD 433/2/1/19.
58. Baldwin explained the episode in a letter of 14 Mar. to Mrs Davidson, which is printed in Middlemas and Barnes, *Baldwin*, p. 263. Churchill finally won the seat in Oct. 1924.
59. 8 Nov. 1924, Jones, *Whitehall Diary*, I, p. 303.
60. Roy Jenkins, *Baldwin* (London, 1994), p. 85.
61. 30 May 1929, diary entry by Hankey, quoted in Phillip Williamson, *Stanley Baldwin: Conservative Leadership and National Values* (Cambridge, 1999), p. 166.
62. Tomes, *Balfour and Foreign Policy*: pp. 265–7.
63. 14 Mar. 1925, AB diary, AJBP/NAS GD 433/2/136; 9 Feb. 1925, Balfour memorandum, AJBP/NAS GD 433/2/136. See also Tomes, *Balfour and Foreign Policy*, pp. 265–7.
64. Mrs Dugdale did not accompany her uncle, but her sister, Mrs Joan Lascelles, did. The two sisters disagreed bitterly over the nature of Zionism, and Baffy's enthusiasm for the movement is obvious in her own writings. In an undated letter to Lady Betty Balfour, Mrs Lascelles insisted that her sister 'depicts our visit there quite incorrectly'. AJBP/NAS GD 433/2/166. An unidentified reader noted on the envelope, 'Joan was equally biased again[st] the Jews & Zionism as Baffy was for them.'
65. Viscount Samuel, *Memoirs* (London, 1945), p. 175. On 2 Apr., Balfour also inaugurated the Einstein–Balfour Physics Institute.
66. The French authorities had apparently assured Samuel that no difficulties were anticipated, but Weizmann expected trouble. Ibid., and 8 Mar. 1926, Weizmann to Vera Weizmann, Joshua Freundlich, ed., *The Letters and Papers of Chaim Weizmann*, vol. XII, series A (Jerusalem, 1977), pp. 472–3.
67. Dugdale, *Balfour*, II, pp. 367–70; Weizmann, *Trial and Error*, p. 400.
68. Balfour, *Speeches on Zionism*, p. 128.
69. Balfour's advice regarding a suitable chairman was sought by the secretary of the Research Council, Sir Walter Fletcher, who finally recommended Balfour himself. 24 Nov. 1924, Fletcher to AJB, AJBP/BL Add. MSS. 49753/3.

70. 4th Baron Rayleigh, *Lord Balfour and His Relation to Science* (London, 1930), pp. 33–8.
71. 12 Mar. 1925, AJB to Baldwin, AJBP/BL Add. MSS. 49694/1–3. He cautioned Baldwin, 'I may add that I do not think [Curzon's] enthusiasms naturally take a scientific direction.'
72. Rayleigh, *Balfour and His Relation to Science*, pp. 40–45.
73. 18 June 1925, Barnes and Nicholson, eds., *Amery Diaries*, I, p. 414.
74. *Proceedings of the British Academy, 1924–25* (London, 1927).
75. British Library Sound Archives, NP 10755W BD 1.
76. James Neidpath, *The Singapore Naval Base and the Defence of Britain's Empire* (Oxford, 1981), ch. 2; Judd, *Balfour and the British Empire*, p. 90.
77. The cornerstone of the Locarno agreements was a mutual non-aggression pact between Germany, France and Belgium, with Britain and Italy as guarantors. Chamberlain did not consider Balfour so rigid an opponent as Curzon had been, but did single him out as one of the principal sceptics. 28 Nov. 1925, A. Chamberlain to I. Chamberlain, ACP AC 5/1/370. On the completion of the treaty, however, Balfour wrote a generous letter of congratulations to the Foreign Secretary. 16 Oct. 1925, ACP AC 37/24.
78. 10 May 1926, Jones, *Whitehall Diary*, II, pp. 44–7; 10 May 1926, Barnes and Nicholson, eds., *Amery Diaries*, I, pp. 451–2. See also Koss, *Political Press*, II, p. 682.
79. Baldwin first requested simply that Balfour 'take part' in the conference. 21 Aug. 1926, Baldwin to AJB, AJBP/BL Add. MSS. 49694/4. In his memoirs, Amery recalled suggesting to Baldwin that he call on Balfour to chair the committee, but Baldwin's biographers disagree: L. S. Amery, *My Political Life* (3 vols., London, 1953–5), II, p. 384; Middlemas and Barnes, *Baldwin*, p. 365. It was not until 12 October that Hankey alerted Balfour that he would probably be asked to chair the committee. Roskill, *Hankey*, II, p. 427.
80. 21 Oct. 1926, Barnes and Nicholson, eds., *Amery Diaries*, I, p. 473. Informal use of the terms 'Dominion' and 'Commonwealth' preceded their appearance in statute.
81. See Tomes, *Balfour and Foreign Policy*, pp. 82–3.
82. He had already addressed this in the Lords on 27 July 1926, three months before the Conference. See also Judd, *Balfour and the Empire*, p. 332.
83. Dugdale, *Balfour*, II, p. 378.
84. Tomes, *Balfour and Foreign Policy*, p. 84. Denis Judd offered a different view: *Balfour and the British Empire*, p. 332.
85. AJBP/BL Add. MSS. 49753/53–61.
86. 12 June 1927, Hankey to AB, AJBP/BL Add. MSS. 49832/294–5; 28–9 Oct. 1926, Barnes and Nicholson, eds., *Amery Diaries*, I, p. 475. Chamberlain, Amery and Birkenhead were also present at these meetings in the Privy Council chambers. Hankey served as secretary.
87. Birkenhead, the India Secretary, also offered a version. There is little doubt

that Amery played a part in crafting the final text, though Balfour's patience was tried by the energetic and pushy Colonial Secretary. Balfour remarked to Chamberlain at one point that Amery's interventions were so annoying that he 'could hardly keep from screaming'. 7 Nov. 1926, A. Chamberlain to I. Chamberlain, ACP AC 5/1/399.

88. See 29 Oct. 1926, Barnes and Nicholson, eds., *Amery Diaries*, I, p. 475.

89. Tomes, *Balfour and Foreign Policy*, pp. 86–7. See 12 June 1927, Hankey to AB, AJBP/BL Add. MSS. 49832/294, 296–312.

90. Cmd 2768 (1926). See Judd, *Balfour and the Empire*, pp. 333–4.

91. 24 Nov. 1926, AJBP/BL Add. MSS. 49832/292–3.

92. 2 Nov. 1926, TP, V/2.

93. Bennett, *Margot*, pp. 353–4. Asquith had been ennobled as Earl of Oxford and Asquith in 1925, and had suffered a series of strokes not long before this encounter. He died in Feb. 1928.

94. Dutton, *Austen Chamberlain*, pp. 272–3. See his Cabinet paper of 11 Jan. 1927, AJBP/BL Add. MSS. 49689/249–52, and 10, 11 Jan. 1927, AJB to Baldwin, SBP 115/188, 191.

95. SBP 115/188.

96. 11 Jan. 1927, Balfour memorandum, SBP 115/192–5.

97. 1 Dec. 1927, CAB 27/355. See Mackay, *Balfour*, p. 349.

98. AJBP/BL Add. MSS. 49833/396–9. The description of Balfour's medical condition draws upon this record by Lord Dawson.

99. 7 Feb. 1928, AJB to Lady Weymss, AJBP/NAS GD 433/2/229/6/8; 27 Jan. 1928, AJB to Baldwin, SBP 163/9–10.

100. Ridley and Percy, eds., *Balfour–Elcho Letters*, p. 352.

101. In 1927, a collection of his speeches, *Opinions and Arguments from Speeches and Addresses of the Earl of Balfour*, was edited by Mrs Dugdale and published by Hodder & Stoughton. Balfour noted in the preface that he had played no part in the choice or editing of the documents and had no idea whether they might have been his own selections, as he had no intention of reading them.

102. 31 Dec. 1922, AJBP/BL Add. MSS. 49836/81–2; Add. MSS. 49833/396–9.

103. 25 July 1928, RA PS/GV/O 2178/1.

104. 31 July 1928, BB to Frank Balfour, AJBP/NAS GD 433/377/60–61; 2 July 1928, Churchill to Sir William Bull, WBP 5/21. The author of the plan was Lady Astor.

105. With more than 300 contributors, the fund exceeded the cost of the Rolls-Royce by £1865 13s. 0d., which was presented to Balfour for his personal use. 25, 26 July 1928, Derby to AJB, AJBP/BL Add. MSS. 49744/283, 285.

106. 25 July 1928, Vincent, ed., *Crawford Papers*, p. 527.

107. 30 July 1925. Barnes and Nicholson, eds., *Amery Diaries*, I, p. 417.

108. Dugdale, *Balfour*, II, pp. 396–8.

109. 30 Oct. 1928, SBP 163/15–16.

110. 7 Sept. 1928, SBP 163/11. The photograph was of a rather rumpled Austen Chamberlain.

111. Alice Balfour's comment on the visit was: 'Hang the woman.' 27, 28 Sept. 1928, BD to BB, AJBP/NAS GD 433/2/378/30–32, 33–6.
112. 15 Sept. 1928, AB to Baldwin, SBP 163/14.
113. 1 Jan. 1929, SBP 164/5.
114. Tom Jones noted in his diary that to Baldwin, this meant those 'older than myself'. 5 Mar. 1929, Jones, *Whitehall Diary*, II, p. 174.
115. 25 Mar. 1929, AJBP/BL Add. MSS. 49694/12–13.
116. Hankey accompanied Balfour on the journey from Fisher's Hill. Apr. 1932, 'Notes of conversation between M. P. A. Hankey and Mrs Dugdale at Roland Gardens', AJBP/BL Add. MSS. 49833/337–8.
117. He expressed the same sentiment to Hankey. Ibid.
118. 7 May 1929, AJB to ME, AJBP/NAS 433/2/229/17.
119. 27 May 1929, BB to FB, AJBP/NAS 433/2/379/57–9; 27 May 1929, GB to Baldwin, SBP 164/6; AJBP/BL Add. MSS. 49833/396–9.
120. Feb. 1932[?] 'An Old partner' wrote to Mrs Dugdale that on 27 July 1929 Balfour had arranged to receive the results of this tournament between British, American and Canadian senior players. AJBP/BL Add. MSS. 49833/297–306. Balfour had been president of the Senior Golfers Society since 1926. 7 Dec. 1926, A. C. M. Croome to AJB, AJBP/NAS GD 433/2/23/90–92.
121. J. Balfour, 'Palm Sunday Case'. See also Egremont, *Balfour*, p. 338. The author of this essay, Jean Balfour, the daughter-in-law of Gerald and later Countess of Balfour, was present at these events and apparently was herself also a 'believer'.
122. 21 June 1929, BD to BB, AJBP/NAS GD 433/2/379/72–3; Dugdale, *Balfour*, II, p. 400.
123. 13–15 Jan. 1940, Jones, *Diary with Letters*, p. 447; 9 Feb. 1930, Jones, *Whitehall Diary*, II, p. 244. Yet there was real affection between Balfour and Chamberlain, and the latter recalled Balfour as 'the last man to whom I looked up in the political world'. 24 Mar. 1933, A. Chamberlain to H. Chamberlain, ACP AC 5/1/495.
124. N.d., memorandum by BB, AJBP/NAS GD 433/2/381/28.
125. The recollection was that of Margot Asquith. 28 May 1906, Blunt, *Diaries*, II, p. 145. Balfour told Lloyd George that he anticipated a 'great experience'. 21 Nov. 1931, Cross, ed., *Life with Lloyd George*, p. 50. In Jan. 1930, weeks before his death, he wondered to Lady Wemyss what the passage would be like: 'HOW', he asked, 'am I to shuffle off the mortal coil?' C. Asquith, *Remember and Be Glad*, p. 33.
126. AJBP/NAS GD 433/2/381/33; 19 Mar. 1933, GB to Baldwin, SBP 165/13.
127. Many of these are preserved in his papers, AJBP/BL Add. MSS. 49831 and AJBP/NAS 433/2/381.
128. 20 Mar. 1920, BB to FB, AJBP/NAS 433/2/38/134.
129. *Observer*, 23 Mar. 1930.
130. Ibid.; Dugdale, *Balfour*, II, pp. 411–12; Egremont, *Balfour*, p. 339.
131. 'Easter Day' 1922, FB to Frank Balfour, AJBP/NAS GD 433/2/367/71.
132. 2 June 1930, AJBP/NAS GD 433/2/386/53–60. See also Harris,

Whittingehame House, pp. 109–10.

133. For the later history of the house and its resurrection see Harris, *Whittingehame House*, pp. 110–24.

134. 9 Nov. 1931, A. Chamberlain to BD, AJBP/BL Add. MSS. 49833/151–6.

135. Chamberlain continued briefly as Lord President after Churchill succeeded him as premier in 1940, and Home, as Sir Alec Douglas-Home, served as prime minister for only one year (1963–4) and later served as Foreign Secretary under Edward Heath (1970–73).

136. See, for example, Raymond, *Balfour*, p. 212.

137. See the correspondence of July 1927 over his 'air pollution' statements and the annoyance they caused to the coal industry. AJBP/BL Add. MSS. 49755/80–88.

138. David Dilks, *Neville Chamberlain*, vol. 1: *Pioneering and Reform, 1869–1929* (Cambridge, 1984), p. 288. Balfour, as Chamberlain once said of him, is said to have spoken of the future 'appeasement' prime minister as having a 'heart like a stone'. Self, ed., *Neville Chamberlain Diary Letters*, I, p. 9.

139. Raymond, *Balfour*, p. 212.

140. 15 Apr. 1929, A. Chamberlain to BD, AJBP/NAS GD 433/2/379/48.

Bibliographic Note

This study is based upon a number of manuscript collections, public and private, upon the contemporary newspaper press and the *Parliamentary Debates*, and upon various published sources. Not surprisingly, a number of studies of Arthur James Balfour have appeared over the past century (all in London, unless otherwise noted), beginning with Bernard Alderson, *Arthur James Balfour: The Man and His Work* (1903) and the more critical E. T. Raymond [Edward Raymond Thompson], *Mr Balfour: A Biography* (1920). Two brief and very personal recollections were published in 1930, the year of Balfour's death: one by his sometime political secretary, Sir Ian Malcolm, *Lord Balfour: A Memory*, and the other by a nephew, the 4th Baron Rayleigh, *Lord Balfour and His Relation to Science*. The two-volume 'official' life, *Arthur James Balfour, First Earl of Balfour* (1936) was written by Balfour's niece, Blanche E. C. Dugdale. Mrs Dugdale loved and admired her uncle, and late in his life she acted as his secretary, editor and confidante. For many years she had noted her conversations with Balfour, and she had access not only to his papers, but to the man and to his friends and colleagues, most of whom she had known since her childhood. Still an irreplaceable resource, her work is highly coloured and must be read with caution; and the warning of Jane Ridley and Clayre Percy should be borne in mind: 'The Balfour she paints is the adored, brilliant, benevolent long-legged uncle of her childhood.' The same may be said of her charming *Family Homespun* (1930). A harder-edged family memoir is that of Balfour's sister-in-law Lady Frances Balfour, *Ne Obliviscaris* (n.d. [1930]). The first 'modern' biography, Kenneth Young, *Arthur James Balfour: The Happy Life of the Politician, Prime Minister, Statesman, and Philosopher* (1963), is a 'good read' but is often misleading. A brief and more academic biography by an American historian, Sydney Zebel, delivers quite effectively what its title promises: *Balfour: A Political Biography* (1973); while Lord Egremont's excellent *Arthur James Balfour* (1980) was the first study to make effective use of the Balfour–Elcho correspondence and is particularly insightful regarding his life beyond Westminster. More recently, Ruddock F. Mackay has published *Balfour: Intellectual Statesman* (1985), the great strength of which, despite the title, lies in its exhaustive treatment of Balfour's defence and foreign-policy thinking. As this is written, a new brief life is soon to be published: E. H. H. Green, *Balfour*.

The Letters of Arthur Balfour and Lady Elcho, 1885–1917 (1992), edited by Jane Ridley and Clayre Percy, is invaluable. The same may be said of Robin Harcourt Williams, ed., *The Salisbury–Balfour Correspondence, 1869–1892* (1988). Among the 'Balfour and . . .' books that examine his career in regard to certain major political questions is Denis Judd, *Balfour and the British Empire: A Study in Imperial Evolution* (1968), as are two studies of Balfour's long connection to 'John Bull's other Island': Catherine B. Shannon, *Arthur J. Balfour and Ireland, 1874–1922* (Washington, DC, 1988), which is very critical of his Irish policy; and David R. C. Hudson, *The Ireland That We Made: Arthur and Gerald Balfour's Contributions to the Origins of Modern Ireland* (Akron, O., 2003), which finds more positive aspects in it. Alfred Gollin, *Balfour's Burden: Arthur Balfour and Imperial Preference* (1965) and Roy Jenkins, *Mr Balfour's Poodle, An Account of the Struggle between the House of Lords and the Government of Mr Asquith* (1954) deal with two of the great crises faced by Balfour during his party leadership. More recently, Jason Tomes has published an excellent study, the title of which tells all: *Balfour and Foreign Policy: The International Thought of a Conservative Statesman* (1997). Difficult to classify, but necessary all the same, is Paul Harris, *Life in a Scottish Country House: The Story of A. J. Balfour and Whittingehame House* (Whittingehame, 1989). Two books, Jane Abdy and Charlotte Gere, *The Souls* (1984) and Angela Lambert, *Unquiet Souls* (1984) are helpful in understanding the social circle which he dominated. An exhaustive index of all published Balfouriana is Eugene L. Rasor, *Arthur James Balfour, 1848–1930: Historiography and Annotated Bibliography* (Westport, Conn., 1998). Of course, no serious book dealing with the politics and society of his time does not deal in some way with Arthur Balfour.

Balfour published much throughout his life, and his books include *A Defence of Philosophic Doubt* (1879), *The Foundations of Belief* (1895), *Theism and Humanism: Being the Gifford Lectures, 1914* (1915) and *Theism and Thought: Second Course of Gifford Lectures, 1922–1923* (1923). Several edited collections of his writings and speeches, including some excerpts from these works, include Wilfrid M. Short, ed., *The Mind of Arthur James Balfour: Selections from His Non-Political Writings, Speeches, and Addresses, 1879–1917* (1918), Israel

Cohen, ed., *Speeches on Zionism* (1928) and Blanche Dudgale, ed., *Opinions and Arguments from Speeches and Addresses of the Earl of Balfour, 1910–1927* (1927). Late in his life he agreed to write his autobiography, but, as his health rapidly declined, he was able only to dictate a few chapters to Mrs Dugdale, and this was published as *Chapters of Autobiography* (1930).

The purpose of the endnote references is not only to identify the origins of quotations or to provide evidence in support of the author's reasoning, but also to aid the reader who wishes to pursue further the matters raised in this book. Perhaps this will be accepted as a justification for the plenitude of the notes and a plea for the forgiveness of those who understandably tire of reading notes that begin: 'See . . .' or 'In this regard . . .'

Documentary sources consulted include the Prime Ministers' official papers and those of the Cabinet and several government departments including the Admiralty, the Treasury, and the Foreign and Irish Offices, as well as the *Parliamentary Debates*. All quotations of parliamentary speeches are taken from this official publication, unless otherwise noted. The major sources of this study are the Balfour papers in the British Library and the Balfour family papers in the National Archives of Scotland. Also of prime importance are the papers of his private secretary of many years, John Satterfield Sandars (Bodleian Library, Oxford), who retained in his possession much of Balfour's pre-war political correspondence. The letters Balfour exchanged over four decades with Lady Elcho, photocopies of which I was permitted to read, also provide useful insights into his character.

The author regrets that, due to one circumstance or another, several collections of papers were unavailable at the time of writing. Many others were, however, and among the archival sources consulted were the papers of Aretas Akers-Douglas, Kent Record Office, Maidstone; Lord Alverstone, British Library; H. O. Arnold-Forster, British Library; Lord Ashbourne, House of Lords Record Office; H. H. Asquith, Bodleian Library, Oxford; Lord Avebury, British Library; Stanley Baldwin, Cambridge University Library; Lord Battersea, British Library; Lord Beaverbrook, House of Lords Record Office; Oscar Browning, King's College, Cambridge; Sir William Bull, Churchill College, Cambridge; Sir Henry Campbell-Bannerman, British Library; Lord Carnarvon, British Library; Sir Edward Carson, Public Record Office of Northern Ireland; Lord Robert Cecil, British Library and Hatfield House; Austen Chamberlain, University Library, Birmingham; Joseph Chamberlain, University Library, Birmingham; Neville Chamberlain, University Library, Birmingham; Lord Chandos (Lyttelton Papers), Churchill College, Cambridge; Sir George Sydenham Clarke, British Library; Richard

Assheton Cross, British Library; Lord Randolph Churchill (Chartwell Trust Papers), Churchill College, Cambridge; Winston S. Churchill (Chartwell Trust Papers), Churchill College, Cambridge; Lord Curzon, British Library; Lord D'Abernon, British Library; J. C. C. Davidson, House of Lords Record Office; Geoffrey Dawson [Robinson], British Library; Lord Derby, Liverpool Public Library; Sir Charles Dilke, British Library; King Edward VII, Royal Archives, Windsor; Lord Esher, Churchill College, Cambridge; Sir John Fisher, Cambridge University Library; J. L. Garvin, Harry Ransom Humanities Research Center, University of Texas; King George V, Royal Archives; Mary Gladstone [Drew], British Library; William Ewart Gladstone, British Library; Sir Arthur Griffith-Boscawen, Bodleian Library, Oxford; Richard Burden Haldane, National Library of Scotland, Edinburgh; Sir Maurice Hankey, Churchill College, Cambridge; Lord Hardinge of Penshurst, Cambridge University Library; Lord Halsbury, British Library; Sir Edward Hamilton, British Library; Sir Samuel Hoare, Cambridge University Library; Sir Edward Hutton, British Library; E. B. Iwan-Müller, British Library; Lord Jellicoe, British Library; Lord Kitchener, National Archives, London; Lord Knollys, Royal Archives; Lord Lansdowne, British Library; Andrew Bonar Law, House of Lords Record Office; Sir Sidney Lee, British Library; David Lloyd George, House of Lords Records Office; Lord Londonderry, Public Record Office of Northern Ireland, Belfast; Walter Long, British Library; Wiltshire Record Office; Sir Antony MacDonnell, Bodleian Library, Oxford; Leopold Maxse, West Sussex Record Office; Lord Midleton (Brodrick Papers), National Archives, London; Lord Milner, Bodleian Library, Oxford; Lord Northcliffe, British Library; Sir Stafford Northcote, British Library; Ralph Spencer Paget, British Library; Sir Horace Plunkett, Plunkett Foundation, Oxford; Lord Riddell, British Library; Charles Thomson Ritchie, British Library; Lord Roberts, National Army Museum, London; 3rd and 4th Marquesses of Salisbury, Hatfield House, Hertfordshire; 2nd Earl of Selborne, Bodleian Library, Oxford; George Bernard Shaw, British Library; J. St Loe Strachey, House of Lords Record Office; Lord Stamfordham, Royal Archives; Henry Wickham Steed, British Library; Sir Arthur Steel-Maitland, National Archives of Scotland; A. J. Sylvester, National Library of Wales; Lord Templewood, Cambridge University Library; Queen Victoria, Royal Archives; Lord Willoughby de Broke, House of Lords Record Office; Sir Henry Wilson, National Army Museum, London; F. S. Wrench, British Library.

Index

Acland-Hood, Alexander (*later* 1st
 Baron St Audries), 180, 230, 249,
 250; gathers information on party
 sentiment toward tariffs; 215;
 predicts Unionist victory, January
 1910, 242
Agar-Robartes, Thomas: proposes
 Ulster exclusion from Home Rule,
 277
Aitken, William Maxwell *see*
 Beaverbrook, 1st Baron
Akers-Douglas, Aretas (*later* 1st
 Viscount Chilston; 'Alec'), 58, 165,
 181, 221, 230; becomes Home
 Secretary, 173; advises AJB on
 'Lloyd George memorandum', 245
Amery, Leopold Stennett, 355, 361,
 362, 370, 373; opposes Churchill's
 election, 367
Apostles, Cambridge, 19, 20
Arnold-Forster, Hugh Oakley:
 becomes Secretary of State for War,
 180; unsuccessful plan for Army
 reform, 181–5
Ashbourne, Edward Gibson, 1st Baron
 (Lord Chancellor of Ireland): AJB
 clashes with, 78
Ashley, William James, 206
Asquith, Lady Cynthia (Cynthia
 Charteris): recalls life at
 Whittingehame, 10
Asquith, Herbert Henry, 119, 133, 238;
 becomes PM, 236; calls for January
 1910 election, 242; government

dependent on Irish National Party
 from January 1910, 242; and
 Parliament Act of 1911, 243,
 251–2; at 1910 Constitutional
 Conference, 244; introduces third
 Home Rule bill, 275; secret talks
 with Bonar Law, 278; meets
 Carson, 279; and Curragh incident,
 181; and 1914 Buckingham Palace
 Conference, 283–4; insists on
 passing and suspending Home
 Rule Act, August 1914, 284–5;
 appoints War Council, 290; forms
 coalition government, 298–9;
 forms Dardanelles Committee, 302;
 forms War Committee, 304; passes
 'Bachelors Bill', 306; downfall of
 government, 315–23; unwillingness
 to forgive AJB for fall of
 government, 322; and 'Coupon
 Election', 340; declining health,
 373
Asquith, Margot (Margaret Tennant):
 friend and fellow 'Soul', 116;
 rumours of betrothal to AJB,
 121–2; marvels at AJB's
 youthfulness, 373

Balcarres, 10th Earl of (*later* 27th Earl
 of Crawford), 132; becomes Chief
 Whip, 249; and AJB's position as
 leader in 1910, 255; learns AJB will
 resign leadership, 256–7; refuses to
 serve under Bonar Law, 355–6

465

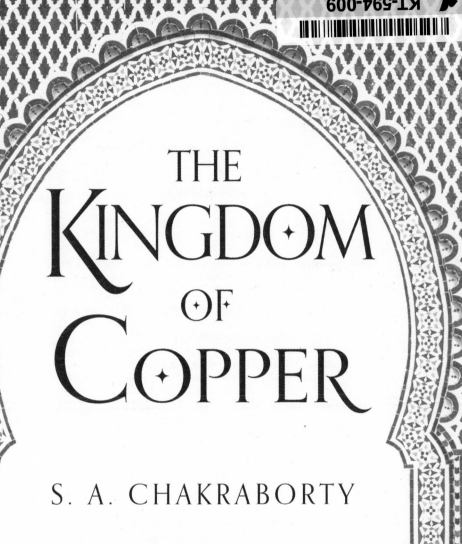

THE
KINGDOM
OF
COPPER

S. A. CHAKRABORTY

Book Two of the
Daevabad Trilogy

HARPER
Voyager

Harper*Voyager*
An imprint of HarperCollins*Publishers* Ltd
1 London Bridge Street
London SE1 9GF

www.harpercollins.co.uk

First published by HarperCollins*Publishers* 2019
1

HB ISBN: 978-0-00823944-2
TPB ISBN: 978-0-00-823945-9

Designed by Paula Russell Szafranski
Map copyright © Nicolette Caven
Half title and chapter opener art © Shutterstock.com

Printed and bound in the UK by
CPI Group (UK) Ltd, Croydon CR0 4YY

MIX
Paper from
responsible sources
FSC C007454

THE KINGDOM OF COPPER

ALSO BY S. A. CHAKRABORTY

The City of Brass

FOR SHAMIK

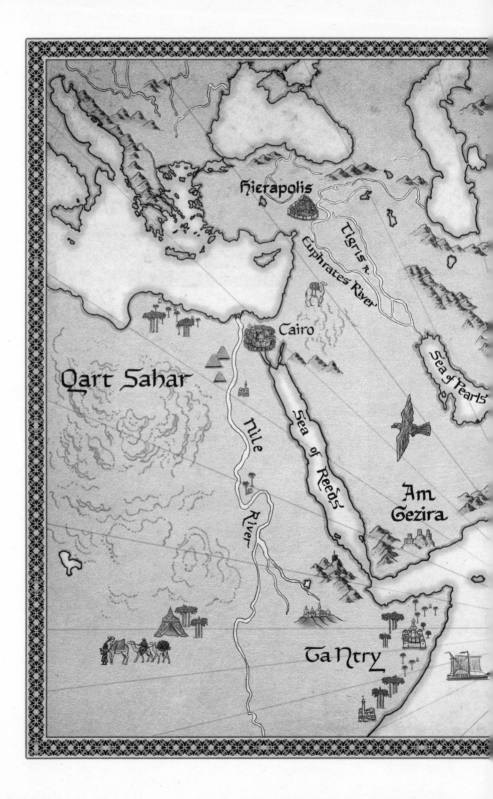

Hierapolis

Tigris R.

Euphrates River

Cairo

Qart Sahar

Sea of Pearls

Nile

Sea of Reeds

River

Am
Gezira

Ta Ntry

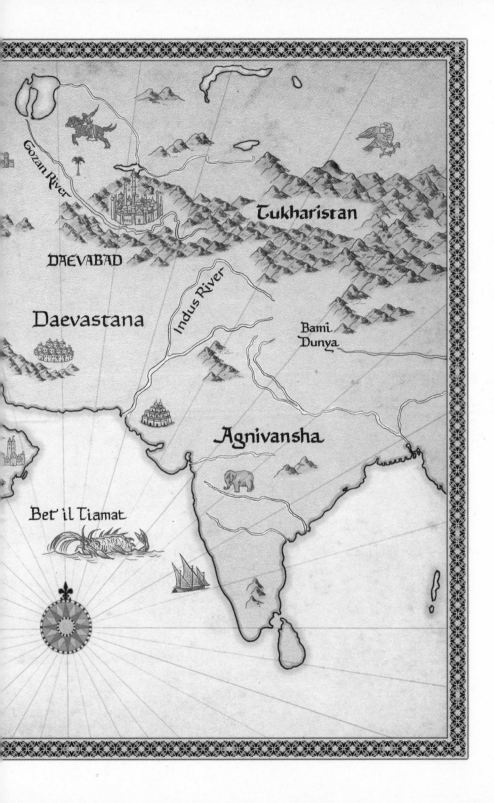

Gozan River

Tukharistan

DAEVABAD

Indus River

Daevastana

Bami
Dunya

Agnivansha

Bet' il Tiamat

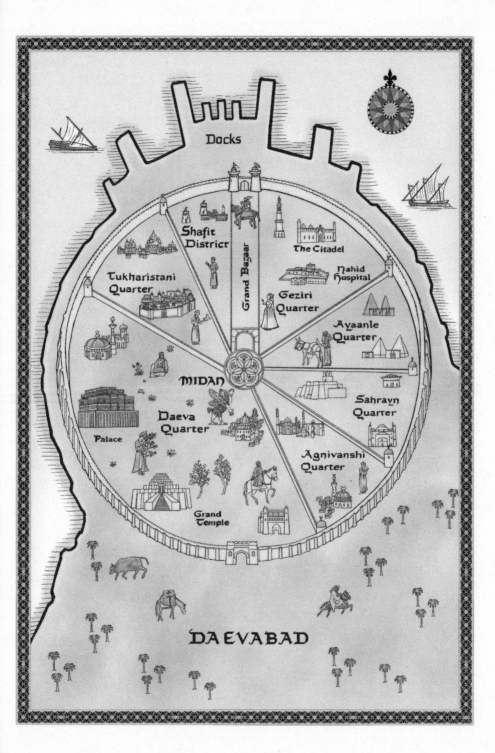

Docks

Shafit
District

The Citadel

Tukharistani
Quarter

Grand Bazaar

Nahid
Hospital

Geziri
Quarter

Ayaanle
Quarter

MIDAN

Sahrayn
Quarter

Daeva
Quarter

Palace

Agnivanshi
Quarter

Grand
Temple

DAEVABAD

PROLOGUE

ALI

Alizayd al Qahtani didn't make it a month with his caravan.

"Run, my prince, run!" the sole Ayaanle member of his traveling party cried as he staggered into Ali's tent one night when they were camped along a southern bend of the Euphrates. Before the man could say more, a blood-dark blade burst from his chest.

Ali flew to his feet. His weapons already at hand, he slashed the back of the tent open with a strike of his zulfiqar and fled into the darkness.

They pursued him on horseback, but the Euphrates glistened close ahead, black as the star-drenched night reflected in the river's coursing surface. Praying his weapons were secure, Ali plunged into the water as the first arrows flew, one whistling past his ear.

The cold water was a shock, but Ali swam fast, the motion as instinctual as walking, faster than he ever had, with a grace that would have taken him aback had he not been preoccupied with saving his life. Arrows struck the water around him, following his path, and so he dived deep, the water growing murky. The Euphrates was wide, and it took him time to cross, to push through waterweeds and fight the fierce current trying to drag him downstream.

It was only when he was staggering up the opposite bank that the sick realization swept over him: he had not needed to emerge for air the entire time.

Ali gulped, shivering as a cold breeze stole through his wet dishdasha. Nausea rose in his chest, but there was little time to contemplate what had happened in the river—not when mounted archers were pacing on the other side. His tent was aflame, but the rest of the camp looked untouched and eerily still, as though a quiet command had been passed among the other travelers in his party to ignore the screams they might hear tonight.

Ali had been betrayed. And he was not waiting around to find out if either the assassins or his traitorous companions could cross the river. He stumbled to his feet and ran for his life, racing headlong toward the opposite horizon.

Dawn had broken by the time his legs finally gave out. He collapsed, landing hard on the golden sand. The river was long gone. In every direction was desert, the sky a bright, hot bowl turned upside down.

Ali's gaze darted across the still landscape as he fought for breath, but he was alone. Relief and fear warred through him. He was *alone*—with a vast desert before him and enemies at his back, his only possessions his zulfiqar and khanjar. He had no food, no water, no shelter. He hadn't even had time to grab the turban and sandals that might have protected him from the heat.

He was doomed.

You were already doomed, you fool. Your father made that clear. Ali's exile from Daevabad was a death sentence, one obvious to anyone with knowledge of the politics of his tribe. Did he really think he could fight it? That his death would be easy? If his father had wanted to be merciful, he would have had his youngest son strangled in his sleep within the city's walls.

For the first time, a twinge of hate clawed up in Ali's heart. He didn't deserve this. He had tried to help his city and his family, and Ghassan wasn't even generous enough to give him a clean death.

Angry tears pricked his eyes. Ali wiped them away roughly, feeling disgusted. No, this wouldn't be how things ended for him, weeping tears of self-pity and cursing his family as he wasted away in some unknown patch of sand. He was Geziri. When the time came, Ali would die dry-eyed, with the declaration of faith on his lips and a blade in his hand.

He fixed his eyes southwest, in the direction of his homeland, the direction he'd prayed his entire life, and dug his hands in the golden sand. Ali went through the motions to cleanse himself for prayer, the motions he'd made multiple times a day since his mother had first shown him how.

When he finished, he raised his palms, closing his eyes and catching the sharp scent of the sand and salt clinging to his skin. *Guide me*, he begged. *Protect those I was forced to leave behind and when my time comes*—his throat thickened—*when my time comes, please have more mercy on me than my father did.*

Ali touched his fingers to his brow. And then he rose to his feet.

Having nothing but the sun to guide him through the unbroken expanse of sand, Ali followed its relentless path across the sky, ignoring and then growing accustomed to its merciless heat upon his shoulders. The hot sand scorched his bare feet—and then it didn't. He was a djinn, and though he couldn't drift and dance as smoke among the dunes the way his ancestors had done before Suleiman's blessing, the desert would not kill him. He walked each day until exhaustion overtook him, only stopping to pray and sleep. He let his mind—his despair at how completely he'd ruined his life—drift away under the white, bright sun.

Hunger gnawed at him. Water was no problem—Ali had not thirsted since the marid took him. He tried hard not to think about the implication of that, to ignore the newly restless part of his mind that delighted in the dampness—he refused to call it sweat—beading on his skin and dripping down his limbs.

He could not say how long he'd been walking when the landscape finally changed, rocky cliffs emerging from the sandy dunes like massive, grasping fingers. Ali scoured the craggy bluffs for any sign of food. He'd heard rural Geziris were able to conjure entire feasts from human scraps, but Ali had never been taught such magic. He was a prince raised to be a Qaid, surrounded by servants his entire privileged life. He had no idea how to survive on his own.

Desperate and starving, he ate any bit of greenery he could find down to the roots. It was a mistake. The following morning, he awoke violently ill. Ash crumbled from his skin, and he vomited until all that came up was a fiery black substance that burned the ground.

Hoping to find a bit of shade in which to recover, Ali tried to climb down from the cliffs, but he was so dizzy that his vision blurred and the path danced before him. He lost his footing on the loose gravel almost immediately and slipped, tumbling down a sharp incline.

He landed hard in a stony crevasse, smashing his left shoulder into a protruding rock. There was a wet pop, and a searing heat burst down his arm.

Ali gasped. He tried to shift and then yelped, a sharp pain shooting through his shoulder. He sucked for air through his teeth, biting back a curse as the muscles in his arm spasmed.

Get up. You will die here if you do not get up. But Ali's weakened limbs refused to obey. Blood trickled from his nose, filling his mouth as he stared helplessly at the stark cliffs outlined against the bright sky. A glance at the crevasse revealed nothing but sand and stones. It was—rather fittingly—a dead place.

He choked back a sob. There were worse ways to die, he knew. He could have been caught and tortured by his family's enemies or hacked apart by assassins eager to claim bloody "proof" of their victory. But God forgive him, Ali was not ready to die.

You are Geziri. A believer in the Most Merciful. Do not dishonor yourself now. Shaking, Ali squeezed his eyes against the pain, trying to find some peace in the holy passages he'd memorized so long ago. But it was difficult. The faces of those he'd left behind in Daevabad— the brother whose trust he'd finally lost, the friend whose love he'd killed, the father who'd sentenced him to death for a crime he hadn't committed—kept breaking through the encroaching darkness, their voices taunting him as he slowly slipped away.

He woke to an impossibly foul substance being forced down his throat.

Ali's eyes shot open and he gagged, his mouth full of something crunchy and metallic and *wrong*. His vision swam, slowly focusing on the silhouette of a broad-shouldered man squatting beside him. The man's face came to him in patches: a nose that had been broken more than once, a matted black beard, hooded gray eyes.

Geziri eyes.

The man laid a heavy hand on Ali's brow and spooned another thick helping of the disgusting gruel into his mouth. "Eat up, little prince."

Ali choked. "W-what is that?" His voice was barely a whisper in his parched throat.

The other djinn beamed. "Oryx blood and ground locusts."

Ali's stomach immediately rebelled. He turned his head to

throw up, but the man clamped his hand over Ali's mouth and massaged his throat, forcing the revolting mixture back down.

"Aye, do not be doing that. What kind of man turns down food that his host has so thoughtfully prepared?"

"Daevabadis." A second voice spoke up, and Ali glanced down at his feet, catching sight of a woman with thick black braids and a face that might have been carved from stone. "No manners." She held up Ali's zulfiqar and khanjar. "Lovely blades."

The man held up a gnarled black root. "Did you eat something like this?" When Ali nodded, he snorted. "Fool. You're lucky not to be a pile of ash right now." He shoved another spoonful of the bloody gristle at Ali. "Eat. You'll need your strength for the journey home."

Ali pushed it weakly away, still dazed and now thoroughly confused. A breeze swept through the crevasse, drying the dampness that clung to his skin, and he shivered. "Home?" he repeated.

"Bir Nabat," the man said as if it was the most obvious thing in the world. "Home. It is but a week's travel west."

Ali tried to shake his head, but his neck and shoulders had gone stiff. "I can't," he rasped out. "I . . . I'm going south." South was the only direction he could think to go; the Qahtani family originally hailed from the forbidding mountain chain along Am Gezira's humid southern coast, and it was the only place he could think to find allies.

"*South?*" The man laughed. "You are mostly dead and you think to cross Am Gezira?" He thrust another spoonful into Ali's mouth. "There are assassins looking for you in every shadow of this land. Word is the fire worshippers will make rich the man who kills Alizayd al Qahtani."

"Which is what *we* should be doing, Lubayd," the other raider cut in. She nodded rudely at the gruel. "Not wasting our provisions on a southern brat."

Ali swallowed back the vile concoction with difficulty, narrowing his eyes at her. "You'd kill a fellow Geziri for foreign coins?"

"I'd kill a Qahtani for free."

Ali started at the hostility in her voice. The man—Lubayd—sighed and shot her an annoyed look before turning back to Ali. "You'll forgive Aqisa here, prince, but it's not a good time to be visiting our land." He put down the clay cup. "We haven't seen a drop of rain in years. Our spring is drying up, we're running out of food, our babies and old folk are dying . . . So we send messages to Daevabad pleading for help. And do you know what our king says, our fellow Geziri king?"

"*Nothing.*" Aqisa spat at the ground. "Your father doesn't even respond. So do not speak of tribal ties to me, al Qahtani."

Ali was too tired to be frightened by the hatred in her face. He eyed the zulfiqar in her hands again. He kept his blade sharp; at least this ordeal would finally end quickly should they choose to execute him with it.

He choked back another wave of bile, the oryx blood thick in his throat. "Well . . . ," he started weakly. "In that case I agree. You needn't waste that on me." He nodded at Lubayd's gruel.

There was a long moment of silence. Then Lubayd burst into laughter, the sound ringing out across the crevasse.

He was still laughing when he grabbed Ali's injured arm without warning and pulled it firmly straight.

Ali cried out, black spots blossoming across his vision. But as his shoulder slid back into place, the searing pain immediately lessened. His fingers tingled, sensation returning to his numb hand in excruciating waves.

Lubayd grinned. He removed his ghutra, the cloth headdress worn by northern Geziri djinn, and quickly fashioned it into a sling. Then he hauled Ali to his feet by his good arm. "Keep your sense of humor, boy. You're going to need it."

A massive white oryx waited patiently at the mouth of the crevasse; a line of dried blood crossed one flank. Ignoring Ali's protests, Lubayd shoved him up onto the animal's back. Ali clutched its long horns, watching as Lubayd wrestled his zulfiqar away from Aqisa.

He dropped it in Ali's lap. "Let that shoulder heal and perhaps you'll swing this again."

Ali gave the blade an incredulous look. "But I thought . . ."

"We'd be killing you?" Lubayd shook his head. "No. Not yet, anyway. Not while you are doing *that*." He motioned back to the crevasse.

Ali followed his gaze. His mouth fell open.

It wasn't sweat that had soaked his robe. A miniature oasis had sprung up around him while he lay dying. A spring gurgled through the rocks where his head had been, trickling down a path shrouded with new moss. A second spring bubbled up through the sand, filling the depression his body had left. Bright green shoots covered a bloody patch of gravel, their unfurling leaves wet with dew.

Ali took a sharp breath, scenting the fresh moisture on the desert air. The potential.

"I have no idea how you did that, Alizayd al Qahtani," Lubayd said. "But if you can draw water into a barren patch of sand in Am Gezira, well . . ." He winked. "I'd say you're worth far more than a few foreign coins."

NAHRI

It was very quiet inside Emir Muntadhir al Qahtani's apartment.

Banu Nahri e-Nahid paced the room, her bare toes sinking into the sumptuous carpet. Upon a mirrored table, a bottle of wine rested beside a jade cup carved in the shape of a shedu. The wine had been brought in by the calm-eyed servants who'd helped

Nahri out of her heavy wedding clothes; perhaps they'd noticed the Banu Nahida's trembling and thought it would help.

She stared at the bottle now. It looked delicate. It would be easy to break it, easier still to conceal a glass shard under the pillows of the large bed she was trying not to look at and end this evening in a far more permanent way.

And then you will die. Ghassan would put a thousand of her tribesmen to the sword, make Nahri watch each one, and then throw her to his karkadann.

She tore her gaze from the bottle. A breeze came from the open windows, and she shivered. She'd been dressed in a delicate blue silk shift and soft hooded robe, neither of which did much to ward off the chill. All that was left of the overly elaborate outfit in which she'd been wed was her marriage mask. Made of finely carved ebony and secured by copper clasps and chains, the mask was engraved with her and Muntadhir's names. It was to be burned upon consummation, the ash marking their bodies the next morning proof of the marriage's validity. It was—according to the excited Geziri noblewomen teasing her earlier at the wedding dinner—a beloved tradition of their tribe.

Nahri didn't share their excitement. She'd been sweating since she entered the room, and the mask kept sticking to her damp skin. She pulled it slightly loose, trying to let the breeze cool her flushed cheeks. She caught the reflection of her movement in the massive bronze-edged mirror across the room and averted her eyes. However fine the clothes and mask, they were Geziri, and Nahri had no desire to see herself in the garb of her enemy.

They're not your enemy, she reminded herself. "Enemy" was Dara's word, and she was not going to think about Dara. Not tonight. She couldn't. It would break her—and the last Banu Nahida of Daevabad was not going to break. She'd signed her wedding contract with a steady hand and toasted Ghassan without trembling, smiling warmly at the king who'd threatened her with the murder of Daeva children and forced her to disown her Afshin with the crudest of charges. If she could handle all of that, she could handle whatever happened in this room.

Nahri turned to cross the bedroom again. Muntadhir's vast apartment was located on one of the upper levels of the enormous ziggurat at the heart of Daevabad's palace complex. It was filled with art: paintings on silk screens, delicate tapestries, and finely wrought vases, all of which had been carefully displayed and all of which seemed to carry an aura of magic. She could easily envision Muntadhir in this wondrous room, lounging with a cup of expensive wine and some cosmopolitan courtesan, quoting poetry and bantering about the useless pleasures of life that Nahri had neither the time nor inclination to pursue. There was not a book in sight. Not in this room, nor in the rest of the apartment she'd been guided through.

She stopped to stare at the closest painting, a miniature of two dancers conjuring flamelike flowers that sparked and flashed like hearts of ruby as they twirled.

I have nothing in common with this man. Nahri couldn't imagine the splendor in which Muntadhir had been raised, couldn't imagine being surrounded by the accumulated knowledge of millennia and not bothering to learn how to read. The only thing she shared with her new husband was one awful night upon a burning ship.

The bedroom door opened.

Nahri instinctively stepped back from the painting, pulling her hood low. There was a soft crash from outside, followed by a curse, and then Muntadhir entered.

He wasn't alone; indeed, she suspected he might not have made it alone, for he was leaning heavily on a steward, and she could practically smell the wine on his breath from across the room. A pair of female servants followed, and Nahri swallowed as they helped him out of his robe, unwinding his turban with a number of what sounded like teasing jests in Geziriyya, before leading him to the bed.

He sat heavily on the edge, looking drunk and somewhat stunned to find himself there. Heaped with cloudlike linens, the bed was big enough to fit a family of ten—and given the rumors she'd heard whispered about her husband, she suspected he'd filled it on many an occasion. Frankincense smoldered in a corner burner beside a chalice of sweetened milk mixed with apple leaves—a traditional Daeva drink brewed for new brides hoping to conceive. That, at least, would *not* be happening—Nisreen had assured her. One did not assist Nahid healers for two centuries without learning a number of nearly foolproof methods to prevent pregnancy.

Even so, Nahri's heart beat faster as the servants left, closing the door softly behind them. Tension filled the air, thick and heavy and at awkward odds with the sounds of celebration in the garden below.

Muntadhir finally glanced up, meeting her eyes. Candlelight played on his face. He might not have had Dara's literally magical beauty, but he was a strikingly handsome man, a charismatic man, she'd heard, one who laughed easily and smiled often . . . at least with people who weren't her. His thick black hair was cut short, his beard stylishly trimmed. He'd worn his royal regalia for the wedding, the gold-trimmed ebony robe and patterned blue, purple, and gold silk turban that were the hallmarks of the ruling al Qahtani family, but he was dressed now in a crisp white dishdasha edged with tiny pearls. The only thing detracting from his careful appearance was a thin scar dividing his left eyebrow—a remnant from Dara's scourge.

They stared at each other for a long moment, neither one moving. She saw that beneath the edge of drunken exhaustion, he too looked nervous.

Finally he spoke. "You're not going to give me plague sores, are you?"

Nahri narrowed her eyes. "Excuse me?"

"Plague sores." Muntadhir swallowed, kneading the embroidered covering on the bed. "That's what your mother used to do to men who looked at her too long."

Nahri hated that the words stung. She wasn't a romantic—on the contrary, she prided herself on her pragmatism and her ability to set aside her emotions—that's what had led her to this room, after all. But it was still her *wedding night*, and she might have hoped for a word of kindness from her new husband; for a man eager to touch her, rather than one worried she would curse him with some sort of magical disease.

She let her robe drop to the floor without ceremony. "Let's get this over with." She approached the bed, fumbling with the delicate copper fixtures holding her marriage mask in place.

"Be careful!" Muntadhir's hand shot out, but he jerked it back when he brushed her fingers. "Forgive me," he said quickly. "It's just—the mask clips were my mother's."

Nahri's hands stilled. No one in the palace ever spoke of Muntadhir's mother, Ghassan's long-dead first wife. "They were?"

He nodded, taking the marriage mask from her hands and deftly unhooking the clips. In comparison to the opulent room and the glittering jewelry they were both wearing, the clips were rather plain, but Muntadhir held them as if he'd just been handed Suleiman's seal ring.

"They've been in her family for centuries," he explained, running his thumb over the fine filigree work. "She always made me promise to have my own wife and daughter wear them." His lips quirked into a sad smile. "She said they brought good fortune and the best of sons."

Nahri hesitated and then decided to press forward; long-lost mothers might be the only topic they had in common. "How old were you—"

"Young," Muntadhir cut in, his voice a little raw, as if the question caused him pain. "She'd been bitten by a nasnas out in Am Gezira when she was a child, and the poison stayed with her. She'd have the occasional reaction, but Manizheh could always treat it." His expression darkened. "Until one summer Manizheh decided dawdling in Zariaspa was more important than saving her queen."

Nahri tensed at the bitterness lingering in his words. So much for a connection between them. "I see," she said stiffly.

Muntadhir seemed to notice. A flush came to his cheeks. "I'm sorry. I shouldn't have said that to you."

"It's fine," Nahri replied, though in truth she was regretting this marriage more with each passing moment. "You've never hid how you feel about my family. What was it you called me to your father? The *lying Nahid whore*? The one who seduced your brother and ordered my Afshin to attack your men."

Muntadhir's gray eyes flashed with regret before he dropped his gaze. "That was a mistake," he said, defending himself weakly. "My best friend and my little brother were at death's door." He rose to his feet, moving toward the wine. "I wasn't thinking straight."

Nahri dropped to sit on the bed, crossing her legs under the silk shift. It was a pretty thing, the fabric so thin it was nearly sheer, chased through with impossibly fine gold embroidery and adorned with delicate ivory beads. At another time—with another person—she might have delighted in the teasing way it brushed her bare skin.

She was decidedly not feeling that way now. She glared at Muntadhir, incredulous that he believed such an excuse sufficient justification for his actions.

He choked on his wine. "That's not helping me forget about plague sores," he said between coughs.

Nahri rolled her eyes. "For God's sake, I'm not going to hurt you. I can't. Your father would murder a hundred Daevas if I so much as put a scratch on you." She rubbed her head and then held out a hand for the wine. Maybe a drink *would* make this more bearable. "Pass that over."

He poured her a cup, and Nahri drank it down, her lips puckering at the sour taste. "That's awful."

Muntadhir looked wounded. "That's an antique ice wine from Zariaspa. It's priceless, one of the rarest vintages in the world."

"It tastes like grape juice that's been passed through a rotting fish."

"A rotting fish . . . ," he repeated faintly. He rubbed his forehead. "Well . . . what do you like to drink then, if not wine?"

Nahri paused but then answered honestly, seeing little harm in it. "Karkade. It's a tea made from hibiscus flowers." The lump grew in her throat. "It reminds me of home."

"Calicut?"

She frowned. "What?"

"Isn't that where you're from?"

"No," she replied. "I'm from Cairo."

"Oh." He looked a bit nonplussed. "Are they close?"

Not at all. Nahri tried not to cringe. He was supposed to be her husband, and he didn't even know where she was from, the land whose essence still flowed in her blood and beat in her heart. Cairo, the city she missed so fiercely it took her breath away at times.

I don't want this. The realization, swift and urgent, swept through her. Nahri had learned the hard way not to trust a soul in Daevabad. How could she share a bed with this self-centered man who knew nothing of her?

Muntadhir was watching her. His gray eyes softened. "You look like you're about to be sick."

She did flinch now. Maybe he wasn't completely blind. "I'm fine," she lied.

"You don't look fine," he countered, reaching for her shoulder. "You're trembling." His fingers brushed her skin, and Nahri tensed, fighting the urge to jerk away.

Muntadhir dropped his hand as though he'd been burned. "Are *you* afraid of *me*?" he asked, sounding shocked.

"No." Nahri's cheeks burned with embarrassment, even as she bristled. "It's just . . . I haven't done this before."

"What, slept with someone you hate?" His wry smile vanished when she bit her lip. "Oh. *Oh*," he added. "I had assumed that you and Darayavahoush—"

"No," Nahri said quickly. She couldn't hear that sentence completed. "Things weren't like that between us. And I don't want to talk about him. Not with you."

Muntadhir's mouth tightened. "Fine."

Silence grew between them again, punctuated by the shouts of laughter that drifted in from the open window.

"Glad to know everyone's so happy we're uniting our tribes," Nahri muttered darkly.

Muntadhir glanced at her. "Is that why you agreed to this?"

"I *agreed*"—her voice turned sarcastic on the word—"because I knew I would otherwise be forced to marry you. I figured I might as well go willingly and take your father for every coin of dowry I could. And maybe one day convince you to overthrow him." It probably wasn't the wisest response, but Nahri was finding it harder and harder to care what her new husband thought.

The color abruptly left Muntadhir's face. He swallowed and then tossed back the rest of his wine before turning to cross the room. He opened the door, speaking in Geziriyya to whoever was on the other side. Nahri inwardly cursed the slip of her tongue. Her feelings toward Muntadhir aside, Ghassan had been hell-bent on marrying them, and if Nahri ruined this, the king would no doubt find some ghastly way to punish her.

"What are you doing?" she asked when he returned, anxiety rising in her voice.

"Getting you a glass of your strange flower tea."

Nahri blinked in surprise. "You don't have to do that."

"I want to." He met her gaze. "Because, quite frankly, you terrify me, wife, and I wouldn't mind staying on your good side." He retrieved the marriage mask from the bed. "But you can stop shaking. I'm not going to hurt you, Nahri. I'm not that kind of man. I'm not going to lay another finger on you tonight."

She eyed the mask. It was starting to smolder. She cleared her throat. "But people will be expecting . . ."

The mask burst into cinders in his hands, and she jumped. "Hold out your hand," he said, dumping a fistful of ash into her palm when she did so. He then ran his ash-covered fingers through his hair and around the collar of his tunic, wiping them on his white dishdasha.

"There," he deadpanned. "The marriage has been consummated." He jerked his head at the bed. "I've been told I toss and turn terribly in my sleep. It will look like we've been doing our part for peace between our tribes all night long."

Heat filled her face at that, and Muntadhir grinned. "Believe it or not, it's nice to know *something* makes you anxious. Manizheh never showed any emotion, and it was terrifying." His voice grew gentler. "We'll need to do this eventually. There will be people watching us, waiting for an heir. But we'll take it slow. It doesn't have to be a horrible ordeal." His eyes twinkled in amusement. "For all the handwringing that surrounds it, the bedroom *can* be a rather enjoyable place."

A knock interrupted them, which was a blessing, for despite growing up on the streets of Cairo, Nahri didn't have a retort for that.

Muntadhir crossed back to the door and returned with a silver platter upon which a rose quartz pitcher rested. He placed it on the table next to the bed. "Your karkade." He pulled back the sheets, collapsing into the small mountain of pillows. "Now if I'm not needed, I'm going to sleep. I'd forgotten how much dancing Daeva men did at weddings."

The worry inside her unknotted slightly. Nahri poured herself a glass of karkade, and, ignoring her instinct to retreat to one of the low couches arranged near the fireplace, carefully slipped into the bed as well. She took a sip of her tea, savoring the cool tang.

The familiar tang. But the first memory that came to Nahri wasn't of a café in Egypt, it was of Daevabad's Royal Library, sitting across from a smiling prince who'd known the difference between Calicut and Cairo quite well. The prince whose knowledge of the human world had drawn Nahri to him in a way she hadn't realized was dangerous until it was too late.

"Muntadhir, can I ask you something?" The words burst from her before she could think better of them.

His voice came back to her, already husky from sleep. "Yes?"

"Why wasn't Ali at the wedding?

Muntadhir's body instantly tensed. "He's busy with his garrison in Am Gezira."

His garrison. Yes, that's what every Geziri said, almost down to the word, when asked about Alizayd al Qahtani.

But secrets were difficult to keep in Daevabad's royal harem. Which is why Nahri had heard rumors that Zaynab, Ali and Muntadhir's sister, had cried herself to sleep every night for weeks after her little brother was sent away. Zaynab, who had looked haunted ever since, even at the wedding festivities this evening.

The real question slipped from her. "Is he dead?" she whispered.

Muntadhir didn't respond right away, and in the silence Nahri felt a tangle of conflicting emotions settle into her chest. But then her husband cleared his throat. "No." The word sounded careful. Deliberate. "Though if you don't mind, I would rather not discuss him. And, Nahri, about what you said before . . ." He looked at her, his eyes heavy with an emotion she couldn't quite decipher. "You should know that when it comes down to it, I'm a Qahtani. My father is my king. I will always be loyal to that first."

The warning was clear in his words, uttered in a voice that had lost all hint of intimacy. This was the emir of Daevabad speaking now, and he turned his back to her without waiting for a response.

Nahri set her glass down with a thud, feeling the slight warmth that had risen between them turn to ice. Annoyance sparked in her chest.

One of the tapestries across the room shuddered in response. The shadows falling across Muntadhir's form, outlining the palace window, suddenly lengthened. Sharpened.

Neither surprised Nahri. Such things had been happening lately, the ancient palace seeming to awaken to the fact that a Nahid dwelled within its walls again.

DARA

In the crimson light of a sun that never set, Darayavahoush e-Afshin slumbered.

It was not true sleep, of course, but something deeper. Quieter. There were no dreams of missed opportunities and unrequited love, nor nightmares of blood-drenched cities and merciless human masters. He lay on the felt blanket his mother had woven for him as a boy, in the shade of a cedar glen. Through the trees, he caught glimpses of a dazzling garden, one that occasionally tugged at his attention.

But not now. Dara did not entirely know where he was, nor did it seem to matter. The air smelled of his home, of meals with his family and the sacred smoke of fire altars. His eyes fluttered open briefly now and then before the sounds of birdsong and a distant lute lulled him back toward sleep. It was all Dara wanted to do. To rest until the weariness finally slipped from his bones. Until the scent of blood left his memory.

A small hand nudged his shoulder.

Dara smiled. "Coming to check on me again, sister?"

He opened his eyes. Tamima knelt at his side, grinning a gap-toothed smile. A shroud draped his little sister's small form, her black hair neatly plaited. Tamima looked far different than she had when Dara had first set eyes on her. When he had arrived in the glen, her shroud had been drenched in blood, her skin carved and scored with names written in Tukharistani script. It was a sight that had made him wild; he'd torn the glen apart with his bare hands again and again until he finally collapsed in her small arms.

But her marks had been fading ever since, along with the black tattoo on his own body, the one that looked like rungs on a twisting ladder.

Tamima dug her bare toes into the grass. "They are waiting to talk to you in the garden."

Apprehension stole through him. Dara suspected he knew all too well the judgment that awaited him in that place. "I am not ready," he replied.

"It is not a fate to fear, brother."

Dara squeezed his eyes shut. "You do not know the things I have done."

"Then confess them and free yourself of their weight."

"I cannot," he whispered. "If I start, Tamima . . . they will drown me. They—"

A burst of heat suddenly seared his left hand, and Dara gasped, the pain taking him by surprise. It was a sensation he'd started to forget, but the burn vanished as quickly as it had come. He raised his hand.

A battered iron and emerald ring was on his finger.

Dara stared at it, baffled. He pushed to a sitting position, the heavy mantle of drowsiness falling from his body like a cloak.

The glen's stillness ebbed away, a cold breeze sweeping aside the smells of home and sending the cedar leaves dancing. Dara shivered. The wind seemed like a thing alive, pulling at his limbs and tousling his hair.

He was on his feet before he realized it.

Tamima grabbed his hand. "No, Daru," she pleaded. "Don't go. Not again. You're finally so close."

Startled, he glanced at his sister. "What?"

As if in response, the shadows in the cedar grove deepened, emerald and black writhing and twisting together. Whatever magic this was . . . it was intoxicating, tugging hard at his soul, the ring pulsing against his finger like a beating heart.

It was suddenly obvious. Of course, Dara would go. It was his duty, and he was a good Afshin.

He obeyed.

He pulled free of his sister's hand. "I will come back," he said. "I promise."

Tamima was weeping. "You always say that."

But his sister's sobs grew distant as Dara walked deeper into the grove. The sound of birdsong vanished, replaced by a low humming buzz that set his nerves on edge. The air seemed to close in around him, uncomfortably hot. The tug came again from his hand, the ring smoldering.

And then he was seized. *Stolen*, an unseen force snatching him like a rukh and dragging him into its maw.

The cedar glen vanished, replaced by utter blackness. Nothingness. A blazing, tearing pain ripped through him, worse than any sensation he could imagine, a thousand knives seeming to shred every fiber of his body as he was pulled, *dragged* through a substance thicker than mud. Disassembled and reformed from pieces as sharp as broken glass.

A presence thundered to life in his breast, pounding like a drum. Rushing liquid swirled through new veins, lubricating the growing muscles, and a smothering heaviness settled upon his chest. He choked, his mouth reforming to draw air into his lungs. His hearing returned, bringing with it screams.

His screams.

Memories slammed into him. A woman shouting his name, whispering his name. Black eyes and a sly smile, her mouth on his as their bodies pressed together in a darkened cave. Those same eyes filled with shock, with betrayal, in a ruined infirmary. A drowned man covered in scales and tentacles looming over him, a rusting blade in his dripping hand.

Dara's eyes shot open, but he saw only blackness. The pain was fading but everything felt wrong, his body both too light and yet too real, pulsing in a way he hadn't experienced in decades. Centuries. He choked again, gasping as he tried to remember how to breathe.

A hand clamped down on his shoulder, and a wave of warmth and calm surged into his body. The pain vanished, his heart slowing to a steady beat.

Relief flooded through him. Dara would know the healing touch of a Nahid anywhere. "*Nahri*," he breathed. Tears burned his eyes. "Oh, Nahri, I am sorry. I am so sorry. I never meant—"

The words died in his mouth. He'd caught sight of his hand.

It was fire-bright, tipped in deadly sharp claws.

Before he could scream, a woman's face swam into view. *Nahri*. No, not Nahri, though Dara could see the ghost of her in the woman's expression. This Daeva was older, her face slightly lined. Silver stole through the black hair roughly shorn at her shoulders.

She looked almost as shocked as Dara felt. Delighted—but shocked. She reached up to stroke his cheek. "It worked," she whispered. "It finally worked."

Dara stared down in horror at his burning hands. The hated emerald slave ring glittered back. "Why do I look like this?" His voice broke in panic. "Have the ifrit—"

"No," the woman assured him quickly. "You're free of the ifrit, Darayavahoush. You're free of *everything*."

That answered nothing. Dara gaped at the incomprehensible sight of his fiery skin, dread rising in his heart. In no world he knew did djinn and daevas look as he did now, even when brought back from slavery.

In a distant corner of his mind, Dara could still hear his sister begging him to return to the garden of his ancestors. *Tamima*. Grief rushed through him, and tears streamed down his cheeks, sizzling against his hot skin.

He shuddered. The magic coursing through his blood felt raw: new and ragged and uncontrollable. He drew a sharp breath, and the walls of the tent they were in undulated wildly.

The woman grabbed his hand. "Calm yourself, Afshin," she said. "You are safe. You are free."

"*What am I?*" He glanced again at his claws, sick at the sight. "What have you done to me?"

She blinked, looking taken aback by the despair in his voice. "I've made you a marvel. A miracle. The first daeva to be freed of Suleiman's curse in three thousand years."

Suleiman's curse. He stared at her in disbelief, the words echoing in his head. That wasn't possible. That . . . that was *abominable*. His people honored Suleiman. They obeyed his code.

Dara had killed for that code.

He shot to his feet. The ground shook beneath him, the tent walls flapping madly in a gust of hot wind. He staggered outside.

"Afshin!"

He gasped. He had been expecting the darkly lush mountains of his island city, but instead, Dara faced a desert, vast and empty. And then with horror, he recognized it. Recognized the line of salt cliffs and the single rocky tower that stood sentinel in the distance.

The Dasht-e Loot. The desert in southern Daevastana so hot and inhospitable that birds dropped dead from the sky while flying over it. At the height of the Daeva rebellion, Dara had lured Zaydi al Qahtani to the Dasht-e Loot. He'd caught and killed Zaydi's son in a battle that should have finally turned the war in the Daevas' favor.

But that was not how things had ended for Dara in the Dasht-e Loot.

A cackling laugh brought him sharply to the present.

"Well, there is a wager I have lost . . ." The voice behind him was smoothly clever, pulled from the worst of Dara's memories. "The Nahid actually did it."

Dara whirled around, blinking in the sudden brightness. Three ifrit were before him, waiting in the crumbling ruins of what might have once been a human palace, now lost to time and the elements. The same ifrit who'd hunted him and Nahri across the Gozan River, a desperate encounter they'd barely survived.

Their leader—Aeshma, Dara remembered—dropped from a broken wall, sauntering forward with a grin. "He even looks like us," he teased. "I suspect that's a shock."

"It's a pity." The ifrit who spoke next was a woman. "I liked the look of him before." She gave him a sly smile, holding up a battered metal helmet. "What do you think, Darayavahoush? Want to see if it still fits?"

Dara's eyes locked on the helmet. It had gone bluish-green with rust, but he instantly recognized the ragged edge of the brass shedu wings that sprouted from its sides. Shedu feathers, passed down from father to son, had once lined the helmet's crest. Dara could still remember shivering the first time he had touched them.

With rising horror, he looked again at the crumbling bricks. At the dark hole they enclosed, a black void upon the moonlit sand. It was the well down which he'd been callously thrown centuries ago to be drowned and remade, his soul enslaved by the ifrit now casually spinning his helmet on one finger.

Dara jerked back, clutching his head. None of this made any sense, but it all suggested something unfathomable. Unconscionable.

Desperate, he reached for the first person on his mind. "N-nahri," he stammered. He'd left her screaming his name upon the burning boat, surrounded by their enemies.

Aeshma rolled his eyes. "I did tell you he would ask for her first. The Afshins are like dogs for their Nahids, loyal no matter how many times they're whipped." He turned his attention back to Dara. "Your little healer is in Daevabad."

Daevabad. His city. His Banu Nahida. The betrayal in her dark eyes, her hands on his face as she begged him to run away.

A choked cry came from his throat, and heat consumed him. He whirled around, not certain where he was going. Only knowing that he needed to get back to Daevabad.

And then in a crack of thunder and flash of scalding fire, the desert was gone.

Dara blinked. Then he reeled. He stood upon a rocky shore, a swiftly coursing river gleaming darkly beside it. On the opposite bank, limestone cliffs rose against the night sky, glowing faintly.

The Gozan River. How he had gotten here from the Dasht-e Loot in the blink of an eye was not a thing Dara could begin to comprehend—but it didn't matter. Not now. The only thing that mattered was returning to Daevabad and saving Nahri from the destruction he'd wrought.

Dara rushed forward. The invisible threshold that hid Dae-vabad away from the rest of the world was mere moments from the riverbank. He had crossed it countless times in his mortal life, returning from hunting trips with his father and his assign-ments as a young soldier. It was a curtain that fell instantly for anyone with even a drop of daeva blood, revealing the misty green mountains that surrounded the city's cursed lake.

But as he stood there now, nothing happened.

Panic swept him. This couldn't be. Dara tried again, criss-crossing the plain and running the length of the river, struggling to find the veil.

On what must have been the hundredth attempt, Dara crashed to his knees. He wailed, flames bursting from his hands.

There was a crack of thunder and then the sound of running feet and Aeshma's annoyed sigh.

A woman knelt quietly at his side. The Daeva woman whose face he'd awoken to, the one who resembled Nahri. A long moment of silence stretched between them, broken only by Dara's ragged breaths.

He finally spoke. "Am I in hell?" he whispered, giving voice to the fear that gnawed at his heart, the uncertainty that had kept him from taking his sister's hand to enter the garden. "Is this punishment for the things I've done?"

"No, Darayavahoush, you are not in hell."

The soft assurance in her calm voice encouraged him to con-tinue, and so he did. "I cannot cross the threshold," he choked out. "I cannot even find it. I have been damned. I have been turned away from my home and—"

The woman gripped his shoulder, the powerful magic in her touch stealing his words. "You have not been damned," she said firmly. "You cannot cross the threshold because you don't carry Suleiman's curse. Because you are free."

Dara shook his head. "I do not understand."

"You will." She took his chin in her hands, and Dara found himself turning to look at her, feeling strangely compelled by the urgency in her dark eyes. "You've been granted more power than any daeva in millennia. We will find a way to return you to Daevabad, I promise." Her grip tightened on his chin. "And when we do, Darayavahoush . . . we are going to *take* it. We're going to save our people. We're going to save Nahri."

Dara stared at her, desperate for the chance her words offered. "Who are you?" he whispered.

Her mouth curved in a smile familiar enough to break his heart. "My name is Banu Manizheh."

1

NAHRI

Nahri closed her eyes, lifting her face to the sun and enjoying its heat on her skin. She inhaled, savoring the earthy smell of the distant mountains and the fresh breeze off the lake.

"They're late," Muntadhir complained. "They're always late. I think they like the sight of us waiting in the sun."

Zaynab snorted. "Dhiru, you haven't been on time for a single event in your life. Is this truly a fight you wish to pick?"

Nahri ignored their bickering, taking another deep breath of the crisp air and reveling in the stillness. It was rare she was allowed such freedom, and she intended to savor what she could of it. She'd learned the hard way that she had no other choice.

The first time Nahri had attempted sneaking out of the palace had been shortly after the night on the boat. She had been desperate for a distraction, aching to wander parts of the city she'd yet to visit, places where thoughts of Dara wouldn't haunt her.

In response, Ghassan had her maid Dunoor brought out before her. He hexed the girl's tongue for not reporting the Banu Nahida's absence, stealing her ability to ever speak again.

The second time, Nahri had been moved by a surge of defiance. She and Muntadhir were soon to be wed. She was the Banu Nahida. Who was Ghassan to lock her away in her ancestor's city? She had taken better care, making sure her companions had alibis and using the palace itself to cloak her in shadows and guide her through the most unused of corridors.

Still, Ghassan had found out. He dragged in the sleeping gate guard she'd tiptoed past and had the man scourged before her until there was not a strip of unbloodied skin on his back.

The third time, Nahri hadn't even been sneaking around. Newly married to Muntadhir, she had merely decided to walk back to the palace from the Grand Temple on a sunny day, instead of taking her guarded litter. She'd never imagined Ghassan—now her father-in-law—would care. On the way, she'd stopped inside a small café in the Daeva Quarter, passing a lovely few moments chatting with its surprised and delighted proprietors.

The following day Ghassan had the couple brought to the palace. This time, he didn't have to harm anyone. Nahri had no sooner seen their frightened faces than she dropped to her knees and swore never to go anywhere without permission again.

Which meant she now never turned away a chance to escape the palace walls. Aside from the royal siblings' squabbling and the cry of a hawk, the lake was entirely silent, the air wrapping her in a blessed, heavy peace.

Her relief didn't go unnoticed.

"Your wife looks like someone just released her from a century in prison," Zaynab muttered from a few paces away. She kept her voice low, but Nahri had a talent for listening to whispers. "Even I'm starting to feel bad for her, and one of the vines in her garden ripped my cup from my hand the last time we had tea."

Muntadhir shushed his sister. "I'm certain she didn't mean it. Sometimes that just . . . happens when she's around."

"I heard one of the shedu statues bit a soldier who slapped her assistant."

"Maybe he shouldn't have slapped her assistant." Muntadhir's whisper turned sharper. "But enough of such gossip. I don't want Abba hearing things like that."

Nahri smiled beneath her veil, pleasantly surprised by his defense. Despite being married now for nearly five years, Muntadhir rarely defended her against his family.

She opened her eyes, admiring the view before her. It was a beautiful day, one of the few in which not a single cloud marred the bright, fathomless blue of Daevabad's sky. The three of them were waiting at the front of the city's once grand port. Though the docks were still serviceable, the rest of the port was in ruins and apparently had been for centuries. Weeds grew through the cracked paving stones and the decorative granite columns lay smashed. The only hint of the port's ancient grandeur was behind her, in the gleaming brass facades of her ancestors on the city's mighty walls.

Ahead was the lake, the misty-green mountains of the opposite shore melting into a thin, pebbly beach. The lake itself was still, its murky water cursed long ago by the marid during some forgotten feud with the Nahid Council. It was a curse Nahri tried very hard not to think about. Nor did she let her gaze drift southward to where the high cliffs beneath the palace met the dark water. What had happened on that stretch of the lake five years ago was a thing she didn't dwell on.

The air shimmered and sparked, pulling Nahri's attention to the center of the lake.

The Ayaanle had arrived.

The ship that emerged from the veil looked like something out of a fairy tale, slipping through the mists with a grace that belied its size. Nahri had grown up along the Nile and was used to boats, to the thicket of sleek feluccas, fishing canoes, and loaded trade transports that glided over the wide river in a ceaseless flow. But this ship was nothing like any of those. It looked large enough to fit hundreds, its dark teak dazzling in the sunlight as it floated lightly upon the lake. Teal banners adorned with the icons of studded golden pyramids and starry silver salt tablets flew from the masts. Its many amber-colored sails—and Nahri counted at least a dozen—dwarfed the glimmering decks. Segmented and ribbed, the sails looked more like wings than anything that belonged on a boat, and they shivered and undulated in the wind like living things.

Awed, Nahri drew closer to the Qahtani siblings. "How did they get a *ship* here?" The only land beyond the magical threshold that embraced Daevabad's vast lake and misty mountains was composed of immense stretches of rocky desert.

"Because it's not just any ship." Zaynab grinned. "It's a sandship. The Sahrayn invented them. They're careful to keep the magic behind them a secret, but a skilled captain can fly across the world with one of those." She sighed, her gaze admiring and rueful. "The Sahrayn charge the Ayaanle a *fortune* to use them, but they do make a statement."

Muntadhir didn't look as impressed by the lovely ship. "Interesting that the Ayaanle can afford such a thing when Ta Ntry's taxes have been chronically short."

Nahri's gaze flickered to her husband's face. Though Muntadhir had never directly spoken to her of Daevabad's economic problems, they were obvious to everyone—especially the Banu Nahida who healed the training injuries of soldiers as they griped about reduced rations and undid the hexes the increasingly frazzled Treasury secretaries had begun hurling at one another. Fortunately, the downturn had yet to largely affect her Daevas—mostly because they'd cut themselves off from trading with the other tribes after Ghassan had tacitly allowed the Daeva stalls to be destroyed and their merchants harassed in the Grand Bazaar after Dara's death. Why take the risk of trading with djinn if none would stand up to protect them?

The Ayaanle ship drifted nearer, its sails fanning out as deckhands in brightly striped linen and thick gold ornaments dashed about the boat. On the top deck, a chimeralike creature with a feline body covered in ruby scales strained at a golden harness, flashing horns that shone like diamonds and whipping a serpentine tail.

The ship had no sooner docked than a knot of passengers made their way toward the royal party. Among them was a man dressed in voluminous teal robes and a silver turban that wrapped his head and neck.

"Emir Muntadhir." He smiled and bowed low. "Peace be upon you."

"And upon you peace," Muntadhir returned politely. "Rise."

The Ayaanle man did so, aiming what seemed to be a far sincerer grin at Zaynab. "Little princess, how you've grown!" He laughed. "You do this old coin-changer a great honor, coming to greet me yourself."

"The honor is mine," Zaynab assured him with a grace Nahri would never have the patience to emulate. "I pray your journey went well?"

"God be praised." The man turned to Nahri, his gold eyes lighting in surprise. "Is this the Nahid girl?" He blinked, and Nahri didn't miss the way he stepped back ever so slightly.

"This is my wife," Muntadhir corrected, his voice considerably cooler.

Nahri met the man's eyes, drawing up as she pulled her chador close. "I am the Banu Nahida," she said through her veil. "I hear you are called Abul Dawanik."

He bowed. "You hear correctly." His gaze didn't leave her, the examination making her skin crawl. He shook his head. "Astonishing. I never imagined I'd meet a real Nahid."

Nahri gritted her teeth. "Occasionally we're allowed out to terrify the populace."

Muntadhir cleared his throat. "I have made room for your men and your cargo at the royal caravanserai. I would be happy to escort you there myself."

Abul Dawanik sighed. "Alas, there's little cargo. My people needed more time to prepare the tax caravan."

Muntadhir's civil mask didn't waver, but Nahri sensed his heartbeat pick up. "That was not the arrangement we agreed on." The warning in his voice was so reminiscent of Ghassan, her skin prickled. "You are aware of how close Navasatem is, yes? It is a bit difficult to plan a once-in-a-century celebration when tax payments are consistently late."

Abul Dawanik threw him a wounded look. "Straight to all this talk of money, Emir? The Geziri hospitality I'm used to typically involves chattering about polite nonsense for at least another ten minutes."

Muntadhir's response was direct. "Perhaps you would prefer my father's company to mine."

Abul Dawanik didn't look cowed; if anything, Nahri saw a hint of slyness in his expression before he responded. "No need for threats, Your Highness. The caravan is but a few weeks behind me." His eyes twinkled. "No doubt you will enjoy what it brings you."

From behind the city walls, the adhan sounded, calling the faithful to noon prayer. It rose and fell in distant waves as new muezzins picked it up, and Nahri fought a familiar twinge of homesickness. The adhan always made her think of Cairo.

"Dhiru, surely this can wait," Zaynab said, clearly trying to alleviate the tension between the two men. "Abul Dawanik is our guest. He has had a long journey. Why don't the two of you go pray together and then visit the caravanserai? I can take Nahri back to the palace."

Muntadhir didn't look pleased, but he didn't protest. "Do you mind?" he asked Nahri courteously.

Do I have a choice? Zaynab's bearers were already bringing their litter over, the pretty cage that would return Nahri to her gilded prison. "Of course not," she muttered, turning away from the lake to follow her sister-in-law.

They didn't talk much on the way back. Zaynab appeared absorbed in her thoughts, and Nahri was happy to rest her eyes before returning to the bustling infirmary.

But the litter shuddered to a stop too soon. Nahri jolted from her half doze and rubbed her eyes, frowning as she caught sight of Zaynab hastily pulling off some of her jewelry. Nahri watched as she piled it on the cushion beside her, and then from beneath the brocade-covered seat, retrieved two plain cotton abayas, pulling one over her silk gown.

"Are we being robbed?" Nahri asked, half-hoping it might be true. Being robbed would mean a delay in returning to the palace and Ghassan's constant, watchful presence.

Zaynab neatly wrapped a dark shawl around her hair. "Of course not. I'm going for a walk."

"A *walk*?"

"You're not the only one who wants to escape sometimes, and I take my opportunities when they arise." Zaynab tossed the second abaya at Nahri. "Quick, put this on. And keep your face veiled."

Nahri stared at her in surprise. "You want me to come?"

Zaynab eyed her. "I've known you for five years. I am not leaving you alone with my jewelry."

Nahri hesitated, tempted. But the terrified faces of the people Ghassan had punished in her place immediately flooded her mind, and her heart seized in fear. "I can't. Your father—"

Zaynab's expression softened. "He hasn't caught me yet. And I'll take the responsibility if he does today, I swear." She beckoned Nahri forward. "Come. You look like you need this even more than I do."

Nahri quickly considered her options. Ghassan did have a soft spot for his only daughter, so after another moment of indecision, temptation won out. She pulled free her most visibly royal jewels, slipped into the garment Zaynab had offered her, and followed her out of the litter.

With a quiet word and a knowing wink between the princess and one of her guards—Nahri sensed this was a well-honed routine—the two women were pulled into the crush of pedestrians. Nahri had been to the Geziri Quarter plenty of times with Muntadhir to visit his relatives, but she hadn't seen anything beyond the curtains of the litters in which they traveled and the sumptuous interiors of mansions. Palace women were not expected to mix with commoners, let alone wander the city streets.

At first glance, the Quarter looked small—despite a Geziri family ruling the city, most of their tribesmen were said to prefer the rugged terrain of their homeland. But it was a pleasant glance, nonetheless. Windtowers loomed far above, sending lake-fresh breezes past neat rows of tall brick buildings, their pale facades adorned with copper shutters and white stucco filigree. Ahead was the market, protected from the hot sun by woven reed mats and a glistening water channel cut into the main street, filled with enchanted ice. Across from the market was the quarter's main mosque, and next to the mosque was a large floating pavilion, shaded by date and citrus trees, where families feasted on dark halwa, coffee, and other treats from the market.

And over it all loomed the stark tower of the Citadel. The home of the Royal Guard, the Citadel threw shadows over the Geziri Quarter and the neighboring Grand Bazaar, jutting up against the brass walls that separated Daevabad from its deadly lake. Nisreen had once told her—in one of her many dark warnings about the Geziris—that the Citadel had been the first structure Zaydi al Qahtani built upon seizing Daevabad from the Nahid Council. He'd ruled from there for years, leaving the palace a deserted ruin stained with the blood of her ancestors.

Zaynab chose that moment to take her arm, pulling her toward the market, and Nahri happily let herself be towed. Almost unconsciously, she palmed a ripe orange from a fruit stand as they passed. Stealing it was probably reckless, but there was something so freeing about strolling crowded city streets. It might not be Cairo, but the rustle of impatient passersby, the aroma of street food, and knots of men emerging from the mosque were familiar enough to briefly ease her homesickness. She was anonymous again for the first time in years, and it was delightful.

They slowed to a stroll once they entered the shadowed depths of the market. Nahri looked around, dazzled. A glassworker was turning hot sand into a speckled bottle with her fiery hands while across the lane a wooden loom worked by itself, bright woolen threads wrapping and twisting to pattern a half-completed prayer mat. From a stall packed with flowers came a rich aroma, a perfumer sprinkling rosewater and musk over a glittering tray of molten ambergris. Next door, a pair of hunting cheetahs in jeweled collars lounged on elevated cushions, sharing a storefront with squawking firebirds.

Zaynab stopped to stroke the large cats while Nahri wandered ahead. Down an adjacent lane was a row of booksellers, and she immediately headed for them, captivated by the volumes laid out in rows on rugs and tables. While a few books had an aura of magic, their covers bound in scales and pages shimmering gently, the majority looked human-made. Nahri wasn't surprised; of all the djinn tribes, the Geziris were said to be closest to the humans with whom they silently shared their land.

She browsed the nearest stall. Most of the books were in Arabic, and the sight sent an odd pang through her. It was the first language she'd learned to read, and a skill she could never entirely divorce in her mind from the young prince who'd taught her. Not wanting to think of Ali, she glanced idly at the next table. A book with a sketch of a trio of pyramids rested in its center.

Nahri was there the next moment, reaching for the book like she might have grabbed a long-lost friend in an embrace. They were Giza's famed Pyramids, all right, and as she flipped through the pages, she recognized more of Cairo's distinctive landmarks: the twin minarets of the Bab Zuweila gate and the vast interior of the Ibn Tulun mosque. There were women in the black dresses Nahri had once worn gathering water from the Nile, and men sorting piles of sugarcane.

"You have a good eye, miss." An older Geziri man ambled forth. "That's one of my newest human acquisitions, and I've never seen anything like it. A Sahrayn trader picked it up crossing the Nile."

Nahri ran her hands over the first page. The book was written in a script she'd never seen. "What language is this?"

The man shrugged. "I'm not certain. The lettering appears similar to some of the old Latin texts I have. The trader who picked it up didn't stay in Egypt long; he said it looked as though the humans were engaged in some sort of war."

Some sort of war. Her fingers pressed harder on the book. Egypt had been freshly subjugated by the French when Nahri left, ruled by the Ottomans before that—it was seemingly Nahri's destiny to belong to an occupied people wherever she went. "How much do you want for this?"

"Three dinars."

Nahri narrowed her eyes at him. "Three *dinars*? Do I look as though I'm made of gold?"

The man seemed shocked. "That . . . that is the price, miss."

"Maybe for someone else," she said scornfully, masking her glee while feigning insult. "I won't give you a coin over ten dirhams."

He gaped. "But that's not how we—"

Zaynab was suddenly there, seizing Nahri's arm in a tight grip. "What are you *doing*?"

Nahri rolled her eyes. "It's called bargaining, sister dear. I'm sure you've never had to do such a thing but—"

"Geziris do not *bargain* in our community markets." Zaynab's words dripped with revulsion. "It breeds discord."

Nahri was scandalized. "So you just pay whatever they ask?" She couldn't believe she'd married into such a naive people. "What if they're cheating you?"

Zaynab was already handing three gold coins to the bookseller. "Perhaps it would be better to stop thinking that everyone is cheating you, no?" She pulled Nahri away and pushed the book into her hands. "And stop making a scene. The point is to *not* get caught."

Nahri clutched the book to her chest, a little abashed. "I'll pay you back."

"Don't insult me." Zaynab's voice turned gentler. "You're not the first outspoken fool for whom I've bought overpriced human books on this street."

Nahri darted a look at the princess. She wanted to press her as much as she wanted to change the subject. And that, in essence, was how she felt about Alizayd al Qahtani.

Let it go. There were plenty of other ways to pester her sister-in-law. "I'm hearing rumors you're being courted by a noble from Malacca," she said brightly as they resumed walking.

Zaynab drew to a stop. "Where did you hear that?"

"I like to converse with my patients."

The princess shook her head. "Your patients should learn to hold their tongues. *You* should learn to hold your tongue. Surely,

I deserve that much for buying your book about odd human buildings."

"Do you not want to marry him?" Nahri asked, peeling the orange she'd stolen.

"Of course, I don't want to marry him," Zaynab replied. "Malacca is across the sea. I'd never see my family." Disdain entered her voice. "Besides which, he has three other wives, a dozen children, and is approaching his second century."

"So refuse the match."

"That's my father's decision." Zaynab's expression tightened. "And my suitor is a very wealthy man."

Ah. Muntadhir's concerns about the state of the city's treasury suddenly made more sense. "Can't your mother object?" she asked. Queen Hatset thoroughly intimidated Nahri, and she couldn't imagine the woman allowing her only daughter to be packed off to Malacca for any amount of gold.

Zaynab seemed to hesitate. "My mother has a more important battle to fight right now."

They'd wandered down a quieter street that ran past the Citadel. Its heavy stone walls loomed high overhead, blocking the blue sky in a way that made Nahri feel nervous and small. Through a pair of open doors came the sound of laughter and the distinctive sizzling clash of zulfiqar blades.

Not certain how to respond, she handed Zaynab half of her orange. "I'm sorry."

Zaynab stared at the fruit, uncertainty blooming in her gray-gold eyes. "You and my brother were enemies when you married," she said haltingly. "Sometimes it seems like you *still* are. How . . . how did you . . . ?"

"You find a way." The words unfurled from a hard place within Nahri, one that she'd retreated to countless times since she'd been plucked from the Nile and dropped in Cairo, alone and afraid. "You'd be amazed by the things a person can do to survive."

Zaynab looked taken aback. "You make me feel as though I should tell Muntadhir to keep a blade under his pillow."

"I'd advise against your brother keeping anything sharp in his bed," Nahri said as they continued walking. "Considering the number of visitors—" She choked, the orange falling from her fingers as a wave of coldness stole through her.

Zaynab instantly stopped. "Are you all right?"

Nahri barely heard the question. It felt as though an unseen hand had grasped her chin, turning her head to stare down the gloomy street they'd just passed. Tucked between the Citadel and the mottled brass of the city's outer walls, it looked as though the block had been razed centuries ago. Weeds and dirt covered the broken paving stones and scorch marks scarred the bare stone walls. At the very end was a crumbling brick complex. Broken windows faced the street, the black spaces looking like missing teeth in a gaping mouth. Beyond the front portico were the lush tops of wildly overgrown trees. Ivy covered the buildings, strangling columns and dangling over smashed windows like so many nooses.

Nahri took a few steps in and then inhaled sharply, a buzz racing down her skin. She'd swear the heavy shadows had lifted slightly when she moved.

She turned to see Zaynab had followed her. "What is this place?" she asked, her voice echoing against the stone.

Zaynab gave the complex a skeptical glance. "A ruin? I'm not exactly an expert when it comes to moldering buildings in a three-thousand-year-old city."

The street warmed beneath Nahri's feet, hot enough to feel through her sandals. "I need to go in there."

"You need to do *what*?"

But Nahri was already walking, thoughts of the princess, even fears of Ghassan's gruesome punishments all falling away. She felt almost compelled, her gaze locked on the mysterious complex.

She stopped outside a pair of large brass doors. Pictograms were carved into their surface—a leaping oryx and a ship's prow, a Daeva fire altar and a pair of scales—and magic all but simmered off the brass. Though Nahri couldn't imagine anyone living in such a place, she raised a hand to knock.

Her knuckles hadn't even grazed the surface when the door swung open with a groan, revealing a yawning black hole.

There was no one on the other side.

Zaynab had caught up. "Oh, absolutely not," she said. "You're with the wrong Qahtani if you think I'm about to go wandering into this haunted wreck."

Nahri swallowed. Had she been back in Egypt, this might have been the start of a tale told to frighten children, one of mysterious ruins and terrifying djinn.

Except she was technically the terrifying djinn, and the icy grip the building had on her heart had only tightened. It was reckless; it was an impulse that made no sense—but she was going inside.

"Then stay out here." Nahri dodged Zaynab's hand and ducked inside.

The darkness instantly swallowed her. "Naar," she whispered. Flames blossomed in her palm, throwing light on what must have once been a grand entrance chamber. Remnants of paint clung to the walls, outlining the forms of winged bulls and prancing phoenixes. Pockmarks were everywhere, places gems had likely been pried from the walls.

She stepped forward, raising her flames. Her eyes widened.

In fragments and shadows, the Nahids' creation story spread on the wall before her. Suleiman's ancient temple rising over the heads of its laboring daeva workers. A woman with pointed ears kneeling in a blue-and-gold chador at the feet of a human king. As Nahri stared in wonder at the mural, she'd swear the figures started to move and merge: a scattering of glazed paint becom-

THE KINGDOM OF COPPER   ✧   41

ing a flock of soaring shedus, the bare line drawing of veiled Nahid healers mixing potions filling with color. The faint sound of marching boots and cheering spectators whispered in her ear as a parade of archers trooped by, wearing ceremonial helmets crested with swaying feathers.

Nahri gasped, and as she did, the flame twirled away from her palm, pinpricks of light dancing away to illuminate the rest of the chamber. It was a burst of unconscious magic, the kind she associated with the palace, the royal heart of the Nahids whose power still coursed in her blood.

The murals abruptly stopped moving. Zaynab had entered and was gingerly picking her way over the debris littering the floor.

"I think this place belonged to my family," Nahri whispered, awed.

Zaynab gave the room a wary look. "To be fair . . . I believe that could be said of much of Daevabad." Her expression turned exasperated when Nahri glared. "Excuse me if it's difficult to be diplomatic when I'm afraid the building is going to come down at any moment. Now can we *please* leave? My father will have me packed off to Malacca tomorrow if his Nahid gets crushed under a pile of falling bricks."

"I'm not his Nahid, and I'm not leaving until I figure out what this place was." The tingle of magic on Nahri's skin had only increased, the humid heat of the city oppressive in the close chamber. She pulled free her veil, thinking it unlikely they would come upon anyone, and then, ignoring Zaynab's warning, Nahri climbed over one of the crumbling walls.

She landed lightly on her feet in a long, covered corridor, a succession of sandstone arches separating a row of doors from an overgrown courtyard garden. The walkway was in far better shape than the foyer: the floor appeared freshly swept, the wall plastered and covered in swirls of colorful paint.

With a curse, Zaynab followed. "If I've not said it lately, I think I hate you."

"You know, for a magical being, you have a terrible sense of adventure," Nahri replied, touching one of the eddies of paint, a blue swell that looked like a wave. An ebony boat was outlined against it. At her touch, the wave rose as if alive, sending the boat careening down the wall.

Nahri grinned. Thoroughly intrigued, she kept walking, peeking inside the rooms she passed. Save for the occasional broken shelf and rotting bits of carpet, they were all empty.

Until they weren't. Nahri abruptly stopped outside the last room. Cedar shelves bursting with scrolls and books covered the walls, stretching to the distant ceiling. More texts were stacked in precarious, towering piles on the floor.

She was inside before she noticed the floor desk wedged between two of the piles. A figure was hunched over its paper-strewn surface: an elderly looking Ayaanle man in a striped robe that nearly swallowed his wizened body.

"No, no, no . . . ," he muttered in Ntaran, scratching out whatever he'd just written with a charcoal pencil. "That makes *no* sense."

Nahri hesitated. She couldn't imagine what an Ayaanle scholar was doing in a book-stuffed room in a ruined building, but he looked harmless enough. "Peace be upon you," she greeted him.

The man's head snapped up.

His eyes were the color of emeralds.

He blinked rapidly and then yelped, pushing back from his cushion. "Razu!" he cried. "*Razu!*" He snatched up a scroll, raising it like a sword.

Nahri instantly backed away, brandishing her book. "Stay back!" she shouted as Zaynab ran to join her. The princess held a dagger in one hand.

"Oh, Issa, *whatever* is the problem now?"

Nahri and Zaynab both jumped and whirled around. Two women had emerged from the courtyard so swiftly they might have been conjured. One looked Sahrayn, with reddish black locks that fell to the waist of her paint-streaked galabiyya. The taller woman—the one who'd spoken—was Tukharistani, dressed in a dazzling cape of visibly magic design that fell like a mantle of molten copper across her shoulders. Her gaze locked on Nahri. Green eyes again. The same bright hue Dara's had been.

The Ayaanle scholar—Issa—peeked past his door, still wielding his scroll. "It looks human, Razu! I swore they would never take me again!"

"That is no human, Issa." The Tukharistani woman stepped forward. Her brilliant gaze hadn't left Nahri's. "It is you," she whispered. Reverence swept over her face and she dropped to her knees, bringing her fingers together in respect. "Banu Nahida."

"*Banu Nahida?*" Issa repeated. Nahri could see him still trembling. "Are you certain?"

"I am." The Tukharistani woman gestured to an emerald-studded iron cuff on her wrist. "I can feel the tug in my vessel." She touched her chest. "And in my heart," she added softly. "Like I did with Baga Rustam."

"Oh." Issa dropped the scroll. "Oh, dear . . ." He attempted to bow. "Apologies, my lady. One can never be too careful these days."

Zaynab was breathing heavily beside her, her dagger still raised. Nahri reached out and pushed her arm down. Thoroughly mystified, she stared at the strange trio, her gaze darting to each of them in turn. "I'm sorry . . . ," she started, lost for words. "But who are you all?"

The Tukharistani woman rose to her feet. Her silver-and-gold-streaked black hair was held back in an intricate lace net, and her face well-lined; had she been human, Nahri would have guessed she was in her sixties. "I am Razu Qaraqashi," she said. "You have already stumbled into Issa, and this is Elashia," she added, affectionately touching the shoulder of the Sahrayn woman next to her. "We are the last ifrit slaves in Daevabad."

Elashia instantly scowled, and Razu bowed her head. "Forgive me, my love." She glanced back at Nahri. "Elashia does not like to be called a slave."

Nahri fought to keep the shock from her face. Quietly, she let her abilities expand. Small wonder she thought she'd been alone: hers and Zaynab's were the only hearts pounding in the entire complex. The bodies of the djinn before her were entirely silent. Just as Dara's had been.

Because they're not true bodies, Nahri realized, recalling what she knew of the slave curse. The ifrit murdered the djinn they took, and in order to free them, the Nahids conjured new forms, new bodies to house their reclaimed souls. Nahri knew little else about the process; slavery was so feared among the djinn, it was rarely spoken of, as if simply mentioning the word "ifrit" would get one dragged off to a fate considered worse than death.

A fate the three people before her had survived. Nahri opened her mouth, struggling for a response. "What are you doing here?" she finally asked.

"Hiding," Issa responded mournfully. "No one else in Daevabad will have us after what happened to the Afshin. People fear we're liable to go mad and start murdering innocents with ifrit magic. We thought the hospital the safest place."

Nahri blinked. "This was a *hospital*?"

Issa's bright eyes narrowed. "Is it not obvious?" he asked, gesturing inexplicably to the crumbling ruins around them. "Where do you think your ancestors practiced?"

Razu quickly stepped forward. "Why don't you two come with me for some refreshments?" she suggested kindly. "It is not often

I have guests as esteemed as Daevabadi royals." She smiled when Zaynab shrank back. "Do not fear, my princess, it is otherwise a lovely disguise."

With the word "hospital" ringing in her ears, Nahri followed at once. The courtyard was in the same sorry state as the rest of the complex, with roots snaking over its shattered blue and lemon-yellow tiles, yet there was something lovely about its ruin. Dark roses grew lush and wild, their thorny vines twining around a long-fallen shedu statue and the air rich with their fragrance. A pair of bulbuls splashed and sang in a cracked fountain set in front of the cascading boughs of a stand of shade trees.

"Do not mind Issa," Razu said lightly. "His social graces could use some work, but he's a brilliant scholar who's lived an extraordinary life. Before the ifrit took him, he spent centuries traveling the lands of the Nile, visiting their libraries and sending copies of their work back to Daevabad."

"The Nile?" Nahri asked eagerly.

"Indeed." Razu glanced back. "That is right . . . you grew up there. In Alexandria, yes?"

"Cairo," Nahri corrected, her heart giving its familiar lurch.

"Forgive the error. I'm not sure there was a Cairo in my day," Razu mused. "Though I'd heard of Alexandria. All of them." She shook her head. "What a vain, upstart youth Alexander was, naming all those cities after himself. His armies terrified the poor humans in Tukharistan."

Zaynab gasped. "Do you mean to say you lived in the same era as *Alexander the Great*?"

Razu's smile was more enigmatic this time. "Indeed. I'll be twenty-three hundred at this year's generation celebration. Anahid's grandchildren were ruling Daevabad when the ifrit took me."

"But . . . that's not possible," Nahri breathed. "Not for ifrit slaves."

"Ah, I suspect you've been told that we're all driven mad by the experience within a few centuries?" Razu quirked an eyebrow. "Like most things in life, the truth is a bit more complicated. And my particular circumstances were unusual."

"How so?"

"I offered myself to an ifrit." She laughed. "I was a terribly wicked thing with a fondness for tales of lost fortune. We convinced ourselves that we'd find all sorts of legendary treasures if we could recover the powers we'd had before Suleiman."

"You *gave* yourself to the ifrit?" Zaynab sounded scandalized, but Nahri was starting to feel a bit of a kinship for this mysterious hustler.

Razu nodded. "A distant cousin of mine. He was a stubborn fool who refused to submit to Suleiman, but I liked him." She shrugged. "Things were a little . . . gray between our peoples back then." She raised her palm. Three black lines marred the skin. "But it was foolish. I set my masters chasing after fantastical prizes my cousin and I planned to retrieve after I was freed. I was digging through some old tombs with my third human when the entire thing collapsed, killing him and burying my ring under the desert."

She snapped her fingers and a bolt of silk spun out from a basket sitting beneath a neem tree, arching and expanding in the air to form a swing. She motioned for Nahri and Zaynab to sit.

"It took two thousand years for another djinn to stumble upon me. He brought me back to Daevabad, and here I am today." Razu's bright eyes dimmed. "I never did see my ifrit cousin again. I suppose a Nahid or Afshin caught up with him, in the end."

Nahri cleared her throat. "I'm sorry."

Razu nudged her shoulder. "You needn't apologize. I was certainly more fortunate than Issa and Elashia; the few human masters I had never abused me. But when I returned, my world was gone, any descendants lost to history, and the Tukharistan

I knew a legend in the eyes of my own people. It was easier to begin anew in Daevabad. At least until recently." She shook her head. "But here I am rambling about the past . . . what brings *you* two here?"

"Carelessness," Zaynab muttered under her breath.

"I . . . I don't quite know," Nahri confessed. "We were passing by and I felt . . ." She trailed off. "I felt the magic emanating from this place, and it reminded me of the palace." She glanced around wonderingly. "Was this truly a hospital?"

Razu nodded. "It was." With another snap of her fingers, a smoking glass ewer appeared alongside three chalices. She poured Nahri and Zaynab each a glass of a cloud-colored liquid. "I spent some time here as a patient after failing to dodge one of my creditors."

Zaynab took a cautious sip and then promptly spit it most inelegantly back into the cup. "Oh, that's definitely forbidden."

Curious, Nahri tested her own glass, coughing at the intense burn of alcohol as it ran down her throat. "What is this?"

"Soma. The preferred drink of your ancestors." Razu winked. "Regardless of Suleiman's curse, the daevas of my day had yet to entirely lose our wildness."

Whatever soma was, it admittedly left Nahri feeling more relaxed. Zaynab looked ready to bolt, but Nahri was enjoying her time more and more with each allusion to Razu's felonious past. "What was it like back then—when you were a patient, I mean?"

Razu gazed pensively at the hospital. "It was an astonishing place, even in a city as magical as Daevabad. The Nahids must have treated thousands, and it all hummed along like a well-oiled wheel. I'd been hexed with a rather contagious streak of despair, so I was treated in quarantine over there." She tilted her head toward a crumbling wing, then took a sip of her drink. "They took excellent care of us. A bed, a roof, and warm meals? It was almost worth being sick."

Nahri leaned back on her palms, contemplating all that. She knew hospitals fairly well; she'd often snuck into Cairo's most famous—the majestic, old bimaristan in the Qalawun complex—to steal supplies and wander its depths, fantasizing about joining the ranks of the students and physicians crowding its lofty corridors.

She tried to imagine how that bustle would look here, the hospital whole and filled with Nahids. Dozens of healers consulting notes and examining patients. It must have been an extraordinary community.

A Nahid hospital. "I wish I had something like that," she said softly.

Razu grinned, raising her chalice in Nahri's direction. "Consider me your first recruit should you attempt to rebuild."

Zaynab had been tapping her foot, but now she stood. "Nahri, we should go," she warned, motioning to the sky. The sun had disappeared behind the hospital walls.

Nahri touched Razu's hand. "I'm going to try and come back," she promised. "The three of you . . . are you safe here? Is there anything you need?" Though Razu and her companions were probably more capable than Nahri at taking care of themselves, she felt suddenly protective of the three souls her family had freed.

Razu squeezed her hand. "We are fine," she assured her. "Though I do hope you come back. I think the place likes you."

2

ALI

Ali gazed at the edge of the rocky cliff, squinting in the desert's bright sunlight. His heart was beating so fast he could hear it in his ears, his breath coming in ragged bursts. Nervous sweat beaded on his brow, soaking into the cotton ghutra he'd wrapped around his head. He raised his arms, shifting back and forth on his bare feet.

"He's not going to do it," he heard one of the other djinn goad. There were six of them there atop the cliffs bordering the village of Bir Nabat, and they were all fairly young, for what they were doing required the sort of recklessness youth provided. "Little prince isn't risking his royal neck."

"He'll do it," another man shot back—Lubayd, Ali's closest friend in Am Gezira. "He *better* do it." His voice rose. "Ali, brother, I've got coin riding on you. Don't let me down!"

"You shouldn't be gambling," Ali shot back anxiously. He took another shaky breath, trying to work up his courage. This was so dangerous. So unnecessary and foolish, it was almost selfish.

From beyond the cliff, there was the sound of reptilian snuffling, followed by the sharp, unpleasant tang of burnt feathers. Ali whispered a prayer under his breath.

And then he took off, sprinting toward the cliff edge. He ran as fast as he could and when the cliff gave way to air, he kept going, hurling himself into empty space. For one petrifying moment, he was falling, the distant, rock-strewn ground he was about to be dashed upon rushing up . . .

He landed hard on the back of the zahhak that had been roosting along the cliff face. Ali gasped, a thrill racing through his blood as he let out a cry that was equal parts terrified and triumphant.

The zahhak clearly didn't share his enthusiasm. With an offended screech, the flying serpent took to the sky.

Ali lunged for the copper collar that a far more enterprising djinn had slipped over the zahhak's neck years ago, tightening his legs around the creature's sleek, silver-scaled body as he'd been instructed. Four massive wings—misty white and billowing like clouds—beat the air around him, snatching the breath from his lungs. Resembling an overgrown lizard—albeit one with the ability to shoot flames from its fanged mouth when harassed by djinn—this particular zahhak was said to be over four hundred years old and had been nesting in the cliffs outside Bir Nabat for generations, perhaps favoring the familiarity of its nesting spot enough to deal with the antics of the Geziri youth.

One of those youths squeezed his eyes shut now; the rush of the wind and the sight of the ground whizzing beneath him sending another rush of fear into Ali's heart. He clutched the collar, huddling against the zahhak's neck.

Look, you fool. Considering there was a chance this ended with him in pieces on the sand below, Ali might as well appreciate the view.

He opened his eyes. The desert spread before him, great sweeps of red-gold sand stretching to meet the bright blue horizon, broken by proudly jutting stands of rocks, antique formations sculpted by the wind over countless millennia. Jagged paths marked the line of long-vanished wadis, a distant stand of darkly lush palms forming a tiny oasis to the north.

"God be praised," he whispered, awed by the beauty and magnificence of the world below him. He understood now why Lubayd and Aqisa had been goading him into taking part in this most deadly of Bir Nabat's traditions. Ali might have grown up in Daevabad, but he'd never experienced anything as extraordinary as flying like this.

He squinted at the oasis, growing curious as he noticed black tents and movement between the distant trees. A group of no-mads perhaps—the oasis belonged to humans according to custom long set, the djinn of Bir Nabat not daring to take even a cup of water from its wells.

He leaned forward against the creature's neck for a better look, and the zahhak let out a smoky grumble of protest. Ali coughed, his stomach turning at the stench of the creature's breath. The gristle of roasted prey crusted its stained fangs, and though Ali had been warned about the smell, it still left him light-headed.

The zahhak obviously didn't think much of him either. With-out warning, it banked, sending Ali scrambling to keep his grip, and then the creature hurtled back the way they'd come, cutting through the air like a scythe.

Ahead, Ali could see the entrance to Bir Nabat: a forbid-dingly dark, empty doorway built directly into the cliffs. Stark sandstone carvings surrounded it: crumbling eagles perched upon decorative columns and a sharp pattern of steps that rose to meet the sky. The carvings had been done eons ago by Bir Nabat's original human settlers, an ancient group lost to time whose ruined settlement the djinn now called home.

His companions were just below, waving their arms and beating a metal drum to draw the ire of the zahhak. It dived for them, letting out a screech. Steeling himself, Ali waited until the zahhak drew close to his friends, opening its jaws to breathe an angry plume of scarlet fire that they narrowly ducked. Then he jumped.

He tumbled hard to the ground, Aqisa yanking him back just before the zahhak scorched the place he'd landed. With another offended shriek, it soared off, clearly having had enough of djinn for one day.

Lubayd hauled Ali to his feet, clapping his back and letting out a whoop. "I told you he would do it!" He grinned at Ali. "Worth the risk?"

Every part of his body ached, but Ali was too exhilarated to care. "It was amazing," he gushed, trying to catch his breath. He pulled away the ghutra the wind had plastered to his mouth. "And guess what? There's a new group of humans at the—"

Groans interrupted him before he'd even finished the sentence.

"No," Aqisa cut in. "I am not going to spy on humans with you again. You are obsessed."

Ali persisted. "But we could learn something new! You remember the village we explored in the south, the sundial they used to regulate their canals? That was very helpful."

Lubayd handed Ali his weapons back. "I remember the humans chasing us away when they realized they had 'demonic' visitors. They were firing quite a lot of those explosive stick . . . things. And I don't intend to learn if there's iron in those projectiles."

"Those 'explosive stick things' are called rifles," Ali corrected. "And you are all sadly lacking a spirit of enterprise."

They made their way down the rocky ledge that led to the village. Etchings covered the sandstone: letters in an alphabet Ali couldn't read, and carefully hewn drawings of long-vanished animals. In one high corner, an enormous bald man loomed over simple line drawings of figures, stylized flames twisting around his fingers. An original daeva, the village djinn believed, from before Suleiman blessed them. Judging from the figure's wild eyes and sharp teeth, they must have terrorized the human settlers.

Ali and his friends crossed beneath the entrance facade. A pair of djinn were drinking coffee in its shade, ostensibly guarding it. On the rare occasion a curious human got too close, they had charms capable of conjuring rushing winds and blinding sandstorms to frighten them off.

They looked up as Ali and his companions passed. "Did he do it?" one of the guards asked with a smile.

Lubayd wrapped an arm around Ali's shoulders proudly. "You'd think he'd been riding zahhak since he was weaned."

"It was extraordinary," Ali admitted.

The other man laughed. "We'll make a proper northerner out of you yet, Daevabadi."

Ali grinned back. "God willing."

They crossed through the dark chamber, passing the empty tombs of the long-dead human kings and queens who once ruled here—no one would ever give Ali a straight answer as to exactly *where* their bodies had gone and he wasn't sure he wanted to know. Ahead was a plain stone wall. To a casual observer—a human observer—little would mark it as special save the slight glow emanating from its oddly warm surface.

But it was a surface that all but sang to Ali, magic simmering from the rock in comforting waves. He placed his palm upon the wall. "Pataru sawassam," he commanded in Geziriyya.

The wall misted away, revealing the bustling greenery of Bir Nabat. Ali paused, taking a moment to appreciate the newly fertile beauty of the place he'd called home for five years. It was a mesmerizing sight, far different from the famine-stricken shell it had been when he first arrived. Though Bir Nabat had likely been a lush paradise at the time of its founding—the remnants of water catchments and aqueducts, as well as the size and artistry of its human-crafted temples, indicated a time of more frequent rains and a flourishing population—the djinn who'd moved in after had never matched their numbers. They'd gotten by for centuries with a pair of remaining springs and their own scavenging.

But by the time Ali arrived, the springs had dwindled down to almost nothing. Bir Nabat had become a desperate place, a place willing to defy their king and take in the strange young prince they'd found dying in a nearby crevasse. A place willing to overlook the fact that his eyes occasionally gleamed like wet bitumen when he got upset and his limbs were covered in scars no blade could draw. That didn't matter to the Geziris in Bir Nabat. The fact that Ali had uncovered four new springs and two untapped cisterns, enough water to irrigate Bir Nabat for centuries, did. Now small but thriving plots of barley and melons hemmed new homes, more and more people opting to replace tents of smoke and oryx hide with compounds of quarried stone and sandblasted glass. The date trees were healthy, thick and towering to provide cool shade. The village's eastern corner had been given over to orchards: a dozen fig saplings growing strong between citrus trees, all carefully fenced off for protection from Bir Nabat's booming population of goats.

They passed by the village's small market, held in the shadow of the enormous old temple that had been carved into the cliff face, its carefully sculpted columns and pavilions laden with magical goods. Ali smiled, returning the nods and salaams of various djinn merchants, a sense of calm stealing over him.

One of the vendors quickly stepped to block his path. "Ah, sheikh, I've been looking for you."

Ali blinked, pulled from his euphoric daze. It was Reem, a woman from one of the artisan-caste families.

She waved a scroll in front of him "I need you to check this contract for me. I'm telling you . . . that shifty southern slave of Bilqis is cheating me. My enchantments have no equal, and I know I should be seeing higher returns on the baskets I sold him."

"You do realize *I'm* one of those shifty southerners, correct?" Ali pointed out. The Qahtanis originally hailed from Am Gezira's mountainous southern coast—and were rather proud descendants of the djinn servants Suleiman had once gifted Bilqis, the human queen of ancient Saba.

Reem shook her head. "You're Daevabadi. It doesn't count." She paused. "It's actually worse."

Ali sighed and took the contract; between spending the morning digging a new canal and getting tossed around by a zahhak in the afternoon, he was beginning to yearn for his bed. "I'll have a look."

"Bless you, sheikh." Reem turned away.

Ali and his friends kept walking but didn't get far before Bir Nabat's muezzin came huffing over to them.

"Brother Alizayd, peace and blessings upon you!" The muezzin's gray eyes flitted over Ali. "Aye, you look half-dead on your feet."

"Yes. I was about to—"

"Of course, you were. Listen . . ." The muezzin lowered his voice. "Is there any way you could give the khutbah tomorrow? Sheikh Jiyad hasn't been feeling well."

"Doesn't Brother Thabit usually give the sermon in his father's place?"

"Yes, but . . ." The muezzin lowered his voice even further. "I can't deal with another of his rants, brother. I just can't. The last time he gave the khutbah, all he did was ramble about how the music of lutes was leading young people away from prayer."

Ali sighed again. He and Thabit didn't get along, primarily because Thabit fervently believed all the gossip coming out of Daevabad and would rail to anyone who would listen that Ali was an adulterous liar who'd been sent to corrupt them all with "city ways." "He won't be happy when he learns you asked me."

Aqisa snorted. "Yes, he will. It will give him something new to complain about."

"And people enjoy your sermons," the muezzin added quickly. "You choose very lovely topics." His voice turned shrewd. "It is good for their faith."

The man knew how to make an appeal, Ali would grant him that. "All right," he grumbled. "I'll do it."

The muezzin pressed his shoulder. "Thank you."

"You're dealing with Thabit when he hears about this," Ali said to Aqisa, half-stumbling down the path. They had almost reached his home. "You know how much he hates—" Ali broke off.

Two women were waiting for him outside his tent.

"Sisters!" he greeted them, forcing a smile to his face even as he inwardly swore. "Peace be upon you."

"And upon you peace." It was Umm Qays who spoke first, one of the village's stone mages. She gave Ali a wide, oddly sly grin. "How does this day find you?"

Exhausted. "Well, thanks be to God," Ali replied. "And yourselves?"

"Fine. We're fine," Bushra, Umm Qays's daughter spoke up quickly. She was avoiding Ali's eyes, embarrassment visible in her flushed cheeks. "Just passing through!"

"Nonsense." Umm Qays yanked her daughter close, and the young woman gave a small, startled yelp. "My Bushra has just made the loveliest kabsa . . . she is an extraordinarily gifted cook, you know, can conjure up a feast from the barest of bones and a whisper of spice . . . Anyway, her first thought was to set aside a portion for our prince." She beamed at Ali. "A good girl, she is."

Ali blinked, a little taken aback by Umm Qays's enthusiasm. "Ah . . . thank you," he said, catching sight of Lubayd covering his mouth, his eyes bright with amusement. "It is much appreciated."

Umm Qays was peeking in his tent. She tutted in disapproval. "A lonely place this looks, Alizayd al Qahtani. You are a great man. You should have a proper home in the cliffs and someone to return to."

God have mercy, not this again. He stammered out a reply. "I-I thank you for your concern, but really I'm quite content. Being lonely."

"Ah, but you're a young man." Umm Qays clapped his shoulder, giving his upper arm a squeeze. A surprised expression came over her face. "Well, my goodness . . . God be praised for such a thing," she said admiringly. "Certainly, you have *needs*, dear one. It's only natural."

Heat flooded Ali's face—more so when he realized Bushra had slightly lifted her gaze. There was a flicker of appraisal in her eyes that sent nerves fluttering in his stomach—and not entirely unpleasant ones. "I . . ."

Mercifully, Lubayd stepped in. "That's very considerate of you, sisters," he said, taking the dish. "We'll make sure he appreciates it."

Aqisa nodded, her eyes dancing. "It smells delicious."

Umm Qays seemed to recognize temporary defeat. She wagged a finger in Ali's face. "One day." She gestured inside as she left. "By the way, a messenger came by with a package from your sister."

The women were barely around the bend when Lubayd and Aqisa burst into peals of laughter.

"Stop it," Ali hissed. "It's not funny."

"Yes, it is," Aqisa countered, her shoulders shaking. "I could watch that a dozen more times."

Lubayd hooted. "You should have seen his face last week when Sadaf brought him a blanket because she felt his bed 'needed warming.'"

"That's enough." Ali reached for the dish. "Give me that."

Lubayd ducked away. "Oh no, this is my reward for saving you." He held it up, closing his eyes as he inhaled. "Maybe you should marry her. I can intrude upon all your dinners."

"I'm not marrying anyone," Ali returned sharply. "It's too dangerous."

Aqisa rolled her eyes. "You exaggerate. It has been a year since I last saved you from an assassin."

"One who got close enough to do this," Ali argued, arching his neck to reveal the faint pearly scar running across his throat just under the scruff of his beard.

Lubayd waved him off. "He did that and then his own clan caught him, gutted him, and left his body for the zahhak." He gave Ali a pointed look. "There are very few assassins foolish enough to come after the man responsible for half of northern Am Gezira's water supply. You *should* start building a life here. I suspect marriage would vastly improve your temperament."

"Oh, immeasurably so," Aqisa agreed. She glanced up, exchanging a conspiratorial grin with Lubayd. "A pity there is no one in Bir Nabat to his taste . . ."

"You mean someone with black eyes and a penchant for healing?" Lubayd teased, cackling when Ali glared at him.

"You know there's no truth to those idiotic rumors," Ali said. "The Banu Nahida and I were merely friends, and she is married to my brother."

Lubayd shrugged. "I find the idiotic rumors enjoyable. Can you blame people for spinning exciting tales out of what happened to all of you?" His voice took on a dramatic edge. "A mysterious Nahid beauty locked away in the palace, an evil Afshin set to ruin her, an irritable prince exiled to the land of his forefathers . . ."

Ali's temper finally snapped as he reached for the tent flap. "I am not *irritable*. And you're the one spinning most of those tales!"

Lubayd only laughed again. "Go on inside and see what your sister sent you." He glanced at Aqisa, holding up the dish. "Hungry?"

"Very."

Shaking his head, Ali kicked off his sandals and ducked inside his tent. It was small yet cozy, with ample space for the bed cushion one of Lubayd's cousins had mercifully lengthened to Ali's "ludicrous" height. In fact, everything in the room was a gift. He'd arrived in Bir Nabat with only his weapons and the bloodstained dishdasha on his back, and his belongings were a record of his years here: the extra robe and sandals that were the first things he'd scavenged from an abandoned human caravan, the Qur'an that Sheikh Jiyad had given him when Ali started teaching, the pages and pages of notes and drawings he'd taken while observing various irrigation works.

And something new: a sealed copper tube the length of his forearm and wide as a fist, resting upon his neatly folded cushion. One end had been dipped in jet black wax, a familiar signature carved around its perimeter.

With a smile, Ali picked up the tube, peeling off the wax to reveal the blade-sharp pattern it had been protecting. A blood seal, one that ensured none but a blood relation of Zaynab's would be able to open it. It was the most they could do to protect their privacy . . . not that it mattered. The man most likely to have their communication intercepted was their own father and he could easily use his own blood to read their messages. Likely he did.

Ali pressed his arm against the edge. The scroll top smoked away the moment the blades drew blood, and Ali tilted it, emptying the contents onto his cushion.

A bar of gold, a copper armband, and a letter, several pages in length. Attached to the armband was a small note in Zaynab's elegant hand.

For the headaches you keep complaining about. Take good care of this, little brother. The Nahid horribly overcharged me for it.

Ali fingered the armband, eying the gold bar and the letter. *God preserve you, Zaynab.* Bir Nabat might be recovering, but it was still a hard place and that gold would go a long way here. He only hoped sending it hadn't gotten his sister in any trouble. He'd written her multiple times trying to warn her off providing him with supplies, and she'd ignored him, flouting his advice as thoroughly as she defied their father's unofficial decree that no Geziri was to aid him. Zaynab was probably the only one who could get away with such a thing; Ghassan had always been soft-hearted when it came to his daughter.

He fell on his bed cushion, rolling onto his stomach to read the letter, Zaynab's familiar script and barbed observations like a warm hug. He missed his sister terribly; theirs was a relationship he'd been too young and self-righteous to appreciate until now, when it was reduced to the occasional letter. Ali would never see Zaynab again. He wouldn't sit by the canal on a sunny day to share coffee and family gossip, nor be proudly at her side when she married. He'd never meet her future children, the nieces and nephews he would have spoiled and taught to spar in another life.

He also knew it could be worse. Ali thanked God every day he'd landed with the djinn of Bir Nabat rather than in the hands of any of the dozens who'd tried to kill him since. But the ache when he thought of his family never quite went entirely away.

Then maybe you should start building one here. Ali rolled onto his back, basking in the warmth of the sun glowing against the tent. In the distance, he could hear children laughing and birds chirping. Bushra's quiet interest played across his mind, and alone in his tent, Ali would not deny it sent a slight thrill through his body.

Daevabad seemed a world away, his father apparently content to forget him. Would it truly be so terrible to allow himself to settle more permanently here, to quietly seize the kind of domestic life he would have never been allowed as Muntadhir's Qaid?

Dread crept over him. *Yes*, it seemed to answer, swallowing the simple fantasies running through his mind's eye. For in Ali's experience, dreaming of a better future had only ever led to destruction.

3

NAHRI

Well, one thing was clear: her Daeva elders did not share Nahri's enthusiasm about the Nahid hospital.

Nisreen stared at her. "You slipped away from your guards? *Again?* Do you have any idea what Ghassan will do if he finds out?"

"Zaynab made me do it!" Nahri defended herself. Then—realizing it was perhaps a little ungrateful to blame her sister-in-law for an outing she rather enjoyed—she quickly added, "She said she takes such walks often and hasn't been caught yet. And she promised to take the blame if we were."

Kartir looked openly alarmed. The grand priest was normally more indulgent of Nahri's . . . unorthodox ways, but this latest misadventure seemed to have shaken his calm. "And you trust her?" he asked, his wiry brows knitting in worry.

"On this, yes." Nahri's relationship with her sister-in-law was a prickly one, but she recognized a woman eager for a little bit of freedom when she saw one. "Now will the two of you stop fretting over everything? This is exciting! Can you imagine it? A Nahid hospital?"

Kartir and Nisreen shared a look. It was quick, but there was no denying the way the priest's cheeks flushed in guilt.

Nahri was instantly suspicious. "You already know of this place? Why wouldn't you tell me?"

Kartir sighed. "Because what happened to that hospital is neither pleasant nor wise to discuss. I doubt anyone besides the king and a few devoted Daevabadi historians even know anything about it."

Nahri frowned at the vague words. "Then how do you two?"

"Because Banu Manizheh learned of its existence—and of its fate," Nisreen said quietly. "She was always poring over her family's old books. She told us."

"What do you mean, 'its fate'?" When neither replied, Nahri's impatience got the better of her. "Suleiman's eye, must everything be a secret here? I learned more from Razu in five minutes than I have from the two of you in five years!"

"Razu? Baga Rustam's Razu?" Relief lit Kartir's face. "Thank the Creator. I feared the worst when her tavern was burned."

Nahri felt a pang of sorrow for the kind gambler who'd welcomed her so warmly. "I'm the Banu Nahida. I should have known ifrit slaves were being hunted down."

Nisreen and Kartir exchanged another glance. "We thought it best," Nisreen said finally. "You were still so deep in grief over Dara, and I didn't want to burden you with the fate of his fellows."

Nahri flinched at Dara's name; she could not deny she had fallen apart in the weeks after his death. "It still wasn't a decision you should have made on my behalf." She eyed them. "I cannot be Banu Nahida in the Temple and infirmary and then be treated like a child when it comes to political matters you believe upsetting."

"Political matters we think could get you killed," Nisreen corrected bluntly. "There is more room for error in the Temple and infirmary."

"And the hospital?" Nahri pressed. "What political reason could there be to have kept me in the dark about its existence?"

Kartir stared at his hands. "It's not because of its existence, Banu Nahida. It's because of what happened to it during the war."

When he fell silent again, an idea struck Nahri. "If you can't give me a better explanation that that, you'll force me to find a way back. One of the freed djinn was a historian, and I'm sure he knows."

"Absolutely not," Nisreen cut in quickly, but then she sighed, sounding resigned. "The hospital was the first place to fall when Zaydi al Qahtani took Daevabad. The Nahids inside didn't even have a chance to flee back to the palace. The shafit revolted the moment Zaydi's army breached the city walls. They stormed the hospital and murdered every Nahid inside. *Every single one*, Banu Nahri. From elderly pharmacists to apprentices barely out of childhood."

Kartir spoke up, his voice grave as the blood left Nahri's face. "It was said to have been quite brutal. The Geziris had their zulfiqars, of course, but the shafit fought with Rumi fire."

"Rumi fire?" Nahri asked. The term sounded slightly familiar.

"It's a human invention," Nisreen explained. "A substance that sticks like tar and burns even Daeva skin. 'Fire for the fire worshippers,' the shafit were said to have shouted." She dropped her gaze, looking sick. "Some still use it. It's how the djinn thieves who murdered my parents set our family's temple ablaze."

Guilt swept through Nahri, hard and fast. "Oh, Nisreen, I'm sorry. I had no idea."

"It's not your fault," Nisreen replied. "In truth, I suspect what happened at the Nahid hospital was far worse. I didn't read the accounts Banu Manizheh did, but she barely spoke for weeks after finding them."

"There were some indications that it was an act of revenge," Kartir added carefully. "The violence . . . it seemed purposeful."

Nisreen scoffed. "The djinn do not need a reason to be violent. It is their nature."

The priest shook his head. "Let's not pretend our tribe doesn't have blood on its hands, Lady Nisreen. That is not the lesson I would impart to a young Nahid." A shadow passed across his face. "Banu Manizheh used to speak like that. It was not good for her soul."

Nisreen's eyes narrowed. "She had reason to speak as she did, and you know it."

There was a knock on the door. Nisreen instantly fell silent. They might be in the Temple, but one still needed to be wary of speaking ill of the Qahtanis in Daevabad.

But the man who poked his head in was anything but a spy. "Banu Nahida?" Jamshid tented his fingers together in respect. "I'm sorry to interrupt, but the palace sent a litter for you."

Nahri scowled. "Because Creator forbid I spend one unauthorized moment in my own temple." She stood up, glancing at Nisreen. "Are you coming?"

Nisreen shook her head. "I have some matters to finish here." She gave Nahri a stern look. "Please resist the urge to take another side trip, I beg you."

Nahri rolled her eyes. "I bet my own mother would have been less controlling than you."

Nisreen touched her wrist as she passed, an act technically forbidden in the Temple. Her eyes were soft. "But she's *not* here, child, so it's up to us to protect you."

The genuine worry in her face cut through some of Nahri's annoyance. For their many arguments, Nisreen was the closest thing Nahri had to family in Daevabad, and she knew her mentor cared dearly for her. "Fine," she grumbled, bringing her hands together in blessing. "May the fires burn brightly for you both."

"And for you, Banu Nahida," they replied.

"SIDE TRIP?" JAMSHID ASKED ONCE THE DOOR WAS closed. "You have the look of someone freshly scolded."

"A new, rather grisly lesson in Daevabad's history." Nahri made a face. "Just once, I'd like to learn of an event that was nothing but our ancestors conjuring rainbows and dancing in the street together."

"It's a bit more difficult to hold a grudge over the good days."

Nahri wrinkled her nose. "I suppose that's true." She set aside thoughts of the hospital, turning to face him. In the dim light of the corridor, the shadows under Jamshid's eyes were well-pronounced and the planes of his cheekbones and nose stood out sharply. Five years after Dara's attack had nearly killed him, Jamshid was still recovering—at a gruelingly slow pace no one could understand. He was a shadow of the healthy archer Nahri had first seen deftly shooting arrows from upon the back of a charging elephant. "How are you feeling?"

"As though you ask me that question every day, and the answer is always the same?"

"I'm your Banu Nahida," she said as they emerged into the Temple's main prayer hall. It was a vast space, designed to fit thousands of worshippers with rows of decorated columns holding up the distant ceiling and shrines dedicated to the most lionized figures in their tribe's long history lining the walls. "It's my duty."

"I'm fine," he assured her, pausing to look at the bustling temple. "It's crowded here today."

Nahri followed his gaze. The temple was indeed packed, and it seemed like many were travelers: ascetics in worn robes and wide-eyed pilgrim families jostling for space with the usual Daevabadi sophisticates.

"Your father wasn't joking when he said people would start arriving months before Navasatem."

Jamshid nodded. "It's our most important holiday. Another century of freedom from Suleiman's imprisonment . . . a month of celebrating life and honoring our ancestors."

"It's an excuse to shop and drink."

"It's an excuse to shop and drink," Jamshid agreed. "But it's supposed to be an extraordinary spectacle. Competitions and parties of every kind, merchants bringing all the newest and most exciting wares from across the world. Parades, fireworks . . ."

Nahri groaned. "The infirmary is going to be so busy." The djinn took merrymaking seriously and the risks of overindulgence far less. "Do you think your father will be back by then?" Kaveh had left recently to visit the Pramukhs' ancestral estate in Zariaspa, ranting about a union dispute among his herb growers and a particularly pernicious plague of ravenous frogs that had besieged their silver-mint plants.

"Most certainly," Jamshid replied. "He'll be back to help the king with the final preparations."

They kept walking, passing the enormous fire altar. It was beautiful, and Nahri always paused for a moment to admire it, even when she wasn't conducting ceremonies. Central to the Daeva faith, the striking altars had persisted through the centuries and consisted of a basin of purified water with a brazierlike structure rising in its middle. Inside burned a fire of cedarwood, extinguished only upon a devotee's death. The brazier was carefully swept of ash at dawn each day, marking the sun's return, and the glass oil lamps that bobbed in the basin were relit to keep the water at a constant simmer.

A long line of worshippers waited to receive blessings from the priest; Nahri caught the eye of a little girl in a yellow felt dress fidgeting next to her father. She winked and the girl beamed, tugging her father's hand and pointing excitedly.

At her side, Jamshid misstepped. He stumbled, letting out a hiss of pain, but waved Nahri off when she moved to take his arm.

"I can do it," he insisted. He tapped the cane. "I'm hoping to be done with *this* come Navasatem."

"An admirable goal," Nahri said gently, worry rising in her as she studied the stubborn set of his features. "But take care not to exhaust yourself. Your body needs time to heal."

Jamshid made a face. "I suppose being cursed has its draw-backs."

She immediately stopped, turning to look at him. "You're not cursed."

"Do you have a better explanation for why my body reacts so badly to Nahid healing?"

No. Nahri bit her lip. Her skills had come a long way, but her inability to heal Jamshid gnawed at her confidence. "Jamshid . . . I'm still new at this, and Nisreen isn't a Nahid. It's far more likely there's some magical or medical reason that your recovery is taking so long. Blame *me*," she added. "Not yourself."

"I would not dare." They were nearing the shrines that lined the Temple wall. "Though on that note . . . I would like to have another session soon if possible."

"Are you certain? The last time we tried . . ." Nahri trailed off, trying to find a diplomatic way to point out that the last time she'd healed him, he'd barely lasted five minutes before he was screaming in agony and clawing at his skin.

"I know." He kept his gaze averted, as if he was struggling to keep both the hope and despair from his face; unlike many in Daevabad, Jamshid had never struck Nahri as a good liar. "But I'd like to try." His voice dropped. "The emir . . . his father forced him to appoint another captain to his personal guard."

"Oh, Jamshid, it's just a position," Nahri replied. "Surely you know you're Muntadhir's closest companion regardless. He never stops singing your praises."

Jamshid shook his head, stubborn. "I should be protecting him."

"You almost died protecting him."

They came into view of Dara's shrine at that rather inopportune time, and Nahri felt Jamshid tense. Dara's shrine was among the most popular; roses garlanded his brass statue, that of a Daeva warrior on horseback, standing proudly upright in his stirrups to aim an arrow at his pursuers, and offerings littered the floor around the statue's base. No blades were allowed in the temple, so small ceramic tokens depicting a variety of ceremonial weapons—mostly arrows—had been brought instead.

An enormous silver bow hung on the wall behind the statue, and as Nahri gazed at it, a lump rose in her throat. She'd spent a lot of time staring at that bow, though never in the company of a man—a friend—she knew had every right to hate the Afshin who'd wielded it.

But Jamshid wasn't looking at the bow. He was instead squinting at the statue's foot. "Is that a *crocodile*?" he asked, pointing to a small charred skeleton.

Nahri pressed her lips together. "Looks like it. Alizayd the Afshin-slayer." She said the title softly, hating everything about it.

Jamshid looked disgusted. "That's obscene. I am no fan of Alizayd's, but the same sentiment that calls the Ayaanle crocodiles calls us fire worshippers."

"Not everyone shares your tolerance," she replied. "I've seen the skeletons here before. I suppose some people think Dara would enjoy having his murderer burned before him."

"He probably would," Jamshid said darkly. He glanced at her, his expression shifting. "Do you do that often? Come here, I mean?"

Nahri hesitated, uncertain how to respond. Dara was a raw nerve within her, even five years after his death—an emotional bramble that only grew more tangled when she tried to cut through it. Her memories of the grumbling, handsome warrior she'd grown to care for on their journey to Daevabad warred with the knowledge that he was also a war criminal, his hands drenched with the blood of Qui-zi's innocents. Dara had stolen his way into her heart and then he'd shattered it, so desperate to save her despite her own wishes that he'd been willing to risk plunging their world into war.

"No," she finally replied, checking the tremor in her voice. Unlike Jamshid, Nahri was accomplished at hiding her emotions. "I try not to. This isn't a shrine to the Dara I knew."

Jamshid's gaze flickered from the shrine to her. "What do you mean?"

Nahri considered the statue, the warrior caught in action. "He wasn't a legendary Afshin to me. Not originally. Qui-zi, the war, his rebellion . . . he didn't tell me about any of that." She paused. It had been here in the Temple that she and Dara had come closest to speaking aloud of what had grown between them, a fight that had dragged them apart and offered Nahri the first true glimpse of how much the war had stolen from Dara—and how much the loss had warped him. "I don't think he wanted me to know. In the end . . ." Her voice softened. "I don't think that was the man he wanted to be." She flushed. "I'm sorry. I shouldn't be burdening you of all people with this."

"You can burden me," Jamshid said quietly. "It's hard to watch the way this city ruins the ones we love." He sighed and then turned away, leaning on his cane. "We should head back."

Lost in thought, Nahri said nothing as they left the Temple and crossed its manicured grounds to the waiting palanquin. The sun blinked past the distant mountains, vanishing into the green horizon, and from deep inside the temple, a drum began to beat. Across the city, the djinn call to prayer answered it in waves. In marking the departure of the sun, the djinn and Daeva faithful were briefly united.

Once inside the palanquin, she relaxed into the cushions, the rocking motion lulling her toward sleep as they made their way through the Daeva Quarter.

"Tired?" Jamshid asked as she yawned.

"Always. And I had a patient who went late last night. An Agnivanshi weaver who inhaled the vapors she uses to make her carpets fly." Nahri rubbed her temples. "Never a dull day."

Jamshid shook his head, looking amused. "I can help when we get back."

"That would be appreciated. I'll have the kitchens send us up some dinner."

He groaned. "Not your strange human food."

"I like my strange human food," Nahri defended. One of the palace cooks was an old man from Egypt, a shafit with a knack for knowing when to prepare the comforting dishes of her former home. "And anyway—"

From beyond the palanquin, a woman's cry pierced the air. "Let him go! *Please!* I beg you. We did nothing wrong!"

Nahri shot upright. The palanquin lurched to a stop, and she yanked back its brocade curtain. They were still in the Daeva Quarter, on a quiet street that ran past some of the city's oldest and finest homes. In front of the largest, a dozen members of the Royal Guard were rooting through a pile of furnishings. Two Daeva men and a boy who couldn't be out of his teens had been bound and gagged, pushed into kneeling positions on the street.

An older Daeva woman was pleading with the soldiers. "Please, my son is only a boy. He wasn't involved!"

Another soldier exited the smashed and dangling doors of the home. He shouted excitedly in Geziriyya and then tossed a carved wooden chest to the cobblestone street with enough force to break it. Coins and uncut jewels spilled out, glittering on the wet ground.

Nahri leapt from the litter without a second thought. "What in God's name is going on here?" she demanded.

"Banu Nahida!" Relief lit in the woman's wet eyes. "They're accusing my husband and his brother of treason and trying to take my son!" She choked back a sob, switching to Divasti. "It's a lie! All they did was hold a meeting to discuss the new land tax on Daeva properties. The king heard of it and now's he's punishing them for telling the truth!"

Anger surged through Nahri, hot and dangerous. "Where are your orders?" she demanded, turning to the soldiers. "I can't imagine they gave you permission to loot this home."

The officers looked unimpressed by her attempt at authority. "New rules," one replied brusquely. "The Guard now gets a fifth of whatever is confiscated from unbelievers—and that would be you Daevas." His expression darkened. "Strange how everyone in this city is suffering save the fire worshippers."

The Daeva woman dropped to her knees in front of Nahri. "Banu Nahida, please! I told them they could have whatever money and jewelry they want, but don't let them take my family! I'll never see them again once they're in that dungeon."

Jamshid came to their side. "Your family isn't going anywhere," he assured her. He turned to the soldiers, his voice steely. "Send one of your men to the emir. I don't want another hand laid on these people until he's here."

The djinn officer snorted. "I take my orders from the king. Not from the emir and certainly not from some useless Afshin pretender." Cruelty edged his voice as he nodded at Jamshid's cane. "Your new bow isn't quite as intimidating as your old one, Pramukh."

Jamshid jerked back like he'd been slapped, and Nahri stepped forward, enraged on his behalf. "How dare you speak so disrespectfully? He is the grand wazir's son!"

In the blink of an eye, the soldier had his zulfiqar drawn. "His father is not here and neither is your bloody Scourge." He gave Nahri a cold look. "Do not try me, Nahid. The king made his orders clear, and believe me when I say I have little patience for the fire worshipper who loosed her Afshin on my fellows." He raised his zulfiqar, bringing it dangerously close to Jamshid's throat. "So, unless you'd like me to start *executing* Daeva men, I suggest you return to your palanquin."

Nahri froze at the threat—and the implication that accompanied its open hostility. Ghassan had an iron grip on Daevabad: if his soldiers felt comfortable intimidating two of the most powerful Daevas in the city, it was because they weren't worried about being punished.

Jamshid stepped back first, reaching for Nahri's hand. His was cold. "Let's go," he said softly in Divasti. "The sooner we're gone, the sooner I can get word of this to Muntadhir."

Heartsick, Nahri could barely look at the woman. In that moment, though she hated the memory of the warrior Dara, she couldn't help but wish he was here, bringing shedu statues to life and drawing his bow against those who would hurt their people. "I'm sorry," she whispered, cursing her inability to do anything more. "We'll talk to the emir, I promise."

The woman was weeping. "Why bother?" she asked, bitter despair lacing into her voice. The words she spoke next cut Nahri to the core. "If you can't protect yourself, how can you possibly protect the rest of us?"

4

DARA

In the deep quiet of a snowy night, Dara made his way through a black forest.

He did so in complete silence, moving stealthily alongside the five young Daeva men mirroring his every action. They had bound their boots in cloth to muffle their steps and smeared their woolen coats with ash and dirt to mimic the pattern of the skeletal trees and rocky ground. There were magical ways—better ways—to conceal oneself, but what they were doing tonight was as much test as it was mission, and Dara wanted to challenge his young recruits.

He stopped at the next tree, raising a hand to signal his men to do the same. He narrowed his eyes and studied their targets, his breath steaming against the cloth that covered the lower part of his face.

Two Geziri scouts from the Royal Guard, exactly as rumored. Gossip in this desolate part of northern Daevastana had been buzzing with news of them. They had apparently been sent to survey the northern border; his sources had told him it was normal, a routine visit completed every half-century or so to harass the locals about their taxes and remind them of King Ghassan's reach. But Dara had been suspicious of the timing and thus quietly relieved when Banu Manizheh ordered him to bring them to her.

"Would it not be easier to kill them?" had been his only protest. Contrary to the rumors he knew surrounded him, Dara did not relish killing. But neither did he like the prospect of two Geziris learning of his and Manizheh's existence. "This is a dangerous land. I can make it look as though they were attacked by beasts."

Manizheh had shaken her head. "I need them alive." Her expression had grown stern, his Banu Nahida perhaps coming to know him a bit too well in the few years he'd served her. "*Alive*, Darayavahoush. That's nonnegotiable."

Which is why they were here now. It had taken them two weeks to find the scouts, and two days to quietly drive them off course, his men shifting the boundary stones in waves to send the Geziris off the established path to the village of Sugdam and deep into the thick forest that belted the nearby mountains.

The scouts looked miserable, wrapped in furs and felt blankets and huddled together under a hastily erected tarp. Their fire was a weak one, slowly losing the battle against the steady snowfall. The older scout was smoking a pipe, the sweet smell of smoldering qat scenting the air.

But it wasn't pipes Dara was concerned with, nor the khanjar daggers tucked in their belts. After a moment of scanning the camp, he spotted the zulfiqars he'd been looking for on a bed of raised stones just behind the scouts. Their leather scabbards had been wrapped in a layer of felt to protect the blades from the snow, but Dara could see a hilt poking free.

He silently cursed. Skilled zulfiqaris were treasured, and he'd been holding out hope that the king hadn't bothered sending such valuable warriors on what should have been a rather dull mission. Invented during the war against the Nahid Council—or stolen from the angels who guarded Paradise, as the more fanciful stories went—the zulfiqar at first appeared to be a normal scimitar, its copper construction and two-pronged end a bit unusual but otherwise unremarkable.

But well-trained Geziris—and only Geziris—could learn to conjure poisoned flames from the zulfiqar's deadly edge. A single nick of the skin meant death; there was no healing from the wounds, not even by the hand of a Nahid. It was the weapon that had turned the war and ended the rule of his blessed and beloved Nahid Council, killing an untold number of Daevas in the process.

Dara glanced at the warrior nearest him. Mardoniye, one of his youngest. He'd been a member of the Daeva Brigade, the small contingent of Daeva soldiers once allowed to serve in the Royal Guard. They'd been run out of the Citadel after Dara's death on the boat, ordered from their barracks by djinn officers they considered comrades and sent into the Grand Bazaar with only the clothes on their backs. There, they'd been met by a shafit mob. Unarmed and outnumbered, they'd been brutally assaulted, several men killed. Mardoniye still bore Rumi fire burns on his face and arms, remnants of the attack.

Dara swallowed against the worry rising in his chest. He'd made it clear to his men that he would not aid them in capturing the Geziris. He considered it a rare opportunity for them to test their training. But fighting zulfiqaris wasn't the same as fighting regular soldiers.

And yet . . . they needed to learn. They would face zulfiqaris one day, Creator willing. They'd fight Daevabad's fiercest, in a battle that would need to be decisively won.

The thought sent more smoldering heat into Dara's hands. He fought it back with a tremble, this new, raw power he'd yet to entirely master. It simmered beneath his skin, the fire aching to escape. He struggled with it more when he was emotional . . . and the prospect of the young Daevas he'd mentored for years being cut down by the blade of a sand fly certainly made him so.

You've spent a lifetime training warriors. You know they need this. Dara pushed aside his misgivings.

He let out a low hoot, the approximation of an owl. One of the djinn glanced up but only briefly. His men fanned out, their dark eyes darting back to him as they moved. Dara watched as his archers nocked their arrows.

He clicked his tongue, his final signal.

The archers' pitch-soaked arrows burst into conjured flames. The djinn had less than a second to spot them before they shot past, striking the tarp. In the blink of an eye, the entire thing was blazing. The larger Geziri—an older man with a thick salt-and-pepper beard—whirled around to grab the zulfiqars.

Mardoniye was already there. He kicked away the blades and then threw himself on the Geziri. They rolled into the snow, scrabbling at each other.

"Abu Sayf!" The younger scout lunged for his companion—an unwise move that left his back exposed when the rest of Dara's men emerged. They threw a weighted net over his head, dragging him back and ensnaring his arms. In seconds, his khanjar had been ripped away and iron cuffs—meant to dampen his magic—clasped around his wrists.

Mardoniye was still struggling. The Geziri man—Abu Sayf—struck him hard across the face and then lunged to grab a zulfiqar. It burst into flames. He whirled back on Mardoniye.

Dara's bow was off his shoulder, an arrow nocked before he even realized what he was doing. *Let him fight!* the Afshin in him demanded. He could all but hear his father's voice, his uncles' voices, his own. There was no room for mercy in the heat of the battle.

But by the Creator, he did not have it in him to watch another Daeva die. Dara drew back his bow, his index finger on the twitching feather fletch, the string a whispered brush against his cheek.

Mardoniye threw himself at the Geziri's knees with a howl, knocking him into the snow. Another of Dara's archers ran forward, swinging his bow like a club at the Geziri man's hand. Abu Sayf dropped the zulfiqar, and the flames were gone before it hit the ground. The archer struck the djinn hard across the face, and he collapsed.

It was over.

The scouts were secured by the time Dara stomped out their campfire. He quickly checked the unconscious one for a pulse. "He's alive," he confirmed, silently relieved. He nodded at the small camp. "Check their supplies. Burn any documents you find."

The conscious djinn was indignant, straining against his binds. "I don't know what you fire worshippers think you're doing, but we're Royal Guard. This is treason! When my garrison commander learns you interfered with our mission, he'll have you executed!"

Mardoniye kicked at a large sack, and it let out a jingle. "All the coins they've been stealing from our people, I suspect."

"Taxes," the Geziri cut in savagely. "I know you're all half feral out here, but surely you have some basic concept of governance."

Mardoniye scoffed. "Our people were ruling empires while yours were scavenging through human trash, sand fly."

"That's enough." Dara glanced at Mardoniye. "Leave the coins. Leave everything but their weapons and retreat. Take them at least twenty paces away."

The Geziri soldier struggled, trying to twist free as they hauled him to his feet. Dara began unwrapping his headcloth, not wanting it to burn when he shifted. It briefly caught on the slave ring he was still too nervous to remove.

"You're going to hang for this!" the djinn repeated. "You filthy, sister-fucking, fire-worshipping—"

Dara's hand shot out as Mardoniye's eyes flashed again. He knew all too well how quickly tensions built between their peoples. He grabbed the djinn by the throat. "It is a long walk back to our camp," he said flatly. "If you can't be *polite*, I am going to remove your ability to speak."

The djinn's eyes traveled over Dara's now uncovered face, landing on his left cheekbone. That was all it took for the color to leach from his skin.

"No," he whispered. "You're dead. You're dead!"

"I was," Dara agreed coldly. "Now I'm not." He could not keep the edge of bitterness out of his voice. Annoyed, he shoved the Geziri back at his men. "Your camp is about to be attacked by a rukh. Best step away."

The djinn let out a gasp, looking up at the sky. "We're about to be *what*?"

Dara had already turned his back. He waited until the sounds of his men faded away. The distance wasn't only for their protection.

Dara didn't like anyone to see him when he shifted.

He pulled off his coat, setting it aside. Heat rose in hazy waves from his tattooed arms, the snow melting in the air around him before the flakes came close to brushing his skin. He closed his eyes, taking a deep breath as he steeled himself. He hated this part.

Fire burst from his skin, flushed light sweeping down his limbs, washing away the normal brown. His entire body shook violently, and he fell to his knees, his limbs seizing. It had taken him two years to learn how to shift between his original form—that of a typical man of his tribe, albeit an emerald-eyed one—and that of a true daeva, as Manizheh insisted on calling him, the form their people had taken before Suleiman changed them. The form the ifrit still held.

Dara's vision sharpened, the taste of blood filling his mouth as his teeth lengthened into fangs. He always forgot to prepare for that part.

His clawed hands clenched at the icy ground as his raw jittery power settled completely. It only ever happened in this form, a peace he obtained by becoming something he hated. He exhaled, burning embers leaving his mouth, and then he straightened back up.

He raised his hands, smoke swirling up from around them. With a quick snap of his claws across his wrist, a shimmer of golden blood dripped down to merge with the smoke, growing and twisting in the air as he shaped it. Wings and talons, a beak and glittering eyes. He fought for breath, the magic draining him.

"Ajanadivak," he whispered, the command still foreign on his tongue. The original language of the daevas, a language only a handful of ifrit still remembered. They were Manizheh's "allies," pressed into teaching a reluctant Afshin the ancient daeva magic that Suleiman had stripped away.

Fire burst from the rukh, and it let out a screech. It rose in the air, still under Dara's command, destroying the camp in a matter of minutes. He took care to let it crash through the canopy and rake its talons over the tree trunks. To anyone with the misfortune of coming across this place—any members of the Royal Guard looking for their two lost fellows, though Dara doubted they'd ever make it out here—it would appear as though the scouts had been eaten, the fortune in taxes left untouched.

He released the rukh, and it disintegrated, cinders raining over the ground as its hazy form dissipated. With a final burst of magic, Dara shifted back, stifling a gasp of pain. It always hurt, like shoving his body into a tight, barbed cage.

Mardoniye was at his side in moments, reliably loyal. "Your coat, Afshin," he said, offering it out.

Dara took it gratefully. "Thank you," he said, his teeth chattering.

The younger man hesitated. "Are you all right? If you need a hand—"

"I am fine," Dara insisted. It was a lie; he could already feel the black pitch churning in his stomach, a side effect of returning to his mortal body while his new magic still swirled in his veins. But he refused to show such weakness before his men; he would not risk it getting back to Manizheh. If the Banu Nahida had her way, Dara would stay forever in the form he hated. "Go. I'll be along shortly."

He watched, waiting until they were out of view. Then he dropped to his knees again, his stomach heaving, his limbs shaking, as the snow fell silently around him.

THE SIGHT OF THEIR CAMP NEVER FAILED TO EASE Dara's mind, the familiar plumes of smoke promising a hot meal, the gray felt tents that blended into the horizon a warm bed. These were appreciated luxuries for any warrior who'd just spent three days trying hard not to rip the tongue out of a particularly irritating djinn's mouth. Daevas bustled about, hard at work cooking, training, cleaning, and forging weapons. There were about eighty of them, lost souls Manizheh had come upon in her years of wandering: the sole survivors of zahhak attacks and unwanted children, exiles she'd rescued from death and the remnants of the Daeva Brigade. They swore allegiance to her, offering loyalty in an oath that would rot their tongues and hands should they attempt to break it.

He'd shaped about forty of them into warriors, including a

handful of young women. Dara had at first balked at that, finding it unorthodox and improper. Then Banu Manizheh had bluntly pointed out that if he could fight *for* a woman, he could fight beside one, and he had to admit she'd been right. One of the women, Irtemiz, was by far his most talented archer.

But his good mood vanished the second he caught sight of their corral. A new horse was there: a golden mare whose finely tooled saddle hung over the fence.

Dara's heart dropped. He recognized that mare.

Kaveh e-Pramukh had arrived early.

A gasp from behind stole his attention. "This is your camp?" It was Abu Sayf, the zulfiqari who'd nearly killed Mardoniye and yet had oddly proven far less maddening on their return trek than his younger tribesman. He asked the question in fluent Divasti; he'd told Dara that he'd been married to a Daeva woman for decades. His gray eyes scanned the neat row of tents and wagons. "You move," he noted. "Yes, I suppose you would. Easier to stay hidden that way."

Dara met his gaze. "You would do well to keep such observations to yourself."

Abu Sayf's expression dimmed. "What do you plan to do with us?"

I do not know. It was also not a thing Dara could think about—not when the sight of Kaveh's horse was making him so anxious he felt sick.

He glanced at Mardoniye. "See that the djinn are secured, but get them water for washing and something hot to eat." He paused, glancing at his tired band of soldiers. "And do the same for yourselves. Your rest is well earned."

Dara turned toward the main tent. Emotions swirled inside him. What did one say to the father of a man they had nearly killed? Not that Dara had meant to do so; he remembered nothing about his assault on the warship. The time between Nahri's strange wish and Alizayd tumbling into the lake that ill-fated night was shrouded in fog. But he remembered what he'd seen afterward far too well: the body of the kind young man he'd taken under his wing slumped on the boat deck, his back riddled with Dara's arrows.

His stomach fluttering with nerves, Dara coughed outside the tent flap, alerting those inside to his presence before he called out. "Banu Nahida?"

"Come in, Dara."

He ducked inside and immediately starting coughing more as he inhaled the cloud of acrid purple smoke that greeted him—one of Manizheh's many experiments. They lined the enormous slate table she insisted on lugging around with them, her equipment taking up an entire wagon.

She was at the table now, seated on a cushion behind a floating glass flask and holding a long pair of forceps. A lilac-hued liquid boiled inside the flask, giving off the purple smoke.

"Afshin," she greeted him warmly, dropping a small, wriggling silver object into the boiling liquid. There was a metallic squeal, and then she stepped back, pulling aside her facecloth. "Your mission was a success?"

"The Geziri scouts are being secured as we speak," he said, relieved that Kaveh was nowhere to be seen.

Manizheh's brow arched. "Alive?"

Dara scowled. "As requested."

A small smile lit her face. "It is much appreciated. Please tell your men to bring me one of their relics as soon as possible."

"Their relics?" Djinn and Daeva alike all wore relics—a bit of blood, sometimes a baby tooth or lock of hair, often paired with a holy verse or two, all bound in metal and worn on the person. They were safeguards, to be used to bring a soul back into a conjured body should one be enslaved by an ifrit. "What do you want with their . . ."

The question died on his lips. Kaveh e-Pramukh had emerged from the inner room to join them.

Dara just managed to keep his mouth from falling open. He wasn't sure what surprised him more: that Kaveh had stepped out of the small, private chamber in which Manizheh slept, or that the grand wazir looked terrible. He might have aged fifteen years, not five, his face scored by lines and his hair and mustache mostly silver. He was thin, the shadowed swells under his eyes indicating a man who had seen too much and not slept enough.

But by the Creator, did those eyes find him. And when they did, they filled with all the anger and betrayal that had undoubtedly been seething inside him since that night on the boat.

Manizheh caught the wazir's wrist. "Kaveh," she said softly.

The practiced words of regret vanished from Dara's mind. He crossed the room, falling to his knees.

"I am so sorry, Kaveh." The apology tumbled inelegantly from his lips. "I never meant to hurt him. I would have taken a blade to myself had I—"

"Sixty-four," Kaveh cut in coldly.

Dara blinked. "What?"

"Sixty-four. It is the number of Daevas who were killed in the weeks following your death. Some died after being interrogated, innocents who had nothing to do with your flight. Others because they protested what they saw as your unjust murder at the hands of Prince Alizayd. The rest because Ghassan let the shafit attack us, in an effort to muscle our tribe back into compliance." Kaveh's mouth thinned. "If you are going to offer useless words of remorse, you should at least be reminded of the extent of what you're responsible for. My son lives. Others do not."

Dara's face burned. Did Kaveh not think he regretted, down to his marrow, what his actions had led to? That he wasn't reminded of his mistake every day as he watched over the traumatized remnant of the Daeva Brigade?

He gritted his teeth. "So in your eyes I should have stood silently by as Banu Nahri was forced to marry that lecherous sand fly?"

"Yes," Kaveh said bluntly. "That is *exactly* what you should have done. You should have bowed your damn head and taken the governorship in Zariaspa. You could have quietly trained a militia for years in Daevastana while Banu Nahri lulled the Qahtanis into a false sense of peace. Ghassan is not a young man. Alizayd and Muntadhir could have easily been manipulated into warring against each other once Muntadhir took the throne. We could have let the Geziris destroy themselves and then swept in to take over with minimal bloodshed." His eyes flashed. "I told you we had allies and support outside Daevabad because I *trusted* you. Because I didn't want you to do something rash before we were prepared." His voice turned scornful. "I never imagined the supposedly clever Darayavahoush e-Afshin, the rebel who almost beat Zaydi al Qahtani, would risk us all because he wanted to run away."

The fire under Manizheh's flask flared, and with it, Dara's anger. "*I was not running—*"

"That's *enough*," Manizheh cut in, glaring at them both. "Afshin, calm yourself. Kaveh . . ." She shook her head. "Whatever the consequences, Dara acted to protect my daughter from a fate I fought for decades. I cannot fault him for that. And if you think Ghassan wasn't looking for a reason to crack down on the Daevas the instant a Nahid and Afshin strolled through the gates of Daevabad, you clearly do not know him at all." She gave them another sharp look. "Tearing each other apart is not why we are here." She gestured to a heap of floor cushions arranged around her fire altar. "*Sit.*"

Chastened, Dara obeyed, rising to his feet and moving toward the cushions. After a few moments, Kaveh did the same, still glowering.

Manizheh placed herself between them. "Would you conjure some wine?" she asked Dara. "I suspect you could both use it."

Dara was fairly certain that the only thing Kaveh wanted to do with wine was throw it in his face, but he obeyed. With a snap of his fingers, three brass goblets appeared, filled with the dark amber hue of date wine.

He took a sip, trying to calm himself. Causing fires to explode was not going to alleviate Kaveh's concerns about his temper. "How is he?" he asked carefully. "Jamshid. If I may inquire."

Kaveh stared at the altar. "He didn't wake for a full year. It took another for him to be able to sit up and use his hands. He's walking with a cane now, but . . ." His voice broke, his hand trembling so hard he nearly spilled his wine. "He hasn't handled being injured well. He loved being a warrior . . . he wanted to be like *you*."

The words were like a blow. Ashamed, he dropped his gaze, though not before he caught sight of Manizheh. Her hand was clenched around her goblet so tightly that her knuckles were turning white.

She spoke. "He will be all right, Kaveh. I promise you. Jamshid will be healthy and whole and have *everything* that has been denied him."

The intensity in her voice took Dara aback. In the years he'd known her, Manizheh's calm was constant. Rather reassuring, in fact. The type of absolute unflappability he preferred in a leader.

They are friends, he reminded himself. Small surprise she was so protective of Kaveh's son.

Deciding Jamshid was perhaps not the safest subject, Dara moved on, all while quietly working to calm the magic pulsing through his veins. "And how is Banu Nahri?" he asked, forcing a bland distance into his voice.

"Surviving," Kaveh replied. "Ghassan keeps her on a tight leash. All of us. She was wed to Muntadhir less than a year after your death."

"He no doubt forced her," Manizheh said darkly. "As I said, he tried to do the same to me for decades. He was obsessed with uniting our families."

"Well, he certainly underestimated her. She took Ghassan for everything she could during the marriage negotiations." Kaveh sipped his wine. "It was actually a bit frightening to watch. But Creator bless her. She ended up signing the bulk of her dowry over to the Temple. They've been using it for charitable work: a new school for girls, an orphanage, and assistance for the Daevas ruined in the assault on the Grand Bazaar."

"That must make her popular with our people. A clever move," Manizheh assessed softly before her expression turned grim. "And regarding the other part of their marriage . . . Nisreen is keeping an eye on that situation, yes?"

Kaveh cleared his throat. "There will be no child between them."

Dara's insides had been churning as they spoke, but Kaveh's carefully worded response made his skin prickle. It did not sound like Nahri had much of a say in that either.

The words were leaving his mouth before he could stop them. "I think we should tell her the truth about what we are planning. Your daughter," he burst out. "She is smart. Strong-willed. She could be an asset." Dara cleared his throat. "And she did not quite seem to . . . appreciate being left in the dark the last time."

Manizheh was already shaking her head. "She is safe in the dark. Do you have any idea what Ghassan would do to her if our conspiracy were uncovered? Let her innocence protect her a bit longer."

Kaveh spoke up, more hesitant. "I must say Nisreen has been suggesting the same, Banu Nahida. She's grown very close to your daughter and hates lying to her."

"And if Nahri knew, she might be able to better protect herself," Dara persisted.

"Or she might reveal us all," Manizheh countered. "She is young, she is under Ghassan's thumb, and she has already shown a predilection for cutting deals with djinn. We cannot trust her."

Dara stiffened. The rather curt assessment of Nahri offended him, and he struggled not to show it. "Banu Nahida—"

Manizheh raised a hand. "This is not a debate. Neither of you know Ghassan like I do. You do not know the things he is capable of. The ways he finds to punish the ones you love." A flicker of old grief filled her eyes. "Ensuring that he cannot do such things to another generation of Nahids is far more important than my daughter's feelings about being left in the dark. She can yell at me about that when Ghassan is ash."

Dara lowered his gaze, managing a bare nod.

"Perhaps we can discuss our preparations then," Kaveh said. "Navasatem is approaching, and it would be an excellent time to attack. The city will be caught up in the chaos of celebration and the palace's attention focused on the holiday."

"*Navasatem?*" Dara's head jerked up. "Navasatem is less than eight months away. I have forty men."

"So?" Kaveh challenged. "You're free of Suleiman's curse, aren't you? Can you not tear down the Citadel with your hands and let your blood beasts loose on the city? That is what Banu Manizheh has told me you can do. That is the reason you were brought back."

Dara gripped his cup tightly. He knew he was viewed as a weapon—but this unvarnished assessment of his worth still stung. "It is more complicated than that. I am still learning to control my new abilities. And my men need more training."

Manizheh touched his hand. "You are too humble, Daraya-vahoush. I believe you and your warriors are more than ready."

Dara shook his head, not as ready to concede on military matters as he was on personal ones. "We cannot take Daevabad with forty men." He looked between them urgently, willing them to listen. "I spent years before the ifrit killed me contemplating how to best capture the city. Daevabad is a fortress. There is no scaling the walls, and there is no tunneling under them. The Citadel has thousands of soldiers—"

"Conscripts," Kaveh cut in. "Poorly paid and growing more mutinous by the day. At least a dozen Geziri officers defected after Alizayd was sent to Am Gezira."

Thoughts of besieging Daevabad vanished from Dara's mind. "Alizayd al Qahtani is in Am Gezira?"

Kaveh nodded. "Ghassan sent him away within days of your death. I thought it might have been temporary, until things calmed, but he hasn't returned. Not even for Muntadhir's wedding." He took another sip of his wine. "Something is going on, but it's been difficult to discern; the Geziris hold their secrets close." A little relish filled the other man's face. "Admittedly, I was happy to see him fall from favor. He's a fanatic."

"He is more than that," Dara said quietly. A buzz filled his ears, smoke curling around his fingers. Alizayd al Qahtani, the self-righteous brat who'd cut him down. The young warrior whose dangerous combination of deadly skill and unquestioning faith had reminded Dara a little too much of his younger self.

He knew quite well how that had turned out. "He should be dealt with," he said. "Swiftly. Before we attack Daevabad."

Manizheh gave him a skeptical look. "You do not think Ghassan would find it suspicious should his son turn up dead in Am Gezira? Presumably in whatever brutal fashion you're currently imagining?"

"It is worth the risk," Dara argued. "I too was a young warrior in exile when Daevabad fell and my family was slaughtered." He let the implication linger. "I would strongly suggest you not let such an enemy have a chance to grow. And I wouldn't be brutal," he added quickly. "We have time aplenty for me to track him down and get rid of him in a way that would leave nothing for Ghassan to question."

Manizheh shook her head. "We don't have time. If we are to attack during Navasatem, I can't have you spending weeks wandering the Am Gezira wastelands."

"We are not going to be able to attack during Navasatem," Dara said, growing exasperated at their stubbornness. "I cannot yet even cross the threshold to *enter* Daevabad, let alone conquer it."

"The threshold is not the only way to enter Daevabad," Manizheh replied evenly.

"What?" Dara and Kaveh said the word together.

Manizheh took a sip of her wine, seeming to savor their shock. "The ifrit think there might be another way to enter Daevabad . . . one for which you may have Alizayd al Qahtani to thank. Or the creatures pulling his strings anyway."

"The creatures pulling his strings," Dara repeated, his voice growing hollow. He'd told Manizheh everything about that night on the boat. About the magic that had overpowered him and stolen his mind. About the prince who'd climbed out of Daevabad's deadly lake covered in tentacles and scales, whispering a language Dara had never heard, raising a dripping blade. She'd come to the same impossible conclusion. "You don't mean . . ."

"I mean it is time we go speak to the marid." A little heat entered Manizheh's expression. "It is time we get some vengeance for what they have done."

5

ALI

"Sheen," Ali said, marking the letter in the damp sand before him. He glanced up, his gaze turning severe at the sight of two boys tussling in the last row. They immediately stopped, and Ali continued, motioning for his students to copy the letter. They obediently did so, also on the sand. Slates and chalk required resources Bir Nabat didn't have to spare, so he taught his lessons in the cool grove where the canals met and the ground was reliably wet. "Who knows a word that starts with 'sheen'?"

"Sha'b!" a little girl in the center piped up while the boy sitting beside her shot his hand into the air.

"I start with sheen!" he declared. "Shaddad!"

Ali smiled. "That's right. And do you know who you share your name with?"

His sister answered. "Shaddad the Blessed. My grandmother told me."

"And who was Shaddad the Blessed?" he asked, snapping his fingers at the boys who'd been fighting. "Do either of you know?"

The smaller one shrank back while the other's eyes went wide. "Um . . . a king?"

Ali nodded. "The second king after Zaydi the Great."

"Is he the one who fought the marid queen?"

The grove went dead silent at the question. Ali's fingers stilled on the damp sand. "What?"

"The marid queen." It was a little boy named Faisal who'd spoken up, his face earnest. "My abba says one of your ancestors defeated a marid queen, and that's why you can find our water."

The simple words, said so innocently, went through Ali like a poisoned blade, leaving sick dread creeping through his limbs. He'd long suspected quiet rumors circulated in Bir Nabat about his affinities with water, but this was the first time he'd heard himself mentioned in relation to the marid. It was probably nothing; a half-remembered folktale given new life when he started discovering springs.

But it was not a connection he could let linger. "My ancestors never had anything to do with the marid," he said firmly, ignoring the churning in his stomach. "The marid are gone. No one has seen them in centuries."

But he could already see eager curiosity catching ahold of his students. "Is it true they'll steal your soul if you look too long at your reflection in the water?" a little girl asked.

"No," an older one answered before Ali could open his mouth. "But I heard humans used to sacrifice *babies* to them." Her voice rose in fear-tinged excitement. "And if they didn't give them up, the marid would drown their villages."

"*Stop*," one of the youngest boys begged. He looked near tears. "If you talk about them, they'll come for you in the night!"

"That's enough," Ali said, and a few children shrank back,

his words coming out sharper than he'd intended. "Until you've mastered your letters, I don't want to hear anything more about—"

Lubayd ran into the grove.

"Forgive me, brother." His friend bent over, clutching his knees as he caught his breath. "But there is something you need to see."

THE CARAVAN WAS LARGE ENOUGH TO BE VISIBLE FROM a fair distance away. Ali watched it approach from the top of Bir Nabat's cliffs, counting at least twenty camels moving in a steady, snaking line toward the village. As they left the shadow of a massive sand dune, the sun glinted off the pearly white tablets the animals were carrying. Salt.

His stomach plummeted.

"Ayaanle." Lubayd took the word from Ali's mouth, shading his eyes with one hand. "And with a fortune . . . that looks like enough salt to pay a year's taxes." He dropped his hand. "What are they doing *here*?"

At his side, Aqisa crossed her arms. "They cannot be lost; we are weeks' travel from the main trade route." She glanced at Ali. "Do you think they could be your mother's kin?"

They better not be. Though his companions didn't know it, his Ayaanle mother's kin were the ones who'd truly gotten Ali banished from Daevabad. They'd been behind the Tanzeem's decision to recruit him, apparently hoping the shafit militants would eventually convince Ali to seize the throne.

It had been a ludicrous plot, but in the chaos following the Afshin's death, Ghassan wasn't taking the chance of anyone preying on Ali's conflicted sympathies—let alone the powerful lords of Ta Ntry. Except, of course, the Ayaanle were difficult to punish in their wealthy, cosmopolitan homeland across the sea. So it had been Ali who suffered, Ali who was ripped from *his* home and tossed to assassins.

Stop. Ali checked the vitriol swirling within him, ashamed of how easily it had come. It was not the fault of the entire Ayaanle tribe, only a handful of his mother's scheming relatives. For all he knew, the travelers below were perfectly innocent.

Lubayd looked apprehensive. "I hope they brought their own provisions. We won't be able to feed all those camels."

Ali turned away, resting his hand on his zulfiqar. "Let's go ask them."

THE CARAVAN HAD ARRIVED BY THE TIME THEY climbed down from the cliffs, and as Ali waded through the crowd of bleating camels, he realized Lubayd had been right about the fortune they were carrying. It looked like enough salt to provision Daevabad for a year and was most certainly some type of tax payment. Even the glossy, bright-eyed camels appeared costly, the decorated saddles and bindings covering their golden-white hides far finer than was practical.

But Ali didn't see the large delegation he would have expected making small talk with Sheikh Jiyad and his son Thabit. Only a single Ayaanle man stood with them, dressed in the traditional bright teal robes that Ayaanle djinn on state business typically donned, their hue an homage to the colors of the Nile headwater.

The traveler turned around, the gold glittering from his ears and around his neck dazzling in the sunlight. He broke into a wide smile. "Cousin!" He laughed as he took in the sight of Ali. "By the Most High, is it possible a prince is under all those rags?"

The man crossed to him before Ali could offer a response, flabbergasted as he was. He held out his arms as if to pull Ali into an embrace.

Ali's hand dropped to his khanjar. He swiftly stepped back. "I do not hug."

The Ayaanle man grinned. "As friendly as people said you would be." His warm gold eyes shone with amusement. "Peace be upon you either way, Hatset's son." His gaze traveled down Ali's body. "You look awful," he added, switching to Ntaran, the language of his mother's tribe. "What have these people been feeding you? Rocks?"

Offended, Ali drew up, studying the man, but no recognition came to him. "Who are you?" he stammered in Djinnistani. The common tongue felt strange after so long in Am Gezira.

"Who am I?" the man asked. "Musa, of course!" When Ali narrowed his eyes, the other man feigned hurt. "Shams's nephew? Cousin to Ta Khazak Ras on your mother's maternal uncle's side?"

Ali shook his head, the tangled lines of his mother's family confusing him. "Where are the rest of your men?"

"Gone. May God have mercy upon them." Musa touched his heart, his eyes filling with sorrow. "My caravan has been utterly cursed with every type of misfortune and injury, and my last two comrades were forced to return to Ta Ntry due to dire family circumstances last week."

"He lies, brother," Aqisa warned in Geziriyya. "No single man could have brought a caravan of such size here. His fellows are probably hiding in the desert."

Ali eyed Musa again, growing more suspicious. "What is it you want from us?"

Musa chuckled. "Not one to bother with small talk, are you?" He pulled free a small white tablet from his robe and tossed it to Ali.

Ali caught it. He rubbed his thumb over the grainy surface. "What am I supposed to do with a lump of salt?"

"Cursed salt. We bewitch our cargo before crossing Am Gezira, and none but our own can handle it. I suppose the fact that you just did means you're Ayaanle, after all." He grinned as if he had said something enormously witty.

Looking doubtful, Lubayd reached to take the salt from Ali's hands and then let out a yelp. His friend yanked his hand away, both the salt and his skin sizzling from the contact.

Musa wrapped a long arm around Ali's shoulder. "Come, cousin. We should talk."

"ABSOLUTELY NOT," ALI DECLARED. "WHETHER OR NOT Ta Ntry's taxes make it to Daevabad is not my concern."

"Cousin . . . show some compassion for family." Musa sipped his coffee and then made a face, setting it aside. They were in Bir Nabat's central meeting place: a large sandstone chamber in the cliffs, its corners dotted with tall columns wrapped in ribbons of carved snakes.

Musa lounged against a worn cushion, his tale of woe finally complete. Ali kept catching sight of curious children peeking past the entrance. Bir Nabat was extremely isolated; someone like Musa, who flaunted the Ayaanle's legendary wealth so openly in his sumptuous robe and heavy gold ornaments, was probably the most exciting thing to happen since Ali's own arrival.

Musa spread his hands; his rings winked in the firelight. "Are you not headed home for Navasatem anyway? Certainly the king's own son would not miss the generation celebrations."

Navasatem. The word rang in Ali's mind. Originally a Daeva holiday, Navasatem was now when all six tribes celebrated the birth of a new generation. Intended to commemorate the anniversary of their emancipation and reflect upon the lessons taught by Suleiman, it had turned into a frenetic celebration of life itself . . . Indeed, it was an old joke that there was typically a *swell* in life ten months after because so many children were conceived during the wild festivities. Like most devout djinn, Ali had mixed feelings about a full month of feasts, fairs, and wild revelry. Daevabad's clerics—djinn imams and Daeva priests alike—typically spent the time clucking their tongues and admonishing their hungover flock.

And yet, in his previous life, Ali had looked forward to the celebrations for years. Navasatem's martial competitions were legendary and, young age notwithstanding, he'd been determined to enter them, to sweep them, earning his father's admiration and the position his name had already bought: Muntadhir's future Qaid.

Ali took a deep breath. "I am not attending Navasatem."

"But I need you," Musa implored, sounding helpless. "There is no way I can continue on to Daevabad alone."

Ali gave him an incredulous look. "Then you shouldn't have left the main route! You could have found assistance at a proper caravanserai."

"We should kill him and take his cargo," Aqisa suggested in Geziriyya. "The Ayaanle will think he perished in the desert, and the lying fool deserves it."

Lubayd touched her fingers, easing them away from the hilt of her zulfiqar. "People won't think much of our hospitality if we start killing all the guests who lie."

Musa glanced between them. "Am I missing something?"

"Just discussing where we might host you for the evening," Ali said lightly in Djinnistani. He pressed his fingers together. "Just so I'm clear. You left the main route to come to Bir Nabat—an outpost you knew could not afford to host you and your animals—in order to foist your responsibilities upon me?"

Musa shrugged. "I do apologize."

"I see." Ali sat back and gave the circle of djinn a polite smile. "Brothers and sisters," he started. "Forgive the burden, but would you mind giving me a few moments alone with my . . . what did you call yourself again?"

"Your cousin."

"My cousin."

The other djinn rose. Thabit gave him a pointed look. He clearly knew Ali well enough to hear the danger in his voice even if Musa did not. "Do not get blood on the rugs," he warned in Geziriyya. "They are new."

The others were barely gone before Musa let out an over-wrought sigh. "By the Most High, how have you survived for so long in this *backwater*?" He shuddered, picking at the goat that had been prepared for him, a goat one of the villagers had been readying for his daughter's wedding and happily offered when he learned they had a guest. "I didn't think djinn still lived like—ah!" he cried out as Ali grabbed him by his silver-embroidered collar and threw him to the ground.

"Does our hospitality not please you?" Ali asked coldly, draw-ing his zulfiqar.

"Not current—wait, don't!" Musa's gold eyes went bright with terror as flames licked down the copper blade. "Please!"

"Why are you really here?" Ali demanded. "And don't give me any more nonsense about your travel woes."

"I'm here to help you, you wild fool! To provide you with a way to return to Daevabad!"

"*Help me?* Your scheming was the reason I was sent away in the first place!"

Musa held up his hands in surrender. "To be fair . . . that was another branch of the family—stop!" he shrieked, scrambling back as Ali pressed the blade closer. "Are you crazy? I'm your blood! And I'm under guest-right!"

"You are not my guest," Ali countered. "I am not from Bir Nabat. And Am Gezira is a dangerous—what did you call it?—*backwater*?" He spat in offense. "Traders disappear all the time. Especially ones foolish enough to go traipsing about alone with such wealth."

Musa's eyes locked on his. There was determination under the fear. "I made it very clear where I was headed. If my cargo doesn't make it to Daevabad in time to pay for Navasatem, the king will come looking for it." He lifted his chin. "Would you invite such trouble upon your new brothers and sisters?"

Ali stepped back, the flames vanishing from his blade. "I'm not getting drawn into another scheme. And I will kill you myself before you threaten these people."

Musa rolled his eyes. "I was warned you had a temper." He straightened up, brushing the sand off his robe. "And a rather alarmingly close relationship with your zulfiqar." He crossed his arms. "But I'm not leaving without you. A not-inconsiderable amount of risk and cost went into this. Another man might be grateful."

"Find him, then," Ali shot back.

"And that would be it? You'd really go back to picking through human trash and selling dates when I'm offering to help you return to Daevabad before it falls apart?"

"Daevabad is not *falling apart*."

"No?" Musa stepped closer. "Does news from the capital not make it to this forsaken place? Crime is soaring, and the economy is so bad that the Royal Guard can barely afford to feed its soldiers, let alone provision them with proper weapons."

Ali gave him an even look. "And what part did the Ayaanle play in those economic woes?"

Musa spread his hands. "Why should we be fair to a king who exiles our prince? A king who turns his back on his own family's legacy and does nothing as shafit are sold at auction blocks?"

"You're lying." Ali eyed the man with scorn. "Not that your people would care about the shafit or the city. Daevabad is a game to the Ayaanle. You sit in Ta Ntry, counting your gold and playing with other people's lives."

"We care far more than you think." Musa's eyes flashed. "Zaydi al Qahtani wouldn't have taken Daevabad without the Ayaanle. *Your* family would not be royalty without the Ayaanle." His mouth lifted in a slight smile. "And let's be honest . . . rising crime and political corruption do have a tendency to disrupt business."

"And there it is."

"That's not all it is." Musa shook his head. "I don't understand. I thought you'd be thrilled! I'd be heartbroken if I was banished from my home. I know I'd do anything to return to my family. And your family . . ." His voice softened. "They're not doing well."

Apprehension raced down Ali's spine. "What are you talking about?"

"How do *you* think your mother responded to your being exiled? You should be relieved she's restricted herself to a trade war rather than an actual one. I hear your sister is heartbroken, that your brother falls further into drink every day, and your father . . ." Musa paused, and Ali did not miss his calculated tone when he spoke again. "Ghassan's a vengeful man, and his wrath has fallen directly on the shafit he believes stirred you to treason."

Ali flinched, the last line finding its mark. "I can't do anything about any of that," he insisted. "Every time I tried, it hurt the people I cared about. And I have even less power now than I did then."

"*Less* power? Alizayd the Afshin-slayer? The clever prince who has learned to make the desert bloom and travels with a pack of Am Gezira's fiercest warriors?" Musa eyed him. "You underestimate your appeal."

"Probably because I know intimately how much of that is nonsense. I'm not going to Daevabad." Ali crossed to the entrance to beckon his companions back. "My decision is final."

"Alizayd, would you just—" But Musa was wise enough to fall silent as the others joined them.

"My cousin apologizes for abusing the hospitality of Bir Nabat," Ali announced. "He intends to depart at dawn and says we may take a fifth of his inventory to compensate our loss."

Musa whirled on him. "What?" he said hotly in Ntaran. "I certainly did not!"

"I will gut you like a fish," Ali warned in the same tongue before slipping back into Djinnistani: ". . . *to compensate our loss*," he repeated firmly, "and refill the bellies of the children gone hungry while his camels gorge. Additionally, have someone take his provisions and replace them with locusts and dates." He watched as Musa went from incredulous to outraged. "You said you were feeling weak. I suggest a change in diet. Such food has made us very hardy." He clicked his teeth. "You get used to the crunch."

Indignation simmered in Musa's eyes, but he didn't speak. Ali stood, pressing a hand to his heart in the traditional Geziri salute. "If you'll excuse me, I have work to do. I'll wake you at dawn for prayer."

"But of course," Musa said, his voice newly cool. "One must never forget their obligations."

Ali didn't like the look in his eyes, but having made his point, he turned for the exit. "Peace be upon you, cousin."

"And upon you peace, prince."

ALI SLEPT HARD; HE ALWAYS DID HERE. HE DREAMT HE was back in Daevabad on the lovely pavilion overlooking the harem gardens, lost in his books. A cool breeze, a wet breeze, gently swung his hammock. The water soaked through the fabric, through his dishdasha, clammy and cold fingers upon his skin . . .

"Ali!"

Ali's eyes snapped open. His hand flew to his khanjar, the dagger a silver gleam in the dark tent. He caught sight of Lubayd, the other man staying wisely out of reach, and dropped the blade.

It landed with a splash in the pool of water nearly level with his bed cushion. Ali shot up in alarm at the sight of his flooded tent, then flew to his feet, quickly snatching up his books and his notes.

"Come," Lubayd said, already holding open the tent flap. "It looks to be the worst rupture we've had."

The scene outside was mayhem. The water in the courtyard was waist high, and judging from its turbulence, still gushing out of the cistern below. The cairns Ali used to block off the canals were nowhere to be seen, probably washed away.

He swore. "Wake the rest. Anyone with a working pair of hands needs to get down to the fields and orchards. Don't let the soil get oversaturated."

Lubayd nodded, his usual humor vanished. "Don't drown."

Ali pulled off his robe and waded through the courtyard. He made sure Lubayd was gone before he submerged to check on conditions underground. Drowning didn't worry him.

It was the fact that he couldn't that did.

THE SUN WAS WELL RISEN OVER A SOGGY BIR NABAT BY the time the rupture was fixed. Ali was so tired he had to be helped from the cistern. His fingers were swollen from groping the rock, his senses numb from the cold water.

Lubayd pushed a cup of hot coffee into his hands. "We've salvaged what we could. I don't think there was much harm to any crops, but several of the aqueducts will need to be repaired. And there was rather extensive damage to the trellis in the fig orchard."

Ali nodded mutely. Water streamed down his limbs, echoing the cold rage welling inside him. "Where is he?"

Lubayd's reluctant silence confirmed Ali's suspicions. He'd known as soon as he dived into the cistern and found that the rocks limiting the spring had been moved. No Geziri would have swum so deep, and none would have ever dared sabotage a well. But an Ayaanle man who'd been taught to swim as a child? One who'd never gone thirsty? He might have.

"Gone, departed in the chaos," Lubayd finally answered. He cleared his throat. "He left his cargo."

Aqisa dropped down next to them. "We should let it rot in the desert," she said bitterly. "Salvage what we can, sell what we can't, and let the rest sink below the sands. To hell with the Ayaanle. Let them explain to the king."

"They will find a way to blame us," Ali said softly. He stared at his hands. They were shaking. "Stealing from the Treasury is a capital offense."

Lubayd knelt before him. "Then we'll take the damned salt," he said firmly. "Aqisa and I. You'll stay in Am Gezira."

Ali tried to clear the lump growing in his throat. "You can't even touch it." Besides, this was his family's mess; it wasn't right to foist responsibility for dealing with it on the people who'd saved him.

He stood up, feeling unsteady. "I . . . I'll need to organize repairs first." The words made him sick. The life he'd been carefully putting together in Bir Nabat had been turned upside down in a night, carelessly cast aside by outsiders in the name of their own political calculations. "We'll leave for Daevabad tomorrow." The words sounded odd in his mouth, unreal somehow.

Lubayd hesitated. "And your cousin?"

Ali doubted they would find Musa, but it was worth a try. "No man who would sabotage a well is kin of mine. Send a pair of fighters after him."

"And should they find him?"

"Drag him back. I'll deal with him when I return." Ali's hands tightened on his cup. "And I *will* return."

6

NAHRI

"*Ow!* By the Creator, are you doing that on purpose? It didn't hurt nearly as bad last time!"

Nahri ignored her patient's complaint, her attention focused instead on his neatly splayed lower midsection. Metal clamps held open the skin, white-hot to keep the wound clean. The shape-shifter's intestines shimmered a pale silver—or at least they would have shimmered had they not been studded with stubborn bits of rocky growths.

She took a deep breath, centering herself. The infirmary was stifling, and she'd been working on this patient for at least two grueling hours. She had one hand pressed against his flushed skin to dull the pain of the procedure and keep it from killing him. With the other, she manipulated a pair of steel tweezers around the next growth. It was a complicated, time-consuming operation, and sweat beaded her brow.

"Damn it!"

She dropped the stone into a pan. "Stop *turning into a statue*, and you won't have to deal with this." She briefly paused to glare at him. "This is the third time I've had to treat you . . . people are not meant to shift into rocks!"

He looked a little ashamed. "It's very peaceful."

Nahri threw him an exasperated look. "Find another way to relax. I beg you. Stitches!" she called aloud. When there was no response, she glanced over her shoulder. "Nisreen?"

"One moment!"

From across the crowded infirmary, she caught sight of Nisreen dashing between a table piled high with pharmaceutical preparations and another with instruments due for a magical scalding. Nisreen picked up a silver tray, holding it over her head as she navigated the tightly packed cots and huddles of visitors. The infirmary was standing room only, with more people pushed into the garden.

Nahri sighed as Nisreen squeezed between a bouncing Ayaanle artist hexed with exuberance and a Sahrayn metalworker whose skin was covered in smoking pustules. "Imagine if we had a hospital, Nisreen. An enormous hospital with room to breathe and staff to do your busywork."

"A dream," Nisreen replied, setting down her tray. "Your stitches." She paused to admire Nahri's work. "Excellent. I never get tired of seeing how far your skills have progressed."

"I'm barely allowed to leave the infirmary, and I work all day. I'd hope my skills had progressed." But she couldn't entirely hide her smile. Despite the long hours and grueling work, Nahri took great satisfaction in her role as a healer, able to help patients even when she couldn't fix the myriad other problems in her life.

She closed the shapeshifter up quickly with the enchanted thread and then bound the wound, pressing a cup of opium-laced tea into his hands. "Drink and rest."

"Banu Nahida?"

Nahri glanced up. A steward dressed in royal colors peeked in from the doors leading to the garden, his eyes going wide at the sight of her. In the moist heat of the infirmary, Nahri's hair had grown wild, black curls escaping her headscarf. Her apron was splashed with blood and spilled potions. All she needed was a fiery scalpel in one hand to look like one of the mad, murderous Nahids of djinn lore.

"What?" she asked, trying to keep her irritation in check.

The steward bowed. "The emir would like to speak with you."

Nahri gestured to the chaos around her. *"Now?"*

"He is waiting in the garden."

Of course he is. Muntadhir was practiced enough in protocol to know she couldn't entirely snub him if he showed up in person. "Fine," she grumbled. She washed her hands and removed her apron, then followed the steward outside.

Nahri blinked in the bright sunshine. The wild harem garden—more jungle than garden, really—had been pruned back and tamed on the land facing the infirmary by a team of dedicated Daeva horticulturists. They'd been giddy at the assignment, eager to re-create the glorious palace landscapes the Nahids had been famous for, even if only in miniature. The infirmary's grounds were now starred with silver-blue reflecting pools, the walkways lined with perfectly pruned pistachio and apricot trees and lush rosebushes laden with delicate blooms that ranged from a pale, sunny yellow to the deepest of indigos. Though most of the herbs and plants used in her work were grown in Zariaspa on the Pramukh family estates, anything that needed to be fresh when used was planted here, in neatly manicured corner plots bursting with shuddering mandrake bushes and dappled yellow henbane. A marble pavilion overlooked it all, set with carved benches and invitingly plump cushions.

Muntadhir stood there now, his back to her. He must have come from court because he was still dressed in the smoky gold-edged black robe he wore for ceremonial functions, his brightly colored silk turban dazzling in the sun. His hands rested lightly upon the balustrade, the lines of his body commanding as he gazed upon her garden.

"Yes?" she asked brusquely as she stepped into the pavilion.

He glanced back, his gaze traveling down her body. "You look a sight."

"I'm working." She wiped away some of the sweat from her forehead. "What do you need, Muntadhir?"

He turned to face her fully, leaning against the railing. "You didn't come last night."

That was what this visit was about? "I was busy with my patients. And I doubt your bed was cold for long." She couldn't resist adding the last part.

His lips twitched. "This is the third time in a row you've done this, Nahri," he persisted. "You could at least send word instead of leaving me waiting."

Nahri took a deep breath, her patience with Muntadhir—already a thing in short supply—diminishing with each second. "I apologize. Next time I'll send word so you can head straightaway to whatever wine-soaked salon you're frequenting these days. *Now* are we done?"

Muntadhir crossed his arms. "You're in a good mood today. But no, we're not done. Can we talk somewhere more private?" He gestured to the bright citrus trees in the distance. "Your orange grove, perhaps?"

A protective instinct surged in Nahri's heart. The orange grove had been planted long ago by her uncle Rustam, and it was precious to her. While not as talented a healer as her mother, Manizheh, Rustam had been a famed botanist and pharmacist. Even decades after his death, the carefully selected plants within the grove grew strong and healthy, their healing powers more potent and their fragrance headier. Nahri had requested the grove be restored to its original glory, enchanted by the privacy and shade afforded by the glen's thick screen of leaves and brambles, and the feeling of standing on soil once worked by her family's hands.

"I don't let anyone in there," she reminded him. "You know that."

Muntadhir shook his head, used to her stubbornness. "Then let's just walk." He moved toward the steps without waiting for her.

Nahri followed. "What's happened with the Daeva family I told you about?" she asked as they made their way along the snaking path. If Muntadhir was going to pull her away from work, she might as well take advantage of it. "The ones who were abused by the Royal Guard?"

"I'm looking into it."

She stopped. "*Still?* You told me you'd speak to your father last week."

"And I did," Muntadhir replied, sounding annoyed. "I can't exactly go around setting criminals free against the king's command because you and Jamshid are upset. It's more complicated than that." He eyed her. "And the more you interfere, the harder you make it. You know how my father feels about you getting involved in political matters."

The words struck hard, and Nahri drew up. "Fine," she said bitterly. "You can go tell him his warning has been passed on."

Muntadhir grabbed her hand before she could turn away. "I'm not here at his command, Nahri," he protested. "I'm here because I'm your husband. And regardless of how either of us feels about that, I don't want to see you hurt."

He led her toward a shaded bench that faced the canal. It was tucked behind a timeworn neem tree whose boughs curved down in a thick cascade of emerald leaves, effectively curtaining them from view.

He sat, pulling her down beside him. "I hear you had quite the adventure with my sister the other week."

Nahri instantly tensed. "Did your father—"

"No," Muntadhir assured. "Zaynab told me. Yes," he clarified, perhaps noticing the surprise on Nahri's face. "I know about her little jaunts in the Geziri Quarter. I found out about them years ago. She's clever enough to keep herself safe, and her guard knows he can come to me if she's ever in trouble."

"Oh." That took Nahri aback. And oddly enough, it made her a little jealous. The Qahtanis might be her ancestral enemies and a bunch of backstabbing opportunists, but the quiet loyalty between the siblings—borne out of the type of familial love Nahri had never known—filled her with a sad sort of envy.

She pushed it away. "I take it she told you about the hospital?"

"She said she'd never seen you so excited."

Nahri kept her face carefully blank. "It was interesting."

"It was *interesting*?" Muntadhir repeated in disbelief. "You, who barely stops talking about your work in the infirmary, discovered your ancestors' old hospital and a group of freed ifrit slaves, and your only comment is 'It was interesting'?"

Nahri chewed her lip, debating how to respond. The hospital had been far more than interesting, of course. But the fantasies she'd been spinning since her visit seemed a fragile thing, safest kept to herself.

Muntadhir clearly wasn't so easily fooled. He took her hand again. "I wish you would talk to me," he said softly. "I know neither of us wanted this, Nahri, but we could try to make it work. I feel like I have no idea what goes on in your head." His tone was imploring but there was no hiding a hint of exasperation. "You have more walls up than a maze."

Nahri said nothing. Of course, she had walls up. Nearly everyone she knew had betrayed her at least once.

He rubbed his thumb against her palm. Her fingers twitched, and she made a face. "Lots of stitching today, and I think my internal healing abilities have stopped recognizing aching muscles as an abnormality."

"Let me." Muntadhir took her hand in both of his and began to massage it, pressing the joints as though he'd been doing it for years.

Nahri exhaled, some of the tension immediately leaving her sore fingers. "Who taught you how to do this?"

He pulled at her fingers, stretching them out in a way that felt heavenly. "A friend."

"Were you and said friend wearing clothes at the time of this lesson?"

"You know, considering the friend . . . it is rather likely we weren't." He gave her a wicked smile. "Would you like to know what else she taught me?"

Nahri rolled her eyes. "I won't unburden myself to you, so now you're trying to seduce me using knowledge you gained from another woman?"

His grin widened. "Political life has taught me to be creative in my approaches." He brushed his fingers lightly up her wrist, and Nahri couldn't help a slight shiver at his touch. "You're clearly too busy to come to my bed. How else to sustain the peace our marriage alliance was supposed to build?"

"You have no shame; do you know that?" But the edge was gone from her voice. Muntadhir was damnably good at this.

His fingers were tracing delicate patterns on the skin of her wrist, his eyes dancing with mirth. "You don't complain about that when you *do* find your way into my bed."

Heat flooded her cheeks—not all of it from embarrassment. "You've slept with half of Daevabad. I'd hope that would teach you some skill."

"That sounds like a challenge."

The mischief in his expression was not helping with the utterly traitorous unspooling of heat in her belly. "I have work," she protested as he pulled her onto his lap. "At least a dozen patients waiting. And we're in the garden. Someone could . . ."

She trailed off as he pressed his mouth to her neck, lightly kissing her throat.

"No one can see anything," Muntadhir said calmly, his voice sending a brush of warmth against her skin. "And you clearly need to relax. Consider it a professional duty." His hands slipped underneath her tunic. "Surely your patients will be better served by having a Banu Nahida who's not in such a snappish mood."

Nahri sighed, pressing closer to him despite herself. His mouth had moved lower, his beard tickling her collar. "I am *not* snappish . . ."

There was a polite cough from behind the tree, followed by a squeaked "Emir?"

Muntadhir removed neither his hands nor his lips. "*Yes?*"

"Your father wishes to speak with you. He says it's urgent."

Nahri stilled, the mention of Ghassan making her go cold.

Muntadhir sighed. "Of course it is." He pulled away to meet her gaze. "Have dinner with me tonight?" he asked. "I will order your strange flower tea and you can insult my shamelessness to your heart's content."

Nahri had little desire to dine with him but admittedly wouldn't mind continuing what they'd just started. She *had* been under a great deal of stress lately, and she often got more sleep the nights she spent in Muntadhir's room; people usually had to be actively dying for a servant to muster up the courage to interrupt the emir and his wife there.

Besides which, the flicker of hope in his eyes was pulling on the one shred of tenderness left in her heart; for all his flaws—and there were a great number—her husband did not lack in charm. "I'll try," she said, biting back a smile.

He grinned back, looking genuinely pleased. "Excellent." He untangled his limbs from hers.

Nahri hastily straightened her tunic; she was not going back to the infirmary looking like . . . well, like she had just been doing what she had been doing. "Good luck with whatever your father wants."

Muntadhir rolled his eyes. "I am sure it is nothing." He touched his heart. "In peace."

She watched him go, taking a minute to enjoy the fresh air and the trill of birdsong. It was a beautiful day, and her gaze drifted lazily over to the herb garden.

It landed on a shafit man scurrying through the bushes.

Nahri frowned, watching as the fellow hurried past a patch of sage to stop in front of a willow tree. He wiped his brow, looking nervously over his shoulders.

Odd. While there were some shafit among the gardeners, none were allowed to touch the Nahid plants, nor was this particular man familiar. He took a pair of shears from his belt and opened them, as though he meant to cut away one of the branches.

Nahri was on her feet in an instant, her silk slippers and a lifetime of cat burglary disguising the sound of her steps. The man didn't even look up until she was nearly on top of him.

"What do you think you're doing to my tree?" she demanded.

The shafit man jumped up, whirling around so fast that his cap tumbled off. His human-hued hazel eyes went wide with horror.

"Banu Nahida!" he gasped. "I . . . forgive me," he begged, bringing his hands together. "I was just—"

"Hacking at my willow? Yes, I see that." She touched the maimed branch, and a sprinkling of new bark spread beneath her fingers. Nahri had a bit of a talent for botany herself, though she hadn't yet attempted to develop it further, much to Nisreen's chagrin. "Do you know what would happen if someone else had caught . . ." She trailed off, the sight of the man's bare scalp stealing her attention. It was disfigured, his hair long around his temples, but prickly and patched at the top as if recovering from a rushed shave. The flesh there was mottled purple and slightly swollen, surrounding an oddly flat patch in the size and shape of a coin. A half-moon of scar tissue edged the patch—it had been stitched, and skillfully so.

Overwhelmed by curiosity, Nahri reached out and lightly touched the swollen flesh. It was soft—too soft. She let her Nahid senses expand, confirming what seemed impossible.

A small section of the man's skull had been removed beneath the skin.

She gasped. It was healing; she could sense the spark of new bone growth, but even so . . . She dropped her hand. "Did someone *do* this to you?"

The man looked petrified. "I had an accident."

"An accident that neatly bored a hole through your skull and then stitched it shut?" Nahri knelt beside him. "I'm not going to hurt you," she assured him. "I just want to know what happened—and make certain someone isn't going around Daevabad cutting coins out of people's skulls."

"It was nothing like that." He bit his lip, glancing around. "I fell off a roof and cracked my head," he whispered. "The doctors told my wife that blood was swelling under the bone and that removing part of the skull might relieve the pressure and save my life."

Nahri blinked. "The *doctors*?" She looked at the tree he'd been taking the cuttings from. Willow. Of course. Both the leaves and bark were valuable, easily distilled into medicine for aches and pains . . . for *human* aches and pains. "Did they ask you for this as well?"

He shook his head, still trembling. "I offered. I saw a picture in one of their books and thought I remembered seeing a tree like it when I worked on the roof here last year." He gave her an imploring look. "They're good people, and they saved my life. I wanted to help."

Nahri was having trouble containing her excitement. Shafit

doctors who could do surgery and had medical books? "Who?" she asked eagerly. "Who are these doctors?"

He dropped his gaze. "We're not supposed to talk about them."

"I don't mean them any harm." She touched her heart. "I swear on my ancestors' ashes. I'll bring them some willow myself, and more. I have plenty of medicines that are safe for shafit in my apothecary."

The man looked torn. Nahri studied him again, noting his bare feet and ragged galabiyya. His heavily calloused hands.

Hating herself a little, Nahri pulled a gold ring from her pocket. She'd forgotten to remove it before starting work in the infirmary and had settled for slipping it in there. Small rubies, set in a floral pattern, were embedded in its surface.

She placed it in his hand. "A name and a location." His eyes went wide, locking on the ring. "I'm not going to hurt them, I promise. I want to help."

Longing filled his face; Nahri imagined the money a ring like that could fetch would go a long way for a shafit laborer.

"Subhashini Sen," he whispered. "The house with the red door on Sukariyya Street."

Nahri smiled. "Thank you."

A SMALL ARMY OF SERVANTS WAS WAITING FOR NAHRI when she finished her work, and she'd no sooner set foot in the steamy hammam than they descended, taking her blood- and potion-splattered clothes away to be washed and then giving her a thorough scrub, rinsing her skin with rosewater, massaging her limbs with precious oils, and attempting to coax her wild curls into an elegant crown of braids.

Never one content to give up control, Nahri had, however, insisted on picking out her own clothes. Tonight she'd selected a gown cut from the finest linen she'd ever touched. It was sleeveless, falling to her ankles in a pale buttery sheath and held together by an ornate collar of hundreds of beads: lapis lazuli, gold, carnelian, and topaz. It reminded Nahri of home, the pattern looking like one that might have been copied from an ancient temple back in Egypt.

A servant had just finished clasping the delicate collar when another approached, bearing a discreet ivory cosmetics pot. "Would you like me to powder your skin, my lady?" she asked.

Nahri stared at the vessel. An innocent question, but one that always caused her stomach to tighten. Instinctively, she glanced up, catching sight of her reflection in the polished silver mirror perched on her dressing table.

Though the line between the shafit and the purebloods in Daevabad was a hard one, carved by centuries of violence and enshrined in law, the differences in their appearances were not as great as their divide in power suggested. The purebloods had their pointed ears and metal-toned eyes, of course, the color varying by tribe. And their skin had a gleam to it, a shimmer and a haze that reflected the hot, jet-colored blood that simmered in their veins. Depending on ancestry and luck, shafit had a mix of human and djinn features: human hazel eyes paired with perfectly pointed ears, or perhaps the tin-toned gaze of the Agnivanshi without the glimmer to their skin.

And then there was Nahri.

At first glance, there was *nothing* magical about Nahri's appearance. Her ears were as rounded as a human's and her skin an earthy matte brown. Her black eyes were dark, to be certain, but she'd always felt like they lacked the same shining ebony depths that marked one as Daeva. Hers was a face that had once convinced Dara she was a shafit with the barest drop of magical blood in her veins. And it was a face that was apparently a lie, the product of a marid curse—or so the ifrit who'd hunted her had claimed, a claim Ghassan had seized upon in order to publicly declare her a pureblood.

Privately, of course, he'd said something very different. Not that it mattered. Nahri suspected she would never fully discern the truth of her origins. But the laissez-faire approach to her appearance had changed when she married Muntadhir. The future queen of Daevabad was expected to look the part, and so hairdressers arranged her braids to cover the tips of her ears. Ash was mixed into her kohl to make her eyes look darker. And then the cursed ivory pot appeared. It contained an incredibly expensive powder made from the Creator only knew what that when brushed upon her skin gave Nahri the shimmer of a pure-blood for hours.

It was an illusion, a waste of time and an utter facade—and all for a future queen who couldn't even protect her tribesmen from being beaten and robbed in front of her. And the fact that it was her shafit servants who were forced to create an image of the blood purity that circumscribed their lives . . . it made Nahri feel ill. "No," she finally replied, trying not to let her revulsion show. "I don't need that."

There was a knock on the door and then Nisreen entered.

Nahri groaned. "No. I need a night off. Tell whoever it is to heal themselves."

Her mentor gave her a wounded smile. "It is not *always* work that I seek you for." She glanced at Nahri's maids. "Would you mind leaving us?"

They obeyed at once, and Nisreen joined her at the dressing table. "You look very pretty," she said. "That dress is beautiful. Is it new?"

Nahri nodded. "A gift from a Sahrayn seamstress happy to no longer have silver-pox."

"Your husband will be hard-pressed to take his eyes off you in that."

"I suppose," Nahri said, fighting embarrassment. She wasn't sure why she was even bothering. Muntadhir had married her for her name, not her face, and her husband was so constantly surrounded by djinn who were breathtakingly gorgeous—men and women who had voices like angels and smiles that could lure humans to madness—that it seemed a waste of time to even attempt to attract his eye.

Nisreen's gaze darted to the door before she set down the small silver chalice that had been casually concealed in the folds of her shawl. "I've prepared your tea."

Nahri stared at the chalice, the sharp scent of herbs wafting from pale green liquid. They both knew what kind of "tea" it was: the kind Nahri drank only when she visited Muntadhir. "I still worry we're going to get caught."

Nisreen shrugged. "Ghassan probably has his suspicions, but you're a Nahid healer. On this, he's going to have a hard time out-maneuvering you, and it's worth the risk to buy you a bit of time."

"A *bit* of time is all it's buying." Ghassan hadn't overly pressed on the topic of grandchildren yet. Djinn didn't conceive easily, and it was entirely reasonable the emir and his wife had yet to be blessed with an heir. But she doubted he'd hold his tongue for long.

Nisreen must have heard the uncertainty in her voice. "That is enough for now." She pushed the cup into Nahri's hands. "Take things here day by day."

Nahri gulped the tea and then stood, pulling a hooded robe over her dress. "I should go." She was early, but if she left now, she could sneak through the back passages and have a few minutes to herself rather than being escorted by one of Muntadhir's stewardesses.

"I won't delay you." Nisreen stood as well, and when she met Nahri's eyes, there was conviction in her gaze. "Have faith, my lady. Your future here is brighter than you realize."

"You always say that." Nahri sighed. "I wish I had your confidence."

"You will one day," Nisreen promised. She shooed her off. "Go on then. Don't let me keep you."

Nahri did, taking one of the private corridors that led from the harem garden to the royal apartments on the upper level of the palatial ziggurat, a level with an excellent view of Daevabad's lake. All the Qahtanis had quarters up there save Zaynab, who preferred the garden below.

Just as Ali had. The thought came to her unbidden—and unwelcome. She hated thinking about Ali, hated that five years after that night, a sting of humiliation still pierced her when she recalled how her supposed friend had quietly led her and Dara into a deadly trap. The naive young prince should have been the last one capable of duping her, and yet he had.

And she hated that despite everything, part of her still worried about him. For it was damnably clear—no matter what the Qahtanis pretended—that Ali was not merely "leading a garrison" in the peace of his ancestral land. He'd been cast out, and under terms Nahri suspected were rather dire.

She emerged onto the expansive balcony that ran the length of Muntadhir's apartment. Like everything he owned, it was achingly sophisticated, its trellised wooden railings and screens carved in the semblance of a garden, with embroidered panels of silk draped to mimic a tent. Frankincense smoldered inside a fiery brazier across from a pile of brocaded cushions that sat angled toward the best view of the lake.

Cushions that were very much *not* empty. Nahri abruptly stilled, catching sight of Jamshid and Muntadhir sitting across from each other. Jamshid's presence there didn't surprise her— but the fact that they were clearly arguing did.

"Tell your father to send him *back*!" Jamshid was insisting. "Is there any reason he can't drop his damned cargo on the beach and turn right around?"

"I tried." Muntadhir sounded nearly hysterical. "I begged my father, and do you know what he told me?" He let out a choked, humorless laugh. "To go *put an heir in my Nahid wife* if I was so worried about my position. That's all we are to him. Pawns in his damned political game. And now his favorite, sharpest piece is returning."

Nahri frowned in confusion. Pushing aside the guilt she felt for eavesdropping—more on account of Jamshid, her friend, than for the sake of her politician of a husband, who almost certainly had a loyal spy or two installed in her infirmary—she crept closer, tucking herself into a niche between a potted fern and an ornamental carved screen.

She took a deep breath. The palace's magic was as unpredictable as it was powerful, and though Nahri had been quietly working to learn how to better call upon it, doing so was always a risk—she had no doubt that if Ghassan got an inkling of what she was up to, she'd be promptly punished.

But sometimes a little risk was worth it. Nahri focused on the shadows at her feet. *Grow*, she urged, beckoning them closer and allowing her fear of getting caught to expand. *Protect me.*

They did so, the shadows sweeping up to envelop her in a cloak of darkness. Breathing a bit easier, Nahri moved closer to the screen to peer through the cutouts in the wood. The two men were alone, Jamshid seated on the edge of a cushion as he watched Muntadhir with open concern.

Muntadhir shot to his feet, visibly trembling. "His mother's going to kill me." He paced, pulling anxiously at his beard. "The Ayaanle have wanted this for years. He'll no sooner be back in Daevabad than I'll be waking up with a cord around my neck."

"That's not going to happen," Jamshid said sharply. "Muntadhir, you need to calm down and think this—*no*." His hand shot out to grab Muntadhir's as her husband lunged for the bottle of wine on the table. "Stop. That's not going to help you."

Muntadhir offered a broken smile. "I disagree," he said weakly. He looked close to tears. "Wine is reportedly an excellent companion during one's downfall."

"There's not going to be any downfall." Jamshid pulled Muntadhir onto the cushion beside him. "*There's not*," he repeated when Muntadhir looked away. "Muntadhir . . ." Jamshid hesitated, and when he spoke again, there was a wary edge to his voice. "It's a long journey back to Daevabad. A dangerous one. Surely you have people who—"

Muntadhir violently shook his head. "I can't. I don't have that in me." He bit his lip, staring in bitter resignation at the floor. "Not yet anyway." He wiped his eyes and then took a deep breath, as if to compose himself before speaking again. "I'm sorry. I shouldn't burden you with this. God knows you've suffered enough for my family's politics."

"Don't be ridiculous." Jamshid touched Muntadhir's cheek. "I want you to come to me with things like this." He smiled. "To be honest . . . the rest of your companions are fairly useless sycophants."

That drew a laugh from her husband. "Whereas I can always rely on you to honestly insult me."

"And keep you safe." Jamshid's hand had moved to cradle Muntadhir's jaw. "Nothing's going to happen to you, I swear. I won't let it, and I'm obnoxiously honorable about these things."

Muntadhir laughed again. "That I know." He took another breath and then suddenly closed his eyes as if in pain. When he spoke again, his voice was heavy with sorrow. "I miss you."

Jamshid's face twisted, the humor vanishing from his expression. He seemed to realize what he was doing with his hand, his gaze falling to her husband's mouth. "I'm sorry," he whispered. "I didn't mean to—"

The rest of his explanation didn't leave his lips. Because Muntadhir was suddenly kissing him, doing so with a desperation that was clearly returned. Jamshid tangled his hand in Muntadhir's dark hair, pulling him close . . .

And then he pushed him away. "I can't," Jamshid choked out, his entire body shaking. "I'm sorry, but I can't. Not anymore. I told you when you got married. She's my Banu Nahida."

Nahri stepped back from the screen, stunned. Not by the allusion to past intimacy between them—there were times it seemed Muntadhir had literally slept with half the people he knew. But those affairs all seemed so casual—flirtations with various foreign ministers, dalliances with poets and dancing girls.

The anguish radiating off her husband now was *not* casual. Gone was the emir who'd confidently pulled her into his lap in the garden. Muntadhir had rocked back like he'd been punched when Jamshid had pushed him away, and it looked like he was struggling not to cry. Sympathy stole through her. For all the trappings of power and glamour of the court, she could not help but be struck by how utterly lonely this place had made them all.

Muntadhir stared at the ground. "Of course." It sounded like he was fighting to regain his composure. "Then maybe you should go," he added, his voice stiff. "I'm expecting her and I would hate to put you in an uncomfortable position."

Jamshid sighed, pulling himself slowly to his feet. He leaned on his cane, looking resignedly down upon Muntadhir. "Have you had any luck freeing the Daeva men Nahri and I told you about?"

"No," Muntadhir replied, his response far flatter than it had been with her on the topic. "It's difficult to free people when they're guilty of the crime they're charged with."

"It's a crime now to discuss the implications of your father's financial policies in a public setting?"

Muntadhir's head jerked up. "Daevabad is restless enough without such gossip being spread. It hurts morale and causes people to lose faith in their king."

"So does arbitrarily arresting people who happen to have wealth and land that can be confiscated for the Treasury." Jamshid's eyes narrowed. "Of course, by 'people' I mean 'Daevas.' We all know the rest of the tribes aren't suffering the same treatment."

Muntadhir was shaking his head. "He's trying to keep the peace, Jamshid. And let's not pretend your people make that easy."

Jamshid's mouth pressed into a disappointed line. "This isn't you, Muntadhir. And since we've established I'm the only one who's honest with you . . . let me warn you that you're going down the same path you say ruined your father." He turned away. "Give my greetings to Nahri."

"*Jamshid—*"

But he was already leaving, making his way toward the place where Nahri was hiding. Quickly, she retreated to edge of the steps as though she'd just arrived.

"Jamshid!" she said, greeting him with false cheer. "What a lovely surprise!"

He managed a smile, though it didn't meet his eyes. "Banu Nahida," he replied, his voice a little hoarse. "Apologies. I didn't mean to intrude upon your evening."

"It's all right," she said gently, hating the heartbreak still writ clearly across his face. Muntadhir wasn't looking at them; he'd walked to the edge of the balcony, his attention focused on the twinkling fires of the city below. She touched Jamshid's shoulder. "Come see me tomorrow. I have a new poultice I want to try on your back."

He nodded. "Tomorrow." He moved past her, disappearing down into the palace.

Nahri took a few steps forward, feeling uncertain. "Peace be upon you," she called out to her husband. "If it's a bad time . . ."

"Of course not." Muntadhir turned around. Nahri had to give him credit: though he was pale, his face was swept of the emotion that had been there only moments ago. She supposed a few decades in Daevabad's royal court taught one that ability. "Sorry." He cleared his throat. "I was not expecting you so soon."

Obviously. She shrugged. "I finished early."

Muntadhir nodded. "Let me call a servant," he suggested, crossing the balcony. "I'll have them bring some food."

Nahri caught his wrist. "Why don't you sit?" she suggested softly. "I'm not hungry and I thought we could talk first."

They'd no sooner sunk into the cushions than Muntadhir was reaching for the wine bottle. "Would you like some?" he asked, filling his cup to the top.

Nahri watched. She wasn't Jamshid, and she didn't feel comfortable stopping him. "No . . . thank you." He drank back most of his cup and then refilled it. "Is everything well?" she ventured. "The meeting with your father . . ."

Muntadhir winced. "Can we talk about something else? For a little while at least?"

She paused. Nahri was madly curious to discover what he'd been discussing with Ghassan that had led to his fight with Jamshid, but perhaps a change in subject would pull him from his dark mood.

And she certainly had a subject ready to discuss. "Of course. Actually, I came across someone interesting in the garden after you left. A shafit man with a hole in his skull."

Muntadhir choked, coughing a spray of wine into his hand. "You found a *dead shafit in your garden*?"

"Not dead," Nahri corrected lightly. "He looked quite well otherwise. He said a surgeon had done the procedure to save his life. A *shafit surgeon*, Muntadhir." Admiration crept into her voice. "Someone skilled enough to bore a hole in a man's skull, sew it back up, and keep him alive. And it looked *perfect*. I mean, it felt a bit spongy where the bone was gone, but—"

Muntadhir raised a hand, looking slightly ill. "I don't need to hear the details." He glanced at his crimson wine, a little revulsion passing across his face, and then set it down. "So what of it?"

"*What of it?*" Nahri exclaimed. "That speaks to extraordinary talent! That physician might have even trained in the human world. I convinced the man in the garden to give me a name and the street where he works."

"But why would you want such information?" Muntadhir asked, looking perplexed.

"Because I want to find him! For one . . . I *am* the Banu Nahida. I should ensure he's a real doctor and not some . . . con artist taking advantage of desperate shafit." Nahri cleared her throat. "But I'd also just love to meet him. He could be a valuable asset; after all, I still find much of what Yaqub taught me relevant."

Muntadhir seemed even more confused. "Yaqub?"

Her stomach tightened. Nahri wasn't used to talking about her passions, the ones closest to her heart, and Muntadhir's bewilderment wasn't making it easier. "The pharmacist I worked with back in Cairo, Muntadhir. The old man. My friend. I know I've mentioned him to you before."

Muntadhir frowned. "So, you want to find some shafit doctor because you once had a pharmacist friend in the human world?"

Nahri took a deep breath, seeing her opening. Maybe it wasn't the best time, but Muntadhir *had* said he wanted her to talk to him more freely, and right now, her heart was bursting. "Because I want to see if there's a way we can work together . . . Muntadhir, it's so hard being the only healer here," she confessed. "It's *lonely*. The responsibility is crushing. There are times I barely sleep, I barely eat . . ." She checked the emotion growing in her voice. "I thought . . . the old Nahid hospital . . ." She stumbled over her words, trying to explain the dreams that had been spinning in her head since her visit to those ruins. "I wonder if maybe we could rebuild it. Bring in a shafit physician to share the patient load and . . ."

Muntadhir's eyes went wide. "You want to *rebuild* that place?"

Nahri tried not to shrink back at the horrified disbelief in his expression. "You . . . you told me that I could come to you, talk to you—"

"Yes—but about *plausible* things. If you want to bring another Daeva to court or take part in the preparations for Navasatem. What you're suggesting . . ." He sounded shocked. "Zaynab said the building was in a shambles. Do you have any idea of the effort and expense it would take to restore?"

"I know, but I thought—"

Muntadhir stood, pacing in agitation. "And to work along-side *shafit*?" He said the word with thinly veiled disdain. "Absolutely not. My father would never allow it. You shouldn't even be looking for this doctor. You must realize that what he's doing is illegal."

"*Illegal?* How is helping people illegal?"

"The shafit . . ." Muntadhir rubbed the back of his neck, shame creeping across his face. "I mean . . . they're not—*we're* not—supposed to act in a manner that . . . encourages their population to increase."

Nahri was silent for a moment, shock freezing her tongue. "Tell me you don't really believe that," she said, praying he'd misspoken, that she'd imagined the distaste in his voice. "You're a Qahtani. Your ancestors overthrew mine—*slaughtered mine*—to protect the shafit."

"That was a long time ago." Muntadhir looked beseechingly at her. "And the shafit are not the innocents you might imagine. They hate the Daevas, they hate *you*."

She bristled. "Why should they hate me? I was raised in the human world!"

"And then you came back here at the side of a man famous for using a scourge to determine the color of someone's blood," Muntadhir pointed out. "You have a reputation with them, Nahri, like it or not."

Nahri flinched, but let the charges slide past her. This conversation had taken enough of a horrifying turn without bringing her broken Afshin and his bloody crimes into it. "I had nothing to do with Qui-zi," she said, defending herself. "None of us alive today did."

"It doesn't matter." Muntadhir's eyes filled with warning. "Nahri, there's too much history between the Daevas and the shafit. Between *most* of the purebloods and the shafit. You don't understand the hatred they feel for us."

"And *you* do? You've probably never spoken to a shafit in your life!"

"No, but I've seen the human weapons they've smuggled here in hopes of sparking unrest. I've listened to their preachers spout poisonous lies and aim threats toward *your* people just before being executed." A look she couldn't decipher crossed his face. "And believe me when I say I know all too well how clever they are in recruiting others to their cause."

Nahri said nothing. She felt sick—and not because of the reminder that she and the Daevas were in danger.

It was because she suddenly realized her husband—the Qahtani she'd assumed cared little about blood purity—might share the worst prejudices of her tribe. Nahri still didn't know what about her appearance made Ghassan so certain she was both Nahid *and* shafit, but he'd made it clear it was the possession of Suleiman's seal that brought him such insight.

And one day Muntadhir would have it. Would take it and see truly the woman he'd married.

Her heart stuttered. "None of what you're suggesting sounds politically stable, Muntadhir," she said, choosing her words carefully. "If things have gotten so bad, wouldn't it be better to try and work with the shafit? You and I were married to foster peace between the Geziris and the Daevas. Why can't we attempt the same with the mixed-bloods?"

Muntadhir shook his head. "Not like this. I feel bad for the shafit, I do. But theirs is a problem generations in the making, and what you're suggesting is too risky."

Nahri dropped her gaze. She caught sight of the beaded collar of her pretty new dress, and she pulled her robe more tightly over it, suddenly feeling very foolish.

He is never going to be the ally I need. The blunt truth resounded through her: Muntadhir's refusal to address the shafits' persecution and Jamshid's accusations churned in her mind. Oddly enough, Nahri couldn't hate him for it. She too had been beaten down by Ghassan, and she wasn't even his son. There was no denying Muntadhir's anguish over Jamshid and the genuine regret when he'd mentioned—and then promptly dismissed—the shafits' plight.

But Ghassan hadn't worn her down, not yet, not entirely. And she didn't want to bend any further than she already had, even if it meant standing alone.

Muntadhir must have registered the change in her expression. "It's not a no forever," he said quickly. "But it's not the right time to propose something so drastic."

Nahri gritted her teeth. "Because of Navasatem?" If one more thing got blamed on that damned holiday, she was going to burn something.

He shook his head. "No, not because of Navasatem. Because of the reason my father wanted to see me today." His jaw clenched, and his gaze fixed on the distant lake, the black water reflecting the scattered stars overhead. "Because my brother is coming back to Daevabad."

7

DARA

Dara studied the smoky map of Daevabad he'd conjured, using his fingers to spin it this way and that as he thought. "On the chance we *do* find a way to pass the threshold and cross Daevabad's lake, getting into the city itself poses the next problem." He glanced up at his band of warriors. He'd chosen the group carefully: his ten cleverest, the ones he was grooming for leadership. "What would you suggest?"

Irtemiz paced the map, almost stalking it. "Is there a way we could scale the walls?"

Dara shook his head. "The walls cannot be scaled, nor can they be tunneled under or flown over—Anahid herself raised them, may she be blessed."

Mardoniye spoke up, nodding at the city gates. "The gates are poorly defended. The Royal Guard keeps an eye out for boats crossing the lake—not for warriors arriving directly upon the beach from the water itself. We could force our way through."

"And enter directly in the middle of the Grand Bazaar," Dara pointed out.

Mardoniye's eyes flashed with hatred. "Is that a bad thing?" He ran a hand over his scarred face, the skin mottled where it had come into contact with Rumi fire. "I would not mind getting some vengeance for what the shafit did to us."

"Vengeance is not our mission," Dara chided. "And right now we are merely discussing strategy—I want you to *think*. The Grand Bazaar is only blocks from the Citadel." He nodded at the Citadel's tower, looming over the Grand Bazaar from its perch beside the brass wall. "We would have hundreds—thousands—of Royal Guard down on us in minutes. We'd be annihilated before we even reached the palace."

Bahram, another survivor from the Daeva Brigade, spoke next. "We could split up," he suggested. "Half of us stay behind to delay the Guard while you take the lady and the rest to the palace."

A chill went down Dara's spine at how easily he suggested it. "It would be certain death for the warriors left behind."

Bahram met his gaze, his eyes glittering. "We are all prepared to make that sacrifice."

Dara glanced at his group. He didn't doubt Bahram was right. The faces of his young soldiers were fierce with conviction. It should have filled Dara with pleasure. He'd poured himself into their training; he should be proud to stand at their side.

But by the Creator, he had fought at the side of so many young Daevas whose faces had sparked with equal conviction. He'd collected their bodies afterward, consigning them to the flames as martyrs in what was beginning to feel like a war with no end.

He sighed. This one *would* have an end, Dara would make sure of it—but he'd also take greater care with his men. "It would only be a delay. They'd slaughter you and be on the rest of us before we got far."

"What about ghouls?" another man suggested. "The ifrit are our allies now, are they not? One of them was boasting about how he could summon an entire army of ghouls. The skinny one."

Dara's face twisted in disgust at the mention of the ifrit, whom he hated in particular, escalating ways. The remark about them being allies and the memory of their ghouls only fueled his revulsion. Not to mention that Vizaresh—the ifrit they were speaking of now—had once threatened Nahri. Threatened "to grind her soul into dust" for blood-poisoning his brother . . . a threat Dara wouldn't be forgetting anytime soon. "I do not wish to see those foul things in our city," he said shortly.

Irtemiz grinned. "The ghouls or the ifrit?"

Dara snorted. His soldiers were all like family to him, but he had a particular fondness for Irtemiz, whose innate talent with a bow had come a long way under Dara's careful hand and who'd managed to keep her good humor even during the hardest of training sessions.

"Both," he replied. Then he gestured back at the map. "I want you to think about this and discuss solutions with each other while I'm away." Dara didn't quite share Manizheh's confidence that some mysterious meeting with Aeshma and the marid would result in his being able to cross the magical threshold protecting Daevabad, but on the off chance it did, he wanted to be prepared.

"Should we keep practicing with Abu Sayf?"

Dara considered that. He'd managed to convince Abu Sayf to spar with his soldiers . . . well, no, perhaps convince wasn't the right term. He'd threatened to scourge the younger, more irritating Geziri scout to death if the older man didn't comply. They were going to face zulfiqars in their fight to retake Daevabad, and they'd been handed a rare opportunity to learn to fight against them with the two Geziri scouts as their prisoners. Dara had not liked making such a ghastly threat, but there was little he was unwilling to do if it would help prepare his young warriors.

But only under his eye; he didn't trust the Geziris not to try something in his absence. "No. I do not want either of them unchained for even a moment." He dismissed the group. "Now go. I will join you for dinner before I leave."

He raised a hand to sweep the map away as they left, watching the buildings tumble together in a smoky wave. The miniature palace collapsed, the Citadel's tower dissolving over the wall.

Dara stilled. He snapped his fingers, conjuring and then crushing the tower again, letting it topple. It was tall enough that the upper half could crash through the wall, ripping a hole into the heart of the Citadel itself—and creating an entrance into the city.

That is magic beyond me. Manizheh might think him invincible, but Dara was learning that the fantastic tales told about the powers of their mighty ancestors in the time before Suleiman were best taken with a little salt. He was willing to break himself to reclaim Daevabad, but he couldn't afford to exhaust his magic at the very beginning of the invasion.

He tucked the idea away, crossing to the large carpet rolled in one corner. Dara hadn't flown one in years, not since journeying to Daevabad with Nahri. He ran a hand down its woolen length.

I will find a way to get back to you. I promise.

But first Dara had a meeting with the devil himself.

HE AND MANIZHEH FLEW EAST, TRAVELING ACROSS A stunning landscape that spread before them like crumpled silk, emerald hills and dusty plains blending into each other, marked by deep blue lines of twisting rivers and streams. The sight brought Dara a rare peace. Khayzur, the peri who'd once nursed him back to health, had tried to teach Dara to appreciate such moments, to let the solace and beauty of the natural world sweep him away. It had been a difficult lesson to internalize. The first time he'd been brought back, Dara had awakened to the news that his world had died fourteen centuries earlier and that he was nothing but a blood-soaked memory to his people.

Not to everyone. It was impossible to sit on this rug as it cut through the sky and not think of the first days he'd spent with Nahri—days that had driven him to drink. He'd found her very existence a scandal, physical proof one of his blessed Nahids had broken their most sacred code and lain with a human. That she'd been a cunning thief who lied as easily as she breathed seemed proof of every negative stereotype Dara had heard about the shafit.

But then . . . she became so much more. He had felt shockingly free with her—free to be a normal man and not the celebrated Afshin or the despised Scourge, free to exchange flirtatious barbs with a quick-witted, beautiful woman, and delight in the unexpected stirring her magnetic, mocking grin caused in his shuttered heart. All because Nahri *hadn't* known their history. She was the first person Dara had spoken to in centuries who knew nothing about his past—and so he'd been able to leave it behind.

He'd known theirs was foolish affection, had known it couldn't last, and yet Dara had been desperate to keep the worst from her—a decision he still regretted. Had he been honest with Nahri and confessed it all . . . given her a chance to make her own choice . . . he could not help but wonder if she would have chosen to escape Daevabad at his side without him putting a blade to Alizayd al Qahtani's throat.

Not that it mattered now. Nahri had seen exactly what Dara was on the boat that night.

"Are you all right?" Startled, Dara glanced up to find Manizheh watching him, a knowing expression on her face. "You look to be contemplating something weighty."

Dara forced a smile. "You remind me of your ancestors," he said, evading the question. "When I was a child, I used to think they could read minds."

Manizheh laughed, a rare sound. "Nothing so fantastical. But when you spend two centuries attuned to every heartbeat, skin flush, and inhalation that surrounds you, you learn to read people." She gave him a pointed look. "The question remains."

Dara flinched. At first glance, there wasn't much resemblance between Manizheh and her daughter. Manizheh was shorter and more compact, reminding him in no small way of his own mother, a woman who could cook up a meal for fifty, then break a spoon over her knee to stab a man. Manizheh's eyes, though, the sharp black eyes that tugged down slightly at the outer edge—those were Nahri's. And when they lit with challenge, they cut through Dara rather effectively.

"I am fine." He swept his hand toward the distant ground. "Appreciating the scenery."

"It is beautiful," she agreed. "It reminds me of Zariaspa. Rustam and I used to spend summers with the Pramukhs when we were young." Her voice turned wistful. "They were the happiest days of my life. We were always dashing about, climbing mountains, racing simurgh, experimenting with whatever forbidden plants and herbs we could." A sad smile crossed her face. "The closest thing to freedom we experienced."

Dara cocked his head. "Perhaps you are fortunate you did not have an Afshin. That all sounds terribly risky. We never would have permitted it."

Manizheh laughed again. "No, there weren't any legendary guardians around to ruin our fun, and the Pramukhs were fairly indulgent as long as we brought Kaveh along. They seemed not to realize he was equally irresponsible." She saw Dara's skeptical expression and shook her head. "Do not let his stern grand wazir face fool you. He was a mud-splattered country boy when I met him, more accomplished at sneaking out to hunt for fire salamanders than reining in two restless Nahids." She stared into the distance, her eyes dimming. "We weren't permitted to go to Zariaspa as frequently when we were older, and I always missed him."

"I suspect he felt the same," Dara said carefully. He had seen the way Kaveh looked at Manizheh, and no one at camp had missed the fact that their visitor had yet to sleep in the tent they'd prepared for him. *That* had thrown Dara; clearly the prim grand wazir did have a hidden side. "I am surprised you didn't bring him with us."

"Absolutely not," she said at once. "I don't want the ifrit to know anything more than necessary about him."

Dara frowned at the fierceness in her voice. "Why not?"

"Would you die for my daughter, Darayavahoush?"

The question surprised him, and yet the answer was already leaving Dara's lips. "Yes. Of course."

Manizheh gave him a knowing look. "And yet, would you let her die for you? Suffer for you?"

She has already suffered for me. "Not if I could help it," Dara said quietly.

"Precisely. Affection is a weakness for people like us, a thing to be concealed from those who would harm us. A threat to a loved one is a more effective method of control than weeks of torture."

She said the words with such cold certainty that a chill raced down his spine. "You sound as though you speak from experience," he ventured.

"I loved my brother very much," she said, staring into the distance. "The Qahtanis never let me forget it." She dropped her gaze, studying her hands. "I will confess that my desire to attack during Navasatem has a personal edge."

"How so?"

"Because Rustam spent the last one in the dungeons. I lost my temper, said something unwise to Ghassan's father. Khader." The name fell like a curse from her tongue. "An even harder man than his son. I don't remember what it was, petty nonsense from an angry young woman. But Khader took it as a threat. He had my brother dragged from the infirmary and thrown into a lightless cell at the bottom of the palace. They say . . ." She cleared her throat. "They say that the bodies of those who die in the dungeon aren't removed. You lie with corpses." She paused. "Rustam spent the entire month of Navasatem there. He didn't speak for weeks. Even years later . . . he could only sleep if lamps were blazing all night long."

Dara felt sick. He thought unwillingly of his sister's fate. "I am sorry," he said softly.

"As am I. I've learned since that anonymity is far safer for those I love." Her mouth twisted bitterly. "Though not without its own cruel drawbacks."

He hesitated; Manizheh's words indicated something that he couldn't let pass. "Do you not trust the ifrit?" he asked. He'd made his poor opinion of the ifrit clear more than once, but Manizheh never wanted to hear it. "I thought they were your allies."

"They are a means to an end, and I do not trust easily." She leaned back on her palms. "Kaveh is dear to me. I will not have the ifrit learn that."

"Your daughter . . ." Dara's throat constricted. "When I said I would die for her, I hope you know I would do so for any Nahid. It was not because . . ." He grew flustered. "I would not overstep my station."

A glint of amusement lit her face. "How old were you when you died, Afshin? The first time?"

Dara tried to recall. "Thirty?" He shrugged. "It was so long ago, and the last years were difficult. I do not remember exactly."

"That's what I thought."

"I do not understand."

She gave him a wry smile. "At times you speak like a young man who's yet to see a half-century. And as we discussed . . . I am a Nahid with a skill you compared to mind-reading."

Heat filled his cheeks before he could check it, his heart skipping a beat . . . the very signs, of course, that he knew she'd been looking for.

Manizheh shaded her eyes. "Ah, I do believe that is the lake where we are to meet Aeshma. You can take us down."

He flushed again. "Banu Manizheh, I pray you know . . ."

She met his eyes. "Your affections are yours, Afshin." Her gaze turned a little harder. "But do not let them be a weakness. In any way."

Embarrassed, he merely nodded. He raised a hand, and the rug dipped, speeding toward a distant gleam of azure. The lake was enormous—more sea than lake—the water a brilliant aquamarine, the tropical hue at stark odds with the snowcapped mountains ringing its shore.

"Lake Ossounes," Manizheh said. "Aeshma says it's been sacred to the marid for millennia."

Dara gave the lake an apprehensive look. "I am not flying over that much water on a rug."

"We needn't." Manizheh pointed to a thin trail of smoke drifting from the easternmost shore. "I suspect that is him."

They flew closer, zooming over rocky red bluffs and a narrow, marshy beach. It really was a stunning place. Lines of evergreens stood as sentinels against jutting hills and grassy valleys. A few clouds streaked the pale sky, and a hawk circled overhead. The air smelled fresh, promising cold mornings around pine-scented fires.

Longing stole into his heart. Though Dara had been born in Daevabad, this was the type of country he loved. Open skies and staggering vistas. One could take a horse and a bow and disappear into a land like this to sleep under the stars and explore the ruins of kingdoms lost to time.

Ahead, a fire blazed on the beach, the flames licking the air with a bit too much malicious delight.

Dara inhaled, catching the scent of ancient blood and iron. "Aeshma. He is near." Smoke curled from under his collar. "I can smell that foul mace he carries, thick with the blood of our people."

"Perhaps you should shift back into your natural form."

Dara scowled. "This is my natural form."

Manizheh sighed. "It isn't, and you know it. Not anymore. The ifrit have warned you that your magic is too much for this body." She tapped his tattooed arm, the skin pale brown and very much not aflame. "You leave yourself weak."

Their carpet fluttered to the ground. Dara didn't respond, but he didn't shift either. He would do so if and when the marid appeared.

"Ah, there are my erstwhile allies."

At the sound of Aeshma's voice, Dara's hand dropped to the long knife at his side. The bonfire split, and the ifrit strolled through the break with a black-fanged grin.

It was a grin that made Dara sick. That was what he looked like now when he shifted, his fire-bright skin, gold eyes, and clawed hands a mirror of the demons who'd enslaved him. That his ancestors had looked the same before Suleiman's curse was of little comfort. It hadn't been his ancestor's grin he'd seen just before the fetid water of the well closed over his face.

Aeshma sauntered closer, his smile widening as if he could sense Dara's displeasure. He probably could; it was not a thing Dara tried to conceal. Balanced on one shoulder was his mace, a crude metal hammer studded with barbs. Aeshma seemed to enjoy the effect it had on Dara's temper, and took special delight in mentioning the times it had been bathed with Nahid and Afshin blood.

Our allies. Dara's hand curled around the hilt of his knife.

"A knife?" Aeshma clucked his tongue in disappointment. "You could summon a sandstorm that would throw me across the lake if you would leave that useless body behind you." His eyes brightened with viciousness. "And surely if you're going to use a weapon, we might as well get a look at your famous scourge."

Manizheh's hand shot out as the air sparked with heat. *"Afshin,"* she warned him before fixing her attention on Aeshma. "I received your signal, Aeshma. What have you heard?"

"The same whispers and premonitions that started up when you brought your Scourge back to life," the ifrit replied. "My companions have gone burning through all the marid haunts they know without response. But now there's something else . . ." He paused, seeming to savor the moment. "The peris have left the clouds to sing their warnings on the wind. They say the marid have overstepped. That they broke the rules and are to be called to account—punished by the lesser being to whom they owe blood."

Dara stared at him. "Are you drunk?"

Aeshma grinned, his fangs gleaming. "Forgive me, I forget at times one must speak simply to you." His voice slowed to a mocking crawl. "The marid killed you, Afshin. And now they owe you a blood debt."

Dara shook his head. "They might have been involved, but it was a djinn who wielded the blade."

"And?" Manizheh cut in. "Think back on what you've told me of that night. Do you truly believe some al Qahtani brat was capable of cutting you down on his own?"

Dara hesitated. He'd put arrows in the prince's throat and lungs and knocked him into the lake's cursed depths. Alizayd should have been dead twice over and instead he'd climbed back onto the boat looking like some sort of watery wraith. "What do you mean by a blood debt?" he asked.

Aeshma shrugged. "The marid owe you a favor. Which is convenient, because you want to break into their lake."

"It's not their lake. It's ours."

Manizheh laid a hand on Dara's wrist as Aeshma rolled his eyes. "It was once theirs," she said. "The marid helped Anahid build the city. Surely you were taught some of this? It's said that the jeweled stones that pave the Temple grounds were brought by the marid as tribute."

Afshin children were not exactly schooled in the finer points of their people's history, but Dara had heard the story of the Temple's stones. "So how does that get me across the threshold?"

"Forget your threshold," Aeshma said. "Do you imagine water beings crossing deserts and mountains? They use the waters of the world to travel . . . and they once taught your Nahid masters to do the same." Resentment flashed in his eyes. "It made hunting *my* people that much easier. We dared not even go near a pond lest some blood-poisoning Nahid spring from its depths."

"This is madness," Dara declared. "You want me to threaten the marid—the *marid*, beings capable of turning a river into a serpent the size of a mountain—based on the supposed whispers of peris and tales of a legendary magic neither Banu Manizheh nor I were alive to witness." He narrowed his eyes. "You wish to kill us, is that it?"

"If I wanted to kill you, Afshin, believe me I'd have come up with a far simpler method and spared myself your paranoid company," Aeshma replied. "You should be excited! You get to avenge yourself on the marid who killed you! You get to be their Suleiman."

The comparison instantly extinguished Dara's anger, replacing it with dread. "I am no Suleiman." The denial surged from his mouth, his skin prickling at the thought of such blasphemy. "Suleiman was a prophet. He was the man who set our laws and granted us Daevabad and blessed our Nahids—"

Aeshma burst into laughter. "My, you really do rattle that off. I remain forever impressed by the training your Nahid Council beat into you."

"Leave him alone," Manizheh said sharply. She turned back to Dara. "No one is asking you to be Suleiman," she assured him, her voice gentler. "You are our Afshin. That is all we need you to be." The confidence in her eyes helped calm him. "But this blood debt is a good thing. A *blessed* thing. It might get us back to Daevabad. To my daughter."

Nahri. Her face played in his memory. The betrayal in her dark eyes as Dara forced her hand in the infirmary, her screams as he was cut down.

Sixty-four, Kaveh had said coldly. Sixty-four Daevas who died in the chaos Dara had caused.

He swallowed the lump growing in his throat. "How do we summon the marid?"

Violent delight danced across the ifrit's face. "We anger them." He turned away. "Come! I've found something they're going to be *very* upset to lose."

We anger *them?* Dara stayed rooted to the sand. "My lady . . . this could be quite dangerous."

"I know." Manizheh's gaze was locked on the retreating ifrit. "You should shift."

This time, Dara obeyed, letting the magic take him. Fire raced down his limbs, claws and fangs bursting forth. He sheathed the knife, conjuring a new weapon from the smoke that swirled around his hips. He raised it, the familiar handle of the scourge warming in his hand.

It would not hurt to remind Aeshma of what he was capable of.

"Don't believe everything they tell you," Manizheh said, suddenly sounding on edge. "The marid. They are liars." She turned abruptly on her heel, following Aeshma through the flames.

Dara stared at her another moment. *What would they possibly have to tell me?* Bewildered, he followed her, his unease growing.

Behind the veil of smoke, a figure writhed on the sandy beach. His hands and legs were bound, his mouth gagged. He was sobbing against the ball of fabric stuffed in his mouth, his wrists bloody where he'd tried to tear away his binds.

Crimson blood.

Manizheh spoke first. "A human? You plan to use a human to summon the marid?"

"Not just any human," Aeshma explained. "A devotee of the marid—one who was hard to find. Humans have been giving up the old ways, but I spied him conducting rituals at high tide." He inhaled, looking disgusted. "He's theirs. I can smell it."

Dara frowned. He could too, as a matter of fact. "Salt," he said softly. He studied the human. "And something else . . . like a heaviness upon him. Something dark. Deep."

Aeshma nodded, swinging his mace in one hand. "He's been claimed."

Manizheh was staring at the human, her expression unreadable. "And that claim is important to them?"

"Very," Aeshma replied. "There's power in worship, and the marid don't have many followers left. They're going to be very upset to lose one."

The ifrit's plan became horribly clear in Dara's head. "Lose one . . . you cannot mean you intend—"

"*I* do not." Aeshma gave them both a careful look. "If I'm wrong about the blood debt, the marid will be within their rights to slaughter whoever kills their acolyte." He held the mace out to Manizheh. "This risk is yours, Banu Nahida."

Dara instantly stepped between them. "No. Banu Manizheh . . . there—there are rules," he stammered. "Our tribe has always obeyed Suleiman's code; it's what separates us from the djinn. We do not touch humans. We certainly do not kill them!"

She shook her head, grim resignation in her eyes as she reached for the mace. "We have to find a way to get into Daevabad, Afshin. We're running out of time."

Dread clawed up in his chest, but he lowered her hand. "Then

I will do it." This was not a sin he could let his Nahid commit herself.

Manizheh hesitated. Her lips were pressed tight, her spine rigid. And then she nodded, stepping back.

Dara took the mace. He headed for the human, closing himself off from the man's sobs, from the voice screaming inside his own head.

He smashed his skull in with a single strike.

A moment of horrified silence seemed to hang in the air. Then Aeshma spoke, his voice strained. "Burn him. In the water."

Sick to his soul, Dara grabbed the human he'd murdered by his bloody collar and dragged him farther into the shallows. The smell of viscera swept over him. Around the dead man's wrist was a blue string knotted with jade beads. Had someone given that to him? Someone who'd be waiting for him to return?

Demon. The whispered accusations that followed Dara in Daevabad rose in his mind. *Murderer*.

Scourge.

Crimson blood stained the clear water, ballooning out from the body like a storm cloud overtaking the sky. The water simmered against his ankles. Dara hated it. He hated everything about this. Fire poured down his hands, rushing to consume the man's body. For a moment, Dara could not help but wish it would consume him as well.

A high, thin screech tore the air—and then the lake attacked.

The water drew up so fast Dara didn't even have time to move. A wave twice his height lunged for him, towering over him like a ravenous bear . . .

And then the wave fell apart, collapsing around his body with an angry hiss of steam. The water tried again, flattening and then twisting around his legs as if to drag him down and drown him. And again it lurched back, as though it were an animal that had been burned.

"Afshin!" he heard Manizheh cry. "Watch out!"

Dara looked up. His eyes went wide. In the churning depths, a ship was re-forming. Barnacle-covered wooden ribs and broken deck planks rushed together, a skeleton of sunken wrecks. An enormous anchor, the metal orange with rust, flew into place on the bow like some sort of battering ram.

Dara stepped back as the boat rushed forward, his first instinct to protect Manizheh.

"Stand your ground!" Aeshma shouted. "Command it!"

Command it? Too shocked to argue and at an utter loss for how *else* to confront the nightmarish wreck hurtling toward him, Dara found himself raising his hands. "Za marava!" he cried, using the words the ifrit had taught him.

The ship burst into ash. The flakes drifted in the acrid air, falling like snow, and Dara stumbled, shaking badly.

But the lake wasn't done. Water dashed over the dead human, frothing as it doused the flames covering his body.

And then the man stood up.

Water streamed from his limbs, seaweed wrapping his arms and crabs skittering up his legs. Triangular fins spiked from his shoulders, tracing down to meet reptilian clawed hands. Mollusks covered his crushed skull, and scales crept across his bloodied cheeks, a snarled mess of shells and decayed fishing nets replacing his soiled clothing. He straightened his broken neck with an abrupt crack and blinked at them, the whites of his eyes vanished under an oily dark film.

Dara recoiled in horror. "That is what Alizayd looked like," he gasped as Manizheh and Aeshma rejoined him. "By the Creator . . . it really was them."

The dead man eyed them, and the temperature plummeted, the air growing clammy with moisture.

"*Daevas*," it hissed, speaking Divasti in a reedy, whispering voice that set Dara's teeth on edge.

Aeshma stepped forward on the smoking sand. "Marid!" he greeted it, sounding almost cheerful. "So you salt-blooded old fiends *are* still around. I was beginning to fear your sea-beast of a mother had devoured you all."

The marid hissed again, and Dara's skin crawled. The thing before them, a dead, twisted nightmare from the depths of the dark water, seemed wrong in every sense of the word.

It bared a set of reptilian teeth. "You killed my human," it accused him.

"You killed *me*," Dara snapped. He had no doubt now, and fresh fury was coursing through him. "One of you did anyway. And for what? I did nothing to your people!"

"Ours was not the hand that slayed you," the marid corrected, an odd defensiveness creeping into its breathy voice. A muddy snail glided along the scaled fin of its shoulder. "You were killed by a man of your own race."

"So kill him again," Aeshma said casually. "He has murdered your acolyte and set aflame your holy waters. Smash him to bits with another ship. Drown him." The ifrit stepped closer, ignoring the glare Dara threw at him. "But you can't, can you? It's being whispered all around. Your people broke the rules . . ." His tongue darted across his lips, hungry anticipation on his fiery face. "He could burn the world's waters and you could do nothing."

The marid hesitated. "An error was made in taking the boy," it finally said.

"An *error*?" Fire burst from Dara's hands. "You slaughtered me in cold blood and *taking Alizayd* was the error?"

The marid made an angry clicking sound, and a thick fog rose from the water. "Blame your Nahid," it hissed, glaring at Manizheh with hate in the glittering depths of its eyes. "She who was warned, she who seeks to upend what was wrought in blood!" The unnatural fog slid over his skin like a snake and Dara shiv-

ered. "If you could see the destruction you portend, Darayavahoush e-Afshin, you would throw yourself in the sea."

Shock froze Dara's tongue, but Aeshma waved a dismissive
hand. "Ignore it. The marid like to pretend at prophecy, but they
are demented fools whose wits are as scattered as their waters."
His bright golden eyes filled with scorn. "A millennium or two
ago, I remember these shores being lined with shining temples,
a ceaseless horde of humans willing to throw themselves in your
waters and declare you their gods. Your kind laughed as Suleiman punished my people." His face was dark with anger. "I am
glad I have lived to see the same done to you."

The marid hissed again. "This creature is no Suleiman." Its
oily eyes narrowed on Dara. "He is nothing but a blood-soaked
pawn."

"And yet you owe him a debt." Manizheh's cool voice cut
through the charged air like a knife. "A debt you would presumably like to be free of. So perhaps we could have a conversation
instead of arguing over old wars."

The marid tilted its head, considering them. The water at
its feet contracted and surged out, as if the creature was taking a
breath. "Speak," it finally replied.

"We wish to return to Daevabad." Manizheh pointed at Dara.
"My Afshin can no longer cross the mountain threshold, but
there are legends that my ancestors had another way. That they
could slip into the lake as though it were a doorway and reemerge
in whichever waters were on their minds, in any place in the
world their hearts most desired."

"That was magic never meant for daevas. The lake was *ours*.
It was sacred." Hurt crept into the creature's voice. "It was the
birthplace of Tiamat. She enchanted it so that we could pay homage to her from any water."

"Tiamat?" Dara repeated, confused. "As in Bet il Tiamat?
The southern ocean?"

"Not precisely," Aeshma replied. "Tiamat was one of their gods, their mother. A giant sea monster born in the chaos of creation with a penchant for destroying whatever dirt-blood civilizations provoked her ire." He grinned. "She *hated* daevas."

"She had cause to hate daevas," the marid hissed. "Anahid stole her lake. We removed the enchantment when Anahid's descendants grew too weak to control us. They deserved to be torn apart for daring to enter our waters." It turned on Manizheh, snapping its teeth. "And it is not just Daevabad you seek, daughter of Anahid. Do not think us so easily fooled. You are after Suleiman's seal."

Manizheh shrugged, unruffled as ever. "I am after what belongs to me. Daevabad was granted to the Nahids by the Creator, as was Suleiman's seal. Their return is equally ordained." She gestured to Dara. "Why would our greatest warrior be given back to us with such extraordinary abilities if it was not the will of the Creator?"

The marid gestured to its murdered human husk. "This is not the will of the Creator. It is the ill-fated scheme of a power-hungry woman." Its gaze flickered to Dara. "And you are worse. Twice undead and with the blood of thousands on your hands . . . and still you serve those who made you into this abomination."

The sudden charge took Dara aback and then it cut him deep, striking the darkest part of his heart, a shadowed part he dared not touch.

There is a city called Qui-zi.

The calm with which those words had been spoken, by an authority Dara was raised never to doubt. The screams of the people who lived there, the shafit that the Nahid Council had assured him were soulless deceptions. The belief he'd desperately clung to until he'd met a shafit woman—Nahri—whose company made him fear that everything he'd been told about the mixed-bloods was a lie.

Except Nahri wasn't shafit. *That* had been the lie, a deception put in place by the very creature before him. A marid curse, a marid lie.

"*Can* you do it?" he demanded of the marid, abruptly done with these games. "Is it possible for us to travel through the waters back to Daevabad?"

"We will not help a Nahid retake Suleiman's seal."

"That is not what I asked," he said through his teeth. "I asked if you *could*."

The marid drew up. "We do not take commands from fire-born devils."

That was answer enough for Dara.

It took very little to call up the raw power burning bright and angry inside him. Dara had spilled so much blood. It couldn't be for nothing, and if the marid needed to learn that lesson the hard way, so be it.

He scorched the ground in a burst of heat that baked the clay beneath his feet, shaking the entire lake bed. The water churned as it came to a vicious boil, steaming away in gigantic clouds of vapor. More fire poured down his hands, dashing to consume everything that had been safely nestled in the lake's embrace. The waterweeds that had been dancing and the fossilized teeth of creatures lost to time; a pair of writhing eels and the remains of countless fishing boats. A flock of cranes beat a hasty retreat, the frightened cry of birds filling the air.

The marid howled as its sanctuary burned, falling to its knees and screeching in pain as if it had taken the blow itself. Its clawed hands scrabbled at the dust.

Dara approached, kneeling at its side. He took the marid by its chin, its skin like pebbles beneath his fingertips. He forced its oily gaze to meet his. "You take commands from this fire-born devil," he said coldly. "You will obey those commands or I will burn every water you consider sacred, every place your kind has *ever* called home. I will reduce it all to ash and dust and murder every human follower you have left on the wreckage of your shores."

The marid jerked free. It stared at its burning sanctuary. In the puddles that remained, writhing fish were ablaze, looking like a sick parody of a Daeva fire altar.

The marid's gaze lingered on the charred remains of a water snake. "When Suleiman punished your people, he shed no blood. He offered a choice . . . a choice to spend your penance *building a temple to the Creator,* not a command to take part in a war."

The words came far easier to Dara now. "I am no Suleiman."

"No," the marid agreed. "You are not." It seemed to have grown smaller, its teeth and scales dull.

A moment passed, the only sound the crackling of flames. The fire was spreading to the trees, to the evergreen forest he'd briefly longed to escape into.

The marid spoke again, its voice lower. "You will consider the blood debt paid if we let you pass through Daevabad's lake?"

A loud crack from ahead caught his attention. The flames had taken a large tree on the opposite shore. It had stood alone, a towering sentinel, but as Dara watched, it broke, shattering from its base. It fell, landing across the smoking lake like the husk of a bridge.

He went very still. "No. That is not my only price," he said softly. "Before you killed me on the lake, you attacked me at the Gozan. You transformed the river itself into a serpent, a beast as large as a mountain. Could you do that to the lake?"

"Perhaps." The marid tensed. "Briefly. The lake is Tiamat's birthplace. Its waters are not easily controlled." It frowned. "Why would you want to do such a thing?"

Dara's eyes returned to the burning tree. "I want to bring down a tower."

8

ALI

Daevabad's lake stretched before him, a pane of murky green glass.

No ripples played upon the dark water, nor did any leaping fish break its surface. The only movement came from the clumps of dead leaves that floated past. The thick, cold air smelled of earthen decay and lightning, an eerie silence hanging over the boat. The lake looked dead, a place cursed and left abandoned long ago.

Ali knew better.

As if in a trance, he stepped closer to the deck's edge, his skin prickling as he watched the ferry course through the water. Its stern looked like a blunt knife dragged through oil, leaving not a single wave in its wake. They had yet to pass the veil, and with the morning's thick fog, nothing was visible behind them. It felt as though they were suspended in time, the lake endless.

Tell me your name. Ali shivered at the memory, the marid's soft whisper like a finger of ice stroking his spine. The soft buzzing of insects rose in his ears. The water really was so close. It would be nothing to climb over the ship's railing. To trail his hands in its cool depths. To submerge.

Aqisa's hand came down on his wrist. "A little close to the edge, don't you think?"

Ali started, pulled from his daze. He was holding the railing, one foot slightly raised though he had no memory of doing so. And the buzzing sound was gone.

"I . . . did you hear that?" he asked.

"All I hear is Lubayd emptying the contents of his stomach," Aqisa replied, jerking a thumb at their friend as he did just that, violently retching over the boat's railing.

Ali shivered again, rubbing his arms. It felt as though something damp and heavy had been clinging to his skin. "Odd," he muttered.

Lubayd made his staggering way over to them, his face pale. "I hate this blasted thing," he declared. "What kind of djinn sail *boats*? We're fire creatures, for the love of God."

Ali gave him a sympathetic look. "We're almost there, my friend. The veil should be falling before us at any moment."

"And have you a plan yet for when we arrive?" Aqisa asked.

"No?" Ali had sent missives to the palace several times during the journey to Daevabad, suggesting that Ayaanle traders be sent out from the capital to intercept them. He'd even offered to simply leave the cargo on the beach outside the city. Each letter received the same reply, written in the hand of a different scribe. *Your return pleases us.* "I suppose the only thing we can do is wait and see how we're received."

Another hush descended, and this time all three of them went still. The scent of smoke washed over him, along with the familiar tingling as they crossed the veil.

And then Daevabad was towering before them.

The city dwarfed their ship, a lion to a gnat. The thick fog was a mere skirt around its massive, glinting brass walls, and its looming bulk blotted out the sky. Peeking over the wall were the tops of sandblasted glass minarets and delicate floating stupas, ancient mud-brick ziggurats and brightly tiled temples. And guarding all of them was the stark crenellated tower of the Citadel, standing tall and proud as a symbol of Am Gezira.

Lubayd exhaled. *"That's* Daevabad? *That's* where you're from?"

"That's where I'm from," Ali echoed softly. The sight of his old home made him feel as though someone had reached into his chest and turned over his heart. He looked up at the facades of the long-dead Nahids carved into the city's brass walls as the boat drew near. Their distant metal gazes seemed ethereal, bored, the arrival of some exiled sand-fly prince a mere footnote in the long history they'd witnessed. Though the Nahid Council had been overthrown centuries earlier, no one had torn down their statues. The common refrain was that the Qahtanis didn't care: they were so confident and secure in their reign that they weren't bothered by ruined remembrances of the defeated Nahids.

But as with many things in Daevabad, the truth was more complicated. The facades *couldn't* be torn down. Not by anyone. Zaydi's workers had no sooner taken a chisel to their surface than boils broke out across their skin, brass erupting through the fetid wounds until all that was left was ashy bone and puddles of cooling metal.

No one had tried since.

The docks were silent and deserted, save for a pair of cargo dhows and a Sahrayn sandship, the port in even worse repair than it had been when Ali left. Even so, the decay only added to the majesty. It was like stepping into some long-abandoned paradise, a massive world built by beings they could scarcely understand.

"Praise God . . . ," Lubayd whispered as they slid past a statue of a warrior holding a bow twice Ali's height and familiar enough to make his stomach turn. "I did not expect to ever see such a sight in my life."

"I did," Aqisa muttered darkly. "I just assumed we'd have an army behind us when it happened."

A dull ache pounded in Ali's head. "You can't talk like that here," he warned. "Not even in jest. If the wrong person in Daevabad hears you . . ."

Aqisa snorted, caressing the hilt of her khanjar. "I'm not worried." She gave Ali a pointed stare. "I saw how well their future Qaid survived in the desert."

Ali threw her a wounded look.

Lubayd groaned. "Can we delay bloodshed for at least a few days? I didn't cross a cursed lake in a giant wooden bowl so I could be beheaded for treason before I had a chance to sample some royal cuisine."

"That's not the punishment for treason," Ali murmured.

"What's the punishment for treason then?"

"Being trampled to death by a karkadann."

Lubayd paled and this time, Ali knew it wasn't due to seasickness. "Oh," he choked out. "Don't you come from an inventive family?"

Ali returned his gaze to the brass walls. "My father doesn't deal lightly with disloyalty." He ran his thumb over the scar on his neck. "Believe me."

THEY LEFT THE CAMELS AND THE BULK OF THEIR cargo at the caravanserai beside the city gate, Lubayd affectionately cooing into the ears of the animals of which he'd grown fond while Aqisa and Ali waited impatiently. Half-expecting to be arrested the moment they docked, Ali was surprised to find no one waiting for them. Uncertain of what else to do, he ordered two camels loaded with the most precious pieces of the Ayaanle's cargo: trunks of raw gold, cases of finely worked jewelry, and a crate of rare books for the royal library that he'd broken into more than once during the long journey.

The gifts secure, they'd headed for the palace. Ali wrapped one end of his ghutra across his face before they set out; his mixed Ayaanle and Geziri features were not entirely uncommon in cosmopolitan Daevabad, but throw a zulfiqar in the mix, and he might as well shout his name from the rooftops.

The Grand Bazaar was a riot of color and chaos, the crowd thick with arguing shoppers, wide-eyed tourists, and beasts of various magical persuasions. The sound of haggling in a dozen different tongues filled Ali's ears, the competing scents of shafit sweat, djinn smoke, fried sweetmeats, enchanted perfumes, and bins of spices making him heady with nostalgia. He dodged a baby simurgh as it belched a plume of green fire, accidentally stepping on the foot of a Sahrayn woman in a snakeskin cape who cursed him in such vulgar terms they bordered on artistry.

Ali only grinned, his giddiness hidden beneath his ghutra. However he'd been brought back to Daevabad, there was no denying that the spectacle of his old home made his heart beat faster. The mysterious whispers on the lake seemed distant, the prickling in his mind gone for now.

But as they moved deeper into the crowd, the conditions of the bazaar swept away his nostalgia. Never clean to begin with—in fact, Ali had threatened to cut out the tongue of the openly corrupt sanitation minister during his brief tenure as Qaid—Daevabad's streets looked positively filthy now. Rotting garbage collected in piles, and the narrow canals cut into the road to drain away rain and sewage were overflowing with debris. More unsettling was the fact that he saw few members of the Royal Guard patrolling the streets—and those he did see were dressed in threadbare uniforms, the younger ones armed with regular swords instead of the costlier zulfiqars. He pressed on, growing more troubled by the minute. Musa had claimed that Daevabad had fallen upon hard times, but Ali had dismissed it as a means of goading him into returning home.

They were halfway to the midan, crossing a crowded intersection deep in the heart of Daevabad's shafit district, when a child's scream split the air.

Ali stopped, pulling the camel he was leading to a halt. The sound had come from a crude platform standing among the ruins of a stone building. Upon the platform was a Geziri man clad in brightly patterned yellow silk. He was forcing another man, a shafit in a dirty waist-wrap, to the front of the platform.

"*Baba!*" The scream came again, and then a little girl burst from a wooden stockade set behind the platform. She ran to the shafit man, throwing herself in his arms.

Ali stared, struggling to comprehend what was happening. A crowd of djinn stood below the platform, all dressed in rather expensive-looking garb. There were more shafit as well—men, women, and children—trapped behind the stockade, hemmed in by several well-armed djinn.

The shafit man was refusing to let go of his daughter. He was shaking, rubbing her back and whispering into her ear as she sobbed. He stepped back as the guards made a halfhearted attempt to pull his daughter away, glaring at them.

The Geziri djinn crossed his arms over his fine silks and then sighed, striding to the front of the platform.

A too-wide grin came over his face. "How's this pair for you who've not yet had the good fortune to spot some weak-blooded kin? They're both Daevabadi-born and fluent in Djinnistani. And our friend here is a talented cook. We found him running a snack stall in the bazaar. He'd be an asset in the kitchen of *any* long-lost relation."

What? Ali stared in incomprehension at the sight before him.

Aqisa was clearly not as confused. "They're selling them," she whispered in rising horror. "They're *selling* shafit."

"That can't be." Lubayd looked sick all over again. "That . . . that is forbidden. No Geziri would ever . . ."

Ali wordlessly pressed the reins of his camel into Lubayd's hands.

Lubayd grabbed his arm. Ali tried to wrench away, and Lubayd nodded at the line of men guarding the stockade. "*Look*, you rash fool."

Ali stared—but it wasn't because of the guards. Familiar landmarks drew his eye: a pottery shop with a blue-striped door, the distinctive way two of the narrow alleys ran close but never touched, the slightly slumped minaret in the distance. Ali knew this neighborhood. He knew what had once stood here, what the building in ruins before him once was.

It was the mosque at which Sheikh Anas, the martyred former leader of the Tanzeem, had preached.

Ali inhaled, suddenly breathless. His father might as well have twisted a knife in his heart. But he knew the punishment hadn't been directed at the son in faraway Am Gezira; it had been aimed at the shafit whose plight had pushed him into disloyalty . . . the ones being auctioned off before his eyes.

The girl began to cry harder.

"To hell with this," Aqisa snapped, striding forward.

Ali followed her, leaving Lubayd cursing in their wake and struggling with the camels. The Geziri trader must have noticed them because he broke off from his vile pitches, his steel eyes lighting with anticipation.

"By the Most High, you two look like you just blew in from a sandstorm." The trader laughed. "Certainly not my usual customers, but I suppose one can find blood kin anywhere." He lifted a dark brow. "As long as that kin can pay."

Aqisa's hand dropped to her sword. Ali swiftly stepped in front of her. "When did Daevabad start selling its shafit citizens?" he demanded.

"Selling?" The man clucked his tongue. "We're not selling anyone." He sounded aghast. "That would be illegal. We are merely facilitating the search for this man's pureblood family . . . and then taking a fee to support our work." He touched his heart. "Easier to find relatives when he's standing in front of them, no?"

It was a pathetically flimsy cover, and at his side, Aqisa snarled. Ali could only imagine how awful his home must look to his friends. Like many Geziris, the djinn of Bir Nabat kept their mixed-blood relatives with them, ignoring the law that demanded they be brought to Daevabad to live out their lives. The few shafit in Bir Nabat were treated as equals, roles found for them no matter their abilities with magic.

Ali gritted his teeth. "It doesn't look like he desires to find any pureblooded kin," he said. "You said he had a livelihood? Why not let him return to it?"

The trader shrugged. "The shafit are like children. Should we let children choose their fate as well?"

At that, Aqisa elbowed Ali hard in the stomach and then took advantage of his distraction to push him out of her way. She pulled free her khanjar, her eyes flashing. "I should cut out your tongue," she snapped in Geziriyya. "You're a traitor to our tribe, to everything our people stand for!"

The trader raised his hands as several of his guards flanked him. "Nothing we're doing here is illegal," he said, the oily tone leaving his voice. "And I don't need some northern garbage-picker getting everyone riled up . . ."

"What is your price?" The question was poison in Ali's mouth. "The price for the man and his daughter both?"

The trader shrugged in the direction of a djinn in shocking spotted robes. "The gentleman from Agnivansha offered twelve hundred dinars for the girl alone."

Twelve hundred dinars. A disgustingly low amount at which to value a life and yet far more than what he and his companions could muster up. Ali was as poor as the rest of Bir Nabat, his wealth stripped away when his father banished him. The camels they towed were loaded with gifts, but all of it was carefully inventoried, a gift from the Ayaanle to the palace.

Reaching down, Ali pulled his zulfiqar from his robes.

Now the trader did more than flinch. He blanched and stepped back in open fear. "Now, wait a minute. I don't know who you stole that from, but—"

"Would this be enough?" Ali's fingers tightened on the hilt of his beloved blade. Then he swallowed hard and offered it to the trader.

A shrewd look entered the man's eyes. "No," he said bluntly. "Not with all the soldiers trying to pawn them before they desert back to Am Gezira. I'll give you the father, but not the girl."

The shafit man had been watching them haggle in what looked like numb shock. But at the trader's offer, his daughter let out a cry, and the man clutched her close.

"*No.*" The word burst from his mouth. "I won't let you put her back in that cage. I won't let you take her away from me!"

The despair in his voice shoved Ali past his tipping point. "A *Qahtani* zulfiqar." He threw it at the man's feet and then pulled away the ghutra covering his face. "Surely *that* will pay your price?"

The trader's mouth fell open, the golden tone of his skin turning a green Ali hadn't realized was possible. He dropped to his knees. "Prince Alizayd," he gasped. "My God . . . f-forgive me," he stammered. "I would never have spoken with such disrespect had I known it was you."

The crowd parted in a way that reminded Ali of how djinn in Am Gezira jumped from horned vipers. His name carried on the wind, whispers in various tongues rustling through the throng.

Ali tried to ignore them, instead letting a little of his old arrogance leach into his voice. "Come now," he challenged. He jutted his chin at the zulfiqar, heartsick at the thought of giving over the weapon that had kept him alive during his exile. "My personal blade. It's been in my family for generations—certainly this will cover them both?"

A mix of greed and fear flitted across the trader's face. "Is this what you used to kill the Scourge?"

Ali was repulsed by the question. But suspecting it would help sway the man, the lie came easily. "The very blade."

The man grinned. "Then I would say it is very good doing business with you, my prince." He bowed and motioned for Ali to join him. "Please . . . the contracts will only take a moment . . ."

The shafit man was looking at him in stunned disbelief. "But you . . . people say—" His eyes darted toward the crowd of pure-bloods, and he abruptly changed the subject. "Please don't separate us, Your Highness." He hugged his daughter closer. "I beg you. We'll serve however you like, but please don't separate us."

"No," Ali said quickly. "That's not what this is." The trader returned with the contracts, and he read through them before adding his signature. Then he handed them to the shafit father.

The other man looked bewildered. "I don't understand."

"You're free," Ali said. "As you should be." He shot the trader his coldest glare, and the man flinched away. "Those who peddle in lives will be among the first to burn in hell."

"And we shall leave it at that!" Lubayd had finally made his way to them, pulling both bleating camels through the crowd. He shoved the reins into Aqisa's hands and seized the hem of Ali's robe, dragging him off the platform.

Ali glanced around, but the shafit father was gone, vanished into the crowd with his daughter. Ali didn't blame him. He could feel the eyes of the bystanders boring into them as Lubayd started trying to rewrap Ali's ghutra around his face.

"Wh-what are you doing?" Ali demanded as his friend poked him in the eye. "Ow! Will you stop . . ." The words died in his mouth as he spotted the reason he suspected Lubayd was trying to hustle him away.

A dozen members of the Royal Guard had joined them.

Ali stood awkwardly, his ghutra askew, uncertain how to greet his former companions. There was a moment or two of hesitant staring, until one of the officers stepped forward. He brought his hand to his heart and brow in the Geziri salute. "Peace be upon you, Prince Alizayd," he greeted him solemnly. "Your father has asked that I retrieve you."

"IT IS A VERY LOVELY PLACE TO BE EXECUTED, I WILL grant you that," Lubayd said conversationally as they were escorted down a deserted palace corridor. Sweet-smelling purple flowers climbed the columns, dappled sunlight playing through the wooden screens.

"We're not going to be executed," Ali said, trying to keep the feeling that they were walking to their doom from his face.

"They took our weapons," Lubayd pointed out. "Well, they took Aqisa's and my weapons . . . you gave yours away. Brilliant move, by the way."

Ali threw him a dark look.

"In here, my prince." The officer stopped, pulling open a blue-painted door with a pattern of leaping gazelles carved around it. It led to a small courtyard garden, enclosed by high walls of pale cream stone. In the center was a sunken pavilion shadowed by lush palms. Water bubbled merrily in a stone fountain shaped like a star and tiled with sunbursts, and across from it was a carpet laden with silver platters of rainbow-hued pastries and jewel-bright fruit.

"Your father will join you shortly. It is an honor to meet you, my prince." The officer hesitated, then added, "My family is from Hegra. The work you did on our well last year . . . it saved them."

His eyes met Ali's. "I hope you know how fond many of us in the Royal Guard remain of you."

Ali considered the carefully worded statement. "A fondness well returned," he replied. "What is your name, brother?"

The man bowed his head. "Daoud."

"A pleasure to meet you." Ali touched his heart. "Send your people my greetings when next you meet."

"God willing, my prince." He bowed again and then left, pulling the door shut behind him.

Aqisa gave him a look. "Making friends?"

Allies. Though Ali didn't like how swiftly his mind settled on that word. "Something like that."

Ahead, Lubayd had fallen upon the food. He took a bite of a honeyed confection studded with sugared flowers, and his eyes closed in bliss. "This is the best thing I've ever tasted."

"It is likely poisoned," Aqisa said.

"It is worth death."

Ali joined him, his stomach rumbling. It had been years since he'd seen such delicacies. As usual, they'd been piled to impress—an amount not even Ali and his hungry companions would be able to finish. It was a practice he hadn't thought much about when he was younger, but recalling the visible poverty in Daevabad's streets, he suddenly saw it as sinfully wasteful.

The door creaked open. "Little Zaydi!"

Ali glanced up to see a barrel-chested man in an officer's uniform and crimson turban stride into the garden. "Wajed uncle!" he cried happily.

The beaming Qaid pulled Ali into a crushing hug. "By God, boy, is it good to see you again!"

Ali felt some of the tension leave him, or perhaps Wajed's embrace was merely turning him numb. "You too, uncle."

Wajed pushed him back, holding him at arm's length to look him over; there were tears in the older man's eyes, but he laughed, clearly delighted at the sight of Ali. "Where is the gangly boy I taught to swing a zulfiqar? My soldiers were whispering that you resembled Zaydi the Great, striding up to the palace in your rags with your companions in tow."

That was not a comparison Ali suspected would sit well with his father. "I don't think anyone would mistake me for Zaydi the Great," he demurred quickly. "But meet my friends." He took Wajed's arm. "Aqisa, Lubayd . . . this is Wajed al Sabi, the Qaid of the Royal Guard. He all but raised me when I was sent to the Citadel."

Wajed touched his heart. "An honor," he said sincerely. A little emotion crept into the Qaid's gruff voice. "Thank you for protecting him."

Ali heard the creak of the door again. His heart skipping a beat, he glanced back, expecting his father.

But it was Muntadhir who stepped into the sunlight.

Ali froze as his brother met and then held his gaze. Muntadhir looked paler than Ali remembered, shadows dark under his eyes. Two thin scars marked his left brow—a remnant of the Afshin's scourge. But they did little to detract from his appearance. Muntadhir had always been the dashing one, the handsome, rakish prince who won over adoring nobles as swiftly as Ali put them off. He looked striking in the Qahtani royal regalia: the gold-trimmed black robe that swirled like smoke around his feet and the brilliant turban of twisted blue, purple, and gold silk that crowned his head. A length of luminous black Geziri pearls circled his neck and a ruby winked like a drop of human blood from the gold ring on his thumb.

Wajed bowed his head. "Emir Muntadhir," he greeted him respectfully. "Peace be upon you."

"And upon you all peace," Muntadhir returned politely. The familiar sound of his brother's voice sent a wave of emotion crashing through Ali. "Qaid, my father requests that you escort Prince

Alizayd's companions to the Citadel's guest quarters. Please ensure that they want for nothing." He touched his heart and then aimed a dazzling smile at Aqisa and Lubayd. "We are forever grateful for the welcome you provided my brother in your village."

Ali narrowed his eyes at the pleasantly worded lie, but neither Aqisa nor Lubayd responded with their usual sarcasm. Instead, they looked rather awestruck by the sight of Daevabad's emir.

Yes, I suppose he makes for a more gripping image than a soaked, starving prince dying in a crevasse.

Lubayd recovered first. "Is that all right with you, brother?" he asked Ali.

"Of course it is," Muntadhir cut in smoothly. "You'll understand that we're eager to spend some time alone with Prince Alizayd."

Ali didn't miss his brother's aggressive use of "we," a manner of speaking he associated with their father. There was a terseness lurking under Muntadhir's charming words that Ali didn't like. And though it probably didn't bode well for him, he suddenly didn't mind his friends being far away. "You'll look after them?" he asked Wajed.

Wajed nodded. "You have my word, my prince."

It would have to do. Ali trusted Wajed as much as he could trust anyone here. He glanced at Lubayd and Aqisa and attempted a smile. "I'll see you soon, God willing."

"You better," Lubayd replied, snatching another pastry before rising to his feet.

Aqisa pulled him into a quick embrace. Ali went stiff with shock at the utter inappropriateness of it, but then something hard was sliding into the fold of his belt. "Do not die," she hissed in his ear. "Lubayd would be inconsolable."

Fairly certain she'd just passed him God only knew what weapon she'd manage to smuggle into the palace, Ali nodded, silently grateful. "Take care."

Wajed squeezed his shoulder. "Get over to the Citadel when you have a chance. Show my Daevabadi-born brats how we fight back home."

As soon as they left, the temperature seemed to dip, and the politely vacant smile vanished from Muntadhir's face. "Alizayd," he said coolly.

Ali flinched; his brother rarely called him by his formal name. "Dhiru." His voice caught. "It's really good to see you."

Muntadhir's only reaction was a slight grimace, as though he'd bitten into something sour. He turned, ignoring Ali to descend into the pavilion.

Ali tried again. "I know we didn't part under the best circumstances. I'm sorry." His brother said nothing, pouring a cup of wine and sipping it as though Ali wasn't there. Ali persisted. "I hope you've been well. I was sorry to miss your wedding," he added. Despite his efforts, he could hear the stiffness in his words.

At that, Muntadhir looked up. "All the blandly diplomatic things you could blather about, and you go straight to her."

Ali flushed. "I only meant—"

"How's your cousin?"

Ali started. "My what?"

"Your cousin," Muntadhir repeated. "The Ayaanle one who conveniently fell ill and needed you to continue on in his place."

The sarcastic implication that Ali had played a part in Musa's plot set his teeth on edge. "I had nothing to do with that."

"Of course not. One Ayaanle plot gets you sent away, another one brings you back. And there remains Alizayd, innocent and oblivious to it all."

"Come on, Dhiru, surely—"

"Don't call me that," Muntadhir interrupted. "I meant what I told you that night—you must remember, it was just before you brought the ceiling of the infirmary down on my head—I'm done protecting you." He took another sip from his cup. His hands were shaking, and though his voice didn't waver, Muntadhir's gaze flickered away as though the sight of his little brother caused him pain. "I don't *trust* you. I don't trust myself with you. And that's not a weakness I intend to let drag me down."

Stung, Ali struggled for a response, emotions swirling in his chest.

Hurt responded first. "I saved your life. The Afshin . . . the boat . . ."

"I'm well aware." Muntadhir's voice was curt, but this time Ali didn't miss the flicker of emotion in his brother's eyes. "So let me return the favor. Leave."

Ali stared at him. "What?"

"*Leave*," Muntadhir repeated. "Get out of Daevabad before you blunder into something else you don't understand and get a score of innocent people killed." A fierce protectiveness crept into his voice. "And stay away from Zaynab. I know she's been helping you. That ends. I will kill you myself before I let you drag my little sister into one of your messes."

Ali recoiled, struck speechless by the open hate in his brother's face. He hadn't expected Muntadhir to greet him with open arms, but this . . .

It was of course at that moment that the door opened again, and their father entered the courtyard.

Training and a lifetime of being scolded to respect his elders had Ali bowing before he even realized what he was doing, his hand moving from his heart to his brow.

But he caught himself before he let a certain word slip. "My king," he greeted Ghassan solemnly. "Peace be upon you."

"And upon you peace, my child," Ghassan replied.

Ali straightened up, taking in the sight of his father as he approached. Ghassan had aged far more than Ali expected. Stress lines bored deep around the king's eyes, echoing the gaunt shadows under his cheeks. A heaviness seemed to have settled on his shoulders, making him appear, if not frail, at least older. He suddenly seemed like a man who'd lived two centuries, a king who'd seen and done far too much.

Ghassan stared back, gazing at Ali with open relief. He stepped closer, and Ali dropped to one knee, reaching out to take his father's hand and press it to his brow. It wasn't a thing the Qahtanis did in private, but Ali suddenly found himself retreating into formality, wanting the distance that ceremony and ritual provided. "May God preserve your reign," he murmured.

He stood and stepped back, but Ghassan grabbed his wrist. "Stay, boy. Let me look at you a moment longer."

Aware of Muntadhir watching them, Ali tried not to cringe. But when his father touched his face, he could not help but stiffen.

Ghassan must have noticed; there was a brief moment of hurt in his lined eyes, gone in the next instant. "You can sit, Alizayd," he said softly. "I know you've had a long journey."

Ali sat, crossing his legs underneath him. His heart was racing. "I pray you can forgive my sudden return, my king," he rushed on. "Bir Nabat could not sustain the Ayaanle caravan, and when that wretched trader abandoned it, I had little choice. I was the only man who could handle the untreated salt."

"You could have butchered the animals for food and stolen the cargo," Muntadhir suggested casually. "The djinn of Bir Nabat are raiders like the rest of the north, no?"

"No," Ali said, matching his brother's even tone. "We are farmers, and it was a small fortune due to the Treasury. I didn't want the village to land in any trouble."

Ghassan raised a hand. "No explanation is necessary, Alizayd. I suspected your mother's people would cook up some trick eventually to get you back here."

Muntadhir looked at his father in disbelief. "And you really think he played no part in this, Abba?"

"He looks ready to leap from his cushion and jump on the first carpet that will whisk him back to the desert. So no, I do not think he played any part." He poured a cup of wine. "He also sent me a letter from every caravanserai between here and Am Gezira suggesting different ways he could avoid this very encounter."

Ali flushed. "I wanted to be thorough."

"Then let us be thorough." Ghassan motioned to the long-healed scar high upon Ali's cheekbone—the spot where the marid had carved Suleiman's seal into his skin. "That looks worse."

"I took my khanjar to it before I reached Am Gezira," Ali explained. "I didn't want anyone recognizing it."

Muntadhir blanched, and even his father looked slightly taken aback. "That wasn't necessary, Alizayd."

"Being exiled made me no less loyal to maintaining our family's secrets," Ali replied. "I wished to be discreet."

"Discreet?" His brother scoffed. "Alizayd the Afshin-slayer? The hero out battling muwaswas and turning Am Gezira green while his relatives laze about Daevabad's palace? That's what you consider discreet?"

"It was just one muwaswas," Ali defended, recalling the incident with the rampaging magical sandfish quite well. "And I'm hardly turning Am Gezira green. It's simple irrigation work, searching for springs and digging canals and wells."

"And I wonder, how did you find those springs, Alizayd?" his father mused idly. "Those springs locals had never managed to discover themselves?"

Ali hesitated, but there was no lie his father would believe. "I have myself under control. What happened in the infirmary . . . I haven't been like that in years."

Ghassan looked grim. "Then it is a side effect of the marid possession."

Ali pressed his palms against his knees. "It's nothing," he insisted. "And no one there cares. They're too busy trying to survive."

His father didn't seem convinced. "It is still risky."

Ali didn't argue. Of course it was risky, but he hadn't cared. The sight of dying Bir Nabat, the thin bodies of its people, and the children whose hair was streaked with the rust of famine had driven those concerns from his heart.

He met his father's gaze. "Northern Am Gezira had been suffering for years. I wanted to do some good for the people who sheltered me before I was murdered by assassins."

He let the charge lie, and though Ghassan's calm expression slipped slightly, his voice was even when he replied. "And yet you still live."

Resisting the urge to offer a sarcastic apology, Ali responded simply. "All praise is due to God." Muntadhir rolled his eyes, but Ali continued. "I have no desire to play politics in Daevabad. My companions need only a short time to rest, and I intend to make the Ayaanle provision us in exchange for the transport of their goods. We can be gone in a week."

Ghassan smiled. "No. As a matter of fact, Alizayd, you cannot."

Dread snared Ali's heart, but Muntadhir reacted first, straightening up like a shot. "Why not? Do you hear him? He wishes to leave."

"It will look suspicious if he goes back too soon." Ghassan took another sip of his wine. "He hasn't been home in five years and leaves in days? People will talk. And I won't have rumors of our rift spreading. Not with the Ayaanle already meddling."

His brother's face shuttered. "I see." He was gripping his knees as though resisting the urge to throttle someone. Ali, most likely. "Then when *is* he leaving?"

Ghassan tented his hands. "When he has my permission to do so . . . permission I'm granting to you now, Muntadhir. Ask the servant at the gate to retrieve the case from my office on your way. He will know what you mean."

Muntadhir didn't argue. He didn't say another word, in fact. He got to his feet smoothly and departed without looking at Ali again. But Ali watched his brother until he vanished, a lump rising in his throat that he couldn't quite swallow.

Ghassan waited until they were alone before he spoke again. "Forgive him. He's been fighting with his wife more than usual lately, and it puts him in a foul mood."

His wife. Ali wanted to ask after her, but he dared not make the situation worse.

But his father had clearly noticed his reticence. "You used to speak far more freely. And loudly."

Ali stared at his hands. "I was young."

"You are young still. You've not even reached your first quarter century."

Silence fell between them, awkward and charged. He could feel his father studying him, and it sent a prickle down his spine. It wasn't the fear of his youth, Ali realized, but something deeper, more complicated.

It was anger. Ali was angry. He was angry about the cruel sentence his father had handed him and angry that the king was more worried about gossip in Am Gezira than its people going hungry. He was beyond angry at what was happening to Daevabad's shafit in the ghastly ruins of Anas's mosque.

And he was angry that feeling this way about his own father still filled him with shame.

Fortunately, a servant came in at that moment, bearing a plain leather box about the size of a turban case. He bowed and set it at Ghassan's side. As he turned to leave, the king motioned him close and whispered an order in his ear Ali couldn't make out. The man nodded and left.

"I will not keep you, Ali," Ghassan said. "It's a long journey and I can only imagine how eager you are for a hot bath and a soft bed. But I have something that should have been given over to you long ago, in keeping with our traditions." He motioned to the box.

Apprehensive, Ali took it. Aware of his father's keen gaze, he opened it carefully. Nestled inside was a beautifully crafted straight blade—a Daeva blade.

A familiar blade. Ali frowned. "This is Nahri's dagger, isn't it?" She had often worn it at her waist.

"It actually belonged to Darayavahoush," his father replied. "He must have given it to her when he first left Daevabad." Ghassan leaned back in his cushion. "Her room was searched after his death, and I wasn't eager to allow such a weapon to remain in her possession. You killed him. You earned it."

Ali's stomach gave a violent turn. They'd stolen this from Nahri to give to him? As though it was some sort of prize?

"I don't want this." Ali closed the box with a snap and shoved it away. "The marid killed him. They just used me to do it."

"That is a truth not to be repeated," Ghassan warned, his words quiet but sharp. When Ali made no move to touch the box, he sighed. "Do with it as you please, Alizayd. It is yours. Give it to the Daevas if you don't want it. They've a shrine to him in the Grand Temple they think I don't know about." He rose to his feet.

Ali quickly followed. "What Muntadhir asked . . . when *can* I go back to Am Gezira?"

"After Navasatem."

Ali swayed on his feet. His father had to be joking. "Navasatem is not for seven months."

Ghassan shrugged. "There is not a soul in Daevabad who would believe my youngest son—one of the best zulfiqari in our world—would leave before the grandest martial competitions in a century if things were amicable between us. You will stay and celebrate Navasatem with your family. Then we will discuss your leaving."

Ali fought panic. There was no way he could stay in Daeva-bad that long. "Abba," he begged, desperation pulling the word from him. He had not intended to use it with the man who'd sent him to die in the desert. "Please. I have responsibilities in Am Gezira."

"I'm sure you can find responsibilities here," Ghassan said breezily. "There will be plenty to go around with the holiday approaching. And Wajed could always use you in the Citadel." He gave his son a pointed look. "Though he was instructed to thrash you should you get too close to the city gates."

Ali didn't know what to say. He felt like the walls were closing in on him.

Ghassan seemed to take his silence as acquiescence. He touched Ali's shoulder—and then pressed the box containing the Afshin's dagger into his hands. "I intend to hold a feast at the end of the week to welcome you properly. For now, rest. Abu Sara will take you to your quarters."

My quarters? Ali remained speechless. *I still have quarters?* Numbly, he headed for the door.

"Alizayd?"

He glanced back.

"I've arranged to have some other property returned to you as well." There was a note of warning in Ghassan's voice. "Take care not to lose it again."

9
ALI

Ali glanced around his old quarters, dazed. The room looked untouched, books laying haphazardly on the desk where he'd left them five years ago, the clothes he'd rifled through while packing for Am Gezira still strewn across the floor. A crumpled sheet of paper—a letter he'd intended to write Nahri and then abandoned for lack of words—was balled up next to his favorite quill and the nub of candle wax he remembered meaning to replace. Though everything was dusted and freshly swept, it was otherwise clear nothing had changed.

Nothing except Ali. And if Ghassan thought to slip his youngest son back into his old life so easily, he was wrong.

Ali took a deep breath, and as he did, smelled a hint of frankincense and the sour tamarind wine his father preferred. A well-worn cushion sat on the floor where Ali once performed his prayers, and Ali recognized one of his caps laid neatly on its surface. He picked it up, and his father's particular scent came more strongly. The cap was well worried, with creases marring the linen from where it had been repeatedly folded.

He shivered as he continued into the inner room, his sleeping area still as sparse now as it had been five years ago. It was beginning to feel like he was visiting his own grave. He glanced at the bed. He blinked.

Resting on the neatly folded quilt was his zulfiqar.

Ali was across the room in the next moment, dropping the Afshin's knife box to the bed. The zulfiqar was indeed Ali's, the heft and hilt as familiar as his own hand. And if he'd had any doubts, the contracts he'd signed had been resting beneath it.

Marked by a royal scribe nullifying them.

Ali collapsed on the bed as though his knees had been cut out from under him. He scanned the pages, hoping he was wrong, but the evidence was spelled out in clear legal terms before him. The shafit father and daughter had been returned to the Geziri trader.

He shot to his feet. *No.* Those people had been innocent. They weren't Tanzeem fighters, they were no threat to anyone. But as he reached for his zulfiqar, his father's warning came back to him. Ghassan had done this to teach him a lesson. He'd destroyed the lives of two shafit because Ali had dared to interfere.

What would he do if Ali fought?

Ali closed his eyes, nausea rising in his chest as the little girl's tear-streaked face sprang to his mind. *God forgive me.* But it wasn't just her. Sheikh Anas and Rashid, Fatumai and her orphans. The auction block erected from the ruined mosque.

Every person I try to help, he breaks. He breaks us all.

He jerked his hand away from the zulfiqar. His skin was crawling. Ali couldn't stay here. Not in this carefully preserved room. Not in this deadly city where every wrong move of his got someone else hurt.

Abruptly, he thought of Zaynab. Ali dared not get further entangled with his mother, but surely his sister could help him. She could get him out of this.

Muntadhir's warning echoed in his ears, and the flicker of hope that had sparked in his chest at the thought of his sister sputtered out. No, Ali could not risk her. He squeezed his eyes shut, fighting despair. Water was pooling in his hands, a thing that hadn't happened in years.

Breathe. Pull yourself together. He opened his eyes.

His gaze fell on the box.

Ali was across the room in the next breath. He threw open the box, grabbed the dagger, and slipped it into his belt.

To hell with his father's commands.

HE WAS HALFWAY TO THE INFIRMARY BEFORE HE started to wonder if he wasn't being a bit rash.

Ali slowed on the path, one of the many that meandered through the heart of the harem garden. It wasn't as though he was actually planning to *visit* Nahri, he reasoned. Ali would wait for a servant outside the infirmary and then ask to speak to her assistant, Nisreen. He could give Nisreen the dagger and a message, and if Nahri didn't want to see him, that was fine. Completely fine. Hell, maybe Muntadhir would find out and murder him for trying to speak to his wife, and then Ali would no longer have to worry about staying in Daevabad through Navasatem.

He took a deep breath of the humid air, rich with the smell of rain-soaked earth and dew-damp flowers, and his chest unknotted slightly. The mingled sounds of the rushing canal and the water dripping off leaves were as soothing as a lullaby. He sighed, taking a short moment to watch a pair of small, sapphire-colored birds dart through the dark trees. If only the rest of Daevabad could be so peaceful.

A surge of cool moisture wove through his fingers. Startled, Ali glanced down to find a ribbon of fog swirling around his waist. As he watched, it curved over his shoulder like the embrace of a long-missed friend. His eyes went wide. *This* had certainly never happened in Am Gezira. And yet he grinned, enchanted by the sight of the water dancing upon his skin.

His smile vanished as quickly as it had come. He glanced quickly at the greenery around him, but thankfully the path was deserted. The whispers on the boat came back to him, the strange tug of the lake and the speed with which water had beaded from his skin in his room. Ali had not given thought to how much harder it might be to hide his new abilities in misty, water-rich Daevabad.

Then you'd better figure it out. He couldn't get caught. Not here. The villagers of Bir Nabat might be willing to overlook his occasional strangeness—Ali had saved them, after all—but he couldn't take the risk with Daevabad's far more mecurial population. The marid were feared in his world. They were the monsters djinn parents evoked in frightening bedtime stories, the unknowable terror djinn travelers wore amulets to ward against. Growing up, he'd heard a dark tale of a distant Ayaanle relative who'd been thrown in the lake after being unjustly accused of sacrificing a Daeva child to his supposed marid lord.

Suppressing a shudder, Ali continued toward the infirmary. But when he reached the grounds, he stopped short again, amazed at the transformation. The formal gardens for which the Daevas were famous made a beautiful sight, with raised beds of bright herbs bordering trellises heavy with flowers, and fruit trees shading glass birdhouses and gently burbling fountains. At its very center, between two rectangular pools, was a striking orange grove. The trees had been planted close together, the branches carefully manicured and coaxed to intertwine as if to form a ceiling. A little enclosure, he realized, the foliage so thick with plump fruit and snowy white flowers one couldn't see through it.

Charmed, he kept walking, drawn to the place. Whoever had planted it really had done an extraordinary job. It even had an archway pruned from the leaves to create . . .

Ali halted so fast, he almost fell backward. Nahri was very much not in the infirmary. She was here, surrounded by books, as though she'd stepped straight out of his fondest memories.

And more—she looked like she *belonged* here, the royal Banu Nahida in the palace of her ancestors. It had nothing to do with jewels or rich brocade; on the contrary, she was dressed simply in a white tunic that fell to her calves and loose purple trousers. A raw silk chador in shimmering umber was pinned just above her ears with diamond clips, thrown back over her shoulders to reveal the four black braids that fell to her waist.

Are you surprised? What had Ali expected of Nahri? That she'd be a faded version of the sharp woman he'd known, grieving for her lost Afshin, pale from being trapped for long hours in the infirmary? That had not been the Banu Nahida he'd once called a friend.

Ali shut his mouth, suddenly aware that it had fallen open, that he was staring like an addled fool, and that he was *very* much somewhere he shouldn't be. A glance revealed neither guards nor servants nearby. Nahri was alone, perched in a wide swing, an enormous volume open in her lap, notes scattered haphazardly on an embroidered rug below her, along with a tray holding an untouched cup of tea. As Ali watched, she frowned at the text as if it had personally offended her.

And suddenly all he wanted to do was step forward and drop down by her side. To ask her what she was reading and resume their bizarrely companionable friendship of hunting through the catacombs of the Royal Library and arguing about Arabic grammar. Nahri had been a light for him during a very dark time, and Ali hadn't realized until he was standing here quite how much he'd missed her.

Then stop stalking her like a ghoul. Nerves fluttering in his stomach, Ali forced himself to approach. "Sabah el-noor," he greeted softly in the Egyptian dialect she'd been teaching him.

Nahri jumped. The book fell from her lap as her startled black eyes swept his face.

They locked on the zulfiqar at his waist, and the earth buckled beneath his feet.

Ali cried out, stumbling as a root burst from the grass to snake around his ankle. It jerked forward, and Ali fell hard, the back of his head hitting the ground.

Black spots blossomed across his vision. When they cleared, he saw the Banu Nahida standing over him. She did not look pleased. "Well . . . ," Ali started weakly. "Your powers have come a remarkably long way."

The root tightened painfully around his ankle. "What the hell are you doing in my garden?" Nahri demanded.

"I . . ." Ali tried to sit up, but the root held firm. It twisted up his ankle, disappearing under his robe to snake around his calf. The feeling was far too similar to the weeds that had grabbed him under the lake, and he found himself fighting panic. "Forgive me," he blurted out in Arabic. "I only—"

"*Stop.*" The flat word in Djinnistani was like a slap across the face. "Don't you dare speak Arabic to me. I won't hear my language on your lying tongue."

Ali stared at her in shock. "I . . . I'm sorry," he repeated in Djinnistani, the words coming more slowly to him. The root was at his knee now, hairy tendrils sprouting and spreading. His skin crawled, a painful prickle shooting down the scars the marid had left on him.

He squeezed his eyes shut, and water beaded on his brow. *It's just a root. It's just a root.* "Please, can you get that thing off me?" It was taking every bit of strength he had not to reach for his zulfiqar and hack it off. Nahri would probably let the earth swallow him whole if he drew his blade.

"You didn't answer my question. *What are you doing here?*"

Ali opened his eyes. There was no mercy in Nahri's expression. Instead, she was slowly spinning one finger, a mirror of the movement the root was making around his leg.

"I wanted to see you." The words rushed from him as though she'd dosed him with one of her ancestor's truth serums. And it was the truth, he realized. Ali had wanted to see her, Darayavahoush's dagger be damned.

Nahri dropped her hand, and the root released. Ali took a shaky breath, embarrassed by how deeply it had frightened him. By the Most High, he could face assassins armed with arrows and blades and yet a root reduced him to near tears?

"I'm sorry," he said for the third time. "I shouldn't have come here."

"You certainly shouldn't have," she snapped back. "I have one place in Daevabad that's mine, one place not even my husband will set foot in, and here you are." Her face twisted in anger. "But I suppose Alizayd the Afshin-slayer does whatever he likes."

Ali's cheeks burned. "I'm not," he whispered. "You were there. You know what killed him."

Nahri clucked her tongue. "Oh no, I was corrected. Firmly. Your father said he'd murder every Daeva child in the city if I dared utter the word 'marid.'" Tears were brimming in her eyes. "Do you know what he made me say instead? What he made me say Dara tried to do? What you supposedly *interrupted*?"

Her words cut him to the bone. "Nahri . . ."

"*Do you know what he made me say?*"

Ali dropped his gaze. "Yes." The rumors had followed him to Am Gezira—there was a reason, after all, that people had no trouble believing the otherwise mild-mannered prince had killed another man.

"I saved you." She let out a high, humorless laugh. "I healed you with my own hands. More than once, even. And in return, you said *nothing* as we got on that boat, though you knew your father's men would be waiting. My God, I even offered to let you come with us! To escape your father's wrath, to escape this *cage* and see the rest of the world." She hugged her arms around herself, pulling her chador close as if to put a wall between them. "You should be proud, Ali. Not many people can outwit me, but you? You had me believing you were my friend until the very end."

Guilt crashed over him. Ali had no idea she'd felt that way. Though he'd considered her a friend, Nahri had seemed to keep him at a careful distance, and the realization that their relationship had meant more to her—and that he'd destroyed it—made him sick.

He fought for words. "I didn't know what else to do that night, Nahri. Darayavahoush was acting like a madman. He would have started a war!"

She trembled. "He wouldn't have started a war. I wouldn't have let him." Her voice was curt, but it looked like she was struggling to maintain her composure. "Is this enough for you, then? You've seen me. You've intruded upon my privacy to dredge up the worst night of my life. Is there anything else?"

"No, I mean, yes, but . . ." Ali inwardly cursed. It scarcely seemed the right moment to pull out Dara's dagger and admit his father had stolen it and kept it as some sort of war trophy. He tried another tack. "I . . . I tried to write you . . ."

"Yes, your sister gave me your letters." She tapped the ash on her forehead. "They made good fodder for my fire altar."

Ali glanced at the mark. In the shadowy grove, he hadn't noticed it at first, and it surprised him. In the time he'd known her, Nahri had never seemed all that keen on the religious rituals of her people.

She saw him take it in and her eyes lit with challenge. He couldn't blame her. He'd been rather . . . loud when voicing his opinions about the fire cult. A bead of cold sweat dripped down his neck, soaking into the collar of his dishdasha.

Her gaze seemed to trace the movement of the water trickling down his throat. "They're all over you," she whispered. "If you were anyone else, I would have heard your heartbeat, sensed your presence . . ." She raised a hand and he flinched, but thankfully, no plants attacked. Instead, she simply studied him. "They changed you, didn't they? The marid?"

Ali went cold. "No," he insisted, to himself as much as to her. "They did nothing."

"Liar," she taunted softly, and he couldn't keep the anger from his face at that. "Oh, do you not like being called a liar? Is that worse than being a man who strikes a bargain with a water demon?"

"A bargain?" he repeated in disbelief. "You think I *asked* for what happened that night?"

"For aid in killing your people's greatest enemy? For the fame of finally finishing off the man your ancestor couldn't?" Scorn filled her eyes. "Yes, Afshin-slayer, I do."

"Then you're wrong." Ali knew Nahri was upset, but she wasn't the only one whose life had been turned upside down that night. "The marid wouldn't have been able to use me to kill your Afshin if he hadn't knocked me into the lake in the first place. And how they took me, Nahri?" His voice broke. "They *ripped through my mind and made me hallucinate the deaths of everyone I loved.*" He yanked up his sleeve. His scars were stark in the faded sunlight: the ragged marks of triangular teeth and a strip of ruined flesh that twisted around his wrist. "And that's while they were doing this." He was shaking, the memory of the awful visions stealing over him. "Some bargain."

He would swear he saw a flicker of shock on her face, but it lasted only a second. Because between being thrown to the ground and pulling up his sleeve, Ali realized too late what had become visible at his waist.

Nahri's gaze locked on the distinctive hilt of Darayavahoush's dagger. The leaves in the grove shuddered. "What are you doing with that?"

Oh no. "I-I meant to give it to you," Ali said quickly, fumbling to pull the dagger from his waist.

Nahri lunged forward and ripped it from his hands. She ran her fingers over the hilt, gently pressing the carnelian and lapis stones as wetness brimmed in her eyes.

He swallowed, aching to say something. Anything. But no words would erase what was between them. "Nahri . . ."

"*Get out.*" She said it in Arabic, the language that had once been the foundation of their friendship, the one with which he'd taught her to conjure flames. "You want to avoid a war? Then get out of my garden before I bury this in your heart."

10
NAHRI

Nahri sank to her knees as Ali vanished beyond the trees. Dara's dagger was heavy in her hands. *No, like this*, she remembered him correcting her when he taught her how to throw it. Dara's hot fingers grazing her skin, his breath tickling her ear. His laugh on the wind when she swore in frustration.

Tears blurred her eyes. Her fingers curled around the hilt, and she pressed her other fist hard against her mouth, fighting the sob rising in her chest. Ali was probably still close and she'd be damned if he was going to hear her cry.

I should have buried this in his heart anyway. Leave it to Alizayd al Qahtani to intrude upon her one sanctuary in Daevabad and upend all her emotions. She was as angry at his nerve as at her own reaction; Nahri rarely lost her composure so badly. She argued plenty with Muntadhir, she looked forward to the day Ghassan burned on his funeral pyre with open relish, but she didn't weep before them like some sad little girl.

But they hadn't tricked her. Ali had. Despite Nahri's best intentions, she'd fallen for his friendship. She'd liked spending time with someone who shared her intellect and her curiosity, with someone who didn't make her feel self-conscious about her ignorance of the magical world or her human skin. She'd liked *him*, his endearing exuberance when he rattled on about obscure economic theory, and the quiet kindness with which he'd treated the palace's shafit servants.

It was a lie. Everything about him was a lie. Including what he'd just been spouting about the marid. It had to be.

She took a deep breath, unclenching her fist. The stones on the dagger's hilt had left an impression in her palm. Nahri had never expected to see Dara's blade again. In the wake of his death, she'd once asked Ghassan about the dagger, and he said he'd had it melted.

He'd lied. He'd given it as a prize to his son. His Afshin-slaying son.

She wiped her eyes with trembling hands. She hadn't known that Ali was already back. In fact, she'd been making a conscious effort to avoid hearing news of him. Muntadhir's stress—and the increasingly shaky grip he had on his wine consumption—had been all the information she'd needed about his brother's progress toward the city.

Footsteps approached on the other side of the grove. "Banu Nahida?" a female voice squeaked. "Lady Nisreen asked me to retrieve you. She said Jamshid e-Pramukh is waiting."

Nahri sighed, glancing at the book she'd been studying before Alizayd had interrupted her. It was a Nahid text on curses that were said to prevent healing. One of the novitiates at the Grand Temple had found it while sorting their old archives, and Nahri had it brought immediately to her. But the Divasti was so confusing and archaic, she feared she was going to have to send it right back for translation.

Not that Jamshid would wait. He'd been pleading with her for weeks to try healing him again, his desperation mirroring Muntadhir's spiral. Nahri didn't have to ask why. She knew not being able to personally protect Muntadhir as the captain of his guard was killing Jamshid.

She took a deep breath. "I'll be right there." She set the book aside—on top of an Arabic volume about hospitals. Or at least Nahri thought it was about hospitals; she hadn't actually had time to read it. Muntadhir might have shot down her nascent dreams of restoring her ancestors' hospital, but Nahri wasn't ready to give up.

She rose to her feet, slipping the dagger's sheath in her waistband, beneath her gown. She forced herself to put Ali out of mind. To put *Dara* out of mind. Her first responsibility was to her patients, and right now it might be a relief to let work swallow her.

THE INFIRMARY WAS ITS USUAL LIVELY SELF, CROWDED and smelling of sulfur. She passed through the patient area and behind the curtain that sectioned off her private work space. The curtain was slippery in her hands, its silk enchanted to dampen noise on both sides. She could step back here and talk frankly with Nisreen about a poor diagnosis without someone overhearing them.

The curtain could also hide the sounds of a man screaming in pain.

Jamshid and Nisreen were waiting for her, Jamshid lying on a pallet, looking pale but determined.

"May the fires burn brightly for you, Banu Nahida," he greeted her.

"And for you," Nahri returned, bringing her fingertips together. She tied her scarf back to hold her braids and washed her hands in the basin, splashing some cold water on her face.

Nisreen frowned. "Are you all right?" she asked. "Your eyes . . ."

"I'm fine," Nahri lied. "Frustrated." She crossed her arms, deciding to throw the emotions Ali had upset in a different direction. "That book is written in some blasted ancient script I can't decipher. I'll have to send it back to the Grand Temple for a translation."

Jamshid glanced up, his panic clear. "But surely that doesn't mean we can't have a session today?"

Nahri paused. "Nisreen, would you leave us for a moment?"

Nisreen bowed. "Of course, Banu Nahida."

Nahri waited until she was gone to kneel at Jamshid's side. "You're rushing this," she said, as gently as she could. "You shouldn't be. Your body is recovering. It just needs time."

"I don't have time," Jamshid replied. "Not anymore."

"You do," Nahri argued. "You're young, Jamshid. You have decades, centuries before you." She took his hand. "I know you want to be at his side again. Capable of jumping on a horse and firing a dozen arrows. And you will be." She met his gaze. "But you need to accept that it might take years. These sessions . . . I know how badly they hurt you, the toll they take on your body . . ."

"I want to do this," he said stubbornly. "The last time you said you'd gotten close to fixing the damaged nerves you believe are causing most of the weakness in my leg."

God, how Nahri suddenly wished she had another decade in the infirmary behind her, or a senior healer at her side to guide her through this conversation. The look in her patients' eyes when they begged her for certainty was difficult enough when they weren't friends.

She tried another tactic. "Where is Muntadhir? He usually comes with you."

"I told him I changed my mind. He has enough to worry about without seeing me in pain."

By the Creator, he really wasn't making this any easier. "Jamshid—"

"Please." The word cut through her. "I can handle the pain, Nahri. I can handle being bedridden for a few days. If you think it's going to do worse than that, we can stop."

She sighed. "Let me examine you first." She helped him out of the shawl wrapping his shoulders. "Lie back." They had done this so many times, the steps came automatically to them both. She took a blunt brass rod from the tray Nisreen had laid out, running it down his left leg. "Same numb burning?"

Jamshid nodded. "But it's not weak like the right leg. That's what's causing me the most trouble."

Nahri eased him onto his belly. She flinched at the sight of his bare back; she always did. Six scars, the ridged lines marking the spots where Dara's arrows had plunged into him. One had lodged in his spine, another had punctured his right lung.

You should be dead. It was the uneasy conclusion Nahri came to every time she looked at the evidence of his wounds. At a cruel order from Ghassan meant to goad Kaveh into finding Dara's so-called accomplices, Jamshid had been left untreated for a week, the arrows still in his body. He should have died. That he hadn't was a mystery on a par with the fact that he reacted so poorly to her magic.

Her gaze drifted past the small black tattoo on the inside of his shoulder. She had seen it many times, three swirling glyphs. It was a faded ghost of the striking, elaborate tattoos that had decorated Dara's skin—family sigils and clan marks, records of heroic deeds and protective charms. Jamshid had rolled his eyes when she asked about it. Apparently, the custom of the tattoos had mostly died out in the generations of Daevas born after the war, particularly in Daevabad. It was an old-fashioned superstition, he'd jokingly complained, one that gave away his rural roots.

Nahri touched his back, and Jamshid tensed. "Would you like some wine?" she asked. "It might dull the pain."

"I downed three cups just to work up the courage to come here."

Lovely. She took up a length of cloth. "I'd like to bind your hands this time." She gestured for him to grip the posts of the pallet. "Hold on to this. It will give you something to squeeze."

He was trembling now. "You have something I can bite?"

She silently handed him a skinny block of opium-infused cedarwood and then laid her hands on his bare back, glancing over to make sure the curtain was fully closed. "Ready?"

He nodded jerkily.

Nahri closed her eyes.

In seconds, she was there, his body open to her. The beat of his racing heart, pumping simmering ebony blood through a delicate map of veins. The gurgling of stomach acid and other humors. His lungs steadily expanding and contracting like bellows.

Her fingers pressed his skin. She could almost see the nerves of his spine in the blackness of her mind, brilliantly colored, dancing filaments protected by the bony ridges of vertebrae. She moved her fingers lower, tracing the bumpy scar tissue. And not just on the skin, but deeper as well: ruined muscles and frayed nerves.

She took a steadying breath. This much she could do without hurting him. It was only when she acted upon him that his body fought back. Were he anyone else, Nahri could urge those nerves to knit back together, could dissipate the scar tissue that had grown over the muscle, leaving him stiff and in pain. It was powerful magic that exhausted her—she might have needed a few sessions to heal him entirely—but he'd have been back on a horse, bow in hand, years ago.

Nahri concentrated on a small section of the flailing nerves. She steeled herself and then commanded them to reconnect.

Magic slammed into her, raw, protective, and powerful, like a blow to her very mind. Prepared, Nahri fought back, pinning a torn nerve back into place. Jamshid seized beneath her, a grunt escaping his clenched teeth. She ignored it, focusing on the next nerve.

She'd fixed three when he started groaning.

He bucked beneath her, pulling at his bindings. His skin burned under her fingertips, scorching to the touch, every pain receptor firing. Nahri held on, sweat pouring down her face. There were only five nerves left in this particular spot. She reached for another one, her hands shaking. It took strength to fight his body's reaction and perform the magic, strength she was rapidly losing.

One more nerve melded back into place, glowing faintly in her mind's eye. She seized the next.

The block fell from Jamshid's mouth, his shriek cutting the air. Ash was powdering on his skin, and then with a burst of magic, the binds holding his hands erupted into flames.

"Jamshid?" A *very* unwelcome voice spoke from behind her. "*Jamshid!*"

Muntadhir rushed inside. The shock of the interruption threw her, and then whatever power was within Jamshid's body took the opportunity to *actually* throw her, a surge of energy so fierce that Nahri stumbled back, her connection severed.

Jamshid fell still. Despite the pounding in her head, Nahri flew to her feet to check his pulse. It was fast, but it was there. He'd only passed out. She quickly smothered the flames around his wrists.

Enraged, she whirled on Muntadhir. "What the hell were you thinking?" she snapped. "I was making progress!"

Muntadhir looked aghast. "Progress? He was on fire!"

"He's a *djinn*! He can handle a little fire!"

"He's not even supposed to be here!" Muntadhir argued back. "Did you convince him to try this again?"

"Did *I* convince him?" Nahri seethed, fighting to control the emotions rising in her. "No, you fool. He's doing this for you. If you weren't so selfish, you'd see that!"

Muntadhir's eyes flashed. His usual grace had deserted him, his movements jerky as he pulled the shawl over Jamshid. "Then you shouldn't have let him. You're being reckless, so eager to prove yourself that—"

"I was not being *reckless*." It was one thing to fight with Muntadhir about politics and family; she would not have him throwing her doubts about her healing abilities in her face. "I knew what I was doing, and he was prepared. *You're* the one who interrupted."

"You were hurting him!"

"I was healing him!" Her temper broke. "Maybe if you'd shown this concern when your father was willing to let him die, he'd be in better shape!"

The words ripped from her, an accusation that for all their many fights, Nahri had never intended to let slip. She knew too well the fear Ghassan used to keep his people in line, the terror that clawed up in her own throat when she thought of his wrath.

And she knew damn well how Muntadhir felt about Jamshid.

Her husband jerked back like she'd slapped him. Shocked hurt—and a good deal of guilt—flashed across his face, spots of angry color rising in his cheeks.

Nahri instantly regretted her words. "Muntadhir, I only meant—"

He raised a hand, cutting her off as he pointed a shaking finger at Jamshid. "The only reason he's hurt is because of Darayavahoush. Because of *you*. Because a lost little girl from Cairo thought she was living in some sort of fairy tale. And because for all her supposed cleverness, she couldn't see that the dashing hero who saved her was actually its monster. Or maybe she just didn't care." His voice grew colder. "Maybe all he had to do was tell one of his sad stories and bat his pretty green eyes, and you were all too happy to do whatever he wanted."

Nahri stared at him, speechless, the words reverberating in her head. She'd seen Muntadhir drunk before, but Nahri had not known he could be so cruel.

She had not known he could cut her so deep.

She inhaled, shaking with hurt betrayal. *This* was why she had walls up, why she tried to hide away her heart. Because it was clear she couldn't trust a damn soul in this city. Her blood boiled. And who was Muntadhir to say such things to her? *Her?* The Banu Nahida in her own infirmary?

The palace seemed to agree, her ancestors' magic swirling in her blood. The flames in her firepit soared, licking out like they might seize him, this newest incarnation of the sand flies who'd stolen their home.

Then Nahri's rage felt different. Purposeful. She could sense Muntadhir as though she were laying hands upon him. The rapid beat of his heart and the flush in his skin. The very delicate vessels in his throat. The bones and joints that could be commanded to break.

"I think you should leave, Emir." It was Nisreen, standing at the edge of the curtain. When she'd gotten there, Nahri didn't know, but the older Daeva woman had obviously heard enough to be gazing at Muntadhir with barely concealed contempt. "The Banu Nahida is in the middle of treating your companion, and it is better for him that they not be disturbed."

Muntadhir's mouth clamped into a stubborn line. He looked like he had more to say . . . and he was clearly unaware of how close Nahri had come to doing something she might not have been able to take back. But after another moment, he touched Jamshid's hand, briefly sliding his fingers through the other man's. Then, without looking at Nahri or Nisreen, he pushed to his feet, turned, and left.

Nahri exhaled, her entire body shivering as the dark urge left her. "I think . . . I think I could have just killed him."

"He would have deserved it." Nisreen crossed to check on Jamshid, and after another moment, Nahri joined her. His pulse was a little rapid and his skin still hot, but his breathing was slowly returning to normal. "Do not ever let that foul drunk touch you again."

Nahri felt like she was about to be sick. "He's my husband, Nisreen. We're supposed to be working to bring peace between the tribes." Her voice was weak, the words almost laughable.

Nisreen pulled over the ice-filled bucket that had been left next to the pallet, dampening a cloth in the cool water and placing it on Jamshid's back. "I would not overly worry about the future of your marriage," she muttered darkly.

Nahri stared at Jamshid. A wave of despair swept her as she remembered his pleading. She felt so utterly useless. It was all too much: the crush of her responsibilities and her constantly deflected dreams. The deadly dance she was forced to do with Ghassan and the pleading eyes of the Daevas who prayed to her to save them. Nahri had tried, she had. She'd married Muntadhir. But she had nothing left to give.

"I want to go home," she whispered, her eyes growing wet. It was a completely nonsensical desire to have, a pathetically childish urge, and yet her heart ached with a longing for Cairo so strong it stole her breath.

"Nahri . . ." Embarrassed, Nahri tried to turn away, but Nisreen reached for her face, cupping her cheeks. "Child, look at me. *This is your home*." She pulled her into a hug, stroking the back of her head, and Nahri couldn't help but sink into her embrace, the tears finally spilling from her eyes. It was a type of physical affection no one here gave her, and she took it gratefully.

So gratefully in fact that she didn't question the fervor in Nisreen's voice when she continued speaking. "I promise you, my lady. It is going to be all right. You will see."

11

ALI

Ali smashed his zulfiqar into Wajed's, spinning off the momentum to duck Aqisa's blade as it passed over his head.

How did you expect Nahri to react? You gave her no warning and you arrived carrying Darayavahoush's dagger. Did you think she'd invite you to talk about books over tea?

He brought his weapon up to block Wajed's next strike.

I still can't believe she thinks I wanted any of this. After all, Ali didn't exactly *ask* to get kidnapped and shot by her precious Afshin. And he didn't believe for a second that Nahri had gone these five years without learning about Qui-zi and Darayavahoush's other innumerable crimes. How could she still defend him?

He pushed off the Qaid's blade, whirling around to face Aqisa again, narrowly parrying her next blow.

Love—for it was apparent even to Ali, who was typically oblivious to such things, that there had been a bit more than the usual Afshin-to-Nahid devotion between Nahri and that brutish demon of a man. *What a useless, distracting emotion.* How ridiculous to be flashed a pretty smile and lose all sense of—

Aqisa smashed him across the face with the flat part of her sword.

"Ow!" Ali hissed in pain and then lowered his zulfiqar. He touched his cheek, his fingers coming away bloody.

Aqisa snorted. "It isn't wise to spar while distracted."

"I wasn't distracted," he said heatedly.

Wajed lowered his weapon as well. "Yes, you were. I've been training you since you were waist high. I know what you look like when you're not focusing. You, on the other hand . . ." He turned to Aqisa, his expression admiring. "You're excellent with that zulfiqar. You should join the Royal Guard. You'd get your own."

Aqisa snorted again. "I don't take orders well."

Wajed shrugged. "The offer remains." He gestured to the opposite corner of the Citadel courtyard where Lubayd appeared to be holding court before an enthralled group of young recruits, no doubt telling some highly sensationalized tale of the trio's adventures in Am Gezira. "Why don't we take a break and join your loud friend for some coffee?"

Aqisa grinned and headed off, but Wajed held Ali back another moment.

"Are you all right?" he asked, lowering his voice. "I know you, Ali. You're not just distracted, you're holding back. I've seen you get the same look in your eyes when you're training others."

Ali pressed his mouth in a thin line. Wajed had struck closer to the truth than he liked. Ali *was* holding back, though not quite in the way the Qaid meant. And it wasn't only memories of Nahri that were distracting him.

It was the lake. It had been pulling on him since he arrived at the Citadel, drawing Ali to the walls more times than he could count to press his hands against the cool stone, sensing the water on the other side. When he closed his eyes, the whispers he'd heard on the ferry rushed back: an incomprehensible buzz that made his heart pound with an urgency he didn't understand. His marid abilities felt closer—wilder—than they had in years, as though with a single snap of his fingers, he could fill the Citadel's courtyard with a blanket of fog.

None of which he could tell Wajed. Or frankly, anyone at all. "It's nothing," Ali insisted. "I'm just tired."

Wajed eyed him. "Is this about your family?" When Ali grimaced, sympathy flooded the Qaid's face. "You didn't even give the palace a day, Ali. You should go home and try to talk to them."

"I am home," Ali replied. "My father wanted me raised in the Citadel, didn't he?" As he spoke, his gaze caught a pair of guards heading out on duty. Both wore uniforms that had been heavily patched, and only one of them had a zulfiqar.

He shook his head, thinking of Muntadhir's jewelry and the sumptuous platter of pastries. It was clear he wasn't alone in noticing the discrepancy: he'd overheard plenty of grumbling comments since arriving at the Citadel. But while Ali suspected some of Daevabad's economic woes could be traced to the Ayaanles' quiet interfering—Musa had implied as much—he doubted his fellow soldiers knew to look so far. They'd only seen Daevabad's feasting nobles and complacent palace denizens. They certainly didn't seem to blame *him*; Ali had been warmly welcomed back with only a few teasing remarks about the reduced meals of lentils and bread he now shared with them.

Commotion at the main gate caught his attention, and Ali glanced over to see several soldiers scurrying toward the entrance . . . and then promptly backing away in a clumsy mob, a few men tripping over their feet as they dropped their gazes to the ground.

A single woman strode in. Tall, and with a willowy grace Ali recognized immediately, she wore an abaya the color of midnight, embroidered with clusters of diamonds that shone like stars. A long silver shayla had been drawn across her face, concealing all but her gray-gold eyes.

Angry gray-gold eyes. They locked on Ali's face, and then she lifted her hand, gold bangles and pearl rings shimmering in the sunlight, to make a single rude beckoning motion before she abruptly turned around, marching straight back out.

Wajed looked at him. "Was that your sister?" Concern filled his voice. "I hope everything is well. She almost never leaves the palace."

Ali cleared his throat. "I . . . I may have come to the Citadel without stopping to see her and my mother."

Ali hadn't known Daevabad's Qaid—a massively built man who wore two centuries of war scars with pride—could go so pale. "You haven't gone to see your mother?" He drew back as if to physically distance himself from what was about to happen to Ali. "You better not tell her I let you stay here."

"Traitor." Ali scowled but couldn't deny the trickle of fear he felt as he moved to follow his sister.

Zaynab was already seated in the litter by the time he climbed inside. He pulled the curtain closed. "Ukhti, you really didn't—"

His sister slapped him across the face.

"You ungrateful ass," she seethed, yanking her shayla away from her face. "Five years I spend trying to save your life and you can't be bothered to come see me? Then when I finally track you down, you think to greet me with a lecture on *propriety*?" She raised her hand again—a fist this time. "You self-righteous—"

Ali ducked her fist and then reached out and gripped her shoulders. "That's not what this is, Zaynab! I swear!" He let her go.

"Then what is it, brat?" Her eyes narrowed in hurt. "Because I've half a mind to order my bearers to toss you in a trash pit!"

"I didn't want to get you in trouble," Ali rushed on. He reached for her hands. "I owe you my life, Zaynab. And Munta-dhir said—"

"Muntadhir said what?" Zaynab interrupted. Her expression had softened, but anger still simmered in her voice. "Did you care to ask my opinion? Think for a moment that maybe I was perfectly capable of making a decision *without* my older brother's permission?"

"No," Ali confessed. All he'd been thinking about was getting away from the palace before he hurt someone else. And of course, in doing so, he had hurt someone else. "I'm sorry. I panicked. I wasn't thinking and . . ." Zaynab yelped, and Ali abruptly released her hands, realizing he'd been squeezing them. "Sorry," he whispered again.

Zaynab was staring at him, worried alarm replacing the anger in her face as her eyes swept his bloody face and filthy robe. She picked up his hand, running her thumb over his ragged fingernails.

Ali flushed, embarrassed at their state. "I'm trying to stop biting them. It's a nervous tic."

"A nervous tic," she repeated. Her voice was trembling now. "You look terrible, akhi." One of her hands lifted to his cheek, touching the ruined flesh where Suleiman's scar had been carved.

Ali attempted and failed to force a weak smile. "Am Gezira wasn't as welcoming as I'd hoped."

Zaynab flinched. "I thought I'd never see you again. Every time I had a messenger, I feared they were coming to say that you . . . that you . . ." She seemed unable to finish the words, tears brimming in her eyes.

Ali pulled her into a hug. Zaynab clutched him, letting out a choked sob.

"I was so worried about you," she wept. "I'm sorry, Ali. I begged him. I begged Abba every day. If I'd been able to convince him . . ."

"Oh, Zaynab, none of this is your fault." Ali held his sister close. "How could you think that? You are a blessing; your letters and supplies . . . you have no idea how much I needed them. And I'm okay." He pulled back to look at her. "Things were getting better there. And I'm here now, alive and already irritating you." He managed a small smile this time.

She shook her head. "Things aren't okay, Ali. Amma . . . she's so angry."

Ali rolled his eyes "I haven't been back *that* long. How mad could she be?"

"She's not angry at *you*," Zaynab retorted. "Well . . . she is, but that's not what I'm talking about. She's angry at *Abba*. She came back to Daevabad in a rage when she learned what happened to you. She told Abba that she was going to drive him into debt."

Ali could only imagine how that conversation had gone. "We'll talk to her," he assured her. "I'll find a way to fix things. And forget all that for now. Tell me how *you* are." He didn't imagine any of this was easy for Zaynab, being the only one of them still on speaking terms with all of her squabbling relatives.

Zaynab's composure cracked for a moment, but then a serene smile lit her face. "Everything's fine," she said smoothly. "God be praised."

Ali didn't believe that for a moment. "Zaynab . . ."

"Truly," she insisted, though a little of the spark had left her eyes. "You know me . . . the spoiled princess without a care."

Ali shook his head. "You're not that." He grinned. "Well, perhaps a little bit of the first part." He ducked when she tried to swat him.

"I hope you guard your tongue better when you're in front of Amma," Zaynab warned. "She didn't think highly of your dashing back to the Citadel and had some rather choice words to say about the fate that befalls ungrateful sons."

Ali cleared his throat. "Anything . . . specific?" he asked, repressing a shiver.

Zaynab smiled sweetly. "I hope you've been saying your prayers, little brother."

QUEEN HATSET'S SPRAWLING APARTMENTS WERE LO-cated on one of the highest levels of the palatial ziggurat, and Ali could not help but admire the view as they climbed the stairs. The city looked like a toy below, a sprawl of miniature buildings and scurrying ant-size inhabitants.

They ducked through the intricately carved teak door that led to his mother's pavilion, and Ali held his breath. Designed to mimic the enchantments of her beloved homeland, the pavilion first appeared to be the ruins of a once magnificent coral castle, like the many human ones dotting the coast of Ta Ntry. But then with a teasing swirl of smoke and magic, it shimmered back to its glory before his eyes: a lush salon of gem-studded coral archways, lined with planters of rich marsh grasses, emerald palms, and Nile lilies. The pavilion had been a marriage gift from Ghassan, meant to ease the homesickness of his new Ayaanle bride—a gesture that spoke to a kinder version of his father than Ali had known. The air smelled of myrrh, and the sounds of a lute and laughter drifted from behind gently billowing purple and gold linen curtains.

Familiar laughter. Ali steeled himself as they passed the curtain. But whatever he was expecting . . . the scene before him was certainly not it.

Queen Hatset sat on a low couch, half bent over a beautifully carved lapis lazuli game board, chuckling with a shafit man and woman. A little girl sat in her lap, toying with the gold ornaments in his mother's braids.

Ali stared in astonishment. It was the shafit girl and her father from the auction, the ones he'd feared he'd doomed. Here they were, with smiles on their faces, dressed in clothing befitting Ayaanle nobles.

Hatset glanced up. Delight, relief, and not a little bit of mischief lit her gold eyes. "Alu! How lovely to *finally* see you." She patted the little girl's cheek and then handed her to the other woman—her mother, judging from the resemblance. "I've been teaching your friends how to play senet." She rose to her feet gracefully, crossing the pavilion. "It seems I had quite a bit of time on my hands, waiting for you."

Ali was still at a loss for words when his mother reached him. "I . . ."

She pulled him into a fierce hug. "Oh, baba," she whispered, holding him tight. Her cheeks were wet. "God be praised for letting me look upon you again."

Ali was caught off guard by the wave of emotion that swept him upon being in his mother's arms again for the first time in years. Hatset. The woman who'd birthed him, whose family had betrayed him and then schemed to drag him away from the life he was building in Bir Nabat. He should have been furious—and yet as she pulled back to touch his cheek, he felt some of the anger he'd been carrying evaporate. God, but how many times had he looked at her face as a child and held the edge of her shayla, followed her absentmindedly through the harem, and cried for her in Ntaran during his first lonely, frightening nights at the Citadel?

"Peace be upon you, Amma," he managed. The curious gazes of the shafit family brought him back to the present, and Ali stepped away, trying to clamp down on his emotions. "How did you—"

"I heard about their misfortune and decided to help." Hatset glanced back at the shafit family with a smile. "I suggested they join my service here at the palace rather than return to their home. It is safer."

The shafit woman touched her heart. "We are much indebted to you, my queen."

Hatset shook her head and then pulled Ali forward firmly. "Nonsense, sister. It is a crime that you were ever even briefly separated."

The woman blushed, bowing her head. "We'll give you some time with your son."

"Thank you." His mother pushed him into the couch with what seemed like unnecessary force and then glanced at the remaining attendants. "My ladies, would you mind seeing if the kitchens can prepare some proper Ntaran food for my son?" She smiled pleasantly at him. "He looks like an underfed hawk."

"Yes, my queen." They vanished, leaving Ali alone with his mother and sister.

In a second, the two women whirled on him, looming over the couch into which he'd been shoved. Neither looked happy.

Ali immediately raised his hands in a gesture of surrender. "I was going to come see you, I swear."

"Oh? When?" Hatset crossed her arms, her smile gone. "After you'd seen everyone else in Daevabad?"

"It's only been two days," he protested. "It was a long journey. I needed time to recover—"

"And yet you had time to visit your brother's wife."

Ali's mouth dropped. How had his mother known *that*? "Do you have spies among the birds now?"

"I do not share a palace with vengeful Nahids and their apothecary of poisons without knowing what they're up to at all times." Her expression darkened. "And that was not a visit you should have made alone. People talk."

He bit his lip but stayed silent. He couldn't exactly argue with her on that point.

His mother's gaze trailed him, lingering on the scar on his temple. "What is that?"

"Just a scar," Ali said quickly. "I injured myself quarrying rock for Bir Nabat's canals."

Hatset continued studying him. "You look like you just robbed a caravan," she assessed bluntly and then wrinkled her nose. "Smell like it too. Why have you not been to the hammam and changed into something that doesn't have the blood of God only knows who all over it?"

Ali scowled. He had a very good reason for avoiding the hammam: he didn't want anyone catching a glimpse of the scars covering his body. "I like this robe," he said defensively.

Zaynab looked like she was struggling not to laugh. She fell into the seat beside him. "I'm sorry," she rushed to say when Hatset threw her an exasperated glare. "I mean . . . did you think his personality would improve out there?"

"Yes," Hatset replied sharply. "I'd hope after being sent to Am Gezira to die, he'd be sharper. Your appearance shapes your public image, Alizayd, and wandering around Daevabad in bloody rags looking like a lost sheep is not particularly impressive."

A little offended, Ali retorted, "Is that what you're doing with that poor family, then? Dressing them up, parading them around in order to shape your image?"

Hatset narrowed her eyes. "What are their names?"

"What?"

"Their names. What are the names of the people *you* put a target on?" She pressed on when Ali flustered. "You don't know, do you? Then I'll tell you. The woman is Mariam, a shafit from Sumatra. Her husband is Ashok and their daughter is Manat. Despite the city's problems, they've been managing fine. So well, in fact, that Ashok's success in running a food stall attracted the jealousy of one of their neighbors, who gave them up to that foul trader's roaming goons. But Ashok likes cooking, so I've gotten him a position in the palace kitchens and rooms where he may live with his wife while she attends me in the harem and her daughter takes lessons with the other children."

Ali was chastened, but not enough to be unsuspicious. "And why would you do such a thing?"

"Someone needed to fix my son's mistake." When Ali flushed, she continued, "I'm also a believer, and it is a great sin to abuse the shafit. Trust me when I say I find what's happening in Daevabad to be as abhorrent as you do."

"My 'cousin' Musa said a very similar thing before sabotaging my village's well in an effort to force his cargo upon me," Ali replied. "I take it you were behind that as well?"

There was a moment of silence, the two women exchanging a look before Zaynab spoke up, her voice uncharacteristically abashed. "That . . . that might have been my idea." When Ali spun on her, she gave him a helpless look. "I was worried you would never come back! My messengers said it seemed like you were settling in!"

"I was! It was *nice*." Ali couldn't believe what he was hearing. He pressed his hands against his knees, fighting his temper. The plot might have been Zaynab's, but this was a game his mother had started. "But maybe if we're going to speak so *plainly* we can talk about the reason I was sent to Am Gezira in the first place."

His mother actually smiled. It was a little unnerving, seeing that sharp delighted grin he'd been told more than once that he shared. The years had not aged Hatset like they had his father. She was every inch the queen, and she straightened up as if he'd issued her a challenge, adjusting her shayla like it was battle armor.

"Zaynab, my love . . . ," she started slowly, not taking her eyes from Ali. A prickle of fear danced over the nape of his neck. "Would you mind leaving us?"

His sister glanced between them, looking alarmed. "Maybe I should stay."

"You should go." His mother's careful smile didn't waver as she took a seat on the opposite couch, but her voice had an authoritative edge. "Your brother clearly has some things he'd like to say to me."

Zaynab sighed and stood. "Good luck, akhi." She squeezed his shoulder again and was gone.

"Alu," Hatset said, in a tone that made Ali fairly certain he was about to be slapped again, "I know you're not insinuating that the woman who carried and birthed you, enormous potato head and all, was involved in that idiotic conspiracy with the Tanzeem."

Ali swallowed. "Abba said they had Ayaanle backers," he said, defending himself. "That one of them was your cousin—"

"Indeed, one of them was. *Was*," his mother repeated, the deadly intent clear in her voice. "I don't deal lightly with those who risk the lives of the ones I love. And on some half-baked scheme at that." She rolled her eyes. "A revolution. How unnecessarily bloody."

"You sound more annoyed by the *method* than by the idea of treason."

"And?" Hatset picked up a fragrant cup of tea from a nearby table, taking a sip. "You're looking at the wrong person if you expect me to defend your father's rule. He's been going astray for years. You clearly agreed with that assessment if you were willing to join the Tanzeem."

He winced, her words finding their mark. He had disagreed—violently—with his father's handling of the shafit. He still very much did. "I was just trying to help the shafit," he insisted. "There was nothing political in it."

His mother gave him an almost pitying look. "There is nothing nonpolitical about someone named 'Zaydi al Qahtani' trying to help the shafit."

At that, Ali dropped his gaze. His name didn't feel like an inspiration these days—it felt like a burden. "He was certainly better at it than I."

Hatset sighed and then moved to sit beside him. "You are still so much the boy I remember," she said, her voice softer. "From the time you could walk, you'd follow me through the harem, babbling about everything you could see. The smallest things would fill you with delight, with wonder . . . The other women declared you the most curious child they'd ever encountered. The sweetest." Her eyes flashed with old betrayal. "Then Ghassan took you from me. They locked you away in the Citadel, put a zulfiqar in your hand, and taught you to be your brother's weapon." Her voice hitched on the last word. "But still I see that innocence in you. That goodness."

Ali didn't know what to say to that. He ran his fingers over the striped blue silk of the couch. It felt soft as a rosebud, far finer than anything he'd sat on in Am Gezira, and yet that was where he ached to be, assassins be damned. A place where helping others was a simple matter of digging a well. "That goodness has gotten me nowhere in Daevabad. Everyone I try to help ends up worse off."

"You don't stop fighting a war just because you're losing battles, Alizayd. You change tactics. Surely, that's a lesson you learned in the Citadel."

Ali shook his head. They were veering too close to a conversation he didn't want to have. "There's no war to be won here. Not by me. Abba wanted to teach me a lesson, and I've learned it. I'll stay in the Citadel with a zulfiqar in my hand and my mouth firmly shut until Navasatem."

"While down the street, shafit are auctioned off like cattle?" Hatset challenged. "While your brothers in the Royal Guard are reduced to training with blunt knives and eating spoiled food so nobles can feast and dance during the holiday?"

"*I can't help them.* And you're hardly innocent in this," Ali accused. "Do you think I don't know the games the Ayaanle are playing with Daevabad's economy?"

Hatset returned his glare. "You are far too clever to believe the Ayaanle are the only reason for Daevabad's financial problems. We are a scapegoat; a slight diminishment in taxes does not do the damage I know you've seen. Keeping a third of the population in slavery and squalor does. Oppressing another third to the point where they self-segregate does." Her tone grew intent. "People do not thrive under tyrants, Alizayd; they do not come up with innovations when they're busy trying to stay alive, or offer creative ideas when error is punished by the hooves of a karkadann."

Ali rose to his feet, wishing he could refute her words. "Go tell these things to Muntadhir. He is the emir."

"Muntadhir doesn't have it in him to act." Hatset's voice was surprisingly kind. "I like your brother. He is the most charming man I know, and he too has a good heart. But your father has carved his beliefs into Muntadhir deeper than you realize. He will reign as Ghassan does: so afraid of his people that he crushes them."

Ali paced, fighting the water that wanted to burst from his hands. "And what would you have me do, Amma?"

"*Help* him," Hatset insisted. "You don't need to be a weapon to be an asset."

He was already shaking his head. "Muntadhir hates me," he said bitterly, the blunt statement salting the wound his brother had inflicted when Ali first returned. "He's not going to listen to anything I say."

"He doesn't hate you. He's hurt, he's lost, and he's lashing out. But those are dangerous impulses when a man has as much power as your brother, and he's going down a path from which he might not be able to return." Her voice darkened. "And that path, Alu? It might present you with choices far worse than talking to him."

Ali was suddenly conscious of the water in the pitcher on the table next to him, in the fountains lining the pavilion, and in the pipes under the floor. It pulled on him, feeding off his mounting agitation.

"I can't talk about this right now, Amma." He ran his hands over his face, pulling at his beard.

Hatset stilled. "What is that on your wrist?"

Ali glanced down, his heart skipping as he realized the sleeve of his damn robe had fallen back once more. He kicked himself. After his encounter with Nahri, he'd sworn he'd find something new to wear. But uniforms at the Citadel had been scarce, and he hated to inconvenience the already struggling men.

Hatset was on her feet and at his side before Ali could respond; he hadn't actually realized his mother could move so quickly. She grabbed his arm. Ali tried to pull back, but not wanting to hurt her—and underestimating her strength—he was not fast enough to block her before she'd shoved the sleeve back to his shoulder.

She gasped, pressing the bumpy edge of the scar that wrapped his wrist. "Where did you get this?" she asked, alarm rising in her voice.

Ali panicked. "Am-Am Gezira," he stammered. "It's nothing. An old injury."

Her gaze trailed his body again. "You haven't been to the hammam . . . ," she said, echoing her earlier words. "Nor taken off this filthy robe." Her eyes darted to his. "Alu . . . are there more of these scars on your body?"

Ali's stomach dropped. She'd asked the question far too knowingly.

"Take it off." His mother was pulling the robe from his shoulders before he could move. Underneath, he wore a sleeve-less tunic and a waist-wrap that came to his calves.

Hatset inhaled. She grabbed his arms, examining the scars that crossed his skin. Her fingers lingered at the ragged line crocodile teeth had torn just below his collarbone, and then she picked up his hand, touching the seared impression of a large fishing hook. Horror filled her eyes. "Alizayd, *how did you get these?*"

Ali trembled, torn between the promise he'd made to his father not to speak of that night and his desperate desire to know what had happened to him beneath the lake's dark water. Ghassan had implied that the Ayaanle had an ancient tie to the marid—that they'd used them to aid in the conquest of Daevabad—and during his darkest days, Ali had been terribly tempted to find someone from his mother's homeland and beg for information.

He said no one could know. Abba said no one could ever know.

Hatset must have seen the indecision warring in his expression. "Alu, look at me." She took his face between her hands, forcing him to meet her gaze. "I know you don't trust me. I know we have our differences. But this? This goes beyond all that. I need you to tell me the truth. *Where did you get these scars?*"

He stared into her warm gold eyes—the eyes that had comforted Ali since he was a child skinning his elbows while climbing trees in the harem—and the truth tumbled out. "The lake," he said, his voice the barest of whispers. "I fell in the lake."

"The lake?" she repeated. "*Daevabad's* lake?" Her eyes went wide. "Your fight with the Afshin. I heard he knocked you overboard, but that you caught yourself before you reached the water."

Ali shook his head. "Not quite," he replied, his throat catching.

She took a deep breath. "Oh, baba . . . here I am discussing politics . . ." She held on to his hands. "Tell me what happened."

Ali shook his head. "I don't remember much. Darayavahoush shot me. I lost my balance and fell in the water. There was something in it, some sort of presence tearing at me, tearing through my mind, and when it saw the Afshin . . ." He shuddered. "Whatever it was, it was so *angry*, Amma. It said it needed my name."

"Your name?" Hatset's voice rose. "Did you give it?"

He nodded, ashamed. "It forced these visions upon me. Dae-vabad destroyed, all of you murdered . . ." His voice broke. "It made me see them again and again, all while it attached itself to me, biting and ripping at my skin. Zaynab and Muntadhir were screaming for me to save them, to give my name and I . . . I broke." He could barely say the last words.

Hatset pulled him into a hug. "You didn't break, child," she insisted, stroking his back. "You couldn't have fought them."

Nerves fluttered in his stomach. "You know what it was, then?"

His mother nodded, pulling back to touch the hooked scar in his palm. "I'm Ayaanle. I know what leaves these marks."

The word lay unsaid between them another moment, and then Ali couldn't bear it. "It was a marid, wasn't it? A marid did this."

He didn't miss the way her gold eyes flickered around the pavilion before she replied—that she did so for this and not while discussing treason was telling. And not reassuring. "Yes." She let go of his hands. "What happened after you gave your name?"

Ali swallowed. "It took over me. Muntadhir said it looked like I was possessed, that I was speaking a strange language." He bit his lip. "It used me to kill Darayavahoush, but I don't remember any-thing between giving my name and waking up in the infirmary."

"The infirmary?" His mother's voice was sharp. "Does that Nahid girl know—"

"No." The danger in the question and a tug of old loyalty pushed the lie from his lips. "She wasn't there. Only Abba and Muntadhir know what happened."

Hatset's eyes narrowed. "Your father knew the marid did all this to you and *still* he sent you to Am Gezira?"

Ali grimaced but could not deny the relief coursing through him. It felt so good to finally talk about all this with someone who knew more, someone who could help him. "I'm not sure I would have survived Am Gezira if the marid hadn't possessed me."

She frowned. "What do you mean?"

He looked at her in surprise. "My abilities, Amma. You must realize that's what's behind my irrigation work."

Too late, he recognized the horror crossing her face. "Your *abilities*?" she repeated.

His heart raced at the shock in her voice. "My . . . my abilities with water. Abba said the Ayaanle had a relationship with the marid. You recognized their marks . . ." Desperate hope clawed up in Ali's chest. "That means this happens to djinn back in Ta Ntry, doesn't it?"

"No, baba . . ." Hatset took his hands in hers again. "Not like this. We find . . ." She cleared her throat. "We find bodies, love. Bodies with marks like yours. Djinn fishermen who stay out past sundown, human children lured to the riverbank. They're murdered, drowned, and drained."

Ali reeled. *Bodies?* "But I thought . . ." He choked on the words. "Didn't our ancestors revere the marid?"

Hatset shook her head. "I don't know what was between our ancestors, but the marid have been a terror as long as I've been alive. We keep it to ourselves; we'd rather handle our own business than invite foreign soldiers into Ta Ntry. And the attacks are rare. We've learned to avoid the places they like."

Ali was struggling to comprehend what he was hearing. "Then how did I survive?"

His mother—his always savvy mother—looked equally at a loss. "I don't know."

A door hinge creaked, and Ali yanked his robe back on so fast he heard some of the stitches tear. By the time a pair of servants joined them, Hatset's face was calm; but he didn't miss the grief with which she'd watched him move.

She offered a small smile to the servants as they set down a tray of covered silver platters. "Thank you."

They removed the tops, and Ali's heart and stomach gave a leap at the familiar smells of the Ntaran dishes he'd loved as a child. Fried plaintains and anise-spiced rice, fish steamed in banana leaf with ginger and grated coconut, and syrupy dumplings.

"I remember your favorites," Hatset said softly when they were alone again. "A mother doesn't forget something like that."

Ali didn't respond. He didn't know what to say. The answers he'd wanted for years about the marid had left worse questions and more mysteries in their wake. What happened to him wasn't something that happened to other Ayaanle. The marid were a terror in Ta Ntry, monsters to be feared.

Monsters who had saved him. Ali shifted, completely on edge. The possession in the lake had been vicious, but his abilities after had felt . . . calming. The solace when he ran his hands through a canal, the near playfulness with which new springs bubbled beneath his feet. What was that all supposed to mean?

His mother touched his wrist. "Alu, it's okay," she said, breaking the silence. "You're alive. That's all that matters now. Whatever the marid did to you . . . it's over."

"That's just it, Amma . . . it's not over," Ali said softly. "It's getting worse. Ever since I came back to Daevabad . . . I feel like these things are *inside* me, slipping over my skin, whispering in my head . . . and if I lose control . . ." He shivered. "People used to kill djinn they suspected of cavorting with the marid."

"That's not going to happen," she declared firmly. "Not to you. I'll take care of this."

Ali bit his lip, wanting to believe her but seeing little way out of a mess it was clear neither of them understood. "How?"

"First, we fix . . . this," she said, waving a hand over his body. "You'll use my hammam from now on. Send the servants away with one of your rants about modesty, and they'll have no problem letting you bathe alone. I also have an Agnivanshi tailor I trust completely. I'll tell him your scars are from the Afshin and you want them hidden. I'm sure he can design you some new clothes to do so."

"Alizayd the Afshin-slayer," he repeated grimly. "How fortunate that I'm known for killing a man who liked to scourge his opponents."

"It's a stroke of fortune I'll take," Hatset replied. "In the meantime, I'm going to reach out to a scholar I'm acquainted with. He can be a bit . . . *difficult*. But he probably knows more about the marid than anyone else alive."

Hope rose in Ali's voice. "And you think he can help us?"

"It's worth a try. For now, put this business with the marid out of your mind. And *eat*." Hatset pushed the platters at him. "I'd like to have you looking like less of a wraith by week's end."

Ali picked up a pitcher of rosewater to rinse his hands. "Why by week's end?"

"Because that's when your father is holding a feast to celebrate your return."

Ali scowled, plucking a bit of rice and stew from the plate with his fingers. "I wish he'd hold a feast to send me somewhere that isn't a marid-haunted island surrounded by a cursed lake."

"He's not going to be sending you anywhere if I have any say in it." She poured a cup of tamarind juice and pushed it in his direction. "I just got you back, baba." Her voice was fierce. "And if I have to fight some marid to keep you, so be it."

12
NAHRI

Because a lost little girl from Cairo thought she was living in some sort of fairy tale. And because for all her supposed cleverness, she couldn't see that the dashing hero who saved her was its monster.

Nahri closed her eyes, quietly obeying the whispered commands of the servants painting her face. Muntadhir's cruel taunt played ceaselessly in her mind; she'd been thinking about his words for days now, the accusation all the more haunting because for the life of her, Nahri could not help but fear it contained a kernel of truth.

One of her maids approached with a selection of ornate hair combs shaped like various birds. "Which would you like, my lady?"

Nahri stared at the jeweled combs, too glum to even silently assess their value. Her braids were already undone, her black curls spilling wildly to her waist. She touched her hair, twisting one lock around a finger. "It's fine like this."

Two of her maids exchanged nervous looks, and from the corner of the room where she'd been watching Nahri dress with open concern, Nisreen coughed.

"My lady, with all respect . . . between your hair and the dress, you do not quite appear to be going to a ceremonial event," her mentor said delicately.

No, I probably look like I'm about to visit my husband's bed, which is ironic because I'm damn well never doing that again. Nahri had again chosen to wear the sleeveless linen gown with the elaborate beaded collar that reminded her of Egypt. The prospect of interacting with the Qahtanis left her anxious and she wanted to cling to something familiar.

And she didn't really care what anyone else thought about it. "I'm going like this. It's a Geziri feast, and there won't be any men in the women's section to see me either way."

Nisreen sighed, perhaps recognizing defeat. "I take it I am still to come up with some sort of emergency so that you can leave early?"

"Please." Nahri couldn't entirely snub the feast, but she could make sure she spent as little time there as possible. "Did you happen to notice if Jamshid left?"

"He did. He insisted on helping me restock the apothecary shelves and then departed. I told him he needed another day to recover, but—"

"But he wants to be at Muntadhir's side." Nahri waited until the maids had left to finish the sentence. "Muntadhir doesn't deserve him."

"I don't disagree." When Nahri moved to stand, Nisreen touched her shoulder. "You'll take care with the queen tonight?"

"I always do." It was the truth; Nahri evaded Hatset like she owed the older woman money. From what Nahri had observed, the queen was Ghassan's equal in cunning and resource, but whereas the king desired Nahri as an ally—in name at least—Hatset wanted nothing to do with her, treating her with the wary disdain someone might show an ill-mannered dog.

Which was fine with Nahri, especially tonight. She would steal a few minutes to eat—possibly *actually* steal one of the gold carving knives used during state functions just to make herself feel better—and then be gone without having to talk to either of the Qahtani princes.

Draping a snow-white chador embroidered with sunbursts of sapphires over her head, she followed a female steward through the open corridor that led to the formal gardens in front of Ghassan's throne room. Globes of enchanted flames in rainbow-bright hues nestled in the fruit trees, and fine carpets embroidered with hunting scenes had been laid upon the trimmed grass. Tiny jade hummingbirds glittered as they sang and swooped between delicate copper feeders, their song mingling with the strumming of lutes. The air was fragrant with jasmine, musk, and roasted meat. The last made her stomach rumble sadly; Nahri hadn't touched meat since committing to her role as Banu Nahida.

Directly ahead was an enormous tent constructed with swaths of silver silk that shimmered under the moonlight. The steward pulled aside one of the pearly curtains, and Nahri stepped inside the perfumed interior.

Its opulence was a mockery of the tents the nomadic Geziris would have once called home. Stunning hand-loomed rugs in a riot of colors lay thick upon the ground, and an illusionist had conjured up a constellation of miniature fireworks to swirl and sparkle overhead. Fire burned in wide, open golden lamps—the djinn had a strong aversion to the small, closed ones often used as slave vessels by the ifrit.

The tent was warm and packed; Nahri slipped out of her chador, handing it off to a waiting attendant and blinking as her eyes adjusted to the crowded, firelit interior. Past the bustle

of servants and guests lingering near the entrance, she caught
a glimpse of Queen Hatset and Princess Zaynab holding court
on a raised marble dais scattered with ebony and gold cushions.
Cursing the etiquette that required her to greet them first, Nahri
made her way across the floor. She was determined to ignore the
raised eyebrows she knew her dress would attract, so she refused
to look at the other women . . . which meant she realized too late
that many had pulled their various shaylas and veils over their
heads.

The reason why sat between his mother and sister.

It took Nahri a moment to recognize the finely dressed young
man in the robes of an Ayaanle noble as the traitorous former
friend she'd contemplated murdering in her garden a few days
ago. Gone were the filthy traveling robe and ragged ghutra. Over
a rich, black dishdasha trimmed with pale moonstone beads, Ali
wore a grass-green robe patterned in silver ikat, a cheerfully
colored garment deeply uncharacteristic of the taciturn prince. A
beautiful silver turban crowned his head, wrapped in the Geziri
style that revealed the copper relic bolted to his ear.

Ali looked equally taken aback by the sight of Nahri, his
shocked gaze traveling from her uncovered head down her bare
arms. She heard him take a sharp breath, and she bristled; given
Ali's conservative views, he probably thought the dress even more
inappropriate than Nisreen had.

"Banu Nahida," Hatset greeted her, beckoning Nahri closer
with a hand that sparkled with golden rings. "There you are.
Come, join us!"

Nahri approached, bowing her head as she brought her hands
together. "Peace be upon you all," she said, in her best attempt at
ingratiating politeness.

"And upon you peace, dear daughter." Hatset gave her a warm
smile. The royal women looked stunning, as usual. Hatset wore
a silk abaya dyed in saffron and crimson, the fabric shimmering

like a flame under a midnight-colored shayla trimmed in Geziri pearls. Zaynab—who could drive men to their knees dressed in an ill-fitting sack—was clad in a gown that looked like a waterfall had come to life and decided to worship her, a cascade of teal, emerald, and cobalt blue held together by a collar of real lotus flowers. "I was beginning to fear something might have happened to you when you didn't arrive with your husband."

The words were said with far too much intent, but Nahri wasn't surprised: there seemed to be very little Hatset didn't know about the domestic happenings of the palace. Nahri had no doubt a few of her maids were in the queen's employ—and that news of her argument with Muntadhir had already been relayed.

But Nahri was not discussing her marital woes with this woman. She feigned a smile. "Forgive my tardiness. I had a patient."

Hatset's golden eyes twinkled. "No apology necessary." She gestured to Nahri's dress. "That is quite lovely. A little different, to be sure, but very beautiful." Her voice took on a teasing tone. "Alu, doesn't she look pretty?" she asked her son.

Ali's gaze was darting everywhere but at Nahri. "I, er, yes," he stammered. "I should go. The men will be expecting me."

Hatset grabbed his wrist. "Remember to talk to people . . . and about things *other* than hadith and economics, for the love of God, Alizayd. Tell some exciting stories about Am Gezira."

Ali rose to his feet. Nahri hated to admit such a thing, but he looked striking in his new clothes, the beautifully dyed robe highlighting his haughty features and luminous dark skin. She supposed that's what happened when you let your mother dress you.

He kept his gaze on the floor as he passed her. "In peace," he said softly.

"Go jump in the lake," she returned under her breath in Arabic. She saw him tense but he didn't stop.

Hatset smiled as she watched him walk away, her expression both proud and fiercely protective.

Of course she's proud; she's probably been conspiring to get him back here for years. Nahri had been turning over in her mind the conversation she'd overheard between Muntadhir and Jamshid since her run-in with Ali. She wondered if there was any truth to her husband's concerns about the deadly intentions of the "mother" she now knew was Hatset.

The queen's gaze shifted back to Nahri. "Dear one, why are you still standing? Sit," she commanded, gesturing to the cushion next to Zaynab. "My daughter has already accidentally knocked aside the tent panel in front of us to improve our view. And you always hide yourself away at these things." She nodded at the platters surrounding them. "I've had the kitchens bring out some vegetarian dishes for you."

Nahri went from baffled to suspicious in one fell swoop. Hatset was clearly up to something—so much so that the queen was barely attempting to hide it with her question about Muntadhir and her exuberant friendliness. And the rather obvious comment to Ali about her dress.

Nahri's cheeks suddenly burned. Oh, no . . . she was not letting herself get dragged between the estranged brothers that way. She had enough problems of her own. But neither could she be rude. Hatset was the queen—wealthy, powerful, and with as much of an iron fist when it came to the harem as her husband held over the city. Daevabad's royal harem was enormously influential; here marriages between their world's most powerful families were debated, and here posts and contracts were given out that changed lives . . . all under the watchful eye of the djinn queen.

So when Hatset again gestured to the cushion next to Zaynab, Nahri sat.

"I take it you knock aside tent panels with the same frequency that your empty litter dallies in the Geziri bazaar?" she whispered to her sister-in-law. Zaynab rolled her eyes, and Nahri continued, gesturing at the platters of fruit and pastries spread before her.

"This reminds me of the first time we met. I mean . . . before you purposely got me so intoxicated I passed out."

Zaynab shrugged. "I was trying to be a good host," she said airily. "How was I to know the potency of such forbidden substances?"

Nahri shook her head, stealing a glance through the billowing tent partitions at the men's section. The jeweled stakes pinning the silk had indeed been knocked aside in front of them, giving Nahri a fairly good view. Ahead, the Qahtani men sat with their closest retainers on a beautiful white jade platform that floated upon the lush grass. The platform was stunning, its edges carved with an assortment of leaping oryxes, sly-eyed sphinxes, and soaring simurghs. Precious stones and gems highlighted the length of a horn, the sweep of a tail, and the delicate array of feathers on a wing. The men reclined upon silk cushions, wine cups and spun glass water pipes scattered about them.

At the center of course, was Ghassan al Qahtani. Nahri's skin prickled as she looked at the djinn king. It always did—there was far too much history between them. The man who held her life in his hands, who controlled her as thoroughly as if he'd locked her away, her chains the lives of the Daevas and friends he would destroy if she so much as thought about stepping out of line.

He looked calm and as inscrutable as ever, dressed in royal robes and his striking silk turban—a turban Nahri couldn't look at without recalling the cold way he'd revealed the truth about Dara and Qui-zi to her on that rain-soaked pavilion five years ago. Early in her marriage, Nahri had quietly asked Muntadhir to take his off before they were alone—a request he had granted without comment and one he'd religiously followed.

Her gaze went to him now. She hadn't spoken to her husband since their fight in the infirmary, and seeing him there, dressed in the same official robes and turban as his father, deepened her unease. Jamshid was at his side, of course, their knees brushing, but there were others as well, most of whom Nahri recognized. Wealthy, well-connected men all of them . . . but they were also Muntadhir's friends, true ones. One appeared to be telling Muntadhir a story, while another passed him a water pipe.

It looked as though they were trying to keep his spirits up—or perhaps distract him from the other side of the platform, where Ali had taken a seat. Though he lacked his older brother's dazzling array of jewelry, the starkness of his attire seemed to elevate him. At Ali's left were several officers from the Royal Guard, along with a thickly bearded man with an infectious grin and a severe-eyed woman in male dress. On his right, the Qaid appeared to be telling a story at which Ghassan gave a hearty laugh. Ali remained silent, his gaze flitting between his companions and a large glass pitcher of water on the rug before him.

And though it was a beautiful night in an enchanted garden, filled with guests who looked like they might have stepped from the pages of a book of legends, Nahri had a sense of foreboding. The things Muntadhir had whispered to Jamshid, whatever Hatset was up to . . . Nahri could see it playing out in the scene before her. Daevabad's sophisticated elites—the literati noblemen and wealthy traders—had flocked to Muntadhir. The rougher men who wielded blades, and the ones who could stand before the Friday crowds and fill their hearts with holy purpose . . . they were with Ali.

And if those brothers remained divided, if those groups turned on each other . . . Nahri didn't see it ending well for her people—for any of them.

Her stomach rumbled. Impending civil war or not, there was little Nahri could do to save her tribe on an empty stomach. Not particularly caring about etiquette, she pulled over a tiled glass dish of knafeh and a reed platter of fruit, fully determined to gorge herself on cheese pastry and melon.

The nape of her neck prickled. Nahri glanced back up.

Through the narrow opening, Ali was watching her.

She met his troubled gray eyes. Nahri typically tried to close herself off from her abilities in crowds like this, the competing heartbeats and gurgling humors an irritating distraction. But for a moment she let them expand.

Ali stood out like a spot on the eye, a deep silence in the ocean of sounds.

You're my friend, she remembered him declaring the first time she'd saved his life, with the utter confidence the haze of opium had instilled. *A light*, he'd added when he begged her not to follow Dara.

Annoyed by the unwanted, unsettling feeling the memory caused, she snatched up one of the serving knives. Still holding his gaze, she plunged it deep into a piece of melon, then began carving it with surgical precision. Ali drew up, looking both startled and somehow still snobbish. Nahri glared, and he finally looked away.

Ahead, Ghassan clapped his hands. Nahri watched as he gazed warmly at the crowd.

"My friends, I thank you for honoring my family with your presence here tonight." He beamed at Ali. "And I thank God for allowing me the joy of seeing my youngest again. It is a blessing whose value I didn't quite realize until he came striding into my palace dressed like some northern raider."

That brought a chuckle to the mostly Geziri crowd, and Ghassan continued. "Prince Alizayd, of course, wanted none of this. If he had his way, we'd share a single platter of dates and perhaps a pot of the coffee I hear he now brews himself." Ghassan's voice turned teasing. "Then he would likely give us a lecture on the benefit of estate taxes."

Ali's companions burst into laughter at that. Muntadhir was clenching his wine cup, and Nahri didn't miss the quiet way Jamshid lowered her husband's hand.

"I will, however, save you from such a thing," Ghassan said. "Indeed, I've something else planned. My chefs have been furiously attempting to outdo each other in advance of Navasatem, so I issued them a challenge this evening. Prepare their finest dish, and my son will choose the best cook to design the menu for the generation celebrations."

Nahri grew a bit intrigued at that. Five years in Daevabad had yet to completely inure her to its marvels, and she was sure whatever the royal chefs conjured would be magnificent indeed. She watched as more servants wound their way through the royal platform, some pouring rosewater over the hands of the men while others refilled cups. Turning away a wine bearer, Ali beckoned politely to a young man holding a glass pitcher icy with condensation.

Before the servant could reach the prince, Jamshid stopped him, holding out his arm in a slightly rude—or perhaps inebriated—manner. He took the pitcher and poured his own glass of what Nahri recognized as tamarind juice, before pushing it back at the other man. He took a sip and then set his cup down, reaching out to quickly squeeze Muntadhir's knee.

Ghassan clapped his hands again and then Nahri wasn't looking at Jamshid.

Because a damned boat had joined them.

Carved from teak and large enough to fit the royal family, the boat swept in on a wave of conjured smoke, a miniature version of the great sewn ships said to sail the Indian Ocean. On its silk sail, the emblem of the Sahrayn tribe had been painted, and indeed the man accompanying it was Sahrayn, his striped hood thrown back to reveal red-streaked black hair.

He bowed low. "Majesty, Your Royal Highnesses, peace be upon you all."

"And upon you peace," Ghassan replied, looking bemused. "An impressive presentation. What do you have for us, then?"

"The finest of delicacies from Qart Sahar: cave eels. They are found only in the deepest, most forbidden cisterns of the Sahara. We capture them alive, bringing them back in great vats of saltwater, and then prepare them in a scented broth of the most delicate perfumes and preserved vinegars." He beamed, gesturing to the boat . . . no, to the vat, Nahri realized, catching sight of several sinuous shapes churning in the dark liquid filling the bottom. "They have been swimming in there a whole fortnight."

The look on Ali's face was almost enough to make the whole evening worth it. He choked on his tamarind juice. "Swimming . . . they're still *alive*?"

"But of course." The Sahrayn chef gave him a puzzled look. "The thrashing makes the meat sweeter."

Muntadhir finally smiled. "Sahrayn eels. Now that is an honor, brother." He took a sip of his wine. "I believe the first bite belongs to you."

The chef beamed again, looking ready to burst with pride. "Shall I, my prince?"

Ali looked ill but motioned for him to continue.

The chef plunged a glittering brass trident into the vat, provoking a metallic shriek that drew startled yelps from the audience. The eel was still squirming as he quickly spun it into a nest and then placed it gingerly on a brightly patterned tile. He presented it to Ali with a flourish.

Muntadhir was watching with open delight on his face, and Nahri had to admit that in this, she and her husband were united.

Ali took the tile and choked down a bite of eel, swallowing hard before he spoke. "It's . . . it's very good," he said weakly. "It certainly tastes like it did a lot of thrashing."

There were tears in the chef's eyes. "I will carry your compliments to my grave," he wept.

The next two competitors did not offer quite the same level of presentation, though the diners looked considerably more pleased by the skewers of minced rukh kebab—Nahri could only imagine how someone had caught one of those—grilled with golden Tukharistani apples, studded with whole spices, and served while still aflame.

They were removing the largest platter of kabsa Nahri had ever seen, a shrewd move made by the Geziri chef who probably suspected a prince living in the countryside might long for comfort food after some of the competition's more "creative" dishes, when Ghassan frowned.

"Strange," he said. "I did not see the competitor from Agni—"

A simurgh soared into the garden with a shriek.

The glittering firebird—twice the size of a camel—swept over the crowd, its smoking wings setting an apricot tree aflame. By the time it fluttered to the ground, half the men had reached for their weapons.

"Hah! It worked!" A grinning Agnivanshi man with a singed mustache joined them. "Peace be upon you, my king and princes! How do you like my creation?"

Nahri watched hands slowly move away from dagger hilts. And then she clapped in delight when she realized what the man meant. The simurgh wasn't a simurgh, not really. It was a composite, constructed from what appeared to be a dizzying array of sweets in every color of creation.

The chef looked inordinately proud of himself. "A little different, I know . . . but what is the purpose of Navasatem if not to celebrate the sweetness of relief from Suleiman's servitude?"

Even the king looked dazzled. "I'll grant you points for creativity," Ghassan offered. He glanced at Ali. "What say you?"

Ali had risen to his feet to better examine the simurgh. "A stunning enchantment," he confessed. "I've never seen anything like this."

"You've never tasted anything like this either," the chef said smoothly. He tapped the simurgh's glass eye and it fell neatly into his hands, a waiting platter. He made a swift selection and then bowed as it was passed toward the prince.

Ali smiled, biting into crumbly pastry covered in silver foil. Appreciation lit his face. "That is delicious," he admitted.

The Agnivanshi chef shot a triumphant look at his competitors as Ali took a sip from his goblet and then tried another sweet. But this time, he frowned, reaching for his throat. He hooked his fingers around the collar of his dishdasha, tugging at the stiff fabric.

"You'll excuse me," he said. "I think I just . . ." He reached for his cup and then stumbled, knocking it over.

Ghassan straightened up, a look Nahri had never seen in his eyes. "Alizayd?"

Coughing, Ali didn't answer. His other hand went to his throat, and as the confusion in his expression turned to panic, his eyes met Nahri's again through the tent panel.

There was no anger there, no accusation. Just pained regret that sent a wave of cold dread through her before Ali even fell to his knees.

He gasped, and with the sound, Nahri was back on the boat, back in that horrible night five years ago. Dara had gasped like that, a hushed sound of true fear—an emotion she hadn't thought her Afshin could feel—as he fell to *his* knees. His beautiful eyes had met hers and then he'd gasped, his body crumbling into dust as she screamed.

From the corner of her eye, she saw Hatset fly to her feet. "Alizayd!"

And then it was chaos.

Ali collapsed, choking and clawing at his throat. Hatset burst through the tent, propriety abandoned as she raced to her son's side. Zaynab screamed, but before she could lunge forward, a pair of female guards descended, nearly knocking Nahri aside in their effort to pull the princess to safety. The Royal Guard was doing the same on the men's side, soldiers hustling a stunned Muntadhir back. The Qaid drew his zulfiqar and then actually grabbed Ghassan, locking him in a tight, protective grip.

No one stopped Hatset. Well, one of the guards tried, and she smashed the heavy goblet she was holding into his face, then dropped at Ali's side, shouting his name.

Nahri didn't move. She could see Dara's tear-streaked face before hers. *"Come with me. We'll leave, travel the world."*

His ashes on her hands. His ashes on the wet robe of his killer.

Everything seemed to go very still; the screams of the crowd faded, the thud of running feet fell away. A man was dying before her. It was a scene she knew well from the infirmary, one of desperate family members and scrambling aides. Nahri had learned not to hesitate, learned to shut her emotions off. She was a healer, a Nahid. The doctor she always wanted to be.

And in her dreams—her foolish dreams of being an apprentice to the great physicians in Istanbul, of taking her place in one of Cairo's famed hospitals—in those dreams, she was not the kind of doctor to sit and watch a man die.

She jumped to her feet.

She was halfway to Ali, close enough to see the shimmering silver vapors escaping the gashes he'd clawed in his skin, when Suleiman's seal crashed down upon her.

Nahri swooned, fighting for air herself, weak and bewildered by the sudden clash of incomprehensible languages. She spotted the seal glowing on Ghassan's face and then Hatset whirled on her, brandishing the goblet. Nahri froze.

Ali started screaming.

Blood blossomed from his mouth, from his throat and neck, silver shards emerging from his skin in bloody bursts. The silver vapors, Nahri realized. They'd turned to solid metal the instant Ghassan called upon the seal; their misty form must have been magical.

Ghassan had just killed his son trying to save him.

Nahri ran. "Lift the seal!" she shouted. "You're killing him!" Ali was seizing as he clutched his shredded throat. She dropped beside Hatset, snatching up one of the silver shards and holding it before the terrified queen. "Look for yourself! Did you not just see this change?"

Hatset glanced wildly between the shard and her dying son. She turned on Ghassan. "Lift it!"

The seal was gone in an instant, Nahri's powers surging back through her. "Help me turn him over!" she shouted as Ali's companions rushed to join them. She thrust a finger down his throat until he gagged and then pounded his back, black blood mingling with the silver gushing from his mouth. "Get me a board! I need to get him to the infirmary immediate—"

A blade whipped past her face.

Nahri jerked back, but it hadn't been meant for her. There was a heavy thump and then a muffled scream as the servant who'd served Ali's juice fell dead at the garden's entrance, the khanjar belonging to Ali's female companion buried in his back.

She didn't have long to dwell on it. Ali's eyes snapped open as they laid him on a stretched portion of cloth.

They were as black as oil. As black as they'd been when the marid took him.

Hatset clamped a hand over them, a little too fast. "The infirmary," she agreed in a shaky voice.

13

NAHRI

It took the rest of the night to save him. Though he'd vomited up most of the poison, what remained was pernicious, racing through his blood to whirl into solid form as it burst through his skin seeking air. Nahri would no sooner lance, clean, and heal a silver boil than another would bloom. By the time she was finished, Ali was a bloody wreck, and silver-soaked rags lay everywhere.

Fighting a wave of exhaustion, Nahri pressed a hand upon his damp brow. She closed her eyes, and that strange sensation rushed back: a deep, impenetrably dark curtain through which she could barely detect the thud of his heart. The scent of salt, of a cold and utterly alien presence.

But no hint of the destructive poison. She sat back, wiping her own brow and taking a deep breath. A violent tremor went through her body. It was a sensation that often overtook her after a particularly terrifying bit of Nahid healing, her nerves catching up only after she was done.

"He is all right?" Ali's friend—Lubayd, as he'd introduced himself—spoke up. He was the only one in the room with her, her own bedroom. Ghassan had commandeered it, insisting on privacy for his son, and in response, Nahri had kicked both him and Hatset out, declaring that she couldn't work with Ali's worried parents hovering over her.

"I think so." She hoped so anyway. She had dealt with poisonings—both intentional and not—plenty of times since arriving in Daevabad, but nothing that worked with such speed and deadliness. Though it was obvious the silver vapors would have eventually choked him, the way they'd turned to metal shards when Ghassan had used Suleiman's seal . . . that was a diabolical bit of cruelty, and Nahri had no idea who might have devised something so vicious.

Looking relieved, Lubayd nodded and retreated to a corner of the room while Nahri returned to her work, leaning closer to Ali to examine one of the wounds on his chest. The poison had burst perilously close to his heart there.

She frowned, catching sight of a bumpy ridge of skin above the wound. A scar. A meandering, savage line as if some sort of spiked vine had crawled across his chest before being ripped away.

Her stomach knotted. Before she could think twice, Nahri yanked close a basin Nisreen had filled with water, dampened a cloth, and wiped away the blood that covered his limbs.

The scars were everywhere.

A ragged line of puncture marks on his shoulder where teeth the size of her thumb had pierced him. The imprint of a fishing hook in his left palm and whirls of ruined flesh that called to mind waterweeds and tentacles. Pocked divots over his stomach, like fish had attempted to feast on him.

She covered her mouth, horrified. The memory of him climbing back onto the boat came to her: his body covered in lake detritus, a crocodile snout clamped on his shoulder, fishing hooks snarled in his skin. Nahri had thought him already dead, and she'd been so panicked that she and Dara were about to follow that she'd given little thought to what had happened to him. The stories about "Alizayd the Afshin-slayer" gallivanting across Am Gezira certainly made it sound like he was fine. And Nahri hadn't seen him again after the boat.

But Nisreen had. She'd treated Ali . . . and she'd never said anything about this.

Nahri stepped away from the bed, beckoning for Lubayd to follow as she passed. "We should give the king and queen a moment with him."

Hatset and Ghassan were standing on opposite sides of the pavilion outside her room, neither one looking at the other. Zaynab and Muntadhir were sitting on the bench between them, Muntadhir holding one of his sister's hands.

"Is he all right?" Hatset's voice shook slightly.

"For now," Nahri answered. "I've stopped the bleeding and there's no trace of the poison left. That I can detect," she clarified.

Ghassan looked as though he'd aged a half-century. "Do you know what it was?"

"No," she said flatly. This wasn't an answer she could risk massaging. "I have no idea what that was. I've never seen or read of anything like that." She hesitated, remembering the fleeing cupbearer—and the thrown dagger that had interrupted that flight. "I don't suppose his cupbearer . . ."

The king shook his head, grim. "Dead before he could be questioned. One of Alizayd's companions acted a bit too rashly."

"I daresay those companions and their rashness are probably the only reason our son is still alive." Hatset's voice was sharper that Nahri had ever heard it.

Muntadhir rose to his feet. "So he'll live?"

Nahri forced herself to meet her husband's eyes, not missing the tangle of emotion in them. "He'll survive this."

"All right." Muntadhir's voice was low and troubled enough that Nahri saw Hatset narrow her eyes at him. He didn't seem to notice, instead turning abruptly away and disappearing down the steps that led to the garden.

Zaynab hurried after him. "Dhiru . . ."

Ghassan sighed, watching them for a moment before turning back to Nahri. "May we see him?"

"Yes. I need to prepare a tonic for his throat. But don't wake him. He lost a lot of blood. I don't even think he should be moved. Let him stay here for at least a few days."

The king nodded, heading toward her room. But Hatset caught Nahri's wrist.

"Do you truly know nothing about this poison?" she asked. "Nothing in your mother's old notes?"

"We're healers, not assassins," Nahri shot back. "And I'd be a fool to get involved with anything like this."

"I'm not accusing you," Hatset said, a little of the edge leaving her voice. "I just want to make sure if you think of anything—*suspect* anything—you come to me, Banu Nahida." Her expression grew intent. "I am not my husband," she added softly. "I reward loyalty—I don't terrorize people into it. And I'll not forget what you did for my son tonight."

She let go of Nahri's wrist, following Ghassan without another word. Her mind spinning, Nahri continued on to the infirmary.

Nisreen was already at work on the tonic, transferring a spoonful of bright orange, freshly ground salamander skin from a stone mortar into a honey-colored potion simmering in a glass flask suspended over an open flame. A puff of smoke burst from the flask and then the mixture turned crimson, uncomfortably close to the color of human blood.

"I started without you," Nisreen called over her shoulder. "I figured you could use the help. It just needs another moment or two to simmer."

Nahri's stomach tightened. Reliable Nisreen, always two steps ahead of what Nahri needed. Her mentor and closest confidante.

The only person left in Daevabad that she thought she could trust.

She joined her, pressing her hands against the worktable and fighting the emotion bubbling up inside her. "You lied to me," Nahri said quietly.

Nisreen glanced up, looking taken aback. "What?"

"You lied to me about Ali. After Dara's de—after that night on the boat." Her voice was unsteady. "You said Ali was fine. You said he had *scratches*." She gave Nisreen an incredulous stare. "There's not a patch of skin on him bigger than my palm that isn't scarred."

Nisreen stiffened. "You'll forgive me not thinking much of his wounds when Dara and a dozen other Daevas lay dead, and Ghassan was contemplating executing you."

Nahri shook her head. "You should have told me. You dismissed me when I tried to talk about that night, you had me doubting my very memories . . ."

"Because I didn't want them to consume you!" Nisreen put down the mortar, turning her full attention on Nahri. "My lady, you were singing to shadows and cutting open your wrists to try and bring Dara back. You didn't need to know more."

Nahri flinched at the blunt depiction of her grief, but Nisreen's last words still set her blood boiling. "Whether or not I needed to know more was not your decision to make. Not with this, not with the hospital, not with *anything*." She threw up her hands. "Nisreen, I can't have this. I need at least one person in this cursed city I can trust, one person who will tell me the truth no matter what."

Nisreen's dark eyes flicked away. When she spoke again, her voice was soft with both pity and disgust. "I didn't know what to tell you, Nahri. He was barely recognizable as a djinn when they brought him in. He was hissing and spitting like a snake, shrieking in some language no one could recognize. The things clinging to his skin attacked us as we removed them. We had to tie him down after he tried to strangle his own father!"

Nahri's eyes widened, but Nisreen clearly wasn't done. "What do you think brought down the ceiling of your infirmary?" She jerked her head up. "It was Alizayd, whatever was *in* Alizayd." Nisreen lowered her voice further. "I assisted your mother and uncle for a century and a half, and I witnessed things I could never have imagined, but, Banu Nahri . . . nothing comes close to what I saw happen to Alizayd al Qahtani." She reached for the simmering glass flask with a gloved hand and poured the potion into a jade cup that she then thrust at Nahri. "His friendship was a weakness you should have never permitted yourself and now he's a threat you barely understand."

Nahri made no move to take the cup. "Taste it."

Nisreen stared at her. "What?"

"Taste it." Nahri jerked her head toward the door. "Or get out of my infirmary."

Without dropping her gaze, Nisreen lifted the cup to her mouth and took a sip. She put it back down with a thud. "I would never risk you like that, Banu Nahida. *Never.*"

"Do you know who might have been capable of making that poison?"

Nisreen's black gaze didn't so much as waver. "No."

Nahri took the cup. Her hands were shaking. "Would you tell me if you did? Or would that be another truth I'm not capable of handling?"

Nisreen sighed. "Nahri . . ."

But she was already walking away.

LUBAYD WAS ON THE PAVILION STEPS, SOME DISTANCE from the entrance to her bedroom.

"I wouldn't interrupt them if I were you," he warned.

Nahri brushed past. "They're the ones interrupting me." She continued toward her room but paused at the curtained door, stepping into the shadow of a rose lattice. She could hear the voices of the royal couple inside.

"—should burn in hell for sentencing your child to such a fate. He was *eighteen*, Ghassan. Eighteen and you sent him to die in Am Gezira after some lake demon tortured him!"

"Do you think I wanted to?" Ghassan hissed. "I have three children, Hatset. I have thirty *thousand* times as many subjects. Daevabad comes first. I have always told you that. You should have concerned yourself with his safety before your relatives and their dirt-blooded friends attempted to lure him into treason!"

Nahri stood utterly still, well aware that the two most powerful people in Daevabad were having an argument it seemed to be courting death to overhear. But she couldn't make herself turn away.

And Hatset wasn't done. "*Daevabad comes first*," she repeated. "Fine words for a king doing his best to destroy everything our ancestors fought for. You're letting the shafit be sold off to the highest bidder while your emir drinks himself into an early grave."

"Muntadhir is not *drinking himself into a grave*," Ghassan said, defending his son. "He has always been more capable than you grant him. He's making peace with the Daevas, a peace long overdue."

"This isn't peace!" Rage and exasperation warred in Hatset's voice. "When will you realize that? The Daevas don't want your peace; they want us *gone*. Manizheh despised you, your grand wazir would cut your throat in your sleep if he could, and that girl you bullied into marrying Muntadhir is not going to forget what you've done to her. The moment she gets pregnant, *you'll* be the one poisoned. She and the Pramukhs will shuffle Muntadhir off into an opium den, and just like that, we'll be under Nahid rule again." Warning laced into her voice. "And the Daevas will pay us back in blood for everything your family has done to them."

Nahri stepped back, her hand going to her mouth in shock. The queen had just neatly and horribly pulled together the strands of a future Nahri hardly dared consider—and the tapestry it created when presented by the other side was awful. A calculated scheme of revenge, when Nahri only wanted justice for her tribe.

Justice was what Dara wanted too, wasn't it? And look at the price he was willing to pay for it. Nahri swallowed, her legs feeling a bit unsteady.

Ghassan raised his voice. "And this is why Alizayd talks and acts the way he does. Why he recklessly throws himself into aiding every shafit he comes across. Because of you."

"Because he wants to fix things, and all you've ever told him to do is shut his mouth and wield a weapon. I've heard the stories coming out of Am Gezira. He has done more good for people there in five years than you have in fifty."

Scorn filled Ghassan's voice. "It is not his leadership in Am Gezira that you desire, wife. Do not think I am so naive. And I will not have you interfere again. The next time you overstep, I *will* send you back to Ta Ntry. For good. You will never see either of your children again."

There was a moment of silence before the queen responded. "And that, Ghassan?" Her voice was chillingly quiet. "That you would reach for such a threat with the mother of your children? That is why people hate you." Nahri heard the door open. "And it breaks my heart when I remember the man you used to be."

The door shut. Nahri leaned in and peered through the roses, catching sight of Ghassan staring at his unconscious son. He inhaled sharply and then was gone, sweeping out in a swirl of black robes.

Nahri was shaking as she entered her room. *I should have been more aggressive in my dowry demands*, she suddenly thought. Because she had *not* been paid enough to marry into this family.

She returned to Ali's side. His chest was rising and falling in the light of her fireplace, reminding her of the first time she'd healed him. The quiet night she'd accidentally killed her first patient and then saved a prince, the first time she'd had to grudgingly admit to herself that the man she insisted was only a mark was becoming the closest thing she had to a friend.

Nahri squeezed her eyes shut. Ali and Nisreen. Muntadhir. *Dara.* Everyone she let get a glimpse past the walls Muntadhir had accused her of keeping around her heart had lied to her or used her. Nahri had once quietly feared that it was her, that growing up alone on Cairo's streets with abilities that terrified everyone had broken her, shaped her into a person who didn't know how to forge a genuine bond.

But it wasn't her. Or at least not *just* her. It was Daevabad. Daevabad had crushed everyone in it, from its tyrant king to the shafit laborer scurrying through her garden. Fear and hate ruled the city—built up by centuries of spilled blood and the resulting grievances. It was a place where everyone was so busy trying to survive and ensure their loved ones survived that there was no room to build new trust.

She let out a breath, opening her eyes to see Ali stir in his sleep. A pained grimace creased his face, breath rasping in his throat. The sight shook away her dark thoughts and reminded her of the potion still clutched in her hand. Her work was not done.

She pulled a cushioned stool closer. Besides his scars, Ali looked like he'd lived a rougher life in Am Gezira than she would have imagined, his body lean and wiry and his nails bitten low. She frowned as she caught sight of another mark just under his jaw. Rather than the ragged imprints the marid left, this one was a clean slash.

It looks like someone tried to cut his throat. Though Nahri couldn't imagine who would be foolish enough to attempt to assassinate a Qahtani prince in the depths of Am Gezira. She reached out and touched his chin, his skin clammy beneath her fingertips as she turned his head to examine a mottled patch of scar tissue on his temple. She could no longer make out the lines of the eight-pointed star that had been carved there—a version of Suleiman's seal, apparently by way of the marid—but she hadn't forgotten the sight of it flashing on his face that night.

She stared at him. *What did they do to you?* And perhaps a question that burned even more—*why?* Why had the marid been so determined to come after Dara?

Movement near her hand caught her eye. Nahri started. The potion in the cup was moving, the liquid's surface rippling like it was being struck by invisible drops.

Ali's eyes fluttered open, his gaze dazed and feverish. He tried to draw a breath and then coughed, pain twisting his face.

Nahri reacted immediately. "Drink this," she commanded, sliding her hand under his head to raise him up. "*No*, don't try to talk," she added as he moved his lips. "Your throat was shredded. Even you can hold your tongue for a moment."

She helped him finish the contents of the cup. Ali was shivering violently, and she eased him back onto the pillow when he was done. "Does anything feel sharp in your body?" she asked. "Anything like a buzzing beneath your skin?"

"No," he croaked. "What-what happened?"

"Someone tried to poison you. Obviously."

Despair swept his face. "Oh," he whispered, his gaze dropping to his hands. "Even in Daevabad then," he added with a soft bitterness that took her aback. The tonic was clearly doing its job, his voice smoother though filled with misery. "I thought they might stop."

Nahri frowned. "Who might stop?"

Ali shook his head stiffly. "It doesn't matter." He glanced up, worry flashing in his eyes. "Was anyone else hurt? My mother—"

"Your mother is fine." That was a lie, of course. Hatset had watched her son almost die in her arms. "No one else was hurt, but your cupbearer was killed trying to escape."

Ali looked pained. "I wish they had not done that. He was only a boy." He covered his mouth as he began to cough again, his hand coming away flecked with blood.

Nahri refilled the cup with water from her pitcher. "Drink," she said, pressing it into his hands. "I suspect your throat will be raw for the next few days. I've done what I could, but the poison was a powerful one."

He took a sip, but his eyes didn't leave her face. "I thought you had done it," he said quietly.

She drew back, annoyed that the accusation hurt. "Yes, I know. You and everyone else. Your people don't make secret what they think of me."

Guilt blossomed in his eyes. "I didn't mean it like that." He lowered the cup, running his thumb against the edge. "I only meant that I wouldn't have blamed you if you wanted me dead."

"Wanting you dead and actually killing you are very different things," she said sharply. "And I'm no murderer."

"No, you're not," Ali said. "You're a healer." He met her eyes again. "Thank you for saving my life." He bit his lip, a little desperate humor creeping across his face. "I think this is the fourth time."

Nahri struggled to remain expressionless, cursing the part of her heart that wanted to soften at his words. His breathing ragged and his eyes bright with pain, Ali didn't look the "Afshin-slayer" right now; he looked sick and weak—a patient who needed her. An old friend who missed her.

A weakness. Not trusting her emotions, Nahri abruptly stood up. "It's my duty," she said brusquely. "Nothing more." She turned for the door. "A servant will bring you fresh clothing. I have other patients."

"Nahri, wait," he rasped. "Please."

Hating herself, she stopped. "I'm not doing this with you, Ali."

"What if I told you that you were right?"

Nahri glanced back at him. "What?"

Ali stared her, his expression beseeching. "You were right. About that night, about the boat." Shame filled his face. "I did know the Royal Guard would be waiting for us."

She shook her head. "Glad to know you're just as brutal when being honest as you are when lying."

He tried to push up, wincing in pain. "I didn't know what else to do, Nahri. I'd never fought someone who could use magic the way Darayavahoush did. I'd never *heard* of someone who could use magic the way he did. But I knew . . . so much else about him." Sick regret crossed his face. "All those books I didn't want you to read. If he had taken you, if he had killed me—our people would have gone to war." Ali shuddered. "And I knew all too well the kinds of things he did during wars."

Do you know why he's called the Scourge of Qui-zi? The regret that hung on Dara like a cloak, the open fear his name had provoked. "He wouldn't have started another war," she tried to insist, her voice hoarse. "I wouldn't have let him." But even as she said it, she knew she didn't quite believe it. There was a reason Muntadhir's accusation had struck so close to the bone.

Because on that awful night, a desperate Dara had shown how far he would go. He had forced her hand in a way she hadn't considered him capable of, with a reckless violence that had stunned her.

And a small part of her still wondered if she should have seen it coming.

"I couldn't take that risk." Ali's face was drawn, a sheen of dampness on his brow. "You're not the only one with a duty."

Silence fell between them. Nahri struggled to maintain her composure, hating that Ali's haunted confession touched her. She almost wanted to believe him. To believe that the boy who'd taught her to conjure a flame was real, and that the man he'd become was not manipulating her yet again, to believe that not everyone and everything in this miserable city had to be second-guessed.

A weakness. Nahri shuttered the thought, ignoring the loneliness that pierced her chest upon doing so. "And the rest?"

He blinked. "The rest?"

"The marid," she prompted, steadying her voice.

He stared at her in disbelief, turning his palms to reveal his scars. "You can't believe I wanted this."

"What did the *marid* want? Why did they use you to kill Dara?"

Ali shivered. "We weren't exactly having a conversation down there. They were showing me things . . . the destruction of Daevabad, of Am Gezira. They said he was going to do it. Showed him doing it . . . but it didn't look like him."

Nahri narrowed her eyes. "What do you mean?"

Ali frowned as though he were trying to remember. "They showed him turning into something else. His skin and eyes were like fire, his hands black claws . . ."

A chill went down her spine at the description. "They showed Dara becoming an *ifrit*?"

"I don't know," Ali replied. "I try not to think about that night."

You're not the only one. Nahri stared at him, a wary, charged tension filling the space between them. She felt raw, the dredged-up details of that awful night—a night she tried so hard not to dwell on—leaving her more exposed than she liked.

But it was a vulnerability she could see echoed in Ali's face, and though her heart was warning her to get out of this room, she couldn't turn away an opportunity to learn more about the dangerous rift she feared was growing in the family that controlled her life.

"Why are you back in Daevabad, Alizayd?" she asked baldly.

Ali hesitated but answered. "An Ayaanle trader, a cousin of mine, fell ill while crossing Am Gezira." He shrugged—a poor attempt at casualness. "I offered to do him the favor of taking his cargo, thinking I'd enjoy the opportunity to celebrate Navasatem with my family."

"Surely you can lie better than that."

He flushed. "That's the reason I'm here. There's nothing more to it."

Nahri drew closer. "Your mother seems to think there's more to it. *Muntadhir* seems to think there's more to it."

Ali's gaze shot to hers. "I could never hurt my brother."

That lay between them for another long moment, Nahri crossing her arms and holding his gaze until he looked away, still a little shamefaced.

His attention fell on the books stacked haphazardly on the table next to her bed. He cleared his throat. "Er . . . are you reading anything interesting?"

Nahri rolled her eyes at the blatantly obvious attempt to change the subject. "Nothing that concerns you." And nothing that should have concerned her. She was never going to rebuild the hospital, let alone find some mysterious shafit surgeon to work with her.

Clueless as usual, Ali didn't seem to pick up on the malice in her voice. "Who is ibn Butlan?" he asked, leaning close to read from the Arabic scrawled on the top book. "*The Banquet of the Physicians*?"

She reached possessively for the armful of books. "Mind your own business. Were you not just weeping about how many times I've saved your life? Surely you owe me some privacy."

That shut him up, but as Nahri crossed to dump the books on her couch, something clicked into place in her head.

Ali *did* owe her. She turned over Ghassan and Hatset's argument. He was reckless when it came to the shafit, so self-righteous about helping them that he flung himself into things without thinking them through.

She straightened up, turning to him. "You know the shafit neighborhoods."

His eyebrows knit together in confusion. "Yes . . . I mean, I suppose so."

She tried to tamp down the excitement swirling in her chest. No. This was a fool's quest. If Nahri had any sense, she'd be staying away from Ali and holding her tongue about the hospital.

And will you do so forever? Was Nahri going to let Ghassan destroy her ability to hope for a better future, to harden her into the threat Hatset suggested she would one day become? Was that the life she wanted in Daevabad?

Ali drew back. "Why are you looking at me like that? It is alarming."

She scowled. "I'm not looking at you like anything. You don't know me." She snatched the cup. "I'm going to get you some food. Touch my books again and I'll put ice spiders in your coffee. And don't die."

Confusion rippled across his face. "I don't understand."

"You owe me a debt, al Qahtani." Nahri strode off, yanking her door open. "I don't intend to let it go unpaid."

14

DARA

They were holding the Geziri scouts in a crude hut of lashed branches that Dara took care to keep wet and covered in snow. He had originally conjured their prisoners a small tent, a place that would have been warmer, but the pair had returned the favor by setting the felt aflame in the middle of the night and arming themselves with the support beams, breaking the bones of two of his warriors in an attempt to flee. Whatever else they were, the Geziris were a wily people, used to finding ways to survive in inhospitable environments, and Dara would not grant them another chance to escape.

His boots crunching on the snow as he approached the hut, Dara called out a warning. "Abu Sayf, tell your fellow that if he greets me with a rock again, I'm going to shove it down his throat."

There was a flurry of conversation in Geziriyya inside at that, Abu Sayf sounding weary and exasperated and the younger one—who still refused to give his name—irritable before Abu Sayf spoke. "Come in, Afshin."

Dara ducked inside, blinking in the dim light. It was fetid and cold, and smelled of unwashed men and blood. After their last escapade, the djinn were kept in irons and given blankets only during the coldest nights. And while Dara understood the need for security measures, the crude conditions made him increasingly uneasy. He had not taken Abu Sayf and his companion on the field of battle as combatants. They were scouts: a young man on what Dara suspected was his first posting, and an old warrior with one foot in retirement.

"Ah, look, it's the devil himself," the younger djinn said heatedly as Dara entered. He looked feverish but was glaring with as much hate as he could muster.

Dara matched his glare and then knelt, putting down the platter he'd been carrying and shoving it toward the younger man's feet. "Breakfast." He glanced at Abu Sayf. "How are you today?"

"A little stiff," Abu Sayf confessed. "Your warriors are getting better."

"A thing I have to thank you for."

The younger Geziri snorted. "Thank? You told him you'd flay me alive if he didn't spar with your band of traitors."

Abu Sayf shot the other djinn a look, adding something in their incomprehensible language before nodding at the tray. "This is for us?"

"It is for him." Dara crossed to Abu Sayf and struck his irons off. "Come with me. A walk will ease your limbs."

Dara led the other man out and toward his own tent, a fittingly bare place for a man who belonged nowhere. He rekindled his fire with a snap of his fingers and waved for Abu Sayf to sit upon the carpet.

The Geziri did so, rubbing his hands before the fire. "Thank you."

"It is nothing," Dara returned, taking a seat across from him. He snapped his fingers again, conjuring a platter of steaming stew and hot bread. The burst of magic while in his mortal form made his head pound, but he felt the other man deserved it. This was the first time he'd invited Abu Sayf to his tent, but not the first time they'd shared conversation. He might have been an enemy, but Abu Sayf's fluency in Divasti and his two centuries serving in the djinn army made him an easy companion. Dara had great affection for his young recruits and was deeply loyal to Manizheh—but Suleiman's eye, sometimes he just wanted to gaze upon the mountains and exchange a few words about horses with an old man who was equally weary of war.

Dara passed over a cloak. "Take this. It has been cold." He shook his head. "I wish you would let me conjure you a proper tent. Your companion is an idiot."

Abu Sayf pulled over the stew, ripping off a piece of the bread. "I prefer to stay with my tribesman. He is not handling this well." A weary sadness fell over his face. "He misses his family. He learned just before we were posted that his wife was pregnant with their firstborn." He glanced at Dara. "She is in Daevabad. He fears for her."

Dara pushed away a stab of guilt. Warriors left wives behind all the time; it was part of their duty. "If she were back in Am Gezira, where you all belong, she would be plenty safe," he offered, forcing a conviction he didn't entirely feel into his voice.

Abu Sayf didn't take the bait. He never did. Dara suspected he was a soldier through and through and didn't care to defend politics in which he had little voice. "Your Banu Nahida came to take blood again," he said instead. "And she hasn't returned my friend's relic."

At that Dara reached for his goblet, watching it fill with date wine at his silent command. "I am certain it is nothing." In truth, he didn't know what Manizheh was doing with the relics, and her secrecy was starting to grate on him.

"Your men say she intends to experiment on us. To boil us alive and grind our bones for her potions." Fear crept into the other man's voice. "They say she can capture a soul like the ifrit and bind it away so it never sees Paradise."

Dara kept his face blank, but annoyance with his soldiers—and with himself for not checking their behavior sooner—sparked in his chest. Animosity toward the djinn and shafit ran high in their camp: many of Manizheh's followers had suffered at their hands, after all. Admittedly, Dara hadn't thought much of it when he was first brought back. During his own rebellion fourteen centuries ago, he and his fellow survivors had expressed similar hatred—and carried out darker acts of vengeance. But they'd been raw with grief over the sack of Daevabad and desperate to save what was left of their tribe. That was not the situation his people were in today.

He cleared his throat. "I'm sorry to hear they've been harassing you. Believe me when I say I'll speak to them." He sighed, looking to change the subject. "May I ask what has kept you in this part of Daevastana for so long? You said you've lived here a half-century now, yes? This does not seem an ideal posting for a man from the desert."

Abu Sayf smiled slightly. "I have come to find the snow lovely even if the cold remains brutal. And my wife's parents are here."

"You could have taken a posting in Daevabad and brought them with you."

The other man chuckled. "You have never had in-laws if you say something so easily."

The comment threw him. "No," Dara said. "I was never married."

"No one ever caught your eye?"

"Someone did," he said softly. "But I could not offer the future that she deserved."

Abu Sayf shrugged. "Then you will have to take my opinion on the matter of in-laws. And regardless, I did not wish to take a posting in Daevabad. It would have led to orders I do not care for."

Dara met his gaze. "You speak from experience."

The other man nodded. "I fought in King Khader's war when I was young."

"Khader was Ghassan's father, no?"

"Correct. The western half of Qart Sahar tried to secede during his reign, about two hundred years ago."

Dara rolled his eyes. "The Sahrayn have a habit of that. They tried to do the same just before I was born."

Abu Sayf's mouth quirked. "To be fair . . . I do believe secession was somewhat in fashion in your time."

He grunted. Had another djinn said that to him, Dara would have been irked, but considering Abu Sayf was his prisoner, he held his tongue. "Fair point. You fought the Sahrayn, then?"

"I'm not sure 'fought' is the best description," Abu Sayf replied. "We were sent to crush them, to terrorize a set of tiny villages on the coast." He shook his head. "Amazing places. They built directly from the sand of the seabed, blasting it into glass to create homes along the cliffs. If you pulled up the rugs, you could watch fish swim beneath your feet, and the way the glass glittered in the sun when we first arrived . . ." Wistfulness filled his eyes. "We destroyed them all, of course. Burned their ships, threw their bound leaders into the sea, and took back the boys for the Guard. Khader was a hard man."

"You were following orders."

"I suppose," Abu Sayf said quietly. "Never seemed right, though. It took us *months* to get out there, and I never really understood what kind of threat some little villages on the edge of the world could present to Daevabad. Why they had anything to do with Daevabad."

Dara shifted, not liking the fact that he'd essentially been backed into defending a Qahtani. "Surely if you wonder why Daevabad rules a distant Sahrayn village you should wonder why a Geziri family commands a Daeva city?"

"I suppose I never really thought of Daevabad as a Daeva city." Abu Sayf looked almost surprised. "Feels like the center of our world should belong to us all."

Before Dara could respond, there was the sound of running outside his tent. He shot to his feet.

Mardoniye appeared at the entrance the next instant, out of breath. "Come quickly, Afshin. There has been a letter from home."

15
ALI

"Okay, we're here," Ali said, throwing out his arm to prevent Nahri from slipping past. "Now will you tell me why you *had* to visit Sukariyya Street?"

Nahri was the very image of calmness at his side, her dark eyes studying the bustling shafit neighborhood like a hunter might survey its prey. "The house with the red door," she remarked softly under her breath.

Perplexed, Ali followed her gaze to a narrow, three-story wooden house that looked like it had been crammed between the two larger stone buildings on either side of it. A small open porch fronted the house, surrounding a red door painted with orange flowers. It was a cloudy afternoon, and shadows swallowed the building, obscuring it in gloom.

His unease instantly grew. The windows were boarded over, but with enough cracks that one could easily spy on the street from the inside, and a man sat on the steps of the neighboring building, reading a pamphlet with a bit too much studied disinterest. At a café across the street, two others sat ostensibly playing backgammon, their gazes occasionally flitting over to the red door.

Ali wasn't Citadel-trained for nothing. "It's being watched."

"Why do you think I brought you?" Nahri asked. A strangled sound of disbelief left his mouth, and she threw him a scornful look. "By the Most High, could you stop acting so jumpy?"

He stared at her. *"Someone tried to murder me a week ago."*

Nahri rolled her eyes. "Let's go." She was off without another word.

Aghast, Ali watched as she strode purposefully towards the guarded house. Admittedly, there was little to give her away. Dressed in a rough-spun abaya and shawl, Nahri blended into the crowd of gossiping shafit shoppers and arguing laborers with ease.

Certainly a different look from the gold dress she wore to the feast. Ali's face abruptly filled with heat. No, he was not thinking about that dress. Not again. Instead, he hurried after her, cursing himself for getting dragged into whatever mysterious business Nahri claimed to have in the shafit district. He still wasn't sure what foolishness had made him agree to this; the days since he'd been poisoned were nothing but a pain-wracked blur of his mother's hovering, endless questions from the Royal Guard's investigators, and increasingly foul-tasting potions from the Banu Nahida.

She probably hexed you into agreeing. The Nahids could do that, couldn't they? Because surely not even Ali was reckless enough to sneak his sister-in-law out of the palace—*and* to agree to take the blame if they were found out—without being hexed.

By the time he caught up, Nahri was walking with a hand on her lower belly. There was suddenly a bump there, and her bag was gone from her shoulder. When she'd slipped it under her abaya,

God only knew, but she was sniffling by the time they neared the house. She wiped her eyes, a feigned limp affecting her walk.

The man next door dropped his pamphlet and rose to his feet, stepping in her path. "Can I help you, sister?"

Nahri nodded. "Peace be upon you," she greeted him. "I . . ." She sucked in her breath, clutching her exaggerated belly. "I'm sorry. My cousin said there was someone here . . . someone who helps women."

The man's gaze swept over them. "If indeed your cousin said such a thing, you'd know to bring her so she could vouch for you." He stared at Ali. "Is this your husband?"

"I didn't tell her it was I who needed help." Nahri lowered her voice. "And this isn't my husband."

The blood left Ali's face. "I—"

Nahri's hand darted out and she grasped his arm in a viselike grip. "Please . . ." She gasped, curling in on herself. "I'm in a lot of pain."

The man flushed, glancing helplessly down the street. "Oh, all right . . ." He crossed the porch, swiftly pulling open the red door. "Come quick."

Ali's heart raced, his mind screaming warnings of entrapment—this was, after all, not the first time he'd been tricked into entering a crumbling shafit building—but Nahri was already dragging him up the steps. They creaked underfoot, the wood soft from Daevabad's misty air. The shafit man shut the door behind them, throwing them into a gloomy darkness.

They were standing in a fairly simple entrance hall, with lacquered wooden walls and two doors. There were no windows, but the ceiling had been left open to the cloudy sky, making it feel as though they'd been dropped into a pit. The only other light came from a small oil lamp that sat burning next to a platter piled with sweets, in front of a garlanded rice-paper painting of a well-armed woman sitting astride a roaring tiger.

His patience with Nahri abruptly vanished. Someone had tried to kill him less than a week ago. He was drawing a line at lurking in some mysterious shafit house while pretending he'd impregnated his brother's wife.

Ali turned on her, selecting his words carefully. "My *dear*," he started. "Would you please explain what we're doing here?"

Nahri was gazing about the foyer with open curiosity. "We're here to meet a shafit doctor named Subhashini Sen. This is where he works."

The man who'd brought them in abruptly straightened up. "*He?*" Suspicion blossomed across his face, and he reached for his waist.

Ali was faster. He drew his zulfiqar in a breath, and the shafit man stepped back, his hand frozen on a wooden baton. He opened his mouth.

"Don't scream," Nahri said quickly. "Please. We don't mean anyone here harm. I only want to talk to the doctor."

The man's gaze darted nervously to the door on his left. "I . . . you can't."

Nahri looked baffled. "Excuse me?"

The shafit man swallowed. "You don't understand . . . she's very particular."

Curiosity lit Nahri's eyes. She must have also noticed the door the shafit man glanced at—because she was reaching for the handle in the next moment.

Ali panicked, not thinking. "Nahri, wait, don't—"

The shafit man's mouth fell open. "*Nahri?*"

God preserve me. Ali charged after her as she slipped into the room. Discretion be damned, they were getting out of here.

A clipped female voice with a thick Daevabadi accent cut him off the moment he passed the threshold.

"I have told all of you . . . at least a dozen times . . . if you interrupt me while I'm doing this procedure, I'm going to perform it on you next."

Ali froze. Not so much at the warning, but at the sight of its source. A shafit woman in a plain cotton sari knelt before them at the side of an elderly man lying on a cushion.

She had a needle inserted in his eye.

Aghast at the grisly sight, Ali opened his mouth to protest, but Nahri clapped a hand over it before he could speak.

"Don't," she whispered. She'd drawn back her veil, revealing the open delight dancing across her features.

The shafit guard joined them, wringing his hands. "Forgive me, Doctor Sen. I would never have interrupted you. Only . . ." He glanced nervously between Ali and Nahri, his eyes seeming to trace Ali's height and his zulfiqar anew. "You appear to have some guests from the palace."

The doctor hesitated. But only for a moment, and neither her hands nor attention so much as twitched. "Whether that's true or some symptom of madness, all of you can take a seat *right now*. I still have part of this cataract to remove."

There was no room for disobedience in the woman's stern voice. Ali backed up as quickly as the guard, dropping into one of the low couches lining the wall. He looked around the room. Full of light from an adjoining courtyard and copious lanterns, it was large enough to fit perhaps a dozen people. Three pallets were set low on the ground, the two not being used loosely covered in crisp linen. Cupboards lined one wall, and beside them a desk faced the courtyard, stacked high with books.

Nahri, of course, had ignored the doctor's command, and Ali watched helplessly as she drifted toward the desk and began flipping through a book, a grin on her face. He'd seen that look back when they'd been friends: when she'd read her first sentence correctly and when they'd gazed upon the moon through a human telescope, ruminating on the source of its shadows. Her desire to learn had been one of the things that had drawn him to her, a thing they had in common. He had not, however, expected

it to lead them to a shafit doctor in one of the city's more dangerous neighborhoods.

The sound of a crying infant broke the silence. The door
creaked open again, the wailing growing louder.

"Subha, love, are you already done, then?" A new voice, a
man's low rumble. "The baby is hungry, but she won't eat any of
the . . . *oh*." The man trailed off as he stepped into the infirmary.

The newcomer was enormous, easily one of the largest men Ali
had ever see. A mop of messy black curls fell past his shoulders,
and his nose looked like it had been broken multiple times. Ali
instantly raised his zulfiqar, but far from being armed, the man
held only a wooden spoon and a small baby.

Ali lowered his weapon with some embarrassment. Maybe
Nahri had a point about him being jumpy.

"And that's the last of it," the doctor announced, setting down
her needle and sitting back. She reached for a tin of salve and
then quickly bandaged the man's eyes. "You'll be keeping this on
for a full week, understand? Don't pester it."

She rose to her feet. The doctor looked younger than Ali
would have expected, but that might have been thanks to her
djinn blood, which was quite apparent. Though her dark brown
skin didn't have the telltale shine of a pureblood, her ears were as
peaked as his own and there was only a glimmer of brown in her
Agnivanshi-tin eyes. Her dark hair was plaited in a thick braid
that fell to her waist, a line of vermilion neatly set in the part.

She wiped her hands on a cloth tucked into her waistband and
then looked them over, a muscle working in her cheek. It was an
appraising gaze, one that flickered from the crying baby to linger
on Ali and Nahri before returning to the child.

Far from ruffled, she appeared unimpressed and rather irritated. "Manka . . . ," she started, and the doorman's head snapped
up. "I want you to help Hunayn to the recovery room. Parimal,
bring the baby here."

Both men instantly obeyed, one helping the groggy patient out while the other handed the baby over. The doctor took her child, her gaze not once leaving Ali and Nahri's faces as she re-arranged her sari over her chest and the baby's sobs turned to happy suckling.

Ali swallowed, fixing his gaze upon the opposite wall. Nahri didn't seem bothered by any of this; she was still standing at the desk with a book in her hand.

The doctor narrowed her eyes, glaring at the Banu Nahida. "If you wouldn't mind . . ."

"But of course." Nahri set down the book and then took a seat next to Ali. "Was that cataract surgery you were doing?"

"Yes." The woman's voice stayed clipped. She took a seat on a wooden stool across from them. "And it's a complicated, delicate procedure . . . one I don't like interrupted."

"We're sorry," Ali rushed to say. "We didn't mean to barge in."

The woman's expression didn't change. He tried not to squirm; it felt like being confronted by Hatset crossed with the most terrifying of his old tutors.

The doctor pursed her lips, nodding at the zulfiqar. "Mind putting that away?"

He flushed. "Of course." He quickly sheathed the sword and then pulled down his face covering. It didn't seem right to intrude upon these people and remain anonymous. He cleared his throat. "Peace be upon you," he offered weakly.

Parimal's eyes went wide. *"Prince Alizayd?"* His gaze darted to Nahri. "Does that mean you're—"

"Daevabad's newest Nahid?" the doctor cut in, her voice filled with scorn. "Seems likely. So are the two of you here to shut us down, then? Planning to haul me off to the bronze boat for try-ing to help my people?"

The mention of the bronze boat sent ice into his veins; Ali had once been forced to do just that to a number of shafit caught in a riot his father had engineered to provoke the Tanzeem. "No," he said quickly. "Absolutely not."

"He's right," Nahri said. "I only wanted to meet you. I came across one of your patients recently. A man with a hole in his skull, like someone had cut—"

"Drilled." Nahri blinked and the doctor pressed on, her voice cold. "It is called a trepanation. If you believe yourself a healer, you should use the correct terms."

Ali felt Nahri tense slightly at his side, but her voice stayed calm. "Drilled, then. He claimed you were a physician, and I wanted to see if that was true."

"Did you?" The doctor's brows knit together in incredulity. "Is the little girl who makes potions for good luck and tickles away bad humors with a simurgh feather here to assess my training?"

Ali's mouth went dry.

Nahri bristled. "I'd daresay what I do is a bit more advanced than that."

The doctor lifted her chin. "Go on, then, make your examination. You've already intruded, and I don't suppose we can protest." She jerked her head at Ali. "That's why you brought your prince, no?"

"I'm not her prince," Ali corrected swiftly, glaring when Nahri threw him an annoyed look. "I said I'd take you to Sukariyya Street," he said, defending himself. "Not sneak you into some doctor's house by pretending that we . . . that you . . ." Very unhelpfully, the memory of Nahri's gold dress appeared again in his mind, and mortified heat stole over his face. "Never mind," he stammered.

"Traitor," Nahri said, her tone withering as she added something even less kind in Arabic. But it was clear neither Ali's desertion nor the doctor's hostility would stop her. She rose to her feet, crossing to the bookshelf.

"This is an impressive collection . . . ," she remarked, longing in her voice. She pulled two volumes loose. "Ibn Sina, al Razi . . . where did you get all this?"

"My father was a physician in the human world." The doctor gestured to her pointed ears. "Unlike me, he could pass, and so he did. He traveled and studied wherever he liked. Delhi, Istanbul, Cairo, Marrakesh. He was two hundred and fifty when some loathsome Sahrayn bounty hunter found him in Mauritania and dragged him to Daevabad." Her eyes lingered on the books. "He brought everything he could."

Nahri looked even more awed. "Your father spent *two hundred years* studying medicine in the human world?" When the doctor nodded, she pressed on. "Where is he now?"

The doctor swallowed hard before responding. "He died last year. A stroke."

The eagerness faded from Nahri's face. She carefully put the book back. "I'm sorry."

"As am I. It was a loss for my community." There was no self-pity in the doctor's voice. "He trained a few of us. My husband and I are the best."

Parimal shook his head. "I'm a glorified bonesetter. Subha is the best." There was affectionate pride in his voice. "Even her father said so, and that man did not compliment easily."

"Do the other doctors he trained practice here as well?" Nahri asked.

"No. It's not worth the risk. Purebloods would rather we die from coughs than live to procreate." Subha's grip on her baby tightened. "The Royal Guard comes in here and any number of my instruments could land me in prison under the weapons ban." She scowled. "Nor are the shafit entirely innocent. These are desperate times, and there are people who believe we're rich. I had a talented surgeon from Mombasa working here until a band of thieves kidnapped his daughter. He sold everything he owned to ransom her back and then fled. They were going to try and smuggle themselves out of the city." Her face fell. "I've heard nothing since. Many of the boats don't make it."

The boats? Ali stilled. Daevabad wasn't an easy place to escape. The courage—the desperation—it must take to load one's family onto a rickety smuggler's boat and pray it made it across the murderous waters . . .

We have failed them. We have utterly failed them. He took in the little family before him, remembering the shafit his mother had saved. There were thousands more like them in Daevabad, men and women and children whose potential and prospects had been coldly curtailed to suit the political needs of the city in which they had no choice but to live.

Lost in his thoughts, Ali only noticed Nahri reaching for a cabinet door when Parimal lunged forward.

"Wait, Banu Nahida, don't—"

But she'd already opened it. Ali heard her breath catch. "I take it this is for protection from those kidnappers, then?" she asked, pulling out a hefty metallic object.

It took Ali a moment to recognize it, and when he did, his blood ran cold.

It was a pistol.

"Nahri, put that down," he said. "Right now."

She threw him an irritated look. "Oh, give me some credit. I'm not going to shoot myself."

"It is a tool of iron and gunpowder and you are the Banu Nahida of Daevabad." When she frowned, looking confused, his voice broke in alarm. "It explodes, Nahri! We are literally creatures of fire; we don't go near gunpowder!"

"Ah." She swallowed and then set it back down, carefully easing the door shut. "Probably best to be careful, then."

"It's mine alone," Parimal said quickly, an obvious lie. "Subha knew nothing."

"You shouldn't have that here," Ali warned. "It's incredibly dangerous. And if you got caught?" He looked between the two. "Shafit possession of even a small amount of gunpowder is punished with execution." Granted, Ali suspected that was a punishment driven by fear of the shafit as much as it was of gunpowder—no pureblooded djinn wanted a weapon around that the shafit could handle with more finesse. "Add a pistol? This entire block would be leveled."

Subha gave him a wary look. "Is that a warning or a charge?"

"A warning," he replied, meeting her eyes. "One I'd beg you heed."

Nahri returned to his side, her swagger gone. "I'm sorry," she said softly. "Truly. I wasn't sure what to think when I saw that man. I've heard rumors of how desperate the shafit are, and I know how easily people can prey upon that type of fear."

Subha stiffened. "That you would think such a thing of me says far more about you."

Nahri winced. "You're probably right." She dropped her gaze, looking uncharacteristically chastened, and then reached for her bag. "I . . . I brought you something. Healing herbs and willow bark from my garden. I thought you could use them." She offered the bag.

The doctor made no move to take it. "You must know nothing of your family's history if you think I'd ever give 'medicine' prepared by a Nahid to a shafit." Her eyes narrowed. "Is that why you're here? To spread some new disease among us?"

Nahri recoiled. "Of course not!" Genuine shock filled her voice, tugging at Ali's heart. "I . . . I wanted to help."

"Help?" The doctor glared. "You broke into my practice because you wanted to *help*?"

"Because I wanted to see if we could work together," Nahri rushed. "On a project I'd like to propose to the king."

Subha was staring at the Banu Nahida as if she'd sprouted another head. "You want to work with *me*? On a project you intend to propose to the king of Daevabad?"

"Yes."

The doctor's gaze somehow grew even more incredulous. "Which is . . . ?"

Nahri pressed her hands together. "I want to build a hospital."

Ali gaped at her. She might as well have said she wished to throw herself before a karkadann.

"You want to build a hospital?" the doctor repeated blankly.

"Well, not so much *build* one as rebuild one," Nahri explained quickly. "My ancestors ran a hospital before the war, but it's in ruins now. I'd like to restore and reopen it."

The *Nahid hospital*? Certainly she couldn't mean . . . Ali shuddered, searching for a response. "You want to recover the Nahid hospital? The one near the Citadel?"

She looked at him with surprise. "*You* know about that place?"

Ali fought very hard to keep his face composed. There was nothing in Nahri's voice that suggested she'd asked the question in anything other than innocence. He dared a glance at Subha, but she looked lost.

He cleared his throat. "I . . . er . . . might have heard a thing or two about it."

"A thing or two?" Nahri pressed, eyeing him closely.

More. But what Ali knew about that hospital—about what had been done there before the war, and the brutal, bloody way the Nahids had been punished for it—those facts were not widely known and certainly not ones he was about to share. Especially with an already arguing Nahid and shafit.

He shifted uncomfortably. "Why don't you tell us more about your plan?"

Her eyes stayed on his, heavy with scrutiny for another moment, but then she sighed, turning back to Subha. "A single cramped infirmary is no place to treat the entirety of Daevabad's population. I want to start seeing people who *didn't* have to pay a bribe to gain access to me. And when I reopen the hospital, I want it open to all."

Subha narrowed her eyes. "To all?"

"To all," Nahri repeated. "Regardless of blood."

"Then you're delusional. Or you're lying. Such a thing would never be permitted. The king would forbid it, your priests would die of shock and horror . . ."

"It will take some convincing," Nahri cut in lightly. "I know. But I think we can make it work." She pointed at the bookshelf. "There are more books like that in the Royal Library; I've read them. I healed people in the human world for years, and I know the value in those methods. There are still plenty of times I prefer ginger and sage to zahhak blood and incantations." She gave Subha an imploring look. "That's why I came to find you. I thought we could work together."

Ali sat back, stunned. Across from him, Parimal appeared equally astonished.

Subha's expression turned colder. "And should I bring to this hospital a shafit man dying of a stroke . . ." Her voice trembled slightly, but her words were precise. "An ailment I suspect you could heal with a single touch . . . are you going to lay hands on him, Banu Nahida? In the presence of witnesses, of your pureblood fellows, would you use Nahid magic on a mixed-blood?"

Nahri hesitated, a wash of color sweeping over her face. "I think . . . initially . . . it might be better if we treated our own."

The shafit doctor laughed. It was bitter and utterly without humor. "You don't even see it, do you?"

"Subha . . . ," Parimal cut in, his voice thick with warning.

"Let her speak," Nahri interrupted. "I want to hear what she has to say."

"Then you will. You say you mean us no harm?" Subha's eyes flashed. "You are the very essence of harm, Nahid. You're the leader of the tribe—the faith—that calls us soulless, and the last descendant of a family that culled shafit for centuries as though we were rats. You were the companion of the Scourge of Qui-zi, a butcher who could have filled the lake with the shafit blood he spilt. You have the arrogance to burst into my infirmary—my *home*—uninvited, to inspect me as though you are my superior. And now you sit there offering pretty dreams of hospitals while I am wondering how to get my child out of this room alive. Why would I *ever* work with you?"

Thunderous silence followed Subha's fiery words. Ali felt the urge to speak up for Nahri, knowing her intentions had been good. But he also knew the doctor was right. He had seen first-hand the destruction that pureblood blunderings could cause the shafit.

A muscle worked in Nahri's cheek. "I apologize for the manner of my arrival," she said stiffly. "But my intent is sincere. I might be a Nahid and a Daeva, but I want to help the shafit."

"Then go to your Temple, renounce your ancestors' beliefs in front of the rest of your people, and declare us equals," Subha challenged. "If you want to help the shafit, deal with your Daevas first."

Nahri rubbed her head, looking resigned. "I can't do that. Not yet. I'd lose their support and be of use to no one." Subha snorted and Nahri glared at her, appearing angry now. "The shafit are hardly innocent in all of this," she retorted, heat creeping into her voice. "Do you know what happened to the Daevas caught in the Grand Bazaar after Dara's death? The shafit fell upon them like beasts, hurling Rumi fire and—"

"*Beasts?*" Subha snapped. "Ah, yes, because that's what we are to you. Ravaging animals who need to be controlled!"

"It isn't a terrible idea." The words slipped from Ali's mouth before he could think, and when both women whirled on him, he fought to stay composed. He was nearly as surprised as they were that he was speaking . . . but it *wasn't* a terrible idea. It was . . . actually sort of brilliant. "I mean, if my father approved this, and you proceeded carefully, I think the Daevas and the shafit working together would be extraordinary. And to build a hospital, something Daevabad could truly use? It would be an incredible achievement."

He caught Nahri's gaze then. Her eyes swam with an emotion he couldn't decipher . . . but she didn't look entirely pleased by his sudden support.

Nor did Subha. "So, you're also a part of this plan?" she asked him.

"No," Nahri said flatly. "He isn't."

"Then you're not good at convincing people to work with you, Nahid," Subha replied, putting her daughter against her shoulder to burp her. "With him at your side, I might actually believe some of this newfound concern you seem to have for the shafit."

"You'd work with *him*?" Nahri repeated in outraged disbelief. "You do realize it's his father currently persecuting your people?"

"I'm quite aware," Subha retorted. "There's also not a shafit in Daevabad who doesn't know how the prince feels about it." She turned her attention back to Ali. "I heard about the father and daughter you saved from the traffickers. People say they're living like nobles in the palace now."

Ali stared at her, his heart dropping. For the first time he thought he might have seen a flicker of interest in Subha's eyes, but he couldn't bear the thought of lying to her.

"They were very nearly returned to that trafficker because I wasn't careful enough. I think the Banu Nahida's plan is admirable, I do. But when things go wrong in Daevabad . . ." He gestured between Nahri and himself. "People like us rarely pay the same price as the shafit."

Subha paused. "It seems neither of you are good at convincing others to work with you," she said calmly.

Nahri swore under her breath, but Ali held his ground. "A partnership founded in deceit is no partnership at all. I would not wish to lie and bring you into danger unwarned."

Parimal reached out to touch a lock of the baby's curly hair. "It might be a good idea," he said softly to Subha. "Your father used to dream about building a hospital here."

Ali glanced at Nahri. "Well?"

She looked murderous. "What do *you* know about building hospitals?"

"What do you know about building anything?" he asked. "Have you given thought to how to collect and administer the funds needed to restore a ruined, ancient complex? It's going to be incredibly expensive. Time-consuming. Will you be assessing contracts and hiring hundreds of workers in between patients at the infirmary?"

Nahri's glare only intensified. "Those were some very pretty words about founding relationships in deceit."

Ali flinched, their fight in the garden coming back to him. "You said I owe you," he replied carefully. "Let me pay my debt. Please."

Whether or not that resonated, Ali couldn't tell. Nahri drew up, the emotion vanishing from her face as she turned back to Subha. "Fine, he's with me. Is that enough for you?"

"No," the doctor said bluntly. "Get the king's permission. Get money and draw up actual plans." She nodded at the door. "And don't come back until you do. I won't have my family caught up in this mess otherwise."

Ali stood. "Forgive us for our intrusion," he apologized in a rasp; his still-healing throat didn't seem to appreciate all the arguing he'd just done. "We'll be in touch soon, God willing." He snapped his fingers, trying to get Nahri's attention. She'd turned back to the desk and its treasures, not seeming particularly eager to leave. "*Nahri.*"

She dropped her hand from the book she'd been reaching for. "Oh, fine." She touched her heart, offering an exaggerated bow. "I look forward to speaking again, Doctor, and hearing what new invective you have to hurl upon my ancestors and tribe."

"An endless supply, I assure you," Subha responded.

Ali ushered Nahri out before she could reply. His hands were shaking as he secured the tail of his turban across his face and then pulled the outer door closed behind them. Then he leaned hard against it, the full meaning of what he'd just agreed to hitting him.

Nahri didn't seem as bothered. She was gazing upon the busy shafit neighborhood below. And though she'd pulled her niqab back over her face, as a man swept past carrying a board of steaming bread, she inhaled, and the cloth pulled close against her lips in a way Ali cursed himself for noticing.

She glanced back. "This doesn't make us friends again," she said, her voice sharp.

"What?" he stammered, thrown by the bald statement.

"Us working together . . . it doesn't mean we're friends."

He was more stung than he wanted to admit. "Fine," he replied, unable to check the snippiness in his tone. "I have other friends."

"Sure you do." She crossed her arms over her abaya. "What did Subha mean when she mentioned that shafit family and traffickers? Surely things haven't gotten that bad here?"

"It's a long story." Ali rubbed his aching throat. "But don't worry. I suspect Doctor Sen will be more than happy to tell it to you, among other things."

Nahri made a face. "If we can even do this. How do you propose we start?" she asked. "Since you seemed so convinced of your skills inside."

Ali sighed. "We need to talk to my family."

16

DARA

Dara sat in shocked silence in Manizheh's tent, attempting to process what Kaveh had just read aloud from the scroll. "Your son poisoned *Alizayd al Qahtani*?" he repeated. "Your son? Jamshid?"

Kaveh glared at him. "Yes."

Dara blinked. The words in the letter Kaveh held did not match Dara's memory of the merry, kindhearted young archer with a regrettably sincere attachment to his Qahtani oppressors. "But he is so loyal to them."

"He's loyal to *one* of them," Kaveh corrected. "Creator curse that bloody emir. Muntadhir's probably been in a drunken, paranoid spiral since his brother returned. Jamshid *would* do something foolish to help him." He threw an annoyed look at Dara. "You might remember whose life Jamshid took six arrows to save."

"Saving a life and taking one are very different matters." A concern Dara didn't like was shaping up in his mind. "And how would he even know *how* to poison someone?"

Kaveh raked a hand through his hair. "The Temple libraries, I suspect. He's always been quite taken with Nahid lore. He used to get in trouble when he was a novitiate for sneaking into their archives." His eyes darted to Manizheh. "Nisreen said this looked somewhat similar to . . ."

"To one of my experiments?" Manizheh finished. "It is, though I doubt anyone but she would recognize that. Jamshid must have stumbled upon some of my old notes." She crossed her arms, her expression grave. "Does she think anyone else suspects him?"

Kaveh shook his head. "No. They believe it was his cupbearer, and the boy was killed in the melee, though she warned they were still interrogating the kitchen staff. She also said that if . . . that if Jamshid fell under suspicion, she was prepared to take the blame."

Dara was stunned. "*What?* Forgive me, but why should she? It is your son who is at fault, and foolishly so. What if his ingredients are followed back to the infirmary? Nahri might be blamed!"

Manizheh took a deep breath. "You are certain this letter was not traced in any way?"

Kaveh spread his hands. "We took all the precautions you taught us. She was only to contact me in an emergency. And respectfully, Banu Nahida—we are running low on time." He nodded at her worktable. "Your experiments . . . have you had luck figuring out how to limit—"

"It doesn't matter. Not anymore." Manizheh exhaled. "Tell me our plans once again," she commanded.

"We cross into the city and take the Royal Guard with the assistance of the marid and the ifrit," Dara answered automatically. "A contingent of my men stay behind with Vizaresh and his ghouls"—he had to fight to keep the distaste from his voice—"while we continue on to the palace." He glanced between them. "You told me you have a plan for taking care of the king?"

"Yes," Manizheh said briskly.

Dara paused. Manizheh had been cagey about this for months, and while he didn't want to step out of bounds, he felt now would be a good time to understand the full scope of their plans. "My lady, I am your Afshin; it might be helpful if you would tell me more." His voice rose in warning. "We don't know how my magic might react to Suleiman's seal. If the king is able to cripple me—"

"Ghassan al Qahtani will be dead before either of us sets foot in the palace. It's being arranged, and I will be in a position to tell you more in a few days. But speaking of Suleiman's seal . . ." Her gaze flickered from Dara to Kaveh. "Have you learned anything more about the ring?"

The grand wazir's face fell. "No, my lady. I have bribed and cajoled everyone I know, from concubines to scholars. Nothing. There is no one ring he wears consistently, and there are no records of how it's passed to a new owner. A historian was executed last year simply for attempting to research the seal's origins."

Manizheh grimaced. "I fared no better, and I spent decades scouring the Temple archives. There are no texts, no records."

"Nothing?" Dara repeated. "How is that possible?" The success of their plan hinged on Manizheh taking possession of Suleiman's seal ring. Without it . . .

"Zaydi al Qahtani probably had all the records burned when he took the throne," Manizheh said bitterly. "But I remember Ghassan going into seclusion for a few days after his father's funeral. When he reappeared, he looked as though he'd been ill—and the seal mark was on his face." She paused, considering this. "He never left the city again. He used to enjoy hunting in the lands beyond the Gozan when he was young. But after he became king, he never strayed farther than the mountains inside the threshold."

Kaveh nodded. "The seal ring may be tied to Daevabad—it's certainly never been used to stop any wars outside the city." He glanced at Dara. "Unless things were different in your day?"

"No," Dara replied slowly. "The members of the Nahid Council would pass it among each other, taking turns serving with it." He thought hard, trying to recall what he remembered—it always hurt to think about his old life. "But I only knew that because of the mark on their face. I do not recall ever seeing a ring."

After another moment, Manizheh spoke again. "Then we need his son. We'll have to make sure Muntadhir survives the initial siege so he can tell us how to take the seal. He's Ghassan's successor. He must know." She eyed Kaveh. "Can you find a way to do this?"

Kaveh looked apprehensive. "I don't think that's information Muntadhir is going to give up easily . . . particularly in the wake of his father's death."

"And I don't think it's going to be difficult to force Ghassan's wastrel son to talk," Manizheh countered. "I imagine the very prospect of being alone in a room with Dara will have him spilling any number of royal secrets."

Dara dropped his gaze, his stomach tightening. Not that he should be surprised she'd use him as a threat. He was the Scourge of Qui-zi, after all. No one—least of all the man Nahri had been forced to wed—would want to be on the receiving end of his supposed vengeance.

Kaveh's face seemed to momentarily display equal misgivings, but then the other man bowed. "Understood, Banu Nahida."

"Good. Kaveh, I would like you to prepare for your journey back to Daevabad. If there's a conflict brewing between those sand-fly princes, make sure our people—not to mention our respective children—stay out of it. Dara will enchant a carpet for you and teach you how to fly it." Manizheh turned back to her worktable. "I need to finish this."

Dara followed Kaveh out of the tent, grabbing his sleeve as soon as they were clear. "We need to talk."

Kaveh threw him an annoyed look. "Surely you can teach me how to fly one of your Creator-forsaken tapestries later."

"It is not about that." He pulled Kaveh toward his tent. This was not a discussion he wanted anyone to overhear—nor a topic he suspected Kaveh would take well to.

Kaveh half stumbled inside and then glanced around Dara's tent, his expression souring further. "Do you sleep surrounded by weapons? Do you truly not have a single personal possession that doesn't deal death?"

"I have what I require." Dara crossed his arms over his chest. "But we are not here to discuss my belongings."

"Then what do you want, Afshin?"

"I want to know if Jamshid's loyalty to Muntadhir is going to be a problem."

Kaveh's eyes flashed. "My son is a loyal Daeva, and considering what you did to him, you have some nerve questioning anything he does."

"I am Banu Manizheh's Afshin," Dara said flatly. "I am in charge of her military conquest and the future security of our city . . . so yes, Kaveh, I need to know if a well-connected, well-trained former soldier—*who just poisoned Muntadhir's political rival*—is going to be a problem."

An expression of pure hostility swept over Kaveh's face. "I am done with this conversation." He turned on his heel.

Dara took a deep breath, hating himself for what he was about to do. "My slave abilities came back to me that night . . . before the boat," he called out as Kaveh reached the tent flap. "It was brief—quite frankly, I still don't know what happened. But when I was in that dancer's salon, I felt a surge of magic, and then I could see her desires, her wishes all spread before me." Dara paused. "She had at least a dozen. Fame, money, a leisurely retirement with a lovesick Muntadhir. But when I saw into Muntadhir's mind next . . . it was not the dancer who occupied it."

Kaveh halted, his hands in fists at his sides.

"There was no throne either, Kaveh," Dara said. "No riches, no women, no dreams of being king. Muntadhir's only desire was your son at his side."

The other man was trembling, his back still turned.

Dara continued, his voice low. "I mean Jamshid absolutely no harm, I swear to you. I swear on the Nahids," he added. "And what we say here never has to leave this tent. But, Kaveh . . ." His tone grew imploring. "Banu Manizheh is relying on us both. We need to be able to talk about this."

A long moment of silence stretched between them, the cheerful chatter and clash of his sparring men beyond the tent at odds with the tension rising inside it.

And then Kaveh spoke. "He did nothing," he whispered. "Jamshid took six arrows for him and all Muntadhir did was hold his hand while his father let my boy suffer." He turned around, looking haunted—and old, as though the very memory had aged him. "How do you do that to someone you claim to love?"

Dara unwittingly thought of Nahri, and he didn't have an answer for the man. Suddenly, he felt quite old himself. "How long"—he cleared his throat, suspecting it still wouldn't take much for Kaveh to storm out—"have they been involved with each other?"

Kaveh's face crumpled. "At least ten years," he confessed softly. "If not longer. He was careful to hide it from me in the beginning. I suspect he feared I would disapprove."

"Such a fear is understandable," Dara said, quietly sympathetic. "People have often looked askance at such relationships."

Kaveh shook his head. "It wasn't that. I mean . . . it was in part, but our name and our wealth would have shielded him from the worst. *I* would have shielded him," he said, his voice growing fiercer. "His happiness and safety are my concerns, not the gossip of others." He sighed. "*Muntadhir* was the problem. Jamshid thinks because he is charming and speaks Divasti and loves wine and entertains his cosmopolitan court that he is different. He is not. Muntadhir is Geziri to the core and will always be loyal to his father and his family first. Jamshid refuses to see that, no matter how many times that man breaks his heart."

Dara sat on his cushion. He patted the pillow next to him, and Kaveh fell into it, still looking half reluctant. "Does Banu Manizheh know?"

"No," Kaveh said quickly. "I would not trouble her with this." He rubbed his silvering temples. "I can keep Jamshid away during the invasion and for those first few days—I'll lock him up if need be. But when he finds out about Muntadhir—about what happens after Manizheh gets what she needs . . ." He shook his head, his eyes dimming. "He'll never forgive me for that."

"Then blame me," Dara offered, his stomach twisting even as he said it. "Tell him Muntadhir was to be kept alive as a hostage, and I killed him in anger." He looked away. "It is what everyone expects from me anyway." Dara might as well use it to quietly ease the grief between the Pramukhs. He'd already hurt them enough.

Kaveh stared at his hands, twisting the gold ring on his thumb. "I don't know that it matters," he said finally. "I'm about to become one of the most infamous traitors in our history. I don't think Jamshid will ever look at me the same way again, regardless of what happens to Muntadhir. I don't think anyone will."

"I wish I could tell you that it becomes easier." Dara's gaze swept over his tent, the accumulated weapons that were his only possessions. His only identity in this world. "I suppose our reputations are small prices to pay if it means our people will be safe."

"Small consolation if our loved ones never speak to us again." He glanced at Dara. "Do you think she'll forgive you?"

Dara knew who Kaveh meant, and he knew all too well the answer, deep in his heart. "No," he said honestly. "I do not think

Nahri will ever forgive me. But she'll be safe with the rest of our people and reunited with her mother. That is all that matters."

For the first time since he'd seen Kaveh again, there was a hint of sympathy in the other man's voice. "I think they'll get along well," he said softly. "Nahri has always reminded me of her mother. So much so that it hurts at times. As a girl, Manizheh delighted in her cleverness exactly the way Nahri does. She was sharp, she was charming, she had a smile like a weapon." Tears came to his eyes. "When Nahri claimed to be her daughter, it felt like someone stole my breath."

"I can imagine," Dara said. "You thought she was dead after all."

Kaveh shook his head, his expression turning grim. "I knew Manizheh was alive."

"But . . ." Dara thought back to what Kaveh had told him. "You said you were the one who found her body . . . you were so upset . . ."

"Because that part was true," Kaveh replied. "All of it. I *was* the one who found Manizheh and Rustam's traveling party after they vanished. The fire-scorched plain, the torn remains of their companions. Manizheh—or the woman I thought was Manizheh—and Rustam with their heads . . ." He trailed off, his voice shaking. "I brought their bodies back to Daevabad. It was the first time I saw the city, the first time I met Ghassan . . ." Kaveh wiped his eyes. "I remember almost nothing of it. Had it not been for Jamshid, I would have thrown myself on her funeral pyre."

Dara was stunned. "I don't understand."

"She planned for me to find them." Kaveh's expression was vacant. "She knew I was the only one Ghassan would believe and hoped my obvious grief would protect her from his pursuit. Those are the lengths that demon pushed her to."

Dara stared at him, completely lost for words. He could not imagine coming upon the body of the woman he loved in such a way; he probably *would* have thrown himself on the funeral pyre, though knowing his cursed fate, someone would have found a way to drag him back. And the fact that Manizheh had done such a thing to Kaveh—a man she clearly loved—spoke to a dark ruthlessness he hadn't thought she possessed.

Then another thought struck him. "Kaveh, if Manizheh was able to feign her own death in such a manner, you do not think Rustam . . ."

Kaveh shook his head. "It was the first thing I asked her when we met again. All she would tell me was that he attempted a magic he should not have. She does not speak of him otherwise." He paused, old grief crossing his face. "They were very close, Dara. Sometimes it seemed like Rustam was the only one who could keep her feet on the ground."

Dara thought of his own sister. Tamima's bright smile and constant mischief. The brutal way she'd been killed—punished in Dara's stead.

And now he was about to introduce more brutality, more bloodshed into their world. Guilt wrapped his heart, constricting his throat. "You should try to do what you can to pull Jamshid and Nahri away from the Qahtanis, Kaveh. From all of them," he clarified, having little doubt Alizayd was already trying to worm his way back into Nahri's good graces. "It will make what is to come easier."

Silence fell between them again until Kaveh finally asked, "Can you do it, Afshin? Can you truly take the city? Because this . . . we cannot go through all of this again."

"Yes," Dara said quietly. He had no choice. "But if I may ask something of you?"

"What?"

"I am not certain of my fate after the conquest. I am not certain . . ." He paused, struggling for the right words. "I know what I am to people in this generation. What I did to Jamshid, to

Nahri . . . There may come a day that Manizheh will find it easier to rule if the 'Scourge of Qui-zi' is not at her side. But you will be there."

"What are you asking, Afshin?"

That Kaveh did not protest such a future spoke volumes, but Dara pushed aside the sickness rising within him. "Do not let her become like them," he rushed on. "Manizheh trusts you. She'll listen to your guidance. Do not let her become like Ghassan." Silently, in his heart, he added the words he could not yet speak. *Do not let her become like her ancestors, the ones who made me into a Scourge.*

Kaveh stiffened, a little of his usual hostility returning. "She won't be another Ghassan. She never could be." His voice was shaky; this was the man who loved Manizheh and spent his nights at her side, not the cautious grand wazir. "But frankly, I would not blame her if she wanted some vengeance." He rose to his feet, not seeming to realize his words had just sent Dara's heart to the floor. "I should go."

Dara could barely speak. He nodded instead, and Kaveh swept out, the tent flap blowing in the cold wind.

This war is never going to end. Dara stared at his weapons again, and then closed his eyes, taking a deep breath of the snow-scented air.

Why do you make those? The memory of Khayzur came to him. After finding Dara, the peri had taken him to the desolate icy mountains he called home. Dara had been a wreck in those early years after slavery, his soul shattered, his memory a blood-colored mosaic of violence and death. Before he could even recall his own name, he had taken to making weapons out of everything he found. Fallen branches became spears, rocks were chipped into blades. It was an instinct Dara hadn't understood, and he hadn't been able to answer Khayzur's gentle quizzing. None of the peri's questions made sense. *Who are you? What did you like? What makes you happy?*

Confused, Dara had simply stared at him. *I am an Afshin*, he'd reply each time—as though that answered everything. It took years for him to remember the better parts of his life. Afternoons with his family and galloping on horseback across the plains surrounding the Gozan. The dreams he'd harbored before his name became a curse, and the way Daevabad had hummed with magic during feast days.

By then, Khayzur's questions had changed. *Would you like to go back?* The peri had suggested a dozen different ways. They could attempt to remove his Afshin mark and Dara could settle in a distant Daeva village under a new name. He'd never lose the emerald in his eyes, but his people treaded lightly around former ifrit slaves. He might have made a life for himself.

And yet—he had never wanted to. He remembered too much of the war. Too much of what his duty had cost him. Dara had to be dragged back to his people, and that was a truth he hadn't even told Nahri.

And now here he was again, with his weapons and his cause.

It will end, he tried to tell himself, pushing away memories of Khayzur.

Dara would make sure.

17

NAHRI

It should have been a lovely morning. They'd gathered at a pavilion high upon the palace wall, the same place Ali and Nahri had once stargazed. The sun was warm, and there was not a cloud in the sky, the lake stretching like a cool glass mirror below them.

A plush embroidered rug deeper than Nahri's hand and large enough to sit fifty had been laid out under painted silk awnings and spread with a sumptuous feast. Every fruit one might imagine lay spread before them, from slivers of golden mango and bright persimmon to gleaming silver cherries that made a distinctly metallic crunch when chewed and trembling crimson custard apples whose similarity to a beating heart made Nahri shudder. Delicate pastries of creamed honey, sweetened cheese, and roasted nuts shared space between bowls of yoghurt strained and shaped into herb-brushed balls and platters of spiced semolina porridge.

And even better, a dish of fried fava beans with onions, eggs, and country bread, an unexpected delight indicating that the quiet old Egyptian cook who served in the palace kitchens had a hand in the morning's meal. In the earliest and darkest months after Dara's death, Nahri had noticed a number of dishes from her old home making their way into her meals. Nothing fancy, but rather, the comfort fare and street food she most loved. During a bout of homesickness, Nahri had once tried to find the cook, a meeting that hadn't gone well. The man had burst into tears when she smilingly introduced herself, his fellows in the kitchen later telling her that he rarely spoke and was considered slightly touched in the head. Nahri had dared not intrude upon him again, but he'd kept quietly preparing food for her, often slipping small tokens next to her dishes: a garland of jasmine, a reed folded to resemble a felucca, a carved wooden bangle. The gifts charmed her as much as they saddened her: reminders of the way Daevabad walled her off from a former countryman.

"Did Muntadhir tell you we found a troupe of conjurers, Abba?" Zaynab asked, pulling Nahri from her thoughts. The princess had been valiantly trying to make small talk with them all since they sat down, a task Nahri didn't envy. Muntadhir was sitting across from her, so stiff he might have been embalmed, and Hatset was slapping Ali's hand every time he reached for a dish without letting her try it first, because "your father's tasters are clearly useless." "They're excellent," Zaynab continued. "They summoned up a whole menagerie of birds that sang the loveliest of melodies. They'll be perfect for Navasatem."

"I hope they've signed a contract, then," Ghassan said lightly. Oddly enough, the djinn king seemed contentedly amused by this barbed family breakfast. "The last few Eids, I've found the entertainers I've hired suddenly lured away to Ta Ntry by promises of fees that are mysteriously always twice the amount we'd agreed to."

Hatset smiled, passing another loaded plate to Ali. "Alu-baba, enough with all those scrolls," she chided, gesturing at the pile of papers next to Ali. "What work could you possibly already have?"

"I suspect those scrolls have to do with his reason for arranging all this," Ghassan said knowingly, taking a sip of his coffee.

Muntadhir straightened up even further. "You didn't tell me Alizayd arranged this."

"I didn't want you finding a reason not to attend." Ghassan shrugged. "And waking before noon for once will not harm you." He turned back to his youngest. "How are you feeling?"

"Fully recovered," Ali said smoothly, touching his heart with a nod in Nahri's direction. "A thing I owe entirely to the Banu Nahida."

Ghassan's attention turned to her. "And has the Banu Nahida made any progress in discovering more about the poison used?"

Nahri forced herself to meet his gaze. Ghassan was her captor, and she never forgot it—but right now, she needed him on her side. "Regretfully, no. Nisreen thinks it might have been something in his tamarind juice designed to react to the sugar in the sweets. The prince is known to favor the drink in place of wine."

Muntadhir snorted. "I suppose that's what you get for being so obnoxious about your beliefs."

Ali's eyes flashed. "And how very interesting, akhi, that it was always you who was loudest about mocking me for them."

Hatset cut in. "Have you learned anything more about the poison?" she demanded, staring at Ghassan. "You told me you were having the kitchen staff questioned."

"And I am," Ghassan replied tersely. "Wajed is overseeing the investigation himself."

The queen held her husband's eye another moment, looking unimpressed, but then glanced at her son. "Why don't you tell us why you've brought us here?"

Ali cleared his throat. "It's not actually me alone. While I've been recovering, the Banu Nahida and I have been discussing working together on a very promising project. Her infirmary . . . it's very crowded."

He stopped as if this explained everything, and seeing confusion on their faces, Nahri swept in, silently cursing her partner. "I want to build a hospital," she said plainly.

"*We*," Ali muttered, tapping on his mountain of scrolls. "What?" he asked defensively when she gave him an annoyed look. "I didn't fiddle with numbers all week just so you can cut me out."

Muntadhir set his cup down so hard that the dark plum liquid inside sloshed out. It did not look like juice. "Of course you went to him. I try to talk sense into you, and your response is to race to your blockhead of a tutor the minute he comes riding back—"

"Should it make a *difference*," Ghassan interrupted, with a look that silenced them all, "I would like to hear them out." He turned to Nahri. "You want to build a hospital?"

Nahri nodded, trying to ignore the daggers Muntadhir was shooting at her from his eyes. "Well, not so much build a new one as restore an old one. I hear the complex my ancestors once used remains near the Citadel."

Ghassan's gaze was so calmly appraising it made the hairs on the back of her neck rise. "And where, dear daughter, did you hear such a thing?"

Her heart skipped a beat; she had to tread carefully or some poor Daeva would suffer for it, of that she had no doubt. "A book," she lied, trying to keep the strain from her voice. "And some rumors."

Zaynab was blinking at her with barely concealed alarm, Muntadhir studying the rug as though it were the most fascinating one he'd ever seen. Nahri prayed they'd stay silent.

"A book," Ghassan repeated. "And some rumors."

"Indeed," Nahri replied, rushing on as if she hadn't noticed the suspicion in his voice. "The descriptions of the hospital in its heyday are extraordinary." She casually picked up her teacup.

"I've also heard a trio of djinn freed from ifrit slavery are living in the remains."

"That's quite a lot of information to glean from some rumors."

Help came from a very unexpected direction. "Oh, stop menacing the poor girl, Ghassan," Hatset interrupted. "She's not wrong. I know about those former slaves as well."

Nahri stared at her. "You *do*?"

Hatset nodded. "One of them is a kinsman of mine." Nahri didn't miss the quick dart of her eyes to Ali. "A brilliant scholar—but a deeply eccentric man. He refuses to return to Ta Ntry, so I keep an eye on him and make sure he doesn't starve himself. I've met the two women there as well. The eldest, Razu, can spin some rather exciting tales of the hospital's past. Their magic is quite formidable, and I suspect she and her partner would be happy to help restore the place."

Nahri swallowed as the queen looked at her; there was far too much knowing in her eyes. But Nahri also suspected Hatset wouldn't betray her—not with Ali at her side. "That's my hope as well."

Ghassan was studying his family with open suspicion, but he let it go, returning his attention to Nahri. "That sounds like an admirable fantasy, Banu Nahida, but even if you had a building, you're barely able to keep up with your patients now. How could you possibly treat an entire hospital's worth?"

Nahri was prepared for the question. Her mind had been turning since she'd left the Sens. Subha's father had arrived alone in Daevabad with two centuries of medical knowledge and used it to train others. Surely, Nahri could do the same. "I'll have help," she explained. "I want to start teaching students."

Genuine surprise lit the king's face. "Students? I was under the impression most of the healing you do couldn't be accomplished by someone without your blood."

"A lot can't," Nahri admitted. "But many of the basics can. With proper training, I could shift some of my workload to others. We could see more people, and I could let them stay on to properly recover instead of booting them out of the infirmary as quickly as possible."

Ghassan took a sip of his coffee. "And earn some acclaim from your tribe, no doubt, for recovering an institution once so important to the Daevas."

"This isn't about tribal politics or pride," Nahri argued. "And I don't intend to only teach Daevas; I'll take students from any background if they're bright and willing."

"And between your duties in the infirmary now and teaching students, when exactly are you going to have time to oversee the rebuilding of a ruined, ancient hospital? Not to mention the cost . . . ah." His eyes narrowed on Ali. "The 'we.' A preposterously expensive public works project. Little wonder you have involved yourself."

"You did tell me to find something to do," Ali replied, a petty edge in his voice. Nahri clenched her teacup, resisting the urge to hurl it at his head. If she could check her temper, so could he. "But it wouldn't be preposterously expensive if handled correctly," Ali continued, gesturing to the armful of scrolls he'd brought. "I've been running estimates with people at the Treasury, and we've devised numerous proposals." He plucked up one of the fatter scrolls. "I know how important financials are, so I haven't spared any details."

Ghassan held up a hand. "Spare the details. We will be sitting here until Navasatem if I let you start talking about the specifics. I can have my own accountants check your proposals later." He tilted his head. "I am, after all, quite aware of your cleverness when it comes to numbers."

The words hung between them for a moment. Unwilling to

let whatever drama swirled around her in-laws eclipse her hospital, Nahri spoke quickly. "I'm willing to offer a portion of my dowry as well, enough to cover the materials and room and board for an initial class of twenty students. And once we start seeing patients, we can charge those who can pay on a sliding scale."

"I also thought the queen might assist me in meeting with the Ayaanle trade envoy," Ali added. "Should Ta Ntry find a way to make restitutions for its unfortunate tax situation, we could use the revenue to fix a lot of things in Daevabad."

Hatset raised her palms, smiling sweetly. "It can be difficult to predict financial matters."

Ali returned her smile. "Not when they can be audited, Amma," he said pleasantly.

Hatset drew up, looking taken aback, and Nahri saw a far more genuine smile spread across Ghassan's face.

But it was not a pleasure that erased his skepticism. "And the staffing cost?" he asked. "However formidable their magic, a handful of freed djinn are not going to be able to build and maintain a complex of that size."

Before Nahri could respond, Ali spoke up again. "I had been thinking in another direction." He toyed with a length of prayer beads looped around his wrist. "I'd like to tear down the shafit . . . *exchange* . . . in the Grand Bazaar and reuse its materials, as well as free those being held there. I'll offer them—and any shafit qualified and interested—employment in the hospital restoration."

Nahri blinked, surprised but pleased at the suggestion. She wasn't sure what exchange Ali was talking about—though the naked disdain in his voice made clear his opinion of it. But Subha's accusations about Nahri's complicity in the oppression of Daevabad's shafit had struck deep. Nahri *didn't* know much about the lives of a people she quietly belonged to, but this seemed like a good way to help some of them.

But Ghassan's expression had darkened. "I thought you'd learned to be warier about getting involved with the shafit, Alizayd."

"It's not just him," Muntadhir cut in. His gaze locked on hers. "And I suspect that's not all they want. This has to do with that shafit physician you were so eager to track down, doesn't it?" He turned back to his father. "She came to me with this weeks ago, talking about how she wanted to start working with shafit doctors and treating shafit patients."

Shock fell across the pavilion, so thick she could almost feel it. Zaynab dropped her cup, the queen taking a sharp breath.

Nahri silently cursed; it wasn't enough for Muntadhir to disagree, apparently. He also needed to undermine her by rudely letting slip a risky plan she'd wanted to be far more precise in proposing.

Ghassan recovered first. "You intend to *heal* shafit?"

Nahri answered honestly, though she loathed the words. "No. Not myself . . . not at first. We'd work and study alongside each other, the djinn using magic and the shafit using human techniques. I'm hoping it might prove a fresh start for the Daevas and the shafit, and that maybe, in the future, we'll be able to cross those lines."

Ghassan shook his head. "Your priests would never approve of such a thing. I am not certain *I* approve of such a thing. The first time a shafit doctor hurts a Daeva—or the reverse—people will be rioting in the streets."

"Or they might learn to get along a bit better." It was the queen, still looking slightly taken aback, though her words were encouraging. "It is the Banu Nahida who is proposing this project. The Daevas are obliged to obey her, are they not?" She shrugged lightly, as though the conversation hadn't turned fraught. "It is her responsibility and her risk if she wants to provoke them."

"Your support is appreciated," Nahri replied, checking her sarcasm. "I figured we could start the rebuilding effort first—of that I am certain my people would approve. I will go to the priests afterward and tell them of my plans regarding the shafit. *Tell* them," she clarified. "I'll listen to their concerns, but as the queen pointed out, I am the Banu Nahida. What I wish to share of my abilities at my hospital is my decision."

Ghassan leaned back. "If we're speaking so frankly . . . what do *we* get out of this? You're asking me to lay out money and risk to restore a monument to your ancestors . . . people who, as you may recall, were the enemies of mine." He arched a dark eyebrow. "The health of Daevabadis aside, I am not naive to the fact that this empowers you, not me."

"But what if it was truly a joint project?" Zaynab spoke this time, softly at first, though her voice grew more assured as she continued. "An extension of your outreach to the Daevas, Abba. It would be greatly symbolic, especially in light of the generation celebrations." She smiled at her father. "Maybe we could even try to finish it in time for Navasatem? You could open it yourself, as a crowning achievement for your rule."

Ghassan inclined his head, but at his daughter's warm smile, his expression had softened. "A rather plain appeal to vanity, Zaynab."

"Because I know you well," she teased. "Peace between the tribes is why you wished to see Muntadhir and Nahri marry, isn't it? Perhaps he could even go with her to the Temple to seek the priests' blessing."

Nahri had to work to keep her expression neutral at that. She was glad for Zaynab's support, but she knew how protective her people were of their customs. "Only Daevas are permitted to enter the Temple. It's been that way for centuries."

Hatset gave her a pointed look. "If you're willing to take djinn money for your hospital, Banu Nahida, I think you'd be willing to let one of us darken the doorstep of your Temple." She laid a hand on her son's shoulder. "But it should be Alizayd. He is the one who wishes to partner with you."

"It should be Muntadhir," Zaynab corrected, pleasantly firm. "He is her husband, and his history is a bit less . . . complicated . . . when it comes to the Daevas." She plucked a pink milk-sweet from one of the silver platters, taking a delicate bite. "Would it not be good to see them work together, Abba? I think it would do much to quell all this unnecessary and divisive talk from some of the other tribes."

Nahri did not miss the sugary smile Zaynab aimed at her mother . . . nor the way Hatset carefully nodded once, not so much in agreement, but in quiet approval of her daughter's maneuvering.

Muntadhir was looking at the three women with outrage. "Me? I don't even agree with this! Why do I have to convince the priests of anything?"

"I'll do the convincing," Nahri said sharply. She wasn't letting Muntadhir ruin this. "You might even enjoy it," she added quickly, trying for more tact. "Jamshid gives a wonderful tour."

Her husband glowered in response but stayed silent.

Ghassan seemed to study her again. It was the same look she'd seen when he'd welcomed her to Daevabad. The same look he'd worn the first time they'd negotiated her betrothal, the look of a gambler willing to bet a great deal if the risk was carefully calculated.

The first time she'd seen that expression it had set her at ease; Nahri had always preferred pragmatists. But now it made her skin crawl. Because she'd seen what Ghassan was capable of when his gambles didn't pay off.

"Yes," he finally said, and her heart skipped. "You may proceed. With *extreme* caution. I intend to be consulted on every development and every snag." He wagged his finger in Ali's direction. "You, in particular, are to be careful. I know how passionate you get about all of this. You are to build a hospital, not start climbing up on minbars and giving the masses sermons about equality, understand?"

Ali's eyes flashed and Nahri did not miss the quick way Zaynab "accidentally" struck his knee, reaching rather purposefully for a serving knife. "Yes, Abba," Ali said hoarsely. "I understand."

"Good. Then you may tell your priests you have my blessing, Banu Nahida, and take Muntadhir with you. But you are to make it clear this is your idea, not ours. I won't have any Daeva spreading rumors that we dragged them into this."

She nodded. "Understood."

The king regarded them all. "This pleases me," he declared, rising to his feet. "It will be good for Daevabad to see us working together in peace." He hesitated and then snapped his fingers at Ali. "Come, Alizayd. If you're going to brag about your financial acumen, you might as well help me. I've a meeting with a particularly slippery governor from Agnivansha and could use you."

Ali looked uncertain, but after a nudge from his mother, he stood. Nahri started to do the same.

Muntadhir's hand fell lightly on her wrist. "*Sit,*" he hissed under his breath.

With a quick glance between them, Zaynab rose hastily. Nahri didn't blame her; Muntadhir's handsome face was furious, a vein jumping in his temple. "Enjoy the Temple, akhi," she teased.

"About that . . ." Hatset pulled Zaynab close. "Take a walk with me, daughter."

The door leading to the steps closed, and then they were alone, save for the wind and the gulls.

Muntadhir turned to her, a shaft of sunshine illuminating the tired shadows under his eyes. It looked as though he hadn't slept in days. "Is this because of our fight?" he demanded. "Are you really ready to throw in with Alizayd and his lunatic ideas because of what I said?"

Nahri's temper flared. "I'm not *throwing in* with anyone. I'm doing this for myself and for my people. And as you'll recall, I came to you first. I tried to talk to you about these things—things close to my heart—and you dismissed me." She fought to keep the bitterness from her voice. "I suppose I shouldn't have been surprised. You made plain what you think of the foolish girl from Cairo."

He pressed his lips into a grim line, dropping his gaze. The moment stretched, silent and tense.

"I shouldn't have said that," he finally said. "I'm sorry. I was upset about Jamshid, and about Ali returning . . ."

"I've had enough of men hurting me because they were upset." Her voice was hard, so much so that Muntadhir looked startled. But Nahri didn't care. She rose to her feet, placing her chador over her head. "I won't have it from the man I call my husband. Not anymore."

Muntadhir's eyes darted to hers. "What are you saying?"

Nahri paused. What *was* she saying? As in Cairo, divorce was permissible in Daevabad—and rather widely practiced considering djinn life-spans and temperaments. But Nahri and Muntadhir were royals, their marriage blessed by Ghassan himself. It wasn't as though she could run to a judge down the street with her grievances.

But there were lines her husband wouldn't cross, and he'd made one of them clear on their wedding night.

"I'm doing this, Muntadhir. For my people, for myself—with or without you. I want to build this hospital. I want to see if there's a way to make peace with the shafit. If you'd like to join me, I will gladly welcome you to my people's Temple. If you cannot bring yourself to visit me there . . ." She paused, choosing her words carefully. "I'm not sure you should be visiting me anywhere."

Stunned incredulity crossed his face, and Nahri turned away. He could stew on the implications of that for a time.

Her hand was on the door when he finally responded.

"He is so much more dangerous than you realize." Nahri glanced back, and Muntadhir continued, his voice low. "I understand, believe it or not. I know you. I know Ali. I suspect you really were friends. I bet it was nice. The palace can be a lonely place, after all. And I know damn well he cared about you."

Nahri stilled.

"And that's just it, Nahri. He does care . . . recklessly so. Passionately so. About the shafit. About his village in Am Gezira. He cares so much he's willing to risk himself and everyone around him, unwilling to accept a shade of gray or a lesser evil in service to a greater good." Warning laced into his voice. "My brother would die for his causes. But he's a prince of Daevabad, so he's not the one who pays that price. Other people do. And you have an entire tribe of such people to protect."

Nahri twisted the edge of her chador in her fists, wishing she could say he was wrong. Except Ali had risked incurring his father's wrath to sneak out of the palace with her because he'd felt guilty. He'd all but warned Subha off working with them because he didn't want to lie. They'd come here today to beg a favor from the king, and he'd been rude, brimming with his usual self-righteousness.

It doesn't matter. Nahri had set herself on this path for the right reasons, and she now had the resources to try and bring her dream to fruition. Ali was a means to an end, and she wouldn't let him be a weakness again.

She opened the door. "Nisreen is expecting me in the infirmary," she said, forcing a steadiness she didn't feel into her voice. "I'll send word when we're visiting the Grand Temple."

NAHRI ALMOST GROANED WHEN SHE SAW JAMSHID waiting in the private section of the infirmary. She didn't need him begging for another healing session or talking about

Muntadhir right now. But then she noticed the anxiety that was all but radiating off his body, one leg jiggling while he passed his cane nervously back and forth between his hands. Nisreen paced before him, her expression harried.

Odd. Nisreen typically doted on him. Nahri frowned as she approached. "Everything all right?"

Jamshid glanced up, his eyes too bright above the shadows lingering under them. "Banu Nahida!" His voice sounded oddly strained. "May the fires burn brightly for you." He cleared his throat. "Of course everything is all right." He blinked at Nisreen. "Everything is all right?"

Nisreen glowered at him. "I certainly hope so."

Nahri looked between the two of them. "Is something wrong at home? Has there been news of your father?"

Nisreen shook her head. "Nothing is wrong. But as a matter of fact, I did recently write to his father. Just after the prince's feast," she added, and Jamshid flushed. "Creator willing, he'll be headed back to Daevabad soon."

Let him delay. Nahri didn't think the powerful—and rather orthodox—Daeva grand wazir was going to think much of her plans for the hospital or the shafit.

Which meant she'd need to set them in motion quickly. "That's good, then. But since you're both here, I want to talk." She took a seat across from Jamshid and motioned for Nisreen to do so as well. "I've just gotten back from meeting with the Qahtanis . . ." She took a deep breath. "We're going to rebuild the Nahid hospital."

It took a moment for her words to land, and then Jamshid's face lit up in intrigue as swiftly as Nisreen's darkened.

"There's a Nahid hospital?" he asked brightly.

"There's an ancient ruin soaked in the blood of your ancestors," Nisreen cut in. She stared at Nahri in shock. "You told *Ghassan* about your visit?"

"I left that part out, actually," Nahri said lightly. "But yes, we're going to restore it. The king agreed."

"Who exactly is 'we,' my lady?" Nisreen asked, though it was clear she already knew the answer.

"The Qahtanis, of course," Nahri replied, deciding it was best not to be precise.

"You're going to rebuild the Nahid hospital with the Qahtanis?" Nisreen repeated faintly. "*Now?*"

Nahri nodded. "We're hoping to have it open in time for Navasatem." That seemed wildly optimistic to her, but if that was the price for Ghassan's blessing, she and Ali would have to find a way to get it done. "I want to change things around here. We'll rebuild the hospital, hire the freed djinn currently living there, start training apprentices . . ." She grinned, hopeful in a way she hadn't been for a very long time. A little happy, even.

"Delay it," Nisreen said bluntly. "Don't do this. Not now. Things are too tense."

Nahri felt some of her spirits drain; she'd hoped her mentor would share at least a touch of her excitement. "I can't. Ghassan only agreed so we could present it as a tribal unity gesture for the celebrations. And anyway, I don't want to delay it," she added, a little hurt. "I thought you'd be thrilled."

"That all sounds extraordinary," Jamshid enthused. "I didn't know about the hospital, but I'd love to see it."

"I'd like to have you do more," Nahri replied. "I want to make you my first student."

His cane clattered to the floor. "What?" he whispered.

Nahri bent to pick it up and then smiled. "You're smart. You're excellent with the other patients here, and you've been a great help already." She touched his hand. "Join me, Jamshid. It might not be the way you originally thought to serve our tribe . . . But I think you'd be a wonderful healer."

He took a deep breath; he seemed stunned by the offer. "I . . ." His gaze darted to Nisreen. "If Nisreen does not object . . ."

Nisreen had the look of a woman wondering what she had done to deserve her current misfortune. "I . . . Yes. I think Jamshid might have quite the . . . knack for healing." She cleared her throat. "Though *perhaps* he might exercise a bit more caution when putting away ingredients in the apothecary—and when reading old texts." She returned her gaze to Nahri. "It seems Jamshid came across some of Manizheh's notes archived in the Temple."

"Really?" Nahri asked. "I'd love to see them."

Jamshid paled. "I . . . I'll try to find them again."

Nahri grinned. "Then I think this would be perfect for you! Though it won't be easy," she warned. "I don't have a lot of time, and neither will you. You'll need to all but take up residence in this place, reading and studying every second you're not working. You might hate me by the end."

"Never." He gripped her hand. "When do I start?"

"There's one more thing before you say yes." She glanced at Nisreen. Her assistant looked like she was fighting panic, which Nahri thought a complete overreaction—Nisreen couldn't hate the Qahtanis so much that she wouldn't want a hospital. "Nisreen, would you mind leaving us? I'd like to speak with Jamshid alone for a moment."

Nisreen let out a huffed sound. "Would it matter if I did mind?" She rose to her feet. "A hospital with the Qahtanis before Navasatem . . . The Creator have mercy . . ."

"What is this 'one thing'?" Jamshid asked, pulling her attention back to him. "Not sure I like the sound of it," he teased.

"It's a sizable one thing," she confessed. "And I'll need you to keep it to yourself for now." She lowered her voice. "I intend to open the hospital to all. Regardless of their blood."

Confusion wrinkled Jamshid's brow. "But . . . that's forbidden. You . . . you can't mean to heal mixed-bloods, Banu Nahida. You could lose your magic that way."

The remark—a prejudice she'd heard uttered by many a fearful Daeva—stung no less for having been said in earnest ignorance. "That's not true," she said firmly. "I'm proof that it isn't. I healed humans for years in Egypt before coming to Daevabad, and it never affected my magic."

He must have heard the heat in her response, for he drew back. "Forgive me. I didn't mean to doubt you."

She shook her head. If she couldn't handle Jamshid's doubt, she wouldn't survive the reactions from the priests at the Grand Temple. "No, I want you to question me. I'm hoping you can help me convince the rest of our tribe. You're a Temple-trained noble, the son of the grand wazir . . . what could sway someone like you to support this?"

He drummed his fingers against his leg. "I'm not certain you could. Let alone what Suleiman's law says about sharing magic with them . . . the shafit despise us. You know what they did to the Daevas they caught after Dara's death. They'd probably murder us all in our beds if they could."

"Does that not make peace sound rather desirable?"

He sighed. "I don't see how that's possible. Look to our history. Whenever the shafit rise, we're the ones who pay a price."

"Jamshid, have you ever even had a conversation with a shafit lasting longer than ten minutes?"

He had the grace to blush. "We're not supposed to interact with the human-blooded."

"No, what we're not supposed to do is creep through the human world, seducing virgins and starting wars. It doesn't say anywhere that we can't talk to them." He fell silent but didn't look convinced. "*Speak*, Jamshid," she pressed. "Call me a fool, a tyrant, but say something."

She saw him swallow. "Why should we have to?" he burst out. "This is *our* home. We're not the ones responsible for the shafit. Let the djinn build them hospitals. Why should we be the ones to offer this peace when they've done nothing to deserve it?"

"Because it *is* our home," she said gently. "And there's got to be a better way to protect it, to protect all of us. Do you have any idea the size of the shafit neighborhoods, Jamshid? How crowded they are? There are probably more shafit in Daevabad than the rest of the djinn tribes put together, and we can't rely on the Qahtanis to keep us from each other's throats forever." These were thoughts that had been swirling in her head for five years, solidifying more and more each day. "Doing so leaves us vulnerable."

He seemed to contemplate that. "That'll be your argument," he finally said. "People are afraid. Convince them that this is the best way to ensure our safety."

I can do that. "Excellent. Now, I should be starting my rounds."

His face lit up. "Wonderful! May I . . ."

She laughed. "Oh, no." She pointed to the nearest desk. Well, Nahri knew it was a desk. At the moment, its surface wasn't visible: it was entirely covered in stacks upon stacks of books, messy notes, pens, inkpots, and empty teacups. "You aren't touching any of my patients. Work your way through those books first and then we'll talk."

Jamshid's eyes went wide. "All of them?"

"All of them." She pulled over a blank piece of parchment. "Write your attendants and have them send over some of your things." She nodded to the couch. "That's yours. Feel free to make yourself comfortable here."

He looked dazed, but still eager. "Thank you, Banu Nahida. I hope you know how much this means to me."

She winked. "We'll see if you're still saying that in a month."

She moved toward the curtain, but then stopped and looked back. "Jamshid?"

He glanced up.

"You . . . you should know that Muntadhir doesn't support this. He thinks I'm being reckless, and I'm sure he'll have words about how I'm going to be the downfall of Daevabad the next time you see him." She paused. If Muntadhir had turned to Jamshid when he found out his brother was returning, she had no doubt he'd do the same after their conversation on the terrace. "If that puts you in an awkward position . . ."

"You're my Banu Nahida." He hesitated, and Nahri could see warring loyalties play across his face. Oddly enough, the way it made his dark eyes crease struck her as familiar. "And I'm Daeva first. You have my support." He gave her a hopeful smile. "Maybe I can convince him to do the same."

A mix of relief and guilt flared in her. Nahri didn't want to put Jamshid in the middle of her marriage, but she would take every advantage she could get. And truthfully, it was clear he was already there. "That would be appreciated." She nodded at the books and grinned. "Now get to work."

18
NAHRI

Two weeks after her barbed family breakfast, Nahri found herself back in the hospital, watching Razu with rapt attention. "Beautiful," she said admiringly, as the ancient Tukharistani gambler swapped the jewels again, a sleight of hand that betrayed nothing as Razu set down a brilliant glass gem in front of her—a pretty bauble, but certainly not the ruby that had vanished. "And it's not magic?"

"Not at all," Razu replied. "One cannot overly rely on magic. What if your hands were bound in iron, and you needed to hide away the key you'd snatched?"

"Is that a situation you've found yourself in?"

The other woman gave her a cryptic smile. "Of course not. I am a . . . what are we telling your law-abiding friends again?"

"A former trader from Tukharistan who ran a respectable inn."

Razu laughed. "Respectability was the last thing my old tavern was known for." She sighed. "I am telling you . . . a couple glasses of my soma and your doctor and prince will be agreeing to your every suggestion."

Nahri shook her head. She was fairly certain a single sip of Razu's soma would knock Ali out cold, and Subha would probably think they were poisoning her. "Let's try a more orthodox approach first. Though I would not be averse to you teaching me how to do that," she said, pointing to the glass gem.

"I am at my Banu Nahida's service," Razu replied, placing the gem in Nahri's palm and adjusting her fingers. "So you twist your hand like this and . . ."

From the other side of the courtyard came a disapproving cluck. Elashia, the freed djinn from Qart Sahar, was painting a turtle she'd carved from cedarwood. Nahri had brought her the paints, an act that had been greeted with wet eyes and a fierce hug.

But right now Elashia was looking at Razu with open disapproval. "What?" Razu asked. "The child wants to learn a skill. Who am I to deny her?" When Elashia turned back around with a sigh, Razu flashed Nahri a conspiratorial smile. "When she is out of sight, I will teach you a spell to give even a rock the appearance of a jewel."

But Nahri's gaze was still on the Sahrayn woman. "Does she ever speak?" she asked softly, switching to Razu's archaic dialect of Tukharistani.

Sadness swept the older djinn's face. "Not often. Sometimes with me, when we are alone, but it took years. She was freed decades ago, but she never speaks of her time in slavery. A companion of mine brought her to my tavern after finding her living on the streets, and she's been with me since. Rustam told me once he believed his grandfather freed her, and that she had been enslaved for nearly five hundred years. She is a gentle soul," she added as Elashia blew on the turtle and then let it go, smiling as it came to life and tottered along the edge of the fountain. "I cannot imagine how she survived."

Nahri watched her, but it wasn't Elashia she saw in her mind's eye. It was Dara, whose captivity had been three times as long as

Elashia's. However, Dara had remembered almost nothing of his imprisonment—and the few recollections they'd shared together had been ghastly enough that he'd confessed to being relieved such memories were gone. Nahri hadn't agreed at the time—it seemed appalling to lose such a huge portion of one's life. But maybe there had been a mercy in it she hadn't realized, one of the few Dara had enjoyed.

A crashing came from the entrance. "I take it your friends are here," Razu said.

Nahri rose to her feet. "I would not call us friends."

Ali and Subha entered the courtyard. They couldn't have looked more different: the djinn prince was smiling, his eyes bright with anticipation as he gazed about the ruins. In contrast, apprehension was written in every line of Subha's body, from her pursed lips to her tightly crossed arms.

"Peace be upon you all," Ali said in greeting, touching his heart as he caught sight of them. He was in plain Geziri dress today: a white dishdasha that fell to his sandaled feet and a charcoal-colored turban, his zulfiqar and khanjar tucked into a pale green belt. On one shoulder, he was carrying a leather bag full of scrolls.

"And upon you peace." Nahri turned to Subha, offering a polite bow. "Doctor Sen, it is lovely to see you again. Razu, this is Doctor Subhashini Sen and Prince Alizayd al Qahtani."

"An honor," Razu said, bringing her left hand to her brow. "I am Razu Qaraqashi, and this is Elashia. You'll excuse our third companion for hiding in his room. Issa does not do well with guests."

Ali made his way forward. "Did you see the seals on the door?" he asked eagerly.

Nahri thought back to the carved pictograms she'd noticed when she first found the hospital. "Yes. Why? What are they?"

"The old tribal sigils," Ali explained. "They were used before we had a shared written language. The great scholar Grumbates once said—"

"Can we not have a history lesson right now? *Another* one?" Subha clarified, in a tone that made Nahri suspect the walk to the hospital in the company of the chatty prince had been a long one. Her gaze darted around the courtyard like she expected some sort of magical beast to leap out and attack. "Well . . . it certainly looks like this place has been abandoned for fourteen centuries."

"Nothing we can't fix." Nahri plastered a grin on her face. She was determined to win over the other healer today. "Would you like some refreshments before we take a tour? Tea?"

"I'm fine," Subha replied, her expression displeased. "Let's just get this over with."

The blunt refusal of her hospitality ruffled something very deep in the Egyptian part of her heart, but Nahri stayed polite. "Certainly."

Ali stepped in. "I tracked down the hospital's old plans and had a Daeva architect at the Royal Library go through them with me to draw up notes for us to follow."

Nahri was taken aback. "That was a good idea."

"Yes. It is almost as if history lessons are useful," he sniffed, plucking out one of his scrolls and spreading it before them. "This was always a courtyard. The architect said there were notes about it containing a garden."

Nahri nodded. "I'd like to keep it that way. I know my patients in the infirmary enjoy the occasional chance to walk around my gardens now. It lifts their spirits." She glanced at Subha. "Does that seem correct to you?"

The doctor narrowed her eyes. "You did see where I worked, yes? Do you imagine us getting some air near the local uncollected trash piles?"

Nahri flushed. She was itching to find a commonality with this fellow female healer, a physician who, in the brief time Nahri

had watched her, seemed to have an abundance of the professional confidence Nahri was still pretending at. She doubted
Subha shook like a leaf before new procedures, or desperately
prayed she didn't kill someone every time she performed surgery.

Ali was peering at his notes. "According to this . . . that
domed chamber there was used for humoral disorders of air. It
says that tethers were set in the floor to prevent people from
injuring themselves while floating . . ."

"And that?" Nahri prompted, pointing to a line of crumbling
columns. She suspected Subha was not ready to discuss rooms
designed to enclose flying djinn. "It looks like a corridor."

"It is. It leads to a surgical wing."

That sounded more promising. "Let's start there."

The three of them headed down the twisting path. The dirt
was soft underfoot, the sun shining in bright swaths through the
overgrown trees. The air smelled of old stone and fresh rain. It
was humid, and Nahri fanned herself with an edge of her linen
chador.

The silence between them was heavy. Awkward. And try as she
might, Nahri couldn't forget that the last time Daevas, Geziris,
and shafit had been together in this place, they had all been brutally killing one another.

"I've been discussing funding options with the Treasury," Ali
said, an oddly pleased smile playing across his mouth. "And after
a visit from my companion Aqisa, I find the Ayaanle trade envoy
suddenly far more eager to offer financial assistance."

Subha shook her head, glancing about in dismay. "I cannot
imagine turning this into a functioning hospital in six months.
With several miracles, perhaps you could do it in six years."

A golden-brown monkey chose that particular moment to
leap over their heads with a screech, jumping from the trees
to land upon a broken pillar. It glared at them as it munched a
mushy apricot.

"We'll, ah, have the monkeys cleared out right away," Nahri said, mortified.

The corridor came to an abrupt stop. The surgical wing was enclosed by thick brass walls that towered overhead, and the one in front of them was covered in scorch marks, the brass melted into an impenetrable barrier.

Nahri touched one of the marks. "I don't think we'll be getting in there."

Ali stepped back, shading his eyes. "It looks as though part of the roof has collapsed. I can climb up and see."

"You're not going to be able to—" But Ali was gone before the words left her mouth, his fingers hooking around handholds she couldn't see.

Subha watched him scale the wall. "If he breaks his neck, I am not taking responsibility."

"You were never here." Nahri sighed as Ali pulled himself on the roof and vanished out of sight. "Your daughter is with your husband today?" she asked, determined to continue the conversation.

"I do typically advise that infants steer clear of decaying ruins."

Nahri had to bite her tongue to keep from saying something sarcastic in return. She was reaching the end of her diplomatic rope. "What's her name?"

"Chandra." Subha said, her face softening slightly.

"That's very pretty," Nahri replied. "She looked healthy too. Strong, mashallah. She's doing all right?"

Subha nodded. "She was born earlier than I'd like, but she's thriving." Her eyes dimmed. "I've seen it go the other way too many times."

Nahri had too, both in Cairo and in Daevabad. "I had one last week," she said quietly. "A woman from out in northern Daevastana rushed here after being bitten by a basilisk. She was in her last month of pregnancy, and she and her husband had been trying for decades. I was able to save her, but the child . . . a basilisk bite is terribly poisonous and I had no good way to administer the antidote. He was stillborn." Her throat tightened at the memory. "The parents . . . I don't think they quite understood."

"They never do. Not really. Grief clouds the mind, makes people say terrible things."

Nahri paused. "Does . . ." She cleared her throat, suddenly embarrassed. "Does it get easier?"

Subha finally met her gaze, her tin-toned eyes understanding if not warm. "Yes . . . and no. You learn to distance yourself from it. It's work; your feelings don't matter. If anything, they can interfere." She sighed. "Trust me . . . one day you'll go from witnessing the worst of tragedies to smiling and playing with your child in the space of an hour, and you'll wonder if that's for the best." She gazed upon the ruined hospital. "The work is what matters. You fix what you can and keep yourself whole enough to move on to the next patient."

The words resonated through Nahri, her mind drifting to another patient: the only one she couldn't heal. "Could I ask you something else?"

Subha nodded briefly.

"Is there anything you recommend for spinal injuries? For a man struggling to walk?"

"Is this about your friend, the grand wazir's son?" When Nahri's eyes widened in surprise, Subha tilted her head. "I do my research before agreeing to work with someone."

"It's about him," Nahri admitted. "Actually, you'll probably meet him soon. He's my apprentice now. But he took several arrows to the back five years ago, and I haven't been able to heal him. He's getting better slowly with exercise and rest but . . ." She paused. "It feels like a failure on my part."

Subha looked contemplative, perhaps the medical nature of

the conversation drawing her out. "I can examine him if he's willing. There are some therapies I know that might work."

Before Nahri could respond, Ali leapt down to join them, landing so silently that she jumped and Subha yelped.

His expression didn't inspire much hope. "Well . . . the good news is, it does indeed look like this was a surgical wing. There are even some tools scattered about."

"What sort of tools?" Nahri asked, her curiosity kindled.

"Hard to say. Much of it is underwater. It appears that a basement collapsed." Ali paused. "And there are snakes. Lot of them."

Subha sighed. "This is madness. You are never going to be able to restore this place."

Nahri hesitated, resignation beginning to seep through her. "Maybe you're right."

"Nonsense," Ali declared, drawing up when Subha glared at him. "Don't tell me the two of you are ready to give up so soon. Did you think this would be easy?"

"I didn't think it would be *impossible*," Nahri countered. "Look around, Ali. Do you have any idea how many people we would need to even get started?"

"I will by the end of the week," he said confidently. "And lots of work is not a bad thing—it means we need lots of workers. It means new jobs and training for hundreds, people who will then have money for food and school and shelter. This project is an opportunity. One we haven't had in generations."

Subha made a face. "You sound like a politician."

He grinned. "And you sound like a pessimist. But that doesn't mean we can't work together."

"But the money, Ali," Nahri replied. "And the *timing* . . ."

He made a dismissive gesture. "I can get the money." An eager glint entered his eye. "I could have trade guilds built around waqfs and increase the tax on luxury imports . . ." Perhaps seeing that the two healers looked lost, he stopped. "Never mind. The two of you tell me what a hospital needs, and I'll worry about getting it done." He turned around without waiting for a response. "Now come. The plans say that building ahead was once the apothecary."

Subha blinked, looking a little bewildered, but she followed Ali, muttering under her breath about youth. Nahri was equally taken aback—but also grateful. Their personal history aside, maybe partnering with Ali wasn't the worst idea. He certainly seemed confident.

They continued down the weed-covered path, pushing aside wet palm fronds and glistening spider webs. Columns lay smashed on the ground, half swallowed by thick, twisting vines, and a large black snake sunned itself on the remains of a small pavilion.

They crossed under a forbidding arch and into the darkened chamber of the ancient apothecary. Nahri blinked as her eyes adjusted to the loss of light. Whatever floor had been there was long gone, swallowed by dirt, and only scattered sections of broken masonry were left behind. The distant ceiling had likely once been beautiful; blue and gold bits of tile still clung to its delicately carved and stuccoed surface. A swallow's nest had been built into one elaborate cornice.

A burst of light briefly blinded her. Nahri glanced back to see that Subha had conjured a dancing pair of flames in one hand.

A challenge lit her face at Nahri's astonishment. "Surely you know there are shafit capable of magic?"

Better than you would imagine. "Ah, of course," Nahri said weakly. "I'd been told that." She turned to study the room. The opposite wall was covered in hundreds of drawers. Though rusted over now, they were linked in a clever structure of metal and marble, their contents held behind securely fastened brass doors. Dozens were still clamped shut, their scrollwork surfaces tarnished by green and red rust.

"Care to see what mysterious magical ingredients look like after being locked away for fourteen centuries?" Nahri jested.

"I would rather not," Subha replied, knocking Ali's hand away when the prince reached for one of the handles. "*No.* The two of you can sate your curiosity when I'm gone."

Nahri hid a smile. The doctor still looked exasperated, but Nahri would take that over openly hostile. "I think there will be more than enough room for all our supplies here."

"I suspect so, considering my pharmaceuticals fit inside a single chest," Subha replied. "I usually have to send patients to buy their own medicines for me to prepare. It's an expense we can't spare."

"You won't have to pay another coin yourself," Nahri said smoothly. "Well, as long as our royal backer remains so sure of himself." She smiled sweetly at him, relishing his glower.

A metal glint caught her eye from the ground. Remembering Ali's comments about seeing tools in the surgical wing, Nahri knelt. Whatever it was was partially buried, half hidden behind a tree root that had burst through the floor and littered the broken tile with mounds of dark soil.

"What's that?" Subha asked when Nahri reached for it.

"It looks like a scalpel," Nahri replied, brushing the dirt away. "But it's stuck."

Ali leaned over her. "Pull a bit harder."

"I *am* pulling hard." Nahri gave another determined yank, and the blade abruptly came free, bursting out of the dirt with a spray of dark soil—and the skeletal hand still holding it.

Nahri dropped it, falling backward with a startled shriek. Ali grabbed her arm, yanking her back as his other hand went to his zulfiqar.

Subha peered past them. "Is that a *hand*?" Her eyes went wide with horror.

Ali quickly let Nahri go. "This place was destroyed during the war," he said haltingly. Guilt flashed in his eyes. "Maybe . . . maybe not all those killed were put to rest."

"Obviously not," Nahri said acidly. Had Subha not been there, she would have had far sharper words, but Nahri didn't dare start fighting about the war in front of the already apprehensive doctor.

It was Subha, however, who continued. "It seems a terrible thing to attack a place like this," she said grimly. "No matter how just a war's cause."

Ali was staring at the bones. "Maybe that's not all that happened here."

"And what exactly do you think happened here that justified destroying a hospital and slaughtering its healers?" Nahri shot back, infuriated by his response.

"I didn't say it was justified," Ali defended. "Just that there might be more to the story."

"I think I've had enough of this particular story," Subha interrupted, looking ill. "Why don't we move on and leave digging in the floors to people who can properly take care of these remains?"

Remains. The word seemed cold, clinical. *Family*, Nahri silently corrected, knowing there was a good chance the person murdered here still clutching a scalpel had been a Nahid. She removed her chador, draping it carefully over the bones. She'd come back here with Kartir.

By the time she straightened up, Subha was already through the apothecary door, but Ali was not.

Nahri grabbed his wrist bfore he could leave. "Is there something about this place you're not telling me?"

His gaze darted away. "You're better off not knowing."

Nahri tightened her grip. "Don't you dare condescend to me like that. Wasn't that your reasoning when it came to Dara as well? All those books I wasn't 'prepared' for? How did that turn out for you?"

Ali jerked free. "Everyone knew about Darayavahoush, Nahri. They just couldn't agree if he was a monster or a hero. What led to this?" He tilted his head to take in the dim room. "It was buried. And if you want a new beginning, it should stay buried."

19

DARA

"We'll attack the second night of Navasatem," Dara said as they gazed at the map he'd conjured: a section of Daevabad's narrow beach, the city walls and looming Citadel tower just behind it. "It is a new moon then and will be lightless. The Royal Guard will not see us coming until their tower is crashing through the lake."

"That's the night after the parade, correct?" Mardoniye asked. "Are you sure that's wise?"

Kaveh nodded. "I may not have witnessed a Navasatem in Daevabad, but I've heard plenty about the first day of celebrations. The drinking starts at dawn and doesn't stop until after the competitions in the arena. By midnight, half the city will be passed out in their beds. We'll take the djinn unaware and the majority of the Daevas will be at home."

"And Nahri will be in the infirmary, yes?" Dara asked. "You are certain Nisreen can keep her safe?"

"For the twentieth time, yes, Afshin," Kaveh sighed. "She will bar the infirmary doors at the first sight of your rather . . . creative sign."

Dara wasn't convinced. "Nahri is not the type to be confined against her will."

Kaveh gave him an even stare. "Nisreen has spent years at her side. I'm certain she can handle this."

And I'm certain she has no idea the Nahid under her charge once made a living getting in and out of locked places undetected. Uneasy, Dara glanced at Mardoniye. "Would you go see if Banu Manizheh is ready to join us?" he asked. She had barely left her tent in the past few days, working at a feverish pace on her experiments.

The young soldier nodded, rising to his feet and heading off across the camp. The sky was a pale pink through the dark trees. The snows had finally melted and the dew-damp earth glistened under the sun's first rays. His archers had already left to go practice with their horses in the valley below, and another pair of warriors was leading a yawning Abu Sayf out to their sparring ring. Dara quickly checked to make sure the zulfiqars were still sheathed on the other side of the ring. He had made it clear to his soldiers they were only to practice with Abu Sayf in his presence.

Aeshma snorted, drawing Dara's attention. "I still cannot believe they celebrate what Suleiman did to us," he said to Vizaresh.

Dara's mood instantly darkened. The ifrit had returned to their camp yesterday, and each hour in their presence was more trying. "We celebrate freedom from his bondage," he shot back. "You remember . . . the part where our ancestors obeyed and thus didn't have their magic permanently taken away. And surely you must have once celebrated *some* sort of festivities."

Aeshma looked wistful. "The humans in my land would occasionally sacrifice virgins in my name. They screamed terribly, but the music was enjoyable."

Dara briefly closed his eyes. "Forget the question. But speaking of the attack . . . are the two of *you* prepared? The ghouls will be handled?"

Vizaresh inclined his head. "I'm well-accomplished at such a thing."

"Accomplished enough to keep them from attacking my warriors?"

He nodded. "I will be at the beach with them myself."

That didn't make Dara feel much better. He hated the idea of separating his small militia and leaving a group of his untested warriors on the opposite side of the city. But he had no choice.

Aeshma grinned. "If you're worried, Afshin, I'm sure Qandisha would be happy to join us. She misses you terribly."

The campfire snapped loudly in response.

Kaveh glanced at him. "Who is Qandisha?"

Dara focused on his breath, staring at the flames as he tried to steady the magic surging through his limbs. "The ifrit who enslaved me."

Vizaresh clucked his tongue. "I was very jealous," he confessed. "I never managed to enslave someone so powerful."

Dara cracked his knuckles loudly. "Yes, what a pity."

Kaveh frowned. "This Qandisha is not working with Banu Manizheh?"

"She was, but then *he* wouldn't allow it," Aeshma mocked, tilting his head toward Dara. "He fell to his knees and begged his Nahid to send Qandisha away. Said it was his only condition. Though I can't imagine why." Aeshma licked his teeth. "After all, she's the only one who remembers what you did as a slave. And you must be curious. *Fourteen* centuries' worth of memories . . ." He leaned in. "Think of all the delightful desires you must have fulfilled."

Dara's hand dropped to his knife. "Give me a reason, Aeshma," he seethed.

Aeshma's eyes danced. "Only a joke, dear Afshin."

He didn't get a chance to respond. There was a startled cry from behind him, a thud, and the unmistakable sound of two bodies colliding.

And then the terrible hiss of a zulfiqar flaring to life.

Dara was whirling around, a conjured bow in his hands before he had taken another breath. The scene came to him in pieces. An exhausted Manizheh emerging from her tent. Abu Sayf's two guards on the ground, the fiery zulfiqar in the Geziri man's hands as he lunged toward her . . .

Dara's arrow flew, but Abu Sayf was prepared, raising a plank of wood with a speed and skill that took Dara by surprise. This was *not* the man who'd been sparring with his soldiers. He shot again, a cry rising from his throat as Abu Sayf rushed forward.

Mardoniye flung himself between the Geziri scout and Manizheh, parrying the zulfiqar's strike with his sword, the iron hissing against the conjured flames. He pushed Abu Sayf back, barely meeting the next blow as he inadvertently stepped between Dara and a clean shot.

But it was clear who was the better swordsman . . . and Mardoniye wasn't able to block Abu Sayf's next thrust.

The zulfiqar went straight through his stomach.

Dara was running for them the next moment, his magic surging, ice and snow melting beneath his feet. Abu Sayf pulled the zulfiqar out of Mardoniye and the Daeva man collapsed. He raised it over Manizheh . . .

She snapped her fingers.

Dara heard the bones in Abu Sayf's hand shatter from ten paces away. Abu Sayf cried out in pain, dropping the zulfiqar as Manizheh stared down at him, cold hatred in her dark eyes. By the time Dara reached them, his soldiers had pinned the Geziri. His hand was horrifically broken, the fingers splayed and pointing in different directions.

Dara dropped to Mardoniye's side. A sheen had swept the young man's eyes, his face already pale. His wound was a ghastly, gaping hole, black blood spreading in a pool beneath him. Though a few tendrils of the zulfiqar's telltale greenish-black poison were snaking across his skin, Dara knew that wouldn't be what took him.

Manizheh had gone right to work, ripping open the young warrior's coat. She pressed her hands against his stomach and closed her eyes.

Nothing happened. Nothing would happen, Dara knew. No one—not even a Nahid—healed from a zulfiqar blow.

Manizheh gasped, a choked sound of angry disbelief in her throat as she pressed harder.

Dara touched her hand. "My lady . . ." Her eyes darted to his, wilder than Dara had ever seen them, and he shook his head.

Mardoniye cried out in pain, clutching Dara's hand. "It hurts," he whispered, tears trickling down his cheeks. "Oh, Creator, please."

Dara took him gently into his arms. "Close your eyes," he soothed. "The pain will be gone soon, my friend. You fought well." His throat constricted. The words came automatically to him; he'd done this awful duty so many times.

Blood was trickling from Mardoniye's mouth. "My mother . . ."

"Your mother will be brought to live at my palace, her every need seen to." Manizheh reached out to bless Mardoniye's brow. "I will take her myself to visit your shrine at the temple. You saved my life, child, and for that your eyes will next open in Paradise."

Dara brought his lips to Mardoniye's ear. "It's beautiful," he whispered. "There's a garden, a peaceful grove of cedars where you'll wait with your loved ones . . ." His voice finally cracked, tears brimming in his eyes as Mardoniye jerked and then grew still, hot blood slowly soaking Dara's clothes.

"He's gone," Manizheh said softly.

Dara closed Mardoniye's eyes, gently laying him back on the bloody snow. *Forgive me, my friend.*

He rose to his feet, pulling free the knife he wore at his waist. Flames were licking down his arms and flickering in his eyes before he even approached Abu Sayf. The Geziri man was bloody, his nose broken, held fast by four of Dara's warriors.

Rage tore through him. The knife in his hand transformed, smoking away to reveal a scourge.

"Tell me why I should not flay you piece by piece right now," Dara hissed. "Why I should not do the same to your companion and make you listen as he screams for death?"

Abu Sayf met his eyes, a mix of defeat and grim determination in his expression. "Because you would have done the same thing in my place. Do you think we don't know who you *are*? What your Nahid is doing with our blood and our relics? Do you think we don't know what you have planned for Daevabad?"

"It is not your city," Dara snapped. "I treated you with kindness and this is how you repay me?"

Incredulity crossed Abu Sayf's face. "You cannot be that naive, Afshin. You threatened to torture the young warrior in my care if I didn't train *yours* to murder my kinsmen. Do you think a few shared meals and conversations erase that?"

"I think you are a liar from a tribe of liars." When Dara rushed on, he knew it was not just Abu Sayf he was angry at. "A horde of sand flies who lie and manipulate and feign friendship to gain trust." He raised his scourge. "I think it should be your tongue I take first."

"No." Manizheh's voice cut through the air.

Dara whirled around. "He killed Mardoniye! He would have killed you!" He was nearly as furious with himself as he was with Abu Sayf. Dara should never have allowed this. He knew how dangerous the Geziris were and yet he'd let them remain at camp, let himself be lulled into complacency by Abu Sayf's fluent

Divasti and the comfort of swapping stories with a fellow warrior. And now Mardoniye was dead.

"I am killing him, Banu Nahida," Dara said flatly, the defiance easy for once. "This is a matter of war you do not understand."

Manizheh's eyes flashed. "Do not dare condescend to me, Darayavahoush. Lower your weapon. I will not ask again." She turned to Kaveh without waiting for a response. "Retrieve the serum and the relic from my tent. And I want the other Geziri brought out."

Dara was instantly chastened. "Banu Nahida, I merely meant—"

"I do not care what you meant." Her gaze leveled on him. "You may be dear to me, Darayavahoush, but I am not as ignorant of our history as my daughter. You obey *my* commands. But if it helps . . ." She brushed past him. "I don't plan to leave these men alive."

Kaveh returned. "Here you are, my lady," he said, handing her a small glass bottle stoppered with red wax.

Dara's men returned the next moment, dragging the second Geziri scout as he struggled and swore. He went still the moment he saw Abu Sayf, their gray gazes locking. A look of understanding passed between them.

Of course, you fool. They've probably been plotting this, laughing behind your back at your weaknesses. Again, he cursed himself for underestimating them. His younger self wouldn't have. His younger self would have killed them in the forest.

Manizheh handed the relic to one of his men. "Put it back in his ear. Then tie them . . . here and here," she said, indicating a pair of trees about ten paces apart.

The younger scout was losing his fight against panic. He thrashed out as they shoved the relic back into his ear, his eyes wild.

"Hamza," Abu Sayf spoke softly. "Do not give them that."

A tear ran down the other man's cheek, but he stopped fighting.

Mardoniye, Dara reminded himself. He turned from the frightened Geziri to Manizheh. "What is that?" he asked, looking at the bottle.

"The other part of our plan. A potion I've been working on for decades. A way to kill a man who might be well-guarded. A way too swift to stop."

Dara drew up. "A way to kill Ghassan?"

Manizheh's gaze seemed distant. "Among others." She removed the top from the flask.

A wispy copper vapor rose out, dancing and darting in the air like a thing alive. It seemed to hesitate, to search.

And then, without warning, it dove for Abu Sayf.

The older scout jerked back as the vapor rushed past his face, swarming his copper relic. It dissolved in the blink of an eye, the liquid metal shimmering in a coppery haze that vanished into his ear.

There was a moment of startled, horrified shock on his face, and then he howled, clutching his head.

"Abu Sayf!" the younger djinn cried out.

The other man didn't respond. Blood was streaming from his eyes, ears, and nose, mixed with the coppery vapors.

Kaveh gasped, covering his mouth. "Is that . . . is that what my Jamshid . . ."

"I suspect Jamshid found an earlier version of my notes," Manizheh replied. "This is far more advanced." She fell briefly silent as Abu Sayf grew still, his unseeing eyes fixed on the sky, and then she swallowed loud enough for Dara to hear. "It's attracted to Geziri relics and grows upon consuming them, pressing upon the brain until it kills its bearer."

Dara couldn't take his eyes off Abu Sayf. His bloody body was twisted, his face frozen in a mask of anguish. Manizheh's explanation sent a chill through him, extinguishing the flames swirling over his limbs.

He tried to recover some semblance of his wits. "But it is magic. If you tried this on Ghassan, he would just use the seal."

"It works as well without magic." She pulled free her scalpel. "If you remove the magic as Nahid blood does, as Suleiman's seal does . . ." She cut her thumb, squeezing out a drop of black blood. It landed on a tendril of vapor rising from Abu Sayf's corpse, and a jagged shard of copper fell instantly to the bloody snow. ". . . that's what you get in your skull."

The other scout was still trying to twist free of his binds as he yelled in Geziriyya. And then he started to scream.

The vapor was creeping toward his feet.

"No!" he cried as it wrapped around his body, winding toward his ear. "No—"

His scream cut off, and this time Dara did glance away, fixing his gaze on Mardoniye's body until the second scout fell silent.

"Well," Manizheh said grimly. There was no triumph in her voice. "I suppose it works."

At his side, Kaveh swayed. Dara steadied him, putting a hand on his shoulder. "You want me to give this to Ghassan?" the wazir said hoarsely.

Manizheh nodded. "Vizaresh has designed one of his old rings so that a false jewel may be filled with the vapor. You need merely break it in Ghassan's presence. It will kill every Geziri in the room."

It will kill every Geziri in the room. Kaveh looked like he was about to be sick, and Dara didn't blame him.

Even so, he spoke up. "I can do it. The grand wazir need not risk himself."

"He does," Manizheh countered, though the quiet worry was audible in her voice. "We don't know if Ghassan will be able to use Suleiman's seal on you, Dara. We can't risk finding out. He needs to be dead before you step into the palace, and Kaveh's position ensures him easy and relatively unguarded access."

"But—"

"I will do it." Kaveh's voice was no less frightened, but it was determined. "For what he did to Jamshid, I will do it."

Dara's stomach tightened. He stared at the dead scouts, the cool earth steaming as their copper-flecked blood spread. So this was what Manizheh had been working on so diligently the past few months.

Did you think this wouldn't be vicious? Dara knew war. He knew—more than anyone alive—just what the Nahids could be capable of.

But by the Creator, did he hate seeing this violence claim her.

It claimed Mardoniye as well, he reminded himself. *It claimed Nahri and Jamshid.* Ghassan had been terrorizing and killing Daevas for years. If victory for his people meant the king and a few of his guards died painfully, that was not a cost Dara would protest. He would end this war and ensure Manizheh never had to resort to anything like this again.

He cleared his throat. "It sounds as if you should pack, Kaveh. Now, if you will both excuse me . . ." He headed for Mardoniye's body. "I have a warrior to put to rest."

DARA BUILT MARDONIYE'S FUNERAL PYRE WITH HIS own hands and stayed at its side until it was reduced to ash, the smoldering remains throwing a weak light into the dark night. Dara was alone by then; Manizheh had overseen rites and then left to see Kaveh off, while Dara ordered the rest of his soldiers to continue with their duties. He could tell they were shaken—for all their devotion and training, few had witnessed the kind of fighting that led to a man bleeding out on the snow, and he could see the unspoken question in their eyes. Would they too end up this way in Daevabad?

Dara hated that he couldn't tell them no.

A touch upon his shoulder startled him. He glanced back. "Irtemiz?"

The young archer stepped closer. "We thought one of us should check on you," she said softly. Her gaze fell on the smoking pyre. "I still can't believe he's gone." Her voice trembled. "I should have had my bow on hand all the time, like you say . . ."

"It is not your fault," Dara said firmly. "The sand fly was likely waiting for such an opportunity." He pressed her shoulder. "Besides, he blocked my arrows, and surely, you are not suggesting you're better than your teacher?" He feigned offense.

That drew a small, sad smile from her lips. "Give me another decade." Her smile faded. "There . . . there was something else we thought you should see."

Dara frowned at her tone. "Show me."

She led him through the dark trees, their boots crunching on the ground. "Bahram first noticed it when he took the horses out. He said it stretched as far as he could see."

They emerged from the tree line, the valley spreading flat before them. The river was a gleaming ribbon of moonlight that would have normally outshone the surrounding plain.

But the spring grass was not dark. It was glowing with a warm copper hue that exactly matched Manizheh's vapor, a low fog of death clinging to the earth.

"Bahram . . . he rode out far, Afshin. He said it's everywhere." She swallowed. "We haven't told the Banu Nahida yet. We weren't certain it was our place, but surely . . . surely, this does not mean . . ." She trailed off, unable to voice the same awful fear snaring Dara's heart.

"There must be some explanation," he finally replied. "I will talk to her."

He went straight to Manizheh's tent, ignoring the stares of his warriors and the chuckles of the ifrit at their roaring fire. Despite the late hour, she was clearly awake; the light of oil lamps shone through the felt and he could smell the tang of freshly brewed tea.

"Banu Manizheh?" he called. "May I speak to you?"

She appeared a moment later, her familiar chador replaced by a thick woolen shawl. She was clearly readying herself for bed; her silvering black braids had been undone and she looked surprised to see him.

"Afshin," she greeted him, her eyes concerned as they swept his face. "What's wrong?"

Dara flushed, ashamed to have come upon her in such a manner. "Forgive my intrusion. But this is a matter best discussed privately."

"Then come in." She held open the tent flap. "Take some tea with me. And sit. This has been a terrible day."

The affection in her voice set him at ease, stilling some of the dread rising in his heart. He slipped off his boots and hung his cloak before taking a seat on one of the cushions. On the other side of the tent, the curtain partitioning off the small area where she slept was drawn back.

One of Kaveh's caps was still there. Dara looked away from it, feeling like he'd seen something not meant for his eyes. "The grand wazir departed safely?"

"Right after the funeral," she replied, pouring the tea. "He wanted to get some distance covered before the sun set."

Dara took the cup she handed him. "Kaveh is a quicker flier than I would have imagined," he said. "There must be some truth to those stories you tell of racing horses around Zariaspa."

Manizheh took a seat across from him. "He is eager to get back to Daevabad. He's been worried about Jamshid since we received Nisreen's letter." Manizheh took a sip of her drink. "But something tells me Kaveh is not the reason you are here."

"No. Not quite." Dara set down his tea. "My lady, my riders brought something to my attention I think you should know about. The copper vapor that killed the scouts . . . it appears to have spread. It looks fainter to my eye, but it's everywhere, hovering just above the ground as far as the river valley."

Manizheh's expression didn't waver. "And?"

The clipped response set his heart racing. "You said that it is attracted to Geziri relics, that it grows upon consuming them . . ." His voice caught. "Banu Nahida . . . when does it *stop*?"

She met his gaze. "I don't know. That's what I've been working on all these months: I've been trying to find a way to contain its spread and the length of time that it's potent." Her eyes dimmed. "But I haven't had much success, and we are out of time."

"You're going to let Kaveh release that in the palace," Dara whispered. He fought for control as the implication swept through him. "Banu Manizheh . . . there must be hundreds of Geziris in the palace. The scholars in the library, secretaries and attendants. The women and children in the harem. Ghassan's daughter. They all wear relics. If he lets this loose in the middle of the night . . . it could kill every Geziri there."

Manizheh quietly set her cup of tea down, and her silence sent him reeling.

No. Creator, no. "Not just the palace." A gasp left his lips. "You think this could kill every Geziri in Daevabad."

There was no mistaking the soft edge of despair in her voice when she replied, "I think that more likely than not." But then her black eyes hardened. "And what of it? How many Daevas died when Zaydi al Qahtani took Daevabad? How many of your friends and relatives, Afshin?" Scorn filled her voice. "The sand flies are not complete fools. At least a few will figure out what is happening and take out their relics. Which is why the timing must be perfect."

A voice was screaming inside his head, but Dara felt no heat, no magic aching to escape his skin. He was colder than he had ever been. "Do not do this," he said, his entire body shaking. "Do not start your reign with this much blood on your hands."

"I have no choice." When Dara looked away, Manizheh pressed on, her voice growing firmer. "This is how we win. And we *must* win. If Ghassan lives, if our victory is anything less than completely decisive, he will annihilate us. He will not rest until every trace of our people is destroyed. You are mourning Mardoniye? You must realize how many more of your warriors will survive if there are no soldiers left to fight by the time we reach the palace."

"You will make us monsters." The ice around his heart shattered, and Dara began to lose the fight with his emotions. "That is what we are if you let this happen . . . and Banu Nahida, that's not a reputation you'll ever lose." He looked at her, beseeching. "I beg you, my lady. These are innocents. *Children.* Travelers coming to celebrate Navasatem . . ." His memories were stealing over him. This was all too familiar.

Merchants. Traders. Weavers whose finely embroidered silk ran with blood just a touch too crimson. Children who didn't realize the human brown in their eyes sealed their fate. The calm commands and coldly reasoned explanations of another generation of Nahids.

The fabled city of Qui-zi reduced to smoking ruins. The screams and smell of earthy blood that would never leave his memories.

"Then we will be monsters," Manizheh declared. "I will pay that price to end this war."

"It won't end it," Dara argued, desperate. "We will have every Geziri capable of picking up a blade at the banks of the Gozan when they learn we slaughtered their kinsmen without provocation. They will fight us until the Day of Judge—"

"Then I will release this poison into their homeland." Dara jerked back, and Manizheh continued. "Let the djinn tribes know the price for defiance. I do not want this death on my hands, but if it will stifle the rebellions of the Sahrayn and the cunning of the Ayaanle, I will take it. Let the fate of the Geziris weigh on the minds of the Tukharistanis who still curse your name and the Agnivanshis who think their wide rivers protect them."

"You sound like Ghassan," Dara accused her.

Her eyes flashed in anger. "Then maybe he was right to rule so," she said bitterly. "But at least this time, it won't be my family and tribe living in fear."

"Until the next war," he said, unable to check the savage resentment rising in him. "Which I assume I'll be dragged back for, should I happen to die here." He rose to his feet. "You were to be better than this. Better than the Qahtanis. Better than your ancestors!"

He crossed the tent, reaching for his cloak.

"Where are you going?" Manizheh demanded sharply.

Dara shoved on his boots. "To stop Kaveh."

"Absolutely not. You are under *my* command, Darayavahoush."

"I said I'd help you retake Daevabad—not commit another Qui-zi." He reached for the tent flap.

It burst into flames and a searing pain shot down his arm. Dara cried out, more in shock than hurt as he whirled back around.

Manizheh snapped her fingers, and the pain vanished. "We are not done with our conversation," she seethed. "I have risked and lost too much to see my plans fail now because a warrior with more blood on his hands than I can even imagine momentarily grew a conscience." Her expression was cold. "If you have ever called yourself an Afshin, you will sit back down right now."

Dara stared at her in disbelief. "This is not you, Banu Manizheh."

"You do not know me, Darayavahoush. You do not know what you've already cost me."

"What *I've* cost *you*?" The charge was almost laughable. Dara beat a fist against his chest. "*Do you think I want to be here?*" Anger swirled into his heart, and then it was breaking free—the line he'd sworn he'd never cross, the resentment that festered in the darkest part of his soul. "I do not want any of this! Your family destroyed my life—my honor, my reputation! You had me carry out one of the worst crimes in our history, and when it blew up in your faces, you blamed me!"

She glared. "I wasn't the one who put a scourge in your hand."

"No, you are just the one who brought me back. Twice." Tears blurred his eyes. "I was with my sister. I was at *peace*."

Her eyes were blazing now. "You don't get to pine for peace with your family after what you did to mine."

"Your daughter would never agree to *any* of this."

"I'm not talking about my daughter." Manizheh's gaze pinned him. He'd swear he could feel her magic, the ghost of fingers around his throat, a barbed tightness in his chest. "I'm talking about my son."

Confusion coursed through him. "Your son?" But before the word fully left his mouth, Dara's gaze fell upon Kaveh's cap beside her bedroll. He recalled her fierce words about keeping those she loved hidden . . .

He thought, very suddenly, of the kindhearted young man he'd left riddled with arrows.

"No," Dara whispered. "He . . . he has no abilities." Dara couldn't even say his name; it would make the horrified suspicion racing through his mind all too real. "He said his mother was a servant. That she died when he was born . . ."

"He was misinformed," Manizheh said brusquely. "He has no mother because if the Qahtanis ever learned of such a thing, he would have been forced into the same cage I was trapped in. He has no abilities because when he was less than a week old, I had to *brand my infant child* with a tattoo that would inhibit them. In order to give him a life, a peaceful future in the Zariaspa that I loved, I had no choice but to to cut him off from his very birthright." Manizheh's voice was trembling. "Jamshid e-Pramukh is my son."

Dara inhaled, fighting for breath, for words. "That cannot be."

"He's my son," Manizheh repeated. "Your Baga Nahid, should such a thing mean anything to you." She sounded more hurt than angry now. "And because of your heedlessness when it came to my daughter, you nearly killed him. You stole from him the only future he ever wanted and left him wracked with such physical pain Kaveh says there are days he can't leave his bed." Her expression twisted. "What is the punishment for that, Afshin? For sending arrows into a man you should have greeted with your face in the dust?"

Dara was suddenly sitting, though he had little recollection of doing so. His knees felt weak, his head heavy.

Manizheh clearly wasn't done. "I wasn't going to tell you, you know. Not until after we'd won. Until he was safe and I'd burned that damned mark from his back. I thought you'd suffered enough. I feared the guilt might break you."

He could see the truth of that in her eyes, and that did break him—that, and the realization that Manizheh had spent these years Jamshid needed her most at the side of the man who'd injured him. "I am sorry," he whispered.

"I don't want your apology," Manizheh snapped. "I want my children. I want my city. I want the throne, and the seal Zaydi al Qahtani stole from my ancestors. I want my generation of Daevas to stop suffering because of the actions of yours. And quite frankly, Afshin, I do not give a damn if you approve of my methods."

Dara ran his hands through his hair. "There has to be a better way." He could hear the plea in his voice.

"There isn't. Your warriors swore oaths to me. If you go after Kaveh, we will be gone when you return. I will take them to Daevabad, release the poison myself, and hope it kills Ghassan before he realizes what's happening and has Nahri, Jamshid, and every Daeva he can get his hands on slaughtered." She stared at him. "Or you can help me."

Dara's hands curled into fists. He felt more trapped than he had in years, as though a net he'd unknowingly stepped into had snapped up around him. And, Creator forgive him, he could not see a way to escape that wouldn't kill more people he loved.

He dropped his gaze, briefly closing his eyes. *Forgive me, Tamima,* he prayed softly. Manizheh might be right. This brutal act might be enough to force the other tribes into a more permanent submission.

But for standing at her side while she committed it, Dara did not imagine he would ever again see the garden where his sister waited for him.

He opened his eyes. His soul was heavy as iron. "My soldiers are asking questions," he said slowly. "And I do not want this guilt on their consciences." He fixed his gaze on his Nahid and bowed his head once again. "What would you have me tell them?"

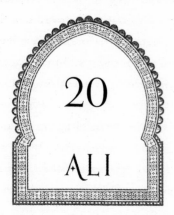

20

ALI

"Take the bricks as well," Ali said, shading his eyes against the bright sun to scan the mound of rubble that his workers had unearthed while ripping up the platform erected over Sheikh Anas's ruined mosque. "We'll find a way to reuse them."

One of the men tugged a piece of rotting textile from the pile of debris. "Looks like old carpeting." He tossed it at Ali's feet. "Probably not worth saving, no?"

Ali's eyes locked on the tattered fragment; what remained of the carpet's geometric pattern was instantly familiar. Ali had prayed upon that carpet, had sat in rapturous silence as he listened to Sheikh Anas's thunderous sermons.

"No," he said, his throat thickening at the memory of his murdered sheikh. "Probably not."

A heavy hand dropped on his shoulder, startling him from his thoughts. "The women and children are off with Aqisa," Lubayd announced. "Tents are waiting for them outside the hospital and that grumpy doctor of yours is going to examine them."

"That grumpy doctor has a name," Ali replied wearily. "And I would recommend not getting on her bad side. But thank you."

Lubayd squinted at him. "Everything all right, brother? You don't look well."

Ali sighed, turning away from the carpet. "This isn't an easy place to be." He glanced across the street where a few of the shafit men they'd freed were eating food his sister had sent over from the palace kitchens. Freshly arrived—or rather dragged—to Daevabad from the human world, they had no other homes to return to. "And these aren't easy stories to hear."

Lubayd followed his gaze. "I'd like to toss the purebloods who oversaw this place in the lake. A bunch of thieves and thugs—stealing jewelry, harassing women, beating the men who talked back." He shook his head. "And under the guise of helping shafit newcomers find family. What a rotten scheme."

"Not just newcomers," Ali pointed out. "I've been speaking to plenty of people who were kidnapped and pressed into service, like the father and daughter we first came upon."

"And you said it was a Geziri man at the top, correct? Tariq al whatever?" Lubayd looked disgusted. "Shameful. Such behavior goes against everything we've fought for."

"Money changes people," Ali said. "And I think quite a lot was made here."

They started walking. "Speaking of money, are we threatening any more rich folk today?" Lubayd asked.

Ali shook his head, wiping the dust from his face with the end of his turban. "Not threatening—correcting a fiscal deficit. But no, not today. I've hammered out a repayment plan with Abul Dawanik," he said, naming the Ayaanle trade envoy. "Their first payment should be in the Treasury by month's end, and he agreed to make immediate arrangements to cover the costs of new

uniforms for the Royal Guard and zulfiqars for the cadets. Their
rations should be improved soon as well. Turns out the official in
charge of contracting meals for the Citadel was taking a cut from
the money he was granted. His secretary figured it out but was too
afraid to approach my father."

"I take it that secretary now has his job?"

Ali smiled. "And my eternal gratitude."

Lubayd clucked his tongue. "Do you ever rest between these
tasks? You *do* know most people sleep at night, yes? They don't
just hunch over pages of numbers and mutter to themselves."

"I like working hard," Ali retorted. "It keeps my mind off
things."

"This seems like the kind of place where you should probably
keep your mind *on* things." Lubayd gestured at a trio of djinn
pulling partitions from the wreckage. "Soldiers?"

"Friends from when I was a cadet. They had the day off and
wanted to help."

"I suspect they're not the only ones." Lubayd lowered his
voice. "I've been hearing whispers again, the kind you asked me
to keep an ear out for."

Ali stopped. "From the Guard?"

Lubayd nodded. "A lot of soldiers think fondly of you, Ali.
Very fondly. And when those new uniforms and rations show up at
the Citadel, people are going to know you're behind them."

Ali paused. "Good."

Lubayd started. "*Good?*"

"My father spent five years making it clear he didn't care
whether I lived or died," Ali said, defending himself. "Should
I pretend I'm not pleased people like me . . . particularly when
those people are the ones with weapons?"

His friend assessed him shrewdly. "I might not be some
Daevabadi courtier, Ali, but even *I* know what it looks like when
bitter second sons start making friends with the military." Intent

laced into his voice. "That wasn't the plan, remember? The plan was to return to Am Gezira with your head still attached to your neck. With *my* head still attached to *my* neck."

The sound of horses—at least a half dozen, their hooves striking the cobbled stones with speed—interrupted them. Ali glanced up, ready to chide whoever it was for riding at such a pace in the crowded plaza.

The words died on his tongue. It was Muntadhir—and he looked furious. Just behind him rode a coterie of his companions, the wealthy dilettantes who orbited him like particularly useless moons. They stood out in this neighborhood, one of Daevabad's poorest, their jewels glinting in the sun and their vibrant silks gaudy.

Despite the crowd, Muntadhir was across the plaza in moments; he'd always been an excellent horseman. When they reached Ali, his mount came to an effortless stop, as if it could read its rider's thoughts. It was a beautiful animal, silver spots scattered across its ebony hide like a spray of stars in the night sky.

Ali tensed. He wasn't expecting his brother. On the contrary, Muntadhir had been avoiding Ali's increasingly desperate attempts to talk to him with admirable success. His brother ignored him when they were at court and had obviously enlisted his formidable—and loyal—staff in ensuring they were never alone. Ali would no sooner corner him after a meeting than a steward would magically appear to usher Muntadhir off on some "urgent" unspecified errand.

"Emir," Ali greeted, uneasy. Every instinct was warning him to tread carefully. "Peace be upon you."

"Peace is the last thing you've brought me," Muntadhir snapped. He threw a thick scroll at Ali, which Ali instinctively caught. "Is this a joke?"

Baffled, Ali unfurled the scroll. He recognized it at once . . . mostly because he'd thrown it himself, hours earlier, at the men he'd found forcing a new group of stolen shafit into the foul pens Ali's workers had just finished tearing down. It was a royal proclamation declaring the area was now the property of the king, and that any shafit in the vicinity were free to leave.

He frowned. "How did you get this?"

"Strange you should ask: it was given to *my cousin* this morning by one of his servants."

A terrible chill descended over Ali. "Tariq al Ubari is your *cousin*? One of your *relatives* was responsible for this place?"

A Geziri man emerged from Muntadhir's crowd of sparkling friends. He sat in a gilded saddle upon a beautiful red stallion, wearing a fine brocade coat woven with silver thread and jade beads. Ropes of pearls lined his neck, the largest ending in a gold brooch the size of Ali's fist, encrusted with rubies in the shape of a zahhak.

Ali instantly disliked him. "You're Tariq al Ubari, I take it?" he asked.

"Cousin to our emir, God preserve him," Tariq declared coolly, matching Ali's disdain. "Queen Saffiyeh, may her soul rest in peace, and I shared a third great-great-uncle."

Oh. The mention of Muntadhir's mother landed like a heavy stone between them. Ali tried to maintain his calm, and he could see Muntadhir struggling to do the same. His brother rarely spoke about his mother. Ali had never known her—she'd died before he was born, when Muntadhir himself was still a child. But he'd heard she and Muntadhir had been very close, and he'd always known his brother was deeply affected by her loss.

Looking at Tariq of the third great-great-uncle, Ali suspected he knew as well, and was only too happy to take advantage of that grief. Anger stirred in Ali's heart. He didn't need another reason to hate the man behind this abominable place, but the fact that he was so obviously using Muntadhir made his hatred burn a hundred times hotter.

Still, the situation before him was delicate. If Tariq had been a closer relation, Ali would have recognized the name and acted with more discretion. God knew things were already strained enough between him and Muntadhir.

He stepped closer to his brother's horse. "Why didn't you say something sooner?"

Muntadhir flushed. "I wasn't aware. Do you know all your relatives' personal assets?"

"I know none of them made a business of selling shafit like slaves." Ali hissed the words under his breath, but clearly not quietly enough, for Tariq drew up.

"*Slaves?*" Tariq rolled his eyes, the word coming in a condescending drawl. "By the Most High, we're all aware of how sensitive you are when it comes to the shafit, Prince Alizayd, but there were no *slaves* here. God forbid such a thing. There were shafit looking for work, and for their pureblooded kin."

Ali couldn't believe the man's gall. "Looking for work?" he asked incredulously. "The first time I came upon this place, your men were auctioning off a child as she screamed for her father!"

Muntadhir turned toward Tariq in shock. "Is that true?"

Ali had to hand it to Tariq—the man didn't so much as flinch. "Of course not." He touched his heart. "Come, Emir, you know me. And you know how the shafit like to exaggerate their woes . . . particularly before a man known to have an open purse and susceptible heart." He shook his head. "I have no doubt they have been filling your poor brother's ears with all sorts of tales of beatings and abuse."

Lubayd threw out a hand, stopping Ali before he lunged forward. But he couldn't stop Ali's tongue. "You lying snake—"

"Enough," Muntadhir snapped. "Both of you." His brother now looked more annoyed than shaken, the doubt that had flashed in his eyes when Ali mentioned the girl already gone. "We didn't come here to fight, Alizayd. The order came from Abba, and Tariq doesn't plan to contest it. But he wants to be properly compensated."

Ali gritted his teeth. "He was. I outlined terms in the scroll."

"A hundred dinars?" Tariq mocked. "That's nothing. Oh, wait, forgive me . . . *and* passage to Mecca," he added sarcastically. "Clearly more an order than an offer."

It was costing every bit of self-control Ali had not to drag this man from his horse. Had Muntadhir not been there, he probably would have. Feeling water begin to pool in his hands, he quickly clenched his fists; he dared not lose control here. "It is a great honor to be allowed to retire to Mecca," he said in an even voice. "We only allow a handful of new djinn to enter the holy city each year; there are those who would weep for such a prize."

"Well, I'm not one of them," Tariq retorted. "My life and my business are in Daevabad. I'm not leaving, and I insist you properly compensate me."

"I can leave you to the shafit you claim to have been assisting in 'finding jobs and kin,'" Ali suggested coldly. "Would that be proper compensation?"

"*No*," Muntadhir said flatly, his eyes flashing as his cousin paled. "Though if you threaten him again, we're going to be having a very different conversation." He stared at Ali. "This man is my kin," he said, his voice low and laced with purpose. "He's under my protection. Do not dishonor me by treating him so disdainfully. There must be some sort of compromise we can agree to."

Ali met his gaze. He understood quite well the Geziri notions of pride and honor his brother was attempting to appeal to.

But that wasn't the only code their tribe held dear.

"There's no compromise to be made here, Dhiru," Ali replied. "I'm not giving this man another coin. We cannot spare them. You are asking me to take bread out of the mouths of the soldiers who guard your life and bricks from the hospital intended to treat your citizens so an already rich man—a man who twisted our most sacred beliefs—can have his pride soothed?" Ali shook his head. "I will not."

A little too late, Ali realized that much of the crowd had gone quiet and that his words had carried. More people were gathering to watch, shafit and working-class djinn locals from the surrounding neighborhoods, people who were staring at the emir and his overdressed companions with open resentment.

Muntadhir seemed to notice as well. His gray eyes flickered across the growing mob, and Ali saw his hands twitch on the reins.

Tariq pressed on, arrogant. "A very pretty speech to your supporters, Prince Alizayd. I suppose it doesn't matter that it rests on the lies of a bunch of ungrateful dirt-bloods and will ruin one of your kinsmen, a man who escorted the emir's own mother to Daevabad." He stared down his nose at Ali, and when he spoke again, his words were precise. "Perhaps a rather clear lesson to us all in how little family means to you."

Ali was biting his tongue so hard it hurt. He could only thank God it was a dry, sunny day—otherwise he was fairly certain he'd be learning new, murderous things to do with rain. "The shafit aren't lying. I saw with my own eyes—"

"Oh?" Tariq interrupted. "Where are the whips then, Prince Alizayd? The chains and these crying children you claim I have so terribly mistreated?"

"I've sent them away to be cared for." Ali motioned to the debris. "There's no evidence because we've been here since dawn. But you can be damn sure I took down the name of every shafit you abused here, and I'd be happy to present their testimony."

"After you've gilded their tongues, you mean," Tariq snorted. "It is the Ayaanle way, after all."

Ali abruptly lost the battle he'd been waging with his temper. His hand dropped to his khanjar. "Would you like to settle things *our* way?" he hissed in Geziriyya. "You should be *fleeing* to Mecca. If you had any fear of God, you would spend the rest of your days repenting for the evil you've done here before you burn in hellfire for all—"

"*Enough.*" Muntadhir's voice cracked across the plaza. "Draw that blade, Alizayd, and I'll have you arrested. *No.*" He held up a hand, cutting off Tariq when he opened his mouth. "I've heard enough from both of you. Return to your home, cousin. There's obviously no negotiation to be made here. I'll take care of you and your wife myself." He nodded to the rest of his men. "Let's go."

Ali dropped his hand from his khanjar. "Dhiru, I only meant—"

"I know what you meant. And I told you not to call me that." Muntadhir suddenly looked exhausted, fed up and disgusted with the entire situation. "My God, and to think she almost convinced me to support this madness . . ." He shook his head. "Perhaps I should be grateful for this, in a way."

"Grateful for what?" Ali ventured, even as his stomach twisted in apprehension.

"Grateful for the reminder that you will always choose your beliefs over your family. Which is fine—enjoy having the shafit as your only ally." Muntadhir touched his brow before turning his horse away. "See how far that takes you in Daevabad, little brother."

21

NAHRI

Nahri pounded again on the door to her husband's apartment. "Muntadhir, I don't care who's in there or what you're drinking, open up. We need to go."

There was no response.

Her frustration reached dangerous levels. She knew her husband and early mornings were no companions, but it had taken her weeks to arrange this visit to the Grand Temple, and they were already running late.

She banged on the door again. "If I have to drag you out of bed—"

The door abruptly opened. Nahri nearly tumbled in, narrowly catching herself.

"Banu Nahida . . ." Muntadhir leaned heavily against the door frame. "Wife," he clarified, lifting a jade wine cup to his lips. "Always so impatient."

Nahri stared at him, completely lost for words. Muntadhir was half dressed, wearing what appeared to be a woman's shawl wrapped around his waist and the dramatically peaked court cap of a Tukharistani noble.

A burst of laughter behind him caught her attention, and Nahri glanced past his shoulder to see two dazzling women lounging in similar states of disarray. One was smoking from a water pipe while the second—dressed in nothing but Muntadhir's court turban wrapped in a way it was certainly *not* intended—rearranged game pieces.

Nahri inhaled, fighting the sudden desire to burn the room down. "Muntadhir," she said, her jaw clenching, "do you not remember that we're supposed to be visiting the Grand Temple today?"

"You know . . . I did remember, as a matter of fact." Muntadhir drained his cup.

Nahri threw up her hands. "Then what is *this*? I can't take you to my people's holiest place while you're drunk and wearing your courtesan's scarf!"

"I'm not going."

Nahri blinked. "Excuse me?"

"I'm not going. I already told you: I think this plan to hire and treat shafit is madness."

"But . . . but you agreed to come today. And your father told you to!" Her voice rose in alarm.

"Ah, there you are wrong," Muntadhir declared, wagging a finger in her face. "He did not order such a thing specifically. He said you had our support." He shrugged. "So tell your priests that you do."

"They're not going to believe me! And if you don't show up, they're going to think there's a reason." She shook her head. "I can't risk another excuse for them to oppose me. They'll take this an insult."

Muntadhir snorted. "They'll be relieved. You're the only Daeva who wants to see a Qahtani in your temple."

The other women laughed in the background again, one throwing dice, and Nahri flinched. "Why are you doing this?" she whispered. "Do you really hate me so much?"

His disinterested expression slipped. "I don't hate you, Nahri. But you're going down a path I can't support, with a partner who destroys everything he touches. I will not sit with my future subjects in a place they hold sacred and make promises I don't believe in."

"You could have told me that last week!"

Muntadhir inclined his head. "Last week, Alizayd had yet to threaten my cousin with hellfire in front of a mob of angry mixed-bloods."

Nahri grabbed his wrist. "He did *what*?"

"I did try to warn you. Go ask your sheikh about it. Hell, ask *him* to go to the Temple with you. I'm sure it would be most entertaining." Muntadhir removed his arm from her grasp and then shut the door in her face.

For a full breath, Nahri stood there stunned. Then she slammed her fists against the door. "MUNTADHIR!"

It stayed closed. As her fury grew, a few cracks appeared in the carved wood and the hinges began to smoke.

No. Nahri stepped back. She'd be damned if she was going to humiliate herself begging her drunken wretch of a husband to keep his word. But damn the bloody princes and their idiotic arguments!

She whirled around, charging down the hall. If Alizayd al Qahtani's recklessness ruined her plans today, she *was* going to poison him.

The door to Ali's apartment was closed when she arrived, and a soldier rose to his feet as she approached. Out of patience and with the palace's magic whirling in her blood, Nahri had no sooner snapped her fingers then a corner brazier unfurled, tossing its fiery contents to the floor and snaking around the soldier's ankle. It yanked him to the ground, and the door burst open before her.

She stepped in and then paused, for a moment not certain she'd entered the correct room. Ali's apartment was in chaos. A half-dozen floor desks were being used by harassed-looking secretaries, and scrolls and record books were everywhere, as were people, pushing papers around and arguing in multiple languages.

Ali's irate voice drifted to her from across the room. "—and I told you I've already awarded the contract. I don't care who your boss's uncle is; that's not how I do things. The hospital's plumbing is being installed by a guild *without* a history of hexing their competition."

She made her way toward him, dodging several startled scribes. Ali noticed her approach at once and quickly straightened up . . . so swiftly, in fact, that he upset an ink bottle across his pale blue dishdasha.

"Banu Nahida, p-peace be upon you," he stammered, dabbing at the ink. "Er, aren't you supposed to be at the Grand Temple?"

"I was supposed to be, yes." She pushed away the edge of her chador to poke a finger at his chest. "With my husband. That is what my people and priests are expecting. And yet my *husband* is now in his cups, entertaining company that is definitely not me, and he's saying *you're* responsible. That you were shouting in the streets about how his cousin was going to burn in hell." She jabbed him again. "Do the two of you not have a *single* grain of sense between you?"

Ali's expression instantly grew stormy. "I didn't say he was *going* to burn in hell," he defended. "I suggested he repent before that happened."

Nahri felt the floor shift beneath her feet. She closed her eyes for a minute, willing herself to be calm. "Alizayd. I spent weeks fighting with the priests to allow this visit. If he doesn't come, they'll view it as a slight. And if they view it as a slight—if they don't think I have your family's support—then how do you think they're going to react when I announce I want to overturn *centuries of tradition* to work alongside shafit? I'm staking my reputation on this hospital. If it fails because you can't keep your mouth shut, hellfire is going to be the least of your problems."

She'd swear the air sparked as the threat left her lips, and she didn't miss the speed at which several of the nearest djinn backed away.

Ali swallowed. "I'll fix it. I swear. Go to the Temple and wait for him."

NAHRI WAS NOT FEELING OPTIMISTIC.

At her side, Jamshid shifted. "I wish you'd let me go talk to him."

She shook her head. "This is between me and Muntadhir. And you shouldn't be solving his problems for him all the time, Jamshid."

He sighed, readjusting his cap. Like Nahri, he was in his Temple attire, bloody and ash-stained hospital smocks traded for silk chadors and coats. "Did you tell Nisreen the truth about why we were coming here?"

Nahri shifted on her feet. "No," she confessed. Nisreen had stayed behind to oversee the infirmary, a thing for which Nahri was secretly relieved. She didn't need another voice arguing against her. "We . . . we have not been seeing eye to eye on much lately."

"She doesn't strike me as the type to enjoy being left in the dark," Jamshid observed mildly.

Nahri grimaced. She didn't like the tension that had grown between her and her mentor, but neither did she know how to fix it.

Jamshid glanced at the gate. "Speaking of unhappy elders, I should probably tell you that my father is—"

The clattering of hooves cut him off. Nahri glanced up to see a rider in an ebony robe cantering toward them. Relief flared in her chest.

It lasted only a moment. Because that rider was *not* her husband.

Ali was at their side in seconds, looking, well, rather damn princely on a magnificent gray stallion. He was dressed in royal colors, the first time she'd ever seen him so, the gold-trimmed black robe smoking around his ankles, the brilliant blue, purple, and gold turban wrapped around his head. He'd shaved his scruffy beard into a semblance of order and was even wearing jewelry—a strand of pearls looping his neck, and a heavy silver ring crowned with one of the famed pink diamonds of Ta Ntry on his left thumb.

Nahri gawked at him. "You're not Muntadhir."

"I am not," he agreed, sliding from the horse. He must have prepared in a hurry; he smelled of freshly burned agarwood, and there were drops of water still clinging to his neck. "My brother remains indisposed."

Jamshid was looking at Ali with open hostility. "Are those his clothes?"

"He doesn't seem to need them today." Ali glanced back, peering in the direction from which he'd come. "Where is she?" he asked, seemingly to himself. "She was right behind me . . ."

Jamshid stepped between them. "Nahri, you can't bring him into the Temple," he warned, switching to Divasti. "People *burn him in effigy* in the Temple!"

Nahri didn't get a chance to respond. Another rider had joined them, one even more surprising than Ali.

"Peace be upon you," Zaynab said in a gallant tone as she dismounted. "A lovely day, isn't it?'

Nahri's mouth actually fell open. The Qahtani princess looked even more dazzling than her brother, in billowy gold riding pants beneath a brightly striped indigo tunic. She wore her black shayla lightly, under a headdress of glittering sapphires, her face partially obscured by a silver Geziri mask. Jewels winked from each of her fingers.

Zaynab took her brother's hand, turning a winning smile toward the Daevas who'd gathered to gawk. There was no denying the royal siblings made for an extraordinary sight, something Zaynab seemed to be relishing.

"What-what are you doing here?" Nahri managed to ask.

Zaynab shrugged. "Ali came running and said you needed Qahtanis to help sway your priests. Now you have some. Even better, you have me." Her tone was sugar sweet. "If you're not aware, the two of you"—she motioned between Ali and Nahri—"are rather abrasive." Her gaze slid past Nahri. "Jamshid!" she said warmly. "How are you? How is your father?"

Some of the anger left Jamshid's face at Zaynab's aggressive goodwill. "We are well, Princess. Thank you for asking." He darted a look at Nahri. "Actually, on the matter of my father . . . he is here."

Nahri closed her eyes. This was all beginning to feel like a terrible dream. "Your father is back? Kaveh's *here*?"

Jamshid nodded, swallowing. "He typically goes straight to the Temple after a journey, to thank the Creator for ensuring his safety."

"What a lovely tradition," Zaynab said cheerfully, aiming a sharp look at her brother. At the mention of Kaveh, Ali's face had twisted like he'd sucked on a lemon. "Isn't that right, Alizayd?"

Ali offered something that might have been a nod. "Yes. Lovely."

"Shall we go?" Zaynab said, stepping between the men. "Jamshid, would you give me a tour? Ali and Nahri likely have many extremely boring things to discuss."

"Your *sister*?" Nahri hissed as soon as Jamshid and Zaynab moved out of earshot.

Ali looked at her helplessly. "*Kaveh?*"

"That's a surprise to me as well," she said grimly. "He's very orthodox. He will argue against this."

"And he won't like seeing me here," Ali warned. "We . . . we do not have the most amicable history."

"You and Kaveh?" she asked sarcastically. "I can't imagine why not." She sighed, glancing at the Temple Gates. For all her fears, bringing Alizayd al Qahtani into the Temple was not nearly as bad as saying she intended to work alongside shafit. "Leave your weapons in my litter."

Ali's hand went to the hilt of his zulfiqar like an overprotective mother might clutch a child. "Why?"

"We don't allow weapons in the Temple. *None*," she added, sensing this was a thing to be clear upon with the warrior prince before her.

"Fine," he muttered, removing his zulfiqar and khanjar and placing them delicately inside Nahri's litter. He freed a small knife from a holster around his ankle and then a spike from his sleeve. He turned back, the sunlight glinting off the copper relic in his ear. "Let's go."

Zaynab and Jamshid were already halfway down the main path, Zaynab's lilting voice carrying back to them. The Temple grounds were crowded as usual, with local Daevabadis strolling the manicured grounds and extended families of pilgrims seated on rugs spread under shade trees. People had stopped to look at Zaynab, excitedly peeking and pointing in the princess's direction.

The sight of Ali provoked a very different reaction. Nahri heard a couple of gasps, catching sight of narrowed eyes and open horror.

She ignored it. She straightened her shoulders and tipped her chin up. She would not show weakness today.

Ali gazed upon the Temple complex with visible appreciation, seeming not to notice the hostility around him. "This is beautiful," he said admiringly as they passed a row of towering cedars. "These trees look like they've been here since Anahid's time." He knelt, running his fingers over one of the brightly colored stone disks that made up the Temple's pathways. "And I've never seen anything like these."

"They're from the lake," Nahri explained. "Supposedly the marid brought them up as tribute."

"The marid?" He sounded startled as he straightened up, holding the stone. It was the bright orange of a setting sun, flecked with bits of crimson. "I didn't realize . . ."

The stone in his hand abruptly brightened, shimmering as if under a pale sea.

Nahri knocked it out of his hand.

Ali's eyes were wide. "I-I'm sorry."

"It's fine." Nahri dared a glance around them. People were watching, of course, but it didn't seem anyone had noticed.

She heard Ali swallow. "Do the stones do that often?" he asked hopefully.

"Never, as far as I'm aware." She gave him a sharp look. "Then again, considering the source of these stones . . ."

He cleared his throat, silencing her. "Can we not talk about that here?"

He had a point. "Fine. But don't touch anything else." Nahri paused, recalling just who she was about to bring into the Temple. "And maybe don't say anything. At all."

A disgruntled expression crossed his face, but he remained silent as they caught up with Jamshid and Zaynab at the Temple's entrance.

Zaynab's eyes were shining. "An extraordinary place," she enthused. "Jamshid has been giving me a wonderful tour. Did you know he was once a novitiate here, Ali?"

Ali nodded. "Muntadhir told me you had trained for the priesthood." He looked curious. "What made you leave it for the Guard?"

Jamshid's face was stony. "I wanted to be more proactive in defending my people."

Zaynab swiftly took her brother's arm. "Why don't we go inside?"

As Jamshid led them into the Temple, the healer in Nahri could not help but note that he seemed to be leaning on his cane a bit less. Perhaps the session Muntadhir had interrupted had done some good after all.

"These are our shrines," Jamshid explained, "dedicated to our most honored ancestors." He glanced back at Ali. "I do believe your people killed a number of them."

"A favor they returned more than once, as I recall," Ali replied acidly.

"Maybe we could rehash the war later," Nahri suggested, walking faster. "The longer I am away from the infirmary, the higher the chance of an emergency occurring."

But at her side, Ali suddenly went still. She turned to look at him and saw his gaze was locked on the last shrine. It drew the eye, of course; it was the most popular in the Temple, garlanded with flowers and offerings.

Nahri heard his breath catch. "Is that—"

"Darayavahoush's?" Kaveh's voice rang out from behind them, and then the grand wazir was striding up, still dressed in his traveling cloak. "It is, indeed." He brought his hands up in blessing. "Darayavahoush e-Afshin, the last great defender of the Daeva people and guardian to the Nahids. May he rest in the shade of the Creator."

Nahri saw Jamshid flinch out of the corner of her eye, but he was quiet, obviously loyal to his tribe first in the face of their visitors.

"Grand Wazir," she greeted diplomatically. "May the fires burn brightly for you."

"And for you, Banu Nahida," Kaveh replied. "Princess Zaynab, peace be upon you. An honor and a surprise to see you here." He turned to Ali, the warmth vanishing from his face. "Prince Alizayd," he said flatly. "You returned from Am Gezira."

Ali didn't seem to notice the rudeness. His gaze hadn't left Dara's shrine, and it looked like he was struggling to keep his composure. His eyes flickered to the bow at the back, and then Nahri saw him stiffen. She couldn't blame him—she'd seen Jamshid react the same way to the replica of the weapon that had nearly taken his life.

And then Ali stepped closer, his gaze falling to the base of Dara's statue. Nahri's heart sank. *No. Not today.*

Ali picked up an object from among the pile of tokens. Charred and blackened though it was, its reptilian features were instantly recognizable.

Zaynab softly gasped, the skeleton perhaps too much even for her. "Is that a crocodile?" she asked, her voice laced with anger.

Nahri held her breath. Ali twitched, and she silently cursed whoever had left it. This was it. He was going to explode, he was going to say something so offensive that the priests would want him tossed out, and her plans for the shafit were going to be over before she'd even proposed them.

"I take it this is meant for me?" Ali asked after a moment of silence.

Kaveh spoke first. "I do believe that was the intent." At his side, Jamshid looked ashamed.

"Ali . . . ," Nahri began.

But he was already putting it back. Not on the ground, but at the feet of Dara's stone horse—its hooves stomping the carved sand flies she had no doubt the sharp-eyed prince noticed.

He brought his fingers together. "Then to Darayavahoush e-Afshin," he said, only the faintest hint of sarcasm in his exaggerated politeness. "The best and most terrifying warrior this crocodile has ever fought." He turned back around, flashing an almost frightening smile at Kaveh. "Come, Grand Wazir," he said, throwing his arm around the other man and pulling him close. "It has been too long since we've shared each other's company, and I know our brilliant Banu Nahida is eager to tell you her plans."

ACROSS FROM HER, KARTIR WAS WRINGING HIS HANDS, the elderly priest paler than she'd ever seen. They'd met in a windowless inner chamber with high walls, torches throwing light on the icons of her ancestors that ringed the room. It felt as though even they were staring down disapprovingly at her.

"Shafit? You intend to work with *shafit*?" Kartir finally asked after she finished laying out her plans for the hospital. It sounded as though he were begging her to contradict him.

"I do," Nahri replied. "I have already partnered with one. A physician with far more training and experience than I. She and her husband are incredible practitioners."

"They are *dirt-bloods*," one of the priestesses all but spat in Divasti. "The un-souled spawn of lecherous djinn and humans."

Nahri was suddenly grateful neither Ali nor Zaynab shared their older brother's fluency in the Daeva tongue. "They are as innocent in their creation as you and I." Heat filled her voice. "You forget I was raised in the human world. I will not hear abuse thrown at those who share their blood."

Kartir brought his hands together in a gesture of peace, glaring admonishingly at the priestess. "Nor shall I. Those sentiments do not have a place in the Temple. But, Banu Nahida . . . ," he added, staring at her beseechingly, "please understand that what you suggest is impossible. You cannot use your abilities on a shafit. It is forbidden." Fear filled his dark eyes. "It is said that Nahids lose their abilities upon touching a shafit."

Nahri kept her face composed, but the words hurt. This from the gentle man who'd taught her about their religion, who'd placed Anahid's original altar in her hands and put her doubts and fears to rest on more than one occasion—even he harbored the same prejudices as the rest of her people. As Dara had. As her husband did. As nearly everyone who was dear to her did, in fact.

"An incorrect assumption," she said finally. "But I don't intend to heal shafit myself," she clarified, forcing the despicable words from her tongue. "We'd work and study alongside each other, that's all."

Another priest spoke up. "It is a violation of Suleiman's code to interact with them in any way!"

Nahri was not unaware of Kaveh looking on, the grand wazir's disapproval plain but unvoiced for now; she suspected he was waiting for the right time to strike. "It is not a violation of Suleiman's code," she argued, switching to Djinnistani for Ali and Zaynab's benefit. "It is another interpretation."

"Another interpretation?" Kartir repeated weakly.

"Yes," she replied, her voice firm. "We are in Daevabad, my friends. A protected magical city, hidden from humans. What we do here, how we treat those with their blood, it has no bearing on the human world beyond our gates. Treating those *already in our world* with respect and kindness does not counteract Suleiman's order that we leave humanity alone."

"Does it not?" Kartir asked. "Would it not be condoning such future interactions?"

"No," Nahri said flatly, continuing in Djinnistani. "Whether or not a djinn obeys the law outside our gates is a separate issue from how we treat those inside them." Her voice rose. "Have any of you been to the shafit districts? There are children wading in

sewage and mothers dying in childbirth. How can you call yourselves servants of the Creator and think such a thing is permissible?"

That seemed to land, Kartir looking slightly chastened. Ali
was staring at her with open pride.

It didn't go unnoticed, and Kaveh finally spoke. "The prince
has put these things in your head," he declared in Divasti. "My
lady, he is a known radical. You mustn't let his fanaticism about
the shafit sway you."

"I need no man to put ideas in my head," Nahri retorted.
"You speak out of turn, Kaveh e-Pramukh."

He tented his hands. "I meant no disrespect, Banu Nahida."
But there was no apology in his voice; it was the way one would
speak to a child, and it grated on her. "What you're suggesting
sounds lovely, it indicates a good heart—"

"It indicates a woman who learned her lesson when Ghassan
lifted his protection from our tribe after Dara's death," Nahri
said in Divasti. "It is kindness as much as pragmatism that moves
me. We will never be safe in Daevabad unless we have peace with
the shafit. You must see this. They are nearly as numerous in the
city as we are. Relying on the djinn to keep us from each other's
throats is foolish. It leaves us weak and at their mercy."

"It is out of necessity," Kaveh argued. "My lady, respectfully . . .
you are very young. I have seen plenty of overtures of peace to both
the djinn and the shafit in my life. They have never ended well."

"That's my choice to make."

"And yet you're asking our blessing," Kartir pointed out
gently. "Are you not?"

Nahri hesitated, her gaze drifting to the icons of her ancestors. The Temple whose construction Anahid had overseen, the
people she'd knit back together after Suleiman cursed them.

"I am not," she said, letting the words fall in Djinnistani as
she gazed at the elders around her. "I am informing you as a
matter of respect. It is my hospital. They are my abilities, and I do

not require your permission. I am the Banu Nahida, and believe it or not, *Kaveh*," she said, deliberately leaving out his title, "in my few years in Daevabad, I've learned the meaning and the history behind that title. You would not dare question my ancestors."

Stunned silence met that. The grand wazir stared at her in shock, and a few of the priests drew back.

"Yet the Nahids ruled as a *council*," Kartir pointed out, undeterred. "Your ancestors discussed things among themselves and with their priests and advisors. They did not rule as kings accountable to no one." He looked at neither al Qahtani as he said this, but the implication was there.

"And they were overthrown, Kartir," she replied. "And we have been fighting ever since. It's time to try something new."

"I think it is obvious where the Banu Nahida stands." Kaveh's voice was curt.

"And I." Jamshid hadn't spoken since they entered the room, but he did now, looking his father in the eye. "She has my support, Baba."

Kaveh glanced at the two of them, his gaze inscrutable. "Then I suppose the matter has been decided. If you don't mind . . ." He rose to his feet. "I have had quite a long journey."

His words seemed to disband the meeting, and though Nahri was irked he'd been the one to do so, she was also relieved. She'd made her decision clear, and even if the priests didn't like it, they hardly seemed willing to openly defy her.

Kartir spoke up one more time. "The procession. If you want our support in this, surely you can grant us your presence in that."

Nahri bit back a groan. She should have known it wouldn't be so easy. "Please don't make me do that."

Ali frowned. "Do what?"

"They want to dress me up like Anahid and put me in some parade for Navasatem." She threw Kartir a desperate look. "It's embarrassing."

"It is fun," he clarified with a smile. "The Daeva procession is a favorite part of Navasatem, and it's been centuries since we've have a Nahid to join."

"You had my mother."

He eyed her. "Do the stories I've told you of Banu Manizheh make it seem like she was the type to take part in such a thing?" His face turned beseeching. "Please. Do it for your people."

Nahri sighed, guilt nagging at her. "Fine. If you will support my hospital, I will dress in a costume and smile like a fool." She feigned a glare. "You're slyer than I would have thought."

The elderly priest touched his heart. "The sacrifices one makes for their tribe," he teased.

They left the sanctuary after that, making their way out of the Temple. Sunspots danced across Nahri's vision as they emerged into the bright afternoon light.

Ali paused on the steps. "This place really is lovely," he said, gazing at the lily-dappled reflecting pools. A breeze brought the scent of the cedar trees lining the perimeter. "Thank you for allowing us to visit. The circumstances aside—it was an honor." He cleared his throat. "And I'm sorry about those circumstances. I'm going to try to be more careful, I promise."

"Yes. In turn, thank you for not strangling the grand wazir." But then remembering the chaos of his apartment, Nahri added, a bit reluctantly, "And thank you for the work you've been doing with the hospital. It hasn't gone unnoticed."

Ali turned to look at her, a surprised grin lighting his face. "Was that a compliment?"

"No," she said, forcing a grumpiness she didn't feel into her voice. "It's a simple statement of fact."

They began crossing the garden. "So," Ali continued, a playful edge in his voice, "what is this about dressing up in an Anahid costume?"

She looked up, eyeing him severely. "Don't start, al Qahtani.

Not when you've been admiring your reflection in every shiny surface we've passed since you got off your horse."

Mortification swept the humor off his face. "Was it that obvious?" he whispered.

Nahri paused, savoring his embarrassment. "Only to anyone who looked your way." She smiled sweetly. "So, everyone."

Ali cringed, reaching out to touch his turban. "I never expected to wear this," he said softly. "I couldn't help but wonder how it looked."

"Good luck with that excuse when Muntadhir learns you stole it." Admittedly, Ali did cut a striking figure in the turban, the dazzling gold stripes picking up a warmth in his gray eyes. Still, Nahri didn't like it on him. "It doesn't suit you," she said, as much to herself as to Ali.

"No," he replied tonelessly. "I suppose of the two of us, Muntadhir looks more like what people expect of a Qahtani prince."

She realized too late the double meaning of her words. "Oh, no, Ali. That's not what I meant. Not at all." Every time Nahri pinned her chador over her human-round ears, she had the same feelings about her appearance not matching expectations, and it made her sick to think she might have implied the same to someone else. "It's just I hate that turban. I hate what it represents. The war, Qui-zi . . . it seems so rooted in the worst parts of our past."

Ali stopped, turning to face her fully. "No, I don't suppose a Banu Nahida who just defied a group of men with a collective millennium on her *would* think highly of such a tradition." He smiled, shaking his head. "Your people are blessed to have you as their leader. I hope you know that." He said the words warmly, with what seemed to be all the friendly sincerity in the world.

Nahri's response was immediate. "Maybe one day *your* people will have me as their leader."

She'd meant it as a challenge, and indeed, Ali jerked back, looking slightly startled. But then he broke into a slow grin, his eyes glinting with dark amusement.

"Well, then I guess I better get back to building your hospital." He touched his heart and brow in the Geziri salute, clearly biting back a laugh. "Peace be upon you, Banu Nahida."

Nahri didn't reply—nor did Ali wait for her to do so. Instead he turned away, heading toward Zaynab, who was already waiting at the gate.

Nahri watched him go, suddenly aware of how many other Daevas were doing the same—and the quiet scrutiny with which she suspected many had just observed their interaction.

She let her expression turn severe and she stared at the crowd until people began hastily resuming their own activities. Nahri meant what she'd told the priests; she was going to do this her way, and a good Banu Nahida couldn't show weakness.

So Nahri would make sure she had none.

22

ALI

Ali grinned as he pressed the pump handle with one hand. A rush of cold water splashed to the ground. "Your son's new specialty," he joked to the woman across from him.

Hatset's golden eyes traced the spray of mud across his dishdasha. "When I envisioned a brighter future for you, baba, you looked distinctly . . . cleaner."

"I like getting my hands dirty." Ali straightened up, wiping his fingers on a rag tucked into his belt. "But what do you think?" he asked, gesturing to the line of bustling workshops in front of the hospital.

"I'm impressed," his mother replied. "Then again, considering the fortune you've shaken out of my tribe since you returned to Daevabad, I'd hope to be impressed."

Ali touched his heart in mock offense. "Ah, what happened to all your words about doing good for my city?" He winked. "Did you think it would be cheap?"

She shook her head, but she was smiling, her gaze lingering on a group of children sitting in the workcamp's school. "It is worth the cost. I'm proud of you. A little exasperated, but still proud."

They continued toward the hospital, and Ali nodded in greeting to a pair of carpenters hammering cabinetry. "It's the shafit doing most of the work," he replied. "I feel more like a glorified task manager than anything; my biggest problem is finding a job for everyone who wants to join us. It's been astonishing to see what people have done with such an opportunity. And in only a few months!"

"A nice thing to watch your beliefs about the shafit made manifest, I take it?"

Ali nodded fervently. "Nothing would make me happier than seeing this place thrive. Let everyone with pretensions of blood purity see what the shafit have accomplished here." He clasped his hands behind his back, toying with his prayer beads. "I wish I could get Abba to see this. We'd have more security investing in the shafit than beating them into obedience."

"Then it sounds as though you should stop pining over this Bir Nabat of yours and work on convincing your father to let you stay in Daevabad." Hatset looked at him intently as they entered the hospital. "The kind of change you want takes time and patience, child. You consider yourself some sort of farmer now, don't you? Do you toss seeds upon the ground only to abandon them in hopes they'll grow untended?"

Ali held his tongue at that. And not just because of the workers bustling around them, but because in truth, with every passing day in Daevabad, he wasn't quite sure what he wanted.

Hatset let out a surprised exclamation as they stepped into the main corridor. "Well, isn't this lovely," she said, admiring the vivid murals Elashia had painted on the walls: dazzling sandships darting through the dunes and the lush oases of Qart Sahar alongside images of its craggy bluffs and azure seas.

"You should see what happens when Nahri passes through," Ali said. "The paintings come alive, the waves crashing over the beach, the trees blooming. The Nahid magic in this place is incredible."

"Yes, it's becoming more and more clear she's cast quite the spell," Hatset said lightly.

Ali leaned over one of the balustrades to check the day's progress. At first glance, the hospital's heart was barely recognizable from the wild, weed-strewn ruin Nahri had first shown him. The feral garden had been transformed into a small slice of paradise, along whose tiled paths visitors and patients might amble, enjoying the sweet-smelling water of the fountains and the coolness of the palms' shade. The interior walls had been rebuilt, and woodworkers were putting together a glasswork roof that would maximize the amount of natural light allowed into the rooms. The main examination chamber was done, awaiting furnishings and cabinetry.

"Prince Alizayd!"

A voice caught his attention, and Ali glanced across the courtyard to see a group of shafit seamstresses seated among a pile of embroidered curtains. A woman who looked to be around his age had risen to her feet, a shy smile on her face.

She continued speaking when their gazes met, a blush rising in her cheeks. "I'm so sorry to bother you, Your Highness. But if you're around later, we were thinking . . ." She gestured to the other women and several giggled. "We hoped you might be able to help us hang these curtains."

"I . . . of course," Ali replied, slightly puzzled by the request. "Let me know when you're ready."

She smiled again, and Ali could not help but note it was to a rather fetching effect. "We'll be sure to hunt you down." She resumed her seat, whispering to her companions.

"It's fascinating," his mother said dryly, "that in this entire magical complex full of building equipment, the only way to hang curtains is to rely on an unmarried, overly tall, handsome young prince."

Ali quickly pulled his gaze from the young women. "I'm sure they meant nothing like that."

Hatset snorted. "Not even you're that naive." She wound her arm through his as they kept walking. "But you know . . . it wouldn't be the worst idea for you to burn a marriage mask with a nice shafit girl. Maybe then you'd actually *visit* your bed instead of working yourself to death."

Embarassed heat swept his face so fast Ali felt he might actually burst into flames. "*Amma . . .*"

"What? Am I not permitted to want some happiness for my only son?"

He was already shaking his head. "You know I'm not allowed to marry."

"No, what you're not allowed is a gaudy ceremony with a noblewoman who could offer you political allies and heirs that might compete with Muntadhir's—which is why I'm not suggesting that." She studied him, her eyes soft. "But I worry about you, baba. You seem lonely. If you would like either Zaynab or me to make inquiries—"

"No," Ali said, trying to keep the ache from his voice. His mother's assessment wasn't wrong—it was simply a part of his life he tried not to dwell on. Growing up as Muntadhir's future Qaid, Ali had attempted to steel himself for what that future would look like—a violent, lonely life in the Citadel for Ali; wealth, a family, and the throne for Muntadhir. Ali had found it easier not to think about the things he'd be denied, the luxuries reserved for his brother.

But those were oaths he'd made as a child, too young to understand their cost. Not that it mattered now. Ali would never be Qaid, and he could not pretend resentment hadn't worked its way into his heart. But there was nothing to be done about it. He'd meant what he said to Lubayd and Aqisa when they teased him about marriage: he would not make vows to an innocent woman if he didn't think he could live up to them, and right now, he was barely capable of protecting himself.

His mother was still looking at him expectantly. "Can we discuss this another time?" he asked. "Perhaps on a day we're *not* trying to force a meeting with a temperamental scholar?"

Hatset rolled her eyes. "There's not going to be any forcing, my dear. I've been dealing with Ustadh Issa for years."

Ali was glad she was so confident. He'd been shocked to learn the Ayaanle scholar his mother hoped could tell them more about the marid and the batty old man barricaded in a room at the hospital were one and the same. Ali had yet to even set eyes on him; upon learning strangers would be entering the hospital, he'd filled the corridor outside his quarters with all manner of magical traps. Finally, after several workers had been bitten by hexed books, Nahri and Razu—the only people Issa would speak to—had been able to negotiate a compromise: no one would be permitted near his room, and in return, he'd stop cursing the corridor.

"We should have asked Nahri to come," Ali said again. "Issa likes her, and she's very skilled at prying information out of people."

His mother gave him a dark look. "You best make sure she's not prying information out of *you*. That woman is the kind of ally you keep at knife's length." They stopped outside the scholar's locked door, and Hatset knocked. "Ustadh Is—"

She hadn't even finished the word when Ali felt a whisper of magic. He yanked his mother back—just before a saber, made from what looked like disassembled astrolabes, sliced across the door frame.

Ali swore in Geziriyya, but Hatset merely shook her head. "Ustadh, now really," she lectured in Ntaran. "We've discussed

being more sociable." A crafty note entered her voice. "Besides . . .
I have a gift for you."

The door abruptly cracked open, but only a handbreadth. Ali
jumped as a pair of emerald-bright eyes appeared in the gloomy
dark.

"Queen Hatset?" Even Issa's voice sounded ancient.

His mother pulled a tiny ash-colored sack from her robe. "I
do believe you were interested in this for your experiments when
last we met?"

Ali inhaled, recognizing the sharp smell. "Gunpowder? You're
going to give him gunpowder? For his *experiments*?"

Hatset shushed him. "A brief chat, Issa," she said smoothly.
"A very brief, *very* confidential chat."

The scholar's luminous eyes darted between them. "There
are no humans with you?"

"We have been over this a hundred times, Ustadh. There are
no humans in Daevabad."

The door swung open, the sack of gunpowder vanishing
from his mother's hand faster than Ali's eyes could track.

"Come, come!" Issa ushered them in, slamming the door
closed when they passed the threshold, whispering what sounded
like an unreasonable number of locking charms under his breath.

Ali was regretting their decision to come here with each passing
moment, but he followed his mother into the cavernous chamber.
Books were stacked to the ceiling and scrolls stuffed into shelves
Issa seemed to have magicked together from salvaged bits of the
infirmary's ruins. A long row of dusty stained-glass windows threw
gloomy light onto a low table crowded with gleaming metal instruments, pieces of parchment, and burning candles. A cot lay tucked
between two towering piles of books and behind a section of the
floor studded with broken glass, as though the scholar feared being
attacked while he slept. Only one small corner of the room was kept
neat, a pair of floor cushions framing a striped ottoman that had

been carefully set with a silver tray that held a teapot, glasses, and, judging from the smell, several of the cardamom-spiced sweets Nahri was fond of.

We really should have brought her, Ali thought again, guilt gnawing at him. God knew he was already keeping enough secrets from Nahri.

The scholar returned to a well-worn pillow on the floor, folding his skinny limbs beneath him like some sort of gangly bird. As a resurrected formerly enslaved djinn, Issa's age was impossible to guess. His face was well lined and his fuzzy brows and beard were entirely snow white. And the disapproving expression on his face was . . . oddly familiar.

"Do I know you?" Ali asked slowly, studying the man.

Issa's green eyes flickered over him. "Yes," he said shortly. "I threw you out of a history lecture once for asking too many questions." He tilted his head. "You were much smaller."

"That was *you*?" The memory came to Ali immediately—not many tutors had dared treat one of Ghassan's sons with such disrespect. Ali had been young, no older than ten, but the man he remembered tossing him out had been a forbidding, furious scholar in fine robes . . . nothing like the frail old man before him. "I don't understand. If you had a position at the Royal Library, what are you doing here?"

Pain filled the scholar's bright eyes. "I was forced to resign."

Hatset took a seat across from Issa, motioning for Ali to do the same. "After the Afshin's rampage, there was a lot of violence directed at the rest of city's formerly enslaved djinn. Most fled the city, but Issa is too stubborn." She shook her head. "I wish you would return home, my friend. You would be more comfortable in Ta Ntry."

Issa scowled. "I am too old for journeying. And I hate boats." He threw an irritated glance in Ali's direction. "The hospital made for a perfectly fine home until this one's workers arrived.

They hammer constantly." He sounded wounded. *"And* they scared away the chimera living in the basement."

Ali was incredulous. "It tried to *eat* someone."

"It was a rare specimen!"

Hatset quickly interjected. "Since you bring up rare specimens . . . we are here to speak to you about another elusive creature. The marid."

Issa's expression changed, alarm sweeping away his cantankerousness. "What could you possibly want to know about the marid?"

"The old tales," Hatset replied calmly. "They've become little more than a legend for my generation of Ayaanle. However, I've heard encounters with the marid were far more common in your time."

"Consider it a blessing they've all but vanished." Issa's expression darkened further. "It is not wise to discuss the marid with our youth, my queen. Particularly overly ambitious ones who ask too many questions." He gave a disgruntled nod in Ali's direction.

His mother persisted. "It's not mere curiosity, Ustadh. We need your help."

Issa shook his head. "I spent my career traveling the length of the Nile and saw more djinn than I care to remember destroyed by their fascination with the marid. I thanked God when I learned it was a madness your generation had forgotten, and it's not one I'll rekindle."

"We're not asking you to rekindle anything," Hatset replied. "And we're not the ones who reached out first—" She grabbed Ali's wrist, swiftly undoing the button that held the sleeve of his dishdasha flush and pushed it back, revealing his scars. "It's the marid who came to us."

Issa's green eyes locked on Ali's scars. He inhaled, straightening up like a shot.

Then he slapped Ali across the face. "Fool!" he shouted. "Apostate! How dare you make a pact with them? What ghastly abomination did you commit to convince them to spare you, Alizayd al Qahtani?"

Ali reeled back, ducking a second blow. "I didn't make a pact with anyone!"

"Liar!" Issa wagged an angry finger in his face. "Do you think I don't know about your previous snooping?"

"My what?" Ali sputtered. "What in God's name are you going on about?"

"I think I'd like to know as well," Hatset said sharply. "Preferably before you start beating my son again."

Issa stormed across the room. With a burst of fiery sparks, a locked chest popped out of the air, landing with a dusty thud. Issa threw it open and plucked out a papyrus scroll, waving it like a sword. "Remember this?"

Ali scowled. "No. Do you have any idea how many scrolls I've seen in my life?"

Issa unfurled it, spreading it on the table. "And how many of those were guides to summoning a marid?" he asked knowingly, as if he'd caught Ali out.

Thoroughly confused, Ali stepped closer. A brilliant blue river had been painted on the scroll. It was a map, he realized. A map of the Nile, from what he could interpret of the roughly drawn borders. That was all he could make out; though there were notations, they were written in a script consisting of bizarre, entirely incomprehensible pictograms.

And then Ali remembered. "This is the map Nahri and I found in the catacombs of the Royal Library."

Issa glared. "So you *do* admit you were trying contact the marid?"

"Of course not!" Ali was rapidly losing patience with this hot-tempered old man. "The Banu Nahida and I were looking into the story that the marid supposedly cursed her appearance and left her in Egypt. We heard this scroll was written by the last djinn to see one in the area. I couldn't read it, so I sent it off for translation." He narrowed his eyes on Issa. "To you, most likely."

Hatset cut in. "Would you please tell me what it is about this map that has you so upset, Ustadh?"

"It's not just a map," Issa replied. "It's an evil thing, meant to serve as a guide to the desperate." He jabbed a gnarled finger at one set of notations. "These mark places on the river believed to be sacred to the marid, and the notes detail what was done—what was *sacrificed*—to call upon them at that particular spot."

Hatset's eyes flashed. "When you say 'sacrifice' . . . surely you don't mean—"

"I mean exactly as I say," Issa cut in. "Blood must be offered to call upon them."

Ali was horrified. "Ustadh Issa, neither Nahri nor I knew anything of this. I've never been to the Nile. And I never desired *any* contact with the marid, let alone sacrificed someone to them!"

"He fell in the lake, Ustadh," Hatset explained. "It was an accident. He said the marid tortured him into giving up his name, and then they used him to kill the Afshin."

Ali whirled on her. "*Amma*—"

She waved him down. "We need to know."

Issa was staring at Ali in shock. "A marid used you to kill another djinn? They *possessed* you? But that makes no sense . . . possession is an acolyte's last act."

Revulsion swept him. "What are you talking about?"

"It's a pact," Issa replied. "A partnership . . . though not a particularly balanced one. If a marid accepts your sacrifice, you're brought under its protection. And they'll give you almost anything you could desire during your mortal life. But in the end? The acolyte owes their lifeblood. And the marid possess them to take it." His eyes swept over Ali. "You don't survive such a thing."

Ali went entirely cold. "I am no marid's *acolyte*." The word left his lips with a savage denial. "I am a believer in God. I would never commit the blasphemy you're suggesting. And I certainly never made any sacrifice," he added, growing heated even as his mother placed a hand on his shoulder. "Those demons tortured me and forced me to hallucinate the deaths of everyone I loved!"

Issa inclined his head, studying Ali as though he were some sort of equation. "But you did give them your name?"

Ali's shoulders slumped. Not for the first time, he cursed the moment he'd broken under the water. "Yes."

"Then that might have been all they needed—they're clever creatures and God knows they've had centuries to learn how to twist the rules." Issa tapped his chin, looking perplexed. "But I don't understand *why*. Plotting the murder of a Daeva—a lesser being—would be risky, even if they used a fellow djinn to do it."

Hatset frowned. "Do they have a quarrel that you know of with the Daevas?"

"It's said the marid cursed the lake after a falling-out with the Nahid Council," Issa replied. "But that must have been over two thousand years ago. As far as I know, they haven't been seen in Daevabad since."

Ali's skin tingled. That, he knew, was not at all true. In the aftermath of his possession, Ali had said the same thing to his father and had been quietly told the marid had indeed been seen—at the side of Zaydi al Qahtani's Ayaanle allies.

But he held his tongue. He'd sworn to his father, sworn on their tribe and his blood, not to reveal that information. Even the slightest whisper that his ancestors had conspired with the marid to overthrow the Nahids would rock the foundations of their rule. Zaydi al Qahtani had taken a throne even he believed God had originally granted to the Anahid and her descendants; his reasons and his methods for doing so had to remain above reproach. And if Hatset and Issa didn't already know, Ali wasn't saying anything.

"How do I get rid of it?" he asked brusquely.

Issa stared at him. "Get rid of what?"

"My connection with the marid. These . . . whispers in my head," Ali rushed on, feeling his control start to fray. "My abilities. I want it all gone."

"Your *abilities*?" the scholar repeated in astonishment. "What abilities?"

Ali abruptly let go of the magic he'd been holding back. Water burst from his hands, a fog swirling around his feet. "*This*," he exhaled.

The scholar scurried back. "Oh," he whispered. "That." He blinked rapidly. "That is new."

"No," Hatset said. "It's not." She gave Ali an apologetic look as he whirled around. "A slight—a *very* slight—affinity with water magic runs in our family. It shows up occasionally in our children and usually vanishes by the time they're in their teens. And it's nothing like what you've told me you can do," she added when Ali's eyes went wide. "A toddler having a tantrum might upset a water pitcher from across the room. Zaynab used to spin little water spouts in drinking cups when she didn't think I was watching her."

Ali gasped. "*Zaynab?* Zaynab has these abilities?"

"Not anymore," Hatset said firmly. "She was very young at the time. She probably doesn't even remember them. I would punish her terribly when I caught her." His mother shook her head, looking grim. "I was so frightened someone would see her." She glanced back at him. "But I never considered it of you. You were so Geziri, even as child. And once you joined the Citadel, you were so loyal to their code . . ."

"You feared I would tell," Ali finished when his mother trailed off. He felt sick. He couldn't even say she was wrong.

There were times when he was a child that he was so determined to prove himself true to his father and brother's tribe, so rigid in his conception of faith, that yes, he would have let slip an Ayaanle secret, and it shamed him. He abruptly sat down, running his wet hands over his face. "But why didn't you say anything when I first told you about the marid possession?"

Her words were gentle. "Alu, you were panicking. You'd been in Daevabad less than a week. It wasn't the time."

Issa was looking between them as though he were suddenly very sorry he'd let them in. "*Stop that*," he warned, waving a hand at the ribbon of fog curling around Ali's waist. "Do you have any idea what would happen if someone saw you doing that? I had a mob chase me from the palace just for these emerald eyes!"

"Then help me," Ali begged, struggling to rein back the water. "Please. It's getting harder to control."

"I don't know how to help you," Issa replied, sounding flabbergasted. He glanced at Hatset, for the first time looking slightly chastened. "Forgive me, my queen. I don't know what you were expecting, but I have never come across anything like this. You should take him back to Ta Ntry. He'd be safer and your family might have answers."

"I cannot take him back to Ta Ntry," his mother said plainly. "Things are too tense in the palace. His father and brother will think I'm preparing him for a coup, and if either of them got wind of this?" She nodded at the still lingering fog. "I do not trust them. Ghassan puts the stability of this city before everything else."

Issa shook his head. "Queen Hatset . . ."

"Please." The word cut through the air. "He is my only son, Ustadh," she pressed. "I will get you everything that's ever been written about the marid. I will get you copies of my family records. All I ask is that you look for a way to help us." Her voice turned a little crafty. "And come now, it must be decades since you've had a good mystery on your hands."

"You might not like the answers," Issa pointed out.

Ill with dread, Ali's gaze had fallen to the floor. Still, he could sense the weight of their stares, the worry radiating from his mother.

Hatset spoke again. "I don't think we have a choice."

THOUGH HIS MOTHER HAD ENDED THEIR MEETING with a firm order for Ali to stay calm and let her and Issa handle things, their conversation at the hospital haunted him. In response, Ali threw himself deeper into his work, trying desperately to ignore the whispers that ran through his mind when he bathed and the fact that the rain—which had not abated in days—came down more heavily each time he lost his temper. He hadn't been sleeping much, and now when he did close his eyes, his dreams were plagued with images of a burning lake and ruined ships, of scaled limbs dragging him beneath muddy waters and cold green eyes narrowing over an arrow's shaft. Ali would wake shivering and drenched in sweat, feeling as though someone had just been whispering a warning in his ear.

The effect it was having on his behavior did not go unnoticed.

"Alizayd." His father snapped his fingers in front of Ali's face as they exited the throne room after court. "*Alizayd?*"

Ali blinked, pulled from his daze. "Yes?"

Ghassan eyed him. "Are you all right?" he asked, a little concern in his voice. "I thought for certain you'd have sharp words for the moneychanger from Garama."

Ali could remember neither a moneychanger nor Garama. "Sorry. I'm just tired."

His father narrowed his eyes. "Problems at the hospital?"

"Not at all," Ali said quickly. "Our work there continues smoothly and we should be on track, God willing, to open by Navasatem."

"Excellent." Ghassan clapped his back as they came around the corner. "Take care not to entirely overwork yourself. Ah . . . but speaking of someone who could stand to overwork himself— Muntadhir," he greeted as his eldest son came into view. "I do hope you have an excuse for missing court."

Muntadhir touched his heart and brow. "Peace be upon you, my king," he said, ignoring Ali. "I do indeed. May we speak inside?"

Ali tried to step away, but Ghassan caught his wrist. "No. You can spare a few minutes. Don't think I've not noticed the two of you avoiding each other. It is deeply childish."

Ali flushed and Muntadhir drew up, giving Ali a short, disdainful glance as though he were some sort of irritating bug before sweeping into the office—which was good because Ali did indeed feel a sudden childish urge to coax the water fountain outside his father's office into ruining the expensive cloak draping his brother's shoulders.

To say things had soured between the princes since Ali visited the Daeva temple in Muntadhir's stead was an understatement. Despite their best efforts, Ali and Zaynab hadn't been able to sneak Muntadhir's regalia back into his wardrobe without getting caught, and Muntadhir—sporting a freshly bruised jaw, no doubt courtesy of their father—had thoroughly upbraided them, shouting at his younger siblings until Zaynab had been on the verge of tears and Ali on the verge of making the bottles of liquid intoxicants scattered about the room explode.

He hadn't tried approaching his brother again. It felt like Muntadhir was constantly watching him, studying him with a ruthless calm that left Ali uneasy and more than a little heartsick. Any hope he had of reconciling with the older brother he'd once adored, the brother he still loved, was beginning to fade away.

Even so, he followed, having little other choice.

"—what do you mean you've solved the problem of the southern Geziri sheikhs?" Ghassan was asking. He'd seated himself at his desk and Muntadhir was standing across from him. "Because unless you've managed to conjure up an additional caravanserai, I don't know how we're going to accommodate a thousand unexpected arrivals."

"I just met with the steward in charge of the palace grounds," Muntadhir replied. "I think we should set up a travelers' camp in the front gardens. The Daevas will be horrified, of course, and it would take some time to restore the grounds afterward, but it could be done beautifully: conjured silk tents between the palms, a water garden and courtyard where we could have merchants selling traditional crafts and maybe a storyteller and some musicians performing the old epics." He smiled hesitantly. "I thought it might be a nice homage to our roots—and the sheikhs could hardly claim offense if we put them next to our own palace."

A wistful expression had drifted across his father's face. "That is an excellent suggestion. Very good, Muntadhir. I'm impressed. You've been doing fine work with the Navasatem preparations."

Muntadhir smiled fully, perhaps the most genuine smile Ali had seen cross his face in months, as though a load had been lifted from his shoulders. "Thank you, Abba," he said sincerely. "I hope only to make you proud and honor our name."

"I am certain you do." Ghassan tented his hands. "However, *after* the holiday, Muntadhir, I expect you to turn your attention and charm back to your wife."

The brief pleasure that had bloomed in his brother's face vanished. "My wife and I are fine."

Ghassan eyed him. "This is my palace, Emir. I know everything that goes on within its walls, which means I'm aware you and Nahri haven't visited each other's beds in over four months.

I married the two of you to *unify* our tribes, understand? It's been nearly five years. I had two children by Hatset in less time."

Ali cleared his throat. "Can I . . . leave?"

Neither man looked at him. Muntadhir was staring at their father's desk, a muscle working in his jaw. "These matters take time, Abba," he said finally.

"They're *taking time* because you spend your nights with everyone who isn't your wife, something I've warned you about more than once. Should another person—another Daeva—be distracting you from your duties . . . well, that person can easily be removed."

Muntadhir's head jerked up, and Ali started at the barely checked fury in his brother's face. "There's no one distracting me," Muntadhir snapped. He was gripping Ghassan's desk so hard his knuckles had turned white. "And I am well aware of my duties; you've been beating their importance into me since I was a child."

Ghassan's eyes blazed. "Should you find your position burdensome, Emir," he started coldly, "I have another who can replace you, one I suspect would happily take over your marital duties and whose company your wife already prefers."

Ali's ears burned at the insinuation. "That's not what—"

Disdain twisted Muntadhir's face. "My wife prefers Queen Hatset's endless purse and a fool she can manipulate into building her hospital." He turned to look at Ali. "And after it's completed, she'll have no use for either."

The cruel words landed, piercing something insecure and vulnerable deep in Ali's heart. "She is worth ten of you," he responded, hurt surging forward and crashing past his self control. "What she's doing is brilliant and brave, and you couldn't even pull yourself from your courtesans long enough to visit—"

The office door burst inward, slamming hard against the wall. Ali spun, unsheathing his zulfiqar as he moved between his family and the doorway. But it was only Wajed who appeared, looking stressed and alarmed.

"Abu Muntadhir," he greeted Ghassan in Geziriyya. Somewhere behind him, Ali could hear a woman wailing, her cries echoing through the corridor. "Forgive me, there's been a terrible crime."

"My lady, please!" Ali stiffened at the sound of Kaveh's voice. "You cannot go before the king like this!"

"Yes, I can!" a woman shouted. "It is my right as a citizen!" A string of Divasti followed, broken by sobbing.

Ghassan stood up as a Daeva woman in a blood-soaked chador came stumbling into sight. Kaveh was at her side, pale and tense, as were a handful of other Daevas and two members of the Royal Guard.

"What's going on?" Ghassan demanded, switching to Djinnistani.

Kaveh stepped forward as the woman sank to her knees in front of them, crying into her hands. "Forgive my tribeswoman, my king," he pleaded. "She lost her wits begging to come before you."

"She is welcome to come before me," Ghassan replied. Ali could hear true concern in his voice. "My dear woman, whatever has happened? Are you hurt? I can have the Banu Nahida summoned . . ."

The woman began to cry harder. "It is too late for that. My husband is already dead. They took him, they cut his throat."

Wajed looked grim. "A few of my men found them. Her husband . . ." He shook his head. "It was bad."

"Did you catch them?" Ali asked quickly.

Wajed paused. "No. It . . . we found them near the Geziri Quarter. They'd gone to shop for pearls and . . ."

"This didn't happen in the Geziri Quarter," Kaveh snapped. "I know where you found them, Qaid."

Ghassan's voice was intent. "Who attacked you, my lady?"

"*Shafit*," she spat. "We wanted to see the Nahid hospital, but we didn't get halfway through their workcamp before these filthy men were pulling at our clothes and dragging us into a back alley. They threatened . . . they threatened to dishonor me. Parvez begged them, told them he would give them everything we had . . ." She shook her head as if to dispel the image, and her veil briefly fell from her face.

Shocked recognition stole through Ali, and his gaze darted to the grand wazir. No. It wasn't possible.

Muntadhir had crossed the office to pour a glass of water from the pitcher on the windowsill. He returned and pressed it into the woman's hands with a few soft words of Divasti. She took a shaky breath, wiped her eyes, and then drank.

And with that second glimpse of her face, Ali was certain. He'd seen this woman twice before. Both had been rather memorable occasions. The first time had been at the Daeva tavern he'd visited with Anas, where she'd been laughing and gambling with a group of courtesans. The second time had been at his apartment; she'd been waiting in his bed after his first morning in court, sent to "welcome" him to the palace.

A "welcome" arranged by Kaveh e-Pramukh.

It was Kaveh who spoke next. "I tried to warn the Banu Nahida about that camp," he said, his voice rising as he wrung his hands. "The dirt-bloods are dangerous. It is unnatural to work with them, and now they have killed a Daeva man in broad daylight. The whole place should be torn down."

Ali cleared his throat, fighting for calm. "Were there any witnesses?"

Kaveh eyed him incredulously. "Is her word not enough?"

Not when you're involved. But Ali didn't say that; instead touching his heart and speaking truly, "I meant no offense toward your employee, Grand Wazir. But it could help us catch—"

"I am not his *employee*," the woman declared. "What is that supposed to mean? I am a woman of noble blood! I belonged to none but my Parvez!"

Ali opened his mouth, but Ghassan held up a hand. "*Were* there witnesses? I do not doubt your account, my lady. But it would help us find the perpetrators."

Wajed shook his head. "No witnesses, my king. None who would speak to us anyway, though it was fairly chaotic when we arrived." He hesitated and then added, "A rather *large* number of Daevas were gathering to demand whoever did this be found and held accountable."

Alarm sparked in Ali. "The shafit in that camp are under our protection. There are hundreds of women and children there."

"They have no business being there," Kaveh retorted. "This is your fault. You whispered your poisonous opinions into my Banu Nahida's ear, and now a Daeva man is dead."

Suspicion gripped Ali. Kaveh had made his opposition to Nahri working with the shafit clear at the Grand Temple. But surely he couldn't be so hateful as to plot something like this. . . .

Aware of how tenuous the situation was, Ali switched to Geziriyya so that the Daevas couldn't understand him. "Abba, I know that woman," he said softly. "*Kaveh* knows that woman. He arranged for her to come visit my bedroom when I first moved back into the palace." Ghassan's eyes flickered to his, his face not betraying a hint of emotion, and Ali pressed on. "Muntadhir, surely you recognize her. You were there too. If she were to re-move her veil, I know you would remember her."

Muntadhir stared at him, seeming to contemplate the situation.

And then a ruthless calm swept his face. "I have made very clear how I feel about your judgment regarding the shafit." He abruptly squared his shoulders, calculated outrage twisting his face. "And I am *not* going to ask this poor woman to disrobe because you think she's a prostitute!"

His final words—uttered in Djinnistani rather than Geziriyya—cracked across the room. Kaveh gasped, and the woman let out a shrill cry.

Ali whirled around, seeing horror in the faces of the growing number of people who'd been drawn by the woman's wails. "I-I didn't say that," he stammered, stunned by Muntadhir's betrayal. "I only meant—"

"How dare you?" Kaveh accused. "Have you no shame, Prince Alizayd? Do you hate the Daevas so much that you'd dishonor a weeping woman while her husband's blood still stains her hands?"

"That's not what I meant!"

Muntadhir deftly brushed past him to kneel at the woman's side. "We will find and punish whoever did this," he promised, sincerity in every line of his handsome face. He glanced back at Ghassan. "Kaveh is right, Abba. I have tried to warn you and Nahri both. The shafit are dangerous, and something like this was bound to happen. Ali is delusional. His fanaticism has been infecting everyone around him."

Ali gaped at him. "*Dhiru* . . ."

"Alizayd, leave us," Ghassan said curtly. "You and your companions are confined to the palace until I say otherwise." His eyes flashed. "*Understand?* Directly to your apartment; I will not have you further enflame this situation."

Before Ali could protest, his brother grabbed him, dragging him toward the doors. "Abba, don't!" he cried. "You heard Wajed, there's a mob growing. Those people are innocent!"

Ghassan didn't even look at him. "It will be handled."

Muntadhir shoved him out, pushing Ali hard enough to knock him off balance. "Is there any situation you can't make worse?" he snapped in Geziriyya.

"You lied," Ali accused, shaking with emotion. "I know you—"

"You know *nothing* about me." Muntadhir's voice was low and venomous. "You have no idea what this position has cost me. And I'll be damned if I'm going to lose it to some shafit-obsessed zealot who can't hold his tongue."

He slammed the door in Ali's face.

Ali staggered back, fury in his heart. He wanted to rip open the door and drag his brother through it. He had never before felt such a physical need to hit someone.

The delicate water table—a new, rather lovely addition to the corridor, a beautifully conjured construct featuring painted crystal birds that appeared to flit as they bathed in the still waters of a mosaic pool—promptly exploded, the water sizzling into mist.

Ali barely noticed. *It will be handled*, his father had said. What did that mean? Ali thought of his workers and their families facing a Daeva mob, of Subha and her little daughter. He wasn't supposed to be reckless, not anymore. But how could he let violence befall the people he'd sworn to protect? He knew his father's politics; Ghassan wasn't going to risk the fallout of letting the Royal Guard loose on mourning Daevas just to protect the shafit.

But there was someone else those Daevas might listen to. Nerves fluttered in Ali's chest. Muntadhir would kill him, if Ghassan didn't first.

It doesn't matter. Not now. Ali jumped to his feet and ran for the infirmary.

23
NAHRI

Daeva or not, Nahri was fairly certain she was never going to like horses.

As if hearing her thoughts, their mount put on a burst of speed, dashing around the next corner at a breakneck pace. Squeezing her eyes shut, Nahri tightened her grip around Ali's waist.

He let out a choked sound of protest. "I don't understand why you couldn't take your own horse," he said for what seemed like the tenth time. "It would have been more appropriate."

"This is faster," she said defensively, not wanting to admit her shortcomings as a rider. It was a skill other Daevas prided themselves on. "Muntadhir's always going on about how much he loves this horse. He says it's the fastest in Daevabad."

Ali groaned. "You might have told me it was his favorite *before* we stole it."

Her temper flared. "Maybe you should have worried about that before bursting into my infirmary ranting about conspiracies."

"But you believe me?" Ali asked, hoping rising in his voice.

I believe Kaveh is up to no good. The grand wazir had made his hostility to the shafit clear, though Nahri wasn't sure she believed he could have plotted such a vile act. There had always been something she hadn't quite trusted about him, but he didn't seem to be a cruel man.

She settled for a different answer. "It's such a monumentally absurd story—even for you—to concoct that I'm assuming there's a chance it's the truth."

"How gracious of you," Ali muttered.

They ducked to avoid a low-hanging line of laundry. They were taking a back passage through the Geziri Quarter that Ali believed was faster, and the windowless expanses of the broad stone mansions loomed up around them, the faint scent of refuse clinging to the air. The horse jumped a wide drainage canal, and Nahri swore, hugging Ali tighter to hook her fingers around his weapons belt. That was an item she knew he'd keep secure.

She heard him murmur a prayer under his breath. "Do you have to do that?" she hissed into his ear, fighting embarrassment. Nahri was not going to pretend the prince was the most . . . objectionable person to hold tight. She was a grown woman; she could quietly note the positive effects daily sparring might have on a man without getting worked up about it. *Ali* was the one making this unnecessarily awkward. "You know, for someone with such a clear recollection of one of Kaveh's courtesans, you're acting pretty prim."

Ali sputtered. "I didn't do anything with his courtesans!" he said, defending himself. "I would never. Forgive me for remembering a face!"

She felt mildly insulted at the heat in his voice. "Do you have something against Daeva women?"

"I . . . no, of course not," he stammered back. Ali shifted as if to put space between their bodies, but another lunge of the horse sent them hard against each other. "Can we . . . can we not talk about this right now?"

Nahri rolled her eyes but let it go. Fighting with Ali wasn't going to help her face down a Daeva mob.

Nerves fluttered in her stomach. Nahri knew the Daevas listened to her—and she had a fair amount of confidence in her ability to persuade—but the prospect of confronting an angry crowd scared even her.

It won't be like that, she tried to assure herself. *You'll swear on your family's name to see justice done and then order them to go home.* The most important thing was to prevent this from spiraling out of control.

It wasn't long before the alley began to widen. They turned another corner, and Ali slowed the horse. Just past an open archway, Nahri caught a glimpse of the street. The horse's clattering hooves softened.

The sound was immediately replaced by wailing. Nahri inhaled sharply, smelling blood and smoke on the warm air. Ali spurred the horse out of the alley, a choked cry of denial on his lips . . .

They were too late.

THERE WAS NO DAEVA MOB. NO CORDON OF ROYAL Guard trying to establish order. Instead what had been a happy, lively neighborhood of workshops and new homes this morning had been reduced to smoldering husks. The air was choked with smoke, a gray haze obscuring much of the camp.

"No," Ali begged softly as he slid from the horse. "God, no . . ."

Nahri jumped off after him. She could hear a baby crying, and sick with fear for Subha's family, she lunged forward.

Ali caught her wrist. "Nahri . . ." His voice was heavy with emotion. "We're alone. If people blame you, if they want revenge . . ."

"Then they want revenge." Nahri glared at him. "Let me go—and don't ever try to stop me again."

He dropped her wrist as if it had burned him. "I'm sorry."

"Good. Come on."

They entered the camp silently.

Smoking workshops and tents loomed around them; one of the pumps Ali had installed had been smashed and was going wild, spraying water in a wide arc. The muddy road had been churned up by hooves and it sucked at her slippers as she passed smashed furniture and broken pots. And yet, it looked like most of the damage was confined to the main thoroughfare, a small mercy; perhaps the Daevas who attacked had been too frightened to get off their horses or venture into the narrow side lanes. Shafit, shocked and covered in dust and blood, were salvaging what they could from their ruined homes, while others simply sat in stunned disbelief.

A hush descended as more and more people recognized them. Ahead she saw a small group of shafit gathered around a prone form on the ground. A body.

Nahri stumbled. Burned beyond recognition, it looked like it might have been a young man, his gaping mouth trapped in a permanent scream.

"They burned him alive."

Nahri whirled around to see Subha. The shafit physician was filthy, her clothes and skin coated in ash, a bloody apron tied around her waist. "A boy younger than you," she spat at Ali. "A boy who could barely string two words together. I would know. I delivered him myself and unwrapped the cord that was around his neck . . ." She trailed off, looking anguished as she tore her gaze from the murdered youth. "Of course, that was after they set fire to our homes and smashed through our workshops. When they rode down those who would not answer their questions and beat those who didn't speak quickly enough. And when that boy couldn't answer, they decided he was their culprit. He did *nothing*." Her voice broke as she raised an accusing finger at both of them. "We came here to help you. To build *your* hospital under *your* protection."

"And we failed you." There were tears in Ali's eyes, though his voice didn't shake. "I'm so sorry, Subha, from the depths of my soul."

The doctor shook her head. "Your words won't bring him back, Alizayd al Qahtani."

Nahri couldn't look away from the murdered boy. "Where are your injured?" she asked softly.

Subha jerked her head toward the remains of a makeshift tent, a tattered tarp all that protected the two dozen or so bloodied people lying in its shade. "Over there. Parimal is bringing more supplies."

"I don't need supplies." Nahri approached the group. A boy lay alone on a dirty blanket closest to her. He seemed to be in shock; his lip was split and his jaw bloodied and bruised. He clutched a second, blood-soaked blanket to his abdomen.

Nahri knelt and pulled it away. He'd been stabbed, very nearly disemboweled. It was a miracle he wasn't already dead. Purple swelling ballooned the skin, and she could smell torn intestine. Subha couldn't help him, even with supplies.

But Nahri could. She took a deep breath, aware of the step she was about to take and what it would mean.

And then she laid her hands upon his body.

Heal. The skin immediately twisted beneath her fingertips, the swelling vanishing, the torn muscles and flesh rushing back together. The young man let out a strangled gasp, and she felt his racing heartbeat even out. Nahri opened her eyes, meeting Subha's stunned expression.

She cleared her throat. "Who's next?"

BY THE TIME THE CALL TO MAGHRIB PRAYER ECHOED across Daevabad, Nahri had lost track of how many shafit she had healed. The injuries were brutal: broken bones, crushed limbs, and gruesome burns. From what Nahri could gather, the rampage had been short but savagely effective: a mob of riders racing through and throwing conjured balls of fire before seizing and murdering the young man they declared guilty.

Twenty-three were dead, a number that likely would have been twice as high without her intervention, and the fact that a third of the camp had fled into the hospital, taking refuge behind the doors that the Daeva raiders hadn't dared pass. "Why didn't everyone do so?" Nahri had asked.

"The men said they rode in the name of the Nahids," had been Subha's blunt answer. "We weren't sure a Nahid hospital was safe."

Nahri hadn't inquired further. And by the time she was done—her last patient a six-year-old with a skull fracture who'd been found in the arms of her dead father—Nahri was drained in every manner a person could be.

She sat back from the girl and took several deep breaths, trying to steady herself. But the acrid smell of smoke and blood turned her stomach. Her vision blurred, and she squinted, trying to see past a wave of dizziness.

Subha put a hand on her shoulder. "Easy," she said as Nahri swayed. "You look ready to faint." She pressed a waterskin into her hands. "Drink."

Nahri took it gladly and drank, pouring some into her hands to splash onto her face. "We will catch and punish the men who did this," she promised. "I swear."

The other doctor didn't even bother to feign a nod. "Maybe in another world."

Too late, Nahri registered the sound of hoofbeats. There were a few alarmed cries, and Nahri dropped the waterskin as she whirled around, half fearing the mob had returned.

It was almost worse. It was Ghassan.

The king wasn't alone, of course. The Qaid and a contingent of the Royal Guard, all very well armed, were behind him, as were Muntadhir and Kaveh. Her blood raged at the sight of the grand wazir. If Kaveh had a hand in the attack that had led to this awful reprisal, he would pay. Nahri would make damn sure of it. But she'd also be careful—she wasn't going to shout accusations she couldn't prove like Ali had and then have them used against her.

She straightened up. "Subha, your family is in the hospital?"

The other doctor nodded. "They're with Razu."

"Good." Nahri wiped her hands on her smock. "Would you join them? I think it best you not draw the king's attention right now."

Subha hesitated. "And you?"

"I need to put some men in their place."

But Ghassan didn't even glance her way as Nahri ducked out of the tent and approached. He was off his horse and striding across the bloody cobblestones straight for his son, as if there was no one else in the street.

Ali seemed to notice a half-moment too late. Covered in blood and dust, he had not stopped moving since they arrived, doing whatever the shafit asked of him: cleaning debris, repairing tents, distributing blankets.

He raised his hands. "Abba—"

Ghassan struck him across the face with the metal hilt of his khanjar.

The crack echoed across the street, the camp going silent at the sound. Nahri heard Ali gasp, and then his father hit him again and he staggered back, blood streaming down his face.

"On your knees," Ghassan snapped, pushing Ali to the ground when he didn't move fast enough. He unsheathed his zulfiqar.

Horrified, Nahri ran toward them, but Muntadhir was faster, jumping from his horse and striding forward. "Abba, wait—"

"*Do it.*" Ali's voice, wracked with anguish, cut his brother off. He spat blood and then glared at his father, his eyes blazing. "End this *facade*," he choked, his voice breaking on the word. "Just do it!"

Ghassan's hand stayed on the zulfiqar. "You disobeyed me," he accused. "I told you I would handle things. How dare you come here? How dare you risk your brother's wife?"

"Because your way of handling things is to let people die! To let everyone who is not us spend so much time fighting each other that they can't oppose you!"

The charge hung in the air like a lit match. People were staring in visible shock at the Qahtani men.

It looked as if it took Ghassan every bit of self-control he had to lower his zulfiqar. He spun around, turning his back on his son and motioning to the Royal Guard. "Take Prince Alizayd to the dungeon. Perhaps a few months sleeping with the corpses of those who've defied me will teach him to hold his tongue. And then tear the rest of this place down."

Nahri stepped directly in his path. "Absolutely not."

Ghassan gave her an annoyed look. "Stand down, Banu Nahri," he said condescendingly. "I do not have the patience for one of your self-important speeches right now. Let your husband punish you as he sees fit."

It was exactly the wrong thing to say.

The ground below her feet gave a single, angry jolt. There were a few cries of surprise as some of the horses were startled and reared. Filthy and fed up, Nahri barely noticed. Energy was crackling down her limbs, the city pulsing angrily in her blood. She had not come to this place—to the hospital they'd rebuilt on the bones of their slaughtered ancestors—to be brushed aside. She had not publicly broken her people's most deeply held taboo to be told to "stand down."

"No," she said flatly. "You won't be tearing this place down.

No one's touching my hospital and no one's dragging my partner off to rot in the dungeon."

Ghassan looked incredulous—and then his face hardened in a way that had once turned her blood to ice. "I beg your pardon?"

A whisper rustled through the group behind them, and then Kaveh came forward, looking aghast.

"Tell me it's not true," he implored. "They are saying you healed a shafit here with your own hands. Tell me they're lying."

"I healed about fifty," she corrected coldly. Before he could respond, Nahri raised her scalpel and cut a deep gash into her palm. Barely three drops had fallen to the dust before the wound closed. "And yet seemingly the Creator has not seen fit to take my abilities."

Kaveh looked horrified. "But at the Temple, you promised—"

"A promise like that means nothing when people are dying. My tribe committed a heinous crime—one whose source you and I will *definitely* be discussing. For now, I did what I could to rectify it." She shook her head in disgust. "Do you understand? What happened was a tragedy that *you* let spin out of control. A few criminals attack an innocent couple and that justifies a war in the streets? Is that who we are?" She gave Ghassan a defiant look but chose her next words carefully. "What happened to the king who was ready to move us past all this?"

It was both a challenge and an opportunity, and Nahri prayed they'd seize on the latter. She couldn't read Kaveh's expression; she suddenly wondered if she'd ever read anything about him correctly.

But Ghassan . . . his expression was one of open appraisal. As though he was seeing her for the first time.

Nahri met his stare. "I have dealt with you fairly at every turn, King Ghassan," she said, lowering her voice. "I renounced my Afshin. I married your son. I *bow my head* while you sit on a shedu throne. But if you try to take this from me, I will rip this city and your family apart."

Ghassan narrowed his eyes and drew nearer; it took every ounce of courage Nahri had not to step back.

"You cannot be so foolish as to threaten me," he said, softly enough that only she could hear. "I could reveal you as shafit right here."

Nahri didn't drop her gaze. And then in a single, petrifying moment, she decided to call his bluff. Nahri could read a mark, djinn king or not, and she was still willing to bet Ghassan al Qahtani would rather be known as the king who united their tribes than the one who destroyed the last Nahid.

"Then do it," she challenged, keeping her voice equally low. "Let us see who the Daevas believe now. Who your children believe. I've kept my word. Do this and it will be *you* acting in bad faith, not I."

Perhaps moved to interfere by the deadly expression brewing on his father's face, Muntadhir approached. He looked sick, his horrified eyes tracing the blood-spattered street and smoldering buildings. "Abba, it's been a long day. Let me take her back to the palace."

"That sounds like an excellent suggestion." Ghassan didn't take his eyes off her. "You're correct, Banu Nahida," he continued, his voice diplomatic. "You *have* acted in good faith, and I'm certain your actions here were only intended to save lives." He shrugged. "Perhaps one day the Daevas will even forget you completely disobeyed Suleiman's code to do so."

Nahri refused to flinch. "My hospital?"

"You may keep your little project, but you won't be returning to it until it's completed." Ghassan shot a glance at Ali, still kneeling on the ground. "Nor will you be *leaving* it unless it is at my command. A contingent of the Guard—and not ones your mother has managed to pay off—will arrest you if you try." He looked between Ali and Nahri. "I think it's best we put some distance into this . . . partnership. Should you need to discuss the work, you may communicate through a messenger . . . one I assure you will be very much in my service."

Muntadhir grabbed her hand, pulling her away. "Understood," he said quickly, perhaps seeing the defiance still bright in her eyes. "Nahri, let's—"

"I'm not done," Ghassan cut in, his voice freezing her blood. But his attention was back on Ali. "The Banu Nahida may have acted in good faith, but you did not. You disobeyed me, Alizayd, and I am not unaware as to who's been whispering in your ear and putting gold in your hands. That ends today."

Ali shot to his feet, his eyes burning. "Excuse me?"

Ghassan stared back at his son. "You've made clear your life means nothing to you, but you can't act so heedlessly and not expect to hurt others." His expression sharpened. "So you can be the one to tell your sister she'll never see her mother again." He turned on his heel, striding back to his horse. "Kaveh, arrange a ship. Queen Hatset will be leaving for Ta Ntry tomorrow."

24

DARA

The lake Dara had ravaged six months ago was already recovering. The gash he'd torn into its bed was barely visible, hidden beneath a sinuous net of sea-green waterweeds that reached out and twisted across opposite ends to knit together like lace. The surrounding trees were blackened, skeletal things, and the beach itself was dusted with ash and littered with the tiny bones of various aquatic creatures. But the water was returning, cool, blue, and smooth as glass, even if it only came to his knees.

"Did you think it would not heal?"

Dara shuddered at the sound of the marid's raspy voice. Though they'd been told to return here, he hadn't been certain what they'd find.

"I thought it might take more time," Dara confessed, clasping his hands behind his back as he gazed at the horizon.

"Water is unstoppable. Eternal. It always returns. *We* return." The marid fixed its dead eyes on him. It was still in the form of its murdered human acolyte, the body now reduced to salt-bleached bones and rotting gristle in the places where it wasn't armored with shell and scales. "Water brings down mountains and nurtures new life. Fire burns out."

Dara returned his gaze, unimpressed. "You know, I grew up on stories where the marid appeared as fetching mermaids or terrifying sea dragons. This decaying corpse is quite the disappointment."

"You could offer yourself to me," the marid replied smoothly, its coat of shells clacking together in the biting wind. "Give me your name, daeva, and I'll show you anything you wish. Your lost world and slain family. Your Nahid girl."

A finger of ice brushed his spine. "What do you know of any Nahid girl?"

"She was in the mind and memories of the daeva we took."

"The daeva you took . . ." Dara's eyes narrowed. "You mean the boy you used to murder me?" His mouth twisted. "Alizayd al Qahtani is no daeva."

The marid seemed to still, even the shells and bones falling silent. "Why would you say such a thing?"

"He is a djinn. At least, that is what his fool tribe call themselves."

"I see," the marid said, after another moment of considered silence. "No matter. Djinn, daeva . . . you are all the same, short-sighted and as destructive as the element that smolders in your hearts." It ran its bony hands through the water, making tiny ripples dance. "You will leave my home soon, yes?"

"That is the plan. But if you try to deceive me, I assume you understand what I'll do." Dara pinned the marid with his gaze.

"You've made your intent clear." A pair of tiny silver fish darted between its hands. "We will return you to your city, Darayavahoush e-Afshin. I pray you content yourself with spilling blood there and never return to our waters."

Dara refused to let the words land. "And the lake? You will be able to re-create the enchantment I asked about?"

The marid cocked its head. "We will bring down your stone tower. And then understand we are done. We will bear no more responsibility for what your people do."

Dara nodded. "Good." He turned away, the wet sand sucking at his boots as he headed back to the camp they'd pitched on a grassy bluff set back from the water. At Dara's suggestion, they had packed up and left their mountain encampment less than a week after Mardoniye's death. Though the mist of copper vapor had been fading by then, its very existence had provoked questions among his men that he couldn't answer. So they'd moved, biding the final weeks before Navasatem here.

And now the generation celebrations began in three days. In three days, they would enter this water and be transported back to Daevabad. In three days, he would be home. In three days, he would see Nahri.

In three days, you will once again have the blood of thousands on your hands.

He closed his eyes, trying to shut away the thought. Dara had never pictured feeling such despair on the eve of a conquest he'd desired for centuries. Certainly not back when he was the Scourge of Qui-zi, the cunning Afshin who'd bedeviled Zaydi al Qahtani for years. That man had been a dashing rebel, a passionate leader who'd picked up the shattered pieces of his tribe and knit his people back together with promises of a better future. Of a day when they would sweep into Daevabad as victors and seat a Nahid on the shedu throne. Back then, he'd had quieter dreams for himself as well. Fleeting fantasies of re-claiming his family's house, taking a wife and raising children of his own.

None of those dreams would ever be now, and for what Dara had done—for what he was about to do—he had no right to them. But Nahri and Jamshid would have such dreams. His soldiers would. Their children would be the first Daevas in centuries to grow up without a foreigner's foot pressed down on their necks.

He had to believe it.

The sun blinked crimson behind the mountains, and a deep, rhythmic drumming came from the firelit camp, a welcome distraction from his grim thoughts. Their group was gathering while Manizheh prepared for sunset ceremonies at a makeshift fire altar. It was little more than a brass bowl set atop a circle of rocks, and Dara could not help but think wistfully of the magnificent gleaming altar back in Daevabad's Grand Temple.

He joined the line of weary soldiers, plunging his hands into the fiery ash in the brazier and sweeping it over his arms. There was a subdued air to the gathering, but that didn't surprise him. Mardoniye's death had been the first time most of his warriors had witnessed what a zulfiqar could truly do. Add the whispers he was trying to quash surrounding the vapor that had killed the Geziri scouts, and it made for a tense, grim atmosphere within the camp.

Manizheh caught his eye, beckoning him closer. "Did you find the marid?" she asked.

He wrinkled his nose. "Decomposing on the rocks on the opposite shore and no less self-righteous. But they are ready to assist us. I made clear the consequences should they betray us."

"Yes, I have no doubt you made yourself quite clear." Manizheh's black eyes twinkled. She had returned to treating Dara with her typical warm affection the very morning after they fought. And why not? She had won, after all, putting him firmly back in his place with a few swift words. "And are you ready?"

His response was automatic. "I am always ready to serve the Daevas."

Manizheh touched his hand. Dara caught his breath at the burst of magic, a sweep of calm similar to a drunken ease surging through him. "Your loyalty will be rewarded, my friend," she replied softly. "I know we've had our disagreements, and I see you standing on the edge of bleakness. But our people will know what you've done for them. *All* of them." Her voice was intent. "We are indebted to you, and for that I promise you, Dara . . . I will see you find some happiness."

Dara blinked, the feelings he'd tried to suppress on his walk back rising and churning within him. "I do not deserve happiness," he whispered.

"That's not true." She touched his cheek. "Have *faith*, Darayavahoush e-Afshin. You are a blessing, our people's salvation."

Emotions warred in his heart. By the Creator, did he want to seize her words. To throw himself back into that belief wholeheartedly, the faith that had once come so easily and now seemed impossible to grasp.

Then force yourself to. Dara stared at Manizheh. Her worn chador and the battered brass bowl before her might have been a far cry from the splendid ceremonial garb and dazzling silver altar found in the Grand Temple, but she was still the Banu Nahida—Suleiman's chosen, the Creator's chosen.

He managed some conviction. "I shall try," he promised. "Actually . . . I would like to do something for you all after the ceremony. A gift, to brighten your spirits."

"That sounds delightful." She nodded to the rest of their group, seated on the grass. "Join your fellows. I would speak to you all."

Dara took a seat next to Irtemiz. Manizheh raised a hand in blessing, and he bowed his head in unison with the rest, bringing together his hands. The emerald on his ring caught the dying light, gleaming past the soot coating his fingers. He watched as Manizheh went through the sacred motions, pouring fresh oil in the glass lamps bobbing along the simmering water and lighting them with a stick of burning cedar. She pressed it to her brow, marking her forehead with its sacred ash. She closed her eyes, her lips moving in silent prayer.

And then she stepped forward.

"You all look terrible," she said flatly. The shoulders of a few of the surrounding Daevas slumped at her words. But then her mouth quirked in a rare true smile. "That's all right," she added gently. "You're entitled to feel terrible. You've followed me on what must seem a fool's dream and you've done so with an obedience that will earn you admittance into the Creator's eternal gardens. You've held your tongues when you must have so many questions." She gazed at them, letting her eyes fall on each man and woman in turn. "And for that you have my promise, my children . . . whether in this world or the next, you and yours will be provided for. Our people will speak of your names in stories and light tribute to your icons in the Grand Temple.

"But not yet." She moved past the altar. "I suspect some of you worry we are rushing this. That we are resorting to dark and cruel methods. That to attack when people are celebrating a cherished holiday is wrong.

"My answer is: we are out of time. With each passing day, Ghassan's persecution of our people worsens. His soldiers have taken to rampaging through our lands and looting our homes. To speak against him is to invite death. And were that not enough, Kaveh tells me that his half-tribe son, the radical who dares call himself 'Afshin-slayer,' has returned to Daevabad to further rile up his dirt-blooded supporters."

Dara tensed. That was *not* what Kaveh had said, and though Dara was not blind to what she was trying to do, the ease with which she spun the lie reminded him far too much of the current occupant of Daevabad's throne.

Manizheh continued. "Another time, this news might please me. Indeed, little would delight me more than to see the Qahtanis ripped apart by their own bloody fanaticism. But that is not how sand flies operate. They mob and they swarm and they devour. Their violence will spread. It *has* spread. It will envelop our city in chaos." Her voice was low and intense. "And the Daevas will pay the price. *We always do*. The icons of too many martyrs already line the Grand Temple, and those of you in the Daeva Brigade witnessed firsthand the savagery of the shafit when you were thrown out of the Citadel."

Manizheh gestured to the last rays of the vanished sun and then knelt, gathering a handful of sand. "This is *our* land. From the Sea of Pearls to the dust of the plains and the mountains of Daevabad, Suleiman granted it to our tribe, to those who served him most faithfully. Our ancestors spun a city out of magic—pure *Daeva* magic—to create a wonder unlike the world had ever seen. We pulled an island out of the depths of a marid-haunted lake and filled it with libraries and pleasure gardens. Winged lions flew over its skies and in its streets, our women and children walked in absolute safety.

"You've heard the Afshin's stories. The *glory* Daevabad once was. The marvel. We invited the other tribes to partake, we tried to teach them, to guide them, and yet they turned on us." Her eyes flashed, and she released the dust. "They betrayed us in the worst of ways: they *stole* our city. And then, not content with breaking Suleiman's law in their land, they let their shafit spawn defile ours. To this day, they keep these pitiful creatures around to wait on them hand and foot. Or worse! They pass them off as djinn children, irrevocably polluting their bloodlines and risking us all."

She shook her head, sadness sweeping her face. "And yet for so long, I saw no way out. The city would call to me, call to my brother, Rustam, with a strength that made our hearts ache. But it seemed dangerous to even dream of a better future. For the safety of us all, I bowed my head as Ghassan al Qahtani lounged on the throne of my ancestors. And then . . ." She paused. "Then the Creator granted me a sign impossible to ignore."

Manizheh beckoned for Dara to rise. He did so, coming to her side.

She laid a hand on his shoulder. "Darayavahoush e-Afshin. Our greatest warrior, the man who made Zaydi al Qahtani himself tremble. Returned to us, freed of Suleiman's curse, as mighty as our legendary forbearers. My people, if you are looking for proof of the Creator's favor, it is here in Dara. We have difficult days ahead. We may be forced to acts in ways that seem brutal. But I assure you . . . it is all necessary."

Manizheh fell momentarily silent, perhaps gauging the impact of her words. Dara saw some of the faces before him shining with wonder, but not all. Many looked uncertain, anxious.

He could help her with that.

He took a deep breath. The pragmatic thing would have been to leave his favored form, but the thought of doing so before their entire camp shamed him, and so instead he raised his hands, letting the heat dance from them in smoky golden waves.

They touched the fire altar first and the jumbled rocks melted together into a shining marble base, the battered bowl shifting into a proper silver vessel, glimmering as it formed from the dying sunlight. The smoke swirled around Manizheh, turning her plain garments into the delicate blue-and-white silks of ceremonial dress before cresting over the rest of their followers.

Dara closed his eyes. In the blackness of his mind, he dreamed of his lost city. Sharing meals and laughter with his Afshin cousins between training sessions. Holidays spent with his sister, sneaking tastes of their favorite dishes while his mother and aunts cooked. Racing his horse across the plains outside the Gozan River with his closest companions, the wind whistling past them. Not a single person in those memories had survived the sack of Daevabad. He gave magic to the yearning in his heart, to the ache he expected would always be there.

There were gasps. Dara opened his eyes, fighting a swoon as the magic drained him.

The Daevas were now seated upon the finest of carpets, spun from green wool the color of spring grass, tiny living flowers woven into the shimmering threads. The men wore matching uniforms, the patterned gray-and-black coats and striped leggings the same ones his Afshin cousins had donned. A feast was spread on white linen behind them, and Dara could tell from a single sniff of the air that the dishes were his family's recipes. The plain felt tents had been replaced by a ring of silk structures that billowed in the air like smoke, and in a marble-screened corral, dozens of ebony horses with flashing golden eyes pranced and snorted.

No, not just pranced. Dara's gaze locked on the horses. They had *wings*—four undulating wings each, darker than night and moving like shadows. The Afshin in him saw the immediate benefit in the marvelous creatures: they would speed his soldiers more swiftly to the palace. But in his heart, oh, the traitorous part of his heart . . . how he suddenly wished to steal one and flee this madness.

Manizheh gripped his shoulder, seizing upon her followers' visible awe. "*Look*," she urged, her voice carrying on the still air. "Look at this wonder, this sign of the Creator's blessing! We are going to Daevabad. *We are taking it back.*" Her voice rang out, echoing against the growing dark. "We will rip the Citadel from its moorings and the Qahtanis from their beds. I will not rest until those who have hurt us, those who threaten our women and children in the city that is *ours*—by the Creator's decree!—have been thrown in the lake, their bodies swallowed by its waters." Smoke was curling from her collar. "We will greet the next generation as leaders of all djinn, as Suleiman intended!"

A youth near the front stepped forward, throwing himself into prostration before Manizheh.

"For the Nahids!" he cried. "For the Lady!"

Those nearest followed suit, falling in a wave before Manizheh. Dara tried to picture Nahri and Jamshid at her side, the young Nahids not only safe but wrapped in the glorious heritage they'd been too long denied.

But the sick burning was already sweeping through him. He choked it down as Manizheh's gaze lit on him, expectation—and a slight challenge—in her eyes.

He fell to his knees in obedience. "For the Nahids," he murmured.

Satisfied triumph filled her voice. "Come, my people. We will take our blessings and then enjoy the feast our Afshin has conjured. Be merry! Celebrate what we are about to do!"

Dara stepped back, fighting to keep from stumbling and struggling for a lie that would allow him to escape before his weakness was noticed. "The horses . . . ," he blurted out, aware that it was a thin excuse. "If you don't mind . . ."

He staggered away. Fortunately, the rest of the Daevas were busy swarming Manizheh and Dara spotted enough jugs of wine as he passed the feast that he suspected no one would miss him for some time. He slipped between the tents, letting the encroaching dusk swallow him. But he barely made it four more steps before he fell to his hands and knees, retching.

His vision blurred. He closed his eyes, the drums beating painfully in his head as he clutched at the dirt.

Transform, you fool. Dara could not recover from the magic he'd just done in his mortal form. He tried to shift, desperate to pull the fire that pulsed in his heart over his shivering limbs.

Nothing happened. Stars were blossoming before his eyes, a metallic ringing in his ears. Panicking, he tried again.

The heat came . . . but it wasn't fire that wrapped his limbs. It was an airy whisper of nothingness.

And then Dara was gone. Weightless. Formless, and yet more alive than he'd ever been. He could taste the buzz of an approaching storm on the air and savor the comforting heat from the campfires. The murmur of creatures unseen seemed to call to him, the world glimmering and moving with shadows and shapes and an utter wild freedom that urged him to fly . . .

He slammed back into his body, flames flickering over his skin. He lay there, his hands over his face.

"Suleiman's eye," he whispered, stunned. "What was that?" Dara knew he should have been terrified, but the brief sensation had been *intoxicating*.

His people's legends flooded his mind. Stories of shapeshifting, of traveling across the desert as nothing more than a hot wind. Is that what he had just done? Had just been?

He sat up. Dara wasn't exhausted or sick now; he felt almost giddy. Raw, as though he'd touched a spark of energy, and it was still coursing through him. He wanted to try it again, to see what it might feel like to fly along the cold wind and race over the snow-dusted peaks.

Laughter and music from the feast caught his ear, a reminder of his people, as insistent as a leash.

But for perhaps the first time in his life, Dara didn't think about his responsibilities to his people. Bewitched and seduced, he grabbed for the magic again.

He was gone even faster this time, the weight of his body vanishing. He spun, laughing to himself as soil and leaves swirled and danced around him. He felt vast and yet remarkably light, the breeze carrying him away the moment he allowed it. In seconds, the lake was nothing but a gleaming mirror of moonlight far below.

And by the Creator . . . the glory spread before him. The forbidding mountains now looked inviting, their sharp peaks and ominous shadows a maze to dash through, to explore. He could sense the very heat seeping through the ground's thick crust, the sea of molten rock flowing beneath the earth, sizzling where it met water and wind. It all pulsed with activity, with life, with an untamed energy and freedom that he suddenly desired more than anything else.

He wasn't alone. There were other beings like him, in this state of formlessness. Dara could sense them, could hear whispered invitations and teasing laughter. It would be nothing to take the ghost of a hand, to race off and travel realms he hadn't known existed.

Dara hesitated, longing tearing through him. But what if he couldn't return? What if he couldn't find his way back when his people needed him most?

Manizheh's resolve—her threat—closed around him. He could see her unleashing the poison and failing to take the city. He could see an enraged Ghassan ripping away his copper relic before it killed him and then seizing Nahri by her hair. Dragging her before her mother and plunging a zulfiqar through her heart.

Fear, thick and choking, snared him, and with it, a panicked wish to return. This Dara did with far less grace, shifting back into his mortal form while still airborne. He slammed into the ground so hard it knocked the air from his lungs.

Gasping and wracked with pain, Dara wasn't sure how long he lay there, blinking at the thick cluster of stars above, before a chuckle drew his attention.

"Well . . . ," a familiar voice drawled. "I suppose it took you long enough to learn that." Vizaresh stepped forward, peering over his body. "Need some help?" he offered lightly, extending a clawed hand. "I suggest next time you land before shifting."

Dara was so stunned he actually let the ifrit help him into a seated position, leaning heavily against the trunk of a dead tree. "What was that?" he whispered.

"What we once were." Yearning filled Vizaresh's voice. "What we were once capable of."

"But . . ." Dara fought for words. No speech seemed worthy of the magic he'd just experienced. "But it was so . . . peaceful. So beautiful."

The ifrit narrowed his yellow eyes. "Why should that surprise you?"

"Because that's not what our stories say," Dara replied. "The original daevas were troublemakers. Tricksters who deceived and hunted humans for their own—"

"Oh, forget the damn humans for once." Exasperation creased Vizaresh's fiery visage. "Your people are obsessed. For all your laws about staying clear of humanity, your kind are just like them now, with your petty politics and constant wars. This—" He gripped Dara's hand, and with a surge of magic, it turned to flame. "*This* is how you were made. You were created to burn, to exist between worlds—not to form yourself into armies and pledge your lives to leaders who would toss them away."

The words struck too close to the misgivings Dara tried to keep buried. "Banu Manizheh is not tossing our lives away," he defended her sharply. "We have a duty to save our people."

Vizaresh chuckled. "Ah, Darayavahoush, there are always people to save. And always cunning men and women around who find a way to take advantage of that duty and harness it into power. If you were wise—if you were a true daeva—you would have laughed in the face of your Manizheh the moment she brought you back and vanished on the next wind. You would be *enjoying* this, enjoying the possibility of all the lovely new things you could learn."

Dara caught his breath against the sharp tug of longing in his chest. "A purposeless, lonely existence," he said, forcing disdain he did not entirely feel into his voice.

"A life of wandering, of wonderment," Vizaresh corrected, hunger in his eyes. "Do you think I don't know what you just experienced? There are worlds you can't see as a mortal, beings and realms and kingdoms beyond your comprehension. We took mates when we desired companionship, parted amicably when it was time to travel the winds again. There were entire centuries my feet didn't touch the ground." His voice grew nostalgic, a smile curving his lips. "Though admittedly when they did, it *was* typically because of the lure of human entertainment."

"Such entertainment brought the wrath of one of the Creator's prophets upon you," Dara pointed out. "It cost you this existence you paint so lovingly."

Vizaresh shook his head. "Dallying with the occasional human was not why Suleiman punished us. Not the entire reason anyway."

"Then what was the reason?"

The ifrit gave him a wicked smile. "Are you asking questions now? I thought all you did was obey."

Dara checked his temper. He might despise the ifrit, but in a small way, he was beginning to understand them—or at least, to understand how it felt to be the last of your kind.

And he was truly curious as to what Vizaresh had to say. "And I thought *you* wanted me to learn new things," he said archly. "Unless this is all bluster and you know nothing."

Vizaresh's eyes danced. "What will you give me for telling you?"

Dara grinned. "I won't smash you against a mountain."

"Always so violent, Darayavahoush." Vizaresh regarded him, pulling and twisting at a length of flame between his hands as if it were a toy. Abruptly, he dropped to sit across from Dara. "Fine, I will tell you why Suleiman cursed us. It was not for playing with humans—it was because we warred with the marid *over* those humans."

Dara frowned. This was not a story he'd ever heard before. "We went to war with the marid over *humans*?"

"We did," Vizaresh replied. "Think, Darayavahoush. How did Aeshma summon the marid of this lake?"

"He had me kill one of its acolytes," Dara said slowly. "A human acolyte. He said the marid would be obliged to respond."

"Precisely."

"Precisely what?"

Vizaresh leaned in close, as though confiding a secret. "Bargains, Darayavahoush. Debts. A human summons me to poison a rival and later I take their corpse as a ghoul. A village with dying crops offers the blood of one of its screaming members to the river, and the marid promptly flood it, filling their fields with rich silt."

Dara drew back. "You speak of evil things."

"I'd not thought you so sensitive, Scourge." When Dara glared, he shrugged. "Believe it or not, I once agreed with you. I was content with my own innate magic, but not all daevas felt similarly. They enjoyed the thrall of human devotion and encouraged it where they could. And the marid did *not* like that."

"Why not?"

Vizaresh toyed with the battered bronze chain he wore around his neck. "The marid are ancient creatures, older even than daevas. The human practices that fed them were established before humans even began raising cities. And when some of those humans began to prefer *us*?" He clucked his tongue. "The marid have an appetite for vengeance that rivals that of your Nahids and Qahtanis. If a human turned from them to beg intercession from a daeva, they'd drown its entire village. In retaliation, our people started doing the same." He let out an exaggerated sigh. "Flood and burn down a few too many cities and suddenly you're getting dragged before some ranting human prophet in possession of a magic ring."

Dara tried to take that all in. "If that's true, it sounds like the punishment was rather deserved. But I do not understand . . . if the marid were also responsible, why were they not disciplined?"

Vizaresh flashed him a mocking grin, his lips pulling back over his curved fangs. "Who says they weren't?" He seemed delighted at Dara's confusion. "You would make for a better companion if you were clever. I would laugh to see the chaos a true daeva would wreak in your position."

I would cause no chaos. I would leave. Dara shoved the thought away as soon as it came. "I'm not like you." His gaze caught on the chain Vizaresh was still fingering, and his irritation sparked. "And were *you* clever, you would not wear that in my presence."

"This?" The ifrit pulled the chain free from his bronze chest plate. Three iron rings hung from its length, crowned with emeralds that winked with unnatural malice. "Trust me, Darayavahoush, I am not fool enough to touch one of your followers even if they should beg it of me." He caressed the rings. "These are empty now, but they have saved me during bleaker centuries."

"Enslaving the souls of fellow daeva *saved* you?"

True anger flashed in the ifrit's eyes for the first time. "They were not my fellows," he snapped. "They were weak, mewling things who threw their allegiance to the family of so-called healers, the Nahid blood poisoners who hunted my *true* fellows." He sniffed. "They should have been glad for the power I gave them; it was a taste of what we once were."

Dara's skin crawled at Vizaresh's words, but he was thankful for it. What was he doing letting Vizaresh fill his mind with dreams and likely lies that would pull him away from Manizheh? Was Dara so foolish as to forget how deceptive the ifrit could be?

He rose to his feet. "I may not remember much of my time in slavery, but I assure you I was not *glad* to be forced to wield magic—no matter how powerful—in the service of violent human whims. It was despicable."

He walked away, not waiting for Vizaresh's response. Ahead, Dara could hear laughter and music from the feast beyond the tents. Night had fallen, a thin sliver of moon and thick cluster of stars making the pale tents and bone-white beach glow with reflected celestial light. The scent of spiced rice with sour cherries and sweet pistachio porridge—his family's recipes—sent a newly sharp ache into his heart. Suleiman's eye, how was it possible to still miss them so much?

A closer—rather drunken—giggle caught his ear.

"—what will you do for it?" It was Irtemiz, teasingly holding a bottle of wine behind her back. Bahram's arms were around her waist as they staggered into view, but the young man went pale when he noticed Dara.

"Afshin!" He stepped away from Irtemiz so fast he half stumbled. "I, er, we didn't mean to intrude upon you. Your brooding." His eyes went bright with embarrassment. "Not brooding! That's not what I meant. Not that there's anything wrong with—"

Dara waved him off, admittedly a little chastened. "It is fine." He eyed them, noting that Irtemiz's coat was already open and Bahram's belt missing. "Are the two of you not enjoying the feast?"

Irtemiz offered a weak smile, color rising in her cheeks. "Just taking a walk?" she offered. "You know, to better . . . er, prepare ourselves for such heavy food."

Dara snorted. Another time, he might have tried to put an end to such trysts—he didn't need lovers' spats among his soldiers. But considering the deadly mission that loomed in just a few days, he decided there was no harm in it. "Choose another direction to walk. Vizaresh is lurking back that way." Though he was slightly disgruntled, he could not help but add, "There is a lovely cove if you follow the eastern beach."

Bahram looked mortified, but Irtemiz grinned, her dark eyes sparkling with mirth. She grabbed the young man's hand. "You heard our Afshin." Laughing, she dragged Bahram off.

Dara watched them go. A quiet sadness stole into his soul as he stood alone. His fellows suddenly seemed so young, so different.

This is not my world. It was clearer to him than it ever had been before. He cared for these people, loved them, but the world he was from had vanished. And it wasn't coming back. He would always be slightly apart.

Like the ifrit. Dara hated the comparison but knew it was an apt one. The ifrit were monsters, no doubt, but it could not have been easy to watch their world destroyed and remade, to spend millennia trying to recapture it while steadily, one by one, they perished.

Dara was not ready to perish. He closed his eyes, remembering the giddy sensation of being weightless and the way the dark mountains seemed to beckon. This time he couldn't tamp down the longing in his heart, so he let it remain, laced under a new veneer of determination. Forget the games of the ifrit and the marid's long-lost secrets—they belonged to a past he wouldn't let claim him again.

Dara would end this war for his people and see them safe.

Then perhaps, it would be time to discover what else the world offered.

25
ALI

Ali gazed upon the room that was to be Nahri's office with quiet approval. The completed window seat had been placed in the cozy alcove overlooking the street this morning, and he sank down upon the cushioned bench, pleased at how comfortable it was. Shelves within easy reach lined the alcove—this place would be perfect for reading.

I hope she likes it. Ali gazed beyond the room, past the balcony that overlooked the hospital's inner courtyard. The sounds of construction—the final stages—came to his ears. *I hope this hospital is worth the price we paid for it.*

He sighed, turning to peer through the wooden screen that looked out at the street below. It was as close as Ali could get to the slowly recovering shafit workcamp—his father had made clear he would personally double the death toll from the attack if Ali so much as opened his mouth about it.

There was a knock and then Lubayd called out from beyond the archway. "Can I come in? Or do you need a minute?"

Ali rolled his eyes. "Come in." He turned away from the window. "Aye, not with your *pipe*," he scolded. He chased the other man back through the archway, waving the offensive fumes away. "You'll stink the place up!"

Lubayd's eyes twinkled with amusement. "Well, aren't you protective of your little Nahid's sanctuary?"

"I'm protective over everything here," Ali shot back, unable to check the defensive heat in his voice. Knowing Lubayd to be merciless in his teasing when he spotted weakness, Ali quickly changed the subject. "You shouldn't be smoking in the hospital anyway. Doctor Sen said she'd toss you out the next time she caught you."

Lubayd inhaled. "What is life without risk?" He tilted his head toward the stairs. "Come. Aqisa is back from the palace and waiting for you."

Ali followed him out, returning the various salaams and nods of workers as they passed through the hospital complex. His home and prison for the past two months, the hospital was now all but complete. Attendants were preparing for tomorrow's opening ceremony, rolling out embroidered silk carpets and conjuring delicate floating lanterns. A few musicians had arrived to practice, and the steady beat of a goblet drum echoed through the courtyard.

He caught sight of Razu and Elashia sitting in a swing deep in the shade of a lime tree. Ali touched his brow in greeting as he passed, but neither woman appeared to notice him. Razu was tucking one of the tree's silky white flowers behind Elashia's ear, the ever-silent Sahrayn woman giving her a small smile.

It must be nice to have such a close friendship, he thought reflectively. Ali had Lubayd and Aqisa, of course, and they were truer and more loyal friends than he deserved. But even they had to be kept at an arm's length; his many secrets were too dangerous to reveal entirely.

Aqisa was waiting in the shadow of the large foyer, dressed in plain robes, her braids tied up and bundled under a turban. "You look dreadful," she greeted him bluntly.

"It's the eyes," Lubayd agreed. "And the shambling walk. Were he a bit bonier, he'd make a convincing ghoul."

Ali glowered at them. Between his nightmares and the race to finish the hospital, he was barely sleeping, and he was not unaware his appearance reflected such a thing. "It's good to see you too, Aqisa. How are things at the palace?"

"Fine." Aqisa crossed her arms, leaning against the wall. "Your sister sends her greetings."

His heart twisted. The last time Ali had seen Zaynab was when he'd been forced to break the news of their mother's imminent banishment. Though Hatset had remained grimly calm, telling them both to be strong—and that she'd be back, no matter Ghassan's orders—Zaynab had broken down in front of him for the first time in his life. "Why couldn't you have just listened to him?" she'd wept as Ali was forcibly escorted back out. "Why couldn't you have held your tongue for once?"

Ali swallowed the lump in his throat. "Is she okay?"

"No," Aqisa said flatly. "But she's surviving and is stronger than you give her credit for."

He winced at the rebuke, hoping she was right. "And you've had no issues getting in and out of the harem? I worry you're risking yourself."

Aqisa actually laughed. "Not in the slightest. You may forget it at times, but I *am* a woman. The harem exists to keep out strange, dangerous men; the guards barely pay me any mind." She caressed the hilt of her khanjar. "If I do not point it out often enough, your gender can be remarkably stupid." The humor left her face. "No luck with the infirmary, however."

"Still guarded?" Ali asked.

"Day and night, by two dozen of your father's most loyal men."

Two dozen men? A wave of sick fear—his constant companion since the attack—rolled through him. He was even more worried for Nahri than he was for himself; despite their strained relationship, Ali suspected his father was still unwilling to directly execute his own son. But Nahri wasn't his blood, and Ali had never seen *anyone* publicly challenge Ghassan the way she had in the ruins of the shafit camp. He could still remember her—small in comparison to his father, exhausted and covered in ash, but thoroughly defiant, heat rippling through the air when she spoke, the stone street shivering with magic.

It was one of the bravest acts he'd ever witnessed. And it petrified him, for Ali knew all too well how his father handled threats.

Ali turned on his heel, pacing. It was driving him mad to be locked up here, trapped on the other side of the city from his sister and Nahri. A sheen of dampness erupted down his back, and he shivered. Between the day's rain and his roiling emotions, Ali was struggling to check his water abilities.

Automatically, his gaze went to the corridor that led to Issa's room. At Hatset's request, the Ayaanle scholar had stayed behind to continue looking into Ali's "problem." But Ali wasn't optimistic. He didn't have his mother's touch with the erratic old man, and the last time he'd tried to check on Issa's progress, he'd found the scholar surrounded by a massive circle of parchment forming a family tree of what must have been every person even tangentially related to Ali. He'd rather impatiently asked what in God's name his ancestry had to do with getting the marid out of his head, and Issa had in turn hurled a globe *at* his head, rudely suggesting that as an alternative.

A shadow fell across them, the shape of a large man stepping into the shaft of sunlight coming from the garden. "Prince

Alizayd," a deep voice rumbled. "I believe your father made his orders clear."

Ali scowled, turning to glare at Abu Nuwas, the senior Geziri officer sent to "watch over" him. "I'm not trying to escape," he said acidly. "Surely, standing near the entrance is permitted?"

Abu Nuwas gave him a surly look. "A woman is looking for you in the eastern wing."

"Did she give you a name? This place is crawling with people."

"I am not your secretary." Abu Nuwas sniffed. "Some grandmotherly-looking shafit." He turned away without another word.

"Oh, don't be rude," Lubayd said when Ali rolled his eyes. "He's only following your father's orders." He blew out a ring of smoke. "And I rather like that one. We got drunk together a few weeks ago. He's an excellent poet."

Ali gaped. "Abu Nuwas is a *poet*?"

"Oh, yes. Wonderfully scandalous stuff. You'd hate it."

Aqisa shook her head. "Is there anyone in this city you haven't befriended? Last time we were at the Citadel, there were grown warriors fighting to take you out for lunch."

"The emir's fancy crowd won't have me," Lubayd replied. "They think I'm a barbarian. But regular Geziri folk, soldiers . . ." He grinned. "Everyone likes a storyteller."

Ali rubbed his temples. Most of Lubayd's "stories" were tales meant to bolster Ali's reputation. He hated it, but his friend only doubled his efforts when Ali asked him to stop. "Let me go see about this woman."

The eastern wing was fairly quiet when Ali arrived, with only a pair of tile workers finishing a last stretch of wall and a small, older woman in a faded floral headscarf standing near the railing overlooking the garden, leaning heavily on a cane. Assuming she was the woman Abu Nuwas had meant, Ali crossed to her. Maybe she *was* someone's grandmother; it would not be the first time an older relative had come here searching for work for a ne'er-do-well youth.

"Peace be upon you," Ali called out as he approached. "How may I—"

She turned to face him, and Ali abruptly stopped talking.

"Brother Alizayd . . ." Sister Fatumai, once the proud leader of the Tanzeem, stared back at him, her familiar brown eyes sharp as knives and simmering with anger. "It's been a long time."

"I'M SORRY TO HEAR YOU'RE HAVING TROUBLE WITH supplies," Ali said loudly as he led Sister Fatumai away from the curious workers, ushering her toward a room packed with fresh linens. He was almost impressed he could lie considering how rattled he was, but knowing the spies his father had filled the hospital with, he had little choice. "Let's see what we can spare . . ."

He ushered the Tanzeem leader into the room, and after quickly checking to make sure they were alone, shoved the door closed and whispered a locking enchantment under his breath. A half-filled oil lamp had been left on one of the shelves, and Ali quickly lit it. The conjured flame danced down the wick, throwing weak light across the small chamber.

He turned to face her, breathing hard. "S-sister Fatumai," Ali stammered. "I . . . I'm so sorry. When I heard what happened to Rashid . . . and saw Sheikh Anas's masjid . . . I assumed—"

"That I was dead?" Fatumai offered. "A fair assumption; your father certainly tried his best. And honestly, I thought the same of you when you left for Am Gezira. I figured it was a story told to hide the truth of your execution."

"You're not far from the truth." He swallowed. "The orphanage?"

"It's gone," Fatumai replied. "We tried to evacuate when Rashid was arrested, but the Royal Guard caught up with the last group. They sold the youngest as servants and executed the rest."

Her gaze grew cold. "My niece was one of the ones they murdered. You might remember her," she added, accusation lacing into her voice. "She made you tea when you visited."

Ali braced himself on the wall, finding it hard to breathe. "My God . . . I'm so sorry, sister."

"As am I," she said softly. "She was a good woman. Engaged to marry Rashid," she added, leaning against the wall as well. "Perhaps a small consolation that they entered Paradise as martyrs together."

Ali stared at the ground, ashamed.

She must have noticed. "Does such speech bother you now? You were once one of Sheikh Anas's most devout students, but I know faith is a garment worn carelessly by those who live in the palace."

"I never lost my faith." Ali said the words quietly, but there was a challenge in them. He'd only met Sister Fatumai after Rashid, another member of the Tanzeem, had tricked him into visiting their safe house, an orphanage in the Tukharistani Quarter. It was a visit designed to guilt the wealthy prince into funding them, a tour to show him sick and hungry orphans . . . but conveniently *not* the weapons he'd learned they were also purchasing with his money. Ali had never gone back; the Tanzeem's use of violence—possibly against innocent Daevabadis—was not a line he would cross.

He changed the subject. "Would you like to sit? Can I get you something to drink?"

"I did not come here to enjoy Geziri hospitality, Prince Alizayd." She shifted on her feet. Beneath the tired exterior and silver hair, there was steel in Fatumai, and it chastened him as much as it concerned him. There had been heart in the Tanzeem. They'd saved and sheltered shafit children, put books in hands and bread in mouths. Ali didn't doubt for a second that they were believers, as God-fearing as he was.

He also didn't doubt that quite a few of them had blood on their hands. "Are the rest of the children safe?"

She laughed, a hard sound. "You really don't know your father, do you?"

Ali almost couldn't bring himself to ask the question. "What do you mean?"

"Do you think it mattered to Ghassan that some were children?" She clucked her tongue. "Oh no, Brother Alizayd. We were a *danger*. A threat to be tracked down and exterminated. We came into his home and stole the heart of his youngest, so he sent his soldiers tearing through the shafit district in pursuit of us. Of anyone related to us. Family, neighbors, friends—he killed scores. We were so desperate to escape we tried to flee Daevabad itself."

"Flee Daevabad? You were able to hire a smuggler?"

"'Hire' is not the word I'd use," she said, a deadly finality in her voice. "Not that it mattered. I volunteered to stay behind with those who were too young for such travel and the ones who had too much magical blood to be able to pass in the human world." Her voice quivered. "The rest . . . I kissed their brows and wiped their tears . . . and watched as your father's firebirds burned the boat."

Ali reeled. *"What?"*

"I'd rather not repeat it if you don't mind," she said flatly. "Hearing their screams as the lake tore them apart was bad enough. I suppose your father thought it was worth it to take out the handful of Tanzeem fighters who were with them."

Ali abruptly sat down. He couldn't help it. He knew his father had done some awful things, but sinking a ship full of fleeing child refugees was pure evil. It didn't matter who Ghassan had been hunting.

He should not be king. The blunt, treasonous thought burst into Ali's head in a moment of terrible clarity. It suddenly seemed simple, the loyalty and complicated love for his father that Ali had long struggled with snipped away as someone might cut a strained rope.

Fatumai paced farther into the chamber, oblivious to his pain or perhaps rightfully uncaring about the prince having a breakdown on the floor. She ran her hands along the stacked supplies. "A lively, organized place this seems," she commented. "You have done extraordinary work, work that has truly changed the lives of innumerable shafit. Ironic, in a way, that it happened here."

That immediately pulled him from his thoughts. "Meaning?"

She glanced back. "Oh, come, brother, let us not pretend. I am certain you know what once happened to the shafit in this so-called hospital. Your namesake certainly did, though it is absent from the songs spun about his mighty deeds." She shrugged. "I suppose there's little glory in tales of plague and vengeance."

Her words were far too precise to be a mistake. "Who told you?" he asked haltingly.

"Anas, of course. Do you think you're the only one with a skill for combing through old texts?" She leveled her gaze on Ali. "He thought it was a story that should be spread far more widely."

Ali closed his eyes, his hands clenching into fists. "It belongs to the past, sister."

"It belongs to the present," Fatumai returned sharply. "It is a warning of what the Daevas are capable of. What your *Nahid* is capable of."

His eyes shot open. "What we are *all* rather capable of. It was not Daevas who murdered your children on the lake. Nor was it Daevas who burned this place to the ground and slaughtered everyone inside fourteen centuries ago."

She stared at him. "And why, brother? Tell me why the Geziris and shafit torched this place with such fury."

Ali couldn't look away and yet he couldn't not answer. "Because the Nahid Council experimented on shafit here," he confessed softly.

"Not just experimented," Fatumai corrected. "They created a poison here. A pox that could be mixed with paint. Paint that could be applied to what, exactly, my warrior friend?"

"Scabbards," he answered softly, sickness rising in his chest. "Their soldiers' scabbards."

"Their *Geziri* soldiers," she clarified. "Let's get our facts straight. For that's all the Nahid Council said your tribe was good for. Fighting and, well . . . we'll not say the impolite term, but *making* more soldiers to fill the ranks." She met Ali's stony gaze. "But the pox wasn't designed to kill the purebloods who wore those scabbards, was it?"

Water was pooling in his hands again. "No," he whispered. "It wasn't."

"That's right, it didn't do a damn thing to those soldiers," Sister Fatumai replied, a savage edge rising in her voice. "They happily headed home to Am Gezira, that insolent, restless little province. One filled with too many shafit, and too many djinn relatives who would spirit them away into the desert when Daeva officials came to drag them to Daevabad." She tilted her head. "Zaydi al Qahtani had a shafit family, didn't he? His first family?"

Ali's voice was thick. "He did."

"And what happened when *he* returned home on leave? When he let his children play with his sword? When he removed his scabbard and touched the beloved wife he hadn't seen in months?"

"He woke beside their bodies the next morning." Ali's gaze flickered unwillingly to the hilt of his own sword. Ali had read of their fate in a misplaced biography when he was a child, and it had given him nightmares for weeks. To see the people you loved most dead at the hands of a contagion you'd unknowingly given to them . . . it was something that would drive a man mad. Would drive a man to return to his garrison and put his khanjar through the throat of his Daeva commander. To lead a revolt that would reshape their world and ally them with the marid against his fire-blooded fellows.

To perhaps, in the dark quiet of his soul, purposely allow the slaughter of a hospital.

Fatumai was studying him. "You've told no one of this, have you? Afraid your shafit friends would rightfully run your Banu Nahida out?"

Her words struck—but that hadn't been the reason. The excitement in Nahri's voice, the cautious interest he'd seen from Subha when they first visited . . . Ali hadn't had the heart to destroy those things. And for what? To point out for the hundredth time the ghastly acts their people had committed so long ago?

"No, I wasn't afraid. I was *tired*." Ali's voice broke on the word. "I'm tired of everyone in this city feeding on vengeance. I'm tired of teaching our children to hate and fear other children because their parents are our enemies. And I'm sick and tired of acting like the only way to save our people is to cut down all who might oppose us, as if our enemies won't return the favor the instant power shifts."

She drew up. "Bold words for the son of a tyrant."

Ali shook his head. "What do you want from me?" he asked wearily.

She gave him a sad smile. "Nothing, Prince Alizayd. Respectfully, all that would make me trust you again would be seeing your father dead by your hand. I am finished with the politics of this city. I have ten remaining children who depend on me. I will not risk them."

"Then why are you here?"

Fatumai touched a tray of tools. "I came to pass on a warning."

Ali tensed. "What warning?"

"Your little speech about vengeance, Alizayd. There are shafit who don't long to work at your hospital, ones who would make the

Tanzeem look like Daeva sympathizers. People whose anger could bring this city to its knees and who would never forgive a Nahid for the past, no matter how many shafit she heals. I've lost some of my older children to them. They watched their friends die on the lake, their neighbors sold on that auction block, and they want nothing more than to see you so-called purebloods suffer. And your Nahid should fear them."

Ali was on his feet the next moment, but Fatumai held up a hand. "There are whispers that an attack will happen during Navasatem," she explained. "I will not reveal who I learned it from, so do not ask."

"What kind of attack?" Ali asked in horror.

"I don't know. It is a rumor and a thin one. I only pass it on because the thought of what the Daevas and the Royal Guard would do to us in retribution terrifies me." She turned to go, her cane tapping the stone floor.

"Sister, wait. Please!"

Fatumai was already pulling open the door. "That is all I know, Alizayd al Qahtani. Do with it what you will."

Ali paused, a thousand responses hovering on his lips.

The one that made it through was a surprise to him. "The little girl we saved. The girl from Turan's tavern. Is she all right?"

The cold grief in Fatumai's eyes told him the truth before she uttered the words.

"She was on the boat your father burned."

NIGHT HAD FALLEN, THE SKY IN THE WINDOW BEHIND Ghassan the silver-purple color of twilight and heavy with fog from the day's warm rain. Ali had all but paced holes in the hospital's courtyard before realizing that, however little he wished to see his father, security for Navasatem rested here.

Ghassan looked unconvinced. "An attack during Navasatem? Who told you this?"

"A friend," Ali said flatly. "One I will not be able to track down again. And she knew nothing more anyway."

Ghassan sighed. "I'll pass your concerns to Wajed."

Ali stared at him. "That's it?"

His father threw up his hands. "What else would you have me do? Do you know how many vague threats we get about the Daevas? About Nahri? Especially after the attack in your workcamp?"

"So increase her security. Cancel the procession. Cancel anything during which she'll be exposed!"

Ghassan shook his head. "I will not be canceling any Daeva celebrations on your word. I care not to hear Kaveh screeching about it." A vaguely hostile expression flitted across his face. "Besides . . . Nahri seems to think rather highly of herself lately. Why should I protect someone who so openly challenges me?"

"Because it's your duty!" Ali said, aghast. "You are her king. Her *father-in-law*."

Ghassan scoffed. "Considering the state of their marriage, I am hardly that."

Ali couldn't believe what he was hearing. "She's a woman under our roof. Her protection is part of our highest code, our most sacred—"

"And I will *speak to Wajed*," Ghassan interjected, in a tone that indicated the conversation was over. He rose to his feet, making his way to the windowsill. "But on another matter, your timing is good. The hospital is ready for tomorrow's opening ceremony?"

"Yes," Ali said, not bothering to conceal the bitterness in his voice. "I can report to the dungeon after it's over if you like."

Ghassan picked up a black velvet case that had been resting near the window. "That's not where I'm sending you, Alizayd."

There was a grim decisiveness to his voice that put Ali on edge instantly. "Where are you sending me?"

Ghassan opened the case, staring at whatever lay inside. "I had this made for you," he said softly. "When you first returned to Daevabad. I had hoped, I had even prayed, that we might find a way past all this as a family." He pulled free a magnificent length of dyed silk, patterned blue, purple, and gold twisting together over its shimmering surface.

A turban. A royal turban like the one Muntadhir wore. Ali's breath caught.

Ghassan ran his fingers over the silk. "I wanted to see you wear this during Navasatem. I wanted . . . so much to have you at my side once again."

At my side. Ali fought to keep his face blank. Because for the first time in his life, those simple words—that reminder of his duty as a Geziri son, the offer of one of the most privileged and safe positions in their world . . .

It filled him with absolute revulsion.

There was a tremor in his voice when he finally spoke. "What do you plan to do with me, Abba?"

Ghassan met his gaze, a storm of emotion in his gray eyes. "I do not know, Alizayd. I am near equally torn between declaring you my emir and having you executed." When Ali's eyes widened, he pressed on. "Yes. You are beyond capable for the position. It's true you lack in diplomacy, but you have a keener command of military matters and the city's economy than your brother ever will." He dropped the turban cloth. "You are also the most reckless and morally inflexible person I have ever come across, perhaps the greatest danger to Daevabad's stability since a lost Nahid strolled in with an Afshin at her side."

His father came around the desk, and Ali found himself stepping back, the air sharp and dangerous between them. And, God forgive him—as Ghassan moved, Ali's gaze fell on the dagger at his father's waist.

Zaydi al Qahtani's rebellion had started with a dagger through a throat. It would be so simple. So quick. Ali would be executed, he'd probably go to hell for killing his own father, but Daevabad's tyrant would be gone.

And then Muntadhir would take the throne. He could see his brother doing so, panicked, grieving, and paranoid. He'd almost certainly lash out, arresting and executing anyone associated with Ali.

Ali forced himself to look into his father's eyes. "I've only ever tried to act in Daevabad's interest." He wasn't sure whether he was speaking to his father or the dark urge in his mind.

"And now I'm going to invite you to act in your own," Ghassan said, seemingly unaware of the deadly thoughts swirling within his son. "I'm sending you back to Am Gezira after Navasatem."

Whatever Ali had expected . . . it was not that. "What?" he repeated faintly.

"I'm sending you back. You will formally renounce your titles and find a way to thoroughly sabotage your relationship with the Ayaanle, but you will otherwise return with my blessing. You may marry a local woman and tend to your crops and your canals with whatever children God grants you."

"Is this a trick?" Ali was too stunned to even be diplomatic.

"No," Ghassan said bluntly. "It is the last resort of a man who does not wish to execute his son." He looked almost imploringly at Ali. "I know not how to get you to bend, Alizayd. I have threatened you, I have killed your shafit allies, banished your mother, sent you to be hunted by assassins . . . and still you defy me. I am hoping your heart proves weaker than your sense of righteousness . . . or perhaps wiser."

Before Ali could stop himself, he saw Bir Nabat in his mind. His students and his fields, himself laughing over coffee with Lubayd and Aqisa.

A wife. A family. A *life*—one away from Daevabad's blood-soaked history and marid-haunted lake.

Ali felt like he'd been punched in the stomach. "And if I refuse?"

Ghassan looked exasperated. "It is not an offer, Alizayd. You are going. For God's sake . . ." A desperate note entered his voice. "Will you let me give at least one of my children some happiness? You wanted to go back, didn't you?"

He had. Desperately. Part of Ali still did. But he'd be leaving his home to a king he no longer believed deserved to rule it.

"Do not offer me this," he begged. "Please."

Ali's warring desires must have been plain on his face, because a quiet remorse swept his father's. "I suppose I've forgotten there are situations for which kindness is the most powerful weapon."

Ali was shaking. "Abba . . ."

But his father was already leading him out. "My men will take you back to the hospital. Your conditions remain."

"Wait, please—"

This time, the door closed softly in his face.

26

NAHRI

Nahri crossed her arms, staring skeptically at the saddle that had been placed on the stack of cushions piled before her. "Absolutely not."

"But it's safe!" Jamshid persisted. Clutching the handholds set in the saddle's frame, he hauled himself into the seat. "Look." He gestured to the raised back. "It's designed to compensate for the weakness in my lower body. I can bind my legs and use a crop to ride."

She shook her head. "You'll fall and break your neck. And a *crop*? You can't control a horse with some stick alone."

Jamshid eyed her. "My dear Banu Nahida . . . I say this with the utmost respect, but you are perhaps the last person in Daevabad I would take riding advice from." Nahri scowled, and he laughed. "Come now . . . I thought you'd be pleased. I got the design from that shafit doctor of yours. We're exchanging skills!" he teased. "Isn't that what you wanted?"

"No! I thought we might try some of her therapies so that in a few years you would be back on a horse *without* the need for a stick."

"I'm pretty sure the Navasatem procession will be over by then." Jamshid shifted in the saddle, looking pleased with himself. "This shall do nicely. Oh, what?" he asked when she glared at him. "You're not my mother. I don't need your permission." He brought his hands together as if holding imaginary reins. "I'm your elder anyway."

"I'm your Banu Nahida!" she argued back. "I could . . . I could . . ." She trailed off, thinking fast.

Jamshid—the former priest in training—turned to face her. "You could do what?" he asked politely, his eyes dancing. "I mean, what precisely could you do, according to the protocols of our faith?"

"Let him be." Nisreen's soft voice interrupted them, and Nahri glanced back to see her mentor standing at the curtain. Her eyes were locked on Jamshid, her face shining with warmth. "You should ride in the Navasatem procession if that's what you desire. It does my heart good to see you like this—even if your current stallion leaves much to be desired," she added, nodding to the stack of cushions.

Nahri sighed, but before she could respond, the sound of retching came from across the infirmary.

Jamshid glanced over. "It looks like Seyyida Mhaqal is sick again."

"Then you better get over there," Nahri replied. "If you have time to construct horses out of cushions, my brilliant apprentice, you have time to deal with fireworms."

He made a face but slipped from the saddle, heading for the sick patient. He didn't take his cane, and Nahri could not help but feel a quiet sense of triumph as he made his way steadily across the room. It might not be happening as quickly as Jamshid liked, but he *was* getting better.

She glanced at Nisreen, wanting to share her happiness. But Nisreen quickly dropped her gaze, collecting the glasswork Nahri had been using to prepare potions earlier.

Nahri moved to stop her. "I can do that. You shouldn't have to clean up after me."

"I don't mind."

But Nahri did. She pulled the pair of beakers from Nisreen's hands and set them down, taking the other woman's arm. "Come."

Nisreen made a startled sound. "But—"

"No *but*. You and I need to talk." She snatched up one of the bottles of soma that Razu had gifted her; it was proving a rather effective pain management technique. "Jamshid," she called. "You're in charge of the infirmary."

His eyes went wide over the bucket he was trying to maneuver beneath Seyyida Mhaqal. Curly gold fireworms clung to his wrists. "I'm what?"

"We'll be right outside." She escorted Nisreen to the balcony, pulling her to a bench, and pressing the bottle of soma into her hands. "Drink."

Nisreen looked indignant. "I beg your pardon?"

"*Drink*," Nahri repeated. "You and I clearly have some things to say to each other, and this will make it easier."

Nisreen took a delicate sip, making a face. "You have been spending too much time with djinn, to be acting thus."

"See? Aren't you happy you got that off your chest?" Nahri asked. "Tell me I've ruined my reputation. That the priests are saying I've strayed and Kaveh is calling me a traitor." Her voice grew slightly desperate. "None of you can meet my eyes nor want to talk to me, so surely that's what's being said."

"Banu Nahri . . ." Nisreen sighed—and then took another swig of the soma. "I don't know what you want me to say. You laid hands on dozens of shafit in broad daylight. You broke Suleiman's code."

"*To save lives*," Nahri said, defending herself fiercely. "The lives of innocent people attacked by members of our tribe."

Nisreen shook her head. "It is not always as simple as that."

"Then you think I'm wrong?" Nahri asked, trying to keep the tremble from her voice. "Is that why you've barely been speaking to me?"

"No, child, I don't think you're wrong." Nisreen touched Nahri's hand. "I think you're brilliant and courageous and your heart is in the right place. If I hold my tongue, it's because you share your mother's stubborn streak and I would rather serve quietly at your side than lose you altogether."

"You make me sound like Ghassan," Nahri replied, stung.

Nisreen passed over the bottle. "You did ask."

Nahri took a long drink of the soma, wincing as it burned down her throat. "I think I went too far with him," she confessed; Ghassan's cold eyes as he gazed at her in the ravaged workcamp were a thing not easily forgotten. "The king, I mean. I challenged him. I had to do it, but . . ." She paused, remembering his threat to reveal her as a shafit. "I don't think he's going to let it pass unpunished."

Nisreen's expression darkened. "Did he threaten you?"

"He doesn't need to. Not directly. Though I suspect he sent Hatset away in warning to me, as well as to Ali. A reminder of the place of queens and princesses in his court, no matter how powerful their family." Nahri's lips thinned in distaste. "Right now, he and I hold each other in check, but should things shift . . ." She took another swig of the soma, her head beginning to swim. "I'm so tired of this, Nisreen. All this plotting and scheming just to keep breathing. It feels like I'm treading water . . . and, God, do I want to rest."

That lay between them for a few long moments. Nahri stared at the garden, the setting sun throwing it in shadow. The air smelled rich, the soil wet from the day's unexpected rain. The soma in her veins tingled pleasantly.

A tickle at her wrist drew her attention, and Nahri glanced down to see a morning glory's tender vine nudging her arm. She opened her palm, one of the bright pink flowers blooming in her hand.

"The palace magic has been responding to you more often," Nisreen said softly. "Since that day."

"It probably likes me picking fights with the Qahtanis."

"I would not be surprised." Nisreen sighed. "But on that . . . things will get better here. I promise. Your hospital is nearly complete. And though I don't agree with your involving the shafit, you've brought back something vital, something incredibly important to our people." She lowered her voice. "And for what you've done for Jamshid, you should be blessed. It was the right thing to take him under your wing."

Nahri let go of the flower, still glum. "I hope so."

Nisreen touched her cheek. "It was." Her eyes turned intent. "I'm proud of you, Nahri. Perhaps in all our disagreements, that's not a thing I've made clear, but I am. You're a good Banu Nahida. A good . . . what is your human word? Doctor?" She smiled. "I think your ancestors would be proud too. A little horrified . . . but proud."

Nahri blinked, her eyes suddenly damp. "I think that's the nicest thing you've ever said to me."

"Happy Navasatem," the other woman offered dryly.

"Happy Navasatem," Nahri repeated, raising the bottle. "To the start of a new generation," she added, trying to stifle the slight slur in her voice.

Nisreen pulled the bottle from her hands. "I think that's enough."

Nahri let her take it, working up the courage to ask her next question. "You said I was stubborn . . . do you—do you think I'm being too proud?"

"I don't understand."

Nahri stared at her hands, feeling self-conscious. "If I had any sense, I'd be patching things up with Muntadhir. I'd be *returning* to Muntadhir. I'd find a way to give Ghassan the grandchild he wants."

Nisreen hesitated. "That strikes me as a terrible reason to bring a child into this world."

"It's the pragmatic one. And that's what I'm supposed to be," Nahri pointed out, bitterness stealing into her voice. "Pragmatic. Heartless. That's how you survive in this place. It's how I've survived everything."

Nisreen's voice was soft. "But what do *you* want, Nahri? What does your heart want?"

Nahri laughed, the sound slightly hysterical. "I don't know." She looked at Nisreen. "When I try to imagine my future here, Nisreen, I see nothing. I feel like the very act of envisioning the things that make me happy will destroy them."

Nisreen was looking at her with open sympathy. "Oh, Banu Nahida, don't think like that. Listen, Navasatem begins tomorrow. Enjoy it. Enjoy your hospital and the parade. Ghassan will be too busy overseeing everything to scheme." She paused. "Try not to fret over your future with the Qahtanis. Let's get through the next few days, and we can sit and discuss all this after." Her voice caught. "I promise you . . . things are going to be different very soon."

Nahri managed a nod, Nisreen's calm words dissipating some of the fear that gripped her heart. They always did; Nisreen had been a steadying presence at Nahri's side since her first day in Daevabad. She'd saved her from the various plots of the harem and guided Nahri's trembling hands through countless procedures. She'd rinsed Dara's ashes from Nahri's tear-streaked face and quietly told her what to expect on her wedding night.

And yet it suddenly struck Nahri that for all the times she'd unburdened herself to Nisreen, there was still so little she knew about her mentor. "Nisreen, can I ask you something?"

"Of course."

"Are *you* happy here?"

Nisreen looked surprised by the question. "What do you mean?"

"I mean . . ." Nahri wrung her hands. "Do you ever regret staying in Daevabad after my mother healed you?" Her voice gentled. "I know you lost your parents in the attack on your village. But you could have returned home and had your own family instead of serving mine."

Nisreen grew very still, her gaze contemplative. "I would be lying if I said there weren't times I feared I'd taken the wrong path. That I never dreamed of something else, never mourned the other lives I might have lived. I don't think that's an uncertainty anyone loses." She took a sip of the soma. "But I've led an astonishing life here. I've worked alongside Nahid healers, witnessing the most miraculous, incredible things magic is capable of. I've saved lives and consoled the dying." She smiled again, taking Nahri's hand. "I've taught the next generation." Her eyes grew wondrous, seeming to gaze into a distance Nahri couldn't see. "And there are even greater things to come."

"Does that mean you plan to stay?" Nahri asked, a mix of jest and hope in her voice. "Because I could really use another Daeva at my side."

Nisreen squeezed Nahri's hand. "I will always be at your side."

SITTING STIFFLY WITH MUNTADHIR IN THE MASSIVE throne room, Nahri watched the oil in the tall glass cylinder burn low.

A hush had descended upon the crowd below, an expectant and excited buzz. Though court had been held as usual, the day's business was done with a wink, the petitions getting silly as was apparently the custom on the last day of a generation. The throne room was packed, eager crowds spilling out into the entrance gardens.

Nahri was struggling to share their excitement. For one, she'd drunk a little too much soma last night and her head was still swimming. But worse was being in the throne room itself. It was here she'd been forced to denounce Dara, and the more she learned about her people, the more obvious the room's Daeva design became. The open pavilion and manicured gardens so similar to those of the Grand Temple; the elegant columns carved with Nahids riding shedu, archers sporting ash marks, and dancers pouring wine. The green marble floor cut through with canals of rushing ice water brought to mind the green plains and cold mountains of Daevastana, not Am Gezira's golden sands. And then there was the throne itself, the magnificent, bejeweled seat carved to imitate the mighty shedu her ancestors had once tamed.

To be a Nahid in the throne room was to have her family's stolen heritage thrust in her face while she was forced to bow down before the thieves. And it was a humiliation she hated.

She could feel Ghassan's gaze on her now, and she tried to bring a happier expression to her face. It was tiring to play the part of the joyful royal wife when she hadn't spoken to her husband in weeks and she was fairly certain her father-in-law was contemplating assassinating her.

Standing at Ghassan's side was Kaveh. Ever diplomatic, the grand wazir had greeted her warmly when she arrived. Nahri had smiled back, even as she considered trying to brew up one of her ancestors' truth serums to slip into his wine. Nahri wasn't certain if Ali's accusations about Kaveh's complicity in the workcamp attack were true, but her instincts told her there was more ruthless cunning behind Kaveh's politely loyal mask than she had previously suspected. Not that she knew what to do about it. Nahri meant what she'd said to Subha: she was determined to find some justice for the camp's victims. But under virtual imprisonment in the palace infirmary—Ghassan would not even let her go to the Temple to speak to her people—she wasn't sure how to accomplish that.

She looked around the chamber once more. Ali was missing, an absence that concerned her. Per Ghassan's orders, they hadn't seen each other since that day, though they'd been exchanging letters through the king's messenger fairly often. In a petty move, they'd resorted to writing out their words in Egyptian Arabic, but Ali's messages were all business: hospital updates and construction news. As far as anyone could tell, he'd been brought into line, chastened by his mother's banishment and his own confinement in the hospital.

Nahri didn't believe that for a minute.

There was a flicker of light, and then a cheer broke out across the room, drawing her attention back to the now extinguished cylinder.

Ghassan rose to his feet. "I call to a close the twenty-ninth generation of Suleiman's Blessing!"

A roar of approval greeted his words, cheers and ululations ringing across the chamber. Sparks flew as people clapped—an already drunk few cackling as they sent up glittering conjured fireworks.

Ghassan lifted his hand. "Go home, my people. Sleep at least one night before we all lose ourselves in merriment." He smiled—for once it looked a little forced—and turned away.

Nahri stood—or tried to. Her aching head protested and she winced, her hand going to her temple.

Muntadhir caught her shoulder. "Are you all right?" he asked, sounding at least half concerned.

"Fine," she muttered, though she let him help her.

He hesitated. "Preparations for the parade tomorrow are going well?"

Nahri blinked. "They are . . ."

"Good." He bit his lip. "Nahri . . . I expect the next few days will be a whirlwind for us both, but if possible, I would like to take you up on your offer to visit the Grand Temple."

She crossed her arms. "So you can stand me up again?"

"I won't, I promise. I shouldn't have before." She raised a skeptical brow at the half apology and he made an annoyed sound in his throat. "All right, Jamshid has been harassing me to make peace with you, and this seems like a good first step."

Nahri considered that, her conversation with Nisreen running through her mind. She wasn't sure how she wanted to proceed with Muntadhir, but visiting the Temple with her husband didn't mean she had to jump back into bed with him. "All right."

A whisper of magic fluttered through the throne room, setting the hairs on the back of her neck on end. The air suddenly warmed, movement near the floor drawing her gaze.

Her eyes went wide. The water in the nearest fountain, a pretty stone octagon covered in starlike mirrored tiles, was boiling.

There was a startled cry behind her. She whirled around to see djinn hastily backing away from the trench fountains lining the perimeter walls. Water was boiling in those fountains as well, the enchanted ice floating in their depths steaming away so quickly that a white haze rose from the floor.

It lasted only seconds. There was a whistling, cracking sound as the scorching water let out enormous clouds of steam and then abruptly drained away, vanishing into jagged gashes at the bottom of the fountains.

Muntadhir had drawn closer. "Please tell me that was you," he whispered.

"No," she replied, her voice shaking. In fact, the familiar warmth of the palace magic seemed briefly gone. "But the palace does that sometimes, doesn't it?"

Muntadhir looked uneasy. "Of course." He cleared his throat. "Magic is unpredictable, after all."

Nervous laughter was breaking out across the throne room, the odd moment already dismissed by the majority of the festive crowd. Ghassan was gone, but Nahri spotted Kaveh standing beside the throne. He was staring at the smoking fountain closest to him.

And he was smiling.

It was grim and it was brief, but there was no denying his expression and the cold pleasure in it sent ice snaking around her heart.

Truth serum, she decided. As soon as the holiday was over. She touched Muntadhir's hand. "I'll see you at the hospital party tonight?"

"I wouldn't miss it for the world."

27

ALI

Ali's head was pounding as he stumbled into his small room at the hospital. The late afternoon light burned his eyes through the window, so he yanked the curtains shut, exhausted from supervising preparations for tonight's opening.

A mountain of paperwork greeted him on the desk. He picked up the first piece of parchment. It was an invitation from one of the Sahrayn trade ministers, a suggestion they meet after Navasatem to discuss some thoughts Ali had on restoring the city's port.

Bitterness swept through him, hard and fast. There would be no "after Navasatem" for Ali.

The words swam before him. Ali was exhausted. He'd pushed himself to the breaking point trying to fix things in Daevabad and now none of it mattered. He was being tossed out either way.

He dropped the letter and then collapsed onto his bed cushion. *It does matter*, he tried to tell himself. The hospital was complete, wasn't it? Ali could at least give Nahri and Subha that.

He closed his eyes, stretching out his limbs. It felt heavenly to lie flat and still for a moment, the allure of sleep tempting. Irresistible.

Just let yourself rest. That's what everyone had been telling him to do anyway. He took a deep breath, settling deeper into the cushion as sleep stole over him, wrapping him in a peace as cool and still as water . . .

The lake is quiet when he arrives, emerging from the silty current that brought him here. The chill of it is a shock, a sharp departure from the warmer waters he prefers. Though this lake is sacred to his people, the Great Tiamat's dazzling cloak of shed scales lining the bottom, it is not his home. Home is the vast twining river that cuts through desert and jungle alike, with waterfalls that crash into hidden pools and a spread of delta that blossoms to greet the sea.

He moves with the current, cutting through a school of rainbow-hued fish. Where are the rest of his people? The lake should be thick with marid, scaled hands and tentacled limbs grasping him in welcome, sharing new memories in quiet communion.

He breaks the water's surface. The air is still, laden with the fog that drifts over the lake like an ever-present storm cloud. Rain-soaked emerald mountains loom in the distance, melting into a pebbly beach.

A crowded beach. His kin have swarmed it, hissing and snapping teeth and beaks and claws. On the shore itself is a sight he has never seen in this holy place: a group of humans, protected by a thick band of fire.

Disbelief washes through him. No humans should be able to cross into this realm. None should be able to, save the marid. He swims closer. The dryness encroaching upon his skin hurts. The fire before him is already changing the atmosphere, sapping the air of its life-giving moisture.

A ripple dances over the lake's surface when the other marid spot him, and he is pulled forward on a current. As he is embraced, he opens his mind to his people,

offering them memories of the rich flood he gifted his humans last season in exchange for the boats and fishermen he devoured.

The visions they offer in return are not as pleasant. Through the eyes of his kin,
he sees the mysterious invaders arriving on the beach, crossing over the threshold as
though it were nothing. He sees one of them accidentally venture past the fire's safety
and then tastes its flesh when it is dragged into the water, seized by tendrils of seaweed
and drowned, its memories consumed for information. What those memories reveal
is shocking.

The invaders are not humans. They are daevas.

Such a thing should be impossible. The daevas are supposed to be gone, van-
quished by the human prophet-king Suleiman a century earlier. He studies them again
from the waterline. Suleiman has changed them, has taken the fire from their skin and
left them shadows of the fiends they once were.

One moves. Anger swirls inside him as he recognizes her from the dead daeva's
memories. It is Anahita the thief; a so-called healer who'd spent centuries luring away
the marid's human worshippers. She's been reduced to a slip of a thing, a ragged young
woman with unruly black curls barely checked by the faded shawl draped over her
head. As he watches, she lights a stick of cedar from a brass bowl of flames and presses
it to the brow of her dead fellow, her lips moving as if in prayer.

Then she stands, her attention turning to the lake. She steps over the protective
ring of fire.

Water snakes, his elders and mates, instantly rush at her. They hiss at her bare,
mud-splattered feet, twining around her ankles.

Anahita hisses back, "Be still."

He freezes, along with the rest of his kin. For her words come out in the marid's
tongue, a language no daeva should be able to speak.

Anahita continues. "You know now what we are . . . trust that I know you as
well." Her eyes burn. "I know the scaled wraiths who caught the feet of wading children in the Euphrates, the ones who swallowed merchant ships as a passing curiosity. I
know you . . . and Suleiman knew you too. Knew what you did." She raises her small
chin. A dark mark stands out on her cheek, a stylized star with eight points. "And he
tasked me with bringing you to heel."

Her arrogance is too much. His kin swarm the shore, churning the lake into waves that flash pointed teeth and sharp silver spines. Creatures from times forgotten, from when the world was simply fire and water. Plated fish and massive snout-nosed crocodiles.

"Fool," another marid whispers. "We will drag you into our depths and extinguish everything that you are."

Anahita smiles. "No," she replies. "You won't." The star symbol on her cheek flashes.

The world breaks.

The sky shatters into smoking pieces that dissipate like dust in water as the veil comes falling down, revealing a painfully azure sky from the realm beyond. The mountains groan as dunes of golden sand rush to swallow them, their life snuffed out.

The lake is next, evaporating from around them in a hot mist. He screams as pain wracks his body, and the holiest of their waters vanishes in the blink of an eye. The creatures of their domain—their fish and their snakes and their eels—shriek and die twitching. Sprawled on the cracked mud, he watches Anahita stride towards the lake's center.

"Here," Anahita declares as the earth buckles before her, rocks and debris racing to pile upon one another. She climbs them, a path smoothing before her feet. She glances back and the mark on her face abruptly stops glowing. "This is where we will build our city."

The lake dashes back. The sky and the mountains reassemble. He slips gratefully into the water, longing to fully immerse himself in its depths, to soothe his wounds by burrowing into the cold mud at the bottom. But there is something new, something dead and oppressive, in the heart of their sacred lake.

An island, growing to dwarf the woman who stands on a rocky precipice. Anahita closes her eyes, her fingers spinning a hot wind into a smoky boat that she blows back to her followers. She makes her way down to the new shore and then sits, lifting her face to the sun—now bright as it has never been before. She trails one hand through the water. A shining black-and-gold pearl winks from a brass ring upon her finger, and a searing pain tears through him when it dips beneath the lake's surface.

Anahita must see their helpless rage, for she speaks again. "You are being called to account as my people were by Suleiman. You will aid in the construction of my city, let my people sail unimpeded, and in return we shall have peace."

The lake sparks with heat, a crackle of lightning splitting the blue sky. It strikes the beach, consuming the daeva they killed in a blast of sacred fire.

"But know this." The flames reflect in Anahita's black eyes. "If you take another daeva life, I will destroy you."

Dead fish dot the lake. Horror is rising through his people. He senses lesser marid hurrying to the bottom, spring sprites and pond guardians desperate to escape into the streams that run far below the earth, below mountains and plains, and deserts and seas.

Streams that are steadily closing up, trapping them here with this daeva demon.

But he is no spring sprite. His is the river of salt and gold and he will not see his people subjugated. He calls to the lake, urging it to fight, to swallow these invaders whole.

Scaled hands grab him, tentacles wrapping his limbs. NO. It is a command, the voices of the lake's elders weaving together into a collective. GO. BEFORE SHE SEES YOU.

He tries to wrestle free, but it is useless. They are dragging him down, using the dying shreds of their magic to wrench open one last portal. He is shoved through.

FIND A WAY TO SAVE US. He gets a final glimpse of the dark lake, the pleading eyes of his people. THEY ARE COMING BACK.

"Ali, wake up. Wake up!"

Ali howled in rage, lashing out at the creatures holding him. "Get off me!" he hissed, his voice coming out in a breathless, slippery tongue. *"GET OFF ME."*

"Lubayd, *shut him up.*" It was Aqisa, barring the door, her dagger drawn.

"Prince Alizayd!" There was knocking on the door. "Is everything all right?"

Aqisa swore out loud and then yanked her turban away, her black braids spilling to her shoulders. Concealing the dagger behind her back, she pulled open the door just enough to reveal her face. "We do not wish to be interrupted," she said brusquely and then slammed it shut.

Ali writhed against the hand Lubayd had clamped over his mouth. Water was pouring from his skin, tears streaming down his face.

"Ali, brother." Lubayd was trembling as he held Ali down. A gash marred his cheek, four straight lines as though claws had swept across his face. "*Stop.*"

Still shaking, Ali managed a nod and Lubayd dropped his hand. "They were burning the lake," Ali wept, the marid's raw grief still roiling within him.

Lubayd looked bewildered and afraid. "What?"

"The lake. The marid. They were in my head and—"

Lubayd's hand instantly went back to Ali's mouth. "I didn't hear that."

Ali pulled free. "You don't understand . . ."

"No, *you* don't understand." Lubayd jerked his head toward the rest of the room.

His small bedroom was in chaos. It looked like a tropical storm had blown through, leaving the curtains in wet tatters and a pool of glimmering water on the floor. Most of his belongings were soaked, and a foggy mist clung to the bed.

Ali's hand went to his mouth in shock and then he recoiled, smelling blood on his fingertips.

Horrified, Ali looked again at Lubayd's face. "Did I . . ."

Lubayd nodded. "You . . . you were screaming in your sleep. Shouting in some language I've never—"

"No, he wasn't." Aqisa's voice was sharp. Intent. "You had a nightmare, understand?" She headed for the windows, tugging down the ruined curtains and letting them drop to the floor. "Lubayd, help me clean this up."

Nausea rose swift and punishing in Ali's stomach. The air smelled of salt, and a cold sweat broke out across his brow. The nightmare was growing murkier by the minute, but he could still feel the marid's despair, its ache to get back to its people.

They are coming back. Those were the only words he remembered and the warning echoed in his head, dread he didn't understand wrapping tight around his heart. "Something's wrong," he whispered. "Something is going to happen."

"Yes, you're going to get thrown in the lake if you don't shut your mouth." Aqisa shoved aside the wet curtain she was using to mop the floor and then tossed her turban cloth to Lubayd. "Wipe that blood off your face." She looked between the men. "No one can see this, understand? *Nothing happened.* We're not in Bir Nabat and this isn't some new spring we can all pretend you were lucky enough to discover."

The words pierced Ali's daze, upending the delicate dance he and his friends usually did around this subject. "What?" he whispered.

Lubayd was stuffing ruined papers into a dripping cloth sack. "Ali, brother, come on. There was a damn oasis bubbling beneath your body when we found you in the desert. There are times you don't emerge from the water in the cistern back home for hours."

"I—I didn't think you noticed," Ali stammered as fear sent his heart racing. "Neither of you ever spoke—"

"Because these are not things to be discussed," Aqisa said bluntly. "Those . . . creatures. You cannot speak of them, Ali. You certainly can't run around shouting that they're *in your head.*"

Lubayd spoke up again, looking almost apologetic. "Ali, I don't spin my wild stories just to annoy you. I do it so people don't spread *other* stories about you, understand? Tales that might not have a happy ending."

Ali stared at them. He didn't know what to say. Explanations, apologies, they ran through his mind, leaving him at a loss.

The adhan came then, calling the faithful to maghrib prayer. Across the city, Ali knew court would be ending, his father announcing the official beginning to Navasatem as the sun dipped below the horizon.

Aqisa straightened up, coming around the bed cushion with a garment bag. "These are the clothes your sister sent you for tonight's ceremony." She dropped it in his lap. "Get dressed. Forget what we discussed here. You're about to have your family and every gossiping, back-stabbing noble in this city crawling through these corridors. You can't be trembling like a leaf and rambling about the marid." She eyed him. "It was a nightmare, brother. Say it."

"It was a nightmare," he repeated, his voice hollow. He'd been having them for months, hadn't he? He was overworked, he was exhausted. Was it any surprise that a dream might have been more visceral today? More gut-wrenching? That his water abilities might have reacted accordingly?

It was a nightmare. Only a nightmare. It had to be.

28

NAHRI

The festivities were in full swing by the time Nahri arrived at the hospital, the complex vibrant with the magical frenzy the djinn excelled at. Bewitched glass dragonflies with wings of colorful conjured fire flitted through the air, and the fountains flowed with date wine. A trio of musicians played instruments that looked as if they'd been fished from an aquatic kingdom: the drums were made from the bellies of impossibly large shells, the sitar carved from pale driftwood and strung with sea silk. A life-size brass automaton in the shape of a sly-eyed dancer crushed sugarcane into juice, the liquid pouring from one glittering, outstretched hand. A banquet had been set up in one of the chambers, the aroma of spices carrying on the warm air.

The crowd of merrymakers was no less impressive. Nobles from the city's oldest families and merchants from the richest mingled and argued with political elites in the garden courtyard, while Daevabad's most popular poets and artists gossiped and challenged each other to impromptu competitions from satin cushions. Everyone was dressed in their enchanted finest: fragrant capes of living flowers, sparkling scarves of harnessed lightning, and glittering robes of mirrored beads.

Muntadhir and Nahri were immediately swept into the packed courtyard. Her husband, of course, was in his element, surrounded by obsequious nobles and loyal friends. At the fringe of the circle, Nahri stood up on her toes in a vain effort to see the completed hospital over the heads of laughing partygoers and dashing servants. She thought she might have caught a glimpse of Razu dealing twinkling playing cards before a group of enthralled onlookers, but deciding to respect whatever scheme the other woman had devised, Nahri stayed put.

That was not the case, however, when Nahri finally saw Subha, scowling at the crowd from beneath a shadowed archway.

"Emir, if you'll excuse me a moment . . ." Distracted by an Agnivanshi minister's exaggerated tale of simurgh hunting, Muntadhir offered what might have been a nod, and Nahri slipped away, winding through the mob until she reached Subha's side.

"Doctor Sen!" she greeted her affectionately. "You look as happy as I expected."

Subha shook her head. "I cannot believe we rushed to complete this place for a party." She glared at a pair of giggling Geziri noblewomen. "If they break anything . . ."

"Ali wrote to assure me all the equipment would be safely packed away." Nahri grinned. "The two of you must like working together. Neither of you have any sense of fun." She laughed when the other healer threw her a dirty look. "Though you do look lovely." Nahri gestured to Subha's clothes, a deep purple sari patterned in maroon and gold diamonds. "This is very pretty."

"Do you know that when you speak, you sound like a fruit peddler trying to sell me overripe produce?"

"One person's overripe is another person's sweet," Nahri said dryly.

Subha shook her head, but her grumpiness took on a slightly warmer edge. "You're quite a sight yourself," she said, nodding at Nahri's attire. "Are the Daevas making gowns of gold now?"

Nahri brushed her thumb over the thickly embroidered sleeve. "Seems like it—and it's as heavy as you might imagine. I'll be eager to trade it for a medical smock as soon as we can start seeing patients here."

Subha's expression softened. "I never imagined working in a place like this. Parimal and I have taken to touring the apothecary and supply closets just to admire how well stocked everything is . . ." Her tone grew a little sad. "I wish my father could have been here."

"We'll do his legacy proud," Nahri said sincerely. "I'm hoping you can share some of his wisdom when it comes to training apprentices. And on that note . . . Jamshid!" she called out, seeing him approaching. "Come! Join us."

Jamshid smiled, offering a bow as he brought his hands together in blessing. "May the fires burn brightly for you both."

Nahri glanced at Subha. "I heard I have you to thank for that dangerous saddle he's insisting on using."

"You did wish us to exchange skills."

Nahri shook her head, managing not to roll her eyes. "Where's the final member of our team?"

Subha's face fell. "I don't know. I haven't seen the prince since this afternoon. I wouldn't be surprised if he finally fell asleep somewhere. He seems determined to work himself to death."

"And what a shame that would be," Jamshid murmured.

Subha suddenly smiled, her gaze fixing on her husband as he emerged from a door on the other side of the courtyard carrying their daughter. The baby's dark eyes went wide and mesmerized at the sight of the magical feast.

Nahri nudged her shoulder. "Go say hi. We'll catch up later." As Subha moved away, Nahri turned to Jamshid. "You really don't like Ali, do you?" This was not the first time she'd seen him react negatively to mentions of the prince.

Jamshid hesitated. "No," he said. "I do not. I didn't mind him when he was younger—he was always intense, but he was Muntadhir's little brother, and Muntadhir adored him. But that night you saved him . . ." His voice lowered. "Nahri, he made me throw a man into the lake. A man I'm not certain was even dead."

"A man who tried to assassinate him," Nahri pointed out. "A shafit. Do you have any idea what Ghassan would have done if he found out a shafit nearly killed his son?"

Jamshid looked unconvinced. "I still don't like him being in Daevabad. I don't like the effect he's had on Muntadhir, and I worry . . ." He pressed his lips into a thin line. "He's a very ambitious man."

Nahri could not deny that Ali's return had sent her husband into a spiral, but she wasn't sure it was a justified one. "Muntadhir is going to be king, Jamshid. And he is a better politician than you give him credit for. Though if you're so concerned about his well-being . . ." Her voice turned crafty. "Perhaps you might go distract him a bit."

Jamshid eyed her knowingly. "You're trying to get away."

"I'm the Banu Nahida. I have a Creator-given right to explore my own hospital."

He exhaled, but it was a feigned grouchiness. "Go on then," he said, inclining his head toward the opposite corridor. "Now, when no one's looking."

Nahri brought her hands up in blessing. "May the fires burn *very* brightly for you."

The corridor he suggested was empty. Nahri quickly slipped off her sandals so her footsteps wouldn't be heard and had no sooner pressed a bare sole to the cool marble floor than the pale walls lit up, glowing softly in the dark as if to lead the way.

She grinned. Wouldn't that be convenient when she had a patient emergency in the middle of the night? She traced her hands along the wall, the rosy hue brightening where her fingers made contact. Her hospital—her ancestors' hospital—was restored. A dream she'd been almost too nervous to voice six months ago had been realized and now stood gleaming in the moonlight, Daevabad's most powerful citizens laughing within its rooms. It all seemed so outrageous, so audaciously hopeful, that it scared her.

Stop. Nisreen's calm words came back to her. Nahri could enjoy a night of happiness. Her many problems would still be there in the morning, whether or not she took a few hours to savor this rare success.

She wandered on, following a twisting staircase she was fairly certain led to the hospital's library. The sounds of celebration faded behind her; she was obviously the only fool creeping through empty hallways instead of enjoying the party.

She emerged in the library, a wide, airy room with lecture space for dozens of students. A wall of shelves had been built into the opposite side, and Nahri went to them, curious to see what volumes had been collected.

Then she stopped. Across the library was a small archway, tiled in a black-and-white pattern reminiscent of Cairo's buildings. Odd. She didn't remember seeing this room on any of the plans. Intrigued, she crossed to investigate.

Her breath caught the moment she stepped over the threshold. It wasn't just the archway that was reminiscent of Egypt.

It was *everything.*

A mashrabiya that might have been plucked from Cairo's heart overlooked the street, the cozy window seat covered in red and gold cushions, its intricate wooden screens hiding a private nook. Brightly embroidered tapestries—identical to the ones she'd seen in the markets back home—adorned the walls, and a stunning teak desk inlaid with glinting vines of mother-of-pearl anchored the room. Miniature reeds and bright purple-blue Nile lotus blooms grew lush within a raised marble fountain that lined the wall, the clear water inside passing over warm brown stones.

A glimmer of silver moved in the shadows of the mashrabiya. "Nahri?" a sleepy voice asked.

She jumped in surprise. "*Ali?*" She shivered. Restored or not, the dark, empty hospital was still an eerie place to stumble upon someone unexpectedly.

She opened her palm, conjuring a handful of flames. Small wonder she hadn't seen Ali: he was seated deep in the window box, pressed against the wooden screen as though he'd been gazing out at the street. Nahri frowned. Though he was dressed in a formal dishdasha, his head was uncovered and he looked . . . well, terrible. His face was gray, his eyes almost feverish.

She stepped closer. "Are you all right?"

Ali sat up. His movements were slow, bone-weary exhaustion written into every line of his body. "I'm fine," he murmured. He scrubbed his hands over his face. "Sorry, I wasn't expecting anyone to come up here."

"Well, you picked a poor time for a nap," she said lightly. "You might remember there's a party going on downstairs."

He blinked, still looking dazed. "Of course. The opening celebration."

Nahri studied him again. "Are you *sure* you're all right?"

"I'm sure," he replied quickly. "I just haven't been sleeping well. Nightmares." He rose to his feet, stepping into the light. "But I'm glad you found me. I was actually hoping to . . ." His gray eyes went wide, tracing over her. "Oh," he whispered. "You . . . you look—" He abruptly shut his mouth, averting his gaze. "Sorry . . . so, ah, how do you like your office?"

She stared at him in confusion. "My *office*?"

He inclined his head. "Your office. I thought you might like somewhere private to steal away between patients. Like the orange grove you have at the palace infirmary. The one I, er, intruded upon," he added, embarrassment in his voice.

Nahri's mouth fell open. "You built this place? For *me*?"

"I'd say the entire hospital is for you, but yes." Ali drifted closer, running his hands through the water in the fountain. "I came across a few shafit artisans from Egypt and told them to let their imaginations run wild." He glanced back with a small smile. "You always did seem so fond of your old land."

My old land. Nahri gazed at the mashrabiya again; in that moment, if she squinted just the right way, she could almost imagine being home. Could imagine hearing men joking in Cairo's distinctive cadence and smelling the spices and herbs of Yaqub's apothecary.

Homesickness rose inside her, sharp and fast. "I miss it so much," she confessed. "I keep thinking I'll stop, that I feel more settled here . . ." She leaned against the desk. "But there are days I'd do almost anything to go home. Even if it was just for an afternoon. A few hours of joking with people in my language and sitting next to the Nile. Of being anonymous in the streets and bartering for oranges. We had the best fruit, you know," she added, her throat catching. "Nothing in Daevabad tastes as sweet."

Ali was looking at her with open sympathy. "I'm sorry."

She shook her head, embarrassed to find herself fighting tears. "Forget it," she said, roughly wiping her eyes. "By God, you must think I'm mad, pining for human citrus when I'm surrounded by every luxury the magical world contains."

"I don't think you're mad." Ali assured her, crossing to join her at the desk. "They're your roots. They're what make you who you are. That isn't something you should have to cut away."

Nahri tipped the flames in her hand into a lamp on the desk. How much easier things would be if that were true here. Struggling to tamp down her emotions, she glanced around her office again. It really was lovely, the tapestries glowing in the light of the flickering lamp. A fresco had been painted on the opposite wall, a replica of a scene she might have seen in one of Egypt's ancient temples.

It touched her more than she thought possible. "Thank you," she finally said. "This . . . this was incredibly kind of of you."

Ali shrugged. "I was happy to do it." He smiled again, the shadows in his tired face lessening slightly. "As you are fond of pointing out—I *do* owe you."

"You'll always owe me," she said, pushing up to sit on the desk. "I have a talent for extending the debts of powerful people indefinitely."

His grin widened. "That I believe." But then his smile faded. "I'm happy to finally see you again. I've been worried about you."

"I'm fine," Nahri said, forcing indifference into her voice. She'd already been emotional enough in discussing her nostalgia for Egypt. "Besides, I'm not the one falling asleep in empty offices. How have *you* been? Your mother . . ."

Pain flashed in his eyes. "We're both still alive," he replied. "Which is more than I can say for a lot of people here."

If that wasn't the bitter truth. Nahri sighed. "For what it's worth, I think we were right to intervene. A lot more people would have died if you hadn't brought me to the camp when you did."

"I know. I just hate that choosing to do the right thing in Daevabad always seems to come with a steep price." His face fell. "Zaynab . . . she decided not to come tonight. I don't think she'll forgive me for our mother's banishment."

Genuine sympathy swept through her. "Oh, Ali, I'm sure that's not true." Nahri reached out to touch the sleeve of his dishdasha; it was an elegant pale silver, chased through with midnight-colored stripes and belted with a teal sash. "After all, she was clearly the one who picked this out."

Ali groaned. "Is it that obvious?"

"Yes. The only time you're not wearing something stark and streaked with dirt, it's because someone else has dressed you." Embarrassment colored his face again, and she laughed. "It's a compliment, Ali. You look nice."

"You look incredible." The words seemed to slip unthinkingly from his mouth, and when she met his gaze, a little startled by the emotion in his voice, he looked away. "Your garments, I mean," he explained quickly. "The headdress. It's very . . . intricate."

"It's very heavy," Nahri complained, reaching up to touch the gold diadem holding her shimmering black chador in place. The smoky fabric was enchanted to appear as though it were smoldering, the ruby and diamond ornaments glittering like fire. She lifted the diadem free, placing it beside her on the desk, and then slid her fingers under the chador to rub the aching spot where the metal had pressed. Catching sight of Ali watching her, she scolded him. "Oh, don't you judge. Your turbans are probably light as a feather in comparison to this thing."

"I . . . I'm not judging." He stepped back from the desk, clearing his throat. "Though while you're here, do you mind telling me what's being done to protect you given that threat?"

It took Nahri a moment to process his words, taken aback by the abrupt change in subject. "Threat? What threat?"

"The one from my shafit acquaintance." When she squinted in confusion, alarm flashed in Ali's face. "The one I passed on to my father. Surely he told you."

"This is the first I've heard."

"The first you've *heard*?" Anger crossed his face. "Is the king here? Did you see him below?"

"Not yet, but—wait!" She grabbed Ali's wrist when he turned

for the door. "Will you stop trying to get tossed in the dungeons?" She pulled him back. "Tell me about this threat."

"A woman I know said she heard some shafit were planning to attack you during Navasatem."

She waited for him to elaborate, but he stayed silent. "And that's it?" she asked. "Nothing more?"

"Isn't that enough?" Ali sounded incredulous.

Nahri looked him in the eye. "No. Ali, I get threats every day. My entire tribe does. But Kaveh, Muntadhir, and Wajed have been harping about security for an entire year, and they've told me their plans. Kaveh panics over everything, and Muntadhir is my husband. I trust them, on this issue at least."

Ali looked unconvinced. "It only takes a few angry people. And after what happened in the workcamp, Nahri, there are a *lot* of angry people."

"I'll be well guarded," she assured him. "I promise."

He sighed. "Would you at least consider having Aqisa join you tomorrow for the procession? I'd offer to come myself, but I don't think your people would like it."

Nahri pondered that, trying to imagine the reaction Ali's fierce friend from rural Am Gezira would have on the crowd of mostly city-raised Daevas. Not to mention what it might suggest to Muntadhir. "Ali . . ."

"Please."

She let go of his wrist, raising her hands in defeat. "Fine. As long as she keeps her dagger on her person unless I give the order." She frowned again. With the moonlight falling on his face, she could see that Ali was trembling. "Ali, what's really going on? You're acting even stranger than usual."

He actually laughed, the sound hollow, and then ran his hands over his face. "It's been a rough few days."

Nahri hesitated. They weren't supposed to be friends, not

anymore. But the despair radiating from the prince tugged at her heart. Despite the circle of companions and family that surrounded him, it was obvious Ali had secrets. And Nahri knew all too well secrets were a burden lonely to bear.

And he *had* built her this lovely office. "Do you want to talk about it?" she asked.

His gaze darted to her, the desperation in his eyes unmissable. "Yes," he said hoarsely. "No. I don't know. I wouldn't even know where to start."

She pulled him toward the cushioned seat next to the screened window. "How about by sitting?" She sat across from him, pulling up her knees. "Is this about your father?"

Ali let out a deep sigh. "Part of it is. He's sending me back to Am Gezira."

"You're going back to Am Gezira?" she repeated in surprise. Ali certainly hadn't been acting like a man going anywhere; he seemed to have a thousand plans for the future of Daevabad. "For how long?"

"Forever?" His voice broke, as if he'd tried to make a joke out of it and failed. "My father doesn't want me stirring up any more trouble. I'm to give up my titles and go back to the village I was living in after Navasatem." Ali's shoulders slumped. "He told me to marry and have a family. To have a peaceful life that doesn't include fomenting dissent in Daevabad."

Both his words and the unexpected jolt of emotion in her chest at the thought of his leaving threw her wildly off balance. She struggled to find the right response. "The village . . . Bir Nabat?"

He looked surprised. "I didn't think you'd remember the name."

Nahri rolled her eyes. "There's not a soul working at the hospital who hasn't heard you wax poetic about the ruins and canals of Bir Nabat." She shook her head. "But I don't understand why you wouldn't want to go back. You clearly love it there. Your letters were always—"

Ali started. "You read my letters?"

Nahri knew she couldn't hide her slip. She let out a huff of frustration at both herself and him. "I . . . All right, I read them. They were interesting," she said, defending herself. "You put in information about local healing plants and stories about the humans to lure me in."

A sad half-smile twisted his mouth. "I wish I was even half as subversive as you think I am. I'd do a lot better in Daevabad."

"But you have a chance to *leave* Daevabad." She nudged his shoulder when he scowled. "So why do you look so upset? You get to have a *life*. A peaceful one, in a place you love."

Ali was silent for several heartbeats, his gaze fixed on the floor. "Because this is my home, Nahri, and I . . ." He squeezed his eyes shut, like whatever he was about to say caused him pain. "I don't think I can leave it while my father still rules."

Nahri would swear the temperature in the room plummeted. She jerked back, instinctively glancing around, but they were alone. She was already shaking her head, the fear Ghassan had carved into her an instinctual response.

"Ali, you can't talk like that," she whispered. "Not here. Not ever."

Ali looked back at her, beseeching. "Nahri, you know it's true. He's done terrible things. He's going to keep doing terrible things. That's the only way he knows—"

Nahri actually clapped her hand over his mouth. "Stop," she hissed, her eyes darting around the room. They might be alone, but God only knew the form Ghassan's spies took. "We're already in his sights. *I'm* already in his sights. Was what he did at the shafit camp not enough to convince you to back down?"

He pushed her hand away. "No," he said fervently. "It did the opposite. A good king wouldn't have allowed that bloodshed.

A good king would ensure justice for both the Daevas and the shafit, so that people didn't resort to taking vengeance into their own hands."

"Do you know how naive you sound?" Nahri said desperately. "People aren't that virtuous. And you can't fight him. He is capable of things you can't imagine. He'll destroy you."

Ali's eyes blazed. "Aren't there some things worth that risk?"

All of Muntadhir's warnings about his younger brother came flooding back to her. "No," she said, her voice so cutting she barely recognized it. "Because a hundred others will pay the price for your risk."

Bitterness creased his face. "Then how do we fight, Nahri? Because I know you want better for Daevabad. I heard you in the Temple, I watched *you* confront my father." He gestured to the rest of the room. "Was not the whole point of building the hospital to move forward?"

"The hospital was meant to be a *step*," she countered. "It was meant to provide a foundation to build some peace and security between the Daevas and shafit for the day your father *doesn't* have his boot on our neck. We're not there, Ali. Not yet."

"And how many more people will die while we wait for that day?"

Their gazes locked. There was nothing but conviction in the warm gray of his eyes. No cunning, no deception.

It terrified her. Because whatever history was between them, Nahri did not think she had it in her to watch the kind man who'd built her this office, this quiet homage to the home she still loved—the man who'd taught her to read and helped her summon flames for the first time—be executed in the arena.

Nahri sat back down. "Ali, you say you owe me your life," she started, fighting a tremble in her voice. "I'm going to collect on that debt. Go back to Am Gezira."

He let out an exasperated sigh, turning away. "Nahri . . ."

She reached out, taking his chin in one hand and forcing him to look back at her. He visibly jumped at her touch, his eyes going wide.

"Take your father's offer," she said firmly. "You can help people in Am Gezira without getting killed. Marry some woman who will love to hear you ramble about canals, and have a whole band of children you'll undoubtedly be too strict with." She cupped his cheek, her thumb brushing his beard. She didn't miss the sudden racing of his heart.

Nor the sadness rising in her own.

Ali seemed speechless, his eyes flickering nervously across her face. It would have to do. She stood up, dropping her hand as she stepped away, the sudden sting of tears in her eyes. "Go steal some happiness for yourself, my friend," she said softly. "Trust me when I say the chance doesn't always come back."

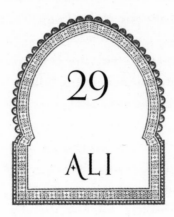

29

ALI

"So you still haven't told me where you were last night," Lubayd
said as they made their way to the arena. "Aqisa and I were looking for you at the celebration."

"I didn't go," Ali replied. "I didn't feel up to it."

Lubayd halted in his tracks. "Another nightmare?"

"No," Ali said quickly, hating the fear in his friend's expression. "No nightmares. But I was exhausted and didn't trust myself
not to say something inflammatory to my father. Or my brother."
He made a sour face as they kept walking. "To anyone really."

"Well, then I'm glad you slept in and avoided getting arrested.
Though you did miss quite the party." He stretched, cracking his
neck. "Is Aqisa meeting us at the arena?"

"Later. I asked her to guard the Banu Nahida during the parade this morning."

"That's the one meant to reenact Anahid's arrival in Daevabad, right?" Lubayd snorted. "In that case, will you and your lit-

tle healer be fighting to the death at some point to represent the latter half of our history?"

Ali flinched at the joke. *Go back to Am Gezira, Ali. Steal some happiness for yourself.* Ali had been replaying those words and the memory of Nahri's hand cradling his jaw in his mind since last night. Which—he had to give credit to her—had rather effectively interrupted his brewing thoughts of rebellion.

He closed his eyes. God forgive him, she had looked so beautiful last night. After not seeing her for weeks, Ali had been struck speechless at the sight of her standing in the darkness of that quiet room, dressed in the finery of her ancestors. She'd looked like a legend brought to life, and for the first time, he'd been nervous—truly nervous—in her presence, struggling not to stare as she smiled her sharp smile and slid her fingers under her chador. And when she'd touched his face . . .

Muntadhir's wife. She's Muntadhir's wife.

As if his thoughts had the power to conjure, a familiar laugh sounded ahead, one whose lightheartedness cut through Ali like a knife.

"—I'm not mocking you," Muntadhir teased. "I think the 'Suleiman just threw me across the world look' has its appeal. Your rags even smell!" Muntadhir laughed again. "It's all very authentic."

"Oh, be quiet," he heard Jamshid return. "There's more where these rags came from and your steward owes me a favor. I'll have them used to line your fancy turban."

Ali peered around the corner. Muntadhir and Jamshid were across the corridor, framed together in a sunlit arch. He frowned, shading his eyes against the sudden brightness. For half a second, he'd swear he saw his brother's hands on Jamshid's collar, his face inclined toward his neck as though jokingly smelling him, but then Ali blinked, sunspots blossoming across his vision, and the two men were apart, neither looking very pleased to see him.

"Alizayd." His brother's disdainful gaze flickered up and down Ali's rumpled dishdasha. "Late night?"

Muntadhir always seemed to know a new way to make him feel small. His brother was immaculately turned out as usual in his ebony robes and brilliant royal turban. He'd looked even more stylish last night, dressed in an ikat-patterned waistcloth and brilliant sapphire tunic. Ali had seen him at the party, had watched from an upper balcony after Nahri left as his brother laughed and caroused like he'd built the hospital himself.

"As always," Ali replied acidly.

Jamshid's eyes flashed at his tone. The Daeva man was indeed dressed in rags, his black tunic torn and smeared with ash and his pants with unfired brick dust—a nod to the human temple that Suleiman had ordered their ancestors to build.

Muntadhir cleared his throat. "Jamshid, why don't you head to the procession? We'll meet later." He squeezed the other man's shoulder. "I still want to see that saddle."

Jamshid nodded. "Until then, Emir-joon."

He left, and Muntadhir ignored Ali, sweeping through the entrance that led to the arena's royal viewing platform.

Lubayd snickered. "I suppose emirs don't like to be interrupted, same as everyone else."

Ali was baffled by the amusement in his friend's voice. "What do you mean?"

"Well, you know . . ." Lubayd stopped and studied Ali. "Oh . . . you don't know." Spots of color rose in his cheeks. "Forget it," he said, turning to follow Muntadhir.

"What don't I know?" Ali asked, but Lubayd ignored him, suddenly very interested in the spectacle below. To be fair, it was a sight: a half-dozen Daeva archers were competing, putting on a show to amuse the packed crowd while they waited for the procession to arrive.

Lubayd whistled. "Wow," he said, watching as a mounted Daeva archer on a silver stallion raced across the sand, aiming a flaming arrow at a hollow gourd mounted on a high pole. The gourd was stuffed with kindling and painted with pitch; it burst into flames, and the crowd cheered. "They really are demons with those bows."

Ali glowered. "I'm well aware."

"Alizayd." Ghassan's voice rang across the pavilion just as Ali was about to take a seat with a few of the officers from the Royal Guard. His father was at the front, of course, leaning against a silk-covered bolster, a jade cup of ruby-colored wine at hand. "Come here."

Lubayd grabbed his wrist before he could move. "Careful," he warned. "You seem a little surlier than usual this morning."

Ali didn't respond. It was true he didn't trust himself to say anything to his father, but he had no choice other than to make his way to the front. Muntadhir was already seated, flashing his charming grin at a pretty servant as she passed. She stopped with a blush and smile to pour him a cup of wine.

He makes that look so easy. Not that Ali wanted to go around enticing attractive women into pouring him wine—every part of that was forbidden. But he knew Muntadhir wouldn't have been reduced to a stammering wreck in front of Nahri last night. And as he watched his brother, Ali was unable to deny the jealousy clawing in his chest. Muntadhir had leaned over to whisper in the cupbearer's ear, and she giggled, playfully bumping him with her shoulder.

You have a wife. A beautiful, brilliant wife. Though Ali supposed when everything else was offered to you on a silver platter, beautiful, brilliant wives weren't blessings to be cherished.

"Everything going well with the procession?" Ghassan asked Muntadhir, paying no attention to Ali as he sat down stiffly on a plain prayer mat, forgoing the soft cushions closer to the pair.

Muntadhir nodded, taking a sip of his wine as the cupbearer

456 ✧ S. A CHAKRABORTY

moved away. "The priests and Nahri led dawn ceremonies at the lake. Kaveh was to make sure they all boarded their chariots, and Jamshid just left to escort them here with another group of archers." A small smile broke his face. "He's riding today."

"And security for the procession?" Ghassan pressed. "Did you speak with Wajed?"

"I did. He assured me he has soldiers lining the parade route and that no shafit would be permitted to join."

Ali struggled not to roll his eyes. Of course, banning the shafit from the festivities would be the type of "security" the palace enacted. Though Ali supposed he should be happy his brother and not his father was overseeing Navasatem. Ghassan probably would have chosen to execute on sight any shafit who strayed within five blocks of the procession route.

All too aware he was in the exact mood that Lubayd had warned him to guard against, Ali tried to direct his attention to the arena. The Daeva archers were dressed in the age-old style of their ancestors, dashing about as if they were part horse themselves in wildly striped felt leggings, dazzling saffron coats, and horned silver helms. They rose to stand in painted saddles as they galloped in sweeping arcs and intricate formations, ornaments flashing in their horses' manes as they drew back stylized silver bows.

Unease pooled in Ali's stomach. Though not Afshins themselves—Darayavahoush's family had been wiped out in the war—the men below were the clearest inheritors of his legacy. One of the men let a scythe-ended arrow fly at a target, and Ali could not help but cringe. He didn't know which kind of arrows Darayavahoush had shot through his throat, but he'd bet one of them was down below.

"Not to your taste, Zaydi?" Muntadhir was watching him.

The sarcasm with which his brother spoke his nickname cut

deep, and then the punch of another arrow tearing through a target made his stomach clench. "Not quite," he said through his teeth.

"And yet to hear it, you're the finest warrior in Daevabad." Muntadhir's tone was light, but malice lurked underneath it. "The great Afshin-slayer."

"I never trained much with the bow. You know that." Ali had learned to use one, of course, but he was meant to be Qaid, and archery took time, time Wajed had preferred Ali spend on the zulfiqar and strategy. The Daeva men before him had likely been in saddles since they were five, given toy bows at the same age.

A servant came by with coffee, and Ali gratefully took a cup.

"You look as though you need that," Ghassan commented. "I was surprised not to see you at the hospital's opening last night."

Ali cleared his throat. "I wasn't feeling well."

"Unfortunate," Ghassan said. "I have to say I was pleased; it's an impressive complex. Regardless of your recent behavior, you and Banu Nahri have done fine work."

Ali checked the resentment growing inside him, knowing he'd be smarter to take advantage of his father's seemingly amicable mood. "I am glad to hear that." He took another sip of his coffee, savoring the bitter, cardamom-scented tang. "On a related note, I was wondering if you'd seen my proposal."

"You'll have to be more specific," Ghassan replied. "I think I have fifty proposals from you on my desk at the moment."

"The one giving official recognition to the shafit guilds in the workcamp. I'd like them to be able to compete for government contract—"

"My God, do you *ever* stop?" Muntadhir cut in rudely. "Can we not have a day's break from your yammering about the economy and the shafit?"

Ghassan raised a hand before Ali could speak. "Let him be.

As it is, he's not wrong to be thinking about the economy." He cleared his throat, his gaze going a little distant. "I've received an offer for Zaynab's hand."

Ali instantly tensed; there was nothing he liked in the careful way his father had delivered that news. "From who?" he demanded, not caring that he sounded curt.

"Nasir Ishak."

Ali blinked. *"Who?"*

"Nasir Ishak." Muntadhir had gone pale as he repeated the name. "He's a spice merchant from Malacca."

"He's more than a spice merchant," Ghassan corrected. "He's king of the djinn in those islands in all but name. Daevabad's control has always been tenuous there."

Malacca. Ali looked between his father and brother. They couldn't be serious. "Daevabad's control is tenuous there because it's *across the ocean*. Zaynab will be lucky to visit here once a century!"

Neither man answered him. Muntadhir looked like he was fighting to keep his composure. "You told me you had decided against his offer, Abba," he said.

"That was before . . . recent events." Ghassan's mouth thinned in displeasure. "We need to start looking beyond Ta Ntry for allies and resources. Nasir is an opportunity we can ill afford to turn away."

"Does Zaynab get a say in this?" Ali could hear the edge in his voice, but this was too much. Was this another reason his mother had been banished? So that she wouldn't be able to protest her daughter being shipped across the sea to fill the Treasury's coffers?

"I've spoken with Zaynab about this possibility," Ghassan replied tersely. "I would never force her. I would never have to. She takes her loyalty and duty to our family far more seriously than you, Alizayd. And quite frankly, your stunt in the shaft camp and your mother taking half the Ayaanle delegation back to Ta Ntry has forced my hand." He turned back to Muntadhir. "Nasir is arriving next week for the holiday. I'd like you to spend time with him and get to know what kind of man he is before I decide anything."

His brother stared at his hands, emotions warring on his face. Ali watched him, silently begging: *Say something. Anything. Give some sign that you can stand up to him, that you won't become him.*

Muntadhir cleared his throat. "I'll talk to him."

"Coward." The moment the word slipped from his lips, Ali knew it wasn't fair. But he didn't care.

Muntadhir stared at him in shock. "What did you just say to me?"

"I said you're a—" From below, another arrow struck the target, making a solid thunk as it tore through the flesh of the gourd. Ali instinctively flinched, the moment stealing his words.

Ghassan had drawn up, glaring at Ali with open contempt. "Have you lost all sense of honor?" he hissed under his breath. "I should have you lashed for speaking with such disrespect."

"No," Muntadhir said sharply. "I can handle this, Abba. I should have already."

Without another word, his brother rose to his feet and turned to face the packed pavilion. He aimed a dazzling smile at the crowd, the change in his expression so sudden it was as though someone had snuffed out a candle.

"Friends!" he called out. The Qahtani men had been speaking quietly in Geziriyya, but Muntadhir raised his voice, switching to Djinnistani. "The great Afshin-slayer is anxious to show his skills, and I do believe you deserve a spectacle."

An expectant hush fell across the crowd, and Ali suddenly realized just how many people were watching them: nobles always eager to witness some drama from Daevabad's royals.

And Muntadhir knew how to draw their attention. "So I'd

like to issue my little brother a challenge . . ." He gestured to the archers below. "Beat me."

Ali stared at him in incomprehension. "You want to compete with *me*? In the arena?"

"I do." Muntadhir put his wine cup down with a flourish, his eyes dancing as if this were all a joke. "Come on, Afshin-slayer," he goaded when Ali didn't move. "Surely you're not afraid?" Without waiting for a response, Muntadhir laughed and headed for the steps.

The eyes of the rest of pavilion were on Ali, expectant. Muntadhir might have done it in jest, but he'd issued a challenge, and Ali would lose face if he didn't address it—especially one so seemingly innocent.

Ali rose to his feet slowly.

Ghassan gave him a warning look, but Ali knew he wouldn't interfere; Geziri men didn't back down from such a public contest, and princes in the line of succession certainly did not. "Remember yourself," he said simply.

Remember what? That I was always meant to be beneath him? Or that I was meant to be his weapon—one who could defeat any man?

Lubayd was at his elbow in a second. "Why do you look like you just swallowed a locust?" he whispered. "You can shoot an arrow better than that gold-draped fool, can't you?"

Ali swallowed, not wanting to confirm his weakness. "I-I was shot, Lubayd. By the Afshin," he stammered, the memories coming to him in a swift punch. "It was bad. I haven't touched a bow since."

Lubayd blanched, but there was no time for him to respond. Muntadhir was already joining the Daeva riders. They grinned as he greeted them in the Divasti that Ali couldn't speak, gesturing back toward Ali with laughter. God only knew what Muntadhir was saying to them. They were probably his friends, the wealthy nobles with whom he liked to wine and dine in the salons of courtesans and poets. A world that didn't look kindly upon men like Ali.

And though he knew he'd provoked his brother, a hurt Ali rarely acknowledged made itself known, the knot of resentment and jealousy he tried so hard to disavow threatening to come undone. The times he'd forced himself to smile when Muntadhir's companions teased him growing up, asking how many men he'd killed at the Citadel and if it was really true he'd never touched a woman. The countless family celebrations that ended with Muntadhir sleeping in a silken bed at the palace and Ali on the floor of his barracks.

Stop. Because of those barracks, the arena right here is your home. Muntadhir and his friends couldn't take that from him. Archery might not be Ali's specialty, but surely he could beat his spoiled, soft brother.

One of the riders slipped from his saddle, and without missing a beat, Muntadhir swung into his place. His brother was the better horseman, that Ali knew. Ali could ride well enough but had never shared Muntadhir's love for the sport. His brother kept his own stable and had probably spent countless hours racing outside the city walls, laughing and trying stunts with Jamshid—who was an even more talented rider—while Ali labored at the Citadel.

Muntadhir's horse cantered up. "Why so glum, Zaydi?" His brother laughed, spreading his arms. "This is your thing, isn't it? You used to talk when you were a kid about these martial competitions. How you would sweep them and earn your place as my Qaid. I'd think the greatest warrior in Daevabad would be smiling right now." Muntadhir drew nearer, his grin fading. "Or maybe you've been intruding upon *my* world for so long—insinuating yourself with my wife, embarrassing me before Abba—that you've forgotten your place." He said the final words in Geziriyya, his voice low. "Maybe you need a reminder."

It was the wrong thing to say. Ali glared back even as the other

Daeva men rode up, joking in Divasti as their horses circled him, kicking sand. "I spent my childhood training to serve you," he shot back. "I'd say I know my place quite well; I was never permitted to have another. Something I suspect Zaynab is about to learn as well."

He'd swear uncertainty flickered in his brother's eyes, but then Muntadhir shrugged, looking nonchalant. "So let's begin." He wheeled his horse around and raised his voice so the crowd could hear him. "I was just telling my companions here that I think it is time a few sand flies tried their hand at this." His brother winked, flashing a mesmerizing smile at the thousands of djinn arrayed in the arena seats. He was the dashing emir again, and Ali heard more than a few women sigh. "Try to contain your laughter, my people, I beg you."

Another Daeva came riding out, carrying a long, wrapped parcel. "Here you are, Emir."

"Excellent," Muntadhir replied. He addressed the crowd again. "I heard the Daevas have a weapon that I thought my brother might like to see. Our dear Zaydi does love his history." He took the parcel, pulling free the cloth and then holding it out to Ali.

Ali felt a catch in his throat. It was the bow from the Afshin's shrine. The exact replica of the weapon with which Darayavahoush had shot him.

"Do you like it, akhi?" Muntadhir asked, a soft edge of cruelty in his voice. "Takes a little getting used to but . . ." He abruptly raised it, drawing the string back in Ali's direction.

Ali jerked, the motion throwing him back into that night. The silver bow glittering in the light of the burning ship, Darayavahoush's cold green eyes locked on him. The searing pain, the blood in his mouth choking his scream as he tried to grab Muntadhir's hand.

He stared at Muntadhir now, seeing a stranger instead of his brother. "May I borrow a horse?" he asked coldly.

The Daevas brought him one at once, and Ali pulled himself into the saddle. The animal danced nervously beneath him, and he tightened his legs as it reared. They'd probably given him the worst-tempered one they had.

"I think maybe he does not like crocodiles," one of the Daevas mocked.

Another time Muntadhir would have harshly rebuked the man for such words, Ali knew. Now his brother just chuckled along.

"Ah, let us give Zaydi a minute to get used to riding a horse again. A bit different from the oryxes in his village." Muntadhir pulled free an arrow. "I should like to try this bow out."

His brother was off like a shot, the sand churning in his wake. As he neared the target, he raised the bow, leaning slightly sideways to aim an arrow upward.

It hit the exact center of the target, the enchanted pitch bursting into a sparkle of blue flames.

Ali's mouth fell open. That had been no lucky shot. The audience's applause was thunderous, their surprised delight clear. Where in God's name had Muntadhir learned to do that?

The answer came to him just as quickly. *Jamshid.* Ali swore under his breath. Of course Muntadhir knew how to shoot; his best friend had been one of the best archers in Daevabad—he'd trained with the Afshin himself.

Muntadhir must have seen the shock in Ali's face, for triumph blossomed in his own. "I suppose you don't know everything, after all." He tossed Ali the bow. "Your turn, little brother."

Ali caught the bow, his sandals slipping in the stirrups. But as the horse stepped nervously, Ali realized it wasn't just his sandals slipping, it was the entire saddle. It hadn't been tightened enough.

He bit his lip. If he dismounted to check it, he was going to look either paranoid or as if he didn't trust the Daevas who'd saddled the horse in the first place.

Just get this over with. Ali pressed his heels to the horse ever so slightly. It seemed to work for a moment, the horse moving at a slow canter. But then it picked up speed, galloping madly toward the target.

You can do this, he told himself desperately. He could ride and fight with a sword; a bow was only a bit more complicated.

He tightened his legs again. Ali's hands were steady as he nocked an arrow and raised the bow. But he'd never been taught how to adjust for the movement of the horse, and the arrow went embarrassingly off target.

Ali's cheeks burned as the Daeva men laughed. The mood was openly hostile now; they were clearly enjoying the spectacle of the sand fly who'd murdered their beloved Afshin being humiliated by his own kin with a weapon they cherished.

Muntadhir took the bow from him. "It was a good attempt, Zaydi," he offered with mocking sincerity. His eyes glittered. "Shall we try it backward?"

"Whatever you wish, Emir," Ali hissed.

Muntadhir rode off yet again. Even Ali had to admit his brother cut a striking figure, his black robe billowing behind him like smoky wings, the brilliant colors of the royal turban glimmering in the sunlight. He executed the move with the same ease, rising in his saddle as if he were the damned Afshin himself, turning backward and again striking the target. The arena burst into more applause, a few ululations coming from a knot of Geziris close to the ground. Ali recognized Muntadhir's cousin, Tariq, among them.

Ali glanced at the screened balcony above the royal platform. Was Zaynab there? His heart twisted. He could only imagine how his sister felt watching this after trying so hard to make peace between her brothers.

Muntadhir tossed the bow at him with more force than necessary. "Good luck."

"Fuck you." The crude words slipped from Ali's mouth in a flash of anger, and he saw Muntadhir startle.

And then smile yet again, a glimmer of spite in his brother's eyes. "Oh, do you not enjoy being embarrassed, Zaydi? That's odd, as you don't seem to mind doing it to me."

Ali didn't take the bait, riding off without another word. He couldn't ride as well as Muntadhir, he knew that. But he could turn around and aim a damn arrow. Drawing back on the bow, he whirled to face the target.

He did so too fast . . . and his saddle slid free.

Ali fell with it, dropping the bow and pulling his feet from the stirrups. The spookish horse reacted the exact way he imagined the Daevas had hoped for, putting on a burst of speed as the saddle slipped further. He saw a blur of hooves, the ground too close to his face. Several people screamed.

And then it was over. Ali landed hard on his back, rolling to narrowly avoid being trampled as the horse bolted away. He gasped, the air knocked clear from his lungs.

Muntadhir leaped lightly from his horse to retrieve the bow from where Ali had dropped it. "Are you all right?" he drawled.

Ali climbed to his feet, biting back a hiss of pain. He could taste blood in his mouth from where he'd bitten his tongue.

He spat it at the ground. "I'm fine." He wrenched the bow from his brother's hands, picking up the arrow from where it had fallen in the dust. He marched toward the target.

Muntadhir followed, staying at his shoulders. "I am surprised you haven't trained more on the bow. You know how your Banu Nahida loves her archers."

The pointed words struck much deeper than they should have. "That has nothing to do with me," he said heatedly.

"No?" Muntadhir retorted softly in Geziriyya. "Because I can give you some pointers. Brother to brother."

"I don't need your advice on how to shoot an arrow."

"Who says I was talking about archery?" Muntadhir continued as Ali drew back the bowstring. His voice was deadly quiet, his words again for Ali alone. "I was talking about Nahri."

Ali sent the arrow hurtling into the wall. A wave of laughter greeted his blunder, but Ali barely noticed. His face burning at the insinuation, he whirled on his brother. But Muntadhir was already there, taking the bow back.

He hit the target dead center, barely taking his gaze from Ali's. "I do believe I win." He shrugged. "I suppose it's fortuitous you're not going to be my Qaid after all."

Ali had no words. He was more hurt than he thought he could ever be, feeling younger and more naive than he had in years.

Muntadhir was already turning away, as if to return to the platform.

Ali stalked after him, keeping his gaze down and defeated though rage burned in his heart. Muntadhir wanted to see the Citadel-trained part of him?

Very well.

The two of them were only out of eyesight for a second, in the shadow of the stairwell, but it was enough. Ali lunged at his brother, shoving a hand against his mouth before he could scream and kicking open the door to a weapons' closet he knew was located under the stairs. He pushed Muntadhir inside, pulling the door closed behind them.

Muntadhir stumbled back, glaring. "Oh, have you something to say to me, hypocrite? Going to give me a lecture on righteousness while you—"

Ali punched him in the face.

His heart wasn't entirely in it, but the blow was enough to make Muntadhir reel. His brother swore, reaching for his khanjar.

Ali knocked it out of his hands but made no move to take it. Instead, he shoved Muntadhir hard into the opposite wall. "What, isn't this what I'm supposed to be?" he hissed. "Your weapon?"

But he'd underestimated his brother's own anger. Muntadhir wrenched free and threw himself on Ali.

They fell to the dirt, and Ali's fighter instincts swept over him; he'd spent too many years battling for his life in Am Gezira to not immediately react. He rolled, snatching up the khanjar and pinning Muntadhir to the ground.

He had the blade at his brother's throat before he realized what he was doing.

Muntadhir seized his wrist when Ali moved to jerk back. His gray eyes were wild. "Go on," he goaded, bringing the blade closer to his neck. "Do it. Abba will be so proud." His voice broke. "He'll make you emir, he'll give you Nahri. All the things you pretend you don't want."

Shaking, Ali fought for a response. "I . . . I don't—"

The door burst open, Lubayd and Zaynab framed in the dusty light. Ali immediately dropped the khanjar, but it was too late. His sister took one look at them sprawled on the floor, and her eyes flashed in a mix of fury and disappointment that would have made their mother proud. "Thank you for helping me find my brothers," she said flatly to Lubayd. "If you wouldn't mind permitting us a moment . . ."

Lubayd was already backing through the door. "Happily!" He pulled it closed behind him.

Zaynab took a deep breath. "*Get off of each other this instant.*" When both princes promptly separated, she continued, her voice seething, "Now would one of you *please* explain what in God's name just happened in the arena?"

Muntadhir glared at him. "Zaydi found out about Nasir and lost his mind."

"Someone had to," Ali snapped back. "And don't you act all innocent! Do you think I don't know my saddle was loosened? You could have killed me!"

"I didn't touch your damned saddle!" Muntadhir shot back,

climbing to his feet. "Don't make an enemy of half the city and then be surprised when people try to sabotage you." Fresh outrage crossed his face. "And you have some nerve accusing me of anything. I've tried to tell you a dozen times to back off and then you go and call me a coward to Abba's face when all I'm doing is trying to clean up your mess!"

"I was trying to stand up for Zaynab, and for that, you embarrassed me in front of the entire arena!" Hurt rose in Ali's voice. "You insulted Nahri, you let your friends call me a *crocodile* . . ." Even saying it stung. "My God, is this what Abba has turned you into? Have you been imitating him so long that cruelty is now your first instinct?"

"Alizayd, enough," Zaynab said when Muntadhir jerked back as though Ali had slapped him. "Can *Zaynab* get a word in edgewise, since apparently *my* future is the one that sparked this latest fight?"

"Sorry," Ali muttered, falling silent.

"Many thanks," she said acidly. She sighed, peeling back the veil she'd worn in front of Lubayd. Guilt rose in Ali's chest. His sister looked exhausted, more than he'd ever seen before. "I know about Nasir, Ali. I don't like it, but I don't need you running your mouth about it before even speaking with me." She glanced at Muntadhir. "What did Abba say?"

"That he's arriving this week," Muntadhir replied glumly. "He told me to spend time with him and find out what sort of man he is."

A muscle worked in Zaynab's cheek. "Maybe you can let me know as well."

"And that's *it*?" Ali asked. "That's all either of you are prepared to do?"

Muntadhir glared at him. "You'll forgive me for not taking political advice from someone who's been living in a village for five years and whose foot is all but attached to his mouth." His expression twisted. "Do you think I *want* to become like him, Zaydi? Do you have any idea of what *I've* had to give up?" He laced his hands behind his head, pacing. "Daevabad is a tinderbox, and the only way Abba keeps it from exploding is by holding it tight. By making sure everyone knows that if they risk its safety, they risk the lives of everyone they love."

"But that's not who you are, Dhiru," Ali protested. "And that's not the only way to rule."

"No? Maybe we should try it your way, then?" Muntadhir turned back, his gaze cutting through Ali. "Because I think *you're* more like Abba than you want to admit. But where Abba wants stability, you want justice. *Your* version of justice—even if you have to drag us there kicking and screaming. And let me tell you, little brother . . . I'm getting pretty damn clear eyed where you're concerned. You're enjoying the favor of a lot of angry people with weapons and grievances in this city . . . and how convenient, then, that you have the Ayaanle ready and willing to financially support you."

"The *Ayaanle*," Zaynab said, her voice biting, "are a great deal more nuanced than you give us credit for, and this one in particular has been scrambling to make peace between you two idiots for months." She closed her eyes, rubbing her temples. "But things were getting worse in Daevabad before Ali came back, Dhiru. I know you don't want to see it, but they were."

Muntadhir threw up his hands. "And what would you have me do? Ruin a financial alliance we need because my sister will be lonely? Make Alizayd my Qaid again and rightfully lose all my supporters for handing my army to a fanatic?" His words rang with true desperation. "Tell me how to fix this between us because I don't see a way."

Ali cleared the lump growing in his throat. "We're not the problem." He hesitated, his mind racing. The cold realization he'd had with Fatumai after learning what his father had done to the Tanzeem children. His conversation with Nahri last night. All the charges Muntadhir had neatly laid out. There was really only one thing it led to, a conclusion clear as glass.

He met his brother's and sister's expectant eyes. "Abba needs to be replaced."

There was a moment of silent shock and then Zaynab let out a choked, aghast sound he'd never before heard from his ever-refined sister.

Muntadhir stared at him before dropping his head into his hands. "I can't believe it. I can't believe you actually found a way to make this conversation worse." His voice was muffled through his fingers.

"Just listen to me," Ali rushed on. "He's been going astray for years. I understand his concerns about Daevabad's stability, but there is only so long this tactic of trampling anything that opposes him can work. You can't build anything on a cracked foundation."

"And now you're talking like a poet," Muntadhir moaned. "You really have lost your mind."

"I'm tired of watching innocent people die," Ali said bluntly. "I'm tired of being complicit in such suffering. The Daevas, the shafit . . . do you know he had a boat full of refugee children burned merely to execute a few Tanzeem fighters? That he ignored a threat I passed on regarding Nahri's safety because he said she was growing arrogant?" He glanced at Zaynab, knowing his sister shared at least a few of his views. "He's crossed too many lines. He shouldn't be king."

Zaynab's face was conflicted, but she took a deep breath. "Ali's not entirely wrong, Dhiru."

Muntadhir groaned. "Oh, Zaynab, not you too." He crossed the floor to start rifling through one of the supply chests, pulling free a small silver bottle and ripping open the top. "Is this liquor? Because I want to be completely intoxicated when Abba gets wind that his children are plotting a coup in a fucking closet."

"That's weapons polish," Ali said quickly.

Zaynab crossed to Muntadhir's side, knocking the bottle out of his hands when he seemed to still be evaluating it. "Stop. Just listen for a moment," she insisted. "Between the three of us, we might have the support. If we presented a united front, Abba would be hard-pressed to oppose us. We'd need to get the majority of the nobles and the bulk of the Citadel on our side, but I suspect those whose hearts aren't amenable might find their purses are."

"Do you think we could do that?" Ali asked. "We've already spent a fair bit on the hospital."

"Little brother, you'd be surprised how far the illusion of wealth will take you even if the deliverance of such promise takes longer," Zaynab said archly.

"Ayaanle gold," Muntadhir cut in sarcastically. "Well, I suppose I know which way the throne will be swinging."

"It won't." Ideas were coming together in Ali's head as he spoke. "I don't know who should rule or how, but there have to be voices besides ours shaping Daevabad's future. Maybe more than one voice." He paused, thinking fast. "The Nahids . . . they had a council. Perhaps we could try something like that."

Zaynab's response was sharp. "There are a lot of voices in Daevabad who don't think very fondly of us, Ali. You start giving power away and we could end up getting chased back to Am Gezira."

"*Enough.*" Muntadhir shushed them, darting a glance around. "*Stop scheming.* You're going to get yourselves killed, and for nothing. There's no overthrowing Abba unless you can take Suleiman's seal ring from him. Do you have any idea how to do that?"

"No?" Ali confessed. He hadn't thought of the seal ring. "I

mean, he doesn't wear it on his hand. I figured he kept it in a vault or . . ."

"It's in his heart," Muntadhir said bluntly.

Ali's mouth fell open. That was not a possibility that had occurred to him.

Zaynab recovered first. "His *heart*? The seal is *in* his heart?"

"Yes." Muntadhir looked between them, his expression grave. "Do you understand? There's no taking Suleiman's seal unless you're willing to kill our father for it. Is that a price you'd pay?"

Ali struggled to push that shocking information aside. "Suleiman's seal shouldn't matter. Not for this. Stripping your citizens of their magic isn't a power a political leader should have. The seal was meant to help the Nahids heal their people and fight the ifrit. And when it comes time for it to be passed again . . . the person that ring belongs to isn't in this room, and you both know it."

It was Zaynab's turn to groan. She pinched the bridge of her nose, looking exasperated. "Ali . . ."

Muntadhir gestured rudely between them. "Now do you believe me?" he asked Zaynab. "I told you he was smitten with her."

"I'm not smitten with her!"

There was a pounding on the door and then it abruptly opened, revealing Lubayd again.

"Ali, Emir Muntadhir!" he gasped, leaning on his knees and fighting for breath. "You need to come quickly."

Ali shot to his feet. "What's wrong?"

"There's been an attack on the Daeva procession."

30
NAHRI

Nahri wouldn't have admitted it to him, but *maybe* Kartir had a point about the Navasatem procession being fun.

"Anahid!" came another cry from below her. "Anahid the Blessed!"

Nahri smiled bashfully from underneath her chador, making a blessing over the crowd. "May the fires burn brightly for you!" she shouted back.

It was an almost unbelievably lovely morning, with not a cloud in the bright blue sky. Nisreen and a coterie of laughing Daeva women had awoken her hours before dawn with milk-sweets and pepper-scented tea, pulling her from bed despite Nahri's weary protests and dressing her in a soft, simple gown of undyed linen. Before the sun had risen, they'd joined an excited and growing throng of Daevas at the city's docks in order to wait for the sunrise. As the first pale rays crossed the sky, they'd lit colorful boat-shaped oil lamps of translucent waxed paper, setting them adrift on the lake—glowing a pale pink in the dawn sun—and transforming the water into an enormous, dazzling altar.

The joy of the crowd had been infectious. Children chased each other, gleefully smearing wet handfuls of the muddy mortar that signified the temple their ancestors had built for Suleiman across arms and faces, while boisterous vendors hawked the sugared barley cakes and rich plum beer traditionally consumed for the holiday.

Chanting and singing, they'd made their way to the chariots that would carry the procession to the palace. They'd been constructed in secret; it was Daeva tradition that the chariots were designed and built by older Daevas and ridden by youth: a literal celebration of the next generation. There were thirty in total, one to signify each century of freedom, and they were utterly spectacular. Because her tribe was not one for half measures, the vehicles were also enormous, resembling moving towers more than anything else, with room for dozens of riders, and wheels twice the height of a man. Each was dedicated to an aspect of Daeva life: one boasted a grove of jeweled cherry trees, golden trunks peeking out from beneath a canopy of carved jade leaves and gleaming ruby fruit, while the one behind hers spun with cavorting brass horses. Their quicksilver eyes flashed, white jasmine blossoms heavy in the rich black tassels of their manes.

Nahri's chariot was the largest, and embarrassingly so, crafted to look like the boat Anahid might have once sailed across the lake. A blue-and-white silk flag billowed above Nahri's head, and standing proud at the stern was a magnificent carved wooden shedu. She was currently sitting on it, cajoled and harassed into doing so by the ring of thrilled little girls at her feet. Traditionally one of them would have stood in for Anahid, but Nahri's attempts to convince them to do the same this time had been met only with disappointed pouts.

But her people's delight was infectious, so embarrassment

aside, Nahri was having a good time, a thing her warm cheeks and silly grin betrayed. She waved to the crowds on the street, bringing her hands together in blessing as she passed by groups of cheering Daevas.

"This is not what I was told to expect," Aqisa groused from Nahri's side, picking at one of the many garlands of flowers the little girls had—at first timidly and then with great exuberance when the warrior woman didn't stop them—draped around her neck.

Nahri bit back a laugh at the sight of the pink blossoms tangled across Ali's terrifying friend. "Don't they celebrate Navasatem in Am Gezira?"

The other woman cast a dismayed look at a pair of drunk young men on the float behind them. They were giggling madly, spinning around the brass horses, each with a bottle of plum beer in hand. "We do not celebrate anything in such a manner."

"Ah," Nahri said softly. "Small wonder Ali likes it there."

"You are enjoying yourself?" she heard Nisreen call from below. Nisreen was riding alongside the chariots with the rest of the Daeva elders, their horses draped in shimmering cloth the color of the rising sun.

Nahri leaned over to shout down to her. "You might have mentioned I'd be seated on a shedu," she complained. "Ghassan is going to burn something when he sees this."

Nisreen shook her head. "It's all in good fun. The first night of the new moon is always the wildest." She nodded at the drunken youths. "By this evening, more Daevas than not will look like them. It doesn't leave us much of a threat to the king."

Nahri sighed. "I look forward to spending all night tending to their injuries." She'd already found herself contemplating how quickly she would be able to get to the young men behind her when one of them inevitably fell and cracked his skull open.

"I'd say that's a fair possibility. But we have Jamshid in the infirmary with us tonight, and we'll make sure none of us leave." Nisreen paused. "Maybe you could ask that shafit healer you're collaborating with to join us. She could bring her family."

Nahri glanced down in surprise. "You want me to ask Subha and her family to spend the night in the infirmary?" It seemed a bizarre request, especially considering the source.

"I think it's a smart idea. We could use the extra hands, and you've mentioned her child is still nursing."

Nahri considered that. It would be good to have Subha's help, and she'd been wanting to show the doctor the infirmary anyway. "I'll send her a message when we get back to the palace."

She straightened back up, peering at the street ahead and trying to get her bearings. It looked like they were almost at the midan.

Nearly out of the shafit district. Nahri flushed, hating how quickly the thought—and the relief—had come. Ali's worry had seemed sincere, but it was difficult to parse out his warning from the *rest* of their conversation, and that was a subject she refused to think about today.

Even so, she glanced around at the crowd. It was mostly Daeva, though there were plenty of purebloods from the djinn tribes pressed against the barricades, spinning starry sparklers and sharing cakes and beer. A line of soldiers separated them from the shafit onlookers, many of whom were also cheering but were held far back.

Guilt stabbed at her. That wasn't right, regardless of the threat. Nahri would have to see if there wasn't some sort of bonus celebration she could put together for the shafit to make up for it.

She shifted on the wooden shedu, pulling her chador past her rounded ears. It was unusually and mercifully light—no heavy gold ornaments draped over her head today. Stitched together from layers of silk so delicate they were nearly transparent and dyed in a beautiful array of colors, the chador was meant to give the appearance of shedu wings. Nahri lifted her face to the sun, listening to the delighted chatter of the Daeva children around her.

I wish Dara could have seen this. The thought rose in her head unbidden and unexpected, and yet oddly enough did not fill her with the tumultuous mix of emotions that memories of Dara usually did. She and Dara might have been of very different minds about the future, but she could not help but hope the Afshin would have been proud to see her sitting upon a wooden shedu today.

Movement caught her eyes ahead; a line of Daeva riders was approaching to join the procession. Nahri grinned as she recognized Jamshid among them. She waved, catching his eye, and he lifted his cap in acknowledgment, gesturing with a wide, giddy smile at the horse beneath him.

A loud bang sounded, an explosive rumble both strange and distantly familiar. God only knew what it was. Some Daeva had probably conjured a set of flying drums.

The noise came again, and this time there was a shout—and then a scream, accompanied by a burst of white smoke from the balcony directly across the street.

A dark projectile smashed into the carved balustrade above her head.

Nahri shouted in surprise, shielding her head from a rain of wooden shards. There was movement on the balcony, a glint of metal and then another explosion of white smoke.

Aqisa yanked her off the shedu. "Get down!" she cried, throwing herself over Nahri.

In the next moment, the shedu shattered, another projectile hitting the head with enough force to cleave it off. Stunned and with Aqisa pinning her hard against the wooden deck, Nahri lay still. She heard more screaming and then another cracking sound.

Gunfire, she finally recognized, her memories of Cairo catching up to her. The hulking Turkish cannons, the deadly French muskets . . . not things an Egyptian girl like her, living on the streets and already evading the authorities, would have ever touched, but weapons she'd seen and heard many times. The type of weapons barely known to djinn, she recalled, remembering Ali's fear when she'd handled the pistol at the Sens.

There was another shot, this one hitting the base of the juggernaut.

They're targeting me, Nahri realized. She tried to push Aqisa off, to no avail. "They're after me!" she shouted. "You need to get the children away!"

An object crashed to the wooden deck an arm's length from her face. Some sort of cracked ceramic jug, with a fiery rag stuffed in one end. Nahri caught the eye-watering smell of pine and tar as a dark sludge seeped out. It touched the flames.

The fireball that exploded was enough to sear her face. Instinctively, Nahri rolled, dragging a shocked Aqisa to her feet. The pieces came together horribly in her head, the pitch-filled pots and wild flames immediately familiar from her people's worst stories about the shafit.

"Rumi fire!" she screamed, trying to grab the little girls. Another jar struck the street, fire engulfing a pair of riders so quickly they didn't even have time to scream. "Run!"

And then it was chaos. The surrounding crowds broke, people pushing and shoving to get away from the spreading flames. Nahri heard the Royal Guard shouting, trying to impose order as their zulfiqars flashed in the light.

Nahri choked down her panic. They had to save the children. She and Aqisa swiftly led them to the other side of the chariot. Daevas on horseback had already thrown up ropes, men climbing to help them down.

Aqisa grabbed her collar. "Water!" she said urgently. "Where is the nearest pump?"

Nahri shook her head, coughing as she tried to think. "Water doesn't work on Rumi fire."

"Then what *does* work?"

"Sand," she whispered, gazing in rising horror at the damp stone streets and wooden buildings surrounding her. Sand was the only thing misty Daevabad didn't have in abundance.

Aqisa abruptly yanked her back again as a metal ball slammed into the wood where Nahri's head had just been. "They're up there," she warned, jerking her head toward a balcony. "Three of them."

Nahri dared a quick peek. A trio of men were hunched inside the screened structure, two of them armed with what looked like muskets.

Rage burned through her. From the corner of her eye, she spotted an Agnivanshi soldier with a bow quickly climbing the jeweled trees of the chariot next to hers. He pulled himself onto one of the branches, nocking an arrow in the same movement.

There was a shout, and then one of the attackers fell from the balcony, an arrow buried in his back. The archer turned for the other men.

A blast of a musket brought him down. As Nahri cried out, the soldier fell dead to the ground, the bow tumbling from his hands.

"Get down, Nahri!" Nisreen yelled, drawing her attention back as another shot splintered off the deck and the last of the children were spirited away.

Nahri jumped, Aqisa urging her into a sprint as the chariot cracked in half from the heat of the spreading flames.

A knot of Daevas pulled her into their midst. Nisreen was there, ripping Nahri's distinctive chador off. "Get the Banu Nahida away," she ordered.

"No, wait—" Nahri tried to protest as hands pushed her onto a horse. Through a break in the crowd, she spotted Jamshid. He was riding hard—dangerously hard—one hand clutching his saddle while he dipped to reach for the bow on the ground . . .

A clay jar of Rumi fire struck him directly in the back.

"*Jamshid!*" Nahri lunged forward as he toppled from the horse. His coat was on fire, flames dancing over his back. "No!"

Everything seemed to slow. A riderless horse galloped past, and the smell of smoke and blood thickened on the air. Nahri caught herself from swooning, the sudden presence of torn bodies, broken bones, and slowing hearts threatening to overwhelm her Nahid senses. The streets her ancestors had carefully laid down were burning, engulfing fleeing parade-goers. Ahead, Jamshid was rolling in a vain attempt to put out the fire spreading across his coat.

Fury and desperation rose inside her. Nahri shoved free of the Daevas trying to wrestle her away.

"Jamshid!" Sheer determination brought her to his side as he writhed on the ground. Not caring if she risked herself, Nahri grabbed the unburnt edge of his collar and wrenched the burning jacket off him.

He screamed, the smoldering fabric taking a good part of the skin on his upper back with it, leaving his flesh bloody and exposed. But it was better than being consumed by Rumi fire— not that it mattered; the two of them were surrounded now, the flames hungrily licking up the surrounding buildings.

A heavy object crashed to the ground before her: the remains of the burning shedu she'd ridden to emulate her ancestors. But as Nahri watched the chaos around her, helplessness threatened to suffocate her. Nahri was no Anahid. She had no Afshin.

She had no idea how to save her people.

Afshin . . . like a burst of light, one of her last memories of Cairo came to her: the warrior with striking green eyes, whose name she had not yet known, standing amid the tombs of her human home, raising his arms to conjure a storm.

A *sand*storm. Nahri caught her breath. *Creator, please*, she prayed. *Help me save my city.*

She inhaled, bowing her head. Acting on instinct, she tried to see the city as she might have seen a patient, tried to visualize the dirt between its cobblestones and the dust gathering in every corner.

She *pulled*. The wind immediately picked up, lashing her braids against her face, but she could still sense resistance, her hold on the magic just a touch too weak. She cried out in frustration.

"Nahri," Jamshid breathed, his voice hoarse as he clutched her hand. "Nahri, I don't feel right . . ." He choked, his fingers tightening on her own.

A raw punch of magic hit her so hard she nearly fell back. She gasped, reeling as she tried to maintain her control. It was both familiar and not, a jolt as if she'd plunged her hands into a vat of ice. It raced through her veins with a wild madness, like a creature too long caged.

And it was the exact push that she needed. Nahri didn't hesitate, her eyes locking on the burning streets. *Heal*, she commanded, pulling hard.

Every speck of sand in her family's city rushed to her.

It whirled into a racing funnel of smothering dust. She exhaled and it collapsed, raining down to cover the street and the ruined chariots, blowing into dunes against the buildings and coating the bodies of fleeing and burning djinn and Daevas alike. Extinguishing the fire as thoroughly as if she'd dunked a candle into a pool of water.

It did the same to Nahri. Her hold on the magic collapsed, and she reeled, exhaustion sweeping her as black spots burst across her vision.

"Banu Nahida!"

Nahri blinked, catching sight of Nisreen racing toward her, still holding her bright chador. At her side, Jamshid struggled to sit up, his shirt hanging in scorched tatters across his chest.

And across his perfectly healed back.

Nahri was gaping at his unmarred skin when there was another crack of the musket. Jamshid shoved her down.

But the shot hadn't been aimed at them.

The time between seeing Nisreen racing toward them and seeing her mentor fall seemed to take hours, as if to effectively sear itself on her mind's eye. Nahri tore away from Jamshid, lunging to Nisreen's side without recalling moving.

"Nisreen!" Black blood was already soaking through her tunic. Nahri ripped it open.

She went completely still at the sight of the stomach wound. It was ghastly, the human weapon damaging the other woman's flesh in a way Nahri hadn't thought possible in the magical world.

Oh God . . . Not wasting a moment, Nahri laid her hand against the blood—and then immediately jerked it back as a searing pain slashed across her palm. The smell, the burn . . .

The attackers had used iron bullets.

There was a cry and then the remaining men on the balcony fell to the ground, their bodies riddled with arrows. Nahri barely noticed. Her heart in her throat, she ignored the pain to lay hands on her mentor again. *Heal*, she begged. *Heal!*

A bloody scrape on Nisreen's cheek instantly did, but from the bullet wound, nothing. The bullet itself stood out like an angry scar against the rest of Nisreen's body, a cold, alien intrusion.

Jamshid sank down next to her, dropping the bow. "What can I do?" he cried.

I don't know. Terrified, Nahri searched Nisreen's face; she needed Nisreen to guide her through this. She needed Nisreen, period. Tears filled her eyes as she took in the blood at the corner of her teacher's mouth, the black eyes that were filled with nearly as much shock as pain.

The answer came to her in an instant. "I need pliers!" she screamed to the crowd. "A spike, a blade, something!"

"Nahri . . ." Nisreen's voice came in a heartbreaking whisper. She coughed, more blood dripping from her mouth. "Nahri . . . listen . . ."

Blood was soaking through Nahri's clothes. Someone, Nahri didn't even care who, thrust the handle of a knife into her hand. "I'm sorry, Nisreen," she whispered. "This is probably going to hurt."

Jamshid had taken Nisreen's head in his lap. With quiet horror, Nahri realized he was praying softly, giving her last rites.

Nahri refused to accept that. She banished her emotions. She ignored the tears running down her cheeks and the steady, horrible slowing of Nisreen's heart.

"Nahri," Nisreen whispered. "Nahri . . . your—"

Nahri inserted the knife, her hands mercifully steady. "I have it!" With a rush of blood, she pulled free the bullet. But the movement cost her. Nisreen shuddered, her eyes brightening in pain.

And then, even as Nahri spread her fingers across the wound, Nisreen's heart stopped. Roaring in anger, Nahri let loose the magic she had left, commanding it to restart, for the torn vessels and frayed flesh to connect.

Nothing.

Jamshid burst in tears. "Her heart," he sobbed.

No. Nahri stared at her mentor in dull disbelief. Nisreen couldn't be dead. The woman who had taught her how to heal could not be the one person she couldn't help. The woman who, for all their many, *many* fights, had been the closest thing to a mother Nahri had ever had.

"Nisreen," she whispered. "*Please.*" She tried again, magic rushing from her hands, but it did nothing. Nisreen's heart was still, blood and muscles slowing as the bright pulses in her head steadily blinked out—Nahri's abilities telling her clearly what her heart wanted to deny.

Nisreen was gone.

31

ALI

Ali ripped the hospital door open, grabbing the first person he saw. "The Banu Nahida! Where is she?"

A bloodied Parimal started, nearly dropping a tray of supplies. Ali quickly let him go.

Parimal's expression was grave. "In the main chamber. She's unharmed, but it's bad, Prince. Many are dead."

That Ali knew. He and Muntadhir had rushed to the procession but the streets had been in turmoil, and they'd finally arrived to learn Nahri was already back at the hospital treating victims.

Muntadhir had stayed behind to assist Jamshid in restoring some order while Ali continued to the hospital, passing the ruins of the celebration turned to carnage with growing despair. The dead lay where they'd fallen, their bodies still being shrouded. Ali had counted at least fifty.

One of the dead, Jamshid grimly told them, had already been

quietly taken to the Grand Temple, her still form covered in the Banu Nahida's own chador. Nisreen's name landed hard in Ali's heart, the scope of the violence done today unimaginable.

"May I ask . . ." Parimal was staring at him, looking sick and hesitant. "The attackers . . . were they identified?"

Ali met his gaze, all too aware of what Parimal was really asking. It had been the same awful prayer in the darkest part of Ali's heart.

"They were shafit," he said softly. "All of them."

Parimal's shoulders dropped, his expression crumpling. "Oh no," he whispered. "It's terrible, but I'd hoped . . ."

"I know," Ali cleared his throat. "Where is she?"

Parimal nodded to his left. "The main examination room."

Ali hurried off, through the halls whose construction he'd personally overseen. He'd looked forward to seeing the hospital operational, but God . . . not like this.

The chamber was packed, the hundred pallets full and more patients lying on woolen blankets on the floor. The vast majority were Daeva. He caught sight of Nahri bent over a crying young boy being held by his mother. She had a pair of forceps in her hands and seemed to be removing bits of wooden shrapnel from his skin. He watched her set aside the forceps and touch the little boy's face before pushing slowly to her feet, exhaustion in every line of her body. She turned around.

Her eyes had no sooner met his than Nahri's face crumpled in grief. Heartsick, Ali rushed to her side. She trembled, shaking her head and looking like it was taking every bit of strength she had not to cry.

"I can't," she choked out. "Not here."

Wordlessly, Ali took her hand. She didn't resist, letting him lead her out of the room and into the garden. They had barely closed the door when she broke down sobbing.

"They killed Nisreen," she wept. "They shot her and I couldn't do anything. I couldn't . . ."

Ali pulled her into his arms. She started to cry harder and they sank slowly to the floor.

"She taught me everything," Nahri gasped through her sobs. "*Everything*. And I couldn't do a damned thing to save her." She shook violently against him. "She was scared, Ali. I could see it in her eyes."

"I'm so sorry, Nahri," he whispered, at a loss for anything else to say. "I'm so, so sorry." Not knowing what else to do, he simply held her as she cried, her tears soaking through his dishdasha. He ached to do something, *anything*, that would make this better.

He wasn't sure how long they'd been sitting there when the call to asr prayer came. Ali closed his wet eyes, letting the muezzins' call wash over him. It put a little steadiness back into his spirit. Today's attack was awful, but the adhan was still being sung. Time wasn't stopping in Daevabad, and it would be up to them to make sure this tragedy didn't shatter the city.

The adhan seemed to bring Nahri back to herself as well. She took a shaky breath, pulling away to wipe her eyes.

She stared at her hands, looking utterly lost. "I don't know what to say to them," she murmured, seemingly as much to herself as to Ali. "I told my people we could trust the shafit. But we were just attacked with human weapons, with Rumi fire, when we were celebrating *our* holiday in *our* city." Her voice was hollow. "How can I call myself a Banu Nahida if I can't protect my own people?"

Ali reached out, taking her chin in his hands. "Nahri, you're not responsible for this. Not in any way. A few twisted souls exploited a security weakness that, to be honest, we should have prepared for the first time those damnable weapons showed up in this city. It has no bearing on your outreach to the shafit, no bearing on your position as Banu Nahida. You saved lives," he assured her. "I heard what you did to put out the fire. You think anyone but a Banu Nahida could have done that?"

Nahri didn't appear to hear him, lost in whatever darkness clouded her mind. "This can't happen again," she muttered. "Never again." Her expression abruptly sharpened, her eyes fixing on his. "The woman who warned you . . . where is she? I want to talk to her."

Ali shook his head. "She knew nothing more."

"She clearly knew enough!" She jerked free of his hands. "Maybe you couldn't get any more information from her, but I bet I can."

The vengeance in her voice unsettled him. "She wasn't behind this, Nahri. And I couldn't find her if I tried."

"Then what's her name? I'll have my people search for her if you won't."

Ice crept over Ali's skin. Right now, he would have done almost anything to help Nahri . . . but he couldn't give her that. He bit his lip, fighting for words. "Nahri, I know you're grieving—"

"*You know?*" She shoved away from him. "What do you know about grief?" Her wet eyes flashed. "Who have *you* lost, Ali? Who's died in your arms? Who have you begged to come back, to look at you one last time?" She staggered to her feet. "The Daevas bleed, the shafit bleed, and there the Geziris stand. Safe in their deserts back home, secure in the palace here."

Ali opened and closed his mouth, but that was not a charge he could dispute. "Nahri, please," he begged. "We . . . we'll fix this."

"And what if we can't?" Her voice cracked in exhaustion. "What if Daevabad is just broken in a way that can't be repaired?"

He shook his head. "I refuse to believe that."

Nahri just stared at him. The anger was gone, replaced by a pity that made him feel even worse. "You should leave, Alizayd.

Escape this awful place while you still can." Bitterness creased her features. "I know I would." She turned for the door. "I need to get back to my patients."

"Nahri, wait!" Ali shot to his feet, desperate. "*Please*. I'll make this right. I swear to God."

She pushed past him. "You can't make this right." She wrenched open the door. "Go back to Am Gezira."

LUBAYD AND AQISA WERE WAITING FOR HIM WHEN ALI left the hospital.

Lubayd took one look at him and then grabbed Ali's arm. "Is she okay?"

Ali's mouth was dry. "She's alive."

Go back to Am Gezira. Suddenly, in a moment of weakness, Ali wanted nothing other than that. It would be easy. The city was in chaos; the three of them could slip out in an instant. His father wouldn't blame him—he had told Ali to leave and would probably be quietly relieved he didn't have to force his son to obey his wishes. Ali could be back in Bir Nabat in weeks, away from Daevabad and its constant bloody heartache.

He rubbed his eyes. Ahead, the sight of the shafit camp caught his eye. It had been rebuilt—expanded—after the attack and was bustling now with tense workers streaming into and out of the hospital.

Sick fear crept into his heart. The Daevas had attacked this place before, killing a score for the death of a single man.

What would they do to the shafit for the destruction wrought today?

They could go to war. It was his father's constant concern, Ali knew. The Daevas and the shafit made up the majority of Daevabad, thoroughly outnumbering the rest of the djinn, and the Royal Guard might not be able to stop them. Ghassan might not even be inclined to let them *try* and stop them. Ali knew their world's cold calculus; the Guard would be sent to watch over the other quarters, to keep the purebloods of the djinn tribes safe while the "fire worshippers" and the "dirt-bloods" had their final fight.

But his first instinct will be to stop this. To brutally stamp out anything that might escalate.

The door opened again, Subha stepping out to join them.

The doctor took a deep breath. "I didn't think I'd ever see worse than the attack on the camp," she confessed by way of greeting. "I can't imagine the demons who planned such a thing. To attack a parade full of children . . ."

They were children themselves only a few years ago. Ali knew in his heart this traced back to the Tanzeem. The few twisted souls who'd watched their sheikh murdered, their orphanage burned, and then their adopted brothers and sisters die on Daevabad's lake, just as Sister Fatumai had said.

"I think we've got the survivors out of danger for now," Subha continued, her expression heavy. "I wish I'd been there," she said softly. "Lady Nisreen . . . I probably could have gotten the bullet out."

"Please don't tell Nahri that," Ali said quickly.

Subha shook her head. "I can tell you it's already on her mind. When you lose a patient like that, you never stop wondering what you could have done differently. And if it's someone you love . . ."

Ali flinched. "Will you stay with her?" he asked. "With Nahri?"

"Where are you headed?"

He hesitated, trying to think. "The Citadel," he finally decided. He wasn't welcome at the hospital and didn't trust his father not to lock him up if he returned to the palace. "I want to see what we can do to keep people from each other's throats while we figure out who's responsible for this."

Aqisa narrowed her eyes. "Are you allowed at the Citadel?"

Ali took a deep breath. "I think we're about to learn exactly how popular I am with the Royal Guard."

THE SOLDIERS AT THE GATE CERTAINLY DIDN'T STOP him from entering; indeed, there was open relief on the faces of a few.

"Prince Alizayd," the first man greeted him. "Peace be upon you."

"And upon you peace," Ali replied. "Is the Qaid here?"

The man shook his head. "You just missed him heading back to the palace." He paused. "He seemed upset. He went tearing out of here with a few of his most senior officers."

Ali's stomach dropped, uncertain what to think about that. He nodded and then continued on, striding into the heart of the Citadel, the place that in many ways had been a truer home to him than the palace. Its tower stood proud, stark against the setting sun.

A knot of Geziri officers were just inside, arguing loudly over a scroll. Ali recognized all of them, particularly Daoud, the officer who'd made a point of thanking him for his effort with his village's well when he first arrived in Daevabad.

"Prince Alizayd, thank God," the man said when he caught sight of Ali.

Ali made his way over cautiously, raising a hand to stop Lubayd and Aqisa from following him. He was here as a soldier now, not as a civilian from outer Am Gezira. "The Qaid has gone to the palace?"

Daoud nodded. "We received orders from the king that troubled him."

"What orders?" Ali asked, instantly concerned.

Barghash, one of the louder, brasher captains spoke up. "He wants us to raze the neighborhood in which the attack took place. It is unnecessary. We found the shafit who lived in the apartments with their throats cut. The attackers must have killed them. And the attackers themselves are dead! We've been asked to slaughter scores of shafit for no reason other than—"

"That's enough," Abu Nuwas interrupted. "You took an oath when you joined the Guard to obey the king."

"That's not quite the oath he took," Ali corrected. "He pledged to serve God and the security of his people. And the shafit are also our people."

Abu Nuwas gave him an annoyed look. "Respectfully, Prince Alizayd, you hold no rank here. You are not even supposed to *be* here. I can have you escorted to the palace if you like."

The threat was clear, and Ali saw more than a few men bristle . . . though their barbed glances were not for him.

Ali paused, seeing Muntadhir and Zaynab in his mind. Their father.

Bir Nabat and the life he might have lived.

God forgive me. God guide me. "I'm very sorry, Abu Nuwas," he said quietly. Ali's hand dropped to his khanjar. "But I'm not going back to the palace."

He cracked the other man across the skull with the hilt of the blade.

Abu Nuwas fell unconscious to the dust. Two of the officers immediately went for their zulfiqars, but they were outnumbered, the remaining officers and several infantrymen lunging forward and restraining them.

"Please make sure he's all right," Ali continued, keeping his voice calm. He picked up the scroll from the ground, his eyes scanning the repulsive order, his father's signature clear on the bottom.

It burst into flames in his hand, and Ali dropped it to the ground.

He gazed at the shocked soldiers around him. "I didn't join the Royal Guard to murder innocents," he said flatly. "And our ancestors certainly didn't come to Daevabad to raze shafit homes while their children sleep inside." He raised his voice. "We *keep the peace*, understand? That's all that's happening right now."

There was a moment of hesitation among the men. Ali's heart raced. Aqisa reached for her blade . . .

And then Daoud nodded, swiftly making the Geziri salute. "Your prince has issued a command," he declared. "Draw up!"

The soldiers in the courtyard, slowly at first and then moving at the speed with which they would have obeyed Wajed, took their places.

Daoud bowed. "What would you have us do?"

"We need to secure the shafit district. I won't have anyone seeking vengeance tonight. The gates to the midan will need to be closed and fortified—fast. I'll need to send a message to the king." *And to my siblings*, he added silently, praying he'd made more headway than he thought while arguing with them in the closet.

"What about the Geziri Quarter?" Daoud asked. "There are no gates separating us from the shafit."

"I know." Ali took a deep breath, considering his options and suddenly wishing he'd done a bit more scheming with Zaynab. He fidgeted with the prayer beads around his wrist. Whose support *could* he count on?

His fingers stilled on the beads. "I need you to get me every Geziri muezzin you can find."

32
NAHRI

You're a good Banu Nahida.

Nisreen's words from the other night rang in Nahri's mind as she stared at the sink. *A good Banu Nahida.* The shock in her mentor's face, the way the spark—the jesting and the weary patience, everything that made her Nisreen—had vanished from her dark eyes, the hands that had guided Nahri's now growing cold in the quiet of the Grand Temple.

"You need a break." Subha's voice yanked her from her thoughts. She threw a towel at Nahri. "You could have washed your hands a hundred times for how long you've been standing here staring at the water."

Nahri shook her head, drying her hands and retying her apron. "I'm fine."

"I'm not asking." Nahri glanced at the other doctor, startled, and saw only determination in her eyes. "You wished to work with another healer? Fine, then I'm acting on behalf of our patients. You are not fit to treat anyone right now."

Before Nahri could protest, the doctor took her by the arm, all but depositing her in a low couch. A cup of tea and platter of food waited on a nearby table.

Subha nodded to it. "The camp workers have been bringing food and clothing by. They thought your people could use it."

The gesture moved her. "That was kind," she said softly. She picked up the tea, too weary to resist, and took a sip.

Subha sat beside her. She sighed, wiping a line of ash from her sweat-streaked brow. "If I've not said it yet, I'm terribly sorry." She shook her head. "I spoke a bit with Lady Nisreen last night." A small smile played on her lips. "It was only slightly confrontational; in all, she seemed very capable and quite kind."

Nahri stared at her tea. "She taught me everything I know about the Nahid sciences." Emotion rose in her voice. "She was the closest thing to family I had in Daevabad, and I couldn't save her."

Subha touched her hand. "Don't lose yourself in what you might have done for a patient, especially not one you loved." She cleared her throat. "Trust that I speak from experience. After my father . . . I felt useless. I wasted weeks on self-pity and grief. You don't have weeks. Your people need you now."

Nahri nodded, finding relief in the direct words. They were certainly more useful than weeping on Ali's shoulder in the garden.

A weakness. That's what Nisreen had called Ali, and clearly she'd been right. Had Nahri been the Banu Nahida her people needed, she would have forced the name of that informant from Ali's lips.

"Banu Nahida?" A familiar voice called from the knot of people bustling about the entrance to the exam chamber.

Jamshid. Someone must have given him a shirt, but it was covered in blood and ash, and he looked as exhausted as Nahri felt. His gaze fell on hers, and then he was across the room in seconds, with such swift agility that Nahri nearly dropped her teacup. Forget the burns, Jamshid wasn't even *limping*.

"*Jamshid?*" She gaped, looking him up and down. Closer now, she could see he was trembling, his eyes bright with barely checked panic.

Subha frowned. "Nahri said you were struck with Rumi fire and badly burned." She rose to her feet, reaching for him. "Would you like us to—"

He jerked back. "I'm fine," he said hoarsely. "Quite, quite fine," he added, sounding slightly hysterical. "How are you?"

Nahri stared at him. He certainly didn't *sound* fine. "We're doing what we can," she replied. "Are they finished at the procession site?"

Jamshid nodded. "The final count is eighty-six dead," he said softly. "Muntadhir and the king were leaving when I did. They only found the three attackers."

"Nearly a hundred people dead at the hands of *three*?" Nahri put down her tea, her hands shaking. "I don't understand how this could happen."

"It never has before," Jamshid said, his voice sorrowful. "I don't think anyone expected anything like this."

Nahri shook her head. "I'm glad to have been present when Daevabad's people discovered a new low in slaughtering one another."

Jamshid stepped closer, laying a hand on her shoulder. "I'm so sorry about Nisreen, Nahri." He blinked back tears. "I can't even really believe it. It's difficult to imagine returning to the infirmary and not seeing her there."

Nahri struggled to keep her voice from thickening. "We'll have to manage. Our people need us."

He flushed. "You're right, of course. But Nahri . . . if things are under control here, do you have a minute to talk? Alone?" he clarified, nodding to the corridor.

"Of course." Nahri stood. "If you'll excuse me, Doctor Sen."

The moment they were outside, Jamshid whirled on her. "Nahri, are you sure it was Rumi fire in those containers?"

Nahri was as taken aback by the question as she was by the fear in his eyes. "Yes? I mean, what else could have burned like that?"

He was wringing his hands. "Do you think there could have been anything else in it? Some sort of . . . I don't know . . . healing serum?"

She blinked. "Because of your back?" In the chaos of the attack and Nisreen's death, Nahri had hardly given thought to how swiftly Jamshid's burns had vanished.

He'd gone pale. "No, not just because of my back . . ." His mouth opened and closed as if he was struggling for words. "Nahri, you're going to think I'm mad, but—"

"Banu Nahida!" It was Razu this time. "You need to come quickly," she said, switching to Tukharistani. "This one's father is throwing a fit outside."

Jamshid spun on Razu. "Then tell him to wait!"

The words had no sooner left Jamshid's lips than he gasped, clapping a hand over his mouth. Nahri's eyes went wide. He'd just spoken in a perfect imitation of Razu's ancient dialect of Tukharistani—a language she'd heard not a soul save Razu and herself speak.

"Jamshid, how did you—"

"Jamshid!" Kaveh came racing into the corridor. "Banu Nahida! Come, there's no time to waste!"

Jamshid still looked too astonished to speak, so Nahri did. "What's going on?"

Kaveh was pale. "It's the emir."

JAMSHID WAS IN FULL PANIC AS THEY GALLOPED TOward the midan, whatever he'd been trying to tell her clearly gone from his mind. "What do you mean, he collapsed?" he demanded of Kaveh again, shouting over the clatter of hooves.

"I am telling you all that I know," Kaveh replied. "He wanted to stop and visit with survivors outside the Grand Temple, and then he passed out. We brought him inside, and I came for you as soon as I could."

Nahri tightened her legs around her horse, clutching the reins as the Geziri Quarter passed by in a blur. "Why would you not bring him to the infirmary or the hospital?"

"I'm sorry, we weren't thinking."

They passed through the Geziri Gate. The midan was eerie in its emptiness, like many of the streets had been, glowing faintly in the deepening night. It should have been filled with celebrations, with Daevas who'd had a bit too much plum beer dancing on the fountains and children conjuring fireworks.

Instead it was entirely still, the smell of burned flesh and smoke hanging on the dusty air. A handcart selling delicate garlands of blown-glass flowers lay abandoned on its side. Nahri feared there was a good chance its owner lay under one of the eighty-six blood-soaked shrouds outside the Temple.

The sound of chanting suddenly drew her ear. Nahri raised a hand, slowing her horse. It was the singsong intonation of the call to prayer . . . except isha prayer had already been called. It wasn't in Arabic either, she realized.

"Is that Geziriyya?" Jamshid whispered. "Why would the muezzins be calling in Geziriyya? And why now?"

Kaveh had grown paler. "I think we should get to the Temple." He spurred his horse toward the Daeva Gate, the two shedu statues throwing bizarre shadows against the midan's copper walls.

They hadn't gotten halfway across when a line of horsemen moved to intercept them. "Grand Wazir!" a man called. "Stop."

The Qaid, Nahri realized, recognizing him. Six members of the Royal Guard stood with him, armed with scythes and zulfiqars, and as Nahri watched, another four archers stepped out from the other gates. Their bows were not yet drawn, but a whisper of fear went through her anyway.

"What is the meaning of this?" she demanded. "Let us pass. I need to get to the Grand Temple and make sure my husband is still breathing!"

Wajed frowned. "Your husband is nowhere near the Grand Temple. Emir Muntadhir is at the palace. I saw him just before we left."

Jamshid pushed forward on his horse, seemingly heedless of the way the soldiers instantly moved their hands to their blades. "Is he all right? My father said he had taken ill at the Grand Temple."

Baffled confusion on Wajed's face, and a flush of guilt on Kaveh's, were all Nahri needed. "Did you lie to us?" she demanded, whirling on the grand wazir. "Why in God's name would you do such a thing?"

Kaveh shrank back, looking ashamed. "I'm sorry," he said hurriedly. "I needed to get you to safety, and Muntadhir was the only way I could think of to get you both to leave the hospital."

Jamshid drew up, looking shocked and wounded. "How could you let me think he was hurt?"

"I'm sorry, my son. I had no—"

Wajed interrupted. "It doesn't matter. None of you will be going to the Grand Temple. I have orders to have the two of you escorted to the palace," he said with a nod to Kaveh and Nahri. He hesitated, looking weary and worn down for a minute, before he continued. "Jamshid, you're to come with me."

Kaveh instantly edged in front of his son and Nahri. "I beg your pardon?"

The call came again, haunting waves of Geziriyya breaking the tense silence. Wajed stiffened, a muscle working in his face, as if whatever was being said caused him pain. He wasn't the only one. Half the men were Geziri, and they too looked visibly unsettled.

One went further, the sole Geziri archer standing in the frame of the neighboring Tukharistani Gate. He shouted something in their language. Wajed returned a terse response.

The archer clearly wasn't mollified. He argued back, gesturing at them and then at the gate that led back to the shafit neighborhoods. Nahri had no clue as to what he was saying, but it was seeming to resonate. The other Geziris shifted uncomfortably, a couple darting uncertain glances at each other.

Abruptly, the archer threw down his bow. He turned on his heel, but he didn't get far because with a single curt word from Wajed, another soldier shot him dead.

Nahri gasped, and Jamshid drew his sword, instantly moving closer to her.

But the Qaid wasn't looking at them, he was glaring at his men. "That is the penalty for treason, understand? There will be no arrests and no forgiveness. I do not care what you hear." He eyed the soldiers. "We take commands from only one man in Daevabad."

"What in the Creator's name is going on, Wajed?" Nahri demanded again. She, Kaveh, and Jamshid had drawn as close as they could on horseback.

"You can direct your questions to the king when you see him." Wajed hesitated. "Forgive me, Banu Nahida, but I have my orders."

He raised a hand, and the rest of the archers drew their bows, their arrows targeted on the Daevas.

"Wait!" Nahri cried. "What are you doing?"

Wajed drew a pair of iron-laced binds from his belt. "As I said, the king has requested that you and Kaveh be taken to him. Jamshid is to come with me."

"*No.*" Kaveh sounded desperate. "Ghassan isn't taking my son. Not again."

"Then I have instructions to shoot the three of you dead," Wajed said quietly. "Starting with the Banu Nahida."

Jamshid slid from his saddle. "Take me," he said immediately, dropping his sword to the ground. "Don't hurt them."

"No! Wajed, *please*, I beg you," Kaveh beseeched. "Just let him stay with me. We're no threat to you. Surely whatever Ghassan has to say to me and Nahri . . ."

"I have my orders, Kaveh," Wajed cut in, not ungently. "Take him," he said to his men and then glanced at her. "And I'd suggest you keep any possible sandstorms to yourself. We're all rather quick with our weapons." He tossed the iron cuffs to her. "You'll be putting those on if you care about their lives."

Kaveh lunged for his son. "Jamshid!"

A soldier hit him hard across the back of his skull with the flat of his blade, and Kaveh crumpled to the ground.

"Baba!" Jamshid sprang for his father but hadn't taken two steps before a pair of men grabbed him, pressing a knife to his throat.

"Your choice, Banu Nahida," Wajed said.

Jamshid's worried gaze darted between his father's slumped form and Nahri. "Let them take me, Nahri. Please. I can take care of myself."

No. Thinking quickly, she spun back on Wajed. "I want to speak to my husband," she insisted. "The emir would never permit this!"

"The emir does not command me," Wajed replied. "The cuffs. *Now*," he clarified as the knife pressed harder into Jamshid's throat.

Nahri cursed under her breath but slipped them on. The iron burned against her skin, her magic not gone, but deadened. A pair of soldiers instantly descended upon her, binding her wrists tightly so that she couldn't take the cuffs off.

Nahri glared at Wajed. "I will kill your king if you hurt him. I swear it to you, Qaid, on my ancestors' ashes. I will kill your king and then I will kill you."

Wajed merely inclined his head. Another pair of soldiers was binding Jamshid's hands.

"I'm going to get you out," she declared. "I promise. I'll get word to Muntadhir."

Jamshid swallowed. "Take care of yourself first. Please, Banu Nahida!" he shouted as they pulled him away. "We need you alive."

33

ALI

From a window at the top of the Citadel's stone tower, Ali surveyed the lake below. On this moonless night, it was darker than usual, a perfectly still pane of black reflecting the sky. In the distance, a narrow band of golden beach was all that separated it from the equally dark mountains.

He inhaled, the crisp air bracing. "The gates are closed?"

"Yes, my prince," Daoud replied. "The shafit district is as secure as possible. The gate in the Grand Bazaar has been sealed with magic and fortified with iron bars. Our people did the same." He cleared his throat. "The recitation of your speech by the muezzins had quite an effect."

The recitation of my speech will be the first charge they read at my trial. Ali had ordered his father's cruel plans revealed to the entire Geziri Quarter: sung by its muezzins and cried out by every imam and sheikh who knew him—respected clerics whose word would be trusted. The plans were followed by a far simpler call:

Ghassan al Qahtani asks that you abide the slaughter of our shafit kin.

Zaydi al Qahtani asks you to stop it.

His plan very much had the desired effect . . . more than even Ali had anticipated. Whether his people were feeling nostalgic for the proud cause that had brought them to Daevabad, fed up with corruption, or simply believed the Afshin-slayer who'd wandered their land digging wells and breaking bread with their relatives was the right man to follow, Ali couldn't say. But they had revolted, Geziri men and women spilling into the streets and seizing any soldiers who tried to stop them from going to the shafit district. Both neighborhoods were now under his control, a mix of soldiers loyal to Ali and well-armed civilians taking up positions throughout.

"The hospital?" he asked, disquiet rising in his heart. "Was the Banu Nahida . . ."

"She had just left," Daoud replied. "With the grand wazir and his son. They apparently went rushing out in some haste. We have soldiers positioned outside the hospital, but per your orders, none will go inside. The freed slave Razu is guarding the entrance and threatening to turn anyone who crosses her into a spider." The man said these words with a nervous glance, as if expecting Razu to pop out and transform him into an insect right then and there.

"Good. Make it known that if a single Daeva is harmed tonight by one of our men, I'll execute the perpetrator myself." The thought of the wounded Daevas still inside the hospital made Ali sick. He couldn't imagine how terrified they must have been to learn they were trapped in the building while the surrounding neighborhoods rebelled under the leadership of the "Afshin-slayer."

Ali's gaze fell on Wajed's desk. Needing access to its wealth of city maps, Ali had taken over the Qaid's office, but doing so felt like carving out a piece of his heart. He could not stand in this room without recalling the hours he'd spent staging battles with rocks and sticks as a young child while the Qaid worked above him. He'd read every book in here and examined every battle diagram, Wajed quizzing him with a far gentler affection than his own father ever had.

He will never forgive me for this, Ali knew. Wajed was loyal to the end, his father's closest companion since their shared childhood.

He turned to Lubayd. "Do you really think Aqisa can sneak into the harem?"

"I think Aqisa can do pretty much anything she sets her mind to," Lubayd replied. "Probably better than you or I."

Good. Ali needed Aqisa to get his letter to Zaynab; his sister would at least try to help him, this he knew. "God willing, my sister can convince Muntadhir to support us."

"And then?" Lubayd crossed his arms. "*You've* taken the Citadel. Why are you going to hand it back to anyone, let alone the brother you've been fighting with for months?" His gaze grew pointed. "People aren't taking to the street to make Muntadhir king, Ali."

"And I'm not doing this to be king. I want my brother and sister on my side. I *need* them on my side." For Ali was fairly certain his father had a plan in place on the chance Ali rebelled and took the Citadel. He'd made his opposition to the king quite clear and it was no secret he was well liked by the soldiers with whom he'd grown up. He knew his father; there was no way Ghassan hadn't come up with a strategy to defuse him.

But for Muntadhir, his devoutly loyal emir? For the Princess Zaynab, the proclaimed light of his eyes? Ali suspected his father's reaction would be murkier, slower, and emotional. Ali might have taken the Citadel, but success lay with his siblings. His *life* lay with his siblings. He'd offered terms to his father—a letter outlining the steps he wanted to take to ensure security while they investigated the attack—but Ali knew the moment he ordered the muezzins to reveal Ghassan's plans for the shafit that there was no going back. His father would not forgive such a breach in loyalty.

"I pray your brother has better sense than you." It was Abu Nuwas, bound on the floor and very angry. Ali had brought him up in what he suspected would be a futile effort to learn what his father might do next. "You brash fool. You should have gone to your father yourself rather than having those charges read aloud. That is not our people's way."

"I'd say a fair number of Geziris disagree with you," Ali argued. "As well as the majority of the Guard."

Abu Nuwas snorted. "You offered to double their salaries. I'd avoid the moral high ground if I were you, Prince Alizayd."

"My father erred when he chose to let his army go hungry rather than force the rich to pay their share." Ali drummed his fingers on the desk, restless. There was not much to do besides wait for a response from the palace, and yet every minute dragged like an hour.

You should enjoy them, he thought darkly. *There is a strong possibility they will be your last.* He paced before the wide window, contemplating his options. It had to be near midnight.

A pair of flies flew lazily past his face. Ali batted them away, but movement caught his eye outside the window, along with a growing buzz. He stepped over to the sill.

Lubayd joined him. "What is *that*?"

Ali didn't respond. He was just as astonished as his friend. What appeared to be hundreds, perhaps even thousands, of flies were swarming above the lake, buzzing and zipping as they rose steadily higher in the air, moving in skittering bursts toward the city.

A few more flew through the window. Lubayd caught one in his hands and then shook it hard to stun it. It fell to the stone sill.

"It looks like a sand fly, like one of the ones from back home." Lubayd poked it and the fly crumbled into ash. "A *conjured* sand fly?"

Ali frowned, running a finger over the remains. "Who would bother conjuring up an enormous swarm of sand flies?" Was this some sort of bizarre Navasatem tradition he wasn't aware of? He leaned out the window to watch as the last of the flies made their way past the lake and into the city itself.

Then he froze. Hidden by the twitching mass of flies overhead, something *else* had begun to move that had no business doing so. Ali opened his mouth to call out.

A presence thundered to life in his head.

He dropped to his knees with a gasp, the world going gray. He clutched his skull, crying out in pain as sweat erupted across his body. A scream that was not a scream, an urgent warning in a language without words, hissed in his mind, urging him to run, to swim, to flee.

It was gone nearly as quickly as it came. Lubayd was holding him, calling his name as he braced himself on the windowsill.

"What happened?" he demanded, shaking Ali's shoulder. "Brother, talk to me!"

Abruptly, all the flies in the room fell dead, a rain of ash tumbling around them. Ali barely noticed, his gaze locked on the window.

The lake was moving.

The dead water shivered, shaking off its stillness as the lake danced, small swells and currents playing on its surface. Ali blinked, convinced his eyes were playing tricks on him.

"Ali, say something!"

"The lake," he whispered. "They're back."

"Who's back? What are you . . ." Lubayd trailed off. "What in God's name is *that*?" he cried.

The water was rising.

It lifted from the earth in an undulating mass, a body of rushing black liquid that pulled from the shore, leaving behind a muddy bed of jagged crevasses and the bones of ancient shipwrecks. It rose higher and higher, blocking the stars and mountains to tower over the city.

The rough outline of a reptilian head formed, its mouth opening to reveal glistening fangs. The bellowing roar that followed shook Ali to his bones, drowning out the alarmed cries from the sentries below.

He was too shocked to do anything other than stare in disbelief at the utter impossibility before him.

They turned the Gozan River into a beast, a serpent the size of a mountain that rose to howl at the moon. The seemingly ridiculous story of a now-dead Afshin and the girl who declared herself Manizheh's daughter ran through Ali's head as the lake-beast howled at the sky.

And then it abruptly turned, its terrifying visage aimed directly at the Citadel.

"Run!" Lubayd shouted, dragging him to his feet. "Get out!"

There was a violent tearing, and then the floor buckled beneath him. The room spun and Ali tumbled through the air.

He slammed hard against the opposite wall, the wind knocked from his lungs. He caught a glimmer through the window, the black water rushing up . . .

And then Ali crashed into darkness.

34

NAHRI

Nahri glared at the guards. "I'm excellent with faces," she warned. "Be assured I won't forget yours."

One of the men snickered. "Good luck getting out of those binds."

Fuming, Nahri returned to pacing the low stone parapet. She and a still unconscious Kaveh e-Pramukh had been dragged back to the palace and deposited at a pavilion high upon the walls overlooking the lake to await the king. It was the same place she had once stargazed with Ali, though there was no hint of the fine furnishings and sumptuous feast she remembered. Instead they were alone with four Geziri warriors bristling with weapons, warriors whose eyes had yet to leave her.

She stopped at the edge, staring over the distant, deadly water as she tried to shift the iron cuffs lower, wincing at the burn. But far worse than the pain was her feeling of helplessness. She and Kaveh had been here for what felt like hours, Nahri watching the sky grow an inky black while Jamshid was taken God only knew where.

The still lake caught her eye. Had it not been cursed, she might have been tempted to jump for her freedom. It was a long fall that would likely break a bone or two, but she was a Nahid. She could always heal.

Except that it is cursed and will tear you into a thousand pieces. Frustrated, Nahri turned back, fighting the urge to burn something.

The look on her face must have been obvious. "Watch yourself, fire worshipper," one of the guards warned. "Believe me when I say none of us have patience for the Scourge's whore."

Nahri straightened up like a shot. "Call me that again and I'll see you dead before dawn."

He instantly moved forward, his hand dropping to the hilt of his zulfiqar before one of his fellows hissed a warning in Geziriyya, pulling him back.

"Banu Nahida?" Kaveh's voice was weak from where he lay slumped against the wall.

Forgetting the Geziri guard, Nahri hurried to the grand wazir's side. His eyes had blinked open, and he looked dazed. Unable to heal him, Nahri had settled for ripping a strip of cloth from his shirt and binding it around his head. Blood had soaked through the cloth in black splotches.

"Are you okay?" she asked urgently.

He touched his head and winced. "I . . . I think so." He sat up slowly. "What . . . where is Jamshid?"

"I don't know," Nahri confessed. "Wajed took him from the midan, and we've been up here since then."

Kaveh drew up, alarm flashing across his face. "What time is it?"

"Midnight, perhaps? Why?" she asked when alarm flashed across his eyes.

"Midnight?" he whispered. "Creator, no. I have to find him."

He grabbed her shoulder with his bound hands, and Nahri jumped at the breach in etiquette. "I need you to think, Nahri. Did they say anything about where they might be taking Jamshid? Anything at all?" His face looked gaunt in the dim light. "It wasn't the Citadel, was it?"

She jerked free. "I don't know. And you're not the only one with questions. Why did you lie about Muntadhir being hurt?"

Kaveh looked only slightly remorseful. "Because I needed you and Jamshid somewhere safe tonight. Lady Nisreen . . . she was supposed to stay with the two of you in the infirmary, but . . ." Sorrow creased his features. "The Grand Temple seemed the next safest option."

"Are you worried the shafit are planning another attack?"

Kaveh shook his head. He was toying with a ring on his hand, a gold band crowned with what appeared to be a copper-striped agate. "No, Banu Nahri. Not the shafit."

The door opened just then, the guards bowing their heads as Ghassan entered the pavilion. Nahri drew back, dread coursing through her. There was open rage in his eyes—an expression that contrasted sharply with the weary slump of his shoulders, and one that sent a shiver down her spine. Ghassan al Qahtani was not a man who easily betrayed his emotions.

He drew to a stop, looking coldly down at the Daevas on the ground. "Leave us," he snapped to the guards.

The soldiers were gone the next moment, closing the door behind them.

Nahri struggled to her feet. "What do you want?" she demanded. "How dare you drag us here when our people are wounded and grieving because of a lapse in *your* security?"

Ghassan tossed a scroll at her feet. "Are you responsible for this?" he asked.

Nahri picked it up. She recognized Ali's handwriting immediately. She read it . . . and then she read it again, convinced she'd misunderstood. The well-thought-out plans to spearhead an investigation into today's attacks and ensure security for the city until passions had died down.

The calm assurances that he would return his father's army when he was convinced there would be no retribution against the shafit.

Nahri stared at the words, willing them to rearrange. *You fool. You could have gone to Am Gezira. You could have found some doting wife and lived a peaceful life.*

"What?" Kaveh prompted, sounding worried. "What is it?"

Nahri dropped the scroll. "Ali took the Citadel."

Kaveh gasped. "He did *what*?"

Ghassan cut in. "The question remains, Banu Nahida. Are you and my son working together?"

"No," she said acidly. "Believe it or not, I did not have much time today between shrouding the dead and treating burned children to participate in a coup."

"Is that why you dragged us here?" Kaveh demanded, glaring at the king. "You've lost control of your fanatical son—a danger you should have dealt with years ago—and you're trying to pin the blame on us?"

Ghassan's eyes lit with challenge. "Oh, has my simpering grand wazir finally grown a spine? A rather rich accusation, Kaveh, considering the part you played in inflaming people's passions." His face grew stormy. "Did you think I wouldn't follow up on Ali's suspicions about the attack on the shafit camp? Did you think you could light a spark like that in this city—*my* city—and not have it explode in your face?"

Nahri's stomach dropped. It was one thing to hear the accusation from Ali—he could be a little overwrought—but the certainty in Ghassan's voice and the flush in Kaveh's cheeks confirmed what her heart had wanted to deny. She might not have trusted the grand wazir, but he was a fellow Daeva, a friend of Nisreen's, and Jamshid's father.

"You faked the attack on the Daeva couple," she whispered. "Didn't you?"

Kaveh's face was bright red. "You and Jamshid needed to see the truth about the shafit, and it would have happened sooner or later on its own—it has today! How can you possibly defend the dirt-bloods after what they did to the procession? They have no business being anywhere near your ancestors' hospital; they have no place in our world at all!"

Nahri jerked back like she'd been slapped.

But Kaveh wasn't done. He glared at Ghassan. "Nor do you. Daevabad has not seen a day of peace since Zaydi al Qahtani bathed it in Daeva blood, and you are as treacherous as your barbarian forefather." Emotion ripped through his voice. "I almost believed it, you know. Your act. The king who wished to unite our tribes." Nahri watched as angry tears filled his eyes. "It was a lie. Twenty years I served you; my son took half a dozen arrows to save yours, and you *used his life* to threaten me." He spat at Ghassan's feet. "Do not pretend you care for *anyone* but your own, you filthy sand fly."

Nahri instinctively took a step back. No one spoke to Ghassan like that. He did not brook the slightest dissent, let alone open insults from an upstart Daeva wazir.

That Ghassan smiled instead of opening Kaveh's throat was petrifying.

"You've wanted to say that for a long time, haven't you?" the king drawled. "Look at you, all full of spite and indignation . . . as if I have not accommodated your tribe's frivolous grievances again and again. As if *I* wasn't the one to lift you and your son out of your sad lives as petty provincial nobles." He crossed his arms. "Let me return the favor, Kaveh, for there is something I have also *long* wanted to tell you."

"Enough of this," Nahri interrupted. Jamshid was missing and Ali was in open revolt; she wasn't wasting time over whatever history Ghassan and Kaveh shared. "What do you want, Ghassan? And where is Jamshid?"

"Jamshid . . ." Ghassan's eyes glittered. "Now, oddly enough, there is a Daeva I like. Certainly more loyal than either of you, though I can't imagine from whom he inherited such wisdom. It clearly doesn't run in his family."

At her side, Kaveh tensed and Nahri frowned. "What's that supposed to mean?"

Ghassan paced closer, reminding her uncomfortably of a hawk stalking something small and fragile. "Did it never strike you as strange how confident I was of your identity, Banu Nahri? So *immediately* confident?"

"You told me I resemble Manizheh," Nahri said slowly.

The king clucked his tongue. "But enough that I'd make a scene in court having only spotted you from a distance?" He glanced at Kaveh. "What do you think, Grand Wazir? It seems you knew Manizheh *very well*. Does our Nahri resemble her strongly?"

Kaveh looked like he was having a hard time breathing, let alone answering. His hands were clenched into tight fists, his knuckles pale and bloodless. "Yes," he whispered.

Ghassan's eyes flashed in triumph. "Oh, come now, you can lie better than that. Not that it matters. She has something else. Something her mother had, something her uncle had. Not that either of them was aware of it. Bit embarrassing actually." He tapped the black mark on his temple, Suleiman's eight-pointed star. "You think you own a thing, and well . . ."

A frisson of danger tingled across her skin. Hating that she was playing into his game but seeing no way out, she pressed. "Why don't you try speaking straight for once?"

"Suleiman's seal, child. You bear a shadow of his mark . . . right here." Ghassan reached out to touch the side of her face, and

Nahri jerked away. "To me, it is clear as day." The king turned back to Kaveh, his gray eyes simmering with triumph and something else, something vicious and vindictive. "They all bear it, Grand Wazir. Every single person with Nahid blood. Manizheh. Rustam. Nahri." He paused, seeming to savor the moment. "Your Jamshid."

Kaveh shot to his feet.

"Sit back down," Ghassan snapped. The cruel humor was gone from his voice in an instant, the merciless cold of a despot replacing it. "Or the only place Jamshid—your Baga Nahid—will end up is in a shroud."

Nahri reeled, her hand going to her mouth. "Jamshid is a *Nahid*?" Bewildered and shocked, she struggled for words. "But he has no . . ."

Abilities. The word died on her tongue. Jamshid's desperate questions about the Rumi fire that had burned him and his abruptly healed wounds. The ancient Tukharistani he'd spoken to Razu . . . and the raw burst of power Nahri had felt when he clutched her hand and she summoned a sandstorm.

Jamshid was a Nahid. Nahri's eyes were suddenly wet. Jamshid was *family*.

And there was no way he knew it; he wasn't that good of a liar. She whirled on Kaveh. He'd dropped back to the ground at Ghassan's command but looked no less fierce. "You hid it from him," she accused. "How could you?"

Kaveh was shaking now, rocking back and forth. "I had to protect him from Ghassan. It was the only way."

The king scoffed. "Fine job you did of that; I knew that boy was a Nahid the moment you brought him to my court. The rest was rather easy to figure out." Hostility leached into his voice. "The summer of his birth was when Saffiyeh died. The summer Manizheh ignored my pleas to return to Daevabad early to save her queen."

"Saffiyeh was never her queen," Kaveh shot back. "And Manizheh got barely a week with her own child before she was forced to return to you once again."

"It was clearly enough time for her to do something to conceal Jamshid's abilities, wasn't it?" Malice twisted Ghassan's face. "She always considered herself so clever . . . and yet her son might have used those abilities when Darayavahoush turned on him. An irony in that: the last Baga Nahid nearly killed by his Afshin, all while trying to save a Qahtani."

Nahri looked away, heartsick. Dara probably would have thrown himself on his own sword if he'd known that truth. She leaned against the parapet, her legs suddenly weak. Ghassan and Kaveh were still arguing, and Nahri knew she should be paying attention, but suddenly all she wanted to do was escape this awful palace and find her brother.

"You should be grateful," Ghassan was saying. "I gave the two of you a life here. Wealthy, respected, powerful . . ."

"As long as we danced to your tune," Kaveh snapped. "Forget *our* desires, *our* ambitions; everything is in thrall to Ghassan al Qahtani's grand plans." His voice was cruel. "And you wonder why Manizheh refused you."

"I suspect the reason she refused me—however disappointing—sits in front of me now." Ghassan was eying Kaveh dismissively, but there was a resentment in his gray gaze that he couldn't entirely mask. "Manizheh clearly had a peculiar . . . taste."

Nahri's patience abruptly vanished. "Oh, get over yourselves," she hissed. "I'm not standing here listening to some old men bicker about a long-lost love. *Where is my brother?*"

Ghassan's expression darkened, but he answered. "Somewhere secure. Where he'll be staying, with people I trust, until the city is calm again."

"Until you beat us back into obedience, you mean," Nahri

said bitterly. "I've been down this path with you before. Why don't you just tell us what you want?"

Ghassan shook his head. "Direct as always, Banu Nahri . . . But I know your people. Right now, I imagine a good number of Daevas are hungry for shafit blood, and it's clear the shafit feel similarly. So let us settle things down." He turned to Kaveh. "You'll be taking the blame. You will confess to faking the camp assault and arming the shafit who attacked your procession."

"I had *nothing* to do with what happened to the procession," Kaveh said heatedly. "I would never!"

"I don't care," Ghassan said flatly. "You will take responsibility. The ruined grand wazir, driven to destruction by his own twisted fanaticism. You will confess to plotting against your Banu Nahida, and after unburdening yourself so, Kaveh . . . ." He nodded coolly toward the wall. "You will take your own life."

Kaveh's eyes went wide, and Nahri swiftly stepped forward. "I'm not going to let you—"

"I am not done." Something different, more complicated to read, flickered across Ghassan's face. "For your part, Banu Nahida, I am going to need you to send a letter to my youngest and inform him that you have been arrested and charged with being his co-conspirator in an attempted coup. And that you will be executed tomorrow at dawn should he not surrender."

Nahri felt the blood drain from her face. "*What?*"

Ghassan waved her off. "Believe it or not, I would rather not involve you, but I know my son. Ali might be happy to martyr himself, but I have no doubt he will no sooner see that letter in your handwriting than throw himself at my feet."

"And then?" she pressed. "What do you intend to do with him?"

The cold humor vanished from Ghassan's face. "He will be the one executed for treason."

No. Nahri exhaled, pressing her hands into fists. "I'm not going to help you trap him," she replied. "I'm glad he's taken the Citadel. I hope he takes the palace next!"

"He's not going to be able to take it by dawn," Ghassan said evenly. "And you'll not only write that letter, I'll have you dragged to the midan so you can weep for him to save you if necessary. Or I'll kill your brother."

Nahri recoiled. "You wouldn't." Her voice was shaking. "You wouldn't do that to Muntadhir."

Ghassan's brows lifted in faint surprise. "Not one to miss much, are you? Though, yes, Banu Nahida, I would. Indeed, Muntadhir would be wise to learn to keep his heart closer. He risks himself with such affections in this world."

"What would you even know about affection?" Kaveh cut in, his eyes wild. "You're a monster. You and your father used Manizheh's love for her brother to control her and now you plan to do the same to her daughter?" Kaveh glared at Ghassan. "How could you ever claim to care for her?"

Ghassan rolled his eyes. "Save me the false pieties, Kaveh. You've too much blood on your hands."

But Kaveh's words were the reminder that Nahri needed.

She closed her eyes. She'd tried so hard to wall herself off from the king, to mask her vulnerabilities and make sure there was no chink in the armor she drew around herself. He already had the fate of her tribe in one fist, had used the threat of violence against them to force her into obedience more than once for years.

But her efforts hadn't mattered. Because he had always had something so much closer. Precious. He'd built a chink into her armor from the start, and Nahri had never even known it was there.

She tried to think. If Ali had taken the Citadel, this was no mere palace revolt; the bulk of the Royal Guard was now out of

Ghassan's hands. She remembered the haunting waves of Geziriyya drifting over the air, recalling what she knew of Daevabad's neighborhoods. Ali could already be in control of the Geziri Quarter. The shafit district.

She opened her eyes. "You think he can do it, don't you?" she asked Ghassan. "You think Ali can beat you."

The king's eyes narrowed. "You're very out of your depth, Banu Nahida."

Nahri smiled; she felt sick. "I'm not. I used to be very good at this, you know. Reading a mark, spotting weaknesses. You and I actually have that in common." Her throat hitched. "And Jamshid . . . I bet you savored that secret." She inclined her head toward Kaveh. "I bet you delighted in it every time you saw him, contemplating the ways you could revenge yourself on the man who had the love of the woman you wanted. You wouldn't give that up easily."

Ghassan drew up. The king's face was calm, but Nahri didn't miss the heat in his voice. "None of this posturing will get your brother back any sooner."

I'm sorry, Jamshid. I'm so sorry. Nahri exhaled, fighting the deep, awful sadness wrapping her heart. "I won't help you."

Ghassan's eyes flashed. "I beg your pardon?"

"I won't help you," she repeated, hating herself. "I won't let you use my brother against me. Not for any reason."

Ghassan abruptly stepped closer. "If you don't do this, Banu Nahida, I'm going to kill him. I'm going to do it slowly and I will make you watch. So you may as well do us all the favor of simply obeying now."

Kaveh scrambled up, alarm twisting his expression. "Banu Nahri—"

Ghassan backhanded him across the face. The king was obviously stronger than he looked; the blow sent Kaveh sprawling to the floor, a burst of blood on his mouth.

Nahri gasped. But the casual, brutal violence only made her more determined. Ghassan was a monster. But he was a desperate one, and Nahri trembled to think what he would do to Daevabad in the wake of a failed coup.

Which meant she'd have to do all she could to make sure it didn't fail. "You're wasting your time, Ghassan. I'm not going to break. This city beats in my family's blood. In my blood." Her voice shook slightly. "In my brother's blood. And if the last Nahids need to die to save it . . ." She stilled her trembling, lifting her chin in defiance. "Then we'll have served our people well."

Ghassan stared at her for a very long moment. His expression wasn't inscrutable now, and he didn't bother arguing with her. Nahri had read her mark.

And she knew he was about to destroy her for it.

He stepped back. "I'm going to tell Jamshid who he really is," he said. "Then I'm going to tell him how his sister, having grown tired of sleeping with the man he loves, betrayed them both to save a man he hates." The words were crude—the last attempt of an angry old man who'd traded decency for a throne that was about to be wrenched away by his own blood. "Then I will finish the job your Afshin started and have your brother scourged to death."

"No, Ghassan, wait!" Kaveh threw himself before the king. "She didn't mean it. She'll write the letter—ah!" He cried out as Ghassan kicked him in the face, stepping around his body and reaching for the door.

With a wail, Kaveh smashed his hand against the stone. Nahri heard a sharp crack, his ring shattering.

A strange coppery haze burst from the broken gem.

In the time it took Nahri to draw a quick breath, the vapor had bloomed to engulf the grand wazir.

"Kaveh, what is that?" she asked sharply as copper tendrils darted out like a dancer's hand, reaching, searching. There was something familiar about the movement, about the metallic shimmer.

The king briefly glanced back, looking more annoyed than anything.

The vapor rushed at the copper relic bolted through his ear.

It instantly melted, and Ghassan cried out, clasping his head as the liquid metal surged into his ear. Suleiman's seal flashed on his cheek, and Nahri swooned, her magic gone.

But it didn't last. The king's eyes went wide and still as a haze of copper veiled their gray depths.

Then Ghassan al Qahtani fell dead at her feet.

Her abilities slammed back into her. Nahri covered her mouth with a startled cry, staring in shock as copper-flecked black blood poured from the king's ears, mouth, and nose.

"By the Most High, Kaveh," she whispered. "What have you done?"

"What had to be done." Kaveh was already crossing to Ghassan's body, stepping into the pool of spreading blood without hesitation. He retrieved the king's khanjar, quickly using it to slice through the binds on his wrists. "We don't have much time," he warned. "We need to find Jamshid and secure Muntadhir."

Nahri stared at him. Had he lost his mind? Ghassan's guards were just outside the door. They weren't getting away, let alone finding Jamshid and "securing" Muntadhir, whatever that meant. "Kaveh, I think—"

"I do not care what you think." The barely checked hostility in his voice shocked her. "Respectfully . . ." It sounded like he was struggling not to shout. "You're not the one making decisions tonight. A thing that is clearly for the best." He glanced at her, his eyes simmering with anger. "You will answer for the choice you just made. Not tonight. Not to me . . . but you will answer."

A fly buzzed past her ear. Nahri barely noticed; she was speechless. Then another swept past her face, brushing her cheek.

Kaveh turned to look at the sky. More flies were coming, a swarm from the direction of the lake.

Grim determination swept his features. "It is time."

There was an angry shout from beyond the closed door.

Nahri instantly recognized the voice. "Muntadhir!" She lunged for the door. His father might be lying in a pool of blood on the ground, but right now Nahri trusted her estranged husband far more than the mad wazir who'd orchestrated a riot and assassinated a king.

"Nahri?" Muntadhir's voice was muffled through the door, but from his tone, he was clearly arguing with the guards on the other side.

Kaveh shoved himself between Nahri and the door. "Muntadhir cannot come in, Banu Nahri. He cannot be exposed to this."

"Exposed to *what*?" she cried. "The fact that you just murdered his father?"

But as she tried to wrestle past him, she suddenly spotted what Kaveh meant.

A coppery haze was reforming above the dead king. Glittering particles, like minuscule metal stars, swirled up from Ghassan's pooling blood, forming a cloud twice the size of the one that had escaped Kaveh's shattered ring.

Nahri instantly backed away, but the vapor flowed harmlessly past her and Kaveh, separating and undulating around her waist like a wave. The flies zipped over them all, dozens now.

Muntadhir broke down the door.

"I don't care what he said!" he shouted, trying to shove past a pair of guards. "She's my damned wife and . . ." Muntadhir recoiled, his eyes locking on his father's bloody body. *"Abba?"*

The guards reacted more swiftly. "My king!" Two flew to Ghassan, the other two going for Nahri and Kaveh. Muntadhir didn't move from the door frame, falling heavily against it as if it was all that was keeping him on his feet.

The flies suddenly flickered into flashes of fire, dissolving into a rain of ash.

"Muntadhir, I didn't do it!" Nahri cried as one of the guards grabbed her. "I swear! I had nothing to do with this!"

A roar broke the air, a scream like the crash of ocean waves and the bellow of a crocodile. It sounded dully distant, but it set every hair on her body on end.

Nahri had heard that roar before.

The vapor struck again.

The guards who'd gone to Ghassan screamed, clutching their heads. The soldier who'd seized her dropped her arm and backed away with a cry, but he wasn't fast enough. His relic dashed into his ear with vindictive speed. He shrieked in pain, clawing at his face.

"No." Kaveh's horrified whisper cut through the wails. His gaze locked on Muntadhir, still framed against the door. "This wasn't how it was supposed to happen!"

Muntadhir's eyes went bright with fear.

Nahri didn't hesitate. She shot to her feet, running across the pavilion as the coppery cloud, now tripled in size, flew at her husband.

"Banu Nahida, wait!" Kaveh cried. "You don't—"

She didn't hear what else he had to say. The vapor just behind her, Nahri threw herself at Muntadhir.

35

NAHRI

Too late, Nahri remembered that the door opened on to a staircase.

Muntadhir grunted as she hit him hard in the stomach and
then he cried out as he lost his balance. They tumbled down the
stairs, various limbs bashing against the dusty stone before they
landed in a heap at the bottom.

Pinned beneath her, Muntadhir swore. Nahri gasped, the
wind knocked from her lungs. Her abilities were still dulled from
the iron cuffs, and she was bruised and battered, a searing pain
running down her left wrist.

Muntadhir blinked and then his eyes went wide, locking on
something past her shoulder. "Run!" he cried, scrambling to his
feet and yanking her up.

They fled. "Your relic!" Nahri wheezed. In the opposite corridor from the one they'd taken, someone cried out in Geziriyya.

Then, chillingly, the wail abruptly cut out into silence. "Take out your relic!"

He reached for it as they ran, his fingers fumbling.

Nahri glanced over her shoulder, horrified to see the coppery haze lapping toward them like a hungry, malevolent wave. "Muntadhir!"

He yanked it out, hurling the copper bolt away just as the vapor engulfed them. Nahri held her breath, terrified. And then it passed, rushing down the corridor.

Muntadhir fell to his knees, shaking so hard Nahri could hear his teeth rattling. "What the hell was that?" he gasped.

Her heart was pounding, the echo throbbing in her head. "I have no idea."

Tears were running down his face. "My father . . . *Kaveh*. I'll kill him." He staggered to his feet and turned back toward the way they had come, one hand braced on the wall.

Nahri moved to block him. "That's not what's important right now."

He glared at her, suspicion crossing his face. "Did you—"

"No!" she snapped. "Really, Muntadhir? I just threw myself down a stairwell to save you."

He flushed. "I'm sorry. I just . . . he . . ." His voice cracked, and he wiped his eyes roughly.

The grief laced in his words dulled her temper. "I know." She cleared her throat, holding her bound wrists out. "Would you get this off me?"

He pulled free his khanjar, quickly slicing through the cloth binds and helping her out of the iron cuffs. She inhaled, relieved as her powers burned through her veins, her blistered skin and dark bruises instantly healing.

Muntadhir had opened his mouth to speak again when a voice echoed down the hall. "Banu Nahida!"

It was Kaveh.

Nahri clapped a hand over her husband's lips, dragging him into the shadows. "Let's not find out if he has any other tricks up his sleeve," she whispered. "We need to warn the rest of the Geziris in the palace."

Even in the shadows, she could see his face pale. "You think it will spread that far?"

"Did it look like it was stopping?"

"Fuck." It seemed an appropriate answer. "My God, Nahri . . . do you know how many Geziris are in the palace?"

She nodded grimly.

There was a sudden rumble, the floor shuddering beneath their feet. It lasted only a second, and then was gone.

Nahri braced herself. "What was *that*?"

Muntadhir shuddered. "I don't know. It feels like the entire island just shook." He ran a hand nervously over his beard. "That vapor . . . do you have any idea what it might be?"

Nahri shook her head. "No. It looked somewhat similar to the poison used on your brother, though, didn't it?"

"My brother." Her husband's expression darkened and then panic swept his face. "*My sister.*"

"Muntadhir, wait!" Nahri cried.

But he was already running.

ZAYNAB'S APARTMENTS WEREN'T CLOSE, AND BY THE time they made it to the harem garden, Muntadhir and Nahri were both thoroughly out of breath. The scarf she'd tied around her head in the hospital was long gone, her curls plastered to her damp skin.

"Jamshid was always telling me I should exercise more," Muntadhir panted. "I should have listened."

Jamshid. His name was like a knife to her heart.

She darted a look at Muntadhir. Well, there was one situation that had just grown more complicated. "Your father had him arrested," she said.

"I know," Muntadhir replied. "Why do you think I was banging down the door? I heard Wajed took him out of the city. Did my father tell Kaveh where?"

"Out of the *city*? No, your father said nothing about that."

Muntadhir groaned in frustration. "I should have stopped all this sooner. When I heard he had you as well . . ." He trailed off, sounding angry with himself. "Did he at least tell you what he wanted with Jamshid?"

Nahri hesitated. Ghassan might have been a monster, but he was still Muntadhir's father, and Nahri didn't need to add to her husband's grief right now. "Ask me later."

"If we're alive later," Muntadhir muttered. "Ali finally lost his mind, by the way. He seized the Citadel."

"It would seem an excellent night to be in the Citadel instead of the palace."

"Fair point." They crossed under the delicate archway leading to the pavilion that fronted Zaynab's apartment. A rich teak platform floated over the canal, framed by the wispy fronds of slender palm trees.

Zaynab was there, perched on a striped linen couch and examining a scroll. Relief coursed through Nahri, followed swiftly by confusion when she saw who was seated with the princess.

"*Aqisa?*"

Muntadhir marched across the platform. "Of course you're here. Doing my brother's dirty work, I assume?"

Aqisa leaned back, a move that revealed the sword and the khanjar belted at her waist. Looking unbothered, she took a leisurely sip of coffee from the paper-thin porcelain cup in her hand before responding. "He asked me to convey a message."

Zaynab deftly rolled the scroll back up, looking uncharacteristically nervous. "It seems Ali was quite inspired by our last conversation," she said, tripping over the last words. "He wants us to remove Abba."

Muntadhir's face crumpled. "We're beyond that, Zaynab." He sank into the couch beside his sister, gently taking her hand. "Abba is dead."

Zaynab jerked back. "What?" When he didn't say anything further, her hand flew to her mouth. "Oh God . . . please don't tell me Ali—"

"Kaveh." Muntadhir reached for his sister's relic, carefully removing it from her ear. "He unleashed some sort of magical vapor that targets these." He held up the relic before hurling it away into the depths of the garden. "It's bad, Zaynab. I watched it kill four guards in a matter of seconds."

At that, Aqisa ripped out her own relic, sending it flying into the night.

Zaynab had started to cry. "Are you sure? Are you sure he's really dead?"

Muntadhir hugged her tightly. "I'm sorry, ukhti."

Not wanting to intrude on the grieving siblings, Nahri edged closer to Aqisa. "You came from the Citadel? Is Ali all right?"

"He has an army and isn't trapped in a palace with some murderous mist," Aqisa replied. "I'd say he's doing better than we are."

Nahri looked out at the dark garden, her thoughts roiling. The king was dead, the grand wazir was a traitor, the Qaid was gone, and Ali—the only one of them with military experience—was involved in a mutiny across the city.

She took a deep breath. "I . . . I think that leaves us in charge."

The night sky abruptly darkened further—which Nahri thought a rather apt response. But when she glanced up, her mouth went dry. A half-dozen smoky, equine shapes with wings of flashing fire were racing toward the palace.

Aqisa followed her gaze and then grabbed her, pulling her swiftly inside the apartment. Zaynab and Muntadhir were right behind them. As they bolted the door, they heard several thudding crashes and the distant echo of screams.

"I don't think Kaveh is working alone," Muntadhir whispered, his face ashen.

Three pairs of gray-toned eyes settled on her. "I have nothing to do with this," Nahri protested. "My God, do you really think I'd be in your company if I did? Surely you both know me better than that."

"I believe that," Zaynab muttered.

Muntadhir sank to the floor. "Then who *could* he be working with? I've never seen magic like this."

"I don't think that's what's most important right now," Zaynab said softly. There were more shouts from somewhere deep in the palace, and they all went quiet for a moment listening before Zaynab continued. "Nahri . . . could the poison spread to the rest of the city?"

Nahri recalled the wild energy of the vapor that had chased them and nodded slowly. "The Geziri Quarter," she whispered, voicing the fear she could see in Zaynab's eyes. "My God, if it reaches there . . ."

"They need to be warned at once," Aqisa said. "I will go."

"As will I," Zaynab declared.

"Oh no, you won't," Muntadhir replied. "If you think I'm about to let my little sister go dashing off while the city is under attack—"

"Your *little sister* isn't asking permission, and there are people who will believe my word more readily than Aqisa's. And you're needed here. Both of you," Zaynab added, nodding at Nahri. "Dhiru, if Abba is dead, you need to retrieve the seal. Before Kaveh or whoever he's working with figures out how to do so."

"Suleiman's seal?" Nahri repeated. She hadn't even given a thought to that—the king's succession seemed a world away. "Is it with your father?"

Muntadhir looked like he was about to be sick. "Something like that. We'd need to get back to him. To his body."

Aqisa locked eyes with Zaynab. "The chest," she said simply.

Zaynab nodded and beckoned them farther into her apartment. It was as rich and finely appointed as Muntadhir's, though not as cluttered with artwork. Or wine cups.

The princess knelt beside a large, elaborate wooden chest and whispered an unlocking charm over it. As the lid sprang open Nahri peered inside.

It was entirely filled with weapons. Sheathed daggers and scimitars wrapped in silk rested beside an oddly lovely mace, a crossbow, and some sort of barbed, jeweled chain.

Nahri didn't know whose expression was more shocked, hers or Muntadhir's. "My God," she said. "You really are Ali's sister."

"What . . . where did you . . . ," Muntadhir began weakly.

Zaynab looked slightly flustered. "She's been teaching me," she explained, nodding to Aqisa.

The warrior woman was already selecting blades, looking unbothered by Nahri and Muntadhir's reactions. "A Geziri woman her age should have mastered at least three weapons. I have been making up for an abominable lapse in her education." She pressed a sword and the crossbow into Zaynab's hands and then clucked her tongue. "Stop trembling, sister. You'll do fine."

Nahri shook her head, and then considered the chest, knowing well her limitations. Quickly, she pulled out a pair of small daggers, the heft reminding her of something she might have used to cut purses back in Cairo. For a moment, she thought longingly of Dara's blade back in her room.

I wish I'd had a few more knife-throwing lessons with him, she thought. Not to mention that the legendary Afshin would have probably made for a better partner in a palace under siege than her visibly skittish husband.

She took a deep breath. "Anything else?"

Zaynab shook her head. "We'll sound the alarm in the Geziri Quarter and then head to the Citadel to alert Ali. He can lead the Royal Guard back. Warn every Geziri you see in the palace, and tell them to do the same."

Nahri swallowed. It could be hours before Ali returned with the Guard. She and Muntadhir would be on their own—facing God only knew what—until then.

"You can do this," Zaynab said. "You have to." She hugged her brother. "Fight, Dhiru. There will be time for grief, but right now, you're our king, and Daevabad comes first." Her voice grew fierce. "I'll be back with your Qaid."

Muntadhir gave a jerky nod. "God be with you." He glanced at Aqisa. "Please keep my sister safe." He nodded toward the pavilion. "Take the stairs we came from. There's a passage close by that leads to the stables."

Zaynab and Aqisa left swiftly. "Are you ready?" Nahri asked when she and Muntadhir were alone.

He laughed as he strapped a wicked-looking sword to his waist. "Not in the slightest. You?"

"God, no." Nahri grabbed another needle-sharp dagger and flipped it into her sleeve. "Let's go die."

36

ALI

Ali floated peacefully in warm darkness, wrapped tight in the embrace of the water. It smelled of salt and mud, of life, gently teasing and tugging at his clothes. A pebbly soft tendril stroked his cheek while another twined around his ankle.

A throbbing at the back of his head slowly brought him to the present. Dazed, Ali opened his eyes. Darkness surrounded him. He was submerged in water so deep and so clouded by muddy silt that he could barely see. Memories came to him in pieces. The watery beast. The Citadel's tower tumbling through the air . . .

The lake. He was in Daevabad's lake.

Sheer panic tore through him. He thrashed, trying desperately to free himself from whatever held him. His robe, he realized, blindly fumbling. The crumbled remains of some sort of brick wall had pinned it to the lake bed. Ali wrenched it off, kicking madly for the surface. The smell of ash and blood grew thicker on the water, but he ignored it, fighting past floating debris.

He finally broke through. He gasped for breath, pain surging through him.

The lake was in chaos.

Ali might as well have emerged onto a scene from the darkest circle of hell. Screams filled the air, cries for help, for mercy, in all the djinn languages he knew. Layered over them were moans, feral, hungry sounds that Ali couldn't place.

Oh, God . . . and the water. It wasn't just debris that surrounded him, it was bodies. Hundreds of djinn soldiers, floating dead in their uniforms. And when Ali saw the reason, he cried out, tears springing to his eyes.

Daevabad's Citadel—the proud symbol of Zaydi al Qahtani's rebellion, of the Geziri tribe, Ali's home for nearly two decades—had been destroyed.

Its once mighty tower had been ripped from its moorings and dragged into the lake, only a crumbled hump remaining above the water. Jagged gashes, as if from the claws of some massive creature, had raked through the remaining buildings, through the soldiers' barracks and across the training yards, making furrows so deep that the lake had filled them. The rest of the complex was on fire. Ali could see skeletal figures moving against the smoke.

Tears ran silently down his cheeks. "No," he whispered. This was a nightmare, another awful vision from the marid. "Stop this!"

Nothing happened. Ali took in the sight of the bodies again. Djinn murdered by the marid's curse did not remain floating upon the water; they were torn apart and swallowed by its depths, never to be seen again.

The curse on the lake was gone.

"I see someone!"

Ali turned toward the voice to spot a makeshift boat, one of the carved wooden doors of the tower, making its way toward him, crewed by a pair of Ayaanle soldiers wielding broken beams as oars.

"We've got you, brother," one of the soldiers said, hauling him aboard. His golden eyes went wide when he glanced at Ali. "Aye, praise God . . . it's the prince!"

"Bring him over!" Ali heard another man cry from some distance away.

They paddled awkwardly through the water. Ali had to turn away from the sight of the door pushing through the thick clutter of bodies, his fellows in uniform, too many of their faces familiar.

This isn't real. It can't be real. But it didn't feel like one of his visions. There was no alien presence whispering in Ali's head. There was just bewilderment, grief, and carnage.

As they neared the ruins of the Citadel, the remains of the toppled tower grew larger, rising from the lake like a lost island. A shattered section of its exterior shielded the few dozen warriors who'd gathered there. Some were curled around themselves, weeping. But Ali's gaze immediately flew to the ones who were fighting, several soldiers fending off a pair of thin, wraith-like creatures whose tattered shrouds clung wetly to their wasted bodies.

One was Lubayd, swinging his sword wildly. With a disgusted cry, he decapitated one of the leering creatures and kicked the body back into the lake.

Ali could have wept with relief. His best friend, at least, had survived the Citadel's destruction.

"We found the prince!" the Ayaanle soldier at his side cried. "He's alive!"

Lubayd whirled around. He was there by the time they arrived, yanking Ali to his feet and throwing his arms around him in a tight hug.

"Ali, brother, thank God . . . ," he choked out. "I'm sorry . . . the water came so fast, and when I couldn't find you in the room—"

Ali could barely manage a response. "I'm all right," he croaked.

A scream cut the air, a plea in Geziriyya. "No, don't! God, please!"

Ali lurched to the edge of the ruined tower, catching sight of the man who'd cried out: a Geziri soldier who'd managed to make it back to the beach only to be mobbed by the skeletal beings. They surrounded him, dragging him to the sand. Ali saw teeth and nails and mouths bearing down . . .

And then he couldn't watch, his stomach rising. He spun back around as the djinn's guttural cry was cut short.

"They . . . are they—" He couldn't even say the word.

Lubayd nodded. He looked shattered. "They're ghouls. It's what they do."

Ali shook his head in denial. "They can't be ghouls. There are no ifrit in Daevabad to summon ghouls—and certainly no dead humans!"

"Those are ghouls," Lubayd said firmly. "My father and I came upon a pair devouring a human hunter once." He flinched. "It's not a sight one forgets."

Ali felt faint. He took a deep breath; he couldn't fall apart. Not now. "Did anyone see what attacked the Citadel in the first place?"

Lubayd nodded, pointing to a thin Sahrayn man rocking back and forth, his arms wrapped tightly around his knees. "He was the first one out, and the things he's saying . . ." He trailed off, looking nauseated. "You should talk to him."

His heart in his throat, Ali approached the Sahrayn man. He knelt at his side, laying a hand on his shivering arm. "Brother," he started softly. "Can you tell me what you saw?"

The man kept rocking, his eyes bright with terror. "I was keeping watch on my ship," he whispered. "We were moored over there." He pointed to the ruined pier where a broken Sahrayn sandship had been driven up onto the shattered docks. "The lake . . . the water . . . it spun itself into a monster. It attacked the Citadel. Ravaged it, pulling what it could back into its depths." He swallowed, shaking harder. "The force of it threw me in the lake. I thought the curse would kill me . . . When it didn't, I started swimming . . . and then I saw them."

"Saw what?" Ali pressed.

"Warriors," the man whispered. "They came racing out of the lake on the backs of smoky horses with their bows drawn. They started shooting the survivors and then . . . and then . . ." Tears were rolling down his cheeks. "The dead came from the water. They swarmed my boat as I watched." His shoulders shook. "My captain . . ." He started to weep harder. "They tore out his throat with their teeth."

Ali's stomach plummeted, but he forced himself to peer through the darkness at the beach. Yes, he could see an archer now: a racing horse, the glimmer of a silver bow. An arrow went flying . . .

Another scream, and then silence. Fury surged through Ali, burning away his fear and panic. Those were his people out there.

He turned to study the ruined Citadel. And then his heart stopped. A ragged hole had been punched into the wall facing the street.

Ali grabbed the Sahrayn man's arm again. "Did you see anything go through there?" he demanded. *"Are those things in our city?"*

The sailor shook his head. "The ghouls, no . . . but the riders . . ." He nodded. "At least half of them. Once they were past the city walls . . ." His voice turned incredulous. "Prince Alizayd, their horses—they *flew* . . ."

"Where?" Ali demanded. "Where did you see them fly?"

The pity in the man's eyes filled Ali with awful, knowing dread. "The palace, my prince."

Ali shot to his feet. This was no random attack. He couldn't imagine who—or what—was capable of something like this, but he recognized a strategy when he saw one. They'd come for the Guard first, annihilating the djinn army before it could muster to protect the next target: the palace.

My family. "We need to get to the beach," he declared.

The Sahrayn man looked at him as though he'd gone insane. "You won't be able to get to the beach. Those archers are shooting everything that moves, and the few djinn who make it out are being eaten alive by ghouls the moment they step out of the water!"

Ali shook his head. "We cannot let those things into our city." He watched as a soldier dispatched another pair of ghouls when they attempted to climb upon the ruined tower, their gaping mouths full of rotted teeth. The man did so fairly easily, a single sweep of his blazing zulfiqar severing both in two.

They are not invincible, Ali noted. *Not at all.* It was their numbers that gave them an advantage; a single, terrified djinn, exhausted from navigating a gauntlet of arrows, stood no chance against dozens of hungry ghouls.

Across the water, another djinn was attempting to climb onto a floating bit of wreckage. Ali watched helplessly as a torrent of arrows cut him down. A small band of the mysterious archers had set themselves up on a section of broken wall that ran between the water and the ruined Citadel complex. Right now, Ali and his fellow survivors were safe, a shell of the tower curving up to protect them from the archers' view. But he didn't imagine their reprieve would last for long.

He examined the stretch of water separating their small sanctuary from Daevabad's shore. It was a manageable swim if not for the fact that anyone who tried would be visible to the archers the entire time.

A decision settled upon him. "Come here," he said, raising his voice. "All of you."

Ali waited for them to do so, taking advantage of the moment to study the survivors. A mix from all five of the djinn tribes, mostly men. He knew nearly all by face, if not by name—they were all Royal Guard except the Sahrayn sailor. A few cadets, a handful of officers, and the rest infantry. They looked terrified and bewildered and Ali couldn't blame them. They'd trained all their lives as warriors, but their people hadn't seen true war in centuries. Daevabad was supposed to be a refuge from the rest of the magical world: from ghouls and ifrit, from water-beasts capable of dragging down a tower that had stood for centuries.

He took a deep breath, well aware of the near suicidal nature of the counterattack he was about to propose. "I don't know what's happening," he started. "I don't think any of us do. But we're not safe here." He gestured to the mountains, looming far from the distant shore. "The curse might be gone from the lake, but I don't think many of us could make that swim. The mountains are too far away. The city, however, is not."

The Sahrayn sailor shuddered again. "Everyone who's made it to that beach has been slaughtered." His voice rose. "We should just take blades to each other's throats—it's a better fate than being eaten alive."

"They're picking us off," Ali argued. "We stand a better chance if we fight together . . ." He eyed the men around him "Would you stay here only to be killed later? Look at what they did to the Citadel. Do you think that wasn't deliberate? They came after the Royal Guard first, and if you think whatever is attacking us is going to have mercy on a band of stranded survivors, you're a fool."

A Geziri captain with a nasty gash across his face spoke up. "We'd be in view of those archers. They'll see us swimming and have us riddled with arrows before we even get close to the shore."

"Ah, but they won't see me coming." Ali kicked off his sandals. It would be easier to swim without them. "I'll stay under the water until I get to the wall."

The captain stared at him. "Prince Alizayd . . . your courage is admirable, but you can't swim that length underwater. And even if you could, you're just one man. I counted at least a dozen of those warriors and probably a hundred ghouls. It's suicide."

"He can do it." It was Lubayd, his voice intense. He met Ali's gaze, and from the mix of grief and admiration in his friend's eyes, Ali could tell Lubayd knew what he was preparing to do. "He doesn't fight like the rest of us."

Still seeing uncertainty on too many faces, Ali raised his voice. "Daevabad is our home! You all took oaths to defend it, to defend the innocents within who are about to be butchered by the same monsters who just killed so many of our brothers and sisters. You *will* get back to that beach. Gather all the weapons you can. Help each other swim. Paddle on pieces of wood. I don't care how you do it, but get across. *Fight.* Stop those things before they get into the city."

By his last words, a good number of the men were rising to their feet, grim but determined, but not all.

"We'll die," the Sahrayn sailor said hoarsely.

"Then you will die a martyr." Ali glared at those still sitting. "Stand up!" he roared. "Your fellows lie dead, your women and children are defenseless, and you're sitting here weeping for yourselves? Have you no shame?" He paused, meeting each of their gazes in turn. "You all have a choice. You can end this night a hero, with your families safe, or you end it with them in Paradise, their entrance bought with your blood." He drew his zulfiqar, fire blazing down its length. *"STAND UP!"*

Lubayd raised his sword with a wild—and slightly frightened—cry. "Come, you puffed-up city-born brats!" he goaded. "What happened to all the crowing I've been hearing about your bravery? Don't you want to be sung about in the stories they'll tell of this night? Let's go!"

That brought the rest of them to their feet. "Prepare yourselves," Ali ordered. "Be ready to go as soon as they're distracted."

His heart racing, he shoved his zulfiqar back into its sheath, ripping a length from his ruined dishdasha to secure his blades.

Lubayd grabbed his wrist, pulling him close. "Don't you fucking die, Alizayd al Qahtani," he said, pressing his brow to Ali's. "I did not drag your starving ass from a crevasse to see you eaten by ghouls."

Ali fought the tears pricking his eyes; they both knew there was little chance he was making it off the beach alive. "God be with you, my friend."

He turned away. Before he could show the fear coursing through his blood, before the others could see even a second of hesitation, Ali dove into the lake.

He swam deep, the motion throwing him back into his memory of the marid nightmare. Though the water was dark with silt, he caught sight of the lake bed below. It was muddy and gray, a pale imitation from the lush marine plain of his dream.

Could the marid be behind all this? Ali wondered, remembering their rage. Had they returned to take back their home?

He kept swimming. Ali was fast and it wasn't long before he caught sight of the wall he was looking for. He took care to press himself close against it as he silently broke the water's surface.

Voices. Ali listened closer. He wasn't sure what he expected—the gibberish of some unknown demons, the slithering tongue of the marid—but what he heard froze his blood.

It was Divasti.

They were being attacked by *Daevas*? Ali glanced up, past a narrow lip of overhanging rock, and caught a glimpse of a young man. He looked as though he could be a Daeva, dressed in a charcoal-colored coat and black leggings, the dark colors blending perfectly with the shadows.

How in God's name did a band of Daevas come through the lake armed with ghouls and flying horses?

The Daeva man suddenly drew up, his attention narrowing on the lake. He reached for his bow . . .

Ali was out of the water in the next breath. He pulled himself onto the wall before the shocked eyes of the man, drew his zulfiqar, and plunged the fiery blade into the archer's chest.

The man didn't have a chance to scream. Ali shoved him off the end of his zulfiqar and knocked him into the water. He'd turned to face the others before a splash even sounded.

Daevas, three of them. Another archer—a woman with a long black braid—and two men armed with a broadsword and a mace. They looked taken aback by his arrival, aghast at their comrade's death. But not afraid.

And they reacted a *lot* faster than he would have imagined.

The first drew his broadsword, the acrid smell warning Ali of iron before it sparked hard against his zulfiqar. The man danced back, careful to avoid the poisoned flame. It was a move Ali associated with other Geziris, with warriors who'd trained against zulfiqars.

Where had a Daeva man learned *that*?

Ali ducked, narrowly avoiding the studded mace that swung past his face. The Daevas neatly fanned out to surround him, moving in perfect unison without saying a word.

Then the remaining archer hissed in Djinnistani. "It's the Afshin-slayer." She let out a mocking laugh. "Bit of a disingenuous title, sand fly."

The swordsman lunged forward, forcing Ali to block him, and again the mace-bearer used the distraction to attack. This time the mace clipped Ali's shoulder, the studs tearing out a patch of flesh.

Ali gasped at the burn, and one of the Daeva men leered at him. "They'll eat you alive, you know," he said, gesturing to the ghouls below. "Not us, of course. Orders and all. But I bet they smell *your* blood on the air right now. I bet it's making them ravenous."

The three warriors stepped closer, forcing Ali to the edge of the wall. He didn't know who had trained the Daevas, but they'd done a damn good job, the soldiers moving as if they were of one mind.

But then the swordsman pressed too close. Ali dropped, seeing his opening and lunging at the man holding the mace. He caught him clean across one thigh, the poisoned flames leaving a line of swiftly blackening flesh in their wake.

"Bahram!" the archer cried in horror. The man looked shocked, his hand going to the fatal wound. Then he glanced at Ali, his eyes wild.

"For the Banu Nahida," he whispered and rushed forward.

Caught *completely* off guard by the man's declaration, Ali was ill-prepared for his desperate charge. He raised his zulfiqar in defense, but it didn't matter. The man took the strike through the stomach, throwing himself on Ali and sending them both tumbling over the wall.

Ali landed with a bone-jarring impact on the wet sand. A wave passed over his face, and he choked on the water, his shoulder throbbing. His zulfiqar was gone, stuck in the body of the Daeva man he'd killed, now lying deeper in the shallows.

A high-pitched moan had him struggling to his knees, the hungry whines and tongueless shrieks of the undead ghouls growing louder. Ali turned his head.

His eyes went wide. There were scores of ghouls running for him—some bloated corpses of putrefied flesh and bloody teeth, others reduced to skeletons, their clawed hands sharp as knives. And they were only seconds away from closing in. They'd eat him alive, rip him apart, and be waiting for his friends—the few who survived the archer he saw even now nocking an arrow.

No. This couldn't be their fate. His family, his city. Ali thrust his hands into the wet sand, the water surging through his fingers.

"Help me!" he begged, crying out to the marid. The ancient monsters had already used him; he knew their assistance would come with a terrible price, but right now Ali didn't care. "Please!"

Nothing. The water stayed silent and lifeless. The marid were gone.

But in a small corner of his mind, something stirred. Not the alien presence he expected, but one that was familiar and comforting. The part of Ali that delighted in wading through the flooded fields of Bir Nabat and watching the way the water made life bloom. The memory of the little boy whose mother had carefully taught him to swim. The protective instinct that had saved him from countless assassins.

A part of him that he denied, a power that frightened him. For the first time since falling in the lake that awful night . . . Ali embraced it.

When the next wave broke, the world was quiet. Soft and slow and gray. Suddenly, it didn't matter if he didn't have his zulfiqar at hand. If he was outnumbered.

Because Ali had *everything* else. The water at his feet that was like a deadly, angry animal pacing its cage. The moisture in the air that was thick and heady, coating every surface. The veins of underwater streams that were spikes of power and pulsing life and the springs in the rocky cliffs eager to burst their stony prison.

His fingers curved around the hilt of his khanjar. The ghouls surrounding him suddenly seemed insubstantial smoky nothings, the Daevas not much more. They were fire-blooded, true, burning bright.

But fire could be extinguished.

Ali screamed into the night, and the moisture in the air burst around him, pouring down as rain that licked his wounds, soothing and healing his battered body. With a snap of his fingers, he raised a fog to shroud the beach. He heard the archer cry out, surprised by her sudden blindness.

But Ali wasn't blind. He lunged for his zulfiqar, yanking it from the dead man's body just as the ghouls attacked.

With the zulfiqar in one hand and the khanjar in the other, droplets of water spinning off their wet blades, he cut through the crowd of undead. They kept coming, relentless, two new ghouls pushing through for every one he decapitated. A furious flurry of snapping teeth and bony hands, seaweed wrapping their decayed limbs.

The Daevas on the wall above him ran, the heat from their fire-blooded bodies vanishing. There were others; Ali could sense another trio rushing to join them and five already in the remains of the Citadel. Ten in total, that he knew.

Ali could kill ten men. He cut off the head of the ghoul blocking his path, kicked another in the chest, and then raced after the Daevas.

He stopped to fling his khanjar at the closest, catching the man in the back. Ali plunged it deeper when he caught up, twisting the dagger until the man stopped screaming before yanking it free.

Pounding caught his attention. He glanced back through the gloom he'd conjured to see two archers on smoky horseback racing along the water's edge. One drew back his bowstring.

Ali hissed, calling to the lake. Watery fingers snaked around the horses' legs, dragging the archers into the depths as their enchanted mounts disappeared in a spray of mist. He kept running. Two of the fleeing Daevas stopped, perhaps inspired by a burst of courage to stand their ground and defend their fellows.

Ali put his zulfiqar through the heart of the first, his dagger opening the throat of the second.

Seven men left.

But the ghouls caught up with him as he lunged for the wrecked outer wall of the Citadel, snatching him back as he attempted to climb it. There was a blur of bone, the scent of rot and blood overwhelming as they tore into him. Ali screamed as one bit deeply into his already wounded shoulder. They were everywhere, and his hold on the powerful water magic dipped as panic seized him.

Daevabad, Alizayd, his father's voice whispered. *Daevabad comes first.* Bleeding badly, Ali gave more of himself up, embracing the raw magic coursing so wildly within him that it felt like his body would burst.

He was given a gift in return. The sudden awareness of a rich vein of water beneath him, a hidden stream snaking deep, deep under the sand. Ali called to it, yanking it up like a whip.

Stone and sand and water went flying. Ali lashed it at the ghouls, taking out enough to escape the horde. He scrambled over the ruined Citadel wall.

Another pair of Daevas had been left to deal with him, their bravery rewarded with two swift strikes of his zulfiqar that took their heads. Blood was running down his face, torn patches of flesh burning under his tattered dishdasha.

It didn't matter. Ali dashed toward the breach, arrows raining down on him as he navigated the broken courtyard where he'd first learned to fight. The bodies of his fellow djinn were everywhere, some pierced with arrows, some torn apart by ghouls, others simply crushed in the violent mayhem the lake-beast had unleashed upon the complex. Grief and rage flooded his veins, pushing him on. And though the archers might have been able to see in the summoned fog, one nearly struck true, an arrow tearing past his thigh. Ali gasped.

But he didn't stop.

He vaulted over a ruined pile of sandstone, what he dimly recognized as the sunny diwan in which he'd attempted to teach economics to a bored group of cadets. The swordsman who'd mocked him stood there now, shaking as he raised his blade.

"Demon!" the Daeva screamed. "What the hell are y—"

Ali silenced him with his khanjar.

Four left. He inhaled, taking a moment to survey his surroundings. A glance revealed two archers still standing on the Citadel wall, a position from which they'd be able to easily target the soldiers landing on the beach. The remaining two Daevas had swords in their hands. They were steps from the breach in the Citadel wall that led into the city, a mob of ghouls on their heels.

Ali closed his eyes, dropping his blades, sinking to the ground and plunging his hands into one of the pools of water left by the lake's attack. He could feel his fellows in the distance, the last survivors of the Royal Guard staggering out of the water. But none were close to the Citadel. Not yet.

Good. He called to the lake again, feeling it pace in his mind. It was angry. It wanted vengeance on the stone island marring its heart.

Ali was about to let it take a small piece. He beckoned to the waves lashing the wall. *Come.*

They answered.

The water roared as it crashed over the Citadel, dashing the archers against the stone courtyard. It parted as it neared him, rushing past to grab the ghouls and smash them to bits. A single scream rent the air as it swallowed the last Daevas and raced to the breach, eager to devour the rest of the city.

It took everything Ali had to rein it in. There was a howl in his head, and then he was the one screaming, clawing at the ground as he wrenched the lake back the way it had come. The water fell at his feet, surging into the sand and swirling into ruined, rocky crevices.

His hold on the magic disintegrated and Ali collapsed. Blood and sweat poured from him in equal parts as he sprawled on the ground. His ears were ringing, the scars the marid had carved in his body throbbing. His vision briefly blurred as his muscles seized.

And then he was lying still upon the cold, wet ground. The sky was a rich black, the spread of stars beautiful and inviting.

"Alizayd!"

Though Ali heard Lubayd shout his name, his friend seemed a world away. Everything did, save the beckoning stars and the warm blood spreading beneath him.

There was a crack of thunder. Odd, he dimly noticed, as the night sky was cloudless.

"Ali!" Lubayd's face swam into view above his. "Oh, brother, no . . ." He glanced back. "We need help!"

But the ground was already turning cold again, water seeping up through the sand to embrace him. Ali blinked, his mind a degree clearer. The spots dancing before his eyes faded as well— just in time for Ali to notice an oily black smoke rising behind Lubayd. The tendrils danced, twisting together.

Ali tried to croak out his friend's name. "Lu-Lubay—"

Lubayd hushed him. "It's okay, just hold on. We're going to get you to that Nahid of yours, and you'll be fine." He tucked Ali's zulfiqar back in his belt, and a smile cracked across his face, doing little to erase the worry in his eyes. "Don't you be letting this—"

A jarring, crunching sound stole Lubayd's words. His friend's expression froze and then his body jerked slightly as the crunch came again, a terrible sucking noise. Lubayd opened his mouth as if to speak.

Black blood spilled from his lips. A fiery hand shoved him out of the way, and his friend crumpled.

"By the Creator . . . ," a smoky voice drawled. "What are *you*—you lovely, destructive bit of chaos?"

Ali gaped at the creature looming over him, its clawed hand

clutching a bloody war ax. It was a skinny wraith of a thing, with limbs that looked like pressed light and golden eyes that flared and flashed. And there was only one creature in their world that looked like that.

An ifrit. An ifrit had crossed the veil into Daevabad.

The ifrit seized him by the throat, and Ali gasped as he was lifted into the air. It pulled him close, its glittering eyes inches from Ali's face. The smell of blood and ash washed over Ali as the ifrit ran a tongue over its sharp teeth, unmistakable hunger and curiosity in its feral expression.

It inhaled. "Salt," it whispered. "You're the one the marid took, aren't you?" One of its razor-sharp claws pressed hard against his throat, and Ali got the impression it would be nothing for the demon to rip it open. "But this . . ." He gestured to the ruined courtyard and drowned Daevas. "I've never seen *anything* like this." Its other hand ran down Ali's arm, a quick examination. "Nor anything like the magic simmering off you." The fiery eyes gleamed. "I'd love to take you apart, little one. See how that works, layer by layer . . ."

Ali tried to wrench himself free and caught sight of Lubayd's body, his glassy, unseeing eyes fixed on the sky above. With a choked cry of denial, Ali reached for his zulfiqar.

The ifrit's fingers abruptly tightened on his throat. It clucked its tongue disapprovingly. "None of that now."

"Prince Alizayd!"

As Ali grappled with the iron grip the demon had on his throat, he glimpsed a band of men running in the distance: the rest of the survivors from the Royal Guard.

"*Prince?*" the ifrit repeated. He shook his head, disappointed. "A shame. There's another after you, and he's got a temper even *I* won't cross." He sighed. "Hold on. This is most *certainly* going to hurt."

There was no time to react. A searing bolt of heat raced over

Ali, consuming them both in a swirl of fire and sickly green clouds. Thunder crashed in his ear, shaking his very bones. The beach vanished and the cries of his men fell away, replaced by the blur of rooftops and the roar of the wind.

And then it was gone. They crashed, and the ifrit released him. Ali landed hard, sprawled on a stone floor. Disoriented, he tried to stand, but nausea rose, swift and fierce inside his roiling stomach, and it was everything Ali could do not to vomit. Instead, he squeezed his eyes shut, trying to catch his breath.

When he opened them again, the first thing he saw was the familiar doors of his father's office. They'd been torn off their hinges, the room ransacked and set ablaze.

Ali was too late.

The ifrit who'd murdered Lubayd was striding away. Still dizzy, Ali tried to track his movement, the scene coming to him in pieces. A knot of young warriors dressed in the same mottled black uniforms of the Daevas on the beach surrounded another man, their commander perhaps. He stood with his back to Ali, barking out what sounded like orders in Divasti.

An enormous silver bow, horribly familiar, was strung across his broad shoulders.

Ali jerked his head in denial, sure he was dreaming.

"Have I got a prize for *you*," the ifrit crowed to the Daeva commander, jerking a thumb back at Ali. "This is the prince your Banu Nahida is after, yes? The one we're supposed to lock away?"

The Daeva commander whirled around, and Ali's heart stopped. The cold green eyes from his nightmares, the black tattoo that declared his position to the world . . .

"It is not," Darayavahoush e-Afshin said in a low, lethal voice. His eyes blazed, a flicker of fire-yellow beneath the green. "But he will do just fine."

37

DARA

Dara had taken two steps toward Alizayd before he stopped himself, hardly believing the blood-covered Ayaanle man before him could be the self-righteous royal brat he'd sparred with in Daevabad years ago. He'd grown up, losing the childish hint to his features that had stayed Dara's hand from ending that match in a more lethal manner. He also looked terrible, like something Vizaresh might have fished from the lake, half dead. His dishdasha hung in soaked rags, his limbs covered in bleeding gashes and bite marks.

His eyes, though—they were the Geziri gray Dara remembered. His father's eyes, Zaydi al Qahtani's eyes, and if Dara doubted it, the zulfiqar hanging at Alizayd's waist was confirmation enough.

The prince had pushed himself to a sitting position. He seemed thoroughly disoriented, his dazed eyes sweeping over Dara in shock.

"But you're dead," he whispered, sounding stunned. "I killed you."

Anger surged into Dara's blood, and he clenched his hands into smoldering fists. "Remember that, do you?" He was struggling to hold on to his mortal form, aching to submit to the flames that wanted to consume him.

Nahri's hands on his face. *We'll leave. We'll travel the world.* Dara had been close, so close to escaping all this.

And then Alizayd al Qahtani gave himself to the marid.

"Afshin?" the tentative voice of Laleh, his youngest recruit, broke through his haze. "Did you want me to lead my group to the harem?"

Dara exhaled. His soldiers. His duty. "Hold him," he said flatly to Vizaresh. He would deal with Alizayd al Qahtani himself, but only after giving his warriors their orders. "And take that damned zulfiqar off him immediately."

He turned around, briefly squeezing his eyes shut. Instead of the blackness of his closed lids, Dara saw through five sets of eyes, those of the smoky beasts he'd conjured from his blood and let loose with each group of warriors. He caught a reassuring glimpse of Manizheh—who'd insisted on separating from them immediately to head for the infirmary—riding atop the galloping karkadann he'd shaped for her.

The creatures pulled hard on his consciousness, the magic wearing on him. He would need to give up his mortal form soon, even if it was only to recover.

"Break apart," he said in Divasti. "You heard the Banu Nahida. Our first priority is finding the grand wazir and Ghassan's body. Laleh, your group will search the harem. Gushtap, take yours to the pavilion on the roof that Kaveh mentioned." He eyed them. "I expect you to remember yourselves. Do what's necessary to secure the palace and keep our people safe, but no more." He paused. "Such mercy does not extend to any survivors you spot from the Royal Guard. Kill them at once. Do not give them a chance to draw their blades. Do not give *any* man a chance to draw a blade."

Gushtap opened his mouth, saying, "But most men wear weapons."

Dara stared at him. "My order remains."

The other warrior bowed his head. Dara waited until his soldiers had vanished before turning back around.

Vizaresh had taken Alizayd's zulfiqar and was holding it near the prince's throat, though the bleeding djinn didn't look capable of putting up much of a fight; he didn't even look like he could stand. The realization made Dara pause. It was one thing to cut down a hated enemy in combat; executing a wounded young man who could barely keep his eyes open was another matter.

He is dangerous. Rid yourself of him. Dara freed the short sword at his side. And then he abruptly stopped, taking in the sight of the soaked prince more carefully.

Bite marks. He whirled on Vizaresh. "You were supposed to be with my soldiers and your ghouls at the beach. Have they secured what remains of the Citadel?"

Vizaresh shook his head. "Your soldiers are dead," he said bluntly. "And my ghouls are gone. There was no point in staying. The djinn were already retaking the beach."

Dara stared at him in disbelief. He'd looked upon the ruins of the Citadel himself and sent his warriors in with a hundred ghouls. They should have been more than a match for whatever survivors remained. "That cannot be." He narrowed his eyes and then lunged at Vizaresh. "Did *you* abandon them?" he snarled.

The ifrit raised his hands in mock surrender. "No, fool. You've *this* one to blame for killing your warriors," he said, jerking his head in Alizayd's direction. "He had command of the lake as if he were marid himself. I'd never seen anything like it."

Dara reeled. He'd sent a dozen of his best to the beach. He'd sent *Irtemiẓ* to that beach.

And Alizayd al Qahtani had killed them all with marid magic. He shoved Vizaresh aside.

Alizayd finally staggered up, lurching toward the ifrit as if to grab his zulfiqar.

He didn't make it. Dara struck him across the face, hard enough that he heard bones crack. Alizayd fell sprawling to the floor, blood pouring from his shattered nose.

Too angry to hold his form, Dara let his magic loose. Fire swept down his limbs, claws and fangs bursting from his skin. He barely noticed.

Alizayd certainly did. He cried out in shock, crawling backward as Dara approached again. Good. Let Zaydi's spawn die in terror. But it wouldn't be with magic. No, Dara was going to put metal through this man's throat and watch him bleed. He grabbed Alizayd by his torn collar, raising his blade.

"*Wait.*" Vizaresh's voice was so softly urgent that it cut through the haze of Dara's rage.

Dara stopped. "*What?*" he spat, turning to look over his shoulder.

"Would you really kill the man who cut you down before your Nahri and slaughtered your young soldiers?" Vizaresh drawled.

"Yes!" Dara snapped. "That's *exactly* what I'm going to do."

Vizaresh stepped closer. "You'd give your enemy the very peace you've been denied?"

Smoke curled past Dara's hands, heat rising in his face. "Are you looking to join him? I do not have patience for your damned riddles right now, Vizaresh!"

"No riddles, Darayavahoush." Vizaresh pulled the metal chain out from under his bronze chest plate. "Merely another option."

Dara's eyes locked on the emerald rings that hung from the chain. He caught his breath.

"Give him to me," Vizaresh whispered in Divasti. "You know his name, do you not? You can take the killing blow yourself and obey Manizheh, but let me take his soul first." He drew nearer, his voice a low purr. "Take the vengeance you deserve. You've been denied the peace of death. Why should your enemy be granted it at your hands?"

Dara's fingers shook on the knife, his breath coming fast. Manizheh was getting her revenge on Ghassan; why shouldn't Dara have his? Was it any worse than what they were already doing? What he had already done?

Alizayd must have realized something was wrong. His gaze darted between Dara and the ifrit, finally dropping to the chain of slave rings.

His eyes went wide. *Wild*, sheer terror coursing through them. He jerked back with a gasp, trying to tear himself from Dara's grip, but Dara easily held on, pinning him hard to the ground and pressing the blade to his throat.

Alizayd shouted, writhing against them. "Get off me!" he screamed, seemingly heedless of the knife against his neck. "Get off me, you—"

With a single brutal motion, Vizaresh grabbed the prince's head and slammed his skull into the ground. Alizayd instantly fell silent, his dazed eyes rolling back.

Vizaresh let out an annoyed sigh. "I swear, these djinn make even more noise than humans, though I suppose that's what happens when you live too close to those earth-blooded insects." He reached for Alizayd's hand, slipping the ring over his thumb.

"Stop," Dara whispered.

The ifrit glared at him, his fingers still closed around the ring. "You said he wasn't the prince you were after. I have not touched any of your people. You can give me this one."

But if the cold way Vizaresh had smashed the young prince's head into the floor—indeed, as one might swat a fly—had already pulled Dara back to himself, the angry possessiveness in the ifrit's voice made him recoil. Was that how Qandisha had thought of him? A possession, a toy to enjoy, to toss to humans as a plaything, only to delight in the chaos it would cause?

Yes. We are the ancestors of the people who betrayed them. The daevas who chose to humble themselves before Suleiman, to let a human forever transform them. To the ifrit, his people—djinn and Daeva alike—were an anathema. An abomination.

And Dara had been a fool to ever forget that. However he'd been brought back to life, he was no ifrit. He would not allow them to enslave another djinn's soul.

"No," Dara said again, revulsion coursing through him. "Get that disgusting thing off him. *Now*," he demanded when Vizaresh didn't move. Instead of obeying, the ifrit jerked up, his attention caught by something behind them. Dara followed his gaze.

His heart stopped.

38

NAHRI

"Are you sure this leads back to the outer wall?" Nahri whispered as she and Muntadhir crept through the twisting servants' passage. Save for a bit of fire she'd conjured, it was entirely dark.

"I've told you twice," Muntadhir replied snippily. "Which of us spent our entire life here again?"

"Which of us used this to sneak into random bedrooms?" Nahri muttered back, ignoring the annoyed look he threw her. "What, am I wrong?"

He rolled his eyes. "This passage ends soon, but we can take the next corridor all the way to the east end and access the outer steps there."

Nahri nodded. "So, Suleiman's seal . . . ," she started, trying for a light tone. "How do we retrieve it? Do we have to carve it from your father's face or—"

Muntadhir made a choking sound. "My God, Nahri, really?"

"You were the one who got all queasy when you first brought it up!"

He shook his head. "Are you going to stick a dagger in my back and run off the moment I tell you?"

"If you keep saying things like that, very possibly." Nahri sighed. "Can we try being on the same side for *one* night?"

"Fine," Muntadhir grumbled. "I suppose someone else *should* know, all things considered." He took a deep breath. "It has nothing to do with his cheek; the mark shows up there once the ring is taken."

"The ring? Suleiman's seal is on a ring?" Nahri thought back to the jewels she'd seen adorning Ghassan over the past five years. Quietly assessing the valuables another person was wearing was a bit of her specialty. "Is it the ruby he wears on his thumb?" she guessed.

Muntadhir's expression was grim. "It's not on his hand," he replied. "It's in his heart. We have to cut it out and burn it. The ring re-forms from the ash."

Nahri stopped dead in her tracks. "We have to do *what*?"

"Please don't make me repeat it." Muntadhir looked ill. "The ring re-forms, you put it on your hand, and that's that. My father said it can take a few days to recover from the magic. And then you're trapped in Daevabad forever," he added darkly. "Now do you see why I was in no hurry to be king?"

"What do you mean, you're *trapped in Daevabad*?" Nahri asked, her mind racing.

"I didn't ask." When she stared at him in disbelief, he threw up his hands. "Nahri, I don't think I was older than eight when he told me all of this. I was more preoccupied with trying not to be sick in terror than with interrogating him about the exact strings attached to wearing a ring I was supposed to pull from his bloody corpse. What he told me was that the ring can't leave the city. So unless someone is willing to leave their heart be-hind . . ."

"How poetic," she muttered as they continued moving down the dim passageway.

He stopped outside the grimy, barely visible contours of a door. "We're here."

Nahri hovered at his shoulder as he gently eased it open. They stepped into the darkness.

Her face fell. A Geziri woman in a steward's robe lay dead on the stone floor, blood running from her ears.

"The poison has been through here," she said softly. This wasn't the first body they'd found. Though they'd been able to warn a handful of Geziri nobles, they were finding far more dead than alive: soldiers with their zulfiqars still sheathed, a scholar with scrolls scattered around her, and—most heartbreaking—a pair of young boys in feast clothing, clutching unlit sparklers in their hands, tendrils of the hazy copper vapor still clinging to their small feet.

Muntadhir closed the woman's eyes. "I'm going to give Kaveh to the karkadann," he whispered savagely. "I swear on my father's name."

Nahri shivered; she couldn't argue with that. "Let's keep going."

They'd no sooner stood up than Nahri heard footsteps. At least three people were approaching from around the bend. With no time to duck back inside the passage, they swiftly pressed into a darkened niche in the wall. Shadows rushed over them, a protective response from the palace, just as several figures came around the bend.

Her heart dropped. Daevas, all of them. Young and unfamil-iar, they were clad in uniforms of mottled gray and black. They were also quite well-armed, looking more than capable of taking on the emir and his wife. It was a conclusion Muntadhir must have come to as well, for he made no move to confront them and stayed quiet until they had vanished.

Finally, he cleared his throat. "I think your tribe is conducting a coup."

Nahri swallowed. "It does seem that way," she said shakily.

Muntadhir looked down at her. "Still on my side?"

Her gaze fell on the murdered woman. "I'm on the side that doesn't unleash things like that."

They kept walking, following the deserted corridor. Nahri's heart was racing, and she didn't dare speak, especially since it was now clear there were enemies creeping through the palace. An occasional scream or abruptly cut-off warning broke the air, carried through the echoing halls of the labyrinthine royal complex.

A strange buzz swept her skin, and Nahri shivered. It was an oddly familiar feeling, but she couldn't place it. She moved her hand to one of her daggers as they continued. She could hear the beat of her heart in her head, a steady pounding. Like the tap-tap-tap of a warning.

Muntadhir threw out his arm. There was a muffled cry in the distance.

"Get off me!"

He gasped. "Nahri, that sounds like—"

But she was already running. There was the sound of arguing, another voice, but she barely heard it. She threw up her arm as they rounded the corner; the sudden light was blinding after so much time stealing through the dark.

But the light wasn't coming from torches or conjured flames. It was coming from two ifrit who had Ali pinned to the ground.

Nahri jerked to a halt, stifling a scream. Ali was a bloody wreck, lying too still beneath a large ifrit inexplicably dressed in the same uniform as the Daeva soldiers and holding a knife to the prince's throat. A skinnier ifrit in a bronze chest plate was clutching Ali's hand, holding the prince's wrist at what must have been a painful angle.

Both ifrit turned to stare at the royal couple. Nahri gasped when she spotted the green gem gleaming on one of Ali's fingers.

A ring. An emerald slave ring.

The ifrit dressed in Daeva clothing opened his mouth, his eyes flashing brighter. "Nah—"

She didn't let him finish. Fury flooding through her, she dragged her dagger hard across her palm, breaking the skin. Then she charged forward, throwing herself on him without hesitation.

She and the ifrit tumbled backward together, Nahri landing on his chest. She raised the bloody dagger, trying to plunge it into his throat, but he easily knocked it out of her hand, his own knife still in one of his.

She scrambled for it, but he was stronger. He let the knife go and it clattered to the floor as he grabbed her wrists and then rolled her over, pinning her beneath him.

Nahri screamed. The ifrit's fiery eyes met hers, and she caught her breath, startled by what looked like grief swirling in the depths of their alien color.

And then the scorching yellow vanished, his eyes turning the shade of green that haunted her dreams. Black curls sprouted from his smoky scalp, and the fiery light was snuffed from his face, leaving his skin a luminescent light brown. An ebony tattoo marked his temple: an arrow crossed with the wing of a shedu.

Dara stared back at her, his face inches from hers. The scent of cedar and burnt citrus tickled her nose, and then he spoke one word, one word that left his lips like a prayer.

"*Nahri.*"

NAHRI HOWLED, SOMETHING RAW AND SAVAGE RIPPING through her. "Stop!" she screamed, writhing underneath him. "Get rid of that face or I'll kill you!"

He held her hands tight as she attempted to claw at his throat. "Nahri, stop!" the ifrit cried. "It's me, I swear!"

His voice shattered her. God, it even sounded like him. But that was impossible. *Impossible.* Nahri had watched Dara die. She'd raked her hands through his ashes.

This was a trick. An ifrit trick. Her skin crawling at his touch, Nahri tried to twist free again, spotting her bloody dagger near her feet.

"Zaydi!" Muntadhir flew to his brother's side only to be promptly thrown across the corridor by the second ifrit. He smashed hard into one of the delicate fountains, water and glass bursting around him.

Thinking fast and desperate to get the ifrit off her, Nahri brought her knee up hard where his legs met his body.

He gasped, his still-green eyes lighting with pain and surprise, and jerked back enough for her to scramble free. A glance revealed Muntadhir back on his feet, running for Ali as the younger prince slowly rolled over, blood streaming down his face. The second ifrit reached for the war ax hanging across his back . . .

"*STOP!*" The corridor trembled, echoing with the first ifrit's command. "Vizaresh, stand down," he snapped as he climbed to his feet. The second ifrit instantly did so, stepping back from the Qahtani brothers with a splash, the water from the broken fountain puddling at his feet.

The ifrit wearing Dara's guise turned back to Nahri, his gaze imploring. "Nahri," he choked out, her name leaving his mouth like it caused him pain. He took a step toward her, reaching out like he wanted to take her hand.

"Don't touch me!" The sound of his voice was physically painful; it was everything she could do not to cover her ears. "I don't know who you are, but I'll blood-poison you if you don't change your appearance."

The ifrit fell to his knees before her, bringing his hands up in the Daeva blessing. "Nahri, it's me. I swear on my parents' ashes. I found you in a Cairo cemetery. I told you my name in the ruins of Hierapolis." The same hollow grief swirled into his eyes. "You kissed me in the caves above the Gozan." His voice broke. "Twice."

Her heart twisted, fierce denial running through her. "It's not." A sob tore from her chest. "You're dead. *You're dead.* I watched it happen!"

He swallowed, sadness rippling across his face as his haunted eyes drank her in. "I was. But no one seems content to leave me in that state."

Nahri swayed on her feet, jerking back when he moved to help her. Too many pieces were coming together in her head. Kaveh's careful treachery. The well-armed Daeva soldiers.

Dara. The dashing warrior who'd taken her hand in Cairo and spirited her away to a land of legend. Her broken Afshin, driven to destruction by the crushing politics of the city he couldn't save.

He spoke again. "I'm sorry, Nahri." That he seemingly registered whatever little change was in her expression—for Nahri didn't easily give up her mask—was its own proof.

"What *are* you?" she whispered, unable to conceal the horror in her voice. "Are you . . . are you one of *them* now?" She jerked her head toward the ifrit, almost afraid to hear the answer.

"No!" Dara closed the distance between them and took her hands, his fingers hot against hers. Nahri did not have it in her to pull away; it looked like it was costing Dara everything not to grab her and *run* away. "Creator, no! I . . . I am a daeva," he said faintly, as though the words made him ill. "But as our people once were. I am free of Suleiman's curse."

The answer made no sense. *None* of this made any sense. Nahri felt as though she'd stumbled upon a mirage, a mad hallucination.

Dara drew her closer, reaching for her cheek. "I am sorry. I wanted to tell you, to come straight away—" His voice turned desperate. "I could not cross the threshold. I could not come back for you." He rushed on, his words growing more incomprehensible. "But it is going to be okay, I promise you. She is going to set it all right. Our people will be free and—"

"Fuck," Muntadhir swore. "It is you. Only you would come back from the dead a second time and immediately start another damn war."

Dara's eyes flashed, and ice stole into Nahri's heart. "You're working with Kaveh," she whispered. "Does that mean . . ." Her stomach twisted. "The poison killing the Geziris . . ." *No, please no.* "Did you know?"

He dropped his gaze, looking sick with regret. "You were not supposed to see it. You were supposed to be with Nisreen. Safe. Protected." He said the words frantically, as though trying to convince himself as much as her.

Nahri jerked free of his grip. "Nisreen is *dead*." She stared at Dara, aching to see a glimmer of the laughing warrior who'd teased her on a flying carpet and sighed as she kissed him in the quiet dark of a secluded cave. "The things they say about you are true, aren't they?" she asked, her voice thick with rising dread. "About Qui-zi? About the war?"

She wasn't sure what she expected: denial, shame, perhaps overly righteous anger. But the flicker of resentment that flared in his eyes—that took her by surprise.

"Of course they are true," he said tonelessly. He touched the mark on his brow, a grim salute. "I am the weapon the Nahids made me. Nothing more, nothing less, and apparently for all of eternity."

With his usual poor timing, Ali chose that moment to speak. "Oh, yes," he croaked from where he sat on the floor, leaning heavily against his brother. His gray eyes were wild with grief, standing out starkly against his blood-covered face. "You poor, pitiful murdering—"

Muntadhir clapped a hand over Ali's mouth, but it was too late.

Dara whirled on the Qahtani princes. "What did you say to me, you filthy little hypocrite?"

"Nothing," Muntadhir said quickly, clearly struggling to keep his brother's mouth shut.

But Ali had drawn their attention . . . though it wasn't his words that held it.

The water from the broken fountains was *rushing* for him. It streamed across the floor, surging into his bloody clothes, tiny rivulets dancing over his hands. Ali seemed to suck for breath, dipping his head as the air abruptly cooled.

Then he jerked his head back up, the movement unnaturally sharp. An oily black mingled with the gray in his eyes.

There was a moment of shocked silence. "I did try to tell you," the ifrit spoke up, "that there was something a little different about him."

Dara was staring at Ali with naked hate. "It is nothing I cannot handle." He stepped away from Nahri. "Vizaresh, take the emir and the Banu Nahida away. I will join you in a moment." His voice softened. "They do not need to see this."

Nahri sprang up to stop him. "No!"

She didn't even get close. Dara snapped his fingers, and a burst of smoke wrapped her body, tight as rope.

"Dara!" Nahri tripped, falling hard to her knees, stunned that he'd used magic against her. "Dara, stop, I beg you! I *order* you!" she tried, pulling desperately for her own power. There was a rumble from the ancient bricks. *"Afshin!"*

Fire licked down Dara's arms. "I am truly sorry, Nahri," Dara said, and she could hear it, the heartbreak in his voice. "But yours are not the orders I follow anymore." He started after Ali.

Ali staggered to his feet, shoving Muntadhir behind him.

The oily color flashed across his eyes again, and then his zulfiqar flew to his hand, a burst of water behind it like he'd cut through a wave. Flames licked down the copper blade.

Vizaresh hadn't moved to follow Dara's command. He looked between them now, his wary yellow eyes taking in the two warriors.

Then he shook his head. "No, Darayavahoush. You fight this one on your own. I will not quarrel with one the marid have chosen to bless so." Without another word, he vanished in a crack of thunder.

Ali rushed forward. As Nahri cried out, he raised his zulfiqar . . .

And then he fell back, as though he'd smashed into an invisible barrier. He stumbled, looking stunned, but without hesitation, gathered himself and sprang forward again.

This time, the barrier knocked him back completely.

Dara hissed. "Yes, your marid masters couldn't do that either." He lunged at the prince, ripping the zulfiqar from Ali's hands. The flames soaring as if he were a Geziri man himself, Dara swung it up. Nahri screamed again, writhing against the smoky binds as the magic of the palace built in her blood.

Muntadhir hurled himself between Ali and the zulfiqar.

There was the smell of blood and burning flesh. A flash of pain in her husband's eyes and then a wail from Ali, a sound so raw it didn't seem real.

Rage ripped through her. And just like that, her magic was there. The smoky binds that had dared to confine her—*her*, in her own damned palace—abruptly burst apart, and Nahri inhaled, suddenly aware of every brick and stone and mote of dust in the building around her. The walls erected by her ancestors, the floors that had run black with their blood.

The corridor shook, hard enough to send the plaster crumbling from the ceiling. Flames twisted around her fingers, smoke curling past *her* collar. Her clothes flapping madly in the hot breeze spinning out from her body, she raised her hands.

Dara turned to her. She could both see him and *sense* him, standing bright and furious on the edge of her magic.

Nahri threw him across the corridor.

He hit the wall hard enough to leave a dent in the stone and crumpled to the floor. A piece of her heart broke at the sight, still traitorously linked to the man who kept finding new ways to shatter it.

And then Dara got back up.

Their gazes met. Dara looked stunned. Betrayed. And yet, still grimly determined, a warrior committed. He touched the golden blood dripping down his face and then threw his hand out, a wave of black smoke wrapping his body. There was a glimmer of scales and flash of teeth as it doubled in size.

In an explosion of plaster and stone, Nahri brought the ceiling down on him.

She collapsed as the dust rose around her, the magic draining.

Ali's screams brought her back. Pushing aside the grief threatening to tear her open, Nahri staggered to her feet. Muntadhir had fallen to his knees, leaning against his brother. Blood was spreading across his dishdasha.

Nahri ran to him, ripping open the cloth. Tears sprang to her eyes. Had he been attacked with anything but a zulfiqar, Nahri would have breathed a sigh of relief; it was a clean gash stretching across his stomach, and though it was bloody, it wasn't deep.

But none of that mattered. Because the skin around the wound was already a sick blackish green, the color of some awful storm. And it was spreading, delicate tendrils tracing the lines of veins and nerves.

Muntadhir let out a dismayed sound. "Oh," he whispered, his hands shaking as he touched the wound. "Suppose that's ironic."

"No. No, no, no," Ali stammered the word as if the whispered

THE KINGDOM OF COPPER ✦ 567

denial would undo the awful scene before them. "Why did you do that? Dhiru, *why did you do that?*"

Muntadhir reached out to touch his brother's face, the blood from his hands staining Ali's skin. "I'm sorry, akhi," he replied weakly. "I couldn't watch him kill you. Not again."

Tears ran down Ali's face. "It's going to be okay," he stammered. "N-Nahri will heal you."

Muntadhir shook his head. "Don't," he said, clenching his jaw as she reached for him. "We all know you'll be wasting time."

"Would you let me at least *try*?" she begged, her voice breaking on the word.

Muntadhir bit his lip, looking like he was struggling to hide his own fear. He nodded, a small motion.

Nahri instantly spread her hands, concentrating on the pulse and heat of her husband's body, and yet she'd no sooner done so than she realized the futility of it. She couldn't heal his torn flesh and poisoned blood, because she couldn't sense the wound. His body seemed to end where the darkening flesh began, its edges pushing back at her consciousness as it advanced. It was worse than her struggles with Jamshid, worse even than her desperate fight to save Nisreen. Nahri—who'd just thrown a man across the room and conjured a sandstorm—could do nothing to fight the zulfiqar's poison.

Muntadhir gently pushed her hands away. "Nahri, stop. You don't have time for this."

"We have time," Ali cut in. "Just try again. Try harder!"

"*You don't have time.*" Muntadhir's voice was firm. "Zaydi, look at me. I need you to listen and not react. Abba is dead. You need to go with Nahri and retrieve Suleiman's seal. She knows how."

Ali's mouth fell open, but before he could speak, there was a rumble from the pile of debris.

Muntadhir paled. "Impossible. You dropped a damned ceiling on him."

Another rumble seemed to answer, dust and plaster shivering.

Ali reached for his brother. "We need to get you out of here."

"That's not happening." Muntadhir took a steadying breath and then pushed himself into a seated position. He glanced around, his gaze settling on an object glimmering in the dust.

A silver bow.

A hint of vindictiveness flitted across his face. "Nahri, would you hand me that bow and see if you can't find the quiver?"

Feeling sick, she nonetheless complied. She knew in her heart whose bow this was. "What are you doing?" she asked as he staggered to his feet holding the bow, determination and pain etched across his features.

Muntadhir swayed, pulling free his khanjar. He beckoned Ali closer and then shoved it in his brother's belt. "Buying you time." He coughed, then nodded at the khanjar. "Take that and your zulfiqar, akhi. Fight well."

Ali didn't move. He suddenly looked very young. "Dhiru, I . . . I can't leave you," he said, his voice trembling, as if this was something he could argue away. "I'm supposed to protect you," he whispered. "I'm supposed to be your Qaid."

Muntadhir gave him a sad smile. "I'm pretty sure that means you have to do as I say." His expression softened. "It's okay, Zaydi. We're okay." He nocked an arrow, something broken in his face even as he winked. "Hell, I think this means I might even make it to your Paradise."

Tears were running unchecked down Ali's cheeks. Nahri quietly picked up his zulfiqar and then stepped forward, taking his hand. She met Muntadhir's eyes, a look of understanding passing between them. "We'll get Suleiman's seal," she promised. "And I'll find Jamshid. You have my word."

At that, Muntadhir's eyes finally grew damp. "Thank you," he said quietly. "Please tell him . . . " He took a deep breath, rocking back slightly, obviously struggling to gather himself. When his gaze met hers again, there was a mix of regret and apology there. "Please tell him I loved him. Tell him I'm sorry I didn't stand up for him sooner." He wiped his eyes with his sleeve and then drew up, looking away. "Now go. I can count my short reign a success if I manage to convince the two most stubborn people in Daevabad to do something they don't want to do."

Nahri nodded, her own vision clouding as she dragged Ali away.

"Dhiru," he choked out again. "Akhi, please . . ."

The rubble gave a giant shake and then a horrible, heart-wrenchingly familiar—and very angry—roar.

"*Go!*" Muntadhir shouted.

They ran.

39

DARA

Agony, the kind of pain Dara hadn't felt since being dragged back to life, was the first thing he was aware of. Crushed limbs and broken teeth, torn flesh and a throbbing in his head so strong he nearly wanted to succumb back to the blackness.

He twitched his fingers, feeling the rough stone and splintered wood beneath them. His eyes blearily winked open, but Dara saw nothing but darkness. He grunted, trying to free the arm twisted painfully underneath him.

He couldn't move. He was pressed in, crushed from all sides.

Nahri. *She brought the ceiling down on me. She actually brought the* ceiling *down on me.* He'd been shocked by the sight of her looking like some sort of wrathful goddess, smoke twisting around her hands, her black curls blowing wildly in the scorching wind she'd summoned. She'd looked like a Nahid icon he might have bowed to in the Temple.

But the hurt in her eyes, the betrayal . . . that was the woman from Cairo.

You are going to be risking the woman you actually serve if you do not get out of here. The thought of Manizheh and his mission was enough to get Dara moving again, pain be damned. The fate of Daevabad hung in the balance. He inhaled, catching the smoky scent of blood as he struggled to free himself.

His blood. *Creator, no.* Dara closed his eyes, reaching out, but there was nothing.

He'd lost his hold on the conjured blood beasts. Suleiman's eye, there'd been half a dozen. Karkadann and zahhak and rukh. They were mindless, destructive things when they escaped his control, a lesson he'd learned early in his training with the ifrit. And now they were wild at the side of his warriors and Manizheh.

Swearing under his breath, Dara tried to wrench free but only succeeded in shaking the debris nearest him and making his body ache worse.

Embrace what you are, you fool. The brief moments he'd spent in his other form had been an instant balm. Dara needed that power.

The fire sparked in his blood, flushing through his skin. His senses sharpened, claws and fangs sprouting. He touched the crumbling bricks above his head, and they exploded into dust.

He climbed out far more slowly than he liked, his body stiff and the pain still present. It was a frightening reminder: Dara was strong but not invincible. He finally hauled himself out of the ruin, coughing on dust and trying to catch his breath.

An arrow tore through his arm. Dara yelped in surprise, hissing as his hand flew to the wound.

The arrow jutting out of it was one of his own.

A second one flitted past his face, and Dara jerked back just before it went through his eye. He flung himself behind a ruined piece of masonry, peering through the rubble.

Muntadhir al Qahtani was shooting at him with his own bow.

Dara spat in outrage. *How dare that lecherous, dishonorable wretch—*

An arrow flew at his hiding spot.

Dara ducked, cursing out loud. Had he not struck Muntadhir with the zulfiqar? And since when did some sand fly know how to handle a Daeva bow that way?

Gritting his teeth, Dara broke the fletch off the arrow in his arm and then yanked it out, biting back a grunt of pain. His fiery skin closed over the wound, leaving a black scar like a line of charcoal. That it healed was a small relief, but Dara tipped his arrows in iron, and he'd just had a very necessary reminder of the limits of his body. He didn't want to learn what would happen if Muntadhir managed to catch him somewhere more vulnerable than his arm.

Why don't you try shooting in the dark, djinn? Dara pressed his hands to the pile of debris, urging the wood to burst into flame. It burned dark, the oily paints and ancient masonry sending up a choking wall of thick, black smoke that Dara directed toward the emir.

He waited until he heard coughing and then shot to his feet, staying low as he charged. Muntadhir sent another arrow spinning in his direction, but Dara ducked and was wrenching the bow from the other man's hands before he could shoot a second. He used it to backhand the emir across the face, sending him to the floor.

Dara was on him the next second. He banished the smoke. The front of Muntadhir's dishdasha was ripped open and his stomach bloodied, the dark green lines and cracking ash around the wound grisly confirmation that Dara had indeed struck him with the zulfiqar.

Nahri and Alizayd were nowhere to be seen. "Where are they?" Dara demanded. "Your brother and the Banu Nahida?"

Muntadhir spat in his face. "Fuck you, Scourge."

Dara put a knee against Muntadhir's wound, and the emir gasped. *"WHERE ARE THEY?"*

Tears were rolling down the other man's face, but Dara had to give him his due—he held his tongue even as his eyes blazed in pain.

Dara thought fast. Nahri and Alizayd were clever. Where would they go?

"Suleiman's seal," he whispered. Dara immediately drew away his knee, remembering his mission. "Is that where they went? Where is it?"

"In hell," Muntadhir choked out. "Why don't you go look for it? You must be a frequent visitor."

It took all of Dara's self-control not to throttle the other man. He needed Muntadhir's help. And Qahtani or not, Muntadhir had stayed behind with a painful, fatal wound so his little brother and wife could escape.

He leaned closer to Muntadhir. "Your people have lost; I will be catching up with your brother either way. Tell me how to retrieve Suleiman's seal and Alizayd dies quickly. Painlessly. On my honor."

Muntadhir laughed. "You have no honor. You brought an *ifrit* into our city. There are Geziri children who should be lighting fireworks now lying dead in the palace because of you."

Dara recoiled, trying to reach for the justifications Manizheh had offered. "And how many Daeva children died when your people invaded? Far more than the Geziri children who will be lost tonight."

Muntadhir stared at him in shock. "Do you *hear* yourself? What sort of man plots that calculus?" Hate filled his gray eyes. "God, I hope it's her in the end. I hope Nahri puts a goddamned knife through whatever passes for your heart."

Dara looked away. Nahri had certainly seemed capable of

that, glaring at him from across the corridor with flames whipping around her hands as if he were a monster.

She was wrong. She doesn't understand. This mission *had* to be right, it had to succeed. Everything Dara had done for his people, from Qui-zi through tonight's attack, could not be for nothing.

He refocused on Muntadhir. "I know you know what happened to my little sister when Daevabad fell. You took pains to remind me when last we met. Give *your* little brother an easier death."

"I don't believe you," Muntadhir whispered, but Dara's words seemed to have an effect, worry creasing the emir's face. "You hate him. You'll hurt him."

"I'll swear on Nahri's life," Dara replied swiftly. "Tell me how to retrieve Suleiman's seal, and I'll grant Alizayd mercy."

Muntadhir didn't speak, his eyes searching Dara's face. "All right," he finally said. "You'll have to get the ring first." His breathing was becoming more ragged. "The palace library. Go to the catacombs beneath. There's a—" He gave a shuddering cough. "A staircase you'll need to take."

"And then?"

"Follow it. It's quite deep; it will go for a long time. You should feel it getting warmer." Muntadhir grimaced, curling in slightly on his stomach.

"And after?" Dara prompted, growing impatient and a little panicked. He wasn't going to lose time going after Nahri and Alizayd only to have Muntadhir die before giving him an answer.

Muntadhir frowned, looking slightly confused. "Is that not the way back to hell? I assumed you wanted to go home."

Dara's hands were at Muntadhir's throat the next moment. The emir's eyes shone feverishly, locking on Dara's in a last moment of defiance.

Of triumph.

Dara instantly let go. "You . . . you are trying to trick me into killing you."

Muntadhir coughed again, blood flecking his lips. "Astonishing. You must have been quite the brilliant tactician in your—ah!" he screamed as Dara kneed his wound again.

But Dara's heart was racing, his emotions a mess. He didn't have time to waste torturing a dying man for information he was loath to give up.

He drew back his knee, looking again at the smoking green-black edges of Muntadhir's wound. This was not the fatal strike that had felled Mardoniye so quickly. It was the zulfiqar's poison that would take the emir, not the cut itself.

How fortunate then, that Muntadhir had been delivered to a man who knew intimately how long such a death could take. Dara had nursed more friends than he cared to recall through their last moments, easing their seizing limbs and listening to their suffering last gasps as the poison slowly consumed them.

He reached out and snatched Muntadhir's turban, shaking the cloth loose.

"What the hell are you doing?" Muntadhir panted as Dara began binding the wound. "God, can you not even let me die in peace?"

"You're not dying yet." Dara hauled the emir to his feet, ignoring how he shook with pain. "You might not tell *me* how to retrieve Suleiman's seal. But there is another, I suspect, who can make you tell her anything."

40

NAHRI

They ran, Nahri dragging Ali through the dark palace, her only thought to put as much distance as possible between the two of them and whatever it was that Dara had become. Her ancestors' magic pulsed through her blood, offering ready assistance in their flight: stairs rising with their strides and narrow passage-ways bricking up behind them, removing their trail. Another time, Nahri might have marveled at such things.

But Nahri wasn't certain she'd ever marvel at anything in Daevabad again.

At her side, Ali stumbled. "I need to stop," he gasped, leaning heavily against her. Blood was dripping from his broken nose. "There." He pointed down the corridor toward an unassuming wooden door.

Her dagger at the ready, Nahri shoved the door open, and they tumbled into a small sunken courtyard of mirrored foun-

tains and jewel-bright lemon trees. She slammed the door behind them and sank down to catch her breath.

And then it all caught up with her. Nahri squeezed her eyes
shut, but she could still see him. His haunted green eyes above
her, the swirl of smoky magic and the defiant set of his features
right before she brought the ceiling down on him.

Dara.

No, not Dara. Nahri could not think of the Afshin she'd known
and the fiery-visaged monster who'd struck down Muntadhir and
arrived in Daevabad on a wave of death as the same man.

And Muntadhir . . . Nahri pressed a fist to her mouth, choking back a sob.

You can't do this right now. Her husband had put himself before
the deadly Afshin to buy his wife and brother time. Nahri would
honor that sacrifice. She had to.

At her side, Ali had fallen to his knees. A glimmer of copper
caught her eye.

"Oh my God, Ali, *give me that.*" Nahri lunged for the relic in
his ear, pulling it out and flinging it at the trees. She shuddered,
horrified to realize he'd had it in the entire time they were running. Had they come upon the vapor . . .

Pull yourself together. Neither she nor Ali could afford another
mistake.

She laid her hands lightly on his brow and left shoulder. "I'm
going to heal you."

Ali didn't respond. He wasn't even looking at her. His expression was dazed and vacant, his entire body shivering.

Nahri shut her eyes. Her magic felt closer than usual, and the
veil between them, the odd cloak of salty darkness that the marid
possession had drawn over him, immediately dropped. Underneath, he was a mess: his nose shattered, a shoulder sprained and
badly punctured, and two ribs broken between the innumerable

gashes and bites. Nahri commanded them to heal, and Ali caught his breath, grunting as his nose cracked into place. Her power, the healing ability that had denied her twice today, swept out bright and alive.

She let go of him, fighting a wave of exhaustion. "Nice to know I can still do that."

Ali finally stirred. "Thank you," he whispered. He turned to her, tears glistening in his lashes. "My brother . . ."

Nahri violently shook her head. "No. Ali, we don't have time for this . . . *we don't have time for this*," she repeated when he turned away to bury his face in his hands. "Daevabad is under attack. *Your people* are under attack. You need to pull yourself together and fight." She touched his cheek, turning him back to face her. "Please," she begged. "I can't do this alone."

He took one shuddering breath, and then another, briefly squeezing his eyes shut. When he opened them again, there was a touch more resolve in their depths. "Tell me what you know."

"Kaveh unleashed some sort of poisonous vapor similar to what nearly killed you at the feast. It's spreading fast and targets Geziri relics." She lowered her voice. "It's what killed your father."

Ali flinched. "And it's spreading?"

"Fast. We came upon at least three dozen dead so far."

At that, Ali jerked upright. "Zaynab—"

"She's fine," Nahri assured him. "She and Aqisa both. They left to warn the Geziri Quarter and alert the Citadel."

"The Citadel . . ." Ali leaned against the wall. "Nahri, the Citadel is gone."

"What do you mean, it's *gone*?"

"We were attacked first. The lake . . . it rose up like some sort of beast—like what you said happened to you at the Gozan when you first came to Daevabad. It pulled down the Citadel's tower and ripped through the complex. The majority of the Guard is dead." He shivered, silvery drops of liquid beading on his brow. "I woke up in the lake."

"The lake?" Nahri repeated. "Do you think the marid are involved?"

"I think the marid are gone. Their . . . presence . . . feels absent," he clarified, tapping his head. "And the lake's curse was broken. Not that it mattered. The few of us who didn't drown were set upon by ghouls and archers. We were taking the beach when that ifrit grabbed me, but there were fewer than two dozen of us left." Grief swept his face, tears again brimming in his eyes. "The ifrit killed Lubayd."

Nahri swayed. Two dozen survivors. There had to have been hundreds—*thousands* of soldiers in the Citadel. Scores of Geziris in the palace. All dead in a matter of moments.

It's true what they say about you, isn't it? About Qui-zi? About the war? Nahri closed her eyes.

But it wasn't heartbreak coursing through her right now. It was determination. Clearly, the man Nahri knew as Dara was gone—if he'd ever truly existed in the first place. This Dara was the Afshin first, the Scourge. He'd brought a war to Daevabad's doorstep and declared himself a weapon of the Nahids.

But he had no idea what kind of Nahid he'd just set himself against.

Nahri rose to her feet. "We need to retrieve Suleiman's seal," she declared. "It's our only hope of defeating them." She glanced down at Ali, reaching out her hand. "Are you with me?"

Ali took a deep breath but then clasped her hand and climbed to his feet. "Until the end."

"Good. We'll need to find your father's body first," she said, trying not to think about what they'd need to do after that. "Last I saw him, we were on the platform where you took me stargazing."

"We're not far, then. We can take a shortcut through the library." He ran a hand anxiously over his beard and then recoiled, dropping his hand to pull the emerald ring off his thumb.

"Ali, wait!" But Ali had yanked it off and tossed it away before Nahri could finish her protest. She braced herself as it clattered on the tiled floor, half expecting Ali to turn to ash. But he stayed solid, staring at her in surprise.

"What?" he asked.

"*What?*" She threw up her hands and then crossed to retrieve the ring. "What if part of the slave curse is still lingering between you and this, you idiot?"

"It's not," Ali insisted. "They'd barely gotten it on my thumb when you arrived. I think they were arguing about it."

Arguing about it? God, she almost hoped so. She never could have imagined Dara giving another djinn to the ifrit that way. Not even his worst enemy.

"I'd still like to keep it close," she said, slipping the ring into her pocket. She pulled free the zulfiqar she'd awkwardly laced into her belt. "You should probably take this."

Ali looked ill at the sight of the zulfiqar that had struck down his brother. "I'll fight with another weapon."

She leaned forward and pressed it into his hands. "You'll fight with this. It's what you're best at." She met his eyes. "Don't let Muntadhir's death be for nothing, Ali."

Ali's hand closed over the hilt, and then they were moving, him leading her through a door that opened into a long, narrow passageway. It sloped downward, the air growing colder as they descended. Floating balls of conjured fire hissed overhead, setting Nahri's nerves on edge.

Neither of them spoke, but they hadn't been walking long when a boom sounded and the ground shook slightly.

Ali held out a hand to stop her, putting a finger to his lips. There was the unmistakable noise of a heavy object dragging along the dusty stone somewhere behind them.

Nahri tensed. That wasn't all she heard: from beyond the library's silver door at the end of the passageway, a shriek sounded.

"Maybe we should find another way," she whispered, her mouth dry as dust.

The door burst open.

"Zahhak!" A Sahrayn scholar ran at them, his eyes wild, his robes flaming. "*Zahhak!*"

Nahri broke apart from Ali, each of them flattening against the wall as the scholar raced by. The heat from his burning robes seared her face. Nahri turned back, opening her mouth to shout for him to stop . . .

Just in time to see a smoky snake, its body nearly as wide as the corridor, come around the bend. The scholar didn't even have a chance to scream. The snake swallowed him whole, revealing glittering obsidian fangs longer than Nahri's arm.

"Run!" she shrieked, pushing Ali toward the library.

They ran full bore, diving through the door. Ali slammed it shut behind them, shoving himself against the metal as the massive snake crashed against it, rattling the frame.

"Tell your palace to do something about this!" he shouted.

Nahri quickly pressed her hands against the door's decorative metal studs, hard enough to break her skin. She had yet to succeed in completely mastering the palace's magic; it seemed to have its own mind, responding to her emotions with its own distinctive quirk.

"Protect me," she pleaded in Divasti.

Nothing happened.

"Nahri!" Ali cried, his feet slipping as the snake rammed the door again.

"PROTECT ME!" she shouted in Arabic, adding a few choice curses that Yaqub would have lectured her for using. "I command you, damn it!"

Her hands began smoking, and then the silver melted, spooling out to meld the door into the wall. She turned and fell back against the frame, breathing hard.

Her eyes shot open. A creature the size of the Sphinx was careening through the air toward them.

This had to be a nightmare. Not even in enchanted Daevabad did smoky beasts capable of devouring a village fly free. The creature soared on four billowing wings, crimson fire flashing beneath glimmering scales. It had a fanged mouth large enough to swallow a horse and six limbs ending in sharp claws. As Nahri watched, it shrieked, sounding lost as it dived for a fleeing scholar. It caught him in its claws and then flung him hard into the opposite wall as a surge of flames burst from its mouth.

Nahri felt the blood drain from her face. "Is that a dragon?"

At her side, Ali gulped. "It . . . it looks like a zahhak actually." His panicked eyes met hers. "They are not usually that big."

"Oh," Nahri choked out. The zahhak shrieked again and set the lecture alcove next to them ablaze, and they both jumped.

Ali raised a shaking finger at a row of doors on the other side of the massive library. "There's a book lift just beyond there. It goes to the pavilion we want."

Nahri eyed the distance. They were several stories up and the floor of the library was in complete chaos, a maze of broken, burning furniture and fleeing djinn, the zahhak diving at everything that moved.

"That thing will kill us—no," she said, seizing Ali's wrist when he went to lunge in the direction of a young scribe the zahhak had just snatched up. "You run out there now and you're no good to anyone."

A crack drew her attention. The serpent was still bashing the barricaded door and the metal was starting to strain.

"Did anything in your Citadel training prepare you for fighting giant monsters of smoke and flame?"

Ali was staring intently at the eastern wall. "Not at the Citadel . . ." He looked pensive. "What you did to the ceiling back there . . . do you think you can do it to that wall?"

"You want me to bring down the library wall?" Nahri repeated.

"The canal runs behind it. I'm hoping I can use the water to extinguish that thing," he explained as the zahhak veered a little too close.

"*Water?* How do you expect to control . . ." She trailed off, remembering the way he'd summoned his zulfiqar while fighting Dara and registering the guilt in his expression now. "The marid did nothing to you, right? Isn't that what you told me?"

He groaned. "Can we fight about this later?"

Nahri gave the shelves on the eastern wall a forlorn last look. "If we live, you're taking the blame for destroying all those books." She took a deep breath, trying to focus and pull upon the palace's magic like she had in the corridor. It had been a surge of rage and grief over Muntadhir that had finally pushed her abilities.

Across the room, a knot of scholars hiding behind an overturned table on the second floor caught her eye. Entirely innocent men and women, many of whom had fetched her books and patiently instructed her in Daevabad's history. This was her home—this palace now filled with the dead she hadn't been able to protect—and she'd be damned if she was going to let that zahhak take another life under her roof.

Her skin prickled, magic simmering through her blood, tickling at her mind. She inhaled sharply, almost tasting the old stone. She could feel the canal, the cold water pressing hard against the thick wall.

Ali shivered as though she'd touched him. "Is that you?" A glance revealed his eyes had once again been swept by the oily dark film.

She nodded, examining the wall in her mind. The process felt suddenly familiar, much like the way she'd examine an arthritic spine for weak spots, and there were plenty here; the library had been built over two millennia ago. Roots snaked through crumbling bits of brick, rivulets of canal water stretching like grasping tentacles.

She *pulled*, encouraging the weak spots to crumble. She felt the wall shiver, the water churning on the other side. "Help me," she demanded, grabbing Ali's hand. The touch of his skin, cold and unusually clammy, sent an icy jolt down her spine that made the entire wall shake. She could see the water fighting its way in and worked to loosen the stone further.

A small leak sprang first. And then, in the time it took for her heart to skip, an entire section of the wall came down in a burst of broken bricks and surging water.

Nahri's eyes shot open. Had she not been concerned for both her life and the priceless manuscripts being swiftly destroyed, the sudden appearance of a stories-high waterfall in the middle of the library would have been an extraordinary sight. It crashed to the floor, rushing in a turbulent whirlpool of broken furniture and cresting whitecaps.

The spray caught the zahhak as it flew too close. It screeched, aiming a torrent of flames at the thundering water. Ali gasped, lurching back as if the fire caused him physical pain.

His movement attracted the zahhak's attention. The creature abruptly spun in the air and flew straight for them.

"Move!" Nahri grabbed Ali, pulling him out of the way just as the zahhak vaporized the shelves they'd taken shelter behind. "Jump!"

They jumped. The water was cold and swiftly rising, and Nahri was still struggling to her feet, hampered by her wet gown, when Ali shoved her head back under the water just as another fiery plume shot at them.

She emerged, gasping for breath and ducking a broken

wooden beam that rushed by. "Damn it, Ali, you made me break my library. Do something!"

He rose to face the zahhak, moving with a deadly grace, drops of water clinging to his skin like honey. He raised his hands, fixing his gaze on the zahhak as it came flying back at them. With a thunderous crack, the waterfall spun out like a whip across the air and cut the zahhak in two.

Their relief was short-lived. Ali swayed, sagging against her. "The door," he managed as she sent another burst of her own healing magic through him. "The door!"

They hurried on, wading as fast as they could through the makeshift river. Nahri lunged for the handle as the door came into reach.

A spray of arrows thudded into it, narrowly missing her hand.

"Suleiman's eye!" She whirled around. A half-dozen riders on smoky steeds were coming through the library's main entrance, silver bows drawn and ready in their hands.

"Just go!" Ali wrenched open the door and shoved her through. He slammed it shut behind them, piling various pieces of furniture to block it as Nahri caught her breath.

They'd entered a small, perfectly circular chamber. It resembled a well, the ceiling disappearing into the distant gloom. A rickety metal staircase climbed in a spiral around two softly glowing columns of amber light. Baskets overflowing with books and scrolls drifted in their midst, one column taking the baskets up while the other brought them down.

Ali nodded to the steps. "That goes straight to the pavilion." He unsheathed his zulfiqar. "Ready?"

Nahri took a deep breath, and they started climbing. Her heart raced with every shuddering groan of the staircase.

After what seemed like hours but was surely only minutes, they drew to a stop in front of a small wooden portal. "I hear voices," she whispered. "It sounds like Divasti."

He pressed an ear to the door. "At least three men," he agreed softly. "And trust me when I say the Afshin trained his soldiers well."

Nahri quickly considered their options. "Take me captive."

Ali looked at her as though she'd gone mad. "Excuse me?"

She shoved herself into his arms, bringing his khanjar to her throat. "Just play along," she hissed. "Give them a rant about fire worshippers and sin. Your reputation precedes you with my people." She kicked open the door before he could protest, dragging him with her. "Help me!" she cried pitifully in Divasti.

The Daeva warriors whirled around to stare at them. There were three, dressed in the same dark uniforms and armed to the teeth. They certainly looked like men Dara might have trained; one had an arrow aimed at them in a second flat.

Thankfully, Kaveh was nowhere to be seen. "Drop your weapons!" she begged, writhing against Ali's arm. "He'll kill me!"

Ali reacted a bit more smoothly than Nahri found comfortable, pressing the blade closer to her throat with a snarl. "Do it, fire worshippers!" he commanded. "Now! Or I'll gut your precious Banu Nahida!"

The closest Daeva gasped. "Banu Nahri?" he asked, his black eyes going wide. "Is that really you?"

"Yes!" she cried. "Now put down your weapons!"

They glanced at each other uncertainly until the archer swiftly lowered his bow. "Do it," he ordered. "That's Banu Manizheh's daughter."

The other two instantly complied.

"Where is my father?" Ali demanded. "What have you done with him?"

"Nothing, sand fly," one of the Daevas spat. "Why don't you let go of the girl and face us like a man? We threw the bodies of your father's men in the lake, but you still have time to join your Abba."

He stepped aside to reveal the dead king, and Nahri recoiled in horror. Ghassan's body had been abused, bloody boot marks staining his clothes, his jewelry and royal turban stripped away. His glassy, copper-hued gray eyes stared vacantly at the night sky, his face coated in blood.

Ali abruptly released her, and a look of rage unlike any she'd seen from him before, twisted his face.

He'd thrown himself at the Daeva soldiers before she could think to react, his zulfiqar bursting into flames. They moved fast, but they could not quite match the speed of the grief-stricken prince. With a cry he cut through the man who had spoken, yanking the blade free and swinging back to behead the archer who had recognized her.

And with that, Nahri was catapulted back into the night of the boat. The night she'd seen firsthand what Dara was truly capable of, the way he'd torn through the men surrounding him like some instrument of death, impervious to the blood and screams and brutal violence that surrounded him.

She stared at Ali in horror. She couldn't see anything of the bookish prince, the man who was still sometimes too shy to meet her eyes, in the raging warrior before her.

Is this how it starts? Was this how Dara had been undone, his soul stripped away as he watched the slaughter of his family and his tribe, his mind and body forged into a weapon by fury and despair? Is this how he'd been made into a monster who would visit that same violence on a new generation?

And yet Nahri still found herself lunging forward when the last Daeva raised his sword, preparing to strike. Nahri grabbed the man's arm, throwing him off balance as he spun to look at her, his expression one of utter betrayal.

Ali plunged the zulfiqar into his back.

Nahri stepped away, her hand going to her mouth. Her ears were ringing, bile choking her.

"Nahri!" Ali took her face in his hands, his own now wet with the blood of her tribesmen. "Nahri, look at me! Are you hurt?"

It seemed a ludicrous question. Nahri was beyond hurt. Her city was collapsing and the people dearest to her were dying or turning into creatures she couldn't recognize. And suddenly she wanted more than anything to flee. To race down the steps and out of the palace. To get on a boat, a horse, any damn thing that would take her back to the moment in her life before she decided to sing a zar song in Divasti.

The seal. Retrieve the seal and then you can sort all this out. She jerked back from his hands, pulling free one of her daggers as she moved automatically toward Ghassan's body.

Ali followed her, kneeling at his father's side. "I should have been here," he whispered. Tears came to his eyes, and something of the friend she knew returned to his face. "This is all my fault. He was too busy trying to deal with my rebellion to anticipate any of this."

Nahri said nothing. She had no assurances to offer right now. Instead, she cut a slit in Ghassan's bloody dishdasha, straight across the chest.

Ali moved to stop her. "What are you doing?"

"We have to burn his heart," she said, her voice unsteady. "The ring re-forms from the ash."

Ali dropped his hand as if he'd been burned. "What?"

She was able to summon up enough pity to soften her voice. "I'll do it. Between the two of us, I've a bit more experience carving into people's bodies."

He looked sick but didn't argue. "Thank you." He shifted away, taking his father's head in his lap, closing his eyes as he began to softly pray.

Nahri let the quiet Arabic words wash over her—reminding her of Cairo, as always. She worked quickly, cutting through the flesh and muscle of Ghassan's chest. There wasn't as much blood as she would have expected—perhaps since he'd already lost so much.

Not that it mattered. Nahri had been bathed in blood today. She expected its stain would never completely fade.

Even so, it was grim work, and Ali looked ready to pass out by the time she finally plunged her hand into Ghassan's chest. Her fingers closed around his still heart, and Nahri would be lying if she said she didn't feel a small twinge of dark pleasure. The tyrant who had toyed with lives as though they were pawns on a game board. The one who had forced her to marry his son because her own mother had denied him. The one who had threatened her brother's life—more than once.

Unbidden, a burst of heat bloomed in her palm, the dance of a conjured flame. Nahri quickly pulled her hand free, but his heart was already ash.

And clenched in her hand was something hard and hot. Nahri uncurled her fingers, her own heart racing.

The seal ring of the Prophet Suleiman—the ring whose power had reshaped their world and set their people at war—glistened in her bloody palm.

Ali gasped. "My God. Is that really it?"

Nahri let out a shaky breath. "Considering the circumstances . . ." She stared at the ring. As far as jewels went, Nahri wouldn't have necessarily been impressed by this one. There were no fancy gems or worked gold; instead a single battered black pearl crowned a thick dull gold band. The pearl had been carefully carved, something she didn't think possible, the eight-pointed star of Suleiman's seal gleaming from its surface. Etched around it were minuscule characters she couldn't read.

She trembled and she'd swear the ring vibrated in return, pulsing in time with her heart.

She wanted nothing to do with it. She shoved it at Ali. "Take it."

He leapt back. "Absolutely not. That belongs to you."

"But you . . . you're next in line for the throne!"

"And you're Anahid's descendant!" Ali pushed her fingers back over it, though she saw the flash of longing and regret in his eyes. "Suleiman gave it to your family, not mine."

A denial so strong it neared revulsion ran through her. "I can't," she whispered. "I'm not Anahid, Ali, I'm a con artist from Cairo!" And *Cairo* . . . Muntadhir's warning flashed through her mind. He said the ring couldn't leave Daevabad. "I have no business touching something that belonged to a prophet."

"Yes, you do." His expression turned fervent. "I believe in you."

"Have you met *you*?" she burst out. "Your belief is not a mark in my favor! I don't want this," she rushed on, and suddenly it was damnably clear. "If I take that ring, I'll be trapped here. I'll never see my home again!"

Ali looked incredulous. "This *is* your home!"

The door crashed open. Nahri had been so focused on her warring heart that she hadn't heard anyone approaching. Ali yanked his father's robe over the ghastly hole in his chest, and Nahri stumbled back, slipping Suleiman's ring into her pocket just before a group of Daeva warriors burst in.

They abruptly stopped, one holding up a fist as he took in the sight before him: the dead king and the very bloody young people at his feet. "He's up here!" he shouted in Divasti, directing his words to the staircase. "Along with a couple of djinn!"

A couple of djinn . . . no, Nahri supposed right now there was little to mark her out. She rose to her feet, her legs wobbly beneath her. "I am no djinn," she declared as another pair of warriors emerged. "I'm Banu Nahri e-Nahid, and you'll put your weapons down right now."

The man didn't get to respond. Her name was no sooner uttered than a slight figure pushed through the door. It was a Daeva woman, her eyes locked on Nahri. Dressed in a dark uniform, she made for an arresting sight, a silky black chador wrapping her head underneath a silver helmet. A steel sword, its edge bloodied, was tucked into her wide black belt.

She pulled the cloth away from her face, and Nahri nearly crumpled to the ground. It was a face that could be her own in another few decades.

"Nahri . . . ," the woman whispered, black eyes seeming to drink her in. She brought her fingers together. "Oh, child, it has been too long since I've looked upon your face."

THE DAEVA WOMAN CAME CLOSER, HER GAZE NOT leaving Nahri's. Nahri's heart was racing, her head spinning. . . .

The smell of burning papyrus and cries in Arabic. Soft arms pulling her into a tight embrace and water closing over her face. Memories that didn't make sense. Nahri found herself fighting for air, tears that she didn't understand brimming in her eyes.

She raised her dagger. "Don't come any closer!"

She immediately had four bows trained on her. She stepped back, stumbling against the stone parapet, and Ali grabbed her wrist before she lost her balance. The parapet was low here, the knee-high stone wall all that kept her from plunging into the lake.

"Stop!" The woman's curt command snapped like a whip, belying the softness in her voice when she'd spoken to Nahri. "Stand down. You're frightening her." She glared at the warriors and then jerked her head toward the door. "Leave us."

"But, my lady, the Afshin won't be happy to learn—"

"It is *I* you take orders from, not Darayavahoush."

Nahri did not know men could move so fast. They were gone in an instant, clattering down the steps.

Ali pressed closer. "Nahri, who is that?" he whispered.

"I . . . I don't know," she managed. She also didn't know why every Cairo-honed instinct in her was screaming at her to get away.

The woman watched the warriors leave with the sharpness of a general. She shut the door behind them and then pricked her finger on the sharp metal screen.

It surged together, instantly locking.

Nahri gasped. "You're a Nahid."

"I am," the woman replied. A soft, sad smile came to her lips. "You're beautiful," she added, seeming to take Nahri in again. "Marid curse be damned—you still have his eyes. I wondered if you would." Grief filled her face. "Do you . . . do you remember me?"

Nahri wasn't sure *what* she remembered. "I don't think so. I don't know." She knew she shouldn't be confessing anything to the woman who claimed to be in command of the forces attacking the palace, but the fact that she claimed to be a Nahid wasn't doing much for Nahri's wits. "Who are you?"

The same broken smile, the look of someone who'd been through far too much. "My name is Manizheh."

The name, both unbelievable and obvious, punched through her. *Manizheh.*

Ali gasped. "Manizheh?" he repeated. "Your *mother*?"

"Yes," Manizheh said in Djinnistani. She only now seemed to realize Ali was there, her gaze leaving Nahri's for the first time. Her dark eyes scanned him, lingering on his zulfiqar. She blinked, looking taken aback. "Is this Hatset's son?" she asked Nahri, returning to Divasti. "The prince they call Alizayd?" She frowned. "You were to be in the infirmary with Nisreen. What are you doing with him?"

Nahri opened her mouth, still reeling. *Manizheh. My mother.* It seemed even more impossible than Dara rising from the dead.

She fought for words. "He . . . he's my friend." It was a ridiculous answer and yet it was the first that came to her. It also seemed wiser than admitting they were here stealing Suleiman's seal. "What are *you* doing here?" she demanded, feeling a little of her sharpness return. "I was told you were dead. Kaveh told me he found your murdered body decades ago!"

Manizheh's expression turned solemn. "A necessary deception and one I pray you can eventually forgive. You were taken from me as a child by the marid, and I feared I'd lost you forever. When I learned you'd fallen into Ghassan's hands . . . the things I'm sure he has subjected you to . . . I am so sorry, Nahri." She stepped forward as if she wanted to take Nahri's hand and then stopped as Nahri cringed. "But I promise you—you're safe now."

Safe. The word echoed inside her head. *My mother. My brother. Dara.* In the space of a few hours, Nahri had gone from being the only living Nahid to having a whole family of relatives to form a council again, with a damned Afshin to boot.

Her eyes were wet, the constant loneliness she carried in her chest expanding to the point where it was difficult to breathe. This couldn't be possible.

But the brutal evidence was before her. Who else but a Nahid would be capable of creating the poison dealing death to the Geziri tribe? Who else but the Banu Nahida rumored to be the most powerful in centuries would be able to bring Dara back from the dead, to make him obey completely?

Suleiman's seal ring burned in her pocket. It was the only ace Nahri had. Because no matter what this woman said, Nahri did not feel like they were on the same side. She had meant what she said to Muntadhir: she wasn't on the side of anyone who'd arranged for the deaths of so many innocents.

Manizheh raised her hands. "I mean you no harm," she said carefully. She switched to Djinnistani, her voice cooling as she addressed Ali. "Put down your weapons. Surrender yourself to my men, and you won't be hurt."

That had the predicted response, Ali's eyes flashing as he raised his zulfiqar. "I won't surrender to the person who orchestrated the slaughter of my people."

"Then you will die," Manizheh said simply. "You have lost, al Qahtani. Do what you can to save those Geziris left." Her voice turned persuasive. "You have a sister in the palace, and a mother I once knew in Ta Ntry, do you not? Believe me when I say I would rather not inform another woman of her children's deaths."

Ali scoffed. "You mean to make us into pawns." He raised his chin defiantly. "I would rather die."

Nahri had absolutely no doubt that was true; she also had no doubt most of the surviving Geziris would feel similarly. Which meant they needed to get off this damned wall and away from Manizheh.

Take the ring, you fool. She could thrust her hand into her pocket and claim Suleiman's seal for herself in the same time it would take Manizheh to lunge for it.

And then? What if she couldn't call upon it correctly? Nahri was guessing the prophetically granted abilities of a magical ring likely had a learning curve. She and Ali would still be stuck on this pavilion with a vengeful Banu Nahida and a swarm of warriors below.

She stepped between Ali and Manizheh. "And that's what you're after?" she demanded. "If we surrendered . . . could you contain the poison?"

Manizheh spread her hands, stepping closer. "But of course." Her gaze returned to Nahri. "But I'm not after *your* surrender, daughter. Why would I be?" She took another step toward them, but stilled as she spotted Ghassan's body.

Her entire expression changed as her eyes swept his face. "Suleiman's mark is gone from his brow."

Nahri glanced down. Manizheh spoke the truth; the black tattoo that had once marked Ghassan's face had vanished.

"Did you take the seal?" Manizheh demanded. Her voice had shifted, barely concealed desire evident beneath her words. "Where is it?" When neither one of them responded, she pursed her mouth in a thin line, looking like she was growing exasperated with their defiance. The expression was almost maternal. "Please do not make me ask again."

"You're not getting it," Ali burst out. "I don't care who you claim to be. You're a monster. You brought ghouls and ifrit into our city; you have the blood of thousands on your—"

Manizheh snapped her fingers.

There was an audible pop, and then Ali cried out, collapsing as he clutched his left knee.

"Ali!" Nahri spun, reaching for him.

"If you try to heal him, I'll break his neck next." The cold threat sliced the air, and Nahri instantly dropped her hand, startled. "Forgive me," Manizheh said, seeming sincere. "This is not at all how I wanted our first meeting to go, but I will not have you interfere. I have planned too many decades for this." She glanced again at Ali. "Do not make me torture you before her eyes. The ring. Now."

"He doesn't have it!" Nahri shoved her hand in her pocket, her fingers running over the two rings there before plucking one out. She thrust her fist over the parapet, letting the ring dangle precariously from her finger. "And unless you're willing to spend the next century searching the lake for this, I'd leave him alone."

Manizheh drew back, studying Nahri. "You won't do it."

Nahri raised a brow. "You don't know me."

"But I do." Manizheh's tone was imploring. "Nahri, you're my daughter . . . do you imagine I've not sought stories of you from every Daevabadi I've met? Dara himself can hardly stop speaking of you. Your bravery, your cleverness . . . In truth a more devoted man I've rarely met. A dangerous thing in our world," she added delicately. "To make plain your affections. A truth Ghassan was always too willing to make cruelly clear to me."

Nahri didn't know what to say. Manizheh's words about Dara felt like salt on a wound, and she could feel the other woman reading her, evaluating her every flinch. Ali was still clutching his knee, breathing heavily against the pain.

Her mother came nearer. "Ghassan's done that to you as well, hasn't he? It's the only way he had to control women like us. I *know* you, Nahri. I know what it's like to have ambitions, to be the cleverest in the room—and have those ambitions crushed. To have men who are less than you bully and threaten you into a place you know you don't belong. I've heard of the extraordinary strides you've made in just a few years. The things I could teach you; you'd be a goddess. You'd never have to lower your head again."

Their gazes met, and Nahri could not deny the surge of longing in her heart. She thought of the countless times she'd bowed to Ghassan while he sat on her ancestors' throne. The way Muntadhir had dismissed her dreams for the hospital and Kaveh had condescended to her in the Temple.

The smoky binds Dara had dared conjure to hold her. The magic that had raged through her blood in response.

Nahri took a deep breath. *This is my home.*

"Why don't we compromise?" she suggested. "You want the Nahids in charge again? Fine. I'm a Nahid. *I'll* take Suleiman's seal. Surely, I can negotiate a peace more effectively than a woman who abandoned her tribe and returned only to plot the slaughter of another."

Manizheh stiffened. "No," she said. "You can't."

"Why not?" Nahri asked archly. "This is about what's best for the Daevas, isn't it?"

"You misunderstand me, daughter," Manizheh replied, and Nahri inwardly swore because try as she could to read it, there was nothing in this woman's face that gave her thoughts away.

"You cannot take the seal yourself because you are not—entirely—daeva. You're shafit, Nahri. You have human blood."

Nahri stared at her in silence. Because with those words—those utterly confident words—Nahri knew the woman before her was not lying about being her mother. It was a secret only Ghassan had known, the truth he said Suleiman's seal made clear.

"What do you mean, she's *shafit*?" Ali gasped from the ground.

Nahri didn't respond; she didn't know what to say.

"It's all right," Manizheh assured her gently as she approached them. "It's not a thing anyone else need ever know. But you cannot take that seal. Possessing it will kill you. You simply aren't strong enough."

Nahri jerked back. "I'm strong enough to use Nahid magic."

"But enough to wield Suleiman's seal?" Manizheh pressed. "To be the bearer of the object that reshaped our world?" She shook her head. "It will tear you apart, my daughter."

Nahri fell silent. *She's lying. She has to be.* But by the Most High, if Manizheh hadn't struck doubt into her soul.

"Nahri." It was Ali. "Nahri, look at me." She did, feeling dazed. This was all too much. "She's lying. Suleiman himself had human blood."

"Suleiman was a prophet," Manizheh cut in, echoing with brutal effectiveness the insecurity that Nahri herself had expressed. "And no one asked you to involve yourself in a Nahid matter, djinn. I have spent longer than you've been alive reading every text that ever mentioned that seal ring. And all of them are clear on this point."

"And that's rather convenient, I'd say," he shot back. He stared up at Nahri, beseeching. "Don't listen to her. Take the—ah!" He yelped in pain, his hands wrenching from his shattered knee.

Manizheh snapped her fingers again, and Ali's hands jerked to the khanjar at his waist.

"What-what are you doing to me?" he cried as his fingers

cracked around the dagger's hilt. Beneath his tattered sleeves, the muscles in his wrists were seizing, the khanjar coming free in shuddering, spasming movements.

My God . . . *Manizheh* was doing that? Without even touching him? Instinctively Nahri sought to pull on the magic of the palace.

She didn't so much as make a stone shiver before her connection was abruptly severed. The loss was like a blow, a coldness seeping over her.

"Don't, child," Manizheh warned. "I have far more experience than you." She brought her hands together. "I do not wish this. But if you don't hand the ring over right now, I will kill him."

The khanjar was nearing Ali's throat. He wriggled against it, a line of blood appearing below his jaw. His eyes were bright with pain, sweat running down his face.

Nahri was frozen in horror. She could feel Manizheh's magic wrapping around her, teasing at the muscles in her own hand. Nahri was not capable of *anything* like that—she didn't know how to *fight* someone capable of anything like that.

But she knew damned well she couldn't give her Suleiman's seal.

Manizheh spoke again. "They have already lost. We have won—*you* have won. Nahri, hand over the ring. No one else will ever learn you're shafit. Take your place as my daughter, with your brother at your side. Greet the new generation as one of the rightful rulers of this city. With a man who loves you."

Nahri wracked her mind. She didn't know who to believe. But if Manizheh was right, if Nahri took the seal and it killed her, Ali would swiftly follow. And then there'd be no one to stop the woman who'd just slaughtered thousands from gaining control of the most powerful object in their world.

Nahri couldn't risk that. She also knew that, shafit or not, she had her own skills when it came to dealing with people. In going after Nahri the way she had, Manizheh had made clear what she believed her daughter's weaknesses to be.

Nahri could work with that. She took a shaky breath. "You promise you'll let the prince live?" she whispered, her fingers trembling on the ring. "And that no one will ever know I'm a shafit?"

"On our family's honor. I swear."

Nahri bit her lip. "Not even Dara?"

Manizheh's face softened slightly, with both sadness and a little relief. "I'll do my best, child. I have no desire to cause you further pain. Either of you," she added, looking as genuinely moved as Nahri had yet seen her. "Indeed, nothing would please me more than to see you find some happiness together."

Nahri let the words slide past her. That would never happen. "Then take it," she said, tossing the ring at her mother's feet.

Manizheh was as good as her word. The ring had no sooner left Nahri's hand than the khanjar dropped from Ali's throat. Nahri fell to his side as he gasped for breath.

"Why did you do that?" he wheezed.

"Because she was going to kill you." As Manizheh bent to retrieve the ring, Nahri swiftly moved as though to embrace him, taking the opportunity to shove his weapons back in his belt. "Are you sure the curse is off the lake?" she whispered in his ear.

Ali stiffened in her arms. "I . . . yes?"

She pulled him to his feet, keeping her hand on his arm. "Then forgive me, my friend."

Manizheh was straightening up with the ring in her hand. She frowned, studying the emerald. "This is the seal ring?"

"Of course it is," Nahri said airily, pulling the second ring—Suleiman's ring—from her pocket. "Who would lie to their mother?" She shoved the ring onto one of Ali's fingers.

Ali tried to jerk free, but Nahri was fast. Her heart gave a single lurch of regret, and then—just as Manizheh glanced up—she felt the ancient band vanish beneath her fingers.

Shocked betrayal blossomed in her mother's eyes—ah, so Manizheh had emotions after all. But Nahri was not waiting for a response. She grabbed Ali's hand and jumped off the wall.

She heard Manizheh cry her name, but it was too late. The cold night air lashed at her face as they fell, the dark water looking a *lot* farther away than she remembered. She tried to steel herself, all too aware that she was in for a great deal of pain and some temporarily broken bones.

Indeed, she hit hard, the crash of the water against her body a cold, painful thrust like a thousand sharp knives. Her arms flew out, tangling in Ali's as she submerged.

She shuddered with pain, with shock, as the memory Manizheh had triggered came briefly again. The smell of burning papyrus, the screams of a young girl.

The sight of a pair of warm brown eyes just before muddy water closed over her head.

Nahri never broke the surface. Darkness whirled around her, the smell of silt and the sensation of being seized.

There was a single whisper of magic and then everything went black.

41

DARA

Dara was not going to last another minute with Muntadhir al Qahtani.

For an actively dying man, the emir was running his mouth at remarkable speed, gasping out an unending stream of barbs obviously calculated to goad Dara into killing him.

"And our *wedding night*," Muntadhir continued. "Well . . . nights. I mean, they all started to blend together after—"

Dara abruptly pressed his knife to the other man's throat. It was the tenth time he'd done so. "If you do not stop talking," he hissed. "I'm going to start cutting pieces off of you."

Muntadhir blinked, his eyes a dark shadow against his wan face. He'd paled to the color of parchment, ash crumbling on his skin, and the green-black lines of the zulfiqar poisoning— creeping, curling marks—had spread to his throat. He opened his mouth and then winced, falling back against the carpet Dara had enchanted to speed them to Manizheh, a flash of pain in his eyes perhaps stealing whatever obnoxious response he had planned.

No matter—Dara's attention had been captured by a far stranger sight: water was gushing through the corridor they flew down, the unnatural stream growing deeper and wilder the closer they came to the library. He'd raced to the infirmary only to be told that a panicked, rambling Kaveh e-Pramukh had intercepted Manizheh and sent her here.

They soared through the doors, and Dara blinked in alarm. Water was pouring through a jagged hole near the ceiling, crashing against the now flooded library floor. Broken furniture and smoldering books—not to mention the bodies of at least a dozen djinn—lay scattered. Manizheh was nowhere to be seen, but he spotted across the room a knot of the warriors who'd been accompanying her.

Dara was there in seconds, landing the rug as gently as possible on an island of debris and splashing into the water. "Where is the Banu—"

He didn't get to finish the question.

A tremor tore through the palace, the ground beneath him shaking so violently he stumbled. The entire library shuddered, piles of debris collapsing and several of the massive shelves breaking free of the walls.

"Watch out!" Dara cried as a cascade of books and scrolls rained down upon them. Another tremor followed, and a crack ripped across the opposite wall with such force that the floor split.

The quake was over in seconds, an eerie hush hanging over them. The water drained away, surging toward the rent in the floor like an animal fleeing. And then . . . as though someone had blown out a lamp he couldn't see, Dara felt a shift in the air.

With a bone-jarring popping sound, the globes of conjured fire that floated near the ceiling abruptly went out, crashing to the ground. The fluttering black al Qahtani banners grew still, and the door ahead of him flew open. All the doors did, whatever locking enchantments had been set seemingly broken.

A chill went down his spine at the silence, at the odd, empty coldness that had stolen through the room. Dara conjured a handful of flames, the firelight dancing along the scorched and water-stained walls. Ahead, his men appeared to be struggling to do the same, gesturing wildly at the dark.

"Can you conjure flames?" he heard one ask.

"I can't conjure anything!"

A far more shocked cry caught his ear. Dara whirled around. Muntadhir had staggered to his feet, swaying as he held out his arms to gape at his body.

In the dim light of the ruined library, the deadly dark lines of the magical poison that marked the emir's skin were retreating.

Dara's mouth fell open as he watched the utterly impossible sight before him. Like a spider curling in on itself, the poison was leaching away, creeping back from Muntadhir's shoulders and down past his chest. Muntadhir ripped away the cloth binding his stomach just in time to reveal the dark green hue lifting from the wound altogether. And then—with the barest hint of smoke—it vanished entirely.

The emir dropped to his knees with a choked sob. He touched his bloody stomach, weeping with relief.

Dread rose in Dara's heart. Something had just gone *very* wrong. "Bind that man!" he managed to snap at his soldiers. Dara didn't need any more surprises when it came to Muntadhir and weapons. "*Now*. And where is the Banu Nahida?"

One of his men raised a finger toward a darkened set of stairs. "I'm sorry, Afshin," he said, his arm trembling wildly. "She ordered us away when we found Banu Nahri."

Nahri. Muntadhir instantly forgotten, Dara raced through the door and then ducked as the remains of an enchanted pulley system came crashing down around him. Heedless of the destruction, he took the steps two at a time, arriving at another door.

"Banu Nahida!" he called loudly. When there was no response, he kicked the door in.

Manizheh stood alone and very still, her back to him, among a tangle of bodies. Fear clawed up in his throat as Dara forced himself to examine their faces. *No, Creator, no. I beg you.*

But Nahri wasn't among the dead. Instead, they were his own men. They'd been slaughtered, still-smoldering slashes rending their bodies.

A zulfiqar. *Alizayd.* Dara knew it in his bones. And it was entirely his fault. He should have killed the prince the second he had him, instead of letting Vizaresh delay him with fantasies of vengeance.

Mardoniye. His warriors on the beach. Now these three. Dara clenched his fists, fighting the heat aching to burst free. This had all gone so wrong—and not just because of the ifrit.

It had gone wrong because in his heart, Dara had known this invasion was a mistake. It was too rushed and too brutal. They'd allied with creatures he didn't trust and used magic he didn't understand. And he had gone along, had bowed his head in submission to a Nahid again and dismissed the disquiet in his soul. Now it had blown up in his face.

It wasn't even the first time. His own history had taught him nothing.

Manizheh had yet to move. She just stood there, staring at the dark lake. "Banu Manizheh?" he spoke again.

"It's gone." Her voice was an uncharacteristic whisper. "*They're* gone. She gave the seal to that sand fly."

Dara staggered back. "*What?* You can't mean . . ."

"I mean exactly as I say." There was an edge in Manizheh's voice. "I should have known better," she murmured. "I should have known not to trust her. She deceived me, *mocked* me, and then gave Suleiman's seal—our ancestors' seal—back to the people who stole it."

Dara's gaze fell again on the murdered men and for the first time, he felt a sting of true betrayal. How could Nahri have given something so powerful, so precious, to a man she'd watched slaughter her own people?

He swallowed, pushing his roiling emotions down. "Where are they?" he asked, trying to check the tremor in his voice. "Banu Nahida, *where are they*?" he pressed when she didn't answer.

She raised a trembling hand, gesturing to the dark water. "They jumped."

"They did *what*?" Dara was at the parapet in seconds. He saw nothing but the black water below.

"They jumped." Manizheh's voice was bitter. "I tried to reason with her, but that djinn had his claws in her mind."

Dara fell to his knees. He clutched the stone, and a stir of movement caught his eye, small swells and eddies glimmering on the dark lake.

He let out his breath. "The water is moving," he whispered. Dara leaned out farther, examining the distance. Surely, a Nahid healer could survive that fall. If she'd jumped clear of the rocks, if she landed the right way . . .

Hope and grief warred in his chest. *Creator, please . . . let her be alive.* Dara didn't care if she greeted him with a dagger to his heart; after tonight, part of him would welcome it. But this couldn't be how Nahri's story ended.

He rose unsteadily to his feet. "I am going to find her."

Manizheh grabbed his wrist. "Stop."

The flat word, uttered as one might issue a command to some sort of animal, broke the fragile grip he had on his emotions.

"I have done everything you asked!" he choked out, wrenching free of her grip. "I have been your Afshin. I have killed your enemies and bloodied our home. You can grant me a few moments to find out whether she still lives."

Manizheh's eyes lit in outrage, but her voice remained cool. "Nahri isn't what's important right now, Darayavahoush." She abruptly pointed up. "That is."

Dara glanced up.

The sky above the palace was shattering.

It looked like a smoky glass dome cracking, the inky midnight peeling away to reveal the warmer hues of dawn, the glow of a desert sky instead of the murky fog that lurked, ever present, above Daevabad. It was spreading, rippling out across the horizon. And as his gaze followed the falling sky, he noticed rooftop fires were winking out across the city. A camp of travelers' tents, magical creations of silk and smoke, collapsed, as did two conjured marble towers.

Dara was utterly bewildered. "What is going on?" He glanced at Manizheh, but she wasn't looking at him. As Dara watched, she drew her sword, pricking her thumb on the blade. A well of black blood blossomed. And then another.

The color left her face. "My magic . . . it's gone."

Coldness swept him as he watched more fires blink out. The stillness that had fallen over the library, the poison that had drained from the emir . . .

"I do not think it is your magic alone," he whispered. "I think it is all of Daevabad's."

EPILOGUE

Consciousness tickled at Nahri, the rich smell of mud and sweet birdsong pulling her from darkness.

The pain came next, her back and shoulders aching. Her head. Her arms. Everything, really.

And that damned sun. Too bright. Brighter than any sun in Daevabad had any right being. Nahri shaded her eyes with one hand, blinking as she tried to sit up.

Her other hand sank into mud. What in God's name . . . Nahri looked around as sunspots cleared from her eyes. She was sitting in some sort of flooded marsh, waist deep in cloudy water. Just behind her was a grove of tall, bristling palm trees, scrubby greenery growing unchecked over a crumbling mud-brick wall.

Ahead was a wide river, its current languid as it stretched to flow across its floodplains. A narrow emerald band of greenery bordered the opposite bank, beyond which was desert, gleaming golden in the bright sun.

Nahri stared at the river in utter incomprehension. She must have taken a blow to the head. Because she would *swear* that it looked like . . .

"No!" A familiar voice broke the still air, ending in a wail. "*No!*"

Ali. Nahri scrambled to her feet, aching all over. What was wrong with her healing abilities? The mud sucked at her legs, and she clambered past the marsh to firmer land. She caught sight of more ruined structures between the trees: a cracked pigeon coop and the bare brick outlines of what might have once been small homes.

She pushed through a cluster of palm fronds. Just ahead was what looked like a village mosque—one long abandoned. Its minaret was broken, its dome cracked open to the sky.

Relief coursed through her—Ali was inside, his back to her as he peered past the top of the minaret. She staggered forward, her limbs protesting every jolt and her skin crawling. Nahri didn't know where they were—it certainly didn't look like Daevabad—but she felt as though she'd been here before.

She climbed up the ruined minaret's stone steps. Thoroughly out of breath by the time she reached the top, Nahri stumbled forward, reaching for his shoulder as she wheezed out his name. "Ali."

He was sobbing when he spun on her.

Suleiman's seal burned bright on his temple.

The events of the night before came together too fast, too horrible, and then Ali was lunging at her, putting his hands on her shoulders like he never had before.

"You have to take us back!" he begged. Closer now, Nahri could see that his face was feverish, his entire body twitching. "Nahri, please! They have my sister! They have every—*ah*," His voice broke as he clutched at his heart, gasping for air.

"Ali!"

He shoved himself away from her. "I can't control this." The smoky mark of the seal shimmered on his skin. "You should never have given me that ring! You should never have taken us away!"

"I haven't taken us anywhere!"

Ali raised a shaking hand. "Then why are we *here*?"

Nahri glanced where he was pointing. She stood.

The sight before her on the not-so-distant horizon was immediately familiar. The ancient stone mosques and towering minarets. The forts and palaces of long-dead sultans and generals, dynasties lost to time. The countless blocks of multistoried buildings, all an earthy warm brown, a *human* warm brown, that Nahri knew rose over twisting, busy streets of jostling shopkeepers, gossiping coffee drinkers, and racing children. Over apothecaries.

Tears sprang to her eyes. *It's not possible*. Her gaze immediately darted from the city she'd have known anywhere to the swollen river at its banks. The river for which she'd been jokingly named by fishermen who'd plucked her out of it as a child.

On the opposite shore, standing unmoving and eternal against the dawn sky, were the three Pyramids of Giza.

The words came to her in Arabic first, of course. "Ya masr," she whispered softly as the Egyptian sun warmed her cheeks, the scent of the Nile's silt on her skin. "I'm home."

CAST OF CHARACTERS

THE ROYAL FAMILY

Daevabad is currently ruled by the Qahtani family, descendants of Zaydi al Qahtani, the Geziri warrior who led a rebellion to overthrow the Nahid Council and establish equality for the shafit centuries ago.

GHASSAN AL QAHTANI, king of the magical realm, defender of the faith

MUNTADHIR, Ghassan's eldest son from his Geziri first wife, the king's designated successor

HATSET, Ghassan's Ayaanle second wife and queen, hailing from a powerful family in Ta Ntry

ZAYNAB, Ghassan and Hatset's daughter, princess of Daevabad

ALIZAYD, the king's youngest son, banished to Am Gezira for treason

Their Court and Royal Guard

WAJED, Qaid and leader of the djinn army

ABU NUWAS, a Geziri officer

KAVEH E-PRAMUKH, the Daeva grand wazir

JAMSHID, his son and close confidant of Emir Muntadhir

ABUL DAWANIK, a trade envoy from Ta Ntry

ABU SAYF, an old soldier and scout in the Royal Guard

AQISA and LUBAYD, warriors and trackers from Bir Nabat, a village in Am Gezira

THE MOST HIGH AND BLESSED NAHIDS

The original rulers of Daevabad and descendants of Anahid, the Nahids were a family of extraordinary magical healers hailing from the Daeva tribe.

ANAHID, Suleiman's chosen and the original founder of Daevabad

RUSTAM, one of the last Nahid healers and a skilled botanist, murdered by the ifrit

MANIZHEH, Rustam's sister and one of the most powerful Nahid healers in centuries, murdered by the ifrit

NAHRI, her daughter of uncertain parentage, left abandoned as a young child in the human land of Egypt

Their Supporters

DARAYAVAHOUSH, the last descendent of the Afshins, a Daeva military caste family that served at the right hand of the Nahid Council, and known as the Scourge of Qui-zi for his violent acts during the war and later revolt against Zaydi al Qahtani

KARTIR, a Daeva high priest

NISREEN, Manizheh and Rustam's former assistant and Nahri's current mentor

IRTEMIZ, MARDONIYE, and BAHRAM, soldiers

THE SHAFIT

People of mixed human and djinn heritage forced to live in Daevabad, their rights sharply curtailed.

SHEIKH ANAS, former leader of the Tanzeem and Ali's mentor, executed by the king for treason

SISTER FATUMAI, Tanzeem leader who oversaw the group's orphanage and charitable services

SUBHASHINI and PARIMAL SEN, shafit physicians

THE IFRIT

Daevas who refused to submit to Suleiman thousands of years ago and were subsequently cursed; the mortal enemies of the Nahids.

AESHMA, their leader

VIZARESH, the ifrit who first came for Nahri in Cairo

QANDISHA, the ifrit who enslaved and murdered Dara

THE FREED SLAVES OF THE IFRIT

Reviled and persecuted after Dara's rampage and death at Prince Alizayd's hand, only three formerly enslaved djinn remain in Daevabad, freed and resurrected by Nahid healers years ago.

RAZU, a gambler from Tukharistan

ELASHIA, an artist from Qart Sahar

ISSA, a scholar and historian from Ta Ntry

GLOSSARY

Beings of Fire

DAEVA: The ancient term for all fire elementals before the djinn rebellion, as well as the name of the tribe residing in Daevastana, of which Dara and Nahri are both part. Once shapeshifters who lived for millennia, the daevas had their magical abilities sharply curbed by the Prophet Suleiman as a punishment for harming humanity.

DJINN: A human word for "daeva." After Zaydi al Qahtani's rebellion, all his followers, and eventually all daevas, began using this term for their race.

IFRIT: The original daevas who defied Suleiman and were stripped of their abilities. Sworn enemies of the Nahid family, the ifrit revenge themselves by enslaving other djinn to cause chaos among humanity.

SIMURGH: Scaled firebirds that the djinn are fond of racing.

ZAHHAK: A large, flying, fire-breathing lizard-like beast.

Beings of Water

MARID: Extremely powerful water elementals. Near mythical to the djinn, the marid haven't been seen in centuries, though it's rumored the lake surrounding Daevabad was once theirs.

Beings of Air

PERI: Air elementals. More powerful than the djinn—and far more secretive—the peri keep resolutely to themselves.

RUKH: Enormous predatory firebirds that the peri can use for hunting.

SHEDU: Mythical winged lions, an emblem of the Nahid family.

Beings of Earth

GHOULS: The reanimated, cannibalistic corpses of humans who have made deals with the ifrit.

ISHTAS: A small, scaled creature obsessed with organization and footwear.

KARKADANN: A magical beast similar to an enormous rhinoceros with a horn as long as a man.

NASNAS: A venomous creature resembling a bisected human that prowls the deserts of Am Gezira and whose bite causes flesh to wither away.

Languages

DIVASTI: The language of the Daeva tribe.

DJINNISTANI: Daevabad's common tongue, a merchant creole the djinn and shafit use to speak to those outside their tribe.

GEZIRIYYA: The language of the Geziri tribe, which only members of their tribe can speak and understand.

General Terminology

ABAYA: A loose, floor-length, full-sleeved dress worn by women.

ADHAN: The Islamic call to prayer.

AFSHIN: The name of the Daeva warrior family who once served the Nahid Council. Also used as a title.

AKHI: "My brother."

BAGA NAHID: The proper title for male healers of the Nahid family.

BANU NAHIDA: The proper title for female healers of the Nahid family.

CHADOR: An open cloak made from a semicircular cut of fabric, draped over the head and worn by Daeva women.

DIRHAM/DINAR: A type of currency used in Egypt.

DISHDASHA: A floor-length man's tunic, popular among the Geziri.

EMIR: The crown prince and designated heir to the Qahtani throne.

FAJR: The dawn hour/dawn prayer.

GALABIYYA: A traditional Egyptian garment, essentially a floor-length tunic.

GHUTRA: A male headdress.

HAMMAM: A bathhouse.

ISHA: The late evening hour/evening prayer.

MAGHRIB: The sunset hour/sunset prayer.

MIDAN: A plaza/city square.

MIHRAB: A wall niche indicating the direction of prayer.

MUHTASIB: A market inspector.

NAVASATEM: A holiday held once a century to celebrate another generation of freedom from Suleiman's servitude. Originally a Daeva festival, Navasatem is a beloved tradition in Daevabad, attracting djinn from all over the world to take part in weeks of festivals, parades, and competitions.

QAID: The head of the Royal Guard, essentially the top military official in the djinn army.

RAKAT: A unit of prayer.

SHAFIT: People with mixed djinn and human blood.

SHAYLA: A type of women's headscarf.

SHEIKH: A religious educator/leader.

SULEIMAN'S SEAL: The seal ring Suleiman once used to control the djinn, given to the Nahids and later stolen by the Qahtanis. The bearer of Suleiman's ring can nullify any magic.

TALWAR: An Agnivanshi sword.

TANZEEM: A grassroots fundamentalist group in Daevabad dedicated to fighting for shafit rights and religious reform.

UKHTI: "My sister."

ULEMA: A legal body of religious scholars.

WAZIR: A government minister.

ZAR: A traditional ceremony meant to deal with djinn possession.

ZUHR: The noon hour/noon prayer.

ZULFIQAR: The forked copper blades of the Geziri tribe; when inflamed, their poisonous edges destroy even Nahid flesh, making them among the deadliest weapons in this world.

THE SIX TRIBES
OF THE DJINN

THE GEZIRI

Surrounded by water and caught behind the thick band of humanity in the Fertile Crescent, the djinn of Am Gezira awoke from Suleiman's curse to a far different world than their fire-blooded cousins. Retreating to the depths of the Empty Quarter, to the dying cities of the Nabateans and to the forbidding mountains of southern Arabia, the Geziri eventually learned to share the hardships of the land with their human neighbors, becoming fierce protectors of the shafit in the process. From this country of wandering poets and zulfiqar-wielding warriors came Zaydi al Qahtani, the rebel-turned-king who would seize Daevabad and Suleiman's seal from the Nahid family in a war that remade the magical world.

THE AYAANLE

Nestled between the rushing headwaters of the Nile River and the salty coast of Bet il Tiamat lies Ta Ntry, the fabled homeland of the mighty Ayaanle tribe. Rich in gold and salt—and far enough from Daevabad that its deadly politics are more game than risk, the Ayaanle are a people to envy. But behind their gleaming coral mansions and sophisticated salons lurks a history they've begun to forget . . . one that binds them in blood to their Geziri neighbors.

THE DAEVAS

Stretching from the Sea of Pearls across the plains of Persia and the mountains of gold-rich Bactria is mighty Daevastana—and just past its Gozan River lies Daevabad, the hidden city of brass. The ancient seat of the Nahid Council—the famed family of healers who once ruled the magical world—Daevastana is a coveted land, its civilization drawn from the ancient cities of Ur and Susa and the nomadic horsemen of the Saka. A proud people, the Daevas claimed the original name of the djinn race as their own . . . a slight that the other tribes never forget.

THE SAHRAYN

Sprawling from the shores of the Maghreb across the vast depths of the Sahara Desert is Qart Sahar—a land of fables and adventure even to the djinn. An enterprising people not particularly enamored of being ruled by foreigners, the Sahrayn know the mysteries of their country better than any—the still lush rivers that flow in caves deep below the sand dunes and the ancient citadels of human civilizations lost to time and touched by forgotten magic. Skilled sailors, the Sahrayn travel upon ships of conjured smoke and sewn cord over sand and sea alike.

THE AGNIVANSHI

Stretching from the brick bones of old Harappa through the rich plains of the Deccan and misty marshes of the Sundarbans lies Agnivansha. Blessedly lush in every resource that could be dreamed—and separated from their far more volatile neighbors by wide rivers and soaring mountains—Agnivansha is a peaceful land famed for its artisans and jewels . . . and its savvy in staying out of Daevabad's tumultuous politics.

THE TUKHARISTANIS

East of Daevabad, twisting through the peaks of Karakorum Mountains and the vast sands of the Gobi is Tukharistan. Trade is its lifeblood, and in the ruins of forgotten Silk Road kingdoms, the Tukharistanis make their homes. They travel unseen in caravans of smoke and silk along corridors marked by humans millennia ago, carrying with them things of myth: golden apples that cure any disease, jade keys that open worlds unseen, and perfumes that smell of paradise.

ACKNOWLEDGEMENTS

Two years ago, I tentatively sent the first book in what would become the Daevabad Trilogy off for submission. Never in my wildest dreams did I imagine my five-hundred-plus-page homage to the medieval Islamic world would gain the extraordinary reception it has, and as I put the finishing touches on its sequel, I am humbled and grateful for the opportunity I've been given to share the story and characters who've lived in my head with the rest of the world. It has been a journey and one that would have never been possible without an amazing group of readers, fantastic fellow writers, a crack publishing team, an extremely understanding family, and quite frankly, the grace of God.

First, to all the readers, reviewers, bloggers, fan artists, and booksellers who loved and spread the word about my book, thank you. You're what makes this all worth it.

A huge thanks as well to all the amazing scholars and "Twitterstorians" who helped me hone this book, whether by helping me track down incredibly specific views of the Cairo waterfront in the nineteenth century or crafting jokes in Akkadian. Your love of history and willingness to share knowledge with the public sphere is exactly what we need nowadays.

To the amazing Brooklyn Speculative Fiction Writers, particularly Rob Cameron, Jonathan Hernandez, and Cynthia Lovett, who came to my aid when I was in the thick of Book 2 despair . . . you're the absolute best and I look forward to your own books flying off shelves one day.

I've been blessed to make the acquaintance of a truly wonderful number of fellow authors in the past few years whose blurbs, words of advice, or simply sympathetic ears made a world of difference to this fretting rookie. S. K. Ali, Roshani Chokshi, Nicky Drayden, Sarah Beth Durst, Kate Elliot, Kevin Hearne, Robin Hobb, Ausma Zehanat Khan, Khaalidah Muhammad-Ali, Karuna Riazi, Michael J. Sullivan, Shveta Thakrar, Sabaa Tahir, Laini Taylor, Kiersten White . . . I am so, so grateful. Fran Wilde, you are an actual treasure and your mantra has gotten me through so many rough patches.

Jen Azantian, my incredible agent and friend, I owe you more than I can ever say for seeing me through the past two years—and too, Ben, for helping us both out! To my editor, Priyanka Krishnan, I have been honored to work with you, know you, and watch my characters and world come to life under your careful hand. To everyone at Harper Voyager on both sides of the Atlantic, particularly David Pomerico, Pam Jaffee, Caro Perny, Kayleigh Webb, Angela Craft, Natasha Bardon, Jack Renninson, Mumtaz Mustafa, Shawn Nicholls, Mary Ann Petyak, Liate Stehlik, Paula Szafranski, Andrew DiCecco, Shelby Peak, Joe Scalora, and Ronnie Kutys, thank you for taking a chance on me and for all your hard work. To Will Staehle, thank you for knocking it out of the park with another gorgeous cover.

To my wonderful and very forgiving family, who has been

spectacularly supportive as I've grown more absentminded and stressed, thank you so, so much. Mom and Dad, I would never have been able to do this without you. Much gratitude as well to my grandmother and mother-in-law, who helped take care of me while I was injured and trying to finish this book.

To my husband, Shamik, my best friend and first reader, thank you for keeping my feet on the ground and for pushing me when I needed it. I love getting to dream and plot in this weird fictional world you've helped me create. For Alia, my little Nahri-in-training, you are the light in my life, my love, and your stories are even grander than my own.

Finally, to my fellow Muslim fantasy nerds: I wrote this story for you, for us, and I have been incredibly humbled and honored by your response. I thank you, from the bottom of my awkward convert's heart. May we all have the grandest of adventures!